APPLIED PRODUCTION AND OPERATIONS MANAGEMENT

THIRD EDITION

APPLIED PRODUCTION AND OPERATIONS MANAGEMENT

THIRD EDITION

JAMES R. EVANS
University of Cincinnati

DAVID R. ANDERSON
University of Cincinnati

DENNIS J. SWEENEY
University of Cincinnati

THOMAS A. WILLIAMS
Rochester Institute of Technology

WEST PUBLISHING COMPANY

St. Paul
New York
Los Angeles
San Francisco

PRODUCTION CREDITS

Copy and Art Editing   Tage Publishing Services, Inc.
Artist   Tech-Graphics
Text Design   Diane Beasley
Cover Design   Delor Erickson
Composition   Parkwood Composition Service, Inc.
Index   Northwind Editorial Services

COPYRIGHT © 1984, 1987 by WEST PUBLISHING COMPANY
COPYRIGHT © 1990   by WEST PUBLISHING COMPANY
                        50 W. Kellogg Boulevard
                        P.O. Box 64526
                        St. Paul, MN 55164-1003

Printed in the United States of America

97 96 95 94 93 92 91   8 7 6 5 4 3 2

Library of Congress Cataloging-in-Publication Data

Applied production and operations management / James R. Evans . . . [et al.] — 3rd ed.
    p.   cm.
  Bibliography: p.
  Includes index.
  ISBN 0-314-57826-9
  1. Production management. 2. Factory management.   I. Evans,
James R. (James Robert), 1950–
TS155.A62 1990
658.5—dc20   89-35359

CIP
⊗

To Beverly, Cheri, and Robbie

CONTENTS IN BRIEF

CONTENTS

PREFACE

The purpose of this book is to provide students of business administration with a sound understanding of the concepts, techniques, and applications of production and operations management (P/OM). To prepare students for the dynamic business environment in which they will enter, they must have a knowledge of technology and how it can be used effectively to improve an organization's productivity, quality, and competitive position. It is this philosophy that forms the basis for the design of the third edition of this text.

The material presented in this book provides a blend of the managerial issues in P/OM with the technical and quantitative aspects of the discipline. To accomplish this, we emphasize practical applications involving real manufacturing and service organizations throughout the text, as well as through our original *P/OM in Practice* feature.

CHANGES IN THE THIRD EDITION

In this edition, we have made several significant improvements in the organization, presentation, and context of the text. *Every chapter has been updated with new and current material and revised to enhance the readability of the text.* The major changes in this edition are discussed below.

Forecasting has been moved to Part I of the text to emphasize its importance and usefulness throughout P/OM. Materials and inventory management have been integrated into one chapter, and decision models for inventory management is now a separate chapter rather than a supplement. As a result of these changes, we have added a new and expanded chapter on just-in-time production. A new supplement on decision analysis has been added and the former supplement on management science and decision making has been condensed and integrated into Chapter 1.

Organization

Additional changes have been made with regard to pedagogical features. P/OM in Practice cases have been consolidated in the final section of each chapter so as not to disrupt the flow of the text; in addition, discussion questions have been added to each case. Solved numerical examples—many of them new—are now

Presentation

clearly highlighted and descriptively titled for easy reference. Finally, computer output from *The Management Scientist* microcomputer software package is used where appropriate.

Content

We have increased the emphasis on P/OM in service organizations, the importance of P/OM in international competitiveness, and the role of quality in the production of goods and services. Over half of the P/OM in Practice cases have been replaced with new and updated material, many of which first appeared in the literature only over the past three years.

We have made important changes in content in all chapters. An overview of some of these changes are as follows:

- **Chapter 1 Introduction to Production and Operations Management.** This chapter has been rewritten to provide a clearer distinction between manufacturing and services, and an increased emphasis on international competitiveness
- **Chapter 2 Productivity and Quality.** This chapter includes new material on quality management and total quality control.
- **Chapter 3 Forecasting and Time Series Analysis.** We have improved the discussion of the multiplicative time series model.
- **Chapter 4 P/OM and Strategic Planning.** In this chapter, we have provided an expanded discussion of Wheelwright's operations strategy factors and new sections on the manufacturing strategy formation process and service organizations.
- **Chapter 5 Product Design and Development.** We have revised the discussions of the role of product design in strategy, the product life cycle, productivity and quality considerations, and product design for services.
- **Chapter 6 Resource-requirements Planning.** This chapter includes an improved discussion of capacity, strategies for capacity expansion, and applications in service organizations, and provides increased coverage of the learning curve. A supplement on decision analysis has been added.
- **Chapter 7 Facility Location and Distribution Systems Design.** We have added the stepping stone method for solving transportation problems to the supplement for this chapter.
- **Chapter 8 Process Technology and Selection.** Several sections of this chapter have been rewritten for improved clarity, particularly with better focus on the role of strategy and reliability calculations. The important concept of process capability has been added.
- **Chapter 9 Process Design and Facility Layout.** We have included a new section on group technology and design of group layouts. The discussion of assembly line balancing and design for services have been substantially revised. The supplement on waiting lines has been rewritten to improve its presentation.
- **Chapter 10 Automation and Advanced Technology.** This chapter includes new and up-to-date material, particularly with regard to service applications.
- **Chapter 11 Job Design and Work Measurement.** A new section on motivation has been added to this chapter, and the discussion of quality circles has been expanded.
- **Chapter 12 Materials and Inventory Management.** This chapter now includes a new discussion of quality considerations in purchasing.

- **Chapter 13 Decision Models for Inventory Management.** The Silver-Meal heuristic for dynamic lot sizing and a revised discussion of single-period inventory models have been added to this chapter.
- **Chapter 14 Aggregate Production Planning and Master Scheduling.** Increased emphasis on capacity planning in service organizations has been added to this chapter.
- **Chapter 15 Material Requirements Planning.** Several sections have been revised for greater clarity.
- **Chapter 16 Operations Scheduling and Production Activity Control.** The section on batch production scheduling has been revised, and new material on OPT has been included.
- **Chapter 17 Just-in-Time Production.** Just-in-time is now a stand-alone chapter, and the material has been substantially expanded to include more details of JIT components: layout, Kanban, total quality control, and supplier relationships.
- **Chapter 18 Project Planning and Management.** We have included a new discussion of constructing project networks and added the linear programming approach to crashing in the chapter supplement.
- **Chapter 19 Quality Control.** This chapter has undergone a major revision with new sections on inspection, acceptance sampling, control-chart applications, cause-and-effect diagrams, and Pareto diagrams.
- **Chapter 20 Competitive Advantage and World-Class Manufacturing.** Finally, we have added a new concluding chapter that describes the concept of world-class manufacturing and its importance in competitiveness.

Questions and Problems

The number of end-of-chapter questions has been increased by 36 percent; in fact, over 200 of the questions are new. The number of problems has been increased by 64 percent, and nearly half of the almost 400 problems are new. Several new case problems have also been added to the end of selected chapters.

Flexibility

The instructor has substantial flexibility in selecting topics to meet specific course needs. For example, an instructor who wishes to focus on broad managerial issues of P/OM rather than the quantitative techniques involved with operational decisions might use the one-quarter course outline suggested below.

- **Introction** (Chapter 1)
- **Productivity and Quality** (Chapter 2)
- **P/OM and Strategic Planning** (Chapter 4)
- **Product Design and Selection** (Chapter 5)
- **Resource-Requirements Planning** (Chapter 6)
- **Analysis and Design of Production Systems** (selected portions of Chapters 7, 8, 9, 10, and 11)
- **Materials and Inventory Management** (Chapter 12)
- **Aggregate Planning** (Chapter 4)
- **Just-in-Time Production** (Chapter 17)
- **Conclusion** (Chapter 20)

A one-quarter course providing more emphasis on quantitative techniques and management science applications in P/OM might use the following outline:

- **Introduction** (Chapter 1)

- **Productivity and Quality** (Chapter 2)
- **Forecasting** (Chapter 3)
- **Strategic Issues and Production System Design** (selected portions of Chapters 4 through 11 and supplements)
- **Inventory Management and Models** (Chapters 12 and 13)
- **Aggregate Planning** (Chapter 14)
- **Material Requirements Planning** (Chapter 15)
- **Operations Scheduling and Production Activity Control** (Chapter 16)
- **Project Planning** (Chapter 18)
- **Quality Control** (Chapter 19)

One-semester courses can expand in either direction, depending on the instructor's orientation and the students' prerequisite knowledge. However, it is probably not possible to cover all the material in the text in one semester.

ANCILLARIES

A number of ancillaries are available to assist both the instructor and the student.

- **For the Instructor.** A *Solutions Manual,* prepared by the text authors, contains answers to all the questions, problems, and cases found in the text. The problem solutions have been independently checked for accuracy. A new *Test Bank* has been written by Stephen Casper, Indiana University, and is available on WESTEST, a microcomputer test generated program for IBM-PC's[1] and compatibles and the Apple II[2] family of computers. A set of approximately fifty transparency masters is also available.
- **For the Student.** A *Student Study Guide,* prepared by John T. Gutknecht and Robin Garner, Georgia Southern College, is new to this edition. It contains review and discussion questions and other features designed to aid students in mastering this text.

COMPUTER SOFTWARE

The Management Scientist microcomputer software package is available from West Publishing Co., for computer support in solving the more-difficult quantitative problems including forecasting, linear programming, the transportation problem, PERT/CPM, inventory models, and waiting lines. Output from this package is used in the text to illustrate the computer solution for many P/OM applications.

Lotus 1-2-3 Templates for Production and Operations Management, by James R. Evans, Jay Nathan, and Ronald J. Gambo, is a new and revised microcomputer package for solving a variety of P/OM problems on spreadsheets. The templates

---

[1] IBM and IBM-PC are registered trademarks of International Business Machines, Inc.
[2] Apple is a registered trademark of Apple ® Computer.

now have a dynamic expansion capability that allows any size of problem to be solved from menu-driven commands. The software is accompanied by a workbook.

ACKNOWLEDGEMENTS

We would like to express our appreciation to our friends and colleagues who have reviewed portions of the text in this and previous editions and provided many valuable comments. Reviewers for the third edition include:

J. K. Bandyopadhyay	Central Michigan University
Alfred J. Bird	University of Houston
Richard E. Crandall	Appalachian State University
Mark M. Davis	Bentley College
William K. Holstein	State University of New York/Albany
Roger G. Klungle	University of Michigan/Dearborn
Giri Kumar-Tayi	State University of New York/Albany
Charles E. Lienert	Metropolitan State College
Larry Scheuermann	University of Southwestern Louisiana
Margaret F. Shipley	University of Houston/Downtown
Devanath Tirupati	University of Texas/Austin
Scott T. Young	University of Utah

We also wish to thank Mr. J. Douglas Ekings, Chairman of the American Society of Quality Control, for allowing permission to reproduce portions of *Production and Quality* by Ross Johnson and William O. Winchell. Finally, we are indebted to our editors, Dick Fenton, Esther Craig, and Tom Hilt, and others at West Publishing Company for their continued excellent support.

James R. Evans
David R. Anderson
Dennis J. Sweeney
Thomas A. Williams

THE SCOPE OF PRODUCTION AND OPERATIONS MANAGEMENT

I. n Part I of this book we introduce the fundamental concepts of Production/Operations Management (P/OM). The general notion of a production system is discussed in Chapter 1. Included is a brief overview of the various decision areas and questions that operations managers must address. Decision making in P/OM is strongly influenced by the organizational hierarchy. At the top, operations decisions affect the entire firm, and at the lower levels, the decisions of operations managers typically affect only a few people or operations. We note that the hierarchical level in the organization is the primary determinant of the scope of operations planning and decision making. The role of management science and quantitative tools in P/OM is also discussed in Chapter 1.

A discussion of the importance of productivity and quality in P/OM forms the basis for Chapter 2. Improving productivity and enhancing quality are major considerations in operations management decisions. Decisions regarding productivity and quality have a significant impact on cost and profitability. Hence, issues affecting productivity and quality will be addressed throughout the text in conjunction with various P/OM decision areas.

Chapter 3 concludes Part I by addressing the role of forecasting in P/OM. Forecasts of the economy and forecasts of demand for goods and services are important inputs to both long- and short-term P/OM decision making. A variety of forecasting methods and applications are presented in this chapter.

Introduction to Production and Operations Management

Production is the process of converting, or transforming resources into goods or services. Resources include materials, machines, employees, time, and so on. The output of the production process may be manufactured goods, such as automobiles and computers, or services such as health care or financial transactions. The term **operations** describes the set of all activities associated with the production of goods and services. Operations may involve *manufacturing*, in which goods are physically created from material inputs; *transportation*, in which the location of something or someone is changed; *supply*, in which the ownership or possession of goods is changed; or *service*, in which the principal characteristic is the treatment or accommodation of something or someone.

The management of operations—that is, the planning, organizing, and controlling of the production process—and the management of the interface with supporting functions in the organization is called **production/operations management (P/OM)**, or simply, *operations management*. In this text we use these terms interchangeably. The purpose of this chapter is to explain the role and scope of P/OM in manufacturing and service organizations. We shall review the history of the development of P/OM as a discipline, the notion of a production system, fundamental activities associated with P/OM, and the link between P/OM and quantitative tools for making decisions.

1.1 THE IMPORTANCE OF PRODUCTION/OPERATIONS MANAGEMENT

Why is P/OM an important field of study? In recent years, the news media, business periodicals, and books have chronicled a variety of problems that plague American business and lamented the decline of U.S. manufacturing competitiveness in world markets. The number of nonagricultural workers employed in manufacturing has dropped from 35.2 percent in 1947 to 18.7 percent in 1987. Manufacturing plants are routinely shut down. About 5.1 million experienced American workers lost their jobs because of plant closings or employment cutbacks between 1981 and 1986. About half of these involved manufacturing jobs.

Foreign investment in the United States is increasing, and the trade deficit has widened. From 1981 to 1987, the trade balance in manufactured goods dropped from a surplus of $18.1 billion to a deficit of $151 billion.[1] Many industries including machine tools, steel, cameras, copiers, and audio and video equipment have lost market share to foreign competitors. In the automobile industry, for example, the United States produced 48 percent of the world's supply versus Japan's 3 percent in 1960; in 1980 the comparable figures were 20 and 28 percent respectively. Today, Japan supplies over one-third of the world's demand, and other countries, such as Korea, are gaining market share.

Increased capital investment has not helped. Between 1980 and 1985, U.S. companies have poured over $200 billion into new domestic facilities and equipment; $40 billion has been invested in the auto industry alone, and yet the United

---

[1]*Business Week,* 20 April 1987, 56.

States continues to lose ground.[2] At the same time, manufacturing productivity and the quality of goods produced by foreign competitors have continued to improve at a faster rate than that of the United States. Japan's productivity improved a dramatic 68 percent between 1977 and 1986, far outpacing the 26 percent U.S. increase over that same period.[3]

Many believe that reversing the trend in manufacturing competitiveness requires more effective management of operations. The Japanese experience—both in Japan *and in the United States*—suggests that operations management is the key to success. New United Motor Manufacturing, Inc. (NUMMI) is a joint venture between General Motors (GM) and Toyota. In setting up this company, Toyota took an antiquated California assembly plant and transformed it into GM's most efficient factory. Productivity in that plant has been twice the average level in GM plants. There is no special technology; the difference is the way that Toyota managers organize and operate the plant. New products are designed for easy assembly and easy modification; production layout is organized by product needs and not by function; production flow is managed so carefully that inventories are almost nonexistent; quality is the shared responsibility of each worker; and robots and other advanced technology are used for mindless tasks. The Japanese philosophy is to make people an important component of the production process, which leads to mutual trust and loyalty. At Honda of America Manufacturing Co. and Nissan Motor Mfg. USA, results have been similar.[4]

There have been recent reports that the Japanese system at NUMMI is beginning to generate friction among employees, but the success of the plant has caused both U.S. managers and unions to take careful notice. As a result, many companies such as Caterpillar, John Deere, 3M, General Electric, and Ford have adopted and are implementing new approaches to managing operations.

Operations management is now "where the action is." Unfortunately for American industry, finance and marketing have, in recent years, been viewed as more glamorous careers. As a result, only a few of our brightest young people have chosen careers in operations management. There is now a shortage of skilled managers who understand the critical issues in P/OM. The message is clear: "Unless the United States gets its manufacturing operations back in shape—and fast—it could lose any hope of maintaining the foundation on which tomorrow's prosperity rests."[5]

While most of the previous discussion has concerned manufacturing, we cannot ignore operations management in the production of services. The service sector represents the most rapidly growing segment of the workforce. Issues of productivity and quality in providing services have become increasingly important. Today, there are approximately three times as many people employed in the service sector as in manufacturing. In 1945, it was about 50–50. Throughout this book we shall devote considerable attention to the management of service operations.

---

[2]Elizabeth A. Haas, "Breakthrough Manufacturing," *Harvard Business Review*, March–April 1987, 75–81. Copyright 1987 by the President and Fellows of Harvard College; all rights reserved.

[3]"IE Federal Beat," *Industrial Engineering*, February 1989, 12.

[4]"The Difference Japanese Management Makes," *Business Week*, 14 July 1986, 47–50.

[5]*Business Week*, 20 April 1987, 56.

1.2 THE EVOLUTION OF PRODUCTION/OPERATIONS MANAGEMENT

In this section we present a brief historical overview of the development of production/operations management as a discipline, and discuss the challenges that P/OM faces as we approach the twenty-first century.

Historical Perspective

Contemporary P/OM has its roots in the industrial revolution that occurred during the latter part of the eighteenth and early nineteenth centuries in England. Until this time, goods were produced in small shops by craftspeople and their apprentices without the aid of mechanical equipment. During the industrial revolution, however, many new inventions came into being, which allowed goods to be manufactured with greater ease and speed. Among these were Hargreaves's spinning jenny (1770) and Cartwright's power loom (1785), which revolutionized the production of textiles, Watt's steam engine (1785), which provided power for mechanization, and Maudslay's screw-cutting lathe (1797), which helped to establish the metal-fabrication and machine-tool industries. These inventions reduced the need for individual craftspeople and led to the development of modern factories.

Methods of planning and organizing work were also changing. In 1776, British economist Adam Smith advocated the principle that productivity improvement can be obtained through the division of labor—that is, having different workers perform different functions of a job rather than having one worker acquire the skills necessary to perform the entire job. Smith reasoned that this would enable workers to become more proficient in their tasks and that they would be able to develop specialized tools and machines to accomplish their jobs more efficiently. Also, the time lost because of changing jobs would be eliminated. Today although this concept is still widely used in our system of manufacturing, it is being reexamined. Along with division of labor, the concept of interchangeable parts, introduced by Eli Whitney in 1798, paved the way for modern manufacturing. This idea was vital to the success of Henry Ford's assembly line in the early 1900s.

In the early part of the nineteenth century, Charles Babbage refined and extended many of Adam Smith's ideas. He believed that the total cost of a product could be lowered by hiring workers with different skills and paying them according to their expertise. In addition, Babbage investigated managerial and organizational structures, human relations, new-product development, and price-volume-profit relationships in the marketplace. Although his work (1832) was not immediately put into practice, it greatly influenced the development of scientific management theories in later generations.

The era of scientific management began in the United States with Frederick W. Taylor around the turn of the twentieth century. Taylor progressed from a laborer to chief engineer. From this experience, he studied production at the most detailed level, focusing on workers, their methods of work, and wages paid for productivity. He believed that the responsibilities for production should differ between management and labor. Management should be responsible for planning, directing, and organizing work, while workers should be concerned only with carrying out their assigned tasks. Taylor also believed in fostering a spirit of cooperation between management and labor and in selecting the best worker for the job. Taylor proposed a "science of management" based on observation, measurement and analysis of work, improvement in work methods, and economic incentives. As a result, he is often called the "father of scientific management."

Many of Taylor's contemporaries extended and enriched his thinking. Henry Gantt recognized the use of rewards other than wages to promote morale; he developed the now famous Gantt chart for scheduling and monitoring work. Frank and Lillian Gilbreth investigated work planning and employee training. Some of their more important contributions include the development of motion study and job improvement methods.

In the 1930s, as a result of the Hawthorne studies conducted at Western Electric, another viewpoint emerged. The Hawthorne studies were actually motivated by Taylor's work. Elton Mayo, who conducted the studies, sought to determine if a set of working conditions could be created within a factory environment that would maximize worker productivity. One experiment involved changing light intensity and measuring the effect on worker productivity. He found that an increase in light intensity led to higher productivity. However, in trying to replicate the experiments, Mayo discovered that even when light intensity was reduced to previous settings, worker productivity continued to increase, rather than decreasing to previous levels. It seems that the extra attention the workers received by being part of the experiment is what had led to their increased productivity.

The Hawthorne studies caused researchers to recognize that workers were not just another capital asset, as in Taylor's perspective, but that they could be motivated (through extra attention) to increase their productivity. This finding led to behavioral science approaches to increasing productivity through motivation. Researchers, such as Maslow, Herzberg, and McGregor, made important contributions. Today, it is recognized that both the technical approaches to increased efficiency advocated by Taylor and his contemporaries as well as the behavioral science approaches following from the Hawthorne experiments are necessary to increase productivity.

About this time, a group of individuals at Bell Telephone Laboratories were developing new theories and methods of inspection to improve quality. Walter Shewart, George Edwards, Harold Dodge, and others made significant contributions that laid the foundation for modern quality assurance. Today, quality assurance is recognized as being vital to successful operations management.

During World War II, a new discipline arose that has had a significant influence on business and industry. Known as *operations research,* or *management science,* it recognized that many physical situations can be adequately represented by a mathematical *model.* Among the first applications of this approach to operations management was the determination of the optimum size of convoys for transporting military supplies to Europe. Today, management science problems may be as specific as improving the efficiency of a production line or as broad as establishing a long-range corporate strategy involving a combination of financial, marketing, and manufacturing considerations. The development of computers and, more recently, microprocessors, has enhanced the scope of management science activity. Management science techniques are useful tools for aiding P/OM decision making. We shall see a number of examples of this throughout the book.

During the years following World War II, the United States found itself in a dominant position with respect to manufacturing. As a result, operations management was taken for granted and not considered part of strategic business planning. The operations manager's goal was to keep the production line running and efficiency high. Job specialization led to boring, repetitive tasks. At the same time, the Japanese were rebuilding from the devastations of World War II. They embraced new manufacturing approaches and the philosophies of quality assurance that were advocated by two U.S. consultants, W. Edwards Deming and Joseph Juran. Over two decades their quality, productivity, and methods of managing operations substantially improved. Then almost overnight, they penetrated major global markets in a variety of industries.

The space program and research in electronics has led to the development of advanced technology that has revolutionized production during the 1970s and the 1980s. Robotics and microprocessors are but two high-technology developments that are changing the practice of P/OM. Industrial robots, for example, provide companies with the flexibility to introduce new products and change production volumes more frequently. Robots also provide more consistent quality and reduce the cost of materials and labor. Other new technologies such as computer-aided design and manufacturing, and flexible manufacturing systems are now changing the focus of manufacturing strategies.

The rapid growth of the service sector has been a major development in recent years. In 1945, 22.9 million people were employed by service-producing industries and 18.5 million people were employed by goods-producing industries.[6] However, by 1985, 72.5 million people were employed in service-producing industries and 25.0 million people were employed in goods-producing industries. Since 1970 there has been little growth in the number of manufacturing jobs in the United States, but there has been tremendous job growth in the service sector. Today, about three-fourths of us work in service-producing industries.

With the increasing importance of the service sector, the emphasis of P/OM is changing. Many of the scientific and behavioral management approaches, originally developed for manufacturing operations, are being widely applied in service industries. Customer service is playing a more prominent role and information technology is becoming a dominant force as operations managers strive to improve productivity, enhance quality, and increase profitability. New challenges must also be faced. Because of the nature of services it is more difficult to leverage capital investment, and hence productivity increases are more difficult to achieve.

The manufacturing leadership of the United States has been challenged in recent years. In many areas the United States is falling behind Japan, West Germany, and, more recently, countries such as Korea and Malaysia. These countries have begun to dominate world markets in the automobile, steel, electronics, and machine tool industries. Critical reviews and research studies have argued that a principal cause of the United States' decline has been that too much emphasis has been placed on the marketing and financial aspects of strategic decisions. It is now generally recognized that operations management *must* be an integral part of any corporate strategy. Table 1.1 summarizes some of the important historical developments cited.

---

[6]Department of Labor, Bureau of Labor Statistics

TABLE 1.1

Important Historical Developments in P/OM

Industrial Revolution	
Hargreaves's spinning jenny	1770
Cartwright's power loom	1785
Watt's steam engine	1785
Maudslay's screw-cutting lathe	1797
Principle of division of labor	1776
Interchangeable parts	1798
Scientific management	early 20th century
Frederick W. Taylor—work measurement	
Frank and Lillian Gilbreth—methods improvement	
Behavioral studies and quality assurance methods	1930s
Operations research/management science	1940s
Computers	1950s
International competition	1970s
Advanced technology and growth of the service sector	1970s and 1980s
Strategic emphasis on manufacturing and service	1980s

Production has traditionally been characterized by long production runs, stable products and engineering designs, repetitive operations, dedicated equipment, and high direct labor costs. This approach is rapidly changing for a variety of reasons. In his best-selling book, *Megatrends,* (New York: Warner Books, 1982) John Naisbitt notes several important trends affecting society. Among these are shifts from

New Challenges and Opportunities

1. an industrial to an information society
2. forced technology to high technology
3. a national economy to a world economy
4. short-term emphasis to longer-term emphasis
5. centralization to decentralization
6. either/or to multiple options.

We need only look around us to see that the trends Naisbitt recognized are now entrenched in our society. Microcomputers, computer networking, and cable television for example, have brought information technology into our homes. Automation is found in both manufacturing and the production of services (e.g., robots and automated tellers). Pepsi, McDonald's, and Kentucky Fried Chicken, for instance, are found in cities throughout the world. Businesses are taking heed of Dr. W. Edwards Deming's message that a long-term emphasis is necessary for corporate survival, and airline deregulation and the breakup of AT&T are prime examples of decentralization. Manufacturers can no longer afford to be only low-cost producers—multiple objectives such as high quality and rapid product development are crucial to success.

These megatrends have significant importance for operations managers. Highly skilled personnel are needed to design, implement, and manage modern complex production systems. Both products and production processes are changing rapidly. Technological innovations in science and engineering together with increased consumer sophistication, have led to shorter product life cycles. For instance, compact discs have captured a large share of the audio market in three short years. To remain competitive, companies need to be able to respond rapidly to changing market demands.

A renewed emphasis on manufacturing strategy has led to operations managers becoming more involved in long-term strategic planning. There are pressures to significantly reduce investment in inventories and to subcontract components instead of trying to become specialists in a variety of manufacturing tasks. Such trends have led manufacturers to investigate "just-in-time" production and purchasing. Production departments and suppliers are required to deliver components and materials just at the time they are needed and not earlier or later. Implementing these systems requires careful control and coordination to be successful.

The concept of a "focused factory," a term coined by Wickham Skinner, is becoming more prevalent. This is a system in which a single manufacturing plant is organized around a limited set of products and processes and operations managers become expert in these areas. This type of factory permits flexibility and rapid changeover of products.

These current trends in both society and industry pose many difficult questions for operations management. How can emerging technology be evaluated? Should automation be used in a centralized or decentralized fashion? Can we develop organizational mechanisms that permit better coordination between operations managers and the managers of other functional fields? How can we introduce nonfinancial objectives into P/OM decision-making techniques? How can we learn from the Japanese approach which emphasizes the human element through participation and quality circles and the systems approach that integrates people, equipment, and information? Are these concepts suited to U.S. manufacturing? Can they be implemented successfully? How should issues of centralization versus decentralization be resolved?[7] The answers are not evident or easy to find. Finding answers is the challenge to operations management today.

Operations management as it is viewed today has evolved from the traditional practice of industrial management in manufacturing to a broad discipline that has applicability in service and nonmanufacturing activities alike. It is recognized as an important functional area in business curricula.

1.3 PRODUCTION OF GOODS AND SERVICES

The production system is the focus of P/OM activities. Production is the process of converting, or transforming, the resources available to an organization into goods and services. The collection of all interrelated activities and operations involved in producing goods and services is called a **production system**. Figure 1.1, a schematic diagram of a production system, shows that any production system consists of four principal components: inputs, a conversion or creation process, outputs, and managers. Decisions and feedback influence the process.

Inputs to a production system consist of the resources that are used to produce desired outputs, namely finished goods and services. The inputs typically include materials, capital, equipment, personnel, information, and energy. The **conversion**

---

[7] J. G. Miller and M. B. W. Graham, "Production/Operations Management: Agenda for the '80s," *Decision Sciences*, 12 (1981): 547–561. Published by the Decision Sciences Institute.

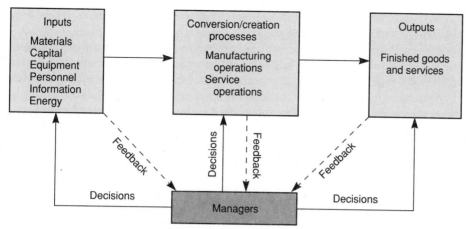

FIGURE 1.1

A Model of a
Production
System

process for manufacturing (which is also known as the creation process for services) is the system of facilities and procedures by which finished goods and services are produced. Operations managers must acquire the inputs, control the conversion or creation process, and ensure that outputs are available at the proper time and place to satisfy demand. Decisions are made to affect productivity, quality, cost control, scheduling, and employee motivation, among others, and to improve the efficiency and effectiveness of the organization. Finally, **feedback** is the process of monitoring the inputs, outputs, and production system performance in order to plan effectively or take corrective action when necessary. Effective feedback requires useful performance measures. Feedback enables an organization to improve the products and services offered and to better meet the demands of the marketplace.

This text is concerned with production systems for both manufacturing and service organizations. Let us describe some of the unique characteristics of these two types of production systems.

The Production System in Manufacturing

Manufactured goods are tangible items that can be transferred from one place to another and can be stored for purchase by a consumer at a later time. For example, goods such as automobiles, home appliances, and packaged foods are usually produced in one location and purchased in another. The principal inputs to manufacturing systems are raw materials and/or the purchased parts that are transformed into finished goods. For instance, these inputs might be crude oils that are converted into gasoline, a block of titanium that is machined into a section of an airplane wing, or a set of plastic parts purchased overseas that are assembled into a toy. Machines and material-handling equipment are important components of manufacturing systems.

Conversion processes in manufacturing typically change the shape of raw materials. For example, drilling and grinding are two metal-removing operations that change the shape of materials. Other manufacturing processes may change the composition or form of the inputs. The conversion of grain into cereal is one example, and assembly operations—which simply combine many individual parts—is another. Large manufacturing systems usually employ several different conversion processes. For example, a producer of industrial machine tools may make the gears and castings, purchase electronic components, and assemble the tools.

Managers in manufacturing organizations generally emphasize technology. How to best control the flow of materials within a plant, how to schedule customer orders and manufacturing operations, and when to upgrade to more advanced technology are among their most important concerns. In controlling manufacturing operations, feedback is essential. For example, managers must obtain information about the status of jobs on the factory floor and adjust schedules when necessary. Feedback on quality is used to determine when to take corrective action such as adjusting a machine, increasing the level of employee training, or improving the design of a product. Table 1.2 provides some examples of production systems in manufacturing.

The Production System in Service Organizations

Service operations are taking on a more important role in operations management because of the fact that the United States is now predominantly a service economy. For many years, more people have been employed in the service sector than in manufacturing. The production of services differs from manufacturing in many ways. Services are intangible and are consumed as they are created. For example, the services of a fire department are produced and used when a fire occurs, and the services of a bus company are used when transportation is provided. What is valued about the service usually involves subjective assessments such as customer satisfaction. This makes it more difficult to measure quantity and quality of output.

Services are generally labor intensive, whereas manufacturing is more capital intensive. For example, patient care in hospitals depends heavily on the performance of nurses, doctors, and other medical staff. Hence, the behavioral aspects of management, much as motivation, are critical in the service sector. The customer and the service worker often must interact for the delivery of the service to be complete. Customers in a fast-food restaurant place orders, carry their food to the table, and even clear the table when they are finished. In recent years, however, the growth of information technology has reduced the labor intensiveness of some service operations. Automatic teller machines and banking by mail,

---

TABLE 1.2   Examples of Manufacturing Systems and Selected Components

System	Inputs	Conversion Process	Outputs	Managers	Feedback
Auto assembly plant	Labor Energy Robots Auto parts	Welding Manual assembly Painting	Automobiles	Supervisors Plant managers	Labor cost Production quantities Quality
Oil refinery	Crude oil Energy Equipment Labor	Chemical reaction Separation	Gasoline Kerosine Other chemical products	Plant manager Chemists	Chemical composition Volume
Computer manufacturer	Chips Circuit boards Purchased parts Labor	Assembly	Computers	Electrical engineers Foremen	Test results Production quantities Unit cost

for instance, have removed some service workers from the picture. While automation reduces the labor intensity it can have an adverse effect on quality. Some would argue that customer satisfaction is decreased because of the lack of personal interaction.

The customer must obtain the services at the time of demand; therefore, services cannot be stored for future use. Manufacturing companies use inventories to provide for future demand. Companies providing services have little opportunity to do this. Even for companies providing services involving tangible goods, such as fast-food restaurants, customers demand fresh products and inventory cannot be held for long. On the other hand, companies producing services are often able to inventory customers through waiting lines. The management of waiting lines is as important to the service industry as the management of inventories is to manufacturing.

Finally, the production of services usually requires a higher degree of customization than that of manufactured goods. A doctor, lawyer, insurance salesman, and even a food-service employee must tailor the service provided to the individual customer.

In the production of services, many inputs are similar to those needed in manufacturing. A fire department needs equipment and skilled fire fighters, and restaurants require food, chefs, waiters, and waitresses. The major output of service systems, however, is intangible. Unlike production systems for goods (manufacturing systems), pure service production systems do not convert raw materials into finished goods; rather, a service is created and made available at a point in time. For example, a professional football game may be produced to be purchased and consumed between 1:00 and 4:00 P.M. on a Sunday afternoon. In other service organizations, such as hospitals, it is the skill and expertise of the staff in caring for the customer that creates satisfaction. The technology used in the service sector is often that which provides information.

Since the customer often interacts with the producer of services, people, rather than equipment, are the driving force in service production. Managers must often focus their attention on people skills of employees rather than on technical issues. High-quality services cannot be provided without extensive feedback on customer satisfaction. The importance attached to feedback is readily apparent; nearly all hotels and restaurants have customer comment cards prominently displayed— and addressed to the president or CEO of the organization!

There are many organizations in which the production of goods and services go hand in hand. Consider, for example, a fast-food restaurant where various food items are converted into consumable products but where the speed and quality of customer service are just as important. We tend *not* to classify such organizations as manufacturing organizations, but rather as service organizations. They compete more on the basis of the services provided than the products sold. It is also important to realize that many manufacturing organizations provide both goods *and* services. An example is a manufacturer of computer equipment who produces the actual hardware and also provides maintenance and repair services.

Service organizations may be for-profit and not-for-profit. Depending on which type, measures of effectiveness differ, and hence P/OM decisions may be focused on different objectives. For instance, the public service objectives of a for-profit hospital may differ from those for a not-for-profit hospital. Table 1.3 provides several examples of service production systems.

TABLE 1.3 Examples of Service Systems and Selected Components

System	Inputs	Conversion Process	Outputs	Managers	Feedback
Hospital	Patients Staff Beds Drugs Medical equipment	Operations Drug administration Health-status monitoring	Healthy individuals Lab results	Chief of staff Head nurse	Response to medication Surgical complications
Restaurant	Meat, vegetables, poultry, fish Customers Food servers Kitchen equipment Utensils	Cooking Meal preparation Serving	Prepared food Happy customers	Head chef Restaurant manager Maitre'd	Customer comments Amount of gratuities
Farm	Land Equipment Seeds Fertilizer	Planting, spraying, harvesting	Fruits Vegetables Grains Meats	Farmer	Yield per acre USDA grade
Post Office	Labor Sorting equipment Trucks	Transporting letters and packages	Mail delivery	Postmasters	Average delivery times Parcels damaged

The Production System and Its Environment

A production system is only one of the components of an organization. Production is affected by and has an impact on decisions in other functional areas of the firm such as finance or marketing. In addition, various external influences affect the overall objectives and policies of a company and have important implications for production. These relationships for a typical firm are illustrated in Figure 1.2.

At the outermost level, external to the firm itself, are several *environmental factors* that influence the overall policies and objectives of the company. Four of the most important environmental factors are economic conditions, government regulation, competition, and technology. *Economic factors* include interest rates, availability of capital, general economic conditions, tax regulations, and economies of scale. For example, oil prices can have a dramatic effect on the product lines of automobile manufacturers. Compliance with *governmental regulations* on pollution controls and environmental impact, can also have an impact on product lines. New product lines require significant retooling and redesign of production processes in the auto industry.

The nature of *competition,* market share, and how the firm reacts to competitive strategies have a significant influence on product lines and other strategic decisions. This has been especially evident in the fast-food industry. You have undoubtedly observed that when a fast-food franchise opens on a well-traveled highway, a variety of other similar operations almost immediately spring up nearby. When a major chain instituted breakfast as part of its normal menu, other national chains developed breakfast menus in order to compete in this new market. This required new consideration in food-production processes and the management of food items and supplies.

New *technology* in manufacturing processes, equipment, or materials can drastically affect product designs and production methods. An excellent illustration

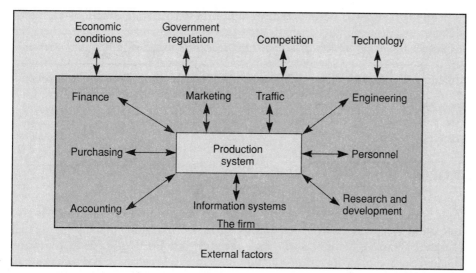

FIGURE 1.2
The Production
System and Its
Environment

of this is the development of solid-state electronics and, more recently, microprocessors in the electronics industry. Manufacturers of mechanical office equipment, cash registers, and other products have been forced to incorporate the new technology in order to stay in business. Thus we see that the production system must react quickly to strategic changes in a firm's business plan.

Within the firm, the production system is influenced by other functional areas. *Finance* is responsible for obtaining funds, controlling their use, analyzing investment opportunities, and insuring that the firm operates on a cost-effective basis and, in most cases, at a profit. Financial decisions affect the choice of manufacturing equipment, use of overtime, cost-control policies, price-volume decisions, and, in fact, nearly all facets of the organization. *Accounting* keeps records on costs and prices that relate to such factors as financial decisions, purchasing, and payroll. Many of these data must be obtained from production managers. *Marketing* is responsible for understanding customer needs, generating and maintaining demand for the firm's products, insuring customer satisfaction, and developing new markets and product potential. Coordination of production and marketing is important in order to use demand forecasts effectively, to project workloads, and to ensure sufficient capacity to handle the demand and deliver finished products on time.

Engineering determines product specifications to meet customer needs, production methods, and other technical specifications. *Personnel and labor relations* recruit and train employees and are responsible for employee morale, wage administration, union negotiations, and so on. Because people are the most important entity in any organization, this function is vital in helping a production system run smoothly. *Research and development* (R & D) investigates new ideas and their potential uses as consumer products. *Purchasing and traffic* are responsible for the acquisition of materials and supplies necessary for production and the distribution of the finished goods to customers, respectively. Entire production lines have been shut down because of the shortage of a 5-cent part, and customers may be lost if products are not shipped and delivered promptly as promised. Finally, *information systems* provide the means for capturing, analyzing, and coordinating the information needs of each of these areas.

Although we focus on the relationship of these corporate functions with production, we do not mean to imply that they are independent of each other. For example, financial considerations affect decisions made in all other functional areas and engineering specifications on materials assist purchasing in identifying qualified suppliers. It is important to realize that these functions are interrelated. Our purpose, however, is not to examine the firm as a complete entity, but rather to focus our attention on the firm's production and operations activities.

1.4 THE ROLE OF OPERATIONS MANAGERS

Appropriate technology and worker skills are key components in the effective operation of a production system. However, a strong argument can be made that it is the operations managers who have the greatest influence on productivity and quality. Sony claims that its production lines in San Diego have the same rate of productivity as their Japanese factories. Workers are different, but operations management standards are the same. After Matsushita Company bought Motorola, they found that American workers could operate to Japanese standards. Hideo Duguira, Honda Motors Executive Vice-President, is quoted in the *Los Angeles Times* as saying: "In any country, the quality of products and productivity of workers depend on management. When Detroit changes its management system, we'll see more powerful American competitors."[8]

Managers of operations perform many different activities. A plant manager, for example, may oversee several departments, such as production control, industrial engineering, and quality control. The problems a plant manager faces might include reducing production bottlenecks, controlling costs, and eliminating lost-time accidents. As another example, a hospital administrator must also manage many departments, such as surgery, X-ray, and outpatient treatment. Such an administrator faces problems of maintaining an adequate staff and ensuring high-quality services. In each of these situations, the manager is concerned with planning, organizing, directing, and controlling productive operations in order to meet the objectives of the organization. These are accomplished by *managing work* (the technical side of P/OM) and by *managing people* (the behavioral side of P/OM). Both are equally important.

The four basic functions of management—planning, organizing, directing, and controlling—are performed by managers at all levels of an organization. **Planning** provides the basis for all future managerial activities by establishing the guidelines and actions that must be taken in order to meet stated objectives, as well as establishing the timing of these actions. **Organizing** is the process of bringing together the resources—personnel, materials, equipment, and capital—necessary to perform planned activities. **Directing** is the process of turning plans into realities by assigning specific tasks and responsibilities to employees, motivating them, and coordinating their efforts. Finally, since planning, organizing and directing are never completely effective, **controlling** is necessary. Controlling includes the evaluation of performance and the application of corrective measures, as nec-

---

[8]Harold, S. Davis, "Management—What We Can Learn From the Japanese," *Production and Inventory Management,* 27, 1 (First Quarter 1986): 85.

Level of	Activity			
Management	Planning	Organizing	Directing	Controlling
Top	High	Low	Low	Moderate
Middle	Moderate	High	Moderate	Moderate
Supervisory	Low	Low	High	High

essary. Table 1.4 shows the relative emphasis of planning, organizing, directing, and controlling at the three major levels of management: top, middle, and supervisory.

Top management is responsible for setting the goals of the organization such as achieving profit, growth, competitive position, or good public relations. Top management makes decisions that affect the long-term future of the organization. The outcomes of such decisions might be the introduction of a new product line or the construction of a new manufacturing facility. The timing and implementation of these decisions are important to the achievement of organizational objectives. Thus effective planning is critical at this level of management. Relatively little organizing and directing occurs at this level, although a moderate level of control is necessary in order to ensure that plans are carried out.

Decisions and plans made by top management specify the goals that middle managers, such as the production manager, must accomplish, as well as the constraints within which they must operate. For instance, in introducing a new product, production managers must acquire the materials and machines to produce the product. Plans at the middle-management level involve a shorter time frame, and more direction is required because a larger number of subordinates frequently report to middle managers.

At the supervisory, or first-line management level, the emphasis is on achieving the short-range goals of the organization. Much of a line manager's time is spent directing production workers, clerks, and other personnel. For instance, warehouse supervisors are responsible for filling and shipping customer orders. They must ensure that orders are filled correctly, packaged properly, and safely loaded onto trucks. Thus their primary effort is spent on directing and controlling operations. In general, planning and organizing are not critical activities for first-line supervisors.

Control is important for providing feedback and linking together the three major levels of management. To accomplish a planned objective, performance must be measured and compared with some standard. For example, top management may be interested in the growth of the market share of a new product; middle management might be concerned with developing an inventory policy for the product; and supervisory management must control the production schedule. If plans are not being accomplished, the reasons for this need to be uncovered and corrective action must be taken.

In general, we see that top management is concerned with long-range plans and decisions, middle management with intermediate-range plans and decisions, and supervisory management with short-range plans and decisions. This observation leads us to a **hierarchical classification** scheme for P/OM activities. Planning and decision-making activities can generally be classified as strategic, tactical, or operational.

Strategic planning and decision making is broad in scope and involves corporate policies and resource-acquisition decisions, such as choosing product lines and distribution and marketing channels, determining required resources, locating and sizing new plants and warehouses, designing manufacturing processes, and so on. Strategic planning involves a long time horizon such as 3–5 years, and a high degree of uncertainty and risk.

Tactical planning and decision making is narrower in scope and involves resource allocation and utilization. In manufacturing organizations, tactical planning normally occurs at the plant level, involves a medium-term time horizon, and a moderate degree of uncertainty and risk. Examples of tactical planning involve the use of capital-intensive equipment to improve production throughput, evaluating resource capacity and demand changes, making 6-month or 1-year production plans, and determining workforce levels.

Finally, **operational planning and decision making** takes place over a short time horizon. There is very little uncertainty and risk. Operational planning involves routine tasks such as scheduling personnel and equipment, controlling inventories and materials, adjusting production rates, adapting to unexpected breakdowns or shortages, and controlling production quality.

These three categories of planning and decision making are hierarchical in nature. That is, strategic plans and decisions made at upper levels in the organization are fed downward and provide the guidelines within which tactical plans and decisions are made. These, in turn, are fed downward and provide guidelines for the operational plans and decisions. Feedback on the results of plans and decisions are fed upward in a similar fashion. With a properly coordinated system, several benefits can accrue to the organization: The system as a whole will work together in a cohesive manner; departments and managers will be able to make plans and decisions that mutually support each other; and objectives, policies, and operational constraints will be better understood by all involved. Part II of this book focuses on strategic issues in P/OM, and in Part III our attention is devoted to tactical and operational issues, primarily in regard to manufacturing planning and control. The next section discusses the specific issues with which operations managers must deal.

1.5 CRITICAL ISSUES IN P/OM

All managers are involved in planning and decision making; that is, they must plan and choose appropriate courses of action to achieve organizational objectives. Objectives such as minimizing production costs, maximizing quality, meeting delivery schedules, speeding up product development, and minimizing capital investment are important considerations for operations managers.

Table 1.5 lists several planning and decision-making areas addressed by operations managers. Fundamental questions in each of these areas are noted. In order to better understand the specific types of questions addressed in Table 1.5, and to provide a better perspective of operations management activities in general, we present two scenarios—one for manufacturing and one for services—that illustrate some of the issues that operations managers must face in these planning and decision-making areas.

Planning and Decision-making Areas	Fundamental Questions
Business planning	What is our strategic business plan? How does operations fit into this plan?
Product design and development	What do we produce?
Resource requirements planning	What facilities, equipment, and personnel do we need?
Facility location and distribution	Where do we produce the product? How should we transport to customers?
Process analysis	What do we need to produce a product?
Process design and facility layout	What is the best way to produce a product?
Automation and advanced technology	What role should computers and other forms of automation play in production?
Job Design	How do people interface with technology?
Inventory policy	What quantities of raw materials and components should be purchased and when?
Aggregate production planning and master production scheduling	When do we produce? How much?
Capacity planning	Is sufficient capacity available? If not, what adjustments can be made?
Material requirements planning	When are materials needed?
Operations scheduling and production activity control	How are personnel and equipment utilized?
Material management	How do we coordinate production plans, capacity decisions, schedules, and materials for maximum effectiveness?
Quality assurance	Do our products meet customers' needs? Are we meeting quality specifications?

P/OM ISSUES IN A MANUFACTURING FIRM

Ricketts Golf Equipment Company is a small manufacturer of golf equipment and supplies. The firm manufactures and distributes gloves, leather grips for golf clubs, wood covers, and so on. Based upon recent marketing studies, Ricketts' management has decided to expand its production facilities to include manufacturing golf bags. This represents a strategic change in the firm's business plan. The vice-president of manufacturing has been given the task of organizing and coordinating the overall production effort.

Let us examine how the planning and decision areas in Table 1.5 relate to this situation.

Product Design and Development

What styles and price ranges should be considered? Of what materials should the golf bags be made? What colors and other features—such as umbrella holders or compartments for shoes—should be included?

Resource-Requirements Planning

Will market demand forecasts warrant the expansion of existing facilities or construction of a new production plant? How much equipment and personnel are necessary in order to meet the forecasted demand?

Facility Location and Distribution

If a new facility is to be constructed, where should it be built? How will the product be distributed to markets? Should Ricketts purchase or lease its trucks? Should public warehouses be used during the peak golfing season?

Process Analysis and Design and Facility Layout

What machines need to be purchased? In what sequence should assembly operations be performed? Where should machines and assembly areas be located in the plant in order to minimize handling? How will materials and finished products be moved from one work center to the next?

Automation and Advanced Technology

Can any process be automated? Is the cost justified? What implications will this technology have for future product changes and other strategic decisions?

Job Design

How should work be assigned to different employees? Do the jobs and work environment meet federal safety regulations? Will the employees be satisfied with their jobs?

Inventory Policy

How many golf bags should be maintained in regional warehouses? How much leather and vinyl should we order and how often?

Aggregate Production Planning and Master Production Scheduling

How are demand forecasts translated into production requirements? Will additional shifts or overtime be needed? Are sufficient labor and equipment available to meet projected demand?

Material-Requirements Planning

For a specific production schedule, when must individual components, such as handles, be ordered so they will be available on time for the final assembly? Will enough capacity be available in order to meet this production schedule?

Operations Scheduling and Production Activity Control

How should the work on each machine be scheduled? What can be done if a machine breaks down? How can an important order be speeded up?

Material Management

Will new control strategies such as "just-in-time" be feasible for the company?

Quality Assurance

Where should the golf bags be inspected during the production process? How can it be determined if a machine needs an adjustment or if bad material was received? How can it be ensured that the final product will be of high quality?

In the Ricketts Golf Equipment Company illustration, we show how the planning and decision areas of Table 1.5 arise in the context of a manufacturing organization. To illustrate how these concepts apply in the service sector, let us consider an application in the transportation industry.

Tri-State Airways (TSA), a financially troubled commuter airline serving the Ohio-Kentucky-Indiana region, was recently acquired by one of the nation's larger domestic airlines. This acquisition was part of the domestic airline's strategic business plan. The acquiring firm believed that some operational improvements in organization, marketing strategies, and equipment could result in a successful commuter operation. In contrast to a manufacturing company, the "product" (service) delivered by the airline is the transportation of people and light cargo between cities. Some of the potential applications of P/OM in reorganizing and operating this airline are given next.

Product Design and Development

Should a new logo or color scheme be considered in order to change Tri-State's image? Should meals be served? If so, what kind? How many flight attendants should there be?

Location and Distribution

Should TSA make changes in its route structure in order to service new cities or discontinue nonprofitable routes? How many flights per day should be made between various cities and how should they be scheduled?

Process Design and Facility Layout

Should new ticketing or baggage-handling procedures be considered? Will changes in office procedures, aircraft maintenance procedures, or work flow improve productivity and reduce costs?

Automation and Advanced Technology

Can optical scanning equipment improve baggage handling and sorting operations? Can computers be used more effectively to schedule flights and allocate equipment among different airports?

Job Design

Can unnecessary work be identified and eliminated? Can certain tasks be made easier for ticket agents and other office personnel? Will rescheduling of flight attendants improve problems of turnover?

Aggregate Production Planning

How many ticket agents are necessary at various times of the month and year? How much baggage-handling equipment is needed? How many telephone lines must be rented?

Inventory Policy

How can supplies of tickets, flight schedules, and office forms be best managed and distributed to airports and branch offices? How many meals should be planned and ordered?

Material-Requirements Planning

Who is responsible for assuring that tickets are sent to customers within 1 week prior to departure? How can peak holiday demands be best handled with the existing work force?

Operations Scheduling

Since phone reservation lines must be staffed 24 hours per day, how should operators be scheduled, vacations planned for, or shifts rotated?

Quality Assurance

How will the quality of service be measured and controlled? How can aircraft reliability be carefully controlled?

The Ricketts Golf Equipment and Tri-State Airways examples show the broad scope of P/OM activities. As a result, you should now be able to identify many of the operations management activities that arise in other manufacturing and service organizations.

1.6 DECISION MAKING AND MANAGEMENT SCIENCE IN P/OM

We have identified the types of issues dealt with by operations managers (see Table 1.5). The best decision-making approach taken in a particular situation depends on the type of problem. Routine, repetitive types of decisions can usually be programmed and solved at lower levels of an organization. Problems that are novel and unstructured usually cannot be programmed and are solved at higher levels of the organization. Eilon[9] has presented a taxonomy of decision-making problems based on two dimensions: replication and frequency. Table 1.6 shows this taxonomy.

Problems in cell 1 are those that recur frequently, and when they do, they are almost identical (a high degree of replication). Since these decisions recur frequently, the economic value of making good decisions is high; since the degree of replication is high, the decision rules can be specified. A P/OM example is the weekly scheduling of jobs in a factory. In such situations, computerized systems using quantitative decision techniques can be justified. Many of the techniques discussed in the chapter supplements are used in these types of situations.

Problems in cell 2 have a high degree of replication, so decision rules can be developed, but because of the low frequency, elaborate decision-making systems usually cannot be justified on economic grounds. Often decision-making authority in these situations is delegated to lower levels of the organization. A P/OM example is the layout of equipment when a new plant is built or an old one is modernized.

Problems in cell 3 are economically important because of frequent recurrence, but the low level of replication makes them unstructured. Thus it is difficult to program this type of decision making. An example is the configuration of a computer system by a computer-equipment manufacturer that meets the needs of a particular customer. Decision-support systems (DSSs) are often effectively applied to this type of problem. A DSS is a computer-based information system designed to provide support to a decision process. Unlike programmed systems

---

[9]Samuel Eilon, "Structuring Unstructured Decisions," *Omega, The International Journal of Management Science*, 13, no. 5 (1985): 369–378.

TABLE 1.6

Types of
Decision-making
Problems

Frequency

	High	Low
High	1	2
Low	3	4

Replication

for problems in cell 1, DSSs are designed for unstructured problems. They can usually be adapted by the user (decision maker) to the problem being solved. A recent development in the artificial intelligence area, expert systems, shows promise for dealing with this type of problem.

Problems in cell 4 are unstructured and cannot be programmed. These are problems best solved by experienced managers with good judgment. Experience with many other problems is helpful in recognizing and structuring the situation. Judgment is necessary in choosing a course of action when the criteria are not certain and the future environment is uncertain. In P/OM, an example of this type of problem is the decision to make a radical change in production facilities by investing in automated manufacturing systems based on high technology.

Over the past few years, many new and important quantitative techniques have been developed as aids to the decision-making process. The emphasis in the use of quantitative techniques in P/OM is not on the techniques per se but rather on the use of these techniques to contribute to better decision making. In this book, our approach is to show how the application of quantitative analysis can help the operations manager make better decisions. Management science techniques are often useful in assisting operations managers address problems in cells 1 and 2. We now explore the role of management science in P/OM.

While a variety of names exist for the body of knowledge and methodology involving quantitative approaches to decision making, two of the most widely known and accepted names are **management science (MS)** and **operations research (OR)**. Operations research is usually associated with mathematical-based problem solving approaches. Management science is a broad discipline that includes all rational approaches to decision making that are based upon an application of scientific methodology. The management science function considers organizational objectives and resources and, by using a scientific problem-solving approach, attempts to establish long- and/or short-range policies and decisions that are in the best interest of the organization. A management science problem may be as specific as improving the efficiency of a production line or as broad as establishing a long-range corporate strategy involving a combination of financial, marketing, and manufacturing considerations. Thus management science techniques can be used at all levels of decision making.

Disciplines such as operations research, decision sciences, information sciences, behavioral sciences, and some aspects of systems analysis are often included under the broad heading of management science. While a precise definition of each of these specific disciplines is not necessary for our purposes, it is important to realize that studies, projects, or analyses employing methodology from one or more of the above scientific disciplines could correctly be called a management science activity.

Often, the terms management science and operations research are used interchangeably or together (MS/OR). Actually, MS/OR may be more broadly defined to include a multidisciplinary scientific approach to decision making. In practice, MS/OR studies are frequently conducted by an MS/OR team, which might consist of a quantitative specialist, an engineer, an accountant, a behavioral scientist, and a manager from the particular problem area being studied (such as, for example, marketing, finance, or manufacturing). While the analysis of a problem situation almost always includes some qualitative considerations, significant portions of most MS/OR studies are based upon quantitative decision-making techniques.

A central theme in the MS/OR approach to decision making is a problem orientation. Nearly all MS/OR projects begin with the recognition of a problem situation that does not have an obvious solution. Quantitative analysts may then be asked to assist in identifying the "best" decision or solution for the problem. Reasons why a quantitative approach might be used in the decision-making process include the following:

1. The problem is complex, and the manager cannot develop a good solution without the aid of quantitative specialists.
2. The problem is very important (for example, a great deal of money is involved), and the manager desires a thorough analysis before attempting a decision.
3. The problem is new, and the manager has no previous experience upon which to draw.
4. The problem is repetitive, and the manager saves time and effort by relying upon quantitative procedures to make the routine decision recommendations.

For example, the scheduling of many jobs in a manufacturing facility can potentially involve millions of solutions. Finding a schedule that meets the objectives is a very difficult task because of the vast number of possibilities. Locating a new factory is an irreversible decision that involves large amounts of capital; management needs to be certain that it makes the best possible decision. Planning for production of an entirely new product involves activities never before performed. Inventories must be continually reordered on a routine basis; quantitative methods can assist in keeping costs low and freeing the manager for more important tasks.

Quantitative Analysis and Decision Making

The role of quantitative analysis in the managerial decision-making process is perhaps best understood by considering the flowchart in Figure 1.3. Note that the process is initiated by the appearance of a problem situation. The manager responsible for making a decision or selecting a course of action will probably make an analysis of the problem that includes a statement of the specific goals or objectives, an identification of all constraints, an evaluation of alternative decisions, and a selection of the apparent "best" decision or solution for the problem. The analysis process employed by the manager may take two basic forms: qualitative and quantitative. The qualitative analysis approach is based primarily upon the manager's judgment and experience. This type of analysis includes the manager's intuitive "feel" for the problem and is more an art than a science. If the manager has had experience with similar problems or if the problem is relatively simple, heavy emphasis may be placed upon a qualitative

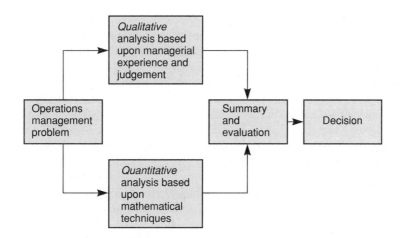

analysis and the final decision made accordingly. However, if the manager has had little experience with similar problems or if the decision problem is sufficiently important and complex, then a quantitative analysis of the problem can be a very important consideration in the manager's final decision. In the quantitative approach to the problem, an analyst will concentrate on the quantitative facts or data associated with the problem and develop mathematical expressions that describe the objectives, constraints, and relationships that exist in the problem. Then, by using one or more quantitative techniques, the analyst provides a decision recommendation based upon the quantitative aspects of the problem.

Both the qualitative and quantitative analysis of a problem provide important information for the manager or decision maker. In many cases, an operations manager may draw upon both sources and, through a comparison and evaluation of the information, make a final decision.

There are several important tools or techniques that have been useful in quantitative analysis for operations management problems. Some of the more popular tools are listed in Table 1.7. These have applications to many P/OM problem situations and are used throughout this book in P/OM decision areas, where they have important applications.

Management science tools have been applied at all levels of decision making. At the strategic level, for example, transportation models are useful in plant location and distribution system design; computer simulation and waiting-line models have been used in manufacturing and service system design and planning

Statistical analysis (sampling, regression, so on)
Computer simulation
Network models (PERT/CPM)
Linear programming
Waiting-line models
Transportation models
Inventory models
Decision trees

TABLE 1.7

Some Useful Quantitative Analysis Tools in P/OM

for long-term capacity. In tactical decision problems, such as inventory control, quantitative techniques are used to determine minimum-cost inventory and storage policies, and linear programming is sometimes used to plan aggregate production over an intermediate-range time horizon. At the operational level, many different quantitative techniques are used to assign jobs to machines, schedule telephone operators and nurses, and route trucks and rail cars. Statistical analysis is used routinely to study quality control problems.

A study by Ford et al. examined the use of MS/OR techniques in production among the 500 largest industrial firms.[10] The study indicated that usage of MS/OR occurs frequently in scheduling, forecasting, advertising, and sales research. These are highly repetitive decisions that occur with high frequency and thus are well suited to quantitative techniques. Regression analysis, linear programming, and simulation are the most utilized methods in a variety of P/OM application areas.

<table>
<tr><td>Mathematical
Models</td><td>

Most applications of management science in P/OM are based on a mathematical model. A **model** is any representation of a real object or situation. Some models are physical replicas of an object, such as an architect's scale model of a new manufacturing plant. Physical replicas are called **iconic models**.

A second classification of models refers to models that are physical in form but do not have the same physical appearance as the object being modeled. Such models are referred to as **analog models**. For example, the layout of machines on a plant floor can be represented by paper cutouts of different colors and sizes.

A third classification of models—the primary types of models we study—refers to models that represent the real situation by a system of symbols and mathematical relationships or expressions. Such models are referred to as **mathematical models**. For instance, operations managers often make use of breakeven analysis to determine how much must be produced and sold before a product becomes profitable. Breakeven analysis is based on mathematical models for cost, revenue, and profit. An example of the use of using break-even analysis is given later in this section.

The purpose or value of any model is that it enables us to draw conclusions about the real situation by studying and analyzing the model. For example, an airplane designer might test an iconic model of a new airplane in a wind tunnel in order to learn about the potential flying characteristics of the full-size airplane. Similarly, a mathematical model may be used to draw conclusions about how much profit will be earned if a specified quantity of a particular product is sold. With both the airplane model and the production examples, an analyst would be able to test and experiment with the model in order to learn about the real situation.

In general, experimenting with models requires less time and is less expensive than experimenting with the real object or situation. Certainly a model airplane is quicker and less expensive to build and study than the full-size airplane. Similarly, a mathematical model of profit allows a quick identification of profit expectations without requiring the manager to wait and see what the profit is

</td></tr>
</table>

---

[10]F. Nelson Ford, David A. Bradbard, William N. Ledbetter, and James F. Cox, "The Use of Operations Research in Production Management," *Production and Inventory Management*, 28, no. 3 (1987): 59–62.

after actually producing and selling a certain number of units. In addition, models have the advantage of reducing the risk associated with the real situation. In particular, bad designs or bad decisions that cause the model airplane to crash or a mathematical model to project a $10,000 loss can be avoided in the real situation.

The accuracy of the conclusions and decisions based on a model are dependent upon how well the model represents the real situation. The more closely the model of the airplane represents the real airplane, the more accurate the conclusions and predictions about the airplane's flight characteristics will be. Similarly, the closer the mathematical model represents the company's true profit-volume relationship, the more accurate the profit projections will be.

Data preparation is an important step in applying management science. In using break-even analysis, for instance, we need to know the price per unit, variable cost per unit, and fixed costs. These are the constants in our problem definition. In many cases, data can be obtained from company records, accounting personnel, and so on. A good computerized information system often assists a manager in obtaining the data necessary to solve a decision problem. In other cases, data may have to be collected by time-study observation or a statistical sampling procedure. Data preparation is often a costly and time-consuming part of the decision process.

Once the model development and data preparation steps have been completed, the model can be solved. In this step, the analyst attempts to identify the values of the decision variables that provide the "best" output for the model. The specific decision-variable value or values providing the best output are referred to as the *optimal solution* for the model. Rarely can this solution be found without the aid of a computer. However, throughout this book we use simple examples to illustrate the essential concepts. You should be aware that real models are usually much larger and complex than the examples we present.

It is important to realize that model development and model solution are not completely separable. While an analyst wants to develop an accurate model or representation of the actual problem situation, the analyst also wants to be able to find a solution to the problem. If we approach the model development step by attempting to find the most accurate and realistic mathematical model, we may find the model so large and complex that it is impossible to obtain a solution. In this case, a simpler and perhaps more easily understood model with a readily available solution procedure is preferred, even if the recommended solution is only a rough approximation of the best decision. As you learn more about the quantitative solution procedures available, you will have a better idea of the types of mathematical models that can be developed and solved.

After a model solution has been obtained, both the quantitative analyst and the manager will be interested in determining how good the solution really is. While the analyst has undoubtedly taken many precautions to develop a realistic model, often the goodness or accuracy of the model cannot be assessed until model solutions are generated. Model testing and validation are frequently conducted with relatively small "test" problems that have known or at least expected solutions. If the model generates the expected solutions and if other output information appears correct, the go-ahead may be given to the use of the model on the full-scale problem. However, if the model test and validation identifies potential problems or inaccuracies inherent in the model, corrective action such as model modification and/or collection of more accurate input data may be taken. Whatever the corrective action, the model solution will not be used in practice until the model has satisfactorily passed testing and validation.

| EXAMPLE | COMPUTING THE BREAK-EVEN POINT FOR A PRODUCT

Eberle Electronics is considering expanding its production facility to manufacture an electrical component. David Rogers, an operations manager, has been asked to determine how many units must be produced and sold in order to break even. The cost for new equipment and installation is $100,000. Each unit produced has a variable cost of $12 per unit and sells for $20.

The equation for total cost is

$$\text{Total cost} = \text{fixed cost} + \text{variable cost}$$

The fixed cost is that portion of total cost not depending on the amount produced. If 1000 units are produced and sold, the total cost is

$$\begin{aligned} \text{Total cost} &= 100,000 + 12(1000) \\ &= \$112,000 \end{aligned}$$

The revenue received from selling 1000 units is $20(1000) = \$20,000$, so at this production level, the firm would incur a loss of $112,000 - \$20,000 = \$92,000$. However, if 20,000 units are produced and sold, the projected profit is

$$20(20,000) - 100,000 - 12(20,000) = \$60,000$$

The amount of sales at which the net profit is zero—or equivalently, when total cost equals total revenue—is called the **break-even point**.

We can find the break-even point by letting x be the sales volume at the break-even point and setting the total revenue equal to total cost. For this example,

$$\begin{aligned} \text{Total cost} &= 100,000 + 12x \\ \text{Total revenue} &= 20x \end{aligned}$$

Thus

$$20x = 100,000 + 12x$$

and hence

$$x = 12,500$$

If sales are less than 12,500 units, the firm will incur a loss; if sales are more than 12,500, then a profit will be realized. This is illustrated in Figure 1.4. This information, when combined with sales forecasts, can assist the manager in deciding whether or not to pursue the expansion.

| EXAMPLE | BREAK-EVEN ANALYSIS FOR CHOOSING BETWEEN TWO PRODUCTION METHODS

Phelps Petroleum Co. must decide between two methods of processing oil at a refinery. Method 1 has fixed costs of $9000 for depreciation, maintenance, and taxes, whereas the fixed costs for method 2 are $11,000. The variable costs depend on the chemical additives used and the heating requirements. These are $.015 and $.010 per barrel, for methods 1 and 2, respectively. Which method is more economical?

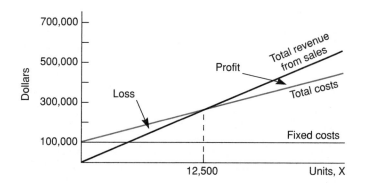

FIGURE 1.4

Break-even
Analysis for
Facility
Expansion
Example

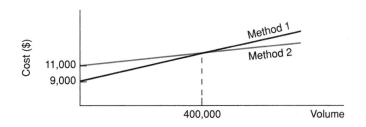

FIGURE 1.5

Break-even
Analysis for Oil
Processing
Alternatives

The break-even point at which both processes are equally preferred is found by setting the total cost of each alternative equal to each other. Let x = number of barrels produced. Thus, we have

$$\text{Total cost for method 1} = \text{total cost for method 2}$$
$$9000 + .015x = 11{,}000 + .010x$$

Solving for x, we get

$$.005x = 2000$$
$$x = 400{,}000 \text{ barrels}$$

Figure 1.5 illustrates the break-even point. We see that if the volume processed is larger than 400,000 barrels, the second method is more economical.

This form of break-even analysis serves to simplify decision-making, especially for repeated decisions such as the case of deciding which machine tool to use for an order.

Since management science is a relatively new discipline, it has not yet been fully integrated into managerial decision making in all levels and all organizations. Many companies cannot afford to maintain a professional staff of management scientists or hire consultants whenever a potential project arises. In many companies, industrial engineers, market research analysts, and other personnel trained in management science perform quantitative analyses. Thus there have been numerous successful applications of management science, particularly at the operational level. Many of the examples presented in this book are typical of ongoing projects in the P/OM area. With the growing use and declining cost of computers and microprocessors, the interest and use of management science in P/OM is continually growing.

Management
Science: Success
and Failure

However, we are not claiming that management science is a magic cure for P/OM problems. There are many reasons why quantitative methods "fail" or are not accepted by managers. Some of the more common reasons include the following:

- *Expectations of the manager and analyst.* Managers may expect the mathematical techniques to provide answers beyond which the method is capable of providing. Also, management scientists may develop models that are too complex to be understood or used correctly by the manager.
- *Limitations of model building.* Many useful models in management science can deal with only a single objective. Decision problems in operations management usually have multiple, conflicting objectives. Many models cannot capture this realism.
- *Time constraints.* Models often require substantial data preparation. There may simply not be enough time to obtain a solution in time for a manager to use it.
- *Dynamic environment.* The operations manager lives in a changing, dynamic world. The solution to a model often solves only a static problem; if not carefully implemented, poor results may occur as conditions change.
- *Resistance to change.* Many traditional managers are reluctant to accept solutions that are provided by mathematical methods and computers. Although this attitude is changing, such skepticism still exists.
- *Preconceived solutions.* Managers may already have preferred alternatives prior to any analysis, quantitative or otherwise. Even though the results of a model may indicate an improved solution, it may be rejected.

Throughout the entire decision-making process, managers and management scientists must work closely together in order to overcome these types of problems.

P/OM IN
PRACTICE

At the end of each chapter, we will include a section entitled "P/OM in Practice" which is designed to present case studies of how operations management principles have been skillfully applied to real problems. These provide valuable insight into the nature of P/OM. As you read these cases, you should consider the technical details of the methods as well as *why* the organization used them and *how* they were implemented. Several questions follow each case to stimulate thought and discussion. The first P/OM in Practice describes the hierarchical nature of planning at International Paper Company. In the second case, we show how operations management activities can improve hospital emergency room services.

HIERARCHICAL PLANNING AT INTERNATIONAL PAPER[11]

I nternational Paper Company (IPCo.) is the world's largest manufacturer of pulp, paper, and paper products and a major producer of lumber and plywood. The company owns over 8.4 million acres

---

[11]Based in part on Paul S. Bender, William D. Northup, and Jeremy F. Shapiro, "Practical Modeling for Resource Management" *Harvard Business Review,* March–April 1981; Copyright © 1981 by

of timberland and has rights over another 11.6 million acres. IPCo. operates an extensive manufacturing system, consisting of two dozen paper mills and more than 100 plants located throughout the world.

Most of IPCo.'s products are commodity items, where price is determined by the market. Thus IPCo.'s relative profitability is chiefly a function of its manufacturing efficiency. In order to keep its mills and plants competitive, the company emphasizes process controls, technological innovation, improvements in operating strategies, research and development in tree genetics and environmental protection, and investments in energy efficiency. Some of the typical problems IPCo. has faced include the following:

- Senior management wishes to develop a long-range plan to meet expected changes in demand for the company's products. Part of the plan involves investing in production capacity for a new product line; management must know whether a new mill should be built and, if so, where and what its capacity should be.
- Shifting product-demand patterns alter demands on the company's woodlands and other primary resource bases. Management needs to know if it should plan to meet changed resource needs through outside purchasing or whether it should begin to invest in new lands and forestation programs to meet anticipated needs. The decision has long-term implications because the trees take a quarter of a century or more to grow.
- The budgets and accounting operations groups must set the annual production standards for the mills in all divisions; the group must also determine a schedule of prices to regulate the transfer of intermediate and final goods within the company. These standards must account for differences in production cost and efficiency among the mills, as well as for varying demand patterns in the markets that the mills serve. On the other hand, the group must try to maximize the overall profit of the company.
- A divisional operations control manager plans the monthly allocation of orders to the mills and machines under the manager's control. This allocation must hold production and distribution costs to a minimum, but at the same time it must come reasonably close to meeting promised delivery dates. The computerized order-processing system that the company and its competitors use has raised customers' expectations for prompt, efficient service. The manager must take into account production efficiencies that vary widely from mill to mill and, within each mill, from product to product. Capacity is already strained at the most efficient mills and, to make matters worse, the costs of energy and warehousing have been changing rapidly. The assignment that would have been optimal only a few months ago no longer looks so good.

To solve problems of this nature effectively, IPCo. organized a resource-allocation systems group to create planning and decision-making tools for efficient resource management. The system developed by this group divides the company's planning problems into strategic, tactical, and operational classes.

The use of the strategic-level planning system begins with long-term projections of demand, costs, supply constraints, capacity restrictions, and other major factors that relate to the company's overall goals and objectives. The results of strategic planning for IPCo. indicate optimal marketing, production, and financial strategies, which are then translated into specific plans for land, facilities, equipment, and materials.

The IPCo. planning system has had more frequent and consistent use at the tactical level, where the planning horizon is on the order of several months to a year. The company uses the tactical planning system on a regular basis to determine yearly profit targets for each business unit as a function of projected demand for various products. The major features of the resulting plans consist of subplans for procurement, production, maintenance, and transportation.

At the operational level, the planning system is used to allocate customer orders to paper mills in order to meet new demands and backorders on a monthly basis. This information is extremely useful in identifying the most profitable marginal business for the company. This hierarchy of IPCo.'s planning effort is summarized in Figure 1.6.

the President and Fellows of Harvard College; all rights reserved. Reprinted with permission of the *Harvard Business Review*. International Paper Co. Annual Report, 1980.

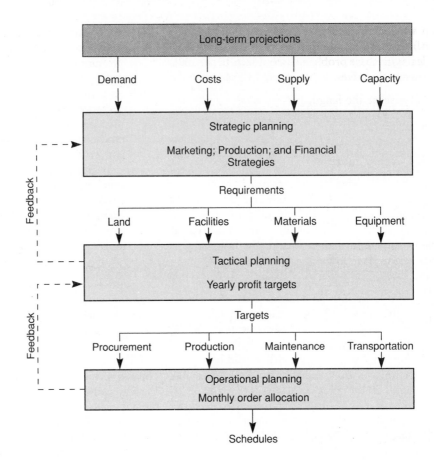

FIGURE 1.6
International Paper Hierarchical Planning System

Long-term projections

Demand   Costs   Supply   Capacity

Strategic planning

Marketing; Production; and Financial Strategies

Feedback

Requirements

Land   Facilities   Materials   Equipment

Tactical planning

Yearly profit targets

Feedback

Targets

Procurement   Production   Maintenance   Transportation

Operational planning

Monthly order allocation

Schedules

QUESTIONS

1. Discuss how the output of the strategic planning system influences the tactical planning system.
2. Given the nature of International Paper's business and the resources used in production, how far into the future do you think they look in doing strategic planning? Why?
3. If you were the divisional operations control manager, in what ways could you increase productivity? Where do you think the biggest potential for savings would be? Would you have more capability to enhance revenues or cut costs? Why?

AN OPERATIONS MANAGEMENT STUDY OF A HOSPITAL EMERGENCY ROOM[12]

I n 1977 the Cottonwood Hospital in Murray, Utah, was treating 40,000 emergency patients per year in a relatively new facility, but was having difficulty treating patients at peak times. In addition, there appeared to be problems regarding information flow and facility design. (The outpatient registration clerk was operating out of a corner in a corridor because the outpatient admissions func-

[12]Adapted from Paul O. Allen and Sidney G. Garrett, "The Emergency Room as a System." Reprinted with permission from *Industrial Engineering* magazine, June 1977. Copyright © Institute of Industrial Engineers, Inc., 25 Technology Park/Atlanta, Norcross, GA 30092.

tion was overlooked in a previous facility expansion!) The hospital administrator authorized a study to deal with these problems in an effort to meet the following objectives:

1. Decrease the length of time a patient spends in the emergency department.
2. Distribute clerical workloads more evenly.
3. Reduce the amount of paperwork.
4. Develop more efficient use of computer applications.
5. Improve communications between departments.
6. Provide a more realistic staffing pattern.
7. Improve patient-hospital relations.

One of the goals of the emergency outpatient operation is to have low patient-waiting times, while at the same time providing steady work flows to doctors, nurses, and ancillary departments. Inefficient paperwork-processing procedures, complex billing procedures, poor staffing patterns, and poor scheduling of patients were determined to be among the factors preventing this goal from being met.

As a result of the study, a number of recommendations were implemented. First, a new layout of clerks, nurses' stations, and waiting areas was designed. This helped to eliminate patient traffic congestion, improved the organization, and simplified admitting procedures. Next, a study of forms used suggested a reduction from six copies to a single form. This alone provided an annual savings of $4000. Third, an analysis of staffing patterns and workloads was conducted, which resulted in changes in work schedules for nurses. This resulted in better service and reduced waiting times.

The job duties of clerks were examined and several jobs were redesigned. This led to job-enrichment benefits, since several jobs became more challenging, and also improved the flow and control of paperwork. Overall, personnel costs were reduced, forms and paperwork were simplified, and revenue was increased through fewer lost charges. The hospital estimated a savings-to-cost ratio for this study of 25 to 1. In addition, increased cooperation between physicians, nurses, and the administration and business office has improved communication throughout the hospital.

From a P/OM perspective, this example shows how several operations management activities can be improved to increase productivity and quality while decreasing costs. In this example, we see that the design of facilities and efficient work procedures were principal goals for Cottonwood Hospital. However, the management of nurses and other medical personnel is just as important, since they actually provide the hospital services.

QUESTIONS

1. Process design and facility layout, job design, capacity planning, scheduling and quality control are the major functions that were addressed. Specify which activities described fall into each of these categories.
2. Discuss how job enrichment can lead to increased productivity and higher quality service.
3. Describe how you think revenue could be increased through fewer lost charges. Does this make sense?

This book is about production and operations management: the variety of activities that are necessary to support the manufacturing of goods and the delivery of services. We have discussed the general nature of these activities and how they are applicable in both manufacturing and service organizations. Because management structure is hierarchical—that is, longer-range and more-important decisions are made at higher levels of the organization—P/OM activities in both manufacturing and service organizations can be classified in this way also. This hierarchical classification provides the structure for this book.

We discussed the role of management science in decision making concerning operations. Two worked-out example problems involving break-even analysis illustrated how mathematical models can assist the operations manager. Two P/OM in Practice cases illustrated how operations management is applied effectively in practice.

SUMMARY

Operations	Operational planning and decision
Production	making
Production/Operations	Production system
Management (P/OM)	Conversion process
Planning	Feedback
Organizing	Management Science/Operations
Directing	Research (MS/OR)
Controlling	Model
Hierarchical classification	Iconic model
Strategic planning and decision	Analog model
making	Mathematical model
Tactical planning and decision	Break-even point
making	

1. Define the term *production*.

2. To which activities does the term *operations* refer? Briefly explain each of these activities, and provide an example of a real company for each.

3. Discuss some of the problems that point to the decline of the competitiveness of U.S. manufacturing firms. Find a recent newspaper or magazine article that further discusses this issue.

4. Briefly trace the history of P/OM and discuss its primary emphasis during each of the last three decades.

5. What are the major components of a production system? Give an example of each.

6. Provide three different examples of manufacturing systems in the same fashion as in Table 1.2.

7. Provide three different examples of service systems in the same fashion as in Table 1.3.

8. A three-way classification of organizations could be: manufactured product versus service, profit versus nonprofit; public versus private. For each of the following organizations, list the categories to which they correspond:
   - a. Water works
   - b. Bank
   - c. Library
   - d. Post office
   - e. Local bar
   - f. Bakery
   - g. Blood bank
   - h. State license plate production
   - i. Church
   - j. Drugstore
   - k. School
   - l. Federal reserve

9. How do service organizations differ from manufacturing organizations? Discuss the principal differences.

10. Explain the role of feedback in service industries, such as fire departments, state legislatures, post offices, charities, and ambulance services.

11. Discuss the major environmental influences on the production system. Which are external and which are internal to the firm?

12. Describe the role of operations managers in P/OM.

13. List at least five activities that each of the following managers would perform regarding the management of people and the management of work.
    a. Plant manager of an automobile assembly plant
    b. Manager of a hamburger franchise
    c. Head chef
    d. Branch manager of a local bank
    e. Warehouse manager

14. Explain the hierarchical classification of planning and decision making.

15. Would the following decisions be classified as strategic, tactical, or operational?
    a. Adding more grocery clerks to checkout counters when lines become long.
    b. Deciding to install a drive-through window in a fast-food restaurant.
    c. Scheduling X-ray equipment for the next day.
    d. Leasing 100,000 square feet of warehouse space for the next month.
    e. Planning a storefront display for the Christmas holiday season.

16. Would you expect a first-line supervisor to be involved in strategic planning? If not, with what level of planning would such a person be involved and why?

17. What are the major planning and decision-making areas that involve operations managers? What important questions are addressed in each area?

18. Explain how the various functions of P/OM might apply in the following situations (in a manner similar to the Ricketts Golf Equipment and Tri-State Airways discussion).
    a. Police services
    b. Street maintenance
    c. University education

19. In terms of frequency and replication, state in which cell of Table 1.6 the following decision problems belong.
    a. The decision by a loan officer to make an automobile loan.
    b. The decision by an admissions officer whether or not a student should be admitted to college.
    c. The decision on whether or not a product should be withdrawn from the market because of consumer-safety considerations.
    d. The decision to buy a new machine to reduce per-unit production costs for a product.

20. Suppose that a manager has a choice between the following two mathematical models of a given situation: (a) a relatively simple model that is a reasonable approximation of the real situation; and (b) a thorough and complex model that is the most accurate mathematical representation of the real situation possible. Why might the model described in (a) be preferred by the manager?

21. A director of material management for a large manufacturing company made the following statement: *All significant problems impacting manufacturing effectiveness really result from one very common problem—incomplete and inaccurate planning, monitoring, and controlling regarding all aspects and phases of the business and manufacturing operations.*
    Do you agree or disagree with this statement? Explain.

1. Clifton Electrical Equipment, Inc. is considering manufacturing electrical switches. Preliminary cost estimates are shown below.

Fixed Costs:	$10,000.00 per year
Unit revenue:	$0.45 per switch
Direct material:	$0.15 per switch
Direct labor:	$0.10 per switch
Overhead:	$0.05 per switch

   a. What is the break-even volume?
   b. If the fixed costs and direct labor are both underestimatd by 10 percent, what is the break-even volume?

2. For a newly designed product, there are two possible technological processes that can be used. The first process has a fixed cost of $6000 and a unit variable cost of $0.85. The second method has a fixed cost of $125,000 and unit variable cost of $0.65. The selling price is proposed to be $1.25 per unit. Under what levels of demand is each process more economical?

3. A nonprofit organization receives a subsidy of $100,000 per year from the city. The unit revenue for the services it provides is $0.75. The unit variable cost is $1.00 and the anual fixed costs are $50,000.
   a. Up to what level will the operations be economical? Use break-even analysis.
   b. If the city is willing to increase its subsidy by another 25 percent, how much additional service can the organization provide if unit revenue is lowered to $0.65?

4. Generally, higher product prices result in a decreased demand, whereas lower product prices result in an increased demand. Letting

$$D = \text{annual demand for a product in units}$$
$$p = \text{price per unit}$$

   assume a firm accepts the following price-demand relationship as being realistic

$$D = 1000 - 20p$$

   where the price (p) must be between $15 and $40.
   a. How many units can the firm sell at the $15 per unit price? At the $40 per unit price?
   b. Show the mathematical model for the total revenue (TR), which is the annual demand multiplied by the unit price.
   c. Based on other considerations, the firm's management will consider only the price alternatives of $20, $25, and $30. Use your model from part (b) to determine the price alternative that will maximize the TR.
   d. What is the expected annual demand and TR using your recommended price?

5. A firm is considering expanding its production operation so that it may introduce a new product into the market. The estimated cost for equipment purchases and installation is $100,000. This $100,000 will be incurred by the company as a "one-time" start-up cost. The variable cost for each unit produced is $12.
   a. Letting x indicate the number of units produced, develop a total cost model.
   b. If the product sells for $20 per unit, develop a total profit model expressed in terms of x, the number of units produced.
   c. If the sales forecast is 10,000 units of the new product, should the firm proceed with the production expansion project?

Productivity and Quality

T he primary objective of an operations manager is to improve operations. This might be accomplished by reducing costs and/or by increasing the quantity and quality of output. For profit-seeking enterprises, such improvements can be translated into increased profitability. For nonprofit organizations, improved operations can be translated into better service and increased customer satisfaction. Although profitability of the firm and customer satisfaction are the ultimate measures of organizational effectiveness, it is not always possible for operations managers to relate decisions directly to these measures.

In this chapter, we focus on two commonly used measures of operations effectiveness: *productivity* and *quality*. Every decision that an operations manager makes, from strategic decisions such as process selection to operational decisions involving shop floor scheduling, has an impact on productivity and quality. Thus, measures of productivity and quality provide a basis for evaluating the effectiveness of operations.

2.1 THE IMPORTANCE OF PRODUCTIVITY AND QUALITY

Historically, American business and industry has focused on increasing output and short-term profits. However, lower cost and higher quality competition from Japan and Europe in many industries has caused U.S. manufacturers to re-examine their priorities. The result has been a shift in focus from maximizing output and short-term profits to increasing productivity and improving quality.

Productivity

Productivity measures to what extent the resources of an organization are being used effectively in transforming inputs to outputs. In other words, productivity is a measure of how well the resources of a firm are used in producing goods and services.

In recent years, productivity has been one of the issues receiving significant attention both within individual organizations and on a national level. Within organizations, productivity concerns have been a leading factor in the increased interest in operations management. National concern about productivity was brought about by the decline in international competitiveness of the United States. Over the period from 1967 to 1974, Japan increased its productivity by 99.6 percent, whereas the United States increased its productivity by only 29.25 percent. In fact, during the 1980s, U.S. productivity declined to the point where our rate of improvement in productivity lagged behind nearly every other industrial nation.

The rate of growth in productivity determines a nation's economic progress. One can argue that the declining competitiveness of the United States can be attributed to the fact that manufacturing productivity has been growing more slowly than its competitors. A low rate of productivity growth spawns a vicious cycle. Fewer units produced leads to higher unit costs for labor, machinery, and energy. These higher unit costs lead to higher prices for goods and services which, in turn, lead to declines in sales volume. Lower sales volumes result in decreased revenues, leading to idle plant capacity, lower employment, and reduced spending on research and development. These reductions in turn cause further declines in productivity, higher costs, increased unemployment, and a decline in the standard of living. Clearly, any nation that wants to remain competitive in an international marketplace cannot allow this situation to occur.

The American Society for Quality Control (ASQC) defines **quality** as "the totality of features and characteristics of a product or service that bears on its ability to satisfy given needs." Quality measures how well a product or service meets customer needs. Similar to productivity, quality has assumed increased importance in recent years.

Although many people associate higher quality with higher prices, this is not always the case. Sears, Roebuck & Co., for instance, has become one of the world's largest retailers by selling quality products at reasonable prices. Similarly, the quality of food and service at many inexpensive restaurants is outstanding.

American consumers in the 1950s and 1960s associated the slogan "Made in Japan" with inferior products. Since the 1970s however, the quality of many American goods has fallen below that of its competitors. For example, a study of the room air conditioning industry showed that the average number of assembly line defects per 100 units manufactured was 63.5 for units produced in the United States versus 0.95 for units produced in Japan. In addition, the U.S. units required an average of 10.5 service calls per 100 units during the first year of warranty while the Japanese units averaged only 0.6 service calls per 100 units.[1] In a 1987 report on automobile quality, *Business Week* observed that the average number of problems reported per 100 cars in the first 60 to 90 days of ownership was between 162 and 180 for automobiles manufactured in the United States. Comparable figures for Japanese and German automobiles were 129 and 152, respectively.[2]

This increase in the quality of foreign products has led consumers to examine their purchasing decisions more carefully. Consumers demand high quality and reliability in goods and services at a fair price. They demand that products function properly and not break or fail under reasonable use, and courts of law have supported this viewpoint. This increased focus on consumerism, strengthened by the activities of Ralph Nader and other consumer-interest groups, has affected the operations of nearly every manufacturing and service organization. This change in consumer behavior especially affects today's technology-oriented businesses, since the more technologically complex a product is, the more opportunity for something to go wrong.

Government safety regulations, product recalls, and the rapid increase in product-liability judgments have changed society's attitude from "let the buyer beware" to "let the producer beware." Business and industry have realized that quality is vital to survival.

---

[1]David A. Garvin, "Quality on the Line," *Harvard Business Review*, September/October 1983, 66–75. Copyright © 1983 by the President and Fellows of Harvard College; all rights reserved.
[2]"The Push for Quality," *Business Week*, 8 June 1987, 131.

The results of a 1987 Gallup survey of top executives showed that executives viewed the task of improving service quality and product quality as the most critical challenge facing companies over the next few years. These executives ranked quality improvement ahead of such issues as productivity, product liability, government regulations, and labor relations. The survey recognized that quality is a major weapon that could be used to restore the United States' competitive position in world markets. Most experts feel that quality has been the dominant factor in the success of the Japanese in world markets. Many U.S. companies agree and have incorporated quality into their strategic planning.

Domestic auto makers are working hard to improve quality. Efforts by Ford, Chrysler, and General Motors at retooling their manufacturing operations, developing new product designs, and devising new promotional campaigns revolve around quality. For example, the "Ford Motor Company Operating Philosophy" is stated simply:

> The operating philosophy of Ford Motor Company is to meet customer needs and expectations by establishing and maintaining an environment which encourages all employees to pursue never-ending improvement in the quality and productivity of products and services throughout the corporation, its supply base and its dealer organizations.

Traditional manufacturing approaches to quality control have been found to be less than satisfactory and are being replaced by improved managerial tools and techniques. Even nonprofit institutions such as hospitals and schools are looking more closely at quality issues. Many organizations are also beginning to feel an increased moral responsibility for product safety and for the efficient use of natural resources. Ironically, it was two U.S. consultants, Drs. W. Edwards Deming and Joseph Juran, who helped educate the Japanese in quality management. Today, U.S. firms are relearning these lessons from Japan.

Poor quality, like poor productivity, decreases the effectiveness of an organization. Poor quality results in additional labor hours needed for rework and often results in material waste. The consequences of these inefficiencies are decreases in productivity, revenue, and profits. Poor productivity, in turn, causes more bottlenecks in processing operations, shipping delays, lower employee morale, increased inspection cost, and low customer satisfaction. In the end, poor quality generally leads to a declining market share.

Quality has been recognized as an issue of national importance. In this regard, the 1983 White House Conference on Productivity, held in Washington, D.C., resulted in 66 recommendations including the following:

- Product and service quality should be targeted as a principal objective of the organization.
- Quality should be integrated into the production and service processes rather than treating it as a separate management or inspection system.
- "Doing it right the first time" should be made a principle of management.
- Quality output should be the standard for evaluating all employees (including managers), and not just volume throughput.
- Quality improvement should be measured and rewarded at all levels of the organization.
- Companies should work with educational institutions to reestablish the concept and importance of quality and productivity among students who will be America's future employees and employers.

Since 1984, October has been designated as National Quality Month in both the United States and Canada. Other nations, such as Great Britain, have also made quality improvement a national goal.

2.2 PRODUCTIVITY MEASUREMENT

In the early 1900s, Frederick W. Taylor and Frank and Lillian Gilbreth studied work methods in order to improve the efficiency of workers. In their studies, efficiency was measured as a ratio of the actual time to perform a task to some predetermined "standard" time. For instance, if a worker was expected to produce 100 units in 8 hours but only produced 96 units, the worker's efficiency was said to be 96 percent.

Historically, the term *efficiency* is derived from concepts of mechanical efficiency. For instance, if a machine can convert 90 percent of its input energy into useful work, then it is said to be 90 percent efficient. Productivity has often been confused with efficiency; however, people now realize that doing unnecessary work efficiently is not productive. Productivity has now taken on the interpretation of effectiveness—"doing the right things efficiently," which is outcome, not output oriented.

Formally we define productivity as the ratio of output of a production process to the input. That is,

$$\text{productivity} = \frac{\text{output}}{\text{input}} \tag{2.1}$$

As output increases for a constant level of input, or as the amount of input decreases for a constant level of output, productivity increases. Thus, a productivity measure describes how well the resources of an organization are being used to produce output.

The way in which output and input are measured can provide very different measures of productivity. Productivity is usually expressed in one of three forms: total productivity, multifactor productivity, and partial factor productivity.

Total productivity measures the ratio of total output to total input.

$$\text{Total productivity} = \frac{\text{total output}}{\text{total input}} \tag{2.2}$$

Total input consists of all resources used in the production of goods and services; for example, total input includes labor, capital, raw materials, and energy. These resources are often converted to dollars so that a single figure can be used as an aggregate measure of total input. Examples of total productivity ratios are tons of steel produced per dollar of input or dollar value of wheat produced per dollar of input. The resources making up total output must be measured in the same units and the resources making up total input must be measured using the same units. However, the total output and total input need not be expressed in the same unit of measurement. For example, total output could be measured in terms of the number of units produced and total input could be measured in dollars.

Total productivity ratios reflect *simultaneous* changes in inputs and outputs. As such, they provide the most inclusive type of index for measuring productivity. However, total productivity ratios do not show the interaction between each

TABLE 2.1 Examples of Partial Productivity Measures

Labor Productivity	Machine Productivity	Capital Productivity	Energy Productivity
Units of output per labor-hour	Units of output per machine-hour	Units of output per dollar input	Units of output per kilowatt-hour
Value added per labor-hour	Tons of output per machine-hour	Dollar output per dollar input	Units of output per energy cost
Dollar output per labor-hour		Inventory turnover ratio (dollar sales per dollar inventory)	Production value per barrel of fuel
Production value per labor-dollar			
Shipments per labor cost			

input and output separately and thus are too broad to be used as a tool for improving specific areas of operations.

Multifactor productivity is the ratio of total output to a subset of inputs.

$$\text{Multifactor productivity} = \frac{\text{total output}}{\text{subset of inputs}} \qquad (2.3)$$

For example, a subset of inputs might consist of only labor and materials, or only labor and capital. The use of a multifactor measure as an index of productivity, however, may ignore important inputs and thus may not accurately reflect overall productivity.

Finally, **partial factor productivity** measures the ratio of total output to a single input.

$$\text{Partial factor productivity} = \frac{\text{total output}}{\text{single input}} \qquad (2.4)$$

The U.S. Government Bureau of Labor Statistics uses "total economic output per total worker-hours expended" as a measure of national productivity; in doing so, the bureau is computing a partial factor productivity measure.

Operations managers generally utilize partial productivity measures—particularly labor-based measures—because the data is more readily available. In addition, since total or multifactor measures provide an aggregate view, partial factor productivity measures are easier to relate to specific processes. However, labor-based measures are affected by the fact that mechanization and automation are not included in the input; thus, when mechanization replaces labor, the risk of misinterpretation exists.

Table 2.1 shows several other examples of commonly used partial productivity measures. These measures can be used in both manufacturing and service organizations. For example, "units of output per labor hour" might represent the number of radios produced per labor hour in a factory or the number of transactions per teller hour in a bank.

EXAMPLE COMPUTING PRODUCTIVITY MEASURES

A division of Miller Chemicals produces water purification crystals for swimming pools. The major inputs used in the production process are labor, raw materials, and energy. The table below shows the amount of output produced and input used for 1988 and 1989.

	1988	1989
Output		
Pounds of crystals	100,000	150,000
Input		
Direct labor hours	20,000	28,000
Direct labor cost	$180,000	$350,000
Energy used	350,000 kWh	400,000 kWh
Energy cost	$ 5,000	$ 6,000
Raw materials used (lb)	120,000	185,000
Raw material cost	$ 30,000	$ 40,000

By dividing the pounds of crystals produced by each input individually, we obtain the following partial productivity measures:

Productivity measure	1988	1989
Output/direct labor-hour	5.000	5.357
Output/direct labor-dollar	.556	.429
Output/kilowatt-hour	.286	.375
Output/energy-dollar	20.000	25.000
Output/pound of raw material	.833	.811
Output/raw material-dollar	3.333	3.750

An example of a multifactor productivity measure would be output per nonlabor dollar. In this example, we would have

1988,

$$\frac{100,000}{\$5,000 + \$30,000} = 2.857 \text{ lb/non-labor dollar}$$

1989,

$$\frac{150,000}{\$6,000 + \$40,000} = 3.261 \text{ lb/non-labor dollar}$$

Thus we see that the output per non-labor dollar was higher in 1989. A total productivity measure can be computed by dividing the total output by the total cost. For 1988, we have

$$\text{Total productivity} = \frac{100,000}{\$20,000 + \$5,000 + \$30,000} = 1.818 \text{ lb/dollar}$$

For 1989 we have

$$\text{Total productivity} = \frac{150,000}{\$28,000 + \$6,000 + \$40,000} = 2.027 \text{ lb/dollar}$$

Productivity in Service Organizations

Many employees in service organizations perform the same tasks as employees in manufacturing organizations. For instance, in many manufacturing firms, employees work on an assembly line; the counterpart in a service organization would be workers who provide services by performing tasks in mail rooms, cafeterias, insurance offices, and so on. Industrial workers may drive lift trucks throughout a manufacturing plant, whereas workers providing services may drive delivery or waste removal vehicles. In both manufacturing and service organizations, productivity is an important issue.

In service organizations, productivity measures such as the number of insurance claims processed per day, the number of letters sorted per hour, the number of miles of roads treated with salt per hour, and so on, can be developed in the same way that their counterparts can be developed in manufacturing organizations.

In other cases, employees in a service organization are knowledge workers who provide consulting, legal services, or health care. In these cases, productivity is more difficult to understand and to measure. In manufacturing organizations, the physical inputs and outputs are easy to identify, and the value of the outputs is easy to measure. With knowledge-based services, the inputs and outputs are often intangible and, as a result, are difficult to measure.

Productivity measures in service organizations, particularly nonprofit organizations, are often stated as **benefit/cost ratios**. For example, consider a transportation agency that promotes carpooling, van-pooling, and other forms of shared rides. To assess the productivity of such a service function, we might use productivity measures such as

$$\frac{\text{Annual reduction in passenger miles}}{\text{Annual program costs}}$$

or

$$\frac{\text{Annual gallons of gasoline saved}}{\text{Annual program costs}}$$

Often, however, it is difficult to define benefits and to develop ways of measuring them. Nevertheless, there are a wealth of opportunities for applying the principles of operations management to improve productivity in health organizations, food services, criminal justice, the travel and leisure industry, and other service organizations.

The problems of productivity measurement are compounded by the job characteristics in service organizations. They are further compounded by the fact that the work performed is often more costly; technology oftentimes has not had a large impact on efficiency; the work is difficult to define and describe; service employees are not used to thinking in terms of costs and benefits; and the employees are generally resistant to change.

Productivity Indicators

In some service organizations it is difficult to measure output because no tangible goods are produced. In such cases, **productivity indicators** such as

$$\frac{\text{Lost sales dollars}}{\text{Number of customer complaints}}$$

and

$$\frac{\text{Number of employees}}{\text{Number of customers served}}$$

are useful. Although these ratios are not output/input measures per se, they can assist managers in tracking productivity.

White-collar workers represent the fastest growing segment of the work force. A study by the management consulting firm of Theodore Barry and Associates found that the average white-collar worker is almost 10 percent less productive than the typical blue-collar worker.[3] The study discovered that the major problems causing this low rate of productivity were the absence of adequate management supervision, poor coordination among functional areas of business, and the lack of precise objectives in the organizations. White-collar work represents an important area for productivity improvement, but unfortunately, one of the least understood.

White Collar
Productivity

Productivity is more difficult to measure for white-collar jobs, yet some companies, such as IBM, have developed useful measurement systems.[4] IBM has divided service work into about 130 different logical elements. For each of these elements, they measure head count against a base. For instance, they measure the number of secretaries against the base of the number of salaried exempt employees and janitors against a base of the square footage of the office area that is serviced. These ratios are plotted for each of the 130 factors. Each manager can compare his or her own performance on each factor for current and past years and relative to others in the organization. The system has stimulated a significant amount of improvement in white-collar productivity.

2.3 USING PRODUCTIVITY MEASURES

Productivity measures are used in a variety of ways.

1. Productivity measures can be used to compare the overall performance of the firm with competitors or similar firms.
2. Productivity measures enable mangement to control the performance of the firm by controlling the performance of individual sectors of the firm, either by function or product.
3. Productivity measures can be used to compare the relative benefits accruing from the use of differing inputs, or varying proportions of the same inputs.
4. Productivity measures can be used for internal management purposes, such as collective bargaining with unions.[5]

---

[3]"Study Explores Declining Productivity of White Collar Workers," *Industrial Engineering*, 13, no. 10 (October 1981): 4.

[4]D. C. Burnham, "Productivity: An Overview," in Gavriel Salvendy, ed., *Handbook of Industrial Engineering*, New York: John Wiley & Sons, 1982.

[5]J. Teague and S. Eilon, "Productivity Measurement: A Brief Survey," Imperial College of Science and Technology, London, 1973.

Productivity measures provide the operations manager with an indication of how to improve productivity: either increase the numerator of the productivity measure, decrease the denominator, or both. For example, consider the labor productivity measure given by the number of units produced per labor-hour. If, for a fixed number of labor hours, the output can be increased, or if, for a fixed number of units of output, labor can be reduced, then productivity will be improved. This might be accomplished through increased automation, improving employee motivation, new work methods, or wage-incentive programs.

Within a single time period, productivity measures can be used to compare similar operations within the same firm, or to compare the firm's performance with industry-wide data, and/or to compare similar firms. For example, a chain of fried chicken restaurants can use productivity data to compare different franchises, and/or to compare its productivity with that of competitors.

Productivity Indexes

Since productivity is a relative measure, it must be *compared* to something in order to be meaningful. The numerical values of productivity measures do not provide useful information by themselves; comparative values across time or similar businesses do. For individual firms, comparisons are usually made using historical productivity data; historical productivity data permits a firm to observe how its performance changes over time. The use of historical data also permits management to measure the impact of certain decisions, such as the introduction of new processes, equipment, worker motivation techniques, and so forth.

Productivity indexes are measures used to assist managers in comparing productivity measured in some base year to productivity measured at the current time. A productivity index is simply the ratio of a productivity measure in some time period to the base period. For instance, if the base-period productivity is computed to be 1.25 and the next period's productivity is 1.18, the ratio 1.18/1.25 = .944 indicates that productivity has decreased to 94.4% of the base period value. By tracking such indices over time, managers can evaluate the success (or lack of success) of various projects and decisions.

EXAMPLE | COMPUTING PRODUCTIVITY INDEXES

Let us consider the Miller Chemicals Company example discussed in the previous section. The productivity measures that we computed for 1988 and 1989 are

Productivity measure	1988	1989
Output/direct labor hour	5.000	5.357
Output/direct labor dollar	.556	.429
Output/kilowatt hour	.286	.375
Output/energy dollar	20.000	25.000
Output/pound of raw material	.833	.811
Output/raw material dollar	3.333	3.750

If we use 1988 as a base period, we may compute a productivity index for 1989 by dividing each productivity measure for 1989 by its 1988 value. For example, the 1989 productivity index for output/direct labor hour is $5.357 \div 5.000 = 1.071$. This indicates that productivity has increased by 7.1 percent. These productivity indexes are summarized below.

Productivity measure	1988	1989	1989 Index
Output/direct labor hour	5.000	5.360	1.071
Output/direct labor dollar	.556	.429	.772
Output/kilowatt hour	.286	.375	1.311
Output/energy dollar	20.000	25.000	1.250
Output/pound of raw material	.833	.811	.974
Output/raw material dollar	3.333	3.750	1.125

How would you interpret these indexes?

Total or multifactor productivity measures are generally preferable to partial measures. The reason for this is that focusing on productivity improvement in a narrow portion of an organization may actually decrease overall productivity. This can be seen by a simple example. Suppose that productivity is measured by

$$\frac{\text{Total units produced}}{\text{Total labor cost} + \text{total equipment cost}} \qquad (2.5)$$

Let us assume that 10,000 units are being produced currently, with annual labor and equipment costs of $50,000 and $25,000, respectively. Thus using (2.5), the measure of productivity is

$$\frac{10,000}{\$50,000 + \$25,000} = .133 \text{ units of output per dollar input}$$

Labor productivity, however, is measured for this example as

$$\frac{10,000}{\$50,000} = .20 \text{ units of output per labor-dollar}$$

Suppose that a $10,000 reduction in labor can be achieved by investing in a more advanced machine. Labor productivity will increase to

$$\frac{10,000}{\$40,000} = .25 \text{ units of output per labor-dollar}$$

Thus, from a partial productivity perspective, it would appear that this investment is attractive. If, however, the annual cost with the new equipment increases to $40,000, then (2.5) would be

$$\frac{10,000}{\$40,000 + \$40,000} = .125 \text{ units of output per dollar input}$$

and hence overall productivity would actually decrease. It is necessary, therefore, to examine the simultaneous effects of all changes on productivity.

Productivity measures are statistics; as with all statistics, it is easy to misuse them or to mask information unintentionally. Consider, for example, an employee earning $18,000 per year, who produces 1000 units of output per year. A trainee of lesser skill is hired at $10,000 to assist this employee, and together they produce 1700 units per year. A partial measure of labor productivity is

$$\frac{\text{Number of units produced per year}}{\text{Labor years}} = \frac{1700}{2}$$

$$= 850 \text{ units of output per labor-year}$$

Because the current (one person) system has a labor productivity value of 1000, we conclude that productivity has decreased in terms of average output per worker. However, suppose that labor productivity is measured as number of units produced per dollar input. For the one-person system, the labor productivity is equal to

$$\frac{\text{Number of units}}{\text{Dollar input}} = \frac{1000}{\$18,000} = .056 \text{ units per labor-dollar}$$

Computing this same measure with the trainee, the labor productivity is $1700 \div \$28,000 = .061$. On this basis, hiring the trainee resulted in about a 9 percent improvement in productivity. In this situation, it is better to use the units per dollar input productivity measure since it takes into account the *relative* value of the inputs; that is, the difference in wages implies a difference in skill level. The first measure, on the other hand, implicitly assumes that each labor-year is equivalent. The point of these illustrations is that we must be very careful when using partial productivity measures.

Productivity Improvement

There are several ways in which operations managers can improve productivity. These may be classified as follows:

1. *Improving efficiency* by lowering total operating costs, generating savings in labor and machine time, and reducing waste.
2. *Improving effectiveness* by better decision making, communication, organizational design, and staffing.
3. *Achieving higher performance* by increasing quality, reducing accidents and lost time, and minimizing equipment breakdowns.
4. *Developing better organizational health* by improving morale, satisfaction, and cooperation.

Technology plays an important role in productivity improvement. **Technology** is the set of processes, tools, methods, and procedures used in the production of goods and services. **Hard technology** involves the application of computers, sensors, robots, and other mechanical and electronic aids. The use of hard technology such as robotic welding and painting, automated assembly, and computer-integrated manufacturing is revolutionizing many industries and significantly improving productivity. For example, mail-processing operations at the U.S. Postal Service have been improved through automation by employing optical character readers and bar-code sorters. The new equipment can sort letters at 10,000 letters per hour, compared to present manual and mechanized methods, which range from 900 to 1800 pieces per hour. This new automation, in conjunction with address improvement and the ZIP + 4 code, is projected to save over 19,000 work years and over $900 million annually.[6]

Soft technology refers to the application of computer software and other techniques that support managers of manufacturing and service organizations. Examples of soft technology include office-automation software such as word processing packages, database management systems, and manufacturing resource-management software. An example of the benefits of such technology occurred at the American Hospital Supply Company,[7] where computer links to customers and suppliers were set up so that hospitals could directly enter orders via computer terminals. This enabled the company to reduce inventories, improve customer service, and get better terms from suppliers for higher volumes. Even more important, it often locked out rival distributors that did not have direct pipelines to hospitals. As a result, their market share dramatically increased. Throughout this text we shall see many other examples of the use of technology in manufacturing and service organizations.

Productivity improvement also often results from behavioral changes. Emphasis on quality, workplace cleanliness, employee involvement in decision making, more responsibility for tools, and performance measurement encourage employee participation in process improvement.

Several examples of productivity improvements are cited by the consulting firm of KPMG Peat Marwick, a major public accounting and consulting firm.[8]

- A U.S. railroad company that was on the verge of bankruptcy undertook a massive and urgently needed reorganization. Over a period of three years, Peat Marwick's consulting teams suggested approaches for streamlining operations, eliminating excess inventory, and reducing manpower needs. The implementation of these productivity improvements resulted in a $111 million reduction in annual operating costs.
- A major Canadian manufacturer of wire rope products was experiencing a downward trend in profits. To help reverse this trend, the existing layout of several manufacturing facilities was analyzed and redesigned for cost effectiveness. Warehousing and distribution cost analyses also pinpointed operating weaknesses in these areas; recommendations for this problem area focused on the development of alternative supply mechanisms. Implementation of these and other recommendations dramatically repositioned the firm for improved operations and profits.
- After a corporate merger and reorganization, the productivity of a French manufacturer of machine tools dropped so much that it was unable to achieve its business plan objectives. An analysis of productivity in the assembly shop showed that a major cause of the problem was inconsistent flow of supplies. A series of improvements resulted in a 23 percent increase in productivity within three months, with 86 percent of all ordered parts arriving on time.

[6]Lane G. Camp, "IEs Evaluate Productivity Improvement Efforts in Own Organizations and Across U.S.," *Industrial Engineering,* 17, no. 1 (January 1985): 84.

[7]*Business Week,* 14 October 1985, 109.

[8]"Operations Management for Productivity and Quality: A Worldwide Challenge," KPMG Peat Marwick, 1987.

Many opportunities for productivity improvement also exist in service organizations. Improvements in the production of services are often realized as a result of reducing errors, decreasing task difficulty, improving response time, better space utilization, and improving communications. Improvements in the scheduling of police patrol units, more efficient routing of snow removal vehicles, and improvements in mail sorting as a result of using advanced technology to read ZIP codes are some examples for service organizations, these types of improvements usually involve the redesign of the service process. Throughout this book we shall see many other examples of how productivity can be improved for services.

2.4 MANAGEMENT OF QUALITY

We defined quality as "the totality of features and characteristics of a product or service that bears on its ability to satisfy given needs." The management of quality involves two types of decisions: *strategic decisions* that influence the ability to satisfy customer needs and determine the role of quality within the organization, and *operational decisions,* which define the day to day operations by which quality control is conducted. In this section we discuss the role of strategic decisions in the management of quality; in Chapter 19 we focus on the role of operational decisions.

Customer needs must be the driving force behind quality management. A quality product or service must meet customer requirements and expectations; these requirements and expectations include the following attributes:[9]

1. performance: a product's primary operating characteristics
2. features: the "bells and whistles" of the product
3. reliability: the probability of a product operating properly over a specified period of time under stated conditions of use
4. durability: the amount of use one gets from a product before it physically deteriorates or until replacement is preferable
5. serviceability: the speed, courtesy, and competence of repair
6. aesthetics: how a product looks, feels, sounds, tastes, or smells.

If a product or service meets the needs of the customer, we commonly say that it is "fit for use."

Individuals who design and develop goods and services must understand customer needs and translate these into specifications for the goods and services. For example, a firm that makes computer chips must determine what product specifications its customers require. As an illustration of what these product specifications might be, suppose that the distance between pins on a computer chip was specified to be .095 ± .005 inches. This means that the allowable

---

[9]David A. Garvin, "What Does Product Quality Really Mean?" *Sloan Management Review*, 26, no. 1, (1984): 25–43.

distance between pins must be between .090 and .100 inches in order to meet the customer requirements and expectations. As an example of specifications for a service, consider the case of an airline company attempting to design its service facilities to meet customer expectations. Suppose a survey of airline passengers has led the airline company to conclude that airline passengers should not wait more than 10 minutes before their baggage is delivered to the baggage claim area. The company could then design its baggage claim service to meet this customer expectation.

Once the product or service specifications are developed, it is up to operations managers to assure that these specifications are met during manufacturing or delivery of services. From this perspective, quality is often defined as "conformance to specifications." Figure 2.1 summarizes this simple and practical view of quality.

Quality assurance refers to the entire system of policies, procedures, and guidelines established by an organization in order to achieve and maintain quality. Quality assurance consists of two principal functions: quality engineering and quality control. The aim of **quality engineering** is to include quality in the design of products and processes and to predict potential quality problems prior to production. In subsequent chapters, we discuss several aspects of quality engineering. **Quality control** involves making a series of planned measurements in order to determine if quality standards are being met. If they are not, quality control also includes taking corrective and/or preventive action in order to achieve and maintain conformance. Statistical techniques are extremely useful in quality control; these statistical procedures are discussed in Chapter 19.

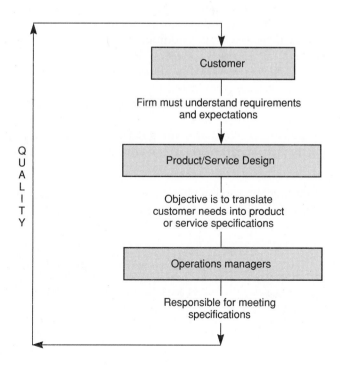

FIGURE 2.1

Customer-driven Quality Cycle

An internal quality survey conducted at Polaroid identified seven major areas of concern within the corporation.[10]

1. Quality was too often entered downstream, that is, at final assembly, rather than in the design and development stages.
2. Customer needs and sources of satisfaction were not well understood.
3. Quality was not an important issue until it became a problem.
4. Management seemed willing to sacrifice quality when cost or scheduling conflicted.
5. Operators were not sufficiently trained in their jobs and in quality.
6. Quality problems were observed with vendors.
7. Quality costs were determined to be high.

These issues involve *people, technology, information,* and *management.* Polaroid's response to them was a comprehensive and integrated quality strategy.

Polaroid's experience is not unique. Effective quality management must be a total, company-wide effort that is aimed at the avoidance of problems through (1) the planning and engineering of products, processes, and methods, (2) the identification of problems that inevitably arise, (3) the correction of these problems, and (4) the commitment to continuously improve quality performance. The term *total quality control* was coined by A. V. Feigenbaum to denote this approach to effective quality management.[11] To accomplish these goals, manufacturing and service organizations require strong management and leadership, technical skills for problem identification, and problem-solving methodologies for improving quality.

The Japanese have adopted Feigenbaum's concept and strongly emphasize total quality control. They are using the concept very successfully to compete in world markets. This has led many American managers to investigate how this concept might improve their quality and competitiveness.

In the Japanese approach to quality, the responsibility for achieving quality rests not with the quality-control department, or top management, but with the production workers themselves[12] In addition, the Japanese are devoted to the goal of *no defectives,* as opposed to tolerating some acceptable percentage of defects. They have achieved remarkable success. The keys to their success lie in the philosophy of prevention, not detection, and the type of production and quality-control systems they have developed. In this section, we briefly discuss this philosophy.

The Japanese are committed to preventing defects at the source of production and not searching for them after the fact. Several principles underly this commitment.

Process Control

In the Japanese approach to total quality control, every work station is a control point, and workers, not inspectors, are responsible for doing the inspection.

---

[10]Harold S. Page. "A Quality Strategy for the '80s," *Quality Progress,* 16, no. 11, (November 1983): 16–21.

[11]A. V. Feigenbaum, *Total Quality Control,* 3d ed., New York: McGraw-Hill, 1983.

[12]This discussion is adapted from Richard J. Schonberger, "Production Workers Bear Major Quality Responsibility in Japanese Industry." Reprinted with permission from *Industrial Engineering* magazine, December, 1982. Copyright Institute of Industrial Engineers, 25 Technology Park/Atlanta, Norcross, GA 30092.

Visible, Measurable Quality

The Japanese want quality to be measurable and *visible*—even to the untrained eye. Quality records are expressed in easy-to-understand charts and diagrams and displayed on chalkboards and signs throughout the factory. This displays and recognizes the achievements of the workers.

Insistence on Compliance

Both production managers and purchasing agents insist that quality goods be produced with an acceptable quality level.

Line-Stop Authority

Workers have the authority to stop a production line when a problem is recognized. Except in certain food and drug plants, this is rarely done in the West.

Self-Correction of Errors

Rework is the responsibility of those who made bad items. Workers may have to work late to correct their mistakes; thus they usually make sure that their production is good.

100 Percent Checking

One hundred percent checking for quality problems, especially in finished goods, is emphasized.

To support this philosophy, several ancillary concepts are a fundamental part of Japanese production systems. The quality-control function, as a separate entity, is minimized in importance. Except where technically difficult inspections are necessary, quality is left to the production workers. Kawasaki has quality control inspectors assigned to check goods imported from the United States, but not those produced in Japan; they are presumed to be good!

Small production lot sizes help identify defectives and their causes quickly, before a large number of parts have been produced. Scheduling is always at less than full capacity to allow production to slow or stop for quality problems and still meet production goals. Cleanliness and preventive maintenance are strictly followed in Japanese plants. Workers check their machines each morning before beginning production, and many workers perform their own preventive maintenance and janitorial work.

Japanese supervisors and workers are trained in statistical quality control and use control charts and histograms with ease as a means of detecting quality problems. Perhaps the biggest difference in statistical control is the fact that random sampling is not used. We have said that most parts are 100 percent inspected. When this cannot be done, the Japanese inspect the first piece and the last piece. The rationale is that if both the first and last pieces are good, then the process probably did not change. Therefore, the sample size is equal to two.

It should be pointed out that these developments did not take place overnight. Beginning around 1950, it took 10 years to train management and another 10 years to train supervisors and workers in this philosophy. However, the West has taken notice, and many efforts are underway to improve quality performance to the level that Japan has achieved.

Total quality control requires achieving objectives more efficiently at every level of the company. Consequently, quality is the responsibility of everyone in the organization from production line operators to the chief executive officer. It is the machine operators, the assembly line workers, the ticket agents, the nurses, and the waitresses who build in the quality of products and services; thus first-line supervisors play an important role in ensuring total quality control. They must not only motivate employees to develop a quality consciousness, but also direct them in how to use effective quality control procedures, locate quality problems, and eliminate sources of error on the shop floor. In a total quality control effort, middle management must plan, coordinate, execute and monitor quality policy, and top management must commit the resources necessary to ensure that the quality programs are carried out at all levels of the organization. Human relations and information transfer are important means for ensuring the successful implementation of a total quality system.

One company, Yokogawa-Hewlett-Packard (YHP), shows the results of a five-year program of total quality control throughout an organization.[13] In fact, YHP has won the coveted Deming Prize as a result of its quality program. Some of the improvements that were made included the following:

- Assembly defects dropped from .4 percent to .04 percent.
- Wave soldering defects decreased from .4 percent to .003 percent.
- Lead time needed to manufacture products dropped from two months to two weeks.
- Warranty costs dropped from 6.5 percent of every thousand dollars of value produced to slightly more than one percent.
- R&D cycle time dropped from five years to about two and one-half years.
- Redesign time (hours spent on design during the production phase) dropped sevenfold.
- Overlooked market needs (desirable design features identified *after* market introduction) dropped ninefold.

Productivity rose 91 percent, profit rose 177 percent, and market share increased 214 percent. At the same time, manufacturing costs dropped 42 percent, the failure rate dropped 60 percent, and inventory was reduced 64 percent.

In general, the YHP case is an excellent example of how a strategic focus on total quality control can maximize the attainment of a company's key objectives—profit and growth.

Quality in Service Organizations

Important quality characteristics for service organizations are accuracy, speed, completeness, consistency, and availability. Quality assurance systems based on manufacturing system analogies are often applicable in setting technical standards for many services. For instance, standards might be set for the fraction of lights operating correctly in a hotel lobby, an airline might have a standard that doors must be opened within 70 seconds of parking the plane, a phone company might specify that a dial tone should be obtained within 3 seconds, and so on. On the other hand, service organizations also have special requirements that quality assurance systems based on manufacturing cannot fulfill.

The customer interaction necessary in providing services adds several dimensions to the notion of quality. Carol King suggests several issues that service

---

[13]Adapted from John A. Young, "The Quality Focus at Hewlett-Packard," *The Journal of Business Strategy,* 5, no. 3, (Winter 1985): 6–9. Reprinted with permission form *Journal of Business Strategy,* Warren Gorham & Lamont, Inc., 210 South Street, Boston, MA 02111. All rights reserved.

organizations should consider when instituting quality assurance systems: customer perceptions, company image, friendliness, training, subjective evaluation, and so on.[14] The quality of human interaction is a vital factor in many service transactions. For instance, banks have found that the friendliness of tellers is a factor in retaining depositors. Company image is a major factor in shaping customer expectations for a service and in setting standards by which customers evaluate that service. A breakdown in image can be as harmful as a breakdown in the delivery of the service itself.

Setting service standards and measuring them may be difficult, because many quality characteristics of services cannot be measured objectively. Quality levels in manufacturing systems are often measured in terms of such things as the amount of scrap and rework generated; quality levels in service systems cannot usually be measured in terms of such hard data. Often standards must be set judgementally and tested for satisfactory levels. Customer attitudes and employee competence must be considered. Because perceptions will vary by individual, setting standards can be a difficult task.

Another concern with services is that quality control activity may be required at times, or in places, where supervision and control personnel are not present. Work must often be performed at the customer's location. Hence more training of employees and "self management" are necessary.

The differences among service organizations create distinct challenges for quality assurance. Measuring the quality of services delivered demands an understanding of the behavioral sciences as well as technical sciences such as statistics. Many firms such as Walt Disney Co., Marriott Hotels, and Delta Airlines have recognized this and have developed quality assurance programs which have resulted in a reputation for their organizations as providing excellent service.

2.5 QUALITY COST MEASUREMENT AND ANALYSIS

Quality costs are any costs that would not occur if perfect quality could be achieved. That is, each time work must be redone—for example, remanufacturing a defective item or retesting an assembly—the cost of quality increases. Many such costs are overlooked or not recognized because traditional accounting systems are not designed to identify them.

Managers find quality cost information valuable for a number of reasons.[15]

1. Dollars can be added meaningfully across departments and/or products and compared to other dollar measures to gain an understanding of the financial significance of lack of quality.
2. Quality cost information helps management identify quality problems and opportunities that might otherwise go unnoticed.
3. Quality cost information helps managers evaluate the relative importance of quality problems and provides a guide as to which to tackle first.

---

[14]Carol A. King, "Service Quality Assurance Is Different," *Quality Progress*, 18, no. 6, (1985) 14–18.

[15]Wayne J. Morse, Harold P. Roth, and Kay M. Poston, *Measuring, Planning and Controlling Quality Costs*, Montvale, NJ: National Association of Accountants, 1987, 17–18.

4. Quality cost information can be used to demonstrate the financial potential of quality improvement programs and aid in obtaining the funds needed for quality improvement projects by quantifying the probable financial impact of the improvement programs.

5. Quality costs can help to evaluate the organization's success in achieving quality objectives.

Quality Cost Categories

Quality costs can be organized into four major categories: prevention costs, appraisal costs, internal failure costs, and external failure costs. **Prevention costs** are those costs expended in an effort to keep nonconforming products or services from occurring and reaching the customer. **Appraisal costs** are those expended on maintaining quality levels through measurement and analysis of data in order to detect and correct problems. **Internal failure costs** result from unsatisfactory quality that is found prior to the delivery of a product or service to the customer; **external failure costs** are those that occur after poor-quality products or services reach the customer. The specific sources of these costs are discussed next.

Prevention Costs

Quality-planning costs are those associated with the time spent planning, designing, and implementing the total quality control system. These costs include salaries and development costs for the establishment of manufacturing controls, costs for establishing procedures, and costs incurred in setting up instructions for testing and inspection, reliability studies, new equipment design, and so on. *Process-control costs* include costs spent on the analysis of production processes in order to improve their operations and the implementation of process-control plans. *Information-systems costs* involve salaries expended developing data requirements and quality measurements. *Training costs* are those associated with developing and operating formal training programs or attending seminars on quality assurance. *General-management costs* include those for clerical staff, supplies, and communications related to quality efforts.

Appraisal Costs

Test and inspection costs are those associated with testing and inspecting incoming materials, work in process, and finished goods, including salaries for inspectors, supervisors, and other personnel as well as the cost of equipment. *Costs of maintaining instruments* include the costs associated with calibration of gauge and test equipment, repair, and so on. *Process-control costs* include time spent by operators in gathering and analyzing quality measurements.

Internal Failure Costs

Scrap and rework costs include material, labor, and overhead associated with production losses. *Costs of corrective action* arise from time spent determining the causes of failure and correcting production problems. *Downgrading costs* include lost revenue as a result of selling a product at a lower price because it does not meet specifications but is still usable.

External Failure Costs

Costs of customer complaints and returns include the costs of investigating complaints and taking corrective action. *Product-recall costs* are those of administration and direct production costs of making adjustments. *Warranty claim costs* include the cost of repair or replacement of products during warranty periods. Finally, *product-liability costs* involving legal action and settlements are a major source of external failure costs.

It is estimated that from 60 to 90 percent of total quality costs are the result of internal and external failure problems, both of which are not easily controllable by management. In the past, the typical reaction to high failure costs has been to increase inspection; this approach, however, leads to higher appraisal costs. While external failures will be reduced with this approach, the costs of internal failures can rise. The overall result is little, if any, improvement in quality or profitability.

The key to improving quality and profitability is *prevention*. Better prevention of poor quality will clearly reduce internal failure costs since fewer defective items will be made; external failure costs will also be reduced. In addition, less appraisal will be required since the products will be made correctly the first time. Since production is usually viewed in the short run, it is difficult to establish such a strategic orientation. This is another reason why quality efforts must be well planned and why quality costs must be understood at every organizational level. Quality costs are both a management responsibility and a technical responsibility.

One of the more interesting approaches to preventing quality problems involves working with suppliers of purchased material in order to improve *their* quality. The Japanese have been very successful following this approach; in fact, Japanese manufacturers often provide free assistance to their suppliers in developing quality-assurance programs or solving quality problems. The reasons are quite simple; if a manufacturer knows that its suppliers are producing quality products, then less effort will have to be spent on verifying the quality of incoming material and reworking or scrapping defectives that may be found in later stages of production. U.S. automakers are now working more closely with suppliers and are beginning to insist on sound quality practice throughout their organizations.

Using Quality Cost Information

The purpose of quality-cost measurement and analysis is to determine the cost of maintaining a certain level of quality. Such activity is necessary to provide feedback to management on the performance of quality assurance and to assist management in identifying opportunities for quality improvement and cost reduction. Quality costs are often reported by product line, department, work center, operator, or defect classification. The problem with attempting to collect and measure quality costs is that many costs involve different departments or functions within an organization and are difficult to measure.

Many quality-cost data are available from an organization's accounting system. Items such as time sheets, expense reports, and purchase orders are typical data sources. The chief drawback is that such data are rarely available in the categories required for quality-cost analysis. New data-processing techniques, such as database management systems are helping to overcome such problems.

Quality costs themselves provide little managerial information, since they may vary due to such factors as production volume or seasonality. Thus **quality-cost indexes** are usually used to analyze quality-cost data. Such indexes are computed by dividing a cost for a current time period by a base-period value. Typical measurement bases are *labor, manufacturing cost, sales,* and *units of product*. Several examples are given next.

Labor-base Index

A typical quality-cost index is total quality cost per direct labor-hour. Direct labor data is easily obtained from accounting. This index will change as a result of changes in technology; thus one must be careful in using it over long periods of time.

Cost-base Index

Total quality cost per manufacturing-cost dollar is a common cost-base index. Manufacturing cost includes direct labor, material, and overhead costs, which are usually available from accounting. Cost indexes are not affected by price fluctuations or by changes in the level of automation.

Sales-base Index

Total quality cost per sales dollar is a popular index. However, this measure is generally unsatisfactory for short-term analysis since sales usually lag behind production and are subject to seasonal variations. In addition, this index is affected by changes in the selling price.

Unit-base Index

A commonly used unit-base index is total quality cost per unit of production. This is an acceptable index if production lines are similar; however it is a poor measure of quality costs if there is a high diversity of products. In this case, an alternative index of quality costs per equivalent unit of output is often used. To obtain this index, different product lines are weighted to approximate a "standard" or "average" product, which is used as a common base.

All of the above quality-cost indexes, although used extensively in practice, have a fundamental problem. A change in the denominator can appear to be a change in the level of quality assurance or productivity alone. For instance, if direct labor is decreased through productivity improvements, the quality-cost index will increase even if there is no change in quality. Also, the inclusion of overhead in manufacturing cost, which is often common, is certain to distort results. Nevertheless, use of such indexes is common for comparing quality costs over time.

Generally, sales bases are the most popular, followed by cost, labor, and unit bases.[16] Quality-cost data can be broken down by product lines, by process, by department, by work center, over time, and by cost category. This makes data analysis much more convenient and useful to management.

Quality costs can be used in several ways in decision making. They can be used as a measurement tool for performance reporting in the accounting sense, for planning and budgeting, or in the evaluation of strategic goals. However, the most important application of quality-cost data is to identify quality problems.

Statistical quality cost information tells managers only where the potential for cost reduction and quality-cost improvement lies; it does not tell them what the problems are. It is up to the managers and engineers to uncover the sources of problems and determine appropriate corrective action. For instance, a steady rise in internal failure costs and decline in appraisal costs might indicate that there is a problem in assembly, a problem with the maintenance of testing equipment,

---

[16]Edward Sullivan and Debra A. Owens, "Catching a Glimpse of Quality Costs Today," *Quality Progress,* 16, no. 12 (December 1983): 21–24.

or a lack of proper inspection of purchased materials. The high external failure costs will probably be viewed closely by top management since this might adversely affect the company's reputation.

COMPUTING AND INTERPRETING QUALITY COST INDEXES

EXAMPLE

Digital Time Corporation (DTC) produces a high volume of inexpensive quartz watches and finer desk clocks. DTC is primarily an assembly operation, with quartz crystals imported from Japan and other materials from domestic suppliers. The desk clocks are made from oak, which is cut and stained in the plant. This process is labor-intensive. Therefore, a measurement base of direct labor cost has been chosen. DTC recently implemented a quality-cost program, and the first year's results in dollars are given in Table 2.2. This table gives an accounting report of quality costs by quarter for each product and cost category.

Using direct labor as the base, the quality cost index is computed as

$$\text{Quality-cost index} = \frac{\text{total quality costs}}{\text{direct labor costs}} (100)$$

The multiplication by 100 converts the index to a percentage. Thus, for example, to compute the quality-cost index for watches in the first quarter, we see from Table 2.2 that total quality costs are $54 thousand and direct labor costs are $35 thousand. The quality-cost index for this case is computed as follows:

$$\text{quality-cost index} = \frac{54}{35} (100) = 154.3$$

If we compute the quality cost index for each product and each quarter, we have

Quarter	Watch	Clock
1	154.3	162.2
2	185.7	181.4
3	187.5	248.9
4	193.3	252.7

We see that for watches, the quality-cost indexes have increased from 154.3 percent of direct labor costs to 193.3 percent over the four quarters considered.

Cost category	Quarter 1 Watch	Quarter 1 Clock	Quarter 2 Watch	Quarter 2 Clock	Quarter 3 Watch	Quarter 3 Clock	Quarter 4 Watch	Quarter 4 Clock
Prevention	2	4	2	4	2	4	2	4
Appraisal	10	20	13	31	16	22	9	24
Internal failure	19	106	16	107	23	194	17	195
External failure	23	16	21	14	34	14	30	12
Total quality costs	54	146	52	156	75	234	58	235
Direct labor	35	90	28	86	40	94	30	93

TABLE 2.2
Quality-cost Data for DTC (in thousands of dollars)

TABLE 2.3
Quality Indexes
by Cost Category

Cost Category	Watches				Clocks			
	Quarter							
	1	2	3	4	1	2	3	4
Prevention	5.7	7.1	5.0	6.7	4.4	4.7	4.3	4.3
Appraisal	28.6	46.4	40.0	30.0	22.2	36.0	23.4	25.8
Internal failure	54.3	57.1	57.5	56.7	117.8	124.4	206.4	209.7
External failure	65.7	75.0	85.0	100.0	17.8	16.3	14.9	12.9

Table 2.3 provides a breakdown of quality costs per direct labor cost by category for the DTC example. For example, in quarter 1 the prevention costs for watches were $2000 and the direct labor costs were $35,000 (see Table 2.2); thus, the cost index is ($2000 ÷ 35,000)100 = 5.7 percent. As with productivity indexes, examination of trends often provides useful information to managers. With regard to watches, for instance, we see that prevention and internal failure costs have remained steady over the four quarters. Appraisal costs initially rose during the second quarter, possibly because of start up of a new quality program, and have since steadily declined. A major problem, however, appears to be growing with regard to external failure costs. For clocks, all costs except internal failure have remained relatively constant. We also see that internal failure costs have taken a significant jump between the second and third quarters. This frequently occurs when quality costs first begin to be monitored. As efforts to control quality increase, prevention costs should increase substantially, appraisal costs should level off, and failure costs should decline.

Refer to Table 2.2. For the fourth quarter, the external failure costs for watches were $30,000. Thus, for this quarter, ($30,000 ÷ $58,000)100 = 51.7 percent of all quality costs are accounted for by external failure costs; we find that for clocks, internal failure costs comprise 29 percent of the total. Information such as this enables managers to direct their attention to problem areas that will yield the greatest improvement per dollar expended. For example, a 10 percent improvement in internal failure costs for watches will only improve total costs by 2.9 percent, whereas the same percentage improvement in external failure costs will result in a 5.2 percent overall reduction. The high external failure costs for watches during the third and fourth quarters might suggest that a different supplier was used and that poor materials were not discovered, since the appraisal and prevention costs are low. The fact that prevention costs are very low for both products indicates that perhaps the quality-assurance function was not well planned.

Quality Costs in Service Organizations

In manufacturing organizations, quality costs are primarily product-oriented; in service organizations however, they are generally labor dependent. Since quality in service organizations depends in a large part on employee-customer interaction, appraisal costs tend to account for a higher percentage of total quality costs than they do in manufacturing. In addition, internal failure costs tend to be much lower for service organizations since there is little opportunity to correct an error before it reaches the customer.

External failure costs can become an extremely significant out-of-pocket expense to consumers of services. For example, a family moving from one city to another may have to pay additional costs for lodging and meals because the moving van does not arrive on the day promised; a doctor's prescription needs to be changed because of faulty diagnosis and the patient pays for unnecessary drugs; a computer billing error requires several phone calls, letters, and copies of cancelled checks to correct, and so on. Service organizations need to be quite sensitive to these quality issues. However, the intangible nature of output makes quality cost accounting for services very difficult.

2.6 THE PRODUCTIVITY-QUALITY CONNECTION

Productivity and quality are closely related. Although productivity improvement is frequently associated with improvements in technology, such as automation and specialization, technology improvements cannot solve all productivity problems. Unfortunately, many operations managers believe that quality improvements will result in decreased productivity, since an improved product may take more hours to produce and cost more; thus, their attitudes toward quality improvement may be adversely biased. Given the fact that most operations managers are evaluated on the basis of cost and quantity of output, this point of view is understandable.

In this book *Quality Is Free,* (New York: McGraw-Hill, 1979) Phil Crosby states that building quality into a product does not cost the company more because of the savings in rework, scrap, and servicing the product after the sale, as well as the benefits of customer satisfaction and repeat sales. He states further that if features are added to improve fitness for use, fewer repairs are necessary, and the customer is pleased. Even though adding a feature may require a manufacturer to charge a premium price, the product cost over its lifetime may actually be lowered. IBM, Caterpillar, Michelin, Procter & Gamble, and Ford are some of the many companies that use this concept of quality in their overall strategy.

In a similar fashion, Dr. W. Edwards Deming, in his book *Out of the Crisis,* (Cambridge, MA: MIT Center for Advanced Engineering Studies, 1986), states that improvement of quality transfers wasted man-hours and machine-time into the manufacture of good product and better service. Management in some Japanese companies observed as early as 1948 and 1949 that improvement of quality naturally and inevitably begets improvement of productivity. Once management in Japan adopted the chain reaction illustrated in Figure 2.2, quality became everyone's aim.

It is true that improvements in *product* quality can lead to lower productivity since an improved product may take more labor hours and cost more. Decreasing the speed of service in order to provide better attention to customers has similar results. However, such improvements have more important, lasting effects on market share and profitability. For instance, improved products can bring about a reduction in liability, make it become easier to introduce new products and react to competition, and offer the potential for better advertising strategies that will further enhance a firm's reputation. Also, improved product design may eliminate unnecessary parts and processing operations, thus reducing inputs and increasing productivity.

FIGURE 2.2
The Deming
Chain Reaction

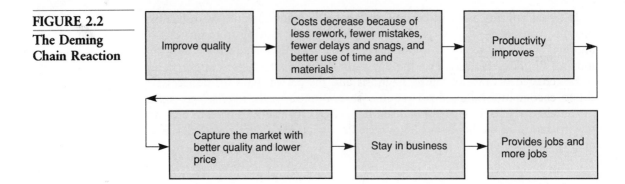

Improvements in *process* quality can easily lead to improvements in productivity. Leonard and Sasser provide some examples:[17]

- One company's installation of a new "clean room" reduced contaminants on printed circuit boards and boosted output by almost 35 percent.
- Elimination of rework stations at one television factory forced assembly workers to find and solve their own quality mistakes. These adjustments resulted in an increased production rate per hour of direct labor and in the elimination of thousands of dollars of rework costs.
- One company using precision assembly equipment designed components that would not fit together unless they were "right." This arrangement raised production rates as well as distribution efficiencies. It also improved the productivity of the sales force, since it no longer had to spend time collecting, boxing, and replacing returned components.

In general, process quality improvement reduces rework and other operating losses, decreases labor and material costs, provides improved managerial control of operations, smoother production flow, better employee morale, and improved return on investment.

Economic
Impacts of
Productivity
and Quality
Improvement

Ultimately, management in a profit-making organization is evaluated by investors and stockholders on the basis of the organization's long-run profitability. Even though the performance of managers of nonprofit organizations is not measured on profitability, such managers must ensure that costs remain in balance relative to the benefits incurred. Thus both profit and not-for-profit organizations must be concerned with economic performance.

Profitability is a function of revenue and cost. Revenue depends on the selling price and the sales volume; cost is the value of the inputs or resources used to produce the outputs. Since operations managers are responsible for transforming inputs into outputs, productivity and quality decisions made by operations managers directly affect revenue, cost, and profitability.

To understand better the relationship between inputs, the transformation process, outputs, productivity, and quality, consider the basic definition of profit.

---

[17]Frank S. Leonard and W. Earl Sasser, "The Incline of Quality," *Harvard Business Review*, 60, no. 5 (September/October 1982): 163–171.

$$\text{Profit} = \text{revenue} - \text{cost}$$

Clearly profit is positive if revenue is greater than cost. Some of the factors that can change and alter profitability are

1. a change in the selling price of the product or service
2. a change in the amount of product or service sold
3. a change in the unit cost of resources
4. a change in the quantity of resources used per unit of output.

Suppose for a moment that the cost of materials or other resources increases. A firm can offset such an increase in cost by increasing the selling price of the product or service and hopefully the revenue. However, in the presence of competition, an increase in price may be accompanied by a decrease in sales, and as a result may not achieve the desired increase in revenue. Thus, if profitability is to be maintained, the firm may try to offset the increased cost of resources by attempting to increase the output per unit of resource used. Doing so provides an improvement in productivity. An alternative approach to maintaining or increasing profits is to improve the quality of the product so as to be able to command a higher price or increased market share. Therefore, profitability is sensitive to changes in both productivity and quality. Improved production quality, resulting in reduced scrap and rework, will reduce manufacturing and service costs, also leading to higher profits. This discussion is summarized in Figure 2.3.

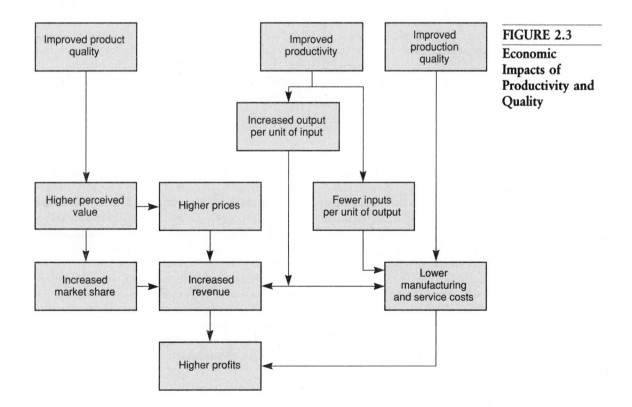

FIGURE 2.3

Economic Impacts of Productivity and Quality

Note: The arrows can be interpreted as meaning "leads to."

The three P/OM in Practice applications illustrate how productivity and quality improvements can be successfully implemented. The first shows how productivity improvements led to increased profitability of Southwest Tube. In a market where little sales growth was possible, improved work methods and better operations management led to dramatic pro-

ductivity increases. The second explains how reduction of quality costs helped Continental Bank improve productivity. The third details the total quality assurance program at Anheuser-Busch. This program has been responsible for the company's quality image.

PRODUCTIVITY IMPROVEMENT AT SOUTHWEST TUBE[18]

B eginning in the late 1970s, Southwest Tube faced major competitive threats in its main product line of small-diameter carbon steel tubing. The market was not expanding and the company's manufacturing capacity was significantly greater than market demand required. As a result of competition, prices were dropping. In addition, manufacturing costs were rising for both labor and raw material.

Commitments for raw materials were made six months to a year in advance, leaving very little that could be done to reduce the raw material cost of finished goods. Management concluded that if the company was going to survive, labor productivity would have to be improved. Four areas needing improvement were identified: manufacturing supervision, absenteeism and turnover, measurement and reporting, and manpower scheduling.

One of the key early improvements in manufacturing supervision involved defining improved staffing levels at manufacturing work centers. This was done in a two-step process: first, using past actual performance, and second, using the results from work measurement studies (see Chapter 11). For example, initial crew size estimates for the weld mill operation indicated that six people should be assigned to operate the mill. Work measurement studies indicated that five people could run the mill if improved work methods were utilized. At the end of three years of continuing improvements in work methods, it was found that three people were able to run a weld mill. Another improvement in manufacturing supervision involved publishing goals for

each production center and then reporting on progress toward meeting those goals. This process provided feedback to workers and helped them understand the need to compare performance to production goals.

In a number of operations, full work crews are needed to run the mill, staff a finishing floor, or move raw material in the yard. When some workers in a crew are absent, new ones must be found to temporarily make up a full crew; this can often lead to reduced productivity since on-the-job training must be conducted for the new crew members. High turnover of employees also caused similar problems. In an attempt to solve the turnover problem, the environment was changed. First, since the plant was old and had a history of poor maintenance and inadequate housekeeping, it was cleaned and painted and the scrap was hauled away. One byproduct of these actions was an improved safety record. Uniforms were provided for manufacturing employees, a job analysis was conducted, and pay scales were altered to establish fair wages and clarify the compensation program. These improvements enabled Southwest Tube to attract a higher quality workforce and this in turn led to a 75 percent reduction in turnover.

Measurement and reporting of manufacturing performance was improved by creating an earned hour per production report. This report gave Southwest Tube management and workers the ability to objectively compare output and productivity against performance targets. Methods improvements were

---

[18]Adapted from James M. Shirley, and Thomas M. Box, "Productivity Gains at Southwest Tube," *Production and Inventory Mangement*, 28, no. 4, (1987): 57–60.

	Cold Draw Department		Weld Mill Department		Table 2.4
Fiscal Year	Labor (1000 hr)	Output (1000 ft)	Labor (1000 hr)	Output (1000 ft)	**Production Results for Southwest Tube**
1980	228	18,269	132	22,434	
1981	234	19,576	157	34,777	
1982	183	17,633	102	26,715	
1983	150	18,870	77	25,227	

identified and implemented throughout the plant. For example, new methods were developed for handling material in the plant to reduce waiting time between work centers.

Production at Southwest tube usually required a three-shift operation, six or seven days per week. The old rotating shift manpower schedule included several negative features: days off were irregular from week to week; shifts rotated every week; and support crews (maintenance, tool room, warehouse, and others) worked different schedules that often resulted in significant gaps in coverage. A new scheduling plan was developed to solve these problems and meet production and labor cost goals. The new schedule called for four 12-hour days followed by three days off. Some of the benefits included double-time pay for the last 8 hours of work each week; one shift supervisor was eliminated; the number of manufacturing employees was reduced; shifts could be stabilized and not require rotation; and a full day for maintenance was available.

One of the questions that arose was "Can workers remain productive through 48 hours of work in physically demanding jobs over a four-day period?" The answer was an unqualified "yes," based on results over a four-year period. Table 2.4 shows some of the changes in output versus labor input. The accident rate was reduced by a factor of two during this same period.

This case shows how attention to people and equipment problems and needs has resulted in significant productivity gains. None of the improvements were easy to implement; in fact, it took more than six months to convince the work force that productivity enhancement was in their best interest. The founder and president of Southwest Tube, F. William Weber, has acclaimed the success of the program and stated publicly that it literally saved the company from bankruptcy.

QUESTIONS

1. How can absenteeism and turnover affect productivity?
2. What did Southwest Tube do in order to reduce absenteeism and turnover?
3. Did scheduling of employees have an effect on productivity at Southwest Tube? Explain.
4. Compute the labor productivity indexes for each year and each department using the data in Table 2.4. How much has productivity increased over this time period?

COST AND PRODUCTIVITY IMPROVEMENT AT THE CONTINENTAL BANK[19]

C ontinental Bank defines quality as the degree to which a service conforms to predetermined standards. Quality is measured in two general ways: (1) adherence to standards and (2) quality costs. For a bank, labor costs make up a major portion of all quality costs. Also, the need for timely processing of financial transactions requires extensive "up-front" and "throughput" quality controls. This is characteristic of all service operations. As a result, appraisal costs for the banking industry tend to account for a much higher percentage of total quality

[19]Adapted from "Quality Costs and Improvements," Charles A. Aubrey, II, and Debra A. Zimbler, *Quality Progress*, 16 no. 12, (December 1983): 16–20.

costs than do corresponding costs in manufacturing firms. Failure costs also tend to be much lower.

A project undertaken in a loan-processing department at Continental Bank provides a good example of the way quality costs can be used. A study showed that "processing holdouts"—computer tickets rejected during daily processing—represented failure costs of more than $2000 per month. Holdouts accounted for 30 percent of all tickets processed. To reprocess the holdouts, the reason for the reject had to be determined, and the tickets were held for next-day processing. The delay prevented the department from updating commercial lending information accurately and promptly—information needed to determine a customer's available credit, the bank's credit exposure, and the bank's financial statements.

The loan-processing area had not been aware of the magnitude of quality costs and, in particular, the holdout problem. The area manger was enthusiastic about starting a quality improvement project. Since the cause of the excessive number of holdouts was unknown, the quality improvement project began with data collection.

In an effort to identify the problem, the area supervisor kept a holdout log. Each holdout was listed by the type of error that caused the reject as well as by the clerk who submitted it. An analysis was performed to determine which errors occurred most frequently and which clerks were responsible for the greatest number of errors. The analysis revealed that three types of errors were primarily responsible for the rejected tickets and that three clerks were responsible for the majority of the errors. The actual production operation was carefully monitored to determine the cause of the high-error rates by certain clerks and the types of errors made. Particular attention was paid to the quality of the incoming information and to the way the clerk transferred the information onto the computer input tickets.

Further, resubmitted tickets were monitored to determine if they were again rejected. Since it was the responsibility of the clerk to determine the cause of the initial rejection and to correct the mistake, a twice-rejected ticket might indicate that the clerk was unsure as to how to correct the error. However, few tickets were rejected twice, indicating that clerks knew how to correct rejected tickets.

Observations identified possible causes of the high-error rates responsible for the rejected tickets. The clerks frequently received incomplete or unclear information, and some of them were unsure about how to proceed. Knowing the need for immediacy, the clerks attempted to process the less-than-perfect information. It appeared that there was not a consistent method of completing input tickets; each clerk had his or her own method. Further, since the supervisor had not been closely monitoring the holdouts, the supervisor was not giving the clerks necessary feedback or suggesting ways to correct the most frequently occurring errors.

These observations suggested several courses of action. Each clerk was required to participate in a training program to ensure that everyone understood section- and ticket-processing procedures. A comprehensive procedures manual was written to accompany the training program and to serve as ready reference for the clerks. Clerks were encouraged to ask the senior clerk or supervisor questions about nonroutine items—prevention and appraisal activities that served to reduce failure costs later.

The clerks were also instructed to reject items that were incomplete or unclear and to return such items to the person who had sent them instead of attempting to process them, hoping they would pass. The supervisor was encouraged to take greater initiative in measuring the frequency and types of errors so that she could resolve or correct potential problems before quality was severely affected. Frequent feedback made the clerks more aware of and more responsible for the quality of their own work.

A productivity measure was developed for the loan-processing department. The numerator specified the tickets processed during the month. The denominator covered the resources incurred to process the tickets which included labor hours, computer run time, and ticket forms. The measure used was

$$\frac{\text{tickets processed}}{\text{labor} + \text{systems} + \text{forms}}$$

Since labor hours, systems, and forms are not expressed in common dimensions and hence could not be added together, a base-period cost was assigned to each resource. The base-period cost of labor was $11.13 per hour, of systems was a fixed $500 per month, and of forms was $.05 each. At the time that quality costs were initially developed, approximately 2080 tickets were processed per month at a cost of $7753. Labor represented $7123, systems $500, and forms $130. The productivity index was calculated to be 26.83.

After the quality improvement project was completed, the productivity index was recalculated to be 31.43, a 17 percent increase, resulting from a 94-hour reduction in labor and 500 fewer forms used. Total quality costs decreased, particularly failure costs. The training and feedback increased the prevention and appraisal activities of both the supervisor and the clerks.

QUESTIONS

1. Why are quality costs an issue for the holdout problem for Continental Bank?

2. How did Continental Bank determine the cause of the excessive number of holdouts?

3. What were some of the factors identified as causing the excessive number of holdouts?

4. What did Continental Bank do to reduce the number of holdouts?

5. Explain how the productivity measure developed for the loan-processing department is used to monitor quality.

QUALITY AND PRODUCTIVITY AT ANHEUSER-BUSCH[20]

Brewing quality beer has been viewed as both an art and a science at Anheuser-Busch for over a century. Protecting that quality image continues to be the company's highest priority in terms of customer service. In fact, August A. Busch, III, chairman and president of Anheuser-Busch, Inc., has said that, "Quality is the single most important unyielding commitment at Anheuser-Busch."

Anheuser-Busch uses what it considers the finest and most costly ingredients available, based on stringent requirements and specifications. All beers are produced according to its traditional "Old World" brewing method, a long, natural process taking up to thirty days or longer, that is probably the most costly brewing process in the industry. While it has chosen not to use *chemical* advances to cut corners in brewing, Anheuser-Busch has always been innovative in the use of science to promote quality. Today the company's traditional brewing process is strictly maintained using modern technology in a rigorous program of quality assurance.

Tasting provides the final quality judgment. "Flavor panels" meet daily at each of the company's eleven breweries to judge the aroma, appearance, and taste of beer. In addition, samples from each brewery are regularly flown to the company's headquarters for test evaluation by a panel of expert brewmasters.

Anheuser-Busch works closely with its wholesale and retail network to ensure that quality, taste, and freshness are protected throughout the distribution system. To assure this, the company offers extensive training to its wholesalers in the proper handling of beer, proper storage temperature, methods to stack products in the warehouse, and proper delivery procedures. Wholesalers, in turn, extend quality control training to their retail customers wherever it is legal. Many distributors equip their warehouses with special seminar rooms designed specifically for training.

Anheuser-Busch provides many services designed to improve the productivity of its wholesalers and to help retail accounts build sales and profitability. They offer more than forty different programs related to productivity and efficiency. For example, they offer a detailed analysis of wholesalers' operations—examining every facet of the business from deployment of sales personnel to a review of expenses by department. Computerized routing assists distributors in minimizing their travel time during delivery. The routing system can also be used to help determine the best site for a satellite warehouse location based on the number and location of existing accounts, distribution costs, and related factors.

The company also offers retail accounts a unique computerized shelf-management system. This system is designed to minimize out-of-stock costs, decrease restocking labor costs, and organize products for ease of consumer selection. To ensure that distributors maintain the highest level of service, the company requires that personal visits be made to

[20]Adapted from William L. Rammes, "Making Friends is Our Business," in Jay W. Spechler, Ed. *When America Does It Right: Case Studies in Service Quality,* Norcross GA: Industrial Engineering and Management Press, 1988, p. 29–37. Copyright 1988 Institute of Industrial Engineers, 25 Technology Park/Atlanta, Norcross, GA 30092. Reprinted with permission.

retail accounts on a periodic basis. This enables wholesaler management to monitor the performance of their sales and delivery personnel, and to address any special retailer issues or concerns.

QUESTIONS

1. What does Anheuser-Busch do to ensure that their beers meet quality specifications for taste?

2. How does Anheuser-Busch ensure that the quality, taste, and freshness are protected throughout the distribution system?
3. What types of programs does Anheuser-Busch offer to improve the productivity of its wholesalers?
4. Why does Anheuser-Busch require distributors to make personal visits to retail accounts on a regular basis?

SUMMARY

In this chapter we have presented an introduction to the issues that face manufacturing and service organizations with regard to productivity and quality. After defining productivity as a ratio of output produced to a specified set of inputs, we showed that productivity measures can be used to assist managers in making decisions that will improve operations. Since quality measures how well a product or service meets customer needs, the costs associated with quality can impact both short- and long-term profitability. Although quality-cost analysis can help pinpoint the source of quality problems, the prevention of quality problems is the best long-term strategy.

The fact that productivity and quality are treated in the second chapter of this text is meant to convey their overall importance to the field of P/OM. Indeed, the very future of American industry depends upon the extent to which American firms are able to institute effective systems for increasing productivity and improving quality.

As Shetty and Buehler point out, "Making companies productive and competitive is the ultimate responsibility of the manager."[21] For profit-making enterprises this translates into increased profitability, and for nonprofit organizations this means better service and increased customer satisfaction. Operations managers are faced with many challenges relating to productivity and quality, including the following:

- effectively managing technology in order to improve productivity and quality
- providing workers with adequate knowledge and the tools needed to improve productivity and quality
- motivating workers to improve productivity and quality.

Productivity and quality issues should be foremost in the minds of operations managers in their daily decision-making activities.

KEY TERMS

Productivity
Quality
Total productivity
Multifactor productivity
Partial factor productivity
Productivity indicator
Benefit/cost ratios

Productivity indexes
Technology
Hard technology
Soft technology
Quality assurance
Quality engineering
Quality control

---

[21]Y.K. Shetty, and V.M. Buehler, *Productivity and Quality Through Science and Technology,* Quorum Books, New York: 1988.

Quality costs
Prevention costs
Appraisal costs

Internal failure costs
External failure costs
Quality-cost index

1. Define the term *productivity*. Why is productivity important to a nation as a whole?

2. What is the ASQC definition of *quality*? Explain this definition in your own words.

3. Discuss the principal reasons why quality has become a critical issue in manufacturing and service organizations?

4. What are some of the consequences of low productivity growth and poor quality?

5. Explain the differences in productivity measurement between total productivity, multifactor productivity, and partial factor productivity.

6. What is a *productivity indicator*? How does it differ from the formal definition of productivity?

7. How does productivity measurement differ between manufacturing and service organizations?

8. List some applications of productivity measurement.

9. Identify specific productivity and quality measures that would be useful in each of the following operations:
   a. Hotel
   b. Post office
   c. Department store
   d. Bus system
   e. Emergency room

10. Why are total or multifactor productivity measures preferable to partial productivity measures?

11. How can operations management help to improve productivity in an organization?

12. What do we mean by the terms *hard technology* and *soft technology*?

13. List the major customer requirements and expectations that relate to quality.

14. Why is quality often defined as "conformance to specifications"?

15. What are *quality assurance, quality control,* and *quality engineering*? How do these activities relate to one another?

16. What does the term *total quality control* mean? How have Japanese manufacturers implemented this concept?

17. Explain the differences between manufacturing and service organizations with respect to quality.

18. List several reasons why quality cost information is important to managers.

19. Discuss the four principal types of costs that relate to quality and give several examples of each.

20. Explain how quality cost indexes can be used as a managerial tool.

21. What is the relationship between productivity and quality?

22. Explain the "Deming Chain Reaction."

23. Explain how improved quality and productivity can lead to higher profits.

24. Consider the following scenarios.[22] Discuss the productivity/quality interaction in these situations and suggest steps that mangement might take to improve the situations.

   a. An organization inspects incoming resources when they are received, inspects at key partial product-completion stages, and inspects at the final product level. Unacceptable output at each stage is rejected and dealt with accordingly or appropriately. Rework is possible and those defects identified and correctable are taken care of.

   b. A group of five spray painters on an assembly line operate with basic job training but with little feedback as to the actual outcomes resulting from their efforts. Inspectors down the line, isolated from the line personnel, evaluate the output from the painting department based upon specific quality attributes (runs, too-wide or too-narrow shading stripes, and so on).

   c. A firm is committed to achieving high quality in the goods and services it produces. The quality-control department has convinced management that in order to accomplish this, all goods and services produced must be inspected. A significant amount of effort and other resources has been devoted to building and developing a large quality organization that emphasizes inspection, correction, and zero defects.

PROBLEMS

1. Productivity measures for a manufacturing plant over a 6-month period are as follows:

Month	January	Febuary	March	April	May	June
Productivity	1.38	1.42	1.49	1.50	1.30	1.25

Using January as the base period, compute a productivity index for February to June and comment on what these productivity indices tell about the productivity trend.

2. The data in the table at top of page 71 are available for the first two quarters of the current year.

   Using total dollar measures of input and output, compare the total profit and productivity achieved for the two quarters. How does the productivity during the second quarter compare to the productivity during the first quarter? Use partial factor productivity to identify what might be done to improve productivity and profitability during the third quarter.

---

[22]Adapted from "Productivity and Quality: What is the Connection" D. Scott Sink and J. Bert Keats, 1982 Fall Industrial Engineering Conference Proceedings, Norcross, Georgia, Institute of Industrial Engineers, pp. 227–283.

	First Quarter	Second Quarter
Unit selling price	$20.00	$21.00
Total units sold	10,000	8,500
Labor hours	9,000	7,750
Labor cost/hour	$10.00	$10.00
Material usage (lb)	5,000	4,500
Material cost/pound	$15.00	$15.50
Other costs	$20,000	$18,000

3. A manufacturing firm uses two measures of productivity.
   a. Total sales/Total inputs
   b. Total sales/Total labor inputs
   Given the following data for the last three years, calculate the productivity ratios. How would you interpret the results? All figures are in dollars.

	Year 1	Year 2	Year 3
Sales	110	129	124
Materials	62	73	71
Labor	28	33	28
Overhead	8	12	10

4. Total productivity is often expressed as

$$\underbrace{\frac{\text{Total output}}{\text{Total input}} = \frac{\text{total output}}{\underset{\substack{\text{labor} \\ \text{productivity}}}{\text{labor}}} \cdot \frac{\text{labor}}{\underset{\substack{\text{labor} \\ \text{intensity}}}{\text{total input}}}}$$

Compute total productivity for the following data.

Year	Labor Productivity	Labor Intensity
1980	2.0	.5
1981	2.2	.5
1982	2.7	.5
1983	3.4	.4
1984	3.8	.4
1985	3.7	.4
1986	4.0	.37

How would you analyze this information?

5. A department consists of three types of employees: laborers earning $4.00 per hour, machine operators earning $9.00 per hour, and machinists earning

$14.00 per hour. For a certain job, over two periods, the following data were collected:

Type of Employee	Number of Labor Hours Worked	
	Period 1	Period 2
Laborer	20	16
Machine operator	12	16
Machinist	6	9

Output increased by 20 percent in period 2 as compared to period 1. How has productivity changed? (First consider how to *measure* it!)

6. A hamburger factory produces 50,000 hamburgers each week. The equipment used will remain productive for three years and costs $5000. The labor cost per year is $8000.
   a. What is the productivity measure of units of output per dollar input averaged over the 3-year period?
   b. We have the option of a more expensive machine for $10,000 whose operating life is five years. Labor cost will be reduced to $4000 per year. Should we consider purchasing this machine (using productivity arguments alone)?

7. A major airlines is attempting to evaluate the effect of recent changes it has made in scheduling flights between New York City and Los Angeles. Data available are as follows:

	Number of Flights	Number of Passengers
Month prior to schedule change	20	8,335
Month after schedule change	24	10,608

   a. Using passengers per flight as a productivity indicator, comment on the apparent effect of the schedule change.
   b. Suggest another measure of productivity that the airline may want to consider.

8. A fast-food restaurant has a drive-through window and during peak lunch times can handle a maximum of 80 cars per hour with one person taking orders, assembling them, and acting as a cashier. The average sale per order is $2.50. A proposal has been made to add two additional workers and divide the tasks among them. One will take orders, the second will assemble them, and the third will act as cashier. With this system it is estimated that 120 cars per hour can be serviced. All workers earn the minimum wage. Use productivity arguments to recommend whether or not to change the current system.

9. A computer software firm provides a 20 ft by 30 ft office for its six systems' analysts and plans to hire two additional employees. In order to maintain a

100-square-foot working space per employee, expansion is being considered. The cost of expansion is $40 per square foot with annual maintenance costs of $4 per square foot. The useful life of floor space is 20 years. By how much should employee productivity increase to justify the additonal expenditure? The current salary of the systems' analysts is $25,000.

10. A small restaurant has 10 employees. Five hundred customers visit the restaurant each day. What is the productivity indicator, employees per customers served for each year?

Year	Average Number of Customers Per Day	Number of Employees
1981	500	10
1982	600	10
1983	700	10
1984	800	12
1985	950	15
1986 (Jan–June)	1100	18

Comment on the productivity indicator.

11. RIDESHARE program sounded like a good service to the community; but the program cost increased every year. The following table indicates the program cost, annual gallons of gasoline saved, and average gasoline cost for that year. Do you think the RIDESHARE program should be continued?

Year	Program Cost ($)	Annual Gallons of Gasoline Saved	Average Cost of Gasoline Per Gallon ($)
1981	50,000	100,000	1.20
1982	65,000	125,000	1.10
1983	70,000	140,000	1.15
1984	80,000	150,000	1.10
1985	90,000	160,000	1.05

12. Analyze the following cost data. What implications does this data suggest to management? (Figures represent percentages of quality costs by product.)

	Product		
	A	B	C
Total sales	$537,280	$233,600	$397,120
External failure costs	42%	20%	20%
Internal failure costs	45%	25%	45%
Appraisal costs	12%	52%	30%
Prevention costs	1%	3%	5%

13. Compute a sales dollar-index base to analyze the accompanying quality-cost information and summarize your findings and conclusions in a memo to management.

	Quarter			
	1	2	3	4
Total sales	$4120.0	$4206.0	4454.0	$4106.0
External failure costs	40.8	42.2	42.8	28.6
Internal failure costs	168.2	172.4	184.4	66.4
Appraisal costs	64.2	67.0	74.4	166.2
Prevention costs	28.4	29.2	30.2	40.2

14. Prepare a graph or chart showing the different quality-cost categories and percentages for a printing company.

Cost Element	Amount
Proofreading	$710,000
Quality planning	10,000
Press downtime	405,000
Bindery waste	75,000
Checking and inspection	60,000
Customer-complaint remakes	40,000
Printing plate revisions	40,000
Quality-improvement projects	20,000
Other waste	55,000
Correction of typographical errors	300,000

15. During the evaluation of the performance of a quality-assurance department, the following cost data were collected for a 1-month period.

Prevention costs: $ 3,500
Appraisal costs: 8,000
Internal failure costs: 12,000
External failure costs: 10,000

During a previous 1-month period, a quality-cost index of .505 had been assigned to the departmental performance. If these cost data apply to a month in which 6000 hours of direct labor had been used at an average cost of $12.00 per hour, compute the quality-cost index for the 1-month period and comment on the performance of the quality-assurance department compared to the previous 1-month period.

16. A transmission manufacturer has estimated prevention and appraisal costs to be

$$90 + 8x$$

where x is the percent (not decimal fraction) of items inspected. Similarly, the internal and external failure costs are estimated by the function

$$\frac{4000}{x} + 2(100 - x)$$

Graph the prevention and appraisal cost function, the failure cost function, and the total cost function. Find the optimum level of quality inspection using any method you desire.

17. The following cost functions apply for a quality control system where p is the percentage of the parts inspected:

Prevention and appraisal costs: $120 + 7p$
Internal and external failure costs: $2000/p + 4(50 - p)$

What is the optimum level of inspection? If the level of inspection is reduced by 25 percent from this level, by what percent does the total cost increase?

18. The following table represents four possible combinations of outcomes of a production process and quality actions that can be taken.

OUTCOME

	Standards being met	Performance is unsatisfactory
Leave operations alone	A	B
Investigate and correct if necessary	C	D

a. Which situations are correct and which are erroneous?
b. Suppose that the following costs apply:

Prevention costs: $30 per hour
Appraisal costs: $10 per unit
Internal failure costs: $80 per unit
External failure costs: $200 per unit

The process produces 10 units per hour. Current quality-control policy is to inspect and test 10 percent of units produced. Based on past history, 20 percent of the units need rework if performance standards of the process are not being met. What is the cost of each situation on an hourly basis?

Forecasting and Time Series Analysis

A critical aspect of managing any organization is planning for the future. Indeed, the long-run success of any organization is closely related to how well management is able to foresee the future and develop appropriate strategies. Good judgment, intuition, and an awareness of the state of the economy may give a manager a rough idea, or "feeling," of what is likely to happen in the future. However, it is often difficult to convert this feeling into hard data, such as next quarter's sales volume or next year's raw-material cost per unit. Nevertheless, forecasts must be developed if a company is to develop effective short- and long-range plans.

Suppose that we have been asked to provide quarterly estimates of the sales volume for a particular product during the coming 1-year period. Production schedules, raw-material purchasing plans, inventory policies, and sales quotas will all be affected by the quarterly estimates we provide. Consequently, poor estimates may result in poor planning and hence result in increased costs for the firm. How should we go about providing the quarterly sales volume estimates?

We certainly want to review the actual sales data for the product in past periods. Suppose that we have actual sales data for each quarter over the past three years. From these historical data we can identify the general level of sales and determine whether or not there is any trend such as an increase or decrease in sales volume over time. A further review of the data might reveal a seasonal pattern, such as peak sales volume during the third quarter of each year and sales volume bottoming out during the first quarter. By reviewing historical data over time we are in a better position to understand the pattern of the past sales and hence better able to predict future sales for the product.

In this chapter, we discuss the problem of forecasting product sales and other variables of interest to operations managers. By having a better knowledge of the future, managers can make better decisions, which can improve productivity.

3.1 THE ROLE OF FORECASTING IN P/OM

In order to plan for the future and make effective decisions, *forecasts* of future demand are required at all levels of decision making. Operations managers need estimates of the demand for goods and services for time horizons ranging from one day to several years.

Long-range sales forecasts are required to plan for the expansion of production and distribution facilities and to determine future needs for equipment and labor. For example, if product sales are expected to grow at an annual rate of 30 percent, then operations managers must plan on increasing production capacity extensively. The long lead time necessary to construct new facilities means that plans for capacity expansion must be made well in advance.

Intermediate-range sales forecasts over a 3- to 12-month period are needed in order to plan work force levels, allocate budgets among product divisions, and establish purchasing policies. Such forecasts may help a purchasing department negotiate a substantial discount by contracting to order a large amount of a certain material or component over the next year. Such forecasts can also be used by personnel departments in planning for future hiring, employee training, and so on.

Short-range forecasts are used by operations managers to plan production schedules and assign workers to jobs. They are also used to determine short-term capacity requirements and are used by shipping departments in planning transportation needs and establishing delivery schedules.

Many different types of forecasts are made in an organization. Consider a consumer products company, such as Procter & Gamble or Colgate-Palmolive, which makes many different products in varying sizes. Long-range forecasts might be expressed in total sales dollars for use in financial planning by top management. At lower organizational levels, managers of different product groups need aggregate forecasts of total sales volume for their products in units of measurement that are more meaningful to them (for example, pounds a certain type of soap) in order to establish production plans. Finally, managers of individual manufacturing facilities need forecasts by brand size—for instance, the number of 64-ounce boxes of Tide—in order to plan material usage and production schedules. These forecasts must be consistent across organizational levels in order to be effective planning aids. In addition, special forecasts—such as forecasts of material and production costs, prices, and so on—may be required for new products and promotional items. We see then, that forecasts may be of many different types and in different units of measurement, depending on their purpose.

Good forecasts can help operations managers make better decisions in an uncertain environment, and bad forecasts can lead to bankruptcy. Forecasting demand for complex and rapidly changing high-technology products such as personal computers, software, robotics, and telecommunication products is especially difficult. Experience has shown that most forecasts for such products have been overly optimistic. For example, actual sales of personal computers in the early 1980s was only about 45 percent of that forecasted.[1] Similar forecasting errors have been found for other technology-based products. The consequences can be devastating as businesses plan for sales expectations that are not realized. In 1983–84, forecasters predicted strong long-term sales growth for semiconductor chips; as a result, many companies built new plants costing up to $500

---

[1]David R. Wheeler and Charles J. Shelley, "Toward More Realistic Forecasts for High-Technology Products," *Journal of Business and Industrial Marketing*, 2, no. 3, (Summer 1987) 55.

million. As the plants opened, demand fell sharply and the companies struggled to survive.

Forecasting demand for services is just as important as forecasting product demand, especially when heavy capital investment is needed to provide the service. For example, airlines need forecasts of demand for air travel to plan for purchases of airplanes. Operations managers in the travel and tourism industry make seasonal forecasts of demand, university administrators require enrollment forecasts, city planners need forecasts of population trends in order to plan highways and mass transit systems, and restaurants need forecasts in order to be able to plan for food purchases.

Forecasting in Service Organizations

Service organizations have some unique characteristics that impact forecasting. For instance, the demand for many services, such as in the airline and hotel industries, is highly seasonal. Demand for services may also vary with the day of the week or time of the day. Grocery stores, banks, and other similar organizations need very short term forecasts to plan for variations in demand. Forecast information is needed for workshift scheduling, vehicle routing, and other operating decisions.

Many firms that provide customized services find it easy to forecast the number of customers that will demand service in a particular time period, but find it quite difficult to forecast the mix of services that will be required or the time it will take to provide those services. Thus, special forecasts of service mix are needed.

3.2 A CLASSIFICATION OF FORECASTING METHODS

There are many different techniques used in forecasting. Which technique should be used depends on the variable being forecast and the length of the time horizon over which the forecast is to be made. If we are forecasting weekly sales of a product, then it is reasonable to assume that recent trends will probably continue on into the near future. Thus a technique that uses historical data to make a forecast will probably be useful.

On the other hand, suppose that we are asked to forecast the length of time until a current technology becomes obsolete (for example, slide rules are now obsolete as a result of electronic calculators, mechanical cash registers have rapidly disappeared because of microprocessors, and typewriters are being replaced by word processors). Certainly past data cannot provide a basis for forecasting obsolescence. Such forecasts must be based to a large extent on the opinions and expertise of those knowledgeable about changing technology.

Forecasting weekly sales and product obsolescence are two examples that provide a basic distinction between the various approaches to forecasting. Figure 3.1 provides a classification of forecasting methods. Forecasting methods can be classified as *statistical* or *judgmental*. The basis for statistical forecasting methods is the assumption that the future will be an extrapolation of the past. Statistical forecasting methods are classified as either *time series models* or *casual* (regression) *models*. Time series models can be further broken down into *trend projection, trend projection adjusted for seasonal influences,* and *smoothing methods.*

FIGURE 3.1   A Classification of Forecasting Methods

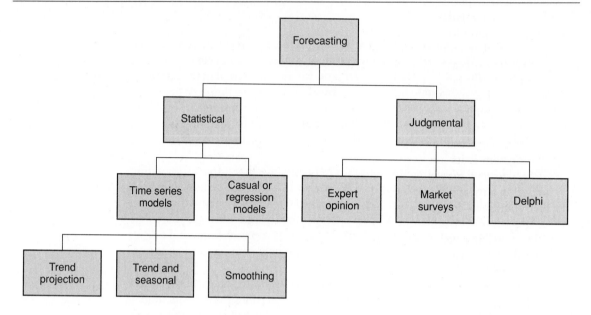

Judgmental forecasting methods include *expert opinion, market surveys,* and the *Delphi method.*

For strategic forecasting of new technology or other variables for which no historical data are available, judgmental forecasting is used. When historical data are available, trend projections and regression models are useful techniques, especially for long-range forecasts. For intermediate-range forecasting, particularly when there are seasonal effects present, the trend and seasonal methods are often used. Finally, smoothing methods are the most common techniques for short-range forecasting.

3.3 JUDGMENTAL FORECASTING

One would be a poor business forecaster if predictions were made solely on the basis of historical data. The demand for products and services is affected by a variety of factors such as interest rates, inflation, and other economic conditions. Actions of competitors and government regulations also have an impact. One interesting illustration of judgmental forecasting occurred during the recession in the mid-1970s. All economic indicators pointed toward a future period of low demand for a manufacturer of machine tools. However, company forecasters recognized that recent government regulations concerning automobile-pollution control would require the auto industry to update its current technology by purchasing new tools. As a result, this machine-tool company was prepared for the new business.

Some techniques that are commonly used to arrive at judgmental forecasts are expert opinion, market surveys, and the Delphi method. Forecasting by *expert opinion* simply consists of gathering judgments and opinions of key personnel based on their experience and knowledge of the situation. For instance, sales people who have regular personal contacts with customers are in a good position to estimate demand for their customers over a future time period. Regional sales managers can then subjectively modify this information and aggregate it to develop broader forecasts. For example, a particular salesperson might always overestimate his or her sales forecast; it would probably be adjusted downward by the regional manager. Or, it may be recognized that a certain new product seems to be catching on in California. Recognizing that California often sets a trend for the rest of the nation, an expert might increase estimates in other regions. Though such forecasts are sometimes very inaccurate, the advantage of using expert judgment is its low cost in comparison to other methods.

Market surveys may utilize questionnaires, telephone contacts, or personal interviews as a means of gathering data. Market surveys are most often used in strategic planning—for instance, in obtaining new product information. Extensive statistical analysis is usually applied to survey results in order to test hypotheses regarding consumer behavior. The cost of such surveys is high due to labor costs, postage, low response rates, and post-survey processing. These surveys are also highly subject to bias.

A third subjective approach to forecasting is called the **Delphi method**. This is a group technique in which a panel of experts are individually questioned about their perceptions of future events. The experts do not meet as a group, however, in order to avoid the danger of consensus being reached because of dominant personality factors. Instead, the responses and supporting arguments of each individual are summarized by an outside party and returned to the experts along with further questions. This process iterates until a consensus is reached by the group; it usually only takes a few rounds. The Delphi method is useful for long-range forecasting and in predicting technological changes. The following example shows the benefits that were derived by one company in using this technique.

American Hoist and Derrick is a manufacturer of construction equipment, with annual sales of several million dollars.[2] Their sales forecast is an actual planning figure and is used to develop the master production schedule, cash flow projections, and work-force plans. One of the important components of their forecasting process is the use of the Delphi method of judgmental forecasting.

Top management wanted an accurate 5-year forecast of their sales in order to plan for expansion of production capacity. The Delphi method was used in conjunction with regression models and exponential smoothing in order to generate a forecast. A panel of 23 key personnel was established, consisting of those who had been making subjective forecasts, those who had been using them or were affected by the forecasts, and those who had a strong knowledge of the market and corporate sales. Three rounds of the Delphi method were performed, each requesting estimates of

- gross national product
- onstruction equipment industry shipments

---

[2]Adapted from Shankar Basu and Roger Schroeder, "Incorporating Judgments in Sales Forecasts: Applicating the Delphi Method at American Hoist and Derrick," *Interfaces* 7, no. 3 (June 1977): 18–27. Reprinted by permission of The Institute of Management Sciences, 290 Westminster Street, Providence, Rhode Island 02903, USA. Copyright 1977.

- American Hoist and Derrick construction equipment group shipments
- American Hoist and Derrick corporate value of shipments.

As the Delphi technique progressed, responses for each round were collected, analyzed, and summarized, and reported back to the panel. In the third-round questionnaire, not only were the responses of the first two rounds included, but—in addition,—related facts, figures, and views of external experts were sent.

As a result of the Delphi experiment, the sales forecast error was less than .33 percent; in the following year the error was under 4 percent. This was considerable improvement over previous forecast errors of plus or minus 20 percent. In fact, the Delphi forecasts were more accurate than regression models or exponential smoothing which had forecast errors of 10 to 15 percent. An additional result of the exercise was educational in nature. Managers developed a uniform outlook on business conditions and corporate sales volume and thus had a common base for decision making.

3.4 STATISTICAL FORECASTING: TIME SERIES MODELS

Statistical methods of forecasting are based on the analysis of historical data called a times series. Formally, a **time series** is a set of observations measured at successive points in time or over successive periods of time. For example, if we are asked to provide quarterly estimates of sales volume, then we are working with time period data. Data such as the prices of common stocks or amounts of working capital are measured at successive points in time.

In order to explain the pattern of behavior of the data in a time series it is often helpful to think to the time series as consisting of several components. The usual assumption is that four separate components—trend, cyclical, seasonal, and irregular—combine to make the time series take on specific values. Let us look more closely at each of these components of a time series.

Trend
Component

In time series analysis the measurements may be taken every hour, day, week, month, or year or at any other regular interval.[3] Although time series data generally exhibit random fluctuations, the time series may still show gradual shifts or movements to relatively higher or lower values over a longer period of time. This gradual shifting of the time series, which is usually because of long-term factors such as changes in the population, changes in demographic characteristics of the population, changes in technology, and changes in consumer preferences, is referred to as the **trend** in the time series.

For example, a manufacturer of photographic equipment may see substantial month-to-month variability in the number of cameras sold. However, in reviewing the sales over the past 10 to 15 years, this manufacturer may find a gradual increase in the annual sales volume. Suppose that the sales volume was approx-

---

[3]We restrict our attention here to time series where the values of the series are recorded at equal intervals. Treatment of cases where the observations are not made at equal intervals is beyond the scope of this text.

imately 1800 cameras per month in 1975, 2200 cameras per month in 1980, and 2600 cameras per month in 1985. While actual month-to-month sales volumes may vary substantially, this gradual growth is sales over time shows an upward trend for the time series. Figure 3.2 shows a straight line that may be good approximation of the trend in the sales data. While the trend for camera sales appears to be linear and increasing over time, sometimes the trend in a time series is better described by other patterns.

Figure 3.3 shows some other possible time series trend patterns. In (a) we see a nonlinear trend. This curve describes a time series showing very little growth initially, followed by a period of rapid growth, and then a leveling off. This might be a good approximation to sales for a product from introduction through a growth period and into a period of market saturation. The linear decreasing trend in (b) is useful for time series displaying a steady decrease over time. The horizontal line in (c) is used for a time series that does not show any consistent increase or decrease over time. It is actually the case of no trend.

Cyclical Component

While a time series may exhibit a gradual shifting or trend pattern over long periods of time, we cannot expect all future values of the time series to be exactly on the trend line. In fact, time series often show alternating sequences of points below and above the trend line. Any regular pattern or sequence of points above and below the trend line is attributable to the **cyclical component** of the time series. Figure 3.4 shows the graph of a time series with an obvious cyclical component. The observations are taken at intervals one year apart.

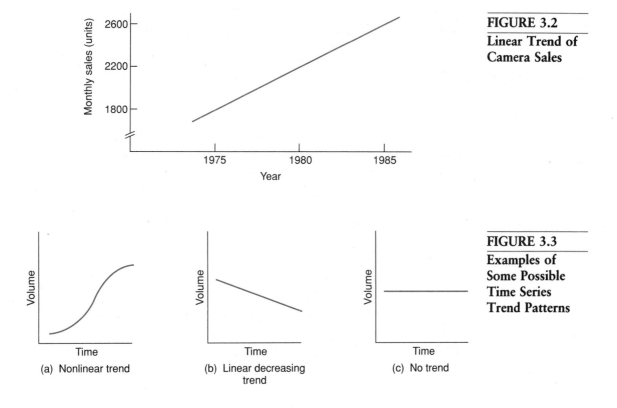

FIGURE 3.2
Linear Trend of Camera Sales

FIGURE 3.3
Examples of Some Possible Time Series Trend Patterns

FIGURE 3.4

Trend and
Cyclical
Components of a
Time Series
(Data Points Are
One Year Apart)

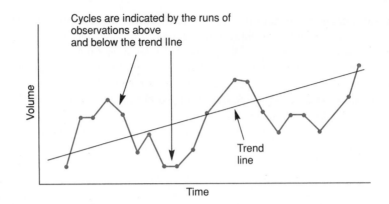

Cycles are indicated by the runs of observations above and below the trend line

Trend line

Volume

Time

Many time series exhibit cyclical behavior with regular runs of observations below and above the trend line. The general belief is that this component of the time series often reflects multiyear cyclical movements in the economy. For example, periods of moderate inflation followed by periods of rapid inflation can lead to many time series that alternate below and above a generally increasing trend line (e.g., housing costs). Many time series in the late 1970s and early 1980s displayed this type of behavior.

Seasonal Component

While the trend and cyclical components of a time series are identified by analyzing multiyear movements in historical data, many time series show a regular pattern of variability within 1-year periods. For example, a manufacturer of swimming pools expects low sales activity in the fall and winter months, with peak sales occurring in the spring and summer months. Manufacturers of snow removal equipment and heavy clothing, however, expect just the opposite yearly pattern. It should not be surprising that the component of the time series that represents the variability in the data because of seasonal influences is called the **seasonal component**. While we generally think of seasonal movement in a time series as occurring within one year, the seasonal component can also be used to represent any repeating pattern that is less than one year in duration. For example, daily traffic volume data show within-the-day "seasonal" behavior, with peak levels during rush hours, moderate flow during the rest of the day and early evening, and light flow from midnight to early morning.

Irregular Component

The **irregular component** of the time series is the residual or "catch-all" factor that accounts for the deviation of the actual time series value from what we would expect given the effects of the trend, cyclical, and seasonal components. It accounts for the random variability in the time series. The irregular component is caused by the short term, unanticipated, and nonrecurring factors that affect the time series. Since this component accounts for the random variability in the time series, it is unpredictable. We cannot attempt to predict its impact on the time series in advance.

Because of the irregular component, *forecasts are never 100 percent accurate*. This is crucial for operations managers to remember when using forecasts in decision making. The best we can hope for is to identify the pattern and use it to provide good estimates for future values.

3.5 LONG-RANGE FORECASTING USING TREND PROJECTION

Long-range forecasts are generally used for business planning purposes for determining long-term capacity requirements for capital investment analysis. The size of facilities, the amount of equipment to purchase, and personnel training for future needs depend on good long-range forecasts.

In this section we will see how to forecast the values of a time series that exhibits a long-term linear trend. Specifically, let us consider the time series data for bicycle sales of a particular manufacturer over the past 10 years, as shown in Table 3.1 and Figure 3.5. Note that 21,600 bicycles were sold in the first year, 22,900 were sold in year 2, and so on; in year 10, the most recent year, 31,400 bicycles were sold. Although the graph in Figure 3.5 shows some up and down movement over the past 10 years, the time series seems to have an overall increasing or upward trend in the number of bicycles sold.

We do not want the trend component of a time series to follow each and every "up" and "down" movement. Rather, the trend component should reflect the gradual shifting—in this case, growth—of the time series values. After we view the time series data in Table 3.1 and the graph in Figure 3.5, we might agree that a linear trend as shown in Figure 3.6 has the potential of providing a reasonable description of the long-run movement in the series. Thus we can now concentrate on finding the linear function that best approximates the trend.

For a linear trend, the estimated sales volume expressed as a function of time can be written as

$$T_t = b_0 + b_1 t \tag{3.1}$$

where

T_t = trend value for bicycle sales in period t

b_0 = intercept of the trend line

b_1 = slope of the trend line

t = time in years

Year t	Sales in Thousands Y_t	Year t	Sales in Thousands Y_t
1	21.6	6	27.5
2	22.9	7	31.5
3	25.5	8	29.7
4	21.9	9	28.6
5	23.9	10	31.4

TABLE 3.1

Bicycle Sales Data

FIGURE 3.5
Graph of the
Bicycle Sales
Time Series

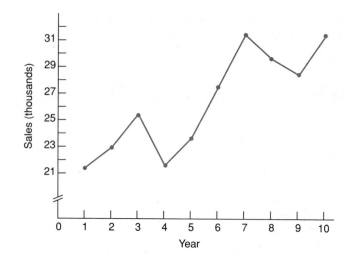

FIGURE 3.6
Trend
Represented by a
Linear Function
for Bicycle Sales

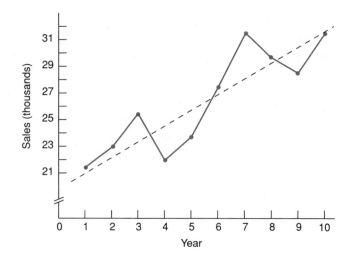

In the linear trend relationship in Equation (3.1) we will let $t = 1$ for the time of the first observation in the time series, $t = 2$ for the time of the second observation, and so on.

The approach most often used to determine the linear function that best approximates the trend is based on a procedure referred to as the least-squares method. The least-squares method identifies the values of b_0 and b_1 that minimize the sum of squared forecast errors. That is, the objective is to determine the values of b_0 and b_1 that minimize

$$\sum_{t=1}^{n} (Y_t - T_t)^2 \qquad (3.2)$$

where

Y_t = actual value of the time series in period t

T_t = forecast or trend value of the time series in period t

n = number of periods

The least-squares method, which is also used for the statistical technique known as regression analysis, is described in most elementary books on statistics. Shown below are the formulas that can be used to compute the value of b_0 and the value of b_1 using this approach.

$$b_1 = \frac{\Sigma t\, Y_t - (\Sigma t\, \Sigma Y_t)/n}{\Sigma t^2 - (\Sigma t)^2/n} \qquad (3.3)$$

$$b_0 = \overline{Y} - b_1 \overline{t} \qquad (3.4)$$

where

$\overline{Y}$ = average value of the time series; that is, $\overline{Y} = \dfrac{\Sigma Y_t}{n}$

$\overline{t}$ = average value of t; that is, $\overline{t} = \dfrac{\Sigma t}{n}$

The above summations are for values of t from 1 through n.

COMPUTING A LINEAR TREND

EXAMPLE

Using Equations (3.3) and (3.4) for b_1 and b_0 and the bicycle sales data of Table 3.1, we have the following calculations:

t	Y_t	tY_t	t^2
1	21.6	21.6	1
2	22.9	45.8	4
3	25.5	76.5	9
4	21.9	87.6	16
5	23.9	119.5	25
6	27.5	165.0	36
7	31.5	220.5	49
8	29.7	237.6	64
9	28.6	257.4	81
10	31.4	314.0	100
Totals 55	264.5	1545.5	385

$$\overline{t} = \frac{55}{10} = 5.5 \text{ years}$$

$$\overline{Y} = \frac{264.5}{10} = 26.45 \text{ thousands}$$

$$b_1 = \frac{1545.5 - (55)(264.5)/10}{385 - (55)^2/10} = \frac{90.75}{82.5} = 1.1$$

$$b_0 = 26.45 - 1.10(5.5) = 20.4$$

Therefore,

$$T_t = 20.4 + 1.1t \qquad (3.5)$$

is the expression for the linear trend component of the bicycle sales time series.

Trend Projections

The slope of 1.1 indicates that over the past 10 years the firm has experienced an average growth in sales of around 1100 units per year. If we assume that the past 10-year trend in sales is a good indicator of the future, then Equation (3.5) can be used to project the trend component of the time series. For example, substituting $t = 11$ into Equation (3.5) yields next year's trend projection, T_{11}, or:

$$T_{11} = 20.4 + 1.1(11) = 32.5$$

Thus, using the trend component, we would forecast sales of 32,500 bicycles next year.

The use of a linear function to model the trend is common. However, as we discussed earlier, sometimes time series exhibit a nonlinear trend. Figure 3.7 shows two common nonlinear trend functions. More advanced texts discuss in detail how to solve for the trend component when a nonlinear function is used and how to decide when to use such a function. For our purposes it is sufficient to note that the analyst should choose the function that provides the best fit to the time series data.

3.6 INTERMEDIATE-RANGE FORECASTING: THE MULTIPLICATIVE TIME SERIES MODEL

Intermediate-range forecasts are used in aggregate production planning. Such forecasts are determined on either a monthly or quarterly basis for product groups, and assist managers in making decisions regarding inventory levels, the

FIGURE 3.7

Some Possible Functional Forms for Nonlinear Trend Patterns

(a) Exponential trend

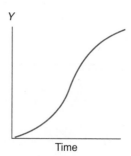

(b) Gompertz growth curve

use of additional shifts, or changes in the work force. Such alternatives are used when demand exhibits seasonal or cyclical fluctuations.

In this section we expand our discussion by showing how to forecast a time series that has both trend and seasonal components. The approach we will take is first to remove the seasonal effect or seasonal component from the time series. This step is referred to as *deseasonalizing* the time series. After deseasonalizing, the time series will have only a trend component. As a result we can use the least-squares method described in the previous section to identify the trend component of the time series. Then, using a trend projection calculation, we will be able to forecast the trend component of the time series in future periods. The final step in developing the forecast will be to incorporate the seasonal component by using a seasonal factor to adjust the trend projection. In this manner we will be able to identify the trend and seasonal components and consider both in forecasting the time series.

In addition to a trend component (T) and a seasonal component (S), we will assume that the time series also has an irregular component (I). The irregular component accounts for any random effects in the time series that cannot be explained by the trend and seasonal components. Using T_t, S_t, and I_t to identify the trend, seasonal, and irregular components at time t, we will assume that the actual time series value, denoted by Y_t, can be described by the following *multiplicative time series model:*

$$Y_t = T_t \times S_t \times I_t \qquad (3.6)$$

In this model T_t is the trend measured in units of the item being forecast. However, the S_t and I_t components are measured in relative terms, with values above 1.00 indicating effects above the normal or average level. Values below 1.00 indicate below-average levels for each component. In order to illustate the use of Equation (3.6) to model a time series, suppose that we have a trend projection of 540 units. In addition, suppose that $S_t = 1.10$ shows a seasonal effect 10 percent above average and $I_t = 0.98$ shows an irregular effect 2 percent below average. Using these values in Equation (3.6), the time series value would be $Y_t = 540(1.10)(0.98) = 582$.

In this section we will illustrate the use of the multiplicative model with trend, seasonal, and irregular components by working with the quarterly data presented in Table 3.2 and Figure 3.8. These data show the television set sales (in thousands of units) for a particular manufacturer over the past four years. We begin by showing how to identify the seasonal component of the time series.

CALCULATING THE SEASONAL INDEXES

EXAMPLE

By referring to Figure 3.8, we can begin to identify a seasonal pattern for the television set sales. Specifically, we observe that sales are lowest in the second quarter of each year, followed by higher sales levels in quarters 3 and 4. The computational procedure used to identify each quarter's seasonal influence requires the identification of the seasonal components, S_t, for each season of the time series.

The computation of seasonal indexes begins with the computation of **moving averages** for the time series. Since we are working with a quarterly television set sales data (four time periods or quarters per year), we will use four data values

TABLE 3.2

Quarterly Data
for Television Set
Sales

Year	Quarter	Sales (1000s)
1	1	4.8
	2	4.1
	3	6.0
	4	6.5
2	1	5.8
	2	5.2
	3	6.8
	4	7.4
3	1	6.0
	2	5.6
	3	7.5
	4	7.8
4	1	6.3
	2	5.9
	3	8.0
	4	8.4

FIGURE 3.8

**Graph of
Quarterly
Television Set
Sales Time Series**

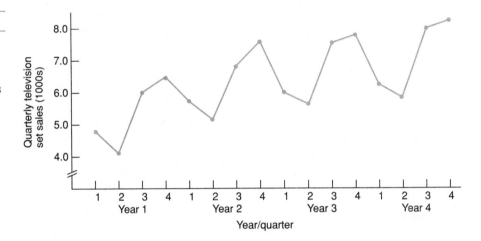

Figure 3.8

Black

in each of the moving averages. For example, the first moving average is simply the average of the first four data values in the time series. Using television set sales for time periods or quarters 1, 2, 3, and 4, the first moving average is as follows:

$$\text{First moving average} = \frac{4.8 + 4.1 + 6.0 + 6.5}{4} = \frac{21.4}{4} = 5.35$$

Note that the moving average calculation for the first four quarters yields the average quarterly sales over the first year of the time series. Continuing the moving average calculation, we next add the 5.8 value for the first quarter of year 2 and drop the oldest value 4.8 for the first quarter of year 1. Thus the second moving average, based on time periods 2, 3, 4, and 5, is

$$\text{Second moving average} = \frac{4.1 + 6.0 + 6.5 + 5.8}{4} = \frac{22.4}{4} = 5.60$$

Similarly, the third moving average calculation is $(6.0 + 6.5 + 5.8 + 5.2)/4 = 5.875$.

Before we proceed with the moving average calculations for the entire time series, let us return to the first moving average calculation, which resulted in a value of 5.35. The 5.35 value represents an average quarterly sales volume (across all seasons) for year 1. As we look back at the calculation of the 5.35 value, perhaps it makes sense to associate 5.35 with the "middle" quarter of the moving average group. However, note that some difficulty in identifying the middle quarter is encountered; with four quarters in the moving average, there is no middle quarter. The 5.35 value corresponds to the end of quarter 2 and the beginning of quarter 3. Similarly, if we go to the next moving average value of 5.60, the middle corresponds to the end of quarter 3 and the beginning of quarter 4.

Recall that the reason for computing moving averages is to isolate the combined seasonal and irregular components. However, the moving average values we have computed do not correspond directly to the original quarters of the time series. We can resolve this difficulty by using the midpoints between successive moving average values. For example, since 5.35 corresponds to the beginning of quarter 3 and 5.60 corresponds to the end of quarter 3, we will use $(5.35 + 5.60)/2 = 5.475$ as the moving average value for quarter 3. Similarly, we associate a moving average value of $(5.60 + 5.875)/2 = 5.738$ with quarter 4. What results is called a centered moving average. A complete summary of the centered moving average calculations for the television set sales data is shown in Table 3.3.

Let us pause for a moment to consider what the moving averages in Table 3.3 tell us about this time series. A plot of the actual time series values and the corresponding centered moving average is shown in Figure 3.9. Note particularly how the centered moving average values tend to "smooth out" the fluctuations in the time series. Since the moving average values are for four quarters of data, they do not include the fluctuations because of seasonal influences. Each point in the centered moving average represents what the value of the time series would be if there were no seasonal or irregular influence.

By dividing each time series observation by the corresponding centered moving average value, we can identify the seasonal-irregular effect in the time series. For

Year	Quarter	Sales	Four-Quarter Moving Average	Centered Moving Average
1	1	4.8		
	2	4.1		
			5.350	
	3	6.0		5.475
			5.600	
	4	6.5		5.738
			5.875	
2	1	5.8		5.975
			6.075	
	2	5.2		6.188
			6.300	
	3	6.8		6.325
			6.350	
	4	7.4		6.400
			6.450	
3	1	6.0		6.538
			6.625	
	2	5.6		6.675
			6.725	
	3	7.5		6.763
			6.800	
	4	7.8		6.838
			6.875	
4	1	6.3		6.938
			7.000	
	2	5.9		7.075
			7.150	
	3	8.0		
	4	8.4		

TABLE 3.3

Centered Moving Average Calculations for the Television Set Sales Time Series

FIGURE 3.9

Graph ot
Quarterly
Television Set
Sales Time Series
and Centered
Moving Average

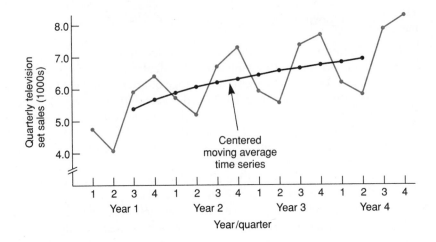

example, the third quarter of year 1 shows $6.0/5.475 = 1.096$ as the combined seasonal-irregular component. The resulting seasonal-irregular values for the entire time series values are summarized in Table 3.4.

Consider the third quarter. The results from years 1, 2, and 3 show third-quarter values of 1.096, 1.075, and 1.109, respectively. Thus in all cases the seasonal-irregular component appears to have an above average influence in the third quarter. Since the year-to-year fluctuations in the seasonal-irregular component can be attributed primarily to the irregular component, we can average the computed values to eliminate the irregular influence and obtain an estimate of the third-quarter seasonal influence.

$$\text{Seasonal effect of third quarter} = \frac{1.096 + 1.075 + 1.109}{3} = 1.09$$

TABLE 3.4

Seasonal-
Irregular Factors
for the Television
Set Sales Time
Series

Year	Quarter	Sales (1000s)	Centered Moving Average	Seasonal-Irregular Component
1	1	4.8		
	2	4.1		
	3	6.0	5.475	1.096
	4	6.5	5.738	1.133
2	1	5.8	5.975	0.971
	2	5.2	6.188	0.840
	3	6.8	6.325	1.075
	4	7.4	6.400	1.156
3	1	6.0	6.538	0.918
	2	5.6	6.675	0.839
	3	7.5	6.763	1.109
	4	7.8	6.838	1.141
4	1	6.3	6.938	0.908
	2	5.9	7.075	0.834
	3	8.0		
	4	8.4		

We refer to 1.09 as the *seasonal index* for the third quarter. In Table 3.5 we summarize the calculations involved in computing the seasonal indexes for the television set sales time series. Thus we see that the seasonal indexes for all four quarters are as follows: quarter 1, 0.93; quarter 2, 0.84; quarter 3, 1.09; and quarter 4, 1.14.

Interpretation of the values in Table 3.5 provides some observations about the "seasonal" component in television set sales. The best sales quarter is the fourth quarter, with sales averaging 14 percent above the average quarterly level. The worst, or slowest, sales quarter is the second quarter; its seasonal index of 0.84 shows that sales averages 16 percent below the average quarterly sales. The seasonal component corresponds nicely to the intuitive expectation that television-viewing interest and thus television purchase patterns tend to peak in the fourth quarter, with its coming winter season and fewer outdoor activities. The low second-quarter sales reflect the reduced television interest resulting from the spring and presummer activities of the potential customers.

One final adjustment is sometimes necessary in computing the seasonal index. The multiplicative model requires that the average seasonal index equal 1.00; that is, the sum of the four seasonal indexes in Table 3.5 should equal 4.00. This is necessary if the seasonal effects are to even out over the year, as they must. The average of the seasonal indexes in our example is equal to 1.00, and hence this type of adjustment is not necessary. In other cases a slight adjustment may be necessary. The adjustment can be made by simply multiplying each seasonal index by the number of seasons divided by the sum of the unadjusted seasonal indexes. For example, for quarterly data we would multiply each seasonal index by 4/(sum of the unadjusted seasonal indexes). Some of the problems at the end of the chapter will require this adjustment in order to obtain the appropriate seasonal indexes.

Often the purpose of finding seasonal indexes is to remove the seasonal effects from a time series. This process is referred to as *deseasonalizing* the time series. Economic time series adjusted for seasonal variations (deseasonalized time series) are often reported in publications such as the *Survey of Current Business* and the *Wall Street Journal*. Using the notation of the multiplicative model, we have

Deseasonalizing the Time Series

$$Y_t = T_t \times S_t \times I_t$$

By dividing each time series observation by the corresponding seasonal index, we have removed the effect of season from the time series. The result is called the **deseasonalized time series**. The deseasonalized time series for television set

Quarter	Seasonal-Irregular Component Values ($S_t I_t$)	Seasonal Index (S_t)
1	0.971, 0.918, 0.908	0.93
2	0.840, 0.839, 0.834	0.84
3	1.096, 1.075, 1.109	1.09
4	1.133, 1.156, 1.141	1.14

TABLE 3.5

Seasonal Index Calculations for the Television Set Sales Time Series

sales is summarized in Table 3.6. A graph of the deseasonalized television set sales time series is shown in Figure 3.10.

Looking at Figure 3.10, we see that while the graph shows some up and down movement over the past 16 quarters, the time series seems to have an upward linear trend. Now, to identify this trend we can use the same procedure we introduced for identifying trend when forecasting with annual data. In this case, since we have deseasonalized the data, quarterly sales values can be used. Thus for a linear trend the estimated sales volume expressed as a function of time can be written

$$T_t = b_0 + b_1 t$$

where

T_t = trend value for television set sales in period t

b_0 = intercept of the trend line

b_1 = slope of the trend line

As before, we will let $t = 1$ for the time of the first observation in the time series, $t = 2$ for the time of the second observation, and so on. Thus for the deseasonalized television set sales time series, $t = 1$ corresponds to the first deseasonalized quarterly sales value and $t = 16$ corresponds to the most recent deseasonalized quarterly sales value. The formulas for computing the value of b_0 and the value of b_1 are shown again as

$$b_1 = \frac{\Sigma \, tY_t - (\Sigma \, t \, \Sigma \, Y_t)/n}{\Sigma \, t^2 - (\Sigma \, t)^2/n}$$

$$b_0 = \overline{Y} - b_1 \overline{t}$$

Note, however, that Y_t now refers to the deseasonalized time series value at time t and not the actual value of the time series.

TABLE 3.6			Sales (1000s) (Y_t)	Seasonal Index (S_t)	Deseasonalized Sales ($Y_t/S_t = T_t I_t$)
Deseasonalized Time Series for Television Set Sales	Year	Quarter			
	1	1	4.8	0.93	5.16
		2	4.1	0.84	4.88
		3	6.0	1.09	5.50
		4	6.5	1.14	5.70
	2	1	5.8	0.93	6.24
		2	5.2	0.84	6.19
		3	6.8	1.09	6.24
		4	7.4	1.14	6.49
	3	1	6.0	0.93	6.45
		2	5.6	0.84	6.67
		3	7.5	1.09	6.88
		4	7.8	1.14	6.84
	4	1	6.3	0.93	6.77
		2	5.9	0.84	7.02
		3	8.0	1.09	7.34
		4	8.4	1.14	7.37

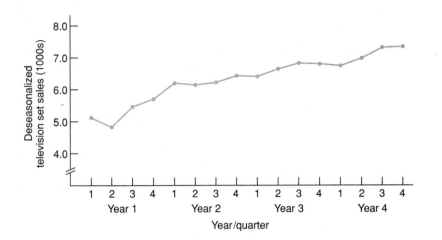

FIGURE 3.10

Deseasonalized
Television Set
Sales Time Series

USING THE DESEASONALIZED TIME SERIES TO
IDENTIFY TREND

EXAMPLE

Using the given relationships for b_0 and b_1 and the deseasonalized sales data of
Table 3.6, we have the following calculations:

t	Y_t (deseasonalized)	tY_t	t^2
1	5.16	5.16	1
2	4.88	9.76	4
3	5.50	16.50	9
4	5.70	22.80	16
5	6.24	31.20	25
6	6.19	37.14	36
7	6.24	43.68	49
8	6.49	51.92	64
9	6.45	58.05	81
10	6.67	66.70	100
11	6.88	75.68	121
12	6.84	82.08	144
13	6.77	88.01	169
14	7.02	98.28	196
15	7.34	110.10	225
16	7.37	117.92	256
Totals 136	101.74	914.98	1496

$$\bar{t} = \frac{136}{16} = 8.5$$

$$\bar{Y} = \frac{101.74}{16} = 6.359$$

$$b_1 = \frac{914.98 - (136)(101.74)/16}{1496 - (136)^2/16} = \frac{50.19}{340} = 0.148$$

$$b_0 = 6.359 - 0.148(8.5) = 5.101$$

Therefore,

$$T_t = 5.101 + 0.148t$$

is the expression for the linear trend component of the time series.

The slope of 0.148 indicates that over the past 16 quarters, the firm has experienced an average deseasonalized growth in sales of around 148 sets per quarter. If we assume that the past 16-quarter trend in sales data is a reasonably good indictor of the future, then this equation can be used to project the trend component of the time series for future quarters. For example, substituting $t; = 17$ into the equation yields next quarter's trend projection, T_{17}.

$$T_{17} = 5.101 + 0.148(17) = 7.617$$

Using the trend component only, we would forecast sales of 7617 television sets for the next quarter. In a similar fashion, if we were to use the trend component only, we would forecast sales of 7765, 7913, and 8061 television sets in quarters 18, 19, and 20, respectively.

Now that we have a forecast of sales for each of the next four quarters based on trend, we must adjust these forecasts to account for the effect of season.

EXAMPLE	

SEASONAL ADJUSTMENTS

For example, since the seasonal index for the first quarter is 0.93, the forecast for the first quarter of year 5 can be obtained by multiplying the forecast based on trend ($T_{17} = 7617$) times the seasonal index (0.93). Thus the forecast for the next quarter is 7617(0.93) = 7084. Table 3.7 shows the quarterly forecast for quarters 17, 18, 19, and 20. The quarterly forecasts show the high-volume fourth quarter with a 9190 unit forecast, while the low-volume second quarter has a 6523 unit forecast.

Models Based on Monthly Data

The television set sales example provided in this section used quarterly data to illustrate the computation of seasonal indexes with relatively few computations. Many businesses use monthly rather than quarterly forecasts. In such cases the procedures introduced in this section can be applied with minor modifications. First, a 12-month moving average replaces the four-quarter moving average; second, 12 monthly seasonal indexes, rather than four quarterly seasonal indexes, will need to be computed. Other than these changes, the computational and

TABLE 3.7

Quarter-by-Quarter Short-range Forecasts for the Television Set Sales Time Series

Year	Quarter	Trend Forecast	Seasonal Index (see Table 3.5)	Quarterly Forecast
5	1	7617	0.93	(7617)(0.93) = 7084
	2	7765	0.84	(7765)(0.84) = 6523
	3	7913	1.09	(7913)(1.09) = 8625
	4	8061	1.14	(8061)(1.14) = 9190

forecasting procedures are identical. Problem 8 at the end of the chapter asks you to develop monthly seasonal indexes for a situation requiring monthly forecasts.

Mathematically the multiplicative model of Equation (3.6) can be expanded to include a cyclical component as follows:

Cyclical Component

$$Y_t = T_t \times C_t \times S_t \times I_t \qquad (3.7)$$

Just as with the seasonal component, the cyclical component is expressed as a percent of trend. As mentioned in Section 3.4, this component is attributable to multiyear cycles in the time series. It is analogous to the seasonal component, but over a longer period of time. However, because of the length of time involved and the varying length of cycles, it is often difficult to obtain enough relevant data to estimate the cyclical component. We leave further discussion of the cyclical component to texts on forecasting methods.

3.7 SHORT-RANGE FORECASTING USING SMOOTHING METHODS

Short-range forecasting is usually needed for individual products in order to develop detailed production schedules or worker requirements. Over a short time period, trend, seasonal, or cyclical components are not very important. In this section we discuss forecasting techniques that are appropriate for a fairly stable time series, one that exhibits no significant trend, cyclical, or seasonal effects. In such situations the objective of the forecasting method is to "smooth out" the irregular component of the time series through some type of averaging process.

In the previous section, we introduced the method of moving averages as a step in the computation of seasonal indexes for a time series. The moving average associated with any time period is simply an average of the *most recent n data values* in the time series. Mathematically, the moving average calculation is made as follows:

Moving Averages

$$\text{Moving average} = \frac{\Sigma \ (\text{most recent } n \text{ data values})}{n} \qquad (3.8)$$

The term "moving" average is based on the fact that as a new observation becomes available for the time series, the new observation replaces the oldest observation in Equation (3.8) and a new moving average is computed. Thus, the data in the moving average changes or "moves" with each new observation for the time series. In short-range forecasting, the moving average for one period is used as the forecast for the next period.

FORECASTING WITH MOVING AVERAGES

EXAMPLE

To illustrate the moving averages method, consider the 12 weeks of data presented in Table 3.8 and Figure 3.11. These data show the number of gallons of gasoline sold by a gasoline distributor in Bennington, Vermont, over the past 12 weeks.

TABLE 3.8
Gasoline Sales
Time Series

Week	Sales (1000s of gallons)	Week	Sales (1000s of gallons)
1	17	7	20
2	21	8	18
3	19	9	22
4	23	10	20
5	18	11	15
6	16	12	22

FIGURE 3.11

Graph of Gasoline Sales Time Series

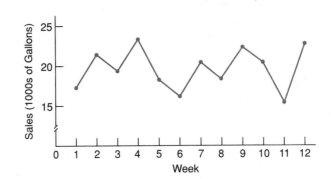

In order to use moving averages to forecast the gasoline sales time series, we must first select the number of data values to be included in the moving average. As an example, let us compute forecasts based on a 3-week moving average. The moving average calculation for the first three weeks of the gasoline sales time series is as follows:

$$\text{Moving average (weeks 1–3)} = \frac{17 + 21 + 19}{3} = 19$$

This moving average value is then used as the forecast for week 4. Since the actual value observed in week 4 is 23, we see that the **forecast error** in week 4 is $23 - 19 = 4$. In general, the forecast error is the difference between the observed value of the time series and the forecast.

The calculation for the second 3-week moving average is shown below.

$$\text{Moving average (weeks 2–4)} = \frac{21 + 19 + 23}{3} = 21$$

This moving average provides a forecast for week 5 of 21. The error associated with this forecast is $18 - 21 = -3$. Thus we see that the forecast error can be positive or negative depending on whether the forecast is too low or too high.

A complete summary of the 3-week moving average calculations for the gasoline sales time series is shown in Table 3.9 and Figure 3.12.

Mean Square Error

An important consideration in using any forecasting method is the accuracy of the forecast. Clearly, we would like the forecast errors to be small. The last two

Week	Time Series Value	Moving Average Forecast	Forecast Error	(Error)²
1	17			
2	21			
3	19			
4	23	19	4	16
5	18	21	−3	9
6	16	20	−4	16
7	20	19	1	1
8	18	18	0	0
9	22	18	4	16
10	20	20	0	0
11	15	20	−5	25
12	22	19	3	9
		Totals	0	92

TABLE 3.9

Summary of Three-Week Moving Average Calculations

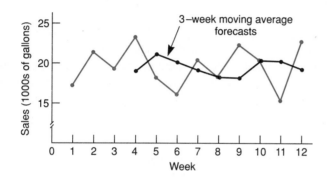

FIGURE 3.12

Graph of Gasoline Sales Time Series and 3-Week Moving Average Forecasts

columns of Table 3.9, which contain the forecast errors and the forecast errors squared, can be used to develop measures of accuracy.

One measure of forecast accuracy you might think of using would be to simply sum the forecast errors over time. The problem with this measure is that if the errors are random (as they should be if our choice of forecasting method is appropriate), some errors will be positive and some errors will be negative, resulting in a sum near zero regardless of the size of the individual errors. Referring to Table 3.9, we see that the sum of forecast errors for the gasoline sales time series is zero. This difficulty can be avoided by squaring each of the individual forecast errors.

For the gasoline sales time series we can use the last column of Table 3.9 to compute the average of the sum of the squared errors. Doing so, we obtain

$$\text{Average of the sum of squared errors} = \frac{92}{9} = 10.22$$

This average of the sum of squared errors is commonly referred to as the **mean square error (MSE)**. The mean square error is an often-used measure of the accuracy of a forecasting method and the one we will use in this chapter.

As we indicated previously, in order to use the moving averages method we must first select the number of data values to be included in the moving average. It should not be too surprising that, for a particular time series, different length moving averages will differ in their ability to forecast the time series accurately. One possible approach to choosing the best length is to use trial and error to identify the length that minimizes the MSE measure of forecast accuracy. Then, if we are willing to assume that the length which is best for the past will also be best for the future, we would forecast the next value in the time series using the number of data values that minimized the MSE for the historical time series. Problem 13 at the end of the chapter will ask you to consider 4-week and 5-week moving averages for the gasoline sales data. A comparison of the mean square error for each will indicate the number of weeks of data you may want to include in the moving average calculation.

Weighted Moving Averages

In the moving averages method each observation in the moving average calculation receives the same weight. One possible variation, known as *weighted moving averages*, involves selecting different weights for each data value and then computing a weighted mean as the forecast. In most cases the most recent observation receives the most weight, and the weight decreases for older data values. For example, using the gasoline sales time series, let us illustrate the computation of a weighted 3-week moving average, where the most recent observation receives a weight three times as great as that given the oldest observation, and the next oldest observation receives a weight twice as great as the oldest. The weighted moving average forecast for week 4 would be computed as follows:

$$\text{Weighted moving average forecast for week 4} = \tfrac{3}{6}(19) + \tfrac{2}{6}(21) + \tfrac{1}{6}(17)$$
$$= 19.33$$

Note that for the weighted moving average the sum of the weights is equal to 1. This was also true for the simple moving average, where each weight was ⅓. However, recall that the simple or unweighted moving average provided a forecast of 19. Problem 14 at the end of the chapter asks you to calculate the remaining values for the 3-week weighted moving average and compare the forecast accuracy with what we have obtained for the unweighted moving average.

Exponential Smoothing

Exponential smoothing is a forecasting technique that uses a weighted average of past time series values in order to forecast the value of the time series in the next period. The basic exponential smoothing model is as follows:

$$F_{t+1} = \alpha Y_t + (1 - \alpha)F_t \tag{3.9}$$

where

$$F_{t+1} = \text{forecast of the time series for period } t + 1$$
$$Y_t = \text{actual value of the time series in period } t$$
$$F_t = \text{forecast of the time series for period } t$$
$$\alpha = \textbf{smoothing constant } (0 \leqslant \alpha \leqslant 1)$$

To see that the forecast for any period is a weighted average of *all the previous actual values* for the time series, suppose that we have a time series consisting of three periods of data: Y_1, Y_2, and Y_3. To get the exponential smoothing calculations started, we let F_1 equal the actual value of the time series in period 1; that is, $F_1 = Y_1$. Hence the forecast for period 2 is written as follows:

$$
\begin{aligned}
F_2 &= \alpha Y_1 + (1 - \alpha)F_1 \\
&= \alpha Y_1 + (1 - \alpha)Y_1 \\
&= Y_1
\end{aligned}
$$

In general, then, the exponential smoothing forecast for period 2 is equal to the actual value of the time series in period 1.

To obtain the forecast for period 3, we substitute $F_2 = Y_1$ in the expression for F_3; the result is

$$
F_3 = \alpha Y_2 + (1 - \alpha)Y_1
$$

Finally, substituting this expression for F_3 in the expression for F_4, we obtain

$$
\begin{aligned}
F_4 &= \alpha Y_3 + (1 - \alpha)[\alpha Y_2 + (1 - \alpha)Y_1] \\
&= \alpha Y_3 + \alpha(1 - \alpha)Y_2 + (1 - \alpha)^2 Y_1
\end{aligned}
$$

Hence we see that F_4 is a weighted average of the first three time series values. The sum of the coefficients or weights for Y_1, Y_2, and Y_3 will always equal 1. A similar argument can be made to show that any forecast F_{t+1} is a weighted average of the previous t time series values.

An advantage of exponential smoothing is that it is a simple procedure and requires very little historical data for its use. Once the smoothing constant α has been selected, only two pieces of information are required in order to compute the forecast for the next period. Referring to Equation (3.9), we see that with a given α we can compute the forecast for period $t + 1$ simply by knowing the actual and forecast time series values for period t, that is, Y_t and F_t.

FORECASTING WITH EXPONENTIAL SMOOTHING

EXAMPLE

To illustrate the exponential smoothing approach to forecasting, consider the gasoline sales time series presented previously in Table 3.8 and Figure 3.11. As we indicated in the discussion above, the exponential smoothing forecast for period 2 is equal to the actual value of the time series in period 1. Thus, with $Y_1 = 17$, we will set $F_2 = 17$ to get the exponential smoothing computations started. Referring to the time series data in Table 3.8, we find an actual time series value in period 2 of $Y_2 = 21$. Thus period 2 has a forecast error of $21 - 17 = 4$.

Continuing with the exponential smoothing computations provides the following forecast for period 3:

$$
F_3 = 0.2Y_2 + 0.8F_2 = 0.2(21) + 0.8(17) = 17.8
$$

Once the actual time series value in period 3, $Y_3 = 19$, is known, we can generate a forecast for period 4 as follows:

$$
F_4 = 0.2Y_3 + 0.8F_3 = 0.2(19) + 0.8(17.8) = 18.04
$$

By continuing the exponential smoothing calculations we are able to determine the weekly forecast values and the corresponding weekly forecast errors, as shown in Table 3.10. Note that we have not shown an exponential smoothing forecast or the forecast error for period 1, because F_1 was set equal to Y_1 in order to begin the smoothing computations. For week 12, we have $Y_{12} = 22$ and $F_{12} = 18.48$. Can you use this information to generate a forecast for week 13 before the actual value of week 13 becomes known? Using the exponential smoothing model, we have

$$F_{13} = 0.2Y_{12} + 0.8F_{12} = 0.2(22) + 0.8(18.48) = 19.18$$

Thus the exponential smoothing forecast of the amount sold in week 13 is 19.18, or 19,180 gallons of gasoline. With this forecast the firm can make plans and decisions accordingly. The accuracy of the forecast will not be known until the firm conducts its business through week 13. However, the exponential smoothing model has provided a good forecast for the unknown 13th-week gasoline sales volume. Figure 3.13 shows the plot of the actual and the forecast time series values. Note in particular how the forecasts "smooth out" the irregular fluctuations in the time series.

In the preceding smoothing calculations we used a smoothing constant of $\alpha = 0.2$, although any value of α between 0 and 1 is acceptable. However, some values will yield better forecasts than others. Some insight into choosing a good value for α can be obtained by rewriting the basic exponential smoothing model as follows:

$$F_{t+1} = \alpha Y_t + (1 - \alpha)F_t$$
$$F_{t+1} = \alpha Y_t + F_t - \alpha F_t$$
$$F_{t+1} = \underbrace{F_t}_{} + \alpha \underbrace{(Y_t - F_t)}_{} \qquad (3.10)$$

$$\underset{\text{in period } t}{\uparrow \text{ Forecast}} \qquad \underset{\text{in period } t}{\uparrow \text{ Forecast error}}$$

TABLE 3.10	Week t	Time Series Value Y_t	Exponential Smoothing Forecast F_t	Forecast Error $Y_t - F_t$
Summary of the Exponential Smoothing Forecasts and Forecast Errors for Gasoline Sales with Smoothing Constant $\alpha = 0.2$	1	17		
	2	21	17.00	4.00
	3	19	17.80	1.20
	4	23	18.04	4.96
	5	18	19.03	−1.03
	6	16	18.83	−2.83
	7	20	18.26	1.74
	8	18	18.61	−0.61
	9	22	18.49	3.51
	10	20	19.19	0.81
	11	15	19.35	−4.35
	12	22	18.48	3.52

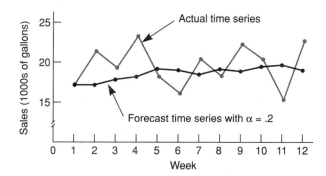

Thus we see that the new forecast F_{t+1} is equal to the previous forecast F_t plus an adjustment, which is α times the most recent forecast error, $Y_t - F_t$. That is, the forecast in period $t + 1$ is obtained by adjusting the forecast in period t by a fraction of the forecast error. If the time series is very volatile and contains substantial random variability, a small value of the smoothing constant is preferred. The reason for this choice is that since much of the forecast error is because of random variability, we do not want to overreact and adjust the forecasts too quickly. For a fairly stable time series with relatively little random variability, larger values of the smoothing constant have the advantage of quickly adjusting the forecasts when forecasting errors occur and therefore allowing the forecast to react faster to changing conditions.

The criterion we will use to determine a desirable value for the smoothing constant α is the same as the criterion we proposed earlier for determining the number of periods of data to include in the moving averages calculation. That is, we choose the value of α that minimizes the mean square error (MSE).

A summary of the mean square error calculations for the exponential smoothing forecast of gasoline sales with $\alpha = 0.2$ is shown in Table 3.11. Note that there is one less squared error term than the number of time periods, because we had no past values with which to make a forecast for period 1.

Microcomputer programs of exponential smoothing models can be very helpful in terms of identifying a good value for the smoothing constant. Such programs enable the user to input the historical data once and then check the forecasting accuracy for a variety of values for the smoothing constant. In Figure 3.14 we show the results obtained for $\alpha = 0.2$ using the forecasting module of *The Management Scientist*[4] software package. In addition to the forecast and forecast error for each time series value, the output provides the mean square error measure of accuracy and the forecast for the next period in the time series.

Would a different value of α have provided better results in terms of a lower MSE value? Perhaps the most straightforward way to answer this question is simply to try another value for α. We will then compare its mean square error with the MSE value of 8.98 obtained using a smoothing constant of 0.2.

The exponential smoothing results with $\alpha = 0.3$ are shown in Table 3.12. With MSE = 9.35, we see that for the current data set a smoothing constant of

[4]*The Management Scientist: A Microcomputer Software Package,* 1989. (Anderson, Sweeney, and Williams). St. Paul, MN: (West Publ. Co.).

TABLE 3.11

Mean Square Error Computations for Forecasting Gasoline Sales with $\alpha = 0.2$

Week t	Time Series Value Y_t	Forecast F_t	Forecast Error $Y_t - F_t$	Squared Error $(Y_t - F_t)^2$
1	17			
2	21	17.00	4.00	16.00
3	19	17.80	1.20	1.44
4	23	18.04	4.96	24.60
5	18	19.03	−1.03	1.06
6	16	18.83	−2.83	8.01
7	20	18.26	1.74	3.03
8	18	18.61	−0.61	0.37
9	22	18.49	3.51	12.32
10	20	19.19	0.81	0.66
11	15	19.35	−4.35	18.92
12	22	18.48	3.52	12.39
			Total	98.80

Mean square error (MSE) = $\dfrac{98.80}{11}$ = 8.98

FIGURE 3.14

Exponential Smoothing Output from *The Management Scientist* Software Package

```
FORECASTING WITH EXPONENTIAL SMOOTHING
****************************************

THE SMOOTHING CONSTANT IS .2


TIME PERIOD        TIME SERIES VALUE        FORECAST        FORECAST ERROR
===========        =================        ========        ==============

    1                     17
    2                     21                 17.00                4.00
    3                     19                 17.80                1.20
    4                     23                 18.04                4.96
    5                     18                 19.03               -1.03
    6                     16                 18.83               -2.83
    7                     20                 18.26                1.74
    8                     18                 18.61               -0.61
    9                     22                 18.49                3.51
   10                     20                 19.19                0.81
   11                     15                 19.35               -4.35
   12                     22                 18.48                3.52


        THE MEAN SQUARE ERROR              8.98


        THE FORECAST FOR PERIOD 13       19.18
```

$\alpha = 0.3$ results in less forecast accuracy than a smoothing constant of $\alpha = 0.2$. Thus we would be inclined to prefer the original smoothing constant of 0.2. With a trial-and-error calculation with other values of α, a "good" value for the smoothing constant can be found. This value can be used in the exponential smoothing model to provide forecasts for the future. At a later date, after a number of new time series observations have been obtained, it is good practice

Week t	Time Series Value Y_t	Forecast F_t	Forecast Error $Y_t - F_t$	Squared Error $(Y_t - F_t)^2$
1	17	17.00		
2	21	17.00	4.00	16.00
3	19	18.20	0.80	0.64
4	23	18.44	4.56	20.79
5	18	19.81	−1.81	3.28
6	16	19.27	−3.27	10.69
7	20	18.29	1.71	2.92
8	18	18.80	−0.80	0.64
9	22	18.56	3.44	11.83
10	20	19.59	0.41	0.17
11	15	19.71	−4.71	22.18
12	22	18.30	3.70	13.69
			Total	102.83

$$\text{Mean square error (MSE)} = \frac{102.83}{11} = 9.35$$

to analyze the newly collected time series data to see if the smoothing constant should be revised to provide better forecasting results.

Another commonly used measure of forecast accuracy is the **mean absolute deviation (MAD)**. This measure is simply the average of the sum of the absolute deviations for all the forecast errors. Using the errors in Table 3.11, we obtain

$$
\begin{aligned}
\text{MAD} &= \frac{\Sigma |Y_t - F_t|}{11} \\
&= \frac{4.00 + 1.20 + \cdots + 4.35 + 3.52}{11} \\
&= \frac{28.56}{11} = 2.596
\end{aligned}
$$

One major difference between MSE and MAD is that the MSE measure is influenced much more by large forecast errors than by small errors (since for the MSE measure, the errors are squared). The selection of the best measure of forecasting accuracy is not a simple matter. Indeed, forecasting experts often disagree as to which measure should be used.

MAD, however, is useful in *tracking* a forecast; that is, monitoring the forecast to determine if the forecasting technique being used remains adequate. The tracking method most often used is to compute a moving sum of forecast errors divided by the MAD; that is

$$\text{Tracking signal} = \frac{\Sigma(Y_t - F_t)}{\text{MAD}}$$

where both the sum of forecast errors and MAD are computed over the last n periods.

Mean Absolute Deviation and Tracking Signals

COMPUTING A TRACKING SIGNAL

Let us illustrate this for $n = 6$ using the data in Table 3.11. The first tracking signal that we can compute is after week 7. Summing the forecast errors for weeks 2–7 yields 8.04. The mean absolute deviation for this period is 15.76/6 = 2.63. Therefore, the tracking signal in period 7 is 8.04/2.63 = 3.06. Continuing in this fashion for weeks 8–12, we find the following:

Week t	$\Sigma(Y_t - F_t)$	MAD	Tracking Signal
8	3.43	12.37/6 = 2.06	1.67
9	5.74	14.68/6 = 2.45	2.34
10	1.59	10.53/6 = 1.76	.90
11	− 1.73	13.85/6 = 2.31	− .75
12	4.62	14.54/6 = 2.42	1.91

Generally, if the tracking signal is within limits such as − 3 to 3 or − 5 to 5 (defined subjectively), then the forecast is considered good. If, however, the tracking signal exceeds one limit, then the forecaster should examine the demand pattern and forecasting technique chosen. Tracking in this manner is appropriate for all forecasting, not just for exponential smoothing.

3.8 FORECASTING WITH REGRESSION MODELS

Causal forecasting models utilize time series related to the variable being forecast in an effort to better explain the cause of a time series behavior. Regression analysis is the tool most often used in developing these causal models.

Regression analysis is a statistical technique that can be used to develop forecasts based on the relationship between two or more variables. In regression notation and terminology, we let y indicate the *dependent* or *response* variable. This is the variable whose value we wish to forecast. The forecast of y will be based on one or more *independent* or *predictor* variables denoted by $x_1, x_2, \ldots, x_n$. If we can obtain a sample of data for all variables involved, regression analysis will provide an equation that can be used to forecast the value of y given the values of $x_1, x_2, \ldots, x_n$. In this section we restrict our attention to regression models involving one independent variable.

DEVELOPING A REGRESSION MODEL FOR FORECASTING

To demonstrate the use of regression analysis in forecasting, let us consider the sales forecasting problem faced by Armand's Pizza, Inc. Armand's Pizza, Inc. is a chain of Italian-food restaurants located in a five-state area. The most successful locations for Armand's have been near college campuses. Prior to opening a new restaurant, Armand's management requires a forecast of the yearly sales revenues.

Such an estimate is used in planning the appropriate restaurant capacity, making initial staffing decisions, and deciding whether the potential revenue justifies the cost of operation. Since no past data are available on sales at a new store, Armand's cannot use time series data to develop the forecast.

Armand's management believes that annual sales revenue is related to the size of the student population on the nearby campus. On an intuitive basis, management believes that restaurants located near large campuses generate more revenue than those located near small campuses. If a relationship can be established between sales revenue and the size of the campus population, Armand's can use the size of the campus population to predict revenues for the new restaurant. To evaluate the relationship between annual sales y and student population x, Armand's collected data from a sample of 10 of its restaurants located near college campuses. These data are summarized in Table 3.13. For example, we see that restaurant 1, with $y = 58$ and $x = 2$, had \$58,000 in sales revenue and was located near a campus with 2000 students.

Figure 3.15 shows graphically the data presented in Table 3.13. The size of the student population is shown on the horizontal axis, with annual sales on the vertical axis. A graph such as this is known as a *scatter diagram*. The usual practice is to plot the independent variable on the horizontal axis and the de-

Restaurant	y = Annual Sales ($1000s)	x = Student Population (1000s)
1	58	2
2	105	6
3	88	8
4	118	8
5	117	12
6	137	16
7	157	20
8	169	20
9	149	22
10	202	26

TABLE 3.13

Data on Student Population and Annual Sales for 10 Armand's Restaurants

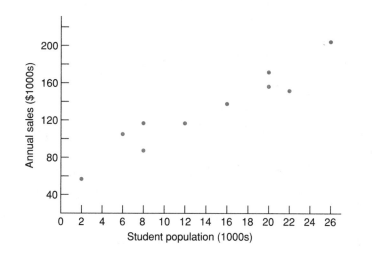

FIGURE 3.15

Scatter Diagram of Annual Sales versus Student Population

pendent variable on the vertical axis. The advantage of a scatter diagram is that it provides an overview of the data and enables us to draw preliminary conclusions about a possible relationship between the variables.

What preliminary conclusions can we draw from Figure 3.15? It appears that low sales volumes are associated with small student populations and higher sales volumes are associated with larger student populations. It also appears that the relationship between the two variables can be approximated by a straight line. In Figure 3.16 we have drawn a straight line through the data that appear to provide a good linear approximation of the relationship between the variables. However, observe that the relationship is not perfect. Indeed, few if any of the data items fall exactly on the line. However, if we can develop the mathematical expression for this line, we may be able to use it to predict or forecast the value of y corresponding to each possible value of x. We will refer to the resulting equation of the line as the *estimated regression equation.*

Using the least-squares method of estimation, we can develop the following estimated regression equation:

$$\hat{y} = b_0 + b_1 x \tag{3.11}$$

where

$\hat{y}$ = estimated value of the dependent variable (sales revenue $)
b_0 = intercept of the estimated regression equation
b_1 = slope of the estimated regression equation
x = value of the independent variable (student population)

Using the sample data, the intercept b_0 and slope b_1 can be computed using the following expressions:

$$b_1 = \frac{\Sigma\, x_i y_i - (\Sigma\, x_i\, \Sigma\, y_i)/n}{\Sigma\, x_i^2 - (\Sigma\, x_i)^2/n} \tag{3.12}$$

$$b_0 = \bar{y} - b_1 \bar{x} \tag{3.13}$$

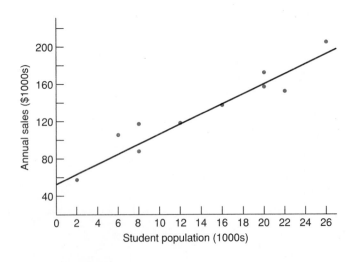

FIGURE 3.16

Straight-Line Approximation

where

x_i = value of the independent variable for the ith observation

y_i = value of the dependent variable for the ith observation

$\bar{x}$ = mean value for the independent variable

$\bar{y}$ = mean value for the dependent variable

n = total number of observations

Some of the calculations necessary to develop the least-squares estimated regression equation for the Armand's Pizza problem are shown in Table 3.14. In our example there are 10 restaurants or observations; hence $n = 10$. Using (3.12) and (3.13), we can now compute the slope and intercept of the estimated regression equation for Armand's Restaurants. The calculation of the slope b_1 proceeds as follows:

$$b_1 = \frac{\Sigma x_i y_i - (\Sigma x_i \, \Sigma y_i)/n}{\Sigma x_i^2 - (\Sigma x_i)^2/n}$$

$$= \frac{21{,}040 - (140)(1{,}300)/10}{2528 - (140)^2/10}$$

$$= \frac{2840}{568}$$

$$= 5$$

The calculation of the y intercept b_0 is as follows:

$$\bar{x} = \frac{\Sigma x_i}{n} = \frac{140}{10} = 14$$

$$\bar{y} = \frac{\Sigma y_i}{n} = \frac{1300}{10} = 130$$

$$b_0 = \bar{y} - b_1 \bar{x}$$

$$= 130 - 5(14)$$

$$= 60$$

Restaurant (i)	y_i	x_i	$x_i y_i$	x_i^2
1	58	2	116	4
2	105	6	630	36
3	88	8	704	64
4	118	8	944	64
5	117	12	1,404	144
6	137	16	2,192	256
7	157	20	3,140	400
8	169	20	3,380	400
9	149	22	3,278	484
10	202	26	5,252	767
Totals	1,300	140	21,040	2,528

TABLE 3.14

Calculations Necessary to Develop the Least-Squares Estimated Regression Equation for Armand's Pizza

Figure 3.17

Graph of the Estimated Regression Equation for Armand's Pizza: $\hat{y} = 60 + 5x$

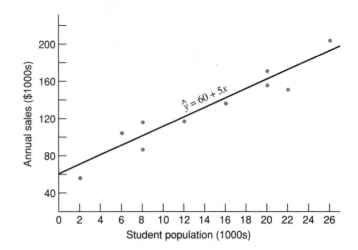

Thus the estimated regression equation found by using the method of least squares is

$$\hat{y} = 60 + 5x$$

In Figure 3.17 we show the graph of this equation.

The slope of the estimated regression equation ($b_1 = 5$) is positive, implying that as student population increases, annual sales increase. In fact we can conclude (since sales are measured in $1000s and student population in 1000s) that an increase in the student population of 1000 is associated with an increase of $5000 in expected annual sales; that is, sales are expected to increase by $5.00 per student.

If we believe that the least-squares estimated regression equation adequately describes the relationship between x and y, then it would seem reasonable to use the estimated regression equation to forecast the value of y for a given value of x. For example, if we wanted to forecast annual sales for a new restaurant location near a campus with 16,000 students, we would compute

$$\hat{y} = 60 + 5(16)$$
$$= 140$$

Hence we would forecast sales of $140,000 per year.

3.9 FORECASTING IN PRACTICE

The basic steps in forecasting are

1. Preliminary data analysis
2. Determination of quantitative and/or qualitative forecasts
3. Evaluation and determination of a final forecast
4. Control and feedback

Figure 3.18 illustrates this process. The first step to successful forecasting is to understand the purpose of the forecast. For instance, if a sales forecast is required

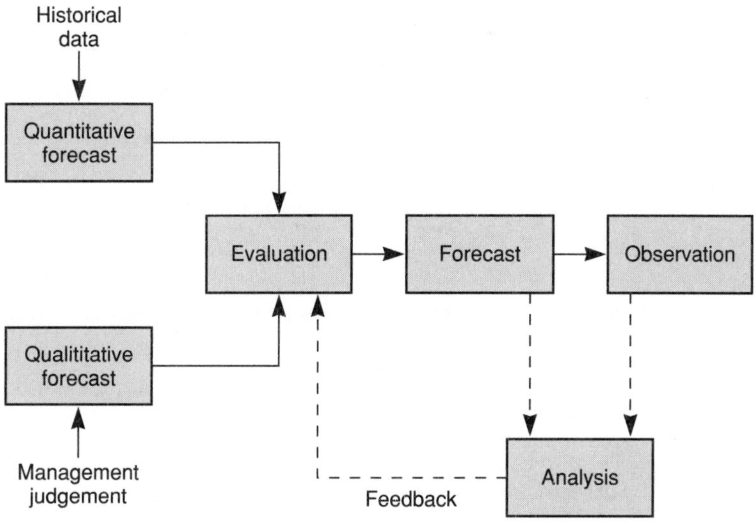

Figure 3.18
The Forecasting
System

by financial personnel for determining capital investment strategies, then a long (2–5-year) time horizon is necessary. Such forecasts should be made for aggregate groups of items, since these forecasts are usually more accurate than if individual item forecasts are added together. These forecasts would probably be measured in dollars. On the other hand, production personnel who need forecasts for procurement of materials and scheduling need short-term forecasts for individual items. Dollar values would not be appropriate; rather, the forecasts should be made in terms of units of production.

If historical data are available, they should be first plotted over time using a scatter diagram (as in Figure 3.15). From this, we can ask questions such as: Is there an upward or downward trend? Is there significant variation about the trend line? Can extreme values (or outliers) be explained? Is there any evidence of seasonality? Answers to such questions assist forecasters in choosing a suitable method.

The choice of a forecasting method depends on several criteria. Among these are the time span for which the forecast is being made, the frequency of updating the forecast, data requirements, accuracy, level of aggregation, and quantitative skills required. The time span is one of the most critical. We have seen different techniques that are applicable for long-range, intermediate-range, and short-range forecasts. The frequency of updating or deriving new forecasts is also important. For example, the Delphi method takes considerable time to implement and thus would not be appropriate for forecasts that require frequent updating.

All forecasters desire accuracy, but not all forecasting methods provide the same degree of accuracy. Also, one may wish to sacrifice some accuracy to satisfy other criteria. The level of aggregation will often dictate the appropriate method. Forecasting the total amount of soap to produce over the next planning period is certainly different than forecasting the amount of each individual product to produce. Aggregate forecasts are generally much easier to develop, while detailed forecasts require more time and resources.

Finally, different forecasting methods require different levels of technical ability and understanding of mathematical principles and assumptions. One of the

TABLE 3.15 Comparison of Forecasting Techniques

Criteria	Expert Opinion	Market Surveys	Delphi	Trend	Trend and Seasonal	Smoothing	Regression
				Forecasting Technique			
Time span	Short/ medium	Medium	Medium/ long	Short/ medium/ long	Short/ medium	Short/ medium	Short/ medium/ long
Ability to update	Rather easily	Somewhat difficult	Difficult	Easy	Easy	Easy	Easy
Data require- ments	Very little	Little	None	Detailed	Detailed	Detailed	Detailed
Accuracy	Usually good	Good	Good for long term	Good	Good	Good	Good if strong and stable rela- tionship
Level of aggrega- tion	Aggregate forecasts	Aggregate forecasts	Limited detail	Detailed	Detailed	Detailed	Aggregate/ detailed
Technical skills	Minimal	Some required	Minimal	High	High	Medium	High

most dangerous things a manager can do is to use a method that he or she does not understand. Table 3.15 summarizes the relative differences among the various methods that we have discussed in this chapter.

P/OM IN PRACTICE

The P/OM in Practice here show how long- and short-range forecasts are used in practice. The first describes how Cincinnati Gas and Electric uses an econometric model to forecast annual energy consumption. The second involves very short-range forecasting (30 minutes into the future) to learn about the demand for checkers at a supermarket. This case illustrates the use of regression models for forecasting.

FORECASTING AT THE CINCINNATI GAS & ELECTRIC COMPANY[5]

The Cincinnati Gas Light and Coke Company was chartered by the State of Ohio on April 3, 1837. Under this charter the company manufactured gas by distillation of coal and sold it for lighting purposes. During the last quarter of the nineteenth century the company successfully marketed gas for lighting, heating, and cooking and as fuel for gas engines.

In 1901 the Cincinnati Gas Light and Coke Company and the Cincinnati Electric Light Company merged to form The Cincinnati Gas & Electric Company (CG&E). This new company was able to

---

[5]The authors are indebted to Dr. Richard Evans, The Cincinnati Gas & Electric Company, Cincinnati, Ohio, for providing this application.

shift from manufactured gas to natural gas and adopt the rapidly emerging technologies in generating and distributing electricity. CG&E operated as a subsidiary of the Columbia Gas Electric Company from 1909 until 1944.

Today CG&E is a privately owned public utility serving approximately 370,000 gas customers and 600,000 electric customers. The company's service area covers approximately 3000 square miles in and around the Greater Cincinnati area.

As in any modern company, forecasting at CG&E is an integral part of operating and managing the business. Depending on the decision to be made, the forecasting techniques used range from judgment and graphical trend projections to sophisticated multiple regression models.

Forecasting in the utility industry offers some unique perspectives compared to other industries. Since there are no finished-goods or in-process inventories of electricity, this product must be generated to meet the instantaneous requirements of the customers. Electrical shortages are not just lost sales, but "brownouts" or "blackouts." This situation places an unusual burden on the utility forecaster. On the positive side, the demand for energy and the sale of energy is more predictable than for many other products. Also, unlike the situation in a multiproduct firm, a great amount of forecasting effort and expertise can be concentrated on the two products: gas and electricity.

The two types of forecasts discussed in this section are the long-range forecasts of electric peak load and electric energy. The largest observed electric demand for any given period, such as an hour, a day, a month, or a year, is defined as the peak load. The cumulative amount of energy generated and used over the period of an hour is referred to as electric energy.

Until the mid-1970s the seasonal pattern of both electric energy and electric peak load were very regular; the time series for both of these exhibited a fairly steady exponential growth. Business cycles had little noticeable effect on either. Perhaps the most serious shift in the behavior of these time series came from the increasing installation of air conditioning units in the Greater Cincinnati area. This fact caused an accelerated growth in the trend component and also in the relative magnitude of the summer peaks. Nevertheless, the two time series were very regular and generally quite predictable.

Trend projection was the most popular method used to forecast electric energy and electric peak load. The forecast accuracy was quite acceptable and even enviable when compared to forecast errors experienced in other industries.

In the mid-1970s a variety of actions by the government, the off-and-on energy shortages, and price signals to the consumer began to affect the consumption of electric energy. As a result the behavior of the peak load and electric energy time series became more and more unpredictable. Hence a simple trend projection forecasting model was no longer adequate. As a result a special forecasting model—referred to as an econometric model—was developed by CG&E to better account for the behavior of these time series.

The purpose of the econometric model is to forecast the annual energy consumption by residential, commercial, and industrial classes of service. These forecasts are then used to develop forecasts of summer and winter peak loads. First energy consumption in the industrial and commercial classes is forecast. For an assumed level of economic activity, the projection of electric energy is made along with a forecast of employment in the area. The employment forecast is converted to a forecast of adult population through the use of unemployment rates and labor force participation rates. Household forecasts are then developed through the use of demographic statistics on the average number of persons per household. The resulting forecast of households is used as an indicator of residential customers.

A number of economic and demographic time series are used in the construction of the above econometric model. Simply speaking, the entire forecasting system is a compilation of several statistically verified multiple regression equations.

The forecast of the annual electric peak load guides the timing decisions for constructing future generating units. The financial impact of these decisions is great. For example, the last generating unit built by the company cost nearly $600 million, and the interest rate on a recent first mortgage bond was 16 percent. At this rate, annual interest costs would be nearly $100 million. Obviously, a timing decision that leads to having the unit available no sooner than necessary is crucial.

The energy forecasts are important in other ways also. For example, purchases of coal and nuclear fuel for the generating units are based on the forecast levels of energy needed. The revenue from the electric operations of the company is determined from forecasted sales, which in turn enters into the planning of rate changes and external financing. These planning and decision-making processes are among the most important management activities in the company. It is imperative that the decision makers have the best forecast information available to assist them in arriving at these decisions.

QUESTIONS

1. Describe some of the unique perspectives associated with forecasting in the utility industry as compared with other industries.

2. Until the mid-1970s, what type of forecasting procedure was used by CG&E? What necessitated a change?

3. Briefly describe CG&E's current approach to forecasting.

4. What are the benefits of accurate forecasts for CG&E?

A FORECASTING MODEL FOR GROCERY STORE CHECKOUT SERVICES[6]

Customer service is a critical aspect in the management of grocery stores. Because of highly variable demand, store managers must make frequent short-term decisions about staffing checkout counters. The number of checkers at any point in time can be adjusted by the store manager in order to control the length of the waiting lines, and hence, customer waiting time. It is usually possible to assign an employee who is working in another part of the store—the produce department, for example—to work temporarily at a checkout counter during periods of high demand.

One large grocery chain was investigating the use of a laser-based scanner at the doors of the store to count arriving and departing customers. Company management wanted to use this information to forecast demand at the checkout counters about 30 minutes into the future in order to make staffing adjustments before long lines developed.

Figure 3.19 shows a schematic diagram of the system operation. Customers enter the store, shop, wait in line at one of several checkout counters, and then depart from the store. The uncertainty in arrival rates at the checkout counters is from not knowing how long customers will shop. Clearly if the store arrival time and shopping time were known, the time at which a customer arrives at the checkout counter could be computed.

A forecasting model was developed based on the assumption that the demand for checkout services is closely related to the number of shoppers in the store. The larger the population of shoppers, the larger will be the demand for checkout services. If the probability distribution of shopping times is relatively stable, then the number of customers demanding checkout service will be proportional to the number of customers in the store. Over a one-week period, data on store arrivals, departures, lengths of checkout lines, and the number of checkers working at the end of fixed time intervals were collected. In effect, these provided "snapshots" of the state of the store over time. By keeping a running

FIGURE 3.19

Grocery Store Customer Flow

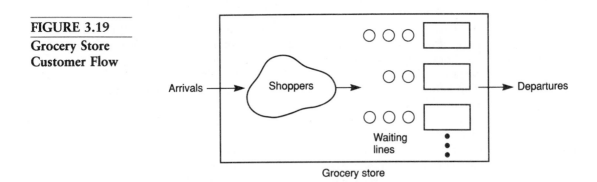

[6]This case is adapted from an actual project in which one of the authors was involved.

total of arrivals less departures, the number of customers in the store at any point in time can be computed easily.

From the arrival-departure data, a variable representing checkout service demand in any given period was created as follows. Let

y = number of customers demanding checkout service during a time period

Q = number of customers in line at the end of the period

C = number of checkers working at the end of the period

d = number of departures during a time period

An estimate for the demand during a given time period is given by

$$y = d + Q + C$$

The rationale for this equation is that the demand is equal to the number of departures (who actually obtained service), plus the number waiting to be served (current demand), plus the number of checkers (assuming that all are busy).

The first analysis conducted was an investigation of demand fluctuation over time. Figure 3.20 is an example of data collected during one day. In general, demand follows a bimodal distribution with peaks at roughly noon and 6 P.M. each day. The next step was to identify quantities that would effectively predict demand for future time periods. Intuition would dictate that the number of customers in the store in earlier periods would be of importance. Likewise the arrival rate of customers would be a significant variable. Figure 3.21 shows demand as a function of the number of arrivals to the store three-time periods earlier (each period was 15 minutes, so this provides demand data for 30 to 45 minutes in the future). From this figure, we see that as the number of arriving customers increases, so also does demand for checkout services. This relationship was not surprising. What was surprising was the highly linear relationship that existed

for many of the days. This indicated that regression models might work extremely well.

The choice of prediction variables was determined by intuition, the strong relationships suggested by the data, and by extensive analysis of certain statistical measures of model adequacy. The model that was ultimately developed used $y(t + 3)$, that is, the demand three time periods into the future, as the dependent variable, with the following independent variables:

$N(t)$ = the number of customers in the store in period t

$N(t - 1)$ = the number of customers in the store in period $t - 1$

$a(t)$ = the number of customers arriving in period t

Thus, if t is the time period 2:15–2:30, the model includes the number of customers in the store at 1:30–1:45 and 1:15–1:30, and the number of arrivals during 1:30–1:45. Therefore a forecast for 2:15–2:30 can be made at 1:45. An example of the actual model for one day was

$$y(t + 3) = .34431 - .12760 \, N(t)$$
$$+ .31627 \, N(t - 1) + .90634 \, a(t)$$

The coefficient of determination, R^2, was .80 indicating that a high percentage of the variation in demand was explained by the variables that were chosen.

QUESTIONS

1. How did the grocery store determine the number of customers in the store at any point in time?
2. What were the independent variables in the regression model?
3. Do you think an exponential smoothing model might do a better job of predicting demand for checkout services? Why or why not?
4. How much lead time does the store manager have to get the appropriate number of checkers to the checkout counter? Do you think the lead time is sufficient?

SUMMARY

The purpose of this chapter is to provide an introduction to the basic methods of forecasting and time series analysis in production and operations management. Both statistical and judgmental forecasting procedures are necessary in order to make effective decisions. Typical subjective methods include expert opinion, market surveys, and the Delphi method.

FIGURE 3.20

Example of
Customer
Demand
Distribution
During a Day

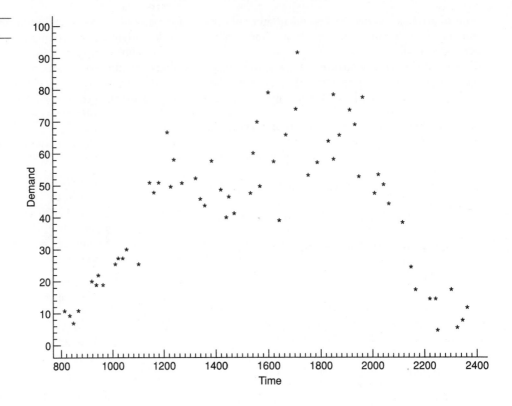

FIGURE 3.21

Example of
Customer
Demand Three
Time Periods in
the Future

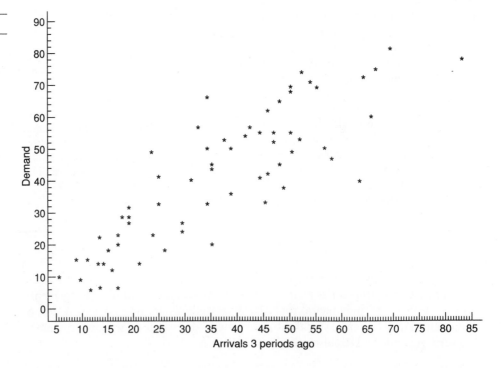

We showed that in order to explain the behavior of a time series, it is often helpful to think of the time series as consisting of four separate components: trend, cyclical, seasonal, and irregular. By isolating these components and measuring their apparent effect, it is possible to forecast future values of the time series.

When the time series exhibits only a long-term trend, we showed how regression analysis could be used to make trend projections. When both trend and seasonal influences are significant, we showed how moving averages could be used to isolate the effects of the two factors and prepare better forecasts.

We discussed how smoothing methods can be used to forecast a time series that exhibits no significant trend, seasonal, or cyclical effect. The exponential smoothing method is a technique that uses a weighted average of past time series values to compute a forecast.

Finally, regression analysis was described as a procedure for developing so-called causal forecasting methods. A causal forecasting method is one that relates the time series value (dependent variable) to other independent variables that are believed to explain (cause) the time series behavior.

Forecasts must be monitored and analyzed by managers. Forecast error is one measure that assists managers in evaluating a forecasting technique. Adaptive smoothing is often used to react to changes in the environment.

It is important to realize that time series analysis and forecasting is a major field in its own right. In this chapter we have just scratched the surface of the field of time series and forecasting methodolgy.

Delphi method
Time series
Trend
Cyclical component
Seasonal component
Irregular component
Moving averages

Deseasonalized time series
Forecast error
Mean square error (MSE)
Exponential smoothing
Smoothing constant
Mean absolute deviation (MAD)
Causal forecasting models

1. Why is forecasting an important technique in P/OM?

2. Explain the uses of forecasting in long-range, intermediate-range, and short-range decision making. What forecasting techniques are often used for each of these time horizons?

3. How does forecasting in service organizations differ from manufacturing organizations?

4. Briefly summarize the classification scheme of forecasting methods presented in this chapter.

5. Discuss the difference between statistical and judgmental forecasting methods. What circumstances would warrant one over the other?

6. Illustrate, by examples of typical applications, the various types of judgmental forecasting techniques often used.

7. What is a *time series?*

8. What are the components of a time series? Briefly explain each.

9. Explain the concept of *moving average.*

10. Explain the philosophy behind *exponential smoothing.*

11. Explain the two basic approaches for measuring forecast accuracy.

12. Explain the concept of a *tracking signal.*

13. What is a *causal forecasting model?*

14. Describe the basic steps in forecasting methodology.

15. How are statistical and judgmental forecasts used together in practice?

16. What criteria are important in choosing a forecasting method?

17. Contrast the differences between expert opinion and smoothing methods according to the criteria used to answer question 16.

PROBLEMS

1. Average attendance figures at home football games for a major university show the following 7-year pattern:

Year	1	2	3	4	5	6	7
Attendance	28,000	30,000	31,500	30,400	30,500	32,200	30,800

Develop the linear trend expression for this time series. Use the trend expression to forecast attendance for year 8.

2. The president of a small manufacturing firm has been concerned about the continual growth in manufacturing costs over the past several years. Shown below is a time series of the cost per unit for the firm's leading product over the past eight years.

Year	1	2	3	4	5	6	7	8
Cost/Unit ($)	20.00	24.50	28.20	27.50	26.60	30.00	31.00	36.00

a. Show a graph of this time series. Does a linear trend appear to exist?

b. Develop a linear trend expression for the above time series. What is the average cost increase that the firm has been realizing per year?

3. The enrollment data for a state college for the past six years are shown below:

Year	1	2	3	4	5	6
Enrollment	20,500	20,200	19,500	19,000	19,100	18,800

Develop a linear trend expression and comment on what is happening to enrollment at this institution. Use the trend expression to forecast enrollment for year 7.

4. Canton Supplies, Inc. is a service firm that employs approximately 100 individuals. Because of the necessity of meeting monthly cash obligations, man-

agement of Canton Supplies would like to develop a forecast of monthly cash requirements. Because of a recent change in operating policy, only the past seven months of data were considered to be relevant. Develop a linear trend expression for the historical data shown below. Use the trend expression to develop a forecast of cash requirements for each of the next 2 months.

Month	1	2	3	4	5	6	7
Cash Required ($1000)	205	212	218	224	230	240	246

5. The Costello Music Company has been in business five years. During this time the sale of electric organs has grown from 12 units in the first year to 76 units in the most recent year. Fred Costello, the firm's owner, would like to develop a forecast of organ sales for the coming year. The historical data are shown below

Year	1	2	3	4	5
Sales	12	28	34	50	76

   a. Show a graph of this time series. Does a linear trend appear to exist?
   b. Develop a linear trend expression for the above time series. What is the average increase in sales that the firm has been realizing per year?

6. Hudson Marine has been an authorized dealer for C&D marine radios for the past seven years. The number of radios sold each year is shown below

Year	1	2	3	4	5	6	7
Number Sold	35	50	75	90	105	110	130

   a. Show a graph of this time series. Does a linear trend appear to exist?
   b. Develop a linear trend for the above time series.
   c. Use the linear trend developed in part (b) and prepare a forecast for annual sales in year 8.

7. The quarterly sales data for a college textbook over the past three years are as follows:

	Year 1	Year 2	Year 3
Quarter 1	1690	1800	1850
Quarter 2	940	900	1100
Quarter 3	2625	2900	2930
Quarter 4	2500	2360	2615

   a. Show the four-quarter moving average values for this time series. Plot both the original time series and the moving averages on the same graph.
   b. Compute seasonal indexes for the four quarters.
   c. When does the textbook publisher experience the largest seasonal effect? Does this appear reasonable? Explain.

8. Identify the monthly seasonal indexes for the following three years of expenses for a six-unit apartment house in southern Florida. Use a 12-month moving average calculation.

Month	Year 1	Year 2	Year 3
January	170	180	195
February	180	205	210
March	205	215	230
April	230	245	280
May	240	265	290
June	315	330	390
July	360	400	420
August	290	335	330
September	240	260	290
October	240	270	295
November	230	255	280
December	195	220	250

9. Refer to the Hudson Marine problem presented in problem 6. Suppose that the quarterly sales values for the seven years of historical data are as follows:

	Quarter 1	Quarter 2	Quarter 3	Quarter 4	Total Sales
Year 1	6	15	10	4	35
Year 2	10	18	15	7	50
Year 3	14	26	23	12	75
Year 4	19	28	25	18	90
Year 5	22	34	28	21	105
Year 6	24	36	30	20	110
Year 7	28	40	35	27	130

a. Show the four-quarter moving average values for this time series. Plot both the original time series and the moving average series on the same graph.
b. Compute the seasonal indexes for the four quarters.
c. When does Hudson Marine experience the largest seasonal effect? Does this seem reasonable? Explain.

10. Consider the Costello Music Company problem presented in problem 5. The quarterly sales data are shown below

	Quarter 1	Quarter 2	Quarter 3	Quarter 4	Total Yearly Sales
Year 1	4	2	1	5	12
Year 2	6	4	4	14	28
Year 3	10	3	5	16	34
Year 4	12	9	7	22	50
Year 5	18	10	13	35	76

a. Compute the seasonal indexes for the four quarters.

b. When does Costello Music experience the largest seasonal effect? Does this appear reasonable? Explain.

11. Refer to the Hudson Marine data presented in problem 9.

a. Deseasonalize the data and use the deseasonalized time series to identify the trend.

b. Use the results of part (a) to develop a quarterly forecast for next year based on trend.

c. Use the seasonal indexes developed in problem 9 to adjust the forecasts developed in part (b) to account for the effect of season.

12. Consider the Costello Music Company time series presented in problem 10.

a. Deseasonalize the data and use the deseasonalized time series to identify the trend.

b. Use the results of part (a) to develop a quarterly forecast for next year based on trend.

c. Use the seasonal indexes developed in problem 10 to adjust the forecasts developed in part (b) to account for the effect of season.

13. Refer to the gasoline sales time series data in Table 3.8.

a. Compute 4- and 5-week moving averages for the time series.

b. Compute the mean square error (MSE) for the 4- and 5-week moving average forecasts.

c. What appears to be the best number of weeks of past data to use in the moving average computation? Remember that the MSE for the 3-week moving average is 10.22.

14. Refer again to the gasoline sales time series data in Table 3.8.

a. Using a weight of ½ for the most recent observation, ⅓ for the second most recent, and ⅙ for the third most recent, compute a 3-week weighted moving average for the time series.

b. Compute the mean square error for the weighted moving average in part (a). Do you prefer this weighted moving average to the unweighted moving average? Remember that the MSE for the unweighted moving average is 10.22.

15. A retail store records the number of units of customer demand during each sales period. Use the following demand data and develop 3-period and 4-period moving average forecasts. Compute the MSE for each. Which number of periods provides the better moving average forecast?

Period	1	2	3	4	5	6	7	8	9	10	11	12
Demand	86	93	88	89	92	94	91	93	96	97	93	95

16. Use the demand data in problem 15 to develop 3-period weighted moving averages forecasts. Use weights of ½ for the most recent demand, ⅓ for one period before most recent demand and ⅙ for two periods before most recent demand. How does this forecasting method compare to the 3-period and 4-period moving averages forecasts in problem 15?

17. Use the gasoline sales time series data from Table 3.8 to compute the exponential smoothing forecasts using $\alpha = 0.1$. Using the mean square error criterion, would you prefer a smoothing constant of $\alpha = 0.1$ or $\alpha = 0.2$ for the gasoline sales time series?

18. Using a smoothing constant of $\alpha = 0.2$, Equation (3.9) shows that the forecast for the 13th week of the gasoline sales data from Table 3.8 is given by $F_{13} = 0.2Y_{12} + 0.8F_{12}$. However, the forecast for week 12 is given by $F_{12} = 0.2Y_{11} + 0.8F_{11}$. Thus we could combine these two results to show that the forecast for the 13th week can be written

$$F_{13} = 0.2Y_{12} + 0.8(0.2Y_{11} + 0.8F_{11}) = 0.2Y_{12} + 0.16Y_{11} + 0.64F_{11}$$

   a. Making use of the fact that $F_{11} = 0.2Y_{10} + 0.8F_{10}$ (and similar expressions for F_{10} and F_9), continue to expand the expression for F_{13} until it is written in terms of the past data values Y_{12}, Y_{11}, Y_{10}, Y_9, Y_8, and the forecast for period 8.
   b. Refer to the coefficients or weights for the past data Y_{12}, Y_{11}, Y_{10}, Y_9, and Y_8; what observation do you make about how exponential smoothing weights past data values in arriving at new forecasts? Compare this weighting pattern with the weighting pattern of the moving averages method.

19. The following time series shows the sales of a particular product over the past 12 months:

Month	1	2	3	4	5	6	7	8	9	10	11	12
Sales	105	135	120	105	90	120	145	140	100	80	100	110

Use $\alpha = 0.3$ to compute the exponential smoothing values for the time series.

20. Analyze the forecasting errors for the time series in problem 19 by using a smoothing constant of 0.5. Does a smoothing constant of 0.3 or 0.5 appear to provide the better forecasts?

21. The number of component parts used in a production process each week in the last 10 weeks showed the following:

Week	Parts	Week	Parts
1	200	6	210
2	350	7	280
3	250	8	350
4	360	9	290
5	250	10	320

Use a smoothing constant of 0.25 to develop the exponential smoothing values for this time series. Indicate your forecast for next week.

22. A chain of grocery stores experienced the following weekly demand (cases) for a particular brand of automatic-dishwasher detergent:

Week	1	2	3	4	5	6	7	8	9	10
Demand	22	18	23	21	17	24	20	19	18	21

Use exponential smoothing with $\alpha = 0.2$ in order to develop a forecast for week 11.

23. United Dairies, Inc. supplies milk to several independent grocers throughout Dade County in Florida. Management of United Dairies would like to develop a forecast of the number of half-gallons of milk sold per week. Sales data for the past 12 weeks are as follows:

Week	1	2	3	4	5	6	7	8	9	10	11	12
Sales (units)	2750	3100	3250	2800	2900	3050	3300	3100	2950	3000	3200	3150

Use the above 12 weeks of data and exponential smoothing with $\alpha = 0.4$ to develop a forecast of demand for the 13th week.

24. Consider the following six-period demand data.

Period	1	2	3	4	5	6
Demand	121	133	146	157	169	183

a. Develop the linear trend model.
b. Develop the exponential smoothing forecasts with $\alpha = 0.3$ and $\alpha = 0.4$.
c. Which model provides the best forecasts? Discuss.
d. What is the forecast for period 7?

25. Use the gasoline sales data and exponential smoothing forecasts shown in Table 3.12 ($\alpha = 0.3$).
a. Compute the mean absolute deviation (MAD) measure of forecast accuracy.
b. The exponential smoothing forecasts for $\alpha = 0.2$ and $\alpha = 0.3$ provided the following MSE measures of forecast accuracy:

α	MSE
0.2	8.98
0.3	9.35

The MAD measure for $\alpha = 0.2$ is 2.596. Using the results of part (a) above, does the MAD criterion also support the use of $\alpha = 0.2$ as the better smoothing constant.
c. Using the data in Table 3.12, compute the tracking signal for weeks 7 to 12 using $n = 6$.

26. Use the demand data in problem 15 with the 3-period and 4-period moving average forecasts.
a. Compute the MAD for the 3-period and 4-period forecasts. Which method is better using the MAD criterion?
b. Using $n = 6$, compute the tracking signal for periods 7 to 12. Compare the tracking signal results for 3-period and 4-period moving average forecasts.

27. Eddie's Restaurants collected the following data on the relationship between advertising and sales at a sample of five restaurants:

Advertising Expenditures ($1000s)	1.0	4.0	6.0	10.0	14.0
Sales ($1000s)	19.0	44.0	40.0	52.0	53.0

a. Let x equal advertising expenditures ($1000s) and y equal sales ($1000s). Use the method of least squares to develop a straight-line approximation to the relationship between the two variables.
b. Use the equation developed in part (a) to forecast sales for an advertising expenditure of $8000.

28. The management of a chain of fast-food restaurants would like to investigate the relationship between the daily sales volume of a company restaurant and the number of competitor restaurants within a 1-mile radius of the firm's restaurant. The following data have been collected:

Number of Competitors Within 1 Mile	1	1	2	3	3	4	5	5
Sales ($)	3600	3300	3100	2900	2700	2500	2300	2000

a. Develop the least-squares estimated regression equation that relates daily sales volume to the number of competitor restaurants within a 1-mile radius.
b. Use the estimated regression equation developed in part (a) to forecast the daily sales volume for a particular company restaurant that has four competitors within a 1-mile radius.

29. In a manufacturing process the assembly-line speed (feet/minute) was thought to affect the number of defective parts found during the inspection process. To test this theory, management devised a situation where the same batch of parts was inspected visually at a variety of line speeds. The following data were collected:

Line Speed	20	20	40	30	60	40
Number of Defective Parts Found	21	19	15	16	14	17

a. Develop the estimated regression equation that relates line speed to the number of defective parts found.
b. Use the equation developed in part (a) to forecast the number of defective parts found for a line speed of 50 feet per minute.

30. An automobile parts dealer notices that demand for wiper blades is related to the amount of rainfall received during a given month. He has collected the following data relating the number of inches of rainfall during various months and the sales during the corresponding period.

Rainfall	3.1	4.0	2.0	8.1	6.3	7.2
Number of Wipers Sold	72	79	62	152	124	136

a. Develop a regression equation for a causal forecasting model.
b. For a projected rainfall of 5 inches, how many wipers can be expected to be sold?

The Vintage Restaurant is located on Captiva Island, a resort community near Fort Meyers, Florida. The restaurant, which is owned and operated by Karen Payne, has just completed its third year of operation. During this period of time Karen has sought to establish a reputation for the restaurant as a high-quality dining establishment that specializes in fresh seafood. The efforts made by Karen and her staff have proved successful, and her restaurant has become one of the best and fastest-growing restaurants on the island.

Karen has concluded that in order to plan better for the growth of the restaurant in the future, it is necessary to develop a system that will enable her to forecast food and beverage sales by month for up to 1 year in advance. Karen has available data on the total food and beverage sales that were realized during the previous 3 years of operation. These data are provided in Table 3.16.

Perform an analysis of the sales data for the Vintage Restaurant. Prepare a report for Karen that summarizes your findings, forecasts, and recommendations. Include information on the following:

1. A graph of the time series.
2. An analysis of the seasonality of the data. Include the seasonal indexes for each month and comment on the high-seasonal and low-seasonal sales months. Do the seasonal indexes make intuitive sense? Discuss.

Month	First Year	Second Year	Third Year
January	242	263	282
February	235	238	255
March	232	247	265
April	178	193	205
May	184	193	210
June	140	149	160
July	145	157	166
August	152	161	174
September	110	122	126
October	130	130	148
November	152	167	173
December	206	230	235

TABLE 3.16

Food and Beverage Sales for the Vintage Restaurant ($1000s)

STRATEGY AND DESIGN IN P/OM

I ssues of strategy and design involve broad corporate objectives and long time horizons. In this part of the text, we examine the role of production and operations management in corporate strategy and the fundamental issues involved in designing effective production systems. Strategic plans become the basis for action at lower levels of an organization and a framework for future decision making. Taking a long-range view of operations helps to intergrate decision making among various functional units of an organization and to avoid "patchwork" solutions to problems.

Chapter 4 discusses the importance of operations in strategic planning and how it relates to strategic financial and marketing objectives. In Chapter 5, we discuss product design issues and their impact on the production process. Chapter 6 is concerned with planning for providing the resources that an organization needs to accomplish its production goals. Facility location and distribution system design is the subject of Chapter 7. In that chapter, we look at how location decisions affect production and strategic objectives. Chapters 8 and 9 deal with process technology and design. Issues such as what production processes and equipment should be selected and how they should be designed into an effective system are addressed. Finally, in Chapter 10 we discuss the role and importance of automation.

P/OM and Strategic Planning

Strategic planning involves the determination of the long-term goals, policies, and plans for an organization. The purpose of this chapter is to provide an introduction to strategic planning and its role in P/OM. At a conference on strategic planning, a representative from IBM stated that "a strategic planning problem is one the firm must live with for over five years."[1] Although the length of the time horizon depends upon many factors, including the type of industry, in general, strategic planning involves issues that have a long-run impact on the firm.

In Chapters 1 and 2 we discussed the importance of competiveness as the key to long-term growth and survival in today's global economy. Corporate strategy—the result of strategic planning—is an important determinant of competitiveness. The three basic components of corporate strategy are the *marketing and sales strategy,* the *design strategy,* and the *operations strategy.*

The marketing and sales strategy defines the markets in which a firm will compete, identifies consumer needs in those markets, and determines the timing and extent of new product introductions. The design strategy determines how the firm will match its technological capability with market needs in order to develop specifications for competitively priced goods and services. Finally, the **operations strategy** sets parameters for how the firm's resources will be converted into goods and services that meet the design specifications.

Because corporate strategy has traditionally emphasized marketing and financial considerations, the operations strategy has received the least amount of high-level attention. In fact, in some organizations, operations has not even been considered to be a factor in the corporate strategy. Consequently, operations managers have often been placed in the position of having to react to strategic plans that were developed from primarily financial and marketing perspectives. In many cases, this has led to inefficient operations. Recently, however, top management has recognized that operations strategy is vitally important to an organization's long-run success. In this chapter, we explore the importance and scope of operations strategy. As we study individual P/OM topics in succeeding chapters, we shall relate them to the strategic issues discussed in this chapter. Finally, in the concluding chapter of this book we will reexamine the topic of operations strategy in light of the whole spectrum of P/OM.

4.1 THE IMPORTANCE OF OPERATIONS STRATEGY

Although U.S. technology is the best in the world, we have recently seen many domestic industries struggling to compete with foreign manufacturers. For example, in 1970 the United States was the largest manufacturer of bicycles in the world; by 1980 Japan was number one, and in 1988 Taiwan had taken over as the leader. Television sets, computer chips, and other electronic products and

---

[1]Cited in D. J. Sweeney, "A Practical Evaluation of the Potential of Mixed Integer Programming as a Strategic Planning Tool," presented at The Future of Optimization Models for Strategic Planning, Oct. 28–29, 1982, Center for Corporate Economics and Strategy at Duke University.

devices from Japan now dominate U.S. markets. Japanese and European automobiles, German machine tools, steel from Japan and Korea, and many other products have made significant penetration into domestic markets. More capital investment is not by itself the answer. Even though the U.S. auto industry invested $40 billion in capital improvements between 1980 and 1985, it continues to lose ground. For instance, in 1981 Japan's automakers were producing subcompacts at a cost $1500 less than Detroit; by 1986 the gap had widened to $1800.[2]

Why has the United States lost much of its domestic market for products that were originally invented and developed here? As we noted in Chapter 2, the decline in productivity growth is often cited as a factor. Other factors often cited are excessive government regulations and taxes, union-labor conflicts, the deterioration of the U.S. work ethic, the energy crisis, and inflation. However, these are not the only reasons for the decline in the rate of U.S. productivity growth and international competitiveness.

Studies of business successes and failures in America, Asia, and Europe have suggested that a critical factor in the decline in the rate of growth of productivity and competitiveness is poor management practice. Specifically, Hayes and Wheelwright[3] suggest that there are three management practices that have contributed to the decline of U.S. industry: (1) an emphasis on analytical detachment and strategic elegance over hands-on experience and well-managed line operations; (2) a focus on short-term results rather than longer-term goals and capabilities; and (3) an emphasis on the management of marketing and financial resources at the expense of manufacturing and technological resources. They raise important questions that relate directly to P/OM and the ability of top management to understand the role of P/OM as a competitive weapon.

Management performance has traditionally been evaluated on the basis of financial measures such as return on investment (ROI), and short-term results have often overshadowed long-term issues such as quality and customer satisfaction. Many companies base capital investment decisions on ROI computations and seek a payback on invested funds only from savings generated. This approach ignores the potential long-run benefits from factors such as increased quality, greater flexibility, faster market response time and increased customer satisfaction. Although these types of long-run benefits are often difficult to quantify, they have a significant effect on the firm's profitability.

Business Week relates a case in point.[4] Cone Drive Operations, Inc., a manufacturer of heavy-duty gears, was losing profits and customers because of high inventory costs and late deliveries. In 1980, the company decided to overhaul its entire operations through computerization. A proposed $2 million computer integrated manufacturing system was difficult to justify through labor savings alone, especially for a company with only $26 million in annual sales. Nevertheless, the company made the investment. Instead of justifying the decision based upon conventional financial considerations, the company's investment decision

[2]Elizabeth A. Haas, "Breakthrough Manufacturing," *Harvard Business Review*, (March–April, 1987) 75. Copyright 1987 by the President and Fellows of Harvard College; all rights reserved.

[3]Robert H. Hayes and Steven C. Wheelwright, *Restoring our Competitive Edge: Competing Through Manufacturing*, New York: John Wiley & Sons, 1984. Copyright © 1984. Reprinted by permission of John Wiley & Sons, Inc.

[4]"How the New Math of Productivity Adds Up," *Business Week*, 6 June, 1988, 103–114.

was based on *expected improvements* in delivery time and corporate image. The company clearly made the right move. The project paid for itself with new business and nonlabor savings in just one year. Deliveries are now 95 percent on time, inventories are 60 percent lower, and special orders and new products take only 15 percent as long to handle.

Top-management career paths in the United States have usually been through financial and marketing positions rather than operations. As a result, many top managers have focused their attention on distribution, advertising, and market segmentation instead of improving operations.

Japanese and European management philosophies and practices differ from those of U.S. companies in many ways. For instance, in the United States manufacturing has long been managed in isolation, reacting to policies set forth by top management, most of whom have financial or marketing backgrounds. Unfortunately, strategists with primarily marketing and financial backgrounds may not fully comprehend the implications that their strategies have on manufacturing processes and procedures. For example, a change in strategy that places greater emphasis on product innovation will result in the development of many new and different products. This puts increased demands on the production capacity and labor skills required to support increased product diversity. Additional investment in inventories would be needed, delivery schedules would change, and so on. Unless the transition is carefully planned, major production problems could result. Even simple changes in product mix, dictated by marketing considerations, can have a significant impact on production. Most of the top managers of foreign competitors, on the other hand, have risen from the ranks of engineering and manufacturing and consequently view manufacturing as an integral part of their corporate strategy.

The Japanese and Europeans have committed themselves to developing new technologies and production systems that have resulted in products with low cost and high quality and reliability. This has given them a competitive advantage in world markets. As a result of the studies of Skinner, Hayes and Wheelwright, and others, U.S. corporations have recently begun to see the links between operations and other strategic business functions such as marketing and finance. Operations strategy is now viewed as a major competitive weapon.

4.2 THE HIERARCHICAL NATURE OF STRATEGIC PLANNING

As we stated in the introduction to this chapter, *strategic planning* involves the determination of the long-term goals, policies, and plans for an organization. It includes defining the basic philosophy of the organization, identifying its competitive advantage and growth direction, determining the products and services to be provided, and planning for the acquisition and allocation of critical resources. Strategic planning involves a long time horizon, such as three, five, or even up to ten years, both to implement plans and to observe their impact. Strategic plans and decisions should be consistently applied throughout the organization. In practice, this is often difficult to do, since many decisions cause conflict among different functional units of the organization. Perhaps the most frequent source of conflict is between marketing and production. Marketing managers want a wide line of products and short delivery times; this requires short production runs and fast product changeover, all of which can degrade productivity and result in higher production costs. Hence, if operations managers are evaluated on short-run performance measures such as quarterly costs or productivity increases, conflicts arise. Strategic planning is therefore necessary to resolve such conflicts and provide an organizational focus.

Strategy is the result of a series of hierarchical decisions about goals, directions, and resources. Figure 4.1 illustrates this hierarchical process. A **corporate strategy** is necessary to define the businesses in which the corporation will participate and develop plans for the acquisition and allocation of resources among these businesses. A corporate strategy includes all the components shown in Figure 4.1. To develop a sound corporate strategy, the firm must first understand environmental factors such as customer demand, labor supply, material sources, capital sources, the company's strengths and weaknesses, and the competitor's strengths and weaknesses. The businesses in which the firm will participate, often called **strategic business units** (SBUs), are usually defined as families of products having similar characteristics or methods of production. Strategic business units might be organized along broad material or process lines, such as steel, glass, plastics, or machine tools, or by consumer-product segments, such as health-care products, foods, and so on.

Corporate strategic planning addresses such questions as these: Is the business profitable? Should we invest in new facilities and equipment to enhance current operations? Should we sell some businesses to provide cash for other opportun-

FIGURE 4.1   Hierarchical Levels of Strategic Planning

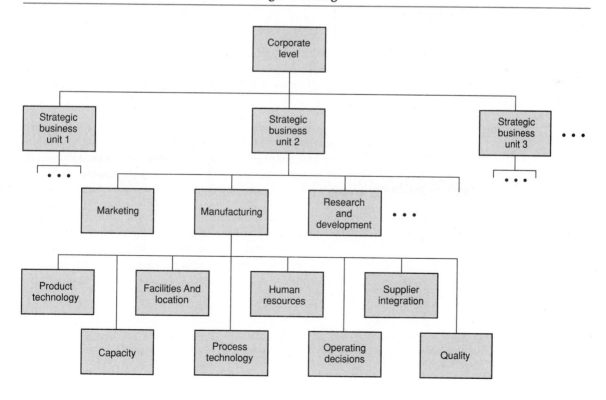

ities? Corporate strategies for growth might revolve around acquiring or merging competing retail outlets, distribution centers, raw-material suppliers, component suppliers, or competing producers, or they might involve developing new product lines within the firm.

At the next hierarchical level, strategic plans defined by SBUs define how the businesses relate to the overall corporate strategy and the basis of achieving and maintaining competitive advantage. The major decisions involve which products and markets to pursue and how best to compete in these markets. Should emphasis be on price, quality, speed of delivery, or service? Should distribution be centralized or decentralized? Answers to such questions depend on the nature of the business and define the business strategy.

4.3 A CLASSIFICATION OF BUSINESSES ACCORDING TO CORPORATE STRATEGY

Richardson, Taylor, and Gordon characterize six types of businesses according to the different corporate strategies that have been observed.[5]

Technological Frontiersmen

Research and development-driven firms on the leading edge of product technology are referred to as technological frontiersmen. Their ability to innovate and introduce new products is a key factor of success. Markets are abandoned when the product becomes price-competitive and profit margins fall, and product performance is the major selling feature. Hewlett-Packard is an example of this type of company.

Technology Exploiters

Technology exploiters are firms that introduce new products and continue to manufacture them throughout the product life-cycle, even when price competition becomes severe. Texas Instruments is a good example of this type of company.

Technological Servicepeople

These firms, also on the leading edge of product technology, provide custom service on complex systems for low-volume customers and markets. Such firms must be extremely flexible and adaptable in order to respond to customer needs. The Canadian division of Litton Industries exhibits these characteristics.

Customizers

Customizers are firms that do little innovation themselves; instead, they take product designs from customers and produce custom products on a low-volume basis. Because of the wide variety of work performed, they must have considerable flexibility for changes in volume and product specifications. Hughes Aircraft's Satellite Division is one example.

---

[5]Reprinted by permission of P.R. Richardson, A. J. Taylor, and J. R. M. Gordon, "A Strategic Approach to Evaluating Manufacturing Performance," *Interfaces,* 15, no. 6 (November–December 1985): 15–27. Copyright © 1985 The Institute of Management Sciences, 290 Westminster Street, Providence, Rhode Island, 02903, USA.

Cost-minimizing Customizers

These firms manufacture low-volume mature products to individual customer designs. Such firms' competitive advantage is in design and process engineering. Price competition is an important factor in marketing products. Many shipyards are examples of this type of business.

Cost-minimizers

These firms are high-volume producers with skills in low-cost production of mature products. High productivity and high-capacity utilization are necessary to compete. Zenith competes on this basis.

The objectives of these various businesses differ greatly. So also do the factors that are important for success. Table 4.1 lists the factors needed to compete successfully for each of these types of businesses. Clearly the manufacturing implications are also different. Strategies developed for each strategic business unit drive functional strategies in marketing, finance, research and development, and, of course, manufacturing. Marketing decisions for low-cost/high-volume firms would differ from those for innovative firms with customized products. Financial strategies, research and development, and manufacturing strategies would also differ.

As an illustration of how corporate strategy varies by type of business, let us contrast Hewlett-Packard, a technological frontiersman, with Texas Instruments, a technological exploiter.[6] Texas Instruments prefers to pursue competitive advantages based on larger, more standard markets and a long-term, low-cost position. Hewlett-Packard, on the other hand, seeks competitive advantages in selected smaller markets based on unique, high value, functional performance. Texas Instruments enters markets early, expands and consolidates its position,

---

[6]Adapted from Steven C. Wheelwright, "Strategy, Management, and Strategic Planning Approaches," *Interfaces*, 14, no. 1, (January–February, 1984) 19–33.

TABLE 4.1

Key Success Factors for Different Types of Businesses

Technological frontiersmen
Outstanding product research, design, and development
High-product quality
Ability to introduce new products continuously

Technology exploiters
Rapid price reduction as production reaches high volume
Substantial skills in product development and design
Ability to introduce new products
High-product quality
Cost-minimization skills

Technological servicepeople
Excellence in product design
High-product quality and quality assurance
Flexibility to customer-specification changes

Cost-minimizing customizers
Low prices
Cost minimization (often without the benefit of high-volume production)
Delivery on schedule
Flexibility to volume and specification changes

Cost minimizers
Low price
High-volume, low-cost production
Rapid delivery

Source: Richardson, Taylor, and Gordon, "Strategic Approach."

and achieves a dominant market share when the product matures. Hewlett-Packard creates new markets and exits or introduces other new products as cost-conscious competitors enter the market. Texas Instruments emphasizes cost reduction in order to build volume while Hewlett-Packard adds features in order to hold prices longer, thus achieving higher profit margins and earlier returns on investment.

These corporate strategies are reflected in the operations decisions that each company makes. For example, Texas Instruments uses capital intensive and cost-effective production processes such as assembly lines, staffed with lower-skilled assemblers. Hewlett-Packard uses more flexible processes employing higher-skilled assemblers who produce in lower volumes. Texas Instruments uses more industrial engineers in order to improve productivity while Hewlett-Packard uses more product engineers in order to develop new performance features for its products. Texas Instruments makes more of its components, while Hewlett-Packard purchases more. Clearly Texas Instruments' operations strategy would not work as well for Hewlett-Packard, and vice-versa. What is important is that the operations strategy chosen by each firm must support the overall corporate strategy.

Functional strategies (marketing, finance, operations) must be vertically coordinated with the strategic plans of the business unit and be consistent with higher level strategies. Vertical integration is accomplished through hierarchical decision making. Strategies must also be coordinated horizontally across functional lines. Horizontal coordination is the more difficult task and the area in which more cooperation is necessary.

4.4 MANUFACTURING STRATEGY

In manufacturing organizations, operations strategy is usually referred to as **manufacturing strategy**. Referring back to Table 1.5, which lists the fundamental planning and decision-making areas in operations management, it is easy to see that developing a manufacturing strategy involves a variety of choices and trade-offs. For example, in choosing a facility location, should we locate closer to suppliers or to customers? Should we use primarily manual labor or invest in automation and other advanced technology? Answers to such questions define the manufacturing strategy of the organization.

Wheelwright suggests that the most important performance criteria on which manufacturing strategy should be based are *efficiency, dependability, quality,* and *flexibility.*[7] Efficiency considerations include both cost and capital efficiency; efficiency is usually measured with indexes such as return on sales, inventory turnover, and return on assets. Generally, the emphasis is on minimizing investment and maximizing return. Dependability considerations involve a company's ability to meet delivery dates at promised prices. Dependability involves not only the capability to stock end products and produce to order deadlines, but also the ability to manufacture replacement parts quickly. Quality, as we have discussed in Chapter 2, is measured by how well a product or service meets customer's

---

[7]Steven C. Wheelwright, "Reflecting Corporate Strategy in Manufacturing Decisions," *Business Horizons,* February 1978, 57–66.

needs. High quality can keep a product competitive even at higher prices. Finally, flexibility is the ability to react to market changes by introducing new products and changing production volumes.

While efficiency is the most often used performance criterion, the lack of attention to the other three criteria in developing an operations strategy has led to the demise of many companies. An operations strategy that supports corporate business objectives is necessary in order to evaluate tradeoffs, discover opportunities, set priorities, and provide the resources necessary to meet objectives.

Table 4.1 shows the different manufacturing capabilities needed to support different types of businesses. On one hand, the technological-frontiersmen show a need for high quality, high flexibility, and product variety. At the other extreme, the cost minimizers require low cost, high product availability, and high-volume production. Table 4.2 summarizes these different needs along the dimensions of volume, variety, and degree of innovation.

Technological frontiersmen require a system with flexible technology capable of producing new and complex products specified by customer orders. Cost minimizers, on the other hand, require an efficient system design based on smooth product flow on a make-to-stock basis. An example presented by Hales[8] illustrates some of the essential components of manufacturing strategy for IBM through the life cycle of a typical product that ultimately has high-volume and low-cost objectives.

- *Early manufacturing involvement in*
  Design
  Process verification
  Sourcing (make/buy) decisions
- *Design for automation by*
  Minimizing the number of parts
  Eliminating fasteners
  Self-alignment, no adjustments
  Symmetrical where possible
  Avoiding parts that interfere

---

[8]H. Lee Hales, "Time Has Come for Long-Range Planning of Facilities Strategies in Electronic Industries." Reprinted from *Industrial Engineering* magazine, April 1985. Copyright Institute of Industrial Engineers, 25 Technology Park/Atlanta, Norcross, GA 30092.

Type of Business	Volume	Variety	Degree of Innovation
Technological frontiersmen	Medium	Medium	High
Technological exploiters	Medium	Low	High
Technological servicepeople	Low	High	High
Customizers	Low	High	Low
Cost-minimizing customizers	Low	Medium	Medium
Cost minimizers	High	Low	Low

TABLE 4.2

Different Manufacturing Needs

Rigid, stiff parts
Close tolerances
One-sided assembly
- *Limited models and features*
  Stable product design
  Group engineering changes for the "model year"
  Customization of the product in distribution centers
- *Building to plan*
  Finished goods owned by sales
  Continuous flow manufacturing
  Supplier integration
  Zero defects
  Reduction of work-in-process inventory
  Multiskilled, focused team
- *Defect-free at shipment*

Notice the planned involvement of manufacturing in design of the products, development of production processes, and design of quality-assurance systems, and how all the components of this strategy relate to the ultimate objectives of high volume and low cost. For instance, automated production helps to achieve a high volume of production; customizing in distribution centers eliminates the need for high product variety in the manufacturing function itself and reduces cost of maintaining high manufacturing inventories.

Components of Manufacturing Strategy

Referring to Figure 4.1, we may define eight major components of manufacturing strategy: product technology, capacity, facilities and location, process technology, human resources, operating decisions, integration of suppliers, and quality. Let us discuss each of these in turn.

Product Technology

In the examples discussed earlier, we saw that products range from those that are custom-made to those that are manufactured in high volume. Custom products are unique, and cost is generally not an important issue. On-time delivery, quality, and the capability to design and manufacture different products are factors that determine success. On the other hand, companies that manufacture high-volume types of products usually benefit most from standardization in design, low manufacturing cost, and high availability of the product through inventories and distribution channels. Thus it is important that product designers understand the nature of the manufacturing process and its implications for design.

Some products, such as soft drinks and household cleaners, have long product-life cycles; others, such as sophisticated electronics products (for example, personal-computer printers) have very short life cycles. Marketing strategies to renew or extend product-life cycles often depend on introducing technological improvements in the product. These strategies must be coordinated with manufacturing for success. Chapter 5 discusses the role of the product-life cycle and other aspects of product development in more detail.

Capacity

Capacity, a measure of the amount of output that can be produced over a period of time, is an important resource that a firm can control. There are many strategic decisions that a firm must make regarding capacity. These involve the amount of capacity to have, timing of capacity changes, and the type of capacity. For example, what is the economic effect of expanding an existing plant versus building a new facility or having one large facility versus several small ones? Do decisions regarding capacity make a difference if the product is well established or new? How does a firm make capacity decisions to deal with cyclic variations in demand? How does a firm best take advantage of economies of scale in planning capacity? Capacity decisions are discussed thoroughly in Chapter 6.

Facilities and Location

Facilities and their locations are closely related to capacity decisions. Management must trade off economies associated with centralized production facilities with distribution costs and customer service. For instance, oil companies often locate processing plants near supplies of crude oil in order to achieve economies of scale. Individual distribution outlets are located much closer to customers. Decisions on how to structure product groups within plants, what types of processes to develop, and what volume to produce are important, especially in rapidly changing industries. For instance, in the semiconductor industry, small, low-volume plants are built for new products with considerable risk, whereas high-volume plants are used for stable and mature products. Chapter 7 focuses on these issues.

Process Technology

A process-oriented system employing general-purpose equipment allows for high flexibility in manufacturing different products. A product-oriented system, with special-purpose equipment and dedicated to the production of one or a few products, provides high volume and low unit costs.

Automation is making process decisions quite difficult, primarily because highly automated plants are very expensive. For example, the John Deere Company spent $500 million on their automated Waterloo, Iowa, plant, and General Electric spent over $300 million in automation improvements alone in their Erie, Pennsylvania, facility. Moreover, automation changes the manufacturing cost structure, labor requirements, and the ability to deliver products. For instance, robotics allows greater product variety and the flexibility to change products and adjust to volume changes without additional capital expenditures. It generally results in lower costs for materials, scrap, labor, and supervision and yields improved quality. Process technology and automation are the subjects of Chapters 8, 9, and 10.

Human Resources

The management of the work force has important long-term implications for manufacturing strategy. Long-term commitments made to unions to solve short-term problems have come back to haunt many companies. For instance, wage concessions made in the U.S. steel industry have contributed to many of the current problems facing that industry. In addition, union protection of multiple job classifications have reduced work force flexibility and made it difficult to increase productivity and introduce automation in the United States.

The relationship between people and machines presents special challenges for organizations facing increased automation. Automation increases the need for skilled technicians, and consequently the design of work systems, training, motivation, and compensation become important manufacturing considerations.

Questions that must be addressed include: Should jobs be created for generalists or specialists? What degree of supervision is appropriate? Should emphasis be placed on work measurement and standards? These are difficult questions to answer in today's technological age. In Chapter 11 we address many of these issues.

Operating Decisions

How operations are planned and controlled affect productivity and the ability to deliver goods on time. While actual decisions are more of a tactical and operational nature, the policies used for making such decisions have long-term effects. New philosophies and techniques for manufacturing planning and control have been developed in recent years. The Japanese have popularized the notion of zero inventories and just-in-time purchasing and production; W. Edwards Deming has advocated increased worker control over quality, and the Japanese have proven this successful. Today's managers must carefully consider such philosophies and techniques in view of their strategic implications. Chapters 12 through 16 focus on these topics.

Integration of Suppliers

This aspect of strategy involves the level of materials control between suppliers and manufacturers. Should we make components or purchase them from external suppliers? Should we acquire suppliers or merge with them? Should we use one or several suppliers? Questions of quality, delivery, and proprietary knowledge enter into such decisions.

Increased integration of suppliers, or "cooperative strategy," requires more complex control by operations managers. Rather than working in a competitive purchasing environment as in the United States, Japanese firms approach supplier relations much differently. They often work with only one or a few suppliers in an atmosphere of mutual dependence and trust. They help in training their suppliers in methods of quality control. In return, they expect 100 percent delivery of materials and components when needed. This supports their operational policy of just-in-time production (discussed in Chapter 17).

Quality

In Chapter 2 we discussed the eight principal dimensions of quality: performance, features, reliability, conformance, durability, serviceability, aesthetics, and perceived quality. These multiple dimensions of quality imply that goods and services can be differentiated in many ways. Note, however, that a company should not necessarily attempt to be the best for each of these dimensions. In fact, some products or services can be improved on one dimension only if they become worse on another; for example, speed versus fuel economy in automobiles. Such trade-offs make quality an important dimension of a manufacturing strategy.

To illustrate this, Garvin describes the differences between Steinway & Sons and Yamaha, two of the leading manufacturers of pianos.[9] Steinway & Sons' pianos have been the industry leader because of their even voicing, sweetness of their registers, the duration of their tone, their long lives, and fine cabinet work. Each of their pianos are handcrafted, and unique in sound and style. Yamaha

---

[9]David A. Garvin, *Managing Quality: The Strategic and Competitive Edge,* New York: The Free Press, 1988.

has developed a reputation for manufacturing quality pianos in a very short time. This was done by emphasizing reliability and conformance (low on Steinway's list), rather than artistry and uniqueness. In contrast to Steinway & Sons, Yamaha's pianos are produced on an assembly line. Further issues of quality control are discussed in Chapter 19.

Manufacturing strategy should have a clear and consistent objective. Often, managers make decisions without realizing the consequences that may occur. Wickham Skinner[10], for instance, relates the following history of one company:

The Focused Factory

> American Printed Circuit Company (APC) was a small company which had been growing rapidly and successfully. Its printed circuits were custom-built in lots of 1 to 100 for about 20 principal customers and were used for engineering tests and development work. APC's process consisted of about 15 operations using simple equipment, such as hand-dipping tanks, drill presses, and manual touch-ups. There was considerable variation in the sequence and processes for different products. Delivery was a major element for success and price was not a key factor.
>
> APC's president accepted an order from a large computer company to manufacture 20,000 printed circuit boards—a new product for the company—at a price equivalent to about one third of its average mix of products. APC made the decision to produce these circuit boards in order to build volume, broaden the company's range of markets, and diversify the line. The new product was produced in the existing plant.
>
> The result was disastrous. The old products were no longer delivered on time. The costs of the new printed circuit boards were substantially in excess of the bid price. The quality on all items suffered as the organization frantically attempted to meet deliveries. Old customers grew bitter over missed deliveries, and the new customer returned one third of the merchandise for below-spec quality. Such heavy losses ensued that the APC company had to recapitalize. Subsequently, the ownership of the company changed hands.

Skinner suggests that many companies, such as APC, attempt to do too many things within one plant and one organization. Using the rationale of economies of scale, they add products, markets, technologies, and support staff that often tend to conflict and compete against one another. In other words, there is a *lack of focus* in the companies' operations.

Noting that there are many ways for an organization to compete besides producing at low cost, that a factory cannot perform well on every yardstick, and that simplicity and repetition breed competence, Skinner has advocated the concept of the *focused factory*. His basic tenet is that a factory that focuses on a narrow product mix for a particular market niche will outperform the conventional plant, which accepts a broader mission. By focusing plant and equipment on a limited task, costs and overhead are likely to be lower. Moreover, the factory can better meet strategic and other functional goals.

Skinner further suggests that a firm must first understand the realities of its technology and economics. Then they must centralize the factory's focus on relative competitive ability, avoid the tendency to add staff and overhead and let each manufacturing unit work on a limited task instead of the usual complex

---

[10]Reprinted by permission of *Harvard Business Review*. "The Focused Factory," by Wickham Skinner, (May–June 1974): 113–121. Copyright © 1974 by the President and Fellows of Harvard College; all rights reserved.

mix of conflicting objectives, products, and technologies. Such a strategy can improve customer service and competitive position sufficiently to cover the higher investment required to focus a factory.

4.5 FORMULATING AND IMPLEMENTING A MANUFACTURING STRATEGY

Booz Allen and Hamilton, Inc., a management consulting firm, has developed and implemented manufacturing strategies for a variety of firms.[11] Figure 4.2 illustrates the general process of developing a manufacturing strategy. The purpose of this process is to determine an "ideal" manufacturing strategy to meet the firm's goals and objectives and then to compare the current manufacturing operations and policies to this ideal. In this fashion, "gaps" and strategies for improvement can be identified. The final step in the process is an evaluation of those alternative strategies and planning for their implementation in order to establish a strategic manufacturing plan.

The process of developing manufacturing strategy can be described as follows:

1. Understand business objectives in terms of market growth, product strategy, and competitive environment. These are part of the business plan. For example, are the objectives to increase market share or maintain the current share of the market? Is the firm oriented toward product innovation or are product lines relatively stable?

2. Determine *strategic manufacturing units* to segment similar groups of products through analysis of key product, market, and manufacturing characteristics.

3. Establish manufacturing missions based on critical market-success factors. (This is similar to the scheme of Richardson, Taylor, and Gordon that we discussed earlier in this chapter.)

4. Establish directional objectives for technology, vertical integration, factory focus, and operating-control policies to support the strategic manufacturing units.

5. Establish the current manufacturing base line, defining the resources available, technology employed, and the managerial organization and philosophy.

6. Determine internal and external measures of performance, such as capacity utilization, operating costs, throughput, profitability, productivity, quality, dependability, and flexibility.

7. Compare manufacturing base-line performance to the strategic mission to determine "gaps" and improvement alternatives. Table 4.3 gives some examples of gaps and possible alternatives for a low-volume firm with a mission of high service levels and a high degree of manufacturing flexibility.

8. Evaluate the costs, benefits, and risks with each alternative and the impact on long-term competitive advantage to establish an integrated strategy.

---

[11]Adapted from Robert J. Mayer and Jack Moore, "Applying Manufacturing Strategy Concepts to Practice," in *Strategic Management of Operations,* S. Wheelwright, R. Schroeder, and J. Meredith, eds., Operations Management Association, OMA Publication P83WH1, September 1983, pp. 45–50.

FIGURE 4.2 Manufacturing Strategy Development Process

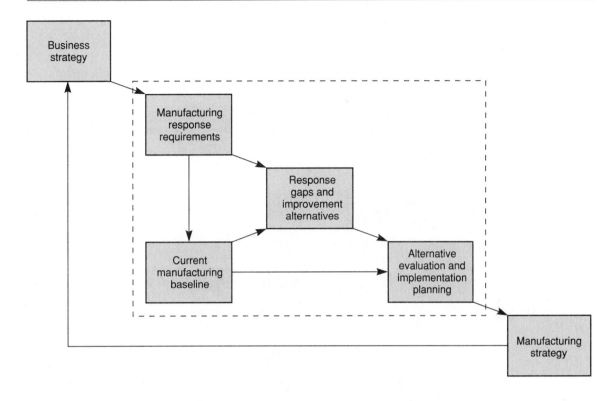

Two disguised examples of this process at work and the results are given next.

Autoparts, Inc.

In 1979 Autoparts, Inc., had annual sales of over $400 million. They produced domestic U.S. automotive parts equipment with many products serving a large number of customers. Autoparts, Inc., had a commanding position in its market but was losing its share of a market that was experiencing a significant downturn.

The company's objectives were to maintain their share of the market and to improve their operating margins. The key issues were product cost, reducing or improving the manageability of operations, and selectively adding capacity. Autoparts served three market segments with three different competitive success requirements, as shown in Figure 4.3. Using the process described earlier to develop

Gaps	Alternatives
Making too many of the product's parts	Reduce degree of integration by selective outsourcing
Overuse of dedicated equipment for some components	Use numerical controlled, computer-aided design and computer-aided manufacturing technologies
Skilled labor not always available	Reduce complexity of the processes
Poor customer delivery status	Upgrade order entry or manufacturing systems

TABLE 4.3

Some Examples of Gaps and Improvement Alternatives

FIGURE 4.3 Market Segments Identified for Autoparts, Inc.

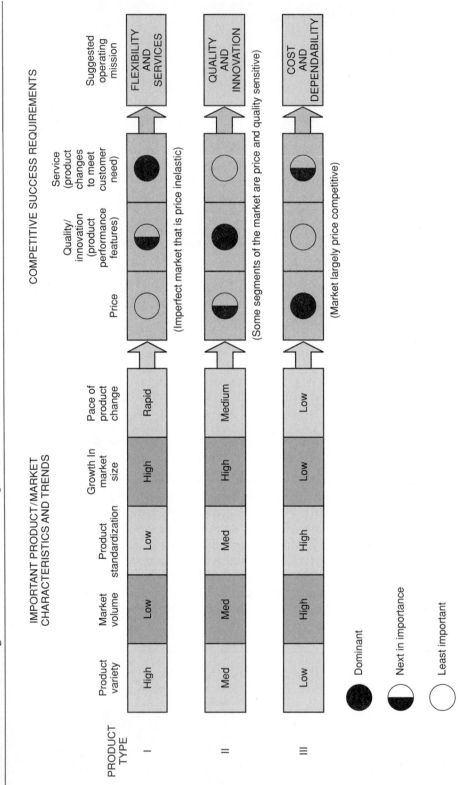

Source: Mayer and Moore, "Applying Manufacturing Strategy Concepts."

the ideal manufacturing strategy and compare it to current operations, gaps were identified in process technology, the degree of supplier integration, and management infrastructure.

Changes were recommended in the processes, organization structure, and the type of management controls. Furthermore, a deployment strategy called for the segmentation of core businesses from the noncore business and the addition of satellite plants. The main manufacturing plant concentrated on fabrication of parts and components with assembly in outlying satellite plants. The strategy produced a potential of $7 million direct-cost annual savings, significantly increased the company's flexibility to meet changing product and service demands, and provided the necessary capacity to meet the changing market demands.

Sweetsmell, Inc.

Sweetsmell, Inc., manufactures house-care, personal-care, and industrial products with one large manufacturing plant in the Midwest; annual sales are approximately $1 million. Its manufacturing capability was becoming strained and the company was not certain where to add additional facilities.

Sixty percent of the firm's house-care and personal-care products were in a mature or declining market; however, its industrial-products markets were growing and thus consuming a greater share of the production resources. Sweetsmell's objectives were to increase its share of the personal-care market and to improve its operating margins. The key issues were where to expand capacity and how to increase the "managability" of operations.

The company produced products in five different manufacturing product segments, each of which had distinct operating missions and key success factors (see Figure 4.4). With this recognition, it was possible to establish important directional objectives for manufacturing technology, the degree of integration, management-operating philosophy and management-control systems, that is, the "ideal" strategy. The strategy devised called for a high volume, centrally located facility, a separate satellite plant for low-volume products, a facility to support the specialized industrial products, and a set of facilities to support regional manufacturing products. The results of this strategy realigned products among facilities to achieve focus on volume and process technology that greatly reduced the complexity of managing manufacturing, improving both service and operating margins.

The process of developing manufacturing strategy recommended by Booz Allen and Hamilton is a good one, but not all firms are sophisticated enough to be employing such a strategy.

A conference held in 1988 at the University of North Carolina focused on the following question, "How is manufacturing strategy formulated and implemented in practice?"[12] Six firms participated representing computer equipment and electronics, telecommunications, furniture, electrical submersible pumps, valves, and pharmaceuticals. The conference led to several interesting conclusions.

Manufacturing strategy was a relatively new activity for each of the firms that participated in the conference; many had started only within the previous five

---

[12]Adapted from Ann S. Maruchek and Ronald T. Pannesi, "The Manufacturing Strategy Process: Principles and Practice," Graduate School of Business Administration, University of North Carolina, Chapel Hill, NC 27599.

FIGURE 4.4   Market Segments Identified for Sweetsmell, Inc.

PRODUCT SEGMENTATION

Product Segment	Description	Applicable S.C. Johnson Products	IMPORTANT PRODUCT/MARKET CHARACTERISTICS						COMPETITIVE SUCCESS REQUIREMENTS			Operating Mission
			Product Variety	Market Volume	Market Volatility	Scope of Market	Product Life Cycle	Pace of Product Introduction	Price	Product Performance	Market Response	
I	HIGH VOLUME STABLE PRODUCTS	• Floor care • Furniture care • Some insecticides and repellents • Some laundry care • Some air fresheners	Low	Medium-High	Low	National	Middle/End	Low	Next in importance	Dominant	Least in importance	Reliability and Cost
II	HIGH VOLUME RAPID MARKET RESPONSE	• Hair care • Skin care • Some rug care and laundry care • Items in early stages of life cycles	High	High	High	National	Beginning	High	Least in importance	Next in importance	Dominant	Flexibility and Responsiveness
III	LOW VOLUME PRODUCTS UNDER FIVE GALLONS	• Some insecticides • Automotive • Small percentage • Commercial products	High	Low	Low	National	Middle/End	Medium	Least in importance	Dominant	Next in importance	Reliability and Flexibility
IV	FIVE GALLON OR MORE BULK PACKAGE GENERAL APPLICATION	• Five gallons and above floor care, cleaners, etc. • Innobulk type items • General metal working lubricants • Agricultural	Medium	Medium	Low	Regional	Beginning-Middle	Medium	Dominant	Least in importance	Next in importance	Cost and Service
V	SPECIALIZED APPLICATION BULK PRODUCTS - CUSTOMER SPECIFIC	• Unique application polymers • Special metal working lubricants	High	Medium-High	Low	Regional	Beginning-Middle	Low-Medium	Dominant	Least in importance	Next in importance	Innovation and Cost

● Dominant
◑ Next in importance
○ Least in importance

← Definition of Success Factors →

• PRICE - The sensitivity to price in the marketplace

• PRODUCT PERFORMANCE - The degree to which superior product performance can enhance the competitive advantage

• MARKET RESPONSE - The importance of serving with consistent reliability and to be capable of meeting changing customer needs

Source: Mayer and Moore, "Applying Manufacturing Strategy Concepts."

years. There was considerable confusion between the terms "strategy" and "tactics." Strategy was viewed as a broad framework for planning, and tactics were viewed as the specific means of achieving the strategy. Thus, in many of the firms the manufacturing objectives were really tactics in achieving a strategy. All of the firms categorized the bases of competition along the dimensions of cost (efficiency), quality, delivery, and flexibility. Quality was at or near the top of every list.

All of the firms followed the top-down hierarchical structure of decision making (discussed in Chapter 1) in formulating manufacturing strategy. Corporate strategy was formulated in support of corporate goals and objectives. This provided the basis for all functional strategies of the firm. Although the role of manufacturing has long been viewed as reactive with respect to corporate strategy, many of the firms reported that manufacturing was taking a more proactive role in identifying manufacturing strengths that could provide a competitive advantage for the firm. In each of the firms, the evaluation of manufacturing strengths and weaknesses and the external and internal environmental analyses form the basis for strategy formulation. Either formally or informally, some assessment is made of current industry conditions, the firm's manufacturing capability, and resource deployment. In all cases, manufacturing strategies are closely tied to marketing strategies either formally or informally through common goals and objectives. In many cases, the marketing strategy is an input to the manufacturing strategy formulation process.

Among the various components of manufacturing strategy, facilities, vertical integration, organization, and capacity were generally constrained by corporate decisions and treated as "givens" in the manufacturing strategy formulation process. The major focus areas were process choice/technology, quality, manufacturing planning and control systems, and people. Process choice, quality, and people were the most emphasized.

Finally, the formulation of manufacturing strategy was always a group effort. Although the head of manufacturing operations had the ultimate responsibility for manufacturing strategy, the formulation process involved multiple people, and in some cases, multiple functions.

4.6 OPERATIONS STRATEGY IN SERVICE ORGANIZATIONS

Services are the major product of organizations such as airlines, banks, law firms, hotels, and restaurants. Ways of providing those services often differ greatly from the ways manufacturing organizations make products. Research and development, for example, deals with ways of doing things rather than physical objects such as products. Thus, it is more difficult to predict the effects of new services or technologies such as drive-through windows, electronic banking, and so on. A significant difference is that there are usually fewer economies of scale in the production of services than in manufacturing. For example, a fast-food restaurant cannot usually increase its competitive advantage by simply adding capacity to an existing unit; instead, it must expand into new locations or offer new products and services. McDonald's, for example, was the first to take advantage of *unused* capacity by offering breakfast; simply expanding its physical facilities would not have had such an impact. However, expanding usage of the existing facilities during off peak time was very profitable.

The eight major elements of manufacturing strategy from Figure 4.1 are also relevant to service organizations, although their relative importance may vary. For instance, in considering product technology, should sandwiches be made to customers' orders (as at Wendy's) or made to one specification and stored (as at McDonald's)? Is capacity the right kind? An airline might consider changing from large jets (which may provide economies of scale) to smaller jets and more frequent flights (which may provide a greater degree of customer service). Location is an important strategic consideration for many service organizations such as restaurants and hotels. For instance, should a motel locate in a downtown area or along an expressway? In the area of process technology, there is much debate on whether hamburgers should be broiled or fried. As another example, should a bank use automatic tellers or people? Professional service organizations, such as law firms, train and manage their work force differently than fast-food restaurants. How workers are trained is an important human resource issue in producing services. Finally, the issue of supplier integration is still important; consider, for example, a fast-food corporation trying to decide whether or not it should raise its own cattle or rely on external suppliers.

It is easy to see that service organizations must address similar questions to those manufacturers address. By examining these areas in conjunction with overall corporate objectives, effective service strategies can be developed.

Most services are produced and marketed at the same place and time and often by the same person. This is certainly true in banks, insurance companies, and many other service organizations. Drawing upon this observation, Heskett coined the term "strategic service vision" in defining a service strategy that integrates both marketing and operations.[13] A strategic service vision focuses on four basic elements.

1. identification of a target market segment
2. development of a service concept to address targeted customers' needs
3. design of an operating strategy to support the service concept
4. design of a service delivery system to support the operating strategy

Identification of a target market segment concerns understanding the characteristics of various market segments, their importance, the needs of customers in these segments, and how well these needs are currently being served. The service concept design should consider what elements of the service are to be provided for customers, how they are perceived by the customers, and how they should be designed, delivered, or marketed. The operating strategy involves identifying which components—operations, financing, marketing, human resources, and so on—are the most important, and on which the most effort will be concentrated. It also involves how quality and cost will be controlled, and what results will be expected. Finally, the design of the service delivery system should define the role of people, technology, capacity, equipment, and procedures in the strategy; in

---

[13]James L. Heskett, "Lessons in the Service Sector," *Harvard Business Review,* March–April 1987, 118–126. Copyright 1987 by the President and Fellows of Harvard College; all rights reserved.

addition, it should determine the extent to which the service design helps ensure quality standards and differentiates the service from the competition.

Chase has suggested that it is the extent of customer contact that distinguishes service industries from manufacturing industries.[14] Customer contact refers to the physical presence of the customer in the system. The extent of contact is the percentage of time the customer must be in the system relative to the total time it takes to serve him or her. Systems in which this percentage is high are called *high-contact systems;* those in which it is low are called *low-contact systems.* Many low-contact systems, such as check processing at a bank, can be treated as quasi-manufacturing systems, since most of the principles and concepts used in manufacturing apply. Service systems with high-customer contact are more difficult to control and design than those with low-customer contact. Table 4.4 lists areas of service strategy that have important implications in the design of the service delivery system in high-contact systems versus low-contact systems.

---

[14]Richard B. Chase, "Where Does the Customer Fit in a Service Operation?" *Harvard Business Review,* (November–December 1978): 137–142. Copyright 1978 by the President and Fellows of Harvard College; all rights reserved.

Table 4.4   Major Design Considerations in High- and Low-contact Systems

Decision	High-Contact System	Low-Contact System
Facility location	Operations must be near the customer.	Operations may be placed near supply, transportation, or labor.
Facility layout	Facility should accommodate the customer's physical and psychological needs and expectations.	Facility should enhance production.
Product design	Environment as well as the physical product define the nature of the service.	Customer is not in the service environment so the product can be defined by fewer attributes.
Process design	Stages of production process have a direct immediate effect on the customer.	Customer is not involved in the majority of processing steps.
Scheduling	Customer is in the production schedule and must be accommodated.	Customer is concerned mainly with completion dates.
Production planning	Orders cannot be stored, so smoothing production flow will result in loss of business.	Both backlogging and production smoothing are possible.
Worker skills	Direct work force comprises a major part of the service product and so must be able to interact well with the public.	Direct work force need only have technical skills.
Quality control	Quality standards are often in the eye of the beholder and hence variable.	Quality standards are generally measurable and hence fixed.
Time standards	Service time depends on customer needs, and therefore time standards are inherently loose.	Work is performed on customer surrogates (e.g., forms), and time standards can be tight.
Wage payment	Variable output requires time-based wage systems.	"Fixable" output permits output-based wage systems.
Capacity planning	To avoid lost sales, capacity must be set to match peak demand.	Storable output permits setting capacity at some average demand level.
Forecasting	Forecasts are short term, time-oriented.	Forecasts are long term, output-oriented.

Let us examine the implications of high-contact and low-contact systems on the four major performance criteria for operations: efficiency, quality, flexibility, and dependability. Efficiency is of more concern to low-contact systems because of the importance of equipment and technology. In high-contact systems, control is more important and cost reduction through economies of scale is more difficult to achieve. Low-contact systems are more amenable to statistical methods of process-quality control similar to those used in manufacturing. The presence of the customer makes quality control more difficult for high-contact systems. Training and motivation of employees are the principal means of quality assurance.

Flexibility is important in high-contact systems. The use of computer technology, for example, can greatly increase the flexibility of a service operation by providing more time for people to work with customers, hence providing the capability to respond faster and more flexibly to a wider range of customer demands. Dependability is achieved through careful scheduling and inventory control. For high contact systems, scheduling emphasis is on personnel, while for low contact systems the emphasis is on scheduling tasks and jobs. Scheduling personnel to be available for providing service is more difficult because of uncertainties in customer demand. Personnel must be available when the customer is present. To some extent, "customer inventory" can be controlled in high-contact systems through appointments and reservation scheduling, which improves the dependability of service delivery. Proper scheduling of jobs in low contact systems can improve dependability.

In developing a service strategy, Chase suggests answering several questions.

1. What kind of operating system do you have? That is, what is the extent of customer contact? Time-study and work-measurement techniques are often useful in making this assessment and obtaining some quantitative measures.
2. Are your operating procedures geared to your present structure? For example, is employee compensation matched to the nature of the system—high-contact systems based on time and low-contact systems based on output?
3. Can you realign your operations to reduce unnecessary direct-customer service? Can some tasks be taken away from high-contact employees? Can the work force be organized into high- and low-contact groups?
4. Can you take advantage of the efficiencies offered by low-contact operations? Can scheduling or forecasting techniques that have proven useful in manufacturing settings be employed?
5. Can you enhance the customer contact you do provide? This can be accomplished, for instance, by adding workers at peak times, keeping longer business hours, or adding those little "personal touches" to the service.
6. Can you relocate parts of your service operations to lower your facility costs? For example, Fotomat uses small drop-off points, whereas actual film processing is done in larger facilities to take advantage of economies of scale.

Managers of service organizations need to consider such questions in developing long-term strategies. Doing so will lead to more effective service system designs.

As we noted in Chapter 1, service is an important supporting function in manufacturing organizations. Oftentimes, service is viewed as secondary in importance to manufacturing. However, next to the quality of the product itself, service is perhaps the greatest key to profitability. Companies that pay attention to providing superior customer service understand that satisfied customers will produce repeat business. They also know that changing business conditions, new developments in technology, expansions and contractions in the work force, and other factors influence purchasing decisions. They realize that direct, on-going relationships with customers provide an effective service organization that can alert the company to emerging trends.

Companies who have consistently provided superior service have certain elements in common.

1. They establish service goals that support business and product line objectives.
2. They identify and define customer expectations for service quality and responsiveness.
3. They translate customer expectations into clear, deliverable, service features.
4. They set up efficient, responsive, and integrated service delivery systems and organizations.
5. They monitor and control service quality and performance.
6. They provide quick, but cost-effective response to customers' needs.

Developing a service support strategy requires examining operations throughout a company and breaking out those processes and tasks that bear most directly on service. Often, it means restructuring responsibilities and redrawing organization charts. Sometimes, it means breaking management molds and thinking about service in new ways.

One example is a multinational technology company that began to recognize that it was continuing to lose long-standing customers despite its efforts to improve service. With the help of a major consulting firm, it soon became clear that no one within the company had a good picture of their customers' service expectations. Each key manager made specific assumptions about service requirements—none of which was accurate. Additionally, key service departments such as customer and technical support, order processing, billing, and receivables, were focused more on internal procedures and policies than on the customer. Customers often had to speak to three or four people in various departments to have a routine question answered.

After some restructuring, management now has a more customer-focused service system. Internal procedures have been redesigned to emphasize customer needs. Information systems were modified to improve the accessibility of data. Standards were established and tracked religiously by management. A program to monitor customer expectations on an on-going basis was defined and implemented.

---

[15]Adapted from Jeffrey Margolies, "When Good Service *Isn't* Good Enough," *The Price Waterhouse Review*, 32, 3, New York: Price Waterhouse, 1988, 22–31.

In this section we present two examples of operations strategy development in practice. The first example discusses the development and implementation of a manufacturing strategy for a large computer equipment manufacturer, and the second example discusses the process used by a telecommunication's manufacturer in developing an operations strategy.

STRATEGY FORMULATION FOR A COMPUTER EQUIPMENT MANUFACTURER[16]

W ith annual sales of over eight billion dollars and 82,000 employees worldwide, this firm, which is highly decentralized, uses a hierarchical approach where manufacturing strategy is formulated at several levels within the firm as depicted in Figure 4.5. Corporate strategy represents the starting point for manufacturing strategy and for the business plans of the operating units. However, the corporate business plan precedes the corporate strategy. The corporate strategy is reviewed and revised constantly, and therefore, is highly responsive to changes in both the internal and external environments. At the corporate level, broad corporate strategic objectives are formulated which provide a set of expectations for lower level manufacturing strategies.

The corporate strategy and the corporate business plan provide the basis for group-level manufacturing strategy. The responsibility for formulating the group-level manufacturing strategy rests on the manufacturing systems group which is a collection of the manufacturing departments of the various divisions which comprise the group. A fundamental goal in formulation of the group manufacturing strategy is to identify and relate all strategic elements formed at the group level to the other plans and strategies developed at higher levels in the hierarchy. Thus, in addition to the corporate strategy and business plan, the group must respond to its own business plan, the plans of the Corporate Manufacturing Council (in which each group participates) and any ongoing *major* research and development program activities which will involve the group. Initial efforts at manufacturing strategy focus on how the group's manufacturing resources can make a contribution to the higher level plans, and

in particular, how they can provide a competitive advantage.

After potential competitive contributions are defined, each division within the group is polled in order to determine what manufacturing strategy is currently being followed. The approach involves prioritizing the major bases of competition (i.e., quality, cost, availability, and design) for each division. This procedure was validated within the firm by conducting two separate surveys. Each respondent was first asked to rank the competitive variables in importance to the customer, and at a later point in time, the respondent was asked how the variables would be ranked based on their perceived importance in day-to-day operations. The discrepancies in these results provided the basis for evaluating how patterns of decisions were being made. The group looked at categories of resources to decide what was currently being done in manufacturing and what opportunities for change were possible. Specific strategies are formulated for each of the categories of resources in the manufacturing strategy, and in addition, performance measures and tactics for accomplishing the strategy are decided upon.

At lower levels, the process is further refined. A division manufacturing strategy is formulated by establishing strategic objectives that are consistent with the group manufacturing strategy. At the same time, there is an effort to provide an appropriate level of detail to specifically focus the strategy to a particular strategic objective. The process involves defining the strategic objective, creating a specific tactical plan for each strategic objective and then defining specific performance measures for each tactical objective. The process is further refined by

---

[16]Adapted from Marucheck and Pannesi, *op cit.*

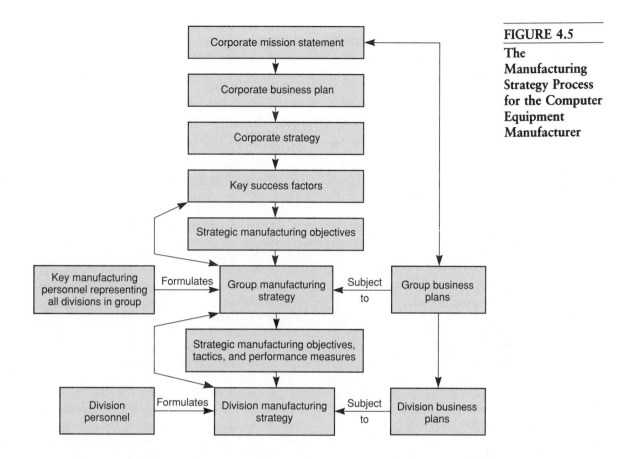

identifying appropriate departmental tactical objectives for each department within the division. With the support of the tactical plans, performance measures, activity plans for implementation of the tactical plans, and supporting organizational plans, implementation can be easily monitored and strategies can be executed.

The firm has been able to exercise considerable flexibility in terms of revising strategy on an ongoing basis. In their hierarchical approach, top management develops strategic directions and objectives while both middle and lower level management indicate what can realistically be accomplished given current resource levels. This information is fed back to top management, who after consideration, may reformulate the strategic objectives. This process may reoccur anytime that business conditions dictate the need for a change.

QUESTIONS

1. Discuss the relationship between the division manufacturing strategy and the group manufacturing strategy. In which ways does one affect the other?
2. Why are the division's polled? How do the results of this polling affect the manufacturing strategy?

STRATEGY FORMULATION FOR A TELECOMMUNICATIONS EQUIPMENT COMPANY[17]

A manufacturer of telecommunications equipment has annual sales of over $5 billion and employs 20,000 people within the United States. The boundaries of operations strategy are more wide ranging

---

[17]Adapted from Marucheck and Pannesi, *op. cit.*

in this firm than in most others. Operations strategy is defined to encompass a strategy for the total product delivery process: product design and development, manufacturing, procurement, order entry, installation, and service. In contrast, the marketing strategy determines which products are to be delivered. Together the two strategies form the business strategy. The process of developing operations strategy is illustrated in Figure 4.6.

The Operations Council, which consists of the directors of operations and/or general managers from all operating groups and divisions as well as all the operations directors at the corporate level, is responsible for developing the operations philosophy and strategy. The Council uses the marketing strategy and an environmental analysis as input to the strategy development process. This process is highly structured and consists of five steps.

The process begins with an evaluation of the effectiveness of operations. Here not only the strengths and weaknesses of the categories as proposed by Hayes and Wheelwright are analyzed but also what is termed "orgware," which includes the organizational metrics, control systems, human resource planning and development, organizational structure, capital investment decisions, plant charters, and corporate culture. The second step is an industry/market analysis which seeks to describe what would have to be included in the strategy for a firm to be successful in the telecommunications industry. The third stage is the development of an operations philosophy which consists of the firm's basic assumptions and beliefs that would precondition a

successful operations strategy. The fourth step is the actual development of the operations strategy which consists of the formulation of a specific strategic objective which would serve as a framework for planning throughout the organization. The strategy is accompanied by an operations methodology which consists of a series of steps designed to execute the strategy and make the product delivery process more effective. The strategy is then encapsulated in a short document which is passed onto senior executives for additional input. The revised strategy is ultimately approved by the president.

Responsibility for strategy implementation also resides with the Operations Council, and specifically with the directors of operations in the operating units. Inherent problems with the strategy are identified by using a strategy—culture compatibility grid, which seeks to identify discrepancies between the behaviors and performance measures required for strategy implementation and those that seem to be currently practiced within the firm. The strategy is documented in the form of a small booklet and a videotape to assist in implementation.

The Council continually reassesses the operations strategy and monitors the status of its implementation with quarterly meetings. Although the strategy is broad enough that it need be revised only every three to five years, or as business conditions dictate, the three-year operating plan is revised annually. The operating plan also contains financial projections, that once approved, the first year of the operating plan automatically becomes the operating budget for the next year. In addition, each business

FIGURE 4.6

Operations Strategy for the Telecommunications Manufacturer

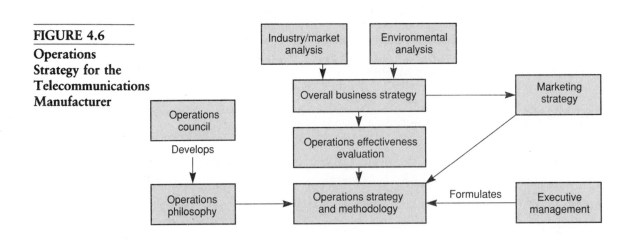

unit also develops a strategic plan from the operations strategy.

1. Discuss the role the operations council plays in strategy formulation.

2. Why do you suppose the firm is interested in "orgware" in conducting an evaluation of the effectiveness of operations?

SUMMARY

Strategic planning involves the long-term determination of goals, policies, and plans for an organization. The outcome of the strategic planning process is a corporate strategy. A corporate strategy involves the definition of businesses in which the corporation will participate and the acquisition and allocation of resources among the businesses. Each strategic business unit must develop strategic plans that support the corporate strategy in marketing, finance, manufacturing, and other functional areas.

Manufacturing strategy involves issues of product technology, capacity, facilities and location, process technology, human resources, operating decisions, integration of suppliers, and quality. A sound manufacturing strategy is essential to strategic planning, particularly in view of international competition in today's marketplace. Manufacturing strategy should support the nature of the strategic business unit, whether its goal is a high level of innovation and flexibility or high volume and low cost. A "focused factory" can better meet strategic goals and marketing objectives.

Strategy is also important in production of services and can be addressed using a similar framework as that of manufacturing. One approach to use in distinguishing service production from manufacturing is the extent of customer contact. The focus of high-contact systems should be significantly different from that of low-contact systems; this dichotomy plays a useful role in developing focused strategies for services.

KEY TERMS

Strategic planning
Operations strategy
Corporate strategy

Strategic business units (SBUs)
Manufacturing strategy

REVIEW/ DISCUSSION QUESTIONS

1. Briefly explain the three components of corporate strategy?

2. What factors are commonly cited as the reasons for the decline in the competitiveness of the United States?

3. What are *strategic business units?*

4. What are the six different types of businesses as defined by the Richardson, Taylor, and Gordon classification of corporate strategy?

5. Describe the key success factors for each of the businesses in the Richardson, Taylor, and Gordon classification.

6. Discuss how corporate strategy at Hewlett-Packard differs from that at Texas Instruments.

7. Define *operations strategy?*

8. Discuss the four most important performance criteria on which manufacturing strategy should be based.

9. What are the major components of manufacturing strategy? Why is each important?

10. Explain the term *focused factory*. What advantages does developing a factory focus have?

11. Explain the approach taken by Booz, Allen, and Hamilton in developing a manufacturing strategy.

12. Discuss the conclusions of the University of North Carolina conference on manufacturing strategy.

13. How does operations strategy in service organizations differ from that of manufacturing?

14. What is a *strategic service vision?*

15. Discuss the importance of customer contact in service organizations. What is the difference between high-contact and low-contact systems?

16. What implications do high-contact and low-contact systems have on efficiency, quality, flexibility, and dependability?

17. How is service strategy important in manufacturing organizations?

18. How might the strategic planning concepts discussed in this chapter be applied to a business school or an individual academic department? Formulate a set of questions and interview your department head or dean.

19. Skinner relates the following scenarios.[18] Explain the problems that each of these companies faced in terms of the manufacturing strategy concepts discussed in this chapter.

    a. Company A entered the combination washer-dryer field after several competitors had failed to achieve successful entries into the field. Company A's executives believed their model would overcome the technical drawbacks that had hurt their competitors and held back the development of any substantial market. The manufacturing managers tooled the new unit on the usual conveyorized assembly line and giant stamping presses used for all company products.

    When the washer-dryer failed in the market, the losses amounted to millions. The plant had been "efficient" in the sense that costs were low. But the tooling and production processes did not meet the demands of the marketplace.

    b. Company B produced five kinds of electronic gear for five different groups of customers; the gear ranged from satellite controls to industrial controls and electronic components. In each market a different task was required

---

[18]W. Skinner, "Manuacturing—Missing Link in Corporate Strategy," *Harvard Business Review* (1969): 136–145. Copyright © 1969 by the President and Fellows of Harvard College; all rights reserved.

of the production function. For instance, in the first market, extremely high reliability was demanded; in the second market, rapid introduction of a stream of new products was demanded; in the third market, low costs were of critical importance for competitive survival.

In spite of these highly diverse and contrasting tasks, production management elected to centralize manufacturing facilities in one plant in order to achieve "economies of scale." The result was a failure to achieve high reliability, economies of scale, or an ability to introduce new products quickly. What happened, in short, was that the demands placed on manufacturing by a competitive strategy were ignored by the production group in order to achieve economies of scale. This production group was obsessed with developing "a total system, fully computerized." The manufacturing program satisfied no single division, and the serious marketing problems that resulted choked company progress.

c. Company C produced plastic molding resins. A new plant under construction was to come on-stream in eight months, doubling production. In the meantime, the company had a much higher volume of orders than it could meet.

In a strategic sense, manufacturing's task was to maximize output to satisfy large, key customers. Yet the plant's production control system was set up—as it had been for years—to minimize costs. As a result, long runs were emphasized. While costs were low, many customers had to wait, and many key buyers were lost. Consequently, when the new plant came on-stream, it was forced to operate at a low volume.

5

Product Design
and Development

Perhaps the most important strategic decision that a firm can make involves the selection and development of new products. In fact, deciding what products should be offered and how they should be positioned in the marketplace will determine the growth, profitability, and future direction of the firm. In this regard, significant competitive advantage can be achieved by having products of superior design. In addition, products that are appealing, reliable, easy to operate, and economical to service give a perception of quality to the consumer. With its breakthrough design for the Taurus-Sable automobiles, the Ford Motor Company showed that a superior product can result in increased sales and higher profits.[1] Other companies, such as Caterpillar Inc. and Black & Decker are winning back customers with innovative new product designs. Modern electronics are responsible for much of the innovations in today's products, and bulky mechanics are being replaced by computer chips which allow radically different product design and function.

A superior product, however, is not the sole criteria for product design. Products also need to be manufactured efficiently and economically. This is where operations management can make substantial contributions to the product-design process. Simplicity of style is often accompanied by simplicity of assembly. This enables lower costs by reducing the assembly time and requiring smaller inventories. The four major strategic criteria—efficiency, quality, dependability, and flexibility—all improve. For example, prior to 1988, IBM had purchased its dot-matrix printers from Japan's Seiko Epson Corp., the world's lowest cost producer. The development of a new printer design, however, enabled IBM to begin manufacturing its own printers at less cost, primarily because the new design had 65 percent fewer parts and reduced assembly time by 90 percent. In a similar manner, General Electric simplified the design of its refrigerator compressor, reducing the number of parts from 51 to 29; this lowered the production cost and cut the failure rate by one-third.[2]

The design of a new product or service begins with the conception of an idea and continues through a variety of development and testing phases until detailed production specifications are determined, production begins, and the product is introduced in the marketplace. Marketing plays a major role in the early stages of product design and development by assessing consumer needs and communicating these to research and development. The operations function is responsible for designing and implementing the production process for the product.

New product decisions affect not only the production system, but other functional areas in the organization as well. For instance, the financial division must raise capital and prepare budgets for research and development of new products and processes, as well as for the other large expenditures that may be necessary. The legal department must review warranty information and assess potential product liability during the product-design process. The purchasing department must interact with the engineering group to determine what materials are required to produce the product so that appropriate vendors can be selected. All these

---

[1]"Smart Design," *Business Week,* 11 April, 1988, 102–108.
[2]Ibid., 105.

activities require good communication and coordination from initial product design through the introduction of the product into the market.

In this chapter we discuss the role of product design and development and the implications they have for production and operations management. We also consider quality and reliability in new product design and development, and issues related to the design of services. The chapter concludes with an overview of current trends and techniques in product design.

5.1 PRODUCT DECISIONS AND BUSINESS STRATEGY

Basically, there are three types of products: custom products, option-oriented products, and standard products.[3] *Custom products,* generally made in small quantities, are designed to meet the customer's specifications. The production cost is relatively high and the assurance of quality requires careful attention at every step in the manufacturing process. Since custom products can only be produced upon demand, the customer must wait for the product to be made.

Option-oriented products are unique configurations of subassemblies that are designed to fit together. The customer participates in choosing the options to be assembled. The subassemblies are made in relatively large quantities; therefore costs are reduced, and quality is easier to achieve because of repetition. Since the manufacturer cannot anticipate all of the configurations a customer may desire, the customer must wait while the product is assembled to the desired configuration.

Standard products are made in larger quantities. The customer has no options to choose from, and quality is easiest to achieve because the product is made the same way every time. Since the manufacturer makes standard products in anticipation of a customer demand, the customer will only have to wait for the product if it is out of stock.

The classification of custom, option-oriented, and standard products are important from a strategic perspective. If a company makes a custom line of products and its competitor offers an equivalent product on an option-oriented or standard basis, then the competitor has an advantage in terms of efficiency, quality, flexibility, and dependability. The implications in the automotive industry are evident. Henry Ford, for example, was one of the first to change the automobile from a custom product to a standard product. Although the standard design and assembly-line process used by Ford greatly reduced production costs, improved quality, and reduced delivery time, the price paid was that no options were available to the consumer. Today, the typical American automobile is the classic option-oriented product. Customers can choose from dozens of colors, seat types, engines, transmissions, tires, and other options. The number of different configurations can easily grow into the hundreds of thousands. The Japanese approach is to design and manufacture cars with very limited options; those options that are available are put on by the dealer, not in the manufacturing plant. This

---

[3]This discussion is adapted from Charles A Horne, "Product Strategy and the Competitive Advantage," *P&IM Review with APICS News,* 7, no. 12, (December 1987): 38–41. Reprinted with permission, The American Production and Inventory Control Society, Inc.

decision provides a distinct cost advantage and enables the Japanese factory to achieve higher levels of productivity.

The advantages of standard products go beyond manufacturing. Standard products also simplify purchasing and customer service. For example, orders of components will be more consistent in terms of what is ordered, and shipments can be scheduled more frequently, resulting in lower inventories.

In the fast-food industry, we see similar strategic choices. McDonald's, for example, produces a standard product and achieves an advantage in terms of service delivery. Burger King and Wendy's, on the other hand, produce option-oriented products. While the selection is greater at Burger King and Wendy's, these companies sacrifice speed of service. Neither the standard nor the option-oriented approach is necessarily better; each firm must decide what strategic tradeoffs must be made with each approach and select the approach that best fits their corporate strategy.

Products often begin as custom products and over time, become standard products. The ability to guide products along this progression determines a company's success. This leads us to a discussion of the product life cycle.

Figure 5.1 depicts a graph of sales volume versus time for a typical new product. This graph is referred to as the **life-cycle curve**. This curve shows that when a product is first introduced, sales begin to grow slowly, and then there is a period of rapid growth as the product gains acceptance and markets for it develop (assuming, of course, the product survives the initial phase). During the growth phase, new consumers are being made aware of the product through advertising, and the product becomes competitive with other brands. This phase is followed by a period of maturity, in which demand levels off and no new distribution channels are available. The product design becomes standardized, causing competitors to focus marketing strategies more on offering the best price for a similar product than on offering a significantly better product for a similar price. Finally, the product may begin to lose appeal as substitute products are introduced and become more popular. This is the decline phase. At this point the product is either discontinued or replaced by a modified or an entirely new product.

Many essential consumer goods, such as soaps, cleaners, and canned foods, exhibit long and almost never-ending phases of maturity, never reaching the decline phase in Figure 5.1. For such products, advertising and minor product improvements play a key role in maintaining sales volume, particularly in the face of new competition, and preventing the product from entering the decline

**The Product
Life Cycle**

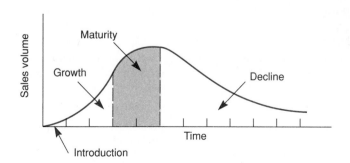

FIGURE 5.1

**Product Life-
cycle Curve**

phase in the life cycle. As a typical example, Levitt[4] discusses some marketing strategies for expanding sales. Jell-O was a unique product when it was first introduced in the market. As other brands appeared and competition increased, some of the strategies used to increase sales of Jell-O included the following:

- Promotion of more frequent usage. Jell-O increased the number of flavors, thereby giving the consumer greater variety.
- Variations of usage. Recipes for using Jell-O in salads and in combination with other products (such as Dream Whip) appear frequently.
- Expansion of the market to new users. The low-calorie features of Jell-O were designed to attract the weight-control market.
- Completely new uses. Unflavored gelatin has been promoted as a strengthening agent for fingernails and as a food for houseplants.

Though Jell-O was never replaced, the *uses* for Jell-O were expanded, thus extending its product life cycle. We see, then, that marketing can have a significant effect on the product life cycle.

A product's life cycle has important implications for operations. When a product is first introduced, design changes are frequent, focusing on changes that will make the product more innovative. Thus operations managers must maintain a high degree of flexibility in order to be responsive to these design changes, and the workforce must be highly skilled in order to quickly adapt to changing production requirements. During this stage the product is produced in small volumes, and hence high-capital investment in production facilities is usually not required.

As the growth stage develops and sales volume increases, manufacturing must have the ability to meet the growing demand. Operations is driven by the market and the focus is on process innovation. Production volume increases, and capacity growth and utilization become critical. As products mature, manufacturing must focus more on improving productivity and minimizing costs. Less production flexibility is needed as the product becomes more standardized, although some product innovation is possible and often desirable in order to maintain market share. The firm must invest in efficient and high-volume production facilities.

It is clear that operations must constantly review its focus in order to meet its strategic goals and objectives as each product moves through its life cycle. To further illustrate this point, let us reconsider Skinner's example of the printed circuit board company discussed in Chapter 4. If APC wants to get into the higher volume end of the business, then it must introduce a new process that will focus more on cost rather than on flexibility and speed of service. The operation will necessarily become less flexible, but will provide the customer with a lower cost product. Conversely, if APC does not want to move into an expanding market, then it should not accept business in that segment. To do so will only be at the detriment of the existing business. In the long run, if the new process is not compatible, the market will erode because the company will not be able to compete on a cost basis. Simultaneously, the inclusion of high-volume orders into the present process negatively affects existing orders because longer delivery times will result.

---

[4]Theodore Levitt, "Exploit the Product Life Cycle," *Harvard Business Review,* 43 (November–December 1965). Copyright 1965 by the President and Fellows of Harvard College. All rights reserved.

5.2 PRODUCTIVITY AND QUALITY CONSIDERATIONS IN PRODUCT DESIGN

The complexity of products has changed dramatically over the last several decades. "Traditional" products such as bicycles, hand tools, and hydraulic pumps have simpler designs and manufacturing processes than do "modern" products, which frequently involve the use of sophisticated electronics. For instance, a single state-of-the-art integrated circuit may involve over 200 manufacturing steps. Some of the major differences between traditional and modern products are listed in Table 5.1 As a result of these differences, operations managers must consider carefully the integration of design and production in order to achieve high productivity and quality.

A product's design must include the determination of the technical specifications that meet a customer's needs. Operations personnel must document the process specifications that determine how the product is to be made, the controls that will monitor incoming materials and purchased parts, the controls for monitoring the manufacturing process itself, the packaging and distribution of the product, and "what the customer sees," including instruction manuals and service policies.

Conformance to specifications is the responsibility of purchasing and manufacturing. If purchased parts are used, methods for checking their conformance to specifications are needed. Poor manufacturing methods may result in a product with low quality and frequent breakdowns. Packaging and distribution are important to assure that the product reaches the customer in good operating condition. This must also be considered during the initial design phase. Finally, the

Aspects of Products	Traditional	Modern	TABLE 5.1
			Aspects of Traditional versus Modern Products
Simplicity	Simple, static	Complex, dynamic	
Precision	Low	High	
Need for interchangeability	Limited	Extensive	
Consumables or durables	Mainly consumables	Mainly durables	
Environment in which used	Natural	Unnatural	
User understanding of product	High	Low	
Importance to human health, safety, and continuity of life	Seldom important	Often important	
Life-cycle cost to user	Similar to purchase price	Much greater than purchase price	
Life of a new design	Long; decades, even centuries	Short; less than a decade	
Scientific basis of design	Largely empirical	Largely scientific	
Basis of reliability, maintainability, etc.	Vague: "best effort"	Quantified	
Volume of production	Usually low	Often high	
Usual cause of field failures	Manufacturing errors	Design weaknesses	

Source: J. M. Juran and Frank M. Gryna, Jr., *Quality Planning and Analysis*, 2d Ed. (New York: McGraw-Hill, 1980), p. 190; used with permission.

quality of user manuals and after-the-sale service is critical to a successful product. Many personal computers were not successful when introduced simply because users, particularly those without a technical background, could not understand the instruction manuals.

Product designers often treat their tasks in isolation without considering the cost and capability of manufacturing the product, testing it, and servicing it after the sale. Many manufacturing problems, such as excessive scrap and defective parts, arise because of poor coordination between manufacturing and design engineers. For example, the choice of a manufacturing process, such as casting molten metal to specifications versus removing metal from a rough casting, affects the structural properties of the finished good and, consequently, design standards.

Setting inappropriate tolerances can also cause serious manufacturing problems and result in a high rate of defects. For instance, in one company, a bearing seat had to be machined on a large part costing over $1,000. Because of the precision tolerance specified by design engineers, one or two parts per month had to be scrapped when the tolerance was exceeded. A study undertaken by the quality manager revealed that the bearings being used did not require such precise tolerances. When the tolerance was relaxed, the problem disappeared. This one design change resulted in approximately $20,000 in savings per year.

This case illustrates that design must be coordinated with manufacturing to produce products of consistent quality with minimum waste. For example, it is typical for a company to replace failing parts during product testing by more expensive counterparts. This action only increases manufacturing cost. The alternative is to *redesign* the product around the less expensive parts. A Japanese watchmaker, for example, found that using expensive quartz crystals was not necessary to achieve high accuracy. The use of an inexpensive capacitor was found to compensate for variations in cheaper crystals and still achieve high accuracy.

Design for Quality and Productivity	The term **quality engineering** refers to the process of designing quality into a product and predicting potential quality problems prior to production. Quality engineering is concerned with the plans, procedures, and methods for design and evaluation of quality. AT&T, for example, has come to realize the importance of quality engineering in product and process design.[5] It is not enough just to manufacture a product that meets design specifications; the product must also be easy to manufacture and insensitive to variability on the factory floor. To illustrate this point, consider the situation that AT&T faced when they developed an integrated circuit for amplifying voice signals. As originally designed, the circuit had to be manufactured very precisely to avoid variations in the strength of the signal. Such a circuit would have been costly to make because of stringent quality controls that are needed during the manufacturing process. But AT&T's engineers, after testing and analyzing the design, realized that if the resistance of the circuit were reduced—a minor change with no associated costs—the circuit would be far less sensitive to manufacturing variations. The result was a 40 percent improvement in quality.

---

[5]John Mayo, "Process Design as Important as Product Design," *Wall Street Journal,* 29 October 1984, 29.

Many aspects of product design can adversely affect quality and productivity.[6] Some parts may be designed with features that are difficult to fabricate repeatedly or with tolerances that are unnecessarily tight. Some parts may lack details for self-alignment or features that prevent insertion in the wrong orientation. In other cases, parts may be so fragile or so susceptible to corrosion or contamination that a fraction of the parts may be damaged in shipping or by internal handling. Sometimes a design, because of lack of refinement, simply has more parts than are really needed to perform the desired functions, so there is a greater chance of assembly error. Thus, problems of poor design may show up as errors, poor yield, damage, or functional failure in fabrication, assembly, test, transport, and end use.

A product's design affects quality in two major areas: at the supplier's plant and in the manufacturer's own plant. A frequent cause of supplier quality problems is incomplete or inaccurate specification of the item to be provided by the supplier. This often occurs with custom parts because of either weakness in the design process, engineers who do not follow set procedures, or sloppiness in the procurement and purchasing process. The greater the number of different parts and the more suppliers involved, the more likely it is that a supplier will receive an inaccurate or incomplete parts specification. Such problems can be reduced by designing a product around preferred parts (those already approved based on their reliability and qualified source of supply), minimizing the number of parts in the design, and procuring parts from a minimum number of vendors.

In manufacturing and assembly, many of the same problems described above for a supplier can occur. In addition, there will be problems in the area of assembly and test. For instance, designs with numerous parts may cause part mixups, missing parts, and more test failures. If some parts are similar but not identical, the chances of an assembler's using the wrong part are increased. Parts without details to prevent insertion in the wrong orientation may be assembled improperly. Complicated assembly steps or tricky joining processes may lead to incorrect, incomplete, unreliable, or otherwise faulty assemblies. Finally, the designer's failure to consider conditions to which parts will be exposed during assembly such as temperature, humidity, vibration, static electricity, and dust may lead to failures during testing. Table 5.2 illustrates various design guidelines that affect quality, yield, and cost.

Quite recently, an approach to design developed by Japan's Genichi Taguchi has received considerable attention. Taguchi's premise is simple: Instead of constantly directing effort in *controlling* a production process to assure consistent quality, *design* the product to achieve high quality despite the variations that will occur on the production line. Taguchi's approach is based on the use of statistically designed experiments to optimize the design and manufacturing process. His methods are being incorporated into computer-aided design systems. ITT Corporation has used Taguchi's technique to cut defects by more than half, saving $60 million in the first two years.[7]

---

[6]Adapted from Douglas Daetz, "The Effect of Product Design on Product Quality and Product Cost," *Quality Progress,* June 1987, pp. 63–67. Copyright © 1987, Hewlett-Packard Co. All rights reserved. Reprinted with permission.

[7]"How to Make It Right the First Time," *Business Week,* 8 June 1987, 142.

TABLE 5.2

Design Guidelines for Productivity and Quality Improvement

Minimize number of parts		
• Fewer part and assembly drawings	→	Less volume of drawings and instructions to control
• Less complicated assemblies	→	Lower assembly error rate
• Fewer parts to hold to required quality characteristics	→	Higher consistency of part quality
• Fewer parts to fail	→	Higher reliability
Minimize number of part numbers		
• Fewer variations of like parts	→	Lower assembly error rate
Design for robustness (Taguchi method)		
• Low sensitivity to component variability	→	Higher first-pass yield
	→	Less degradation of performance with time
Eliminate adjustments		
• No assembly adjustment errors	→	Higher first-pass yield
• Eliminates adjustable components with high-failure rates	→	Lower failure rate
Make assembly easy and foolproof		
• Parts cannot be assembled wrong	→	Lower assembly error rate
• Obvious when parts are missing	→	Lower assembly error rate
• Assembly tooling designed into part	→	Lower assembly error rate
• Parts are self-securing	→	Lower assembly error rate
• No "force fitting" of parts	→	Less damage to parts, better serviceability
Use repeatable, well-understood processes		
• Part quality easy to control	→	Higher part yield
• Assembly quality easy to control	→	Higher assembly yield
Choose parts that can survive process operations		
• Less damage to parts	→	Higher yield
• Less degradation of parts	→	Higher reliability
Design for efficient and adequate testing		
• Less mistaking "good" for "bad" product and vice versa	→	Truer assessment of quality, less unnecessary rework
Lay out parts for reliable process completion		
• Less damage to parts during handling and assembly	→	Higher yield, higher reliability
Eliminate engineering changes on released products		
• Fewer errors due to changeovers and multiple revisions/versions	→	Lower assembly error rate

Source: Douglas Daetz, "The Effect of Product Design on Product Quality and Product Cost," *Quality Progress*, June 1987. Copyright © 1987 Hewlett-Packard Company. All rights Reserved. Reprinted with Permission.

5.3 THE PRODUCT-DEVELOPMENT PROCESS

In order to illustrate how a typical new product comes into existence, let us consider the case of Bergstein Sports Equipment (BSE). Mark Schroer, a university student and a member of the tennis team, strings rackets part time at a local club in order to earn extra money. He would prefer to operate his own business at home, but professional tennis racket-stringing machines are rather large, heavy, and expensive. Stringing machines consist of a vise that holds the racket in place while strings are installed, a tensioner that enables the correct tension to be applied, and clamps to hold the strings while they are being tied. Having had considerable experience stringing rackets, Mark has developed some ideas for a new home racket stringer. He approached Bob Bergstein, president of Bergstein Sports Equipment, a local manufacturer of tennis equipment and other sporting goods. Bob expressed interest in Mark's idea.

This scenario illustrates the first step in developing any new product: an idea. However, a good idea does not necessarily indicate a successful product. A significant amount of development effort is necessary before a product can be produced and made available to the consumer. This effort is described by the **product-development process** given in Figure 5.2. This process consists of idea

---

FIGURE 5.2   The Product-Development Process

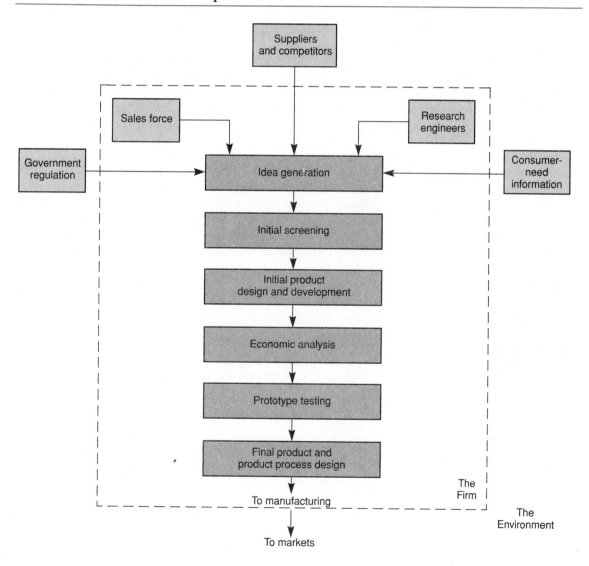

generation, initial screening, product design and development, initial economic analysis, prototytpe testing, and final product and production process design. At each of these stages, a potential product idea may be scrapped. In fact, the lifetime of new product ideas has been found to follow a survival curve similar to the one in Figure 5.3.

Many ideas are immediately rejected because of marketing factors, for being technically infeasible, or because it is concluded they are impractical to produce. Others are eliminated because of budgetary considerations or for not meeting corporate goals and objectives. Product ideas that survive the initial screening may later be eliminated during a formal economic analysis. An idea may even become obsolete during the initial design and development stage because of a new technological discovery, and testing of prototypes may uncover serious problems that cannot be technically or economically corrected. Finally, even if the product survives test marketing and is introduced into the marketplace, it may not be a commercial success. Sometimes this is the result of external influences, such as competition or economic factors. Often it is the result of ineffective planning of marketing strategies, inherent technological problems, or poor management in general. Product development, therefore, needs to be systematic in order to be effective.

The product-development process depicted by Figure 5.2 is presented from the perspective of a manufactured product, but similar steps must be followed in developing new services. In Section 5.4 we discuss some of the similarities and differences in the development processes for manufactured goods and services. Let us consider the stages in the product-planning process in more detail.

Idea Generation Ideas for new products can arise from a variety of sources internal and external to the firm. Many ideas come from customers or employees who feel they have a better idea. Although Bergstein Sports Equipment is a hypothetical example, numerous "basement inventors" have developed successful products. For instance, Howard Head invented the oversize Prince tennis racket in order to improve his own game. More often than not, however, new-product ideas are developed within the firm.

FIGURE 5.3
Survival Curve of New Product Ideas

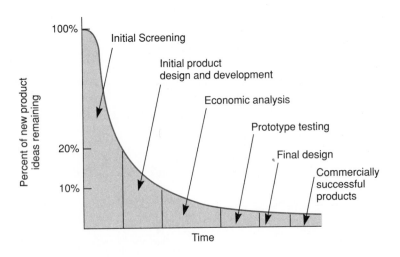

PART TWO   STRATEGY AND DESIGN IN P/OM

There are two principal sources for generating ideas: user needs and techno-logical developments. A product is useless if nobody wants it. Manufacturers are always trying to develop new products that meet the needs and demands of consumers. An example is the development of small cars and cheaper alternative modes of transportation, such as mopeds. Many "fad" items are also developed in response to consumer demand.

The second source of new product ideas is new technology. In the 1970s, for example, the development of semiconductors, microchips, and microprocessors revolutionized the electronics industry. This led to many improvements in the design and function of numerous items, such as television sets and business machines. These new innovations replaced products based on older technologies. Also, entirely new products, such as home video equipment, electronic games, and many others, were created.

Research and development (R&D) plays an important role in developing new products and advancing technology. The purpose of R&D is to generate new ideas and concepts and to develop these ideas and concepts into useful products. R&D performs three functions

- *Pure research*. Knowledge-oriented research with a goal of developing new ideas or concepts but with no specific product or application in mind.
- *Applied research*. Problem-oriented research dedicated to discovering new concepts, ideas, and materials with specific commercial applications.
- *Development*. Product-oriented research, concerned with translating re-search ideas into products.

Pure research is more likely to be carried on at major scientific and technical universities. Such research is usually supported by various government agencies, such as the National Science Foundation, Office of Naval Research, Air Force Office of Scientific Research, Department of Transportation, and so on. The Department of Defense also supports pure research at high-technology corpo-rations that produce products with potential military applications. In addition, many large consumer-oriented companies conduct pure research in hopes that new scientific discoveries will have profitable commercial applications. Many coalitions exist between industry, government, and universities that are designed to improve the state of the art of science and technology.

Applied research and **development** are undertaken by most profit-making cor-porations. Many large firms in such industries as electronics, consumer products, chemicals, pharmaceuticals, aircraft, automotive, and machine tools have exten-sive R&D groups. Often R&D effort is spread throughout the organization. A typical organization for R&D efforts for large firms with many diverse product lines is shown in Figure 5.4. Basic research to develop new business areas is carried on in a central research laboratory. For example, a consumer-products company might investigate entering the commercial drug market. For current product lines, individual R&D groups conduct research on improvements such as new flavors for food products. In such an R&D organization, there is usually also a group that monitors government policy and regulations. New research information is fed back to development groups in functional product areas, who are responsible for developing the idea to the point of production. A company that produces paper towels, for example, may discover a new formula or process to increase the absorbency of the paper towels. This information would be com-municated to the paper-products division for further development and might result in new products, such as diapers.

FIGURE 5.4   Information Flow in a Typical R&D Organization

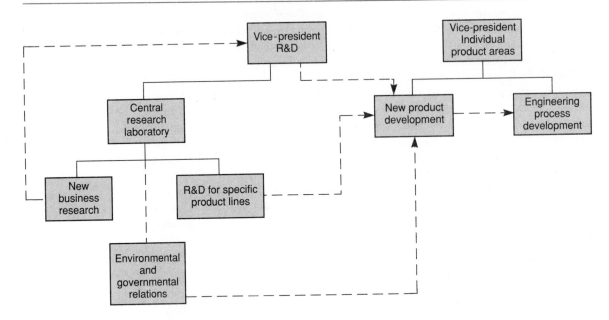

There is a high cost involved in performing R&D. Expensive equipment and highly qualified personnel are required. In addition, there is a high risk involved. For each successful R&D project, there are many failures. Nonetheless, the average payoff from the small number of successes may far outweigh the investment loss from the unsuccessful projects.

Screening

The purpose of screening is to eliminate ideas that do not appear to have a high potential for success and thus avoid expensive development costs. It is not uncommon for development costs to run as high as 50 to 60 percent of the total cost of producing a new product. Generally, three major criteria are used in initial screening: product development criteria, market criteria, and financial criteria. The fundamental questions considered for each of these criteria are listed below.

Criteria	Fundamental Questions
Product development	Is the product new or simply an imitation? Can we produce it with existing facilities? Is it technically feasible? Will there be any patent or other legal problems?
Market	What is the current market for this product? Is it expected to grow? What is the competition? How will this product affect our existing product line?
Financial	What will the return on investment be? How will this product contribute to overall profitability? How will development and production affect our cash flow?

In order to develop a quantitative assessment of product success based upon the criteria listed, a **scoring model** is often used. To develop a scoring model, each of the criteria is broken down into a set of attributes. For example, attributes of product development usually include the length of time required to develop the product, experience of the firm in producing similar products, length of product life, materials availability, and equipment. Several levels for each attribute are determined, and a value or score is assigned to each. Thus product-development time might be measured as (1) less than six months, (2) six months to one year, (3) one to two years, or (4) more than two years. The scores assigned each level reflect the relative benefits of that level. The results of the scoring model are then reviewed by top management for evaluation.

USING A SCORING MODEL FOR NEW PRODUCT JUSTIFICATION

A scoring model for the BSE example is shown in Table 5.3. Knowledgeable experts within the organization choose specific values for each level. Summing the maximum and minimum scores for all attributes within each criterion and adding the scores that were checked for the BSE example we have the following:

Criteria	Maximum Possible Score	Minimum Possible Score	Total Score
Product Development	+10	−10	+5
Market	+12	−12	0
Financial	+ 4	− 4	+3
			+8

Based on these rather rough estimates, we see that this new product idea ranks high with respect to product development criteria, average with respect to market criteria, and high with respect to financial criteria. After extensive discussions, the consensus among top managers at BSE was that the product had a very good potential for success. Thus the product development group was given the authority to continue with the project.

A scoring model such as the one we have presented is essentially a judgmental forecasting technique. The use of such a model helps top management conveniently summarize important variables and provides a means for analysis and discussion in the initial screening process. However, it is important to realize that the actual scores chosen are more often the result of analyses by operations managers at lower levels in the organization.

The scoring model we have illustrated for BSE assumes that all the attributes of all criteria have equal importance. This assumption can be easily modified by weighting the values. For example, if it is felt that return on investment is twice as important as capital outlay, the scores for return on investment could be multiplied by two in Table 5.3. Such an approach helps managers to quantify the relative importance of many different criteria. This model also assumes independence of the various criteria. If they are not independent, then it is more difficult to arrive at scores that reflect the dependencies.

TABLE 5.3

**Scoring Model
for Bergstein
Sports Equipment**

Criteria	Level		Score
	Product Development		
1. Development time	Less than 6 months	✓	+2
	6 months to 1 year	—	+1
	1–2 years	—	−1
	More than 2 years	—	−2
2. Experience	Considerable	—	+2
	Some	—	+1
	Little	✓	−1
	None	—	−2
3. Length of product life	More than 8 years	✓	+2
	5–8 years	—	+1
	3–5 years	—	−1
	3 or less	—	−2
4. Materials	Available inside firm	—	+2
	Available outside	✓	+1
	Limited availability inside	—	−1
	Limited availability outside	—	−2
5. Equipment	Present equipment usable	—	+2
	Some new equipment	✓	+1
	Mostly new equipment	—	−1
	New production facility	—	−2
	Market		
6. Marketability	Current customers	—	+2
	Mostly current customers	✓	+1
	Some current customers	—	−1
	All new customers	—	−2
7. Stability	High stable	✓	+2
	Fairly stable	—	+1
	Unsteady	—	−1
	Highly volatile	—	−2
8. Trend	New market	—	+2
	Growing	✓	+1
	Stationary	—	−1
	Decreasing	—	−2
9. Advertising	Little required	—	+2
	Moderate requirements	—	+1
	High requirements	—	−1
	Extensive	✓	−2
10. Competition	None	—	+2
	One or two	—	+1
	Several	✓	−1
	High competitive	—	−2
11. Demand	Stable	—	+2
	Subject to business cycle	—	+1
	Seasonal	✓	−1
	Seasonal and subject to business cycle	—	−2
	Financial		
12. Return on investment	30% or more	✓	+2
	25–30%	—	+1
	20–25%	—	−1
	Less than 20%	—	−2
13. Capital Outlay	Low	—	+2
	Moderate	✓	+1
	High	—	−1
	Extensive	—	−2

During the initial product design and development phase, product designers must be concerned with the operational characteristics of the product as well as its quality and reliability. For example, in the BSE case, designers would have to consider different methods for applying string tension, using clamps, and so on to develop a product that is easy to set up and use, strings rackets to the desired tension, and will not easily break. As another example, restaurant chefs and researchers in the kitchens of the major food manufacturers spend hours testing and developing new recipes.

The design of a product includes much more than simply a physical description of the item. Three factors must be taken into account: (1) the function of the product; (2) technical requirements and specifications; and (3) the economics of production and distribution.

Functional Influences

In order to be a commercial success, a product must be functional and appeal to consumers. Some of the important design considerations that relate to a product's function and appeal are:

- size, weight, and appearance
- safety
- quality and reliability
- product life, service, and maintenance.

The size and weight of items are important to the consumer. For example, an aluminum ladder is often preferred to a wood ladder because it is easier to carry. A lightweight chain saw might be chosen by a homeowner who cuts firewood once a year, whereas someone who sells wood for a living would require a heavy-duty chain saw. The flak-jacket used in football to protect injured quarterbacks was designed to be light and not bulky.

The appearance of a product—namely, the color, style, or pattern—is usually an important consideration in product acceptance. Many food items, for instance, are artificially colored solely for consumer appeal. The stylings of a Corvette and a Cadillac are designed to appeal to different groups of consumers.

Over recent years, consumers have become more aware and demanding of safety in products. Product-liability lawsuits and governmental regulations have made safety a prime consideration in product design. Volvo has used safety as an effective marketing strategy for its automobiles. Fires and other tragedies have resulted in critical evaluation of the design and operation of facilities in the hotel industry.

Products produced by different manufacturers are expected to differ in quality, a perception that often leads to the old adage "you get what you pay for." Not all products are designed to be of high quality. For example, high-class service in a restaurant might be oriented toward achieving a four- or five-star rating in the Mobil Travel Guide, while another restaurant might not consider this important. While this may be true of many consumable goods, quality and reliability are essential for products with high safety requirements, such as aircraft engines. The materials used in manufactured goods and the method of production affect the quality and reliability of a product. It is the responsibility of operations managers to ensure that these characteristics are achieved during production.

Product lifetimes and the cost of service and required maintenance are important considerations for most consumers. For example, radial tires have a much longer life than ordinary bias-ply tires. Good repair records and the length of intervals between required maintenance are criteria used in selecting new automobiles. New manufactured products often facilitate the design of services to repair and maintain the new product. For instance, the growth of video cassette recorders created the need for skilled repairpeople. A firm must consider the availability of service in new product decisions.

Technological Influences

Technical requirements in product design include the selection of the materials and component parts to be used and the manufacturing methods to be employed. Materials must be chosen to satisfy the functional requirements of the product. For instance, certain materials can be machined to much closer tolerances than others; thus, parts that require close tolerances must be made from the appropriate material. Different materials may require different manufacturing methods. For example, in aircraft production, many parts are made from aluminum or titanium. Titanium cannot be processed on many conventional machines. In addition, it costs more and has different performance characteristics than aluminum. Thus knowledge of the engineering properties of materials is essential to the designer.

Economic Influences

The price that a consumer must pay for a product depends on the direct and indirect costs of manufacturing and distribution. Products are targeted toward specific markets. Mercedes-Benz automobiles, for example, are marketed to individuals with high incomes, while many other models of automobiles are marketed to individuals with average incomes. It would make little sense for a company to produce a product for mass consumer appeal if the costs of manufacturing and distributing the product are very high. Therefore, product designers have to consider the costs of manufacturing and distributing the product during the design phase in order to produce a functional product at a reasonable cost.

Two techniques that assist in reducing costs associated with product design and development are *value engineering (VE)* and *value analysis (VA)*. These techniques involve analyzing the function of every component of a product, system, or service in order to determine how that function can be accomplished most economically without degrading the quality of the product or service.[8] **Value engineering** is focused on making certain that each element of a product design serves a necessary function. This occurs before production and therefore represents a cost prevention technique. **Value analysis** examines existing product specifications and requirements and is a cost reduction technique. VE/VA consist of asking fundamental questions about a product, such as the following:

1. What are the functions of a particular component? Are they necessary? Can they be accomplished in a different way?
2. What materials are used? Can a less-costly material be substituted?
3. How much material is wasted during manufacturing? Can this be reduced by changing the design?

These types of questions are no different than those a good operations manager would ask in analyzing the productivity of an operation such as material handling

[8]Vincent G. Reuter, "What Good are Value Analysis Programs?" *Business Horizons,* 29, no. 2, (1986): 73–79.

in a warehouse. Operations managers who think in terms of productivity improvement can provide important input to product designers. Consider, for instance, the handling and transportation of finished goods. Bulky items that can be assembled by the consumer, such as backyard swing sets or wheelbarrows, are often packaged and shipped unassembled in smaller containers in order to reduce the cost of assembly and distribution. Product designers must therefore realize that design is not strictly an engineering function, but a function that incorporates ideas and knowledge from all areas of the firm.

The benefits of value engineering and value analysis programs include not only cost reduction, but increased sales volume through improved product value, improved product performance and reliability, improved quality and product maintainability, improved delivery through faster production flow, improved productivity, and increased innovation and creativity of human resources. Often these improvements result in a product that merits a higher selling price, thus leading to increased profit.

All too often, pressures of reducing costs cause the designer to overlook other important objectives such as reliability, safety, serviceability, issues of human factors, and so on. To ensure that all important design objectives are accounted for, many companies have instituted formal **design reviews** during the product-planning process. The purpose of a design review is to stimulate discussion, raise questions, and generate new ideas and solutions to problems, the outcome of which is a better product. Design reviews help to facilitate standardization and reduce the costs of frequent design changes by anticipating problems before they occur.

Design reviews should be planned, scheduled, and documented and should involve all aspects of the production system. Generally, there are three major design reviews: *preliminary, intermediate,* and *final.* The preliminary design review establishes early communication between marketing, engineering, manufacturing, and purchasing and provides a better means of coordinating their activities. It usually involves higher levels of management and concentrates on strategic issues in design that relate to customer requirements, and thus the ultimate quality of the product. Included in a preliminary design review are:

- product function
- product value and appearance
- marketing considerations
- make or buy decisions
- environmental conditions and product testing
- reliability requirements
- liability issues
- scheduling of the design and development process.

After the design is well established, an intermediate review takes place to study the design in much more detail; the purpose is to identify potential problems and suggest corrective action. Personnel at lower levels of the organization are more heavily involved at this stage. Finally, just prior to actual production of the product, a final review is held. Material lists, drawings, and other detailed design information are studied with the purpose of preventing costly changes after production startup.

A design-review process usually includes a **failure mode and effects analysis (FMEA).** This technique consists of answering questions such as: How could a component fail? What would the consequences be? Generally, each component of a product is listed along with the way in which it may fail, the cause of failure, the effect or consequence of this failure, and how it can be corrected by improving the design. For instance, in a table lamp, one of the components is the socket. A typical FMEA for this component might be:

Failure:	cracked socket
Causes:	excessive heat
	forcing bulb
	bumping
Effects:	may cause shock
Correction:	use improved materials

An FMEA can uncover serious design problems prior to manufacturing and improve the quality and reliability of a product considerably.

Economic Analysis

Scoring models provide a rough, quantitative measurement of product potential. The purpose of economic analysis is to determine more specific quantitative measures of profitability and return on investment. A formal economic analysis is necessary in order to decide whether or not to commit further resources toward development of an idea.

In order to perform a formal economic analysis, an accurate estimate of demand is required. Thus forecasting is an important tool in the product-development process. Both statistical and judgmental forecasting techniques are often used. For example, statistical forecasts of industry sales prepared by the government, trade associations, or private marketing research companies often provide information on future trends for product lines. Judgmental estimates of market share can be incorporated with such forecasts to determine an estimate of product demand. Market research personnel have considerable experience in sales estimation and can usually provide this information.

In addition to demand forecasts, estimates of production costs must be obtained. Engineering and accounting are responsible for estimating manufacturing costs, costs of materials, supplies, personnel, equipment, depreciation, and other indirect operating expenses. Finally, the selling price of the product must be estimated in order to compute financial measures such as rate of return, payback period, and net present value. These can then be analyzed by top management in order to make a go/no-go decision. Break-even analysis is a useful tool for estimating the economic impact of a new product.

EXAMPLE | BREAK-EVEN ANALYSIS FOR NEW PRODUCT JUSTIFICATION

Let us illustrate the use of break-even analysis for the BSE example. Suppose that the marketing department estimates that 4000 stringers can be sold on an annual basis. This estimate is based on current trends in the sports and leisure industry, projections of racket sales, and growth of USTA-registered[9] professionals, who

---

[9]United States Tennis Association.

would most likely purchase a home stringer. The engineering and accounting departments at BSE have estimated that production costs would be as follows:

Variable costs per unit
  Manufacturing $55
  Selling and administrative   5
  Total variable costs $60

Fixed costs
  Manufacturing $350,000
  Selling and administrative 100,000
  Total fixed costs $450,000

Other stringers are priced from $90 to $250. In order to capture the projected share of the market, BSE would like to keep the selling price at $150. If we let S represent total sales of the stringer, then the total cost (TC) is estimated to be

$$TC = 450,000 + 60S$$

At a selling price of $150, the total revenue ($TR$) is

$$TR = 150S$$

These functions are illustrated on the graph in Figure 5.5. Since annual sales are estimated to be 4000 units, the break-even point of 5000 units will be reached after the product is on the market 1¼ years. In the judgment of BSE management, this indicated a sound investment. Therefore, it was decided to proceed with development of the product.

Prototype Testing

Once a product has been designed, a prototype is usually constructed to test its physical properties or use under actual operating conditions. Even though the initial design phase may consist of numerous computer calculations and design checks, actual testing is important in order to uncover any problems and correct them prior to full-scale production. Auto manufacturers, for instance, perform extensive road tests on new models; similar experiments are performed on tires, airplanes, and sports equipment. Prototype testing for many consumer products, such as food or laundry products, may consist of consumer panels, which judge

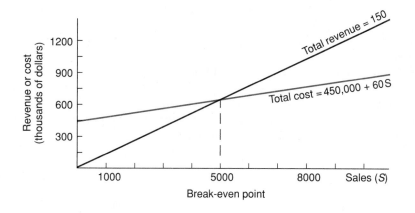

FIGURE 5.5

Break-even Analysis for the BSE Example

the product as "typical" consumers. In the BSE example, several local professionals could try a prototype stringer and judge its value according to criteria such as the time necessary to prepare a racket for stringing, the ease of use, and accuracy of tension after the racket is strung.

Final Product and Production-process Design

Prototype testing may indicate certain changes in the preliminary design. During the final design phase, these changes are incorporated into the design specifications. Drawings are made, and plans for production are initiated. It is during this time that production processes are selected and many detailed problems in operations management are resolved. We address these issues in more detail in later chapters.

New Perspectives on Product Development: The Taurus-Sable Success Story

The product development process that we have just described was formalized in the 1950–1960s. It is essentially a serial process in that marketing first determines customers' needs and develops a product concept. This is passed on to engineers who develop technical specifications for the conceptual design. Manufacturing is then handed the task of producing according to these specifications. Finally, the sales force is told to sell the product.

This approach is still predominant in many companies. Ford, however, took a radical new approach to product development in designing the Ford Taurus and Mercury Sable line of automobiles.[10] Recognizing that the company was not competitive on quality in the international marketplace, Ford threw out its traditional product development organizational structure. "Team Taurus" took a program management approach in which representatives from all the various units—planning, design, engineering, and manufacturing—worked together as a group. Communication was dramatically improved and many problems were resolved much earlier in the process. For instance, manufacturing suggested changes in design that resulted in higher productivity and better quality.

Other changes included "reverse engineering" in which other companies' cars were dissembled to learn how they were designed. Comprehensive market surveys were conducted to determine customers' wants and preferences. Ford asked assembly-line workers for their advice even before the car was designed. For example, workers complained that they had trouble installing doors because the body panels were made up of too many pieces. Designers reduced the number of panels from eight to two. One worker suggested that all bolts have the same head size so they would not have to constantly change wrenches. These examples clearly illustrate the importance of operations in product design and development and their impacts on both quality and productivity.

The Taurus and Sable have been one of Ford's biggest success stories since the Mustang, and have established new levels of quality both in the United States and abroad. Chrysler and General Motors have moved toward similar program management styles of product development.

---

[10] "How Ford Hit the Bull's-Eye With Taurus," *Business Week,* 30 June, 1986, 69–70.

5.4 PRODUCT DESIGN AND DEVELOPMENT FOR SERVICES

To this point we have concentrated on the design and development of manufactured products. The product development process also applies to the design and development of services. Services begin as ideas to satisfy some unfulfilled need. Initial screening is performed to determine market potential and feasibility; prototype design, analysis, and testing are carried out, leading to the final design. The differences between manufacturing and service system design involve the degree of customer focus and human interaction. Service design requires significantly more interaction between the system and the customer; this demands more flexibility and rapid response.

Several important differences which have critical implications for quality of service must be recognized. In manufacturing, it is straightforward to determine technical specifications for a product. Similar specifications are more difficult to define for services because they must reflect characteristics such as behavior and image. Specifications are required, however, so that service employees will know what is expected in their work, and to ensure that a consistent high-quality service will be provided for the customers.

The development of technical specifications for services should follow the same approach as for manufactured goods; that is, customer expectations and requirements must be converted into quantitative standards during design. These standards will then guide the design process and can be used later to develop quality control procedures. For example, the purpose of an airline carrier is to provide quality service to its customers as measured by schedule performance, baggage-handling performance, and so on. Standards might be developed for the percentage of on-time flights and the number of baggage irregularities per 10,000 passengers. While 100 percent conformance is the goal, more realistic targets might be specified for operating personnel, such as 85 percent of international flights and 90 percent of domestic flights arriving on time. The baggage handling goal might be stated as no more than 12 baggage irregularities per 10,000 passengers.

Second, services cannot be inventoried like tangible goods; services must be made available to the customer on demand. Major quality considerations must be planned and designed into the service just as it should be with manufactured products; however, finished goods may be *inspected* prior to being released from the factory. For services, this cannot be done. Thus internal failure costs of quality that were discussed in Chapter 2 do not apply; only external failure costs are important for services.

Third, a great deal of variation exists in service delivery. For manufactured products, conformance to standards can be closely monitored and controlled. The quality of services, on the other hand, depends on the skill and training of personnel who produce the services, and is more difficult to set standards on service performance and to ensure consistent quality. For example, meals on an airline can be carefully checked to ensure consistent quality, but service may vary considerably with different flight crews.

Since services are more labor-intensive than manufacturing, many aspects of service design are easier. As services move through their life cycles, service designs can be altered far more easily and quickly. For example, the size of a factory or number of machines constrains manufacturing capacity. Services, however, can easily change capacity; for instance, grocery stores can add or remove grocery clerks, and banks can do the same with bank tellers. The distance between the customer and the service can be easily changed, as illustrated by banks that build low cost branch offices that are closer to their customers. In manufacturing, this is generally not practical. Service procedures such as cash only sales can be altered by allowing credit or charge cards, and higher volumes can be handled by transferring some activity to the customer; for example, hospitals often require patients to fill out preadmission forms at home rather than at the hospital upon arrival. Services can also standardize operations more easily; for instance, gasoline stations can drop their full service operation or reduce the number of different goods or services that are provided.

Designing Services

A service product is a *process;* that is, a method of doing things. The design of the service is the specification of how the service should be delivered. This is done by specifying in detail the sequence of steps involved in the service delivery. This technique is similar to methods that we shall study for manufacturing process design in Chapter 8. Once these specifications have been developed, they can become the basis for job descriptions, employee-training programs, and performance measurement. As design tools, they enable management to study and analyze services prior to implementation in order to improve quality and productivity.

A service specification is usually depicted as a flow chart. Such a graphical representation provides an excellent communication device for visualizing and understanding the service operation. Figure 5.6 is an example of a flow chart for a car rental check-in and check-out process. This can be used to consider some fundamental questions about the service design:

1. Are the steps of the process arranged in logical sequence? For instance, might it be possible to prepare and present the billing information to the customer before updating the car status in the computer in order to enable the customer to leave the system faster?
2. Can some steps be eliminated or should others be added in order to improve productivity and quality? Can some be combined? One example might be preparing customer reservations in advance (perhaps by the night clerk when traffic is slow) to eliminate the time required to access the reservation system and receive the customer information while the customer is waiting.
3. Are capacities of each step in balance; that is, do bottlenecks exist for which customers will incur excessive waiting time? For instance, the lack of the proper number of car preparation personnel might lead to a backlog after preliminary inspection and fewer cars available for customers.
4. At which points might errors occur in the system that would result in customer dissatisfaction and how might these errors be corrected? For example, the car status information in the computer might not match the correct location of the car in the parking lot.
5. At which point should quality be measured? For example, one might use a quality checklist to verify that the car is properly prepared before it is parked in the ready lot.
6. Where interaction with the customer occurs, what procedures and guidelines should employees follow that will present a positive image? For instance, when a customer returns a car, the clerk should greet him or her with a smile and ask if any problems arose. When a customer departs, adequate exit instructions should be provided.

FIGURE 5.6   Flow Chart of Car Rental Check-in and Check-out Process

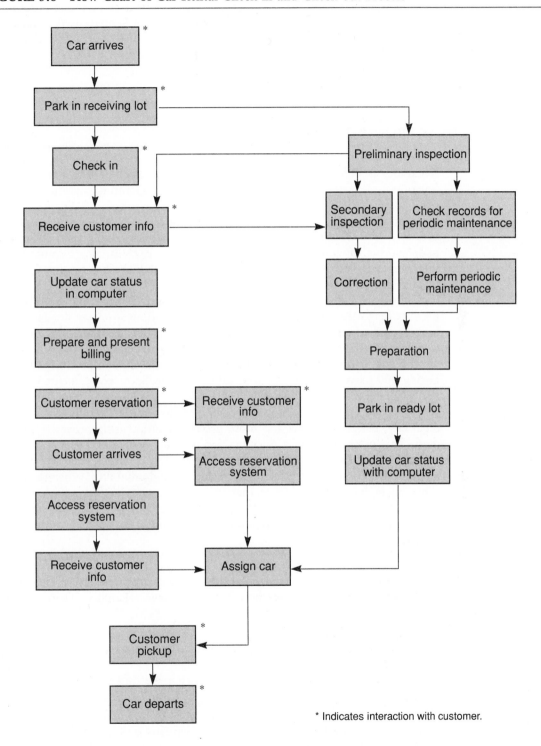

* Indicates interaction with customer.

Source: W. Earl Sasser, R. Paul Olsen, and D. Daryl Wyckoff, *Management of Service Operations, Text, Cases, and Readings,* Needham Heights, MA: Allyn and Bacon, Inc. 1978, p. 74.

This approach allows the service system designer to test alternatives without the actual construction and operation of the system. This is analogous to prototype testing for manufactured goods. Computer simulation is often used to facilitate this process (see the chapter supplement). Also, at the end of this chapter a P/OM in Practice case illustrates the use of simulation in service system design for Burger King Corporation.

5.5 RELIABILITY IN PRODUCT DESIGN

Reliability is defined as the probability that a product performs its intended function for a stated period of time under specified operating conditions. Hence, reliability is a quantitative measure of performance over time. For example, a manufacturer might determine that the reliability of a 48-month automobile battery is .97. This means that 97 out of 100 batteries should last 48 months under normal operating conditions (12,000 miles per year, for instance). With the complexity of modern electronic products, reliability has become a critical issue in design.

Conformance to specifications does not necessarily mean high reliability. A product may meet all the manufacturer's specifications but may not last over a long period of time. Like quality, reliability must be designed into products. Consumers would like products to have 100 percent reliability; indeed, this is a worthy goal for manufacturers. However, it is impossible to produce a product having 100 percent reliability under all conditions. Some components will inevitably fail because of uncontrollable and inherent variations in materials, power surges, or complex interactions of environmental conditions. To achieve high reliability, better materials and more precise manufacturing processes must be used. This often presents a dilemma for product designers, because increased reliability often means higher cost, more weight, and larger size. Management must therefore evaluate trade-offs between cost and reliability. When the cost of achieving high reliability is large, the firm seeking high reliability risks low profits and its competitive position in the marketplace. Low reliability, on the other hand, may damage the firm's reputation and result in lost sales or, even worse, product-liability suits.

Reliability
Engineering

Reliability engineering involves the planning, design, manufacturing, testing, and product-maintenance activities necessary to achieve reliability. These activities parallel those of product design.

- Define customer requirements.
- Define the environment in which the product will be used.
- Determine important economic factors.
- Select components and design to meet reliability and cost criteria.
- Determine reliability for process planning and selection.
- Evaluate reliability of purchased parts and manufactured components.
- Analyze field reliability data and take corrective action.

Testing for reliability is important for a variety of reasons. Test data are often necessary for liability protection, as a means for evaluating designs or vendor reliability and in process planning and selection. Often reliability-test data are required in military contracts. Testing is necessary to evaluate warranties and to avoid high costs related to early field failure. Good testing leads to high reliability and quality.

Figure 5.7 illustrates a typical product-failure rate curve. The performance indicated by this figure is common for electrical components and systems which make up a large portion of modern products. Such curves are usually determined from statistical studies. The curve shows the failure rate (failures per unit time) as a function of time. The **failure rate** λ (the Greek letter lambda) is defined as

Reliability Measurement

$$\text{Failure rate} = \lambda = \frac{\text{number of failures}}{\text{total unit operating hours}}$$

Since total unit operating hours is equal to the number of units tested times the number of hours tested, an equivalent definition of the failure rate is

$$\lambda = \frac{\text{number of failures}}{\sum_{i=1}^{n} \text{operating hours for item i}}$$

where n = number of items tested.

There is a fundamental assumption behind this definition that allows for different interpretations. Since the total unit operating hours equals the number of units tested times the number of hours tested, there is no difference in total unit operating hours between testing 10 units for 100 hours or 1 unit for 1000 hours. In view of Figure 5.7 this would clearly make a difference. This is why time is an important element of the definition of reliability. During a product's useful life, however, the failure rate is assumed constant, and different test lengths during this period of time should show no difference.

To illustrate the computation of λ, suppose that 10 units are tested over a 100-hour period. Four units failed, with 1 unit each failing after 6, 35, 65, and 70 hours; the remaining 6 units performed satisfactorily until the end of the test. The value of the total unit operating hours is computed as follows:

$$
\begin{array}{rcl}
1 \times 6 & = & 6 \\
1 \times 35 & = & 35 \\
1 \times 65 & = & 65 \\
1 \times 70 & = & 70 \\
6 \times 100 & = & \underline{600} \\
& & 776
\end{array}
$$

Therefore, $\lambda = 4/776 = .00515$ failures per hour.

In Figure 5.7, three distinct time periods are evident. The first is the early failure period, sometimes called the **burn-in period**. Weak components resulting from poor manufacturing or quality-control procedures will often lead to a high rate of failure early in a product's life. This usually cannot be detected through normal test procedures. This is particularly true for electronic semiconductors. Such components or products should not be permitted to enter the marketplace. The second phase of the life characteristic curve describes the normal pattern of random failures during a product's **useful life**. This period usually has a relatively

FIGURE 5.7

Failure-rate
Curve

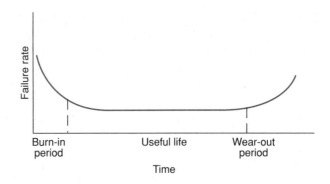

low constant failure rate that is determined by uncontrollable factors such as sudden and unexpected stresses resulting from complex interactions in materials or the environment. These are usually impossible to predict on an individual basis. However, it is possible to model the collective behavior of such failures statistically. Finally, as age takes over, the **wear-out period** begins, and the failure rate increases. You may have experienced such phenomena with automobile components or other consumer products.

Knowing the product-life characteristic curve for a particular product helps management predict behavior and make decisions accordingly. For instance, if it is known that the early failure period for a microprocessor is 60 hours, then one can test the chip for 60 hours (or more) under actual or simulated operating conditions before releasing it to the market. This process is usually called *burn-in* or *debugging*. When products enter the wear-out phase, the probability distribution of remaining life is often described by the normal distribution. This is illustrated in Figure 5.8. If the mean μ and variance σ^2 of product life are known, the normal distribution can be used to calculate the probability that the remaining lifetime will exceed a given value.

EXAMPLE

DETERMINING A MILEAGE WARRANTY POLICY FOR A TIRE COMPANY

The Goodman Tire Company has just developed a new steel-belted radial tire. Since the tire is a new product, Goodman's management believes that the warranty

FIGURE 5.8

Normal Distribution for Product Lifetime During the Wear-out Period

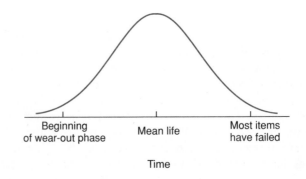

offered with the tire will be an important factor in the acceptance of the product. Before finalizing the warranty policy, Goodman's management would like some information concerning the tire lifetime.

From actual road tests, Goodman's engineering group has estimated that the mean tire mileage is $\mu = 36,500$ miles, and that the standard deviation, σ, is 5000 miles. Suppose that a 40,000-mile warranty is considered. What percentage of tires can be expected to last more than 40,000 miles? This question can be interpreted as trying to find the area of the shaded region in Figure 5.9. At $X = 40,000$, we have

$$z = \frac{X - \mu}{\sigma} = \frac{40,000 - 36,500}{5000} = .70$$

Using Appendix B, we find that this area is $.5000 - .2580 = .2420$. Thus we can conclude that about 24.2 percent of the tires will exceed 40,000 miles. Table 5.4 presents a summary of probabilities that actual mileage will exceed specified warranty values.

How can the Goodman Tire Company use this information? If the warranty is set at 40,000 miles, for example, then 75.8 percent of the tires will wear out before 40,000 miles. The company would have to replace them—not at full value, but with appropriate mileage adjustments. The paperwork and processing in-

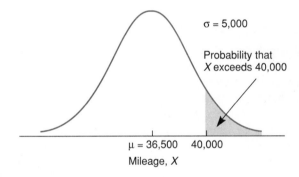

FIGURE 5.9

Goodman Tire Company Mileage Guarantee

Warranty Mileage, X	$z = \dfrac{X - 36,500}{5000}$	Probability That Actual Mileage Exceeds Warranty
31,000	-1.10	.8643
32,000	$-.90$	.8159
33,000	$-.70$	.7580
34,000	$-.50$	.6915
35,000	$-.30$	.6179
36,000	$-.10$	.5398
36,500	.00	.5000
37,000	.10	.4602
38,000	.30	.3821
39,000	.50	.3085
40,000	.70	.2420
41,000	.90	.1841
42,000	1.10	.1357

Table 5.4

Goodman Tire Lifetime Probabilities

volved could result in considerable expense. If a small warranty figure is chosen, such as 32,000 miles, then only 18.41 percent of the tires will be expected to require replacement.

5.6 PROCEDURES AND TRENDS IN PRODUCT DESIGN

Today, products mature more quickly than in the past. In the semiconductor industry, for example, the average life cycle of a product is estimated to be only two years. New technologies frequently appear and manufacturing processes change. The time to create new products, particularly in the electronics industry, must be shortened if firms are to remain competitive. New technology is changing the product design and development process. For example, the determination of consumer needs and purchasing patterns has been assisted by *scanner-based test marketing,* in which selected consumers use identification cards at supermarket checkout counters with laser scanning equipment so that purchasing patterns can be recorded and analyzed by computer.[11]

Several trends are evident in product design. Among these are the use of computers to aid the design process, standardization, modularity, and human factors consideration. These issues will be covered in this section.

Computer-aided Design

Computer-aided design (CAD) has had extensive use in product design and development and enables the designer to interact with the computer in the design process and eliminate formerly time-consuming activities such as drawing blueprints and constructing prototypes (see Photo 5.1). According to Decker,[12] CAD enables design changes to be made with minimal risk, since they have already been "proved" by the system, thus removing a lot of trial and error from the design process. In the Burger King example the computer simulation model was able to evaluate the effect of introducing small specialty sandwiches. If this had not been done, the corporation would have wasted a great deal of money in further product development, not to mention the loss in profits that would have resulted after the new products would have been introduced.

In the design of manufactured products, many companies—such as General Motors—have been using CAD for many years. For example, a common design activity at GM is reducing the weight of a chassis cross member. This used to involve a long wait while prototypes were constructed and tested. If the design was not feasible, the process had to be repeated, sometimes two or three times. Decker estimates that up to 40 to 50 percent of the time involved in design activity is saved through CAD.

CAD systems are based on interactive computer graphics; these systems allow a user to create visual displays on a computer terminal screen. The computer software can manipulate or analyze the image in a variety of ways. For example, it can rotate or turn a three-dimensional representation of an object or dynam-

---

[11]E. J. Tracy, "Testing Time for Test Marketing," *Fortune,* 29 October 1984, 75–76.

[12]Robert W. Decker, "Computer Aided Design and Manufacturing at GM," *Datamation,* 24, no. 5 (May 1978): 159–165.

PHOTO 5.1

This Tektronix 4114 Computer Display Terminal is part of a series of intelligent graphics terminals designed to meet the graphics needs of the engineering and scientific user. Such CAD systems increase productivity by reducing drafting and prototype development in product design. Photo courtesy Tektronix, Inc.

ically show vibration and stress as force is applied. A typical CAD system consists of one or more video terminals connected to a digital computer. The designer uses a *light pen* to draw on the screen or enters data via the keyboard. Figure 5.10 illustrates the use of a light pen in such a system. The designer touches the screen at points 1 and 2 in Figure 5.10(a); the computer responds by drawing a line between the two points, as shown in Figure 5.10(b). Among the major advantages of using CAD are the flexibility in visualization afforded to the designer and the capability of testing the design for engineering feasibility without building a prototype. (Figure 5.11 shows three-dimensional visualizations of a car body, for example.) This is very useful to a designer and provides the same information that a physical model would. However, changes can be made much faster and more cheaply. The designer has the ability to enlarge detailed portions of a design at a stroke of the pen, modify the design and instruct the computer to perform computations on performance and characteristics of the design according to preprogrammed instructions. The user can even tell the computer to print blueprints automatically on a plotter and construct N/C (numerical-controlled) tapes for automated manufacturing.

CAD is also finding many other applications. For instance, transportation-routing problems are well suited to computer-assisted analysis. A typical example involves a furniture store whose fleet of trucks make daily deliveries from a central warehouse. Because each truck can only hold a limited number of items, sched-

FIGURE 5.10
CAD. (a) User touches points 1 and 2 with light pen.
(b) Computer responds with line between points.

(a)

(b)

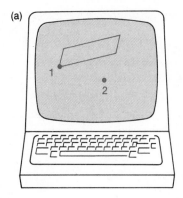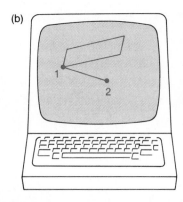

FIGURE 5.11
Three-dimensional Visualizations of a Car Body

uling deliveries is an important task. A CAD system allows the warehouse and delivery points to be represented on a computer terminal screen, and the designer can use a light pen to design routes for the vehicles. The computer can be programmed to respond with an evaluation of the routes from a feasibility and cost basis, as well as to suggest potential improvements. The designer can then modify the routes to improve the schedule.

Graphics can be used in a variety of other ways. For example, the management of an automobile division might plot the density of car ownership on a regional map along with the location of dealerships in order to determine marketing strategies. In a similar fashion, public safety officials can plot the locations of crimes to see their density in city neighborhoods. Graphics allow engineers to speed up the design of physical products and analyze data more efficiently. Through graphics, a manager can communicate complex data to others more easily, observe trends or departures from normal, and acquire information through tables and graphs rather than by sorting through pages of numerical data. Many minicomputer and microcomputer systems available today have graphics software that is easy to learn and use.

Standardization

Standardization refers to the process of specifying product characteristics such as dimensions, composition, quality, or performance. Although individual manufacturers set their own standards for production, we generally think of standardization as applying to an industry as a whole. For example, a standard light bulb designed for home use will fit into any socket, regardless of the manufacturer; 35-millimeter film, whether it be Kodak, Fuji, or Fotomat, will fit in any 35-millimeter camera; and standard 5¼ inch floppy disks can be used with any IBM, Zenith, or AT&T personal computer. Such standards are set by industry in cooperation with the National Bureau of Standards. This is done on a voluntary basis for the convenience and benefit of both the manufacturer and consumer. Other types of standards, such as the automobile emissions standards, are imposed by government regulatory agencies for the purpose of increasing the safety and health of a product's users.

The goal of the American National Standards Institute (ANSI), a nonprofit organization consisting of about 900 companies and 200 trade, technical, professional, labor, and consumer organizations, is to coordinate national standards for industry. There are about 8500 ANSI-approved standards that provide definitions, ratings, terminology and symbols, test methods, and performance and safety requirements for a wide range of products, equipment, materials, components, and systems. For example, the ANSI[13] specifications for outdoor power lawn mower equipment include the following:

- *Starting arrangement.* Must be positioned so the operator need not stand within the angle of discharge opening.
- *Safety interlock system.* Gear shift must be in neutral, mower clutch in neutral or disengaged, and ignition key must be unlocked before engine can be started.
- *Foot pedal materials.* All foot pedal material must be slip resistant.
- *Sound levels.* The sound level must not exceed 95 decibels when a test microphone is located 10 inches to the right and left of the center line of the operator's position, 30 inches above the seat, and 4 inches forward of the seat back rest, when the mower attachment is mounted.

Standardized products offer important benefits to the consumer. They permit the consumer to compare different brands more easily; they reduce the waiting time required to obtain spare parts; and they make repairs much easier. For the manufacturer, standardization reduces the cost of goods by allowing items to be purchased and/or mass-produced in large quantities. For instance, after videotape recorders became popular around 1980, several Japanese and European manufacturers met to discuss international standards for home video equipment. This was brought about by a lack of interchangeability of tapes on various machines. Standardization eliminates some uncertainty on the part of the consumer in selecting a machine and purchasing tapes and assists manufacturers and suppliers in their production efforts. However, it is impossible to set standards during the growth of a new industry such as video recorders or personal computers. To do so would stifle new technological development. With emerging technologies, the latest and most advanced equipment becomes a de facto standard.

Standardization is also important in service industries. In banking, for instance, standardization of checks and magnetic code numbers enables fast and efficient

---

[13]American National Standards Institute, Inc., American National Standard Safety Specifications for Power Lawn Mowers, Lawn and Garden Tractors, and Lawn Tractors, ANSI B71.1-1972, March 31, 1972.

clearing of checks and money transfers between banks. The use of three-letter airport codes assists communication between employees and different airlines. Even computer programming languages are being standardized so that hardware differences will have no effect on the operation of a program.

Standardization plays an important role in assisting manufacturers and service organizations in using their resources efficiently and avoiding needless costs. In the Burger King P/OM in Practice example at the end of this chapter, you will see that standardization of work procedures led to improved productivity and higher profits. The consumer is assured of reliable performance and quality as well as safety in the products and services that are used.

Modular Design

Modular design enables manufacturers to meet different preferences of consumers and yet still take advantage of the low costs of mass production. The principal idea behind modular design is to design and produce manufactured parts and services that can be combined in a large number of ways. For example, many of the options available on automobiles, such as radios, air conditioning, steering wheels, and wheel covers, can be used on a variety of models in a manufacturer's line; it is simply a matter of assembling the proper components for the customer's order. Printed circuit boards are built in modules for television sets; computing equipment is modular in the sense that different input/output devices can be combined with mainframes, disk drives, and so on. The modular trend has reached into the realm of furniture manufacturing and interior design—modular furniture can be arranged to suit unique room arrangements and shelf units can be stacked as needed. In the clothing industry, we see that many coats, vests, and slacks can be purchased as separates for sport outfits or suits.

The number of different designs that can be made with modular components can be calculated using a fundamental counting formula: If there are n_1 components of the first type, n_2 components of the second type, . . ., and n_k components of the kth type, then the number of different designs possible is $n_1 n_2 \cdots n_k$. For example, if a cafeteria offers 4 choices of entrees, 3 vegetables, and 5 different desserts, then a total of $4 \cdot 3 \cdot 5 = 60$ meals can be put together. Wendy's Hamburgers has exploited this in advertising 256 ways of preparing hamburgers (with or without ketchup, onions, mayonnaise, and so forth).

Human Factors in Design

Designers often devote considerable effort in order to incorporate human factors in the design process. By **human factors**, we mean the biomedical, psychosocial, training, and performance considerations associated with a manufactured product or service. For example, the design and location of instruments in jet aircraft and space vehicles have an important impact in a pilot's reaction time during emergencies. Factors in the design of office layouts such as temperature and noise levels can affect worker morale, performance, and communication. Human factors issues that relate to an individual's job are discussed in more detail in Chapter 11.

Many products purchased by consumers have human-factors implications. The consumer should be able to use a product easily and safely without undue strain or effort. Items such as power tools can be dangerous unless they are designed so that the average person who follows instructions and is reasonably careful will not be injured. The Consumer Product Safety Act of 1972 has determined that designers may be liable for faulty designs that lead to accidents. Therefore, it is very important that human-factors considerations be included in product design, labeling, and packaging.

Designing products and services for the handicapped has also received considerable attention in recent years. Building entrances, doors, water fountains, restrooms, and elevators are examples in which a handicapped person's physical capabilities must be taken into account during design. New devices must be developed to assist individuals with visual or hearing impairments to communicate. These areas represent only a few of the challenges in contemporary product design.

P/OM IN PRACTICE

In this section we present two examples that illustrate the role of product design and development. In the first example we discuss how Burger King uses a computer simulation model to evaluate new products and services. In the second example we discuss how Shure Bros., Inc. uses in-house reliability testing to help achieve their goal of marketing products with a long life of useful service.

SIMULATION IN SERVICE DESIGN FOR BURGER KING[14]

B urger King is one of the largest fast-food restaurant chains, having approximately 3000 restaurants across the United States and in other nations. At corporate headquarters in Miami, new products, systems, and procedures are developed; however, franchises (which are owned and operated independently) must be persuaded to adopt them on a cost/benefit basis. That is, the corporation must demonstrate that new products or systems will provide an adequate return on investment.

Many changes have occurred over the years since Burger King was founded in 1954, which necessitated new design of their service facilities. For instance, as the take-out business increased, Burger King was the first system to introduce the drive-through service lane. The "Have It Your Way" concept introduced in 1973 required a change in the kitchen operations from mass production of similar items to food preparation based upon individual customer specifications. In addition, "specialty

sandwiches," which were introduced in 1978, required new equipment and procedures. As these changes were implemented, the original kitchen and work designs required redesign in order to maintain effective levels of customer service.

One example where such a redesign was necessary involved the drive-through system. Figure 5.12 illustrates the activities performed by customers and employees in the original drive-through system. Customers enter the system, wait in line to place an order, order at an outside menu board, wait in line again, pay for the order at the pick-up window, and finally leave. One employee was used to take the order, assemble it, bag it, and collect the money. Burger King had established a standard transaction time of 30 seconds. However, an analysis of a number of restaurants showed that times were averaging 45 seconds. During peak periods, cars could not even join the end of the line and sales were lost. If the transaction time were 45 seconds, then 80 cars

[14]Adapted from William Swart and Luca Donno, "Simulation Modeling Improves Operations, Planning, and Productivity of Fast Food Restaurants," *Interfaces,* 11, no. 6 (December 1981): 35–45. Copyright 1981, The Institute of Management Sciences, 290 Westminster Street, Providence, Rhode Island 02903, USA.

FIGURE 5.12 Burger King Drive-through System

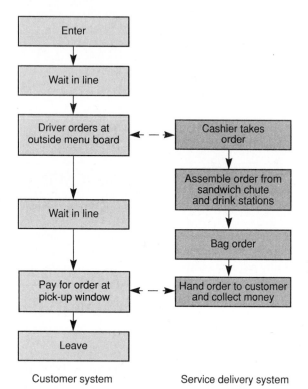

Customer system   Service delivery system

FIGURE 5.13 Modular View of Burger King Restaurants

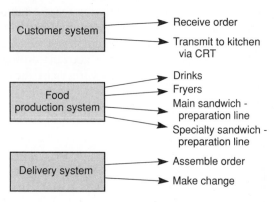

gram in 1979. One of the outputs of this effort was the development of a general-purpose restaurant simulation model. The restaurant was viewed as three interrelated subsystems (Figure 5.13). The simulation model was developed in a modular fashion in order to be flexible and easily modified. This allows minor changes to be made in the model that reflect variations in individual franchise operations or changes in staffing during peak and low demand periods.

The simulation model has been extensively used in evaluating proposed design changes, introductions of new products, and design of new restaurant configurations. For instance, in many restaurants, the distance between the order station and pickup window could only accommodate two or three vehicles. The model was used to determine the best vehicle capacity, which resulted in a drastic reduction in waiting time and an annual increase of over $10,000 per restaurant during the lunch hour.

A second application involved the evaluation of a second drive-through window in series with the first. The model projected a sales benefit of 15 percent during peak lunch hours. After installation in several restaurants, actual benefit was found to be 14 percent, a very close prediction. A third application of the model was to analyze the effect of introducing small specialty sandwiches. The model indicated that the additional preparation time required would not be cost-effective and would actually result in a loss in total sales. The model has also been used to evaluate new restaurant designs. This includes establishing the proper size in a spe-

per hour could be handled. With an average check of $2.44 per order, drive-through sales were limited to a maximum of $195 per hour. If the time could be shortened to 30 seconds, maximum sales could rise to $292 per hour. This represented an annual increase in sales of more than $35,000 per restaurant. The operations research group at corporate headquarters worked with several franchises and devised new work procedures to decrease the transaction time.

The work procedures in Figure 5.12 were separated into distinct tasks. In the new system, one employee does nothing but take orders. A runner/bagger assembles the order, and a third employee acts as a cashier and hands the order to the customer. This seemingly minor modification has significantly increased the productivity and sales in the Burger King chain.

In view of the number of changes that have taken place and escalation of costs, Burger King management developed a productivity improvement pro-

cific location, while emphasizing the human engineering aspects of work methods in the kitchen.

Burger King is an example of an organization that provides both manufactured goods (food items) and service as its major products. Productivity, quality, and profitability issues are integrated into the product design and development process. Computer simulation has proven to be a useful tool in the strategic evaluation of new products and facilities for Burger King.

QUESTIONS

1. What were some of the product and service innovations introduced by Burger King over the years?
2. How has simulation been used to evaluate product and service innovations?
3. What are some of the measures Burger King uses to evaluate changes in the restaurant operation?

TESTING AUDIO COMPONENTS AT SHURE BROS., INC.[15]

T he philosophy at Shure Bros., Inc., is quality-oriented. Microphones and phonograph cartridges are tested for reliability well beyond the warranty period; the goal is to provide long-term service and satisfaction for the customer. Audio transducers, for example, are sensitive and rather fragile devices. A precisely cut and polished diamond weighing only 20 micrograms is attached to the stylus shank, which for some cartridges are formed from .0005-inch beryllium foil. Dynamic microphone coils are wound with fine wire only one-fifth the diameter of a human hair; although their sensitivity ranks them along with the finest of laboratory instruments, they must be able to perform under conditions much less than ideal, in locations all over the world. The reliability problems for Shure Bros., Inc., are made even more difficult because there are four major classes of end use environments for these types of audio components.

- *Home systems.* In the home, potential damage ranges from situations such as accidental dropping of the cartridge onto the turntable or scraping the stylus across the record to using the wrong cleaning agents. There is also the potential for damage because of extremes of temperature and humidity that cannot be easily predicted.
- *Public-address systems.* Microphones are found in environments as diverse as churches, schools, bars, stores, and outdoors. Each of these environments poses potential challenges to the integrity of the microphone, which may be damaged by mishandling or long-term abuse.

Random drops from a height of several feet are not uncommon.
- *Mobile applications.* In vehicles, extremes of heat and cold, vibration, shock, and repeated switch actuation and cable flexing must be considered. Sand and dust are likely to be present. Reliability is critical, as there will probably be no backup available in an emergency road situation.
- *Professional recording and sound reinforcement.* Sound professionals require high degrees of reliability and cannot tolerate a dead or noisy microphone in the middle of a live performance or recording session. Yet repeated set up and tear down during concert tours pose many problems.

Many standardized destructive tests developed by the military, the Electronic Industry Association, and the American Society for Testing and Materials are employed to learn what causes product failure. Specialized environmental tests are also conducted. These tests include

- *Cartridge drop test.* This test simulates the accidental dropping of the tone arm and cartridge onto a moving record. The vertical tracking force is set to the maximum recommended for the unit under test, and the minimum required number of drops is 100. This test simulates abuse in excess of the normal type accidentally given to a stylus.
- *Cartridge scrape test.* This test consists of moving the cartridge mounted in a tone arm

---

[15]Adapted from Roger Franz, "Audio Component Reliability," *Quality* (June 1983): 50–51. Reprinted with permission from QUALITY, a Hitchcock publication.

across a moving record 100 times. The tone arm is pushed down hard enough to bottom out the cartridge.

- *Microphone drop test.* This is an unpackaged test consisting of a random free fall onto the floor. The test height is 6 feet, designed to simulate a fall from a tall shelf or an accidental drop by a very tall person at shoulder height. Ten drops must be sustained without significant loss of performance.
- *Barrel tumble.* A specially constructed barrel is used to tumble small microphones without packaging. This test is designed to simulate the roughest treatment expected in handling or transporting microphones loose in a case.
- *Stair tumble test.* A shipping carton is packed with a dozen units, sealed with tape, and tumbled down 17 steel stairs onto a concrete floor. Ten tumbles must be sustained without loss of function or severe loss of appearance of the

packaging. This test allows for evaluation of possible damage during shipping.
- *Outside weathering test.* This test actually exposes test units to outside weather. It aids in evaluating finishes and the performance of products that might actually be used outside, such as microphones and sound-reinforcement equipment.

These are some examples of in-house reliability testing designed to simulate actual operating conditions. These tests help the company to achieve their goal of marketing products with a long life of useful service.

QUESTIONS

1. What types of tests are conducted on Shure Bros. cartridges?
2. What is the purpose and value of the tests? What quality characteristics are studied from the results of these tests?

SUMMARY

The product-development process consists of idea generation, screening, initial design and development, economic analysis, prototype testing, and final product and process design. Although this process is more often associated with manufactured goods, the product-development process applies equally well to services. For services, however, management is primarily interested in the human interface rather than technical specifications.

New product decisions affect manufacturing strategy, since they put new demands on production. The goals of manufacturing change as products move through their life cycles. The ability to meet design specifications at minimum cost is the operations manager's job. Quality and reliability specifications may require new production processes and close managerial control. In addition, new products may also necessitate additional production capacity. Therefore it is essential that operations managers be involved in the product development process.

Computer-aided design has greatly improved productivity during the design process. Techniques such as computer simulation enable managers to analyze alternate designs without having to construct expensive prototypes. Standardization and modular design have lowered product costs and benefited consumers. In addition, human factors have recently become more important in the design of both goods and services. These considerations have helped corporations to develop better products and to improve productivity within their own organizations.

KEY TERMS

Life-cycle curve
Quality engineering
Product-development process
Pure research

Applied research
Development
Scoring model
Value analysis

Reliability
Failure rate
Burn-in period
Useful life
Wear-out period
Design reviews
Failure mode and effects analysis
 (FMEA)

Computer-aided design (CAD)
Standardization
Modular design
Human factors
Value engineering
Economic analysis
Break-even analysis

1. Why is the selection and development of new products an important strategic decision?

2. How do new product decisions affect production?

3. Explain the difference between custom, option-oriented, and standard products. Of what significance to P/OM is this distinction?

4. Explain the *product life cycle*. What implications does it have for operations?

5. Discuss the differences between "traditional" and "modern" products. Why are these differences significant.

6. How does product design affect quality and productivity? What can be done to improve quality and productivity through product design?

7. What is *quality engineering?* What benefits can it provide?

8. Discuss the general steps in the product-development process. How do they differ for manufactured products versus services?

9. List the major sources of idea generation in product development.

10. Discuss the differences between pure and applied research. What types of organizations would be likely to engage in each type of research?

11. Explain the functions of research and development activities within a firm.

12. Discuss how you might apply a scoring model in selecting a job or purchasing an automobile or new appliance.

13. Choose some product or service with which you are familiar. Develop some typical value-analysis questions for this product or service.

14. Discuss why some products are purposely designed to be lower in overall quality than similar or competing products. That is, why might a firm not want to manufacture a particular product at the product's maximum possible quality level?

15. Explain the concept of failure mode and effects analysis.

16. Choose some manufactured product and perform an **FMEA**.

17. The College of Business at the University of Clifton is considering the development of a new program in actuarial science. Discuss how the product-development process can be applied to this situation. (You may wish to interview some professors in order to obtain better understanding of new-program development at a university.)

18. Discuss the similarities and differences in product design activities between manufacturing and service organizations.

19. Explain the use of flowcharts to design services. What questions should be asked in examining these flowcharts?

20. Construct a flowchart detailing the sequence of steps involved in the following service operations. Use your past experiences as a guide.
    a. Cashing a check at a bank.
    b. Renewing license plates.
    c. Obtaining a new driver's license.
    d. Filling a prescription at a pharmacy.
    Using the questions posed in Section 5.4, discuss how these operations might be analyzed or improved upon.

21. A major bank is trying to decide on the best waiting-line system for its customers. The current method allows customers to wait in individual lines (Figure (a)), whereas the proposed method is to have one line and wait for the next available teller (Figure (b)).

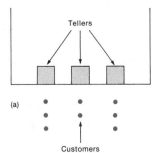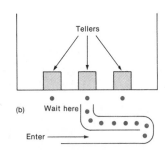

What operational differences are there between these systems? How might this affect customer perceptions or teller productivity? Can simulation be used to analyze these systems? What data would the bank have to collect? Why might simulation be preferable to actually trying the proposed method?

22. Define the term *reliability*. How does it differ from *quality?*

23. Describe the activities associated with reliability engineering.

24. What is the *failure-rate curve* and why is it important to know this curve for a product?

25. About where in the product-development process do you think the Goodman Tire Company is on the basis of the information in Section 5.5?

26. What is *CAD?* How can it help to improve productivity and quality in product design?

27. Explain the term *standardization*. What benefits does standardization have for consumers and producers of goods and services.

28. What do we mean by *human factors?* What impact do human-factors issues have in product design?

1. A manufacturing firm is considering developing a new product for commercial use. During the economic-analysis phase of the product development process, analysts developed two alternatives for manufacturing the product. The alternatives and related cost data are as follows:

■ *Alternative A*. Expand current manufacturing facilities and produce the product at one of the firm's manufacturing plants. Fixed cost of the expansion is estimated at $200,000. Variable manufacturing costs are projected to be $15.00 per unit.

■ *Alternative B*. Purchase the primary component of the product from a supplier and assemble the complete product at one of the firm's manufacturing plants. Since this alternative would not require a facilities expansion, fixed manufacturing, selling, and administrative expenses are estimated to be only $48,000. The purchased primary component would cost $16.00 per unit with an additional $5.00 variable cost per unit to assemble the final product.

a. If the selling price is $25.00 per unit, conduct a break-even analysis for the new product under both alternatives.

b. If the projected volume for the new product were 18,000 units, which production alternative, if any, would you recommend?

c. What would the projected volume need to be before the alternative *not* recommended in part (b) would be the preferred alternative?

2. The O'Neill Shoe Company will produce a special style shoe if the order size is large enough to provide a reasonable profit. For each special style order the company incurs a fixed cost of $1000 for the production setup. The variable cost is $30 per pair, and each pair sells for $40.

a. Let x indicate the number of pair of shoes produced. Develop a mathematical model for the total cost of producing x pairs of shoes.

b. Let P indicate the total profit. Develop a mathematical model for the total profit realized from an order for x pairs of shoes.

c. How large must the shoe order be before O'Neill will break even?

3. Myers Products is considering the introduction of three new products. Existing production facilities will not be able to handle the additional volume at the current time; thus management needs to choose one product to introduce now. The following information has been determined.

Criterion	Minimum Score	Maximum Score	Product I	Product II	Product III
Product development	− 5	+ 5	4	0	−4
Market	−10	+10	2	9	8
Financial	−20	+20	16	14	17
			22	23	21

a. What is the relative importance of the three criteria? How might the actual scores reflect risk?

b. Should the total score be used to choose the product? If not, how should Myers assess this information?

c. Suppose the following additional information is available:

Criterion	Product I	Product II	Product III
Expected annual sales	6,000	9,000	12,000
Contribution to profit per unit	$8	$10	$9
Fixed costs of development	$125,000	$100,000	$180,000
Product lifetime (years)	10	5	12

How might this information affect the decision?

4. A firm is faced with the choice of three new product designs. It uses the following scoring model:

Criteria	Max Score	Min Score	Product 1	Product 2	Product 3
Product development					
Time	+ 5	− 5	+3	−2	0
Material availability	+ 5	− 5	+4	+3	+ 5
Market					
Competition	+10	−10	+7	+6	+ 2
Demand	+10	−10	+7	+5	+ 1
Financial					
Risk	+10	−10	+3	−5	− 9
Returns	+10	−10	+4	+5	+10

a. What is the proportion of weight assigned to Product Development as compared to Marketing and Financial criteria?
b. Which product would be chosen using the above data?
c. If all 3 factors are to be given equal weight, how should the scores be changed?

5. The lifetime of a color television picture tube is normally distributed with a mean of 7.8 years and a standard deviation of 2 years.
a. What is the probability that a picture tube will last more than 10 years?
b. If the firm guarantees the tube for 2 years, what percentage of television sets sold will have to be replaced because of failure in the picture tube?
c. If the firm is willing to replace the picture tubes in a maximum of 1 percent of the television sets sold, what guarantee period can be offered for the picture tubes?

6. The useful life of a computer terminal at a university computer center is known to be normally distributed, with a mean of 3.25 years and a standard deviation of .5 years.
a. Historically, 22 percent of the terminals have had a useful life less than the manufacturer's advertised life. What is the manufacturer's advertised life for the computer terminals?
b. What is the probability that a computer terminal will have a useful life of at least 3 but less than 4 years?

7. A manufacturer of household appliances such as refrigerators, stoves, washers and dryers uses data on product life to establish product guarantee policies

and to evaluate product quality. Assume that a particular appliance has a lifetime that is normally distributed with a mean of 5 years and a standard deviation of 1.3 years.

a. What is the probability that a particular appliance will have a useful life of at least 4 years?

b. What is the probability that a particular appliance will have a useful life of at least 7 years?

c. The manufacturer wants at most 1 percent of the appliances to fail prior to the stated appliance guarantee. Determine the stated guarantee period for the appliance.

8. A component used in aircraft guidance systems has a lifetime that is normally distributed with a standard deviation of 250 hours. Product specifications indicate 98 percent of the components must last at least 1000 hours. What mean lifetime must the component have in order to meet the design specifications?

9. In the testing of 12 light bulbs, the hours of useful life were recorded as follows:

25, 80, 480, 800, 1050, 1225, 1250, 1280, 1300, 1310, 1350, 1500

a. What is the failure rate for 500 hours?

b. What is the failure rate for 1000 hours?

c. What is the failure rate for 1400 hours?

d. Do the given failure-rate data correspond to the general shape of the failure-rate curve shown in Figure 5.7? Explain.

10. In a test on the reliability of an electronic component, a sample of 15 components provided the following data on hours of operation: 14, 42, 48, 120, 350, 580, 880, 905, 940, 948, 988, 995, and 998. Two components were still operating at the end of the thousand-hour test period. The manufacturer has defined the burn-in period as the first 100 hours, the useful life up to 800 hours, and the wear-out period from 800 to 1000 hours. Compute the failure rates at 100 hours, 800 hours and 1000 hours. Do the computations indicate that generally higher failure rates occur during the burn-in and wear-out periods?

SUPPLEMENT TO CHAPTER 5
COMPUTER SIMULATION

S imulation is a technique that is used to describe the behavior of a real-world system over time. Most often this is done using a computer program. Computer simulation is an important tool in P/OM because it can be used to model and analyze an extremely wide variety of practical situations that cannot be approached by other types of economic or management science models. Many practical problems are so complex that it is impossible to determine exact relationships among decision variables. Other practical problems have high levels of uncertainty, which precludes the use of traditional methods of analysis. Simulation modeling can overcome these difficulties.

There are other advantages in using computer simulation. The simulation approach is relatively easy to explain and understand. As a result, management confidence is increased and, consequently, acceptance of the technique is more easily obtained. Software packages exist that consist of specialized simulation programming languages, thus facilitating use by analysts.

Simulation models have been used successfully at all levels of decision making. Corporate simulation models have been used in strategic business planning. The Burger King example introduced in this chapter illustrates the use of simulation in service system design. Simulation is used extensively to analyze and design manufacturing processes, determine inventory policies, and model production control and material management systems. Perhaps one of the biggest advantages of simulation is the ability to perform "what-if" analysis—that is, the ability to change design characteristics or operating rules to determine their impact without changing the actual system. This is one of the key features in Burger King's use of simulation.

In this supplement we introduce the concepts and procedures of computer simulation by studying how the approach can be applied in a waiting-line situation. The system we study is similar to the Burger King P/OM in Practice application and involves the drive-in window operation of the Lincoln Savings Bank.

LINCOLN SAVINGS BANK DRIVE-IN WINDOW PROBLEM

Lincoln Savings Bank has been experiencing difficulty in servicing customers at their Forest Park branch drive-in window during the peak Saturday morning period. Specifically, the branch manager is concerned about long waiting lines that have been forming during this time period and complaints by customers. As a result, the branch manager has suggested that a study be conducted in order to investigate possible alternatives for improving service.

Figure 5S.1 illustrates the physical characteristics of the system. Drivers enter from Beechwood Ave. and drive around the rear entrance to the drive-in window. If cars are already at the window, then the new arrival must wait in line until the drivers ahead have been serviced. Otherwise, the driver proceeds to the window, processes his or her transactions, and leaves. The logic of this process is summarized in the flowchart in Figure 5S.2.

In modeling this system, we study the operation of the drive-in window in terms of what happens during 1-minute time periods. That is, we count the number of arrivals and determine whether or not a customer is being serviced during each 1-minute interval. Then we consider what happens during the next 1-minute interval, and so forth. A simulation model that increments time in fixed intervals is referred to as a **fixed-time simulation model.**[16] During this process, we keep track of such information as the number of cars waiting during each minute, the total number of arrivals, and the total number of cars serviced by the drive-in window. These statistics form the basis for the simulation results, which will be analyzed by the branch manager.

Preliminary Data Analysis

Based on a study of traffic flow, the bank has estimated the probability distribution of customer arrivals to be as shown in Table 5S.1. This probability distribution is believed to be representative of the number of arrivals during the peak business period occurring on

FIGURE 5S.1 Lincoln Savings Bank System Description

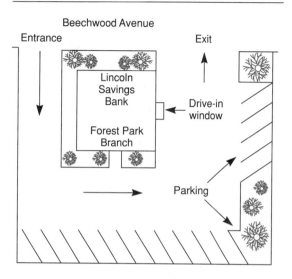

Saturday morning. As the data show, there is a .55 probability of no customers arriving during a given 1-minute period, a .25 probability of one customer arriving during the same 1-minute period, and so on.

Historical data also show that the time to service a customer varies from 1 to 4 minutes. Using this data the bank has estimated the probability distribution of service time to be as shown in Table 5S.2.

Simulation of Customer Arrivals

Before developing the complete simulation model, we concentrate on simulating the number of customers that arrive during any 1-minute period. In simulating

FIGURE 5S.2 Lincoln Savings Bank Drive-in System Operation

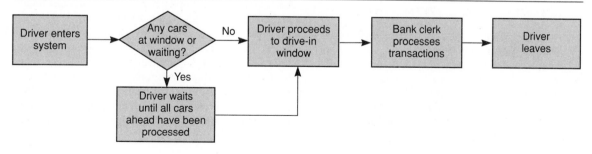

---

[16]Simulation models that increment time based on the occurrence of the next event (time of next arrival, time of next service, and so on) are referred to as *next-event simulation models.*

TABLE 5S.1 Probability Distribution for Customers Arriving at the Lincoln Savings Bank Drive-in Window (1-minute Period)

Number of Customers Arriving	Probability
0	.55
1	.25
2	.15
3	.05
	1.00

TABLE 5S.2 Probability Distribution for Service Time for the Lincoln Savings Bank Drive-in Window

Service Time (Minutes)	Probability
1	.50
2	.30
3	.15
4	.05
	1.00

the customer arrival process for Lincoln Savings Bank, we also demonstrate how the probabilistic component of a real-world process or system is modeled.

The technique used to simulate customer arrivals is based on the use of random numbers. Almost everyone who has been exposed to simple random sampling and basic statistics is familiar with tables of random digits or random numbers.[17] We have included a table of random numbers in Appendix C. Twenty random numbers from the first line of this table are

$$63271 \quad 59986 \quad 71744 \quad 51102$$

The specific digit appearing in a given position is a random selection of the digits 0, 1, 2, . . . , 9, with each digit having an equal chance of selection. The grouping of the numbers in sets of five is simply for the convenience of making the table easier to read.

Suppose we select random numbers from our table in sets of two digits. There are 100 two-digit random numbers from 00 to 99, with each two-digit random number having a $1/100 = .01$ chance of occurring. While we could select two-digit random numbers from any part of the random number table, suppose we start by using the first row of random numbers from Appendix C. The first ten of the two-digit random numbers are

$$63 \quad 27 \quad 15 \quad 99 \quad 86 \quad 71 \quad 74 \quad 45 \quad 11 \quad 02$$

Now let us see how we can simulate the number of customers arriving in a 1-minute period by associating a given number of arrivals with each of these two-digit random numbers. For example, let us consider the possibility of no customers arriving during a 3-minute interval. The probability distribution in Table 5S.1 shows this event to have a .55 probability. Since each of the two-digit random numbers has a .01 probability of occurrence, we can let 55 of the 100 possible two-digit random numbers correspond to no customers arriving. Any 55 numbers from 00 to 99 will do, but for convenience we associate the arrival of 0 customers with the first 55 two-digit numbers: 00, 01, 02, 03, . . . , 54. Thus any time one of these two-digit numbers is observed in a random selection, we will say that no customers arrived during that period. Because the numbers 00 to 54 include 55 percent of the possible two-digit random numbers, we expect the arrival of no customers for any given 1-minute interval to have a probability of .55.

Now consider the possibility of one customer arriving during a 1-minute period, an event which has a .25 probability of occurring (See Table 5S.1). Letting 25 of the 100 two-digit numbers (such as 55, 56, 57, 58, . . . , 79) correspond to a simulated arrival of one customer will provide a .25 probability for one customer arriving. Continuing to assign the number of customers arriving to sets of two-digit numbers according to the probability distribution shown in Table 5S.1 results in the number and customer arrival assignments shown in Table 5S.3.

Using Table 5S.3 and the two-digit random numbers in the first row of Appendix C (63, 27, 15, 99, 86, . . .), we can simulate the number of customers arriving during each 1-minute period. The results for ten such 1-minute periods are shown in Table 5S.4. Note, for example, that the first two-digit random number, 63, is in the interval 55–79; thus, according to Table 5S.3, this corresponds to one customer arriving during the first 1-minute period. The second random number, 27, is in the interval 00–54; thus the number of simulated arrivals during the second period is zero, and so on.

---

[17]See, for example, *A Million Random Digits with 100,000 Normal Deviates,* Rand Corporation, 1955, 1983.

TABLE 5S.3   Random-Number Assignments for the Number of Customers Arriving at the Lincoln Savings Bank Drive-In Window (1-Minute Period)

Interval	Simulated Arrivals	Probability
00–54	0	.55
55–79	1	.25
80–94	2	.15
95–99	3	.05
		1.00

TABLE 5S.5   Random-Number Assignments for the Service Time of Customers of Lincoln Savings Bank Drive-In Window

Interval	Service Time	Probability
00–49	1 minute	.50
50–79	2 minutes	.30
80–94	3 minutes	.15
95–99	4 minutes	.05
		1.00

TABLE 5S.4   Simulated Customer Arrivals at the Lincoln Savings Bank Drive-In Window (Ten 1-Minute Periods)

Period	Random Number	Simulated Customer Arrivals
1	63	1
2	27	0
3	15	0
4	99	3
5	86	2
6	71	1
7	74	1
8	45	0
9	11	0
10	02	0
	Total arrivals (10 minutes)	8

By selecting a two-digit random number for each 1-minute period, we can simulate the number of customer arrivals during that period. In doing so, the simulated probability distribution for the number of customer arrivals is the same as the given probability distribution shown in Table 5S.1. In this manner, the simulation of customer arrivals has the same characteristics as the specified distribution of customer arrivals. Simulations that use a random-number procedure to generate probabilistic inputs such as the number of customer arrivals are referred to as **Monte Carlo simulations.**

For any simulation model it is relatively easy to apply the above random-number procedure to simulate values of a random variable. First develop a table similar to Table 5S.3 by associating an interval of random numbers with each possible value of the random variable. In doing so, be sure that the probability of selecting a random number from each interval is the same as the actual probability associated with the value of the random variable. Then each time a value of the random variable is needed, we simply select a new random number and use the corresponding interval of random numbers to find the value of the random variable. Using a similar procedure, we see that the random-number intervals given in Table 5S.5 can be used to simulate service times for customers stopping at the Lincoln Savings Bank drive-in window.

A SIMULATION MODEL FOR THE LINCOLN SAVINGS BANK DRIVE-IN WINDOW

Now that we know how to simulate the number of customers arriving and the service time, let us proceed with the development of the logic for the Lincoln Bank simulation model. We develop the model in a step-by-step manner. In doing so, we carry out the necessary calculations to demonstrate how the simulation process is working.

Whenever we need to generate a value for the number of customers arriving and/or the service time, we use the random numbers from row 10 of Appendix C. Tables 5S.3 and 5S.5 are used to determine the corresponding number of customer arrivals and the service times. For convenience, the first five two-digit random numbers from row 10 are reproduced here:

81   62   83   61   00

In developing the logic and mathematical relationships for the simulation model, we follow the logic and relationships of the actual operation as closely as possible. To demonstrate the simulation process, we begin with an idle, or empty, system and simulate what happens for each of the first three periods (Figures 5S.3 through 5S.5). Try to follow the logic of the model

and see if you agree with the statements under the column labeled "things that happen."

The flow chart of the simulation model we have been using is shown in Figure 5S.6. Continue to use the random numbers from row 10 of Appendix C and

FIGURE 5S.3   Status of the System for the First 1-minute Simulation Period

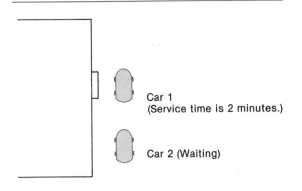

PERIOD 1   (See Figure 5S.3.)

Random Number	Things That Happen
81	Two cars arrive for service; the first car, identified as car 1, gets immediate service.
62	The service time for car 1 is 2 minutes, so this car will not be finished until the end of period 2.

FIGURE 5S.4   Status of the System for the Second 1-minute Simulation Period

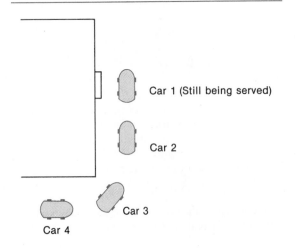

PERIOD 2   (See Figure 5S.4.)

Random Number	Things That Happen
83	Two more cars, identified as cars 3 and 4, arrive for service. The drive-in window is still busy serving the customer from period 1; thus a total of three cars (one waiting plus two new customers) are waiting for service this period.

FIGURE 5S.5   Status of the System for the Third 1-minute Simulation Period

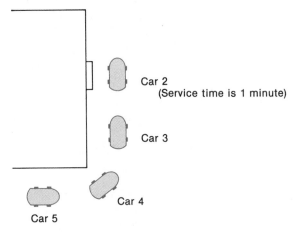

PERIOD 3   (See Figure 5S.5.)

Random Number	Things That Happen
61	One more car, identified as car 5, arrives for service. The service area is free at the beginning of this period, since the customer from period 1 (car 1) has completed service and left the bank.
	One car from the waiting line (car 2) begins service, leaving three cars still awaiting service.
00	The service time for the customer in car 2 is 1 minute and thus car 2 will finish service at the end of this period.

FIGURE 5S.6 Flowchart of the Lincoln Savings Bank Simulation Model

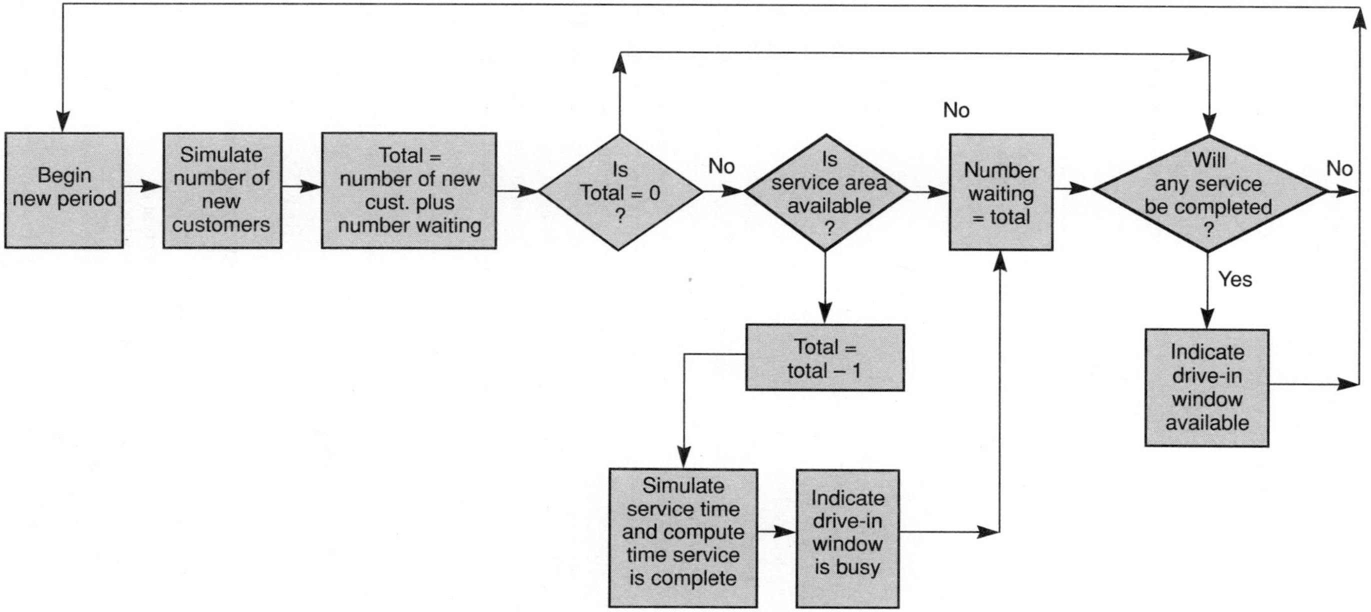

TABLE 5S.6 Simulation Results from Ten 1-minute Periods of Operation for the Lincoln Bank Drive-In Window

Period	Random Number	Number of New Customers	Is Service Area Available?	Random Number	Service Time	Number Waiting	Was Service Completed This Period?
1	81	2	Yes	62	2	1	No
2	83	2	No	—	—	3	Yes
3	61	1	Yes	00	1	3	Yes
4	39	0	Yes	25	1	2	Yes
5	45	0	Yes	68	2	1	No
6	35	0	No	—	—	1	Yes
7	37	0	Yes	63	2	0	No
8	60	1	No	—	—	1	Yes
9	24	0	Yes	21	1	0	Yes
10	98	3	Yes	06	1	2	Yes

see if you can conduct the simulation calculations for the first ten periods of operation. Your simulation results should agree with those shown in Table 5S.6.

At this point we have succeeded in simulating ten periods, or a total of 10 minutes of operation. Although the results in Table 5S.6 do not show evidence of long waiting lines, a 10-minute simulation period is too short a time frame to draw general conclusions about the operation of the drive-in system. In order to take full advantage of the simulation procedure, we must continue to simulate the system's operation for many more time periods. But even for this relatively small simulation problem, continuing the hand simulation computations as we have been doing is unrealistic, if not practically impossible. Thus we look to the computer to provide the computational assistance necessary to conduct the simulation process.

Computer Simulation—Generating Pseudorandom Numbers

If a computer procedure is going to be used to perform the simulation calculations, we need a way for the computer to generate random numbers and values for the probabilistic components of the model. While the computer could be programmed to store random-number tables and then follow the procedure outlined previously, the computer storage space required would result in an inefficient use of computer resources. For this reason, computer simulations make use of mathematical formulas that generate numbers which, for all practical purposes, have the same properties as the numbers selected from random-number tables. These

numbers are called **pseudorandom numbers**. In computer simulations pseudorandom numbers are used in exactly the same way as we used the random numbers selected from random-number tables in our hand simulation.

Most mathematical formulas designed to generate pseudorandom numbers produce numbers from 0 up to, but not including 1. Thus we must consider a somewhat different approach in order to simulate the number of customer arrivals and the service times. We must now associate an interval of pseudorandom numbers with each number of arrivals so that the probability of generating a pseudorandom number in the interval will be equal to the probability of the corresponding number of arrivals. Table 5S.7 shows how this would be done for the number of cars arriving at the Lincoln Savings Bank drive-in window. Note that Table 5S.7 shows a pseudorandom number less than .55 corre-

TABLE 5S.7 Pseudorandom-Number Intervals and the Associated Number of Customers Arriving at the Lincoln Savings Bank Drive-In Window

Interval of Pseudorandom Numbers	Simulated Customer Arrivals	Probability
.00 but less than .55	0	.55
.55 but less than .80	1	.25
.80 but less than .90	2	.15
.90 but less than 1.00	3	.15
		1.00

```
10   REM   THIS PROGRAM SIMULATES          520  REM   UPDATE TOTAL ARRIVALS
20   REM   THE OPERATION OF THE            530  REM   AND NUMBER WAITING
30   REM   LINCOLN SAVINGS BANK            540  REM
40   REM                                   550  TARR = TARR + CAR
50   REM                                   560  WAYT = WAYT + CAR
60   REM   TABLE OF VARIABLES              570  REM
70   REM        TSRV= CUMULATIVE NO.       580  REM   IF NO ONE WAITING SKIP
                                           590  REM   PROCESSING
80   REM             SERVED                600  REM
90   REM        TARR= CUMULATIVE NO.       610  IF WAYT = 0 THEN 950
                                           620  REM
100  REM             OF ARRIVALS           630  REM   IF SERVER BUSY SKIP TO
110  REM        TIME= CURRENT CLOCK        640  REM   SEE IF SERVICE COMPLETE
                                           650  REM
120  REM             TIME                  660  IF SERV = 0 THEN 950
130  REM        WAYT= NO. WAITING          670  REM
140  REM             FOR SERVICE           680  REM   START SERVICE
150  REM        CAR= NO. OF ARRIVLS        690  REM
160  REM             LAST PERIOD           700  WAYT = WAYT - 1
170  REM        ST= SERVICE TIME           710  REM
180  REM        SERV=1 IF SERVR IDLE       720  REM   DETERMINE SERVICE TIME
                                           730  REM
190  REM             0 IF SERVR BUSY       740  RN = RND (1)
                                           750  IF RN < .50 THEN ST = 1
200  REM        RN= RANDOM NUMBER          760  IF RN > .50 AND RN < .80 THEN
210  REM        TCPT= TIME NEXT SER             ST = 2
220  REM             VICE COMPLETED        770  IF RN > .80 AND RN < 95 THEN
                                                ST = 3
230  PRINT "ENTER A NUMBEP BETWEE          780  IF RN > .95 THEN ST = 4
     N 1 AND 100"                          790  REM
240  INPUT N                               800  REM   UPDATE TOTAL NO. SERVED
250  FOR I = 1 TO N
260  RN = RND (1)                          810  TSRV = TSRV + 1
270  NEXT                                  820  REM
280  REM   INITIALIZE                      830  REM   COMPUTE SERVICE
290  TSRV = 0                              840  REM   COMPLETION TIME
300  TARR = 0                              850  REM
310  TIME = 0                              860  TCPT = TIME + ST
320  SERV = 1                              870  REM
330  WAYT = 0                              880  REM   SET SERVER TO BUSY
350  REM   PRINT VALUES                    890  REM
360  PRINT "TIME=    ";TIME,"NO.           900  SERV = 0
     WAIT= ";WAYT                          910  REM
370  PRINT "TOT ARR= ";TAPR,"TOT           920  REM   CHECK FOR SERVICE
     SER=   ";TSRV                         930  REM   COMPLETION
380  PRINT                                 940  REM
390  FOR I = 1 TO 10                       950  IF TCPT < > TIME THEN 1010
400  TIME = TIME + 1                       960  REM
410  REM                                   970  REM   IF COMPLETED, SET
420  REM   CHECK FOR END OF RUN            980  REM   SERVER TO IDLE
430  IF TIME > 180 THEN 1070               990  REM
440  REM                                   1000 SERV = 1
450  REM   FIND NUMBER OF ARRIVALS         1010 NEXT .
460  RN = RND (1)                          1020 REM
470  IF RN < .55 THEN CAR = 0              1030 REM   GO TO PRINT EVERY
480  IF RN > .55 AND RN < .80 THEN         1040 REM   10 TIME UNITS
     CAR = 1                               1050 REM
490  IF RN > .80 AND RN < .90 THEN         1060 GOTO 360
     CAR = 2                               1070 END
500  IF RN > .90 THEN CAR = 3
510  REM
```

sponds to no arrivals, a pseudorandom number greater than or equal to .55 but less than .80 corresponds to one arrival, and so on. Table 5S.8 provides the pseudorandom-number intervals that can be used to simulate the service times for customers.

Computer Simulation—Computer Program and Results

A computer **simulator** is a computer program written to conduct simulation computations. For the Lincoln

Savings Bank simulation, we need a computer program with the logic, as shown in Figure 5S.6. Such a program would perform the calculations and keep track of the simulation results in a form similar to that shown in Table 5S.6. Figure 5S.7 shows a computer program written in the BASIC language that simulates the Lincoln Savings Bank operation.

The Lincoln Savings Bank simulator is designed to produce output that shows the status of the system after every 10 minutes of operation. Actual results from simulating the system for 3 hours—which corresponds to the 9–12 Saturday morning hours—is shown in Table 5S.9. Note that the columns labeled "total num-ber of arrivals" and "total number served" are cumulative figures, whereas the column labeled "number waiting" represents the total number of customers waiting for service at the end of each 10 minutes of operation. Figure 5S.8 shows the simulated growth of the waiting line over time.

FIGURE 5S.8 Simulation Results for Lincoln Savings Bank, One Drive-in Window

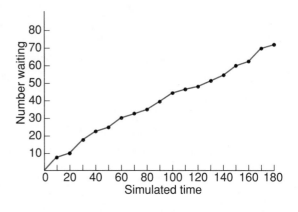

TABLE 5S.8 Pseudorandom-Number Intervals and the Associated Service Times for the Lincoln Savings Bank Customers

Interval of Pseudorandom Numbers	Service Time (Minutes)	Probability
.00 but less than .50	1	.50
.50 but less than .80	2	.30
.80 but less than .95	3	.15
.95 but less than 1.00	4	.05
		1.00

TABLE 5S.9 Computer-simulation Results for Lincoln Savings Bank—One Drive-In Window

Time (Mins.)	Total Number Of Arrivals	Number Waiting	Total Number Served
10	11	8	3
20	18	12	6
30	26	17	9
40	37	25	12
50	43	27	16
60	52	33	19
70	56	34	22
80	63	37	26
90	72	41	31
100	80	47	33
110	86	49	37
120	91	50	41
130	98	54	44
140	105	58	47
150	114	63	51
160	118	65	53
170	125	68	57
180	133	72	61

TABLE 5S.10 Computer-simulation Results—One Drive-in Window with Balking

Time (Mins.)	Total No. Of Arrivals	Number Waiting	Total Number Served	Total Number Balking
10	11	6	3	2
20	18	4	6	8
30	26	4	9	13
40	37	5	12	20
50	43	5	16	22
60	52	4	19	29
70	56	5	22	29
80	63	4	26	33
90	72	3	31	38
100	80	5	33	42
110	86	4	37	45
120	91	4	41	46
130	98	4	44	50
140	105	4	47	54
150	114	4	51	59
160	118	5	53	60
170	125	4	57	64
180	133	4	61	68
		78		

Average number waiting $= \dfrac{78}{18} = 4.33$

Based on these simulation results, we can make the following observations about the behavior of the system. First of all, over the 3-hour period, only $^{61}/_{133}$, or about 46 percent, of all customers have been served by the drive-in window. Secondly, we see that the waiting line grows rapidly; by the end of the simulation, over 70 cars are waiting. Recall for a moment that a primary objective of simulation is to describe the behavior of a real system. Do these results agree with what the bank manager would actually observe? Of course not. In the actual system, a customer would either park and transact business inside the bank or leave and return at another time if the line is too long. An important step in any simulation study is the **validation** of the simulation model. Validation involves verifying that the simulation model accurately represents the real-world system it is designed to simulate.

Models that do not adequately reflect the behavior of the real system cannot be expected to provide worthwhile information. Thus, before implementing any simulation results, the analyst must be sure that a thorough job of model validation has been done.

For the Lincoln Savings Bank, the branch manager has observed that there are seldom more than four or five cars waiting at the drive-in window. Thus it appears that drivers will not join the waiting line (technically, this is called *balking*) if four or more cars are already waiting. The computer program was modified to reflect this. (How would the flowchart in Figure 5S.6 change?) These results are shown in Table 5S.10. The total number balking (cumulative) provides the branch manager with a better measure of customer dissatisfaction.

LINCOLN SAVINGS BANK DRIVE-IN WINDOW—SERVICE ALTERNATIVES

The primary conclusion from the simulation results presented above is that the drive-in window cannot handle the amount of business that is anticipated during the peak Saturday morning period. The simulation model does not determine what the bank should do, but simply how the system behaves. Management must consider alternatives for improving the system. One idea being considered by the vice-president for operations is the addition of a second drive-in window. In order to permit the vice-president for operations to consider this alternative properly, a simulation model was developed for this type of operation. In developing this model it is assumed that the probability distribution for the number of customer arrivals does not change and that the probability distribution for the service time for the second drive-in window is the same as for one drive-in window. In essence customers enter one single waiting line, and the next person in line takes the first drive-in window that becomes available. A diagram of the Lincoln Savings Bank system with two drive-in windows is shown in Figure 5S.9. Table 5S.11 shows the simulation results of 3 hours of simulation for this new system.

These simulation results clearly show the addition of a second drive-in window has improved customer service. In this simulation, $^{132}/_{162}$, or 81 percent, of the customers are serviced by a drive-in window. Comparing these results with Table 5S.10, we see that the average number waiting has decreased from 4.33 to 2.33 and the number of customers balking has decreased from 68 to 25. However, it is questionable whether the cost to construct the new system is justifiable, especially in light of the fact that the one-window system is currently working well in every time period other than Saturday morning. One idea that has been suggested is to keep the one-window system but to restrict the use of the drive-in window on Saturday mornings to customers with one or two transactions. In this way, the length of time to service cus-

FIGURE 5S.9   Lincoln Savings Bank—Two Drive-in Windows

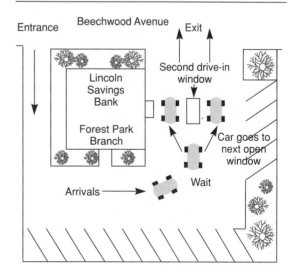

TABLE 5S.11 Computer-simulation Results for Lincoln Savings Bank—Two Drive-in Windows

Time (Mins.)	Total No. Of Arrivals	Number Waiting	Total Number Served	Total Number Balking
10	7	2	5	0
20	20	2	13	5
30	28	4	19	5
40	35	1	26	8
50	43	3	32	8
60	50	3	39	8
70	55	1	46	8
80	67	2	54	11
90	78	3	63	12
100	85	3	70	12
110	93	4	77	12
120	103	4	84	15
130	112	0	93	19
140	118	0	99	19
150	129	0	107	19
160	144	4	115	19
170	153	3	124	25
180	162	3	132	25
		42		

Average number waiting $= \dfrac{42}{18} = 2.33$

TABLE 5S.13 Computer-simulation Results for Lincoln Savings Bank—One Drive-in Window with Balking and Restricted Transactions

Time (Mins.)	Total No. Of Arrivals	Number Waiting	Total Number Served	Total Number Balking
10	11	3	4	4
20	21	5	8	8
30	30	3	13	14
40	40	2	17	21
50	52	6	22	24
60	60	4	27	29
70	64	3	31	30
80	67	2	35	30
90	76	4	39	33
100	84	5	43	36
110	89	4	48	37
120	95	2	53	40
130	105	3	57	45
140	115	6	61	48
150	122	4	66	52
160	130	4	71	55
170	140	5	75	60
180	149	3	80	66
		68		

Average number waiting $= \dfrac{68}{18} = 3.78$

TABLE 5S.12 Probability Distribution for Service Times When Customers are Restricted to One or Two Transactions

Service Time (Minutes)	Probability
1	.70
2	.30

tomers would be reduced and hence more customers could be serviced. Management believes that the probability distribution for service times in this case would be as shown in Table 5S.12. Using this probability distribution for service times, we ran our original simulation (with balking) anew for 3 hours of operation. The results are shown in Table 5S.13.

The simulation results presented in Table 5S.13 indicate that the proposed restriction in terms of the number of transactions allowed does not provide very much improvement over the original system. The av-

erage size of the waiting line is somewhat shorter, but a high proportion of customers still balk. Even though on the surface it would appear that this alternative might remedy the problem, the simulation results prove otherwise. This is useful information for the vice-president for operations before deciding to try such an alternative. This might even result in further dissatisfaction from those customers with more than two transactions. If this dissatisfaction leads to their changing banks, Lincoln Savings Bank could stand to lose far more than the cost of installing another drive-in window. The ultimate recommendation for a solution will most likely require a much more detailed analysis. Nonetheless, the simulation results have provided management with a better understanding of the current system and the effect of two proposed alternatives. Perhaps a creative person could come up with an idea for modifying the existing system that would not have any of the disadvantages of the current proposals. If such an idea occurs, a simulation model could be developed to evaluate its effectiveness.

ADVANTAGES AND DISADVANTAGES OF COMPUTER SIMULATION

A primary advantage of computer simulation is that it is applicable in complex cases where analytical procedures cannot be employed. For example, the Lincoln Savings Bank waiting-line system was sufficiently complex that analytical approaches do not apply, that is, the forms of the probability distributions involved do not satisfy the assumptions of the analytical models. In general, as the number of probabilistic components in the system becomes larger, the more likely it is that simulation will be the best approach.

Another advantage of the simulation approach is that the simulation model and simulator provide a convenient experimental laboratory. Once the computer program has been developed, it is usually relatively easy to experiment with the model. For example, if we wanted to know the effect of a change in the service time distribution we could have simply changed random number intervals and rerun the simulation. The effect of experimental changes in other inputs, such as the probability distributions of customer arrivals, could also be investigated.

Simulation is not without its disadvantages. One obvious disadvantage is that someone must develop the computer program. For large simulation projects, this is usually a substantial undertaking. Hence we should certainly not attempt to develop a simulation model unless the potential gains promise to outweigh the costs of model development. This disadvantage has been reduced in recent years with the development of computer simulation languages such as **GPSS**, **SIMSCRIPT**, **GASP**, and **SLAM**, many of which are available on microcomputers. The use of these languages often leads to considerable savings in time and money as the computer program or simulator is developed.

Another disadvantage of simulation is that it does not guarantee an optimal solution to a problem. We usually select those values of the decision variables to test in the model that have a good chance of being near the optimal solution. However, since it is usually too costly to try all values of the decision variables, and since different simulations may provide different results, there is no guarantee that the best simulation solution found is the overall optimal solution. Nonetheless, the danger of obtaining bad solutions is slight if good judgement is exercised in developing and running the simulation model. The decision maker usually has a good idea of reasonable values to try for the decision variables, and it is usually possible to run the simulation long enough to identify the apparent best decisions.

SUMMARY AND KEY TERMS

Summary

In this supplement we have shown how a complex problem can be analyzed and solved using computer simulation. Based on this simulation model, we can make the following general observations about the simulation approach to decision making:

1. Simulation is most appropriate when the problem is too complex or difficult to solve using another quantitative technique.
2. A model must be developed to represent the various relationships existing in the problem situation.
3. A process such as a random-number procedure must be employed to generate values for the probabilistic components in the model.
4. A bookkeeping procedure must be developed to keep track of what is happening in the simulation process (See Table 5S.6).

5. Because of the numerous calculations required in most simulations, a computer program or simulator is required.
6. The simulation process must be conducted for many days or periods in order to establish the long-run averages for the decision alternatives or other changes in the system.

Simulation should not necessarily be thought of as another technique for finding optimal solutions to problems. However, once a simulation model has been developed, a quantitative analyst may vary certain key design parameters and observe the effect on the output of the computer runs. Through a series of experiments with the simulation model good values may be selected for the key design parameters of the system.

In the example studied in this supplement, the probabilistic components resulted from discrete probability distributions; that is, the random variables involved could take on only a finite number of values. In many computer-simulation experiments, probabilistic components are encountered that follow continuous distributions, such as the normal or exponential probability distributions. The basic simulation approach we have developed in this chapter is still appropriate for these situations. The only difference concerns the method of generating random values from the appropriate continuous probability distributions.

Key Terms

Simulation
Fixed-time simulation model
Monte Carlo simulation
Pseudorandom numbers
Simulator
Validation

PROBLEMS

Most of the problems in this section are designed to enable you to perform simulations with hand calculations. To keep the calculations reasonable, we ask you to consider only a few decision alternatives and relatively short periods of simulation. While this should give you a good understanding of the simulation process, the simulation results will not be sufficient for you to make final conclusions or decisions about the problem situation. If you have access to a computer, we suggest that you develop a computer simulation model for some of the problems. Then, by using the model to test several decision alternatives over a much longer simulated period of time, you will be able to obtain the desired decision-making information.

1. A retail store has experienced the following historical daily demand for a particular product:

Sales (Units)	Frequency (Days)
0	4
1	6
2	14
3	12
4	7
5	5
6	2
Total	50

a. Develop a relative frequency distribution for the given data.
b. Use the random numbers from row 4 of Appendix C to simulate daily sales for a 10-day period.

2. A study was conducted in order to investigate the number of cars arriving at the drive-in window of Community Savings Bank. The following data were collected for 100 randomly selected 5-minute intervals.

Number of Arrivals	Number of Occurrences
0	12
1	24
2	37
3	19
4	8
Total	100

a. Develop a relative frequency distribution for the given data.
b. Use random numbers to simulate the number of customers that arrive between 9:00 A.M. and 9:15 A.M. on a given day.

3. Decca Industries has experienced the following weekly absenteeism frequency over the past 20 weeks:

Number of Employees Absent	Frequency
1	2
2	4
3	7
4	3
5	2
6	2
Total	20 weeks

a. Develop a relative frequency distribution for the given data.
b. Use random numbers to simulate weekly absenteeism for a 15-week period.

4. Charlestown Electric Company is building a new generator for its Mt. Washington plant. Even with good maintenance procedures, the generator will have periodic failures or breakdowns. Historical figures for similar generators indicate that the relative frequency of failures during a year is as follows:

Number of Failures	0	1	2	3
Relative Frequency	.80	.15	.04	.01

Assume that the useful lifetime of the generator is 25 years. Use simulation to estimate the number of breakdowns that will occur in the 25 years of operation. Is it common to have 5 or more consecutive years of operation without a failure?

5. Use row 15 of Appendix C to simulate 15 minutes of operation for the Lincoln Savings Bank application presented in this supplement. Show your simulation results in the format of Table 5S.6.

6. A service technician for a major photocopier company is trained to service two models of copier: the X100 and the Y200. Approximately 60 percent of the technician's service calls are for the X100 and 40 percent are for the Y200. The service time distributions for the two models are as follows:

X100		Y200	
Time (Minutes)	Relative Frequency	Time (Minutes)	Relative Frequency
25	0.50	20	0.40
30	0.25	25	0.40
35	0.15	30	0.10
40	0.10	35	0.10

a. Show the random-number intervals that can be used to simulate the type of machine to be serviced and the length of the service time.
b. Simulate 20 service calls. What is the total service time the technician spends on the 20 calls?

7. Given below are 50 weeks of data showing the number of breakdowns per week for a production line. A simulation of breakdowns will help the production manager better understand production delays and costs resulting from the breakdowns.

Number of Breakdowns	0	1	2	3	4	5
Number of Weeks	2	5	8	22	10	3

a. Develop the relative frequency distribution for the data.
b. Use random numbers to simulate the production breakdowns for a 12-week period.

8. Bushnell's Sand and Gravel (BSG) is a small firm that supplies sand, gravel, and topsoil to contractors and landscaping firms. BSG maintains an inventory of high-quality screened topsoil that is used to supply the weekly orders for two companies: Bath Landscaping Service and Pittsford Lawn Care, Inc. The problem BSG has is to determine how many cubic yards of screened topsoil to have in inventory at the beginning of each week in order to satisfy the needs of both its customers. BSG would like to select the lowest possible inventory level that would have a 0.95 probability of satisfying the combined weekly orders from both customers. The demand distributions for the two customers are as follows:

	Weekly Demand	Relative Frequency
Bath Landscaping	10	0.20
	15	0.35
	20	0.30
	25	0.10
	30	0.05
Pittsford Lawn Care	30	0.20
	40	0.40
	50	0.30
	60	0.10

Simulate 20 weeks of operation for beginning inventories of 70 and of 80 cubic yards. Based on your limited simulation results, how many cubic yards should BSG maintain in inventory? Discuss what you would want to do in a full-scale simulation of this problem.

9. A project has four activities (A, B, C, and D) that must be completed sequentially in order to complete the project. The probability distribution for the time required to complete each of the activities is as follows:

Activity	Activity Times (weeks)	Probability
A	5	0.25
	6	0.30
	7	0.30
	8	0.15
B	3	0.20
	5	0.55
	7	0.25
C	10	0.10
	12	0.25
	14	0.40
	16	0.20
	18	0.05
D	8	0.60
	10	0.40

a. Use a random number procedure to simulate the completion time for each activity. Sum the activity times to establish a completion time for the entire project.
b. Use the simulation procedure developed in part (a) to simulate 20 completions of this project. Show the distribution of completion times and estimate the probability that the project can be completed in 35 weeks or less.

10. A New York City corner newsstand orders 250 copies of the *New York Times* daily. Primarily due to weather conditions, the demand for newspapers varies from day to day. The probability distribution of the demand for newspapers is as follows:

Number of Newspapers	150	175	200	225	250
Probability	0.10	0.30	0.30	0.20	0.10

The newsstand makes a 15-cent profit on every paper sold, but it loses 10 cents on every paper unsold by the end of the day. Use 10 days of simulated results to determine whether the newsstand should order 200, 225, or 250 papers per day. What is the average daily profit that the newsstand can anticipate based on your recommendation?

11. Bristol Bikes, Inc. would like to develop an order quantity and reorder point policy that would minimize the total costs associated with the company's inventory of exercise bikes. The relative frequency distribution for retail demand on a weekly basis is as follows:

Demand	0	1	2	3	4	5
Probability	0.20	0.50	0.10	0.10	0.05	0.05

The relative frequency distribution for lead time is as follows:

Lead Time (weeks)	1	2	3	4
Relative Frequency	0.10	0.25	0.60	0.05

The inventory holding costs are $1 per unit per week, the ordering cost is $20 per order, the shortage cost is $25 per unit, and the beginning inventory is 7 units. Using an order quantity of 12 and a reorder point of 5, simulate 10 weeks of operation of this inventory system.

12. Production requirements at the Karlin Krafts Company have fluctuated over the past few months. The production manager has authorized a simulation study to obtain an estimate of potential daily production requirements in order to better schedule production activities. Historical data on production requirements are presented in the table below.

Daily Production Requirements	Frequency
0	2
100	4
200	7
300	12
400	14
500	5
600	6
	50

a. Determine a relative frequency distribution for the above information.
b. Use the following random numbers to simulate sales for a 6-day period.

21   77   80   20   85   27

13. Paula Williams is currently completing the design for a drive-in movie theater to be located in Big Flats, New York. Paula has purchased the land and is now in the planning stages of determining the number of automobiles to accommodate. Each automobile location requires installing a speaker system at a total cost of $250 per location. Based upon her experience with the five other drive-ins she has been operating for the past 8 years, Paula estimates that the nightly attendance will range from 100 to 500 automobiles with the relative frequencies shown.

Approximate Number of Automobiles	Relative Frequency
100	0.10
200	0.25
300	0.40
400	0.15
500	0.10

a. Simulate 20 days of attendance for capacities of 300, 400, and 500.

b. In the 20 days of simulated operation, how many daily demands of 300 would you have expected? Did you observe this many in your simulation? Should you have? Explain.

c. After considering personnel and other operating costs, the average profit is $1 per car. Using your 20 days of simulated data, what is the average nightly profit for the capacities of 300, 400, and 500? How many days of operation will it take Paula to recover the speaker installation cost if all profits are allocated to this cost?

14. A firm with a national chain of hotels and motels is interested in learning where individuals prefer to stay when on business trips. Three competing hotel and motel chains are included in the study. They are the Marimont Inn, the Harrison Inn, and the Hinton Hotel. The study found that where an individual stays on one trip is a good predictor of where the individual will stay the next trip. However, the study showed that there is also a tendency of individuals to switch from one chain to another. The probabilities of staying at each chain are shown below. For example, if an individual stayed at the Marimont Inn on one trip, there is a .70 probability of staying at the Marimont Inn the next trip, a .10 probability of staying at the Harrison Inn the next trip, and a .20 probability of staying at the Hinton Hotel the next trip. Similar probability values are shown for individuals staying at the Harrison Inn and Hinton Hotel on a particular trip.

Staying At	Probability		
	Marimont	Harrison	Hinton
Marimont	.70	.10	.20
Harrison	.20	.60	.20
Hinton	.15	.05	.80

a. Show the random-number assignments that can be used to simulate the next visit for an individual previously staying at the Marimont, Harrison, and Hinton chains.

b. Develop a flowchart that describes the simulation process for simulating where an individual will stay during a series of business trips.

c. Assume an individual most recently stayed at the Marimont Inn. Simulate where the individual would stay on the next 50 business trips. What percentage of time will the person select each chain? Which appears to be the most popular chain?

d. Repeat the simulation in part (c) starting with an individual most recently staying at the Harrison Inn. Repeat part (c) again with the individual most recently staying at the Hinton Hotel. Which is the most popular chain based on these simulation results?

15. Mt. Washington Garage sells regular and unleaded gasoline. Pump 1, a self-service facility, is used by customers who want to pump their own gas. Pump 2, a full-service facility, is used by customers who are willing to pay a higher cost per gallon in order to have an attendant pump the gas, check the oil, and so on. Both pumps can service one car at a time. Based upon past data, the owner of the garage estimates that 70% of the customers select the self-service pump and 30% want full service. The arrival rate of cars for each minute of operation is given by the following probability distribution:

Number Of Arrivals In 1 Minute Of Operation	Probability
0	.10
1	.20
2	.35
3	.30
4	.05
	1.00

The time to service a car, which depends upon whether the self-service or full-service facility is used, is given by the following probability distribution:

Self-Service Pump		Full-Service Pump	
Service Time (Minutes)	Probability	Service Time (Minutes)	Probability
2	.10	3	.20
3	.20	4	.30
4	.60	5	.35
5	.10	6	.10
	1.00	7	.05
			1.00

Study the operation of the system for 10 minutes using simulation. As part of your analysis consider the following types of questions. What is the average number of cars waiting for service per minute at both facilities? What is the average amount of time a car must wait for service? Prepare a brief report for Mt. Washington Garage that describes your analysis and any conclusions.

16. A medical consulting firm has been asked to determine the facilities required in the X-ray laboratory of a new hospital. In particular, the firm should provide recommendations on the number of X-ray units for the laboratory. How could computer simulation assist in reaching a good decision? What factors would you consider in a simulation model of this problem?

17. Consider a medium-sized community that currently has only one fire station. You have been hired by the city manager to assist in the determination of the best location for a second fire station. What would be your objective for this problem? Explain how computer simulation might be used to evaluate alternative locations and help identify the best location.

18. A bus company is considering adding a new ten-stop route to its operation. The bus will be scheduled to complete the route once each hour. If the company has determined the approximate demand distribution for each location, discuss how simulation might be used to project the hourly profit associated with the new route. If the company can assign a regular bus or a more economical minibus to this route, discuss how simulation might help make this decision. Note that with the minibus the company's management is concerned about being unable to pick up customers if the bus is already carrying its maximum number of riders.

CASE PROBLEM: MACHINE REPAIR

Jerry Masters, president of Pacific Plastics, Inc. (PPI), has become concerned with reports that downtime for PPI'S plastic injection-molding machines has been increasing. The downtime for a machine includes the time the machine must wait for a repair service technician to arrive after a breakdown plus the actual repair time. Currently PPI has three plastic injection-molding machines, which are repaired by one service technician. However, because of an increase in business, PPI is considering the purchase of three additional machines. Jerry is concerned that with the additional machines the downtime problem will increase.

An analysis of historical data shows that the probability of each machine breaking down during 1 hour of operation is 0.10. In addition, the distribution of the repair time for a machine that breaks down is as follows:

Repair Time (hours)	Probability
1	0.20
2	0.35
3	0.25
4	0.15
5	0.05

The loss in revenue associated with a machine being down for 1 hour is $100. PPI pays its service technician $22 per hour, and it is believed that additional service technicians can be hired at the same wage rate.

In reviewing the breakdown problem, Jerry decided that the best way to learn about the machine repair operation would be to simulate the performance of the system. In considering the potential use of simulation, Jerry indicated that PPI must deal with the two conflicting sources of cost: the cost of the service technician(s) and the cost of machine downtime. He indicated that PPI could minimize salaries by employing only one service technician. On the other hand, PPI could minimize the cost of machine downtime by hiring so many service technicians that a machine could be serviced immediately after a breakdown.

Jerry would like to develop a simulation model of the machine repair operation and use it to determine how many service technicians PPI should employ in order to minimize its total cost. When developing the simulation model, you can assume that if a machine has a breakdown, the breakdown can be treated as occurring at the beginning of the hour of operation. Thus, if a machine were to break down in hour 4, it would be considered to break down at the beginning of the hour. If 1 hour was spent waiting for a service technician and the length of time required to service the machine were 2 hours, the machine would be down during hours 4, 5, and 6, then be ready for operation at the beginning of hour 7. You can also assume that the probability of any machine breakdown is independent of the breakdown of any other machine, and that the service times are also independent of other service times.

Prepare a report that discusses the general development of the simulation model, the conclusions that you plan to draw by using the model, and any recommendations that you have regarding the best decision for PPI. Include the following:

1. List the information the simulation model should generate so that the decision can be made about the desired number of service technicians.
2. Set up a flow chart of the machine repair operation for one machine and one service technician.
3. Use a random number table and hand computations to demonstrate the simulation of the machine repair operation with three machines and one service technician. Use a table similar to Table 5S.6 to summarize 10 hours of simulation results.
4. Develop a computer simulation model for the machine repair operation when PPI expands to six machines. Use your simulation results to make a recommendation about the number of service technicians that PPI should employ.

Resource-Requirements Planning

Resource-requirements planning is the process of determining the types and amounts of resources that are required to implement an organization's strategic plan. The goal of resource-requirements planning is to determine the appropriate level of production capacity—as represented by facilities, equipment, and labor—that is required to meet future product demand. In this chapter we focus on capacity planning, facility planning, and labor and equipment planning. In the chapter supplement, we show how decision analysis may be used as a tool in this planning process. Because of its strategic nature, resource-requirements planning involves a joint operations, marketing, and finance effort. Important issues to be considered include:

1. How is the market changing for existing products and how will current and future technological innovations affect operations? How accurately can these trends be forecasted?
2. Can existing facilities accommodate new products and adapt to changing demand for existing products?
3. Should new facilities be built? Should existing ones be modified, expanded, or closed down? What are the financial implications of such decisions?
4. How large should facilities be and where should they be located? Should we have a few large facilities near suppliers or numerous smaller facilities near customers?
5. When should facility changes take place?
6. How much equipment and labor will be required for future operations?

Capacity planning is a crucial element of the operations strategy. The capacity decision has major cost implications and must be made in the face of considerable uncertainty regarding future product demand. A firm must balance the cost of having excess capacity with the potential lost sales from too little capacity. What really complicates the decision is that the capacity plan must be based on long-term forecasts, which are usually uncertain. Other factors to consider include interest rates, technology improvements, construction costs, competition, and government regulations. Products, as we saw in the last chapter, follow a life cycle; thus the resource needs change over time. Capacity planning must therefore account for the forecasted product mix and the aggregate effect of different life cycles on resource requirements. There is usually a high-capital investment and a long time horizon involved in adding resources such as facilities and equipment, and once these decisions are made, they cannot be easily reversed.

Competition and industry trends can significantly affect capacity decisions. If several firms in an industry decide to add capacity at the same time, a supply/demand imbalance is created; in such a situation, the costs due to increased overhead and the lower industry prices resulting from an increase in supply will result in a reduction in profits. Such a situation actually occurred in 1982 in the videotape market, when FUJI Photo Film, Hitachi Maxwell, and TDK collectively increased capacity by 90 percent.[1]

How the issues raised are addressed in the resource-requirements planning process will be discussed.

---

[1] "A Volatile Tape Market has TDK on a Roller Coaster," *Business Week,* 25 July 1983.

6.1 AN OVERVIEW OF THE RESOURCE-REQUIREMENTS PLANNING PROCESS

Figure 6.1 provides an overview of the resource-requirements planning process. The business plan sets the direction of the organization by specifying the types of goods or services that are offered. As a first step in determining the resources required to produce each good or service, the organization must develop a long-range forecast of demand. This forecast should take into account factors such as industry trends, the rate and direction of technological innovation, the likely behavior of competitors, and the impact of international markets and sources of supply.

Forecasts of demand for goods and services must then be translated into a measure of *capacity* needed. For instance, based upon the forecast of product demand, a manufacturing firm concluded that there was a need for 2400 machine hours in the milling department next year; anticipated growth in machine hours needed was expected to be 5 percent per year over the following five years. In another instance, an airline translated a demand forecast for flight services into an estimate of the number of flight attendants required to meet the projected level of demand.

Capacity decisions must be translated into facilities, equipment, and labor plans. Facility needs can be met through the expansion or contraction of existing facilities, by the construction of new facilities, or by closing down old ones. Important questions include: Should a firm have one large facility or several smaller ones? Where should plants, warehouses, and so on be located, and what should the focus of each facility be? (The subject of location is an important issue in itself and is discussed in detail in the next chapter.)

Equipment and labor needs must be assessed and plans developed that are consistent with the capacity and facilities plans. Equipment needs might be met by purchasing additional machines or by replacing old machines with newer and faster technology. Labor needs might be met by hiring new workers or retraining existing employees. Automation issues have an impact on both equipment and labor requirements.

Finally, alternative resource-requirements plans must be evaluated for feasibility and economic impact. Decisions can then be made and implemented. Although we do not discuss the financial issues associated with meeting resource requirements, financial considerations play a key role at all levels of an organi-

FIGURE 6.1   The Resource-Requirements Planning Process

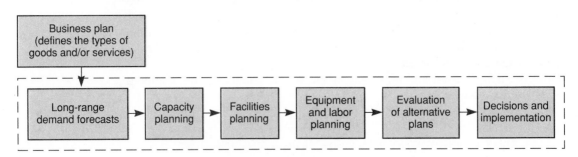

zation and influence the selection among alternative plans. Resource-requirements planning needs to be integrated into financial planning for effective results.

6.2 CAPACITY PLANNING

The central issue in resource-requirements planning is providing adequate capacity. **Capacity**, as defined by the American Production and Inventory Control Society (APICS), is "the highest reasonable output rate which can be achieved with the current product specifications, product mix, work force, plant, and equipment." Actually, there are two distinct ways of viewing capacity. *Design capacity* is the *maximum* possible rate of output that can be achieved, and *effective capacity* (the APICS definition of capacity) is the rate of output that a firm is *capable* of achieving, given process limitations such as preventive maintenance downtime, setup time, and so forth. Thus, effective capacity will be less than design capacity. The *actual output rate* will generally be less than the effective capacity when production losses because of scrap, machine breakdowns, rework, sick time, and so on are taken into account. A simple example will serve to illustrate the differences.

Suppose that a small machine shop, designed to operate one shift per day, five days per week, can produce 500 units per shift with its current equipment, product mix, and workforce. The design capacity of the shop is

$$(500 \text{ units/shift})(1 \text{ shift/day})(5 \text{ days/week}) = 2500 \text{ units/week}$$

If 10 percent of the productive time is used for preventive maintenance and product changeover setups, the effective capacity is .90(2500) = 2250 units/week. However, because of unanticipated machine breakdowns, defective output, material shortages, and other unplanned delays, the actual output might be only 2000 units/week.

Using these concepts, we define

$$\text{Efficiency} = \frac{\text{actual output}}{\text{effective capacity}}$$

and

$$\text{Utilization} = \frac{\text{actual output}}{\text{design capacity}}$$

Thus, the efficiency of the shop in this example would be

$$\text{Efficiency} = \frac{2000}{2250} = .889 \text{ or } 88.9 \text{ percent}$$

and the utilization is

$$\text{Utilization} = \frac{2000}{2500} = .80 \text{ or } 80 \text{ percent}$$

Design capacity cannot be increased unless facilities are expanded (possibly through the use of overtime or extra shifts) or modified. Effective capacity, on the other hand, can often be improved by operational improvements such as improving work methods to reduce set up times or purchasing machines with less maintenance requirements.

From this discussion we see that capacity is influenced by a number of factors: the size and layout of facilities, type of process, speed of equipment, the quality that the process is capable of producing, the mix of products, the size of the workforce, human-factors issues such as the design of work methods, and operations factors such as scheduling.

| The Measurement of Capacity | Capacity can be measured in one of two ways. One measure of capacity is a rate of output per unit of time. The unit of measure selected should be common to the type of product produced. Tons per month and parts per minute are examples. If a plant produces only one type of product, capacity is usually easy to define. In a sugar refinery, for example, a logical measure of capacity is tons of sugar per month (or per day, per week, and so on). However, if more than one product is produced, an output-rate capacity measure may be misleading. To illustrate this, let us consider a small winery. A good measure of capacity is the number of gallons or barrels of wine produced per month. However, red wine takes longer to age than white wine. If the winery is currently producing half red wine and half white wine, and then changes to a 30 to 70 percent mix, the capacity as an output measure would clearly increase, even though the physical facilities and labor have not changed. Hence the product mix of a firm will affect capacity if it is measured in this way. This need not always be the case, however. For example, the capping department of the winery may have a capacity of 6000 bottles per day. Obviously, this does not depend on the type of wine that is produced. |

The second principal method of measuring capacity is in terms of units of input. This is commonly used in service organizations, since the ability to meet demand depends in part on the resources that are available. The concept of output per unit of time is less meaningful for a service organization. An example of an input measure of capacity is the number of beds available in a hospital. This partially determines the amount of service demand that can be accommodated (along with equipment and labor).

As another example of measuring capacity in terms of units of input, consider how universities use student credit hours as a measure of capacity. To illustrate this concept, assume that each professor has a standard teaching load of 12 hours per quarter and that each 3-hour course can have a maximum of 60 students. If a department has 8 faculty members, then its capacity per academic quarter is

(8 faculty members)(4 courses/faculty member)(60 students/course)(3 credit hours) = 5760 student credit hours

This is the maximum amount that the department can effectively teach. Other capacity measures are given in Table 6.1. Both input and output measures are useful in resource-requirements planning. The appropriate measure to use depends on the type of organization and the nature of the product.

When several different operations are performed in sequence, the capacity of the system is determined by the slowest operation, or bottleneck, in the system. Let us suppose that the bottling operation is an intermediate step in the production of a household cleaner. The complete process is shown in Figure 6.2. Suppose that the chemical process can produce at a rate of 2 gallons per minute and that

TABLE 6.1

Capacity
Measures

Output Measures	
Organization	**Measure of Capacity**
Automobile plant	Number of autos/hour
Law firm	Number of cases handled/week
Oil refinery	Barrels of oil/day
Electric company	Megawatts of electricity/hour
Paper producer	Tons of paper/week

Input Measures	
Organization	**Measure of Capacity**
Jet engine plant	Machine hours/month
	Labor hours/month
Airline	Number of seats/flight
Hotel	Number of rooms, number of beds
Grocery store	Number of checkout lines
Warehouse	Cubic feet of space
Tennis club	Number of courts
Department store	Number of square feet

each bottle holds 16 ounces. The bottling department can produce 12 bottles per minute, and the case packer packages 12 bottles per case at a rate of 1.2 cases per minute. If we translate each production rate into bottles per minute, we see that the production rate of the chemical process is

$$(2 \text{ gallons/minute})(8 \text{ bottles/gallon}) = 16 \text{ bottles/minute}$$

The production rate of the bottling department is 12 bottles/minute, and the production rate of the case packer is

$$(1.2 \text{ cases/minute})(12 \text{ bottles/case}) = 14.4 \text{ bottles/minute}$$

Since the bottling rate is the slowest (12 bottles per minute), the capacity of the entire system is 12 bottles per minute. Hence, the bottling process limits system production and is the bottleneck (no pun intended!) in the system. Capacity improvements and investment decisions should be focused on bottleneck operations.

CAPACITY PLANNING FOR A FAST-FOOD RESTAURANT

EXAMPLE

Fast Burger Inc., is building a new restaurant near a busy shopping mall. The restaurant will be open 15 hours per day, 360 days per year. Management has analyzed demand patterns at other Fast Burger restaurants and concluded that the restaurant should have the capacity to handle a peak hourly demand of 1000 customers. Consequently, they would like to determine how many grills, deep fryers and soft drink spouts are needed.

The average customer purchase is

    1 burger (4 ounce hamburger or cheeseburger)
    1 bag of french fries (4 ounces)
    1 soft drink (12 ounces)

FIGURE 6.2

Production
Process for a
Household
Cleaner

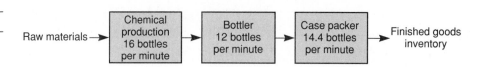

A 36 × 36 inch grill can cook 450 ounces of burgers every 10 minutes and a single basket deep fryer can cook 4 pounds of french fries in 6 minutes, or 40 pounds per hour. Finally, one soft drink spout can dispense 50 ounces of soft drink per minute or 3000 ounces per hour.

To determine the equipment needed to meet peak hourly demand, Fast Burger must translate expected demand in terms of customers per hour into needs for grills, deep fryers, and soft drink spouts. First note that the peak hourly needs for burgers, french fries, and soft drinks are as follows:

Product	Peak Hourly Need (Ounces)
Burgers	4,000
French fries	4,000
Soft drinks	12,000

Since the hourly capacity of a grill is $(450)(6) = 2700$ ounces, the number of grills needed to satisfy a peak hourly demand of 4000 ounces of burgers is

$$\text{Number of grills} = \frac{4000}{2700} = 1.48 \text{ grills}$$

To determine the number of single basket deep fryers needed to meet a peak hourly demand of 4000 ounces of french fries, we must first compute the hourly capacity of the deep fryer.

$$\text{Capacity of the deep fryer} = \frac{4000 \text{ oz/hr}}{16 \text{ oz/lb}} = 250 \text{ lb/hr}$$

Hence, the number of single basket deep fryers needed is $250/40 = 6.25$.

Finally, the number of soft drink spouts needed to satisfy peak demand of 12,000 ounces is

$$\text{Number of soft drink spouts needed} = \frac{12,000}{3000} = 4$$

After reviewing this analysis, management decided to purchase one of the 36 × 36 inch grills and a second smaller 30 × 30 inch grill. A deep fryer capacity of seven baskets was planned for and a five-spout soft drink system was installed. While the above analysis only showed a need for four spouts, management wanted to provide some margin for error, primarily because they felt that the peak hourly demand for soft drinks might have been underestimated.

Strategies for Capacity Planning

Capacity planning strategies involve an assessment of existing capacity, forecasts of future capacity requirements, choice of alternative ways to build capacity, and financial evaluation. Forecasts (see Chapter 3) play a crucial role in capacity strategy. One useful tool in forecasting product demand is the product life cycle, which we discussed in Chapter 5. For firms that are product innovators and whose products have relatively short life cycles, forecasts of aggregate demand can be obtained by combining demand estimates over the product life cycles as shown in Figure 6.3. For stable products that exhibit steady growth, demand estimates can be combined in a similar manner as shown in Figure 6.4.

In developing a long range capacity plan, a firm must make a basic economic tradeoff between the cost of capacity and the opportunity cost of not having adequate capacity. Capacity costs include both the initial investment in facilities and the annual cost of operating and maintaining the facilities. The cost of not having sufficient capacity is the opportunity loss incurred from lost sales and reduced market share. These opportunity costs, however, are very difficult to quantify. Conceptually, at least, the level of capacity should minimize the present value of the total cost as shown in Figure 6.5.

This model assumes that one level of capacity is planned over some planning horizon as opposed to planning capacity on an incremental basis. The advantages of such an approach are that the fixed costs of building and construction need be incurred only once and thus the firm can take advantage of any economies of scale.

However, there are several disadvantages associated with this approach. The firm may not be able to acquire the considerable financial resources required for a major capacity expansion, and substantial risks are involved if forecasts are

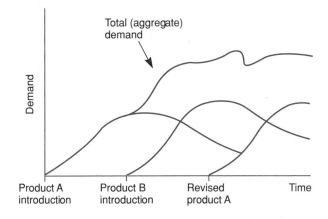

FIGURE 6.3

Determining Aggregate Demand from Life-cycle Curves

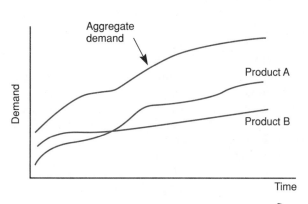

FIGURE 6.4

Aggregate Demand for Steady-growth Products

FIGURE 6.5
Economic Model
of Capacity Cost
Tradeoffs

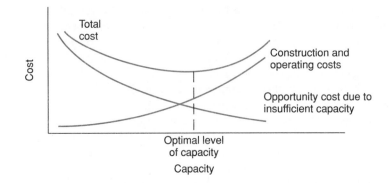

incorrect. Note also, that if aggregate demand exhibits steady growth, the facility will be underutilized for a long period of time since the level of capacity is planned for the end of the time horizon. Other disadvantages involve the fact that new and unforeseen products and technology, government regulations, and other factors affecting capacity needs may alter capacity requirements. The alternative is to view capacity expansion incrementally. Such an approach requires determining the *amount, timing,* and *form* of such capacity changes.

To illustrate capacity expansion decisions, make the following two assumptions: (1) Capacity is assumed to be added in "chunks" or discrete increments, such as five units per change; and (2) demand is steadily increasing. There are three basic options for matching capacity with demand.

Figure 6.6(a) illustrates the strategy of matching capacity additions with demand as closely as possible. When the capacity curve is above the demand curve, the firm has excess capacity; when it is below, there is insufficient capacity to meet demand. During periods of capacity shortage, there are several alternatives. The firm can incur lost sales and possibly lose market position, or it can make short-term capacity expansions through subcontracting, overtime, additional shifts, and so forth. (In Chapter 14 we discuss short-term capacity decisions in further detail.)

In Figure 6.6(b) we show a capacity-expansion policy with the goal of maintaining sufficient capacity so that the chances of not meeting demand are minimized. Since there is always excess capacity, a "cushion" against unexpected demand from large orders or new customers is provided. The additional capacity also provides the firm with the capability of improving customer service, since backorders will rarely occur.

Finally, in Figure 6.6(c) a policy of capacity expansion that lags demand and results in constant capacity shortage is illustrated. Such a strategy requires less investment and provides for high-capacity utilization and thus a higher rate of return on investment. However, it can also reduce long-term profitability through overtime and productivity losses that would undoubtedly occur as the firm scrambles to satisfy demand. In the long run, such a policy can lead to a permanent loss of market position.

With all of these strategies, the firm has the option of making frequent small-capacity increments or fewer large increments. These options are shown in Figure 6.7. The choice should be made from careful economic analysis of the cost and risks associated with excess capacity and capacity shortages. The ability and desire of the firm to make short-term capacity adjustments must also be taken into account. With proprietary technology, for example, it would not be feasible to subcontract.

FIGURE 6.6 Matching Capacity with Demand (a), Excess Capacity Policy (b), and Capacity Shortage Policy (c)

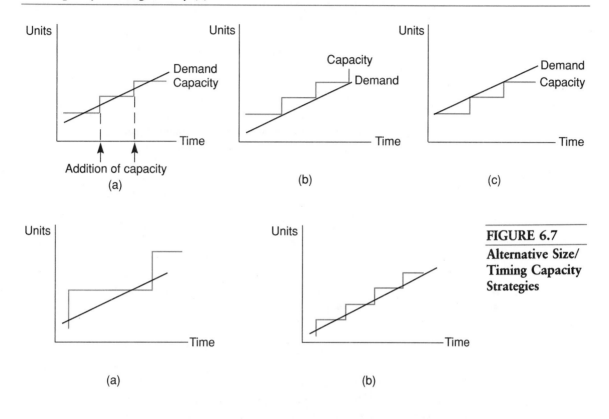

FIGURE 6.7
Alternative Size/ Timing Capacity Strategies

6.3 CAPACITY PLANNING FOR SERVICE ORGANIZATIONS

Capacity planning for the production of services presents a different problem than for manufactured goods. In manufacturing, if demand is cyclical, shortages can usually be avoided by building up inventory during slow periods or arranging to subcontract production with another firm. In some service organizations, such as grocery stores, similar short-term capacity decisions can be made. For example, a store manager might schedule more checkout clerks during the late afternoon and early evening hours to handle increased numbers of shoppers. This approach to managing short-term capacity will be discussed in later chapters. However, we note that the design capacity is limited by the number of checkout counters. These cannot be "inventoried" like manufactured goods. Thus it is important that sufficient capacity be built into the facility to meet peak periods of demand. The need to provide capacity to meet peak-period demand is a dominant consideration in capacity planning for the production of services.

Output measures of capacity for service production are more difficult to interpret and control since the rate at which humans work is more variable than that of machines. Therefore, input measures are more commonly used. While manufacturers forecast demand for physical goods in determining capacity requirements, service organizations must forecast the human behavior involved in providing and receiving services. Hence, there is more uncertainty in the forecasts, and this makes capacity planning more difficult.

As with manufacturing organizations, it is important to balance capacity at various stages of a service process in order to avoid bottlenecks. For service organizations, however, it is probably even more important; that is, although manufactured goods do not complain about waiting, people do!

In deciding to change capacity, service and manufacturing organizations must make similar decisions. They must be concerned with the amount, timing, and form of capacity additions. It is easy to add the wrong kind of capacity for producing services. For instance, to increase passenger capacity and take advantage of economies of scale, some airlines have purchased large (jumbo) jets. This has turned out to be a poor strategic decision when competitors have increased their capacity by flying more frequently with smaller jets. While total capacities were the same in terms of seats per day, the more frequent flight schedules provided better customer service and gained increased market share for the airline providing the service.

Another strategic error made by service organizations is to only increase a portion of its service capacity. For example, if a hotel adds more rooms, it must also increase its capacity in restaurants, meeting rooms, and recreational facilities to accommodate the increased number of guests. In the following example, an application of break-even analysis in making a capacity-expansion decision for a restaurant is illustrated.

| EXAMPLE | ECONOMIC ANALYSIS FOR CAPACITY EXPANSION |

The Myatt House Restaurant presently has a capacity for 100 patrons. Business at lunch is fair, but business for dinner on Tuesday through Saturday is excellent. The owner of the restaurant is considering adding an additional dining room with a seating capacity of 50, which will be used for dinner. The building's owner has agreed to build the addition for an extra $1600 per month in rent. The cost of new decorations and fixtures, amortized over their lifetime, and associated interest expense will amount to $7000 per year. Maintenance and utility costs would rise by $3000 per year. Additional personnel required to support the expansion include a new chef, extra waitresses, and a hostess. Wages for these employees would be $35,000.

The average dinner bill per person is $12 for food and $4 for alcoholic beverages, for a total average bill of $16.00. The food cost is 40 percent and the beverage cost is 25 percent of the average dinner bill. Other miscellaneous expenses vary with sales and are estimated to be 10 percent of the total bill.

Over a period of several weeks a survey was made of the number of people who leave because of long waiting times (no reservations are accepted). Table 6.2 lists these statistics, along with the maximum waiting time that was observed.

Total annual fixed and variable costs are computed as follows:

Fixed Costs
Rent	$19,200
Decorations and fixtures	7,000
Maintenance, utilities	3,000
Wages	35,000
Total fixed costs	$64,200

Day	Average Number of Turnaways	Maximum Waiting Time (Minutes)
Tuesday	10	30
Wednesday	10	30
Thursday	15	40
Friday	40	80
Saturday	45	90
	120	

TABLE 6.2

Statistical Data on Waiting and Turnaways at the Myatt House

Variable Costs

Food cost (40%)	$4.80
Beverage cost (25%)	1.00
Miscellaneous (10%)	1.60
Total variable cost	$7.40

We may now calculate the break-even point for the number of additional customers that can be served. Let x be the number of additional customers. The break-even point is found by equating total revenue to total costs.

$$16.00x = 64,200 + 7.40x$$
$$8.6x = 64,200$$
$$x = 7465 \text{ customers per year}$$

From Table 6.2, we see that the annual average number of customers that leave is $(120)(52) = 6240$, which is below the break-even point. Therefore, on this basis alone, the expansion is not economically attractive.

There are, however, a number of other factors that the owner of the Myatt House should consider before making a decision. For example, many people may not even bother to come on weekends because of the long wait. Thus the number of turnaways may not be the best value to use to compare with the break-even point. Actually, this represents 6240/7465 or about 84 percent of the break-even value. The actual number of additional patrons may be much higher. On the other hand, customer perceptions of the popularity and quality of the restaurant as evidenced by the long waiting lines may be diminished by the expansion. Therefore, as in any decision in operations management, the qualitative considerations must be weighed along with the quantitative analysis.

6.4 FACILITY PLANNING

Capacity expansion can be accomplished in a variety of ways. Old facilities can be expanded and modernized, a single large facility can be built, or several smaller facilities can be built and geographically dispersed. Arguments based on economies of scale are often used to justify large facilities. In general, the per-unit manufacturing costs increase at a slower rate than the production volume. For example, if we let F = the total fixed cost, V = the variable cost per unit, and Q = the production quantity, then

$$\text{Total cost per unit} = \frac{\text{fixed cost} + \text{variable cost}}{\text{total production}} = \frac{F + VQ}{Q}$$

$$= \frac{F}{Q} + V$$

The per-unit variable cost, V, is constant (the same for all production levels). As Q increases, F/Q decreases; that is, fixed costs are spread over more units and hence total cost per unit decreases. However, when capacity is added, the initial increase in the production quantity Q is usually not large enough to offset the additional fixed costs, and thus higher total costs per unit are incurred. However, as production volume increases, and more of the additional capacity is utilized, benefits from economies of scale begin to accrue.

There are also disadvantages to large facilities, or "diseconomies of scale." A larger work force requires more supervisors and managers, leading to a higher level of bureaucracy. As discussed in Chapter 4, large facilities can reduce the focus of the plant and lead to inefficiencies and loss of strategic position. For example, in the electronics industry there are three major areas of production focus: development and prototype manufacturing, component manufacturing, and assembly and test. By focusing each within a single small facility, the firm can achieve many of the advantages discussed in Chapter 4. For instance, development and prototype manufacturing requires high technology and high flexibility to product changeover; component manufacturing needs high volume and limited flexibility; assembly and test should have more specialized and dedicated equipment and high-volume throughput capability. In addition, with one large plant, there is increased vulnerability to natural disasters, strikes, and future reductions in demand. With smaller facilities, a firm can sell off plants much more easily when cash is required or a change in strategic direction occurs.

Estimates of capacity requirements must be translated into more detailed specifications of space, equipment, and labor. Among the most important space considerations are

1. space requirements for machines and handling equipment
2. storage requirements for raw materials, work in process, and finished goods
3. utilities and other plant services
4. personnel services such as restrooms and cafeterias
5. office space.

One of the principal roles of the architect is to work with operations managers to determine space needs. Space requirements are necessary inputs to facility-layout techniques that we discuss in the next chapter.

Equipment and Labor Planning

In order to determine equipment needs for manufactured products, we must begin with an analysis of the items to be produced and the equipment needed to manufacture them. This requires a detailed specification of individual parts and components that make up a product, the method of manufacture, and the sequence of production and assembly steps. From this information, it is possible to determine the processing time p (usually in minutes per piece) for each operation and the efficiency e of the operation, where **efficiency** is a dimensionless quantity defined as the fraction of time that the equipment is operating. This analysis takes into account factors such as setup time on the machine, maintenance, and unexpected failures. The details of this analysis fall under the scope of *process analysis and design* and *work measurement* and are discussed in Chapters 8, 9, and 11.

If the required production is R units per day and there are H hours available each day, then the number of machines required (N), can be calculated by the following formula:

$$N = \frac{pR}{60He} \tag{6.1}$$

That is,

$$N = \text{number of machines required}$$

$$= \frac{(p \text{ minutes/unit})(R \text{ units/day})}{(60 \text{ minutes/hour})(H \text{ hours/day/machine})(e)}$$

This is a very approximate measure of equipment requirements, since it does not include such factors as scrap and rework, changes in product mix, or delays from previous production operations. However, it is useful as a planning tool to determine general equipment requirements.

To illustrate the use of formula (6.1), consider the bottling department of a consumer goods plant that manufactures liquid household cleaners. Each bottling machine can fill 6 bottles per minute at an efficiency of .85. The department works one shift per day (8 hours) and the required production is 5000 bottles per day. The number of bottling machines required to meet this demand is

$$N = \frac{(1/6)(5000)}{60(8)(.85)} = 2.04$$

The required production can be approximately satisfied with two machines.

Equation (6.1) can also be used to estimate labor requirements. For example, suppose that a company is interested in determining the number of quality-control inspectors needed for the final inspection of a product. If each inspector can work at a rate of p minutes per unit at an efficiency e (taking into account fatigue, personal time, and so forth), then Equation (6.1) can be used to determine the number of inspectors required in order to meet a required output rate R.

In service organizations, labor planning is one of the most important aspects of capacity planning. Examples include nurse staffing in hospitals, operator staffing at a telephone switchboard, and the number of grocery clerks at checkout counters. Equation (6.1) usually has to be modified for service organizations, since each person will usually perform a variety of tasks with different times. Also, activities are usually longer in duration, therefore it is generally better to measure activities in hours rather than in minutes.

In general,

$$N = \frac{\sum_{i=1}^{k} p_i R_i}{Te} \tag{6.2}$$

where

> N = labor requirements
>
> k is the number of different activities performed,
>
> p_i = time for activity i,
>
> R_i = workload per unit time for activity i,
>
> T = total time available
>
> e = efficiency factor

EXAMPLE

LABOR PLANNING FOR A SERVICE ORGANIZATION

A social worker performs two major activities. Activity 1 requires 4 hours, whereas activity 2 requires 1.5 hours. Each person is available 40 hours per week and an allowance for personal time and nonroutine activities is 20 percent. Thus the efficiency factor will be $1 - .20 = .80$. The estimated workload is 40 cases per week of type 1 and 60 cases per week of type 2. We let

> p_1 = time for activity 1 = 4 hours
>
> p_2 = time for activity 2 = 1.5 hours
>
> R_1 = number of cases per week of type 1 = 40
>
> R_2 = number of cases per week of type 2 = 60
>
> T = 40 hours per week (This replaces the term $60H$ in Equation 6.1)

Then the staff size required for this agency is calculated as follows:

$$N = \frac{p_1R_1 + p_2R_2}{Te}$$
$$= \frac{4(40) + 1.5(60)}{40(.8)}$$
$$= 7.8125$$

Thus eight workers will be needed to meet the forecasted demand.

6.5 THE LEARNING CURVE

If you have ever learned to type or play a musical instrument, you know that the longer and more often you work at it, the better you become. The same is true in production and assembly operations. This was recognized in the 1920s at Wright-Patterson Air Force Base in the assembly of aircraft. Studies showed that the number of labor hours required to produce the fourth plane was about 80 percent of the amount of time spent on the second; the eighth plane took only 80 percent as much as the fourth; the sixteenth plane 80 percent of the time of the eighth, and so on. This decrease in production time as the numbered produced increases is illustrated in Figure 6.8. As production doubles from x units to $2x$ units, the time per unit of the $2x$th unit is 80 percent of the time of the xth unit. This is called an 80 percent **learning curve**. Such a curve exhibits a steep initial decline and then levels off as workers become more proficient in their tasks.

Defense industries (e.g., the aircraft and electronics industries), which introduce many new and complex products, use learning curves to assist managers in estimating labor requirements and capacity, in determining costs and budget requirements, and in planning and scheduling production. Eighty percent learning curves are generally accepted as a standard, although the ratio of machine work to manual assembly affects the learning percentage. Obviously, no learning takes place if all assembly is done by machine. As a rule of thumb, if the ratio of manual to machine work is 3 to 1 (three-fourths manual), then 80 percent is a good value; if the ratio is 1 to 3, then 90 percent is often used. An even split of manual and machine work would suggest the use of an 85 percent learning curve.

Mathematically, the learning curve is represented by the function

$$y = ax^{-b} \tag{6.3}$$

where

x = number of units produced

a = hours required to produce the first unit

y = time to produce the xth unit

b = constant equal to $\dfrac{-(\ln p)}{(\ln 2)}$ for a $100p$ percent learning curve

Thus for an 80 percent learning curve, $p = .8$ and

$$b = \frac{-(\ln .8)}{\ln(2)} = \frac{-(-.223)}{(.693)} = .322$$

For a 90 percent curve, $p = .9$ and

$$b = \frac{-(\ln .9)}{(\ln 2)} = \frac{-(-.105)}{(.693)} = .152$$

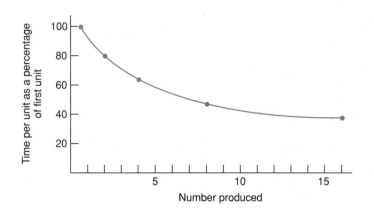

FIGURE 6.8

An 80 Percent Learning Curve

USING THE LEARNING CURVE FOR LABOR PLANNING

Suppose that a manufacturing firm is introducing a new product and has determined that a 90 percent learning curve is applicable. Estimates of demand for the next three years are 50, 75, and 100 units. The time to produce the first unit is estimated to be 3500 hours. Thus the learning curve function is

$$y = 3500x^{-.152}$$

Hence the time to manufacture the second unit will be

$$3500 (2)^{-.152} = 3150 \text{ hours}$$

Table 6.3 gives the cumulative number of hours required to produce the 3-year demand in increments of 25 units. If we assume that each employee works 160 hours per month, or 1920 hours per year, we find that for the first year the firm will require

$$\frac{112,497}{1920} = 59 \text{ employees}$$

to produce this product. In the second year, the labor requirements are

$$\frac{246,160 - 112,497}{1920} = 70 \text{ employees}$$

and for the third year, the labor requirements are

$$\frac{406,112 - 246,160}{1920} = 83 \text{ employees}$$

These are aggregate numbers; at a more detailed planning level, these will vary according to how production is actually scheduled over the year.

Values for learning curve functions can be computed easily through the use of tables. Tables 6.4 and 6.5 present unit values and cumulative values, respectively, for learning curves from 60 percent through 95 percent. To find the time to produce a specific unit, multiply the time for the first unit by the appropriate factor in Table 6.4. For the 90 percent learning curve example presented earlier, the time for the second unit is found by 3500(.9000) = 3150, the time for the third unit would be 3500(.8462) = 2961.7, and so on.

TABLE 6.3

Cumulative Time Required Under Learning

Cumulative Units	Cumulative Hours Required
25	61,996
50	112,497
75	159,164
100	203,494
125	246,160
150	287,545
175	327,894
200	367,374
225	406,112

p	.60	.65	.70	.75	.80	.85	.90	.95
x b	.737	.621	.515	.415	.322	.234	.152	.074
1	1.0000	1.0000	1.0000	1.0000	1.0000	1.0000	1.0000	1.0000
2	0.6000	0.6500	0.7000	0.7500	0.8000	0.8500	0.9000	0.9500
3	0.4450	0.5052	0.5682	0.6338	0.7021	0.7729	0.8462	0.9219
4	0.3600	0.4225	0.4900	0.5625	0.6400	0.7225	0.8100	0.9025
5	0.3054	0.3678	0.4368	0.5127	0.5956	0.6857	0.7830	0.8877
6	0.2670	0.3284	0.3977	0.4754	0.5617	0.6570	0.7616	0.8758
7	0.2383	0.2984	0.3674	0.4459	0.5345	0.6337	0.7439	0.8659
8	0.2160	0.2746	0.3430	0.4219	0.5120	0.6141	0.7290	0.8574
9	0.1980	0.2552	0.3228	0.4017	0.4929	0.5974	0.7161	0.8499
10	0.1832	0.2391	0.3058	0.3846	0.4765	0.5828	0.7047	0.8433
11	0.1708	0.2253	0.2912	0.3696	0.4621	0.5699	0.6946	0.8374
12	0.1602	0.2135	0.2784	0.3565	0.4493	0.5584	0.6854	0.8320
13	0.1510	0.2031	0.2672	0.3449	0.4379	0.5480	0.6771	0.8271
14	0.1430	0.1940	0.2572	0.3344	0.4276	0.5386	0.6696	0.8226
15	0.1359	0.1858	0.2482	0.3250	0.4182	0.5300	0.6626	0.8184
16	0.1296	0.1785	0.2401	0.3164	0.4096	0.5220	0.6561	0.8145
17	0.1239	0.1719	0.2327	0.3085	0.4017	0.5146	0.6501	0.8109
18	0.1188	0.1659	0.2260	0.3013	0.3944	0.5078	0.6445	0.8074
19	0.1142	0.1604	0.2198	0.2946	0.3876	0.5014	0.6392	0.8042
20	0.1099	0.1554	0.2141	0.2884	0.3812	0.4954	0.6342	0.8012
21	0.1061	0.1507	0.2087	0.2826	0.3753	0.4898	0.6295	0.7983
22	0.1025	0.1465	0.2038	0.2772	0.3697	0.4844	0.6251	0.7955
23	0.0992	0.1425	0.1992	0.2722	0.3644	0.4794	0.6209	0.7929
24	0.0961	0.1387	0.1949	0.2674	0.3595	0.4747	0.6169	0.7904
25	0.0933	0.1353	0.1908	0.2629	0.3548	0.4701	0.6131	0.7880
30	0.0815	0.1208	0.1737	0.2437	0.3346	0.4505	0.5963	0.7775
35	0.0728	0.1097	0.1605	0.2286	0.3184	0.4345	0.5825	0.7687
40	0.0660	0.1010	0.1498	0.2163	0.3050	0.4211	0.5708	0.7611
45	0.0605	0.0939	0.1410	0.2060	0.2936	0.4096	0.5607	0.7545
50	0.0560	0.0879	0.1336	0.1972	0.2838	0.3996	0.5518	0.7486
55	0.0522	0.0829	0.1272	0.1895	0.2753	0.3908	0.5438	0.7434
60	0.0489	0.0785	0.1216	0.1828	0.2676	0.3829	0.5367	0.7386
65	0.0461	0.0747	0.1167	0.1768	0.2608	0.3758	0.5302	0.7342
70	0.0437	0.0713	0.1123	0.1715	0.2547	0.3693	0.5243	0.7302
75	0.0415	0.0683	0.1084	0.1666	0.2491	0.3634	0.5188	0.7265
80	0.0396	0.0657	0.1049	0.1622	0.2440	0.3579	0.5137	0.7231
85	0.0379	0.0632	0.1017	0.1582	0.2393	0.3529	0.5090	0.7198
90	0.0363	0.0610	0.0987	0.1545	0.2349	0.3482	0.5046	0.7168
95	0.0349	0.0590	0.0960	0.1511	0.2308	0.3438	0.5005	0.7139
100	0.0336	0.0572	0.0935	0.1479	0.2271	0.3397	0.4966	0.7112
125	0.0285	0.0498	0.0834	0.1348	0.2113	0.3224	0.4800	0.6996
150	0.0249	0.0444	0.0759	0.1250	0.1993	0.3089	0.4669	0.6902
175	0.0222	0.0404	0.0701	0.1172	0.1896	0.2979	0.4561	0.6824
200	0.0201	0.0371	0.0655	0.1109	0.1816	0.2887	0.4469	0.6757
225	0.0185	0.0345	0.0616	0.1056	0.1749	0.2809	0.4390	0.6698
250	0.0171	0.0323	0.0584	0.1011	0.1691	0.2740	0.4320	0.6646
275	0.0159	0.0305	0.0556	0.0972	0.1639	0.2680	0.4258	0.6599
300	0.0149	0.0289	0.0531	0.0937	0.1594	0.2625	0.4202	0.6557
350	0.0133	0.0262	0.0491	0.0879	0.1517	0.2532	0.4105	0.6482
400	0.0121	0.0241	0.0458	0.0832	0.1453	0.2454	0.4022	0.6419
450	0.0111	0.0224	0.0431	0.0792	0.1399	0.2387	0.3951	0.6363
500	0.0103	0.0210	0.0408	0.0758	0.1352	0.2329	0.3888	0.6314
550	0.0096	0.0198	0.0389	0.0729	0.1312	0.2278	0.3832	0.6269
600	0.0090	0.0188	0.0372	0.0703	0.1275	0.2232	0.3782	0.6229
650	0.0085	0.0179	0.0357	0.0680	0.1243	0.2190	0.3736	0.6192
700	0.0080	0.0171	0.0344	0.0659	0.1214	0.2152	0.3694	0.6158
750	0.0076	0.0163	0.0332	0.0641	0.1187	0.2118	0.3656	0.6127
800	0.0073	0.0157	0.0321	0.0624	0.1163	0.2086	0.3620	0.6098
850	0.0069	0.0151	0.0311	0.0608	0.1140	0.2057	0.3587	0.6070
900	0.0067	0.0146	0.0302	0.0594	0.1119	0.2029	0.3556	0.6045

TABLE 6.4

Table of Unit Values for Learning Curves

TABLE 6.5

TABLE 6.5

Table of
Cumulative
Values for
Learning Curves

x p	.60	.65	.70	.75	.80	.85	.90	.95
1	1.0000	1.0000	1.0000	1.0000	1.0000	1.0000	1.0000	1.0000
2	1.6000	1.6500	1.7000	1.7500	1.8000	1.8500	1.9000	1.9500
3	2.0450	2.1552	2.2682	2.3838	2.5021	2.6229	2.7462	2.8719
4	2.4050	2.5777	2.7582	2.9463	3.1421	3.3454	3.5562	3.7744
5	2.7104	2.9455	3.1950	3.4591	3.7377	4.0311	4.3392	4.6621
6	2.9774	3.2739	3.5928	3.9345	4.2994	4.6881	5.1008	5.5380
7	3.2158	3.5723	3.9601	4.3804	4.8339	5.3217	5.8447	6.4039
8	3.4318	3.8469	4.3031	4.8022	5.3459	5.9358	6.5737	7.2612
9	3.6298	4.1021	4.6260	5.2040	5.8389	6.5332	7.2898	8.1112
10	3.8131	4.3412	4.9318	5.5886	6.3154	7.1161	7.9945	8.9545
11	3.9839	4.5665	5.2229	5.9582	6.7775	7.6860	8.6890	9.7919
12	4.1441	4.7800	5.5013	6.3147	7.2268	8.2444	9.3745	10.6239
13	4.2951	4.9831	5.7685	6.6596	7.6647	8.7925	10.0516	11.4511
14	4.4381	5.1770	6.0257	6.9940	8.0923	9.3311	10.7212	12.2736
15	4.5740	5.3628	6.2739	7.3190	8.5105	9.8611	11.3837	13.0921
16	4.7036	5.5413	6.5140	7.6355	8.9201	10.3831	12.0398	13.9066
17	4.8276	5.7132	6.7467	7.9440	9.3218	10.8977	12.6899	14.7174
18	4.9464	5.8791	6.9727	8.2453	9.7162	11.4055	13.3344	15.5249
19	5.0606	6.0396	7.1925	8.5399	10.1037	11.9069	13.9735	16.3291
20	5.1705	6.1950	7.4065	8.8284	10.4849	12.4023	14.6078	17.1302
21	5.2766	6.3457	7.6153	9.1110	10.8602	12.8920	15.2373	17.9285
22	5.3791	6.4922	7.8191	9.3882	11.2299	13.3765	15.8624	18.7241
23	5.4783	6.6346	8.0183	9.6604	11.5943	13.8559	16.4833	19.5170
24	5.5744	6.7734	8.2132	9.9278	11.9538	14.3306	17.1002	20.3074
25	5.6677	6.9086	8.4040	10.1907	12.3086	14.8007	17.7132	21.0955
30	6.0974	7.5398	9.3050	11.4458	14.0199	17.0907	20.7269	25.0032
35	6.4779	8.1095	10.1328	12.6179	15.6428	19.2938	23.6660	28.8636
40	6.8208	8.6312	10.9024	13.7232	17.1935	21.4252	26.5427	32.6838
45	7.1337	9.1143	11.6245	14.7731	18.6835	23.4955	29.3658	36.4692
50	7.4222	9.5654	12.3069	15.7761	20.1217	25.5131	32.1420	40.2239
55	7.6904	9.9896	12.9553	16.7386	21.5147	27.4843	34.8766	43.9511
60	7.9413	10.3906	13.5742	17.6658	22.8678	29.4143	37.5740	47.6535
65	8.1774	10.7715	14.1674	18.5617	24.1853	31.3071	40.2377	51.3333
70	8.4006	11.1347	14.7376	19.4296	25.4708	33.1664	42.8706	54.9924
75	8.6123	11.4823	15.2874	20.2722	26.7273	34.9949	45.4753	58.6323
80	8.8140	11.8158	15.8188	21.0921	27.9572	36.7953	48.0539	62.2544
85	9.0067	12.1367	16.3335	21.8910	29.1628	38.5696	50.6082	65.8599
90	9.1912	12.4461	16.8329	22.6708	30.3459	40.3198	53.1399	69.4498
95	9.3683	12.7451	17.3182	23.4329	31.5081	42.0474	55.6504	73.0250
100	9.5388	13.0345	17.7907	24.1786	32.6508	43.7539	58.1410	76.5864
125	10.3079	14.3614	19.9894	27.6971	38.1131	52.0109	70.3315	94.2095
150	10.9712	15.5326	21.9722	30.9342	43.2335	59.8883	82.1558	111.5730
175	11.5576	16.5883	23.7917	33.9545	48.0859	67.4633	93.6839	128.7232
200	12.0853	17.5541	25.4820	36.8007	52.700	74.7885	104.9641	145.6931
225	12.5665	18.4477	27.0669	39.5029	57.1712	81.9021	116.0319	162.5066
250	13.0098	19.2816	28.5638	42.0833	61.4659	88.8328	126.9144	179.1824
275	13.4216	20.0653	29.9855	44.5588	65.6246	95.6028	137.6327	195.7354
300	13.8068	20.8059	31.3423	46.9427	69.6634	102.2301	148.2040	212.1774
350	14.5112	22.1796	33.8916	51.4760	77.4311	115.1123	168.9593	244.7667
400	15.1451	23.4362	36.2596	55.7477	84.8487	127.5691	189.2677	277.0124
450	15.7230	24.5987	38.4799	59.8030	91.9733	139.6656	209.1935	308.9609
500	16.2555	25.6835	40.5766	63.6753	98.8473	151.4506	228.7851	340.6475
550	16.7500	26.7028	42.5680	67.3900	105.5032	162.9622	248.0809	372.1002
600	17.2125	27.6662	44.4684	70.9671	111.9671	174.2309	267.1118	403.3421
650	17.6474	28.5808	46.2889	74.4225	118.2598	185.2815	285.9030	434.3918
700	18.0583	29.4528	48.0387	77.7693	124.3985	196.1346	304.4757	465.2653
750	18.4482	30.2869	49.7254	81.0183	130.3976	206.8073	322.8479	495.9759
800	18.8193	31.0871	51.3552	84.1786	136.2693	217.3144	341.0347	526.5353
850	19.1737	31.8568	52.9333	87.2580	142.0242	227.6687	359.0497	556.9538
900	19.5131	32.5989	54.4644	90.2631	147.6709	237.8811	376.9043	587.2402

To find the time for a cumulative number of units, we can use Table 6.5. Thus for a 90 percent learning curve, if the time for the first unit is 3500, the time for the first 25 units is 3500(17. 7132) = 61,996. Similarly, the time for the first 100 units would be 3500(58.1410) = 203,494. The values in Table 6.3 were found using this table.

Learning curves can apply to individual operators or in an aggregate sense to the entire process for a new product. Often the terms *improvement curve, experience curve,* or *manufacturing progress function* are used to describe the learning phenomenon in the aggregate context. These curves can be used for cost estimating and pricing, short-term work scheduling, setting manufacturing performance goals, and determining incentive payments for piecework employees. From a strategic perspective, a firm may use the learning curve concept to establish a pricing schedule that does not initially cover cost in order to gain increased market share.

Managers should realize that improvement along a learning curve does not take place automatically. Learning curve theory is more applicable to new products or processes that have a high potential for improvement and the benefits will only be realized when appropriate incentives and effective motivational tools are used. Organizational changes may also have significant effects on learning. Changes in technology or work methods will affect the learning curve, as will the institution of productivity and quality improvement programs.

We summarize this subsection by listing a number of factors that may affect the applicability of the learning curve and/or the amount of learning that takes place.

1. The learning curve does not usually apply to supervisory personnel, skilled craftspeople, or jobs that have nonrepetitive job tasks.
2. A change in the ratio of indirect labor or supervisory talent to direct labor can alter the rate of learning.
3. The institution of incentive systems, bonus plans, zero defect programs, and so on may increase learning.
4. Changes in product design, raw material usage, and/or the production process may significantly alter the learning curve.
5. A contract phaseout may result in a lengthening of production times for the last units produced since employees want to prolong their income period.
6. The lack of proper maintenance of tools and equipment, the nonreplacement of tools, or the aging of equipment can have a negative impact on learning.
7. The transfer of employees may result in the interruption or the regressing back to an earlier stage of the learning curve, or may result in the necessity to begin a new learning curve.

P/OM IN PRACTICE

In this section three examples are presented which illustrate the resource-requirements planning process. In the first example, the process of strategic resource planning at Pfizer, Inc., and the Dow Corning Corporation are discussed. In the second example, we discuss how Champion International

Corporation carried out a study to investigate whether or not it would be worthwhile to invest in improvements to increase the capacity at one of their major pulp and paper facilities. The third example discusses how Recording for the Blind, a national nonprofit service organization, conducted a resource-requirements planning project to examine client needs, resources, and costs.

RESOURCE REQUIREMENTS PLANNING AT PFIZER AND DOW CORNING[2]

O ur first example of resource-requirements planning involves the Easton, Pennsylvania, plant of Pfizer, Inc., which is in Pfizer's Minerals, Pigments, and Metal Division. This plant has annual sales of approximately $15 million, producing iron oxides for pigment, ferrite, magnetic, and other applications. The products are industrial raw materials used in paints, plastics, food, cosmetics, magnetic inks, recording tapes, and other products. The two primary uses are for coloring and for magnetic properties.

The plant employs approximately 250 people and runs 24 hours per day, 7 days per week. The plant produces only 50 end-items, 30 of which account for approximately 90 percent of the volume. The products are produced to stock, with typical inventory levels of 8 weeks finished goods, 4 weeks work-in-process, and 5 weeks raw materials. Total customer-booked orders is typically 3 weeks. About 90 percent of the shipping dates are specified by the customer, and the plant is expected to meet these dates at least 95 percent of the time.

The long-term planning for plant facilities is done on a divisional basis. A computer model converts forecasted product demand over a 10-year horizon into capacity needs by type of production process. These needs are matched against current plant capacities so that capacity additions and cash requirements can be planned. The end result is a pro forma cash flow and profit-loss statement. Changes in the timing of capital additions are tested iteratively, as are different assumptions about the marketplace. This analysis is performed annually, and the result is the long-range resource plan.

The second example of strategic resource planning is for Dow Corning Corporation, a multinaland, Michigan. The company produces silicone materials for both industrial and commercial applications.

Silicones are a unique family of chemical compounds not found in the natural state that exceed the performance of natural synthetic carbon-base polymers. Silicone compounds commonly take the form of fluids, rubber, or plastic resin. The industrial market served by Dow Corning includes applications in manufacturing processes such as silicone fluids, emulsions, rubbers, sealants, and so on. The commercial market served by Dow Corning includes such products as Dow Corning® Bathtub Caulk, Sight Savers® eyeglass cleaners, heat shields for spacecraft, and surgical devices (for example, pacemakers, finger joints for arthritis, and drain valves). In total, the domestic plants produce 4000 packaged end products (including the packaging alternatives), of which 640 represent 90 percent of the sales dollars.

Dow Corning prepares a long-range estimate of production equipment needs covering a 5-year period. This plan is expressed in terms of similar product family groupings called PTUs (process train units). These PTU groupings are not market based, but rather are established by identifying a family of products that have a unique initial raw materials and a common set of processing equipment requirements. In the domestic plants, there are 200 PTU groupings, which aggregate the 4000 product-packaged combinations and 1400 end-product types. These estimates of equipment processing capacities

[2]Adapted from W. L. Berry, T. E. Vollmann, and D. C. Whybark, *Master Production Scheduling: Principles and Practice,* American Production and Inventory Control Society, 1979. Reprinted by permission.

are based on projections of the PTU production rates for individual plants which are prepared by the production planner.

The process involves extrapolating the resource requirements of a given plan using planning ratios between PTUs and resources. The resource plan serves as the basis for the preparation of the long-run capital budget at Dow Corning.

QUESTION

1. What are the differences in Pfizer's approach to resource-requirements planning versus Dow Corning's approach?

PRODUCTION CAPACITY ANALYSIS AT CHAMPION INTERNATIONAL[3]

C hampion International Corporation is one of the largest forest products companies in the world, employing over 41,000 people in the United States, Canada, and Brazil. Champion manages over 3 million acres of timberlands in the United States. Its objective is to maximize the return of the timber base by converting trees into three basic product groups: (1) building materials, such as lumber and plywood; (2) white paper products, including printing and writing grades of white paper; (3) brown paper products, such as liner-board and corrugated containers. Given the highly competitive markets within the forest products industry, survival dictates that Champion must maintain its position as a low-cost producer of quality products. This requires an ambitious capital program to improve the timber base and to build additional modern, cost-effective timber conversion facilities.

An integrated pulp and paper mill is a facility in which wood chips and chemicals are processed in order to produce paper products or dried pulp. To begin with, wood chips are cooked and bleached in the pulp mill; the resulting pulp is piped directly into storage tanks, as shown in Figure 6.9. From the storage tanks the pulp is sent to either the paper mill or a dryer. In the paper mill, the pulp is routed to one or more paper machines which produce the finished paper products. Alternatively, the pulp is sent to a dryer, and the dried pulp is then sold to other paper mills, which do not have the capability of producing their own pulp. The total system, referred to as an integrated pulp and paper mill, is a large facility costing several hundred million dollars.

One of Champion's major pulp and paper facilities is presently comprised of a pulp mill, three paper machines, and a dryer. As the facility developed, it was found that the pulp mill could produce more pulp than the combination of paper machines and the dryer could use. A study was undertaken to determine whether it would be worthwhile to

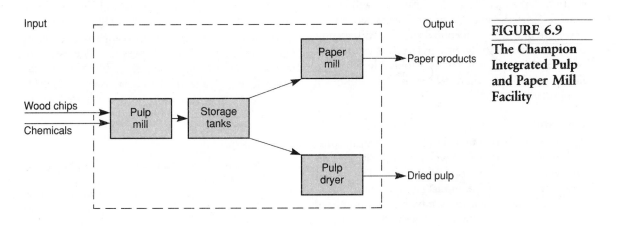

FIGURE 6.9

The Champion Integrated Pulp and Paper Mill Facility

[3]The authors express their appreciation to Bill Griggs and Walter Foody of Champion International for providing this application.

invest in improvements to increase the capacity of the dryer. One of the first questions to be answered in the study was how much additional pulp could be produced and dried, given each possible capacity increase on the dryer.

A simple approach to this question is to look at average flows. For example, the pulp mill has a capacity of 940 tons per day (TPD), the three paper machines together average 650 TPD of pulp use, and the dryer can handle 200 TPD. Based on average flows for each ton of increased dryer capacity, we can produce one more ton of pulp in the pulp mill. Note, however, that this is true only until the capacity of the dryer reaches 290 TPD, after which further improvements to the dryer will have no benefit.

The above analysis is inadequate because it ignores the day-to-day deviations from the average. That is, all of the equipment in the mill is subject to downtime and to variations in efficiency. For example, suppose that on one day, the pulp mill is inoperable for more than the average length of time; on the same day, the paper machines are experiencing less than the usual downtime. In this case there will be very little pulp available for the dryer, regardless of its capacity. This lack of pulp will not "average out" on days when the opposite conditions occur, since there will be far more pulp available than the pulp dryer can handle. Consequently, the pulp storage tanks will become full, and the pulp mill will have to shut down.

Based upon the above analysis, we can conclude that in order not to reduce the production on the paper machines, the ratio of additional pulp production to the increase in dryer capacity will be less than 1. Since the benefits of any investment in the dryer are directly proportional to this ratio, a computer simulation study was undertaken in order to estimate this ratio as precisely as possible. The simulation model that was developed had the following components:

Pulp Mill

The pulp mill was assumed to have an average production rate of 1044 TPD when it is operating, with an average of 10 percent downtime. The actual downtime used in the model in each time period simulated was drawn randomly from a sample of actual downtimes experienced by the pulp mill over several months. Thus one day the pulp mill might be down 2 percent of the time, the next day 20 percent and so on.

Paper Machine

The rate of pulp flow to the paper machines in a time period is a function of the particular type of paper being made and the amount of downtime on the paper machines. In the simulation, the rate of pulp flow was input to the model based on a typical schedule of types of paper to be made. The downtime for each machine was drawn from a sample of actual downtimes.

Pulp Dryer

In each run of the model, downtime on the dryer was drawn from a sample of actual downtimes. The capacity of the dryer was set at different levels in different runs.

Storage Tanks

The connecting link between the pulp mill, the paper machines, and the dryer is the pulp storage tanks. In the model, all pulp produced by the pulp mill is added to the inventory in these tanks. All pulp drawn by the dryer and paper machines is subtracted from this inventory. If the storage tanks are empty, the model must shut down the paper machines. If the tanks are full, the pulp mill must be shut down. The actual rate at which the dryer is operated at any moment must be set by the model (as it is in reality) to try to keep the storage tanks from becoming "too empty" or "too full."

A computer program was developed to simulate the above process. The simulation program was run at various levels of dryer capacity. The simulation results showed that for every TPD of additional pulp capacity, approximately 0.8 TPD of additional pulp could actually be dried without reducing the production on the paper machines. This number was then used by management in comparing the costs and benefits of the capital investment necessary to increase the pulp dryer capacity. Note that if the "average basis" analysis had been used, the benefits of the project would have been overstated by 25 percent.

QUESTIONS

1. Briefly describe the function of an integrated pulp and paper facility.
2. What is the primary reason why Champion conducted a study of its integrated pulp and paper facility?
3. Why is an analysis of average flows inadequate in comparing the costs and benefits of expanding the pulp dryer capacity?

RESOURCE-REQUIREMENTS PLANNING IN A NONPROFIT SERVICE ORGANIZATION[4]

R ecording for the Blind is a national nonprofit service organization that provides recorded educational books on a no charge basis to blind and physically and perceptually handicapped students and professionals. Because the capacity of its former New York location was limited and insufficient for future expansion, the organization moved in 1983 to a new modern-design one-level facility in Princeton, New Jersey. This move led to the design and implementation of an updated, integrated production system utilizing high-technology automated material handling.

A resource-requirements planning project was undertaken to examine present and future client needs, resources, availability of technology, labor requirements, and capital and operational costs. With demand increasing at 8 to 9 percent per year and only 16 percent of its budget coming from federal funds, cost savings was a primary goal. A second goal was to reduce the lead time for duplicating a book and processing an order.

Figure 6.10 shows that the demand pattern for books is seasonal, with peaks in January, June, and September. Low-demand months can be utilized to balance yearly production capacity needs. A standby library was created to store multiple copies of pre-duplicated best sellers. However, only a limited inventory is possible. Five percent of the titles constitute 50 percent of the demand, whereas 95 percent are in a bracket of highly random demand pattern.

To define total capacity requirements for calculating the work-station loads and labor needs, a 3-year (1980–82) demand pattern was analyzed. A production capacity requirement of 450 books per day was established for 1984–85. With a given 95 percent productivity, this yields an average of 427 books/day. The calculations were based on a demand trend of 88 percent growth per year (see Figure 6.11). The actual performance before the move was standing at 74 percent productivity (333 books per day in 1982) with 39 production-line employees. The new system had to provide, at the same cost per book or less, an increase of 28 percent in the daily production average.

New automated equipment and system integra-

tion were the key elements in achieving the organization's objectives. For example, an automated storage and retrieval system was designed for rapid access to the 20,000 most active titles; conveyors were designed to connect all work stations; tape-duplicating machines were modified to double their

FIGURE 6.10 Recording for the Blind Demand Pattern: 5 Years' Average Demand Per Month

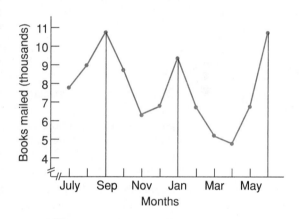

FIGURE 6.11 RFB's Demand Projections to 1990

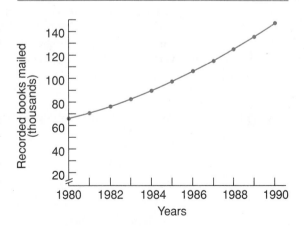

[4]Joseph G. Jarkon and Ravinder Nanda, "Resource Requirement Planning Achieves Production Goals for Non-Profit Organization." Reprinted from *Industrial Engineering* magazine, Oct 1985. Copyright Institute of Industrial Engineers, 25 Technology Park/Atlanta, Norcross, GA 30092.

FIGURE 6.12 Books Produced and Cost Per Book

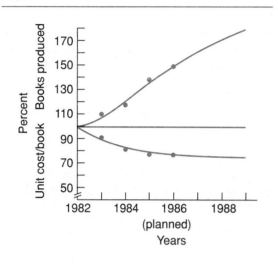

speed; and automated sorting equipment with laser scanners was proposed for use in restocking returned items.

After 2 years' experience with the new system, Recording for the Blind experienced a 21 percent productivity improvement, enabling them to provide 27 percent more books in 1985 than in 1983. Unit costs were reduced by 16 percent and 97 percent of orders were mailed no more than five working days from receipt. These statistics and expected trends are summarized in Figure 6.12.

QUESTIONS

1. Explain how Recording for the Blind determined the production capacity necessary for 1984–85.
2. What actions did Recording for the Blind take that led to a 21 percent productivity increase by 1985? How is productivity measured?

SUMMARY

Resource-requirements planning is the process of determining the types and amounts of resources that are required to implement an organization's strategic plan. Its goal is to determine the appropriate level of production capacity to meet future product demand. This includes determining the proper amount of facilities, equipment, and labor.

Capacity is formally defined as the highest reasonable output rate which can be achieved with the current product specifications, product mix, work force, plant, and equipment. Capacity is measured as either output per unit of time or as units of input. Capacity decisions involve the amount and timing of capacity changes. Capacity strategy is closely tied to customer service goals and long-run profitability and must be carefully addressed. In service organizations it is important that sufficient capacity be built into the design of the facility since capacity cannot be inventoried the same as manufactured goods.

The learning curve provides a means of estimating labor requirements and capacity when learning occurs; however, caution must be taken when using it as various factors can affect its applicability.

KEY TERMS

Resource-requirements planning
Capacity
Efficiency
Learning curve

**REVIEW/
DISCUSSION
QUESTIONS**

1. What is *resource-requirements planning?* Discuss the important issues that are considered in resource-requirements planning.

2. Outline the resource-requirements planning process, focusing on its hierarchical nature.

3. What is the APICS definition of *capacity*?

4. What is the difference between *design capacity* and *effective capacity*?

5. Explain the difference between *efficiency* and *utilization*.

6. Discuss the differences between input measures of capacity and output measures of capacity. Provide some examples of each that are different from Table 6.1.

7. Define capacity measures for
   a. a brewery
   b. a police precinct
   c. a movie theater
   d. a restaurant

8. What is a *bottleneck* in a production process?

9. How can the product life cycle be used for capacity planning?

10. What issues are involved in planning capacity changes? Discuss the common strategies used for capacity expansion.

11. How does capacity planning differ between manufacturing and service organizations?

12. Discuss the important issues involved in facility planning.

13. Explain the principle behind the learning curve. What are some applications of the learning curve?

14. What factors may affect the applicability of the learning curve or the amount of learning that takes place?

15. In using decision analysis for facility expansion (see the chapter supplement), the expected monetary value criterion assumes that decisions are made repeatedly. In practice, facility expansion is only a one-time decision. Comment on the interpretation of decision analysis information in light of these observations.

PROBLEMS

1. The roller coaster at Treasure Island Amusement Park consists of 15 cars, each of which can carry up to 3 passengers. If each run takes 1.5 minutes and the time to unload and load riders is 3.5 minutes, what is the maximum capacity of the system in number of passengers per hour? Would the actual capacity observed actually equal this value? Explain.

2. An automobile transmission-assembly plant normally operates one shift per day, 5 days per week. During each shift, 400 transmissions can be completed. Over the next 4 weeks, the plant has planned shipments according to the following schedule:

Week	1	2	3	4
Shipments	1800	1700	2200	2100

   a. What is the normal capacity?
   b. At what percent of capacity is the plant actually operating?

3. A grocery store has five regular checkout lines and one express line (12 items or less). Based on a sampling study, it takes 11 minutes on the average for

a customer to go through the regular line and 4 minutes to go through the express line. This store is open from 9 A.M. to 9 P.M. daily.

a. What is the store's maximum capacity?
b. What is the capacity if the number of regular checkout lines operating is according to the following schedule? (The express line is always open.)

Hour/Day	Mon	Tue	Wed	Thur	Fri	Sat	Sun
9–12	1	1	1	1	3	5	2
12–4	2	2	2	2	3	5	4
4–6	3	3	3	3	5	3	2
6–9	4	4	4	4	5	3	1

4. The double chair lift at Whiteface Mountain Ski Resort carries two skiers in each chair to the top of the beginner's slope in 2 minutes. The time between loading skiers on one chair until the time the skiers are loaded on the following chair is 15 seconds.

a. What is the normal capacity of the system expressed in terms of number of skiers per hour?
b. If approximately 10 percent of the time only one skier gets on the chair being loaded, will this affect the capacity of the system? Explain.
c. Frequently it is necessary to stop the chair lift temporarily in order to assist beginning skiers in safely getting on and off the chair lift. How could the ski resort's operations manager assess the effect of this situation on the capacity of the lift?

5. A small manufacturer estimates that the demand for a product (in thousands of units) over the next 5 years will be as follows.

Year	1	2	3	4	5
Demand	114	129	131	134	133

Currently the manufacturer has eight machines which work on a 2-shift basis. Twenty days are available for scheduled maintenance of equipment. Each item takes 26 minutes to produce.

a. What is the normal capacity?
b. At what levels will the firm be operating over the next 5 years?
c. If demand above 20 percent of normal capacity for 2 consecutive years warrants purchase of new machines, how many should the firm acquire?

6. A company manufactures 4 products on 3 machines. The production schedule for the next 6 months is given below.

Product	Jan	Feb	Mar	Apr	May	Jun
1	200	0	200	0	200	0
2	100	100	100	100	100	100
3	50	50	50	50	50	50
4	100	0	100	0	100	0

The number of hours each product requires on each machine is given in the following table:

Machine	Product 1	2	3	4
1	0.25	0.15	0.15	0.25
2	0.33	0.2	0.3	0.50
3	0.20	0.3	0.25	0.10

Set up times are roughly 20% of the operation times. The number of machine hours available during the six months are as follows:

Machine	Jan	Feb	Mar	Apr	May	Jun
1	120	60	60	60	60	60
2	180	60	180	60	180	60
3	120	60	120	60	120	60

Determine if there is enough capacity to meet the product demand.

7. Xtech, Inc., makes and sells electronic testing equipment in the industrial market. The two products, called Microtester and Macrotester, are assembled from two components: C1 and C2. Each Microtester is assembled from 2 C1s and 1 C2; each Macrotester is assembled from 2 C1s and 3 C2s. Three machines are used in the production of components C1 and C2. Component C1 requires 1½ hours on machine 1, 2 hours on machine 2, and 1 hour on machine 3. Component C2 requires 1 hour on machine 1, 1½ hours on machine 2, and 3 hours on machine 3. Xtech is projecting annual demand of 3000 units of the Microtester and 2000 units of the Macrotester. Planning is now underway for additional equipment. In particular, management wants to know how many of each of the machines are needed. Experience with the three machines suggests utilization rates of .97, .95, and .92 for machines 1, 2, and 3 respectively. The firm is planning a single shift operation which provides 2000 working hours per year. How many machines of each type are required?

8. A plant manufactures three products, A, B, and C. A drill press is required to perform one operation for each product. Machine operators work at a 75 percent efficiency, and the machines themselves have a 90 percent efficiency. The plant operates one shift, 5 days per week. The operation times for each product are as follows:

Product	A	B	C
Operation Time (Minutes)	5.0	1.85	7.0

Determine the amount of equipment and number of machine operators needed in order to produce 10,000 units per month.

9. Mary Johnson, the tax assessor for Yates County, has estimated that her office must perform 200 property reevaluations per day. Each staff member

assigned to the reevaluation will work an 8-hour day. If it takes a staff member 10 minutes to do a reevaluation and the efficiency of any staff member is .75, how many staff members must be assigned to this project?

10. JR's Income Tax Service is determining its staffing requirements for the next income tax season. Income tax preparers work 50 hours per week from January 15 through April 15. There are two major tasks: preparation of short forms and preparation of long forms. The normal time to prepare a short form is 15 minutes; long forms take 50 minutes if all records are in order. Fifteen percent of customers using the long form have complicated problems that require approximately ½ hour of additional work. The usual mix of customers requiring long versus short forms is 40–60. A personal allowance of 15 percent is given over the 3-month period. JR expects 1000, 3500, and 5000 customers for each of these three months. How many preparers are needed each month to meet this demand?

11. The process for renewing a driver's license at the Archer County Courthouse is as follows:
    1. Fill out application by clerk.
    2. Get picture taken.
    3. Type and process new license.

    It takes an average of 5 minutes to fill out an application, 1 minute to get a picture taken, and 7 minutes to type and process the new license.
    a. If there are 2 clerks and 3 typists, where will the bottleneck in the system be? How many drivers can be processed in 1 hour if the clerks and typists work at 80 percent efficiency?
    b. If 50 drivers are to be processed each hour, how many clerks and typists should be hired?

12. The consumer loan division of a major bank would like to determine the size of the staff they would need in order to be able to process up to 200 loan applications per day. It is estimated that each loan officer can process a loan application in approximately 20 minutes. If the efficiency of a loan officer is .8 and each loan officer works 7 hours each day, how many loan officers would be needed to handle this volume of business?

13. A sporting goods firm has been commissioned to build five sailboats for a Florida resort. The first boat took 6000 labor-hours to build. How many labor-hours will it take to complete the order, assuming that a 90 percent learning curve is applicable? Draw graphs of time per boat and cumulative production time as a function of the number of boats produced.

14. Suppose that a manufacturer of copiers has concluded that a 70 percent learning curve is applicable for the time it takes a beginning service technician to install a copy machine. If the time required to install the first copy machine is estimated to be 4 hours, what is an estimate of the time required by a new technician to install their second and third copiers?

15. A manufacturer has committed to supply 16 units of a particular product in 4 months (i.e., 16 weeks) at a price of $30,000 each. The first unit took 1000 hours to produce. Even though the second unit took only 750 hours to produce, the manufacturer is anxious to know
    a. If the delivery committment of 16 weeks will be met

b. Whether enough labor is available (presently 500 hours were available per week)

c. Whether or not the venture is profitable.

Use learning-curve theory to answer each of these issues. Assume that the material cost per unit = $22,000, labor = $10 per manhour, and overhead = $2000 per week.

16. Operating at an 80 percent learning rate, the first unit took 72 hours to produce. How long will the 32nd unit take?

17. Given the following data:

$$
\begin{array}{ll}
\text{fixed costs for one shift} & = \$60,000 \\
\text{unit variable cost} & = \$7 \\
\text{selling price} & = \$12 \\
\text{number of machines} & = 5 \\
\text{number of working days in year} & = 340 \\
\text{processing time per unit} & = 60 \text{ minutes.}
\end{array}
$$

a. What is the capacity with a single shift?

b. What is the capacity with two shifts? The additional fixed cost for a second shift is $40,000.

c. What is the break-even volume with a single shift operation?

d. What is the maximum revenue with a single shift?

e. What is the break-even volume with a two-shift operation?

f. Draw the break-even chart.

CASE PROBLEM[5]

The Bethesda Hospitals of Cincinnati include Bethesda Oak Hospital, located near the center of the city of Cincinnati, and Bethesda North Hospital, which was built to meet the needs of the population to the north of the city. As part of the strategic planning process, a long-range plan for 1982–87 was developed. The overall goal was stated as maintaining the strength of current operations and continuing to broaden the scope of Bethesda's health-care system. The corporate objectives were threefold:

1. Maintain and improve current services and develop new hospital-based services.
2. Continue to expand the scope of Bethesda's health-care system by diversifying into other health-related services and by acquiring, merging with, managing, or developing affiliations with other health-care organizations.
3. Provide high-quality services at the most reasonable possible cost.

To meet these objectives, some specific goals were defined:

I. *Maintain and Develop Hospital-Based Services*
   A. Medical/Surgical Services—High Priority. Continue to improve existing medical/surgical services, as well as develop new ones in response to community needs. At Oak, it is vital to maintain the volume of routine medical/surgical care along with development of specialty services. At

---

[5]The authors are indebted to E. Anthony Woods for providing the information in this case.

North, growth will be planned as aggressively as financially prudent in order to meet needs of the expanding population in the suburban service area. Comprehensive planning will be undertaken to ensure orderly expansion of North. A major new program in open-heart surgery is also possible.

    B. Cancer Treatment—High Priority. Develop state-of-the-art multidisciplinary cancer treatment program to make cancer care one of the major strategic strengths of Bethesda Oak.

    C. Obstetrics Services—High Priority. Increase Bethesda's share of local obstetrics market and the percentage of patients with private insurance.

    D. Outpatient Services—High Priority. Develop outpatient services at both Oak and North to meet community needs. Major emphasis will be devoted to development of new outpatient facility at North.

    E. Alcoholism Treatment—Medium Priority. Implement treatment program at North.

    F. Mental Health—Medium Priority. Maximize use of existing inpatient psychiatric facilities and develop additional programs to support inpatient treatment.

    G. Geriatric Services—Medium Priority. Implement plan to upgrade facilities and improve financial performance. Develop additional hospital-related geriatric programs as interest within the medical staff grows. Provide these services at reasonable cost.

II. *Expand the Scope of Bethesda's Health-Care System*

    A. Arrangements with Other Health-Care Organizations—High Priority. Seek customers or partners among other health-care organizations for acquisitions, management contracts, shared services, joint ventures, or affiliations.

    B. Sale of Services—Medium Priority. Sell existing or specially developed health services to new customers. These services may include consulting, shared services, clinical services (including laboratory), and health promotion.

    C. Ambulatory Care—High Priority. Coordinate ambulatory care programs into a system that will become a significant source of referrals for Bethesda's hospitals and their medical staffs.

III. *Organizational & Management Development*

    A. Management Development—High Priority.

        1. Develop financial and information systems necessary to operate in a price sensitive competitive environment.

        2. Increase government and community involvement.

        3. Develop management personnel to meet the needs of the organization as it grows. Develop programs to internally train nursing and other health professional personnel to meet the organization's needs.

        4. Evaluate desirability of reorganizing into holding company organization.

    B. Medical Staff Development—High Priority.

        1. Maintain active, well-balanced medical staff. Construct professional office buildings at Oak and North.

2. Continue efforts to develop a residency program affiliated with the University of Cincinnati.

C. Prepaid Insurance Plans—Medium Priority. Monitor development of IPA and HMO insurance plans. Keep medical staff aware of trends in this field. Investigate options for participating in prepaid plans should the Medicare voucher system be adopted.

Discuss how resource requirements planning might be carried out for the Bethesda Hospitals in response to these objectives. Be specific in defining the data and information that need to be obtained, what alternatives management might need to consider, and the expected outcomes of the planning process.

SUPPLEMENT TO CHAPTER 6
DECISION ANALYSIS

R esource-requirements planning involves a large amount of uncertainty, particularly with regard to future demand. **Decision analysis** is a technique that can be used to determine optimal strategies when a decision-maker is faced with several decision alternatives and an uncertain or risk-filled pattern of future events.

Thus, decision analysis is often applied to problems such as strategic resource planning. In this supplement we will introduce the basic concepts and procedures associated with decision analysis, using a capacity expansion problem to illustrate the methodology.

THE EDMUND CHEMICALS COMPANY CAPACITY EXPANSION PROBLEM

In order to illustrate the decision analysis approach, let us consider the problem facing the Edmund Chemicals Company. Edmund Chemicals is a medium-size producer of a variety of industrial chemical products. The company has recently perfected a new synthetic industrial lubricant that will increase tool life for machining operations in metal-fabrication industries. A new plant will be necessary to produce the lubricant on a large scale; however, an expansion of existing facilities will allow production on a smaller scale basis. The management of the company is uncertain about which decision to choose. Clearly, the best decision will depend on future demand. If the demand for the product is high, then the expansion alternative will not provide enough capacity to meet all the demand and profits will be lost. If demand is low and a new plant is built, the excess capacity will substantially reduce the return on investment. With an unstable economy, it is difficult to predict actual demand for the product.

Formulating the Decision Problem

In decision analysis terminology, the future events that are not under the control of the decision maker are

referred to as the **states of nature**. In the Edmund Chemicals example, the two states of nature correspond to a low or a high product acceptance. It is assumed that the list of possible states of nature includes everything that can happen and that the individual states of nature do not overlap; that is, the states of nature are defined so that one and only one of the listed states of nature will occur.

Let

d_1 = decision to expand the existing plant

d_2 = decision to build a new plant

and

s_1 = state of nature corresponding to low-product demand

s_2 = state of nature corresponding to high-product demand

Given the two decision alternatives (d_1, d_2) and the two states of nature (s_1, s_2), which decision should Edmund Chemicals make? In order to answer this question we need information on the profit associated with each combination of a decision alternative and a state of nature. For example, what profit would Edmund Chemicals experience if the firm decided to expand the existing plant (d_1) and product demand was low (s_2)?

We refer to the outcome resulting from making a certain decision and the occurrence of a particular state of nature as the *payoff*. Using the best information available, the management of Edmund Chemicals has estimated the profits or payoffs for the Edmund Chemicals' capacity-planning problem. These estimates are presented in Table 6S.1. A table of this form is referred to as a **payoff table**. In general, entries in a payoff table can be stated in terms of profits, costs, or any other measure of output that may be appropriate for the particular situation being analyzed. The notation that we use for the entries in the payoff table is $V(d_i, s_j)$, which denotes the payoff associated with decision alternative d_i and state of nature s_j. Using this notation, we see that $V(d_2, s_1) = \$100,000$.

Expected Monetary Value Criterion

The identification of the decision alternatives, the states of nature, and the determination of the payoff associated with each decision alternative and state of nature combination are the first three steps in the decision analysis approach. The question we now turn to is the following: How can the decision maker best utilize the information presented in the payoff table to arrive at a decision? The expected-monetary-value (EMV) criterion offers an approach that makes use of probability estimates for the states of nature.

In many situations, good probability estimates can be developed for the states of nature. The EMV criterion requires the analyst to compute the expected value for each decision alternative and then select the alternative yielding the best expected value. Let

$P(s_j)$ = probability of occurrence for state of nature s_j

N = number of possible states of nature

Since one and only one of the N states of nature can occur, the associated probabilities must satisfy the following two conditions:

TABLE 6S.1 Payoff Table for the Edmund Chemicals' Capacity-planning Problem

	States of Nature	
Decision Alternatives	Low Product Demand (s_1)	High Product Demand (s_2)
Expand existing plant (d_1)	$200,000	$300,000
Build new plant (d_2)	$100,000	$400,000

$$P(s_j) \geq 0 \qquad \text{for all states of nature } j$$

$$\sum_{j=1}^{N} P(s_j) = P(s_1) + P(s_2) + \cdots + P(s_N) = 1$$

The EMV for decision alternative d_i is given by

$$\text{EMV}(d_i) = \sum_{j=1}^{N} P(s_j) V(d_i, s_j) \qquad (6S.1)$$

In words, the EMV of a decision alternative is the sum of weighted payoffs for the alternative. The weight for a payoff is the probability of the associated state of nature and, therefore, the probability that the payoff occurs. Let us now return to the Edmund Chemicals' problem to see how the EMV criterion can be applied.

Suppose that management of Edmund Chemicals believes that the probability that market demand will be low is .4 and the probability that market demand will be high is .6. Thus $P(s_1) = .4$ and $P(s_2) = .6$. Using the payoff values $V(d_i, s_j)$ shown in Table 6S.1 and equation (6S.1), expected monetary values for the two decision alternatives can be calculated.

$$\text{EMV } (d_1) = .4 \, (200,000) + .6 \, (300,000)$$
$$= \$260,000$$
$$\text{EMV } (d_2) = .4 \, (100,000) + .6 \, (400,000)$$
$$= \$280,000$$

Thus, according to the EMV criterion, the decision to build a new plant, d_2, with an EMV of $280,000 is the recommended capacity alternative.

DECISION TREES

Although decision problems involving a modest number of decision alternatives and a modest number of states of nature can be analyzed by using payoff tables, they can also be analyzed by using a graphical representation of the decision-making process called a **decision tree**.

Figure 6S.1 shows a decision tree for the Edmund Chemicals' capacity-planning problem. Note that the tree shows the natural, or logical, progression that will occur in the decision-making process. First, the firm must make its decision (d_1 or d_2); then, once the decision is implemented, the state of nature (s_1 or s_2)

occurs. The number at each end point of the tree represents the payoff associated with a particular chain of events. For example, the topmost payoff of 200,000 arises whenever management makes the decision to expand the existing plant (d_1) and product acceptance turns out to be low (s_1). The next lower terminal point of 300,000 is reached when management makes the decision to expand the existing plant (d_1) and the true state of nature turns out to be s_2, high product acceptance. Thus we see that each possible sequence of events is represented for Edmund Chemicals on the decision tree.

Using the general terminology associated with decision trees, we refer to the intersection or junction points of the tree as **nodes** and the arcs or connectors between the nodes as **branches**. Figure 6S.2 shows the Edmund Chemicals' decision tree with the nodes num-

bered 1 to 3 and the branches labeled as decision or state-of-nature branches. When the branches *leaving* a given node are decision branches, we refer to the node as a *decision node*. Decision nodes are denoted by squares. Similarly, when the branches leaving a given node are state-of-nature branches, we refer to the node as a *state-of-nature node*. State-of-nature nodes are denoted by circles. Using this node-labeling procedure, node 1 is a decision node, whereas nodes 2 and 3 are state-of-nature nodes.

At decision nodes, the decision maker selects the particular decision branch (d_1 or d_2) that will be taken. Selecting the best branch is equivalent to making the best decision. However, the state-of-nature branches are not controlled by the decision maker; thus the specific branch followed from a state-of-nature node depends upon the probabilities associated with the branches. Using $P(s_1) = .4$ and $P(s_2) = .6$, we show the Edmund Chemicals' decision tree with state-of-nature branch probabilities in Figure 6S.3.

FIGURE 6S.1 Decision Tree for the Edmund Chemicals' Capacity-planning Problem

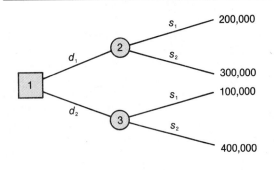

Determining an Optimal Decision Strategy

We now use the branch probabilities and the criterion of expected monetary value to arrive at the optimal decision for Edmund Chemicals. Working *backward* through the decision tree, we first compute the expected monetary value at each state-of-nature node. That is, at each state-of-nature node, we weight the possible payoffs by their chances of occurrence. The expected monetary values for nodes 2 and 3 are computed as follows:

$$\text{EMV (node 2)} = .4 (200,000) + .6 (300,000)$$
$$= 260,000$$
$$\text{EMV (node 3)} = .4 (100,000) + .6 (400,000)$$
$$= 280,000$$

FIGURE 6S.2 Decision Tree for the Edmund Chemicals Problem with Node and Branch Labels

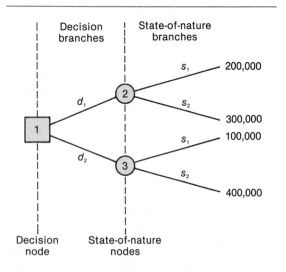

FIGURE 6S.3 Edmund Chemicals Decision Tree with State-of-nature Branch Probabilities

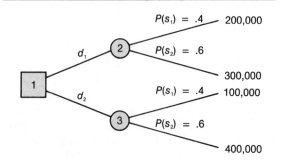

```
BEST DECISION RECOMMENDATION
*****************************

USING THE EXPECTED VALUE CRITERION

  DECISION        CRITERION      RECOMMENDED
 ALTERNATIVE        VALUE         DECISION
 **********       *********      **********

      1          260,000.00
      2          280,000.00          YES
```

FIGURE 6S.4

The Management Scientist Computer Software Solution to the Edmund Chemicals Capacity Planning Problem

We now continue backward through the tree to the decision node. Since the expected monetary values for nodes 2 and 3 are known, the decision maker can view decision node 1 as follows:

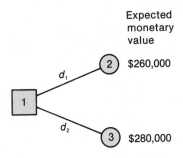

Since the decision maker controls the branch leaving a decision node and since we are trying to maximize expected monetary value, the best decision branch at node 1 is d_2. Thus the decision-tree analysis leads us to recommend d_2, with an expected monetary value of $280,000.

Computer software packages can assist with the solution to decision analysis problems. For example, the solution to capacity planning problem as provided by *The Management Scientist* microcomputer software package is shown in Figure 6S.4. Input to the computer program included the payoff table and the state of nature probabilities. Building a new plant (decision alternative 2) with an expected monetary value of $280,000 is the recommended capacity planning strategy.

SUMMARY AND KEY TERMS

Summary

We have seen how decision trees can be used to analyze a decision under uncertainty. While other decision problems may be substantially more complex than the Edmund Chemicals' problem, if there are a reasonable number of decision alternatives and states of nature, the decision-tree approach outlined in this section can be used. First, the analyst must draw a decision tree consisting of decision and state-of-nature nodes and branches that describe the sequential nature of the problem. Assuming the EMV criterion is to be used, the next step is to determine the probabilities for each of the state-of-nature branches and compute the expected monetary value at each state-of-nature node.

The decision branch leading to the state-of-nature node with the best expected monetary value is then selected. The decision alternative associated with this branch is the best decision using the EMV criterion.

Key Terms

Decision analysis
States of nature
Payoff table
Decision tree
Nodes
Branches

PROBLEMS

1. Southland Corporation's decision to produce a new line of recreational products has resulted in the need to construct either a small plant or a large plant. The decision as to which plant size to select depends on how the marketplace reacts to the new product line. In order to conduct an analysis, marketing management has decided to view the possible long-run demand as either low, medium, or high. The following payoff table shows the projected profit in millions of dollars.

	Long-Run Demand		
Decision	Low	Medium	High
Small plant	150	200	200
Large plant	50	200	500

Construct a decision tree for this problem. Assume that the best estimate of the probability of a low long-run demand is 0.20, a medium long-run demand is 0.15, and high long-run demand is 0.65. What is the recommended decision using the expected monetary value approach?

2. The Gray Corporation is considering constructing a new plant to handle a new product line of synthetic drugs. A large plant and a small plant are being considered. The decision will depend on the long-run average demand. The probability of a high demand is estimated to be .65; moderate demand, .15; and low demand, .20. The payoff table (in thousands of dollars per year over a 10-year horizon) is as follows:

	Long-Run Average Demand		
Decision	High	Medium	Low
Build Large	250	100	25
Build Small	100	100	75

Construct a decision tree for this problem and determine the optimal strategy.

3. For the Gray Corporation in Problem 2, suppose that the facility decision can be time-phased; that is, if a small plant is built, the company will consider expanding it in 3 years if initial demand is high. If the initial demand is moderate or low, then no further decisions will be considered. Revise the decision tree to account for this. (*Hint:* There will be two decision nodes.)

4. For the situation described in Problem 3, suppose that the payoffs for building a small plant initially and then expanding are as follows:

Long-Run Average Demand		
High	Medium	Low
200	90	10

Further, suppose that the probabilities of *initial* demand being high, moderate, or low are .60, .20, and .20, respectively. Also, if the initial demand is high, then the probabilities of long-run average demand being high, moderate, or low are .85, .10, and .05, respectively. Will Gray's decision strategy change in this case?

5. Milford Trucking, located in Chicago, has requests to haul two shipments, one to St. Louis and one to Detroit. Because of a scheduling problem, Milford will be able to accept only one of these assignments. The St. Louis customer has guaranteed a return shipment, but the Detroit customer has not. Thus if Milford accepts the Detroit shipment and cannot find a Detroit-to-Chicago return shipment, the truck will return to Chicago empty. The payoff table showing profit is as follows:

Destination	Return Shipment from Detroit (s_1)	No Return Shipment from Detroit (s_2)
St. Louis (d_1)	2000	2000
Detroit (d_2)	2500	1000

If the probability of a Detroit return shipment is 0.4, what should Milford do?

6. McHuffter Condominiums, Inc., of Pensacola, Florida, recently purchased land near the Gulf of Mexico and is attempting to determine the size of the condominium development it should build. Three sizes of developments are being considered: small d_1, medium d_2, and large d_3. At the same time

an uncertain economy makes it difficult to ascertain the demand for the new condominiums. McHuffter's management realizes that a large development followed by a low demand could be very costly to the company. However, if McHuffter makes a conservative small development decision and then finds a high demand, the firm's profits will be lower than they might have been. With the three levels of demand—low, medium, and high—McHuffter's management has prepared the following payoff table:

	Demand		
Decision	Low	Medium	High
Small	400	400	400
Medium	100	600	600
Large	−300	300	900*
	*Profit in $ × 10^3		

If $P(\text{low}) = 0.20$, $P(\text{medium}) = 0.35$, and $P(\text{high}) = 0.45$, what decision is recommended using the expected monetary value approach?

7. Construct a decision tree for the McHuffter Condominiums problem (Problem 6). What is the expected value at each state-of-nature node? What is the optimal decision?

8. Martin's Service Station is considering investing in a heavy-duty snowplow this fall. Martin has analyzed the situation carefully and feels that this would be a very profitable investment if the snowfall is heavy. A small profit could still be made if the snowfall is moderate, but Martin would lose money if snowfall is light. Specifically, Martin forecasts a profit of $7000 if snowfall is heavy and $2000 if it is moderate, and a $9000 loss if it is light. Based on the weather bureau's long-range forecast, Martin estimates that $P(\text{heavy snowfall}) = 0.4$, $P(\text{moderate snowfall}) = 0.3$, and $P(\text{light snowfall}) = 0.3$.
   a. Prepare a decision tree for Martin's problem.
   b. Using the expected monetary value approach, would you recommend that Martin invest in the snowplow?

9. Refer again to the investment problem faced by Martin's Service Station (Problem 8). Martin can purchase a blade to attach to his service truck that can also be used to plow driveways and parking lots. Since this truck must also be available to start cars, etc., Martin will not be able to generate as much revenue plowing snow if he elects this alternative, but he will keep his loss smaller if there is light snowfall. Under this alternative Martin forecasts a profit of $3500 if snowfall is heavy and $1000 if it is moderate, and a $1500 loss if snowfall is light.
   a. Prepare a new decision tree showing all three alternatives.
   b. Using the expected monetary value approach, what is the optimal decision?

10. The Gorman Manufacturing Company must decide whether it should purchase a component part from a supplier or manufacture the component at its Milan, Michigan, plant. If demand is high, it would be to Gorman's advantage to manufacture the component. However, if demand is low, Gorman's unit manufacturing cost will be high because of underutilization of equipment. The projected profit in thousands of dollars for Gorman's make or buy decision is shown below.

	Demand		
Decision	Low	Medium	High
Manufacture component	−20	40	100
Purchase component	10	45	70

The states of nature have the following probabilities: $P(\text{low demand}) = 0.35$, $P(\text{medium demand}) = 0.35$, and $P(\text{high demand}) = 0.30$. Use a decision tree to recommend a decision.

11. A firm produces a perishable food product at a cost of $10 per case. The product sells for $15 per case. For planning purposes the company is considering possible demands of 100, 200, or 300 cases. If the demand is less than production, the excess production is discarded. If demand is more than production, the firm, in an attempt to maintain a good service image, will satisfy the excess demand with a special production run at a cost of $18 per case. The product, however, always sells at $15 per case.
   a. Set up the payoff table for this problem.
   b. If $P(100) = 0.2$, $P(200) = 0.2$, and $P(300) = 0.6$, should the company produce 100, 200, or 300 cases?

12. Sealcoat, Inc. has a contract with one of its customers to supply a unique liquid chemical product that will be used by the customer in the manufacture of a lubricant for airplane engines. Because of

the chemical process used by Sealcoat, batch sizes for the liquid chemical product must be 1000 pounds. The customer has agreed to adjust manufacturing to the full batch quantities and will order either one, two, or three batches every 3 months. Since an aging process of 1 month exists for the product, Sealcoat will have to make its production (how much to make) decision before the customer places an order. Thus Sealcoat can list the product demand alternatives of 1000, 2000, or 3000 pounds, but the exact demand is unknown.

Sealcoat's manufacturing costs are $150 per pound, and the product sells at the fixed contract price of $200 per pound. If the customer orders more than Sealcoat has produced, Sealcoat has agreed to absorb the added cost of filling the order by purchasing a higher-quality substitute product from another chemical firm. The substitute product, including transportation expenses, will cost Sealcoat $240 per pound. Since the product cannot be stored more than 2 months without spoilage, Sealcoat cannot inventory excess production until the customer's next 3-month order. Therefore, if the customer's current order is less than Sealcoast has produced, the excess production will be reprocessed and is valued at $50 per pound.

The inventory decision in this problem is how much should Sealcoat produce given the above costs and the possible demands of 1000, 2000, or 3000 pounds? Based on historical data and an analysis of the customer's future demands, Sealcoat has assessed the following probability distribution for demand:

Demand	Probability
1000	0.3
2000	0.5
3000	0.2
Total	1.0

a. Develop a payoff table for the Sealcoat problem.
b. How many batches should Sealcoat produce every 3 months?

13. A quality control procedure involves 100 percent inspection of parts received from a supplier. Historical records show that the following defective rates have been observed.

Percent Defective	Probability
0	0.15
1	0.25
2	0.40
3	0.20

The cost to inspect 100 percent of the parts received is $250 for each shipment of 500 parts. If the shipment is not 100 percent inspected, defective parts will cause rework problems later in the production process. The rework cost is $25 for each defective part.

a. Complete the following payoff table, where the entires represent the total cost of inspection and reworking:

	Percent Defective			
Decision	0	1.	2	3
100% inspection	$250	$250	$250	$250
No inspection				

b. The plant manager is considering eliminating the inspection process in order to save the $250 inspection cost per shipment. Do you support this action? Use expected monetary value to justify your answer.
c. Show the decision tree for this problem.

Facility Location and Distribution System Design

T hrough resource-requirements planning, a firm can determine if additional long-range production and/or storage capacity are required. As we suggested in the previous chapter, one alternative for meeting additional capacity requirements is to expand existing facilities. This may not always be possible; for example, there may be insufficient land for expansion. It may not even be desirable; a firm may wish to build a facility closer to its customers in order to provide better service. Thus determining appropriate locations for new facilities such as plants, warehouses, retail stores, and hospitals represents an important strategic decision. In this chapter we present basic concepts and procedures for facility location decisions for both manufacturing and service organizations.

7.1 LOCATION STRATEGY AND CORPORATE OBJECTIVES

Location decisions can have a profound effect on a firm's competitive advantage, and these decisions should be made to support overall business objectives. For example, a firm might choose to locate a plant in a new geographical region in order to reduce distribution costs and create cultural ties between the firm and the local community. By doing so, the firm becomes a part of the community, and the relationships established may attract new business and solidify the firm's market position over distant competitors.

Location decisions can also be a source of problems. Honda of America Manufacturing, Inc., for example, located a new automobile plant near Marysville, Ohio. An important factor in that decision was the state's agreement to build a four-lane highway linking the site to the interstate highway system. Subsequently, the state announced a delay of at least six years in completing the highway.[1] The lack of a good transportation system can cause problems in recruiting labor and delays in delivery of supplies, which may adversely affect manufacturing.

"Bottom-line" criteria in location decisions, such as low costs, low taxes, and low wages, are not always the most important factors in such decisions. Location decisions should relate to overall manufacturing strategy. New facilities require large amounts of capital investment and, once built, cannot easily be moved.

Location decisions also affect the management of operations at lower levels of the organization. For instance, if a manufacturing facility is located far from sources of raw materials, it may take a considerable amount of time to deliver an order, and there will be more uncertainty as to the actual time of delivery. To guard against shortages, higher inventories have to be carried, thus increasing costs. Likewise, if a plant or warehouse is located far from market centers, higher transportation costs are incurred in order to deliver finished goods to customers. The availability of labor and utilities, state and local politics, climate, and other factors all affect the productivity and quality of the production system.

---

[1]"Honda Encounters Some Surprises on the Road to Marysville, Ohio," *Wall Street Journal*, 22 March, 1983.

To help understand the importance of location in meeting strategic objectives, we present an overview of business logistics. **Business logistics** refers to the management of all move-store activities that facilitate product flow to the point of final consumption as well as the information flows that set the product in motion for the purpose of providing adequate levels of customer service at reasonable cost.[2] The key elements of a logistics system, or the production/distribution system, are illustrated in Figure 7.1. These elements are *transportation, inventory,* and *order processing*. Raw materials and components are ordered from suppliers. These must be transported to manufacturing facilities for production into finished goods. Finished goods are generally shipped to regional warehouses (often called *distribution centers*) and finally to retail stores, where they are made available to customers. At each plant, warehouse, and retail store, inventory is maintained in order to meet demand in a reasonable amount of time. As inventory levels diminish, orders are sent to the next higher level for replenishing stock. Customer demand sets the entire process in motion.

In order to create an effective production and distribution system, business logistics planning must coordinate production and marketing efforts. One of the goals of marketing managers is to make a product available to customers at the right place and the right time; thus the decision of where a product is produced and stored is of major importance. Production managers, on the other hand, are concerned with maintaining high productivity and low cost. A product mix that seeks only to satisfy marketing goals may lead to inefficiencies in production. Conversely, decisions that consider only production efficiencies may lead to high distribution costs and low customer service. Since product mix decisions affect transportation costs, customer service, capacity utilization, scheduling, and other factors, both marketing and production criteria should be evaluated. Chrysler Corporation, for instance, routinely uses a computer model to assign automobile production to different assembly plants, while taking into account distribution costs to dealers.[3] The model groups automobile makes and styles into 11 product lines. Almost 5000 individual dealers are aggregated into 550 "trading areas." The computer program determines which product lines should be made at each of 10 assembly plants and also how to ship cars from the plants to trading zones in order to minimize production and distribution costs and also satisfy dealer orders and plant-capacity limitations.

We see, then, that the prime objective of location decisions is to position effectively each element of the production/distribution system with respect to the overall system. A manufacturing facility, for example, must be strategically positioned between its suppliers and its customers (which may be distribution centers or retail outlets). Larger firms have more complex location decisions; they must position both plants and warehouses simultaneously with respect to suppliers, retail outlets, and each other. However, rarely are all these facilities located simultaneously. The more typical case involves locating a new plant with respect to suppliers and a fixed set of warehouses or locating a set of warehouses with respect to manufacturing plants and markets. In this chapter we focus on the location decision for a single facility (such as a plant), the location of warehouses

---

[2]Ronald H. Ballou, *Basic Business Logistics,* Prentice-Hall, Englewood Cliffs, N.J., 1978, p. 9.

[3]"Chrysler Corporation Plant Loading Model," in James S. Dyer and Roy D. Shapiro, *Management Science/Operations Research, Cases and Readings,* New York: John Wiley & Sons, 1982.

FIGURE 7.1   The Production/Distribution System

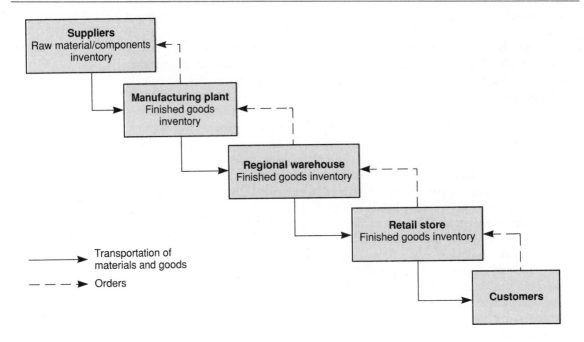

in the distribution system, and the special cases of locating retail, public service, and emergency facilities.

7.2 PLANNING LOCATION STUDIES

Any location study must be carefully planned and implemented. The following are stages of a typical location project:

- *Initial planning*: To determine goals and objectives, relationship to manufacturing strategy, and specific criteria for evaluation.
- *Geographic screening*: To determine candidate locations that meet major location constraints, such as availability of adequate water supplies (in the case of plants that generate a large amount of heat), labor skills, political climate, and so on.
- *Data analysis*: To develop quantitative measures of financial performance and qualitative assessments of the benefits of the candidate location.
- *Evaluation and selection*: To select one or more locations from among the candidates based upon both qualitative and quantitative analysis.

Location Criteria

There are two types of criteria on which location decisions are based: economic factors and noneconomic factors. Economic factors include *facility costs,* such as utilities, insurance, taxes, depreciation, and maintenance, *operating costs,* including fuel, direct labor, and administrative personnel (which may vary considerably by location), and *transportation costs*. Noneconomic factors include the *availability of labor, transportation services*, and *utilities; climate, community environment*, and *quality of life;* and *state and local politics.* Table 7.1 provides a more complete list of important location factors for site selection.

Transportation provides the link between suppliers, plants, warehouses, and retail stores in the logistics system. Once facility locations have been established, management must become involved in detailed decisions concerning how much to ship from each plant to each warehouse and from each warehouse to each retail market. The primary concern in these decisions is with minimizing the delivered cost of a product at its final destination. The delivered cost includes the cost of manufacturing the product at the plant plus transportation and other costs associated with moving the product through the logistics system to its ultimate destination.

In many cases, production costs are about the same at the various plants, and minimizing transportation cost becomes the principal objective. In other cases, production costs may vary considerably, and management's goal is to establish a trade-off between production and transportation costs. This is particularly true when firms establish production operations in foreign countries; usually production costs go down and transportation costs go up. Thus the plant location decision must attempt to minimize combined production and transportation costs.

Some rather simple management science techniques are available for determining a minimum cost production and distribution plan for a given set of plant locations. Often we can use these techniques to determine plant locations that minimize total production and transportation costs. In the supplement to this chapter, we show how the *transportation problem* can be used in cost analysis for plant location decisions. This type of approach is used in many large location studies.

The availability of qualified labor is usually one of the principal noneconomic factors in plant location analysis. There must be a sufficient supply of labor to

TABLE 7.1   Factors for Facility Site Location

Labor Factors	Transportation Factors	Utilities Factors	Climate, Community Environment, and Quality of Life Factors	State and Local Political Factors
Labor supply	Closeness to sources of supply	Water supply	Climate and living conditions	Taxation policies
Labor-management relations	Closeness to markets	Waste disposal	Schools (elementary and high school)	Tax structure
Ability to retain labor force	Adequacy of transportation modes	Power supply	Universities and research facilities	Opportunity for highway advertising
Availability of technical and executive personnel	Costs of transportation	Fuel availability and cost	Community attitude	
Labor rates		Communications	Religious factors	
			Property costs	

meet planned production levels; in addition, workers must have the appropriate skills. Labor-intensive firms may wish to locate where wage rates and costs of training are low. The labor climate may also be important: high turnover necessitates higher costs for hiring and training; absenteeism affects productivity; and local union rules may restrict operations.

The availability of transportation services is also a major consideration. Most companies require some form of trucking service, particularly if they do not own a private fleet. Some firms require rail service in order to receive bulk raw materials and other heavy items, whereas other types of organizations need to be close to water transportation or major airports. Consideration must also be given to the availability of mass transit for employees, particularly if there are many low-paying or part-time jobs.

All production activities require services such as electricity, water, and waste removal. Availability of these types of services and their costs are important factors in deciding on a location, especially if a large quantity of some service is required. For example, chemical processing, paper, and nuclear power companies require large amounts of water for cooling and therefore might consider only those locations near an abundant water supply.

The quality of the environment is important to both the organization and its employees. A favorable climate is good for employee well-being and morale. The proper climate can also reduce energy needs for heating or cooling in certain manufacturing processes. Taxes, the cost of living, and educational and cultural facilities are all important to employees, particularly if they are offered a promotion and transfer to a new location.

Community attitudes toward industry and the local political attitude toward business should also be evaluated. For example, industries that handle high-risk chemicals or radioactive substances are particularly susceptible to unfavorable public reaction and legislation and are less likely to locate in urban areas.

The political attitudes of the state can be either a favorable or unfavorable inducement to locate there. Many states in the United States have enacted legislation in order to attract more industry. Activities such as industrial development programs, revenue bond financing, state industrial loans, and tax inducements can be important in choosing to locate in one state instead of another. Most location decisions are complex, and a variety of noneconomic factors must be included. The most common method for evaluating noneconomic factors in a facility location study is to use a scoring model.

Scoring Models for Facility Location

Scoring models were introduced in Chapter 5 for product selection decisions as a method of dealing with multiple criteria. Applied to facility location, a scoring model consists of a list of major location criteria, each of which is partitioned into several levels. A score is assigned to each level that reflects the relative importance of that criterion. For example, consider the following qualitative factors:

1. Climate
2. Water availability
3. Schools
4. Housing
5. Community attitude
6. Labor laws

An illustrative scoring model is shown in Table 7.2. In this table, the levels for each factor range from 0, representing the worst possible, to either 4 or 5, representing ideal conditions. Notice that the maximum number of points assigned to each factor is different. This implies that higher rated factors are more important than those with lower ratings.

For instance, from Table 7.2, it appears that water availability and housing are of equal importance and of lesser importance than the other criteria. Community attitude carries the most weight and can be viewed as the most important factor in this example. The actual choice of points assigned to different factors is rather subjective and is best done after careful analysis by a group of experienced personnel.

TABLE 7.2

Facility Location Scoring Model

1. Climate

Levels		Score
(0)	Unlivable or prohibitive to planned manufacture; corrective measures cannot change conditions.	0
(1)	Extreme variations in climate conditions; susceptible to violent, destructive storms, floods, and so on.	6
(2)	Wide climate variation; infrequent destructive climatic forces.	12
(3)	Wide climate variations; little likelihood of destructive climatic forces.	18
(4)	Moderate climatic variations; very livable, corrective measures are needed for limited periods of the year.	24
(5)	Ideal for both living and manufacturing. Limited climatic variations.	30

2. Water Availability

Levels		Score
(0)	Unavailable.	0
(1)	Available in small quantities; premium prices; of dubious purity for manufacturing process.	2
(2)	Available in sufficient quantities for households, but not for manufacturing processes.	4
(3)	Available in sufficient quantities for manufacturing, but highly treated.	6
(4)	Available in sufficient quantities and pure enough for proposed manufacturing process.	8
(5)	An abundance for proposed usage; of a very pure nature.	10

3. Schools

Levels		Score
(0)	No schools exist.	0
(1)	Only low-quality public schools through high school level exist.	4
(2)	Only low-quality public schools through high school level, but good private schools exist.	8
(3)	High-quality public schools exist through high school level.	12
(4)	High-quality public schools exist through high school level; excellent private, vocational, and junior colleges exist; colleges or universities are very near.	16
(5)	High-quality public schools exist through high school level; excellent private, vocational, and junior colleges exist; colleges or universities are very near; comprehensive plan for further adult education is available.	20

TABLE 7.2

Continued

4. Housing

Levels		Score
(0)	Nonexistent.	0
(1)	Largely unavailable and of poor quality.	2
(2)	Largely available, but of poor quality.	4
(3)	Available, of acceptable quality and at reasonable rates.	6
(4)	Excellent quality, limited range of types and at reasonable rates.	8
(5)	Excellent quality, wide range of types and at reasonable rates.	10

5. Community Attitude

Levels		Score
(0)	Hostile, bitter, noncooperative	0
(1)	Parasitic in nature.	15
(2)	Noncooperative.	30
(3)	Cooperative.	45
(4)	Friendly and more than cooperative.	60

6. Labor Laws

Levels		Score
(0)	Strict and rigidly enforced.	0
(1)	Strict, but not rigidly enforced.	8
(2)	Work no hardship on employment policy.	15
(3)	Very few and not troublesome.	23
(4)	Nonexistent or of such a nature as to be conducive to good relations.	30

Adapted from R. Reed, *Plant Layout: Factors, Principles, and Techniques,* Irwin, Homewood, Ill., 1961. Used with permission.

EXAMPLE | ## USING A SCORING MODEL FOR FACILITY LOCATION

The Halvorsen Supply Company has identified two sites for a new facility. Using the scoring model in Table 7.2, management has evaluated each site as follows:

Criteria	Site A		Site B	
Climate	Wide variations	18	Ideal climate	30
Water	Sufficient quantity	8	Sufficient; treated	6
Schools	High-quality public	12	Low-quality public	8
Housing	Wide range	10	Acceptable	6
Community	Cooperative	45	Cooperative	45
Labor Laws	No hardship	15	Few; not troublesome	23
Total		108		118

Site B appears to have a slight advantage overall for these factors. However, Site B is better than Site A only in climate and labor laws, but is worse that Site A in water, schools, and housing. These might be important factors in attracting a skilled labor force or in getting managerial personnel to relocate. Other factors such as construction, labor, transportation, and utility costs need to be considered along with these factors. The final approval, however, rests with top management.

7.3 DISTRIBUTION SYSTEM DESIGN

Warehousing plays a crucial role in total distribution design. Consider, for example, a large national grocery chain that manufactures many products under its own name, maintains regional distribution centers, and owns hundreds of retail stores. Such a firm would have a distribution structure similar to that in Figure 7.1. Note that the firm has control over the location of all intermediate components in the logistics system.

Suppose that this firm does not own any warehouses. Then shipments of finished goods would have to be made directly from plants to retail stores. If the factory is located far from its supplies of raw materials, premiums must be paid for transporting these materials to the plant (inbound transportation costs). Also longer delivery times increase the chances of material shortages for production. On the other hand, if the plant is located far from clusters of retail stores, then transportation costs incurred in shipping from the plant to the retail stores (outbound transportation costs) are higher. As before, it takes longer to deliver an order to a retail store. This could result in out-of-stock situations, which reduce the level of customer service. However, the use of warehouses placed close to the markets can provide quick and efficient delivery to retail stores, while still allowing factories to be near suppliers.

Warehouses and distribution centers play an important intermediary role between plants and retail stores. They allow a company to store finished goods for efficient distribution to points of use. For example, suppose that the firm owns several manufacturing plants, which produce a variety of products. Rather than ship small quantities of each product directly from the plants to retail stores, a warehouse can be used for **consolidation** of orders, as shown in Figure 7.2. The economic advantage of such a system lies in the fact that it is often cheaper to ship in truckload (TL) or railcarload (CL) quantities rather than in smaller less-than-truckload (LTL) or less-than-carload (LCL) quantities. Productivity is increased, since transport vehicles are used more efficiently and unit costs are reduced. The following examples illustrate the use of consolidation in both a manufacturing and a service organization.

Western Electric was faced with spiraling costs of distribution, as well as cumbersome inventory control and order processing for 50,000 items used by its field installations.[4] Under the old system, products were warehoused at separate factories and shipped in odd lots to one of 26 service centers, as needed. To reduce costs and improve productivity, Western Electric designed seven regionalized material management centers (MMC). Factory orders are now shipped in

---

[4] "Regionalized Material Management for Best Use of Equipment, Space, and Manpower," Reprinted with permission from *Industrial Engineering* magazine, October 1977. Copyright Institute of Industrial Engineers, 25 Technology Park/Atlanta, Norcross, GA 30092.

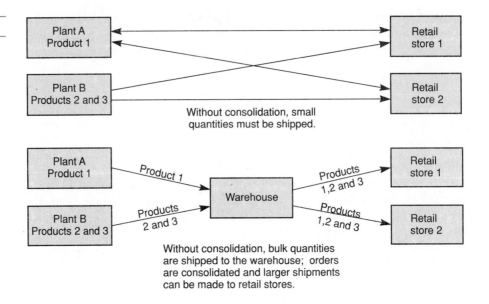

FIGURE 7.2
Product Consolidation

Without consolidation, small quantities must be shipped.

Without consolidation, bulk quantities are shipped to the warehouse; orders are consolidated and larger shipments can be made to retail stores.

truckload lots directly to the MMCs, where orders are processed and consolidated for shipment to individual service centers.

Brodheim and Prastacos describe a similar system for the management of blood.[5] Since blood is a highly perishable item (having only a 21-day lifetime) with uncertain availability and demand, inventory and distribution management are complex activities. The Greater New York Blood Program established a regional blood center responsible for collecting and distributing blood to individual hospital blood banks. A prototype system implemented in Long Island improved utilization, which resulted in an 80 percent waste reduction with annual savings of $500,000. In addition, it has increased the availability of blood to patients and has decreased the number of elective surgeries that were previously postponed because of lack of the right products. Here we see a direct analogy between production and service operations in that surgeries (production) depend greatly on the management and distribution of blood (raw materials). Figure 7.3 illustrates the system analogies between these two examples.

Cost and Service Trade-offs

As the number of distribution centers increases, total transportation costs decline, since the number of long-haul LCL and LTL shipments are reduced. On the other hand, inventory and order-processing costs rise, since more inventory is carried and there is a corresponding increase in paperwork and other administrative costs. These trade-offs are illustrated in Figure 7.4. The optimum number of distribution centers will balance transportation costs with inventory and order-processing costs.

The level of customer service also varies with the number of distribution centers. Many different productivity measures can be used to evaluate customer

---

[5]Reprinted by permission of E. Brodheim and G. P. Prastacos, "The Long Island Blood Distribution System as a Prototype for Regional Blood Management," *Interfaces,* 9, no. 5, (October 1979):3–19. Copyright 1979, The Institute of Management Sciences.

FIGURE 7.3   Examples of Consolidation in Manufacturing and Service Organizations

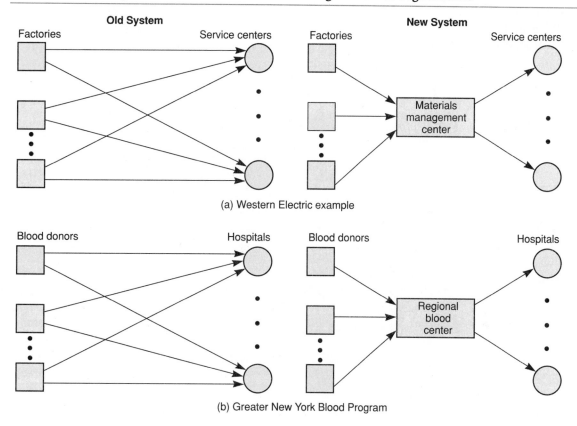

(a) Western Electric example

(b) Greater New York Blood Program

service. Among these are: the average order processing time—that is, the time between receipt of an order at the warehouse and its shipment; the percentage of shipments delivered within x days of order receipt; the percentage of orders that are accurately filled; and the number of damaged items. The first two measures depend on the number and location of warehouses; the second two depend on internal control. The closer warehouses are to retail stores, the shorter is the average time to process and deliver an order. Thus increasing the number of warehouses provides better service, since the average distance to retail stores is shorter. This relationship is shown in Figure 7.5. Comparing this with Figure 7.4, we see that low cost and high customer service are conflicting criteria. Thus the optimum number of warehouses in Figure 7.4 may correspond to an unacceptable level of service. The managers responsible for location decisions must therefore make some difficult decisions in balancing these criteria. This depends to a large extent on the overall goals and objectives of the firm and the firm's customer-service policies.

A number of decisions other than location must be made with regard to warehousing. Some important questions are: Which products should be stored in each warehouse? Should public or private warehouses be used? What types of material-handling equipment should be used? Which customers should be

FIGURE 7.4

Cost Trade-offs in Distribution System Design

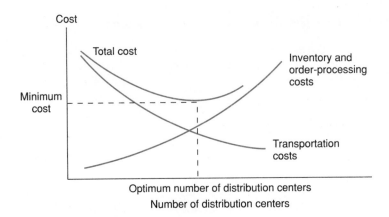

FIGURE 7.5

The Relationship Between Distribution System Design and Customer Service

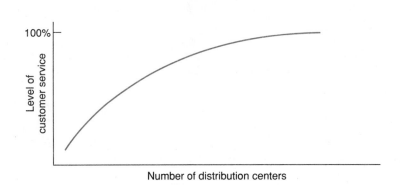

assigned to each warehouse? Proper design of logistics systems requires comprehensive planning and a systems orientation in order to be effective.

7.4 WAREHOUSE LOCATION: THE CENTER-OF-GRAVITY METHOD

In this section, we present a method for determining a location for a single warehouse, (e.g., a consolidation warehouse.) This technique, called the **center-of-gravity method**, is based primarily on cost considerations. Although it does not explicitly address customer-service objectives, the center-of-gravity method can be used to assist managers in balancing cost and service objectives.

The center-of-gravity method takes into account the locations of plants and markets, the volume of goods moved, and transportation costs in arriving at the best location for a single intermediate warehouse. It would seem reasonable to find some "central" location between the plants and customers at which to locate the warehouse. Distance alone should not be the principal criterion, since the volume shipped from one location to another will also affect the cost. The measure we use incorporates both distance and volume, but assumes that cost is directly proportional to each.

The *center of gravity* is defined to be the location that minimizes the weighted distance between the warehouse and its supply and distribution points, where the distance is weighted by the volume supplied or consumed. The first step in this procedure is to place the locations of existing supply and distribution points on a coordinate system. The origin of the coordinate system and scale used are arbitrary, just as long as the relative distances are correctly represented. This can be easily done by placing a grid over an ordinary map. The center of gravity is determined by Equations 7.1 and 7.2.

$$C_x = \frac{\sum_i x_i W_i}{\sum_i W_i} \tag{7.1}$$

$$C_y = \frac{\sum_i y_i W_i}{\sum_i W_i} \tag{7.2}$$

where

C_x = x-coordinate of the center of gravity
C_y = y-coordinate of the center of gravity
x_i = x-coordinate of location i
y_i = y-coordinate of location i
W_i = volume of goods moved to or from location i

We shall illustrate the application of the center-of-gravity method through the following example:

USING THE CENTER-OF-GRAVITY METHOD

Taylor Paper Products is a producer of paper stock used in newspapers and magazines. Taylor's demand is relatively constant and can be forecast rather accurately. The company's two plants are located in Hamilton, Ohio, and Kingsport, Tennessee. These plants distribute paper stock to four major markets: Chicago, Pittsburgh, New York, and Atlanta. The board of directors has authorized the construction of an intermediate warehouse to service these customers.

Coordinates for the plants and markets are shown in Figure 7.6. For example, we see that location 1, Hamilton, is located at the coordinate (58,96). Therefore $x_1 = 58$ and $y_1 = 96$. Data on plant production and market usage rates are given in Table 7.3. For Hamilton, $W_1 = 400$.

Using the data in Table 7.3 and Figure 7.6, we find

$$C_x = \frac{(58)(400) + (80)(300) + (30)(200) + (90)(100) + (127)(300) + (65)(100)}{400 + 300 + 200 + 100 + 300 + 100}$$

$$= 76.3$$

$$C_y = \frac{(96)(400) + (70)(300) + (120)(200) + (110)(100) + (130)(300) + (40)(100)}{400 + 300 + 200 + 100 + 300 + 100}$$

$$= 98.1$$

This location (76.3, 98.1) is shown by the cross on Figure 7.6. By overlaying a map on Figure 7.6, we see that this location is near the border of southern Ohio and West Virginia. Management may use this area to search for an appropriate site.

However, further examination of Figure 7.6 shows that unnecessary movement would be required to ship from the warehouse to Chicago and Atlanta. Perhaps it would be better to ship directly from Kingsport to Atlanta and from Hamilton to Chicago and use a central warehouse to service Pittsburgh and New York. If Table 7.3 is modified to account for this—namely, by removing Atlanta and Chicago and adjusting the plant capacities, we would have

Location	Capacity
1. Hamilton	200
2. Kingsport	200
3. Pittsburgh	100
4. New York	300

The new location has coordinates

$$C_x = \frac{(58)(200) + (80)(200) + (90)(100) + (127)(300)}{200 + 200 + 100 + 300} = 93.4$$

$$C_y = \frac{(96)(200) + (70)(200) + (110)(100) + (130)(300)}{200 + 200 + 100 + 300} = 104$$

This is slightly southeast of Pittsburgh. Taylor Products can use this information in conjunction with actual cost data, estimated service times, and other intangible factors to arrive at a decision, or perhaps investigate other alternatives.

We must caution you that the center-of-gravity method is based on the assumption that transportation rates to and from the warehouse are equal. In locating a warehouse for which inbound transportation costs differ from outbound rates, as is the case in many practical problems, Equations 7.1 and 7.2

FIGURE 7.6

Coordinate Locations of Plants and Customers

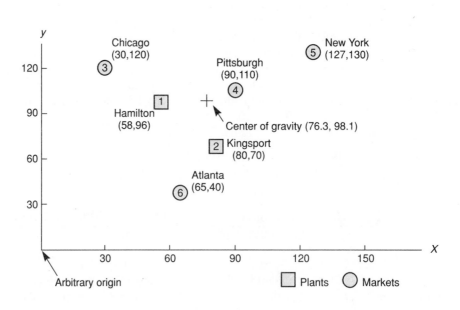

PART TWO   STRATEGY AND DESIGN IN P/OM

	Location	Production/Usage (Tons Per Month)
Plants	1. Hamilton	400
	2. Kingsport	300
Markets	3. Chicago	200
	4. Pittsburgh	100
	5. New York	300
	6. Atlanta	100

TABLE 7.3

Data for Taylor Paper Products Example

must be modified by placing proportionately more weight on the more costly routes.

7.5 COMPUTERIZED LOCATION AND DISTRIBUTION PLANNING

As we have seen, location decisions and transportation decisions are very interdependent. We would obtain poor solutions by considering one but not the other. The most effective planning systems are those that treat location and transportation problems comprehensively. For large companies like Shell Oil, which supplies five products from three refineries to over 100 plants and then distributes these products to over 20,000 customers, such problems are staggering.[6]

Comprehensive computerized logistics-planning systems are available to assist managers in studying strategic logistics problems. Because of the many recent technological developments and advances in distribution, such as containerization, air freight, the use of microprocessors and computers, as well as threats of energy shortages and tight economic policies, many companies are reevaluating their distribution systems. Computerized systems enable managers to determine answers to such questions as: How many warehouses should we have and where should they be located? What size should they be? How should customers be assigned to various warehouses? How much of each product should be sent to each warehouse from each plant? What modes of transportation are most economical? How much savings will result from system improvements? To answer questions such as these, managers must obtain large amounts of data regarding transportation costs, warehousing and inventory-control costs, costs of opening new warehouses, savings from closing existing ones, costs of production, and so on. This requires considerable effort; however, for strategic planning, the benefits are usually great.

One of the most useful applications of computerized distribution-planning systems is investigating the effects of environmental changes and business policies on the distribution system.[7] This is often referred to as asking "what-if?" ques-

---

[6]Thomas K. Zierer, "Applications of Linear and Mixed Integer Programming to Shell's Distribution Network," TIMS/ORSA National Meeting, San Francisco, 1977.

[7]Reprinted by permission of A. M. Geoffrion and R. F. Powers, "Facility Location Analysis Is Just the Beginning," *Interfaces*, 10, no. 2, (April 1980):22–30. Copyright 1980, The Institute of Management Sciences.

tions. A computerized system that allows a manager to study potential changes, whether controllable or otherwise, provides a great deal of information for decision making. Some typical uses of such a system are investigating the effects of the following:

1. changes in demand structure
2. higher fuel costs for transportation
3. transportation strikes, natural disasters, and energy shortages
4. plant-capacity expansion proposals
5. new product lines
6. deletion of product lines
7. price changes
8. new markets
9. transportation using common carriers versus private fleets
10. adding new distribution centers

Many companies are successfully using such systems, based on linear programming models or computer simulation, to plan, design, and evaluate facility location and product-distribution strategies.

For example, in 1971, Hunt-Wesson Foods initiated a comprehensive distribution-planning project.[8] In the previous few years, they had faced distribution center expansion/relocation problems, and management had made a commitment to use a computer-based model that would rebalance the company's entire distribution system. The key decisions involved the relocation of distribution centers, reassignment of customers to the centers, and the determination of how products would flow through the system.

In 1970, Hunt-Wesson manufactured foods at 12 locations and distributed their products through 10 distribution centers by rail and by common and contract truck carriers. The company's policy dictated that each customer be serviced by a single distribution center. This simplified accounting and marketing, made customer inquiries easier to process, and enabled the firm to take advantage of economies of scale through lower bulk-shipping rates. The distribution-planning project was established as a result of continued rapid growth of the company.

The project resulted in the development of a computer-based model involving 17 product groups, 121 customer zones, and 45 potential distribution-center locations. As a result, a variety of options were investigated and changes in the distribution system were implemented in accordance with the analysis. It has been estimated that the use of this model saves the firm $200,000 to $300,000 annually in distribution costs by keeping distribution patterns in synchronization with demand.

---

[8]Complete discussions of this system can be found in: A. Geoffrion and G. Graves: "Multicommodity Distribution System Design by Benders Decomposition," *Management Science* (January 1974); A. Geoffrion, "A Guide to Computer Assisted Methods for Distribution Systems Planning," *Sloan Management Review* (Winter 1975); A. Geoffrion, "Better Distribution Planning With Computer Models," *Harvard Business Review* (July-August 1976), and J. S. Dyer and R. D. Shapiro, "Hunt-Wesson Foods," case study in *Management Science/Operations Research, Cases and Readings,* New York: John Wiley & Sons, 1982.

While the emphasis of this chapter has been on manufacturing facility location decisions, we wish to address some of the significant differences between manufacturing facility location and service facility location. In a manufacturing operation, the location analysis considers distribution costs and customer service. Service facilities, on the other hand, do not have the traditional product distribution channel structure as shown in Figure 7.1. Service facilities are the terminal points in the system at which demand takes place. Either the customer travels to the service facility (as in the case of a hospital), or the service facility travels to the customer (for instance, a mobile library unit). Service facilities generally serve a small geographic area, therefore the principal trade-off is between the number of facilities to have and the travel cost between the facilities and customers. Hence service facility location problems often involve multiple sites.

The criteria for choosing service facility locations differ from those used in manufacturing. For profit-seeking service organizations, perhaps the most important criterion is road access or the availability of public transportation. The visibility of the site from highways, traffic volume around the site, parking, and location of competition are also critical factors. For emergency services such as fire protection and police, response time and reliability are the principal criteria. In this section we discuss location decisions for retail outlets, public service facilities, and emergency facilities.

The major criterion used in locating a retail facility is the volume of demand. For a grocery store or restaurant, this might be measured by dollar sales revenue, whereas for an amusement park, this might be the number of visitors each year. In any case, estimates of demand must be obtained for potential locations.

Retail Facility Location

Consider the situation of a bank, which needs to determine future locations for its automatic teller machines. The success of a site is measured by the number of transactions that take place each month. Thus some way of estimating or predicting this volume is required. The statistical technique of regression analysis can be used to predict demand. In order to use regression analysis for automatic-teller location, we need to specify a set of independent variables that are related to the number of transactions. This can be established through meetings with the bank executives and branch managers in charge of existing sites. The following set of variables are typical:

1. population in a given census tract (census tracts might be chosen as site locations because of their size and the availability of demographic data)
2. median income per census tract
3. median age per census tract
4. median educational level per census tract
5. whether the machine is located at a branch of the bank or a remote location
6. total number of automatic teller cards in a given zip code (from bank records)
7. whether the site was predominantly commercial or residential
8. level of dollar sales per retail establishment (obtained from Bureau of Census publications)

9. traffic counts at the potential site (obtained from the regional planning agency)
10. number of employed persons
11. number of occupied households
12. number of persons between the ages of 20 and 30
13. number of years the machine is in use.

Using data in census tracts corresponding to existing locations of automatic tellers, a regression equation that relates the most important independent variables to the volume of transactions can be developed. The regression model can be used by bank executives to predict the volume of transactions and thus determine good locations for future automatic tellers.

In locating facilities that are oriented toward sales, we see that the principal factors are market related and that the important data are demographic in nature. Other intangible factors that influence retail location are competition, zoning laws, traffic patterns and accessibility, and aesthetic qualities of the location. As in industrial location analysis, a scoring model can be used to rank potential sites.

Public Service Facility Location

Public service facilities include post offices, schools, highways, parks, and so on. One of the major problems in locating such facilities is the lack of easily quantifiable data. How does one define "social cost" or "social benefit"? Some of the typical criteria used in public service location problems include the average distance or time traveled by the users of the facilities and the maximum distance or travel time between the facility and its intended population. Another factor not present in industrial location problems is that public facilities create demand; one would like to locate facilities to serve the largest segment of the population. In this sense, the problem is similar to locating a bank or grocery store, except that profit is not a motivating factor. Cost-benefit analysis is often used to determine public facility location.

Emergency Facility Location

The problem of locating emergency facilities such as fire stations, ambulance stations, and police substations has the objective of minimizing response time from the notification of an emergency to the delivery of service. Usually, the goal is to locate the facility so that the maximum response time to any point of demand is minimized. In practice, such problems are complicated by the random nature of demand, but we shall ignore this issue in order to simplify the discussion. We illustrate this with the problem of locating a fire station in a small township.

EXAMPLE

LOCATING A FIRE STATION

Marymount is a small township on the outskirts of a large city. Currently the township is serviced by the city fire department just outside the township limits. However, costs of purchasing this service have been escalating and the township trustees have decided to organize their own fire department. The township is divided into several zones based upon the geographic structure of the community. The center of each zone, the distance between zones, and the travel time in minutes along the major roads are shown in Figure 7.7.

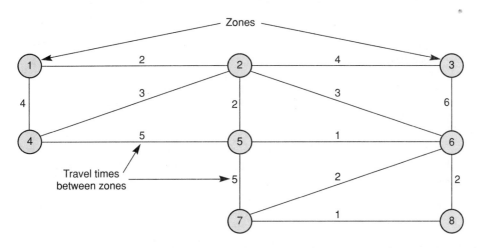

Zones

FIGURE 7.7

Zone Connections for Marymount Township

Travel times between zones

Where should the fire station be located? We first have to decide on an objective for evaluating potential sites. Let us suppose that the goal is to locate the station so that the *maximum* response time to any other zone is the *smallest*. We assume that a route is chosen that corresponds to the shortest time between zones. For instance, suppose the station is located in zone 1. We must determine how long it would take to travel to each of the other zones in the shortest possible time. For our purposes, we do this by inspection of Figure 7.7. You should verify that the shortest travel times from zone 1 to all others are:

Zone	Shortest Time
2	2
3	6
4	4
5	4
6	5
7	7
8	7

For example, the shortest route from zone 1 to zone 7 is to go through zones 2, 5, and 6. The maximum response time from zone 1 to any other zone is 7 minutes. Next, suppose we locate in zone 2. The shortest times from zone 2 to all other zones are

Zone	Shortest Time
1	2
3	4
4	3
5	2
6	3
7	5
8	5

TABLE 7.4

Organization	Weights
Power-generating station	Demand for power at each customer location
Sewage-treatment plant	Volume of sewage arising from each region of a city or county
Waste-disposal facility	Average amount of waste transported from residential neighborhoods and industrial sites

The longest time is 5. Therefore zone 2 is a better location than zone 1 according to this criterion. If we compute the shortest travel times from each zone to every other zone we obtain the following:

From	To								Longest time (min)
	1	2	3	4	5	6	7	8	
1	—	2	6	4	4	5	7	7	7
2	2	—	4	3	2	3	5	5	5
3	6	4	—	7	6	6	8	8	8
4	4	3	7	—	5	6	8	8	8
5	4	2	6	5	—	1	3	3	6
6	5	3	6	6	1	—	2	2	6
7	7	5	8	8	3	2	—	1	8
8	7	5	8	8	3	2	1	—	8

To minimize the longest response time, the fire station should be located in zone 2.

There are several quantitative techniques that are more efficient for large problems than inspecting each possible site individually; however, such techniques are beyond the scope of this text.

The center-of-gravity method can often be used to locate service facilities. Retail outlets, power-generating stations, sewage-treatment plants, and waste-disposal facilities are but a few examples. To illustrate, consider a fast-food chain that is attempting to determine a best location for a new outlet. Customers are drawn from several population centers. The center-of-gravity method can be used, where W_i represents the population of center i. Table 7.4 illustrates examples of weights for other applications.

P/OM IN
PRACTICE

Applications of facility location and distribution system design are presented in this section. In the first P/OM in Practice, a microcomputer-based logistics-planning system, MICRO-LMS, is discussed. A manufacturing example that uses a mathematical model to determine the minimum-cost production-distribution policy with three plants, five ware-

houses, and several market territories is presented. The second P/OM in Practice discusses facility location issues in the service sector by considering the location of a blood bank facility. This application illustrates the use of a scoring model in making the location decision.

MICRO-LMS: A LOGISTICS-PLANNING TOOL[9]

M ICRO-LMS (Logistics Modeling System) is a proprietary product of Optimal Decision Systems, Inc., a firm specializing in logistics software and consulting. MICRO-LMS is a decision-support system that allows managers to address key logistical issues such as these:

1. the number, size, location, and type of facilities
2. supply relationships between facilities and customers
3. the allocation of customer orders to production/ distribution facilities
4. the effect of changes in costs, capacities, and customer demands
5. customer service versus cost trade-offs

The system can actually be used at the strategic, tactical, and operational levels. At the strategic level, the system can be used to evaluate hypothetical facility locations such as new plants or warehouses; at the tactical level it might be used to address the effects of changing costs, capacities, and customer demands on the allocation of orders; at the operational level, it can determine the minimum-cost allocation of customer orders to production and distribution facilities subject to available capacity and customer-service restrictions. The system is being used by such companies as Frito-Lay, AT&T, 3M, and the Popsicle Co.

One of the important features of the system is the method of data generation. MICRO-LMS contains a module that uses corporate historical shipment data to generate customer demands automatically by product and market from an aggregate sales forecast; a module that automatically provides the needed distances between facilities and markets; and a module that automatically provides accurate transportation rates, taking into account current discounts and historical shipment patterns. This feature relieves the user of considerable data-generation effort.

The logistics system is modeled as a network. Suppose that a company has three manufacturing plants, four warehouses, and nine market territories with six products. Management is considering adding a fifth warehouse in Atlanta. Figure 7.8 illustrates the structure of this logistics network. The addition of the new warehouse may result in a redistribution of product flows from the plants and to the markets. Management wishes to determine the minimum-cost distribution policy.

The key input data are the network structure, forecasted customer demand, facility alternatives (locations, types, and capacities), operating costs, inventory costs, transportation costs, and lead times. Other information that must be defined includes demand forecasts, product selling prices, and geographic ZIP-code definitions of market territories.

The system takes these data, and through the use of a mathematical model, determines the minimum-cost product-distribution policy. A summary of the solution that appears on the screen is as follows:

```
PLANT AND FACILITY FLOW:
TOTAL COST =      $180,229.27
```

From	To	Units
PLANT1	CINTI	301
PLANT1	JACKSNV	105
PLANT1	ATLANTA	594
PLANT2	CHICAGO	610
PLANT2	CINTI	390
PLANT3	ATLANTA	406
PLANT3	DENVER	352

Figure 7.9 is an example of one of the many detailed reports that can be generated by the system. Such reports provide the decision maker with specific accounting information by plant, warehouse, and market territory.

One of the principal advantages of computerized logistics modeling is the ability to modify data easily and perform what-if analyses. For example, suppose that management wished to know the effect of increasing the capacity of the proposed Atlanta warehouse and plant 1 by 50 percent. This capacity data

---

[9]Adapted from MICRO-LMS Demonstration Diskette Handbook, Optimal Decision Systems, Inc. 10921 Reed Hartman Highway, Suite 311, Cincinnati, Ohio 45242, 1983. The firm is presently owned by Cleveland Consulting Associates.

FIGURE 7.8
Logistics
Network

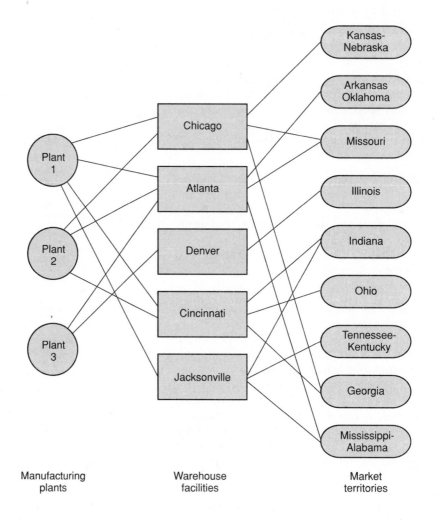

Manufacturing
plants

Warehouse
facilities

Market
territories

can be easily changed in the input files. The new problem can be reoptimized with the resulting solution:

```
PLANT AND FACILITY FLOW:

TOTAL COST =        $179,581.13
-----------------------------------

    From        To        Units
    ----        --        -----
    PLANT1      CINTI        170
    PLANT1      ATLANTA     1330
    PLANT2      CHICAGO      510
    PLANT2      CINTI        490
    PLANT3      DENVER       258
```

By comparing both solutions, the savings are found to be $180,229.27 − $179,581.13 = $648.14 per month. This information can be compared to the cost of providing the additional capacity as well as to the customer-service implications of the new solution. In a similar manner, changes in locations, costs, demand, and so on can be analyzed very easily.

QUESTIONS

1. List some of the logistical issues that the MICRO-LMS system can address.
2. Discuss how the system could be used to evaluate and choose the facility locations for a new plant or warehouse.

FIGURE 7.9 MICRO-LMS Facility Summary Report

10-23-1985 00:00:40 XYZ CORPORATION — LOGISTICS MODELING STUDY FACILITY SUMMARY PAGE: 1

*** TRANSPORTATION COSTS *** *** F A C I L I T Y C O S T S ***

FACILITY	THRUPUT (CWT)†	UTIL-IZATION	INBOUND TOTAL $	INBOUND $/CWT	OUTBOUND TOTAL $	OUTBOUND $/CWT	OPERATING COSTS FIXED	OPERATING COSTS VAR	OPERATING COSTS TOTAL	INVENTORY COSTS FIXED	INVENTORY COSTS VAR	INVENTORY COSTS TOTAL	TOTAL FACILITY COST	TOTAL FACILITY CWT
PLANT1	1000	1.00	1400	1.40	2225	2.23	10000	30	10030	5000	20	5020	18675	18.675
PLANT2	1000	1.00	1270	1.27	2178	2.18	10000	50	10050	5000	30	5030	18528	18.528
PLANT3	758	0.76	1046	1.38	2019	2.66	8000	45	8045	6000	30	6030	17141	22.613
* TOTALS	2758		3716		6422		28000	125	28125	16000	80	16080	54344	19.704
CHICAGO	610	0.61	1336	2.19	4001	6.56	12000	2613	14613	6000	1367	7367	27316	44.780
ATLANTA	1000	1.00	2395	2.40	16289	16.29	11000	2472	13472	5000	1194	6194	38351	38.351
DENVER	352	0.70	841	2.39	3652	10.38	10000	629	10629	4950	382	5332	20454	58.109
CINTI	691	0.69	1622	2.35	4173	6.04	11950	1105	13055	7260	519	7779	26629	38.537
JACKSNV	105	0.21	228	2.17	611	5.82	12565	147	12712	5920	85	6005	19557	186.254
* TOTALS	2758		6422		28726		57515	6966	64481	29130	3548	32678	132307	47.972
* TOTALS	2758		10138		35149		85515	7092	92607	45130	3628	48758	180229	65.348

†cwt stands for ''hundred weight''

LOCATING A BLOOD BANK IN QUEBEC CITY[10]

The Red Cross Blood Donor Clinic and Transfusion Center has been located in downtown Quebec for 20 years. Increases in the population served and improvements in service provided have resulted in additional staff needs and the need for additional equipment. These were not planned for in the original building design, and the present site left no room for expansion; consequently administrators of the Center sought to relocate.

Three main activities influenced the location decision. First, donors may travel to the Center by public or private transportation. Second, the Center delivers blood and blood products throughout the Quebec urban community and eastern Quebec province. Finally, the Center holds mobile blood donor clinics over this same extensive territory.

Early in the study, the following site selection criteria were identified:

1. access to the road network for the mobile clinics and for the blood delivery vehicles so as to increase efficiency, minimize delays, operating costs, and deterioration of blood products in transit
2. the ability to attract a larger group of donors through better visibility or ease of access
3. convenience to both public and private transportation
4. little sensitivity with respect to changes in the population distribution or in the road network
5. ease of travel to and from work for Center employees
6. minimum internal space and lot size
7. acceptability of the site to the management committees and governmental authorities

A variety of data was collected that included population data, donor data, public transport trip data, and delivery data. Several different center-of-gravity models were used to analyze the data. Each of these used differently weighted criteria to identify a recommended location. One model used the population of all donors who attended the Center; another used locations where deliveries were made. In all, ten different models were used. The sites proposed by the different models were evaluated using other qualitative factors. Several alternative locations were proposed based on other factors. Five sites were selected as final candidates for the Center location.

Each of the final sites were evaluated according to four criteria

1. accessibility to the road network
2. accessibility to the public transit network
3. proximity to the centers of gravity
4. availability of a lot or suitable building

Table 7.5 shows the rankings of the five sites on the four criteria. The rankings were converted to "preference weights" using a simple method. The method applied to road access is shown in Table 7.6. A "1" indicates that the row site is preferred to the column site. The weight is the sum of the row entries divided

TABLE 7.5 Ranking of Five Sites on Four Criteria

Site	Road Access	Bus Access	Proximity to Centers of Gravity	Availability of a Lot or Building
A	1	5	1	1
B	3	3	2	1
C	2	2	3	4
D	5	1	4	4
E	4	4	5	1

TABLE 7.6 Preference Weights for Road Access

Site	1	2	3	4	5	Weight
A	—	1	1	1	1	0.4
B	0	—	0	1	1	0.2
C	0	1	—	1	1	0.3
D	0	0	0	—	0	0.0
E	0	0	0	1	—	0.1

[10]Adapted from Price and Turcotte, "Locating a Blood Bank," *Interfaces*, 16, no. 5, (September–October 1986): 17–26, Tables 7, 8 and 9. Reprinted by permission. Copyright (1986) The Institute of Management Sciences, 290 Westminster Street, Providence, Rhode Island 02908, USA.

by the sum of all entries. This method was applied for each of the criteria. Table 7.7 shows the final weightings obtained.

The purpose of the modeling process was not to determine a single optimal solution, but rather to provide good solution alternatives that might be considered by the decision makers. The modeling process also provided justifications for turning down any unsuitable sites that might be suggested during the complex negotiation process that had to be followed before a new site could actually be chosen.

TABLE 7.7   Final Weights and Overall Ranking

Site	Road Access	Bus Access	Proximity to Centers of Gravity	Availability of a Lot or Building	Overall Rank
A	0.4	0	0.4	0.67	1
B	0.2	0.2	0.3	0.67	2
C	0.3	0.3	0.2	0	4
D	0	0.4	0.1	0	5
E	0.1	0.1	0	0.67	3

QUESTIONS

1. Discuss the issues that had the major impact on the location decision for the blood bank.

2. Comment on the differences in location criteria for manufacturing and service sector applications that are evident from this example.

Facility location is an important strategic consideration that affects the success of any organization. Costs of distribution and transportation, as well as the service afforded to the customers, depend on the location of facilities such as factories, warehouses, retail stores, and emergency stations. Location decisions are made after careful evaluation of a variety of quantitative factors, such as costs and anticipated service, as well as many qualitative factors, such as the availability of labor and utilities, climate, and political attitudes. Scoring models are often used to evaluate the intangible factors, while several quantitative techniques— such as the transportation model and center-of-gravity method—are useful in selecting locations to minimize costs. Today, many companies are turning toward computerized planning systems to examine the strategic effects of changes in markets, costs, and availability of materials.

Retail and emergency facility locations require different approaches, since transportation is not the principal consideration. Rather, we are concerned with the location of customer demand and response time. Regression analysis and other quantitative techniques are often used in location analyses of service facilities.

SUMMARY

KEY TERMS

Business logistics
Consolidation
Center-of-gravity method

REVIEW/ DISCUSSION QUESTIONS

1. Explain why location decisions are important to overall business strategy.

2. Define the term *business logistics*. What are its key elements?

3. Describe the stages of a typical location project.

4. Briefly discuss the major economic and noneconomic factors influencing location decisions.

5. What are some of the advantages and disadvantages of scoring models for location analysis?

6. How does consolidation affect cost and service in distribution system?

7. What implications does increasing the number of warehouses have in a distribution system?

8. What role do computerized distribution-planning systems play in strategic decision making?

9. Explain the assumptions behind the center-of-gravity method. Why does it work?

10. Discuss the major differences between manufacturing and service organizations with respect to facility location problems.

11. How do the objectives differ among retail, public service, and emergency facility location problems?

12. Discuss how the center-of-gravity method can be used in service facility location.

13. Discuss some of the reasons why a grocery chain might close one store and open another.

14. What considerations would be important to a bank in selecting a branch location? What information would you want to make the site selection decision?

PROBLEMS

1. An industrialist faced with the choice among four possible locations uses a scoring model as shown below. Which location would be the best?

		Location			
Criteria	Weight	1	2	3	4
Raw material availability	0.2	G	P	OK	VG
Infrastructure	0.1	OK	OK	OK	OK
Transportation costs	0.5	VG	OK	P	OK
Labor relations	0.1	G	VG	P	OK
Quality of life	0.1	G	VG	P	OK

Points VG = Very good: 5 points
G = Good: 4 points
OK = Acceptable: 3 points
P = Poor: 1 point

2. Goslin Chemicals has decided to build a new plant in the sunbelt in order to take advantage of new solar-powered heating units used in chemical production. Three sites have been proposed: Phoenix, Arizona; El Paso, Texas; and Mountain Home, Arkansas.
   a. Construct a scoring model using the criteria in Table 7.2 in which the factors have the priorities
      1. Climate
      2. Water availability

3. Labor laws and community attitude

4. Schools and housing

(Factors having the same priority should have the same rating scale.)

b. Suppose the three sites have ratings given below. Under the system constructed in (a), which seems to be most preferable?

	Level Assigned		
Factor	Phoenix	El Paso	Mountain Home
Climate	5	5	4
Water	3	5	5
Labor	1	2	4
Attitude	3	3	4
Schools	5	3	2
Housing	4	2	3

3. Given the following locational information and volume of material movements from a supply point to several retail outlets, find the optimal location for the supply point using the center of gravity method.

	Location Coordinates		Material
Retail Outlet	x	y	Movements
1	20	5	1200
2	18	15	1800
3	3	16	1600
4	3	4	1100
5	16	20	2000

4. Broderick's Burgers would like to determine the best location for drawing customers from three population centers. The map coordinates of the three centers are given as follows:

$$\text{Population center 1} \quad x_1 = 2, y_1 = 8$$
$$\text{Population center 2} \quad x_2 = 6, y_2 = 6$$
$$\text{Population center 3} \quad x_3 = 1, y_3 = 1$$

a. What location will minimize the total distance from the three centers?

b. Population center 1 is four times as large as center 3, and center 2 is twice as large as center 3. The firm feels that the importance of locating near a population center is proportional to its population. Find the best location under these assumptions.

5. A large metropolitan campus needs to erect a parking garage for students, faculty, and visitors. The garage has a planned capacity of 1000 cars. Based on a survey, it is estimated that 30 percent of the arrivals to campus go to the business school and adjacent buildings; 40 percent go to the engineering

complex; 20 percent to the University Center area, and 10 percent go to the administrative offices (see campus map below). Four potential sites (A, B, C, and D) are being considered. Which one would be best for the new garage?

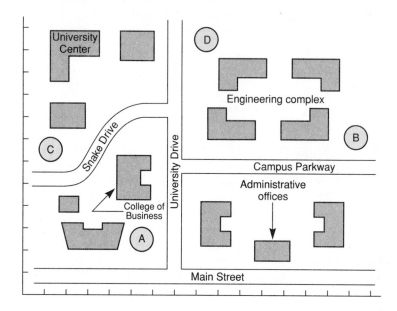

6. A national drug store chain prefers to operate one outlet in a town that has four major market segments. The number of potential customers in each segment along with the coordinates are given below.

Market Segment	Location Coordinates		Number of Customers
	x	y	
1	2	18	1000
2	15	17	800
3	2	2	1500
4	14	2	2200

a. Which would be the best location using the center-of-gravity method?
b. If after five years, half the customers from segment 4 are expected to move to segment 2, where should the drug store shift, if the same criteria is adopted?

7. Microserve provides computer repair service on a contract basis to customers in five sections of the city. The five sections, the number of service contracts in each section, and the x, y coordinates of each section are as shown.

Section	No. of Contracts	Coordinates x	y
Parkview	90	8.0	10.5
Mt. Airy	220	6.7	5.9
Valley	50	12.0	5.2
Norwood	300	15.0	6.3
Southgate	170	11.7	8.3

Use the center-of-gravity method to recommend an ideal location for a service center.

8. In locating an emergency facility which has to cater to six communities, the criterion adopted is minimizing the maximum response time. The travel times between the six communities are indicated in the figure below. Where should the facility be located?

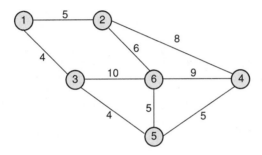

9. In problem 8, if the objective was to choose a location based on *average* response time, which would be the best location?

10. The following data relate to the operating costs of three possible locations for a manufacturing plant.

	Location 1	Location 2	Location 3
Fixed costs	$110,000	$125,000	$150,000
Direct material cost per unit	8.5	8.4	8.6
Direct labor cost per unit	4.2	3.9	3.7
Overhead per unit	1.2	1.1	1.0
Transportation costs per 1000 units	800	1,100	950

a. Which location would minimize the total costs given an annual production of 50,000 units.
b. For what levels of manufacture and distribution would each location be best?

11. A firm has three possible locations for opening warehouses to cater to its five geographically separated market segments. The firm could install one, two

or three warehouses to cater to these markets. The fixed costs of each warehouse location and the transportation costs are given below. What would be the best mix of warehouses? To which market should each warehouse cater to?

Warehouse Location	Fixed Costs	Transportation Costs to Market Segments				
		1	2	3	4	5
1	50	500	1000	2000	2500	600
2	55	1100	400	600	1100	1050
3	45	1200	1025	900	500	850

12. Grave City is considering the relocation of a number of police substations in order to obtain better enforcement in high-crime areas. The locations being considered together with the areas that can be covered from these locations are given in the accompanying table.

Potential Locations For Substations	Areas Covered
A	1, 5, 7
B	1, 2, 5, 7
C	1, 3, 5
D	2, 4, 5
E	3, 4, 6
F	4, 5, 6
G	1, 5, 6, 7

Find the minimum number of locations necessary to provide coverage to all areas. Where should the police substations be located?

13. The Farmington City Council is attempting to choose among three sites as a location for its life squad facility. The city manager has developed the following matrix showing the distance (in miles) from each of the sites to five areas that must be served.

Site	Area Served				
	1	2	3	4	5
A	1.2	1.4	1.4	2.6	1.5
B	1.4	2.2	1.3	2.1	.7
C	2.7	3.2	.8	.9	.7

The number of emergency runs to each of these areas over the past three months are: area 1, 100; area 2, 20; area 3, 100; area 4, 170; area 5, 200.
a. If the council decides to choose the site on the basis of minimizing the longest response time, which site should be selected?

b. If the council decides to minimize the annual cost (in terms of miles traveled) of operating the facility, which site should be selected?

14. Izzy Rizzy's Trick Shop specializes in gag gifts, costumes, and novelties. Izzy owns a store on the south side of Chicago and is considering opening another store on the north side. A sample of 10 customers yielded the following data:

Amount of Sale ($)	17	15	40	20	15	25	20	30	30	35
Age		20	17	32	40	35	21	18	25	36	31

Izzy believes that age is the most important factor for his customers. He is considering three possible locations: one is in the high-rise, near-north side, where many singles in the 25–35 age group reside; the second is near a residential area in which the majority of the population is over 35; and the third is near a college campus. From this data, where should Izzy locate?

15. The city of Binghamton is attempting to determine the best location for an ambulance service facility that can be used for emergency calls throughout the city. The network of zones within the city is shown in the figure below.

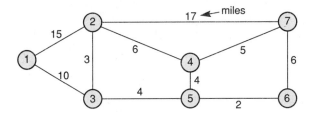

Where should Binghamton locate the service facility such that the maximum distance to any zone is the smallest?

CASE PROBLEM

On January 1, 1979, a change in the branch banking law for the state of Ohio went into effect. Prior to this date, the law permitted a bank to place branches in the county of its principal place of business, but not in other counties. For example, a bank with a charter to operate in Hamilton County could establish numerous branches in Hamilton County but none in Clermont County. (See Figure 7.10.)

The new law allowed banks to establish branches in any county adjacent to a county in which it had a principal place of business. Two counties which are separated only by a body of water are considered adjacent (for example, Ottawa and Erie counties).

This change in the law caused banks and bank holding companies to reexamine their strategy for expansion into new areas. Among other things, this made it possible to establish a principal place of business (PPB) in a county adjacent to a county with a large population, so that branches could be established in the heavily populated county. Since it would ordinarily be cheaper to acquire a PPB in a lightly populated county, such a strategy might be preferred. Of course, there are many other considerations that must also be dealt with by strategic planners.

FIGURE 7.10
Ohio Counties

Questions for Analysis

1. A bank holding company would like to determine in how many counties a charter must be obtained in order to establish branches in every county in the state. Determine the minimum number of charters necessary and identify the counties in which they must be obtained.

2. Assume the holding company already has a charter in Hamilton and Franklin counties. Repeat the analysis in Question 1.

3. Population estimates for each county are given in Table 7.8. Devise a method for selecting locations that will maximize the population that can be served given 3, 4, 5, . . . , n charters are obtained. Discuss how the information can be used in ensuring that short-range and long-range expansion plans are consistent. Obtain a solution for this problem if $n = 3$. How can a computer help in this case?

4. Discuss other information that might be valuable to bank officers in making such strategic decisions.

TABLE 7.8 Population Estimates and Retail Trade for Ohio Counties

County or County Equivalent	Population Estimated 1/1/1977	Total Retail Trade Sales 1975* ($1000)	Ranally Sales Units	County or County Equivalent	Population Estimated 1/1/1977	Total Retail Trade Sales 1975* ($1000)	Ranally Sales Units
Adams	23,200	48,716	81	Lorain	271,600	722,138	1,206
Allen	108,900	334,793	559	Lucas	477,500	1,558,733	2,602
Ashland	43,300	98,332	164	Madison	32,300	64,283	107
Ashtabula	103,900	257,482	430	Mahoning	305,900	869,754	1,452
Athens	49,600	113,585	190	Marion	68,200	200,587	335
Auglaize	42,400	99,368	166	Medina	103,700	224,679	375
Belmont	82,700	223,234	373	Meigs	21,600	47,174	79
Brown	30,700	52,837	88	Mercer	37,900	80,005	134
Butler	248,200	571,987	955	Miami	87,800	212,845	355
Carroll	24,400	48,841	82	Monroe	15,400	25,668	43
Champaign	32,800	49,582	83	Montgomery	582,800	2,013,698	3,362
Clark	153,800	435,876	728	Morgan	13,800	22,114	37
Clermont	112,400	189,292	316	Morrow	25,200	37,445	63
Clinton	32,900	89,332	149	Muskingum	80,900	218,175	364
Columbiana	112,600	260,458	435	Noble	11,400	21,961	37
Coshocton	35,400	74,093	124	Ottawa	39,300	98,758	165
Crawford	49,300	121,419	203	Paulding	20,900	28,072	47
Cuyahoga	1,574,400	4,695,365	7,839	Perry	28,800	45,263	76
Darke	57,100	105,884	177	Pickaway	44,600	90,549	151
Defiance	36,600	118,653	198	Pike	21,000	35,999	60
Delaware	52,400	1,002,889	170	Portage	134,400	284,974	476
Erie	77,500	261,363	436	Preble	36,400	59,657	100
Fairfield	88,600	199,115	332	Putnam	31,200	52,254	87
Fayette	26,700	68,143	114	Richland	130,500	417,161	696
Franklin	875,000	2,941,893	4,911	Ross	60,700	153,819	257
Fulton	34,600	93,300	156	Sandusky	64,100	166,964	279
Gallia	29,100	63,855	107	Scioto	82,600	189,908	317
Geauga	68,600	110,883	185	Seneca	59,900	145,567	243
Greene	125,600	249,589	417	Shelby	40,500	77,257	129
Guernsey	39,900	81,536	136	Stark	386,500	1,096,242	1,830
Hamilton	901,600	2,819,819	4,707	Summit	530,900	1,652,973	2,760
Hancock	61,500	193,891	324	Trumbull	242,900	705,119	1,177
Hardin	32,100	53,799	90	Tuscarawas	81,300	215,630	360
Harrison	18,000	30,977	52	Union	30,400	46,783	78
Henry	27,600	58,354	97	Van Wert	29,500	64,811	108
Highland	32,400	59,882	100	Vinton	10,400	11,005	18
Hocking	22,800	53,454	89	Warren	88,400	153,923	257
Holmes	25,800	48,614	81	Washington	60,100	166,930	279
Huron	52,900	155,031	259	Wayne	91,600	221,018	369
Jackson	29,400	74,939	125	Williams	34,600	82,135	137
Jefferson	93,900	233,044	389	Wood	102,700	304,028	508
Knox	44,300	94,563	158	Wyandot	22,100	45,048	75
Lake	208,200	621,783	1,038	The State	10,781,400	30,104,792	50,263
Lawrence	61,100	138,720	232				
Licking	116,600	280,070	468				
Logan	38,300	96,051	160				

*Source: SRDS Consumer Market Data, 1976.

SUPPLEMENT TO CHAPTER 7
THE TRANSPORTATION
PROBLEM

SETTING UP THE TRANSPORTATION PROBLEM
FINDING AN INITIAL FEASIBLE SOLUTION: THE MINIMUM-COST METHOD
MOVING TO AN OPTIMAL SOLUTION: THE STEPPING-STONE METHOD
MODIFIED DISTRIBUTION (MODI) METHOD
SUMMARY OF THE SOLUTION PROCEDURE FOR THE TRANSPORTATION
PROBLEM
HANDLING SPECIAL SITUATIONS
COMPUTER SOLUTION
SUMMARY AND KEY TERMS
PROBLEMS

T he **transportation problem** arises frequently in planning for the distribution of goods and services from several supply locations to several demand locations. Usually the quantity of goods available at each supply location (*origin*) is limited, and there is a specified quantity of goods needed at each demand location (*destination*). With a variety of shipping routes and differing transportation costs for the routes, the objective is to determine how many units should be shipped from each origin to each destination so that all destination demands are satisfied with a minimum total transportation cost.

In this supplement, we show how to set up a transportation problem and find an optimal solution. The optimal solution to a transportation problem can provide information helpful in making a facility location decision.

Let us consider the problem faced by Foster Generators, Inc. Currently Foster has two plants: one located in Cleveland, Ohio and one located in Bedford, Indiana. Generators produced at the plants (origins) are shipped to distribution centers (destinations) located in Boston; Chicago; St. Louis; and Lexington, Kentucky. Recently, an increase in demand has caused Foster Generators to consider adding a new plant which will provide expanded production capacity. After some study, the location alternatives for the new plant have been reduced to York, Pennsylvania and Clarksville,

Tennessee. To help choose between the two locations, management has asked for information comparing the projected operating costs. If the plant is located in York, management wants to know the minimum shipping costs from the three origins (Cleveland, Bedford, and York) to the four distribution centers. Then finding the minimum shipping cost for the three origins (Cleveland, Bedford, and Clarksville) to the four distribution centers will provide a comparison of transportation costs; this will help determine which location is preferred.

We will illustrate how this shipping cost information can be obtained by solving the transportation problem using the York location alternative. Problem 1 at the end of this supplement will ask you to solve another transportation problem using the Clarksville location alternative. Using a typical one-month planning period, the production capacities at the three plants are as follows:

Origin	Plant	Production Capacity (units)
1	Cleveland	5,000
2	Bedford	6,000
3	York	2,500
	Total	13,500

Forecasts of monthly demand at the four distribution centers are given as follows

Destination	Distribution Center	Demand Forecast (units)
1	Boston	6,000
2	Chicago	4,000
3	St. Louis	2,000
4	Lexington	1,500
	Total	13,500

TABLE 7S.1 Transportation Cost per Unit for the Foster Generators Transportation Problem

	Destination			
Origin	Boston	Chicago	St. Louis	Lexington
Cleveland	3	2	7	6
Bedford	7	5	2	3
York	2	5	4	5

The transportation cost per unit shipped varies for each plant-to-distribution center route. The transportation cost per unit for each route is shown in Table 7S.1.

SETTING UP THE TRANSPORTATION PROBLEM

In order to summarize the transportation problem data conveniently and to keep track of the necessary calculations, a **transportation tableau** is employed. The transportation tableau for the Foster Generators problem is presented in Table 7S.2.

Note that the 12 **cells** in the tableau correspond to the 12 possible shipping routes from the three origins to the four destinations. The entries in the right-hand border of the tableau represent the supply available at each plant, and the entries in the bottom border represent the demand at each distribution center; note also that total supply equals total demand. The entries in the upper right-hand corner of each cell represent the per unit cost of shipping over the corresponding route.

Once the transportation tableau is complete, we can proceed with the calculations necessary to determine the minimum-cost solution. To begin, let us see how we can obtain an initial feasible solution.

FINDING AN INITIAL FEASIBLE SOLUTION: THE MINIMUM-COST METHOD

The **minimum-cost method** for identifying an initial feasible solution requires that we begin by allocating as many units as possible to the minimum-cost route. In Table 7S.2 we see that the Cleveland–Chicago, Bedford–St. Louis, and the York–Boston routes each qualify as the minimum-cost route, since they each have a per unit transportation cost of 2. When ties such as this occur, we will follow the practice of selecting the route over which we can ship the most units. Since this corresponds to shipping 4000 units from Cleveland to Chicago, we write 4000 in the Cleveland–Chicago cell of our transportation tableau. This reduces the supply at Cleveland from 5000 to 1000; hence we cross out the 5000 supply value and replace it with the revised value of 1000. In addition, since shipping 4000 units on this route satisfies the demand at Chicago, we cross out the 4000 Chicago value and replace it with 0. The Chicago demand is now zero. Thus, we eliminate this column from further consideration by drawing a line through the column. Our transportation tableau now appears as shown in Table 7S.3.

Now we look at all unlined cells in order to identify the new minimum-cost route. There is a tie between the Bedford–St. Louis and York–Boston routes. But since more units can be shipped over the York–Boston route, we choose it for the next allocation. This results in an allocation of 2500 units over the York–Boston route. Thus the York supply is reduced to zero, and we eliminate this row from further consideration by drawing a line through it. Continuing this process results in an allocation of 2000 units over the Bedford–St. Louis route and results in the elimination of the

TABLE 7S.2

Transportation Tableau for the Foster Generators Transportation Problem

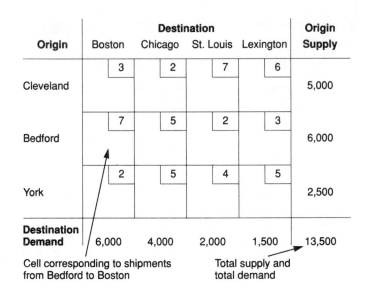

Origin	Destination				Origin Supply
	Boston	Chicago	St. Louis	Lexington	
Cleveland	3	2	7	6	5,000
Bedford	7	5	2	3	6,000
York	2	5	4	5	2,500
Destination Demand	6,000	4,000	2,000	1,500	13,500

Cell corresponding to shipments from Bedford to Boston

Total supply and total demand

TABLE 7S.3

Revised Tableau/ Foster Generators Problem

Origin	Destination				Origin Supply
	Boston	Chicago	St. Louis	Lexington	
Cleveland	3	2 (4,000)	7	6	1,000 ~~5,000~~
Bedford	7	5	2	3	6,000
York	2	5	4	5	2,500
Destination Demand	6,000	~~4,000~~ 0	2,000	1,500	

St. Louis column since its demand goes to zero. The transportation tableau we obtain after carrying out the second and third allocations is shown in Table 7S.4.

We now have two routes that qualify for the minimum-cost route with a value of 3: Cleveland–Boston and Bedford–Lexington. Since a maximum of 1000 units can be shipped over the Cleveland–Boston route as compared with 1500 over the Bedford–Lexington route, we will next allocate 1500 units to the Bedford–Lexington route. Doing so results in a demand of zero at Lexington, and hence this column is eliminated. The next minimum-cost allocation then becomes 100 over the Cleveland–Boston route. The transportation tableau now appears as shown in Table 7S.5.

The only remaining unlined cell is now Bedford–Boston. Allocating 2500 units over this route uses up the remaining supply at Bedford and satisfies all the demand at Boston. The resulting tableau is shown in Table 7S.6.

This solution is feasible, since all the demand is satisfied and all the supply is used. The total transportation cost resulting from this solution is calculated in Table 7S.7.

The method that we discuss in the next section provides an iterative procedure for moving from the initial feasible solution provided by the minimum-cost method to an optimal solution. This method can be implemented only if the initial feasible solution of an

Destination

Origin	Boston	Chicago	St. Louis	Lexington	Origin Supply
Cleveland	3	2 4,000	7	6	1,000 ~~5,000~~
Bedford	7	5	2 2,000	3	4,000 ~~6,000~~
~~York~~	2 ~~2,500~~	5	4	5	0 ~~2,500~~
Destination Demand	~~6,000~~ 3,500	~~4,000~~ 0	~~2,000~~ 0	1,500	

TABLE 7S.4

Revised Tableau/ Foster Generators Problem

Destination

Origin	Boston	Chicago	St. Louis	Lexington	Origin Supply
~~Cleveland~~	3 1,000	2 4,000	7	6	0 ~~1,000~~ ~~5,000~~
Bedford	7	5	2 2,000	3 1,500	2,500 ~~4,000~~ ~~6,000~~
~~York~~	2 ~~2,500~~	5	4	5	0 ~~2,500~~
Destination Demand	~~6,000~~ ~~3,500~~ 2,500	~~4,000~~ 0	~~2,000~~ 0	~~1,500~~ 0	

TABLE 7S.5

Revised Tableau/ Foster Generators Problem

Destination

Origin	Boston	Chicago	St. Louis	Lexington	Origin Supply
~~Cleveland~~	3 1,000	2 4,000	7	6	0 ~~1,000~~ ~~5,000~~
~~Bedford~~	7 2,500	5	2 2,000	3 1,500	0 ~~2,500~~ ~~4,000~~ ~~6,000~~
~~York~~	2 ~~2,500~~	5	4	5	0 ~~2,500~~
Destination Demand	~~6,000~~ ~~3,500~~ ~~2,500~~ 0	~~4,000~~ 0	~~2,000~~ 0	~~1,500~~ 0	

TABLE 7S.6

Revised Tableau/ Foster Generators Problem

TABLE 7S.7
Total Cost of Initial Feasible Solution Using the Minimum-cost Method

Route		Units	Per Unit	Total
From	To	Shipped	Cost ($)	Cost ($)
Cleveland	Boston	1000	3	3,000
Cleveland	Chicago	4000	2	8,000
Bedford	Boston	2500	7	17,500
Bedford	St. Louis	2000	2	4,000
Bedford	Lexington	1500	3	4,500
York	Boston	2500	2	5,000
				42,000

m-origin, n-destination transportation problem utilizes exactly $m + n - 1$ transportation routes. Hence the Foster Generators transportation problem must have $3 + 4 - 1 = 6$ transportation routes in the initial solution. For the Foster Generators problem, the initial feasible solution just found satisfies this condition. However, *to guarantee that the minimum-cost method will always generate initial feasible solutions with $m + n - 1$ routes being assigned shipments, we must modify the method as discussed below.*

Note that when we made our last allocation of 2500 units over the Bedford–Boston route, we simultaneously exhausted all the supply at Bedford and the demand at Boston. In developing an initial feasible solution, the last allocation will always reduce both the remaining row supply and column demand to zero. If this situation were to occur at *any prior iteration,* however, we would obtain an initial feasible solution with less than $m + n - 1$ transportation routes in use. To prevent this from occurring, whenever we reach an iteration that results in the supply at an origin and the demand at a destination being both reduced to zero simultaneously, we must proceed as follows:

1. Eliminate the row and column in question by drawing a line through each.
2. In addition to the assignment to the cell at the intersection of the lined-out row and column, we assign a shipment of zero units to any unoccupied cell in either the lined-out row or column. We treat this cell the same as all other cells to which shipments are assigned.

Summary of the Minimum-cost Method

Before moving on to the second phase of the solution procedure and attempting to improve the initial feasible solution, let us restate the steps of the minimum-cost method for obtaining an initial feasible transportation solution.

Step 1 Identify the cell in the transportation tableau with the lowest cost and assign as many units as possible to this transportation route or cell. In case of a tie, choose the cell over which the most units can be shipped. If ties still exist, choose any of the tied cells.

Step 2 Reduce the row supply and the column demand by the amount assigned to the cell identified in step 1.

Step 3 If *all* row supplies and column demands have been exhausted, then stop; the allocations made will provide an initial feasible solution. Otherwise continue with step 4.

Step 4 If the row supply is now zero, eliminate the row from further consideration by drawing a line through it. If the column demand is now zero, eliminate the column by drawing a line through it. If both a row and column are lined out, make another allocation of 0 units to any unoccupied cell in the lined-out row or column.

Step 5 Continue with step 1 for all unlined rows and columns.

MOVING TO AN OPTIMAL SOLUTION: THE STEPPING-STONE METHOD

The **stepping-stone method** provides an iterative procedure for moving from an initial feasible solution to an optimal solution. We will use the stepping-stone method to evaluate the economics of shipping via transportation routes that are not currently part of the transportation solution. If we can find cost-reducing routes, the current solution will be revised by making shipments via these new routes. By continuing to evaluate the costs associated with routes that are not in the current solution, we will know that we have reached the optimal solution when all routes not in the current solution would increase costs if they were brought into the solution.

To see how the stepping-stone method works, let us return to the initial feasible solution for the Foster Generators problem found by the minimum-cost method (Table 7S.8).

Suppose that we were to allocate 1 unit to the route or cell in row and column 2; that is, ship one unit on the currently unused route from Bedford to Chicago. In order to satisfy the Chicago demand exactly, we would have to reduce the number of units in the Cleveland–Chicago cell to 3999. But then we would have to increase the amount in the Cleveland–Boston cell to 1001 so that the total Cleveland supply of 5000 units could be shipped. Finally, we would reduce the

Bedford–Boston cell by 1 in order to exactly satisfy the Boston demand. Table 7S.9 summarizes the series of adjustments just described.

What is the added or reduced cost that will result from allocating one unit to the Bedford–Chicago route? Let us calculate the net effect of this change. The cost adjustments are as follows:

Changes	Effect on Cost
Add 1 unit to the Bedford–Chicago Route	+5
Reduce the Cleveland–Chicago Route by 1 unit	−2
Add 1 unit to the Cleveland–Boston Route	+3
Reduce the Bedford–Boston Route by 1 unit	−7
Net effect	−1

TABLE 7S.8
Revised Tableau/ Foster Generators Problem

Origin	Destination Boston	Chicago	St. Louis	Lexington	Origin Supply
Cleveland	3 / 1,000	2 / 4,000	7	6	5,000
Bedford	7 / 2,500	5	2 / 2,000	3 / 1,500	6,000
York	2 / 2,500	5	4	5	2,500
Destination Demand	6,000	4,000	2,000	1,500	

TABLE 7S.9
Revised Tableau/ Foster Generators Problem

Origin	Destination Boston	Chicago	St. Louis	Lexington	Origin Supply
Cleveland	3 / 1,001 / ~~1,000~~	2 / 3,999 / ~~4,000~~	7	6	5,000
Bedford	7 / 2,499 / ~~2,500~~	5 / 1	2 / 2,000	3 / 1,500	6,000
York	2 / 2,500	5	4	5	2,500
Destination Demand	6,000	4,000	2,000	1,500	

This analysis shows that the total transportation cost can be reduced by $1 for every unit shipped over the Bedford–Chicago route if corresponding changes are made in other routes as shown.

Before making additions to this new route, let us consider the general procedure for evaluating the costs associated with a new cell or route and then check all currently unused routes to find the best route to add to the current transportation solution.

The method we have just demonstrated for evaluating the Bedford–Chicago route is known as the *stepping-stone method*. Note that in considering the addition of this new route, we evaluated its effect on other routes *currently in the transportation solution,* referred to as *occupied* cells. In total we considered changes in four cells, the new cell and three *current solution* or *occupied* cells. In effect, we can view these four cells as forming a path, or *stepping-stone path,* in the tableau, where the corners of the path are current solution cells. The idea is to view the tableau as a pond with the current solution cells as stones sticking up in the pond. To identify the stepping-stone path for a new cell, we move in horizontal and vertical directions using current solution cells as the stones at the corners of the path by which we can step from stone to stone and return to the new cell we initially started with. To help focus our attention on which occupied cells are part of the current stepping-stone path, we draw each occupied cell in the stepping-stone path as a cylinder; this should help to reinforce the image of these cells as stones sticking up in the pond. Hence, when evaluating the Bedford–Chicago route using the stepping-stone method, we would depict the solution as in Table 7S.10.

In the above stepping-stone path we depicted the sequence of adjustments as proceeding from the Bedford–Chicago cell to the Cleveland–Chicago cell to the Cleveland–Boston cell to the Bedford–Boston cell and then back to the Bedford–Chicago cell; that is, the adjustments were made moving in a counterclockwise fashion. You should convince yourself that exactly the same adjustments appear if we had proceeded in a clockwise direction.

For example, let us consider how to compute the stepping-stone path if we were to use the Cleveland–St. Louis route. The dotted line in the tableau depicted in Table 7S.11 represents the stepping-stone path for the Cleveland–St. Louis route or cell. In terms of a transportation tableau, the stepping-stone path represents the sequence of adjustments that are necessary to maintain a feasible solution, given that one unit is to be shipped through a new or currently unoccupied cell.

Note that in order to carry out the adjustments necessary to increase the flow on the Cleveland–St. Louis route, the corners of the stepping-stone path are established in such a way that as we "jump" from stone to stone on this path we jump over the occupied Cleveland–Chicago cell. This type of situation frequently arises when we determine a stepping-stone path.

After identifying the stepping-stone path for a new cell, we can evaluate the net effect associated with a one-unit addition to the new cell. For example, for the Cleveland–St. Louis cell this would result in the following changes:

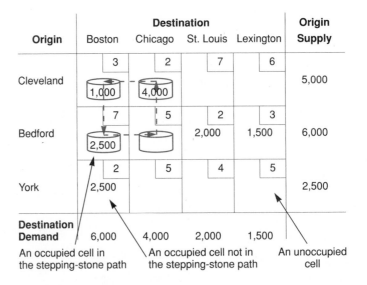

TABLE 7S.10	Destination				Origin
Revised Tableau/ Foster Generators Problem	**Origin**	Boston	Chicago	St. Louis	Lexington	**Supply**

An occupied cell in the stepping-stone path

An occupied cell not in the stepping-stone path

An unoccupied cell

Origin	Destination Boston	Chicago	St. Louis	Lexington	Origin Supply
Cleveland	3 / 1,000	2 / 4,000	7 / (empty)	6	5,000
Bedford	7 / 2,500	5	2 / 2,000	3 / 1,500	6,000
York	2 / 2,500	5	4	5	2,500
Destination Demand	6,000	4,000	2,000	1,500	

TABLE 7S.11

Revised Tableau/ Foster Generators Problem

Changes	Effect on Cost
Add 1 unit to the Cleveland–St. Louis Route	+7
reduce the Bedford–St. Louis Route by 1 unit	−2
Add 1 unit to the Bedford–Boston Route	+7
Reduce the Cleveland–Boston Route by 1 unit	−3
Net effect	+9

Thus we see that the Cleveland–St. Louis route is unattractive; shipping one additonal unit over this route will result in a $9 increase in the total transportation cost.

Finding the stepping-stone path for each possible new cell enables us to identify the cost effect for each new cell or route. Evaluating this cost effect for all possible new cells leads to the transportation tableau in Table 7S.12. The per unit cost effect for each possible new cell is circled in the cell.

On the basis of the calculated per unit changes, we see that the best cell in terms of cost reduction is the Bedford–Chicago cell, with a $1 decrease in cost for every unit shipped on this route. The question now is: How much should we ship over this new route? Since the total cost decreases by $1 per unit shipped, we would like to ship the maximum possible number of units. We know from our previous stepping-stone calculation that each unit shipped over the Bedford–Chicago route results in an increase of one unit shipped from Cleveland to Boston and a decrease of one unit in both the amount shipped from Bedford to Boston (currently 2500) and the amount shipped from Cleveland to Chicago (currently 4000). Because of this the maximum we can ship over the Bedford–Chicago route

is 2500. This results in a reduction of 2500 units on the Cleveland–Chicago route, an increase of 2500 units on the Cleveland–Boston route, and a decrease of 2500 units on the Bedford–Boston route. Table 7S.13 shows this new solution.

Note that the only changes from the previous tableau are located on the stepping-stone path originating in the Bedford–Chicago cell. We can now use the stepping-stone method to recalculate the per unit changes resulting from attempting to add new cells or routes to this new solution. Doing so we get Table 7S.14. Note that the stepping-stone path used to evaluate the York–St. Louis cell is indicated by the dashed line in the tableau.

The per unit change for every possible new cell is now greater than or equal to zero. Thus since there is no new route that will decrease the total cost, we have reached the optimal solution. The optimal solution, together with its total cost, is summarized in Table 7S.15. We see that if the York location is chosen, transportation costs can be expected to run $39,500 per month.

Maintaining $m + n - 1$ Transportation Routes Using the Stepping-stone Method

In the discussion of the minimum-cost method we stated that a requirement of the iterative procedure for finding an optimal solution is that the initial feasible solution must utilize $m + n - 1$ transportation routes. This requirement must also be maintained at each iteration of our stepping-stone solution procedure. Although we had no difficulty with the Foster Generators problem, situations can arise where as a result of making an allocation to a new cell the allocation to more than one of the unoccupied cells is reduced to zero.

TABLE 7S.12
Revised Tableau/ Foster Generators Problem

Origin	Boston	Chicago	St. Louis	Lexington	Origin Supply
Cleveland	3 / 1,000	2 / 4,000	(+9) 7	(+7) 6	5,000
Bedford	7 / 2,500	(-1) 5	2 / 2,000	3 / 1,500	6,000
York	2 / 2,500	(+4) 5	(+7) 4	(+7) 5	2,500
Destination Demand	6,000	4,000	2,000	1,500	

TABLE 7S.13
Revised Tableau/ Foster Generators Problem

Origin	Boston	Chicago	St. Louis	Lexington	Origin Supply
Cleveland	3 / 3,500	2 / 1,500	7	6	5,000
Bedford	7	5 / 2,500	2 / 2,000	3 / 1,500	6,000
York	2 / 2,500	5	4	5	2,500
Destination Demand	6,000	4,000	2,000	1,500	

TABLE 7S.14
Revised Tableau/ Foster Generators Problem

Origin	Boston	Chicago	St. Louis	Lexington	Origin Supply
Cleveland	3 / 3,500	2 / 1,500	(8) 7	(6) 6	5,000
Bedford	(1) 7	5 / 2,500	2 / 2,000	3 / 1,500	6,000
York	2 / 2,500	(4) 5	(6) 4	(6) 5	2,500
Destination Demand	6,000	4,000	2,000	1,500	

Route		Units	Per Unit	Total	
From	To	Shipped	Cost ($)	Cost ($)	
Cleveland	Boston	3500	3	10,500	**TABLE 7S.15**
Cleveland	Chicago	1500	2	3,000	**Optimal Solution**
Bedford	Chicago	2500	5	12,500	**to the Foster**
Bedford	St. Louis	2000	2	4,000	**Generators**
Bedford	Lexington	1500	3	4,500	**Transportation**
York	Boston	2500	2	5,000	**Problem**
				39,500	

This would cause us to have fewer than $m + n - 1$ transportation routes in the current solution. To provide an illustration of such a situation let us consider the following modification of the Foster Generators transportation problem.

Suppose that the original supply at Cleveland were 3500 (instead of 5000) and that the demand at Chicago were 2500 (instead of 4000). The initial feasible solution we would obtain using the minimum-cost method is shown by the tableau in Table 7S.16.

Now if we were to consider shipping 250 units over the Bedford–Chicago route as we did previously, the number of units shipped over the Cleveland–Chicago route would be reduced to zero, the number shipped over the Cleveland–Boston route would be increased to 3500, and the number shipped over the Bedford–Boston route would be reduced to zero. Thus two cells would be simultaneously reduced to zero, and hence in our new solution we would have only five transportation routes being utilized instead of the required

six. To maintain a solution with six transportation routes, then, we arbitrarily select either the Cleveland–Chicago route or the Bedford–Boston route to received a shipment of zero units. Selecting the Bedford-Boston route results in the tableau found in Table 7S.17.

In further computations the Bedford–Boston cell is treated like any other occupied cell. The assignment of a shipment of zero units in cases such as this guarantees that we will always utilize $m + n - 1$ transportation routes at any iteration of the solution procedure.

The most difficult part of the solution procedure we have outlined is the identification of every stepping-stone path so that we can calculate the cost-per-unit change in each new cell. There is an easier way to make these cost-per-unit calculations; it is called the **modified distribution (MODI) method**. Let us demonstrate how this method can be used to calculate the per unit changes for the new or unoccupied cells.

MODIFIED DISTRIBUTION (MODI) METHOD

The MODI method provides a simple approach for determining the best unoccupied cell to bring into solution. This method requires that we define an index u_i for each row of the tableau and an index v_j for each column of the tableau. The values of these indexes are found by requiring that the cost coefficient for each occupied cell equal $u_i + v_j$. If we define c_{ij} to be the per unit cost of shipping from origin i to destination j, then we require that $u_i + v_j = c_{ij}$ for each occupied cell.

Requiring that $u_i + v_j = c_{ij}$ for all the occupied cells in the final tableau of the Foster Generators problem leads to a system of six equations and seven variables.

Cleveland–Boston $u_1 + v_1 = 3$

Cleveland–Chicago $u_1 + v_2 = 2$

Bedford–Chicago $u_2 + v_2 = 5$

Bedford–St. Louis $u_2 + v_3 = 2$

Bedford–Lexington $u_2 + v_4 = 3$

York–Boston $u_3 + v_1 = 2$

Since there is one more variable than equation in the above system, we can set any one of the variables equal to an arbitrary value and then solve for the values of the other variables. We will always set $u_1 = 0$ and then solve for the values of the other variables. Setting $u_1 = 0$, we get the following system of equations:

$$0 + v_1 = 3$$

Origin	Boston	Chicago	St. Louis	Lexington	Origin Supply
Cleveland	3 — 1,000	2 — 2,500	7	6	3,500
Bedford	7 — 2,500	5	2 — 2,000	3 — 1,500	6,000
York	2 — 2,500	5	4	5	2,500
Destination Demand	6,000	4,000	2,000	1,500	

Origin	Boston	Chicago	St. Louis	Lexington	Origin Supply
Cleveland	3 — 3,500	2	7	6	3,500
Bedford	7 — 0	5 — 2,500	2 — 2,000	3 — 1,500	6,000
York	2 — 2,500	5	4	5	2,500
Destination Demand	6,000	4,000	2,000	1,500	

$$0 + v_2 = 2$$
$$u_2 + v_2 = 5$$
$$u_2 + v_3 = 2$$
$$u_2 + v_4 = 3$$
$$u_3 + v_1 = 2$$

Solving these equations leads to the following values for u_1, u_2, u_3, v_1, v_2, v_3, and v_4:

$$u_1 = 0 \quad v_1 = 3$$
$$u_2 = 3 \quad v_2 = 2$$
$$u_3 = -1 \quad v_3 = -1$$
$$v_4 = 0$$

It can be shown that $e_{ij} = c_{ij} - u_i - v_j$ represents the per unit change in total cost resulting from allocating one unit to the unoccupied cell in row i and column j. Rewriting the final tableau for the Foster Generators

problem and replacing the previous marginal information with the values of u_i and v_j, we obtain the table below. Once again the per unit cost effect for each new cell (e_{ij}) has been circled.

u_i	v_j = 3	2	-1	0
0	3 — 3,500	2 — 1,500	⑧ 7	⑥ 6
3	① 7	5 — 2,500	2 — 2,000	3 — 1,500
-1	2 — 2,500	④ 5	⑥ 4	⑥ 5

Note how much easier it is to compute the net changes using the MODI method. For example, $e_{13} = c_{13} - u_1 - v_3 = 7 - 0 - (-1) = 8$ represents the net change in the total cost that would result from allocating one unit to the cell in row 1 and column 3. We also observe that the e_{ij} calculated by the MODI method are exactly the same as the net changes calculated by the stepping-stone method. It is still nec-essary to search for a stepping-stone path to determine which route to remove from the solution once the best route to bring into the solution has been identified. However, it is not necessary to generate a stepping-stone path for any of the other unoccupied cells. Thus, considerable savings in the work required at each iteration can be obtained by employing the MODI method in the calculation of the e_{ij} for each unoccupied cell.

SUMMARY OF THE SOLUTION PROCEDURE FOR THE TRANSPORTATION PROBLEM

In the preceding discussion we showed how the min-imum-cost method can be used to obtain an initial feasible solution to the transportation problem. We then illustrated how the stepping-stone method can be used to determine which route (if any) to bring into the solution, which route to remove from the solution, and the number of units to ship over the new route. Finally, we showed that the MODI method—as com-pared with the stepping-stone method—provides an easier way to determine which route to bring into the solution.

This discussion suggests that we employ the fol-lowing approach to solve the transportation problem: (1) use the minimum-cost method to determine an in-itial feasible solution; (2) use the MODI method to determine which new route (if any) to bring into the solution; and (3) use the stepping-stone method to determine which route to remove from the solution and how many units to ship over the new route. Since we have already provided a summary of the steps needed to carry out the minimum-cost method, we will not repeat the details of this method in summarizing the solution procedure for the transportation problem.

Step 1 Use the minimum-cost method to identify an initial feasible solution consisting of $m + n - 1$ occupied cells.

Step 2 Letting $u_1 = 0$, use the occupied cells of the transportation tableau to compute row in-dexes $u_2, u_3, \ldots$ and column indexes $v_1, v_2, v_3, \ldots$ such that

$$u_i + v_j = c_{ij}$$

for all occupied cells.

Step 3 Compute the cost e_{ij} of adding one unit to each unoccupied cell using the equation

$$e_{ij} = c_{ij} - u_i - v_j$$

Step 4 In a minimization problem, if the per unit changes (e_{ij}'s) for all unoccupied cells are nonnegative, the solution is optimal. How-ever, if negative per unit changes exist, iden-tify the best cell (most negative per unit change) and continue.

Step 5 For the best cell, find the stepping-stone path through the transportation tableau. Label the best cell as cell 1 and number sequentially 2, 3, 4, . . ., the occupied cells on the corners of the stepping-stone path. Determine the even-numbered stepping-stone cell over which the smallest quantity is being shipped. Add this quantity to the new cell and all other odd-numbered cells. Subtract this quantity from all even-numbered cells. If more than one of the currently occupied cells on the stepping-stone path is forced to zero, maintain the require-ment of $m + n - 1$ occupied cells by en-tering a shipment of zero units on one or more of the cells that were forced to zero. Return to step 2.

Let us see how the following special situations are handled with the solution procedure:

1. total supply not equal to total demand
2. maximization objective
3. unacceptable transportation routes

The case where the total supply is not equal to the total demand can be handled easily by the solution procedure if we first introduce a dummy origin or dummy destination. If total supply is greater than total demand, introduce a **dummy destination** with demand exactly equal to the excess of supply over demand. Similarly, if total demand is greater than total supply, introduce a **dummy origin** with supply exactly equal to the excess of demand over supply. In either case, assign cost coefficients of zero to every route into a dummy destination and every route out of a dummy origin. This is because no shipments will actually be made from a dummy origin or to a dummy destination when the solution is implemented.

The solution procedure can also be used to solve maximization problems. The only modification necessary involves the selection of an unoccupied cell to allocate units to. Instead of picking the cell with the most negative e_{ij} value, we pick that cell for which e_{ij} is most positive. That is, we pick the cell that will cause the largest per unit increase in the objective function.

To handle unacceptable transportation routes, we require that unacceptable assignments carry an extremely high cost, denoted M, in order to keep them out of solution. Thus if we have a transportation route from an origin to a destination that for some reason cannot be used, we simply assign this route a per unit cost of M, and thus this route will not enter the solution. Unacceptable routes would be assigned a per unit value of $-M$ in a maximization problem.

Let us now consider another example to show how special situations can be handled. In the process we will also show how production costs can be taken into account in a transportation problem. Suppose that we have three plants (origins) with production capacities as follows:

Plants	Production Capacity
P_1	50
P_2	40
P_3	30
Total	120

We also have demand for the product at three retail outlets (destinations). The demand forecasts for the current planning period are presented below.

Retail Outlets	Forecasted Demand
R_1	45
R_2	15
R_3	30
Total	90

The production cost at each plant is different, and the sales prices at the retail outlets vary. Taking prices, production costs, and shipping costs into consideration, the profits for producing one unit at plant i, shipping it to retail outlet j, and selling it at retail outlet j are presented in Table 7S.18.

We note first that the total production capacity exceeds the total demand at the retail outlets. Thus we must introduce a dummy retail outlet with demand exactly equal to the excess production capacity. We therefore add retail outlet R_4 with a demand of 30 units. The per unit profit for shipping from each plant to retail outlet R_4 is set to zero, since these units will not actually be shipped. To obtain an initial feasible solution, we use the minimum-cost method. However, since this is a maximization problem, the minimum-cost method must be changed to a corresponding maximum-profit method. That is, in general we select the shipping route that will maximize profit instead of minimizing cost. The initial feasible solution obtained using this approach is shown by the tableau in Table 7S.19.

Now let us compute the value of $e_{ij} = c_{ij} - u_i - v_j$, where the value of e_{ij} represents the per unit change in total profit resulting from allocating one unit to the unoccupied cell in row i and column j; Table 7S.20 shows the values of u_i, v_j, and e_{ij} that we obtained.

TABLE 7S.18 Profit Per Unit for Producing at Plant i and Selling at Retail Outlet j

Plants	Retail Outlets R_1	R_2	R_3
P_1	2	8	10
P_2	6	11	6
P_3	12	7	9

Origin	Destination R₁	R₂	R₃	R₄	Origin Supply
P₁	2	8	10 / 30	0 / 20	50
P₂	6 / 15	11 / 15	6	0 / 10	40
P₃	12 / 30	7	9	0	30
Destination Demand	45	15	30	30	

TABLE 7S.19
Initial Feasible Solution

u_i	v_j = 6	11	10	0	Origin Supply
0	⊝4 2	⊝3 8	10 / 30	0 / 20	50
0	6 / 15	11 / 15	⊝4 6	0 / 10	40
6	12 / 30	⊝10 7	⊝7 9	⊝6 0	30
Destination Demand	45	15	30	30	

TABLE 7S.20
Revised Transportation Tableau

Since this is a maximization problem, we look for the cell with the largest positive e_{ij}. However, since each e_{ij} value is negative, introducing any new allocation will only reduce the profit. Thus, the initial solution is optimal. When implementing this solution, we would ship 30 units from plant P_1 to retail outlet R_3, 15 units from P_2 to R_1, 15 units from P_2 to R_2, and 30 units from P_3 to R_1. Thus we are left with an excess supply of 20 units at P_1 and 10 units at P_2.

COMPUTER SOLUTION

Although the solution procedures presented in this supplement make it possible to solve small transportation problems by hand, the amount of computation can become prohibitive for modest-sized problems. Consequently, microcomputer software packages such as *The Management Scientist* have been developed to take advantage of the special network structure of the transportation problem.

To solve a transportation problem such as the Foster Generators problem using the transportation module of *The Management Scientist*, the user must enter the following data:

1. number of origins
2. number of destinations
3. amount of supply at each origin

FIGURE 7S.1 Optimal Solution to the Foster Generators Problem Using *The Management Scientist* Software Package

```
OPTIMAL SHIPMENT SCHEDULE
*************************

SHIP              TO DESTINATION
FROM
ORIGIN      1       2       3       4
******    ****    ****    ****    ****

  1       3500    1500      0       0

  2          0    2500    2000    1500

  3       2500       0       0       0


TOTAL TRANSPORTATION COST     39,500
```

4. amount of demand at each destination
5. per unit cost of shipping from each origin to each destination

A portion of the output for the Foster Generators problem is shown in Figure 7S.1. Note that origin 1 corresponds to Cleveland, origin 2 to Bedford, and origin 3 to York. Similarly, destination 1 corresponds to Boston, destination 2 to Chicago, and so on. The ease of use of such a package makes it an attractive alternative when solving transportation problems.

SUMMARY AND KEY TERMS

Summary

In this supplement we have introduced the transportation problem and its solution procedure. The transportation problem involves determining how many units should be shipped from each of several origins to each of several destinations so that all destination demands are satisfied with a minimum total transportation cost. Setting the problem up in a transportation tableau enabled us to make the computations necessary to arrive at an optimal solution. The minimum-cost method provides the identification of an initial feasible solution. The stepping-stone method and the modified distribution (MODI) method were then presented as procedures to be used to improve the initial solution in order to find the optimal solution.

We also showed how to handle special situations that can occur in transportation problems. The special situations included cases where total supply did not equal total demand, cases where the objective was maximization rather than minimization, and cases where some unacceptable transportation routes existed.

Key Terms

Transportation problem
Transportation tableau
Cell
Minimum-cost method
Stepping-stone method
Modified Distribution (MODI) method
Dummy destination
Dummy origin

PROBLEMS

1. Reconsider the Foster Generators, Inc.'s, transportation and facilities location problem. Assume that the York plant location alternative is replaced by the Clarksville, Tennessee plant location. Using the 2500 units capacity for the Clarksville plant and the unit transportation costs shown below, determine the minimum-cost transportation problem solution if the new plant is located in Clarksville.

Shipping from Clarksville to	Unit Cost
Boston	9
Chicago	6
St. Louis	3
Lexington	3

Compare the total transportation cost using the York plant location and the Clarksville plant location. Which plant location provides the lower cost transportation solution?

2. Consider the following transportation problem.

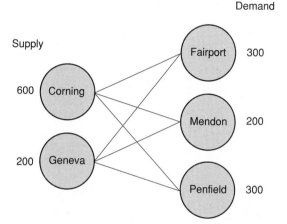

Supply / Demand

The transportation costs per unit are as follows:

	Fairport	Mendon	Penfield
Corning	16	10	14
Geneva	12	12	20

a. Set up the transportation tableau for this problem.
b. Use the minimum-cost method to find an initial feasible solution.
c. Find an optimal solution.

3. A product is produced at three plants and shipped to three warehouses; the transportation costs per unit are shown in Table 7S.21. Find the optimal solution.

TABLE 7S.21 Transportation Costs for Problem 3

	Warehouse			Plant
Plant	W_1	W_2	W_3	Capacity
P_1	20	16	24	300
P_2	10	10	8	500
P_3	12	18	10	100
Warehouse demands	200	400	300	

4. Arnoff Enterprises manufactures the central processing unit (CPU) for a line of personal computers. The CPUs are manufactured in Seattle, Columbus, and New York and shipped to warehouses in Pittsburgh, Mobile, Denver, Los Angeles, and Washington, D.C., for further distribution. The transportation tableau in Table 7S.22 shows the number of CPUs available at each plant and the number of CPUs required by each warehouse. The shipping costs (dollars per unit) are also shown.
a. Determine the amount that should be shipped from each plant to each warehouse in order to minimize the total transportation cost.
b. The Pittsburgh warehouse has just increased its order by 1000 units and Arnoff has authorized the Columbus plant to increase its production by 1000 units. Do you expect this development to lead to an increase or a decrease in the total transportation cost? Solve for the new optimal solution.

5. Consider the minimum cost transportation problem in Table 7S.23.

TABLE 7S.22

Transportation Tableau for Arnoff Enterprises (Problem 4)

Plant	Pittsburgh	Mobile	Warehouse Denver	Los Angeles	Washington	Origin Supply
Seattle	10	20	5	9	10	9,000
Columbus	2	10	8	30	6	4,000
New York	1	20	7	10	4	8,000
Units Required	3,000	5,000	4,000	6,000	3,000	21,000

TABLE 7S.23   Problem 5 Tableau

Origin	Destination Los Angeles	Destination San Francisco	Destination San Diego	Origin Supply
San Jose	4	10	6	100
Las Vegas	8	16	6	300
Tucson	14	18	10	300
Destination Demand	200	300	200	700

a. Find an initial feasible solution.
b. Find an optimal solution.
c. How would the optimal solution change if we must ship 100 units on the Tucson-San Diego route?
d. Because of road construction, the Las Vegas-San Diego route is now unacceptable. Resolve the initial problem with this change.

6. Find the optimal solution to the transportation problem below.

Origin	D_1	D_2	D_3	Origin Supply
O_1	6	8	8	250
O_2	18	12	14	150
O_3	8	12	10	100
Destination Demand	150	200	150	

7. The R.K. Martin Company is in the process of planning for new production facilities and developing a more efficient distribution system design. At present they have one plant at St. Louis with a capacity of 30,000 units. Because of increased demand, management is considering four potential new plant sites: Detroit, Denver, Toledo, and Kansas City. The transportation tableau below sum-

marizes the projected plant capacities, the cost per unit of shipping from each plant to each destination, and the demand forecasts over a 1-year planning horizon.

Origin	Boston	Atlanta	Houston	Capacities
Detroit	5	2	3	30,000
Toledo	4	3	4	20,000
Denver	9	7	5	30,000
Kansas City	10	4	2	40,000
St. Louis	8	4	3	30,000
Destination Demand	30,000	20,000	20,000	

Suppose that the fixed costs of constructing the new plants are

Detroit	$175,000
Toledo	$300,000
Denver	$375,000
Kansas City	$500,000

The R. K. Martin Company would like to minimize the total cost of plant construction and distribution of goods.

a. Explain how the transportation model can be used to make this decision.
b. Suppose that only one additional plant is to be constructed. Determine the best choice.

8. Klein Chemicals, Inc., produces a special oil-base material that is currently in short supply. Four of Klein's customers have already placed orders that in total exceed the combined capacity of Klein's two plants. Klein's management faces the problem of deciding how many units is should supply to each customer. Since the four customers are in different industries, the pricing structure allows different prices to be charged to different customers. However, slightly different production costs at the two plants and varying transportation costs between the plants and customers make a "sell to the highest bidder" strategy unacceptable. After considering price, production costs, and transpor-

tation costs, Klein has established the following profit per unit for each plant-customer alternative.

	Customer			
Plant	D_1	D_2	D_3	D_4
Clifton Springs	$32	$34	$32	$40
Danville	$34	$30	$28	$38

The plant capacities and customer orders are as follows:

Plant	Capacity (Units)	Customer	Orders (Units)
Clifton Springs	5000	D_1	2000
		D_2	5000
Danville	3000	D_3	3000
		D_4	2000

How many units should each plant produce for each customer in order to *maximize* the total profit? Which customer demands will not be met?

9. Sound Electronics, Inc., produces a battery-operated tape recorder at plants located in Martinsville, North Carolina; Plymouth, New York; and Franklin, Missouri. The unit transportation costs for shipments from the three plants to distribution centers in Chicago, Dallas, and New York are as follows:

	To		
From	Chicago	Dallas	New York
Martinsville	1.45	1.60	1.40
Plymouth	1.10	2.25	0.60
Franklin	1.20	1.20	1.80

After considering transportation costs, management has decided not to use the Plymouth-Dallas route. The plant capacities and distributor orders for the next month are as follows:

Plant	Capacity (Units)	Distributor	Order (Units)
Martinsville	400	Chicago	400
Plymouth	600	Dallas	400
Franklin	300	New York	400

Because of different wage scales at the three plants, the unit production cost varies from plant to plant. Assuming that the costs are $29.50 per unit at Martinsville, $31.20 per unit at Plymouth, and $30.35 per unit at Franklin, find the production and distribution plan that minimizes the total production and transportation cost.

The Ace Manufacturing Company has orders for three similar products.

Product	Orders (Units)
A	2000
B	500
C	1200

Three machines are available for the manufacturing operations. All three machines can produce all the products at the same production rate. However, because of varying defect percentages of each product on each machine, the unit costs of the products vary depending on the machine used. Machine capacities for the next week, and the unit costs, are as follows:

Machine	Capacity (Units)
I	1500
II	1500
III	1000

	Product		
Machine	A	B	C
I	$1.00	$1.20	$0.90
II	$1.30	$1.40	$1.20
III	$1.10	$1.00	$1.20

a. Use the transportation model to develop the minimum-cost production schedule for the products and machines.
b. Find an alternate optimal production schedule.

Process Technology and Selection

I n the previous chapter we discussed the problems associated with locating facilities such as plants and warehouses, and designing a firm's overall distribution system. Management must also make strategic decisions concerning both the design of such facilities and the selection of the production processes to be used to convert inputs into goods and services.

Both managerial and technical issues are involved in selecting the production processes to be used. Managerial issues focus on the role of process technology in operations strategy. Can the process help meet the strategic goals and objectives of the organization—quality, flexibility, dependability, and cost—and give the firm a competitive edge? Technical issues concern the choice of equipment and methods for converting inputs to outputs. Factors that must be considered include the short- and long-term economics of the process, the ability of the process to meet design specifications and achieve consistent quality, and the reliability of the process. Because operations managers must be able to evaluate a process in terms of its ability to meet the organization's strategic objectives, operations managers must understand both the technical and the managerial implications of the production processes.

This chapter covers the issues involved in selecting production processes. Since process design for services was discussed in Chapter 5 on product design, our focus here is primarily on manufacturing. In the next chapter we continue this discussion by focusing on the physical design and layout of production processes within a facility.

8.1 PROCESS TECHNOLOGY ISSUES AND OPERATIONS STRATEGY

Process technology consists of the methods and equipment used to manufacture a product or deliver a service, and it is an essential component of an organization's operations strategy. Given the firm's financial resources, processes must be selected that provide the capability to meet a product's design specifications and volume requirements. Processes must also provide sufficient flexibility to respond to market changes and new-product development.

Hayes and Wheelwright[1] suggest that a narrow general management perspective on process technology may be the source of many strategic problems that have surfaced in U.S. manufacturing firms. Table 8.1 summarizes their thoughts concerning the consequences of taking a narrow perspective regarding process technology. Hayes and Wheelwright advocate taking a broader view of process technology. Table 8.2 lists several consequences associated with this broader viewpoint. Taking a broad view of process technology results in top management having greater familiarity with the technology being used, leading to upper level decisions that support an organization's operations strategy. As a result, upper management can better prepare the firm for changes in market conditions.

---

[1]Robert H. Hayes and Steven C. Wheelwright, *Restoring Our Competitive Edge: Competing Through Manufacturing,* New York: John Wiley & Sons, 1984. Copyright © 1984. Reprinted by permission of John Wiley & Sons, Inc.

| Factors Affecting Process Technology Decisions | An important factor affecting process technology decisions is the type of production process. There are three types of process technology: *manual, mechanized,* and *automated.* Manual technology uses no machinery to perform manufacturing or assembly tasks; mechanized technology involves the use of machines under human control; and automated technology uses computers to control the entire process. Although there are now a number of highly automated technology processes, the majority of U.S. factories still depend primarily on mechanized technology. However, automation is becoming increasingly more important as technology continues to evolve. As a result, Chapter 10 focuses solely on this topic. |

A second important factor affecting which type of process technology to use is product design. In Chapter 5 we discussed the importance of coordinating the product design decision with the production process decision. Simplification of product design can often lead to simpler and more effective production processes, and managers are beginning to recognize that product and process design cannot be treated independently.

The variety of products produced at a facility is another important factor in determining what technology should be used. As the product line expands, the technology required to produce different items must also maintain pace. Product proliferation can, however, lead to a lack of focus, as we noted in Chapter 4 in the discussion of the "focused factory." By limiting the number of products and processes, the firm can increase productivity (through specialization and learning) and achieve a competitive advantage.

Volume requirements are also critical factors in process technology decisions. As production volume increases, more specialized equipment is necessary to achieve economies of scale resulting in reduced flexibility to introduce product variations. Process technology must follow a product's life cycle, and must change as the product moves through its various stages.

Finally, quality is an important consideration in selecting process technology. Human work is highly variable and can lead to inconsistent quality. Automated technology, on the other hand, is more consistent and can greatly increase the accuracy and precision of a production process, thus leading to higher quality. The cost of increased automation, however, is reduced flexibility.

Table 8.1 **A Narrow Perspective on Process Technology**	1. Technology is *narrowly defined* and is the responsibility of the technical specialist and lower-level operating manager.
	2. Process technology is *separable* and individual projects can be examined and evaluated in isolation.
	3. Manufacturing-technology decisions relate to *specific products;* the fact that equipment remains in use over several product generations is ignored.
	4. All important issues and decisions can be addressed within the framework of the *capital budgeting process.*
	5. Significant competitive moves come from *major breakthroughs,* not small incremental changes that are largely invisible to top management.
	6. Technical knowledge is in the domain of the *specialist* and is neither required nor useful to general management, which must deal with the big picture.

Source: Adapted from Hayes and Wheelwright, p. 189–191.

Table 8.2
A Broad View of
Process
Technology

1. Process technology is defined in terms of information and material flows, linkages, controls, and potential for improvement and is viewed as a *total system*.
2. Manufacturing technology is an *integrated activity* that cuts across functional boundaries and is continuous over time.
3. Technology is a set of *general capabilities* that meet the firm's current needs as well as future product market strategies.
4. Technology is a product of *holistic decision making* that includes a variety of subjective elements, nonfinancial and financial and long-term as well as short-term.
5. Improvement comes from *incremental efforts* that are difficult for competitors to imitate.
6. Technical competence is essential for *general managers* as well as technical specialists.

Source: Adapted from Hayes and Wheelwright, pp. 192–194.

Firms either produce *in response to* customer orders, or produce *in anticipation of* customer orders. Thus, production systems can usually be classified into one of two general categories: *make-to-order* and *make-to-stock*. Since manufacturers of jet engines produce only in response to orders from aircraft builders, their production system would be classified as make-to-order. Manufacturers of radios and other small appliances, however, build inventories for future sale. Such a production system would be classified as make-to-stock. Restaurants and self-service cafeterias are also examples of make-to-order and make-to-stock systems, respectively.

The focus of operations management activities differs in these two types of systems. For instance, forecasting is relatively easy for make-to-stock items, whereas it is usually more difficult to forecast the demand for make-to-order products. Control of inventories is important in make-to-stock situations, especially in planning for the purchase and delivery of raw materials and components. In make-to-order systems, a larger variety of materials must be maintained because of uncertainty of orders, and finished goods inventory is of little concern. On the other hand, scheduling is very difficult in make-to-order systems because each job may have unique processing characteristics. Scheduling for the production of large quantities of make-to-stock items is generally easier.

We see that make-to-order and make-to-stock production systems differ in two fundamental respects: the *variety* of products made, and the *quantity* of a given product that is produced. Make-to-order production systems typically produce a larger variety of products in smaller quantities than do make-to-stock production systems. Therefore, different production processes are appropriate for each type of system. Production processes are often classified as

- continuous flow
- mass, or assembly line
- batch
- job shop
- project

As we move down the list from continuous flow to project production processes, variety increases while volume decreases.

Continuous-flow production processes are characterized by a high-production volume and a high degree of product standardization. The production of bulk quantities of chemicals, oil, sugar, and other commodity-type items are examples of continuous-flow processes. Such industries use highly specialized and dedicated equipment and often a high degree of automation. Since the equipment is highly specialized, there is little need to change machine setups for different products and the labor skills required are low. Because of the high volume, unit costs are generally low.

Mass or *assembly-line* production processes are used for high-volume production of discrete parts. Usually only a small variety of different products are produced, although there may be many minor model variations. Automobiles, household appliances, electronic calculators, and computers are manufactured with this type of production process. As with continuous-flow production processes, specialized equipment and automation are common. Machine setups are infrequent, labor skill requirements are low, and as a result, unit costs are also low.

Batch or *intermittent production* processes are used for the production of small lot sizes of similar products, such as books, clothing, or wine. The products are made in batches with short production runs, and the same sequence of operations is generally followed.. Such processes usually differ from mass production in the materials used, machine setups, and layout. More labor skills are necessary to set up machines and perform a wider variety of tasks during production. These differences increase unit costs.

Job shop production processes produce a wide variety and small quantity of specialized products. Products are generally customized; each product may follow an entirely different sequence of operations. Job shops are essentially make-to-order systems, whereas continuous flow, mass, and batch production processes are generally make-to-stock processes. Makers of industrial machine tools, small parts suppliers, some pharmaceutical companies, and print shops are examples of organizations that use job shops. More general purpose equipment is used and there is less opportunity for specialized, automated equipment. The labor force must be highly skilled and able to perform a wide variety of tasks on different jobs. Unit production costs are higher than for other production processes.

A *project* production process is one in which a unique item is produced. The construction industry utilizes the project production process. The production of large, complex items such as ships, aircraft, and space vehicles is managed by projects. The products made are assembled at a fixed location and components and subassemblies must be brought to that location. Project network techniques such as PERT/CPM (see Chapter 18) are useful management tools for such production processes. Labor skills and costs are generally high.

Table 8.3 summarizes the basic differences among these five types of production processes. One can see that in selecting the appropriate production process, various trade-offs must be made and that each provides different strategic advantages. This leads us to a discussion of the product-process matrix and its significance in operations strategy.

The Product-Process Matrix

The relationship between process technology and the products that a firm manufactures has important implications for operations strategy. Managers must match process technology to products in order to achieve a competitive advantage. Gold presents an example of the importance of this relationship.[2] Every major

---

[2]Bela Gold, "CAM sets new rules for production," *Harvard Business Review* November-December 1982; 169. Copyright 1982 by the President and Fellows of Harvard College; all rights reserved.

Type of Production Process	Product and Process Characteristics					
	Product Volume	Product Variety	Automation and Specialized Equipment	Frequency of Machine Setup and Change	Labor Skills	Unit Cost
Continuous flow	High	Low	High	Low	Low	Low
Mass production	Medium	Medium	High	Low	Low	Low
Batch	Medium	Medium	Medium	Medium	Medium	Medium
Job shop	Low	High	Low	High	High	High
Project	Low	High	Low	N/A	High	High

TABLE 8.3

Characteristics of Production Processes

piece of equipment in Ford Motor Company's most automated factory was designed to accommodate a narrow range of processing operations. The machines were so tightly wedded to the production of eight-cylinder engines that a shift to six-cylinder engines would have necessitated changes throughout the plant. When market conditions led Ford to opt for the smaller engines, the company reluctantly closed the plant because it could not convert its specialized equipment to a different set of tasks.

In a classic article, Hayes and Wheelwright suggest representing the interaction of product and process structure in a matrix.[3] Figure 8.1 illustrates a **product-process matrix** and some examples of businesses positioned in the matrix. The diagonal of the matrix represents typical matchings of products and processes. For instance, in a commercial printing firm, each job is unique and a job shop process is usually most effective in meeting its needs. Manufacturers of heavy equipment that offer several basic models with a variety of options utilize a batch process in which batches of a given model are produced intermittently. High-volume processes that produce only a few models, such as the assembly of automobiles or appliances, use mass-production and assembly-line processes. Finally, high-volume, commodity-type products, such as oil, paper, or sugar, rely on highly specialized, inflexible, and capital-intensive equipment in a continuous-flow setting.

As one moves down the diagonal of the product-process matrix, the emphasis in both product and process structure moves from high flexibility to low cost. Thus, product and process structure must be jointly reviewed in order to properly focus operations strategy. As products move through their life cycle, processes must be adjusted accordingly.

By positioning a business off the diagonal of the product-process matrix, a company can differentiate itself from its competitors. If this is done intentionally, then it can help to achieve a competitive edge. For example, Rolls-Royce produces a small line of automobiles using a process similar to a job shop rather than the traditional mass-production methods of other automobile manufacturers. However, if a firm drifts off the diagonal unintentionally, then numerous problems

[3]Robert H. Hayes and Steven C. Wheelwright, "Link Manufacturing Process and Product Life Cycles," *Harvard Business Review* January-February 1979; 133–140. Copyright 1979 by the President and Fellows of Harvard College; all rights reserved.

can result. Movement to the right of the diagonal makes it increasingly difficult to coordinate production and marketing. For example, higher volume demands on a job-shop operation result in lost economies of scale that are afforded by batch- and mass-production processes. Production control becomes more complex, and the continual need for product changeovers makes it difficult to maintain high volumes. As one moves down from the diagonal, lower profitability may result since volume remains small but equipment costs increase. Any potential savings in production efficiency from more streamlined processes might be lost from the decreased flexibility the firm would have to meet market demands.

Understanding the product-process matrix can help a firm focus more appropriately on what it does well and achieve "distinctive competence" in a particular area of production. A firm can strategically make decisions to move from its current position and better understand the implications of such decisions and the role and impact of new products in operations strategy as well as justify the reorganization of facilities to provide the focus discussed in Chapter 4. In the

FIGURE 8.1

Product-Process Matrix

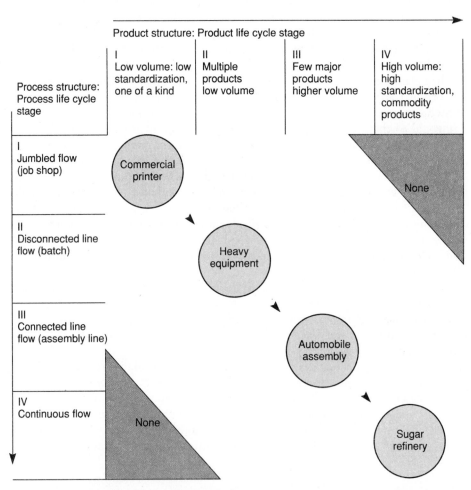

remainder of this chapter we review fundamental issues relating to process technology.

8.2 TECHNICAL ANALYSIS FOR PROCESS SELECTION

Planning for production begins with a thorough analysis and definition of the product to be made. Perhaps the most common way of defining a product is by a drawing. Figure 8.2 is an example of an assembly drawing of a carburetor for a four-cycle lawnmower engine. An **assembly drawing** is an exploded view of the individual components of a product that shows their relationships to one another. A parts list, such as the one shown in Figure 8.3, is also necessary in order to provide detailed technical information that is not found on an assembly drawing. **Parts lists** include information such as part numbers, names, whether the part is manufactured or bought, and a detailed engineering drawing number. In addition, parts lists may contain parts dimensions, material specifications, and other production information.

Detailed engineering drawings (Figure 8.4) provide the necessary technical specifications for in-house operations personnel, as well as for purchasing agents who are authorized to procure the item from a vendor. Such drawings are also useful for inspecting finished parts to determine if they conform to specifications.

The development of drawings and parts lists is also an important activity associated with new-product design. For example, in order to determine whether or not it is feasible to produce the product, drawings and parts lists can be used to determine what materials and machines are required. In addition, if a product needs to be assembled by the consumer, assembly drawings can be used to estimate the effort required. As consumers, we often find assembly drawings packed along with assembly instructions for a product.

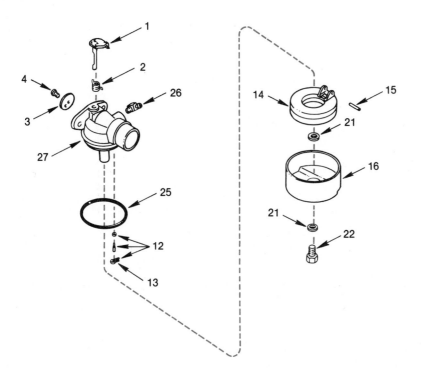

FIGURE 8.2

Assembly Drawing of Lawnmower Carburetor

FIGURE 8.3

Parts List for
Lawnmower
Carburetor

Parts List for Carburetor 631928

REF. NO.	PART NO.	NAME	MAKE OR BUY	DRAWING FILE NO.
1	631615	Throttle shaft and lever assy.	Make	26079
2	630731	Throttle return spring	Buy	26080
3	631616	Throttle shutter	Make	20091
4	650506	Screw slotted washer head	Buy	25030
12	631021	Inlet needle, seat & clip assy.	Make	26026
13	631022	Inlet needle clip	Make	26030
14	631023	Carburetor float	Make	26031
15	631024	Float shaft	Buy	26048
16	631700	Float bowl	Make	26032
21	631334	Bowl-to-body gasket	Buy	26049
22	631617	Float-bowl bolt	Buy	26352
25	631028	Bowl-to-body gasket	Buy	26053
26	631775	Fuel inlet fitting	Make	26054
27	631927	Housing	Make	26058

For the purposes of production planning and control, especially for modern computerized control systems, additional information is necessary. Product structure is usually expressed in a level-by-level hierarchy showing the logical relationships between parts in an assembly. Figure 8.5 illustrates the product structure for the lawnmower carburetor. The first level consists of one housing subassembly, one inlet-needle subassembly, one carburetor float, one float shaft, and one float-bowl subassembly. The second level illustrates the parts or assemblies that comprise the "parent items" at the first level. Thus the float-bowl subassembly is the parent item of one float bowl, one float-bowl bolt, two bowl-to-body gaskets, and one gasket. By including the quantity of each item required in the parts list, we have a *bill of materials (BOM)*. A bill of materials for the lawnmower carburetor is as follows:

Lawnmower carburetor

LEVEL	ITEM	QUANTITY
1	Housing subassembly	1
1	Inlet-needle subassembly	1
1	Carburetor float	1
1	Float shaft	1
1	Float-bowl subassembly	1
2	Throttle subassembly	1
2	Throttle-shutter subassembly	1
2	Fuel inlet fitting	1
2	Housing	1
2	Inlet needle, seat & clip assembly	1
2	Inlet needle clip	1
2	Float bowl	1
2	Float-bowl bolt	1
2	Bowl-to-body gasket	2
2	Gasket	1
3	Throttle shaft and lever assembly	1
3	Throttle return spring	1
3	Throttle shutter	1
3	Screw, slotted washer head	1

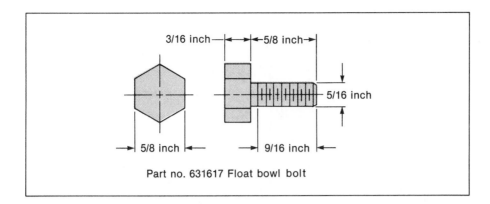

FIGURE 8.4

Detailed
Engineering
Drawing

3/16 inch — — 5/8 inch —

5/16 inch

5/8 inch

9/16 inch

Part no. 631617 Float bowl bolt

BOMs are used by purchasing and operations personnel to determine the amounts of material needed and by finance to cost out the direct material in a product. While this product-structure information describes the logical relationship of parts to one another, it does not specify the *sequence* of assembly.

The assembly sequence is important to know in order to determine which operations are to be performed by an individual worker and the number of work stations that are required. An **assembly chart** is a graphical representation of the order of assembly for a product. An example of an assembly chart for the lawn-mower carburetor (in Figures 8.2 and 8.3) is given in Figure 8.6. The circles at the extreme left correspond to individual parts. As we move to the right, the individual parts are joined together to form subassemblies (denoted by SA-1, SA-2, and so on). Thus parts 1 and 2 constitute subassembly SA-1. Finally, at the extreme right, individual parts and subassemblies are added to partially completed assemblies (A-1, A-2, and so on). The sequence of assembly is from the top to the bottom of the chart. Inspections are often included between assemblies. For instance, SA-1, SA-2 and parts 27 and 26 are put together to form assembly A-1. After an inspection, subassembly SA-3 is added to A-1 to form the housing assembly, A-2.

As a general rule, subassemblies and assemblies should contain a small number of parts and be transportable between work stations. This allows greater flexibility in planning work stations and job assignments. The assembly chart is an important tool in designing layouts for assembly lines. We will discuss methods for assembly-line design in the next chapter.

Assembly charts can also be applied in service organizations. Figure 8.7 presents an illustration of the use of an assembly chart for filing a federal income tax return.

8.3 PRODUCTION PROCESSES AND EQUIPMENT SELECTION

After product specifications and processing requirements have been determined, it is necessary to choose the particular production processes to be used. There are three hierarchical levels of decisions to make: *choice of technology, choice*

FIGURE 8.5   Product Structure for Lawnmower Carburetor

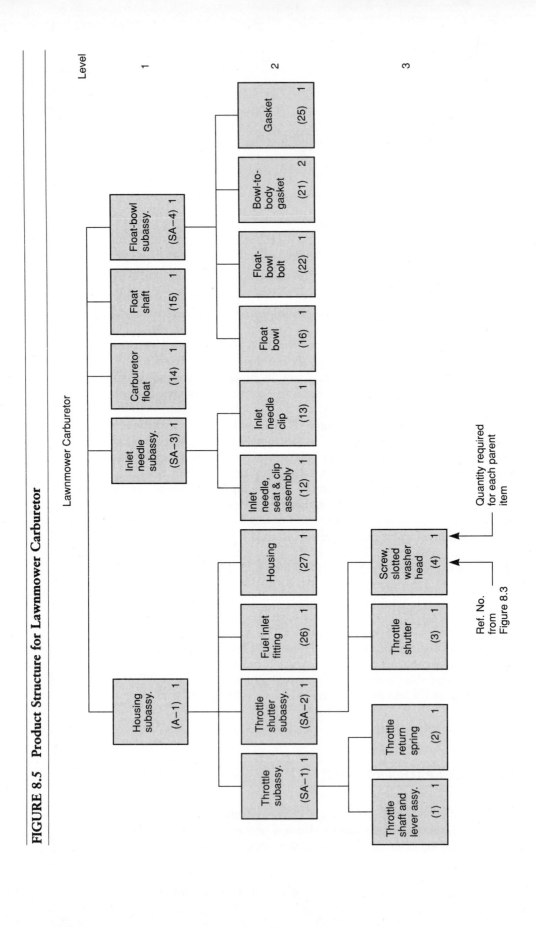

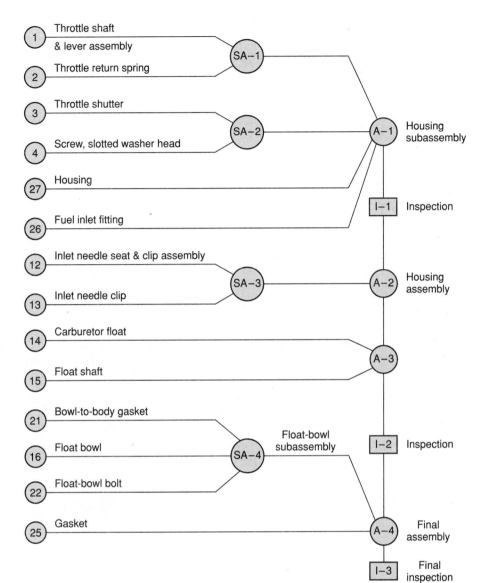

FIGURE 8.6

Assembly Chart for Lawnmower Carburetor

of *production processes,* and *choice of specific equipment.* First, we must deter-mine whether or not the technology exists to produce the product according to the specifications determined by product design and development. This decision is usually made as part of the R&D activity (see Chapter 5). For example, the conceptual design of a military airplane might specify that the wings must with-stand certain stresses and heat factors. Thus one part of the R&D effort would be focused on determining whether or not the materials and processes exist to produce such a product. However, in other situations, it may be obvious that the technology exists, but a decision might have to be made between two ap-proaches; for example, forming techniques or plastics technology. Such decisions, though, are usually made in product design and R&D groups. At the plant level, process and equipment selection become the principal decisions. In order to better

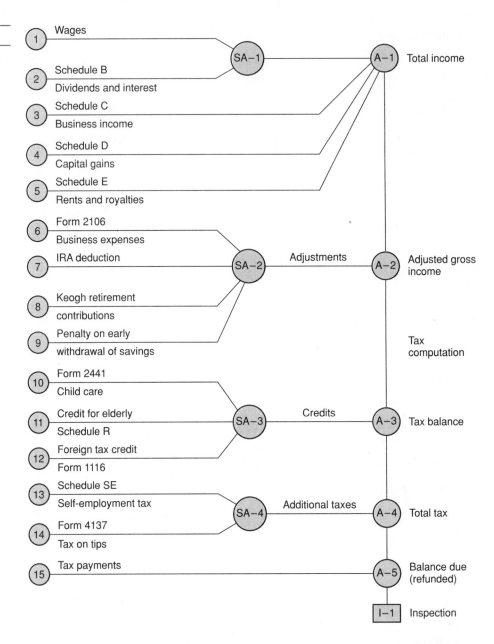

FIGURE 8.7

Assembly Chart for a Simplified Form 1040 Income Tax Return

1	Wages
2	Schedule B Dividends and interest
3	Schedule C Business income
4	Schedule D Capital gains
5	Schedule E Rents and royalties
6	Form 2106 Business expenses
7	IRA deduction
8	Keogh retirement contributions
9	Penalty on early withdrawal of savings
10	Form 2441 Child care
11	Credit for elderly Schedule R
12	Foreign tax credit Form 1116
13	Schedule SE Self-employment tax
14	Form 4137 Tax on tips
15	Tax payments

SA-1

A-1 Total income

SA-2 Adjustments A-2 Adjusted gross income

Tax computation

SA-3 Credits A-3 Tax balance

SA-4 Additional taxes A-4 Total tax

A-5 Balance due (refunded)

I-1 Inspection

understand the process selection decision, let us briefly discuss some of the more common production methods and terminology.

Production Processes

Fabrication is the process of modifying the physical characteristics of materials.[4] A variety of processes can be used for fabrication. These include forming, ma-

[4]Adapted from Don T. Phillips and Rodney J. Heisterberg, "Development of a Generalized Manufacturing Simulator (GEMS)," Report No. GEMS-5-77. Prepared for National Science Foundation, Department of Industrial Engineering, Texas A&M University, December 1, 1977.

chining, heat-treating, surface-treating, and joining processes. Under the general title of *forming processes,* we have the following:

1. *Casting.* Forming objects by putting liquid or viscous material into a prepared mold or form.
2. *Bending.* The process by which bars, rods, wire, tubing, and sheet metal are bent to many shapes in dies.
3. *Rolling.* The process by which metal is squeezed between two revolving rolls.
4. *Extrusion.* Forcing metal (often aluminum) or plastics out through specially formed discs.
5. *Forging.* Forming of metal (usually hot) by individual and intermittent applications of pressure instead of by applying continuous pressure, as in rolling.
6. *Powder metallurgy.* The manufacture of products from finely divided metals and metallic compounds. This is often used for materials with high-melting points.
7. *Spinning.* Forming of metal parts from a flat, rotating disk by applying controlled pressure to one side and causing the metal to flow against a rotating form that is held against the opposite side.
8. *Stamping.* Forcing a hardened steel punch against a flat metal surface.
9. *Wire drawing.* Pulling a rod through several dies of decreasing diameter until the final desired diameter is obtained.

Machining processes consist of removing metal in some fashion from parts that have already been fabricated. Among the most common of these are the following:

1. *Boring.* Enlarging of a hole that has previously been drilled.
2. *Broaching.* Metal removal by means of an elongated tool having a number of successive teeth of increasing size, which cut in a fixed path.
3. *Counterboring.* Enlarging of one end of a drilled hole.
4. *Drilling.* Producing a hole by forcing a rotating drill against it.
5. *Grinding.* Removal of metal by means of a rotating abrasive wheel.
6. *Milling.* Progressive removal of small increments of metal from the workpiece as it is fed slowly to a cutter, which rotates at high speed.
7. *Reaming.* Bringing holes to more-exact size and better finish by slightly enlarging an existing hole.
8. *Shearing.* Cutting of metals in sheet or plate form without the formation of chips or by burning.
9. *Turning.* Producing an external cylindrical or conical surface through the relative action between a rotating workpiece and a longitudinally fed single-point cutting tool.

Heat-treating processes include hardening (heating followed by rapid cooling) and other methods that alter the properties of the materials. *Surface-treating processes* are used to finish an item. This includes buffing to give a higher luster, galvanizing to protect from rust, painting, plating, sandblasting, degreasing, waxing, and so on.

Joining processes are methods for joining different parts together. The most important ones are:

1. *Mechanical joining.* Use of bolts or rivets to join two pieces.
2. *Soldering.* Joining by means of a molten metal or alloy.

3. *Welding.* Joining metals by concentrating heat, pressure, or both at the joint in order to coalesce the adjoining areas.
4. *Adhesive.* Use of glues or other adhesives to join materials.
5. *Snap-in assembly.*

This is by no means an exhaustive list. For example, special processes are used for plastic-injection molding, silicon chip formation, in food and textile processing, and in the chemical industry. However, this list does show the large variety of processes available in metal fabrication, one of our most important industries.

Process Selection	One of the roles of the manufacturing engineer is to select the proper process for producing a given part. This requires a thorough understanding of materials and their properties, existing technology, and the desired properties of the final product. For example, one of the growing areas of current research in manufacturing is high-speed machining (HSM). Cutting speeds depend on the type of material being cut and the cutting tool itself. Typical cutting speeds may be 600 meters per minute for aluminum or 50 meters per minute for titanium alloys; in some cases, speeds may even reach 9000 meters per minute. The manufacturing engineer needs to know the effects of such speeds on the structural properties of the materials being cut, such as stress properties of aircraft wings. Tool life may also be substantially affected by HSM. For example, higher cutting speeds can cause cutting tools to wear out more frequently; production must then be interrupted in order to replace them. Thus financial considerations such as operating costs, labor, and fixed capital expenses weigh heavily in the process selection decision.

Marketing factors, such as volume demanded and product quality, are also important considerations in process selection. The assembly of Rolls Royce automobiles is done by hand with meticulous care (the radiators have the maker's initials carved into them so that they may be repaired by the same person in the event of an accident!), whereas much of the automobile assembly in Japan and the United States is done using industrial robots and other mass-production techniques. Clearly the costs and rate of output differ greatly between these two processes.

In service organizations, process-selection decisions are also important. Printing can be offset or typeset; hamburgers can be broiled or fried. In a department store, credit verification of bank cards can be done by checking the credit card number against a printed list of bad accounts (manual), by calling a special telephone number for authorization (person-machine), or by using automatic verification equipment at the store itself (machine). In designing a waiting-line system for banking services, the process-selection decision is essentially the same as the product-design decisions discussed in Chapter 5, since the product *is* the process itself.

Process selection, then, depends on a variety of economic, quantitative, and qualitative factors, much in the same way as product design. The final decision rests in the selection of specific equipment; this issue is discussed next.

Equipment Selection	The goal of selecting a specific piece of equipment is to provide the required quantity of output from the production process with appropriate quality at the

most economical cost. Constraints on production specifications often limit the available choices. For instance, some products may require a shearing operation, as opposed to a cutting operation. In choosing a computer system for a service organization, memory requirements, speed, and software may limit the feasible alternatives.

Generally, operations personnel have to choose between general-purpose and special-purpose equipment. General-purpose equipment, such as drill presses, lathes, and so on, can be used in a large variety of manufacturing applications. Special-purpose equipment may be limited to only one or two different applications. Thus the major factors to be considered are the *variety of work available, output rate desired,* and *cost.*

For plants that produce a large variety of different products or produce to customer specifications, general-purpose equipment provides greater flexibility, fewer required maintenance skills, and faster setup times. General-purpose equipment is also less likely to become obsolete as new technology is introduced. Special-purpose equipment, on the other hand, generally results in faster production rates because of automated handling or numerical-control features. For manufacturers with only a few product lines and high volume, special-purpose equipment can provide substantial benefits.

There are a number of economic and noneconomic criteria that must be evaluated in selecting a piece of equipment. Economic factors include the following:

1. rate of return on investment
2. budget limitations
3. purchase price
4. installation cost
5. operating expenses
6. training costs
7. labor savings
8. tax implications
9. miscellaneous costs (such as computer software for programmable equipment)

Important noneconomic factors include

1. installation time
2. availability of training
3. productivity improvements
4. vendor service
5. adaptability and flexibility of the equipment

MAKING AN EQUIPMENT SELECTION DECISION

EXAMPLE

The Sterling Equipment Corporation is contemplating the purchase of an industrial robot. Equipment from four vendors has been identified as meeting the basic technical criteria. An economic analysis resulted in the data shown in Table 8.4. In addition, an evaluation of the noneconomic factors resulted in the data shown in Table 8.5.

The plant manager has decided to translate the noneconomic factors into numerical scores, with 1 = Excellent, 2 = Good, 3 = Average, and 4 = Poor. This results in the following evaluation:

	Vendor			
Factor	1	2	3	4
Installation lead time	2	3	1	4
Vendor training	2	4	2	3
Productivity improvement	2	2	2	2
Vendor service	2	1	1	2
Flexibility	1	2	2	1
Total	9	12	8	12

While vendor 3 is slightly better than vendor 1 on the noneconomic criteria, the fact that the net cost was significantly lower for vendor 1 led Sterling to select vendor 1.

The choice of which robot to select in this example was not necessarily straightforward as it is difficult to assess the relative value of economic and noneconomic criteria. As in product selection and facility location, such decisions must be carefully weighed by the management team.

TABLE 8.4

Economic Analysis (All Figures Are Discounted to Present Values)

	Vendor			
Factor	1	2	3	4
Purchase cost	$50,000	$70,000	$55,000	$75,000
Installation cost	2,500	1,000	4,500	0
Operating cost	5,000	6,000	7,500	6,500
Training costs	1,000	0	1,000	1,500
Software costs	1,000	1,000	1,500	2,000
Total costs	59,500	78,000	69,500	85,000
Labor savings	30,000	40,000	30,000	45,000
Tax benefits	1,500	2,000	1,000	2,000
Total savings	31,500	42,000	31,000	47,000
Net total cost	$28,000	$36,000	$38,500	$38,000

TABLE 8.5

Noneconomic Factor Evaluation

	Vendor			
Factor	1	2	3	4
Installation lead time	Good	Average	Excellent	Poor
Vendor training	Good	Poor	Good	Average
Productivity improvement	Good	Good	Good	Good
Vendor service	Good	Excellent	Excellent	Good
Flexibility	Excellent	Good	Good	Excellent

8.4 QUALITY AND RELIABILITY IN PROCESS AND EQUIPMENT SELECTION

One goal of production is to produce output of consistent quality. A critical technical issue in process and equipment selection is the quality of conformance to design specifications that can be achieved from a particular process or piece of individual equipment.

Variation in production output occurs in every process because of the complex interaction of minor variations in materials, tools, machines, operators, and the environment. While one cannot predict such variations individually, their combined effects are generally stable and can be described rather accurately using probability distributions. (In Chapter 19 we will see how to do this.) **Process capability** refers to the range over which the natural variation of a process occurs. It is measured by the proportion of output that can be produced within design specifications.

Process Capability

There are three important components of process-capability analysis: the design specifications, the average value of a process dimension based on actual output from the production process, and the range, or spread, of the variation. A design specification is usually stated as a mean value plus or minus a tolerance. For example, the design specification for the diameter of a metal shaft might be stated as .750 ± .010 inches; thus, the acceptable range for the diameter is between .740 and .760 inches. When the actual diameters of shafts produced by a process are measured, the average value may or may not be .750 inches; similarly, the actual diameters of shafts produced may not fall between the design specifications of .740 and .760 inches.

Figure 8.8 illustrates four possible situations that can arise when the observed variability of a process is compared to design specifications. In Figure 8.8(a), the range of process variation is larger than the design specification; thus it will be impossible for the process to meet specifications a large percentage of the time. Management can either scrap or rework nonconforming parts (100 percent inspection is necessary), invest in a better process with less variation, or change the design specifications. In (b), the process can produce according to specification, although it would require close monitoring to assure that it remains in this position. In (c), the observed variation is tighter than the specifications; this is the ideal situation from a quality control viewpoint since little inspection or control would be necessary. Finally, in (d), the observed variation is the same as the design specification, but the process is off center; thus some nonconforming product should be expected.

Process capability is important both to product designers and manufacturing-process engineers. If product specifications are too tight, the product will be difficult to manufacture. Production personnel will be under pressure and will have to spend a lot of time adjusting the process and inspecting output. Process engineers must also understand the implications of process capability. For example, if a design specification requires a length of metal tubing to be cut to within .1 inch, then a process consisting of a worker using a ruler and a hacksaw will probably result in a large percentage of nonconforming parts because of the worker's inability to provide the desired precision. Hence product design and process selection decisions must be integrated.

FIGURE 8.8

Process
Capability Versus
Design
Specifications

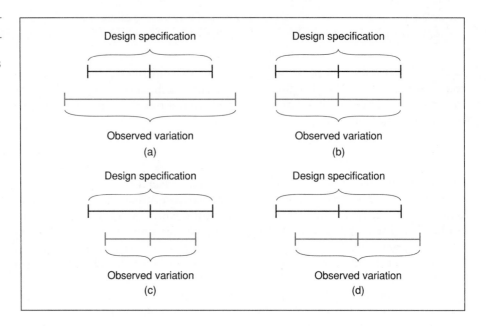

EXAMPLE

EVALUATING PROCESS CAPABILITY

A machining process makes a part having a required dimension of .575 ± .007 inches. Twenty-five parts were selected over a short period of time. The measurements are given below

.557	.574	.573	.575	.576
.556	.587	.578	.565	.577
.576	.578	.577	.582	.576
.564	.573	.579	.573	.572
.580	.584	.580	.578	.574

To determine how well the process can meet the specifications, we first compute the sample mean and standard deviation. The sample mean is $\bar{x} = .57576$ and the sample standard deviation is .00529. From statistics, we know that nearly all the data will lie within three standard deviations from the mean. Therefore, $\bar{x} \pm 3s$ determines the natural variation of this production process; that is, the process capability. We have

$$\bar{x} \pm 3s = .57576 \pm 3(.00529)$$

or

$$.55989 \text{ to } .59163.$$

Since the specifications are .575 ± .007, or .568 to .582, we see that the process capability is rather poor. In fact, if we assume that the process output is normally distributed with mean .57576 and standard deviation .00529, we may compute the percentage of output that will fall out of specification. This is done by transforming the lower and upper specification limits to standard normal values, as shown below:

$$z_L = \frac{.568 - .57576}{.00529} = -1.47$$

$$z_U = \frac{.582 - .57576}{.00529} = 1.18$$

Using Appendix B, we find that 7.08 percent of the output will fall below the lower specification limit, and 1.19 percent of the output will fall above the upper specification limit. This is summarized in Figure 8.9.

Process Reliability

The **reliability** of a production process is the probability that the process will perform satisfactorily over a specified period of time. Thus if we say that the reliability of a process is .85, we mean there is a probability of .85 that the process will not break down over a period of time such as a day, week, or month. A process that has low reliability will increase costs due to frequent maintenance and lower productivity. In this section, we present some quantitative approaches for analyzing the reliability of a production process. Such techniques are useful in selecting equipment and determining the amount of downtime expected. This is necessary in order to plan future production activities.

Many production systems are comprised of several machines, or operations, that are in series but function independently of one another. This is illustrated in Figure 8.10. If one component fails, then the entire system fails. If we know the individual reliability, p_j, for each component j, we can compute the total reliability of an n-component series system, R. We note that the joint probability of n independent events can be computed as the product of the individual probabilities. Thus, if the individual reliabilities are denoted by $p_1, p_2, \ldots p_n$ and the system reliability is denoted by R, then

$$R = p_1 p_2 \ldots p_n \tag{8.1}$$

Other production systems are comprised of several components that are in parallel, but function independently of one another, as illustrated in Figure 8.11.

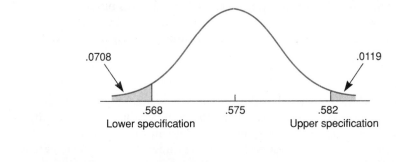

.0708   .0119

.568   .575   .582
Lower specification   Upper specification

FIGURE 8.9

Percentage of Process Output Not Meeting Specifications

FIGURE 8.10

Series Production System

FIGURE 8.11

Parallel
Production
System

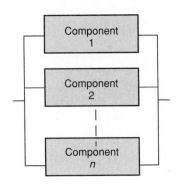

The entire system will fail only if all components fail; this is an example of *redundancy*. The system reliability is computed as

$$R = 1 - (1 - p_1)(1 - p_2) \ldots (1 - p_n) \qquad (8.2)$$

Many systems are a combination of series and parallel components. To compute the reliability of such systems, first compute the reliability of the parallel components using Equation (8.2) and treat the result as a single series component; then use Equation (8.1) to compute the total series reliability. The following example illustrates these calculations.

EXAMPLE

COMPUTING THE RELIABILITY OF AN AUTOMATED PRODUCTION SYSTEM

Figure 8.12 is an example of an automated production system with three operations: turning, milling, and grinding. Individual parts are transformed from the turning center to the milling center, and then to the grinder by a robot; thus if one machine or the robot fails, the entire production process must stop. The probability that any one component of the system will fail, however, does not depend upon any other component of the system.

Conceptually, we can think of the robot and machines in series, as shown in Figure 8.13. The reliability of the system can be computed using Equation (8.1). Thus in Figure 8.13, if we assume that the reliability of the robot, turning center, milling machine, and grinder are .99, .98, .99, and .96, respectively, then the total reliability is

$$R = (.99)(.98)(.99)(.96) = .92$$

Thus there is a .92 probability that the system will be working over a specified period of time. As stated above, this calculation assumes that the probability of failure of each component in the system is independent of the others.

Suppose that the system is redesigned with two grinders that operate in parallel; if one grinder fails, the other grinder may still work and hence the total system will continue to function. Such a system is illustrated in Figure 8.14. Letting p_{g_1} denote the reliability of grinder 1 and p_{g_2} denote the reliability of grinder 2, the probability that *both grinders will fail* is given by $(1 - p_{g_1})(1 - p_{g_2})$. Since

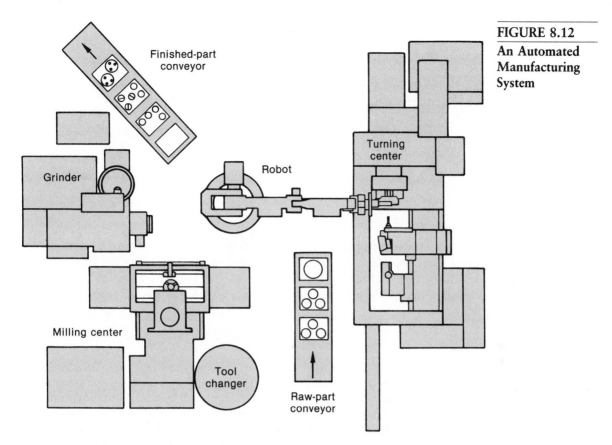

FIGURE 8.12

An Automated
Manufacturing
System

Source: John G. Holmes "Integrating Robots into a Manufacturing System," Reprinted with permission from 1979 Fall Industrial Engineering Conference Proceedings, Copyright Institute of Industrial Engineers, 25 Technology Park/Atlanta, Norcross, GA 30092.

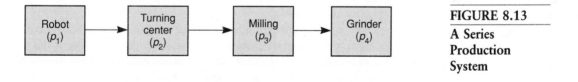

FIGURE 8.13

A Series
Production
System

either both grinders will fail *or* at least one grinder will not fail, we can compute the probability that at least one grinder will not fail, R grinders, as follows

$$R_{\text{grinders}} = 1 - [(1 - p_{g_1})(1 - p_{g_2})]$$

Thus, if each of the grinders has a reliability of 0.96, the reliability of both grinders together is

$$
\begin{aligned}
R_{\text{grinders}} &= 1 - (1 - .96)(1 - .96) \\
&= 1 - .0016 \\
&= .9984
\end{aligned}
$$

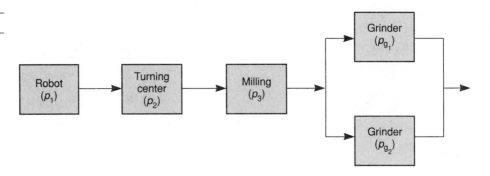

FIGURE 8.14

A Series
Production
System with
Parallel Grinders

Notice that the total grinder reliability has increased considerably by adding the extra machine. Now we may use Equation (8.1) to compute the total system reliability, using .9984 as the reliability of the grinders. Essentially, we have replaced the parallel grinders with one grinder having a reliability of .9984. Thus we have

$$R = (.99)(.98)(.99)(.9984) = .96.$$

Maintenance

In order to achieve specified levels of quality and reliability in manufactured items, maintenance of equipment is necessary. For certain industries, such as airlines and railroads, this may even be regulated by law. With increased automation and more complex equipment in use today, maintenance costs have become a high priority for operations managers. In order to control maintenance costs and not interrupt production, the maintenance effort in an organization must be carefully planned.

The principal objective of maintenance is to ensure that the equipment is in good working condition. This results in improved efficiency of labor, reduction of downtime because of unexpected breakdowns, achievement of planned quantity and quality of output, and a general increase in productivity. An efficient maintenance program also keeps costs down in relation to the level of production.

There are two types of maintenance activities: maintenance because of machine failure and preventive maintenance. Maintenance because of machine failure is unavoidable, although it can be minimized by a preventive maintenance program. Such a program helps to achieve better utilization of the maintenance staff through planned scheduling of maintenance work and can reduce losses because of breakdowns or injury. Determining an appropriate maintenance policy for a piece of equipment should take into account the economic and operational trade-offs involved. The following example illustrates how reliability data can be used in this analysis.

EXAMPLE

DETERMINING A PREVENTIVE MAINTENANCE POLICY

A part of a bathroom-tissue production system is a saw/wrapper machine, which cuts long rolls into smaller pieces and wraps them into packages prior to placing them into cartons. Historical data on the time between failures is presented in

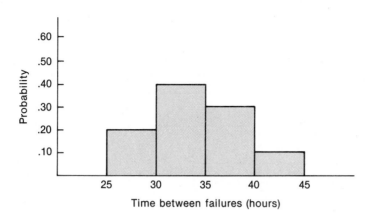

FIGURE 8.15

Histogram of
Time Between
Failures

Figure 8.15. From this information, we can calculate the mean time between failures (MTBF) by multiplying the midpoint of each cell by its associated probability and adding, as shown below.

$$MTBF = 27.5(.20) + 32.5(.40) + 37.5(.30) + 42.5(.10)$$
$$= 34 \text{ hours}$$

Assume that in the current system the machine is repaired only when it fails, at an average cost of $50. The company is considering a preventive maintenance program that will cost $30 for each inspection and adjustment. Should this be done, and if so, how often should preventive maintenance occur?

To find the best policy, we must compute and compare average annual costs for both approaches. Consider, for instance, the current policy. Assuming 260 working days per year and one 8-hour shift per day, there are 2080 hours of available time. If the mean time between failures is 34 hours, then we expect $2080/34 = 61.2$ failures per year. Hence the annual cost will be $(61.2)(\$50) = \$3060$. Now suppose that the machine is inspected and adjusted every 25 hours. If we assume that the time until the next failure after adjustment follows the distribution in Figure 8.15, then the probability of a failure under this policy is zero. However, inspection every 25 hours will occur $2080/25 = 83.2$ times per year, resulting in a preventive maintenance cost of $(83.2)(\$30) = \$2496$. Next suppose we inspect the machine every 30 hours. From Figure 8.15, the probability of a failure occurring before the next inspection is .20. Thus the total expected annual cost will be the cost of inspection, $(\$30)(2080/30) = \$2080$, plus the expected cost of emergency repair $(\$50)(2080/30)(.2) = \$693$; hence the total is $2773. We may perform similar calculations for other maintenance intervals. The results are shown in Table 8.6. Thus we see that a maintenance interval of 25 hours results in a minimal cost policy.

In this example, we see that as the time between inspections increases, the inspection cost decreases, but the failure cost increases. These economic trade-offs are typical of preventive maintenance problems and will generally follow a graph similar to that of Figure 8.16.

The maintenance function can either be a decentralized staff responsibility or a line responsibility reporting to the plant manager. The specific organizational

TABLE 8.6

Maintenance
Cost
Computation

(1) Time Between Inspections	(2) Number of Inspections Per Year	(3) Probability of Failure Before Next Inspection	(4) Preventive Maintenance Cost ($)	(5) Failure Cost ($)	Total Cost ($)
25	83.2	0	2496	0	2496
30	69.3	.2	2080	693	2773
35	59.4	.6	1782	1782	3564
40	52	.9	1560	2340	3900

FIGURE 8.16

Economic Trade-
offs in
Maintenance

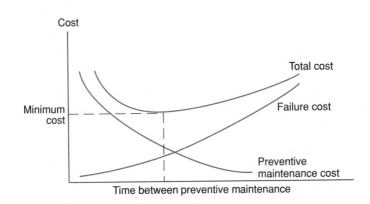

structure usually depends on the demand for maintenance services and the amount of specialization required by the crew. In many service organizations, maintenance is often contracted to an outside firm. This is usually the case with computers or typewriter repair, for example. Control of maintenance work includes scheduling and establishing priorities of work. A formal work order is usually required. This helps to provide information for planning work loads, scheduling maintenance personnel, and collecting historical data for operational and accounting purposes. Scheduling tools that are discussed in Chapter 16, such as Gantt charts, are often used to establish priorities and to control maintenance work.

Cost and performance control are enhanced through the use of standards. Since preventive maintenance is repetitive, standards can easily be developed using traditional work measurement techniques. Through the use of standards, time requirements can be more accurately estimated, thus improving planning and scheduling, and labor efficiency can be more easily measured as a step toward productivity improvement. Chapter 11 discusses the subject of work measurement in more detail.

For large firms with hundreds of pieces of equipment, maintenance management is often automated using a computer. A typical data file might include a description of the equipment, cost data, warranty information, preventive maintenance intervals, standard times, and historical data of maintenance time and costs. Reports of scheduled maintenance activities can be generated on a daily or weekly basis, as can reports on backlogs and delays. In addition, such a data base can provide productivity reports to management and cost reports for accounting and budgeting purposes.

and records against actual performance levels using microprocessors and digital readouts.

As a result of this project, total costs were reduced by more than 10 percent, and 78 percent fewer parts were handled, thus reducing work in process. Most importantly, product-quality improvement goals were exceeded.

QUESTIONS

1. What was the primary reason General Electric began to upgrade and automate its automatic dishwasher production facilities?

2. What method did GE use to reduce production costs and improve quality?
3. Did automation result in the loss of jobs?
4. In their new production facilities, do the workers have more or less control of the production process? Explain.
5. How does GE verify that the final product is meeting specifications?

PROCESS TECHNOLOGY SELECTION FOR OHIO EDISON COMPANY[6]

O hio Edison Company is an investor-owned electric utility headquartered in northeastern Ohio. Ohio Edison and a Pennsylvania subsidiary provide electrical service to over 2 million people. Most of this electricity is generated by coal-fired power plants. In order to meet evolving air-quality standards, Ohio Edison has embarked on a program to replace existing pollution control equipment on most of its generating plants with more efficient equipment. The combination of this program to upgrade air-quality control equipment with the continuing need to construct new generating plants to meet future power requirements has resulted in a large capital investment program. We shall discuss an application of decision analysis to process technology selection.

The flue gas emitted by coal-fired power plants contains small ash particles and sulfur dioxide (SO_2). Federal and state regulatory agencies have established emission limits for both particulates and sulfur dioxide. Recently, Ohio Edison developed a plan to comply with new air-quality standards at one of its largest power plants. This plant consists of seven coal-fired units and constitutes about one-third of the generating capacity of Ohio Edison and the subsidiary company. Most of these units had been constructed in the 1960s. Although all the units had initially been constructed with equipment to control particulate emissions, that equipment was not capable of meeting new particulate emission requirements.

A decision had already been made to burn low-sulfur coal in four of the smaller units (units 1 to 4) at the plant in order to meet SO_2 emission standards. Fabric filters were to be installed on these units to control particulate emissions. Fabric filters, also known as baghouses, use thousands of fabric bags to filter out the particulates; they function in much the same way as a household vacuum cleaner.

It was considered likely, although not certain, that the three larger units (units 5 to 7) at this plant would burn medium- to high-sulfur coal. A method of controlling particulate emissions at these units had not yet been selected. Preliminary studies had narrowed the particulate control equipment choice to a decision between fabric filters and electrostatic precipitators (which remove particulates suspended in the flue gas as charged particles by passing the flue gas through a strong electric field). This decision was affected by a number of uncertainties, including the following:

- Uncertainty in the way some air-quality laws and regulations might be interpreted.
- Certain interpretations could require that either low-sulfur coal or high-sulfur Ohio coal (or neither) be burned in units 5 to 7.
- Potential future changes in air quality laws and regulations.
- An overall plant reliability improvement program was underway at this plant.
- The outcome of this program would affect the operating costs of whichever pollution control technology was installed in these units.
- Construction costs of the equipment were uncertain, particularly since limited space at the

[6]The authors are indebted to Thomas J. Madden and M. S. Hyrnick of Ohio Edison Company, Akron, Ohio, for providing this application.

We present two cases that discuss process technology issues. In the first case, we see how the process technology for automatic dishwashers was improved by General Electric. The new process technology generated substantial improvements in both productivity and quality. The second case illustrates how Ohio Edison Company used decision analysis (see the Supplement to Chapter 6) for selecting among alternative process technologies.

QUALITY IMPROVEMENT THROUGH PROCESS SELECTION AT GENERAL ELECTRIC[5]

To counteract a declining market share in the automatic dishwasher market in the late 1970s, General Electric resolved to build a better quality product at less cost by investing heavily in upgrading and automating its production facilities. GE spent $38 million on advanced automation technology and employee retraining programs in its Louisville, Kentucky, plant. This project incorporated advanced automation, point-of-use manufacturing, and standardized product design to reduce production costs while meeting the highest quality standards ever developed for GE dishwashers.

All new tubs and door liners are made from GE-engineered plastic that will not rust, peel, or chip. The special "Permatuf" compound is trucked to Louisville from another plant. The tubs are fabricated by injection-molding machines and delivered immediately via conveyor (this is an example of point-of-use manufacture) to the tub structure area, where robots and other automated devices perform a 21-step assembly process. A similar process is used for the door liner. Parts are made only as needed, and each one is quality checked before being allowed to continue through the production and assembly process. Simplified, standardized designs further reduce production cost and help ensure consistent quality.

Automation has reduced the number of employees required in some assembly lines from 25 or 30 to 2 people. GE points out, however, that many of these employees were retrained to perform quality audits and other necessary functions. This resulted in upgrading many personnel while it improved product quality and productivity.

After the tub structure is completed, overhead conveyors transport these items to a nonsynchronous assembly line, where much of the hardware is added using semiautomated equipment such as automatic screwdrivers. In a nonsynchronous process, the product stops at each work station and does not move until the employee is finished. After the operation is completed, the employee pulls a green handle overhead and the product is released to join the queue ahead. If the operator cannot complete the job or there is a problem, a yellow handle is pulled and the unit is automatically transported to a repair area. If there is a major problem, a red handle can be pulled that shuts down the entire line, alerting supervisory personnel. By providing the operators with such controls, not only is product movement regulated with less chance of human error, but also the quality of work is individually controlled.

Each step of the automated process is monitored by computer. If a part is not assembled properly, the system will not allow the assembly process to be completed; the unit will be sent automatically to a repair area along with a computer printout of specific repair steps needed.

As an added quality-assurance measure, each day 30 units are pulled at random from the final assembly line just before packing and subjected to extensive technical tests. A GE quality technician gives each unit a visual check and tests all operating parts

---

[5]Adapted from Robert Waterbury, "Automated Quality," Reprinted with permission from *Quality,* Nov. 1983, a Hitchcock publication.

culations or estimates. Probabilities were obtained from existing data or the subjective assessments of knowledgeable persons.

A decision tree similar to that shown in Figure 8.17 was used to generate cumulative probability distributions for the annual revenue requirements outcomes calculated for each of the two particulate control alternatives. Careful study of these results led to the following conclusions:

■ The expected value of annual revenue requirements for the electrostatic precipitator technology was approximately $1 million lower than that for the fabric filters.
■ The fabric filter alternative had a higher "upside risk"—that is, a higher probability of high revenue requirements—than did the precipitator alternative.
■ The precipitator technology had nearly an 80 percent probability of having lower annual revenue requirements than the fabric filters.
■ Although the capital cost of the fabric filter equipment (the cost of installing the equip-

ment) was lower than the precipitator, this was more than offset by the higher operating costs associated with the fabric filter.

These results led Ohio Edison to select the electrostatic precipitator technology for the generating units in question. Had the decision analysis not been performed, the particulate control decision might have been based chiefly on capital cost, a decision measure that would have favored the fabric filter equipment. Decision analysis offers a means for effectively analyzing the uncertainties involved in a decision. Because of this, it is felt that the use of decision analysis methodology in this application resulted in a decision that yielded both lower expected revenue requirements and lower risk.

QUESTIONS
1. Why was decision analysis used in the selection of particulate control equipment for units 5, 6, and 7?
2. List the decision alternatives for the decision analysis problem developed by Ohio Edison.
3. What were the benefits of using decision analysis in this application?

SUMMARY

This chapter has been concerned with preliminary planning for the design of production processes and the selection of equipment. In order to choose the proper technology and equipment, a thorough analysis of the product to be made and the method of production must be conducted. The selection of machines and handling equipment and their arrangement on the shop floor form the basis of production system design, which is addressed in the next chapter.

Quality and reliability are important issues in process analysis. The process selected must be able to produce in conformance to design specifications, and the process itself should be reliable. Proper maintenance is necessary to achieve product quality and process reliability.

Production processes can be classified as continuous flow, mass production, batch, job shops, or project types. The variety of products made and the quantity required are the primary factors used in determining the proper process. The relationship between process technology and product decisions is an important component of manufacturing strategy. The product-process matrix provides a framework for examining this relationship.

KEY TERMS

Process technology
Product-process matrix
Assembly drawing
Parts list

Assembly chart
Fabrication
Process capability
Reliability

REVIEW/ DISCUSSION QUESTIONS

1. Discuss the managerial and technical issues involved in selecting production processes.

2. What do we mean by the term *process technology*?

plant site made it necessary to install the equipment on a massive bridge deck over a four-lane highway immediately adjacent to the power plant.

- The costs associated with replacing the electrical power required to operate the particulate control equipment were uncertain.
- Various uncertain factors, including potential accidents and chronic operating problems that could increase the costs of operating the generating units, were identified. The degree to which each of these factors affected operating costs varied with the choice of technology and with the sulfur content of the coal.

The decision to be made involved a choice between two types of particulate control equipment (fabric filters or electrostatic precipitators) for units 5 to 7. Because of the complexity of the problem, the high degree of uncertainty associated with factors affecting the decision, and the importance (because of the potential reliability and cost impact on Ohio Edison) of the choice, decision analysis was used in the selection process.

The decision measure used to evaluate the outcomes of the particulate technology decision analysis was the annual revenue requirements for the three large units over their remaining lifetime. Revenue requirements are the monies that would have to be collected from the utility customers in order to recover costs resulting from the decision. They include not only direct costs but also the cost of capital and return on investment.

A decision tree was constructed to represent the particulate control decision, its uncertainties and costs. A simplified version of this decision tree is shown in Figure 8.17. The decision and state-of-nature nodes are indicated. Note that to conserve space, a type of shorthand notation is used. The coal sulfur content state-of-nature node should actually be located at the end of each branch of the capital cost state-of-nature node, as the dotted lines indicate. Each of the indicated state-of-nature nodes actually represents several probabilistic cost models or submodels. The total revenue requirements calculated are the sum of the revenue requirements for capital and operating costs. Costs associated with these models were obtained from engineering cal-

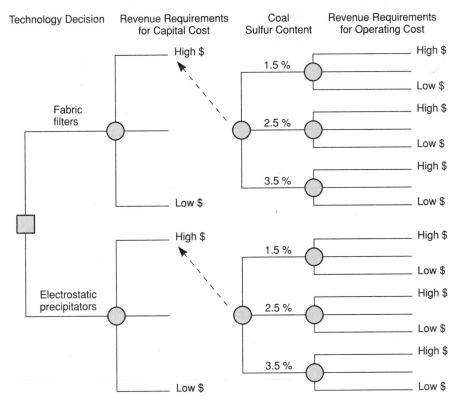

FIGURE 8.17

Simplified Particulate Control Equipment Decision Tree

plant site made it necessary to install the equipment on a massive bridge deck over a four-lane highway immediately adjacent to the power plant.

■ The costs associated with replacing the electrical power required to operate the particulate control equipment were uncertain.

■ Various uncertain factors, including potential accidents and chronic operating problems that could increase the costs of operating the generating units, were identified. The degree to which each of these factors affected operating costs varied with the choice of technology and with the sulfur content of the coal.

The decision to be made involved a choice between two types of particulate control equipment (fabric filters or electrostatic precipitators) for units 5 to 7. Because of the complexity of the problem, the high degree of uncertainty associated with factors affecting the decision, and the importance (because of the potential reliability and cost impact on Ohio Edison) of the choice, decision analysis was used in the selection process.

The decision measure used to evaluate the outcomes of the particulate technology decision analysis was the annual revenue requirements for the three large units over their remaining lifetime. Revenue requirements are the monies that would have to be collected from the utility customers in order to recover costs resulting from the decision. They include not only direct costs but also the cost of capital and return on investment.

A decision tree was constructed to represent the particulate control decision, its uncertainties and costs. A simplified version of this decision tree is shown in Figure 8.17. The decision and state-of-nature nodes are indicated. Note that to conserve space, a type of shorthand notation is used. The coal sulfur content state-of-nature node should actually be located at the end of each branch of the capital cost state-of-nature node, as the dotted lines indicate. Each of the indicated state-of-nature nodes actually represents several probabilistic cost models or submodels. The total revenue requirements calculated are the sum of the revenue requirements for capital and operating costs. Costs associated with these models were obtained from engineering cal-

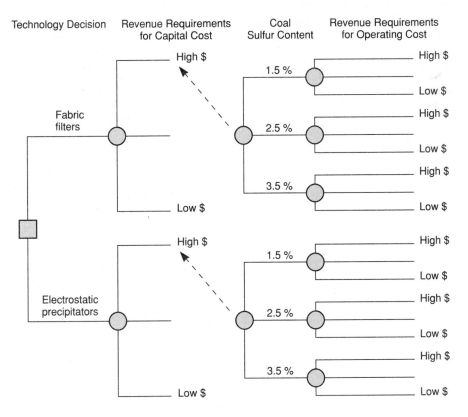

FIGURE 8.17

Simplified Particulate Control Equipment Decision Tree

culations or estimates. Probabilities were obtained from existing data or the subjective assessments of knowledgeable persons.

A decision tree similar to that shown in Figure 8.17 was used to generate cumulative probability distributions for the annual revenue requirements outcomes calculated for each of the two particulate control alternatives. Careful study of these results led to the following conclusions:

- The expected value of annual revenue requirements for the electrostatic precipitator technology was approximately $1 million lower than that for the fabric filters.
- The fabric filter alternative had a higher "upside risk"—that is, a higher probability of high revenue requirements—than did the precipitator alternative.
- The precipitator technology had nearly an 80 percent probability of having lower annual revenue requirements than the fabric filters.
- Although the capital cost of the fabric filter equipment (the cost of installing the equip-

ment) was lower than the precipitator, this was more than offset by the higher operating costs associated with the fabric filter.

These results led Ohio Edison to select the electrostatic precipitator technology for the generating units in question. Had the decision analysis not been performed, the particulate control decision might have been based chiefly on capital cost, a decision measure that would have favored the fabric filter equipment. Decision analysis offers a means for effectively analyzing the uncertainties involved in a decision. Because of this, it is felt that the use of decision analysis methodology in this application resulted in a decision that yielded both lower expected revenue requirements and lower risk.

QUESTIONS
1. Why was decision analysis used in the selection of particulate control equipment for units 5, 6, and 7?
2. List the decision alternatives for the decision analysis problem developed by Ohio Edison.
3. What were the benefits of using decision analysis in this application?

SUMMARY

This chapter has been concerned with preliminary planning for the design of production processes and the selection of equipment. In order to choose the proper technology and equipment, a thorough analysis of the product to be made and the method of production must be conducted. The selection of machines and handling equipment and their arrangement on the shop floor form the basis of production system design, which is addressed in the next chapter.

Quality and reliability are important issues in process analysis. The process selected must be able to produce in conformance to design specifications, and the process itself should be reliable. Proper maintenance is necessary to achieve product quality and process reliability.

Production processes can be classified as continuous flow, mass production, batch, job shops, or project types. The variety of products made and the quantity required are the primary factors used in determining the proper process. The relationship between process technology and product decisions is an important component of manufacturing strategy. The product-process matrix provides a framework for examining this relationship.

KEY TERMS

Process technology
Product-process matrix
Assembly drawing
Parts list

Assembly chart
Fabrication
Process capability
Reliability

REVIEW/ DISCUSSION QUESTIONS

1. Discuss the managerial and technical issues involved in selecting production processes.
2. What do we mean by the term *process technology*?

3. Discuss the "narrow perspective" and "broad view" of process technology as proposed by Hayes and Wheelwright. Why do they advocate the broad view of process technology?

4. Explain the differences between *manual, mechanized,* and *automated* process technology.

5. What factors affect process technology decisions?

6. Explain the difference between *make-to-order* and *make-to-stock* production systems. How do operations management activities differ between these two types of systems?

7. Explain the differences between continuous flow, mass production, batch, job shop, and project processes?

8. Which process—continuous flow, mass production, batch, job shop, or project—would most likely to be used to produce the following?
   a. Telephones   e. Custom machine tools
   b. Gasoline   f. Paper
   c. Cigarettes   g. Many flavors of ice cream
   d. Air-conditioners

9. What is the *product-process matrix?* What implications does it have for operations strategy?

10. Develop a product-process matrix for the following food services. Justify the location you specify for each.
    ■ Fast food
    ■ Family steak house
    ■ Cafeteria
    ■ Traditional restaurant
    ■ Classic French restaurant

11. What information is contained in an *assembly drawing?* How does an assembly drawing differ from a parts list?

12. What information is contained in a *bill of materials?*

13. What is an *assembly chart?* How does it differ from an assembly drawing?

14. List the major types of fabrication processes used in production.

15. How does process selection differ from equipment selection?

16. What economic and noneconomic criteria should be evaluated in selecting equipment?

17. Explain the concept of *process capability?* Why is process capability important to both designers and manufacturing-process engineers?

18. Discuss the importance of reliability in production systems.

19. Discuss the role of maintenance in production operations. What types of maintenance activities are commonly performed?

1. Given the bill of material (Figure 8.18) for an automobile brake assembly, draw an assembly chart. (The bill of material has been drawn in such a way as to illustrate the sequence of activities in the assembly from left to right.)

PROBLEMS

FIGURE 8.18 Bill of Material for Problem 1

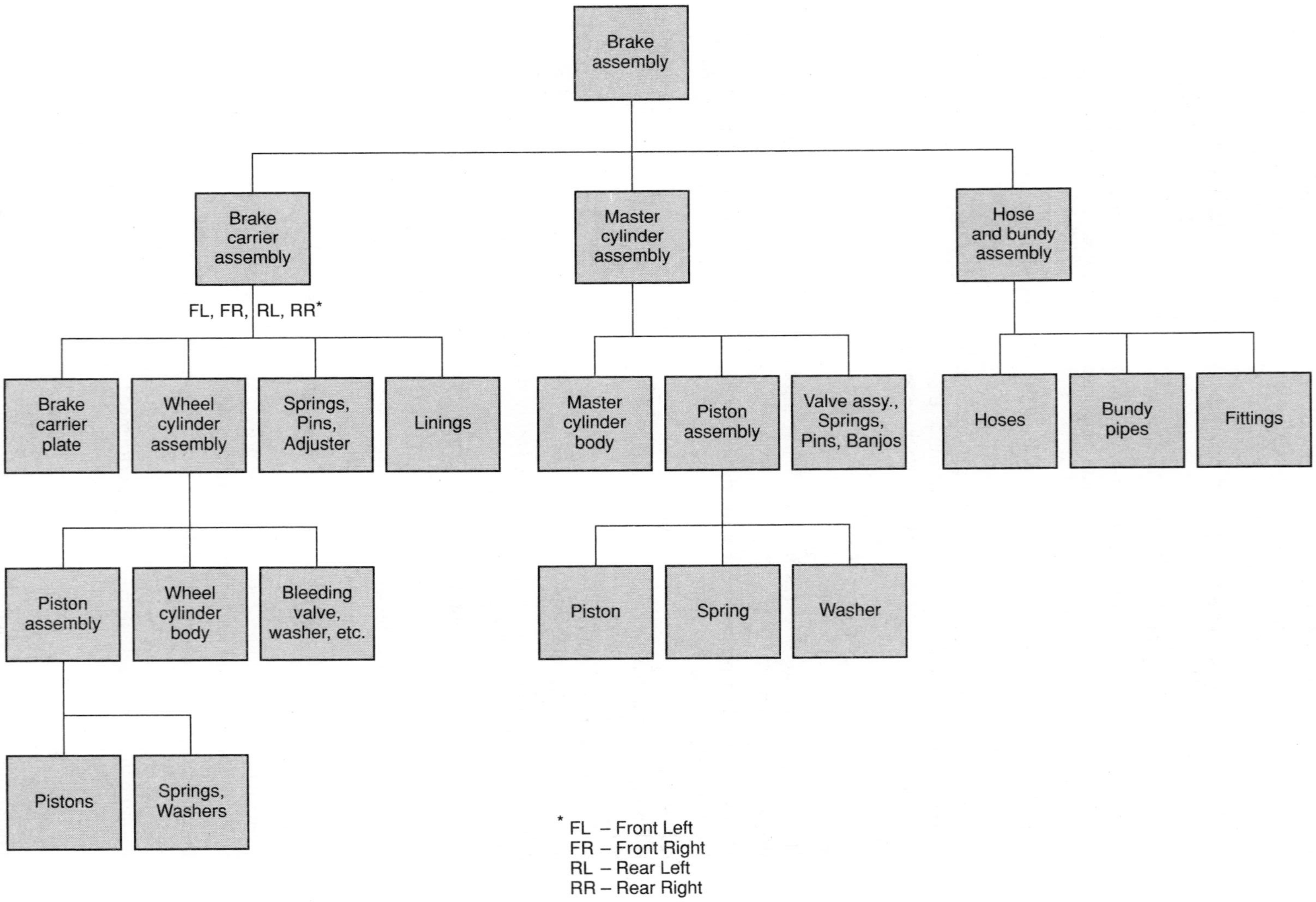

* FL – Front Left
  FR – Front Right
  RL – Rear Left
  RR – Rear Right

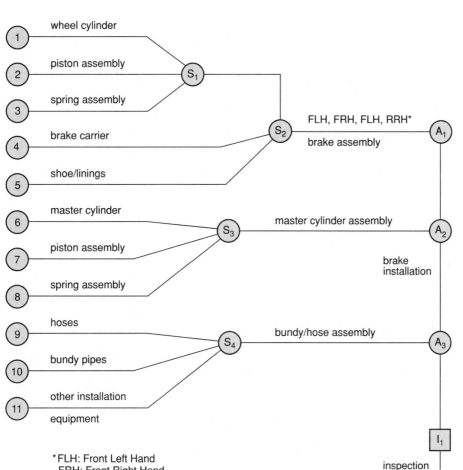

FIGURE 8.19
Assembly Chart

wheel cylinder
① 1

piston assembly
② 2

spring assembly
③ 3

brake carrier
④ 4

shoe/linings
⑤ 5

master cylinder
⑥ 6

piston assembly
⑦ 7

spring assembly
⑧ 8

hoses
⑨ 9

bundy pipes
⑩ 10

other installation
⑪ 11
equipment

S₁

S₂   FLH, FRH, FLH, RRH*
       brake assembly

A₁

S₃   master cylinder assembly   A₂

       brake
       installation

S₄   bundy/hose assembly   A₃

A₁

A₂

A₃

I₁

inspection

*FLH: Front Left Hand
 FRH: Front Right Hand
 RLH: Rear Left Hand
 RRH: Rear Right Hand

2. Given the assembly chart in Figure 8.19, draw the bill of material diagram.

3. Dismantle a small (unusable) object such as a clock and draw an assembly chart for it.

4. Construct an assembly chart for the recipe given below (one of the authors' original creations—try it!).

CHICKEN AND MUSHROOM MORNAY

Mornay sauce (below)
4 chicken breasts, boned and skinned
½ teaspoon salt
¼ teaspoon pepper
flour

4 tablespoons butter
¾ pound fresh mushrooms, sliced
thyme
2 tablespoons dry white wine
½ cup shredded baby Swiss cheese

Prepare Mornay sauce. While sauce is cooking, melt butter over medium heat in skillet. Salt and pepper chicken and dust lightly with flour. Saute chicken about 15 minutes until tender and lightly browned, turning once. Remove chicken to shallow baking dish and keep warm. In butter remaining in skillet, saute mushrooms with a dash of thyme 5 minutes; add wine and cook 1 minute longer. With slotted spoon, remove mushrooms to baking dish with chicken. Top with mornay sauce and grated cheese. Place under broiler 1–2 minutes until cheese melts and is bubbly. Serve with fresh egg noodles.

Mornay sauce

1 cup milk
1 cup chicken broth
1 tablespoon minced onion
1 tablespoon heavy cream
1 bay leaf
2 tablespoons butter

2 tablespoons flour
¼ teaspoon salt
dash pepper
3 tablespoons grated parmesan
   cheese

Bring milk and broth to a boil with the onion and bay leaf. Let stand 10 minutes. Strain. Melt butter in saucepan. Blend in flour and cook 1 minute, stirring constantly. Whisk in the milk mixture gradually, stirring until boiling. Add salt and pepper and cook 15 minutes, stirring often. Blend in cheese and cream.

5. If your state has a personal income tax, construct an assembly chart for your state income tax form.

6. Suppose that the vendor ratings for the Sterling Equipment Corporation example in the chapter were as follows:

| Factor | Vendor | | | |
	1	2	3	4
Installation lead time	Average	Average	Excellent	Poor
Vendor training	Good	Poor	Good	Average
Productivity improvement	Average	Good	Excellent	Good
Vendor service	Average	Excellent	Good	Good
Flexibility	Good	Good	Excellent	Excellent

Would you still choose vendor 1? Why or why not?

7. The natural variation of a process is normally distributed with a mean of 3.0 and a standard deviation of .2. The design specification calls for parts to be manufactured with a dimension of 3.0 ± .3. Evaluate the process capability by computing the proportion of the output that can be produced within the design specification. What percent of the output would have to be scrapped or reworked?

8. The following measurements of the diameter of a piston ring were taken. Based on this limited sample, determine the process capability by computing the mean value and range of the observations. If the design specifications are 54.000 ± .020, how well is the process capable of meeting specifications?

54.030	54.002	54.019	53.992	54.008
53.995	53.992	54.001	54.011	54.004
53.988	54.024	54.021	54.005	54.002
54.002	53.996	53.993	54.015	54.009

9. A machining process produces a part having a required dimension of 0.575 ± .007. Twenty-five samples were measured, and the results are given below. How well can this process meet the specifications?

.571	.575	.573	.576	.576
.578	.575	.574	.571	.574
.576	.573	.571	.577	.575
.579	.577	.575	.570	.575
.574	.576	.579	.575	.576

10. Military radar and missile-detection systems are designed to warn a country against enemy attacks. A system-reliability question deals with the ability of the detection system to identify the attack and perform the warning correctly. Assume that a particular detection system has a .90 probability of detecting a missile attack.
   a. What is the reliability of the system?
   b. Assume two detection systems are installed in the same area and that the system operates satisfactorily if at least one of the two detection systems performs correctly. Assume that the probability of detecting a missile attack is .90 for each system. What is the reliability of the two systems?
   c. If three systems are installed, what is the reliability?
   d. Would you recommend that multiple detection systems be operated simultaneously? Explain.

11. In a complex manufacturing process, three operations are performed in series. Because of the nature of the process, machines frequently fall out of adjustment and must be repaired. To keep the system going, two identical machines are used at each operation; thus if one fails, the other can be used while the first is repaired:

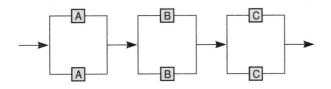

The reliabilities of the machines used in each operation are given below.

Operation	A	B	C
Reliability	.60	.75	.70

   a. Analyze the system reliability, assuming only *one* machine at each operation.
   b. How much is the reliability improved by having two machines at each operation?

12. a. What is the reliability of the following system if the probability of failure of each component is as shown in the figure?

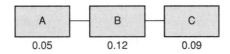

   b. If component B is backed up with another component with a probability = 0.15 what is the overall reliability?

13. A piece of electronic equipment utilized for aviation has the following three elements with reliabilities shown:

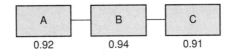

a. What is the reliability of this system?

b. If each of the elements is provided with standby elements with equal reliability, by how much is the overall reliability improved?

c. If the 3 standby elements can function only as a total standby system, what is the overall reliability?

14. Refer to the histogram of the time between failures for the equipment-maintenance example as shown in Figure 8.15. What preventive-maintenance period would you recommend if the preventive-maintenance cost was $50.00 and the average cost for an equipment failure was $30.00? How many breakdowns a year should you expect under your preventive-maintenance program?

15. The MTBF for a computer's central processing unit is normally distributed with a mean of 14 days and a standard deviation of 3 days. Each failure costs the company $500 in lost computing time and repair costs. A shutdown for preventive maintenance can be scheduled during nonpeak times and will cost only $100. As the manager in charge of computer operations, you are to determine if a preventive maintenance program is worthwhile. What is your recommendation?

16. For a particular piece of equipment, the probability of failure during a given week is as follows:

Week of Operation	1	2	3	4	5	6
Probability of Failure	.20	.10	.10	.15	.20	.25

Management is considering a preventive-maintenance program that would be implemented at the end of a given week of production. The production loss and downtime cost associated with an equipment failure is estimated to be $1500.00 per failure. If it costs $100.00 to perform the preventive maintenance, when should the firm implement the preventive maintenance program? What is the total maintenance and failure cost associated with your recommendation and how many failures can be expected each year? Assume 52 weeks of operation per year.

17. Let t denote the number of days of operation before preventive maintenance of a particular piece of equipment. Analysis of historical operating data shows that the annual cost of preventive maintenance is $32,000/t$ and the annual cost of failure is $320t$.

a. Develop an equation that will show the total annual preventive maintenance and failure cost as a function of the time before preventive maintenance, t.

b. Use your answer to part (a) to compute the total cost for a preventive-maintenance period of 5 days.

c. Use trial and error to evaluate the total cost under a variety of values for t. What preventive-maintenance period appears to provide the lowest total cost?

d. Assuming 260 working days per year, what is the cost of each preventive maintenance performed?

18. The probability of breakdown of a particular machine versus the number of hours elapsed after previous maintenance is given below.

Number of Hours After Previous Maintenance	Probability
10	0.01
20	0.05
30	0.15
40	0.15
50	0.15
60	0.15
70	0.20
80	0.14

The number of working days in a year is 250 on a two shift basis. A breakdown costs $350 to repair, and a preventive maintenance costs $150.

a. What is the MTBF?

b. What is the maintenance cost if no preventive maintenance is followed?

c. What is the cost of a preventive-maintenance policy carried out once every 10 hours.

d. Decrease the frequency of preventive maintenance in steps of 10 hours and evaluate total costs. Find the best maintenance policy.

I n the previous chapter we focused on the analysis and selection of production processes. We discussed technological issues involved in producing quality products and the overall choice of processes to match the strategic objectives of the firm. This chapter concentrates on the design of the process and the layout of facilities that provide the means for achieving strategic objectives.

Process design and facility layout are necessary whenever one or more of the following situations occur: (1) a new facility is constructed; (2) there is a significant change in production or throughput volume; (3) new products are introduced; and (4) different processes and equipment are installed.

The physical design of a facility can be an important factor in determining the productivity of an organization. In manufacturing organizations, the objectives of process design and facility layout studies are to improve the flow and control of work, reduce costs because of handling and carrying work-in-process inventory, minimize equipment investment, make the best use of space, and improve employee morale and supervision. Process design and facility layout studies are also useful in service organizations such as libraries, hospitals, restaurants, and banks. In these organizations, the objectives are to minimize customer waiting time, maximize worker productivity, minimize customer travel time, and so on.

Many advantages can be gained from proper attention to process design and facility layout. These include

1. shorter manufacturing cycle times; potentially, 95 percent shorter if material is never put down until the manufacturing process is completed
2. reduce in-process inventory; as with cycle times, a substantial reduction is often possible
3. less floor space required
4. substantially reduced material handling costs
5. simplified scheduling and control systems
6. improved product quality
7. enhanced manufacturing flexibility.

Sun Microsystems provides an illustration of the benefits that can be achieved.[1] Sun, founded in 1982, produces computer workstation products. Sun's manufacturing facility evolved in stages as the company grew and more capacity was needed. As a result, there was no coordinated process design. Materials, paper, and people were everywhere, often in conflicting flow patterns. Things would always get done, but it was due primarily to the effectiveness of the workers rather than an effective process flow. Moreover, the product mix was constantly changing. Consequently, management decided that a new facility was needed. Some of the goals in designing the new facility were

- provide flexibility to meet product changes
- provide high quality through better materials handling and process flow
- provide the ability to track and control materials through computerized systems
- improve employee morale through a pleasant working environment.

---

[1]"Flexibility Helps Company Cope with Rapid Growth," *Modern Materials Handling*, August 1987, 54–56.

The new plant increased on-time delivery performance by 50 percent and dramatically improved quality, even with a higher volume of production.

This chapter begins with a discussion of how process design can be used to determine how the physical resources of a firm can be best utilized.

9.1 PROCESS DESIGN ANALYSIS

The objective of *process design* is to determine how the physical resources of a firm can be best organized and structured. To do this effectively we need a step-by-step description of how products are to be produced. This is usually accomplished using a *process-flow diagram*. For instance, in Figure 9.1 we show a simple process-flow diagram for a printed circuit board assembly. In this figure, each box represents a processing operation. The first processing operation is component placement, followed by soldering, subassembly attachment, test and repair, and final assembly.

Process-flow diagrams provide a general description of the flow of materials and work-in-process. More detailed information is given in route sheets and flow-process charts. An example of a **route sheet** is given in Figure 9.2. Route sheets, like assembly charts, provide important information on the specific operations in the manufacturing process. Generally, a route sheet contains the part name and number, person responsible for the route sheet, operation numbers, descriptions, department, and specific machines to be used. Route sheets, along with assembly drawings and charts, provide complete specifications for manufacturing.

Route sheets, however, do not provide critical information about the movement and handling of the part through the various production stages. A flow-process chart is used to provide this information. A **flow-process chart**, illustrated in Figure 9.3, provides a step-by-step analysis of the sequence of operations, transportations, inspections, storages, and delays, which are the basic elements of any production process. The symbols used are shown in Figure 9.4. Flow-process charts are often used to assist industrial engineers and operations managers in eliminating unnecessary activities. In analyzing a flow-process chart, we should ask questions such as: Can some operations be eliminated or combined? Can transport operations be simplified or eliminated? Why do delays occur? Answers to such questions may lead to changes in work methods, equipment, or even layout and can significantly reduce costs and improve productivity. In the next chapter, we see how similar techniques can be used to design and improve individual jobs.

FIGURE 9.1   Process-flow Diagram for Printed Circuit-Board Assembly

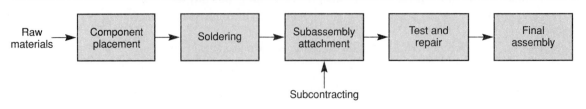

FIGURE 9.2

Route Sheet

Part name	5" Mitre		Date: 1/14/90	
Part number	36025		Issued by: George Johnson	
Operation	Dept	Description	Equipment	
01	07	Shear coil to desired length	480 shear	
02	05	Punch blanks	335 punch press	
03	06	Press hem into blank	334 press	
04	06	Press blanks into form	333 press	
05	06	Press profile into form	332 press	
06	06	Press flange into form	345 press	
07	09	Spot weld	Spot welder	

A **work center** consists of one or more people and/or machines which can be considered as one unit for the purposes of capacity planning and scheduling. For example, a work center can be a single machine or group of machines in one location, a group of workers who perform a similar task or closely related set of tasks such as on an assembly line, or a set of different machines that function together to perform a set of operations on one or more products. In Figure 9.1, for instance, component placement and soldering could be combined into one work center, or test and repair could be split into two distinct work centers. As more work centers are defined, scheduling and control of the production process becomes more difficult, and the data needed for management decision making become more complex. Too few work centers, on the other hand, make it difficult for managers to find bottlenecks and gather the performance and cost data that are needed in order to identify and correct specific problems.

The importance of capacity was discussed in Chapter 6. To plan production schedules effectively, work center capacities must be known. Here, capacity is usually defined as the number of available hours in a given time period, either for machines or labor.

Capacity should include an efficiency factor reflecting downtime for failure and maintenance. For example, suppose that a work center consists of four machines, each of which is used during an 8-hour, one-shift operation; furthermore, suppose that the *efficiency* of each machine is 85 percent (that is, the machines are expected to be available for productive work 85 percent of the time). The capacity of the work center is computed as

(4 machines)(8 hours/shift/machine)(1 shift)(.85) = 27.2 hours

Given the capacity of each work center and the processing requirements per unit manufactured, we can determine the number of units of production that can be achieved over a period of time. Thus, in our previous illustration, if a product requires .8 minutes of processing, the production volume per shift will be

(27.2 hours)(60 minutes/hour)(1 part/.8 minutes) = 2040 parts/shift

FIGURE 9.3 Flow-process Chart

Part name ____5" Mitre____

Part Number ____36025____

Process desc. _____

Charted by ____George Johnson____

Date ____1/14/90____

Summary		No.
Operations		7
Transportations		7
Inspections		
Delays		6
Storages		
Distance traveled		300'

Details of present method	Flow	Comments
1. Slit coils sheared to desired length	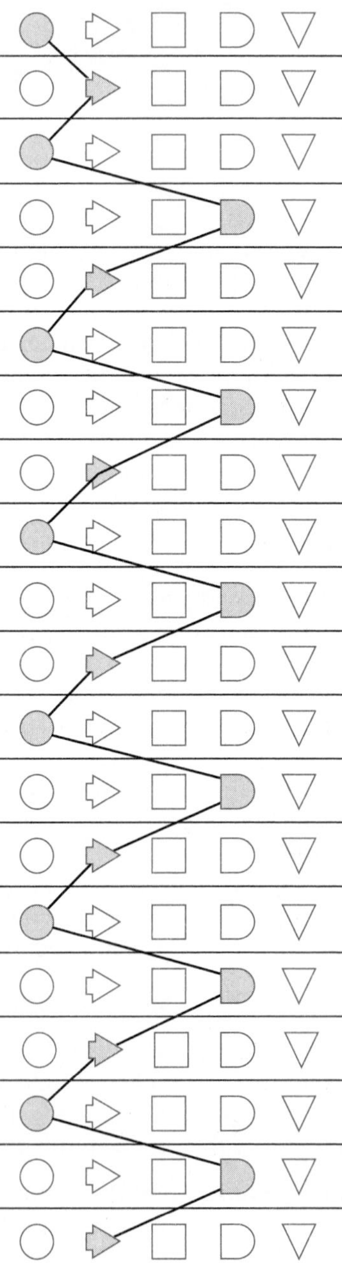	Machine 480
2. To machine 335		30'
3. Blanks punched out and stacked in boxes		
4. In boxes		
5. To machine 334		45'
6. Hem pressed into blanks—parts stacked in boxes		
7. In boxes		
8. To machine 333		40'
9. Blanks pressed into form—parts stacked in boxes		
10. In boxes		
11. To machine 332		10'
12. Profile pressed into form—parts stacked in boxes		
13. In boxes		
14. To machine 345		20'
15. Flange pressed into form—parts stacked in boxes		
16. In boxes		
17. To spot welder machine		80'
18. Parts spot welded and stacked in boxes		
19. In boxes		
20. To storage		75'

Symbol	Meaning	Definition
◯	Operation	A job or task normally performed at one location
▷	Transportation	The movement of an item from one location to another
□	Inspection	The determination of acceptability of an item
D	Delay	A pause or interruption in scheduled work
▽	Storage	Scheduled holding of items before, during, or after production operations

FIGURE 9.4

Flow-process Chart Symbols

From this information and process-flow diagrams, process designers can determine the critical or bottleneck work centers and evaluate the impact of changes in the design of the production process.

Once all required operations are known, the routing of materials and semi-finished product is determined, and work centers are defined, attention may be turned to how to best arrange the physical facilities.

9.2 FACILITY LAYOUT

Facility layout involves the specific arrangement of physical facilities. It affects material flow, handling and maintenance costs, equipment utilization, productivity, production flexibility, management effectiveness, and even employee morale. A good facility layout will enable materials, workers, and information to move efficiently and effectively. Specific objectives of facility layout include the following:

1. minimize delays and material handling
2. maintain flexibility
3. use labor and space effectively
4. promote high employee morale
5. provide for good housekeeping and maintenance

Layout Patterns

Four major types of layout patterns or arrangements are commonly used in designing production processes: product layout, process layout, group layout, and fixed position layout.

Product Layout

Continuous flow, mass production, and batch-processing production processes are usually physically organized by **product layout**. That is, equipment arrangement is based on the sequence of operations performed in production, and products move in a continuous path from one department to the next. An example of an industry that uses a product-layout pattern is the wine-making industry. Figure 9.5 shows a layout pattern that is typical of most wine-making operations.

Because all products move in the same direction, product layouts provide a smooth and logical flow of production and enable the use of specialized handling equipment. Other advantages of product layouts include small in-process inventory, short-unit production time, low material handling, low labor skill requirements, and simple planning and production control systems.

However, there are several disadvantages associated with product layouts. For instance, a breakdown in one machine can cause an entire production line to shut down. In addition, since the layout is determined by the product, a change in product design or the introduction of new products may require major changes in the existing layout; thus flexibility can be limited. Note also that the capacity of the production line is determined by the bottleneck work center. Finally, and perhaps most important, the jobs in a product-layout facility, such as those on a mass production line, may provide little job satisfaction. This is primarily because of the high level of division of labor often required and the monotony that usually results.

Process Layout

A **process layout** consists of a functional grouping of machines or activities that do similar work. For example, all drill presses may be grouped together in one department and all milling machines in another. Depending on their processing requirements, parts may be moved in different sequences among departments (see Figure 9.6). Job shops are an example of firms that use process layouts in order to provide high flexibility in the type of products that can be made and the utilization of equipment and labor. Compared to product layouts, process layouts generally require a lower investment in equipment. In addition, the diversity of jobs inherent in a process layout can lead to increased worker satisfaction.

FIGURE 9.5
Product Layout

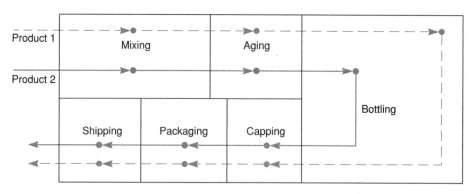

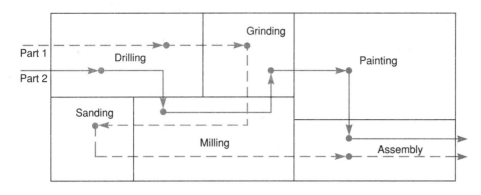

FIGURE 9.6
Process Layout

Some of the limitations of process layouts include (1) high handling and transportation costs, primarily because of the fact that products must be moved frequently between departments; (2) more complicated planning and control systems, because jobs do not always flow in the same direction; (3) longer total production time, because of increased handling between departments; (4) higher in-process inventory, since jobs from several departments may arrive and wait at a particular department; and (5) higher worker skill requirements, since workers must be able to handle the processing requirements for different orders, rather than a standard product.

Group Layout

Process layouts, which dominate batch-production facilities, result in a large number of setups for different parts, as well as high material-handling costs and high work-in-process inventory. Mass-production systems, on the other hand, have few setups and lower handling and work-in-process, since all parts go through the same sequence of processes. The idea of **group technology**, or *cellular manufacturing*, is to classify parts into families so that efficient mass-production-type layouts can be designed for these families of parts.

In a **group layout**, the design is not according to the functional characteristics of machines, but rather by groups of different machines (called *cells*) that are necessary for the production of families of parts. An example of a cell is shown in Figure 9.7. In this figure we see a U-shaped arrangement of machines that is typical of cellular manufacturing. Within this cell, it is easy to see the characteristics of a product layout. Materials move in a straight line fashion from one machine to the next. Three workers are assigned to this cell. One loads incoming parts on the saw, performs final inspection and loads the finished part for transportation out of the cell. A second worker operates the two lathes and the grinder, and a third worker operates the three milling machines.

To illustrate the group technology concept, consider a facility that produces two families of parts. The first group of parts are cylindrical (Figure 9.8a) and require operations on a lathe, milling machine, and drilling machine. The second family are rectangular (Figure 9.8b) and require shearing, milling, and drilling. The traditional process layout shown in Figure 9.9 places shearing machines, lathes, milling machines, and drilling machines in separate departments. As parts from each family pass through milling and drilling departments in batches, new setups on the machines must be performed. The group concept establishes a

FIGURE 9.7   Schematic of a Cell Using Conventional Machine Tools

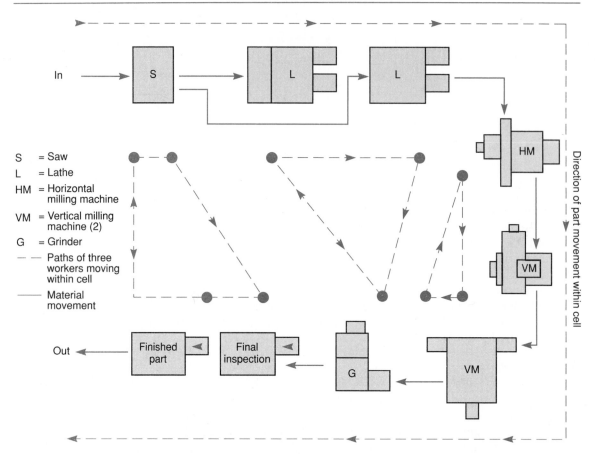

S = Saw
L = Lathe
HM = Horizontal milling machine
VM = Vertical milling machine (2)
G = Grinder
— — Paths of three workers moving within cell
——— Material movement

Source: J. T. Black, "Cellular Manufacturing Systems Reduce Set Up Time, Make Small Lot Production Economical," Reprinted from *Industrial Engineering* magazine, November 1983. Copyright Institute of Industrial Engineers, 25 Technology Park/Atlanta, Norcross, GA 30092.

separate machine group which consists of milling and drilling machines for each part family (Figure 9.10). Since part families have similar features, retooling is much easier; hence setup times are reduced and the system operates in the fashion of a production line.

Group layouts can provide significant benefits. In a traditional process layout, jobs normally experience long delays in traveling between departments and waiting to be processed; in contrast, group layouts reduce waiting and throughput times. Since the work flow is standardized and centrally located in a group layout environment, material handling requirements are also reduced. This reduction enables workers to concentrate on production rather than moving parts between machines.

Quicker response to quality problems within cells can improve the overall level of quality. Since machines are closely linked within a cell, additional floor space becomes available for other productive uses. Because workers have greater responsibility in a cellular manufacturing system, they become more aware of

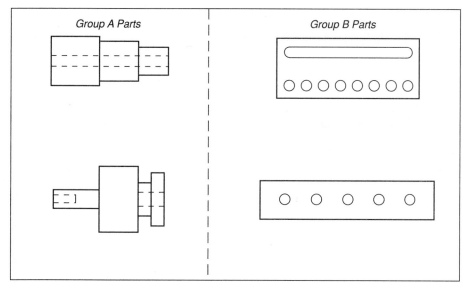

FIGURE 9.8
Two Part
Families

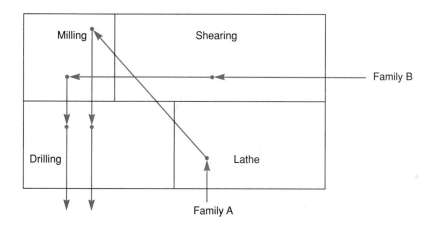

FIGURE 9.9
Process Layout

their contribution to the final product; this increases morale, satisfaction, and ultimately quality and productivity.

The implementation of group technology requires a systematic analysis of the firm's production processes and may take several months to accomplish. It requires an effective information system, a new layout of the facility, and possible equipment changes. However, the savings in setup time and increased production potential may be of significant economic benefit to the firm.

An example at Rockwell's Dallas plant illustrates the improvements that can result from cellular manufacturing.[2] Figure 9.11 shows the situation at the plant

---

[2]Dan L. Shunk, "Group Technology Provides Organized Approach to Realizing Benefits of CIMS." Reprinted from *Industrial Engineering* magazine, April 1985. Copyright Institute of Industrial Engineers, 25 Technology Park/Atlanta, Norcross, GA 30092.

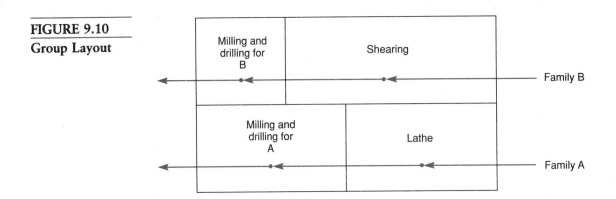

FIGURE 9.10
Group Layout

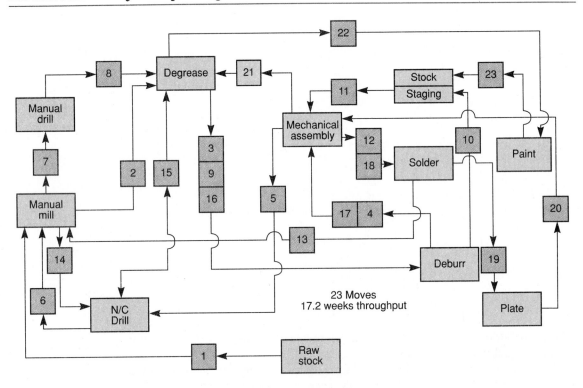

FIGURE 9.11   The Job Shop Arrangement

23 Moves
17.2 weeks throughput

before the cellular approach was implemented. The numbers in the squares indicate the sequence of moves throughout the shop. For example, raw stock first goes to the manual mill, then to degrease, deburr, mechanical assembly, and so on. You can observe from this figure that the movement within the factory was very complex. It took a typical part 23 moves and 17.2 weeks to flow through the fabrication shop prior to assembly. This long lead time forced planners to forecast part requirements and thus created large amounts of in-process inventory. By reviewing all part designs, tooling, and fabrication methods through a group technology part-family analysis, a cell was created that allowed parts to be made with only 9 moves in 2.2 weeks (Figure 9.12). In this figure, the product movement is simplified considerably.

The impact on cost was substantial, but the major impact was in planning. The planner did not have to predict parts requirements; instead, it was possible to make parts in the fabrication shop fast enough that assembly could be supported without inventory buildup.

Fixed-position Layout

The construction of large items, such as heavy machine tools, airplanes, locomotives, and so on, is usually accomplished in one place. Rather than move the item from one work center to another, tools and components are brought to one place for assembly. This **fixed-position layout** is synonymous with the project classification of production processes presented in the previous chapter.

Table 9.1 summarizes the relative features of process, product, and group layouts. It is clear that the basic trade-off in selecting among these layout types is flexibility versus productivity. Process layouts offer high flexibility at the expense of low productivity, while product layouts have limited flexibility with high productivity. Group layouts are designed to balance the advantages of both types.

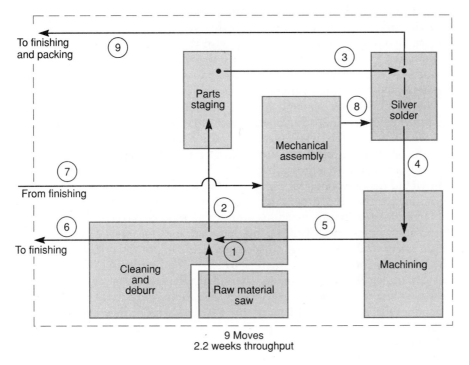

FIGURE 9.12
The Cellular Arrangement

9 Moves
2.2 weeks throughput

TABLE 9.1

Comparison of Basic Layout Patterns

Attribute	Process Layout	Product Layout	Group Layout
Amount of flexibility	High	Low	Moderate
Automation potential	Low	High	Moderate
Type of equipment	General purpose	Highly specialized	Some specialization
Production volume	Low	High	Moderate
Equipment utilization	Low	High	Moderate
Setup costs and requirements	Low	High	Moderate

Layout Issues in Service Organizations

Service organizations must deal with similar issues in selecting appropriate layouts. The basic trade-off between product and process layouts concerns the degree of specialization versus flexibility as well as productivity. Services must consider the volume of demand, range of the types of services offered, degree of personalization of the service, skills of employees, and cost.

Service organizations that need the ability to provide a wide variety of services to customers with differing requirements usually use a process layout. For example, libraries place reference materials, serials, and microfilms into separate areas; hospitals group services by function also, such as maternity, oncology, surgery, and X-ray; and insurance companies have office layouts in which claims, underwriting, and filing are placed in individual departments.

Service organizations that provide highly standardized services tend to use product layouts. For instance, course registration at a college or university is probably set up in a product layout since the registration process is similar for all students. The same is true of customs and immigration checking at airports. In general, whenever little variety and personalization of services is offered, and the volume of demand generally is high, a product layout is used.

Group layouts are less common in service organizations than in manufacturing. However, one example where group layouts are found is in offices. When an office has a typist in each department rather than having a centralized typing pool, it is analogous to a group layout in manufacturing. A typing pool arrangement would be an example of a pure process layout.

Waiting, or the perception of waiting, is an important issue in process design and layout for service organizations. Major fast food chains have made a science of studying waiting lines. Wendy's International, Inc., for instance, assigned eight people solely to discover ways to speed service. One of the critical decisions in process design for services is whether to have one "serpentine" line or several lines in parallel. Waiting customers often feel victimized when another customer in the next line receives service before they do. Studies show that customers prefer serpentine lines—even if it increases their wait—because they are perceived to be fair.

An interesting example of how facility layout can affect waiting perception is that of an airline in the Houston airport. Passengers complained about long delays in the baggage claim area. The solution by the airline was to move the baggage to the farthest carousel from the arrival gates. Though passengers had to walk further and the total time until baggage arrived was the same, the complaints stopped because their waiting time had diminished! The supplement to this chapter deals with some of the technical issues of analyzing waiting lines.

9.3 DESIGN OF PRODUCT LAYOUTS

Continuous flow, assembly line, and many batch processing production processes operate in a similar manner in that products follow a fixed sequence of production operations. These types of product layouts can be classified as *production lines*. A **production line** is a fixed sequence of production stages, each consisting of one or more machines or work stations. In designing production lines, there are often many alternative configurations that can be considered, along with a wide variety of material-handling equipment from which to choose.

A challenging problem in designing a production line involves the determination of the optimum configurations of operators and buffers (queues of work-in-process). Product layouts might have several work stations in series (Figure 9.13a), in parallel (Figure 9.13b), or a combination of both (Figure 9.13c). A major design consideration for production lines is the assignment of operations so that all stages are more or less equally loaded. Consider, for instance, a traditional conveyor-paced production line illustrated in Figure 9.14. In this example, parts move along a conveyor at a rate of one part per minute to three work centers, and each work center performs one of three required operations. The first operation requires 3 minutes per unit; the second, 1 minute per unit; and the third, 2 minutes per unit. The first work center consists of three operators; the second, one operator; and the third, two operators.

The assigned location where a worker performs his or her job is called a *work station;* this could be a machine or a work bench, for example. In Figure 9.14, a worker removes a part from the conveyor and performs some task at his or her work station. The completed part is returned to the conveyor and transported to the next work center. The number of workers at each work center was chosen so that the line is *balanced*. Since three operators work simultaneously at the first work center, on the average one part will be completed each minute. This is also true for the other work centers. Since the parts arrive at a rate of one per minute, parts are also completed at this rate.

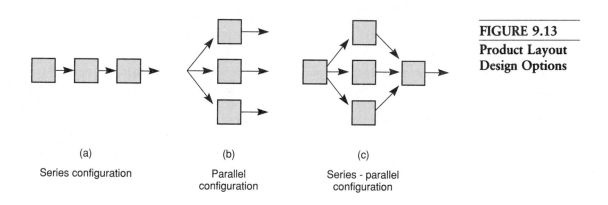

FIGURE 9.13

Product Layout Design Options

(a) Series configuration

(b) Parallel configuration

(c) Series - parallel configuration

FIGURE 9.14

Traditional
Conveyor-Paced
Assembly Line

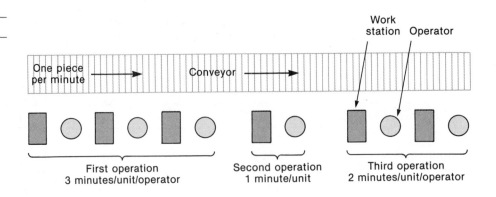

Conveyor-paced production lines such as this work well when there is a low variance in times required to perform the individual operations. If the operations are somewhat complex, thus resulting in higher time variance, operators down the line may not be able to keep up with the flow of parts from the preceding work center or may experience excessive idle time. In addition, conveyor-paced lines provide no worker control, are monotonous, and offer little social interaction. Workers do not identify with the product, and often negative behavioral consequences—and quality problems—result. An alternative is to use unpaced production lines in which work centers are linked by gravity conveyors (where parts simply roll to the end and stop). These act as buffers between the successive operations and eliminate pacing of work tasks. An example is shown in Figure 9.15. These provide more worker autonomy and less of a feeling of being under "control" of mechanization.

In unpaced production lines, however, there are two sources of delay: **flow-blocking delay**, and **lack-of-work delay**. Flow-blocking delay occurs when a work center completes a unit but cannot release it because the in-process storage at the next stage is full. The operator must remain idle until storage space becomes available. Lack-of-work delay occurs whenever one stage completes work and no units are awaiting processing from the previous stage.

The determination of an optimal production-line configuration is a complex task that is often assisted by computer simulation. Queueing, or waiting-line theory, is another quantitative analysis tool that is also often used to analyze production lines and other systems where arrivals and service rates are random. In the supplement to this chapter we discuss waiting-line models and their applications to a service-system situation. Operations management personnel need to work closely with designers and industrial engineers in developing effective systems.

Assembly-line Balancing

Conveyor-paced production lines are commonly used for manual assembly tasks. Because of their importance and widespread use, this section covers the topic of balancing assembly lines. In the traditional conveyor-paced production line illustration (see Figure 9.14) discussed in the previous section, workers were allocated to the three operations so that the line was perfectly balanced. That is, each work center has the same amount of work per operator per unit of time. In realistic situations, such an allocation is usually not possible. Let us now examine the issues involved in balancing assembly lines.

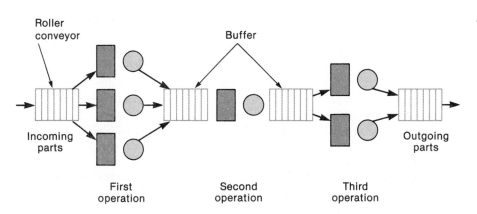

FIGURE 9.15

Unpaced
Assembly Line
with Buffers

For an assembly line, we are given a set of operations to perform and *precedence relations* among the operations. Precedence relations tell the sequence in which operations must be performed. This information can be obtained from an assembly chart which was introduced in Chapter 8. In addition, each operation has a time associated with it. For example, consider the simple three-operation assembly line shown in Figure 9.16. Operation A is first and must be completed before operation B can be performed. After operation B is finished, operation C may be performed. Since all three operations must be performed in order to complete one part, the total time required to complete one part is .5 + .3 + .2 = 1.0 minute. Thus in an 8-hour day, if we assume a 90 percent efficiency in order to account for rest breaks and other delays, a production system in which one operator, who performs each of the three operations in sequence, could produce

$$(1 \text{ part}/1 \text{ min})(60 \text{ minutes per hour})(8 \text{ hours per day})(.9 \text{ efficiency})$$
$$= 432 \text{ parts/day}$$

As an alternative to a one-operator production system, suppose that three operators work on the line, each performing one of the three operations. The first operator can produce 120 parts per hour, since his or her task time is .5 minute. Thus, a total of

$$(1 \text{ part}/.5 \text{ min})(60 \text{ minutes per hour})(8 \text{ hours per day})(.9 \text{ efficiency})$$
$$= 864 \text{ parts/day}$$

could be sent to operator 2. Since the time operator 2 takes is only .3 minutes, he or she could produce

$$(1 \text{ part}/.3 \text{ min})(60 \text{ minutes per hour})(8 \text{ hours per day})(.9 \text{ efficiency})$$
$$= 1440 \text{ parts/day}$$

However, operator 2 cannot do this because the first operator has a lower production rate. This is an example of lack-of-work delay. Thus, even though the third operator can produce

$$(1 \text{ part}/.2 \text{ min})(60 \text{ minutes per hour})(8 \text{ hours per day})(.9 \text{ efficiency})$$
$$= 2160 \text{ parts/day},$$

we see that the maximum output of this three-operator assembly line is 864 parts per day.

A third alternative is to use two work stations. The first operator performs operation A, while the second performs operations B and C. Since each operator takes .5 minutes to perform the assigned duties, the line is in perfect balance and 864 parts per day can be produced. Therefore, we can achieve the same output rate with two operators as we can by using three, thus saving labor cost.

The objective of assembly-line balancing is to assign tasks to individual work stations along to the line in order to minimize labor cost while satisfying precedence constraints and achieving the desired output rate. Typically, one either minimizes the number of work centers for a given production rate, or maximizes the production rate for a given number of work stations.

An important concept in assembly-line balancing is the **cycle time**. The cycle time is the interval between successive parts coming off the assembly line. In the three-operation example as shown in Figure 9.16, if we use only one work station, the cycle time is 1 minute; that is, one completed assembly is produced every minute. If two work stations are used as described above, then the cycle time is .5 minutes. Finally, if three work stations are used, the cycle time is still .5 minutes, because task A is the bottleneck, or slowest operation. The line can only produce one assembly every .5 minutes.

If C is the cycle time in minutes and H is the number of productive minutes available per shift, then the number of parts that can be produced during the shift is given by H/C. In order to produce at least P parts per shift, H/C must be greater than or equal to P. Solving the inequality $H/C \geq P$ for C, we find that $C \leq H/P$ in order to produce at least P parts per shift. For example, in the three-operation illustration, suppose that a production rate of at least 600 units per 8-hour shift is required to meet demand. Furthermore, suppose that we have (8 hours)(60 minutes per hour)(.9 efficiency) = 432 productive minutes per shift. Thus, in order to produce at least 600 units per shift, the cycle time must be no greater than 432/600 = 0.72. This means that the one-station assembly line cannot meet the required production requirements; either the two- or three-station designs must be used. Moreover, the cycle time cannot be smaller than the largest operation time nor larger than the sum of all the operation times. In this example, we have $.5 \leq C \leq 1.0$. This, in addition to the constraint $C \leq H/P$, provides a range of feasible cycle times.

Suppose that we decide to use the three-station configuration in which each task is assigned to a different worker. We see that for each cycle of .5 minutes, station A is always busy, but station B is only busy .3/.5 = .6 or 60 percent of the time. Similarly, station C is only busy .2/.5 or 40 percent of the time. The idle time at each station is equal to the cycle time minus the sum of all the operation times assigned to that station. Thus stations B and C are idle .2 and .3 minutes per cycle, respectively. We may compute the *efficiency* of the entire line using the following formula:

$$\text{Line efficiency} = \frac{\text{sum of all operation times}}{(\text{cycle time})(\text{number of work stations})}$$

FIGURE 9.16

Three-task Assembly-line Balancing Problem

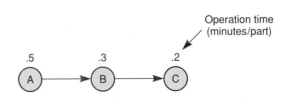

For this example we have

$$\text{Line efficiency} = \frac{1.0}{(.5)(3)} = \frac{1.0}{1.5} = .67 \text{ or } 67 \text{ percent}$$

This tells us that only 67 percent of the available productive capacity is utilized, or equivalently, that the workers will be idle 33 percent of the time on average because of imbalance of the line. One objective of assembly-line balancing is to maximize the line efficiency.

For more complex problems, the number of possible work station configurations can be very large. In the following example we introduce a heuristic procedure that finds a good, but not necessarily the best, solution to the assembly line balancing problem.

BALANCING A CARBURETOR ASSEMBLY LINE

EXAMPLE

Refer back to Figure 8.6 in the previous chapter, which shows an assembly chart for a lawnmower carburetor. From that figure we may define the following operations that must be performed during the assembly process:

1. Assemble throttle shaft and return spring (SA-1).
2. Assemble throttle shutter and screw (SA-2).
3. Assemble SA-1, SA-2, housing, and fuel-inlet fitting (A-1).
4. Inspect (I-1).
5. Assemble inlet-needle assembly and clip (SA-3).
6. Assemble SA-3 with A-1 (housing assembly).
7. Assemble carburetor float and float shaft with housing assembly (A-3).
8. Inspect (I-2).
9. Assemble gasket, float bowl, and bolt (SA-4).
10. Final assembly of SA-4 and gasket with completed housing assembly A-3.
11. Final inspection.

Table 9.2 gives the time for each operation. We may represent the precedence relations of each of these 11 operations as prescribed in the assembly chart by the network in Figure 9.17. For example, the network shows that operations 1

Operation Number	Assembly Time (min.)
1	.4
2	.7
3	.5
4	.7
5	.4
6	.2
7	.1
8	.3
9	.4
10	.5
11	.6
Total	4.8 minutes

TABLE 9.2

Assembly-line Balancing Data

FIGURE 9.17 A Work Station Assignment for Carburetor Assembly

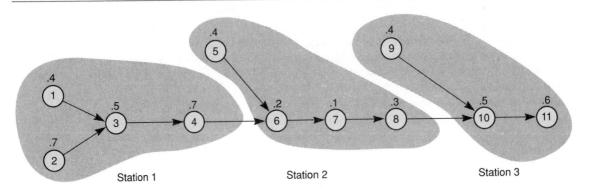

and 2 must be completed before operation 3 may be performed; similarly, operation 3 must precede operation 4.

In designing an assembly line for this product, we might assign operations 1, 2, 3, and 4 to one work station, operations 5, 6, 7, and 8 to a second, and operations 9, 10, and 11 to a third, as shown in Figure 9.17. However, we could not assign operations 1, 2, 3, 4, and 6 to work station 1 and operations 5, 7, and 8 to work station 2, since operation 5 must precede operation 6. If we use only one work station, then the cycle time is 4.8 minutes—the sum of all the processing times. If each operation is assigned to one station, the cycle time is .7, the largest operation time. Thus, feasible cycle times must be between .7 and 4.8 minutes.

For this example, let us suppose that an output rate of 6500 units per week is desired. Operating three shifts per day for 5 days per week amounts to approximately 433 units per shift. Note that at 90 percent efficiency, (.9)(8) = 7.2 productive hours are available; thus the required cycle time is

$$C = \frac{(7.2 \text{ hours/shift})(60 \text{ minutes/hour})}{433 \text{ units/shift}} = .9977 \approx 1.0 \text{ minute/unit}$$

The problem is to assign operations to work stations without violating precedences and exceeding the cycle time of 1.0. We proceed as follows. Start with station 1 and determine which operations can be assigned. In this case, operations 1, 2, 5, and 9 are candidates, since they have no immediate predecessors. We need some rule for choosing among them. Various rules can be used and each may result in a different solution. We will arbitrarily assign elements using the rule *choose the operations with the largest time first*. We therefore assign operation 2 to station 1.

Next, we determine a new set of operations that may be considered for assignment. In general, this set consists of all unassigned operations for which all immediately preceding operations have been assigned. Since operation 1 has not yet been assigned, operation 3 is *not* a candidate. Hence only operations 1, 5, or 9 can be considered at this time. It is impossible to assign operations 1, 5, or 9 to station 1 without violating the cycle time restriction. In this case we move on to station 2.

Station	Operations Assigned		Total Operation Time	Idle Time
1	2		.7	.3
2	1, 3		.9	.1
3	4		.7	.3
4	5, 9, 6		1.0	0
5	7, 8, 10		.9	.1
6	11		.6	.4
		Totals	4.8 minutes	1.2 minutes

TABLE 9.3

Solution to Assembly-line Balancing Problem

At station 2, we may consider assigning either task 1, 5, or 9 first, all of which have times of .4. We break ties by selecting the operation with the smallest operation number. Thus we assign operation 1 to station 2. Each time an operation is assigned to a station, we must determine a new set of candidates. Since all predecessors of operation 3 have now been assigned, we add it to the set of assignable candidates. Thus operations 3, 5, and 9 are the new set. Choosing the largest time first, we assign operation 3 to station 2. The new candidate set consists of operations 4, 5, and 9. We cannot assign any of these to station 2 without exceeding the cycle time, so we move on to station 3.

Continuing in this fashion, we obtain the solution given in Table 9.3.[3] We may compute the line efficiency as

$$\text{Line efficiency} = \frac{\text{sum of all operation times}}{(\text{cycle time})(\text{number of work stations})}$$

$$= \frac{4.8}{(1.0)(6)} = .80$$

1. Determine the cycle time required to meet production quotas.
2. Construct a precedence network for the balancing problem.
3. Choose a set of assignable operations consisting of all unassigned operations for which all immediate predecessors have already been assigned.
4. Assign the operation with the largest time first to a work station if the cycle time would not be exceeded. Break ties by choosing the lowest operation number. Construct a new set of assignable candidates. If no further operations can be assigned, move on to the next work station. Continue in this fashion until all operations have been assigned.

Summary of the Assembly-line Balancing Algorithm

9.4 DESIGN OF PROCESS LAYOUTS

In designing process layouts, we are concerned with the arrangement of departments relative to one another. In designing new layouts, material-handling cost

---

[3]This procedure is a network adaptation of Hoffman's method in "Assembly Line Balancing With a Precedence Matrix," *Management Science*, 9, no. 4 (July 1963).

usually is the principal design criterion. In general, departments with a large number of moves between them should be located close to one another. In order to provide a quantitative basis for the layout analysis, we need to construct a load matrix. A **load matrix** lists the number of moves from one department to another over some time period, such as one year. This information can be obtained from route sheets and planned production schedules.

The handling cost is generally proportional to the distance traveled and the type of equipment used. For example, the cost of transporting materials by forklift truck is higher than using a conveyor because of higher capital investment, maintenance, and labor costs. We assume that the movement of all materials takes place by forklift so that cost will simply be proportional to distance. In general, a wide variety of material-handling equipment can be chosen. The most effective layout-planning methods attempt to integrate the material-handling selection decision with the layout itself. However, such a discussion is beyond the scope of this text.

Clearly the distance traveled depends on the layout. We use the following approach:

1. Design a trial layout.
2. Compute the distances between departments.
3. Multiply the interdepartmental distances by the volume of flow between departments to create a volume-distance matrix, and then compute the total cost.
4. Use the volume-distance matrix created in Step 3 to propose changes in the current layout, then repeat the process (from Step 2) until a satisfactory layout is obtained.

| EXAMPLE | DESIGNING A PROCESS LAYOUT |

Consider the situation facing Home Video Equipment, Inc., (HVE), a California-based company that produces video recording equipment. Increasing sales volume and new product lines have necessitated building a new plant in order to provide more effective distribution to the eastern United States. HVE must determine how the eight major departments needed to produce the video recorders should be laid out. The eight departments and the estimated space needed in each department are as follows:

1. Receiving   1200 square feet
2. Machining   1800 square feet
3. Pressing   2400 square feet
4. Cleaning   600 square feet
5. Plating   1200 square feet
6. Painting   900 square feet
7. Assembly   2400 square feet
8. Shipping   1500 square feet

Table 9.4 shows the annual number of moves between departments. For example, the number of moves from receiving to machining is 200, the number of moves from painting to assembly is 300, and so on.

From Table 9.4 we see that materials move from receiving to either machining or pressing; from machining to either plating, painting, or assembly, and so on.

TABLE 9.4   Load Matrix for HVE, Inc.

From	Receiving	Machining	Pressing	Cleaning	Plating	Painting	Assembly	Shipping
Receiving		200	100					
Machining					350	60	20	
Pressing		150		200	100		250	
Cleaning					500		200	
Plating						50	400	
Painting							300	
Assembly								600

From this information, we may draw a flow chart showing the material movement between departments.

From Figure 9.18, we see that the general direction of material flow is from receiving to machining and pressing to cleaning, plating, and painting, and finally to assembly and shipping. Using this information, we propose an initial layout, shown in Figure 9.19. Remember that this layout is just a rough approximation of the relative shapes and sizes of departments. Detailed architectural designs must account for aisles, support pillars, office space, restrooms, and other service facilities. In order to compute interdepartmental distances, we shall assume that all transportation takes place between department centers (shown by a ● in Figure 9.19) and along the coordinate axes. That is, if departments A and B are

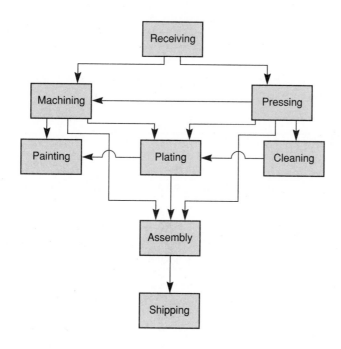

FIGURE 9.18

Material Flow for HVE, Inc.

FIGURE 9.19

Initial Layout
(each block
represents 10 feet
× 10 feet)

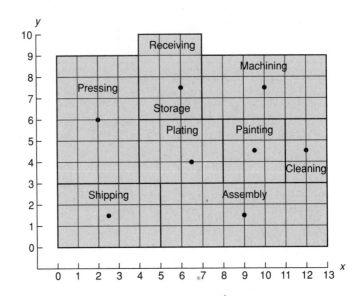

centered at coordinates (x_A, y_A) and (x_B, y_B) respectively, then the distance between them is

$$d_{AB} = |x_A - x_B| + |y_A - y_B|$$

This is most often the case when moving items with trucks along aisles. For this layout, the distance between receiving and storage, whose center is at the point $(5.5, 8)$, and pressing, whose center is at the point $(2, 6)$, is

$$|5.5 - 2| + |8 - 6| = 3.5 + 2 = 5.5$$

Note that the actual distance is 55 feet because of the scale used. The other interdepartmental distances are computed in a similar fashion. If these distances are multiplied by the volume requirements in Table 9.4, we obtain the volume-distance matrix shown in Table 9.5. For example, multiplying the load between receiving and pressing (100) by the distance between the departments (55) yields a volume-distance figure of 5500 as shown in Table 9.5. Since cost is assumed to be proportional to distance, the volume moved times the distance moved is a surrogate measure of cost.

TABLE 9.5 Volume-distance Matrix for Initial Layout

From	Receiving	Machining	Pressing	Cleaning	Plating	Painting	Assembly	Shipping
					To			
Receiving		10,000	5,500					
Machining					24,500	1,800	1,400	
Pressing		14,250		23,000	5,500		28,750	
Cleaning					30,000		12,000	
Plating				Significant		2,000	24,000	
Painting				potential for			12,000	
Assembly				improvement				39,000

Total volume-distance = 251,700

From this table, we see that the largest costs involve transportation between assembly and shipping, pressing and assembly, and cleaning and plating. The initial layout has other disadvantages. For instance, receiving and shipping are on opposite sides of the building. This can cause a problem if rail is used and might also cause problems in constructing access roads. A second proposal, which places these departments on the same side of the building, is shown in Figure 9.20. You should verify that the total volume-distance for this layout is 214,550, which represents a 15 percent reduction over the initial layout. This was gained by moving cleaning adjacent to plating and pressing closer to assembly. However, there is still a high cost involved in moving materials from painting to assembly and from assembly to shipping. In an effort to reduce this, a third alternative, shown in Figure 9.21, was proposed.

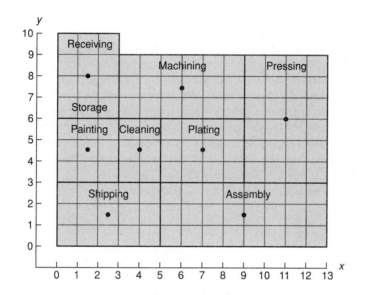

FIGURE 9.20
Second Proposed Layout

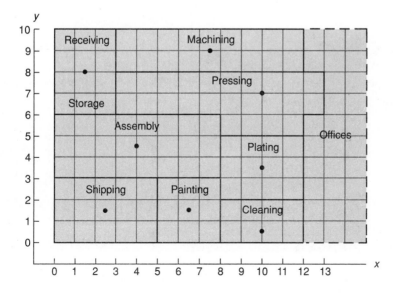

FIGURE 9.21
Third Proposed Layout

This layout has a total volume-distance requirement of 183,650. The basic shapes of the machining and pressing departments have been considerably altered. Shape requirements depend on machine sizes and processing requirements to a large extent and must be taken into account prior to a layout analysis. In addition, office space can be provided on the opposite end of the building from shipping and receiving; thus the building can maintain a rectangular shape.

Because of the large number of factors that must be considered, the trial-and-error approach is often the only way of designing process layouts. This process is often aided by scale models (see Photo 9.1). However, computerized methods can assist the layout planner in this task, which follows.

Computerized
Layout
Planning

From the HVE example in the previous section, it is clear that there are a large number of alternative configurations for a process layout. In fact, there are $n!$ possible arrangements of n departments, irrespective of shape. Thus for the Home Video Equipment example, there are $8! = 40,320$ possible arrangements. This makes finding the best possible layout an extremely difficult task. Several computer packages have been written expressly for facility layout.

These have the advantage of being able to search among a much larger number of potential layouts than could ever possibly be done manually. Despite the capabilities of the computer, no layout program will find optimal solutions for large, realistic problems. Similar to many practical solution procedures in management science, they are heuristic in nature; hopefully, these procedures will find a very good, but not necessarily optimal, solution.

One of the most widely used facility-layout programs is **CRAFT** (Computerized Relative Allocation of Facilities Technique). CRAFT attempts to minimize the

PHOTO 9.1

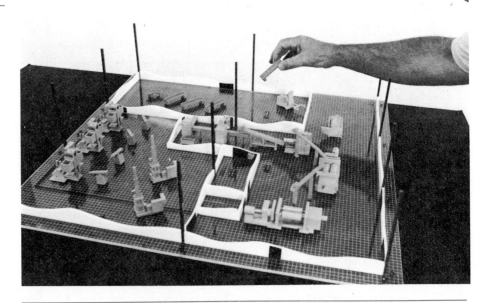

The layout of departments and equipment is often aided by templates or scale models.
Courtesy of "Visual" Industrial Products, Inc.

total material-handling cost in a manner similar to the approach used in the Home Video Equipment example. The user must generate an initial layout and provide data on the volume between departments and the material-handling costs. CRAFT uses the centroid of each department to compute distances and material-handling costs for a particular layout. In an effort to improve the current solution, CRAFT exchanges 2 (in later versions, 3) departments at one time and determines if the total cost has been reduced. If so, it then uses the new solution as a base for determining new potential improvements. A flow chart describing this procedure is given in Figure 9.22. An example of typical output from CRAFT is plotted with block letters, as shown in Figure 9.23. In this figure, each row or column represents 10 feet, and each letter corresponds to a different department. Thus department A is 20 by 60, department B is 30 by 60, and so on.

CRAFT has undergone many revisions and extensions over the years and has been used as a basis for other facility-layout procedures. For instance, CRAFT-M[4] considers the cost of moving an existing department, as well as potential process-improvement cost effects made possible by the move. The concept is to design a layout that will pay for the required costs of rearrangement over the lifetime of the layout as estimated by the user. **COFAD** (COmputerized FAcilities Design) attempts to integrate the material-handling selection decision along with the layout.[5] COFAD iteratively generates new layouts and minimum-cost material-handling systems until no additional savings in cost can be found.

CRAFT has also been modified specifically for office layout planning.[6] The typical data used includes a list of departments, divisions, sections, and subsections in an organization, employee interaction and authority structure, use of duplicating equipment, frequency of meetings and conferences, and visitor traffic. The program analyzes the work group structures of the office employees and generates layouts based on these interactions. It assists the office planner to assign

---

[4]Phillip E. Hicks and Troy E. Cowan, "CRAFT-M for Layout Rearrangement," *Industrial Engineering*, 8, no. 5 (May 1976): 30–35.

[5]James A. Tompkins, "Computerized Facilities Design," Ph.D. dissertation, Purdue University, 1972.

[6]F. Robert Jacobs, John W. Bradford, and Larry P. Ritzman, "Computerized Layout: An Integrated Approach to Special Planning and Communication Requirements," *Industrial Engineering*, 12, no. 7 (July 1980): 56–61.

FIGURE 9.22 CRAFT Logic

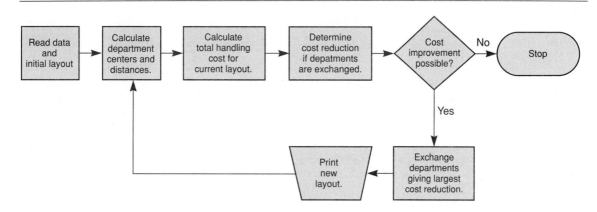

FIGURE 9.23
A Typical
CRAFT Layout

	1	2	3	4	5	6	7	8	9	10	11	12
1	A	A	A	A	A	A	B	B	B	B	B	B
2	A	A	A	A	A	A						B
3	C	C	C	C	C	C	B	B	B	B	B	B
4	C					C	E	E	E	D	D	D
5	C					C	E		E	D	D	D
6	C	C	C	C	C	C	E		E	F	F	F
7	H	H	H	H	H	H	E	E	E	F		F
8	H					H	H	H	H	F	F	F
9	H	H	H	H	H	H	H	H	H	G	G	G
10	G	G	G	G	G	G	G	G	G	G	G	G

departments to floors in a multistory building, and to determine relative arrangements and detailed placement of offices, desks, and equipment.

Other programs that have been extensively used in facilities layout are ALDEP (Automated Layout-DEsign Program) and CORELAP (COmputerized RElationship LAyout Planning). Rather than using material-handling costs as the primary solution, the user constructs a preference table, which specifies how important it is for two departments to be close to one another. These "closeness" ratings are as follows:

A   absolutely necessary
B   especially important
C   important
D   ordinary closeness OK
E   unimportant
F   undesirable

The programs attempt to optimize the total closeness rating of the layout.

Computer graphics is providing a major advance in layout planning. This allows interactive design of layouts in real time and can eliminate some of the disadvantages, such as irregularly shaped departments, that often result from noninteractive computer packages. Graphics programs also allow more details to be incorporated in the process-layout planning effort. Aisles, obstructions, and individual machine arrangement can be considered in interactive graphics programs.

9.5 DESIGN OF GROUP LAYOUTS[7]

The design of group layouts involves three basic steps: selection of part families, selection of machine groupings or cells, and detailed arrangement of the cells.

---

[7]Adapted from Hector H. Guerrero, "Group Technology: I. The Essential Concepts," *Production and Inventory Management*, 28, no. 1, (1987) 62–70 and "Group Technology: II. The Implementation Process," *Production and Inventory Management*, 28, no. 2, (1987) 1–9. Reprinted with permission, The American Production and Inventory Control Society, Inc.

The selection of part families involves grouping parts whose processing requirements are similar. Several sophisticated methods are used to group parts and only the basic concepts will be illustrated.

SELECTING PART FAMILIES AND MACHINE GROUPS IN CELLULAR MANUFACTURING

Let us consider the collection of parts shown in Figure 9.24. Table 9.6 gives the different processing operations that are required for each part. If we examine the parts-processing matrix in Table 9.6, we see that several parts have identical processing requirements. It would be logical to group these into one part family. You should verify that the following part families have identical processing requirements:

Part Family	Parts	Processing Requirements
1	a, f, l	Polish, grind, cut
2	c, e, o	Mill, grind, cut
3	b, d, g	Stamp, grind, cut
4	m, n	Drill, grind, cut
5	h, k	Drill, turn
6	j	Turn, mill
7	i	Drill, turn, mill

These seven part families could be used to define seven cells for a group layout. For example, cell 1 would consist of a polishing machine, grinder, and cutting machine. This may not be a good choice if the equipment is expensive or if sufficient equipment is not available (as would be the case if an existing plant is being redesigned). For instance, suppose that the plant in this example has only two machines of each type. It would be impossible to create the seven cells defined above without significant capital investment, since four cells require grinding, four cells require cutting, and so on. In most situations, it would be very difficult to define cells on the basis of identical processing requirements; the parts that

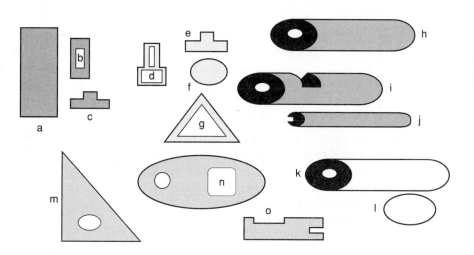

FIGURE 9.24

Group
Technology Parts
Example

TABLE 9.6

Processing
Requirements

Part	Drill	Turn	Stamp	Mill	Polish	Grind	Cut
a					X	X	X
b			X			X	X
c				X		X	X
d			X			X	X
e				X		X	X
f					X	X	X
g			X			X	X
h	X	X					
i	X	X		X			
j		X		X			
k	X	X					
l					X	X	X
m	X					X	X
n	X					X	X
o				X		X	X

make up a part family may share many of the same processing steps, but not necessarily all.

One way to resolve this dilemma is to further combine part families. For example note that if we group milling, cutting, polishing, and grinding into one cell, this cell can process part families 1 and 2. Similarly, part families 3 and 4 can be processed by a cell that contains drilling, stamping, grinding, and cutting. Finally, part families 5, 6, and 7 can be processed with a cell which consists of drilling, turning, and milling. This would yield the following part families and cells:

Part Family	Parts	Cell	Processes
1	a, f, l	1	Polish, grind
2	c, e, o		Cut, mill
3	b, d, g	2	Stamp, grind
4	m, n		Drill, cut
5	h, k	3	Drill, turn
6	j		Mill
7	i		

In this group layout, we have attempted to maximize the utilization of existing equipment. Other criteria which can be used in the design of group layouts are

1. minimizing the number of groups
2. consideration of volume of parts through the machine groups
3. work flow smoothing
4. consideration of future part design and design changes
5. feasibility of particular layout patterns
6. consideration of possible process technology changes
7. labor force skill availability.

The final step in the procedure—designing the detailed layout—is based on considerations similar to those involved in the design of a typical product layout. In general, the number of machines and the bottleneck process will determine the cell capacity, material-handling requirements should be minimized, and there should be an attempt to balance operator workloads as much as possible. The final design must be evaluated with respect to the planned production rates for the family of parts processed by each cell.

9.6 MATERIAL-HANDLING EQUIPMENT

Material handling occurs in all phases of production and ancillary activities. In the receiving department, materials must be unloaded from trucks and railroad cars, moved to inspection, and finally moved to storage. In the storage area or warehouse, materials are usually stored on racks, high-rise shelves, or stacked on pallets. Later, they must be transported to the production floor. During manufacturing itself, materials must be transported between departments, to and from individual workplaces, and to assembly. Finally, the finished products must be packaged and stored for shipping.

Material-handling costs may range from 20 to 80 percent of the total production cost of a product. Thus it is extremely important that handling is considered in the design of manufacturing systems. In this section, we discuss the basic material-handling equipment that is available and then briefly comment on its application.

Material-handling systems can be described by the following categories:

1. Industrial trucks
2. Conveyor systems
3. Cranes
4. Storage and retrieval systems
5. Tractor-trailer systems

Taxonomy of Material-handling Systems[8]

Industrial trucks such as forklifts are the most commonly used type of material-handling equipment. They are basically hand or powered vehicles used for moving mixed loads over various paths with suitable running surfaces and clearances (see Photo 9.2). Their primary function is maneuvering or transporting goods. Industrial trucks are generally used when material is moved on an infrequent basis, movement occurs between many different locations, loads are mixed in size and weight, and most of the operations involve physical handling.

Fixed-path *conveyor systems* are more adaptable to moving a high volume of items than industrial trucks. Conveyors are gravity or powered devices used for moving uniform loads continuously from point to point over fixed paths (see Photo 9.3). The primary functions of conveyors are transportation and storage. Conveyors are generally used when the route does not vary, continuous movement

[8]Don T. Phillips and Rodney J. Heisterberg, "Development of a Generalized Manufacturing Simulator (GEMS)," Report No. GEMS-5-77. Prepared for National Science Foundation, Department of Industrial Engineering, Texas A&M University, December 1, 1977.

PHOTO 9.2

Forklift trucks such as this Raymond Model 31 Reach Truck enable
materials to be stored on high racks, thus increasing space utilization. Lift
trucks are one of the principal means of material movement in factories and
warehouses. Courtesy of The Raymond Corporation.

is required, and automatic sorting, in-process inspection, or in-process storage
is required.

Overhead *cranes* are devices fixed by supporting and guiding rails that are
used to move or transfer material between points within an area. They are
commonly used in operations where the floor-space utilization or the product
characteristics render the use of forklift trucks or conveyors undesirable, where
travel distances and paths are reasonably restricted, and where the products are
bulky, large, or heavy, such as engines, turbines, machine tools, and many aerospace components.

Automated *storage and retrieval systems* are high-technology material handling or storage configurations usually involving computer control, unit loads,
and digital computer interface/control. They are becoming increasingly popular
because of small actual floor-space requirements, although the capital investment
is usually significant. These systems normally fall into two categories; total com-

PHOTO 9.3

Systems of conveyors provide an efficient means for moving in-process inventory between work stations and finished goods from assembly to packaging to shipping. Pictured here are roller conveyors (upper) and a belt conveyor (lower). Courtesy of HYTROL CONVEYOR CO., INC., Manufacturers of Complete Conveying Equipment and Gravity Rack Systems.

puter control with manual overrides and automated picking, or worker-on-board partial computer control.

Tractor-trailer systems are simply powered vehicles that pull a train of trailers, or load-carrying platforms. They offer the advantages of being able to move large volumes of bulky or heavy material over long distances and do not tie up lift trucks, which are primarily used for stacking, loading, and unloading (see Photo 9.4).

A variety of different material-handling equipment is used throughout a plant. In the receiving and shipping activities, forklift trucks, cranes, hoists, and portable conveyors are most often used for unloading transport vehicles and movement to temporary storage. In storage areas and warehouses, forklift trucks are often used to store and retrieve heavy loads. In more-sophisticated, high-volume op-

Application and Selection of Material-Handling Equipment

PHOTO 9.4

At the right of this picture is a Raymond Electote, an automatically controlled, driverless vehicle that is guided by wires embedded in the shop floor. Such systems are useful in transporting loads over medium to long distances and more cost-effective than using forklift trucks with skilled operators. Courtesy of The Raymond Corporation.

erations, automated storage and retrieval systems are used. Material movement in assembly-line systems is often accomplished with conveyors. Production lines and facility layout are more effective if material handling considerations are integrated into the design.

The College-Industry Council on Material Handling Education has developed twenty principles to guide the selection and application of material handling equipment. These are listed in Table 9.7. This list can be of valuable assistance to operations managers and engineers in facility design and layout. Economic justification of material-handling equipment can be carried out in the same manner as that of machines and other equipment that we have previously discussed in Chapter 8.

9.7 DESIGN FOR STORAGE AND WAREHOUSING

Storage refers to the physical aspect of inventory control. Provisions must be made for the storage of raw materials and supplies, tools and equipment, and semifinished and finished goods. Small firms may provide storage space within their own production facilities or in an adjacent warehouse. Larger corporations,

TABLE 9.7

Principles of
Material
Handling

1. *Planning principle.* Plan all material handling and storage activities to obtain maximum overall operating efficiency.
2. *Systems principle.* Integrate as many handling activities as practical into a coordinated system of operations covering vendor, receiving, storage, production, inspection, packaging, warehousing, shipping, transportation, and customer.
3. *Material-flow principle.* Provide an operation sequence and equipment layout optimizing material flow.
4. *Simplification principle.* Simplify handling by reducing, eliminating, or combining unnecessary movements and/or equipment.
5. *Gravity principle.* Utilize gravity to move material wherever practical.
6. *Space-utilization principle.* Make optimum utilization of building cube.
7. *Unit-size principle.* Increase the quantity, size, or weight of unit loads or flow rate.
8. *Mechanization principle.* Mechanize handling operations.
9. *Automation principle.* Provide automation to include production, handling, and storage functions.
10. *Equipment-selection principle.* In selecting handling equipment, consider all aspects of the material handled, the movement, and the method to be used.
11. *Standardization principle.* Standardize handling methods, as well as types and sizes of handling equipment.
12. *Adaptability principle.* Use methods and equipment that can best perform a variety of tasks and applications where special purpose equipment is not justified.
13. *Dead-weight principle.* Reduce ratio of dead weight of mobile handling equipment to load carried.
14. *Utilization principle.* Plan for optimum utilization of handling equipment and labor.
15. *Maintenance principle.* Plan for preventive maintenance and scheduled repairs of all handling equipment.
16. *Obsolescence principle.* Replace obsolete handling methods and equipment when more efficient methods or equipment will improve operations.
17. *Control principle.* Use material handling activities to improve control of production, inventory, and order handling.
18. *Capacity principle.* Use handling equipment to help achieve desired production capacity.
19. *Performance principle.* Determine effectiveness of handling performance in terms of expense per unit handled.
20. *Safety principle.* Provide suitable methods and equipment for safe handling.

William E. Fillmore, "Material Handling Analysis Is Approached from Traditional Points of View." Reprinted with permission from *Industrial Engineering* magazine, April 1981. Copyright Institute of Industrial Engineers, 25 Technology Park/Atlanta, Norcross, GA 30092.

particularly multiplant companies and pure distribution systems such as grocery chains or retail department stores, use warehouses that may be a distance away from actual production or customer locations. This rationale and the location decision were discussed in Chapter 7. In this section, we concentrate on the internal aspects of storage and warehousing.

The principal functions of warehousing include

1. storing inbound shipments
2. transferring items to actual storage
3. order picking and removal from storage
4. packaging and loading for outbound shipping.

In each of these functions, it is clear that material handling plays an important role in the efficient use of warehouse capacity. The same principles of material handling that were presented in the previous section apply to warehouse operations.

Warehouse Design and Arrangement

The design and layout of a warehouse should focus on achieving high productivity in day-to-day activities of material management. These productivity objectives are

1. maximum utilization of space
2. efficient stock location and identification
3. conservation of time, labor, and equipment
4. rapid and easy transfer to and from storage.

Meeting these goals depends on a variety of factors, such as the size and shape of the physical facility, type of material-handling equipment available, placement and arrangement of stock, and the nature and usage of the items. Unless high-rise automated storage and retrieval systems are planned, one-story buildings provide the most usable space per dollar invested. In addition, material-handling requirements are reduced, since elevators and other vertical-movement equipment are far more expensive than horizontal-movement equipment.

Cubic footage should be utilized to its fullest extent (Figure 9.25). **Pallets** or portable platforms are used to take advantage of vertical stacking capability. They can be moved easily by forklift trucks and other handling equipment. Pallets are useful for large quantities or bulk items that are used or ordered in pallet loads. Other storage methods must be used for small items or those that are used infrequently. Typically, racks, shelves, and bins are used for this purpose and items are usually picked by hand.

The arrangement of the warehouse is an important factor in determining productivity. Figure 9.26 illustrates two types of warehouse arrangements in which items move from receiving to shipping in a direct pattern. Figure 9.26(b) has some advantages because travel distances are smaller if items are stored by popularity; it has greater dock flexibility; and shipping and receiving personnel can be centralized.

FIGURE 9.25

Use of Cubic Space

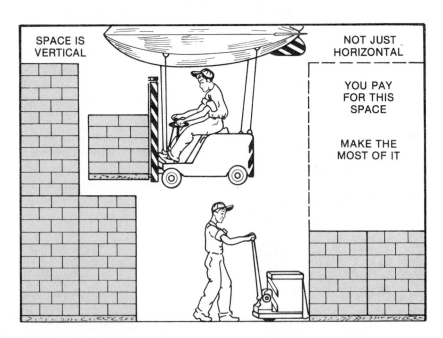

Source: *Warehouse Operations*, General Services Administration, Federal Supply Service, U.S. Government Printing Office, 1969.

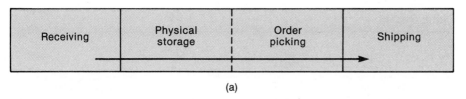

(a)

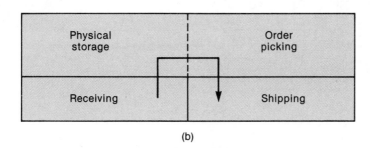

(b)

FIGURE 9.26

Sample
Warehouse
Arrangements

Order picking may or may not be physically separate from actual storage. For example, large furniture warehouses fill individual orders directly from primary storage. However, for a company like Avon, in which orders consist of many small and distinct items, such a practice would be unduly time-consuming. Instead, unit loads of items are moved to order-picking stations, where individual pieces may easily be chosen from bins or racks to fill individual orders. Catalog distribution centers for firms such as Montgomery Ward use this method to reduce order-filling time. You may notice a resemblance between such an arrangement and assembly layouts. Filling orders is indeed a method of assembly, except that each order has a unique makeup. Consequently, similar layout techniques can be used in warehouse design.

A WAREHOUSE ORDER-PICKING SYSTEM

EXAMPLE

We illustrate a typical order-picking system by discussing one used by a major toy manufacturer. At the company's distribution center, large orders are filled by bulk shipment, which are loaded directly onto trucks. Orders consisting of many different products are picked from bins, sent by conveyor to a diverting station (where individual products are sorted by order), and then loaded onto trucks. Figure 9.27 illustrates the basic layout. The order pickers receive orders and labels each morning. Labels are placed on the cartons to indicate to which truck the items are to be diverted. Orders are also sequenced by bin number, so that travel time is minimized. The system has approximately 130 items in 80 bins on each side of the pick line. These are restocked periodically from the main warehouse.

Note that the flow in this arrangement is unidirectional. The receiving docks are at the bottom of the illustration, and products flow upward toward the loading docks. Conveyors are the principal material-handling equipment used. Also, you can observe that gravity is used whenever possible in order to utilize the material-handling equipment effectively.

The arrangement of items in storage depends on a variety of factors. The type of material often dictates special storage considerations. Items subject to dete-

Figure 9.27 Order-picking System

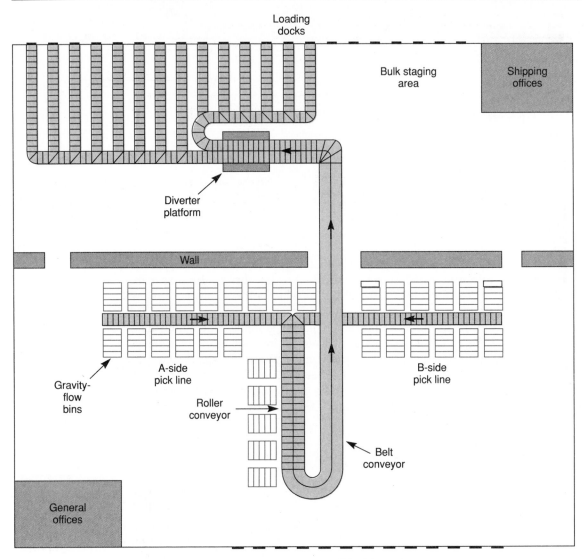

rioration, such as foodstuffs, medical supplies, or paints, must be protected from dampness, insects, or extreme temperatures. These types of items would also require a first-in-first-out (FIFO) retrieval policy. This precludes arrangements that stack items deep along walls or in large containers, where the most easily removed items are those that were most recently stored, a last-in-first-out (LIFO) policy.

Valuable items need special storage locations with security provisions. Hazardous materials require special attention and location. The size, weight, and shape of items affect storage and handling. For example, fragile items cannot be stacked very high, and heavy or bulky items are best stored near the shipping

The design of a warehouse for high productivity often includes a complex system of storage racks, conveyors, and automated storage/retrieval equipment. Photo courtesy of Hytrol Conveyor Co., Inc., Manufacturers of Complete Conveying Equipment & Gravity Rack Systems.

area to reduce handling needs. Product turnover also affects storage and handling. Fast-moving items need to be handled quickly, while slow movers can be stored in less desirable locations or locations that require slower handling (see Photo 9.5).

P/OM IN PRACTICE

In this section we discuss how process design and facility layout concepts were applied by the Southern Technical Institute Library in designing a new layout for the library's workroom. The new layout resulted in a more orderly flow at work and a 367 percent increase in available shelf space.

DESIGN OF A UNIVERSITY LIBRARY WORKROOM[9]

The workroom in the Southern Technical Institute Library processed about 8000 new books each year. All library books had to pass through the workroom in order to be prepared for shelving in

[9]Adapted from Lawrence S. Aft, "Work Methods in the Library." Reprinted with permission from *Industrial Engineering* magazine, November 1973. Copyright Institute of Industrial Engineers, 25 Technology Park/Atlanta, Norcross, GA 30092.

the library's stacks. When the library was built, about 3000 books were processed each year. Since no major additions or remodeling changes were possible, this increase necessitated an evaluation of the existing layout.

A flow-process chart for the production process of cataloging new books is given in Figure 9.28. Figures 9.29 and 9.30 illustrate the current layout and work flow in the workroom. As you can see from the flow diagram, there is unnecessary move-

---

FIGURE 9.28 Flow Process Chart for Library Workroom

Part name _____

Process desc. ___Catalog new book___

Charted by ___P.T.___

Date ___6/21/90___

Summary		
		No.
Operations		6
Transportations		6
Inspections		1
Delays		1
Storages		1
Present distance traveled		153'
Proposed distance traveled		90'

Description		Present/proposed
1. Receive books from outside	⬤ ▷ ☐ D ▽	
2. Move to check-in area	○ ▷ ☐ D ▽	33/12 feet
3. Check if duplication of existing book	⬤ ▷ ☐ D ▽	
4. Move to catalog research area	○ ▷ ☐ D ▽	28/8 feet
5. Catalog—Library of Congress Classification	⬤ ▷ ☐ D ▽	
5a. If no catalog number, move to storage area	○ ▷ ☐ D ▽	26/26 feet
5b. Store until number available	○ ▷ ☐ D ▽	
5c. Move to catalog research area	○ ▷ ☐ D ▽	20/26 feet
5d. Catalog	⬤ ▷ ☐ D ▽	
6. Move to verification area	○ ▷ ☐ D ▽	28/8 feet
7. Verify	○ ▷ ◼ D ▽	
8. Move to pocket and call number application area	○ ▷ ☐ D ▽	18/10 feet
9. Install pocket and date due slip	⬤ ▷ ☐ D ▽	
10. Apply call number	⬤ ▷ ☐ D ▽	
11. Store until shelving	○ ▷ ☐ D ▼	

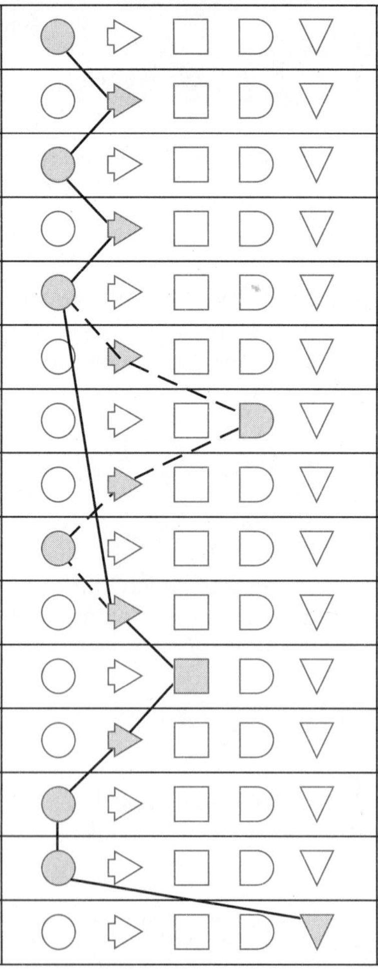

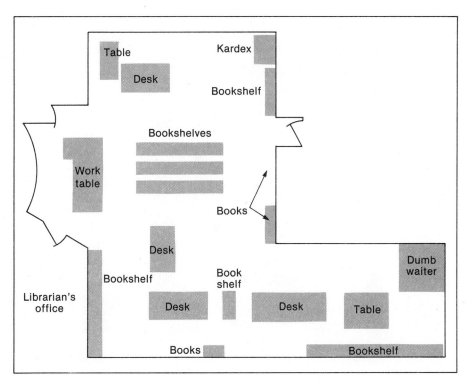

FIGURE 9.29
Original Layout of Library Workroom

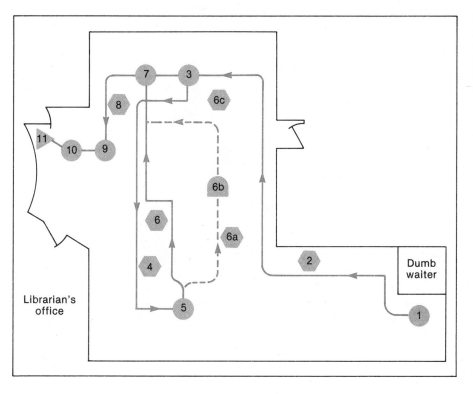

FIGURE 9.30
Original Flow Diagram of Library Workroom

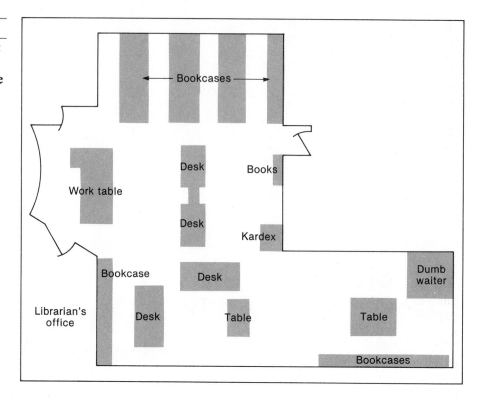

FIGURE 9.31
Proposed Layout of Library Workroom. Note the new location of the bookcases

Bookcases

Desk

Books

Work table

Desk

Kardex

Bookcase

Desk

Dumb waiter

Librarian's office

Desk

Table

Table

Bookcases

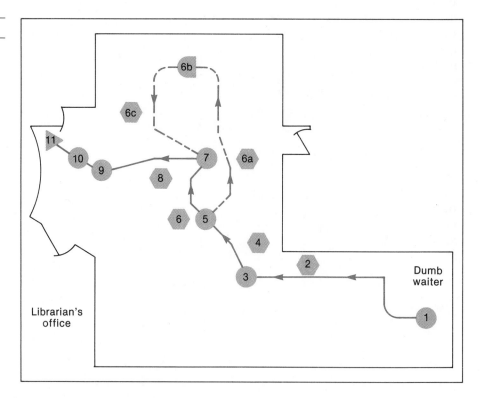

FIGURE 9.32
Flow Diagram for the Proposed Layout of the Library Workroom

6b

6c

11

10

9

7

6a

8

6

5

4

2

3

Dumb waiter

1

Librarian's office

ment back and forth across the workroom. In addition, the main storage shelves constitute a major barrier to the effective flow of materials. From these observations, a new layout was proposed, which results in more orderly flow, shorter distance traveled, and more book storage space. By moving the major storage shelves out of the center of the room and off to one side, not only can additional racks be added, but the density of books in a rack can be increased by decreasing the shelf height from 24 to 12 inches. This corresponds to a 367 percent increase in available shelf space. This is illustrated in Figures 9.31 and 9.32.

In a simple problem as this, layouts can be designed by visual inspection. However, in more-complex industrial situations, handling cost is a major factor. Thus some quantitative analysis would appear to be helpful in process-layout design.

QUESTIONS

1. What was the primary reason the library workroom had to be redesigned?
2. What are some of the problems with the existing layout?
3. What is the major change in the proposed layout? What are the benefits associated with this change?

In this chapter we discussed the essential problems that operations managers face in the design and layout of production processes. Physical facilities can have a significant impact on productivity, efficiency, and cost, and hence, on manufacturing strategy. The major types of layout patterns are process layout, product layout, group layout, and fixed-position layout.

The design and layout of the physical facility depends on a variety of factors, such as the volume and variety of products that are made and the degree of automation and specialization of equipment. Material-handling considerations should be integrated with the layout decision. Designing good layouts is most often a trial-and-error procedure with the goal of obtaining maximum productivity. Various quantitative tools and computerized methods are available to assist production managers in this task. For instance, assembly-line balancing techniques, waiting-line theory, and simulation are useful in designing production lines. Flow-process charts, multiple-activity charts, load-matrix analysis, and computerized layout programs are routinely used for process-layout analysis and design.

SUMMARY

KEY TERMS

Route sheet
Flow-process chart
Work center
Product layout
Process layout
Group technology
Group layout
Fixed-position layout

Production line
Flow-blocking delay
Lack-of-work delay
Cycle time
Load matrix
CRAFT
COFAD
Pallet

REVIEW/ DISCUSSION QUESTIONS

1. Under what conditions are process design and facility layout studies conducted?
2. What are the objectives of process design and facility layout?
3. What advantages can be gained from proper attention to process design and facility layout?

4. What information is contained in *process-flow diagrams, route sheets,* and *flow-process charts?*

5. What is a *work center?*

6. Describe the major types of layout patterns used in production. What are the advantages and disadvantages of each?

7. Discuss the important characteristics of service organizations that impact facility layout activities.

8. What is a *production line?*

9. Contrast the differences between conveyor-paced and nonconveyor-paced production lines.

10. Explain the differences between *flow-blocking delay* and *lack-of-work delay.*

11. What are buffers and why are they necessary?

12. Discuss the important issues involved in assembly-line balancing.

13. Describe the approach used in designing process layouts. Will this guarantee an "optimal" solution? Why or why not?

14. How are computers used in layout planning? Explain how CRAFT develops facility layouts.

15. What criteria are used in designing group layouts? Discuss the general procedure for forming part families and cells.

16. List the major categories of material-handling systems. What capabilities do equipment in each category have?

17. Discuss the principles of material handling. How can these be used in process design and facility layout?

18. What are the primary objectives in designing warehouses?

PROBLEMS

1. Interview a branch manager of a bank in order to find out what happens to a check written on an account in the bank. Based on your interview, construct a route sheet and flow-process chart for the process.

2. A process-flow diagram shows a process with two workstations. Data about the workstation capacities are as follows:

	Workstation	
	1	2
Hours per shift	8	7.5
Number of machines	3	2
Efficiency	88%	94%
Processing time per part	1.5 min	1.0 min

a. What is the capacity per shift for each workstation?
b. What is the capacity per shift for the production system?

3. Consider a production process with two workstations. Workstation 1 contains two machines, operates for 40 hours per week, has a machine efficiency of .85, and has a machine processing time of .40 minutes per part. Your job is to design the second workstation such that the weekly capacity matches the weekly capacity of the first workstation. Each machine used at the second workstation has an efficiency of .90 and requires a time of .75 minutes per part. How many machines and how many hours per week would workstation 2 need to be operated in order to match the capacity of workstation 1? Assume 40 hours per week is the maximum time available for a machine.

4. For the lawnmower carburetor example in Chapter 8, suppose the times for the individual operations are as given:

Operation	Time (Sec.)
SA-1	5
SA-2	5
A-1	30
I-1	10
SA-3	10
A-2	10
A-3	15
I-1	10
SA-4	15
A-4	20
I-3	10

Assume that inspections cannot be performed by production personnel, but only by persons from quality control. Thus inspections separate the assembly operations into three groups. Design production lines (similar to that of Figure 9.11) in order to achieve output rates of 120 per hour and 360 per hour. Will these lines experience any lack of work or flow-blocking delays?

5. A production process consists of four machines in sequence. The production rates of the four machines are 80, 155, 305, and 147 pieces per hour respectively. A normal working day consists of two eight-hour shifts. The desired daily output is 4000 pieces.
   a. Determine the capacity of each machine.
   b. Balance the line, by suitably determining the number of each machine required.
   c. What is the utilization of each machine at the desired production level?

6. Determine appropriate part families and machine groupings for the following part-processing matrix:

	Process				
Part	Turn	Mill 1	Mill 2	Drill	Grind
1	x	x		x	x
2	x	x		x	x
3		x	x	x	x
4	x		x	x	x
5	x	x			
6		x		x	x
7	x	x		x	
8	x		x	x	
9	x	x			x
10			x	x	
11	x	x		x	
12	x		x	x	x
13		x	x	x	x
14	x	x		x	
15	x		x		x
16		x		x	
17	x		x	x	
18	x		x	x	x
19	x		x		
20	x	x		x	x

7. An assembly operation consists of 10 tasks that must be completed in order from task 1 to task 10. The respective task completion times in minutes are as follows: .3, .5, .3, .2, .2, .1, .4, .3, .8, and .2. Assume a 40-hour week, a 92 percent efficiency, and a desired production rate of 1840 units per week.
   a. What is the desired cycle time for the assembly line?
   b. How many workstations will be required and what tasks are to be performed at each station?
   c. What is the line efficiency for this assembly line?

8. Repeat Problem 7 if the production rate is increased to 2760 units per week.

9. Solve the accompanying assembly-line balancing problem for cycle times of 10 and 7.

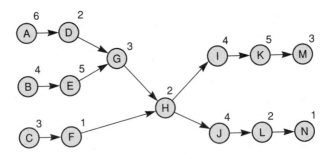

10. We suggested assigning operations to stations on an assembly line by choosing the largest time first among all assignable operations. Solve both the carburetor assembly problem in Section 9.3 and Problem 9 using the rule

choose the assignable operation with the shortest time. How do these rules compare? Can you think of any other rules or procedures to achieve a better balance on these problems?

11. Balance of the following assembly line for: (1) a shift output of 60 pieces; (2) a shift output of 40 pieces. Assume an 8-hour shift and use the rule *"choose the assingable operation with the longest time."* Compute the line efficiency for each case.

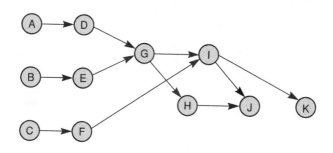

Activity	Precedence	Time (min.)
A	—	5
B	—	3
C	—	2
D	A	3
E	B	4
F	C	6
G	D,E	7
H	F,G	5
I	F,G	6
J	H	4
K	I	3

12. Balance the assembly line in problem 11 using the criterion "choose the assignable operation with the shortest time" and compare the performance of this criterion with the *longest time* rule.

13. From the following list of activities and precedence relations:

Activity	Predecessors	Time Per Piece (min.)
A	—	7
B	—	2
C	A	6
D	A	4
E	B	3
F	B	2
G	D,E	1
H	C	2
I	F	3
J	H,G,I	9

a. Draw the precedence diagram.

b. Balance the assembly line for a shift output of 52 pieces.

c. Determine maximum and minimum cycle times.

14. Raffles Potato Chips manufacturing process consists of (1) chip making, (2) pouching, (3) cartoning, (4) check weighing, and (5) case packing. The rates of each process are as given

Process	Rate (Per min.)	
Chip maker	12000 chips	
Poucher	1000 pouches	(12 chips per pouch)
Cartoner	220 cartons	(6 pouches per carton)
Check weigher	220 cartons	
Case packer	20 cases	(24 cartons per case)

The production line is to be operated on a one-shift basis (8 hours) with 80 minutes lost time per shift for lunch, breaks, start-up, and shutdown. Draw a schematic layout of this system. If 6000 cases per day are to be produced, analyze the equipment utilization. Where do bottlenecks occur?

15. In Problem 14, determine if additional machines can increase production capacity and better balance the lines.

16. Given the following layout of six different departments and the frequency of movements among them along with the distance between each department, determine if less material handling is achieved by switching departments D and F. Assume diagonal distances to be 2 units and horizontal/vertical distances between adjacent departments to be 1.

	Frequency of Movements					
	To					
From	A	B	C	D	E	F
A	0	10	–	5	5	10
B	5	0	–	5	10	5
C	2	10	0	5	5	1
D	5	10	2	0	5	5
E	10	5	0	0	0	5
F	0	10	5	0	5	0

Present layout

A	B
C	D
E	F

Proposed layout

A	B
C	F
E	D

17. Mantel's Metal Products produces a diversified line of metal goods. An analysis of last year's production orders shows that seven groups of products account for over 95 percent of the total business volume. The production routing for these groups are shown below.

		Department Operation Sequence			
Group	Percent Volume by Weight	1	2	3	4
1	20	A	D	E	
2	25	B	C	D	E
3	10	A	D	E	
4	15	C	B	E	
5	10	A	C		
6	8	A	B	D	E
7	8	C	B		

Space requirements for each department are

Receiving	1500 square feet
A	2500 square feet
B	1500 square feet
C	2000 square feet
D	1000 square feet
E	500 square feet
Shipping	1500 square feet

a. Prepare a (percent) volume travel chart using the percentages in the table above. (How does this differ from the type discussed in the text?)
b. By trial and error on graph paper, design a good layout.

18. Using the closeness ratings A–F described in the discussion of ALDEP and CORELAP in Section 9.4, design a layout for the main floor of a new business building from the following information and that given in Figure 9.33.

Function	Space Requirement (Sq Ft)
Main entry	500
Dean's office	300
Student affairs	500
Graduate lounge	400
Auditorium	3000
Large classrooms (5)	900 each
Computer center	2000
Laboratories (2)	600 each
Undergraduate lounge	600
Reading/study rooms (10)	150 each
Vending area	200

19. A factory uses three types of forklift trucks operating at a cost of $30, $20, and $10 per hour respectively. The three types of equipment are housed in

separate stations and the frequency of movement to each department is given below.

Department	Type		
	I	II	III
Turning	10	15	10
Milling	25	15	15
Press shop	30	10	25
Assembly	5	15	30

The distance from each station to the four departments are given below.

From Station	To Department			
	A	B	C	D
1	10	10	5	5
2	5	10	5	10
3	5	5	10	10

The present layout is as follows:

Station 3

A	Assembly	Milling	B
Station 2			
	Press	Turning	
C			D

Station 1

a. What is the present material-handling cost?

b. Is there any advantage in switching assembly and milling departments?

20. Given the following spatial requirements for six departments and also the preference table, design a layout.

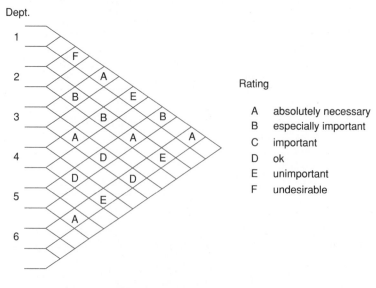

Rating

A absolutely necessary
B especially important
C important
D ok
E unimportant
F undesirable

Department	1	2	3	4	5	6
Area (sq ft)	1500	2000	2000	1000	1500	10000

21. Mercy Hospital is renovating an old wing to house four departments: out-patient services, x-ray lab, physical therapy, and orthopedics. The following matrix gives the distances in feet between each of the existing rooms.

Location	1	2	3	4
1	—	40	60	60
2		—	20	30
3			—	15
4				—

That is, rooms 1 and 2 are 40 feet apart. The average number of trips per day between each location is given below.

Location	Out-patient service	X-ray lab	Physical therapy	Orthopedics
Out-patient service	—	25	42	34
X-ray lab		—	15	55
Physical therapy			—	10
Orthopedics				—

The hospital wishes to locate each department in one of the existing four rooms so as to minimize the sum of the trips × distance. What is the best facility design? How many possible ways of locating the departments are there?

22. What types of material-handling equipment would most likely be selected for the following applications?
    a. Moving packages of disposable diapers to a case packing station.
    b. Transporting automotive transmissions between assembly stations.
    c. Moving furniture from a warehouse to a railroad car.
    d. Transporting a completed heavy machine tool to a test facility in a different, nearby building.
    e. Moving bottles of beer from a filling machine to a capper.

23. A railcar is to be unloaded at a dock, as in the Figure below.

Usable warehouse space

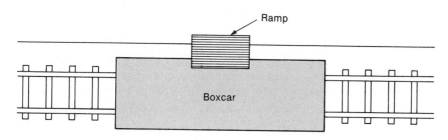

Ramp

Boxcar

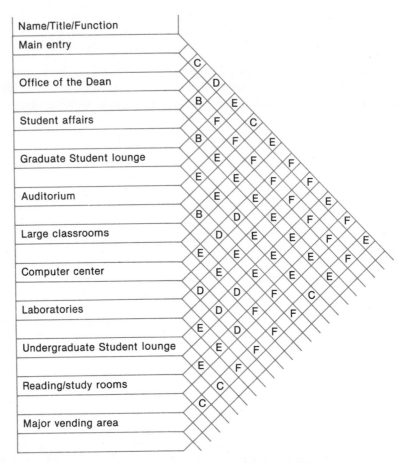

FIGURE 9.33
Preference Table

Develop designs for the following situations. Be sure to state the type of material-handling equipment that should be used, and sketch a design of the receiving and storage areas.

a. Bulk shipments of industrial chemicals on palletized loads.

b. A carload containing consolidated orders of a large variety of products, all of which can easily be moved by hand.

24. A large book publisher located in New York City sells college textbooks across the country. Orders from individual bookstores arrive about 2 months prior to the start of a quarter or semester. The orders for an individual book may be for as few as 5 copies or as many as several hundred. Books are packaged in cases containing 15 to 40 copies, depending on size, and are stored on pallets in a high-rise shelf system and retrieved by high-rise forklifts. Discuss some of the order-processing problems faced by this company, and design a system (with a layout sketch) for filling the orders.

CASE PROBLEM When a patient enters the emergency room at the Children's Hospital Emergency Room in Cincinnati, the parent or guardian accompanying the patient is greeted by a triage nurse or interviewer if a triage nurse is unavailable. An ER registration form is taken from a stack and the triage portion of the form is completed. The nurse then evaluates the medical complaint, takes vital signs, and triages based upon preliminary evaluation. When this is completed, the patient's registration form is placed in the "to be registered" tray according to medical need. The interviewer takes the top form on the tray, calls the parent or guardian, and escorts him or her to an interview room for completion of the data portion of the form. This data is then entered into a computer terminal. The registration form is a six-part document made up of the following:

Copy 1: Medical record
Copies 2 & 3: Patient billing
Copy 4: Primary source of care
Copy 5: Hemophilia and outpatient surgery
Copy 6: Take-home instructions and data control information

For each patient who arrives at the ER, a blue plate is embossed with patient information immediately after the interviewer fills out the registration form and enters the information into the computer. Upon completion of the interview, the parent or guardian is directed to return to the waiting area or the triage area. The interviewer completes the computer work, makes an addressograph plate, imprints all documents, and places the completed paperwork in the "to be seen" tray. At the conclusion of registration, the interviewer will instruct the parent or guardian to stop at the front desk upon discharge of the patient. They will receive a take-home instruction sheet and, if continuing care is required, make an appointment.

Analyze this system using route sheets and/or flow-process charts. Discuss how this information can assist a hospital administrator.

SUPPLEMENT TO CHAPTER 9
WAITING-LINE
MODELS

I n this supplement, we describe how waiting-line models can provide information about the characteristics of a process. In particular, we are interested in how well a new process will serve its intended use. Results from a waiting-line analysis can provide helpful process design and layout information that will insure proper operation when the new process is implemented.

Everyone has experienced situations such as waiting in a line at a supermarket checkout counter, waiting in a line at a teller window of a bank, or waiting in a line of cars at a traffic light. In these and many other situations, *waiting* time is undesirable for all parties concerned. For instance, the customer in a supermarket checkout line can become very annoyed by excessive waiting times. If the manager of the supermarket is concerned about the existence of long waiting lines, one obvious solution would be to add more checkout counters. The added service capability should provide better service and correspondingly shorter customer waiting lines. However, additional supermarket checkout counters will lead to greater costs in terms of additional personnel, equipment, and space requirements. The supermarket waiting-line problem requires the manager to balance the benefits of better service with the added costs involved.

Quantitative models have been developed to help managers understand and make better decisions concerning the operation of waiting lines. *Queueing theory* is the term used to refer to the study of waiting lines. The waiting line is referred to as the *queue*. Thus, in the supermarket example, customers in the waiting line could have been referred to as customers in the queue.

For a given waiting-line system, waiting-line models may be used to identify *operating characteristics*, such as the

1. percentage of time or probability that the service facilities are idle
2. probability of a specific number of units (customers) in the system[1]
3. average number of units in the waiting line
4. average number of units in the system
5. average time a unit spends in the waiting line
6. average time a unit spends in the system (waiting time plus service time)

---

[1] The system includes the waiting line and the service facility.

7. probability that an arriving unit has to wait for service.

Managers who are provided with the above information are better equipped to make decisions that balance desirable service levels with service costs. Let us demonstrate the use of waiting-line models to assist in the design of the airport passenger-security screening process at a new international airport.

WAITING-LINE ANALYSIS OF AIRPORT SECURITY SCREENING

Process design and facility-layout activities are currently being conducted for Airport International in Washington, D.C. One particular area of concern is the design and layout of the airport passenger-security screening system. Security screening consists of two distinct operations: inspecting the passengers' carry-on bags and inspecting the passengers themselves. Both of these operations employ electronic equipment and X-ray devices to speed the inspection process. A waiting-line analysis of the screening system helps determine whether or not the screening systems located at the entrance to each concourse provide adequate service to the airport passengers. Excessive delays and long waiting times at the screening locations would be a serious problem once the airport is put into operation.

In order to develop a waiting-line model for the security screening system, we need to identify some important characteristics of the system: (1) the arrival distribution of the passengers; (2) the service time distribution for the screening operation; and (3) the waiting line, or queue, discipline for the passengers.

Arrival Distribution

Defining the arrival distribution for a waiting line involves determining how many units arrive for service in a given period of time. For example, in the airport passenger-screening process, we are interested in determining the number of passengers arriving at the screening facility during each 1-minute period. Since the number of passengers arriving each minute is not a constant, we need to define a probability distribution that describes the passenger arrivals.

For many waiting lines, the arrivals occurring in a given period of time appear to have a *random pattern*—that is, while we may have a good estimate of the total number of arrivals expected, each arrival is independent of other arrivals and we cannot predict when the arrival will occur. In such cases, operations researchers have found that the Poisson probability distribution provides a good description of the arrival pattern.

The **Poisson probability distribution** is defined as follows:

$$P(x) = \frac{\lambda^x e^{-\lambda}}{x!} \quad \text{for } x = 0, 1, 2, \ldots \quad (9S.1)$$

where, in waiting-line applications,

x = number of arrivals in a specific period of time

λ = average, or expected, number of arrivals for the specific period of time

$e \approx 2.71828$

For the passenger-screening process, the wide variety of flight schedules and the variation in passenger arrivals for the various flights causes the number of passengers requiring screening to vary substantially. For example, data collected from the actual operation of similar screening facilities show that in some instances, 20 to 25 passengers may arrive during a 1-minute period. However, at other times, passenger arrivals may drop to as low as 3 or fewer passengers during a 1-minute period. Since passenger arrivals cannot be controlled and appear to occur in an unpredictable fashion, a random arrival pattern appears to exist. Thus the Poisson probability distribution should provide a good description of the passenger-arrival pattern. Airport planners have projected passenger volume through 1999 and estimate passengers will arrive at an average rate of 9 passengers per minute during the peak activity periods. Using this average, or **mean arrival rate** (λ = 9), we can use the Poisson distribution to compute the probability of x passenger arrivals in a 1-minute period.[2]

$$P(x) = \frac{9^x e^{-9}}{x!} \quad (9S.2)$$

Sample calculations for x = 0, 5, and 10 passenger arrivals during a 1-minute period are as follows:[3]

---

[2] Appendix A provides a table for computing $e^{-\lambda}$.

[3] In computing the values of factorials, ($x!$), $x! = x(x - 1)(x - 2) \ldots (2)(1)$. For example, 5! = 5(4)(3)(2)(1) = 120. Note that 0! is defined to be 1.

$$P(0) = \frac{9^0 e^{-9}}{0!} = .0001$$

$$P(5) = \frac{9^5 e^{-9}}{5!} = .0607$$

$$P(10) = \frac{9^{10} e^{-10}}{10!} = .1186$$

Using the Poisson probability distribution, we expect it to be very rare to have a 1-minute period in which no passengers ($x = 0$) arrive for screening since $P(0) = .0001$. Five passenger arrivals occur with a probability $P(5) = .0607$ and ten passenger arrivals occur with a probability of $P(10) = .1186$. The probabilities for other numbers of passenger arrivals can also be computed. Figure 9S.1 shows the arrival distribution for passengers based on the Poisson distribution.

In the analysis that follows, we use the Poisson distribution to describe the passenger arrivals at the screening facility. You can see that the assumption of a Poisson arrival distribution helps simplify our analysis of the waiting-line problem. In practice you would want to record the actual number of arrivals per time period for several days or weeks and compare the frequency distribution of the observed number of arrivals to the Poisson distribution to see if the Poisson distribution is a good approximation of the arrival distribution for the waiting line.

Service-Time Distribution

A service time probability distribution is needed to describe how long it takes to process a passenger through the screening operation. This length of time is referred to as the *service time* for the passenger. While many passengers will complete the screening process in a relatively short period of time, other passengers will take a long time because of having more carry-on luggage, having the agent request a check of carry-on luggage, having to repeat the walk-through screening because of metal detection such as keys, and so on. Thus we anticipate the service times to vary from passenger to passenger. In the development of waiting-line models, operations researchers have found that the exponential probability distribution often can be used to describe the service time distribution. The **exponential probability distribution** is defined by the expression

$$f(x) = \mu e^{-\mu x} \qquad \text{for } x \geq 0 \qquad (9S.3)$$

In waiting-line applications,

x = service time

μ = average or expected number of units that the service facility can handle in a specific period of time

$e \approx 2.71828$.

If we use an exponential service time distribution, *the probability of a service being completed within a specific period of time, t, is given by*

$$P(\text{service time} \leq t) = 1 - e^{-\mu t} \qquad (9S.4)$$

By collecting data on service times for similar screening systems in operation at other airports, we find that the system can handle an average of 10 passengers per minute. Using a **mean service rate** of $\mu = 10$ in Equation (9S.4), the probability of a screening service being completed within t minutes is

$$P(\text{service time} \leq t) = 1 - e^{-10t}$$

FIGURE 9S.1 Poisson Distribution of Passenger Arrivals

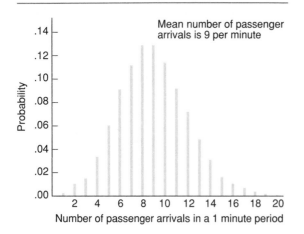

FIGURE 9S.2 Probability That a Passenger Will Be Serviced in t Minutes

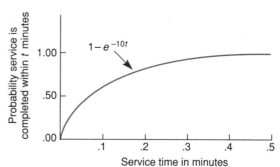

Using this equation, we can compute the probability that a passenger completes the screening process (that is, is serviced) within any specified time t. For example,

$$P(\text{service time} \leq .1 \text{ minutes})$$
$$= 1 - e^{-10(.1)} = 1 - e^{-1} \approx .6321$$

$$P(\text{service time} \leq .25 \text{ minutes})$$
$$= 1 - e^{-10(.25)} = 1 - e^{-2.5} \approx .9179$$

Thus, using the exponential distribution, we would expect 63.21 percent of the passengers to be serviced in 6 seconds or less ($t = .1$ minutes or less) and 91.79 percent in 15 seconds or less ($t = .25$ minutes or less). Using the 15-second time period, we see that relatively few passengers (8.21 percent) require more than 15 seconds to go through the screening operation. Figure 9S.2 shows graphically the probability that t minutes or less will be required to service a passenger.

In the analysis of a specific waiting line, we want to collect data on actual service times to see if the exponential distribution assumption is appropriate. If you find that other service time patterns (such as a

normal service time distribution or a constant service time distribution) exist, the exponential distribution should not be used. For the airport passenger-screening process, we assume that the exponential probability distribution is an appropriate representation of the service times.

Queue Discipline

In describing a waiting line we must define the manner in which the waiting units are ordered for service. For the airport problem, and in general for most customer-oriented waiting lines, the waiting units are ordered on a *first-come, first-served* basis, which is referred to as a FCFS queue discipline. When people wait in line for an elevator, it is usually the last one in line who is the first one serviced (that is, first to leave the elevator). Other types of queue disciplines assign priorities to the waiting units and service the unit with the highest priority first. We will restrict our attention to waiting lines with a FCFS queue discipline.

THE SINGLE-CHANNEL WAITING-LINE MODEL WITH POISSON ARRIVALS AND EXPONENTIAL SERVICE TIMES

The waiting-line model presented in this section can be applied to waiting lines where the following assumptions or conditions exist:

1. The waiting line has a single channel.
2. The pattern of arrivals follows a Poisson probability distribution.
3. The service times follow an exponential probability distribution.
4. The queue discipline is first-come, first-served (FCFS).

Since we have assumed that the above conditions were applicable to the airport problem, we will show how this waiting-line model can be used to analyze the airport security operation.

The quantitative methodology used in the development of most waiting-line models is rather complex. However, our purpose in this chapter is not to provide the theoretical development. Rather we restrict our presentation to showing how the operating characteristics of a waiting-line model can be determined and how this information can be applied to problems such as the one encountered at the screening facility.

Let us begin by reviewing the following notation:

λ = expected number of arrivals per time period (mean arrival rate)

μ = expected number of services possible per time period (mean service rate)

For the airport passenger-screening problem we have already concluded that $\lambda = 9$ passengers per hour and $\mu = 10$ passengers per hour.

Using the assumptions of Poisson arrivals and exponential service times, quantitative analysts have developed the following expressions, which define the operating characteristics of a **single-channel waiting line:**[4]

1. The probability that the service facility is idle (that is, the probability of 0 units in the system):

$$P_0 = \left(1 - \frac{\lambda}{\mu}\right) \qquad (9S.5)$$

2. The probability of n units in the system:

$$P_n = \left(\frac{\lambda}{\mu}\right)^n P_0 \qquad (9S.6)$$

---

[4]These equations apply to the *steady-state* operation of a waiting line, which occurs after a start-up or transient period.

3. The average number of units waiting for service:

$$L_q = \frac{\lambda^2}{\mu(\mu - \lambda)} \qquad (9S.7)$$

4. The average number of units in the system:

$$L = L_q + \frac{\lambda}{\mu} \qquad (9S.8)$$

5. The average time a unit spends waiting for service:

$$W_q = \frac{L_q}{\lambda} \qquad (9S.9)$$

6. The average time a unit spends in the system (waiting time plus service time):

$$W = W_q + \frac{1}{\mu} \qquad (9S.10)$$

7. The probability that an arriving unit has to wait for service:

$$P_w = \frac{\lambda}{\mu} \qquad (9S.11)$$

The values of the mean arrival rate λ and the mean service rate μ are clearly important components in the above formulas. From Equation (9S.11), we see that the ratio of these two values, λ/μ, is simply the probability that an arriving unit has to wait because the server is busy. Thus λ/μ is often referred to as the **utilization factor** for the waiting line.

The formulas for determining the operating characteristics of a single-channel waiting line presented in equations (9S.5) to (9S.11) are applicable only when the utilization factor $\lambda/\mu < 1$. This condition occurs when the mean service rate μ is greater than the mean arrival rate λ, and hence the service rate is sufficient to process or service all arrivals.

Returning to the airport passenger-screening problem, we see that with $\lambda = 9$ and $\mu = 10$, we can use Equations (9S.5) to (9S.11) to determine the operating characteristics of the screening operation. This is done as follows:

$$P_0 = \left(1 - \frac{\lambda}{\mu}\right) = \left(1 - \frac{9}{10}\right) = .10$$

$$L_q = \frac{\lambda^2}{\mu(\mu - \lambda)} = \frac{9^2}{10(10 - 9)} = \frac{81}{10}$$

$$= 8.1 \text{ passengers}$$

$$L = L_q + \frac{\lambda}{\mu} = 8.1 + \frac{9}{10}$$

$$= 9.0 \text{ passengers}$$

$$W_q = \frac{L_q}{\lambda} = \frac{8.1}{9}$$

$$= .9 \text{ minutes per passenger}$$

$$W = W_q + \frac{1}{\mu} = .9 + \frac{1}{10}$$

$$= 1.0 \text{ minutes per passenger}$$

$$P_w = \frac{\lambda}{\mu} = \frac{9}{10} = .90$$

Using the above information, we can learn several important things about the airport passenger-screening operation. In particular, we see that passengers wait an average of .90 minutes (54 seconds) before starting the screening process. With this as the average, many passengers wait even longer than this 54 seconds. In airport operations with passengers rushing to meet plane connections, this waiting time was judged to be undesirably high. In addition, the facts that the average waiting line is 8.1 passengers and that 90 percent of the arriving passengers have to wait for screening are indicators that something should be done to improve the efficiency of the airport passenger-screening operation.

Recall that we are using a waiting-line model to predict the operating characteristics of the airport passenger-screening process under the assumption that

TABLE 9S.1 Waiting-line System Characteristics for the Airport Passenger-screening Process

Characteristic	Mean Arrival Rate, Passengers Per Minute			
	7	8	9	10
Probability screening facility is idle, P_0	.30	.20	.10	.00
Average number of passengers waiting, L_q	1.63	3.20	8.10	*
Average number of passengers in the system, L	2.33	4.00	9.00	*
Average waiting time, W_q	.23	.40	.90	*
Average time a passenger is in the system, W	.33	.50	1.00	*
Probability an arriving passenger has to wait, P_w	.70	.80	.90	1.00

*Time and number of passengers continue to grow larger and larger. Service facility cannot handle arrivals.

passengers arrive at an average rate of 9 passengers per minute and can be serviced at an average rate of 10 passengers per minute. However, what if arrival and service rates differ from these expected values? The waiting-line model is flexible in that it can be readily used to predict operating characteristics under a variety of assumptions about the arrival and service rates.

In terms of the screening service times, we believe that the actual screening time data collected from the operation of similar screening systems is very reliable and that the mean service rate of 10 passengers per minute is realistic. However, at the same time we realize that the mean arrival rate for the passengers is based on airport planners' estimates and, as such, is subject to forecasting errors. Thus the screening process is evaluated under several possible passenger-arrival rates. Using Equations (9S.5) to (9S.11), the operating

characteristics for mean arrival rates of 7, 8, 9, and 10 passengers per minute are shown in Table 9S.1.

What do the data of Table 9S.1 tell us about the design of the airport passenger-screening process? They tell us that if the mean arrival rate drops to as low as 7 passengers per minute, the system functions acceptably. On the average, only 1.63 passengers are waiting and the average waiting time of .23 minutes (approximately 14 seconds) appears acceptable. However, we see the mean arrival rate of 9 passengers provides undesirable waiting characteristics, and if the mean arrival rate increases to 10 passengers per minute, the screening system as proposed is completely inadequate. Based on these results, airport planners need to consider layout and/or design modifications that will improve the efficiency of the passenger-screening process.

If a new screening facility or process can be designed that will improve the passenger service rate, Equations

```
SUMMARY OF A 1 CHANNEL WAITING LINE WITH
********************************************

     MEAN NUMBER OF ARRIVALS = 8

     MEAN NUMBER OF SERVICES = 10


THE PROBABILITY THAT THE CHANNEL IS IDLE                  0.2000

THE AVERAGE NUMBER OF UNITS WAITING FOR SERVICE           3.2000

THE AVERAGE NUMBER OF UNITS IN THE SYSTEM                 4.0000

THE AVERAGE TIME A UNIT SPENDS WAITING FOR SERVICE        0.4000

THE AVERAGE TIME A UNIT SPENDS IN THE SYSTEM              0.5000

THE PROBABILITY THAT AN ARRIVING UNIT HAS TO WAIT         0.8000


SUMMARY OF A 1 CHANNEL WAITING LINE WITH
********************************************

     MEAN NUMBER OF ARRIVALS = 9

     MEAN NUMBER OF SERVICES = 10


THE PROBABILITY THAT THE CHANNEL IS IDLE                  0.1000

THE AVERAGE NUMBER OF UNITS WAITING FOR SERVICE           8.1000

THE AVERAGE NUMBER OF UNITS IN THE SYSTEM                 9.0000

THE AVERAGE TIME A UNIT SPENDS WAITING FOR SERVICE        0.9000

THE AVERAGE TIME A UNIT SPENDS IN THE SYSTEM              1.0000

THE PROBABILITY THAT AN ARRIVING UNIT HAS TO WAIT         0.9000
```

FIGURE 9S.3.

Airport-passenger Screening Waiting-line Characteristics Generated by *The Management Scientist* **Software Package**

(9S.5) to (9S.11) can be used to predict operating characteristics under any revised mean service rate, μ. Developing a table with alternative mean service rates provides the information to determine which, if any, of the screening facility designs can handle the passenger volume acceptably.

Given the information in Table 9S.1, an alternative that we want to evaluate is the expansion of the screening process from a one-channel to a two-channel system. By this we mean that a second identical screening system is installed and the passengers complete the screening process by using one of the two alternative facilities, or channels. We can project the operating characteristics for the screening process with two channels by considering the models that have been developed for multiple-channel waiting lines.

Computer Software packages such as *The Management Scientist* can be used to generate operating characteristics of waiting-line systems. For example, the computer printout shown in Figure 9S.3 provides the characteristics of the airport passenger-screening waiting line for mean arrival rates of 8 and 9 passengers per minute. As you can see, the computer results provide the information previously summarized in Table 9S.1.

THE MULTIPLE-CHANNEL WAITING-LINE MODEL WITH POISSON ARRIVALS AND EXPONENTIAL SERVICE TIMES

A logical extension of the single-channel waiting line is the **multiple-channel waiting line**. By multiple-channel waiting lines we mean that two or more channels or service locations are present. Although items arriving for service wait in a single waiting line, they move to the first available channel to be serviced. The airport passenger screening example involved a single channel. However, a multiple-channel waiting-line model could be applied if an additional screening facility is built so that two passengers can be serviced simultaneously. Arriving passengers would form a single waiting line and wait for either of the two service areas to become available. A diagram of this system is shown in Figure 9S.4.

In this section we present formulas that can be used to compute various operating characteristics for a multiple-channel waiting line. The model we will use can be applied to situations where the following assumptions are met:

1. The waiting line has two or more identical channels.
2. The arrivals are Poisson with a *mean arrival rate* of λ.
3. The service times have an exponential distribution.
4. The *mean service rate* μ is the same for each channel.
5. The arrivals wait in a single waiting line and then move to the first open channel for service.
6. The queue discipline is first-come, first-served (FCFS).

Using these assumptions, operations researchers have developed formulas for determining the operating characteristics of the multiple-channel waiting line.

FIGURE 9S.4

Diagram of Two-channel Airport Screening Facility

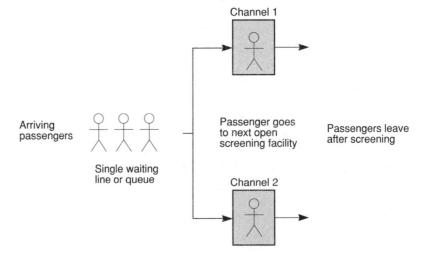

Let

k = number of channels

λ = mean arrival rate for the system

μ = mean service rate for *each* channel

The following equations apply to multiple-channel waiting lines for which the overall mean service rate, $k\mu$, is greater than the mean arrival rate, λ. In such cases, the service rate is sufficient to process or service all arrivals.

1. The probability that all k service channels are idle (that is, the probability of zero units in the system):

$$P_0 = \frac{1}{\left[\displaystyle\sum_{n=0}^{k-1} \frac{(\lambda/\mu)^n}{n!}\right] + \frac{(\lambda/\mu)^k}{(k-1)!}\frac{\mu}{k\mu - \lambda}} \quad (9S.12)$$

2. The probability of n units in the system:

$$P_n = \frac{(\lambda/\mu)^n}{k!\, k^{n-k}} P_0 \quad \text{for } n > k \quad (9S.13)$$

$$P_n = \frac{(\lambda/\mu)^n}{n!} P_0 \quad \text{for } 0 \leq n \leq k \quad (9S.14)$$

3. The average number of units waiting for service:

$$L_q = \frac{(\lambda/\mu)^k \lambda\mu}{(k-1)!(k\mu - \lambda)^2} P_0 \quad (9S.15)$$

4. The average number of units in the system:

$$L = L_q + \frac{\lambda}{\mu} \quad (9S.16)$$

5. The average time a unit spends waiting for service:

$$W_q = \frac{L_q}{\lambda} \quad (9S.17)$$

6. The average time a unit spends in the system (waiting time + service time):

$$W = W_q + \frac{1}{\mu} \quad (9S.18)$$

7. The probability that an arriving unit has to wait for service:

$$P_w = \frac{1}{k!}\left(\frac{\lambda}{\mu}\right)^k \frac{k\mu}{k\mu - \lambda} P_0 \quad (9S.19)$$

While the equations describing the operating characteristics of a multiple-channel waiting line with Poisson arrivals and exponential service times are somewhat more complex than the single-channel equations, they provide the same information and are used exactly as

we used the results from the single-channel model. To simplify the use of Equations (9S.12) to (9S.19), Table 9S.2 shows values of P_0 for selected values of λ/μ. Note that the values provided correspond to cases for which $k\mu > \lambda$ and hence the service rate is sufficient to service all arrivals.

For an application of the multiple-channel waiting-line model we return to the airport passenger-screening

TABLE 9S.2 Values of P_0 for Multiple-channel Waiting Lines with Poisson Arrivals and Exponential Service Times

Ratio λ/μ	Number of Channels (k)			
	2	3	4	5
0.15	0.8605	0.8607	0.8607	0.8607
0.20	0.8182	0.8187	0.8187	0.8187
0.25	0.7778	0.7788	0.7788	0.7788
0.30	0.7391	0.7407	0.7408	0.7408
0.35	0.7021	0.7046	0.7047	0.7047
0.40	0.6667	0.6701	0.6703	0.6703
0.45	0.6327	0.6373	0.6376	0.6376
0.50	0.6000	0.6061	0.6065	0.6065
0.55	0.5686	0.5763	0.5769	0.5769
0.60	0.5385	0.5479	0.5487	0.5488
0.65	0.5094	0.5209	0.5219	0.5220
0.70	0.4815	0.4952	0.4965	0.4966
0.75	0.4545	0.4706	0.4722	0.4724
0.80	0.4286	0.4472	0.4491	0.4493
0.85	0.4035	0.4248	0.4271	0.4274
0.90	0.3793	0.4035	0.4062	0.4065
0.95	0.3559	0.3831	0.3863	0.3867
1.00	0.3333	0.3636	0.3673	0.3678
1.20	0.2500	0.2941	0.3002	0.3011
1.40	0.1765	0.2360	0.2449	0.2463
1.60	0.1111	0.1872	0.1993	0.2014
1.80	0.0526	0.1460	0.1616	0.1646
2.00		0.1111	0.1304	0.1343
2.20		0.0815	0.1046	0.1094
2.40		0.0562	0.0831	0.0889
2.60		0.0345	0.0651	0.0721
2.80		0.0160	0.0521	0.0581
3.00			0.0377	0.0466
3.20			0.0273	0.0372
3.40			0.0186	0.0293
3.60			0.0113	0.0228
3.80			0.0051	0.0174
4.00				0.0130
4.20				0.0093
4.40				0.0063
4.60				0.0038
4.80				0.0017

problem and consider the desirability of expanding the screening facility to provide two screening locations at the entry to the concourse. How does this alternative design compare to the single-channel alternative?

We answer this question by applying Equations (9S.12) to (9S.19) specifically for the two-channel ($k = 2$) waiting line. Using $\lambda = 9$ passengers per minute and $\mu = 10$ passengers per minute for each of the screening facilities, we have the following operating characteristics:

$$P_0 = .3793 \text{ (from Table 9S.2 for } \lambda/\mu = .9 \text{ and } k = 2)$$

$$L_q = \frac{(9/10)^2(9)(10)}{(2-1)!\,(20-9)^2}\,(.3793) = .23 \text{ passengers}$$

$$L = .23 + \frac{9}{10} = 1.13 \text{ passengers}$$

$$W_q = \frac{.23}{9} = .026 \text{ minutes}$$

$$W = .026 + \frac{1}{10} = .126 \text{ minutes}$$

$$P_w = \frac{1}{2!}\left(\frac{9}{10}\right)^2\left(\frac{20}{20-9}\right)(.3793) = .279$$

What is your assessment of the two-channel screening operation? The operating characteristics suggest the two-channel operation will do extremely well in terms of handling the volume of passengers needing service. Specifically, note that the total time in the system is an average of .126 minutes (approximately 8 seconds), which is excellent. The percentage waiting is 27.9 percent, which is acceptable, especially in light of the short average waiting time. In addition, airport planners can use the multiple-channel model to show that even if the mean arrival rate for passengers exceeds the estimated 9 passengers per minute, the two-channel system should operate nicely. As a result of the waiting-line analysis, the two-channel passenger screening system is recommended.

APPLICATIONS OF WAITING-LINE MODELS

Waiting-line models have been applied in a variety of practical situations.[5] In this section we briefly review some of these applications and the benefits that were realized.

Toll Booths Toll-plaza activities at Port Authority tunnels and bridges in New York involve more than 250 traffic officers, whose payroll exceeds $1 million annually. A study was undertaken to balance expenses and employee and customer satisfaction. Specifically, the purposes of the study were to evaluate the grade of service given to customers as a function of traffic volume, to establish optimum standards of service, and to develop a more precise method of controlling expenses and service while providing for toll-collector rest periods.

Data collected included the traffic arrivals at the toll plaza, the number of cars in each toll-lane queue, and the toll-transaction count and times. It was observed that the pattern of arrivals was volume-dependent: Poisson distributed at low volumes, normally distributed at high volumes, and uniformly distributed at peak volumes. The scheduling procedure developed through waiting-line analysis resulted in an immediate yearly savings equivalent to ten times the cost of the study. In addition, the scheduling procedure offered better service to the public and benefits to toll-collection personnel.

Tool Cribs Queuing models were used to determine the optimum number of clerks to station at tool cribs at the Boeing Company. Boeing maintained about 60 tool cribs, scattered among several plants and providing tools required by mechanics. The supervisor wanted to reduce the idle time of the mechanics by increasing the number of crib clerks. Management was not receptive to the idea, since additional crib clerks result in increased labor costs. The best economic solution was obtained from a waiting-line model, which balanced the costs associated with the two conflicting objectives. The model justified a personnel reduction, which resulted in a savings of about $10,000 per month.

Transportation System A queuing model was used to determine the number of trucks required for an

[5]Adapted from G. Kemble Bennett and Brian J. Melloy, "Applying Queuing Theory Helps Minimize Waiting Time and Costs of Available Resources," *Industrial Engineering*, 16, no. 7 (July 1984): 86–91. Copyright Institute of Industrial Engineers, 25 Technology Park/Atlanta, Norcross, GA 30092.

internal transport system at a plant that manufactures electrical appliances. Complaints by the trucks' users that the number of trucks needed to be increased prompted the investigation. The objective was to weigh the cost of an additional truck against the reduction in the cost incurred by the users. A Poisson-arrival, exponential-service, multiple-server model was used. Information was gathered over a period of 17 consecutive two-shift working days. This information included detailed truck-request data and average queuing times.

Model results did not match those of the actual system, however. This led to a discovery of the real cause of the problem: poor communication caused the servers to be idle even as customers waited. When direct communication links between truck user and driver were implemented, the complaints ended, and an additional truck was not needed.

Teller Staffing The Bankers Trust Company of New York used a waiting-line model for teller staffing. The study was motivated by management's concern with rising labor costs and the need to maintain high levels of customer service. Data collection and analysis activity determined that a standard waiting-line model could be used. The output of the model provided management with the appropriate staffing requirements based on the expected customer arrival rate, the average service time, and the service level desired. It was used to establish teller staffing at over 100 branches of Bankers Trust. An average reduction of one teller per branch was realized with a comparable level of service, and the total benefit of the project was estimated to exceed $1 million annually.

Health Care A waiting-line model was used to assist in a cost/benefit analysis of a telemetry system at Long Community Hospital in Greensboro, North Carolina. The telemetric unit is used to monitor ambulatory cardiac patients.

The purpose of the study was to determine the number of units to provide a satisfactory level of patient service while simultaneously maximizing revenue. Records of patient arrival and service times were reviewed to obtain data for the model. The analysis revealed that the current number of units resulted in a loss of approximately $20,000 per year. It was determined that four additional units would not only negate this loss but also reduce patient waiting time by almost 100 percent.

These are but a few of the many practical applications of waiting-line models in production and operations management.

SUMMARY AND KEY TERMS

Summary

Waiting-line problems occur in a variety of practical situations in which customers or other units may wait for service. Queuing, or waiting-line, models have been developed that provide information regarding waiting times, idle times, number of units waiting, and other operating characteristics of the system. This information, along with cost considerations, may be used to assist in making design and layout decisions that will provide the desirable operating characteristics for the system. Typical examples include the design of production lines and the number of repairpeople to have for maintenance activities.

We presented models for single-channel and multiple-channel waiting lines with Poisson arrivals and exponential service times. Specifically, we emphasized how these models could be used for process analysis and selection decisions. If a waiting-line situation exists where the assumptions concerning the arrival and/or service distributions appear inappropriate, a simulation model (see the simulation supplement to Chapter 5) can be used to model the unique features of the system under study. Using the simulation model to project operating characteristics under a variety of design alternatives can provide the information needed for the specific problem under study.

Key Terms

Queuing theory
Queue
Poisson probability distribution
Mean arrival rate
Exponential probability distribution
Mean service rate
Single-channel waiting line
Utilization factor
Multiple-channel waiting line

PROBLEMS

The following waiting-line problems are all based on the assumptions of Poisson arrivals and exponential service times.

1. The reference desk of a large library receives requests for assistance at a mean rate of 10 requests per hour. Assuming that the reference desk has a mean service rate of 12 requests per hour, consider the following questions:
   a. What is the probability that the reference desk is idle?
   b. What is the average number of requests that will be waiting for service?
   c. What is the average waiting time plus service time for a request for assistance?
   d. What is the utilization factor for the reference desk?

2. Trucks using a single-channel loading dock have a mean arrival rate of 12 per day. The loading/unloading rate is 18 per day.
   a. What is the probability that the truck dock will be idle?
   b. What is the average number of trucks waiting for service?
   c. What is the average time a truck waits for the loading or unloading service?
   d. What is the probability that a new arrival will have to wait?

3. A mail-order nursery specializes in European beech trees. New orders, which are processed by a single shipping clerk, have a mean arrival rate of 6 per day and a mean service rate of 8 per day.
   a. What is the average time that an order spends in the queue waiting for the clerk to begin service?
   b. What is the average time that an order spends in the system?

4. Assume trucks arriving for loading/unloading at a truck dock form a single-channel waiting line. The mean arrival rate is four trucks per hour and the mean service rate is five trucks per hour.
   a. What is the probability that the truck dock will be idle?
   b. What is the average number of trucks in the queue?
   c. What is the average number of trucks in the system?
   d. What is the average time a truck spends in the queue waiting for service?
   e. What is the average time a truck spends in the system?

   f. What is the probability that an arriving truck will have to wait?

5. Marty's Barber Shop has one barber. Customers arrive at a rate of 2.2 per hour, and haircuts are given at an average rate of five customers per hour.
   a. What is the probability that the barber is idle?
   b. What is the probability that one customer is receiving a haircut and no one is waiting?
   c. What is the probability that one customer is receiving a haircut and one customer is waiting?
   d. What is the probability that one customer is receiving a haircut and two customers are waiting?
   e. What is the probability that more than two customers are waiting?
   f. What is the average time a customer waits for service?

6. Trosper Tire Company has decided to hire a new mechanic to handle all tire changes for customers ordering a new set of tires. Two mechanics are available for the job. One mechanic has limited experience and can be hired for $7 per hour. It is expected that this mechanic can service an average of three customers per hour. A mechanic with several years of experience is also being considered for the job. This mechanic can service an average of four customers per hour, but must be paid $10 per hour. Assume that customers arrive at the Trosper garage at the rate of two per hour.
   a. Compute waiting-line operating characteristics for each mechanic.
   b. If the company assigns a customer waiting cost of $15 per hour, which mechanic provides the lower operating cost?

7. Agan Interior Design provides home and office decorating assistance for its customers. In normal operation an average of 2.5 customers arrive per hour. One design consultant is available to answer customer questions and make product recommendations. The consultant averages 10 minutes with each customer.
   a. Compute operating characteristics for the customer waiting line.
   b. Service goals dictate that an arriving customer should not wait for service more than an average of 5 minutes. Is this goal being met? What action do you recommend?
   c. If the consultant can reduce the average time spent per customer to 8 minutes, will the service goal be met?

8. Pete's Market is a small local grocery store with only one checkout counter. Assume that shoppers arrive at the checkout lane at an average rate of 15 customers per hour and that the average order takes 3 minutes to ring up and bag. What information would you develop for Pete to aid him in analyzing the current operation? If Pete does not want the average time waiting for service to exceed 5 minutes, what would you tell Pete about the current system?

9. In problem 8 you analyzed the checkout waiting line for Pete's Market. After reviewing the analysis, Pete felt it would be desirable to hire a full-time person to assist in the checkout operation. Pete believed that if the new employee assisted the checkout cashier, average service time could be reduced to 2 minutes. However, Pete was also considering installing a second checkout lane, which could be operated by the new person. This second alternative would provide a two-channel system with the average service time of 3 minutes for each server. Should Pete use the new employee to assist on the current checkout counter or operate a second counter? Justify your recommendation.

10. Keuka Park Savings and Loan currently has one drive-in teller window. The arrival of cars occurs at a mean rate of 10 cars per hour. The mean service rate is 12 cars per hour.
   a. What is the probability that the service facility will be idle?
   b. If you were to drive up to the facility, what is the expected number of cars you would see waiting and being serviced?
   c. What is the average time waiting for service?
   d. What is the probability an arriving car has to wait?
   e. As a potential customer of the system, would you be satisfied with the above waiting-line characteristics? How do you think management could go about assessing the feelings of its customers with respect to the operation of the current system?

11. In order to improve the service to the customer, Keuka Park Savings and Loan (Problem 10) wants to investigate the effect of a second drive-in teller window. Assume a mean arrival rate of 10 cars per hour. In addition, assume a mean service rate of 12 cars per hour for each drive-in window. What effect would the addition of a new teller window have on the system? Does this system appear acceptable?

12. Fore and Aft Marina is a newly planned marina that will be located on the Ohio River near Madison, Indiana. Assume that Fore and Aft decides to build one docking facility and that a mean arrival rate of 5 boats per hour and a mean service rate of 10 boats per hour are expected. Consider the following questions:
   a. What is the probability that the boat dock will be idle?
   b. What is the average number of boats that will be waiting for service?
   c. What is the average time a boat will spend waiting for service?
   d. What is the average time a boat will spend at the dock?
   e. If you were the management of Fore and Aft Marina, would you be satisfied with the service level your system would be providing?

13. Management of the Fore and Aft Marina project in Problem 12 wants to investigate the possibility of adding a second dock. Assume a mean arrival rate of 5 boats per hour for the marina and a mean service rate of 10 boats per hour for each channel.
   a. What is the probability that the boat dock will be idle?
   b. What is the average number of boats that will be waiting for service?
   c. What is the average time a boat will spend waiting for service?
   d. What is the average time a boat will spend at the dock?
   e. If you were the managment of Fore and Aft Marina, would you be satisfied with the service level your system would be providing?

14. The City Beverage Drive-Thru is considering a two-channel system. Cars arrive at the beverage store at the mean rate of 6 per hour. The service rate for each channel is 10 per hour.
   a. What is the probability that both channels are idle?
   b. What is the average number of cars waiting for service?
   c. What is the average time waiting for service?
   d. What is the average time in the system?
   e. What is the probability of having to wait for service?

15. Consider a two-channel waiting line with a mean arrival rate for the system of 50 per hour and a mean service rate of 75 per hour for each channel.
   a. What is the probability that both channels are idle?

b. What is the average number of cars waiting for service?

c. What is the average time waiting for service?

d. What is the average time in the system?

e. What is the probability of having to wait for service?

16. For a two-channel waiting line with a mean arrival rate of 14 per hour and a mean service rate of 10 per hour per channel, determine the probability that an arrival has to wait. What is the probability of waiting if the system is expanded to three channels?

17. Big Al's Quickie Car Wash has two wash areas. Each area can wash 15 cars per hour. Cars arrive at the carwash at the rate of 15 cars per hour on the average, join the waiting line, and select the next open wash area when it becomes available.

a. What is the average time waiting for a wash area?

b. What is the probability that a customer who arrives at the carwash will have to wait?

c. As a customer of Big Al's Quickie Car Wash, do you think the service of the system favors the customer? If you were Al, what would your attitude be relative to this service level?

18. Refer to the Agan Interior Design situation in Problem 7. Again would like to evaluate two alternatives:

1. Use one consultant with an average service time of 8 minutes per customer.

2. Expand to two consultants, each of whom has an average service time of 10 minutes per customer.

If the consultants are paid $16 per hour and the customer waiting time is valued at $25 per hour, should Agan expand to the two-design-consultant system? Explain.

19. A fast-food franchise is currently operating a drive-up window. Orders are placed at an intercom station at the back of the parking lot. After placing an order, the customer pulls up and waits in line at the drive-up window until the cars in front have been served. By hiring a second person to help take and fill orders, management is hoping to improve customer service.

With one person filling orders, the average service time for a drive-up customer is 2 minutes; with a second person working, the average service time can be reduced to 1 minute, 15 seconds. Note that the drive-up window operation with two people is still a single-channel waiting line. However, with the addition of the second person, the average service time can be decreased. Cars arrive at the rate of 24 per hour.

a. Determine the average waiting time in the queue when only one person is working the drive-up window.

b. With only one person working the drive-up window, what percentage of time will that person not be occupied serving customers?

c. Determine the average waiting time when two people are working at the drive-up window.

d. With two persons working the drive-up window, what percentage of time will no one be occupied serving drive-up customers?

e. Would you recommend hiring a second person to work the drive-up window? Justify your answer.

20. Refer to problem 19. Space is available to install a second drive-up window adjacent to the first. Management is considering adding such a window. One person will be assigned to service customers at each window.

a. Determine the average customer waiting time for this two-channel system.

b. What percentage of the time will both windows be idle?

c. Which design would you recommend for providing service at the drive-up window? One attendant at one window? Two attendants at one window? Two attendants and two windows with one attendant at each window?

CASE PROBLEM

Regional Airlines is establishing a new phone system for handling flight reservations. During the 10:00 A.M. to 11:00 A.M. time period, past data show that calls to the ticket agents occur at an average rate of one call every 4.28 minutes. In addition, service time data indicate that an average of 3 minutes will be required to process a call. If a customer calls and the ticket agents are busy, a recorded message tells the customer that the call is being held in the order received and that a ticket agent will be available shortly; the customer will be asked to wait until an agent is free.

Regional Airline's management feels that offering an efficient telephone reservation system is an important part of establishing an image as a service-oriented carrier and, if properly implemented, the system will increase business. However, management also is aware of the fact that a busy or overloaded system with long waiting times may result in negative customer reaction to the point that Regional might even lose business. The cost per hour for a ticket reservation agent is $20. Thus management wants to provide good service, but does not want to overstaff the telephone reservation operation with more agents than are necessary.

At a planning meeting Regional's management team agreed that an acceptable service goal is to immediately answer and process at least 85% of the incoming calls. During the planning meeting, Regional's vice-president of administration pointed out that the historical data show that the average service rate by the agent is faster than the average arrival rate of the telephone calls. His conclusion is that one agent should be able to handle the telephone reservations and still have some idle time. The vice-president of marketing disagreed and felt the company should use at least two agents.

Prepare a report for Regional Airlines, analyzing the telephone reservation operation. Include the following information in your report:

1. A detailed analysis of the operating characteristics of the reservation system with one ticket agent as proposed by the vice-president of administration.
2. A detailed analysis of the operating characteristics of the ticket reservation system based on your recommendation regarding the number of reservation agents Regional should use.
3. The telephone arrival data presented above are for the 10:00 A.M. to 11:00 A.M. time period; however, the arrival rate of incoming calls is expected to change from hour to hour. Describe how your waiting-line analysis could be used to develop a ticket agent staffing plan that would enable the company to provide different levels of staffing for the ticket reservation system at different times during the day. Indicate the information that you would need to develop this staffing plan.

T he state of technology in the United States has grown rapidly since the industrial revolution. Nonetheless, we cannot look back over the last several decades without a sense of awe at the technological progress that has been made, particularly in the areas of electronics and microprocessor technology. Much of this rapid development is a direct result of the space program; it has had an important effect on manufacturing activities, office productivity, service organizations, and nearly every aspect of our daily lives. Among the three primary determinants of total productivity—namely, labor, capital investment, and technology—the one with the most potential for productivity improvement is technology.

Advances in technology have provided industry with dramatic opportunities to increase productivity. For example, the installation of computer-controlled equipment at the Messerschmitt-Bolkow-Blohm factory in Augsburg, West Germany, *reduced* (1) the time to manufacture the Tornado fighter plane from 30 months to 18 months, (2) the number of machines by 44 percent, (3) the number of personnel by 44 percent, and (4) the floor space by 30 percent. The capital investment required to achieve these improvements, however, was $50 million.[1]

The importance of automation and advanced technology in manufacturing and service organizations is due to several factors.

1. Technological innovation and the international nature of competition have increased the need for productivity improvement.
2. A shift from the mass production of standardized products to custom-produced products requires production systems with a high degree of flexibility.
3. Marketing pressures that demand shorter life cycles for products require production systems that are responsive to change.
4. The increasing complexity of products, such as those that integrate microprocessor technology, has made the problems associated with production more difficult.

To accommodate such factors in the manufacturing environment requires production systems that are both responsive and flexible.

In this chapter we introduce some of the important concepts of automation and advanced technology that impact operations management decisions. In order to better understand the role of technology, we begin our discussion by examining the relative roles that humans and machines play in production.

10.1 THE HUMAN-MACHINE INTERFACE

The rapid changes in technology in the last few decades have resulted in machines that are capable of performing tasks that have traditionally been done by people. Robots, for example, have relieved many workers of menial and dangerous tasks such as arc welding or lifting heavy objects. In offices, word processors have

---

[1]Joel G. Goldhar and Mariann Jelinek, "Plan for Economies of Scope" *Harvard Business Review,* November–December 1983, 193–200. Copyright 1983 by the President and Fellows of Harvard College; all rights reserved.

broadened the scope of secretaries' jobs. In one sense, such technological developments have enhanced the role of the worker in production systems. On the other hand, however, increased automation has been a real threat to job security; for instance, totally automated factories are a reality in countries such as Germany and Japan. This presents an interesting dilemma for operations managers: What should be the proper balance between human work and machine work?

During the next decade, automation will significantly change the nature of the work force even further. The decrease in jobs for minimally skilled, direct factory workers will be accompanied by a rapid increase in the demand for highly trained specialists. There will be a larger number of technical, professional, and managerial workers performing irregular, complex, long-cycle activities. Most of the worker's time will be devoted to mental processes, with much less time expended doing physical work. The proper balance of human and machine work will vary among different industries. The selection of automation level and use of human labor for a specific situation should be determined to provide the lowest unit-manufacturing cost (highest productivity) when all input resources—such as materials, labor, and capital—are considered.

The relative roles that human beings and machines have played in production have changed during the course of history. Figure 10.1 illustrates the relative emphasis of people in providing power and control of manufacturing processes. Prior to the industrial revolution, manufacturing tasks were performed primarily by people who provided both the power and control of the production process. Activities such as weaving cloth, forging and bending metal, and picking cotton were labor intensive. As the industrial revolution took effect, machines provided more of the power for manufacturing, but workers retained much of the control of the process. For example, lathes and drill presses required a large amount of operator assistance. Today, numerically controlled machines and robots permit less human involvement in the production process. In service organizations, we also see evidence of this evolution in automatic bank tellers and self-service gasoline pumps. Because of this new technology, job design must place considerable importance on the human-machine interface.

In order to make effective decisions regarding the introduction of new technology, managers need to understand the relative advantages and disadvantages of using humans and machines for work. Table 10.1 lists some of the capabilities

FIGURE 10.1

The Role of
People in
Manufacturing
Throughout
History

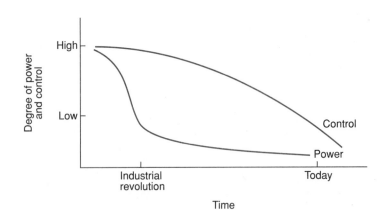

TABLE 10.1 Human versus Machine Capabilities

People		Machines	
Advantages	Disadvantages	Advantages	Disadvantages
Recognize and use information creatively	Relatively poor short-term memories	Precise, accurate, and fast responses	No creative capability
Improvise and adapt to new situations	Cannot perform many tasks simultaneously	Highly reliable for routine tasks	Decision making limited by programmed instructions
Reason by induction	Slow in response	Can perform tasks beyond human capabilities	Cannot adapt to unexpected situations
Make subjective decisions	Difficulty in maintaining consistency in performance	Fast deductive reasoning	Limited perceptual capability
		Store and process large amounts of information	

of people and machines. In general, people can think creatively and adapt to new and unexpected situations much better than machines. Machines, however, are better suited for complex or repetitive tasks requiring precision and speed. The goal of the operations manager is to provide the best synthesis of technology and people.

10.2 ELEMENTS OF AUTOMATION

Automation and advanced technology began in the 1950s with the development of numerically controlled (N/C) machine tools. N/C machining enables the machinist's skills to be duplicated by a computer program that is stored on a computer medium such as punched paper tape. The computer program controls the movements of a tool when making complex shapes. Over time, N/C computer hardware has become smaller and cheaper, computer-controlled software has become more sophisticated, and machine tools have become more complex. This has led to the development of industrial robots, vision systems, and automatic identification systems. The elements of modern automation discussed in this section, form the building blocks for factory automation systems introduced in the next section.

N/C was probably the earliest true CAM (computer-assisted manufacturing) system. Early N/C systems had manufacturing instructions on punched paper tapes. These instructions controlled the operations of a machine tool—for example, movement, drilling, and cutting—and tool changes. Today many systems use computer numerical control (CNC), in which the machine is controlled by a minicomputer. Computer systems will even prepare detailed instructions automatically if the part shape, tools required, and machining information are provided.

Numerical Control

For example, a part might require several holes of various sizes to be drilled. An N/C drill press with an automatic tool changer would automatically position the part to drill holes A, B, C, D, and E, in order, as shown in Figure 10.2. While the part is being repositioned to drill hole F, the tool is automatically changed.

FIGURE 10.2
Drilling Sequence for an N/C Operation

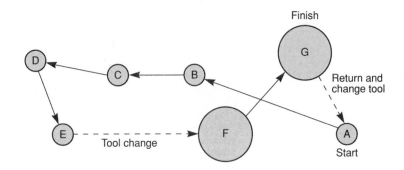

After hole G is drilled, the part is removed by an operator and the machine sets up to begin a new part. The sequence of drilling is programmed so that a minimum time is required to perform all operations. The operator has only to load and unload parts and push a button to begin processing. In this fashion, the operator can tend several N/C machines at one work center.

Computers are also used to create N/C tapes automatically. An interesting system has been developed by Structural Dynamics Research Corporation (SDRC), which specializes in computer-aided engineering. The SDRC HI-PRO system is an integrated N/C tape-preparation system for punching, shearing, and other sheet metal operations.[2] Typically, a supplier receives orders for sheet metal parts of different sizes—for instance, 100 pieces of 1.5-inch by 8-inch, 300 pieces of 6-inch by 10-inch, and so on. These parts are cut from larger sizes of sheet metal on N/C shearing machines. The different parts must be laid out in a manner that will minimize the waste from the larger sheets. Computer programs are used to generate optimal cutting patterns, to plot graphically the patterns for visual verification, and to create automatically an N/C tape for manufacturing. The user need enter only the various stock sizes, part dimensions, and requirements. Thus the cutting patterns and manufacturing are both computer-controlled.

Robotics

A **robot** is a programmable machine designed to handle materials or tools in the performance of a variety of tasks. Industrial robots were first introduced in 1954 when George Devol filed a design with the U.S. Patent Office for a simple pick-and-place robot. Unimation, founded in 1962, was the first industrial-robot company. In 1969, General Motors installed the first robot for spot-welding automobiles.

In 1986, approximately 16,000 industrial robots were in use in the United States; by way of contrast, Japan had approximately 60,000 in use. By the early 1990s, it is estimated that the United States will have between 30,000 and 100,000 robots installed. Some of the reasons why robots have been relatively slow to be applied in the United States have been management resistance to change, the fact that the United States has a plentiful labor supply, human fears associated with being replaced by robots, and a lack of technical knowledge about their uses.

An illustration of an industrial robot is given in Figure 10.3. We see that a robot consists of two major components: a *manipulator,* much like a human arm and wrist that carries a tool to perform work; and a *control system* to provide

---

[2]SDRC Super-Shear, General Electric-CAE International, Inc.

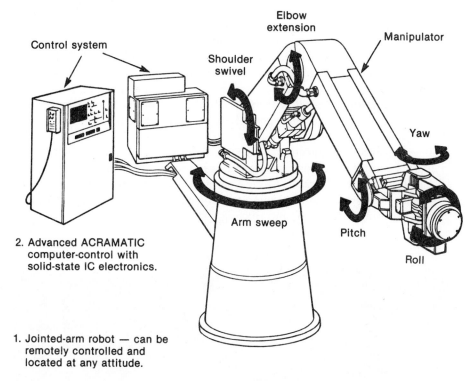

3. Combined hydraulic/electrical power unit built to machine tool quality and standards.

FIGURE 10.3

Cincinnati Milacron Robot System.

Control system

Elbow extension

Manipulator

Shoulder swivel

Yaw

Arm sweep

Pitch

Roll

2. Advanced ACRAMATIC computer-control with solid-state IC electronics.

1. Jointed-arm robot — can be remotely controlled and located at any attitude.

Courtesy Cincinnati Milacron.

the guidance to direct the manipulator to follow a prescribed sequence of operations. The manipulator usually has six basic motions, as illustrated in Figure 10.3:

1. *Shoulder swivel.* Allows vertical movement.
2. *Elbow extension.* Allows radial, or in/out, movement.
3. *Arm sweep.* Provides rotational movement.
4. *Pitch.* Allows the wrist to move up and down.
5. *Roll.* Provides wrist rotation.
6. *Yaw.* Allows the wrist horizontal movement.

Not all robots have the capability of all six motions; some may only have a subset of them. Using computer control, the robot can be "taught" a large number of sequences of motions and operations and even make logical decisions. A principal advantage of a robot is that it can be reprogrammed and transported from one application to another.

Some of the benefits associated with the use of robots are the cost savings which result because of reduced labor requirements, improvements in quality, increased capacity, and more flexibility of low-volume production equipment. In addition, robots never complain!

Robots have been used extensively in the automotive industry. A typical application is spot welding (see Photo 10.1). At General Motors, for example, over 90 percent of the welds are performed by robots. Robots are also used to deliver parts and materials from one area of an automotive plant to another. Great Britain's Motor Industry Research Association has built a robot to test drive automobiles on a rolling dynometer; the robot tests exhaust emissions, fuel economy, and vehicle durability. Robots have been developed to operate an automatic transmission and even drive on an actual road by computer control. Robots are also used for spray painting, machining operations such as drilling and assembly (see Photo 10.2), inspection, and material handling (see Photo 10.3). Robots are especially useful for working with hazardous materials or heavy objects; for instance, in nuclear power plants robots are used to do work in highly radioactive areas.

Robots are finding applications in service industries as well. For example, to help doctors complete tedious brain operations, a robot arm is used to make very precise drill holes into the skull. At the Veterans Administration Medical Center in Palo Alto, California, quadriplegics use a voice-controlled robot to assist them in eating, brushing their teeth, and shaving.

PHOTO 10.1

Finish spot welding of the six versions of the Ford Sierra car body is done by a total of fifty T³-586 Robots installed by Cincinnati Milacron at two fully automated body-assembly plants at Dagenham, England, and Genk, Belgium. More than 300 spot welds are applied to each body shell in a cycle that has Sierra bodies leaving each of four identical lines—two at Dagenham, two at Genk—at a rate of 43 per hour, a total production capability of 172 cars every hour. Courtesy Cincinnati Milacron.

PHOTO 10.2

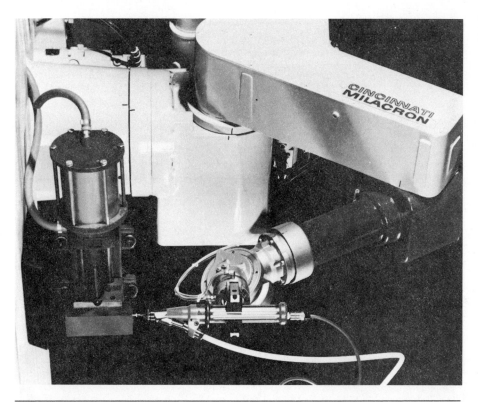

Here Cincinnati Milacron's electric T³-726 Industrial Robot uses an automatic screw driver to insert screws into a workpiece. The ability of the robot to maintain correct tool orientation is essential in this application. Courtesy Cincinnati Milacron.

Robots are not necessarily the perfect solution to every problem. For example, approximately 30,000 Ford Aerostar minivans were recalled because some robots had failed to make certain key welds. At the Campbell Soup Company, every time a certain defect was found in a case of soup, the robot would drop the case. After further analysis, Campbell decided to replace the robot with three human employees. Despite occasional problems such as these, robot technology is continually advancing. It appears that robotics and other forms of automation will help to improve production capability and quality, and will ultimately lead to competitive advantages for the organizations that understand how they can be utilized.

Vision Systems

The Machine Vision Association of the Society of Manufacturing Engineers defines **machine vision systems** as "the use of devices for optical noncontact sensing to automatically receive and interpret an image of a real scene, in order to obtain information and/or control machines or processes." Vision systems consist of a camera and video analyzer, a microcomputer, and a display screen (see Photo 10.4). Computer vision systems can read symbols, identify objects, measure dimensions, and inspect parts for flaws. Thus they are beginning to find extensive use in

PHOTO 10.3

A Milacron T³-586 Robot palletizes heavy aluminum cylinders. Combined weight of the gripper and part is over 250 pounds. Courtesy Cincinnati Milacron.

quality control. In addition, vision systems have numerous applications in material control and other facets of production.[3] Among these are the following:

- *Sortation.* Sorting of parts, assemblies, products, and containers by quantity, size, shape, color, or other characteristics.
- *Packaging.* Determining if containers are properly filled.

---

[3]J. Quinlan, "Those Big, Brainy Eyes," *Material Handling Engineering* 37, no. 7 (1982): 74–81.

PHOTO 10.4

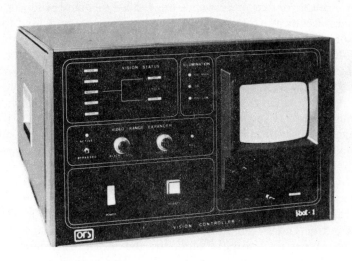

The console of the ORS *i-bot 1* robot vision system and the pneumatic *i-bot g-1* gripper (above) are manufactured by Object Recognition Systems, Inc. of Princeton, New Jersey. The *i-bot 1* vision module and the *i-bot g-1* gripper are integrated in a system that parallels the functions of hand-eye coordination. Courtesy Object Recognition Systems, Inc.

- *Shipping*. Directing containers to proper docks.
- *Bin-picking*. Assisting robots to pick an object out of a group of different-sized parts.
- *Process control*. Finding defects in welding, drilling, assembly, and so on.

The automotive industry was an early user of machine vision systems. In automotive applications, vision systems are used in conjunction with robots to weld body seams of varying widths, tighten imprecisely located bolts, mark identification numbers on engines and transmissions using lasers, and arrange car hoods on racks that have unevenly spaced slots. At a General Motors plant in Lansing, Michigan, for example, a vision-equipped robot system finds the exact location of a dozen lower-suspension-rail bolts and then uses a pneumatic nut-runner attachment to tighten the bolts to precise torque specifications. The system works by visually locating two gauge holes on the underbody of the car. From these two known points, the robot's control computer can calculate the exact locations of the 12 bolts and guide wrench sockets to the bolt heads. The vision feature is needed because the cars can be located as much as three inches fore or aft in the overhead conveyor cradles; a robot not equipped with vision would be lucky to stumble onto the bolts! The system has resulted in more accurate bolt torquing and in less manual rework required downstream on the assembly line.[4]

Vision systems are also used in many other industries besides the automotive industry. For example, vision systems are used to sort fruit by size and volume, and to help in the processing of nuts, grain, potato chips, cookies, pizza, and a variety of other food products. Makers of dishwashers, lawn mower engines, and turbine blades have integrated vision systems into their manufacturing processes. Vision systems are also used to control printing presses and to verify print quality and color. Printing of date and lot code are verified on many products, especially in the pharmaceutical industry, where vision systems are also used for pill formation, sorting, counting, and packaging. To assist in cutting control, the wood products industry uses machine vision to inspect logs for knots and grain direction. In the electronics industry, vision systems are widely applied in the manufacture of integrated circuits and in the final inspection of printed circuit boards.

A recent vision system developed by Global Holonetics Corp. in Iowa is capable of detecting defects as small as cracks in a candy bar or punctured safety seals on medicine bottles on high-speed production lines.[5] This system can process information such as shape, texture, and color, scanning up to 15 items per second.

Automatic Identification Systems

At the operational level of manufacturing, a large amount of data from the shop floor is required in order to provide the information necessary for effective production control. The conventional method of capturing data involves manual recording by supervisors using a clipboard and pencil. This data is then key-entered into a computer system for processing. This method is slow and subject to errors. For instance, typical error rates for handwritten documents are 1 error per 30 pieces of data and for keyboard input, 1 error per 300 pieces of data.

An alternative approach to the conventional method of capturing data involves the use of automatic identification systems. These systems read source data and convert it to a form readable by computers and processors for controlling equipment and generating reports. Error rates for automatic identification systems are as low as 1 in 3 million, and speeds are hundreds of times faster than conventional

---

[4]Stuart F. Brown, "Building Cars with Machines That See," *Popular Science* (October 1985).
[5]"Optical System Flags Defective Products," *Insight,* 6 June 1988, 48.

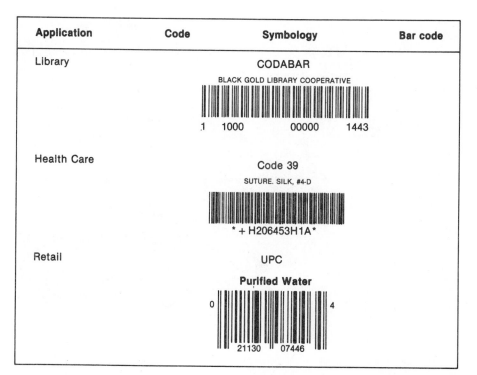

Application	Code	Symbology	Bar code

Library

CODABAR

BLACK GOLD LIBRARY COOPERATIVE

.1   1000   00000   1443

Health Care

Code 39

SUTURE. SILK, #4-D

* + H206453H1A*

Retail

UPC

Purified Water

0   4

21130   07446

FIGURE 10.4

Bar Code Symbology and Applications

Source: R. A. McDonald, "Bar Code Systems Enhance Productivity of Computer Systems With Real Time Mode." Reprinted from *Industrial Engineering* magazine, Nov. 1985. Copyright Institute of Industrial Engineers, 25 Technology Park/Atlanta, Norcross, GA 30092.

methods. Automatic identification systems reduce paperwork, improve accuracy, and provide more timely and useful information than previous methods of data collection.

Examples of automatic identification systems are bar-code scanners and voice-recognition systems. Illustrations of bar codes are given in Figure 10.4. Photo 10.5 shows a typical industrial application. Bar-code scanners read symbols by measuring the width of the bars and spaces and differentiating between symbols by the amount of light reflected. Bar-code scanners are probably the most popular method of automatic identification, and are the fastest and most accurate.

Voice-recognition systems are useful in operations that require a worker to use both eyes and hands for accomplishing a task—for instance, in a receiving and inspection application, in which handling, sorting, and recording of data must all be done simultaneously. One drawback of this technology is that the vocabulary of such systems typically consists of only several hundred words. Some of the benefits of automatic identification systems can be seen through an example of its application at Miles Laboratories.[6]

---

[6]Adapted from Jeff Laurel, "Bar Code Data Collection at Miles Laboratories." Reprinted from *Industrial Engineering* magazine, Nov. 1984. Copyright Institute of Industrial Engineers, 25 Technology Park/Atlanta, Norcross, GA 30092.

PHOTO 10.5

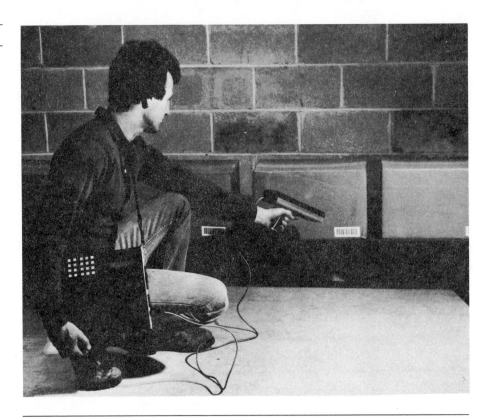

A bar code is automatically read from a package using automatic data-capture equipment. Photo courtesy of W&H Systems.

BENEFITS OF AN AUTOMATIC IDENTIFICATION SYSTEM

The Ames Instrument Division of Miles Laboratories is a manufacturer of biomedical diagnostic equipment. The division grew from a work force of 36 in 1977 to 270 in 1984. As the number of products increased during this growth period, it became more difficult manually to track work-in-progress status. Production workers manually filled out labor tickets, which were reviewed by the supervisors each night and keyed into the data-processing system the next day. The company wanted a simplified reporting system that would make it possible to gather production information directly from the workers and interface with their work-in-process information system.

The company selected a complete bar-code data-collection system using IBM personal computers from Data Collection Systems, Inc., a Minneapolis-based firm. Information on production and indirect labor activity is entered by the production workers from 31 bar-code wanding stations and stored on the internal disk storage of the PC for immediate inquiry and display. From the PC, information is passed on to the main production-control computer system.

Workers at the Miles facility monitor production and indirect labor activity by using the bar-code wanding devices. They read bar code printed on labor tickets from individual operations to identify the job numbers and operations being performed. Badges are wanded with each report to identify the reporting employee.

Workers can enter the data in any sequence desired. The required entries are indicated on templates at the wanding stations, and the data-collection system informs the worker if all required entries have been made. Indirect labor is recorded by the workers through bar-coded menus of indirect charge codes, which are posted at each wanding station.

Time savings of the workers, their supervisors, and clerical personnel has been so extensive that the data-collection system had a payback period of less than 1 year. Improved quality was also recognized as a significant benefit. Specifically, before the bar-code data-collection system was implemented, the operation was experiencing an average of 20 reporting errors per day; these errors had to be corrected by clerical personnel before the production reports could be run. After implementation of the bar-code identification system, an average of only two or three reporting errors per day were found.

10.3 AUTOMATION AND THE "FACTORY OF THE FUTURE"

Computers and automation are drastically changing the fundamental nature of today's factories. The combination of computers and sophisticated multipurpose machine tools produces highly flexible production systems. As we briefly discussed in Chapter 5, computers are being used extensively in engineering and design, referred to as computer-aided design (CAD). In a similar manner, the knowledge base on which production planning and control decisions are made has significantly improved. By combining such knowledge bases with physical process control, *computer-assisted manufacturing* (CAM) was born. Since CAD and CAM systems usually share a common database, integrated systems are called CAD/CAM systems.

Systems that perform multiple functions under computer control are called *flexible manufacturing systems* (FMS). They consist of numerical control (NC) machines linked by automated material-handling devices or robots. The union of CAD/CAM with FMS represents the latest development in manufacturing, which is referred to as *computer-integrated manufacturing* (CIM). In this section we discuss these technologies and their strategic implications for operations management.

Computer-aided Design and Computer-aided Manufacturing

Early CAD systems were basically computer-controlled plotting systems; today's systems revolve around graphics terminals. CAD allows engineers and draftspeople to work in two and three dimensions and utilize color to simplify complex designs. Designers can carry out geometric transformations at high speeds and can obtain the conventional top, side, and front views of a design as well as rotations about any axis and cross sections. This allows, for example, the ability to check for physical mating of parts. In addition, CAD systems allow the storage and retrieval of designs for easy updating and automatic creation of bills of materials and process information for production planning and scheduling systems.

Computer-aided manufacturing (CAM) involves computer control of the manufacturing process, such as determining tool movements and cutting speeds.

N/C is an old form of CAM, whereas robotics is a modern example. CAM provides advantages over conventional manufacturing approaches under many conditions, such as when several different parts with variable or cyclic demands are produced, when frequent design changes are made, when the manufacturing process is complex, when there are multiple machining operations on one part, or when expert operator skills and close control are required. Each machine in a CAM system has the ability to select and manipulate a number of tools according to programmed instructions; thus CAM provides a high degree of flexibility in performing and controlling manufacturing processes.

Caterpillar Corporation, for instance, uses CAM to make components for tractor engine drive assemblies. About a dozen machines stand on both sides of a railroad-like track, along which a transfer device shuttles parts among the work stations where some 30 to 40 machining operations are performed. Operators at entry and exit points clamp the parts on and off the transfer mechanism; the rest of the process is computer-driven. As a second example, an automobile manufacturer uses CAM to weld gasoline tanks. The tanks are five-sided and irregularly shaped, with no two sides being parallel. If the manufacturing operation were manual, someone would have to turn the tank at each stage; with CAM, a complex welding system manufactures the individual sides precisely to specifications.[7] Photo 10.6 illustrates another example of how CAM is used at International Harvester.

The integration of CAD and CAM allows for important coordination between design and manufacturing; this is one of the important issues that was discussed in Chapter 5. Through such integration, the lead time for process planning can be reduced, quality assurance can be improved, and cost savings in tool design and other capital investments can be realized.

Flexible Manufacturing Systems	A **flexible manufacturing system** (FMS) is a logical extension of CAM. An FMS consists of two or more computer-controlled machines linked by handling devices such as robots and transport systems. Computers direct the overall sequence of operations and route the workpiece to the appropriate machine, select and load the proper tools, and control the operations performed by the machine. More than one different workpiece may be machined simultaneously, and many different parts can be processed in random order. Photo 10.7 shows an example of an FMS configuration.

General Electric modernized its locomotive plant in Erie, Pennsylvania, using an FMS. The machining time for engine-frame parts was reduced from 16 days to 16 hours; overall productivity was increased by 240 percent; capacity was increased by 38 percent; and design flexibility was increased as well. Another firm that uses an FMS is Mazak Corporation in Florence, Kentucky, which manufactures machine tools. Their system produces 180 parts, ranging from a few pounds to 3 tons in weight, using only two human operators.

FMSs provide the ability to economically manufacture small to medium volumes of many different parts. As such, these systems have the advantages of the flexibility of a job shop and the high productivity associated with production

---

[7]Bela Gold, "CAM Sets New Rules For Production" *Harvard Business Review* (November–December 1982): 168–174. Copyright 1982 by the President and Fellows of Harvard College; all rights reserved.

PHOTO 10.6

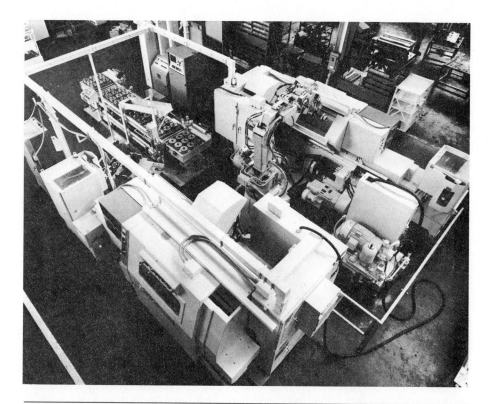

In this production cell at International Harvester's Farmall Division, a Cincinnati Milacron computer-controlled T3 Industrial Robot serves two Milacron Cinturn Series C turning centers. Parts enter the cell as rough castings and leave it completely machined and inspected.
  The sequence of operations is as follows:

1. The T3 Robot takes a part from the pallet on the conveyor to the first turning center (shown). Entering from the rear of the machine, the robot removes the part just machined and loads the part from the pallet.
2. The robot takes the part it just removed from the first machine to an automatic gaging station. If the part is found to be within tolerances at this point, the robot takes it to the second turning center.
3. The robot removes a finished part from the second turning center and loads the part just gaged for a second turning operation.
4. The robot takes the finished part to the gaging station. If the part is good, it is returned to the pallet, the robot picks up another part, and the sequence is repeated.

Loading the turning centers from the rear leaves the fronts of the machines open for operator observation, control access, and tool replacement. Courtesy of Cincinnati Milacron.

lines. A FMS can achieve higher machine utilizations than stand-alone machines because setup times are reduced, parts are handled more efficiently, and several parts are produced simultaneously. Machine utilization can be as high as 85 percent, compared to 50 percent for typical NC machines. Material handling requirements are less, and hence costs are reduced.

A FMS provides more flexibility in dealing with engineering and production schedule changes. Manufacturing lead times are reduced because FMSs result in reduced setup times. This allows a manufacturer to respond quicker to new products and to changes in demand. As you may recall, this is one of the important issues in manufacturing strategy. As demand increases, FMSs can be more easily

PHOTO 10.7

A flexible manufacturing system. Cincinnati Milacron's Variable Mission random-type parts-machining system consists of machining centers with parts being automatically delivered to the machines from load stations and returned to the unload areas when the operations are completed. Tools can also be exchanged automatically at the machines. The system is modular and can be expanded as needed. Productivity is increased by reducing the nonproductive time a part spends on the shop floor. Courtesy Cincinnati Milacron.

expanded in a modular fashion. As a result of shorter lead times, in-process inventory is reduced. Finally, since both machining and material handling are under computer control, operators are needed only to perform necessary loading and unloading operations; this provides a significant cost reduction. All these advantages can only help to increase profitability and the competitive position of the firm.

FMSs, like robots, are not without limitations. FMSs require capital investments that can easily exceed $10 million. Many managers are reluctant to make such an investment, especially since technology advances may make today's FMS obsolete. Because FMSs must be custom-designed to a company's specific needs, it may take several years until the system is installed and running. In addition, the computer software needed to control an FMS is highly complex, and often prone to problems.

Computer-integrated Manufacturing Systems

Today we are beginning to see the complete integration of CAD, CAM, and FMS. These systems are called **computer-integrated manufacturing systems**, or **CIMS**. Computer-integrated manufacturing represents the union of hardware, software, database management, and communications to plan and control production activities from planning and design to manufacturing and distribution.

The primary goal of computer-integrated manufacturing is not to eliminate direct-labor costs, which are typically in the 5 to 15 percent range for most manufactured goods. Instead the benefits of CIM come from automating the flow of information through a factory. This can often save nearly half the total costs attributed to indirect labor, middle management, and other overhead. The cost of quality can also be significantly reduced through the elimination of human error. For example, Allen-Bradley built a totally automated facility costing $15 million to produce electric motor starters. Even though direct labor accounted for only 7 percent of the cost, the new facility reduced total costs by 35 percent.[8] CIM factories offer break-even points as low as 25 or 30 percent of capacity compared to 60 to 65 percent in conventional manufacturing plants. Thus, they offer important advantages for cyclical businesses with costly hiring and training programs.

CIMSs are being used for high-volume, highly standardized production where mass-production technology has traditionally been employed. However, CIMSs allow for much smaller and economically viable batch-production capabilities. A firm can then match its production efforts to a much wider range of demand and create a competitive advantage through rapid response to market changes and new products.

CIMS also provides all the advantages discussed for CAD, CAM, and FMS: shorter design cycles, better quality, reduced waste, better management control, and high equipment utilization. The cost of developing and implementing a fully operational CIM system can be staggering, however, and requires a high degree of management commitment and effort. Many companies are beginning to reap the rewards of carefully planned systems. The development of CIMSs will be a focus of manufacturing throughout the rest of this century.

Successful implementation of automation is not simply the introduction of fancy equipment; many companies tried this and wound up with little to show for it. Such an approach failed primarily because the environment was constantly changing. From such failures a new vision of future manufacturing enterprises is emerging, based on complete reorganization from the ground up, and aided by artificial intelligence (AI) software.

The Road to Automation

Business Week suggests the following steps to automation:[9]

1. Simplify and reorganize the shop floor for optimum efficiency—with no automation, or at least no new automation. While this is done widely and rigorously in Japan, it is often poorly implemented in the United States. Western Europe lags behind both.
2. Create "islands of automation" with robots, flexible manufacturing cells, computer controls, and other advanced shop floor systems. This has been widely implemented in Japan and in the U.S. and is just beginning in Europe.
3. Link the islands of automation together, and to CAD. Many major U.S. companies are doing this. Japan is slightly ahead, while Europe is far behind.
4. Use AI to integrate some operations with CAD and to automate other functions such as production scheduling. This represents the cutting edge

---

[8]"High Tech to the Rescue," *Business Week,* 16 June 1986, 101.
[9]"Smart Factories: America's Turn?" *Business Week,* May 8, 1989, p. 142.

of progressive U.S. companies. It is rare in Japan and almost nonexistent in Europe.

5. Finally, extend AI to all decision-making steps from product planning to customer service. Only a few U.S. companies are exploring this aspect.

The aerospace industry is leading in this process. The B-2 Stealth bomber, produced by Northrup Corporation, was developed using this approach. The use of AI represents an important competitive weapon in the future.

10.4 AUTOMATION IN MATERIALS HANDLING

Automation plays an important role in materials handling applications. In this section we review two major applications of automation in materials handling: automated sorting, and automated storage and retrieval.

Automated Sorting

For many applications in which orders consist of a number of different, small items, manufacturers are turning to automated sortation systems.[10] Such systems consist of conveyors, diverters, and controls to batch order-pick a large volume of merchandise and automatically sort it by store, order, or shipping route. Five components make up an automated sortation system.

1. A subsystem, which receives a mixture of articles from the other parts of the warehouse.
2. A station, where each article is examined and coded by its sorting characteristic.
3. The sortation system itself, which reads the codes and automatically sorts the articles into their proper groups.
4. Receiving stations, where each sorted group accumulates.
5. A computer-controlled coordination mechanism.

An example of an automated sortation system is shown in Figure 10.5. In this type of system, items are pushed off the conveyor into sorting locations. Other systems have trays or bins, which tilt to deposit the items into cartons or onto holding conveyors.

In designing such systems, a number of factors must be taken into account. The most important factors are.

1. nature of items to be sorted: dimensions, weight, and composition
2. number of groupings required
3. throughput capacity: number of articles per hour, number of shifts
4. accumulation capacity at sorting stations
5. building facilities
6. type of coding scheme
7. current operating costs.

---

[10]Adapted from "ACCO Automated Sortation Systems," Bulletin 3320, ACCO Babcock, Inc., Material Handling Group.

FIGURE 10.5 **Automated Sortation System**

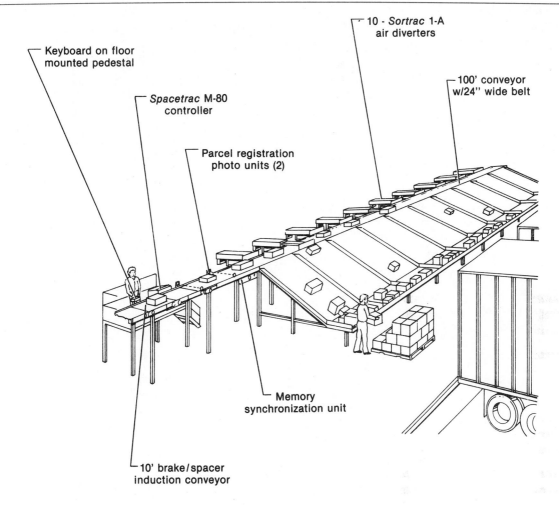

10 - *Sortrac* 1-A
air diverters

Keyboard on floor
mounted pedestal

Spacetrac M-80
controller

100' conveyor
w/24" wide belt

Parcel registration
photo units (2)

Memory
synchronization unit

10' brake/spacer
induction conveyor

Source: ACCO Pre-engineered Sortation System Bulletin 3380. ACCO Babcock, Inc., Material Handling Group.

Automated sorting equipment is often found in such places as post offices, air cargo terminals, mail order distribution centers, airline baggage handling, truck terminals, and publishing houses.

Automated storage and retrieval systems (AS/RS) are designed to provide high material-flow rates through warehouses, particularly for high-volume, unit-load storage. An overhead view of a typical AS/RS is shown in Figure 10.6. Incoming pallets arrive via conveyor and are transferred to a loader at one of the storage aisles. The storage/retrieval (S/R) vehicle then moves both horizontally and vertically to deposit the load in an empty storage location (see Figure 10.7). On the way back, S/R vehicles usually retrieve a required item to be sent to shipping. S/R vehicles may be manually controlled or fully automated. Computer control

Automated Storage and Retrieval Systems

FIGURE 10.6
Overhead View of an AS/RS System

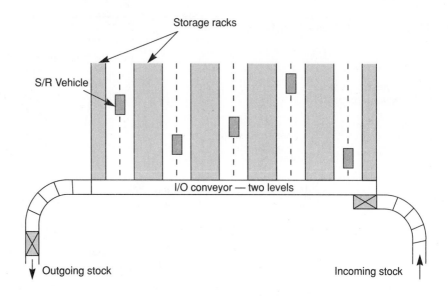

Storage racks

S/R Vehicle

I/O conveyor — two levels

Outgoing stock

Incoming stock

FIGURE 10.7
Floor View of S/R Vehicle

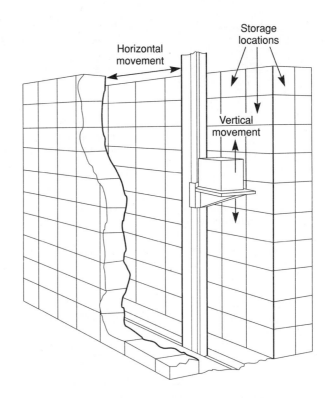

Storage locations

Horizontal movement

Vertical movement

is needed to maintain an up-to-date list of storage locations for efficient retrieval. See Photos 10.8 and 10.9.

Capital investment in AS/RS is high, although the increased productivity and reduction of direct labor are the primary benefits. For example, Delta Airlines installed an automated storage and retrieval system to service maintenance re-

PHOTO 10.8

In a warehousing application, HP 3076A is mounted on wall for storekeeper. As the operator passes the terminal, she inserts into the reader the card that travels with the goods and receives a routing ticket from the printer assigning storage space to the goods. Transaction is recorded by the associated computer. Courtesy of Hewlett Packard.

quests in a timely and efficient manner. Built in 1981, the system cost $1.9 million. Without the system, however, Delta would have required about 30 percent more employees over a five-year period. The system holds 123,000 different parts with a configuration of six aisles. Each aisle contains 46 sections with 28 tray levels, each of which can hold up to 54 different parts. Under the manual system, the retrieval process started with six teletype operators. Once a request had been received by an operator, the operator manually pulled the parts specified on the pick lists. This operation took an average of seven minutes. Under the automated system, the teletype operators are not required; the request or pick list is sent automatically to the station operation and there is less likelihood of "paper error." With the new system, the average time to retrieve a part is down to 30 seconds.

PHOTO 10.9

The Litton® miniload AS/R system completely regulates all phases of small-parts inventory with precise material control. Major system benefits include reduced labor and energy requirements, maximum utilization of available storage cube, and increased productivity. Control can range from manual operation to distributed multicomputer networks, all furnished in-house by Litton UHS. Courtesy of Litton Unit Handling Systems, a division of Litton Systems, Inc.

10.5 AUTOMATION IN THE SERVICE SECTOR

Advanced technology is rapidly becoming an important aspect of service organizations. One popular example is the fast food industry, which is turning toward automation to increase quality and productivity as well as to respond to growing labor shortages. Hardee's, for example, the number three national chain behind

McDonald's and Burger King in 1988, has installed new grills called "top-side cookers" that cook from the top and bottom at the same time so that burgers are fatter and juicier. Arby's Inc., is developing a system that would slice, weigh and move portions of roast beef to a sandwich-making station. Pepsico, Inc., is testing a fully automated soft drink system. In their systems, orders are keyed in at the cash register and are transmitted to a computer in the dispenser. Under computer control, the dispenser drops a cup, fills it with ice and the soft drink, and puts a lid on it. The drink is then moved by conveyor to the server. The system is designed to let workers interact more with the customer rather than spending time filling drinks.

Grocery stores have been using automatic identification equipment for many years at the checkout counters. General retail stores are beginning to adopt this technology. Toys 'R' Us, for instance, will not purchase goods unless they are labeled with Universal Product Codes. Not only does the use of bar-coding save time for customers, but the computer system can automatically adjust the store's inventory records each time an item is sold. Some retailers use similar systems to automatically reorder products when inventories reach predetermined levels. Credit authorizations, which use to take several minutes by telephone, are now accomplished in seconds through computerized authorization systems.

Retail stores are experimenting with other innovative forms of automation. The Dayton Department Store in Minneapolis plans to set up unattended computer terminals, or electronic kiosks, where credit-card customers can charge their purchases themselves. Florsheim shoe stores have similar systems in which a customer can search an electronic catalog of all styles and colors of shoes and place an order. Some automobile dealerships use videodisc systems to allow customers to select and view a car from thousands of possible options.

The Kroger Company is testing self-service automated checkouts in Atlanta. The self-service shopper passes each purchase over a scanner. If he or she forgets to scan a product before putting it on the second conveyor headed toward the bagging area, the belt moves backwards, taking the item back to the customer. A polite videotaped message appears on the computer screen reminding the customer to scan the product; the system even illustrates how to do it correctly. After customers have scanned their groceries, they take their receipts to a central cashier for payment.

The U.S. Postal Service expects to deliver 250 billion pieces of mail per year by 2000. Mail carriers spend about 50 percent of their time placing mail in the proper order for delivery. In 1985, 19 percent of the Postal Service's $29 billion budget was used for manual sorting. The Postal Service is spending approximately $35 million to find ways of exploiting robotics, vision systems and other forms of advanced technology for mail handling. As a first step, the Postal Service plans to purchase 600 optical character recognition systems that can read and sort 5000 pieces of mail per hour. This compares to 800 pieces of mail per hour for a human or 1650 per hour for a mechanical sorter.

Many other applications of computers and advanced technology in the service sector exist. Several other applications are reviewed in selected service industries.[11]

---

[11]Adapted from David A. Collier, "The Service Sector Revolution: The Automation of Services." Reprinted with permission from *Long Range Planning,* 16, no. 6. Copyright 1983, Pergamon Press, Ltd.

Financial Services

Automation in financial services began in the 1930s with mechanical machines that could sort checks into a series of pockets, each containing checks for a particular bank. Today, the IBM 3890 check-processing machine can read, record, and sort up to 2000 magnetic-ink character-recognition checks per minute into as many as 24 pockets. Automatic teller machines (ATMs) provide improved customer service and reduce the costs associated with conventional teller transactions. Electronic fund-transfer systems have emerged and have made possible direct payroll deposit and MasterCard and VISA debit cards, for example. Trust administrators, cash managers, and portfolio managers all routinely make use of computer hardware and software to make complex financial decisions.

Public and Government Services

Automation in the public and government services takes many forms. A few examples include a fixed-sequence robot named Herbie who works as a mechanical messenger in the hallways of the U.S. Justice Department, totally automated systems used to operate fossil- and nuclear-power generating plants, and numerically controlled and intelligent robots used to manufacture and operate cruise missiles.

The "paperless office" involves a wide array of equipment, such as electronic switchboards, word processors, high-speed printers, teleconferencing, electronic mail, and voice-actuated devices. The U.S. Postal Service began its "electronic computer-originated mail" (E-COM) system in 1982. Messages are sent electronically to the receiving post office, where they are printed, enclosed in envelopes, and put into the regular mail stream. At its inception, over 80 corporations and organizations had signed up for this service.

Transportation Services

The principal modes of transportation are air, pipeline, railroad, water, and highway. Air transport is the most automated, as exemplified by baggage conveyors, automatic ticketing machines, and autopilot systems. Pipeline systems are also highly automated, having computer-controlled systems for instrumentation and pumping. Switching systems and computerized railcar tracking systems are examples of automation in the railroad industry. The captain of a 92-ton ore freighter uses a voice-recognition system to change engine speed.

Health Care Services

Health care has quickly adopted automation. Automation can be found in nearly every type of medical technology. Examples include CAT scanners, fetal monitors, laboratory diagnosis, pacemakers, and medical information systems. Computerized "expert systems" act as advisors to physicians in making diagnoses and prescribing treatments.

Education Services

Computers are becoming as basic to the classroom as chalk and blackboards. Computer-assisted instruction (CAI) is changing the way many students learn; they can learn at their own pace and free the teacher of many time-consuming and repetitive tasks. Library research has improved dramatically because of the ability to access computerized bibliographic databases.

Hotel and Motel Services

The operations function of hotels and motels uses electronic reservation systems, message and wake-up systems, and key and lock systems. Many other activities that are not apparent to guests are automation-based, such as automatic ironing machines and automated clean-up, vacuum, wash, and wax machines. Such technologies improve the quality and timeliness of service and reduce operating costs.

Despite computers and the automation of services, productivity actually fell in the finance, real-estate, and insurance industries between 1973 and 1986.[12] Much of the problem was discovered to be caused by the fact that individuals tend to cling to old habits and resist new technology; some get bogged down in extraneous information; and insufficient planning is performed prior to implementation of new technology. For example, one insurance company discovered that even though it had a modern computer system, the clerks still worked as they had under the old system: one specialized in processing surrenders of old policies, another in issuing new policies, and a third in transferring cash values from old to new. By redesigning the *process* to a team effort, significant productivity gains were achieved.

The service sector has traditionally been highly labor-intensive. Automation is clearly changing the way services are offered. In most service industries, this means that fewer jobs will be available and that new skills will be required. These facts cause some serious concern to both labor and management. In the final section of this chapter we address this issue and other impacts of automation.

10.6 IMPACTS OF AUTOMATION

Automation and advanced technology provide many benefits for improving productivity, quality, and competitiveness of manufacturing and service organizations. Let us summarize the principal benefits that are incurred through automation.

- New products can be introduced with smaller lead times because CAD reduces the time required to design and test new ideas.
- Product life cycles are shorter because of the ability to redesign products faster, and because of the rapid pace of technological improvements in manufacturing.
- Quality is improved because of CAD/CAM and improved inspection capabilities such as vision systems. Note, however, that the quality of purchased materials *must* be good in order for automated factories to function without human intervention.
- Work-in-process inventory is reduced because of increased stability in machine operation times. As a result, high machine reliability is required to maintain a constant flow of production.

---

[12]"Service Industries Find Computers Don't Always Raise Productivity," *The Wall Street Journal,* 19 April 1988, 29.

- Machine setup and tool change times are reduced and less costly. As a result, smaller lot sizes can be produced, increasing the plant's flexibility.
- Supervision, energy, and other overhead costs will decrease.
- With less inventory, materials handling, and labor, smaller facilities can achieve the same production output.
- Work becomes more challenging and conceptual as automated equipment performs routine and repetitive tasks.

The implications of automation for employment has been a most serious concern among scholars, legislators, and labor leaders. Whereas many jobs in direct manufacturing will indeed be lost because of automation, economic forecasters have predicted a net increase of about 2.5 million jobs in manufacturing alone by 1990. These jobs, however, will be in new or different industries. The demand for workers to design, operate, maintain, and manage automated systems will increase. The trend toward multiple careers and the development of several different skills over a person's working life will become more widespread; consequently, training and retraining will consume a larger portion of working time.

One consequence of increasing automation appears to be a decline in union membership. The argument for this is that the technically trained worker who will be required to run automated factories of the future does not sense the same need to join the union ranks as his or her former counterpart. Unions have recognized the impact of automation on their members and seem to be dealing with it in a positive fashion. Instead of resisting advances in technology, they are trying to participate in them by bargaining for contracts aimed at retraining and reemploying their members in the new skills that are required for successfully implementing automation. The United Auto Workers union has stated that it recognizes the introduction of new technologies as essential for promoting economic progress that will ultimately benefit its membership. In return, they expect advanced notice of the introduction of new technologies, protection of union workers against displacement, and retraining of members in the new technologies.

Many questions still need to be answered, such as, Who should pay for the cost of retraining displaced workers? Should it be the company, the union, or society as a whole? Will displaced workers be capable of being retrained in areas requiring higher scientific and mathematical skills? History has shown that technological advances in the past have resulted in higher employment and greater economic growth, despite temporary worker displacement. Nevertheless, automation will represent an important challenge to industry and the service sector in the years to come.

P/OM IN PRACTICE

In this section we discuss how automation and advanced technology are utilized by IBM at their Lexington, Kentucky facility. The results show how automation can lead to significant cost savings and at the same time maintain full employment and employee morale.

AUTOMATION FOR QUALITY AND COST EFFECTIVENESS AT IBM[13]

One of the largest automated manufacturing facilities in the world is IBMs Information Products Division in Lexington, Kentucky. The factory occupies nearly one million square feet of floor space and contains conveyors, monorails, automated guided vehicles, automated storage and retrieval systems, and 250 robots working together within a structured computer-integrated manufacturing system.

The Lexington plant, which opened in 1956, was originally designed to manufacture typewriters. When IBM introduced the Personal Computer in 1981, it did not manufacture PC printers. By 1984, Japanese printers accounted for more than 80 percent of U.S. sales. This gave the Japanese cost advantages along with experience in high-volume manufacturing of these products. IBM decided to remain in the typewriter business and also enter the printer market. They concluded that the best way to overcome the cost advantage of Japanese firms was to stay in the United States and automate the Lexington plant. This decision resulted in the investment of more than $300 million in the Lexington plant.

Manufacturing is divided into separate modules, each of which operates similar to a self-contained business run by a separate management team. Typewriters and printers are produced in seven subassembly manufacturing modules: motors, frame paperfeed/transport; covers; electronic cards; keyboards; a final assembly and test module; and a packaging module. Even though the modules are linked together by a computer-integrated manufacturing network and automated material-handling systems, the capability to operate independently is retained so that production can continue in the event of a computer or handling system malfunction.

Both typewriters and printers can be made on the same lines at the same time by an integrated computer system which directs the right parts to the right work stations. The test equipment checks and measures print quality against a wide variety of computerized images and then sends the products to packaging.

The motor module is produced on a continuous flow line that features a mix of hard automation using fixed processes and flexible automation using robots to produce two different motors for the printwheel rotation and the transport of the print carrier. At the end of the line, a robot puts the motors in a test unit that verifies their acceptability, then loads them into eggcrate trays. The trays are stacked automatically, moved to a vertical transfer station, and transported to the frame paperfeed transport subassembly module.

The keyboard module produces the keyboards used in typewriters. The previous generation keyboard, which was manually assembled, had about 370 individual parts and was held together with 65 screws. The new keyboard has 11 parts, no screws and is assembled almost entirely by robots. Automated guided vehicles deliver parts to the keyboard line from an automated storage and retrieval system to the point of use. The new design makes it easy and cost effective to switch production from one model to another. Keybuttons are installed in groups of six of more by several robots. The line turns out a completed keyboard every 30 seconds.

Two testing systems check the mechanical parameters of each key position and the electrical characteristics of every switch. Another system takes a picture of the keyboard and compares it with a picture in computer memory to verify that the keybuttons are free of defects and in the correct locations. Once the keyboards have passed inspection, the automated guided vehicles transport them to buffer storage in the final assembly and test module.

The final assembly and test module produces seven typewriter models and three printer models interchangeably. It includes five miles of conveyors, 27 robotic assembly stations, 17 assembly stations with manual backup, 74 automated support stations, and 12 automated test stations. A computer system controlling the final assembly diverts the carrier either into or around the station, as appropriate. A bar code calls the programs needed to build that par-

---

[13]Adapted from Mehran Sepehri, "IBM's Automated Lexington Factory Focuses on Quality and Cost Effectiveness," *Industrial Engineering,* 19, no. 2, (1987): 66–74. Copyright Institute of Industrial Engineers, 25 Technology Park/Atlanta, Norcross, GA 30092.

ticular product. Therefore, changeover from one model to another in final assembly is done instantaneously.

In the test area immediately following final assembly, another bar-code reader examines the code on the carrier to program the test station for the product model being carried. One test for print quality uses a vision system to examine several printed characters to determine whether their shape, alignment, density, and skew meet specifications. Finished products that pass inspection are delivered to the packaging module.

One of the key features leading to the effectiveness of the facility has been the product design process. In the past, manufacturing was forced to react to new product plans turned out by development engineering. In this facility, the responsibilities for development and manufacturing were combined under a product manager. Designers were forced to anticipate automated assembly and design products that can be manufactured easily. For example, the IBM Selectric System/2000 typewriter is made with a layered design. The parts go together sequentially in one direction—from the bottom up—so that robots can do the job easily. There are many common fasteners, and nearly all screws were eliminated. Detailed parts were combined whenever possible. Self-alignment reference points were designed for locating such things as posts and countersinks. Since robots are not efficient at finding a plug at the end of a wire, integrated packaging and solid connectors had to be used. All these changes improved quality, reducing the repair rate significantly.

IBMs original objective was to produce high-quality, low-cost products, not necessarily to utilize automation. The technology was aquired selectively and some operations remained manual. Groups of manufacturing engineers and automation experts defined several goals and requirements, such as a desired cycle time or quality level for a particular set of operations. These defined objectives for interfaces between stations in manufacturing which provided ground rules for the extent of computer integrated manufacturing.

Senior management supported the project actively with financial and resource commitments. It was recognized that the automation project would not succeed without the cooperation and support of the employees. Therefore, the company instituted a communications program aimed at involving them in the plan. The program explained why the company had no choice but to automate to stay competitive. The employees had to learn about electronic technologies and automated assembly. They were candidly told that their jobs would be profoundly affected. Hundreds of employees were retrained as computer programmers and robotic system technicians. The plant was able to maintain full employment, and employee morale, as measured by an annual opinion survey, actually went up.

As a result of the project, the time to make a typewriter has been cut from four hours to one and significant cost savings have been realized. Customers now have more reliable equipment with additional functions at a lower price. The experience has brought a renewed respect for the importance of manufacturing.

QUESTIONS

1. What factors led IBM to automate their Lexington plant?
2. What are the modules that make up the manufacturing system?
3. Briefly describe the product design process used by IBM in automating the Lexington plant.
4. Briefly explain why IBM was able to automate the plant and still maintain employee morale.

SUMMARY   Automation and advanced technologies are dramatically changing the scope of manufacturing. Beginning with simple numerically controlled machine tools, we have seen the development of industrial robots, vision systems, automated identification systems, computer-aided design and manufacturing, and the recent integration of these technologies into flexible manufacturing and computer-integrated manufacturing systems. These technologies are not limited to manufacturing, as there are many examples of service organizations that have adopted such technologies and adapted them to their operations. While productivity, quality, and profitability are short-term benefits, there are a number of social and ethical concerns that the implementation of automation has raised. The answers are not clear but represent an important challenge to operations managers.

1. Discuss the major factors that have made automation and advanced technology important in manufacturing and service organizations.

2. Explain the relative advantages and disadvantages of humans versus machines and their implications for productivity and quality.

3. Explain the basic features of numerical control.

4. Describe a typical industrial robot. What are some of the common applications of robotics in manufacturing?

5. Discuss the various applications of vision systems in production.

6. How have automatic identification systems improved productivity and quality?

7. Explain the evolution of and differences among CAD, CAM, FMS, and CIMS.

8. Discuss the benefits and limitations of flexible manufacturing systems.

9. Discuss the applications of automation in materials handling.

10. List at least one application of automation in each of the following service industries:
    a. Financial services
    b. Public and government services
    c. Transportation services
    d. Health-care services
    e. Educational services
    f. Hotel and motel services

11. Find at least three new applications of automation in the service sector that are not discussed in this chapter. What impacts on productivity and quality do you think these applications have had?

12. Write a report discussing the changes as a result of automation that have been made in your own college or school of business. What advantages have the faculty and administrators seen as a result?

13. Discuss the impacts of automation on the labor force.

CINCINNATI MILACRON, INC. ROBOT WELDING[13]

Cincinnati Milacron, Inc. is engaged in the design, manufacture and sale of process equipment and systems for industry, along with the supplies and accessories sold for use in those systems. Formed as Cincinnati Screw and Tap Company in 1884,

---

[14]This case was written by James M. Comer and Marianne M. Hill under a grant entitled "Management Issues in High-Technology Manufacturing Industries," from the Cleveland Foundation of Cleveland, Ohio 44114. Used with permission.

the company originally sold screws, taps, and dies. The portion of the company devoted to milling machines was purchased in 1889 and named the Cincinnati Milling Machine Co.

In 1970 the Cincinnati Milling Machine Co. was renamed Cincinnati Milacron. By 1983 the company had eleven plants in the United States and eight overseas, employing some 10,000 people and having annual sales in excess of $500 million. Industry sources in 1983 ranked Cincinnati Milacron first in dollar sales of robotics in the United States although these sales represented less than ten percent of total company sales.

The company has three divisions: Machine Tools, Plastics Processing Machinery, and Industrial Specialty Products. The Machine Tool Division (see Figure 10.8) has a number of departments including Metal Fabrication. The welding shop and the foundry are two parts of the Metal Fabrication Division.

In the late 1960s Cincinnati Milacron had workable robotic technology. One of the first interests of management was the application of this new technology in other corporate divisions. One division that seemed to have a natural fit was in the Metal Fabrication Division because it had many repetitive jobs and the opportunity for significant cost savings.

In the early 1970s the division ignored the robotic technology. They showed no inclination to seek out and use the robots in their operations despite their apparent advantages. The president of Cincinnati Milacron, along with upper management, as an incentive, offered to provide robots without cost or overhead charges to the divisions. Despite this offer, no strong interest was evidenced in their adoption and use.

In the period 1977–79 an executive committee reviewed the entire company's manufacturing processes. One of their decisions was to apply the company's existing expertise in robot welding to the firm's own operations in the Metal Fabrication Division. They told the weld shop that a welding robot would be installed because:

1. other divisions of the company developed and marketed robots including robots for welding and they needed a readily available customer demonstration site. Thus an on-site application could be used as a marketing and selling tool
2. customer specific technological problems could be investigated in-house rather than going outside
3. there were some welding applications in Milacron's manufacturing process that would be improved by the use of robotic welding techniques. For example, Cincinnati Milacron welded box-type enclosures such as hydraulic

FIGURE 10.8

Partial Organizational Design

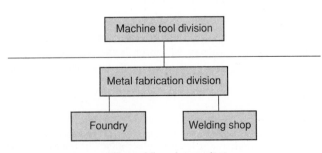

The welding shop project

tanks and electrical cabinets which were particularly appropriate for robotic applications.

Project Development and Implementation

The project was initiated in September 1980 when the feasibility study on the first welding robot indicated the potential for a good return on the investment. The first group that worked on the project consisted of a manager, an engineer who was familiar with welding, and a welder from another division brought in as a technician. None of them were experienced with robot welding.

The year 1981 was spent in the welding shop developing techniques and methods for the robot cell. The project initially experienced resistance by some people in the weld shop. In January 1982 the project was physically moved into the production area where its capabilities were demonstrated to the foundry management and welders alike. By June 1982 this resistance had disappeared with the demonstration of the robot welding hydraulic tanks. The quality, consistency, and speed of the robot dispelled any reluctance to adopt it. A second robot welder was requested by welding shop management and installation completed by January 1983. The third, devoted solely to heavy welding, was put into operation in July 1983.

Initial Situation

Prior to 1980 the welding shop consisted of well trained and closely supervised people hand welding both light (16 gauge to ¼″) and thick (up to 3″) metals. Spot and arc welding were used on the light metals with arc welding exclusively applied to heavier plate metal. Typical welding problems were "warping" (the heat induced from the welding caused the light metals to bend) and "seam tracking" (keeping the weld straight) in the heavy welding. In the manual welding operation when the welder received a job, he would put the parts to be welded on a welding table or the floor, move them around until he achieved the desired angle, and then hold them down with hand clamps or his foot while he performed the necessary welding.

Robot Installation and Workforce

In 1982 when the initial robot welder was installed in the shop, management chose not to use an experienced welder to operate the robot. In fact, a person was selected and trained to operate it who had had no previous welding experience. The reason was quite simply that management knew that experienced welders would find it difficult, if not impossible, to ignore their own training and years of experience and operate the machine accordingly. Training of a new person to the necessary proficiency to operate the robot required about six months, although he could operate the robot adequately with one month's training. On the other hand training of a manual welder to perform simple seam welding required about five to six weeks. Training a welder to interpret engineering drawings and competently assemble a variety of pieces required about one year. The existing workforce of manual welders were promised that only new work would be given to the robots.

Applications of Robot Welding

The company found that the installation of the robot had a number of effects both on the operation of the welding shop as well as in operations upstream and

FIGURE 10.9
Robot Ladder

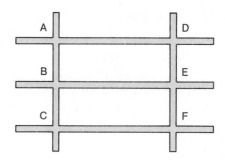

downstream from it. In the welding of tanks, ladders, and cabinets these effects could be readily seen.

Customers of the company used or sold tanks to hold such products as liquids. Previously these tanks were welded by hand on both the inside and the outside of the tanks and, when completed, these welds usually had to be sanded smooth. There were some problems with weld quality on these tanks so this operation was chosen as the first application for robot welding. When the robot first started welding these tanks, it was programmed to weld both the inside and outside just as the manual welder had done. Very quickly, however, management found that the robot was so accurate and steady that only one side had to be welded. This reduced welding cost and production time while increasing the quality of the finished product. The quality was so reliable that pressure and leak testing were no longer necessary. An additional unexpected benefit was that the robot weld was so smooth that it required little or no finishing.

A second instance where the robot proved its value was in the welding of robot ladders (see Figure 10.9). The human welder was instructed to weld in a pattern such as A, E, C, D, B, F so that heat wouldn't build up in one area causing warpage and having to scrap the ladders because they were "out of square." At first, under direct supervision and instruction, the welder would weld the ladder in the proper sequence. An experienced welder typically could do about two to three ladders a day. Without direct supervision, however, welders too often succumbed to the temptation to weld it in the quickest manner such as A, D, E, B, C, F. The result was that the ladder scrappage rate commonly ran as much as 33% of production.

Given the problems in the ladder welding, the robot welder was assigned to weld ladders. The robot, however, did exactly as it was programmed to do time after time with no variation. It was able to weld five ladders a day perfectly and with no scrappage.

In welding box-type enclosures such as electrical cabinets, there is considerable accuracy necessary in the cutting and bending process prior to welding. A sheet of metal is cut in the shape illustrated in Figure 10.10 and the four peninsulas are then bent upward to form a box. The corners must then be welded and finished to have a solid product. When the company relied on hand welding the welder would take the pieces of metal, put them in a convenient spot (usually on the floor!), twist them around to the proper angle by hand or hoist as was needed to complete the job. If the worker saw an improper cut or bend he would "adjust" for the difference by twisting or bending the metal by force. He could also compensate for imperfections by adjusting the welding process.

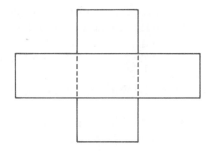

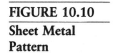

FIGURE 10.10
Sheet Metal
Pattern

A robot is not able to identify imperfections in the metal sheets and make on-the-spot adjustments. Thus the installation of the robot to weld cabinets dictated that a number of changes be made both upstream of the welding operation as well as in the operation itself. First, the company had to design, acquire, and install a complete set of relatively elaborate fixturing to hold the metal parts at precisely the right position and angle every time. Second, when two pieces of metal did not match properly, the robot could not compensate by bending or twisting the metal until it matched as did a human operator. Thus the company had to buy new shears to cut parts more accurately and a new break press to bend the metal more precisely.

In all three operations the robot's speed and accuracy had direct impacts on middle management's planning requirements. For example, management had to be much more accurate in acquiring raw materials as well as maintaining in-process inventory to avoid machine downtime. In addition, materials handling equipment and procedures had to be more closely monitored to insure compatibility with robot operation.

Evaluation

The company conducted a number of post audits of the impact of the robot welding process on shop operation. They were uniformly favorable in that the robot quality was not only higher than the human operator but it was also more consistent. From a marketing and sales perspective however, only three or four general customer tours visited the robot-welding operation. Reportedly no customers or prospective customers requested or were given direct experience with the robot welding process.

As of June 1983 the welding robots were being used solely on new business with none of the existing welders replaced by the technology. Management's objective was to have some eighty percent of Cincinnati Milacron's welding operations performed by robot in the future.

In general, management was extremely pleased with the installation and operation of the robot welding process. Problems arose with the initial installation but these were viewed as minor compared to the improvement in the welding operation.

Questions for Analysis

1. Why did the Metal Fabrication Division managers not seek out the robotic technology even though it offered significant cost advantages and was a "free good"?

2. Why Milacron's upper management did management choose to use a development team that was relatively inexperienced with robotics?
3. Was there anything unusual about the justification for introducing this technology in this case? Why? Was there any implicit reason for the introduction?
4. What changes were caused by this new technology? What can be learned from the results?
5. Does an in-house demonstration site seem to be the best way to market a product/process? What do you expect might have gone wrong? What other alternatives are there? What are the implications of choosing another alternative?
6. What assumption(s) did the firm make when they promised that only "new work" would go to the robot? What are the firm's responsibilities to the welders?

TACTICS AND OPERATIONS IN P/OM

T actical and operational issues in P/OM involve a much shorter time horizon than do strategic and design issues. Tactics and operations deal primarily with the *implementation* of the production system.

In Chapter 11, we discuss job design and work measurement, and the methods for effectively incorporating human skills into the production system. Chapter 12 introduces materials management and inventory policy, and in Chapter 13 we present a variety of quantitative models for inventory analysis and control.

Chapter 14 begins a three-chapter sequence on production planning. Chapter 14 focuses on aggregate production planning and master scheduling. These tools are used to plan levels of future production over a time horizon of several months to a year. These plans must be translated into detailed schedules for the production or purchase of the components that comprise the goods that are produced. Chapter 15, Material Requirements Planning, describes this process of timing production and purchasing, and in Chapter 16 we focus on short-range scheduling issues and production-activity control.

Chapter 17 presents a discussion of just-in-time, an approach to material control that has received considerable interest because it has been successfully used by the Japanese. In Chapter 18 we discuss project management techniques, and finally, in Chapter 19, we address the subject of quality control.

Job Design and Work Measurement

I n previous chapters we have focused on the location and design of the physical facilities that are necessary to support production. Although a significant amount of automation has been incorporated in many factories, human beings still control a large amount of the production process. Therefore, the design of jobs for individual workers is an important issue in P/OM.

By a **job** we mean the set of tasks that an individual performs. **Job design** involves the determination of specific job tasks and responsibilities, the work environment, and the methods by which these tasks will be carried out to meet the goals of production. There are two broad objectives that must be satisfied in job design. One is to meet the goals of productivity and quality in production; the other is to make the job safe, satisfying, and motivating for the individual worker.

Job design has traditionally been viewed principally in the context of blue-collar jobs on the factory floor. The jobs of blue-collar workers are more easily defined and measured than for white-collar workers; work can be divided into specific tasks and performance can be compared to a standard. White-collar work, on the other hand, is more intangible, and outputs are often difficult to define and measure. However, with the increase in the use of high-technology equipment as well as the expanding service sector, the need for blue-collar workers is decreasing. Thus, more attention is being paid to job design for white-collar workers.

In this chapter we focus on the technical and social aspects of job design and the related topic of work measurement. Work measurement is needed in order to know how long it takes for a job to be accomplished. Such information is used to estimate work-force and capacity requirements and is also used to measure performance in production control. It is important that operations managers understand these technical issues and their implications for productivity and quality.

11.1 THE IMPORTANCE OF JOB DESIGN

To better understand the importance of job design in production and operations management, it is useful to examine some history. During the scientific management era of Frederick Taylor, management sought to reduce the cost and increase productivity through increased mechanization and specialization of job tasks. One rationale for this approach was that workers who require fewer skills can be more easily trained. In addition, since little education is required for repetitive work, lower wages can be offered. Thus, proponents of increased mechanization and specialization argued that higher output could be achieved and production could be better controlled.

It has been found that extreme division of labor results in boredom, fatigue, and minimum worker satisfaction. With mechanization, the worker often cannot control the work pace and sees no future opportunities for learning and progress. During the 1930s, as a result of the Western Electric Hawthorne experiments, job designers began to turn their attention to issues of worker satisfaction rather than pure productivity concerns. We briefly touched on some of these issues in Chapter 9 while discussing assembly-line balancing. There, we discussed the importance of including behavioral considerations, along with efficiency, in process design.

The traditional approach to job design, based on division of labor, has made it difficult for many industries to succeed in today's internationally competitive markets. Collective bargaining and unionization, while curing many past ills of manufacturing, have also over the years resulted in restrictive work rules, narrowly defined jobs, and a labor-management schism that impedes cooperation. In many cases, the result has been high costs, poor quality, and reduced flexibility.

The Japanese have taken a different approach based on more broadly defined jobs and labor-management cooperation. For example, when Toyota and General Motors embarked on a joint venture in California, Toyota insisted that the plant be allowed to operate without restrictive job classifications. No more than three assembly-worker job classifications were permitted (as opposed to some 25 in other U.S. plants).[1] More recently, we have seen unions accepting work-rule changes, such as allowing crafts to be combined in task assignments, having equipment operators run more than one machine, restricting "bumping" practices, using job rotation, and so on. These flexible approaches are producing increases in productivity.[2]

Developing effective job designs is a critical task for the operations managers. An effective job design enables a worker to perform his or her task better. Higher levels of productivity and quality and lower costs to the firm can be obtained. Performance is enhanced, and the individual derives greater satisfaction from the work.

Another reason for the importance of job design relates to the cost of job-related injuries. The Bureau of Labor Statistics estimated that there were 5 million work-related injuries in 1980, of which approximately 1 million were back injuries. Industry cost was in the $5 billion to $10 billion range for back injuries alone. The design of the physical workplace can have a significant effect on reducing injuries resulting from poor material handling practices and environmental effects.

Job design techniques can also be used to design jobs that utilize more of the total work force. In the past, physically demanding jobs were designed for young,

---

[1] "UAW Studies Concessions While Seeking Success Formula for GM-Toyota Venture," *Wall Street Journal*, 21 July 1983.

[2] "A Work Revolution in US Industry: More Flexible Rules on the Job are Boosting Productivity," *Business Week*, 16 May 1983.

strong males. By redesigning such jobs, the available labor pool can often be increased, thereby providing the firm with additional flexibility in meeting demand during changes in production volume or when new products are added. Good job design also helps to eliminate causes of human error, thus increasing quality and reducing cost. Finally, the analysis of jobs can help in identifying opportunities for automation improvements.

The resolution of conflicts between the need for technical and economic efficiency and employee satisfaction is the challenge that faces managers in designing jobs. Clearly, efficiency is needed for a firm to remain competitive. However, it is also clear that any organization that has a large percentage of dissatisfied employees cannot be competitive either.

Recent trends in operations suggest that job design is becoming even more important.[3] Direct manufacturing jobs are becoming increasingly mechanized. This means one individual worker can control more of the production process. Just a few workers can often control an automated plant; thus it is critical that the workforce be reliable and dedicated. We are also beginning to see many tasks that cannot be mechanized performed outside of the country where labor costs are lower.

The current trend toward more automation creates more "monitoring" jobs than "doing" jobs. Such jobs can be incompatiable with workers' expectations and education. Workers are becoming more highly educated and their expectations for rewarding work are greater than ever. Today's workforce wants challenge, opportunity, recognition, and respect. Jobs must be designed for people; while mechanization is designed for processing material. The factory of the future depends on the successful integration of mechanization and job design.

11.2 THE SCOPE OF JOB DESIGN

The major elements of job design fall into three categories: *the physical environment, the social or psychological environment,* and *work methods.* The design of the physical environment and the social or psychological environment are in turn the key factors to be considered in developing good work methods.

The physical environment includes the individual's workplace and the surrounding environment. The workplace should be designed to assist and not hinder the worker in task performance. For example, the angle and height of a secretary's chair can have a profound effect on back fatigue and, consequently, job performance. The distance an assembly worker must reach for an object or the size of a visual gauge are additional examples of physiological factors that should be considered. Machines, equipment, and tools should be in good repair, and the worker should have the necessary inputs of materials and information to accomplish his or her task. The working environment should not threaten the health of the worker or distract the worker from accomplishing the tasks of the job. Environmental factors such as lighting, noise, and temperature are factors that affect not only a worker's physical well-being but also his or her psychological and social attitude.

---

[3]Kelvin F. Cross, "The Factory of the Future Depends on Successful Integration of Automation and Job Design," *Industrial Engineering,* 18, no. 1, (1986): 14–18.

The social and psychological environment must provide workers positive motivation to perform their jobs in a quality fashion and achieve a sense of satisfaction. As demonstrated by Maslow, a worker cannot be motivated by pride in one's work unless basic human needs are first satisfied. The worker must have a sense of job security and be compensated on a fair basis. There must be some comprehension of what is expected from the job and how the work fits in the overall scheme of things. Workers need challenges and opportunities for personal growth in their jobs; team concepts and broader responsibilities have become important. Every effort must be made to involve workers in their work and any changes that affect their work. There must be appropriate incentives and rewards for achieving manufacturing goals and objectives and not just for output produced. The work environment has a social structure, with official and unofficial activities, beliefs, and interactions. Job design must address both the formal and informal social structure.

Finally, jobs must be designed to take advantage of the best attributes of the machine and worker; hence the worker must be trained in proper work methods. This not only helps to improve productivity and quality but makes the job easier for the worker and increases satisfaction. The design of work methods involves the reduction of unnecessary movements or the simplification of tasks by using improved tools and fixtures.

These principles apply not only to blue-collar jobs but to white-collar jobs as well, although the emphasis is different. For example, in most white-collar work, the input to the workplace is generally information instead of materials.

The consideration of both the technology of production and the social aspects of the work environment, called the *sociotechnical approach* to job design, has been prevalent since the 1950s. What is sought is a job design that provides for high levels of productivity and quality, while at the same time providing a satisfying job and work environment. The shaded region of Figure 11.1 depicts the type of design we seek when employing the sociotechnical approach. The sociotechnical approach emphasizes the need for integrating the social consequences of work with the traditional cost and quality considerations of production. Considerations such as the costs of employee turnover, training, and absenteeism that might result from a lack of job satisfaction may lead management to sacrifice cost savings in production efficiency in order to achieve greater cost savings in these other areas.

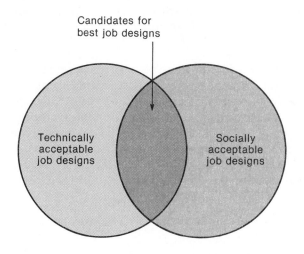

FIGURE 11.1

The Sociotechnical Approach to Job Design

The environment in which a worker performs his or her job is an important consideration for operations management. If not properly designed, the work environment can be distracting and result in reduced productivity. It can even be dangerous to the employees' health. In designing the physical work environment, one must consider both human factors and the surrounding environment.

Principles of Ergonomics

Ergonomics, or **human-factors engineering,** is concerned with improving productivity by designing workplaces, tools, instruments, and so on that take into account the physical capabilities of people. According to Huchingson,[4] the objectives of a human-factors program are to improve human performance by increasing speed, accuracy, and safety; to reduce energy requirements and fatigue; to reduce the amount and cost of training and special skills; to reduce accidents because of human error; and to improve the comfort and acceptance by the user.

Ergonomics is derived from the Greek word for work. Ergonomists suggest that machines be designed to meet the needs of the user. Ergonomics developed as a discipline during World War II when analysts concluded that the death of many pilots was due to the fact that they could not master the complicated controls of their airplanes. The problem continued to grow because as aircraft technology developed, so did the need for more instruments. For instance, the P-51 fighter of 1940 had 21 instruments and the F-100 in 1965 had 46 instruments. In 1980, when the F-15 fighter was introduced, the problem of displaying vital pilot information required 33 basic dials. Because no pilot could simultaneously keep track of this much information, five small cathode-ray tubes (CRTs) were installed in order to highlight only information that was pertinent at the time.

Ergonomics is used in a variety of consumer products. Kodak, for example, has some 40 ergonomists to assist in the design of cameras and copiers as well as improving work in its own factories. The window-level stoplight required in 1986 model cars was the result of ergonomic analysis.

Ergonomics draws information from a variety of disciplines. Among the areas of knowledge that a human-factors specialist must develop are *physical anthropology, work physiology,* and *biomechanics.* Knowledge from these fields is applied to the physical design of workplaces and the development of efficient work methods. Let us first briefly discuss the importance of this knowledge.

Physical Anthropology

Human beings have a wide range of body characteristics, such as height, arm length, and strength. Physical anthropologists provide important input for workplace design by developing statistical profiles on such characteristics. These data are called **anthropometric data.** An example of anthropometric data is given in Table 11.1 for two-handed reach while standing. Typically, these data are presented statistically for different percentiles of the population. For example, the 25th percentile has a depth of reach of 21 inches. This means that at least 25 percent of the population has a maximum reach of 21 inches or less and at least

---

[4]R. Dale Huchingson, *New Horizons for Human Factors in Design,* New York: McGraw-Hill, 1981, p. 7.

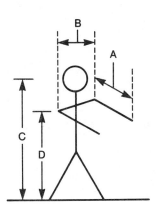

TABLE 11.1
Standing Two-arm Reach (Inches)

Characteristic		Percentile				
		5th	25th	50th	75th	95th
Reach	A	19.25	21.00	22.25	22.75	24.50
Shoulder width	B	15.50	17.00	17.75	18.50	19.50
Height to eye level	C	61.00	63.50	65.25	66.50	69.00
Height to shoulder level	D	52.25	54.75	56.00	57.25	59.00

Source: K. W. Kennedy and B. E. Filler, "Aperature Sizes and Depths of Reach for One- and Two-handed Tasks," Report No. AMRL-TR-66-27, Aerospace Medical Research Labs, Wright Patterson Air Force Base, 1966.

75 percent has a maximum reach of 21 inches or more. Similarly, only 5 percent of the population has a reach of at least 24.5 inches or more. Anthropometric data assist designers in developing workplaces that are comfortable and functional for the operators intended to use them.

Work Physiology and Biomechanics

Work physiology data are usually obtained through experimental observation and measurement. Heart rate and oxygen consumption are monitored and converted into energy use. For example, Table 11.2 illustrates the energy expenditure in kilocalories per minute (a kilocalorie is 1000 calories and is often called the "large calorie"—the layperson's notion of "calorie") associated for various jobs studied at Eastman Kodak. How can this data be applied in job design? Jobs with higher energy demands naturally require more rest. A formula for estimating the amount of rest required for a particular job is[5]

$$ R = \frac{T(K - S)}{K - 1.5} $$

where

R = minutes of rest required
T = total working time in minutes
K = energy expenditure
S = adopted standard of energy expenditure (for example, 2–5 kcal/min)

---

[5]K.F.H. Murrell, *Human Performance in Industry,* New York: Reinhold Publishing Corp., 1965.

<table>
<tr><td rowspan="3">**TABLE 11.2**
Average Energy
Expenditure for
Selected Jobs</td></tr>
</table>

Job	Energy Expenditure (Kilocalories per Minute)
Unload coal cars in power plant	8.0
Handling 38 pounds of chemicals	6.5
Mixing powdered chemicals	6.0
Loading corrugated cartons of product into boxcars	6.0
Tending cartoning machine	5.2
Cleaning production department	4.9
Handling 46-pound cans of chemicals	4.4
Ash removal in power plant (94°F)	4.0
Packing on conveyor	3.7
Unloading rolls of film at slitter windup	3.5
Motion-picture film wrapping	3.0
Coal displacer operator	2.1

Source: H.L. Davis, T.W. Faulkner, and C.I. Miller, "Work Physiology," *Human Factors,* 11, no. 2 (1969): 157–166. Copyright © 1969 by The Human Factors Society, Inc., and reproduced by permission.

Thus if $S = 4$ is used as the energy standard, a worker unloading coal cars in a power plant requires

$$R = \frac{60(8 - 4)}{8 - 1.5} \approx 37$$

minutes of rest for each 60-minute period, while a worker mixing powdered chemicals requires only

$$R = \frac{60(6 - 4)}{6 - 1.5} \approx 27$$

minutes.

Workplace Design

In designing a workplace, three categories of anthropometric data are generally used: the range of visual capability, the reach of arms and legs, and the support of the human body. A number of questions should be addressed.

1. *Who will use the workplace?* Anthropometric data for males and females are different; military personnel have different characteristics than the average citizen.
2. *How will the work be performed?* The number of tools required and the frequency of use and specific work methods often dictate feasible designs.
3. *What must the user see?* The placement of controls or blueprints and the need to see outside the immediate workplace must be considered.
4. *What must the user be able to hear?* The communication requirements with other workers and the need to hear warning sounds may be an important factor.
5. *What must the user be able to reach?* This often determines whether the operator should be seated or standing.

Figure 11.2 illustrates a suggested design of a workplace for an operator seated at a console-type work station (such as a computer terminal or radar screen). This design is appropriate for males in the 5th to 95th percentile range. Note that visual requirements, reach capability, and posture are all addressed in the design.

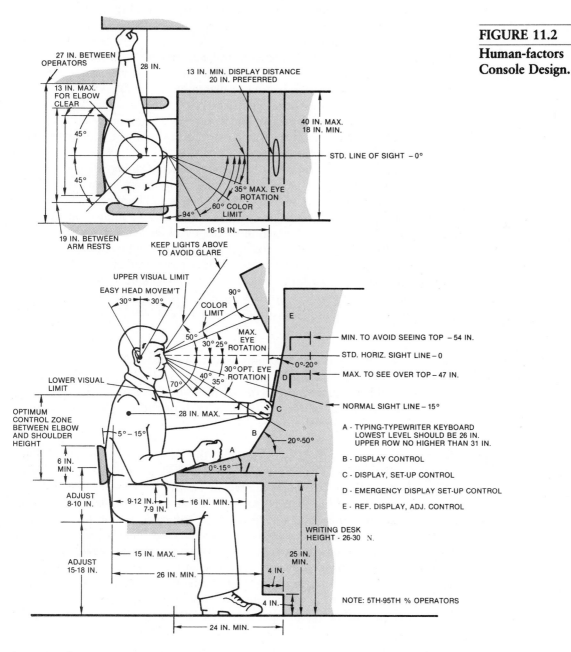

FIGURE 11.2
Human-factors Console Design.

Source: Van Cott and Kinkade, *Human Engineering Guide to Equipment Design,* U.S. Government Printing Office, 1972. Adapted from H. Dreyfuss, *The Measure of Man,* Whitney Library of Design, New York, 1959. Reprinted by permission of The Whitney Library of Design, an imprint of Watson-Guptill Publications.

Workplace Design for Knowledge Workers

The increase in white-collar positions, particularly those often referred to as "knowledge workers," presents special demands on workplace design.[6] What is needed is a work station that facilitates a worker's access to the tools, equipment, material, and information necessary to perform a task. Logical traffic flow from worker to worker, worker to equipment, and worker to other departments is also vital. In addition, a good work station should be automatically self-adjusting (with manual overrides) and should accommodate a wide spectrum of workers with diverse anthropometric measures such as weight, height, and reach.

In its present form, the knowledge-worker's work station may be divided into a series of major components such as seat, desk, storage containers, information storage/retrieval, data-entry equipment, and accessories. A limited number of techniques have been used to evaluate the design of the work seat. Generally, some form of subjective rating is used to determine preferable work seats. The resulting work seats tend to have high back rests, tilt characteristics, mobility via casters, crude height adjustments, and arm rests. The majority do not incorporate ergonomic factors, because all too often, office furniture is designed from a predominantly esthetic point of view.

Information storage and retrieval is of major concern to knowledge workers. Although the most advanced method for such activity is the computer, the majority of white-collar workers still utilize file cabinets and bookcases. Telephones have become critical to knowledge workers. Considerable improvements have been made in the design and function of the telephone, including pushbutton keyboards, call forwarding, conferencing, speed dialing, and computer interface.

There is considerable opportunity for advancing the state of automation with regard to working conditions for knowledge workers. A comprehensive, ergonomics-based design would provide significant benefits in increasing productivity and employee morale. One proposed design is shown in Figure 11.3.

Safety and the Physical Environment

To provide healthy working conditions and reduce hazards in the work environment, the Occupational Safety and Health Act (OSHA) was passed in 1970. As a result of this legislation, the National Institute of Occupational Safety and Health (NIOSH) was formed to enforce standards provided by OSHA. Business and industry are required to abide by OSHA guidelines or face potential fines and penalties.

Industrial safety is a function of the job, the human operator, and the surrounding environment. The job should be designed so that it will be highly unlikely that a worker can injure himself or herself. This means, for instance, that equipment should be designed so that moving parts are guarded or out of reach. At the same time, the worker must be educated in the proper use of equipment and the methods designed to perform the job. Finally, the surrounding environment must be conducive to safety. This might include providing nonslip surfaces, warning signs, or buzzers. Specific environmental factors that can influence productivity and health are lighting, temperature and humidity, and noise.

The type and amount of illumination required depends on the nature of the job. For example, difficult inspection tasks and close assembly work require more

---

[6]Richard L. Shell, O. Geoffrey Okogbaa, and Thomas R. Huston, "The Work Station of the Future for Knowledge Workers," *Industrial Engineering,* 17, no. 8 (August 1985): 55–62. Copyright 1985 Institute of Industrial Engineers, 25 Technology Park/Atlanta, Norcross, GA 30092.

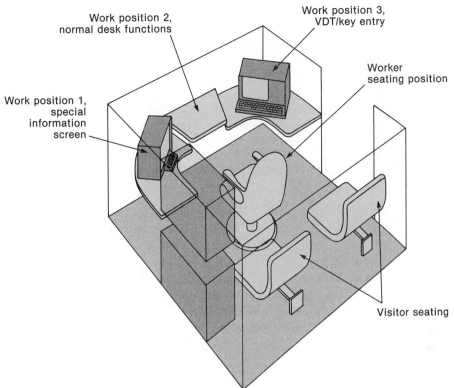

Work position 2, normal desk functions

Work position 3, VDT/key entry

Worker seating position

Work position 1, special information screen

Visitor seating

Source: Shell *et al.*

FIGURE 11.3

Overview of Knowledge-Worker Work Module

light than operating a milling machine or loading crates in a warehouse. Illumination is measured by *footcandles,* a measure of the amount of light generated by an ordinary candle at a distance of 1 foot. There are published guidelines for illumination requirements for different jobs. To illustrate, the *IES Lighting Handbook* (IES, New York, 1972) recommends the illumination for rough bench and machine work to be 50 footcandles, while for extra-fine bench and machine work, the recommended requirement is 1000 footcandles. Similarly, drafting requires 200 footcandles, sorting mail requires 100 footcandles, and so on. The quality characteristics of light also vary. Glare, brightness, contrast, and uniformity may contribute to eye strain and reduce job performance. These factors should be considered in designing individual workplaces as well as offices and factories.

Temperature and humidity affect a person's comfort and can be a very distracting influence on productivity. A temperature in the low 60s might be ideal for lifting boxes in a warehouse in overalls and gloves but may chill a typist's fingers in an office. Because of recent energy considerations, federal and state regulations have set minimum temperatures of 75° to 78° in the summer and maximum temperatures of 65° to 68° in the winter for many buildings. Temperatures beyond these extremes can be uncomfortable or a health hazard. Some jobs require such extremes—for example, in a meat-packing plant or in industrial areas where considerable heat is generated by machinery. A number of alternatives exist for operations managers in situations like these. Some of these include adjusting the humidity (higher temperatures can be tolerated at lower humidity levels); increasing air circulation in high-temperature areas; limiting exposure through rest periods or job rotation; and simply providing adequate protection.

A third environmental factor that is often a problem is noise. Noise levels are measured in decibels. A 10-decibel increase is equivalent to multiplying the sound intensity by 10; that is, decibel levels of 20 and 30 have sound intensities of 100 and 1000, respectively. Intense noise over long periods of time can result in impaired hearing. OSHA has set limits on acceptable noise levels and duration. For example, a worker may sustain a 90-decibel noise level for 9 hours. The worker must be protected from levels exceeding this standard. This can be done by controlling the source of noise, absorbing the sound, increasing the distance from the sound, or providing ear protection. Other noises can simply be annoying; however, we learn to tune out many ordinary sounds. Often, companies provide background music as a means of blending random noises in an office or factory and providing a pleasant atmosphere.

11.4 DESIGN OF THE SOCIAL AND PSYCHOLOGICAL ENVIRONMENT

In addition to the physical comfort and well-being of workers, proper attention must also be paid to behavioral issues. Adequate training and supervision must be provided. Employees must know company policies, rules, and regulations; they must know what is expected of them, be instructed properly in the performance of their job, and be given credit for a job well done and constructive criticism regarding mistakes.

Motivation is of particular importance, and jobs must be designed in such a way as to motivate individuals to perform at peak levels. In this section, we review the behavioral issues of motivation, job enlargement, and job enrichment with emphasis on their importance in job design.

Motivation

Human motivation may be defined as an individual's response to a felt need. Thousands of studies have been performed over the years on human and animal subjects in attempts to understand and refine the concept of motivation. It is an extremely complex phenomenon that is not fully understood.

Many theories of work motivation have been developed by behavioral scientists over the past 75 years. These can be classified as *content* and *process models*. Content models describe how and why people are motivated to work. Two of the best-known content theories are the Hierarchy of Needs theory developed by Abraham Maslow and the Two-Factor theory developed by Frederick Herzberg. You may have studied these in previous management courses.

Process models tend to focus on the dynamic process of how individuals make choices in an effort to obtain desired rewards. Included in this category are the expectancy concepts of Kurt Lewin and E.C. Tolman, B.F. Skinner's reinforcement model, Victor Vroom's valence/expectancy model, and the performance/satisfaction approach of Porter and Lawler. Reviews of these theories can be found in other sources; here we focus very specifically on the motivational aspects of task design.

The Hackman and Oldham model, shown in Figure 11.4, has been proposed to help explain the motivational properties of job design by tying together the technical and human components of a job. This model is an effective operationalization of earlier motivation theories and research studies. It draws heavily on the work of Herzberg and others and has been validated in numerous organizational settings. The model contains four major parts

1. critical psychological states
2. core job characteristics
3. moderating variables
4. outcomes

Three critical psychological states drive the model. Experienced meaningfulness is the psychological need of workers to have the feeling that their work is a significant contribution to the organization and society. Experienced responsibility indicates the need of workers to be accountable for the quality and quantity of their work. Knowledge of results implies that there is a need felt by all workers to know how their work is evaluated and what the results of the evaluation are.

Five core job characteristics have an impact on the critical psychological states. These are

1. Task significance. The degree to which the job gives the participant the feeling that it has a substantial impact on the organization, or the world.
2. Task identity. The degree to which the worker can perceive the task as a whole, identifiable piece of work from start to finish.
3. Skill variety. The degree to which the job requires the worker to have and to use a variety of skills and talents.
4. Autonomy. The degree to which the task permits freedom, independence, and personal control to be exercised over the work.

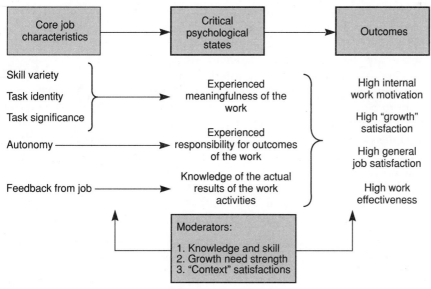

FIGURE 11.4

Complete Job Characteristics Model of Hackman and Oldham

Source: J. Richard Hackman and Greg R. Oldham, *Work Redesign.* Copyright © 1980, Addison-Wesley Publishing Co., Inc., Reading, Massachusetts. Reprinted with permission.

5. Feedback from the job. The degree to which clear, timely information about the effectiveness of individual performance is available.

An example illustrating characteristics of the Hackman and Oldham model is the case of a small Delaware firm that produces space suits for astronauts. The work requires a great deal of hand crafting, using conventional sewing machinery as well as high technology in testing the suits for proper functioning. Task significance and task identity are evident in the workers' ability to see the job as being of extreme importance and as fitting into a complete unit. Skill variety and autonomy are somewhat limited, since conventional sewing techniques must be used and rigid specifications must be precisely followed. However, other motivating aspects of the job may compensate for the lack of these characteristics. Feedback on results is timely and individualized.

Job Enlargement and Enrichment

During the scientific management era, operations managers sought to improve productivity through division of labor and increased specialization. However, for the assembly-line worker who simply tightens bolts all day, there is little challenge or self-esteem in the job. Morale is not high, and workers are often not concerned about quality. As a result, there are often more rejects and scrap, and productivity suffers. In later years, it has been discovered that productivity and quality can be enhanced by making work tasks more important to the worker, by challenging and developing a worker's abilities, by granting increased responsibility, and by allowing the worker to see the results of his or her efforts.

Job enlargement is the reverse of specialization. It is horizontal expansion of the job to give the worker more variety, although not more responsibility. Job enlargement might be accomplished, for example, by giving a production-line worker the task of building an entire product rather than a small subassembly, or it might, for example, be accomplished by job rotation, such as rotating nurses among hospital wards or flight crews on different airline routes. The loss in efficiency of specialization can often be made up in the long run by better motivation, reduced turnover, and lower costs. This increases the *effectiveness* of the firm.

Job enrichment is vertical expansion of job duties to give the worker more responsibility. For instance, an assembly worker may be given the added responsibility of testing a completed assembly; in this fashion he or she acts also as a quality inspector. A prime example of job enrichment is the quality-circle concept to be discussed shortly. By giving a group of workers the responsibility for solving problems of production and quality control, management has increased the variety of skills and abilities that the worker uses, made the job more meaningful, and given the worker more involvement in decision making and feedback.

IBM's philosophy on job design is based on principles put forth by its founder, Thomas J. Watson, Sr. and the past chairperson, Thomas J. Watson, Jr.[7] These principles are summarized in three points.

1. respect for the individual
2. a goal of providing superior customer service

---

[7]Raymond J. Kimber, "IBM Combines High Tech with the Personal Touch," *Quality*, 22, (November 1983): 18–21.

3. a belief of pursuing all tasks with the idea that they can be accomplished in a superior way

During the past 40 years, no IBM employee has been laid off because of a shortage of work. Instead, when employees are no longer needed for one job, they are retrained and reassigned to other departments or divisions. Many years ago, IBM eliminated piecework in all plants. Managers and workers were rated on the basis of their overall contribution to the company rather than solely on the basis of the number of items they produced. IBM uses job enlargement and job enrichment extensively. Whenever possible, workers set up their own machines and perform their own inspection. In jobs that are repetitious, employees are rotated periodically, giving them an opportunity to learn new skills and avoid monotony.

This is not to say that job enlargement and job enrichment are magical cures for problems involving job satisfaction and productivity. Indeed, there have been some sharp criticisms levied against job enrichment. Mitchell Fein[8] notes a number of job-enrichment programs at major corporations that have not been successful and concludes that pay, job security, and work rules are of primary concern to blue-collar workers. Saari and Lahtela[9] suggest that job enrichment may be the cause of increased accidents when proper planning has not occurred. We conclude by stating that there are many pros and cons regarding job enrichment and job enlargement. Dealing with the inexactness and uncertainties of human behavior makes job design all the more difficult for the operations manager.

Work Groups and Employee Involvement

The purpose of job enlargement is to increase the scope of job tasks for an individual worker. One way to do this is to build a *team* of workers that can perform all tasks in the group. This approach has several advantages. First there is considerable flexibility; if one worker is absent, others can perform his or her duties. Teams enhance esprit de corps among the members, thereby improving their attitudes and overall job satisfaction, as well as increase concern for productivity and quality. Also, problem solving is more effective in groups because it tends to lead to higher degrees of creativity.

McManus and Sentore discuss their experiences in team organization at Eaton Corporation Controls Division.[10] In an effort to increase productivity, a "productivity team" was established in the spring of 1979 at one of Eaton's manufacturing plants. The team included several plant engineers, one supervisor, and one hourly assembler. The purpose of the team was to improve the workplace layout at an assembly operation. This was accomplished by reducing reaches, improving parts layouts, and, where necessary, building new containers. The results of the team's efforts was a workplace that led to higher efficiency and an increase in productivity. Later, a second productivity team was formed, consisting of one supervisor and four assemblers. This was in response to the success of the

---

[8]Mitchell Fein, "Job Enrichment: A Reevaluation," *Sloan Management Review,* 15, no. 2 (1974): 69–88.

[9]J. T. Saari and J. Lahtela, "Job Enrichment: Cause of Increased Accidents?" *Industrial Engineering,* 10, no. 10 (1978): 41–45.

[10]Ross McManus and Frank Sentore, "Employee Participation Programs that Improve Productivity and Quality," *Proceedings, 1984 Annual International Industrial Engineering Conference,* Norcross, Georgia: Institute of Industrial Engineers, 1984, pp. 297–299.

first team and interest among other hourly employees. The productivity team concept generated considerable enthusiasm among employees, whose desire to contribute their experience and knowledge with management was evident.

Participative approaches to problem solving, such as work groups, hold the promise of breaking down barriers between labor and management, designers and engineers, line and staff, and other groups that often relate to each other in an adversarial fashion. Participative problem solving approaches have been found to increase worker satisfaction and morale, improve quality, increase productivity, and better develop worker skills.

Today, a number of labels are being applied to various participative team, or employee involvement (EI), approaches used in organizations. Some of these are "quality of worklife (QWL)," "productivity action teams," and "quality circles." While every approach is somewhat unique, all are focused on using the skills, experience, and knowledge of employees to improve productivity and quality. Quality circles, which have had phenomenal success in Japan, is discussed next.

Quality Circles

The term **quality control circles** (QCCs) was coined in Japan in the early 1960s and brought to the United States in the early 1970s. It took five years for the concept to begin to blossom in the United States. QCCs blend participative management approaches with classical problem solving, work simplification, and statistical quality control techniques to improve productivity as well as quality. The term *quality control circles* was shortened to *quality circles* (QCs), which is in common use in the United States.

A **quality circle** is a small group of employees from the same work area who meet regularly and voluntarily to identify, solve, and implement solutions to work-related problems. Quality circles have some unique characteristics.[11]

- Quality circles are small groups, ranging from 4 to 15 members. Eight members is considered the norm.
- All members come from the same shop or work area. This gives the circle its identity.
- The members work under the same supervisor, who is a member of the circle.
- The supervisor is usually, though not always, the leader of the circle. As leader, he or she moderates discussion and promotes consensus. The supervisor does not issue orders or make decisions. The circle members, as a group, make their own decisions.
- Voluntary participation means that everyone has an opportunity to join.
- Circles usually meet once every week on company time, with pay, and in special meeting rooms removed from their normal work area.
- Circle members receive training in the rules of quality circle participation, the mechanics of running a meeting and making management presentations, and techniques of group problem solving.
- Circle members, not management, choose the problems and projects that they will work on, collect all information, analyze the problems, and develop solutions.

---

[11]Philip C. Thompson, *Quality Circles: How To Make Them Work In America,* New York: AMACOM, 1982.

- Technical specialists and management assist circles with information and expertise whenever asked to do so. Circles receive advice and guidance from an adviser who attends all meetings but is not a circle member.
- Management presentations are given to those managers and technical specialists who would normally make the decision on a proposal.

Quality circles were an outgrowth of training received in the 1950s by the Japanese from two consultants in statistical quality control, Dr. W. Edwards Deming and Dr. Joseph Juran. Initially, the training was presented to Japanese engineers and supervisors, which represented the American approach to quality control. However, Japanese philosophy was considerably different. They rely on production workers for much of the planning and creativity necessary in production. Essentially, the Japanese took American concepts of quality control and changed the organizational implementation.

Circles employ brainstorming techniques to generate alternative solutions, look for causes of problems rather than just symptoms, make extensive use of analytical tools such as histograms and cause and effect diagrams, and use presentations and visual aids to present their recommendations to management. Organizationally, communications problems are reduced and resistance to change is minimized. In addition, quality circles develop a cooperative atmosphere, improve worker self-confidence, and develop leadership abilities. The ultimate result is improvement in quality and productivity. A company can operate with less inventory, save money on materials and labor, and reduce defects.

Quality circles represent a significantly different organizational philosophy that grew out of the social atmosphere in Japan. The traditional managerial styles in the United States may not easily lend themselves to this philosophy. Autocratic management does not encourage participation; thus quality circles would never succeed under this approach to management. The successful introduction of quality circles requires support by upper and middle management, cooperation by unions and union leadership, and careful training to ensure that circles will not become gripe sessions.

The quality circle concept is being implemented in many U.S. companies. For example, Ford has called their concept "employee-involvement groups" and has used this idea as an advertising strategy in promoting their commitment to quality. However, in many cases, the quality-circle concept has been advocated more by personnel and human resource people than by quality-control or technical people. The opposite is true in Japan. Some U.S. managers are beginning to recognize that a heavier commitment must be made in training production managers and workers in the statistical, as well as the interpersonal and problem oriented, aspects of quality assurance. This has been one of the factors in the success of the Japanese in improving quality and productivity.

Quality circles are but one component of the Japanese approach to quality. Quality in Japanese manufacturing is based on total involvement from top management down to maintenance personnel. As discussed in Chapter 2 they often refer to this concept as "total quality control," or "company-wide quality control." The responsibility for quality does not belong to a quality-control department, but rather to the production workers themselves. This is the basis for the success of quality circles.

Returning to the Eaton Corporation experience, the transition from productivity teams to quality circles involved greater numbers of hourly personnel and increased the variety of projects available to them. Quality circles were used in workplace and method improvements, tooling and equipment revisions, quality improvements, and scrap reductions. Significant cost savings were realized, and the flow of communication between labor and management has improved. Individuals who would not have thought of contributing their knowledge to management became concerned with quality and productivity.

Wage Incentives   One of the important factors in an individual's psychological perception of work is his or her wages. Lack of adequate wages can easily reduce morale and lower productivity. On the other hand, wage incentives can be a motivating factor in job performance, particularly in difficult economic times. Wage incentives have been found to improve productivity without high capital investment, reduce costs, increase morale, and improve supervisory effectiveness.

A wage incentive plan is designed to reward employees for above-normal performance. One of the earliest and most widely used types of wage incentive plans provides a salary increase or some type of cash bonus. Examples are commission or piece-rate incentive plans. Individual incentive or bonus plans attempt to tie pay directly to individual performance and are generally considered more effective in motivating employees than pay raises or salary increases.

A typical plan might be for a worker to earn an additional 1 percent for every 1 percent above the standard rate. This means that, for example, if an employee works at a rate of 117 percent during a week, he or she will be paid an additional 17 percent above the normal rate. Other plans, called group incentive plans, base incentive earnings on the average efficiency of a group of workers. This type of plan encourages cooperation among workers and appears to be gaining wider acceptance by both employees and employers.

Many individuals believe that financial rewards are not effective motivators for changing behavior in work situations. However, they have been used extensively in business and industry. For example, Lincoln Electric Co. in Cleveland, Ohio, a world leader in arc-welding equipment, initiated a bonus plan in 1934 based on the concepts that

1. each employee's job security is fully protected
2. employees must see increased productivity reflected in increased take-home pay and job security
3. increased productivity and reduced costs are passed on to Lincoln's customers
4. management will continue to use earnings to develop the company and market position.

Since 1934, the company has paid more in annual bonuses than in regular wages, and employees are among the most productive and highest paid in the world.

As another example, a bank in Arkansas initiated an incentive program that has increased productivity as much as 200 percent in some areas. In addition to increased earnings for the employees, absenteeism has been reduced and the employees' morale has risen.

11.5 THE DESIGN OF WORK METHODS

In Chapter 9 we saw how flow-process charts can be used in the analysis and design of production processes. In designing work methods for individual tasks, we use a similar approach, only on a more detailed level. **Motion study** is the analysis of a manual task in sufficient detail to design the task or to make improvements that will result in increased efficiency when performing the work, or less fatigue on the part of the worker. Motion study and methods analysis go hand in hand. That is, improving the motions that a worker uses often requires a redesign of the workplace.

An operation chart is often used to describe a manual task. An **operation chart** is similar to a flow-process chart in that it uses the same symbols for operation, transportation, inspection, storage, and delay; however, in the operation chart, these apply to individual motions of both the left and right hand. For example, an operation might consist of grasping a part from a bin; a transportation might be the process of moving it to another place; and inspection might be holding a part to inspect it; storage could represent the process of holding a part in one hand while the other is performing an operation; and delay occurs when a hand is idle. How can the operation chart be used? A good methods analyst will ask questions such as these: Can any motions be eliminated? Can more simultaneous motions be performed? Will a new layout, use of fixtures, or use of different tools improve the operation? In order to see how an operation chart is constructed and its usefulness, let us consider the following example.

Operation Charts

IMPROVING WORK METHODS USING OPERATION CHARTS　　EXAMPLE

The Freeland Faucet Company manufactures a variety of kitchen and bathroom faucets and other plumbing items. One of the work stations at the shop is for the assembly of stems for bathroom faucets. The components of the assembly are shown in Figure 11.5. The layout of the work station is shown in Figure 11.6. All items are stored in bins on the workbench. The current assembly process proceeds as follows. The operator picks up a housing and stem, and screws the stem into the housing. Next, he or she places a washer into the stem, inserts a screw, and tightens it with the screwdriver. An operation chart for this assembly process is shown in Figure 11.7. To construct this chart, the analyst observes the process, usually several times, noting the simultaneous operations performed by each hand. In this case, we have not broken down the operation into very fine elements. For example, the process of getting a housing actually consists of reach for housing (transport), grasp housing (operation), and move to immediate work area (transport). Such detail is the subject of *micromotion study,* which is briefly discussed later. Since the left hand is moving throughout most of this process,

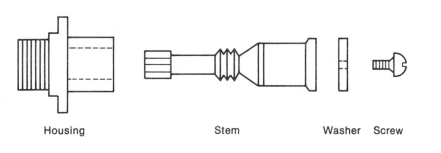

Housing　　　　　　Stem　　　　Washer　Screw

FIGURE 11.5

Assembly of Faucet Stem Component

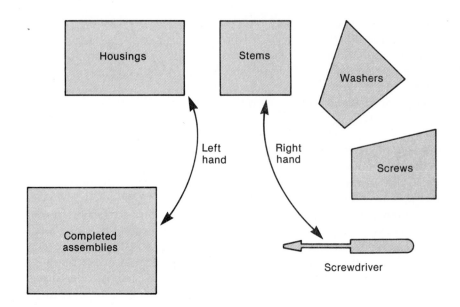

FIGURE 11.6
Work-station
Layout at
Freeland Faucet

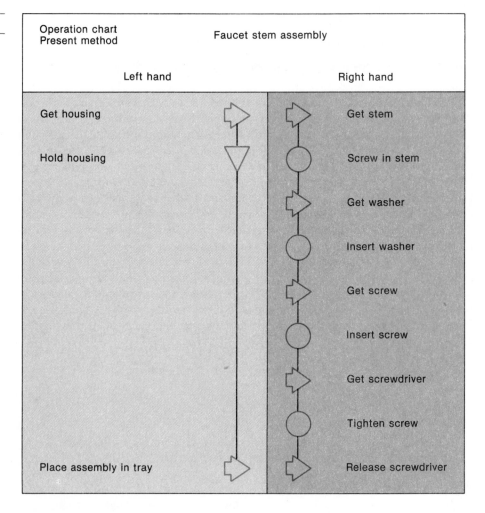

FIGURE 11.7
Operation Chart
for Faucet Stem
Assembly

we have lumped these elements together into one transport operation. Generally, a rough description of the process will suffice in methods analysis. After noticing that the right hand does most of the work, the analyst at Freeland Faucet suggested the new layout and operation sequence shown in Figures 11.8 and 11.9. The fixture is used to hold the housing-stem subassembly while the washer and screw are assembled. In addition, a powered screwdriver hanging from above the work place was suggested. With the assembly in the fixture, the screw head will be pointing up, and the worker need only pull the screwdriver down. This new design allows for freeing of the left hand because of the fixture, increased symmetry of motions, and fewer transportations. The use of the powered screwdriver also reduces arm fatigue. Can you think of other improvements? How will the method change if the fixture is designed to hold several subassemblies?

The concepts used in improving the assembly process for the Freeland Faucet example are embodied in a set of principles of motion economy given in Table 11.3. The origin of these principles dates back to the work of Taylor and the Gilbreths in studying work methods during the scientific management era. Although they seem merely to be common sense, they can be easily overlooked. The easiest way to apply these rules is to study the process by means of an operation chart and ask if any principle is violated. If so, then a means should be designed to correct the method. These rules can apply to industrial work, offices, and nearly any task where productivity can be improved.

Multiple-activity Charts

A device that is often used to analyze worker-machine interaction and suggest possible improvements is a multiple-activity chart. In a **multiple-activity chart**, the activities of each component of a system, such as machines and people, are graphically represented along a vertical time scale.

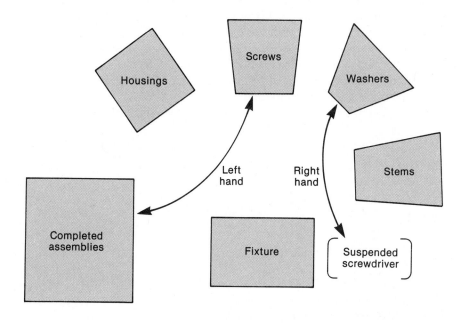

FIGURE 11.8
New Layout for Faucet Stem Assembly

FIGURE 11.9

Operation Chart for Improved Assembly Process

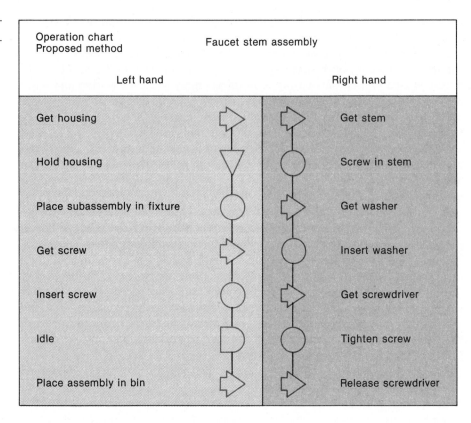

Operation chart Proposed method	Faucet stem assembly	
Left hand		Right hand
Get housing		Get stem
Hold housing		Screw in stem
Place subassembly in fixture		Get washer
Get screw		Insert washer
Insert screw		Get screwdriver
Idle		Tighten screw
Place assembly in bin		Release screwdriver

EXAMPLE

USING A MULTIPLE-ACTIVITY CHART TO IMPROVE PRODUCTIVITY

To illustrate the use of a multiple-activity chart, consider the operation of a numerically controlled drill press. Let us suppose that a worker first inspects and prepares a part for drilling. Next, the part is positioned on the machine. After the drilling is completed, the part is removed and inspected. While the machine is running, the part that was previously drilled is assembled to another component and placed on a cart to be moved to the final assembly department. The times for each operation are given as follows:

Activity	Time (Minutes)
Inspect and prepare new part	3
Position part	2
Machine running	3
Remove part	1
Inspect	2
Assemble	3

A multiple-activity chart for this job is shown in Figure 11.10. We see that the machine is idle for 5 minutes and that the entire cycle takes 11 minutes. Thus only 5.45 parts per hour can be produced.

TABLE 11.3

**Principles of
Motion Economy**

USE OF THE HUMAN BODY

1. The two hands should begin, as well as complete, their motions at the same time.
2. The two hands should not be idle at the same time except during rest periods.
3. Motions of the arms should be made in opposite and symmetrical directions and should be made simultaneously.
4. Hand and body motions should be confined to the lowest classification with which it is possible to perform the work satisfactorily.
5. Momentum should be employed to assist the worker wherever possible, and it should be reduced to a minimum if it must be overcome by muscular effort.
6. Smooth continuous curved motions of the hands are preferable to straight-line motions involving sudden and sharp changes in direction.
7. Ballistic movements are faster, easier, and more accurate than restricted (fixation) or "controlled" movements.
8. Work should be arranged to permit easy and natural rhythm wherever possible.
9. Eye fixations should be as few and as close together as possible.

ARRANGEMENT OF THE WORKPLACE

10. There should be a definite and fixed place for all tools and materials.
11. Tools, materials, and controls should be located close to the point of use.
12. Gravity-feed bins and containers should be used to deliver material close to the point of use.
13. Drop deliveries should be used wherever possible.
14. Materials and tools should be located to permit the best sequence of motions.
15. Provisions should be made for adequate conditions for seeing. Good illumination is the first requirement for satisfactory visual perception.
16. The height of the workplace and the chair should preferably be arranged so that alternate sitting and standing at work are easily possible.
17. A chair of the type and height to permit good posture should be provided for every worker.

DESIGN OF TOOLS AND EQUIPMENT

18. The hands should be relieved of all work that can be done more advantageously by a jig, a fixture, or a foot-operated device.
19. Two or more tools should be combined wherever possible.
20. Tools and materials should be prepositioned whenever possible.
21. Where each finger performs some specific movement, such as in typewriting, the load should be distributed in accordance with the inherent capacities of the fingers.
22. Levers, crossbars, and hand wheels should be located in positions that allow the operator to manipulate them with the least change in body position and with the greatest mechanical advantage.

Source: Ralph M. Barnes, *Motion and Time Study: Design and Measurement of Work,* 6th ed. New York: John Wiley & Sons, Inc., 1968. Copyright © 1968 by John Wiley & Sons. Reprinted by permission.

How can this job be redesigned in order to improve productivity? If possible we would like to reduce the idle time and shorten the cycle time. One possibility is to assign an additional worker to the job. The methods analyst, by trial and error, might arrive at a job design, as shown by the multiple-activity chart in Figure 11.11. With this division of work between the operator and the assistant, the total operation time can be reduced to 6 minutes, thus increasing production to 10 parts per hour. Idle time on the machine is reduced to zero. It must then be determined if the additional production would more than compensate for hiring the additional person. In this way, multiple-activity charts can be used to design and evaluate alternative methods and work assignments.

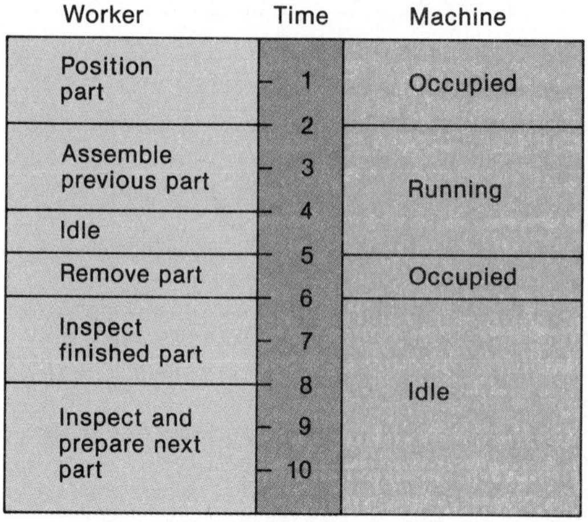

FIGURE 11.10
Multiple-activity
Chart

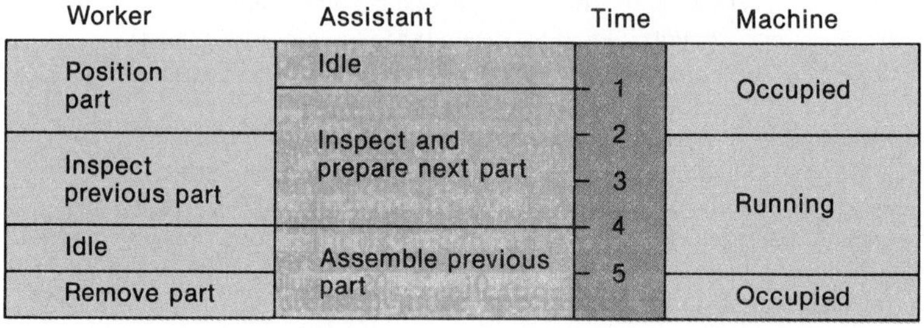

Worker	Time	Machine
Position part	1	Occupied
	2	
Assemble previous part	3	Running
	4	
Idle	5	
Remove part	6	Occupied
Inspect finished part	7	
	8	Idle
Inspect and prepare next part	9	
	10	

FIGURE 11.11
Mutiple-activity
Chart for
Improved Process

Worker	Assistant	Time	Machine
Position part	Idle	1	Occupied
	Inspect and prepare next part	2	
Inspect previous part		3	Running
		4	
Idle	Assemble previous part	5	
Remove part			Occupied

Micromotion Study

Motion study can be performed on a much finer level than the Freeland Faucet example illustrates. Micromotion study involves a very detailed analysis of work elements. This is done by studying the process, either through observation or by taking motion pictures and analyzing them frame by frame, and charting elementary motions called *therbligs* (therblig being an anagram of the name Gilbreth). A **therblig** is one of 17 fundamental motions: search, select, grasp, transport empty, transport loaded, hold, release load, position, preposition, inspect, assemble, disassemble, use, unavoidable delay, avoidable delay, plan, and rest. Therbligs form the basis for certain systems of work measurement that we discuss in the next section. The methods analyst studies the sequence of therbligs, and determines if any of them can be eliminated or shortened, again using the principles of motion economy as guidelines. Because of the detail involved, such studies are costly and usually are not economical except for very short cycle, high-volume production jobs.

Work Simplification

The primary goal of methods analysis in job design is to simplify the work. Motion study, biomechanics, work physiology, and workplace design are all tools for work simplification. Persons trained in industrial engineering or industrial management are usually best suited to perform work simplification studies. However, one must not overlook one of best sources of ideas—the workers themselves.

They are the experts in performing a job but often do not volunteer ideas because they perceive improved methods as a threat to job security or benefits. Operations managers need to gain their confidence and cooperation, often through a formal system of recognition and awards, so that employees take an active role in increasing productivity and quality and reducing costs.

11.6 WORK MEASUREMENT

The purpose of work measurement is to develop time standards for the performance of jobs. A **time standard** is generally defined as the amount of time it takes to perform a task by a trained operator working at a normal pace and using a prescribed method. Some key words in this definition are *trained, normal,* and *method.* To establish usable standards, the operator must be trained to do the job in an efficient manner. Thus methods analysis and motion study should precede work measurement. Work measurement is also a useful tool in evaluating proposed methods' changes. By a normal pace, we mean a pace that can be consistently performed by the average worker without undue fatigue. Here again, work physiology data are helpful in determining what this pace should be.

Work measurement is used for several purposes in organizations. The most common applications of work measurement are

1. estimating work force and capacity requirements
2. determining the cost of production operations for accounting purposes
3. establishing wage incentive systems
4. monitoring worker performance
5. scheduling production.

In each of these applications, management is interested in the length of time necessary to produce an item or, equivalently, the number of items that can be produced over a certain length of time. Time standards allow easy computation of such measures.

There are several techniques for work measurement that we shall discuss. These are estimates based on historical experience, time study, predetermined motion-time data, standard data, and work sampling. Each has certain advantages and disadvantages.

Historical Time Data

Time estimates for different activities can be obtained by statistically analyzing data collected over one or more periods of time. Such estimates are not standards in the true sense of the word, since there is no control over the method or pace. However, if historical estimates are compared over time, any deviations from the average might cause a manager to seek a reason. In this way, historical data can act as a control mechanism.

Historical data are advantageous in that a trained time study person is not required to collect the data. Employees or their supervisors can record output. Without a standard to determine a work pace, production workers themselves are more apt to develop improved methods to make the job easier.

Time Study　　Time study is the development of a standard through observation and analysis of a task using a stopwatch. The general approach to time study can be described as follows:

1. divide the task content into smaller work elements
2. observe the time to perform each element over a number of cycles
3. rate the performance of each work element
4. use the performance rating to determine the normal element time
5. determine allowances for personal time, fatigue, and unavoidable delays
6. determine the standard time.

The first step in performing a time study is to analyze the job content. This is accomplished by using the techniques of motion study that we discussed in the previous section. The second step, timing the work elements, is usually performed by a trained observer with a stopwatch. Most stopwatches used in time study are calibrated in units of .01 minute or .001 hour. Two principal methods are used for operating the stopwatch. The first method, called the *snap-back method,* involves timing each work element from zero; thus the stopwatch must be snapped back to zero after each element is completed. The second method, called *continuous timing,* involves starting the clock at the beginning of each task and recording the cumulative time at the end of each element. After completing the study, the times for each work element can be found by subtraction. Since time is lost in the snap-back method, continuous timing is more accurate.

No person can perform every task in the same amount of time, so several observations must be taken to account for this variability. How do we determine how many cycles should be observed? If we assume that the distribution of element times is normal, then the sample size is determined by the amount of precision that we desire. From statistics we know that when we select a simple random sample that is reasonably large (30 or more), there is a $1 - \alpha$ probability that the value of the sample mean will provide a sampling error of $z_{\alpha/2}$ ($\sigma/\sqrt{n}$) or less, where n is the sample size, σ is the population standard deviation, and $z_{\alpha/2}$ is the value of the standard normal distribution having an area of $\alpha/2$ in the upper tail. See Figure 11.12. Thus if we desire that the size of the sampling error be no more than E—for example, 0.1 or 0.5—we may solve the equation.

$$z_{\alpha/2} \frac{\sigma}{\sqrt{n}} = E$$

for n to obtain

$$n = \frac{(z_{\alpha/2})^2 \sigma^2}{E^2}$$

as the required sample size.

The next step is to rate the operator's performance. A performance rating is the time study analyst's subjective judgment regarding the pace sustained by the worker. One hundred percent is considered a normal pace. A performance rating of 90 percent indicates that the worker is working 10 percent below normal; likewise, a rating of 115 percent indicates a pace or effort that is 15 percent above normal. To rate performance properly, the analyst requires considerable training and experience. One of the most common ways of training time-study analysts in performance rating is to show films of people working at different

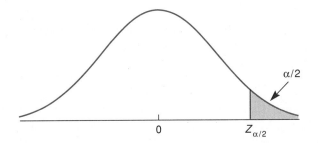

FIGURE 11.12
Standard Normal
Distribution

$\alpha/2$

$$0 \qquad Z_{\alpha/2}$$

work paces with accepted ratings. The analyst can rate the people in the film and compare his or her results with the accepted values. In this way the analyst can develop expertise in judging performance for that specific location.

Once the performance rating of each work element is established, the *normal time* for each element is computed by multiplying the performance rating (expressed as a decimal fraction) by the average element time. The sum of these times is the normal time for the entire operation.

Finally, allowances must be determined. Allowances are made for normal interruptions and factors that are external to the job. Typically, three types of allowances are made.

- *Personal allowance,* such as time for going to the bathroom.
- *Fatigue allowance,* which is time for rest as a result of the physical activity of the job.
- *Delay allowance,* which includes shortage of materials, equipment malfunction, interruptions by supervisors, and so on.

DETERMINING STANDARD TIME THROUGH TIME STUDY | EXAMPLE

We shall illustrate the time-study procedure using the Freeland Faucet Company. We use the operation chart in Figure 11.7 as the basis for developing the time study. However several of the smaller work elements are combined in order to obtain more accuracy. For instance, "get washer" and "insert washer" are combined. We obtain the following set of work elements:

1. get housing and stem
2. screw in stem
3. get and insert washer
4. get and insert screw
5. tighten screw
6. place completed assembly in tray

To determine the sample size for the Freeland Faucet example, suppose that we want to have a 90 percent probability that the value of the sample mean provides a sampling error of .01 minute or less. Further assume that σ is estimated from historical experience to be .02. Therefore, $\alpha = .10$, $z_{.05} = 1.645$, and $E = .01$. We then have

$$n = \frac{(1.645)^2(.02)^2}{(.01)^2} = 10.8$$

A sample size of 11 or more will provide the required precision. (Fractional values of n should always be rounded up to ensure that the precision is at least as good as desired.)

Figure 11.13 illustrates a typical time-study chart when continuous timing is used. The element times are found by subtracting successive cumulative times. These are added and averaged to obtain the mean time for each work element. Performance ratings are given in the second-to-last column. By multiplying the performance rating by the average time, we obtain the normal time for each work element and add them. We next determine allowances to complete the standard time. For the faucet stem assembly, we assume a 5 percent personal allowance, 5 percent fatigue allowance and 10 percent delay allowance. Thus the total allowance is 20 percent.

The standard time for the job is then computed as

$$\text{Standard time} = (\text{normal time})(1 + \text{allowance})$$

where the allowance is expressed as a decimal. For Freeland Faucets, we have

$$\begin{aligned}\text{Standard time} &= (.550)(1 + .2) \\ &= .660 \text{ minutes per part}\end{aligned}$$

Thus, an assembler of faucet stem assemblies can be expected to produce at a rate of $1/.660$ parts per minute, or about 91 parts per hour.

Predetermined Motion-Time Data

An alternative to time study is the use of standard times for work elements that have been predetermined from long periods of observation and analysis. The major advantage of this method is that only motion patterns must be known; in this way, alternatives may be evaluated prior to actually trying them out. In order for such a system to be universally applied, it is necessary to define a basic set of motions into which any task can be decomposed. The set of therbligs that we discussed in reference to micromotion studies is one such example. However, these motions must be refined to account for various degrees of difficulty. For example, grasping a flat washer is more difficult than grasping a 6-inch bolt and thus should be expected to take more time. Since micromotion analysis is necessary in order to apply such systems, these systems are often costly to use.

There are a number of different motion-time systems. One of the best known and most widely used is **MTM (methods-time measurement)**. MTM was developed in 1948 from studies of motion-picture films of assembly operations. The basic elements used in MTM are

1. reach
2. move
3. turn and apply pressure
4. grasp
5. position
6. release
7. disengage
8. eye travel time and eye focus

FIGURE 11.13 Time-study Chart for Freeland Faucet Example

Time Study Chart

Operation: Faucet stem assembly

Date: 7 / 14 / 83
By: KME

Work element		1	2	3	4	5	6	7	8	9	10	11	Sum	Avg	Rating	Normal time
Get housing and stem	Cumulative time	.03	.03	.02	.03	.04	.03	.04	.04	.03	.03	.04	.36	.033	1.00	.033
	Element time	.03	.03	.02	.03	.04	.03	.04	.04	.03	.03	.04				
Screw in stem	Cumulative time	.13	.15	.14	.16	.13	.12	.14	.16	.15	.13	.16	1.21	.110	1.10	.121
	Element time	.10	.12	.12	.13	.09	.09	.10	.12	.12	.10	.12				
Get and insert washer	Cumulative time	.24	.25	.26	.29	.23	.21	.24	.26	.27	.22	.27	1.17	.106	1.00	.106
	Element time	.11	.10	.12	.13	.10	.09	.10	.10	.12	.09	.11				
Get and insert screw	Cumulative time	.32	.33	.36	.38	.33	.30	.32	.33	.37	.31	.35	.96	.087	1.00	.087
	Element time	.08	.08	.10	.09	.10	.09	.08	.07	.10	.09	.08				
Tighten screw	Cumulative time	.48	.50	.54	.53	.50	.45	.51	.52	.58	.49	.51	1.91	.174	.97	.168
	Element time	.16	.17	.18	.15	.17	.15	.19	.19	.21	.18	.16				
Place completed assembly in tray	Cumulative time	.51	.53	.58	.56	.54	.49	.54	.55	.62	.52	.55	.38	.035	1.00	.035
	Element time	.03	.03	.04	.03	.04	.04	.03	.03	.04	.03	.04				
															Sum	.550

Allowances: Personal 5%
　　　　　　 Fatigue 5%
　　　　　　 Delay 10%

Standard Time: .660

9. body, leg, and foot motions

10. simultaneous motions.

Each of these has several subcategories. For example, there are five types of reach:

a. Reach to an object in a fixed location or in the other hand.

b. Reach to an object in a general location.

c. Reach to objects jumbled together.

d. Reach to very small objects.

e. Reach to indefinite location, such as moving the hand out of the way.

Element times are measured in TMUs (time-measurement units), where 1 TMU is .00001 hour, or .0006 minutes. Tables of times have been developed for each subcategory of these elements and for different cases. To illustrate, a reach of 6 inches takes 7.0 TMUs for type a, 8.6 for type c or d, and 8.0 for type e. The analyst must first determine all the basic motions that comprise a task and the subcategory, and then look up the TMUs associated with each. This is very time consuming and is therefore not economical except for highly repetitive tasks. Other systems, such as MTM-2 and MTM-3, are much more condensed and require less application time, though they are less accurate.

Standard Data

For jobs in which there are a large number of repetitive operations with similar characteristics, companies often develop standard data through the use of time studies or predetermined data. The advantage of having standard data is that each job need not undergo a time study. In a sense, then, standard data is applied in a similar manner as predetermined motion-time data, except on a less-detailed level. For instance, an income tax service may develop standard data on the time required to fill out different tax forms. From this data, it is easy to provide an estimate of the cost for a client based on information about the forms required for that client.

Standard data are also useful in estimating times for jobs with different characteristics through regression-type equations. For example, suppose that in a warehouse the standard time required to unload 10-pound boxes from a railcar is 2 minutes per box. Due to increasing allowances for fatigue, suppose this goes up by .10 minutes for each additional 2 pounds. The standard time for a box of weight x is $2 + .05 (x - 10)$. Therefore, if 50 boxes, each weighing 18 pounds, are to be unloaded, the standard time is $50[2 + .05(18 - 10)] = 50(2.4) = 120$ minutes, or 2 hours. Having standard data enables such calculations to be made easily.

Work Sampling

Work sampling is a method of randomly observing work over a period of time in order to obtain a distribution of the activities of an individual or a group of employees. Work sampling has several applications. It can be used to determine the percentage of idle time experienced by people or machines in a job; it can also be used as a means of assessing nonproductive time in order to determine performance ratings or to establish allowances.

Work sampling is based upon the binomial probability distribution because it is concerned with the proportion of time that a certain activity occurs. In the

Example that follows, we try to estimate the proportion of time spent typing. One of the questions that must be answered in a work-sampling study is how large a sample to take. This is similar to the problem of determining the sample size in a time study. From statistics we can say that there is a $1 - \alpha$ probability that the value of the sample proportion will provide a sampling error of $z_{\alpha/2}\sigma_{\bar{p}}$ or less, where $\sigma_{\bar{p}}$ is the standard deviation of the sampling distribution of the population proportion. Now

$$\sigma_{\bar{p}} = \sqrt{\frac{p(1 - p)}{n}}$$

Thus if we wish to have a sampling error of E, then

$$z_{\alpha/2}\sqrt{\frac{p(1 - p)}{n}} = E$$

We may solve this equation for n, obtaining

$$n = \frac{(z_{\alpha/2})^2 p(1 - p)}{E^2}$$

This is the appropriate sample size. We must choose a planning value for the population proportion p. Obviously, p will never be known exactly, since it is the population parameter we are trying to estimate. We may choose a value for p from either past data, a preliminary sample, or a subjective estimate. If p is difficult to determine this way, we may select $p = .5$, since it gives us the largest value for $p(1 - p)$ and therefore provides the largest and most conservative sample size.

Work sampling is useful in studying the content of certain jobs in order to decide upon or justify new equipment. It is particularly useful when the work is irregular and nonrepetitive, as is often the case with service organizations.

CONDUCTING A WORK SAMPLING STUDY

EXAMPLE

Consider the secretarial staff in a college office. The secretaries spend their time on various activities, such as

1. answering the telephone
2. typing new drafts of technical papers
3. revising technical papers
4. talking to students
5. duplicating class handouts
6. other productive activities
7. personal time
8. idle periods.

Suppose that a new word processor is being considered. This will greatly increase productivity of typing and revising technical papers. However, the purchase of the word processor is not justified unless it is used a significant percentage of time. To determine the percentage of time secretaries spend performing these activities, we could observe them at random times and record their activities. If 100 observations are taken, we might have the following results:

Activity	Number Observed
Answering the telephone	14
Typing new drafts	21
Revising papers	7
Talking to students	10
Duplicating	15
Other productive activity	25
Personal	6
Idle	2
	100

The percentage of time spent typing or revising is 21 percent + 7 percent = 28 percent.

To determine the sample size, suppose that we wish to estimate the proportion of time spent typing to within ± .05 with a 95 percent probability. Using the sample size formula,

$$n = \frac{(z_{\alpha/2})^2 \, p(1 - p)}{E^2}$$

we have $E = .05$ and $z_{\alpha/2} = 1.96$. Suppose that the secretary estimates that 40 percent of the time is spent typing. This provides a value for p of .4. Then the sample size is

$$n = \frac{(1.96)^2(.4)(1 - .4)}{(.05)^2} = 368.79$$

Thus a sample of 369 or more observations should be taken. If this is to be done over a 1-week (40-hour) period, it represents approximately 9 observations per hour (9.225, to be exact). The observations should be taken randomly when work is at a normal level (not during the Christmas holidays!).

To take a random sample, we can use the table of random digits in Appendix C. There are several ways to use random digits in deciding when to take observations. For this example, an average of 9.225 observations per hour requires the observations to be spaced, on the average, 6.5 = (60/9.225) minutes apart. We should not take observations exactly 6.5 minutes apart, for then the sample would not be random. Suppose however, observations are between 3 and 10 minutes apart. If these are random, the average is 6.5 minutes. We can use the random digits as follows. Suppose that the first observation is taken at 9:00. We choose numbers from the first row of Appendix C to represent the number of minutes later at which to take the next observation (0 represents 10 minutes, and we discard any 1s or 2s). For instance, the first number is 6; thus we take the next observation at 9:06. The next number is 3, so the third observation is made at 9:09. We discard the 2 and take the next observation 7 minutes later, at 9:16. We see that

Technique	Advantages	Disadvantages
Historical data	Inexpensive Useful for nonrepetitive work	Not a true standard Subject to bias
Time study	Highly accurate Better than historical data since performance is also measured	Requires substantial training of personnel Can be expensive Possible negative reaction by workers
Predetermined data	Jobs can be analyzed without observation Performance rating is not necessary	Like time study, requires training and can be expensive Not appropriate except for short-cycle, highly repetitive work
Standard data	Useful when many time standards must be determined Few disruptions	Requires development of a data base of information
Work sampling	Useful for job analysis and equipment planning Less skill required to perform	Cannot be used to determine accurate standards May require a large number of observations

TABLE 11.4

Work-measurement Techniques

the time required to take a random sample can be significant; this is one of the disadvantages of random sampling.

In choosing a particular method, operations managers must decide the purpose of the work-measurement study and the cost involved. Each of the methods we have described have several relative advantages and disadvantages. These are summarized in Table 11.4. In addition, there are several behavioral aspects to consider. Human beings tend to change their behaviors when being observed. This was verified during the Hawthorne experiments in the 1930s; workers were found to perform better just because they were part of an experiment. Many workers are sensitive to time studies and, as a result, labor relations problems have often occurred. In such cases, predetermined motion-time study is perhaps a better alternative.

Choosing a Work-measurement Technique

P/OM IN PRACTICE

The two P/OM in Practice cases illustrate how good job design can lead to high levels of productivity and job satisfaction. The first describes how Rockwell used ergonomic considerations and group technology to reduce direct manufacturing substantially.

The second describes how a job rotation program and other behavioral improvements led to increased productivity and higher quality at Toyota Motor Company.

PRODUCTIVITY IMPROVEMENT THROUGH ERGONOMICS AT ROCKWELL[12]

A combined effort of applying group technology and ergonomics in production and material-handling systems at the Communication Transmission Systems Division of Rockwell International has resulted in significant improvements in productivity in a sheet-fabrication department. The operation was ergonomically evaluated in three areas.

- material flow between production operations
- material and tool handling at each operation
- job tasks and workplace design

The department consists of typical metal-working machines, such as numerically controlled punch presses, power brakes, shears, deburr machines, and degreasers, which make a wide variety of sheet-metal parts for microwave communications equipment. The problems encountered in the department were the result of a high production volume of parts, large differences in the size of the parts, and the large variety of different parts produced. Part sizes range from 1 inch square to over 6 feet in length.

The large number of different part numbers resulted in an extremely large number of different process routings, machine requirements, and tool setups. Demand was increasing, putting additional strain on production. Management therefore decided to apply group technology and automation to improve the system.

The department was reorganized into various manufacturing cells through group technology. This necessitated a determination of new methods for material or part transport. The ergonomic considerations included muscular work requirements, work heights, noise, and vibration. A number of objectives were established.

1. minimize flow distances and part handling
2. route and move parts using operator or handling system
3. deliver parts to operator work station
4. provide parts at workbench height
5. eliminate lifting of parts
6. minimize manual movement of parts
7. ensure correct body posture
8. reduce static muscular work
9. automate where feasible
10. minimize noise, vibration and any other potential distractions

Various material-transfer methods were evaluated, and three systems were selected. Material carts were selected for adjacent operations to provide a low-cost system that would not require operator lifting and could also be utilized as a workbench. A powered conveyor system was chosen for completed parts because of the longer travel distance. An automatic on-off system was designed using photocells, since the operator has both hands busy when loading the conveyor. In addition, the cart and conveyor were the same height to allow the operator to slide the parts. Heavy or large parts were moved with new skid carts.

The second area of improvement was material-, tool-, and scrap-handling at the operations. The ergonomic objective was to minimize the operator effort necessary to prepare for production and provide work materials at the proper work heights and locations. Setup included the transfer of parts to the workbench, machine setup, disposal of scrap and machine cleanup. Two major improvements were using the material carts as workbenches and designing new tool racks that could be placed at the workplace. Material carts were then pushed into place next to the machine tool itself. Because of this dual use, the carts were specially ordered to be a recommended bench height to allow the operator to sit or stand at the operation.

New tool racks were designed to maximize operator efficiency. Design considerations included work heights depending on tool weight, adequate room to grasp the tools properly, movement directions in relation to the setup requirements, operator efficiency, and elimination of unnatural body positions.

The last phase of the project was the evaluation of job content and design of the workplace. Operators were given total responsibility for quality, which included the evaluation of previous operations and sign-off responsibility. Prior to the change, the work

---

[12]Adapted from John W. Priest, "Ergonomic Changes in Work Place Can Improve the Productivity of Production Operations." Reprinted from *Industrial Engineering* magazine, July 1985. Copyright Institute of Industrial Engineers, 25 Technology Park/Atlanta, Norcross, GA 30092.

was performed by an inspection department. Other changes included job flexibility, increased autonomy for the group, development of quality circles, and direct participation in the design of the operation.

The workplaces were designed to allow the employees to perform the operation in a sitting or standing position. This allowed posture changes, which alternate the stress and strain over different muscular groups. Where possible, adjustable benches and chairs were also provided to allow posture flexibility. Several problems were also identified for hand tools and machine controls. Where feasible, new tools were purchased or existing tools redesigned, and controls that did not meet normal ergonomic standards were changed where possible.

After 6 months of implementation, direct manufacturing costs were reduced by 30 percent (one-third of this due to ergonomics changes, the rest to group technology improvements), a throughput improvement of 65 percent was realized (15 percent due to ergonomics and 50 percent due to group technology), and inventory was reduced by $500,000.

QUESTIONS

1. State how you believe the ergonomics changes in material transfer methods caused reductions in direct manufacturing costs.
2. Explain how the improvements in work methods described here could have led to a reduction in inventory costs.

JOB ENLARGEMENT AND JOB ENRICHMENT AT TOYOTA MOTOR COMPANY[13]

A mong the objectives of Toyota Motor Company are to reduce cost, labor hours, and number of defects by increasing the number of suggestions from workers, promoting quality control circles, and developing worker motivation. Toyota surveyed workers' desires and other factors affecting motivation at their Tsutsumi plant. Major worker desires identified were "to improve oneself through the present job, to work optimistically in their shop, unconcerned with company objectives and aims," and "to overcome various frustrations in the present job such as those caused by excessive direction from a supervisor and needless company regulations." Three factors that strongly influenced motivation were found to be rest time, job rotation, and the number of workers per group. The company also surveyed and analyzed job characteristics and working conditions in the plant. Using the above information, an interesting production system focusing on behavioral characteristics was designed at Toyota and has been operating since 1975.

Because of the fluctuations in demand for different types of cars, the work load in various departments in the plant changes. When the work load for a particular department is low, it is desirable to increase productivity by transferring a number of

the workers in that department to one with an increased work load. Thus, it is necessary that workers be versatile and trained for many different operations. Toyota designed its production system to harmonize these company needs with worker desires.

For example, in order to enhance the worker's desire to improve himself or herself and to overcome frustrations, several features were designed into the new system.

1. enlarging the opportunity for the worker to exhibit his or her ability,
2. offering the opportunity for the workers to learn a wide variety of jobs without restriction,
3. allowing the worker to take breaks freely during working hours,
4. varying the number of workers in a group from 8 to 15, according to shop characteristics

In the shop, whenever worker A wants to take a break or perform another job, he signals the group leader or relief man by tapping him on the shoulder or calling to him. The group leader or relief man then moves to worker A's work station and does worker A's job. While the leader is working, worker A may take a rest or smoke a cigarette. After he has taken a rest, he goes to another worker, B, taps him

---

[13]Adapted from R. Muramatsu, H. Miyazaki, and K. Ishii, "A Successful Application of Job Enlargement/Enrichment at Toyota," *IIE Transactions*, 19, no. 4, (1987): 451–459. Copyright Institute of Industrial Engineers, 25 Technology Park/Atlanta, Norcross, GA 30092.

on the shoulder, or calls for another worker who wants to take a break. If worker B want to rest, he follows the same procedure. Worker B moves from his work station and worker A does worker B's job. If worker B does not want to take a rest, worker A goes to another worker, C, and signals to him with a tap on the shoulder. Worker C then moves from his work station and A takes his place. If worker X wants to take a rest, he calls worker C, worker C goes to worker X's work station after taking a rest and then takes the place of worker X. In this manner, all workers change place until the last worker taps the leader or relief man on the shoulder, and the group leader or relief man then returns to his original position.

Experiments indicate that the rotation time for each group varies from one hour to one and a half hours, depending on the size of the group. In this way, each worker can master a number of different jobs, and all workers are better able to rotate in their jobs freely.

Introducing this system required the effort of both the company and workers. For example, the company offered all workers, who desired it, the opportunity to master different jobs. Workers had to master a large number of different jobs so that they could help each other accomplish the group's tasks.

After implementation of the system, productivity and quality increased, while at the same time, worker's desires were satisfied. For instance, from 1974 to 1980, the percentage of operators with the ability to handle several different jobs increased from 40 to 95; the number of suggestions per year per worker increased from 14 to 50; defects were reduced almost by half; and the time to produce a car fell from 10.9 to 7.6 labor hours.

QUESTIONS

1. In what ways did Toyota provide the opportunity for the worker to learn a wide variety of jobs?
2. Explain how workers were allowed to take breaks freely during working hours without disrupting operations.
3. How does the number of workers in a group affect the rotation time?

SUMMARY

In this chapter we have examined a number of important issues regarding the design of jobs and have developed some useful tools for job analysis and productivity improvement. In considering the role of people in work, operations managers must take a sociotechnical approach; that is, they must consider not only the technical aspects but also the social atmosphere of the job. The specific design factors that must be addressed are the physical workplace, the physical environment, the social environment, and work methods. All these must come together to create an effective job that will meet the organizational objectives of low cost, high productivity and quality, and worker satisfaction. Time and motion study, work measurement, job enlargement and enrichment, and wage incentives are but some of the useful tools that can be applied in job design.

KEY TERMS

Job
Job design
Ergonomics (human-factors engineering)
Anthropometric data
Quality control circles (QCCs)
Quality circle (QC)
Motion study

Operation chart
Multiple-activity chart
Therblig
Time standard
Time study
MTM (methods-time measurement)
Work sampling

1. Define *job design*. How has management viewed job design since the industrial revolution?

2. Why is job design important in P/OM?

3. What aspects of the physical environment, social or psychological environment, and work methods are important in job design?

4. What is the role of ergonomics in job design?

5. Explain the contributions of physical anthropology, work physiology, and biomechanics to ergonomics.

6. What questions should be addressed in designing a workplace for an individual worker?

7. Discuss some of the special needs of knowledge workers with respect to workplace design.

8. What environmental factors should be considered in designing jobs? How does OSHA impact on these decisions?

9. Describe the Hackman and Oldham model of motivation. What implications does it have for operations managers in designing jobs?

10. What are the major differences between job enlargement and job enrichment? Provide at least three examples of each.

11. How can participative approaches to problem solving improve productivity and quality?

12. Describe the characteristics of quality circles. What benefits can result from using quality circles?

13. Describe individual and group wage incentive plans. How important do you think wage incentives are for increasing productivity and quality?

14. What is an *operation chart*? How can it be used to improve work methods?

15. What information is provided in a multiple-activity chart? How can it be used to improve a process?

16. Discuss the principles of motion economy.

17. How does micromotion study differ from the general concept of motion study?

18. Define a *time standard*. How are time standards used in P/OM?

19. Discuss the various approaches to work measurement and their relative advantages and disadvantages.

20. Describe the procedure for developing a time study.

21. What is *work sampling*? Discuss some applications of work sampling in manufacturing and in service organizations.

1. Figure 11.14 illustrates a design for a personal computer work station. Discuss the various ergonomic features of this design. Can you think of any additional features that should be included?

FIGURE 11.14
Workstation Design

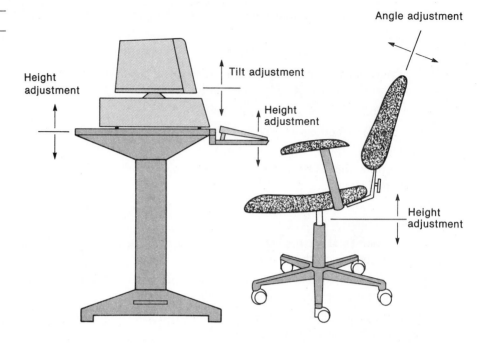

2. Suggest means of job enlargement and job enrichment for the following cases:
   a. An insurance company in which employees specialize in different types of insurance (life, auto, and so on).
   b. A bank in which different personnel perform typing, checking, and correcting.
   c. Maintenance employees assigned to a particular department.
   d. Auto mechanics who specialize in brake work, transmissions, and so on.

3. An Internal Revenue Service employee responsible for the preliminary check of tax returns must determine if the return was mailed by April 15, if the return has been signed, and if the W-2 forms were attached to the return. Thus, there are (2)(2)(2) = 8 possible outcomes corresponding to this task; for example, (return on time–signed–W-2's attached), (return late–signed–W-2's attached), and so on.
   a. Design a work station that could be used to carry out this process.
   b. Construct an operation chart for this process.

4. You have been asked to do the following: (a) Make one copy of a 100-page report; and (b) copy and collate 50 copies of a 4-page memo. Design efficient work methods for doing these tasks and construct an operation chart for each. Be sure to consider the principles of motion economy.

5. Observe someone photocopying a large volume of work at your school. Construct a multiple-activity chart for this activity. Can you suggest any methods improvements?

6. Referring to Figure 11.9, suppose that the worker runs two machines that produce the same part. Develop a multiple-activity chart for this situation, trying to make the best use of both the worker's and the machine's times.

7. For the Freeland Faucet example, develop work methods and an operation chart for the case in which the fixture used in the second method is designed to hold six subassemblies.

8. Observe a classmate replacing the ink cartridge of a ballpoint pen. Perform a micromotion study and construct an operation chart.

9. Finger Lakes Wines, Inc., is a small winery located in Bluff Point, New York. Because of their relatively small volume, they use a manual process for applying labels to filled bottles of wine. The label that appears on the front of the bottle has a picture of the winery and information concerning the type of the wine, its alcoholic content, and so on. The label that appears on the back of the bottle describes the history of the winery and briefly describes the type of wine. Both labels must be moistened slightly before they can be applied. Design an efficient work method for applying the labels and construct an operation chart. Be sure to consider the principles of motion economy.

10. Construct a multiple-activity chart for the case of a worker operating 2 machines making similar components. The loading and unloading times are 20 seconds and the operating time is 45 seconds. What is the utilization of the operator? What is the total output per hour?

11. A machine operator has to operate 2 machines and for each machine, loading and unloading operations are involved. The time for each operation is given below.

Machine 1	Machine 2
loading time = 1.33 minutes	loading time = 2.0 minutes
operation time = 4.00 minutes	operation time = 3.3 minutes
unloading time = 1.00 minute	unloading time = 1.0 minute

Construct a multiple-activity chart showing the operation of the worker and the machines.
a. What is the utilization level of each machine and the worker?
b. What is the cycle time?
c. What is the output per shift?

12. What sample size should be used for the following time studies?
a. There should be a .95 probability that the value of the sample mean be within 2 minutes if the standard deviation is 4 minutes.
b. There should be a 90 percent chance that the sample mean provides an error of .10 minutes or less when the variance is estimated to be .50 minutes.

13. Compute the number of observations required in a work sampling study if there should be a 90 percent chance that the sample mean has an error of
a. 0.15 minutes
b. 0.10 minutes
c. 0.005 minutes

The standard deviation is 0.2 minutes.

14. In a work sampling study, what sample size should be used to provide a 95 percent probability for determining the processing time of a single order form

with an error of 0.05 minutes. There is no estimate of the proportion of time spent on useful work by the clerical staff.

15. Figure 11.15 shows a partially completed time-study worksheet. Determine the standard time for this operation.

16. Compute the normal time for drilling a hole in a steel plate if the following observations (in minutes) have been observed. Use a rating factor of 1.00.

.24	.25	.29	.24	.27
.25	.245	.19	.20	.23

17. Given the following time-study data conducted by continuous time measurement, compute the standard time. Use a fatigue allowance of 20 percent.

Activity	Cycle of Observation					Performance Rating
	1	2	3	4	5	
Get casting	0.21	2.31	4.41	6.45	8.59	0.95
Fix into fixture	0.48	2.59	4.66	6.70	8.86	0.90
Drilling operation	1.52	3.65	5.66	7.74	9.90	1.00
Unload	1.73	3.83	5.91	7.96	10.10	0.95
Inspect	1.98	4.09	6.15	8.21	10.30	0.80
Replace	2.10	4.20	6.25	8.34	10.42	1.10

18. Provide the missing data in the following table:

Actual time	Normal time	Standard time	Performance Rating	Fatigue Allowance
10.6			1.06	20%
7.8	7.2			15%
6.5		7.98	1.05	
		6.92	1.10	15%

19. In a work sampling study conducted on a clerical worker in an office, the employee was found to be working 2700 times out of a total of 3000 observations made over a time span of 240 working hours. The output of the employee was 1800 forms. If a performance rating of 1.05 and an allowance of 15 percent is given, what is the standard output for this task?

20. How many observations should be made in a work-sampling study if it is desired to have an estimate of the proportion of time spent changing tools by a production worker within .10 with a 99 percent probability?

21. Figure 11.16 illustrates the actual activity of a typist in an office word processing pool at Rayburn law offices. The senior partner is considering the purchase of new word-processing software in order to reduce the time spent revising and correcting drafts. Determine the sample size required to estimate the proportion of time spent revising and correcting documents to within 10 percent with a 90 percent probability. An initial estimate is that perhaps 20 percent of the typist's time is spent on this activity. Perform a work-sampling

FIGURE 11.15 Time-study Worksheet

Time Study Chart

Work Element		1	2	3	4	5	6	7	8	9	Sum	Avg	Rating	Normal time
A	Cumulative time	.09	.12	.08	.11	.10	.09	.13	.12	.13			1.05	
	Element time													
B	Cumulative time	.23	.28	.21	.20	.24	.22	.26	.25	.25			1.00	
	Element time													
C	Cumulative time	.46	.49	.46	.44	.47	.47	.49	.46	.48			.90	
	Element time													
D	Cumulative time	.61	.66	.62	.59	.69	.67	.67	.66	.70			.85	
	Element time													
E	Cumulative time	.70	.74	.72	.68	.79	.80	.76	.78	.81			1.00	
	Element time													
F	Cumulative time	1.00	1.02	.98	.99	1.07	1.09	1.02	1.06	1.09			1.10	
	Element time													
													Sum	

Allowances: Personal 5%
Fatigue 5%
Delay 5%

Standard time: _____

FIGURE 11.16 Activity Chart in Rayburn Law Office (Shaded Areas Indicate Time Spent Correcting and Revising Drafts)

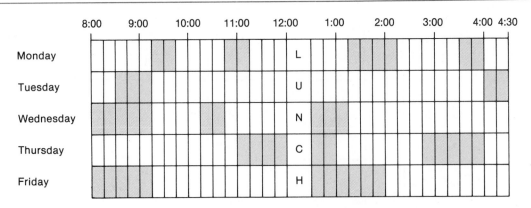

study using Figure 11.16. How do the results compare with the actual proportion?

CASE PROBLEM: CINCINNATI MILACRON CASTING CLEANING[14]

In early 1982, Malcolm Davis, Manager of Manufacturing Process Development of Cincinnati Milacron, Inc., faced a decision regarding the continuation of the robot aided casting cleaning project. Although it had taken much longer than planned to tool and program the robot, it had successfully cleaned two types of castings during December 1981. There was some concern, however, about continuing the development of the cleaning applications for the remainder of the thirty castings in the foundry's medium castings line.

Industry and Company Background

Cincinnati Milacron Inc. is engaged in the design, manufacture, and sale of process equipment and systems for industry, along with the supplies and accessories sold for use in these systems. Incorporated as Cincinnati Screw and Tap Company in 1884, the company originally sold screws, taps, and dies. After discovering a market for milling machines, the portion of the company devoted to these machines was purchased in 1889 and named the Cincinnati Milling Machine Co. The "Cincinnati Milacron" name was adopted in 1970. In 1981 the firm had 19 plants in the United States and 11 overseas, employed over 13,000 people, and had annual sales approaching one billion dollars. Financial data for the years 1974–1981 are found in Table 11.5.

[14]This case was prepared by James M. Comer and Marianne M. Hill as part of a grant from the Cleveland Foundation of Cleveland, Ohio entitled "Management Issues in High-Technology Manufacturing Industries." Used with permission.

TABLE 11.5 Cincinnati Milacron, Inc.

(In Thousands, Except Per-Share Amounts)	1974	1975	1976	1977	1978	1979	1980	1981
Operations Summary								
Sales	$424,760	$431,225	$420,396	$497,073	$592,563	$702,120	$816,402	$934,395
Earnings (loss) from continuing operations	6,390	8,356	7,572	18,357	31,219	52,577	52,441	60,787
Percent of sales	1.5%	1.9%	1.8%	3.7%	5.3%	7.5%	6.4%	6.5%
Percent of average shareholders' equity	4.3%	5.4%	4.8%	10.8%	16.2%	22.8%	18.4%	18.3%
Per common share	.28	.37	.34	.83	1.40	2.34	2.32	2.68
Net earnings (loss)	10,259	9,946	9,991	20,869	33,184	55,439	75,644	60,787
Percent of average shareholders' equity	6.9%	6.4%	6.3%	12.3%	17.2%	24.1%	26.6%	18.3%
Per common share	.47	.45	.45	.95	1.49	2.47	3.35	2.68
Year-End Financial Position								
Working capital	169,132	167,561	160,719	165,436	182,758	206,335	253,923	266,983
Property, plant and equipment—net	95,300	95,379	101,792	109,109	118,864	146,148	156,944	184,440
Total assets	421,560	376,891	393,824	426,422	482,049	570,562	626,696	715,779
Long-term debt and lease obligations	124,076	116,304	110,917	106,919	108,053	108,723	100,786	104,715
Total debt	188,449	149,249	141,635	136,012	136,908	139,340	127,343	126,993
Shareholders' equity	152,356	157,015	161,752	178,065	206,937	253,521	316,145	349,315
Per common share	6.77	6.99	7.20	7.86	9.01	11.03	13.75	15.17
Other data								
Dividends paid to common shareholders	5,044	5,047	5,051	5,809	7,017	9,902	14,571	16,283
Per common share	.2333	.2333	.2333	.2667	.3167	.4416	.6467	.7200
Capital expenditures	26,752	12,029	18,793	22,683	24,922	36,288	43,752	49,655
Depreciation	7,365	7,948	8,886	9,352	10,008	11,748	14,542	17,326
Unfilled orders at year end	346,226	216,166	250,082	320,738	471,231	673,316	698,288	476,856
Employees (average)	14,915	13,369	12,445	13,011	13,379	13,743	13,750	13,602
U.S. plants					16	18	17	19
Overseas plants					14	13	11	11

Source: 1983 Annual Report

The company has three major divisions: machine tools, plastics processing machinery, and industrial specialty products. In 1981, the machine tool group accounted for 68.5 percent of total sales and 78.1 percent of total operating earnings, and the plastics machinery group provided 14.6 percent of total sales and 11.6 percent of operating earnings. The third group, industrial specialty products, accounted for 16.9 percent of sales and 10.3 percent of operating earnings. The five product lines in this group include robots, cutting fluids, grinding wheels, semiconductor materials (silicon epitaxial wafers), and printed circuit board materials. Although industry sources rank Milacron first in dollar sales of robots in the United States, robot sales represent less than 10 percent of total company sales. Table 11.6 shows annual sales and operating earnings for the three-product groups for the years 1978–1981.

A major component of the machine tool division is a large jobbing foundry, which has provided gray and ductile iron castings for the Milacron's machine tools for over 70 years.[15] With recent capacity expansion and modernization facilitating the marketing of castings to other firms, plans are currently underway to change the foundry to a cost center. There are three separate departments in the foundry served by two cupolas and an electric holding furnace producing approximately 2500 different types of castings in lot sizes from 1 to 600 in small, medium, or large sizes. The small castings range in size from 4 ounces to 200 pounds; the medium castings range from 200 to 2000 pounds and account for the largest percentage of iron poured; and, the large castings range from 2000 to 40,000 pounds.

In 1980, foundry shipments dropped significantly from 1979 levels. Even with this decline, iron foundries were the nation's fifth largest manufacturing industry in 1981 and the second largest metal producing industry (surpassed only by rolled steel). Table 11.7 gives gray and ductile iron shipment figures in the United States for the years 1969–1981.

Casting and
Cleaning
Process

Iron castings are made in the following manner: Typically, a pattern is first made which conforms to the external shape of the casting. In the sand molding process, this pattern is then used to form a cavity in the sand which is shaped to the desired contours and dimensions of the casting. Sand is packed firmly around the pattern. After the pattern is removed, cores are set in place; the cores form the interior surface in the casting. The mold is then closed, and the casting is poured. After the iron has solidified, the casting is removed from the mold, the sand is broken away, and the casting is sandblasted. It is then sent to the casting cleaning area to remove all extraneous metal. After final cleaning, it is sent to the paint line. A flowchart of a typical foundry operation is included in Figure 11.17.

Casting cleaning is the most labor intensive operation in the foundry and one of the most difficult to staff. A casting is dumped on the floor in the cleaning area; the casting cleaners stand over it while cleaning and use crowbars and an overhead crane (which is shared among all the men) to move it and turn it over.

---

[15]A glossary of terms used in this case is at the end of the case. Definitions from Charles F. Walton (editor), *Iron Castings Handbook,* Iron Castings Society, Inc., 1981; and J. Gerin Sylvia, *Cast Metals Technology,* Reading, MA: Addison-Wesley Publishing Company, 1972; and *Industrial Robots,* Tech Tran Corporation, Naperville, IL, 1983.

	1978	1979	1980	1981
Machine Tool Group				
Sales	374	449	563	640
Operating Earnings	47	68	89	97
Plastics Machinery Group				
Sales	144	155	129	137
Operating Earnings	19	23	12	14
Industrial Specialty Products Group*				
Sales	75	99	125	158
Operating Earnings	5	13	12	13

TABLE 11.6

Cincinnati Milacron, Inc. Annual Sales and Operating Earnings (In Millions)

*1980–81: Robots, cutting fluids, grinding wheels, semiconductor material, printed circuit board material.
1978–1979 (called Industrial Products): specialty chemicals, cutting fluids, grinding wheels, semiconductor material, printed circuit board material. In these years, robots are included in "Machine Tools."
Source: 1982–1983 Annual Reports

	Gray Iron		Ductile Iron	
	Total (000 Tons)	For Sale	Total	For Sale
1969	14,649	9,206*	1,286	N.A.
1970	12,388	8,146*	1,607	N.A.
1971	11,865	7,909*	1,712	N.A.
1972	13,467	7,153	1,835	1,037
1973	14,801	7,688	2,246	1,320
1974	13,459	7,260	2,203	1,505
1975	10,622	5,235	1,824	1,202
1976	11,923	5,455	2,245	1,405
1977	12,371	5,477	2,736	1,808
1978	13,140	6,316	3,005	1,993
1979	12,512	6,084	2,890	1,865
1980	9,399	4,788	2,400	1,669
1981	9,610	5,063	2,191	1,524
	*Includes ductile iron for sale.			

TABLE 11.7

Shipments (Net Tons) of Ductile Iron and Gray Iron Castings

Source: Bureau of the Census

The system of risers, runners, and gates that created a path for the molten iron to enter the mold cavity is removed. Fins and other protrusions are also trimmed with the use of chisels, grinders, etc. The casting cleaners originally worked under very difficult conditions. The position was viewed by workers primarily as an entre into a desirable organization, since one of the "incentives" of the job was the ability to transfer to another position.

A comprehensive internal study of the foundry was instituted in 1973. The committee investigated forecasted needs, workflows, floor plans, and health and safety concerns in order to develop an effective foundry modernization plan. The plan

Foundry Modernization

FIGURE 11.17 Flow Chart of Foundry Operations

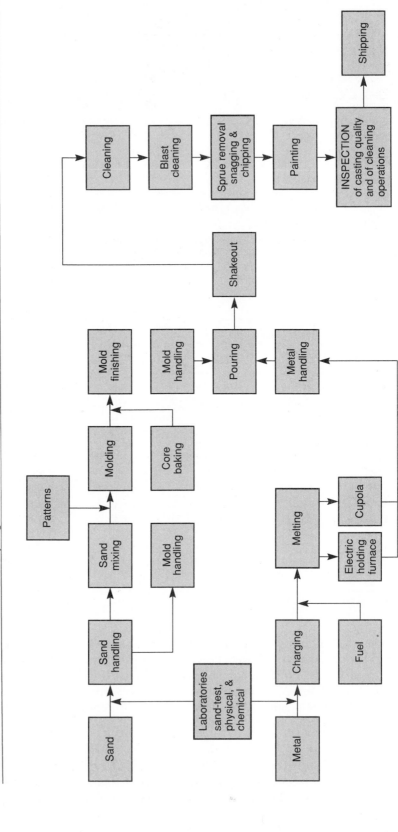

called for the modernization to begin first in the core room, proceed to molding, and then to the cleaning process. It was to start with the small casting line and then move on the medium and large lines. The project began in 1976 and the scheduled completion date for the plan was 1986.

An accident in 1980 caused by a cracked wheel on an old grinder prompted an adjustment to the plan. Four grinders with improved safety features immediately replaced the remaining older ones. Also in 1980, OSHA cited Milacron for unacceptable levels of noise and respirable dust in the cleaning areas.[16]

The modernization project in the cleaning areas specified the installation of "cleaning booths." The first booth was installed in the fall of 1980, and the twelfth was to be completed at the end of 1982, all in the small and medium castings lines. Three-sided booths for large castings are planned for 1986.

Castings enter a cleaning booth on a conveyor, and each booth has its own crane for lifting the casting onto a table. This table both rotates and elevates the casting so that the large grinders can be used. Previously, a 40-pound limit had been placed on castings that could be lifted by human operators. Castings weighing over 40 pounds were left on the floor and smaller grinders were used on them, which greatly increased the cleaning times.

In the booths, the air is circulated and cleaned. Although the air quality in the booths is such that helmet respirators are not needed, they are still worn for two reasons: they greatly reduce potential eye injury, and management wants consistency in the treatment of casting cleaners both in and out of the booths. The booths also provide isolation from noise associated with other cleaners. Although the booths and helmets did not constitute an engineering solution to the dust and noise problems, all OSHA regulations have been satisfied in these areas.

The booths result in a more orderly flow of work, improved material handling, and a decrease in tool repair. Tools are now conveniently located instead of being tossed around the cleaning area. There is also improved "housekeeping" in the booths. Management attributes this to the increased "pride of ownership" on the part of the casting cleaners. The turnover rate of cleaners has subsequently decreased dramatically.

The Introduction of Advanced Manufacturing Technologies

During 1977–79 an executive committee reporting directly to the president was established at Cincinnati Milacron to examine the trend in manufacturing throughout the entire firm. In general, the committee concluded that the company had to modernize and update the way in which they manufactured products in order to stay competitive with the foreign competition. More specifically, studies of the future trends in the work force had indicated that workers would become unavailable for undesirable jobs, such as casting cleaning. Thus, this area was identified for a possible robotic application. Other areas targeted for new technology included the introduction of robotics into the welding shop and the implementation of a computer-aided design (CAD) system.

In early 1980 Malcolm Davis, Manager of Manufacturing Process Development, was assigned the task of investigating and implementing robotic technology for possible use in the casting cleaning process. Manufacturing Process Development is part of the Corporate Facilities and Manufacturing division, which is responsible for the buildings, their contents, and the equipment used in manu-

The Introduction of Advanced Manufacturing Technologies

---

[16]Noise levels are calculated as weighted daily averages of all exposure to noise, including that produced by the worker himself and other workers within hearing range.

facturing. In addition, all new equipment purchases must be approved by this division. Before the robot project, new technology at the foundry had been the responsibility of the group headed by the Foundry Technical Manager.

In September 1980, a development group was physically assigned to the foundry. A robot was delivered to the foundry and the entire project was conducted there. The involvement of the foundry personnel in this project included site selection and preparation (the robot project was carried out fifty feet from the installation of a new cleaning booth) and weekly meetings between the robot development group and the foundry technical group. The superintendent of the foundry joined these meetings once a month.

One of the first tasks was to provide tools for the robot. In the existing cleaning operation, air tools were the standard type used by humans. It was obvious that the robot was capable of handling tools with much greater horsepower, so the search began for existing tools with higher horsepower that could be used by the robot.

During January and February of 1981, the market and literature were searched for potential tools to be used, but nothing was available. Electric motors were ruled out because they were too heavy and the weight-to-horsepower ratio was too great. Hydraulic motors offered the most promise because the weight-to-horsepower ratio is low and the power source can be remote.

Hydraulic tools that were available on the market could not readily be adapted for use by the robot. The development of these tools by an outside supplier was ruled out because of the cost. Cincinnati Milacron decided it would be more effective to purchase hydraulic motors and then develop the tools themselves around the robot application. An outside engineering firm was hired in March 1981 to do the mechanical drawings, and Milacron did the design work and built the tools in-house.

One of the first tools developed was a chisel, but it did not perform as expected. Effort was then directed toward developing grinding tools, burr cutters, and a cutoff wheel. Six tools were developed. It was also necessary to develop a way to change the tools and to then transmit hydraulic power through this tool changer. This was a very extensive endeavor; two iterations of the tool changers were necessary.

Figure 11.18 describes the robot-aided casting cleaning operation. The robot cleaned its first casting in December 1981. Applications were developed for two types of castings. Castings of each type were cleaned continuously.

The standard time to clean the first casting was 20 minutes for the worker and 16 minutes for the robot. Since this was a smaller casting, the robot spent a considerable amount of time changing tools. The robot, though, could work continuously, while the man needed to rest. It was estimated that the robot could complete in three days what it would take the worker five days to do. Although the robot's cleaning was more consistent (e.g., grinding lines were identical on all pieces), the quality of the casting was not assessed as better than that done by the worker.

The second casting cleaned by the robot was larger than the first. The standard time was 36 minutes for the man and 22 minutes for the robot. Since the amount of cleaning was greater (as opposed to tool changing), the robot could use the tool more productively over a longer period of time.

The casting cleaning robot is a point-to-point motion robot. It takes from six hours to three days to program the cleaning of each part and each operation

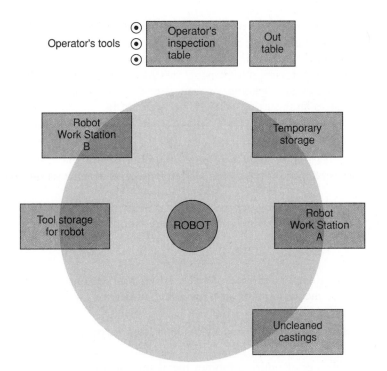

FIGURE 11.18
Casting Cleaning
Robot Operation

requires a separate tape. (In comparison, twelve applications could be stored on a single tape for robot welding operations.) It is estimated that it would take one and a half to two years of programming to have enough parts programmed for the robot to function productively.

An operator, with the help of a crane, would pick up a raw casting and put it on Work Station A (assume a casting is already at B). The robot would clean as many sides as it could at A and then move to Work Station B and work on the one there. Meanwhile, the operator picks up the casting from A and puts it on the temporary storage table and picks up another raw casting and puts it on A. When the robot is through at B, the operator takes the casting from B to the operator's inspection table, and moves the one from temporary storage to Station B. He checks the one on the inspection table to see if anything else needs to be worked on, and if so, he does it. When it is completed, he moves it to the out table.

The robot is busy all of the time. The operator is idle about 20 percent of the time and is moving castings and working 80 percent of the time. If the robot were adopted, production would be rebalanced to keep the man busy for greater periods of time.

Current Situation

Malcolm Davis is thus faced with drafting his recommendation. Although some feel that the need for the robot application is not as great now since the cleaning booths have been installed, Malcolm views the booths as a temporary, transitional measure.

The robotic application to casting is extremely attractive to management because the robot can work in any environment and would qualify as an engineering solution (required by OSHA) to the dust and noise problem. In addition, 12 to 16 undesirable jobs in casting cleaning could be eliminated.

Discussions with the foundry technical manager revealed that he thinks that future directions will focus on improving the quality of casting in order to reduce the amount of necessary cleaning, as well as examining other methods of metal removing, such as laser cutting and plasma arc cutting.

<table>
<tr><td>Questions for
Analysis</td><td>

1. A financial feasibility study was not attempted before the casting cleaning project began. Should it have been? What costs and benefits would have been included?
2. Do the cleaning booths reduce the need for the casting cleaning robot? Explain.
3. If you were Malcolm Davis, what recommendations would you make? Why?

</td></tr>
</table>

Case Glossary

Blast cleaning Removal of sand or oxide scale from castings by the impinging action of sand, metal shot, or grit projected under air, water, or centrifugal pressure.

Captive foundry One that produces castings from its own patterns for its own use.

Casting (Verb) act of pouring molten metal into a mold; (noun) metal object cast to a required shape by pouring or injecting liquid metal into a mold.

Chip (Verb) to remove extraneous metal from a casting by hand or pneumatically operated chisels.

Cleaning The process of removing all metal that does not belong on the final casting, such as gates, fins, runners, and risers; may also include the removal of adhering sand from the casting.

Core A preformed sand aggregate inserted into a mold to shape the interior of the casting or that part of the casting which cannot be shaped by the pattern.

Cupola A vertically cylindrical furnace for melting metal, in direct contact with coke as fuel, by forcing air under pressure through openings near its base.

Fins Thin projections of excess metal on a casting resulting from imperfect mold or core joints.

Gate End of the runner in a model where the rate of flow of molten metal is controlled as it enters the casting or mold cavity.

Gray iron Cast iron which contains a relatively large percentage of the carbon present in the form of flake graphite. The metal has a gray fracture.

Holding furnace Usually a small furnace for maintaining molten metal at the proper pouring temperature, and which is supplied from a large melting unit.

Hydraulic motor An actuator which converts forces from high pressure hydraulic fluid into mechanical shaft rotation.

Jobbing Foundry One which is equipped to economically produce a single casting or in small quantities from a variety of patterns.

Mold The form, made of sand, metal, or refractory material, which contains the cavity into which molten metal is poured to produce a casting of desired shape.

Off-line programming A means of programming a robot by developing a set of instructions on an independent computer and then using the software to control the robot at a later time.

Pattern A form of wood, metal, or other materials, around which molding material is placed to make a mold for casting metals.

Point-to-point motion This is a type of robot motion in which a limited number of points along a path of motion is specified by the controller. The robot moves from point-to-point in a straight line rather than a curved path between points. The latter is often referred to as continuous path motion and requires larger memory because more points are required.

Respirable dust Extremely fine dust; when combined with high levels of quartz silicon, it can be carcinogenic.

Riser A reservoir of molten metal provided to compensate for the contraction of the metal in a casting as it solidifies.

Robot A reprogrammable multifunctional manipulator designed to move material, parts, tools, or specialized devices through variable programmed motion for the performance of a variety of tasks.

Runner The portion of the gate assembly that connects the downgate with the casting ingate or riser.

Snagging Removal of fins and rough places on a casting by means of grinding.

Sprue The vertical portion of the gating system where the molten metal first enters the mold.

Teaching The process of programming a robot to perform a desired sequence of tasks.

Materials and Inventory Management

Materials management involves planning, coordinating, and controlling the acquisition, storage, handling, and movement of raw materials, purchased parts, semifinished goods, supplies, tools, and other materials that are needed in the production process. Any idle goods or materials that are held for future use are called **inventory**. For many organizations, the expenses associated with financing and maintaining inventories are a substantial part of the cost of doing business. In large firms, especially those with many or expensive products, these costs can run into millions of dollars.

Materials and inventory management represents one of the most important functions of P/OM. Materials and inventory managers are faced with the dual problems of maintaining sufficient inventories to meet demand and achieve productivity, while at the same time incurring the lowest possible cost. In this chapter we present the fundamental issues and concepts of materials and inventory management. In the next chapter, we review the basic analytical models and approaches for planning and controlling inventories.

12.1 THE SCOPE AND IMPORTANCE OF MATERIALS AND INVENTORY MANAGEMENT

Figure 12.1 depicts the essential materials-management activities associated with a production system. There are three components: *the management of raw materials and purchased parts* (purchasing, receiving, storage, and retrieval); *the management of finished goods* (packaging and shipping, storage and retrieval in warehouses, and distribution to the customer); *and the management of materials during the conversion process* (handling and storage of work-in-process inventories). All these activities deal with inventory in some form or another.

Inventory is important to a firm from two points of view: financial and operational. First, inventory represents a major financial investment for any company. The cost of maintaining inventories can be large, stemming from transportation, warehousing, and capital costs. Thus, economic forces exert strong pressure to reduce inventories. From a top management perspective, inventories have significant impact on a company's balance sheet and income statement. A common financial measure of liquidity is the *current ratio,* the ratio of current assets to current liabilities. The current ratio is a measure of short-term solvency;

FIGURE 12.1
Materials-
management
Activities

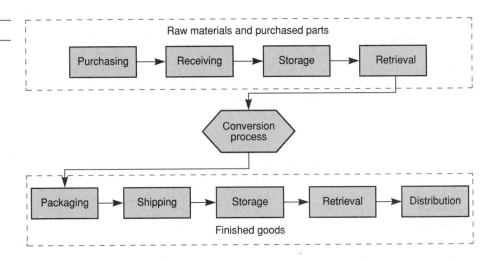

a value of about 2 is considered good. A reduction in inventory lowers current assets, and hence the current ratio, although the capital saved can be used to acquire more productive assets or to reduce liabilities. Better control of inventory can reduce operating expenses. If the "right" inventory is carried, profits can be increased through additional sales revenues.

The length of time that inventory is held determines the amount of investment; the quicker inventory moves through a company, the lower is the average investment. One way of measuring how long inventory is held is to determine how fast it "turns over." The *turn ratio* is computed by dividing the annual production or purchases of an item by the average inventory value. For instance, if the total annual purchases equals $5,000,000 and the average inventory value is $250,000, then the turn ratio is 20. Management seeks to have high turn ratios. Since *return on investment* (ROI) is defined to be the after-tax profit divided by the average investment, it makes financial sense to attempt to reduce inventories. That is, a decrease in average investment will increase the ROI ratio. Thus there are important financial pressures that suggest that inventory investment be held to a minimum.

On the other hand, from an operational perspective, inventory is an important aspect of production operations. There are five different types of inventory that are carried.

1. *Raw materials and purchased parts.* Items purchased from outside suppliers to be used in the production of the finished product; for example, chemicals, sheet metal, transistors, nuts, and bolts.
2. *Components.* Subassemblies or parts that are awaiting final assembly.
3. *Work-in-process.* All materials, semifinished goods, or subassemblies on the production floor in various stages of processing or between operations.
4. *Finished goods.* Final products waiting to be distributed to or purchased by customers.
5. *Supplies.* Items that support production and administrative functions but are not part of the finished product; for instance, tools, office supplies, and so on.

In service organizations, no physical products are made; however, inventories of supplies—such as forms in an insurance company or drugs in a hospital—are essential to the successful operation of the organization.

Although these five classes describe the types of inventories that are maintained, we have not addressed the question of *why* an organization carries inventory. There are five principal reasons. First, it is rarely possible to predict sales levels and production times accurately. Sales may average, 5000 units per month, for example, but may vary between 3500 and 7000 units. An order for raw materials may likewise have an average delivery time of 7 days, but the time may fluctuate between 5 and 15 days. Thus **fluctuation inventories**, most often called **safety stock**, are maintained in order to minimize the effect of such variations. Second, many items have high seasonal demand. It might be impossible to produce enough during a short selling season because of limited production capacity. **Anticipation inventories** are built up during the off-season in order to meet the estimated demand. A third reason for maintaining inventory is to take advantage of economies of scale in production and purchasing. The purchase of large lots often accrues savings through quantity discounts and truckload-discount transportation rates, even though the entire quantity is not required all at once. Such inventory is called **lot-size inventory**. Fourth, a significant amount of stock is usually in transit between various stages in the logistics system. For example, the shipment of goods from factories to regional warehouses by truck or rail may take several days or weeks. This **pipeline inventory** cannot be used until it reaches its destination. Finally, **work-in-process (WIP) inventories** have traditionally been used as buffers between work centers or departments in order to enable the production system to continue operating when machines break down, when vendor shipments are late, or when quality problems reduce the amount of acceptable WIP. However, to respond to market conditions, high WIP inventories can make it more difficult to change product lines, since they must be phased out. Thus, they limit a firm's flexibility as discussed in Chapter 4. Recognizing this, many industries have attempted to reduce the size of their WIP inventories.

Nearly every department in an organization views inventory objectives in a different manner. The marketing department, for instance, prefers high inventory levels in order to provide the best-possible customer service. Purchasing agents tend to buy in large quantities in order to take advantage of quantity discounts and lower freight rates. Similarly, production wants high inventories in order to prevent production delays. On the other hand, as we have discussed, financial personnel seek to minimize inventory investment and warehousing costs. Like all the P/OM decisions we have studied, the most effective policy is to achieve a *balance* among these conflicting objectives.

12.2 FUNCTIONS AND OBJECTIVES OF MATERIALS MANAGEMENT

In this section we present an overview of the materials-management activities illustrated in Figure 12.1. **Purchasing** is responsible for acquiring raw materials, component parts, tools, and any other items from outside suppliers. Purchasing's responsibilities are far broader than simply filling out orders; for example, they may also advise and challenge material specifications from engineering, perform value analyses, or analyze make/buy decisions.

Receiving includes the unloading of inbound goods from transportation vehicles, verifying that proper quantities are received in good condition and satisfy quality standards, and preparing the goods for storage. Quality-control techniques, which we discuss in Chapter 19, play an important role in receiving. The term **stores** is often used to designate the department that physically maintains all inventoried items and issues tools and supplies to production and maintenance.

Packaging and **shipping** departments are responsible for insuring that finished goods are properly packaged to prevent damage, correctly labeled, and loaded onto the right transportation vehicles. **Warehousing** acts as an interface between the plant and the customer and must be capable of filling orders accurately and in a reasonable amount of time. The role of *physical distribution,* often called *traffic,* is to select transportation carriers, manage company-owned fleets, and control interplant movement of materials and goods.

For most organizations the materials-management function has nine major objectives.[1]

1. Obtaining low prices for purchased items and transportation service. With lower operating costs, profits are increased.
2. Maintaining high-inventory turnover, that is, a high ratio of sales to average inventory. When inventories are low in relation to sales, less capital is tied up in inventories. This utilizes capital efficiently and increases return on investment.
3. Achieving low costs for receiving, storage, and inspection. If the receiving and stores departments operate efficiently, their costs can be reduced. Generally, the unit cost of handling material is reduced if materials are received in large quantities; note, however, that this also increases the inventory storage cost.
4. Maintaining reliable delivery and continuity of supply. Disruptions in supply will inevitably increase costs in production and transportation. Continuity of supply is especially important for highly automated processes that are on rigid schedules.
5. Maintaining consistent quality. The materials department is responsible for the quality of materials and services received from outside suppliers. If poor quality items are purchased, significant costs will be incurred later in the production process.
6. Achieving low support personnel costs. The objective of reducing payroll costs whenever possible is common to every department in a firm.
7. Maintaining favorable supplier relations. Manufacturing companies rely heavily on outside suppliers. Sudden changes in demand may require quick response from outside suppliers. Good relations with suppliers can result in extra service, improved attention to quality, and lower costs.
8. Achieving development of personnel. This is important to identify leadership potential within the company for continued success and growth.
9. Keeping adequate records and information. Good records provide important information needed for quality programs, production scheduling, and as an audit trail to discourage corruption and misuse of company assets.

Meeting these objectives requires an effective organization and sound communication among the various managers and supervisors. This is especially difficult, since goals of different functions often conflict. For example, purchasing—in an attempt to maintain low costs—may choose vendors that have poor delivery records. This may potentially affect manufacturing if materials are not received on time. Manufacturing, on the other hand, requires adequate supplies of ma-

---

[1]Dean S. Ammer, *Materials Management,* Homewood, Illinois: Richard D. Irwin, 1974.

terials. This may lead to maintaining higher inventory levels than necessary. If not properly controlled, excessive inventory costs may result. Because of these potential conflicts, many companies centralize their materials-management activities. For instance, Cincinnati Milacron, a large manufacturer of industrial machine tools and other products, has a director of materials management, whose responsibility is to coordinate purchasing, production and capacity planning, inventory control, stockroom activities, and materials handling. With such an organizational structure, personnel must work more closely with each other and cannot resort to "passing the buck."

12.3 SUPPLIERS AND THE PURCHASING FUNCTION

No one can dispute that the vital interests of any company depend upon the satisfactory performance of products and services furnished by its suppliers. Deficiencies in supplied products or services can increase spoilage, reduce sales, delay delivery schedules, and reduce productivity. These in turn have an adverse effect on profits of the company, and may even jeopardize the company's ability to stay in business.

The costs of purchased materials, parts, and components make up a substantial portion of the total direct costs for many companies, though the proportion varies considerably from company to company and from one product to another within any company. There are two primary reasons why firms use suppliers: (1) The supplier can provide materials or parts at a lower cost than if they were produced in-house, or (2) the supplier has knowledge or skills not possessed by the company.

The purchasing department in any organization acts as an interface between suppliers of materials and the production function. Since materials comprise one of the largest sources of cash outlay in any manufacturing firm, their acquisition requires careful management. The responsibilities of a purchasing department include learning the material needs of the organization, selecting suppliers and negotiating price, ensuring delivery, and monitoring cost, quality, and delivery performance. Occasionally the term **procurement** is used to describe the acquisition of goods and services. This is a broader term and includes purchasing, stores, traffic, receiving, and inspection.

Purchasing Objectives and Procedures

The principal goals of purchasing are related to *quality, service, price,* and *vendor relations*. In addition to the obvious necessity of quality purchased parts, the purchasing department must consider vendor reliability, maintenance and return policies, and other aspects of customer service. Moreover, purchasing must continually seek new vendors and products and be able to evaluate their potential to the company. Also, purchasing seeks the best price that is consistent with company quality standards, in order to lower inventory investment and product cost. Good relations with vendors are another goal of purchasing, so that such matters as expediting shipments can be easily accomplished when necessary.

Within the organization, purchasing must maintain good relations and communication with other departments, such as accounting and finance, where budgets are prepared; engineering, where material specifications are set; production, where timely delivery is essential; and legal, where contracts must be reviewed.

To accomplish these goals, purchasing activities are varied. The principal procedures in a purchasing department can be listed as follows:

1. *Receive purchase requisitions.* It is at this time that purchasing receives the authority to buy required materials. **Purchase requisitions** are documents generated by production or inventory control that authorize material purchases. Sufficient lead time must be given so that purchasing can seek out alternative vendors or materials, arrange delivery schedules, and so on.

2. *Review and evaluate requisitions.* It is often the case that specific materials or items requested by engineering or production can be substituted with less costly items or perhaps eliminated altogether. **Value analysis** considers these alternatives by studying the functions of requisitioned material in relation to cost. Value-analysis studies often consider job design and work simplification, as well as the use of alternative materials or components, as means of reducing cost. In addition, such studies may evaluate product appearance and specifications relative to sales appeal.

3. *Select qualified suppliers.* A qualified supplier should be able to (1) provide goods that meet the firm's quality specifications, (2) deliver the goods on time and at an acceptable price, and (3) be able to work cooperatively with the purchasing department when special situations arise, such as changes in specifications or volume, service problems, or other requests. Many companies have *supplier certification programs* that evaluate suppliers according to various criteria such as quality, cost, and delivery. Ford Motor Company suppliers, for example, must meet stringent quality standards in order to be awarded business.

4. *Aggregate and place orders.* Purchasing must select suppliers based on price, quality, delivery performance, and reliability. Sales contacts, buyers' conventions, and trade magazines are the most important sources of information. Consideration must be given to quantity discounts and other price breaks. This requires effective communication with inventory control. Aggregating many orders for one supplier can substantially reduce transportation and handling costs. This is an important function of purchasing.

5. *Follow-up and expedite.* It is important that goods are delivered on schedule for production. Entire production lines have been shut down because of delays in securing a part worth only pennies. Purchasing must monitor deliveries and production schedules and expedite deliveries and schedules when necessary.

6. *Authorize payments.* Purchasing must work closely with receiving and accounting to ensure that all ordered goods are delivered before payment is authorized.

7. *Keep records.* With thousands of products and materials, hundreds of suppliers, requisitions in various stages of review, order processing, and so on, an accurate information system is essential.

In most organizations, there are three classes of purchased items. The first class of items are those of large capital expense that are either purchased on a one-time basis or very infrequently—for example, machine tools, computing equipment, or transportation vehicles. The second class consists of those items purchased in small quantities, infrequently purchased items, and low-cost items, such as typewriter ribbons and other office supplies and small tools. High-volume-use items such as sheet metal or bulk raw materials constitute the third class.

Purchasing procedures often vary, depending on the type of item purchased. For instance, large capital expenditures often require competitive bids based on detailed technical specifications and legal contracts, whereas small items can be ordered by departmental secretaries through catalogs or purchased outright without any formal procedure. In the latter case, payments are usually made from petty-cash funds or small-supplies budgets, thus eliminating unnecessary paperwork and time. High-volume purchases, however, are often handled by **blanket contracts**. With this type of arrangement, a large quantity is contracted for over a long period of time. In such systems, delivery dates are not specified. Instead, as material is needed, release orders are sent out for delivery, perhaps on a monthly or weekly basis. The buyer can take advantage of quantity discounts and be assured of supply in this way.

Often the procured items are complex or perform vital functions in the product; therefore it is important for any company to emphasize the quality of procured items. Because the manufacturing and quality control operations of the supplier are not under the direct control or observation of the buyer, it is necessary to implement tasks and controls to assure the needed quality. When a current supplier is being considered for an order, the quality of products supplied previously becomes a primary consideration. If quality has been inadequate and the supplier shows little interest in improving it, a reorder usually goes to a different supplier.

In the 1980s many U.S. firms changed their supplier relationship to secure improved quality. Where suppliers' quality has substantially improved, companies have then been able to achieve two other goals: (1) eliminate or substantially reduce inventories and (2) eliminate or substantially reduce incoming inspection and testing.

These objectives have been achieved through a number of strategies. First, the total number of suppliers can be reduced, allowing for tighter links with the resulting fewer suppliers. Second, suppliers' experts can be brought in at the early stages of design. Next, long-term contracts can be made so that suppliers are more willing to invest in process and system improvements. The older practice of having many suppliers bid on each order—with the lowest price accepted—is losing favor except on standard items. Many companies are now requiring suppliers to provide evidence, such as quality control charts or test results, showing that manufacturing processes are under tight control. This evidence is then used in eliminating or reducing incoming inspection so that items can go directly to production areas for immediate use. A side benefit is the reduction of inventories and the associated problems of outdated stocks, deterioration, and scrap or rework if design changes are made.

Quality Considerations in Purchasing

12.4 RECEIVING AND SHIPPING

The principal functions of receiving and shipping include deliveries of inbound and outbound freight, inspection, and transfer to and from storage. Efficient processing of materials at these points is essential for effective stock control, production, and customer satisfaction.

Receiving takes delivery of inbound shipments and releases the materials to inventory. The major responsibilities include:

The Receiving Function

1. control and scheduling of deliveries

2. accurate checking and recording of shipments received
3. preparation for handling and storage.

Whenever possible, deliveries should be scheduled to balance the workload throughout the day. For instance, deliveries from local vendors should be requested for the morning hours so that sufficient personnel and equipment are available for processing outbound shipments, which normally peak later in the day. To plan for receiving activities, supervisors should review information due in from purchase orders, bills of lading, or vendor notices of shipment to determine approximate dates of arrival. This enables storage space to be planned for large shipments or expeditious processing of back orders that may be urgently needed by production.

All shipments received should be given a thorough and accurate inspection. Prior to acceptance, each shipment should be physically checked against the freight bill, bill of lading, or other delivery document, as well as the purchase order. Any discrepancies or damage should be noted so that legal recovery of damages can be processed. Quality inspection may be the responsibility of the receiving department or may be performed by a separate quality-control function. In any case, items for which quality control is essential should be tested for acceptance.

Once the materials have been unloaded and accepted, they are prepared for release to storage. This may involve labeling or repacking and palletization. Of course, handling is reduced if items are immediately palletized during the unloading operation.

The Shipping Function	Shipping is responsible for:

Shipping is responsible for:

1. preparation of material for shipment
2. inspection of outgoing freight
3. loading onto transport vehicles.

Proper packaging is essential for delivery of goods on time and in usable condition. Failure to control packing can result in replacement of damaged shipments and unnecessary transportation costs, as well as loss of customer goodwill. The two basic principles of packaging are

1. proper selection of the container or packaging materials
2. use of the best packing methods.

In selecting a container, we must consider factors such as size, weight, shape, fragility, and value of the item and the costs of possible containers. The container should be the smallest size that will adequately protect the item. Items may be packed in boxes, crates, or bundles. Cushioning material is normally used for interior protection. A variety of automated packing machines and fastening systems are available for efficient packaging.

Inspection of outbound shipments is similar to that of checking incoming freight. Any discrepancies must be adjusted or changes made to the shipping documents before the shipments are turned over to the carrier.

Traffic and physical distribution is the movement of goods and materials from the supplier to the customer and is a critical element of materials management. Strategic aspects of physical distribution, such as warehouse location and aggregate transportation strategies, were considered in Chapter 7. Traffic is responsible for the more routine decisions related to physical distribution. Specifically, the role of traffic is to

1. purchase transportation services
2. select the appropriate mode of shipment and specific carrier
3. negotiate transportation rates and contracts
4. trace shipments in transit and expedite them when necessary
5. file claims for damaged goods
6. audit freight bills.

Traffic personnel are also involved in special studies, such as warehouse location or fleet-routing problems. In large multiplant corporations, traffic has the added responsibility for interplant movement of goods.

The purchase of transportation services is a complex decision, since a wide variety of services are available. The critical factors in selecting a mode of transportation are

1. time
2. availability
3. cost
4. dependability
5. capability.

The primary modes of transportation that are available are rail, motor carrier, air, water, and pipeline. Pipelines have limited use and accessibility and are used primarily for such products as oil and natural gas. Similarly, water transportation is limited and most useful in transporting large quantities of bulky items, for instance raw materials such as coal and other ores.

Railroads, motor carriers, and air transport are common carriers that, until recently, have been highly regulated by the federal government. Recent deregulation has increased competition in the marketplace, thus making good traffic management even more important.

A comparison of these three modes of transportation illustrates the important differences between them. These are summarized in Table 12.1. Rail transit is generally slow; boxcars average about 20 miles per hour, primarily due to the

Table 12.1

A Comparison of Transportation Modes

Characteristic	Rail	Truck	Air
Speed	3	2	1*
Accessibility	2	1	3
Cost	1	2	3
Load capability	1	2	3

*The best ranking is a 1.

time spent in classification yards while trains are being consolidated. Many factories and warehouses are not situated near railroad tracks. Consequently, the use of rail transit requires additional handling by truck. Rail transit is used for shipping large volumes of relatively low-value items over long distances. However, rail cars often encounter long delays and are less dependable than other forms of transportation. Motor carriers have high availability and can ship nearly anywhere. Transportation costs are higher, and this mode is used most often for short distances and smaller shipments. Weight and size limitations often limit the capability of trucks for carrying certain loads. Scheduled service is more dependable than rail.

Since rail traffic has limited access, one of the more unique transportation options that has come along over the last several decades is the TOFC (trailer on flat car), referred to as the "piggyback" concept. Semitrailers are removed from the motor unit at the railroad yard and loaded onto flatcars for long-haul distances. Upon reaching their principal destinations, they are removed from the train and hauled over the road to their final destination. This reduces unnecessary handling of goods to and from rail cars and lowers average cost per mile traveled.

Air transportation is highly dependable and very fast; although, like rail, it is much less accessible. Costs are higher, but this mode of transport may be cheaper overall than surface transportation because of reduced needs for packaging. Clearly, air cargo carriers cannot handle very large loads.

In choosing a mode of transit, we must therefore consider factors such as cost, time, weight restrictions, loading and unloading facilities, and carrier reliability. Smaller transit time means less inventory carried if contract terms are f.o.b. origin;[2] more reliable delivery when scheduled results in less chance of a stockout. Characteristics of individual carriers differ within a particular mode. The traffic manager has the responsibility of selecting that carrier who not only gives a good rate but also has proven customer service policies in areas of delivery, damage rates, claims handling, and so on.

We have reviewed the general functions of materials management. In Chapter 17 we will study how materials management activities are integrated into production systems through a concept known as "just-in-time." In the remainder of this chapter, we focus on specific inventory management issues.

12.6 CLASSIFYING INVENTORY PROBLEMS

A large variety of inventory problems exist.[3] For instance, a self-serve gasoline station maintains an inventory of only a few grades of gasoline, whereas an appliance store may carry several hundred different items and brands. Demand for gasoline is relatively constant, while the demand for air-conditioners is highly seasonal and variable. If a gasoline station runs out of gas, a customer will go elsewhere. However, if an appliance store does not have a particular item in stock, the customer may be willing to order the item and wait for delivery. Since

---

[2] F.o.b. means *free on board*. F.o.b. *origin* means that the buyer pays for transportation and owns the goods in transit; f.o.b. *delivered* means that the seller pays for transportation, and title to the goods is turned over the buyer on delivery.

[3] A more complete, technical classification and survey of inventory problems is given in E.A. Silver, "Operations Research in Inventory Management," *Operations Research,* 29 (1981): 628–645.

TABLE 12.2

A Classification
Scheme for
Inventory
Problems

Characteristic	Attributes
Number of items	One or many
Nature of demand	Independent or dependent; deterministic or stochastic; static or dynamic
Number of time periods in planning horizon	One or many
Lead time	Deterministic or stochastic
Stockouts	Backorders or lost sales

the inventory characteristics of the gasoline station and appliance store differ significantly, the proper control of inventories requires different approaches.

One of the first steps in analyzing an inventory problem should be to describe the essential characteristics of the environment and inventory system. Although it is impossible to consider all characteristics here, we address the more important ones. Table 12.2 summarizes inventory problems in terms of the characteristics that may exist.

Number of Items

Many models in inventory control deal with determining the inventory policy for only one item. For organizations with hundreds or thousands of distinct items, applying an inventory model for each item might prove rather difficult. In such cases, items are often aggregated, or partitioned, into groups with similar characteristics or dollar value. It is easier to design effective inventory systems for the control of a small number of aggregate groups of items.

With multiple items, there may be various constraints that affect inventory policy. For instance, there may be a limit on available warehouse space or the amount of money that can be invested in inventory. This makes the determination of optimum inventory levels more difficult. Other interactions may exist among products that must also be considered. For example, certain groups of products tend to be demanded together, such as motor oil and oil filters, certain chemicals, or food items. These must be considered together in developing an inventory policy.

Nature of Demand

Demand can be classified as being either independent or dependent, deterministic and stochastic, and dynamic or static. By *independent demand*, we mean demand that is not influenced by operations but rather by the market. Inventories of finished goods have independent demand characteristics. Items are said to have *dependent demand* if their demand is related to that of another item. For example, a chandelier may consist of a frame and six light bulb sockets. The demand for chandeliers is independent, while the demand for sockets is dependent on the demand for chandeliers.

In many situations, demand is reasonably stable and thus can be accurately forecast. In such cases, demand can be assumed to be known with certainty. We call this *deterministic demand*. In other cases, demand is highly variable and can be specified only by a probability distribution. In this case, we refer to it as *stochastic demand*. In stochastic demand situations, accurate forecasting is more difficult. Such is often the case with one-time sales or seasonal items.

Demand may also fluctuate over time or be stable throughout the year. For instance, food items such as bread or canned goods exhibit relatively stable demand, while the demand for holiday items such as turkeys or hams varies significantly over the year. Stable demand is usually called *static,* while demand that varies over time is referred to as *dynamic demand.*

Number of Time Periods

In some cases, the selling season is relatively short and any leftover items cannot be physically or economically stored until the next season. For example, Christmas trees that have been cut cannot be stored until the following year, and other items, such as seasonal fashions, are sold at a loss simply because there is no storage space or it is uneconomical to keep them for the next year. This "single-period" inventory problem requires a different analysis than problems in which inventory is held from one time period to the next.

Lead Time

Lead time is the amount of time between the placement of an order and when it is received. Lead time may be relatively constant or stochastic (in which case it may be described by some probability distribution). Lead time is affected by transportation carriers. Rail, truck, and air transportation have different characteristics. Thus the lead time for products shipped by air may be less variable than that for rail. We must also include the time to process the order by the vendor or produce it if it is not readily available. A good purchasing system maintains lead-time information that can be used in inventory analysis.

Stockouts

When no stock is available to satisfy the demand for an item, it is either backordered or a lost sale is incurred. Backorders result in additional costs for transportation, expediting, or perhaps buying from another supplier at a higher price. A lost sale has an opportunity cost associated with it, which may include any loss of goodwill and potential future revenue.

From a customer-service viewpoint, we would never want to incur a stockout; indeed, in situations such as blood inventories, stockouts can be tragic. However, in many situations backorders may be economically justified. For instance, with very high-value items such as commercial jet planes, no inventory is carried and a backorder state always exists. Backorders may also be planned in order to smooth demand on the work force. When backorders occur but are not planned, one of several reasons can usually be identified; these include forecast inaccuracies on usage or lead time, unreliable vendor delivery, clerical errors, quality problems, insufficient safety stock, or transportation accidents.

We see that a large number of different inventory situations exist. For example, we may have a single item, independent, deterministic, static-demand problem for several time periods with a stochastic lead time and backorders. Another situation may involve multiple items with independent, stochastic, and static demand for a single time period with deterministic lead time and lost sales. Clearly the inventory policies differ for each of these problems. We cannot discuss every possible case in this book; rather, in Chapter 13 we discuss some fundamental situations that operations managers face and that provide the basis for the analysis of more-complex situations.

12.7 INVENTORY COSTS

Inventory costs fall into four major categories: cost of the items themselves, order-preparation costs, inventory-holding costs, and shortage costs. The cost of maintaining inventory is the principal criterion for determining inventory policy: namely, how much inventory to carry and the frequency of ordering.

The cost of items is often an important consideration when quantity discounts are offered; it may be more economical to purchase large quantities at a lower unit cost. In most cases, however, the cost of the item is constant.

Ordering costs are incurred because of the work involved in placing purchase orders with vendors or organizing for production within a plant. For purchased items, this can include such activities as order processing, forms, selecting vendors, fixed costs of handling by vendors, processing receiving documents, and inspection of goods when they arrive. If a manufactured lot is ordered within a plant, the ordering costs (generally called *setup costs*) include paperwork, machine setup, and start-up scrap. Ordering costs do not depend on the number of items purchased or manufactured, but rather on the number of times that an order is placed.

Inventory-holding or inventory-carrying costs include all expenses incurred because inventory is carried. In this category we include such items as rent, electricity and heat, insurance and taxes, spoilage and obsolescence, and the cost of capital. Rent, utilities, insurance, and so on are fixed costs associated with maintaining the storage facilities and are relatively easy to measure from accounting data. Spoilage and obsolescence costs apply to food and drug items, which may have only a limited shelf life, or to novelty and seasonal items such as toys or Christmas trees. The **cost of capital** invested in inventory normally accounts for the largest component of inventory-holding costs. Cost of capital is the product of the value of a unit of inventory, the length of time held, and an interest rate associated with a dollar tied up in inventory. The interest rate can often be highly volatile and depends upon the prime interest rate, the risk environment of the firm, and management goals for rates of return on investment.[4] For instance, if money is borrowed to finance inventory, an interest charge is incurred. If the firm's own money is used, then there is an opportunity cost associated with not being able to use the money for other productive investments. Since many of these factors are difficult to determine, holding charges are often based substantially on management judgment.

A shortage can either be resolved by a backorder, in which case a customer waits until the item is available, or by a lost sale, in which case the customer purchases the item somewhere else. Backorders incur additional costs for shipping, invoicing, and labor involved in handling the paperwork, receiving the goods, and notifying customers. Lost sales result in lost profit opportunities and possible future loss of revenues which are often referred to as **goodwill costs**.

From this discussion, you may wonder how inventory models can ever be used effectively, since the important inventory costs are difficult to measure. Fortunately, inventory models are generally quite *robust*. By this we mean that even if the costs used are not the correct values but are good approximations, there is generally little variation in the resulting solution recommended by the model. Consequently, even the simplest models have been used successfully in reducing costs in many companies.

There are three primary decisions that must be made in regard to inventory: how to monitor inventory, how much should be ordered, and when should orders be placed. Each of these has an important impact on cost. The more control

---

[4]Everette S. Gardner, "Inventory Theory and the Gods of Olympus," *Interfaces*, 10, no. 4 (1980): 42–45.

placed on monitoring inventory levels, the higher the cost of clerical work and data processing. On the other hand, better control may result in fewer stockouts and improved customer service. The quantity and frequency of ordering also affects inventory costs. If large lots are ordered, then more inventory is carried, on the average. Therefore, fewer orders are placed and ordering costs are low. However, holding costs are high. On the other hand, if frequent, small orders are placed, ordering costs are high, but holding costs are low. These costs must be balanced in order to achieve a minimum-cost inventory policy.

12.8 INVENTORY-MANAGEMENT SYSTEMS

In this section we discuss some of the principal features of inventory system design. We have seen that there are a large variety of different inventory problems, that is, multiple items, dependent or independent demand, and so on, therefore, one type of management system may not be applicable for all inventory problems. Effective inventory control may require a combination of several systems. In this section, we consider aggregate inventory management, systems for independent demand, and physical control of inventories. The control of dependent-demand inventory warrants a separate chapter and is discussed in Chapter 15.

ABC Inventory Analysis

The concept of ABC inventory analysis was first proposed by H.F. Dickie at General Electric in the early 1950s for studying inventories consisting of a large number of different items. The technique has been shown to be a very valuable management tool for identifying and controlling important inventory items. ABC analysis consists of classifying inventory items into three groups, called the **ABC classification**, according to their total annual dollar usage. These groups are defined as follows:

1. *A items.* Those accounting for a large dollar value but a relatively small percentage of total items.
2. *C items.* Those accounting for a small dollar value but a large percentage of total items.
3. *B items.* Those in between A and C.

Typically, A items usually comprise 70 to 80 percent of the total dollar usage while consisting of about 15 to 30 percent of the items, whereas C items account for 5 to 15 percent of the total dollar value and about 50 percent of the items. There is no specific rule on where to make the division between A and B items or between B and C items. The percentages we have given simply serve as a guideline.

EXAMPLE | FINDING AN ABC INVENTORY CLASSIFICATION

Consider the data for 20 inventoried items of a small company, shown in Table 12.3. The last column gives the projected annual dollar usage of each item, which is found by multiplying the annual projected usage based on forecasts (in units) by the unit cost. If the items are ranked in order of annual dollar usage, we can construct Table 12.4. Here, we have also listed the cumulative percentage of items, cumulative dollar usage, and cumulative percent of total dollar usage. Analysis of Table 12.4 indicates that 70 percent of the total dollar usage is

Table 12.3

Usage-cost Data
for Twenty
Inventoried Items

Item Number	Projected Annual Usage	Unit Cost	Projected Annual Dollar Usage
1	1,500	$ 5.00	$ 7,500
2	6,450	20.00	129,000
3	5,000	45.00	225,000
4	200	12.50	2,500
5	20,000	35.00	700,000
6	84	250.00	21,000
7	800	80.00	64,000
8	300	5.00	1,500
9	10,000	35.00	350,000
10	2,000	65.00	130,000
11	5,000	25.00	125,000
12	3,250	125.00	406,250
13	9,000	.50	4,500
14	2,900	10.00	29,000
15	800	15.00	12,000
16	675	200.00	135,000
17	1,470	100.00	147,000
18	8,200	15.00	123,000
19	1,250	.16	200
20	2,500	.20	500

Table 12.4

ABC Analysis
Calculations

	Rank	Item Number	Cumulative Percent of Items	Annual Dollar Usage	Cumulative Dollar Usage	Cumulative Percent of Total
A	1	5	5	$700,000	$ 700,000	26.8
	2	12	10	406,250	1,106,250	42.3
	3	9	15	350,000	1,456,250	55.7
	4	3	20	225,000	1,681,250	64.3
	5	17	25	147,000	1,828,250	70.0
B	6	16	30	135,000	1,963,250	75.1
	7	10	35	130,000	2,093,250	80.1
	8	2	40	129,000	2,222,250	85.1
	9	11	45	125,000	2,347,250	89.8
	10	18	50	123,000	2,470,250	94.5
C	11	7	55	64,000	2,534,250	97.0
	12	14	60	29,000	2,563,250	98.1
	13	6	65	21,000	2,584,250	98.9
	14	15	70	12,000	2,596,250	99.4
	15	1	75	7,500	2,603,750	99.6
	16	13	80	4,500	2,608,250	99.8
	17	4	85	2,500	2,610,750	99.9
	18	8	90	1,500	2,612,250	99.9
	19	20	95	500	2,612,750	99.9
	20	19	100	200	2,612,950	100.0

accounted for by the first five, that is, only 25 percent of the items. In addition, the lowest 50 percent of the items account for only 5.5 percent of the total dollar usage. If we plot the percent of items versus percent dollar usage for our previous example we get the *ABC curve* shown in Figure 12.2, sometimes known as a *Pareto curve*.

An ABC analysis provides the inventory-control manager with some useful information. Since the A items represent a substantial inventory investment, these items need to be closely controlled. This usually involves using the most complete and accurate records, continuous monitoring of inventory levels, frequent accuracy counts, high priorities, and maximum attention paid to order sizes and frequency of ordering. C items, on the other hand, need not be as closely controlled. Large quantities of these items might be ordered to take advantage of quantity or transportation discounts, and inventory levels might simply be checked on a periodic basis without maintaining any formal records. B items fall in the middle; more control should be exercised than for C items, but they do not have to be regarded as critically as those in class A.

Many phenomena besides inventory exhibit the characteristics of ABC curves. Other applications are given in Table 12.5. In each of these cases, the ABC curve provides the manager with data on critical items in the population. For instance, consider the population item "delivery routes" in a distribution situation. ABC analysis can indicate that a small percentage of routes will account for a large percentage of total stops. For these routes, more care in scheduling might be recommended. ABC analysis can thus be useful in many diverse P/OM problems.

Control Systems for Independent Demand

There are two basic types of inventory control systems: a continuous-review system and a periodic-review system.

Inventory position is defined as the amount on hand *plus* any amount on order but not yet received *minus* backorders. In a **continuous-review system**, the inventory position is continuously monitored. Whenever the inventory position falls at or below a level *r*, called the **reorder point**, an order for *Q* units is placed (see Figure 12.3). Values for *Q* and *r* are determined in advance. If the reorder

FIGURE 12.2

ABC Curve

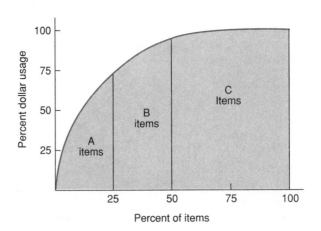

Table 12.5

Applications of
ABC Analysis

Population Item	Ranking Order (Descending Value of Activity per Item)	Coordinates of ABC Plot
Stores in retail chain	Annual dollar sales per store	Cumulative percent of total sales versus percent of ranked stores
Active inventory items	Annual dollar sales per active inventory item	Cumulative percent of total sales versus percent of ranked inventory items
Active inventory items	Dollar inventory investment per inventory item	Cumulative percent of total inventory versus percent of ranked inventory items
Active inventory items	Cubic feet storage required per item	Cumulative percent of total cubic feet versus percent of ranked inventory items
Incoming or outgoing shipments or orders	Cases of merchandise per shipment or order	Cumulative percent of total cases versus percent of ranked shipments or orders
Incoming or outgoing line items on order	Cases per line item	Cumulative percent of total cases versus percent of ranked line items
Delivery routes	Stops per route	Cumulative percent of total stops versus percent of ranked routes
Days	Outgoing or incoming orders per day	Cumulative percent of total orders versus percent of ranked days
Half-hours of day	Numbers of truck arrivals in each half-hour	Cumulative percent of total arrivals versus percent of ranked half-hours

Source: David Herron, "Industrial Engineering Applications of ABC Curves," Reprinted with permission from AIIE Transactions, June 1976. Copyright Institute of Industrial Engineers, 25 Technology Park/Atlanta, Norcross, GA 30092.

decision is based solely on the on-hand inventory level, then orders would be placed continuously as the stock falls below r. This would clearly be incorrect.

You have undoubtedly seen several examples of continuous-review systems. For example, many retail department stores have computerized cash registers, which are tied into an inventory-control system. When the clerk enters the item code number, the computer automatically reduces the inventory level for that unit by one and checks to see if the reorder point has been reached. If so, it signals that a purchase order should be initiated to replenish the stock. Optical scanning devices in grocery stores work in a similar fashion. If computers are not used in such systems, some form of manual system is necessary to monitor daily usage and check whether or not the reorder point has been reached. This requires substantial clerical effort and commitment on the part of users to fill out the proper forms when items are used. This is often a source of errors.

One version of a continuous-review system that eliminates the need for daily reporting and is often used for small parts is called the *two-bin system*. Consider a supply of small parts kept in a bin with a second (full) bin in reserve. When the first bin is empty, a resupply order is placed and the second bin is used. The second bin should contain at least enough material to last during the lead time.

FIGURE 12.3

Operation of a Continuous-review Inventory System

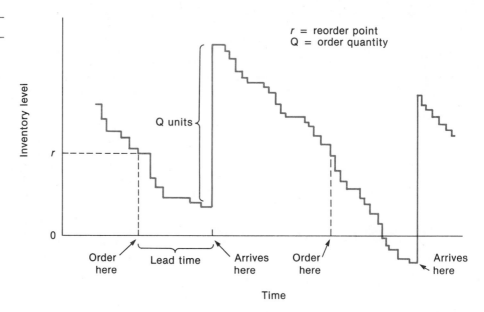

This system is easily implemented by placing a card at the bottom of the bin, which is turned in when the last item is taken. A variation of this system is often found in bookstores, in which the second-to-last copy of a book contains a card with appropriate reorder information; the cashier removes this card when the book is sold.

In **periodic-review systems**, the inventory position is checked only at fixed intervals of time. If the inventory position is at or below the reorder point r when checked, an order is placed for sufficient stock to bring the inventory position *up to R*, called the *reorder level* (see Figure 12.4). Such systems usually involve stock clerks making the rounds and physically checking the inventory levels. Notice that if the lead time is always shorter than the time between reviews, then the reorder point can be based on inventory level rather than inventory position, since there will never be an order outstanding. This makes implementation easier, since the stock clerk need not know what orders are outstanding. Usually the reorder point for each item is identified by a tag on the shelf; the clerk needs only to compare this to the number of items remaining.

The choice of which system to use depends on a variety of factors. Continuous-review systems require that accurate records of inventory positions be maintained. With today's computer systems, this is usually easy to do; however, in some situations it is not economical to monitor inventory continuously when manual records must be updated. Continuous-review systems offer tighter control of inventoried items, since orders may be placed to insure that stockout risks are minimized. Thus, high-value (A) items are usually controlled with continuous-review systems. Periodic-review systems are useful when a large number of items are ordered from the same supplier, since individual orders will be placed at the same time. This allows shipments to be consolidated, resulting in lower freight rates. This type of system is the one most often used in controlling C items.

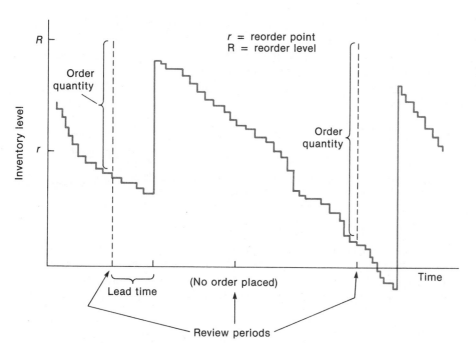

FIGURE 12.4

Operation of a Periodic-review Inventory System

Maintaining a sophisticated, computerized inventory system is worthless if actual inventory levels are not the same as inventory records. Inventory systems tend to accumulate errors over time. These include errors in counting or recording the amount of goods received, misidentification of the goods, theft, and so on. These errors arise from poor design of forms, untrained personnel, carelessness, theft, or poor document control. Therefore, some method of checking the actual physical inventory is necessary. One approach is to shut down the plant or warehouse periodically and count the inventory. The major disadvantages of this method are that productive time is lost and overtime premiums are usually required to accomplish this task during off hours.

An alternative to closing for inventory is known as *cycle counting*. **Cycle counting** is a system for continuous physical counting of inventory throughout the year. It allows scheduling of physical counts to insure that all parts are counted and that higher value parts (A items) are counted more frequently than lower value parts (B or C items). With cycle counting, inventory is counted when orders are placed and received, when the inventory record shows a zero or negative (obviously an error) balance, when the last item is removed from stock, or on a fixed-interval periodic basis.

There are several benefits to cycle counting. Errors can be detected on a more timely basis and causes can be investigated and corrected. Annual physical inventory counts are eliminated, and the loss of productive time is minimized. A high level of inventory accuracy can be achieved on a continuous basis, and the firm can have a correct statement of assets throughout the year. Also, specialized teams of cycle counters are usually established, who become efficient in obtaining good counts, reconciling differences, and finding solutions to system errors.

Cycle Counting

The ABC classification is usually used to determine the frequency of counting. Clearly, errors are more critical for A items since their values are higher. It is recommended that an accuracy of ± 0.2 percent be maintained for A items, ± 1 percent for B items, and ± 5 percent for C items.

An example at FMC Corporation is given by Cantwell.[5] An ABC analysis resulted in the following:

Class	Number of Items	Percent	Value	Percent
A	2,973	8	$41,704,252	87
B	4,155	12	4,292,290	9
C	28,687	80	1,853,364	4

The A items were subdivided into two classes: regular A items and super A items, having unit costs of $1000 or greater. Management policy stated that super A items be counted every month, regular A items, every 2 months, B items, every 4 months, and C items, once a year. The following schedule was established:

Class	Number of Items	Counts per Year	Work Days Between Counts	Days Available	Average Daily Counts
super A	1,173	12	20	15	*
A	1,800	6	40	30	60
B	4,155	3	80	60	70
C	28,687	1	240	180	160

*See explanation in text.

Super A items are each counted once per month resulting in $(1173)(12) = 14,076$ counts per year. Average daily counts for the other classes of items are computed by dividing the number of items by the days available for counting (based on a 20-day work month and excluding one week per month). This all amounts to a total of 66,276 annual counts, or an average of 5500 per month. The FMC warehouse in Bowling Green, Kentucky, where this approach is used, has achieved an inventory accuracy of 99 percent due to the cycle counting program.

P/OM IN PRACTICE

Practical applications of materials and inventory management occur in virtually all manufacturing and service operations. In this section two examples are discussed. In the first example, an automated identification system for managing pharmaceuticals in a large metropolitan hospital is illustrated and in

---

[5]Jim Cantwell, "The How and Why of Cycle Counting: The ABC Method," *Production and Inventory Management*, 26, no. 2 (1985): 50–54. Reprinted with permission, The American Production and Inventory Control Society, Inc.

the second example, an ABC inventory management system is discussed. In both cases, principles of materials and inventory management lead to improvements in costs and efficiencies.

MATERIALS MANAGEMENT WITH AUTOMATED IDENTIFICATION SYSTEMS[6]

The Henry Ford Hospital, located in Detroit, Michigan, is a 1000-bed general medical and surgical teaching institution serving over 1.5 million patients per year. The hospital pharmacy is responsible for procuring and maintaining all medications within the institution. The pharmacy must dispense and bill patients for drugs used. This operation includes bulk supplies such as intravenous solutions as well as patient-specific medications and controlled substances.

The hospital previously used a manual system for tracking, billing, and restocking pharmaceuticals. While the job was getting done, the paperwork became extremely difficult to maintain. The manual keyboard entry of records was both time consuming and prone to error. The tracking of controlled substances and floor stock replacement of bulk items was another major problem area. As a result, the hospital investigated the use of an automatic identification system for pharmaceuticals and related supplies.

Drugs are stored in the pharmacy's main stock room and are distributed upon request to various satellite pharmacies or to the ambulatory clinics throughout the community. A bar-coded inventory system is used to keep track of the inventory in the stockroom by item number. The 2500 different drugs are arranged alphabetically by generic name and the stockroom shelves use bar-code labels which identify the drug item number.

When the stockroom receives a requisition, the clerk responsible for filling the order goes to the stockroom floor with a portable bar code transaction manager and a handheld laser scanner. Each requesting department has a bar-coded cost-center number and drug-quantity number on a preprinted menu which is used for tracking costs. The clerk scans the cost-center number at the beginning of the requisition cycle and then the item number from the

shelf and the quantity issued number. When all requisitions are filled, the clerk uploads the data from the portable scanning unit to an IBM personal computer. The PC creates a file and prints a copy of the data scanned to verify what was actually pulled from the shelf.

At the end of the day, a variety of reports can be created to monitor the work load and the inventory control. All transactions are uploaded to the hospital's mainframe computer which automatically generates a report telling the pharmacy when a particular item needs to be reordered.

The pharmacy replaces floor stock items in each nursing unit on a daily basis. Each nursing unit has a bar-code menu which includes the unit's cost-center number and list of floor stock drugs. When a stockroom clerk visiting each nursing unit's medication storage area sees the minimum acceptable quantity of an item, the clerk scans the menu for the cost-center number, drug item label, and the number label which conveys the type and quantity of item needed and to which station it should be charged. Back in the stockroom, the data are uploaded into the PC which produces a pick list of items for distribution to all stations.

The Henry Ford Hospital has proven the value of automatic identification in several areas of application. Having seen the savings and improvements that are possible through the technology, the hospital is seeking other ways of using it in health care.

QUESTIONS

1. Describe the principal reasons why the Henry Ford Hospital installed an automated identification system for its materials and inventory management.
2. Indicate some of the ways the automated identification system improved the cost and efficiency at the hospital.

---

[6]Adapted from Geoffrey Abdian, "Bar Code Tracking Cuts Data Entry at Henry Ford Hospital," *Industrial Engineering*, 20, no. 10, (1988): 43–45. Copyright Institute of Industrial Engineers, 25 Technology Park/Atlanta, Norcross, GA 30092.

APPLICATION OF ABC INVENTORY ANALYSIS TO HOSPITAL INVENTORY MANAGEMENT[7]

I n recent years, cost containment activities have become particularly important to hospital operations managers, stimulated by major revisions in health care reimbursement policies and significant growth in marketing activities by private sector health care organizations. Recognizing that poor inventory control policies reflect an ineffective use of organizational assets, many hospital managers have sought to institute more systematic approaches to the control of supply inventories.

The ABC classification method was applied to a group of 47 disposable stock keeping units (SKUs), a common term used for inventoried items, in a hospital-based respiratory therapy unit.

Table 12.6 displays the data elements and resulting computed values for the problem, created on a personal computer with a spreadsheet program. The classification listing of SKUs was rank-ordered in accordance with annual dollar usage.

A natural break in the sequential decrease of SKU annual dollar usage is apparent between the tenth SKU (Pleural Drainage Bottles—$2407.50) and the eleventh SKU (Croupette Canopy—$1075.20). This discontinuity provides a logical basis for separating Class A items from those in Class B. Thus, the first 10 SKUs in Table 1 were designated as Class A items. They represent 21.3 percent of all SKUs and account for $38,013.70 of annual usage, or 73.5 percent of the total usage value for all supply items.

The next 13 SKUs, numbers 11 through 23, were assigned to the second category: Class B. A visual inspection of the tabular listing shows slight discontinuities occurring in the annual dollar usage values between items 19 and 20 and again between items 28 and 29. However, informed judgment reflecting the importance of various SKUs in achieving departmental goals was used to identify SKUs 20 through 23 as members of the Class B grouping with SKUs 24 through 28 then being labeled, along with the last 20 SKUs, as Class C items. Although Class C contains over one-half of all inventory items, their total annual usage value amounts to only 8.3 percent of the total expenditures for all disposable supplies during the year. These results are summarized for each of the designated inventory classes in Table 12.7.

Using the ABC classification, three distinct control policies were designed to manage the items.

Policy for Class A Items

In practice, usage for the 10 Class A items was monitored closely and forecasts were updated monthly. Stock replenishment occurred weekly or more frequently, if the reorder point was encountered. Minimum stock levels were established relative to the (1) expected product lead times, (2) availability of substitute SKUs, and (3) SKU criticality. Twice per year these reorder points were reviewed as necessary and revised. A physical inventory was performed weekly to verify recorded stock levels for these SKUs. If several suppliers were available or alternative acceptable products were being distributed, a competitive bidding process was employed.

Policy for Class B Items

The 13 Class B inventory items in the respiratory therapy unit were replenished on a biweekly basis. Some emphasis was placed on negotiating price discounts through blanket order commitments with major suppliers. A reevaluation of safety stock levels for the Class B items produced some reductions when explicit computations of the trade-offs between stockout risk and additional carrying cost were assessed.

Policy for Class C Items

The ordering of the 24 SKUs in Class C was automated. These SKUs were counted and replenished to a preestablished maximum value every two to three months, as time permitted. The two-bin concept was often used to trigger the purchase of an economic order quantity between replenishment points. Limited storage capacity prevented large quantities of C Class items from being ordered. Co-

---

[7]Adapted from Richard A. Reid, "The ABC Method in Hospital Inventory Management: A Practical Approach," *Production and Inventory Management*, 28, no. 4, (1987): 67–70. Reprinted with permission, The American Production and Inventory Control Society, Inc.

TABLE 12.6 An ABC Classification Listing of Disposable SKUs for a Respiratory Therapy Department

Sequential SKU Number	Cumulative % of All SKUs	Total Annual Usage	Average Unit Cost	Annual Dollar Usage	Cumulative Annual Dollar Usge	Cumulative Annual Percent Usage	ABC Inventory Class
1	2.1	117	$49.92	$5,840.64	$5,840.64	11.3	A
2	4.3	27	210.00	5,670.00	11,510.64	22.3	A
3	6.4	212	23.76	5,037.12	16,547.76	32.0	A
4	8.5	172	27.73	4,769.56	21,317.32	41.2	A
5	10.6	60	57.98	3,478.80	24,796.12	48.0	A
6	12.8	94	31.24	2,936.56	27,732.68	53.7	A
7	14.9	100	28.20	2,820.00	30,552.68	59.1	A
8	17.0	48	55.00	2,640.00	33,192.68	64.2	A
9	19.1	33	73.44	2,423.52	35,616.20	68.9	A
10	21.3	15	160.50	2,407.50	38,023.70	73.6	A
11	23.4	210	5.12	1,075.20	39,098.90	75.6	B
12	25.5	50	20.87	1,043.50	40,142.40	77.7	B
13	27.7	12	86.50	1,038.00	41,180.40	79.7	B
14	29.8	8	110.40	883.20	42,063.60	81.4	B
15	31.9	12	71.20	854.40	42,918.00	83.0	B
16	34.0	18	45.00	810.00	43,728.00	84.6	B
17	36.2	48	14.66	703.68	44,431.68	86.0	B
18	38.3	12	49.50	594.00	45,025.68	87.1	B
19	40.4	12	47.50	570.00	45,595.68	88.2	B
20	42.6	8	58.45	467.60	46,063.28	89.1	B
21	44.7	19	24.40	463.60	46,526.88	90.0	B
22	46.8	7	65.00	455.00	46,981.88	90.9	B
23	48.9	5	86.50	432.50	47,414.38	91.7	B
24	51.1	12	33.20	398.40	47,812.78	92.5	C
25	53.2	10	37.05	370.50	48,183.28	93.2	C
26	55.3	10	33.84	338.40	48,521.68	93.9	C
27	57.4	4	84.03	336.12	48,857.80	94.5	C
28	59.6	4	78.40	313.60	49,171.40	95.1	C
29	61.7	2	134.34	268.68	49,440.08	95.6	C
30	63.8	4	56.00	224.00	49,664.08	96.1	C
31	66.0	3	72.00	216.00	49,880.08	96.5	C
32	68.1	4	53.02	212.08	50,092.16	96.9	C
33	70.2	4	49.48	197.92	50,290.08	97.3	C
34	72.3	27	7.07	190.89	50,480.97	97.7	C
35	74.5	3	60.60	181.80	50,662.77	98.0	C
36	76.6	4	40.82	163.28	50,826.05	98.3	C
37	78.7	5	30.00	150.00	50,976.05	98.6	C
38	80.9	2	67.40	134.80	51,110.85	98.9	C
39	83.0	2	59.60	119.20	51,230.05	99.1	C
40	85.1	2	51.68	103.36	51,333.41	99.3	C
41	87.2	4	19.80	79.20	51,412.61	99.5	C
42	89.4	2	37.70	75.40	51,488.01	99.6	C
43	91.5	2	29.89	59.78	51,547.79	99.7	C
44	93.6	1	48.30	48.30	51,596.09	99.8	C
45	95.7	1	34.40	34.40	51,630.49	99.9	C
46	97.9	1	28.80	28.80	51,659.29	99.9	C
47	100.0	3	8.46	25.38	51,684.67	100.0	C

TABLE 12.7 Summary Parameter Values for ABC Inventory Classification Method

ABC Inventory Class	Number of SKU Members	% of Total SKUs	Annual Dollar Usage	% of Annual Dollar Usage
A	10	21.3%	$38,023.70	73.6%
B	13	27.6	9,390.68	18.1
C	24	51.1	4,270.29	8.3
Totals	47	100.0%	$51,684.67	100.0%

ordination of purchases for these SKUs occurred when Class A and B items were being ordered from two major suppliers.

As competition in nonprofit service organizations (such as hospitals) increases, operations managers will need to utilize more cost-minimizing approaches (similar to the ABC method) to aid in policy formulation. Significant cost savings can accrue if managers will allocate appropriate resources to control the important inventory items. Real benefits are available for a reasonable investment of managerial time and energy, especially in designing control procedures for Class A and B items.

QUESTIONS

1. Describe the differences between the inventory policies for the three classes of inventory items.
2. Discuss the value and advantages in terms of how an ABC system improves the materials and inventory management operation.

SUMMARY

Materials management is concerned with the acquisition, storage, handling, and movement of all materials in a production process. Materials-management activities include purchasing, warehousing, receiving and shipping, and physical distribution. These activities are often centralized in order to provide effective planning and control.

Purchasing has objectives of ensuring quality, and obtaining low prices and reliable service from its vendors. They are responsible for reviewing and evaluating requisitions for materials and supplies, selecting vendors, placing orders, and keeping track of shipments outstanding. Good information systems are necessary in order to effectively operate a purchasing department.

The outbound movement of goods from a plant or warehouse is coordinated by traffic and physical distribution activities. The selection of transportation modes and carriers, negotiation of rates, and claims handling are among the most important functions.

In this chapter, we also presented some of the basic concepts of inventory management. Different types of inventory serve different functions, and operations managers need to be concerned with the effective design of inventory systems, focusing on the planning of order quantities and timing of replenishments. The principal characteristics of inventory problems include the number of items, the nature of demand, number of time periods, lead time, and stockout type. Costs include the items themselves, order preparation, holding, and shortage. An effective inventory policy attempts to balance these costs.

ABC analysis is a tool for aggregating items according to value. This technique is useful in establishing guidelines for controlling inventory items according to their importance. For independent demand items, continuous-review and periodic-review systems are often used. Cycle counting is a method for checking physical inventory accuracy.

Materials management
Inventory
Fluctuation inventory
Safety stock
Anticipation inventory
Lot-size inventory
Pipeline inventory
Work-in-process (WIP) inventories
Purchasing
Receiving
Stores
Packaging
Shipping
Warehousing
Procurement
Purchase requisition

Value analysis
Blanket contract
Traffic and physical distribution
Lead time
Ordering cost
Inventory-holding or inventory-carrying costs
Cost of capital
Goodwill cost
ABC classification
Inventory position
Continuous-review system
Reorder point
Periodic-review system
Cycle counting

1. What is *materials management*?

2. What is *inventory*? Define the five major types of inventory.

3. List the objectives of materials management.

4. What are the two principal reasons why firms use suppliers?

5. What are the principal objectives and activities in a purchasing department?

6. What strategies have many companies taken in order to improve the quality of goods received from suppliers?

7. Discuss the major responsibilities of receiving and shipping.

8. Discuss the role of traffic in materials management. What are the critical factors in selecting a mode of transportation?

9. What are the relative advantages and disadvantages among rail, truck, and air for transportation of goods?

10. What are the major factors used in classifying inventory problems?

11. Explain the difference between backorders and lost sales.

12. Define the major costs associated with inventory. How do you think these costs can be determined in practice?

13. Explain the ABC classification for inventory. Of what value is ABC analysis?

14. Discuss how ABC analysis can be used in situations that do not involve inventory.

15. Describe the operation of a continuous-review inventory system.

16. Describe the operation of a periodic-review inventory system.

17. What is cycle counting? How can cycle counting best be implemented?

1. Perform an ABC analysis for the following items. Which items should be classified as A, B, and C items? Draw the ABC curve.

Item	Annual Usage	Unit Value	Item	Annual Usage	Unit Value
1	8,800	68.12	7	112,000	7.59
2	9,800	58.25	8	198,000	3.19
3	23,600	75.25	9	210,000	2.98
4	40,000	53.14	10	168,000	4.27
5	60,000	26.33	11	100,000	9.00
6	165,000	4.52	12	70,00	13.57

2. Develop an ABC curve for the given data. Which items would you classify as A, B, and C?

Item	Annual Usage	Unit Cost	Item	Annual Usage	Unit Cost
1	2400	$ 19.51	11	500	$ 40.50
2	6200	32.60	12	2000	15.40
3	8500	10.20	13	2400	14.60
4	3200	6.80	14	6300	35.80
5	6000	4.50	15	4750	17.30
6	750	55.70	16	2700	51.75
7	8200	3.60	17	1600	42.90
8	9000	44.90	18	1350	25.30
9	5800	35.62	19	5000	67.00
10	820	82.60	20	1000	125.00

3. A&M Industrial Products purchases a variety of parts that are used in small industrial tools. Inventory has not been tightly controlled, and management thinks that costs can be substantially reduced. The following items comprise the inventory of one product line:

Part Number	Annual Demand	Unit Cost	Part Number	Annual Demand	Unit Cost
A367	700	.04	P157	13	3.10
A490	3,850	.70	P232	600	.12
B710	400	.29	R825	15,200	.12
C615	600	.24	S324	20	30.15
C712	7,200	2.60	S404	400	.12
D008	680	51.00	S692	75	12.10
G140	45	100.00	T001	20,000	.005
G147	68,000	.0002	X007	225	.15
K619	2,800	5.25	Y345	8,000	.16
L312	500	1.45	Z958	455	2.56
M582	8,000	.002	Z960	2,000	.001
M813	2,800	.0012			

Perform an ABC analysis of this inventory situation.

4. Given the weekly demand data below, illustrate the operation of a continuous-review inventory system with a reorder point of 75, an order quantity of 100, and a beginning inventory of 125. Lead time is 1 week. All orders are placed at the end of the week. What is the average inventory and number of stockouts?

Week	Demand	Week	Demand
1	25	7	50
2	30	8	35
3	20	9	30
4	40	10	40
5	40	11	20
6	25	12	25

5. For the situation described in problem 4, illustrate the operation of a periodic-review system with a 2-week review period (end of every alternate week), a reorder point of 75 and a reorder level of 150. Initial inventory is 125. What is the average inventory and number of stockouts?

6. The table below gives the daily demand of a certain oil filter at an auto supply store. Illustrate the operation of a continuous-review inventory system by graphing the inventory level versus time if $Q = 40$, $r = 15$, and the lead time is 3 days. Assume that orders are placed at the end of a day and that orders arrive at the beginning of a day. Thus if an order is placed at the end of day 5, it will arrive at the beginning of day 9. Assume that 30 units are on hand at the start of day 1.

Day	Demand	Day	Demand
1	6	14	0
2	8	15	2
3	5	16	4
4	4	17	7
5	5	18	3
6	6	19	5
7	1	20	9
8	1	21	3
9	3	22	6
10	8	23	1
11	8	24	9
12	6	25	1
13	7		

7. For the data given in Problem 6, illustrate the operation of a periodic-review inventory system with a reorder level of 40, a reorder point of 15, and a review period of 5 days.

Decision Models for Inventory Management

A complete discussion of decision models for inventory management would require an entire book, and indeed, several books have been written on this subject. In this chapter we discuss the basic types of quantitative models that are useful in inventory control.

13.1 Economic Order Quantity (EOQ) Model

Undoubtedly the best known and most fundamental inventory model is the **economic order quantity (EOQ)** model, developed in the early 1900s. Several important assumptions are made regarding the EOQ model: We are considering only a single item under continuous review; the entire quantity ordered arrives in the inventory at one point in time; and the demand for the item has a constant, or nearly constant, rate. The condition of **constant demand rate** simply means that the same number of units are taken from inventory each period of time, such as 5 units every day, 25 units every week, 100 units every 4-week period, and so on. We also assume that the lead time is constant and that no stockouts are allowed.

To illustrate the development and use of the EOQ model, let us consider the situation faced by the Holton Drug Company. Holton Drug Company operates a chain of 142 drugstores located throughout Minnesota and northern Wisconsin. From a main warehouse located in St. Paul, Holton supplies the individual drugstores with nearly 1000 different products. The company's historical inventory policy has involved monthly orders placed directly with the manufacturers of the various products. These orders are shipped to the St. Paul warehouse, where they are held in inventory until needed by the various drugstore outlets. With the company's gradual expansion of the number of items carried, the total inventory at the St. Paul warehouse has continued to grow. Consequently, Holton is being faced with a warehouse-capacity problem, where expansion of the warehouse facility is beginning to be viewed as a necessity. In addition, Holton's top management has expressed concern about the sizeable inventory levels and the associated high-inventory costs.

As a result, Holton's inventory manager has been asked to make a detailed cost analysis of the items carried in inventory to see if a better inventory policy can be established. As part of this analysis, the inventory manager has decided to do a detailed study of one product for the purpose of establishing decisions about how much to order and when to order that will result in the lowest possible inventory cost for the product. If the results of the study provide significant cost savings for the product, the inventory analysis will be expanded to include the other products carried by Holton. The inventory manager has selected one of Holton's top-selling products, All-Bright toothpaste, for this study.

The historical demand for All-Bright toothpaste over the past 6 months has been as follows:

Month	Demand (Cases)
1	2,025
2	1,950
3	2,100
4	2,050
5	1,975
6	1,900
Total cases	12,000
Average cases per month	2,000

Strictly speaking, these monthly demand figures do not show a constant demand rate. However, given the relatively low variability exhibited by the monthly demands, inventory planning with a constant rate of 2000 cases per month appears to be acceptable. The number agrees closely with records from the purchasing department, which showed 12 monthly orders placed over the past year for a total of approximately 24,000 cases. Currently, the cost to Holton of All-Bright toothpaste is $12.00 per case.

The how-much-to-order decision involves selecting an order quantity that draws a compromise between (1) keeping small inventories and ordering frequently and (2) keeping large inventories and ordering infrequently. The first alternative would probably result in undesirably high ordering costs, while the second alternative would probably result in undesirably high inventory-holding costs. In order to find an optimal compromise between these conflicting alternatives, let us develop a mathematical model that will show the total cost as the sum of the inventory-holding cost and the ordering cost.[1]

Holton estimates its cost of capital at a rate of 12 percent. Insurance, taxes, breakage, pilferage, and warehouse overhead are estimated to be approximately 6 percent of the value of the inventory. Thus the annual inventory-holding costs are estimated to be 18 percent of the value of the inventory. Since the cost of one case of All-Bright toothpaste is $12.00, the cost of holding, or carrying, one case of All-Bright in inventory for 1 year is .18($12.00) = $2.16. Note that defining the inventory-holding cost as a percentage of the value of the product is convenient because it is easily transferable to other products. For example, a case of Spring bath soap (cost of $17.00 per case) has an annual inventory holding cost of .18($17.00) = $3.06 per case.

The next step in the inventory analysis is to determine the cost of placing an order for All-Bright toothpaste. The cost includes the salaries of the purchasing agents and clerical support staff, transportation costs, and miscellaneous costs such as paper, postage, and telephone costs. After considering all costs associated with ordering, the manager estimates that it costs Holton $38.00 to place an order, regardless of the quantity requested in the order.

---

[1]While management scientists typically refer to "total cost" models for inventory systems, often these models describe only the total *variable*, or *relevant*, costs for the decision being considered. Costs not affected by the how-much-to-order decision are considered to be fixed, or constant, and not included in the model.

With information on product demand (2000 per month, or 24,000 per year), inventory-holding costs ($2.16) and ordering costs ($38.00), we are ready to develop a total cost model to help Holton determine the minimum cost-inventory policy for All-Bright toothpaste. We begin by defining Q to be the size of the order. Thus the decision of how much to order involves trying to determine the value of Q that will minimize the total inventory holding and ordering costs for the product.

The inventory level for All-Bright has a maximum value of Q units when the order of size Q is received from the manufacturer. Holton then supplies its drugstore outlets from this inventory until the inventory is depleted, at which time another shipment of Q units will be received. With the assumption of the constant demand rate of 2000 units per month, the sketch of the inventory level for All-Bright toothpaste is shown in Figure 13.1. Note that the sketch indicates that the average inventory level for the period in question is ½Q. This should appear reasonable, since the maximum inventory level is Q, the minimum is 0, and the inventory level declines at a constant rate over the period.

Figure 13.1 shows the inventory pattern during one order cycle period T. As time goes on, this pattern will repeat. The complete inventory pattern is shown in Figure 13.2. If the average inventory during each cycle is ½Q, the average inventory level over any number of cycles is also ½Q. Thus as long as the time period involved contains an integral number of order cycles, the average inventory for the period will be ½Q.

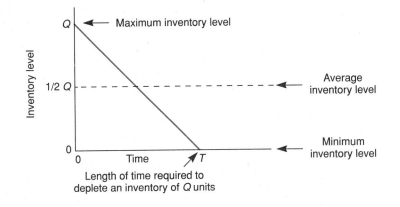

FIGURE 13.1

Sketch of the Inventory Level for All-Bright Toothpaste

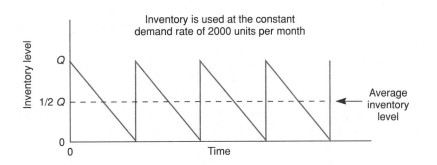

FIGURE 13.2

Inventory Pattern for the EOQ Inventory Decision Model

The inventory-holding cost can be calculated using the average inventory level. That is, we can calculate the inventory-holding cost by multiplying the average inventory by the cost of carrying one unit in inventory for the stated period. The period of time selected for the model is up to you; it could be 1 week, 1 month, 1 year or more. However, since the inventory-carrying costs for many industries and businesses are often expressed as an *annual* percentage or rate, you will probably find most inventory models developed on an *annual cost* basis.

Letting

$$I = \text{annual inventory-carrying charge}$$
$$C = \text{unit cost of the inventory item}$$

the cost of storing one unit in inventory for the year, denoted by C_h, is given by $C_h = IC$. For All-Bright, where I is 18 percent and $C = \$12$ per case, we showed this cost to be $C_h = .18(\$12.00) = \$2.16$. Thus the general equation for annual inventory-holding cost is

$$\begin{array}{c}\text{Annual inventory-}\\\text{holding cost}\end{array} = \left(\begin{array}{c}\text{average}\\\text{inventory}\end{array}\right)\left(\begin{array}{c}\text{annual holding}\\\text{cost}\\\text{per unit}\end{array}\right) = \frac{1}{2}QC_h \quad (13.1)$$

To complete the total cost model, we must now include the ordering cost. The goal is to express this cost in terms of the order quantity Q. Since the inventory-holding cost is expressed on an annual basis, we need to express ordering costs as an annual cost. The first question is how many orders will be placed for All-Bright toothpaste during a 1-year period? Letting D denote the annual demand for the product, we know that by ordering Q units each time we order, we have to place D/Q orders per year. If C_0 is the cost of placing one order, the general expression for the annual ordering cost is

$$\begin{array}{c}\text{Annual ordering}\\\text{cost}\end{array} = \left(\begin{array}{c}\text{number of}\\\text{orders}\\\text{per year}\end{array}\right)\left(\begin{array}{c}\text{cost}\\\text{per}\\\text{order}\end{array}\right) = \left(\frac{D}{Q}\right)C_0 \quad (13.2)$$

Thus the total annual cost—inventory-holding cost given by Equation (13.1) plus ordering cost given by Equation (13.2)—can be expressed as

$$TC = \frac{1}{2}QC_h + \frac{D}{Q}C_0 \quad (13.3)$$

Using the All-Bright toothpaste data with an annual demand of $D = 24,000$ cases, the total-cost model becomes

$$\begin{aligned}TC &= \frac{1}{2}Q(\$2.16) + \frac{24,000}{Q}(\$38.00)\\&= 1.08Q + \frac{912,000}{Q}\end{aligned} \quad (13.4)$$

The development of this total-cost model has gone a long way toward helping solve the inventory problem. We now are able to express the total annual cost as a function of one of the decisions, *how much* should be ordered. Equation (13.3) is the general total-cost equation for inventory situations in which the assumptions of the economic order quantity model are valid.

The next step is to find the order quantity Q that does, in fact, minimize the total cost as stated in Equation (13.4). Using a trial-and-error approach, we can compute the total cost for several possible order quantities. As a starting point, let us use the current purchasing policy for All-Bright, which called for monthly orders of the amount $Q = 2000$. The total annual cost is

Determining an Inventory Policy from the EOQ Model

$$TC = 1.08(2000) + \frac{912,000}{2000} = \$2616.00$$

A trial with an order quantity of $Q = 1600$ shows a total annual cost of

$$TC = 1.08(1600) + \frac{912,000}{1600} = \$2298.00$$

These results, along with other trial order quantities, are shown in Table 13.1. As can be seen, the lowest annual cost-order quantity observed in these calculations is $Q = 800$ cases. A graph of the inventory holding, ordering, and total costs is shown in Figure 13.3.

The advantage of the trial-and-error approach is that it is rather easy to do and provides the cost information for any number of trial order quantities. The disadvantage of this approach, however, is that it does not necessarily provide the minimum cost-order quantity. Referring to the total cost curve in Figure 13.3, it appears that the minimum cost occurs somewhere between 800 units and 1200 units.

By using differential calculus, we can show that the quantity that minimizes the total cost, denoted by Q^*, is given by the formula

$$Q^* = \sqrt{\frac{2DC_0}{C_h}} \tag{13.5}$$

This formula is referred to as the *economic order quantity (EOQ)* formula.

For All-Bright toothpaste, the minimum cost-order quantity as given by Equation (13.5) is

$$Q^* = \sqrt{\frac{2(24,000)(38)}{2.16}} = 919 \text{ cases}$$

Using this order quantity in Equation (13.4) shows that the inventory for All-Bright toothpaste can be handled with a total annual cost of $TC = 1.08(919)$

Order Quantity	Annual Inventory-holding Cost	Annual Ordering Cost	Annual Total Cost
2000	$2160	$ 456	$2616
1600	1728	570	2298
1200	1296	760	2056
800	864	1140	2004
400	432	2280	2712

Table 13.1

Inventory-holding, Ordering, and Total Costs for Various Order Quantities of All-Bright Toothpaste

FIGURE 13.3

Graph of Annual
Inventory-
holding,
Ordering, and
Total Cost for
All-Bright
Toothpaste

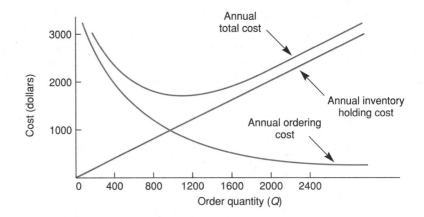

+ 912,000/919 = $1984.90. Recall that the current ordering policy for All-Bright for an order quantity of 2000 units provided a total annual cost of $2616.00. Thus the EOQ analysis has resulted in a $2616.00 − $1984.90 = $631.10, or 24.1 percent, cost reduction. Notice also that the total ordering costs ($992.52) are equal to the total holding costs ($992.38), with the small difference due to rounding. In general, this will always be true for the EOQ model.

Now that we know how much to order, we want to answer the second question of *when* to order. The when-to-order decision is most often expressed in terms of the reorder point.

The manufacturer of All-Bright toothpaste guarantees a 3-day delivery on any order placed by Holton. Considering weekends and holidays, Holton operates 250 days per year. Thus on a daily basis, the annual demand of 24,000 cases corresponds to a daily demand of 24,000/250 = 96 cases. Thus we anticipate

$$(3 \text{ days})(96 \text{ cases per day}) = 288$$

cases of All-Bright to be sold during the three days it takes a new order to reach the Holton warehouse. Since the 3-day delivery period is the lead time for a new order, the 288 cases of demand during this period is referred to as the **lead-time demand**. Thus Holton should order a new shipment of All-Bright toothpaste from the manufacturer when the inventory position reaches a reorder level of 288 cases.

For inventory systems using the constant-demand rate assumption and a fixed lead time, the reorder point is the same as the lead-time demand. The general expression for the reorder point is

$$r = dm \tag{13.6}$$

where

r = reorder point
d = demand per day
m = lead time for a new order in days

The question of how frequently the order should be placed can now be answered. This period between orders is referred to as the **cycle time**. Previously (see Eq. (13.2)), we defined D/Q as the number of orders that are placed in a year. Thus D/Q^* = 24,000/919 = 26 is the number of orders Holton will place for All-Bright toothpaste each year. With 250 working, or operating days per year, Holton should be placing an order approximately every 250/26 = 9.6 days. Thus the cycle time is computed to be 9.6 days. The general expression for cycle time of T days is given by

$$T = \frac{N}{D/Q^*} = \frac{NQ^*}{D} \qquad (13.7)$$

where N = number of days of operation for the year.

Computer Models for Inventory Decisions

Like many other quantitative methods for production and operations management, inventory models can be programmed and made available to inventory managers through the use of computers. The inventory models module of *The Management Scientist* computer software package contains solution procedures for the six different inventory models discussed in this chapter. Using the economic order quantity option of the module, the computer output for the Holton inventory policy is shown in Figure 13.4. Our previously computed economic order of quantity of $Q^* = 919$ provides the minimum-cost inventory policy. The reorder point is shown to be 288. Additional information is provided, including total annual cost, maximum inventory level, average inventory level, number of orders per year, and cycle time. Thus the output provides order quantity and reorder point decision recommendations as well as a variety of additional information that should be helpful to the inventory manager.

Even though substantial time has been spent in arriving at the inventory-carrying charge (18 percent) and ordering cost ($38.00), we should realize that these figures are at best good estimates. Thus we may want to consider how much the order size recommendation would change if the estimated ordering and holding costs had been different. To determine this, we can calculate the recommended order quantity under several different cost conditions. These calculations are shown in Table 13.2. As you can see from the table, the value of Q^* appears relatively stable, even with some variations in the cost estimates. Based on these results, it appears that the best order quantity for All-Bright toothpaste is somewhere

Sensitivity Analysis for the EOQ Model

```
                  INVENTORY POLICY
                  ****************

     OPTIMAL ORDER QUANTITY            918.94
     ANNUAL INVENTORY HOLDING COST    $992.45
     ANNUAL ORDERING COST             $992.45
     TOTAL ANNUAL COST                $1984.90
     MAXIMUM INVENTORY LEVEL          918.94
     AVERAGE INVENTORY LEVEL          459.47
     REORDER POINT                    288.00
     NUMBER OF ORDERS PER YEAR         26.12
     CYCLE TIME (DAYS)                  9.57
```

FIGURE 13.4

Optimal Inventory Policy for All-Bright Toothpaste as Computed by *The Management Scientist* Software Package

Table 13.2

Economic Order Quantities for Several Inventory-holding Cost and Ordering Cost Possibilities

Possible Inventory-holding Cost (Percent)	Possible Cost Per Order	Optimal Order Quantity Q^*	Projected Total Cost Using Q^*	Using $Q = 919$
16	$36	949	$1821	$1822
16	40	1000	1920	1927
20	36	849	2036	2043
20	40	894	2147	2147

around 850 to 1000 cases and definitely not near the current order quantity of 2000 cases. In addition, the projected total costs using Q^* and $Q = 919$, as shown in Table 13.2, indicate that there is very little risk associated with implementing the calculated order quantity of 919 cases. For the worse situations shown in Table 13.2, the total cost using the 919-case order quantity is only $7.00 more expensive than the minimum total cost in the "Using Q^*" column.

From the above analysis we can say that this EOQ model is insensitive to small variation or errors in the cost estimates. This is a property of EOQ models in general, which indicates that if we have at least reasonable estimates of ordering and inventory-holding costs, we should obtain a good approximation of the true minimum cost order quantity.

Using the EOQ Model

The inventory model and analysis has led to a recommended order quantity of 919 units. Is this the final decision, or should the manager's judgment enter into the establishment of the final inventory policy decisions? Although the model has provided us with a good order quantity recommendation, it may not have taken into account all aspects of the inventory situation. As a result, the decision maker should feel free to modify the final order quantity recommendation to meet the unique circumstances of his or her inventory situation.

In the case of All-Bright toothpaste, the order quantity of 919 resulted in a cycle time of 9.6 days. The inventory manager felt that there would be some benefits of establishing a 10-day, or 2-week, cycle time for the item. In particular, the manager was interested in keeping open the possibility that other items could be placed on the 2-week order cycle so that multiple products ordered from the same manufacturer could be handled in one shipment. Thus, in addition to inventory cost savings, there is the possibility of making transportation cost savings also. The adjustment to the 10-day, or 2-week, cycle time increased the recommended order quantity to

$$(10 \text{ days})(96 \text{ cases per day}) = 960 \text{ cases}$$

Using Equation (13.4) and $Q = 960$ units results in a total cost of $1987. Thus the recommended policy has a $2616 - $1987 = $629, or 24 percent, savings over the current inventory policy. If similar savings can be made on a large number of items Holton carries in inventory, the use of the inventory decision model can provide significant benefits to the company.

In addition, at the introduction of the Holton inventory problem, we mentioned that warehouse capacity was becoming a significant problem and that warehouse expansion was being considered. Under the current ordering policy with an order quantity of 2000 cases, the average inventory level should be $Q/2 = 1000$ cases. Under the new policy, the 960-case order quantity results in an average inventory level of $960/2 = 480$ cases. Thus we anticipate a decrease of $1000 - 480 = 520$ cases or a 52 percent decrease in the warehouse space needs. Thus, in addition to providing a cost reduction, the inventory analysis provided by the EOQ model may also decrease the need for an expensive warehouse expansion.

13.2 QUANTITY DISCOUNTS FOR THE EOQ MODEL

Earlier we stated that the cost of the items is an important consideration in many inventory decisions. Letting the purchase cost per unit be denoted by C, the total purchase cost for an annual demand D is CD. In the EOQ model, we assumed that the demand D and the purchase cost C were both constant. Therefore, this portion of the total cost is fixed and is not affected by the order quantity decision. As a consequence we omitted the component of purchase cost from the model.

However, we now want to consider inventory policies for situations where the purchase cost of the item depends upon the quantity ordered. In this case, we want to include the purchase cost in the total-cost model and consider its impact on the optimal order quantity. The most frequently encountered situation where purchase cost of the item depends upon the quantity ordered is when quantity discounts are allowed. **Quantity discounts** occur in numerous businesses and industries, where suppliers provide an incentive for large purchase quantities by offering lower unit costs when items are purchased in larger lots or quantities. This model can also be applied to situations where transportation discounts for shipping in bulk quantities, such as carload or truckload, apply.

Typically, a company offers several discount categories. For example, for every item ordered up to 1000, a base unit price applies; if the order is for 1001 to 2000 items, a discounted unit price (discounted by, perhaps, 2 percent) applies; for every additional item ordered beyond 2000, a larger discount (say, 4 percent) applies. To compute the optimal order quantity, the following, three-step procedure is used.

Step 1. Compute Q^* using the EOQ formula for the unit cost associated with each discount category.

Step 2. For those Q^*'s that are too small to qualify for the assumed discount price, adjust the order quantity upward to the nearest order quantity that will allow the product to be purchased at the assumed price.

If a calculated Q^* for a given price is larger than the *highest* order quantity providing the particular discount price, this discount price need not be considered any further, since it cannot lead to an optimal solution. While this may not be obvious, it does turn out to be a property of the EOQ quantity discount model.

When quantity discounts are considered, the annual purchase cost (annual demand $D \times$ unit cost C) is included in the total-cost model.

$$TC = \frac{Q}{2} C_h + \frac{D}{Q} C_0 + DC \qquad (13.8)$$

Using this total-cost formula we can determine the optimal order quantity for the EOQ discount model in Step 3.

Step 3. For each of the order quantities resulting from Steps 1 and 2, compute the total annual cost using the unit price from the appropriate discount category and Equation (13.8). The order quantity yielding the minimum total annual cost is the optimal order quantity.

We illustrate this procedure with the following example.

DETERMINING AN OPTIMAL ORDER QUANTITY WITH QUANTITY DISCOUNTS

Let us return to the Holton Drug Company example. Holton used the EOQ model to conclude that it should order All-Bright toothpaste in quantities of 960 cases per order. The EOQ recommendation was based on the following information:

Annual demand:	24,000 cases
Cost per case:	$12.00
Inventory-holding charge:	18%
Order Cost:	$38.00

The combined inventory holding and ordering costs for this inventory problem are $1987.

Now let us assume that the manufacturer of All-Bright toothpaste has offered its customers the following quantity discount schedule:

Discount Category	Order Size	Discount	Unit Cost
1	0–3,999	0	$12.00
2	4,000–11,999	3%	11.64
3	12,000 and over	5%	11.40

The 5 percent discount looks attractive; however, the 12,000-case order quantity is substantially more than the current recommendation of 960 cases. Since the greater order quantities require higher inventory-carrying costs, we should prepare a thorough cost analysis before making a final inventory policy decision.

First, we compute Q^* using the EOQ formula. In our preliminary calculations, we use Q_1^* to indicate the order quantity for discount category 1, Q_2^* for discount category 2, and Q_3^* for discount category 3.

Recall the EOQ model $Q^* = \sqrt{2DC_o/C_h}$. In this case,

$$Q_1^* = \sqrt{\frac{2(24,000)(38)}{(.18)(12.00)}} = 919$$

$$Q_2^* = \sqrt{\frac{2(24,000)(38)}{(.18)(11.64)}} = 933$$

$$Q_3^* = \sqrt{\frac{2(24,000)(38)}{(.18)(11.40)}} = 943$$

Since the only differences in the models are slight differences in the inventory-holding costs, the economic order quantities resulting from this step are approximately the same. However, the calculated order quantities are usually not all of the size necessary to qualify for the discount price assumed. In the above case, both Q_2^* and Q_3^* are insufficient order quantities to obtain their assumed unit costs of $11.64 and $11.40, respectively.

Applying Step 2 of the quantity discount method, we adjust Q_2^* and Q_3^* upward since they do not fall within the specified order size in their discount categories. In our example, this causes us to set

$$Q_2^* = 4000$$

and

$$Q_3^* = 12,000$$

The calculations of Step 3 are summarized in Table 13.3. As you can see, a decision to order 4000 units at the 3 percent discount rate yields the minimum-cost solution. While the 12,000-unit order quantity would result in a 5 percent discount, its excessive inventory-holding cost prevents it from being the best decision.

Note that the sum of the inventory and ordering costs with $Q^* = 4000$ is $4190.40 + 228.00 = $4418.40. This portion of the total cost is substantially more than the $1986.80 cost associated with the 960-unit order size. In effect, the quantity discount savings of 3 percent per unit is so great we are willing to operate the inventory system with a substantially higher inventory level and substantially higher inventory-holding cost. Provided we have the space to handle larger inventories, purchasing in larger quantities in order to obtain discounts is economically sound.

13.3 ECONOMIC PRODUCTION LOT-SIZE MODEL

The following inventory decision model is similar to the EOQ model in that we are attempting to determine *how much* we should order or produce and *when* the order should be placed. Again, we make the assumption of a constant demand rate. However, instead of the goods arriving at the warehouse in a shipment of size Q^* as assumed in the EOQ model, we assume that units are supplied to

TABLE 13.3 Total Annual Cost Calculations for the EOQ Model with Quantity Discounts

Category	Unit Cost (C)	Inventory Cost/Unit $C_h = .18(C)$	Order Quantity	Annual Inventory Cost $\frac{1}{2}QC_h$	Annual Ordering Cost $(D/Q)C_0$	Annual Purchase Cost DC	Total Annual Cost
1	$12.00	$2.160	960	$ 1,036.80	$950.00	$228,000.00	$289,986.00
2	11.64	2.0952	4,000	4,190.40	228.00	279,360.00	283,778.40
3	11.40	2.052	12,000	12,312.00	76.00	273,600.00	285,988.00

inventory at a constant rate over several days or several weeks. The assumption of a *constant supply rate* implies that the same number of units are supplied to inventory each period of time (for example, 10 units every day, 50 units every week, and so on). This model is designed for production situations in which once an order is placed, production begins and a constant number of units are added to inventory each day until the production run has been completed.

If we have a production system that produces 50 units per day and we decide to schedule 10 days of production each time we want additional units, we have a $50(10) = 500$-unit production run size. Alternative terminology may refer to the 500 units as the production lot size or lot quantity.

If, in general, we let Q indicate the production lot quantity, our approach to the inventory decisions is similar to the EOQ model; that is, we attempt to build an inventory-holding and ordering-cost model that expresses the total annual cost as a function of the production quantity. Then we attempt to find the quantity that minimizes the total cost.

One other condition that should be mentioned at this time is that the model applies only to production situations in which the production rate is greater than the demand rate. Stated more simply, the production system must be able to satisfy the demand. For example, if the constant demand rate is 2000 units per week, the production rate has to be at least 2000 units per week if we are going to satisfy demand.

Since we have assumed that the production rate exceeds the demand rate, each day during a production run we manufacture more units than we ship. Thus we put the excess production in inventory, resulting in a gradual inventory buildup during the production period. When the production run is completed, the inventory shows a gradual decline until a new production run is started. The inventory pattern for this system is shown in Figure 13.5.

As in the EOQ model, we are now dealing with two costs, the inventory-holding cost and the ordering cost. While the inventory-holding cost is identical to our definition in the EOQ model, the interpretation of the ordering cost is slightly different. In fact, in a production situation the ordering cost may be more correctly referred to as production-setup cost. This cost, which includes labor hours, material, and lost production costs incurred while preparing the production system for operation, is a fixed cost that occurs for every production run, regardless of the production quantity.

Let us begin building our model by attempting to write the inventory-holding cost in terms of our production quantity Q. Again, our approach is to develop

FIGURE 13.5

Inventory Pattern for the Production Lot Size Inventory Model

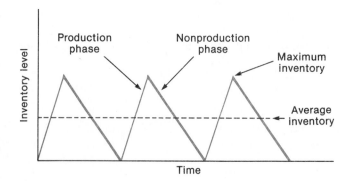

an expression for average inventory and then establish the holding costs associated with the average inventory level. We use a 1-year time period and an annual cost for our model.

We saw in the EOQ model that the average inventory was simply one-half the maximum inventory, or $Q/2$. Since Figure 13.5 shows a constant inventory buildup rate during the production run and a constant inventory depletion rate during the nonproduction period, the average inventory for the production lot-size model will also be one half of the maximum inventory level. However, in this inventory system the production quantity Q does not go into inventory at one point in time, and thus the inventory level never reaches a level of Q units.

Let us see if we can compute the maximum inventory level. First we define the following symbols:

d = daily demand rate for the product
p = daily production rate for the product
t = number of days for a production run

Since we are assuming p is larger than d, the excess production each day is $p - d$, which is the daily rate of inventory buildup. If we run production for t days and place $p - d$ units in inventory each day, the inventory level at the end of the production run will be $(p - d)t$. From Figure 13.5, we can see that the inventory level at the end of the production run is also the maximum inventory level. Thus we can write

$$\text{Maximum inventory} = (p - d)t \tag{13.9}$$

If we know we are producing a production quantity of Q units at a daily production rate of p units, then $Q = pt$, and we can compute the length of the production run t to be

$$t = \frac{Q}{p} \text{ days} \tag{13.10}$$

Thus

$$\text{Maximum inventory} = (p - d)t = (p - d)\left(\frac{Q}{p}\right)$$

$$= \left(1 - \frac{d}{p}\right) Q \tag{13.11}$$

The average inventory, which is one-half of the maximum inventory, is given by

$$\text{Average inventory} = \frac{1}{2}\left(1 - \frac{d}{p}\right) Q \tag{13.12}$$

With an annual inventory holding cost of C_h per unit, the general equation for annual inventory-holding cost is

$$\begin{pmatrix} \text{Annual inventory-} \\ \text{holding cost} \end{pmatrix} = \begin{pmatrix} \text{average} \\ \text{inventory} \end{pmatrix} \begin{pmatrix} \text{annual holding} \\ \text{cost} \\ \text{per unit} \end{pmatrix}$$

$$= \frac{1}{2}\left(1 - \frac{d}{p}\right) QC_h \tag{13.13}$$

If D is the annual demand for the product and C_0 is the setup cost for a production run, then the total annual setup cost, which takes the place of the total annual ordering costs of the EOQ model, is

$$\begin{array}{c} \text{Annual setup} \\ \text{cost} \end{array} = \left(\begin{array}{c} \text{number of production} \\ \text{runs per year} \end{array}\right)\left(\begin{array}{c} \text{setup cost} \\ \text{per run} \end{array}\right)$$

$$= \left(\frac{D}{Q}\right)C_0 \tag{13.14}$$

Thus the total annual cost (TC) model is

$$TC = \frac{1}{2}\left(1 - \frac{d}{p}\right)QC_b + \frac{D}{Q}C_0 \tag{13.15}$$

In this total-cost model, we use the ratio of daily demand to daily production, d/p. Actually this ratio of demand relative to production is the same regardless of the period of time considered. In terms of an annual demand D and an annual production capacity P, the ratio $D/P = d/p$. Substituting D/P for d/p in Equation (13.15) provides the following total annual cost model:

$$TC = \frac{1}{2}\left(1 - \frac{D}{P}\right)QC_b + \frac{D}{Q}C_0 \tag{13.16}$$

Equations (13.15) and (13.16) are equivalent. However, equation (13.16) may be used more frequently, since an *annual cost* model tends to make the analyst think in terms of collecting *annual* demand (D) and *annual* production (P) data rather than daily-rate data.

Given the estimates of the inventory holding cost, C_b, setup cost, C_0, annual demand rate, D, and annual production rate, P, we can use a trial-and-error approach to compute the total annual cost for various lot sizes Q. However, we may also use the minimum-cost formula for Q^*, which has been developed using differential calculus. The equation is

$$Q^* = \sqrt{\frac{2DC_0}{(1 - D/P)C_b}} \tag{13.17}$$

EXAMPLE | DETERMINING THE OPTIMAL PRODUCTION LOT SIZE

Forum Shoes, Inc., produces a basic dress shoe for men, which sells throughout the year at a constant demand rate. Total annual demand for the shoe is 21,000 pairs. Forum's production costs are $22.00 per pair, with annual inventory-holding cost figured at a 16 percent rate. The setup of the production line operation, including cleaning, preparation, and changeover from the previous production operation requires several hours of work, at a cost of $200. On an annual basis, the production capacity for the dress shoes is 50,000 pairs. Given the above demand, production rate, and cost information, what is the recommended production lot size that will minimize the total inventory-holding cost and production-setup cost? Using Equation (13.17), we have

$$Q^* = \sqrt{\frac{2(21,000)(200)}{(1 - 21,000/50,000)(.16)(22)}}$$

$$= \sqrt{\frac{8,400,000}{2.0416}} = 2028 \text{ pairs}$$

Thus production runs, or lot sizes, of 2028 pairs of shoes are recommended for the Forum dress shoes. With 250 days of operation per year, the daily production capacity is 50,000/250 days = 200 shoes. Thus the length of a production run should be scheduled for 2028/200 = 10.14 days. After seeing these results, Forum's inventory manager reduced the production lot size to 2000 pairs because this figure would help scheduling, as the production runs would be for the more convenient 10-day, or 2-week, periods.

Equation (13.16) shows the production lot size of 2000 pairs enables the system to operate with an annual cost of

$$TC = \frac{1}{2}\left(1 - \frac{21,000}{50,000}\right)(2000)(.16)(22) + \frac{21,000}{2000}(200)$$

$$= 2042 + 2100 = \$4142$$

Other relevant data include the fact that a 5-working-day lead time is required to schedule and set up a production run. With daily demand $d = 21,000/250 = 84$ pairs, the reorder point becomes $r = 5(84) = 420$ pairs.

On an annual basis, $D/Q = 21,000/200 = 10.5$ shows that 10 or 11 production runs should be scheduled during the year. The cycle time, or time between production runs, is $T = 250(2000)/21,000 = 24$ working days.

13.4 AN INVENTORY MODEL WITH PLANNED SHORTAGES

In many inventory situations a shortage or stockout—a demand that cannot be supplied from inventory or production—is undesirable and should be avoided if at all possible. However, there are other cases in which it may be desirable—from an economic point of view—to plan for and allow shortages. In practice, these types of situations are most commonly found where the value per unit of the inventory is very high, and hence the inventory-holding cost is high. An example of this type of situation is a new-car dealer's inventory. It is not uncommon for a dealer not to have the specific car you want in stock. However, if you are willing to wait several weeks, the dealer will generally order a car for you.

The specific model developed in this section allows the type of shortage known as a *backorder*. Recall that in a backorder situation, an assumption is made that when a customer places an order and discovers that the supplier is out of stock, the customer does not withdraw the order. Rather, the customer waits until the next shipment arrives, and then the order is filled. Frequently the waiting period in backordering situations will be relatively short and, by promising the customer top priority and immediate delivery when the goods become available, companies can convince customers to wait for the order. In these cases the backorder assumption is valid. If, for a particular product, a firm finds that a shortage causes the customer to withdraw the order and a lost sale results, the backorder model would not be the appropriate inventory decision model.

Using the backorder assumption for shortages, we now develop an extension to the EOQ model presented in Sec. 13.1. The EOQ model assumptions of the goods arriving in inventory all at one time and a constant demand rate for the product will be used. If we let S indicate the amount of the shortage or the number of backorders that have accumulated when a new shipment of size Q is received, then the inventory system for the backorder case has the following characteristics:

1. With S backorders existing when a new shipment of size Q arrives, the S backorders will be shipped to the appropriate customers immediately and the remaining $(Q - S)$ units will be placed in inventory.
2. $Q - S$ will be the maximum inventory level.
3. The inventory cycle of T days will be divided into two distinct phases: t_1 days when inventory is on hand and orders are filled as they occur and t_2 days when there is a stockout and all orders are placed on backorder.

The inventory pattern for this model, where negative inventory represents the number of backorders, is shown in Figure 13.6.

With the inventory pattern now defined, we should be able to proceed with the basic step of all inventory models; namely, the development of a total cost expression. For the inventory model with backorders, we encounter the usual inventory-holding costs and ordering costs. In addition, we incur a backordering cost in terms of labor and special delivery costs directly associated with the handling of the backorders. Another portion of the backorder cost can be expressed as a loss of goodwill with customers due to the fact that customers will have to wait for their orders. Since the *goodwill cost* depends upon how long the customer has to wait, it is customary to adopt the convention of expressing all backorder costs in terms of how much it costs to have a unit on backorder for a stated period of time. This method of computing cost of backorders on a

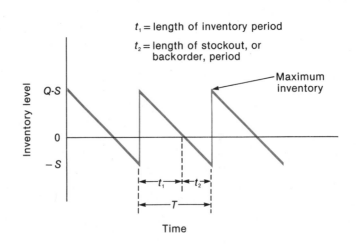

FIGURE 13.6

Inventory Pattern for an Inventory Model with Backorders

t_1 = length of inventory period

t_2 = length of stockout, or backorder, period

time basis is similar to the method we used to compute the inventory-holding cost.

Using this method for approaching backorder costs, we can compute a total annual cost of backorders once the average backorder level and the backorder cost per unit per unit time is known. As you recall, this is the same type of information that is needed to calculate inventory-holding costs.

Admittedly, the backorder cost rate (especially the goodwill cost) is difficult to determine in practice. However, noting that EOQ models are rather insensitive to the cost estimates, we should feel confident that reasonable estimates of the backorder cost will lead to a good approximation of the overall minimum cost inventory decision.

Letting C_b be the cost to maintain one unit on backorder for one year, the three sources of cost in this planned-shortage inventory model can be expressed as follows:

$$\text{Inventory-holding cost} = \frac{(Q - S)^2}{2Q} C_h \qquad (13.18)$$

$$\text{Ordering cost} = \frac{D}{Q} C_0 \qquad (13.19)$$

$$\text{Backordering cost} = \frac{S^2}{2Q} C_b \qquad (13.20)$$

Thus our total annual cost expression (TC) becomes

$$TC = \frac{(Q - S)^2}{2Q} C_h + \frac{D}{Q} C_0 + \frac{S^2}{2Q} C_b \qquad (13.21)$$

Given the cost estimates C_h, C_0, and C_b and the annual demand D, we can begin to determine the minimum cost values for our inventory decisions, Q and S. With two decision components, a trial-and-error approach, while valid, becomes cumbersome. Using calculus, analysts have established the following minimum-cost formulas for the order quantity Q^* and the planned backorders S^*:

$$Q^* = \sqrt{\frac{2DC_0}{C_h} \left(\frac{C_h + C_b}{C_b} \right)} \qquad (13.22)$$

and

$$S^* = Q^* \left(\frac{C_h}{C_h + C_b} \right) \qquad (13.23)$$

DETERMINING THE OPTIMAL ORDER QUANTITY WITH BACKORDERS

EXAMPLE

RCB Electronics Company is concerned about an expensive part used in television repair. The cost of the part is $125 and RCB's inventory-holding rate is 20 percent. The cost to place an order is estimated to be $40. The annual demand, which occurs at a constant rate throughout the year, is 800 parts. Because of the cost of the item, RCB's inventory manager continually seeks ways to reduce the amount of inventory carried for the part. Currently, the inventory policy is based on the EOQ model with

$$Q^* = \sqrt{\frac{2DC_0}{C_h}} = \sqrt{\frac{2(800)(40)}{.20(125)}} = 51 \text{ parts}$$

The total annual cost of inventory holding and ordering has been

$$TC = \frac{1}{2} QC_h + \frac{D}{Q} C_0 = \frac{1}{2}(51)(.20)(125) + \left(\frac{800}{51}\right)(40)$$

$$= \$637.50 + 627.50 = \$1265$$

With an average inventory of $Q/2 = 51/2 = 25.5$ parts evaluated at \$125 each, RCB's inventory manager has expressed a willingness to allow backordering if it will help reduce the $(25.5)(\$125) = \$3187.50$ average inventory investment for the part.

In attempting to develop a cost estimate for a backorder, the manager felt a 1-week cost in the neighborhood of \$1 to \$1.25 per unit would be a reasonable assumption. On an annual basis, a unit backorder cost of \$60 was assigned. Let us use the inventory decision model with planned shortages to see what the effect of backordering would be on RCB's inventory policy.

Using Equations (13.22) and (13.23), the optimal order quantity, Q^*, and the optimal number of backorders, S^*, become

$$Q^* = \sqrt{\frac{2(800)(40)}{.20(125)} \left(\frac{.20(125) + 60}{60}\right)} = 60 \text{ parts}$$

and

$$S^* = 60 \left(\frac{.20(125)}{.20(125) + 60}\right) = 18 \text{ parts}$$

Using Equations (13.18), (13.19), and (13.20), the various costs associated with the inventory policy are:

$$\text{Inventory-holding cost} = \frac{(Q - S)^2}{2Q} C_h$$

$$= \frac{(60 - 18)^2}{2(60)} (.20)(125)$$

$$= \$367.50.$$

$$\text{Ordering Cost} \qquad = \frac{D}{Q} C_0$$

$$= \frac{800}{600} (40) = \$533.33$$

$$\text{Backordering cost} \qquad = \frac{S^2}{2Q} C_b$$

$$= \frac{(18)^2}{2(60)} (60) = \$162.00$$

The total cost is $367.50 + $533.33 + $162.00 = 1062.83, and hence the backordering policy provides a $1265 - $1062.83 = 202.17, or 16 percent, cost reduction when compared to the EOQ model. Let us look more closely to see how this savings has come about. From the above inventory-holding cost calculation, we see that there will be an average of 14.7 units in inventory and that the inventory-holding cost has been reduced from $637.50 to $367.50, a savings of $270. The inventory investment for the 14.7 units is $(14.7)(\$125) = \$1837.50$, which is down $1350 compared to the $3187.50 required by the EOQ model. Thus we see that allowing shortages in the form of backorders enables us to make significant cost reductions in the amount of inventory carried. However, this savings is offset somewhat by the cost associated with the backorders, which is $162.00. An additional savings comes from a reduction in the number of orders placed, which in the above example resulted in a cost reduction of $627.50 - $533.33 = 94.17. The net effect of these cost adjustments is that the backordering does in fact reduce the total cost of the RCB inventory operation.

As a final observation, note that the daily demand for the part is (800 parts)/(250 days) = 3.2 parts per day. Since the maximum number of backorders is 18, we see that the length of the backorder period will be 18/3.2 = 5.6 days. This tells RCBs inventory manager that a person experiencing an out-of-stock situation will have to wait at most 5 to 6 working days (approximately a week) to obtain a part. This waiting period was viewed as being acceptable to RCBs management and the inventory policy with planned shortages was implemented.

13.5 LOT SIZING FOR DYNAMIC DEMAND

One of the fundamental assumptions behind the EOQ model is that demand is constant over time. In many situations, such as when demand is seasonal or orders are placed intermittently, this assumption is unrealistic. In this section we introduce some techniques for dealing with dynamic demand.

The objectives of EOQ are to determine when and how much to order to minimize the total cost of ordering and carrying inventory. Lot-sizing techniques have similar objectives. Usually demand is given in discrete time periods, such as in weeks. The goal of lot sizing is to determine a schedule of orders to minimize total cost.

Suppose that the ordering cost for a particular item is $150 and that it costs $1 per unit per week to store the item in inventory, charged on the end-of-week inventory. The forecast of demand is as follows:

Week	1	2	3	4	5	6	7	8	9	10	11	12
Requirement	20	20	30	40	140	360	500	540	460	80	0	20

We may use the economic order quantity to establish an ordering schedule. The average weekly demand is $(20 + 20 + 30 + \cdots + 0 + 20)/12 = 184.2$. Hence the EOQ is

$$Q^* = \sqrt{2DC_0/C_h} = \sqrt{\frac{2(184.2)\,(150)}{1}} = 235$$

We order 235 units to be available in week 1; this will satisfy demand through week 4 but not through week 5. Continuing in this fashion we arrive at the following schedule. Note that the order quantity must be increased when demand plus the previous week's inventory exceeds the lot size (as occurs in week 7). Of course, one can place additional orders of 235 earlier to cover this demand, but this would only increase the ordering and holding costs.

Week	1	2	3	4	5	6	7	8	9	10	11	12
Demand	20	20	30	40	140	360	500	540	460	80	0	20
Orders	235				235	235	405	540	460	235		
Ending inventory	215	195	165	125	220	95	0	0	0	155	155	135

There are seven orders placed over this 12-week horizon, and the total end-of-week inventory is $(215 + 195 + \ldots + 135) = 1460$ units. Thus, the total cost of this policy is

$$
\begin{aligned}
7 \text{ orders at } \$150 \text{ per order} &= \$1050 \\
1460 \text{ units at } \$1/\text{week} &= \underline{1460} \\
& \$2510
\end{aligned}
$$

Larger inventory-carrying costs than necessary are incurred because of the mismatch between the order quantity and the demand, causing excess inventory to be carried week to week. We now present three alternate methods that overcome some of the difficulties associated with the EOQ approach.

Periodic Order Quantity

The periodic-order-quantity approach is very simple. The economic order quantity is divided by the average demand to yield an *economic time interval* between orders. Orders are placed at these intervals for all known future demands. Since the economic order quantity is 235, the economic time interval is $235/184.2 = 1.3$, or about every 1 to 2 weeks. Using 2-week intervals, orders should be planned as follows:

Week	1	2	3	4	5	6	7	8	9	10	11	12
Demand	20	20	30	40	140	360	500	540	460	80	0	20
Orders	40		70		500		1040		540			20
Ending inventory	20	0	40	0	360	0	540	0	80	0	0	0

Essentially we order to satisfy the next 2 weeks' demand. The total ordering cost is $900 (6 orders × $150), and holding cost is $1040, for a total cost of $1940 over this 12-week horizon. This is a $570 improvement over the EOQ-based policy. Check for yourself to see that the total cost of a one-week periodic order quantity policy is $1650.

Recall that for the EOQ model, the total ordering cost equals the total holding cost for Q^*. The part-period balancing method uses this fact in attempting to balance these costs for dynamic demand. Using the data given above, let us determine how much to order at the beginning of the time horizon. We assume that all orders are multiples of weekly requirements. Thus initially we can order 20 units, 40 units (first 2 weeks' demand), 70 units (first 3 weeks' demand), and so on. Since each order costs $150, we try to order the amount for which holding costs come closest to $150. Suppose we order 20 units, the first week's demand. Since there is no ending inventory, the holding cost is zero.

Next, consider ordering 40 units (2 weeks' demand). The ending inventory in week 1 is 20. At a carrying cost of $1 per unit per week, the total holding cost is $20. In a similar fashion, ordering 70 units results in ending inventories of 50 and 30 in weeks 1 and 2 respectively, and a holding cost of $50(1) + 30(1) = $80. We still have not matched the ordering cost of $150, so we consider the first 4 weeks of demand. If we order 110 units, the holding cost is $90(1) + 70(1) + 40(1) = $200. This is the closest value to the ordering cost of $150; thus we order 110 units initially. This covers the first 4 weeks. To determine the scheduled receipts in week 5 we repeat this procedure, beginning with the demand for week 5, weeks 5 and 6, and so on. You should verify that part-period balancing yields the following solution with total cost of $1240:

Week	1	2	3	4	5	6	7	8	9	10	11	12
Demand	20	20	30	40	140	360	500	540	460	80	0	20
Orders	110				140	360	500	540	560			
Ending inventory	90	70	40	0	0	0	0	0	100	20	20	0

A method that is both computationally efficient and effective in terms of providing very good solutions with dynamic demand was developed by Edward Silver and Harlan Meal.[2] The method is similar to part-period balancing in that we consider ordering one period's demand, then two period's demand, and so on, stopping when the *average cost* per period exceeds that of the previous period. This is best illustrated using the same problem with which we have been working.

First consider ordering only enough to satisfy demand in the first week. There is no holding cost, so the total cost is simply the ordering cost, $150. If we order for the first 2 weeks, the total cost is computed by adding any holding costs to the ordering cost. The ordering cost is $150, and we must carry the second weeks' demand of 20 units for 1 period at a cost of $1 per unit per week, or $20. Thus the total cost is $170. The *average cost per week* is $170/2 = $85. This is *less* than the average cost incurred if we order only one weeks' demand, which is $150. Therefore we continue, considering ordering for the first 3 weeks.

The total cost for ordering 3 weeks' demand, or 70 units, is $150 + 50(1) + 30(1) = $230. Thus the average cost per week is $230/3 = $76.67 which is less

---

[2]E.A. Silver and H.C. Meal, "A Heuristic for Selecting Lot Size Quantities for the Case of a Deterministic Time Varying Demand Rate and Discrete Opportunities for Replenishment," *Production and Inventory Management*, 14, p. 64–74, 1973.

than that of the previous week, $85. Again we continue. If we order 110 units, or 4 weeks' demand, the average cost is

$$\frac{150 + 90(1) + 70(1) + 40(1)}{4} = \$87.5$$

This now is *greater* than the average cost for the first 3 weeks, so we stop and order 70 units, or 3 weeks' demand. Notice that once we find that the average cost for ordering a given number of weeks' demand exceeds that of the previous week, we order enough to fill the demand to the *previous* week, not to the current week under consideration.

Next, we move the time horizon to week 4 and begin the procedure again. If we order only to fill the demand for week 4, the cost is $150. If we consider the demand for weeks 4 and 5, the average cost per week is

$$\frac{150 + 140(1)}{2} = \$145$$

which is less than $150 so we continue. Ordering for weeks 4, 5, and 6, gives an average cost of $336.67 which is greater than $145. Therefore in week 4 we order the demand for weeks 4 and 5, or 180 units.

The complete solution to the example problem using the Silver-Meal heuristic is given in the table that follows. You should verify this solution for weeks 6 through 12. The total cost is $1260.

Week	1	2	3	4	5	6	7	8	9	10	11	12
Demand	20	20	30	40	140	360	500	540	460	80	0	20
Orders	70			180		360	500	540	560			
Ending inventory	50	30	0	140	0	0	0	0	100	20	20	

There are many other lot-sizing methods that have been developed. One method that gives the true minimum total cost is called the *Wagner-Whitin algorithm*. Essentially, the Wagner-Whitin algorithm implicitly evaluates all the possible ways of ordering to meet the demand at minimum total cost. However, it is somewhat more complicated than the other methods we have discussed and is rather time consuming to perform by hand, although it is extremely easy to implement on a computer.[3] The optimal solution to the example problem found by the Wagner-Whitin algorithm turns out to be the same one that was found by the part-period balancing procedure. This is merely a coincidence; in general, part-period balancing will not produce the minimum-cost solution.

A study by one of the authors compared EOQ, part-period balancing, and Silver-Meal heuristics with the Wagner-Whitin algorithm. The results showed that EOQ was over 30 percent higher than the minimum cost schedule; part-period balancing, about 7 percent higher; and Silver-Meal, only about 2 percent higher. In addition, the Silver-Meal heuristic was the fastest in terms of computer time.

---

[3]Evans, James R. "An Efficient Implementation of the Wagner-Whitin Algorithm for Dynamic Lot Sizing," *Journal of Operations Management*, 5, no. 2, (1985): 229–236.

13.6 SERVICE LEVELS AND UNCERTAINTY IN DEMAND

One of the critical assumptions of the EOQ model is that demand is constant. In many cases, demand is *relatively* constant but still fluctuates around an average value. This fluctuation can often be described by a probability distribution. The decision models used to analyze these inventory systems are referred to as *stochastic demand models*. However, even when stochastic demands exist, the inventory manager will be attempting to make the how-much-to-order and/or when-to-order decisions that will enable an efficient operation of the inventory system. Under a minimum-cost objective, the relevant cost components, just as with the EOQ model, are ordering and inventory-holding costs.

Since the level of mathematical sophistication required for an exact formulation of order quantity-reorder point inventory models with stochastic demand is beyond the scope of this text, we restrict our discussion of these inventory decision problems to a heuristic procedure that should provide good, workable solutions without relying upon advanced mathematical techniques. While this solution procedure can be expected to provide only approximations to the optimal inventory decisions, it has been found to yield very good decisions in many practical situations.

Let us consider the case of Southern Office Supplies, Inc., located in Atlanta, Georgia. Southern distributes a wide variety of office supplies and equipment to as many as 500 customers in Atlanta and northern Georgia. In addition, it sells through three retail outlets. Suppose we consider the inventory problem associated with a typing paper product. The paper is purchased in reams from a firm located in Portland, Oregon. Southern would like a recommendation on how much it should order and when it should place an order so that a low-cost inventory operation can be realized. Pertinent facts are that ordering costs are $45.00 per order, one ream of paper costs $3.80, and Southern uses a 20 percent annual inventory-carrying cost rate for its inventory. The inventory-holding cost is $C_h = .20(\$3.80) = \$.76$. With its numerous customers, Southern experiences an uncertain, or stochastic, demand in that the number of orders will vary considerably from day to day and from week to week. While demand is not specifically known, historical sales data indicate that an annual demand of 15,000 reams, while not exact, can be used as a good estimate of the anticipated annual volume.

Although we are in a stochastic demand situation, we have a good estimate of the expected annual volume, 15,000 reams. As an approximation of the best order quantity, we can apply the EOQ model with the expected annual volume substituted for the annual demand, D. In Southern's case, we have

$$Q^* = \sqrt{\frac{2DC_0}{C_h}} = \sqrt{\frac{2(15,000)(45)}{0.76}} = 1333 \text{ reams}$$

When we studied the sensitivity of the EOQ models, we learned that the total cost of operating an inventory system was relatively insensitive to order quantities that were in the neighborhood of Q^*. Using this knowledge, we expect 1333 reams per order to be a good approximation of the optimal order quantity. Even if annual demand were as low as 13,000 or as high as perhaps 17,000 units, an order quantity of 1333 reams should be a relatively good low-cost order size.

Thus, given our best estimate of annual demand at 15,000 reams, we use $\dot{Q}^* =$ 1333. Using this order quantity, Southern can anticipate placing $D/Q^* = 15,000/$ 1333, or approximately 11 orders per year, with slightly over a month between orders.

We now want to establish the reorder point that will trigger the ordering process. Further pertinent data indicate that it usually takes 2 weeks for Southern to receive a new supply of paper from the manufacturer. With a 2-week demand of (15,000 reams/52 weeks) $\times$ 2 = 577 reams, we might first suggest a 577-unit reorder point. However, it now becomes extremely important to consider the probabilities of the various demands. If 577 reams is the average 2-week demand and if the demands are symmetrically distributed about 577, then demand will be more than 577 reams roughly 50 percent of the time. This means Southern would show a stockout before an incoming shipment arrives about 50 percent of the time. This shortage rate would probably be viewed as unacceptably high. To reduce the chances of a stockout, *safety stock* can be carried. Safety stock is simply additional inventory that is carried to guard against short-term fluctuations in demand. The amount of safety stock is related to the reorder point, which in turn determines the probability of a stockout. Let us then see how these factors are related to one another and how an appropriate level of safety stock can be determined.

In order to determine a reorder point for which there is a low likelihood of a stockout, it is necessary to establish a probability distribution for the lead-time demand called the **lead-time demand distribution** and analyze stockout probabilities. Usually, the lead-time demand distribution is assumed to be normal, although any demand probability distribution is acceptable. By collecting historical data on actual demands during the lead-time period, an analyst should be able to determine if the normal distribution or some other probability distribution is the most realistic picture of the lead-time demand distribution.

Given the lead-time demand probability distribution, we can now determine how the reorder point r affects the probability of stocking out of the item. Since stockouts occur whenever the demand during the lead time exceeds the reorder point, we can find the probability of stockout by using the lead-time demand distribution to compute the probability of demand exceeding r.

We can now approach the when-to-order problem by defining a cost per stockout and then attempting to include this cost in a total cost equation. Possibly a more practical approach is to ask management to define an acceptable **service level**, where the service level refers to the probability that the company will not have a stockout during a lead-time period. For example a .95 service level means that there is a 95 percent chance the inventory will be able to satisfy all demand occurring before the next shipment arrives. In other words, there is a .05 probability the firm will experience a stockout during the lead-time period.

If demand for a product is stochastic, a manager who says he or she will never tolerate a stockout is being somewhat unrealistic, because attempting to avoid stockouts completely will require high-reorder points, high-inventory levels, and an associated high inventory-holding cost.

For any situation where a normal probability distribution provides a good approximation of lead-time demand, the general expression for reorder point is as follows:

$$r = \mu + z\sigma \tag{13.24}$$

where

z = the number of standard deviations necessary to achieve
the acceptable service level

μ = expected lead-time demand

σ = standard deviation of lead-time demand

DETERMINING SAFETY STOCK LEVELS

EXAMPLE

Let us return to the Southern Office Supplies situation. Using historical data and some judgment, the lead-time demand distribution for Southern's paper product is assumed to be a normal distribution with a mean of 577 reams and a standard deviation of 100 reams. This distribution is shown in Figure 13.7.

Suppose that Southern's management desires a service level of .95. That is, there is a tolerable 5 percent probability of a stockout during a given lead time period. With 11 orders anticipated per year, the 5 percent level of stockouts means Southern should experience a stockout for this product roughly once every 2 years. Let us consider how we could find the reorder point r that provides this level of service. This situation is shown graphically in Figure 13.8.

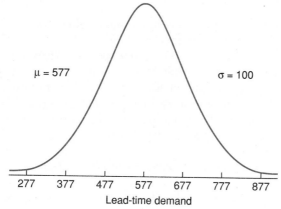

FIGURE 13.7

Distribution of Demand During the Lead Time for Southern Office Supplies, Inc.

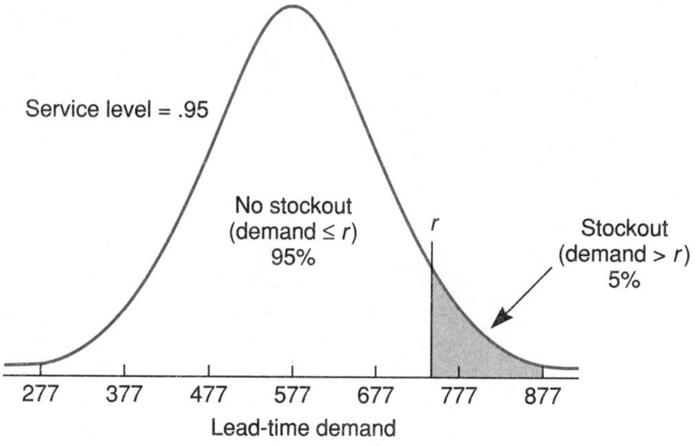

FIGURE 13.8

Reorder Point r That Allows a 5 Percent Chance of Stockout for Southern Office Supplies, Inc.

From the normal distribution tables in Appendix B, we see that an r-value that is 1.645 standard deviations above the mean will allow stockouts 5 percent of the time. Therefore, for the assumed normal distribution for lead-time demand with $\mu = 577$ and $\sigma = 100$, the reorder point r is determined by

$$r = 577 + 1.645(100) \approx 577 + 165 = 742 \text{ reams}$$

In the above computations, we see the reorder point is based on the expected lead-time demand, plus a safety stock of 165 reams.

Thus the recommended inventory decision is to order 1333 reams whenever the inventory position reaches the reorder point of 742. This policy should work to minimize inventory costs and simultaneously satisfy demand with a 5 percent probability of stockout during a lead-time period. The anticipated annual cost for this system is as follows:

Ordering cost	$\left(\dfrac{D}{Q}\right) C_0 = \left(\dfrac{15,000}{1333}\right) 45 =$	\$506
Holding cost, normal inventory	$\left(\dfrac{Q}{2}\right) C_h = \left(\dfrac{1333}{2}\right)(.76) =$	\$507
Holding cost, safety stock	$(165) C_h = (165)(.76) =$	\$125
Total cost		\$1138

If Southern can assume that a known, constant demand rate of 15,000 reams per year exists for the paper product, then $Q^* = 1333$, $r = 577$, and a total annual cost of $506 + $507 = $1013 can be expected. When demand is uncertain and can be expressed only in probabilistic terms, a larger total cost can be expected. The larger cost occurs in the form of larger inventory holding costs due to the fact that more inventory must be maintained in order to prevent frequent stockouts. For Southern this additional inventory, or safety stock, is 165 units, with an additional cost of $125 per year.

In the Southern example, the manager expressed a desire for a service level of .95. Decreasing the service level—and thus increasing the probability of a stock-out—permits a lower safety stock. Thus the manager must make a trade-off between inventory costs and customer service, two conflicting objectives. The values in Table 13.4 illustrate this trade-off by showing what happens to the inventory cost and safety stock level if the manager is willing to consider other service levels. Ultimately the manager has to weigh the added inventory cost with the chance of stockouts in determining an appropriate decision.

TABLE 13.4

Cost/Service Trade-offs for Southern Office Supplies

Service Level	Probability of Stockout	z-Value	Reorder Point r	Safety Stock	Additional Inventory Cost
.99	.01	2.33	810	233	\$177
.95	.05	1.645	742	165	125
.90	.10	1.28	705	128	97
.85	.15	1.04	681	104	79
.80	.20	0.84	661	84	64

In the previous treatment of inventory problems we assumed that the inventory system operates continuously and that we will have many repeating cycles or periods. Furthermore, we assumed that the inventory may be carried for one or more repeat periods and that we will be placing repeat orders for the product in the future. The **single-period inventory model** refers to inventory situations in which *one* order is placed for the product. At the end of the period the product has either sold out or there is a surplus of unsold items which will be sold for a salvage value. The single-period models occur in situations involving seasonal or perishable items that cannot be carried in inventory and sold in future periods. Seasonal clothing (such as bathing suits, winter coats) are typically handled in a single-period manner. In these situations a buyer places one preseason order for each item and then experiences a stockout or holds a clearance sale on the surplus stock at the end of the season. No items are carried in inventory and sold the following year. Newspapers are another example of a product that is ordered one time and is either sold or not sold during the single period. While newspapers are ordered daily, they cannot be carried in inventory and sold in later periods. Thus newspaper orders may be treated as a sequence of single-period models; that is, each day or period is separate, and a single-period inventory decision must be made each period (day). Since we order only once for the period, the only inventory decision we must make is *how much* of the product to order at the start of the period. Because newspaper sales is an excellent example of a single-period situation, the single-period inventory problem is sometimes referred to as the *newsboy problem*.

Obviously, if the demand were known for a single-period inventory situation, the solution would be easy: We would simply order the amount we knew would be demanded. However, in most single-period models the exact demand is not known. In fact, forecasts may show that demand can have a wide variety of values. If we are going to analyze this type of inventory decision problem in a quantitative manner, we will need information about the probabilities associated with the various demand possibilities. Thus the single-period model is another type of probablistic demand model.

Let us show how the method of marginal analysis can be used to determine the optimal order quantity for a single-period inventory model. Marginal analysis addresses the how-much-to-order question by comparing the cost or loss of *ordering one additional unit* with the cost or loss of *not ordering one additional unit*. The costs involved are defined as follows:

c_o = the cost per unit of *overestimating* demand; this cost represents the loss of ordering one additional unit and finding that it cannot be sold.

c_u = the cost per unit of *underestimating* demand; this cost represents the opportunity loss of not ordering one additional unit and finding that it could have been sold.

It can be shown that the optimal order quantity (Q^*) satisfies the following expression:

$$P(\text{demand} \leq Q^*) = \frac{c_u}{c_u + c_o} \qquad (13.25)$$

FINDING AN OPTIMAL SINGLE-PERIOD ORDER QUANTITY

Let us consider a single-period inventory model that could be used to make a how-much-to-order decision for the Johnson Shoe Company. The buyer for the Johnson Shoe Company has decided to order a shoe for men that has just been shown at a buyers' meeting in New York City. The shoe will be part of the company's spring–summer promotion and will be sold through nine retail stores in the Chicago area. Since the shoe is designed for spring and summer months, it cannot be expected to sell in the fall. Johnson plans to hold a special August clearance sale in an attempt to sell all shoes that have not been sold by July 31. The shoes cost $40 per pair and retail for $60 per pair. At the sale price of $30 per pair, it is expected that all surplus shoes can be sold during the August sale. If you were the buyer for the Johnson Shoe Company, how many pairs of the shoes would you order?

An obvious question at this time is, what are the possible levels of demand for the shoe? We will need this information in order to answer the question of how much to order. Let us suppose that the uniform probability distribution shown in Figure 13.9 can be used to describe the demand for the size 10D shoes. In particular, note that the range of demand is from 350 to 650 pairs of shoes with an average or expected demand of 500 pairs of shoes.

The Johnson Shoe Company will incur the cost of overestimating demand whenever it orders too much and has to sell the extra shoes during the August sale. Thus the cost per unit of overestimating demand is equal to the purchase cost per unit minus the August sales price per unit; that is, c_o = $40 − $30 = $10. In other words, Johnson will lose $10 for each pair of shoes that it orders over the quantity demanded. The cost of underestimating demand is the lost profit (opportunity loss) due to the fact that a pair of shoes that could have been sold was not available in inventory. Thus the per-unit cost of underestimating demand is the difference between the regular selling price per unit and the purchase cost per unit; that is, c_u = $60 − $40 = $20. Thus Equation (13.24) shows that the optimal order size for Johnson shoes must satisfy the following condition:

$$P(\text{demand} \leqslant Q^*) = \frac{c_u}{c_u + c_o} = \frac{20}{20 + 10} = \frac{20}{30} = \frac{2}{3}$$

We can find the optimal order quantity Q^* by referring to the assumed probability distribution shown in Figure 13.9 and finding the value of Q that will provide $P(\text{demand} \leqslant Q^*) = \frac{2}{3}$. In order to do this, we note that in the uniform distribution the probability is evenly distributed over the range from 350 to 650 pairs of shoes. Thus we can satisfy the expression for Q^* by moving two-thirds of the

---

FIGURE 13.9

Uniform
Probability
Distribution of
Demand for the
Johnson Shoe
Company Size
10D Shoes

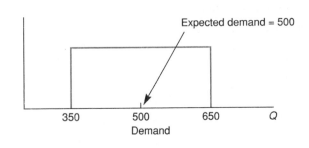

way from 350 to 650. Since this is a range of $650 - 350 = 300$, we move 200 units from 350 toward 650. Doing so provides the optimal order quantity of 550 pairs of size 10D shoes.

We note that in Equation (13.25) the value of $c_u/(c_u + c_o)$ will be equal to 0.50 whenever $c_u = c_o$; in this case we select an order quantity corresponding to the median of the probability distribution of demand. With this choice it is just as likely to have a stockout as a surplus. This makes sense since the costs are equal. Whenever $c_u < c_o$, Equation (13.25) leads to the choice of an order quantity more likely to be less than demand; hence a higher risk of a stockout is present. However, for the Johnson Shoe example, $c_u > c_o$ and the optimal order quantity leads to a higher risk of a surplus. This can be seen from the fact that the order quantity is 50 pairs of shoes over the expected demand of 500 pairs of shoes. Thus the optimal order quantity for Johnson has a probability of a stockout of $\frac{1}{3}$ and a probability of a surplus of $\frac{2}{3}$. This is what we should have expected, since $c_u = 20$ is greater than $c_o = 10$.

In the Johnson Shoe Company example a uniform probability distribution was used to describe the demand for the size 10D shoes. However, any probability distribution of demand may be used for the single-period inventory model. Using the cost of overestimation and underestimation, Equation (13.25) can be used to find the location of Q^* in any appropriate demand probability distribution. For example, suppose that a normal probability distribution with a mean of 500 and a standard deviation of 100 had been a better description of the demand distribution for the size 10D shoes. This probability distribution is shown in Figure 13.10. With $c_u = \$20$ and $c_o = \$10$ as previously computed, Equation (13.24) still shows that the optimal order quantity Q^* must satisfy the requirement that $P(\text{demand} \leq Q^*) = \frac{2}{3}$. We simply use the table of areas under the normal curve (Appendix B) to find the Q^* where this condition is satisfied.

Referring to Figure 13.11, $P(\text{demand} \leq Q^*) = \frac{2}{3}$ requires a 0.1667 area, or probability, between the mean demand of 500 and the optimal order quantity Q^*. From Appendix B we see that the 0.1667 area under the normal curve occurs at $z = 0.43$ standard deviation above the mean. With the mean or expected demand given by $\mu = 500$ and the standard deviation given by $\sigma = 100$, we have

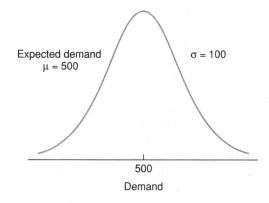

FIGURE 13.10

Normal Probability Distribution of Demand for the Johnson Shoe Company Size 10D Shoes

FIGURE 13.11

Probability
Distribution of
Demand for the
Johnson Shoe
Company
Showing the
Location of the
Optimal Order
Quantity Q*

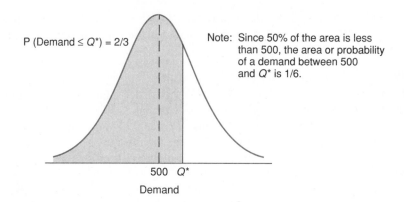

$P\,(\text{Demand} \le Q^*) = 2/3$

Note: Since 50% of the area is less
than 500, the area or probability
of a demand between 500
and Q^* is 1/6.

500 Q^*

Demand

Thus, with the assumed normal probability of demand, Johnson should order 543 pairs of the size 10D shoes in anticipation of customer orders.

In any probabilistic inventory model, the assumption about the probability distribution of demand is critical and can affect the recommended inventory decision. Equation (13.25), which provides the critical probability value, $P(\text{demand} \le Q^*)$, can be applied to any demand probability distribution. Thus, in using quantitative approaches to inventory decision problems with probabilistic demand, we must exercise care in selecting the probability distribution that is the best approximation of reality.

13.8 SIMULATION MODELS FOR INVENTORY ANALYSIS

In this chapter, we have concentrated on inventory decision models that can be applied to a variety of specific inventory systems. By understanding the characteristics of the system and the assumptions of the decision model, we should be able to select and apply an appropriate model to reach low-cost operating policies for the inventory system.

But what happens when the characteristics of an inventory system do not appear to agree with the specific assumptions of the inventory decision model? In this case, there are two alternatives: (1) attempt to develop and use a specially designed decision model that correctly reflects the characteristics of the system; and (2) attempt to develop and experiment with a computer simulation model that will indicate the impact of various decision alternatives on the cost of operating the system. Computer simulation as introduced in the supplement to Chapter 5 is an important decision analysis tool because it has the flexibility to model unique features of the system that are difficult to represent in purely mathematical terms. In the following example, we demonstrate the use of simulation in making inventory policy decisions.

Sound Systems, Inc., is a retail firm that carries high-quality audio equipment, including a well-known stereo radio system for automobiles. While the store's manager has used inventory models to determine how much to order and when to order for many of its products, the manager has become especially concerned about the inventory situation for the stereo system. Demand for the stereos has been relatively low, but it is clearly subject to variability. It has been very difficult to anticipate when and how much the demand for the product will be. On approximately one-half of the days, the store is open for business but no one orders a stereo system. However, about 1 day per month, three or even four orders may occur. If variable demand were the only source of uncertainty, the store manager believes the order quantity and reorder point decision could be based on a stochastic demand model like the one presented previously. However, the auto stereo system inventory problem is further complicated by the fact that the lead time also varies. Historically, the length of the lead time has been anywhere between 1 and 5 days. These lead times have caused the store to run out of inventory on several occasions. Orders received during the out-of-stock period have caused lost sales. Thus, given this situation, the store manager would like to establish order quantity and reorder point decisions that minimize total relevant inventory cost—that is, ordering, holding, and stockout, or shortage, costs.

After an analysis of delivery charges and other costs associated with each order, the store manager was able to estimate an order cost at $40 per order. An analysis of interest, insurance, and other costs of carrying inventory led to an estimate for the holding cost of $.20 per unit per day. Finally, the shortage cost was estimated to be $100 per unit. The total cost of the system is given by the sum of the ordering cost, the holding cost, and the shortage cost. The objective is to find the combination of order quantity and reorder point that will result in the lowest possible total cost.

A first step in the simulation approach to this inventory problem is to develop a model that can be used to simulate the total cost corresponding to a specific order size and reorder point. Then, using this model, the two decision variables can be varied systematically in order to determine what appears to be the lowest cost combination. Let us see what is involved in developing such a model to carry out a 1-day simulation of the inventory process.

Assume that a specific reorder point and order quantity have already been selected. We must begin each day of the simulation by checking whether any ordered inventory has just arrived. If so, the current inventory on hand must be increased by the quantity of goods received. Note that this assumes that orders are received and inventory on hand is updated at the start of each day. If this assumption is not appropriate, a different model, perhaps calling for goods to be received at the end of the day, would have to be developed.

Next, our simulator must generate a value for the daily demand from the appropriate probability distribution. If there is sufficient inventory on hand to meet the daily demand, the inventory on hand will be decreased by the amount of the daily demand. If, however, inventory on hand is not sufficient to satisfy all the demand, we will satisfy as much of the demand as possible. The inventory will then be zero, and a shortage cost will be computed for all unsatisfied demand. In using this procedure we are assuming that if a customer orders more stereo systems than the store has in inventory, the customer will take what is available and shop elsewhere for the remainder of the order. With another audio store only two blocks away, the store manager is sure that unsatisfied demand will result in lost sales, and a goodwill cost for each shortage is appropriate.

After the daily order has been processed by the simulator, the next step is to determine if the ending inventory has reached the reorder point and a new order should be placed. However, prior to placing a new order, we must check to see if the most recent order is outstanding and should be arriving shortly. If so, we do not place an order.[4] Otherwise, an order is placed and the company incurs an ordering cost. If a new order is placed, a lead time must be randomly generated to reflect the time between the placement and the receipt of the goods.

Finally, an inventory holding cost, which is $.20 for each unit in the daily ending inventory, is computed. The sum of the shortage costs, ordering costs, and inventory holding costs becomes the total daily cost for the simulation. Performing the above sequence of operations would complete one day of the simulation. Figure 13.12 depicts this daily simulation process for the auto stereo system operation.

The daily simulation process should be repeated for as many days as are necessary to obtain meaningful results. The output from the simulation will show the total cost involved in using one particular order quantity and reorder point combination. By simulating the inventory operation with different order quantity reorder point combinations, we can compare total operating costs and select the apparent "best" order quantity and reorder point decisions for the stereo systems.

Suppose the store has a complete set of records showing the demand for the auto stereos for the past year (300 days). Furthermore, suppose the records also show the number of days between placement and receipt of each order over the same period. Table 13.5 shows the frequency and relative frequency distributions for demand and lead time.

In order to carry out the simulation steps depicted in Figure 13.12, we must develop the procedure for generating values from the demand and lead-time distributions. As before, we associate with each value of the random variable an interval of pseudorandom numbers such that the probability of generating a pseudorandom number in that interval is the same as the relative frequency of the associated demand and lead time. The intervals of pseudorandom numbers are shown in Tables 13.6 and 13.7.

To appreciate how the simulation method works for this problem, we follow a 10-day simulation of the process. Let us assume that the store manager wants to determine the effect of using an order quantity of 5 units with a reorder point of 3 units. For purposes of starting the simulation, let us assume that we have a beginning inventory of 5 units at the start of day 1 of our 10-day simulation.

TABLE 13.5	Demand			Lead Time		
Frequency and Relative Frequency Distributions for Demand and Lead Time in Sound Systems' Problem	Units	Frequency	Relative Frequency	Days	Frequency	Relative Frequency
	0	150	.50	1	6	.20
	1	75	.25	2	3	.10
	2	45	.15	3	12	.40
	3	15	.05	4	6	.20
	4	15	.05	5	3	.10
		300	1.00		30	1.00

[4]We are assuming that it will never be necessary to have two orders outstanding simultaneously. However, in other simulation models, having several orders outstanding may be an entirely appropriate assumption.

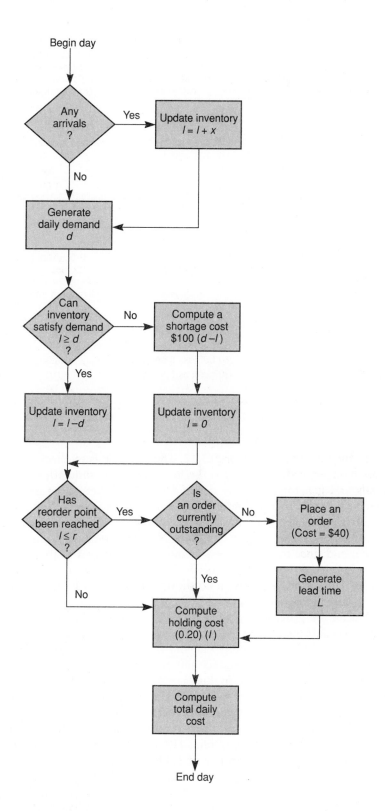

Begin day

Any arrivals ? — Yes → Update inventory $I = I + x$

No

Generate daily demand d

Can inventory satisfy demand $I \geq d$? — No → Compute a shortage cost $\$100 \, (d - I)$

Yes

Update inventory $I = I - d$

Update inventory $I = 0$

Has reorder point been reached $I \leq r$? — Yes → Is an order currently outstanding ? — No → Place an order (Cost = $40)

No

Yes

Generate lead time L

Compute holding cost $(0.20) \, (I)$

Compute total daily cost

End day

TABLE 13.6

Pseudorandom Numbers and Associated Daily Demands for Sound Systems' Auto Stereo Inventory Problem

Daily Demand	Relative Frequency	Interval of Pseudorandom Numbers	Probability of Selecting a Pseudorandom Number in Interval
0	.50	.00 but less than .50	.50
1	.25	.50 but less than .75	.25
2	.15	.75 but less than .90	.15
3	.05	.90 but less than .95	.05
4	.05	.95 but less than 1.00	.05
	1.00		1.00

TABLE 13.7

Pseudorandom Number Intervals and Associated Lead Times for Sound Systems' Auto Stereo Inventory Problem

Lead Time (Days)	Relative Frequency	Interval of Pseudorandom Numbers	Probability of Selecting a Pseudorandom Number in Interval
1	.20	.00 but less than .20	.20
2	.10	.20 but less than .30	.10
3	.40	.30 but less than .70	.40
4	.20	.70 but less than .90	.20
5	.10	.90 but less than 1.00	.10
	1.00		1.00

Refer to the flow chart in Figure 13.12. The first step is to check to see if any shipments have arrived. Since this is the first day of the simulation, we assume no arrivals and generate the daily demand for day 1. Let us assume we use a computer to generate pseudorandom numbers between 0 and .999 and that the first number generated is .093. From Table 13.6, we see that this pseudorandom number corresponds to a demand of 0 units. Note that we have no shortage costs to compute, and since the inventory on hand (5 units) is greater than the reorder point (3 units), we do not place an order. The holding costs for day 1 are computed to be ($.20)5, or $1.00. With no shortages and no ordering, the total cost for day 1 is just the holding cost of $1.00.

To illustrate the process of placing an order, consider day 4. At the start of day 4, the beginning inventory is 4 units. The random number selected to generate daily demand is .528; thus a daily demand of 1 unit is generated. As a result, the ending inventory drops to 3 units and an order for 5 units is placed. Generating another random number, in this case .620, indicates a lead time of 3 days, which means that the new order will be available on day 7. The day 4 costs are ($.20)3 = $.60 for the inventory-holding cost and $40.00 for the ordering cost. Since there was no shortage cost, the total cost for the day was $40.60. Continuing our simulation in this manner, we obtained the computer-generated results shown in Table 13.8. The totals at the bottom of Table 13.8 provide the average holding cost, average ordering cost, average shortage cost, and average total cost for the 10-day simulation. Prior to drawing any firm conclusions based on these limited simulation results, we should run the simulation for many more days. Also we want to test many other order quantity reorder point combinations.

A computer programmer can develop a computer simulation program or simulator to enable the store to explore a variety of order quantities and reorder points for a large number of simulated days. In Table 13.9, we present output from a simulator that was developed to solve inventory problems such as the auto stereos inventory problem. In this simulator, the decision maker has the option of selecting a variety of order quantities and reorder points. For purposes of illustration, the computer simulation output is shown for simulations with order quantities of from 5 units to 50 units in increments of 5 and for reorder points of from 1 to 10 in increments of 1. A total of 1000 days is represented in the simulation of each order quantity reorder point combination.

We see that the results of this computer simulation indicate that the lowest cost solution occurs at an order quantity of 25 units and a reorder point of 6 units; in this case the resulting average total cost is $4.78 per day. After studying these results, the store manager might wish to explore other order quantities near the apparent best order quantity of 25. In Table 13.10 the results of varying the

TABLE 13.8   Computer Simulation Results for 10 Days of Operation of Sound Systems with an Order Quantity of 5 and Reorder Point of 3

Day	Beg Inv	Units Rcvd	Rndm Numb	Units Demd	End Inv	Rndm Numb	Lead Time	Holding Cost	Order Cost	Short Cost	Total Cost
1	5	0	.093	0	5			1.00	.00	.00	1.00
2	5	0	.681	1	4			.80	.00	.00	.80
3	4	0	.292	0	4			.80	.00	.00	.80
4	4	0	.528	1	3	.620	3	.60	40.00	.00	40.60
5	3	0	.866	2	1			.20	.00	.00	.20
6	1	0	.975	4	0			.00	.00	300.00	300.00
7	0	5	.622	1	4			.80	.00	.00	.80
8	4	0	.819	2	2	.939	5	.40	40.00	.00	40.40
9	2	0	.373	0	2			.40	.00	.00	.40
10	2	0	.353	0	2			.40	.00	.00	.40
				Average cost for 10 simulated days				.54	8.00	30.00	38.54

TABLE 13.9   Simulated Average Daily Cost for 1000 Days of Sound Systems' Inventory Problem

Reorder Point	Order Quantity									
	5	10	15	20	25	30	35	40	45	50
1	28.70	16.60	13.16	10.40	10.70	8.32	6.60	8.84	7.96	10.44
2	23.02	11.86	10.92	7.84	7.82	6.88	5.92	7.38	6.40	7.42
3	18.68	11.28	6.74	6.02	6.06	5.68	7.92	6.58	5.80	6.14
4	13.80	8.24	6.94	5.56	6.28	5.58	6.58	6.50	6.74	6.84
5	10.82	6.62	5.70	4.84	5.22	6.48	6.50	5.86	6.36	6.44
6	9.44	5.50	5.38	5.20	(4.78)	5.48	5.86	6.12	6.26	6.68
7	9.44	5.70	5.04	5.20	5.52	5.42	6.12	5.98	6.04	6.56
8	11.00	5.78	5.32	5.00	5.24	5.50	5.98	6.10	6.66	7.12
9	8.72	6.22	5.24	5.24	5.32	5.54	6.10	6.36	6.68	6.98
10	9.36	6.10	5.50	5.44	5.60	5.70	6.36	6.56	6.62	7.44

**TABLE 13.10 Simulated Average Daily Cost for 1000 Days of Sound Systems'
Inventory Problem**

Reorder Point	Order Quantity									
	21	22	23	24	25	26	27	28	29	30
4	5.88	6.04	6.26	5.48	5.78	5.12	5.48	6.14	5.34	6.48
5	5.18	5.16	5.68	5.40	5.32	5.18	5.76	5.14	4.98	5.50
6	5.10	(4.66)	5.74	4.70	5.50	4.90	5.62	5.58	5.22	5.20
7	5.04	4.90	4.94	5.02	5.14	5.24	5.22	5.26	5.24	5.34
8	5.00	5.38	4.96	4.98	5.26	5.14	5.26	5.38	5.38	5.42

order quantity from 21 to 30 in increments of 1 and reorder points from 4 to 8 are shown. The smallest simulated average total cost of $4.66 now occurs when the order quantity is 22 units and the reorder point is 6 units. Note, however, that in this second set of simulation experiments the previously best order quantity of 25 units and reorder point of 6 units has a total cost of $5.50 per day. Since different random numbers were used in the two simulations, different total costs are to be expected. The selection of the "best" order quantity and reorder point is now up to the analyst. What decisions would you make? While you might want to run more or longer simulations, the simulation data of Tables 13.9 and 13.10 indicate that good solutions apparently exist with order quantities around 20 to 25 units and reorder points around 6 or 7 units. Thus while simulation has not guaranteed an optimal solution, it has enabled us to identify apparent low-cost or "near-optimal" decisions for the inventory problem. The final decision for an order quantity and reorder point is based on the store manager's preference from among the good, or near-optimal, solutions.

P/OM IN PRACTICE

A variety of inventory decision models have been presented in this chapter. In each case, the model was based on certain assumptions that enabled optimal order quantity and reorder point decisions to be made. By selecting the appropriate model for a given inventory system, the model can be used to provide low-cost operating policies for the inventory. The following P/OM in Practice describes the uses and value of inventory models at Pfizer Pharmaceuticals.

APPLICATIONS OF INVENTORY MODELS AT PFIZER PHARMACEUTICALS[5]

Pfizer Pharmaceuticals is a vertically integrated company that manufactures key intermediates or chemicals used in its finished products. The company operates in 65 countries with five major busi-

[5]Reprinted by permission of P.P. Kleuthgen and J.C. McGee, "Development and Implementation of an Integrated Inventory Management Program at Pfizer Pharmaceuticals," *Interfaces*, 15, no. 1 (Jan.–Feb. 1985), 69–87. Copyright 1985 The Institute of Management Sciences, 290 Westminster Street, Providence, Rhode Island, 02903, U.S.A.

nesses: agriculture, specialty chemicals, materials science, consumer, and health care (whose pharmaceutical segment accounts for more than 50 percent of the company's sales). In the early 1980s, the combination of high interest rates, rapid growth of the pharmaceutical business, and historically high inventories dictated a more focused approach to managing inventory. Divisional management embarked upon a program to (1) control and improve inventory turnover, (2) understand and manage the forces behind the swings in inventory levels, and (3) improve the accuracy of dollar inventory forecasts and thus improve cash-flow projections.

The initial step in the program was a comprehensive analysis of the inventory management function as it presently existed. It revealed the following problems and opportunities.

1. The lack of an accurate and adequately detailed data base to support the analysis and monitoring of inventory performance confused the management process.
2. Responsibility for inventory management was assigned to several organizations. Raw materials and work-in-process (WIP) inventories were managed at the local plant level, while finished goods inventories were managed and planned by the headquarters production planning and inventory-control (PPIC) function.
3. Inventories were not part of the performance evaluation objectives at the plant level.
4. Inventory data was highly aggregated and did not allow meaningful trend analysis or an understanding of how management intervention affected inventories.
5. Methods for inventory management were not consistent among the different plants.
6. The methods used in inventory management were not "state-of-the-art."
7. Inventory forecasting was manual, time consuming, inaccurate, and not routine.
8. The impact on inventory management of the operating differences between the dosage and organic synthesis phases of production was not clearly understood.
9. Inconsistent definition of different classes of inventories among plants (what belongs in finished goods, WIP, raw materials, and so forth) prevented meaningful interplant comparisons.
10. The quantitative impact of capacity constraints, degree of vertical integration, and product mix on inventory was not fully understood and resulted in inaccurate and counterproductive comparisons between plants and divisions within the company.

The second phase was the development of a plan of action that was proposed to senior management. This plan was summarized as follows.

1. A centralized function for divisional inventory management was needed to assure that appropriate, up-to-date management techniques were developed and applied consistently across the divisional locations.
2. Major inventory categories (such as finished goods, WIP, purchased materials, and so forth) needed to be defined accurately, and inventory data reported consistently throughout the division. This required changes in the divisional inventory accounting and reporting systems.
3. Management science models specifically tailored to the operational needs of dosage and synthesis plants had to be created.
4. Inventories would become part of the objectives in overall performance evaluation at the plant level. This would require a functional reporting system and the definition of quantitative targets against which performance could be measured. These objectives would be set using the output of the models.
5. A computer-based inventory-forecasting system would be designed and implemented to improve the speed and accuracy of all inventory forecasts.

The third phase of the project involved the detailed development of inventory models to be used in the system. Inventory models had to meet several criteria.

1. Output from the models would become the quantitative objective of a performance measurement system.
2. Since local management would have to agree to the objectives, the models needed to be intuitively understandable.
3. Since the new methods were to be phased in over a short period of time, they had to be easy to implement, especially in data processing and programming.
4. All models had to be cost-effective, that is, the expected cost savings in inventory investment had to be greater than the cost of model design and implementation.

Detailed models and techniques were designed and introduced for the following applications:

- finished goods lot sizes and safety stocks
- target WIP inventories in the dosage plants
- organic synthesis "campaign sizes" (run quantities) in the chemical plants
- organic synthesis safety stocks
- inventory forecasting
- purchased materials inventory strategies

The full implementation of the new inventory management program depended on organizational changes and top management support.

1. The PPIC organization was restructured to emphasize the increased focus on inventories. The job of inventory manager was created to provide centralized expertise and to develop state-of-the-art management techniques.
2. A control system was designed that used the output of the models as control parameters. In addition, a reporting system was instituted to track inventory performance, to maintain program visibility, and to identify opportunities for reducing inventory.
3. Routine communication of performance and standards of performance was crucial to the successful implementation of the program. Individual targets for each of the major inventory categories at each plant were agreed upon in advance with local management, insuring that all principals in the organization understood and accepted the objectives. Acceptance of the inventory program was not immediate, particularly given its innovative nature and the initial concern about headquarters becoming more involved in plant matters. As with all such programs, strong commitment from senior management was a must. During development, the PPIC group used this commitment and numerous formal presentations to keep the program visible and to encourage local organizations as progress was made. With this approach, the inventory-management program became a cooperative venture between headquarters and plant management. This ensured a broad base of support, sustained commitment, and an ultimately successful program.

The full design and implementation took only 1.5 worker-years over a period of three calendar years. Several student interns programmed the models, and the full expense for the program totaled less than $100,000.

The main impact was in inventory reductions in the following areas: finished goods lot sizes, $2.9 million; finished goods safety stocks, $5.9 million; purchased materials, $5.8 million; organic synthesis safety stocks, $5.1 million; organic synthesis campaign sizes, $2.1 million; and dosage WIP, $2.1 million; for a total of $23.9 million in inventory reductions.

The positive cash-flow benefit of $23.9 million results in a permanent savings in interest and insurance expenses of $3.6 million per year, estimated at an average, conservative carrying cost of 15 percent. The drop in inventory levels alone resulted in a significant increase in the return on investment for the U.S. pharmaceutical group. Further opportunities for reduction of $7.9 million have been formally included in the 1984 pharmaceutical operating plan, and opportunity for an incremental $8.9 million are targeted for 1985 through 1988.

The increased emphasis on inventory management has been extended to other PPIC areas, which led to some unexpected positive results in customer service, particularly a dramatic decrease in weekly national back orders, from an average of $778,000 in 1980 to $31,000 in 1983. In 1983 customer service jumped to an unprecedented 99.98 percent, a record high for the division and at the leading edge of performance within the U.S. pharmaceutical industry as reported in surveys issued by the industry's trade association. Although the positive impact of decreased back orders is difficult to quantify, it is estimated internally that 10 percent of back orders result in lost sales. By comparing the difference in weekly back orders between 1980 and 1983 and assuming a 10 percent lost sales rate, we estimate increases in sales at $3.8 million per year.

The introduction of the finished-goods model triggered a series of schedule policy changes for high-volume products. They are now campaigned under an optimal policy that reduces total setup costs and increases equipment efficiency and productivity. The impact of these policy changes is a reduction in annual setup costs of $250,000.

Finally, as a result of the improved product supplies, total freight costs were reduced by $280,000 per year: air shipments, formerly needed to avoid stockouts in branch warehouses, were needed to a lesser extent. These savings were estimated by comparing direct freight billings and were not adjusted to reflect the fact that shipping volumes doubled over a period of three years.

The total annual savings directly attributable to the inventory management program are as follows:

Inventory carrying costs	$3,600,000
Increased sales	3,800,000
Savings in setup costs	250,000
Reduced freight costs	280,000
	$7,930,000

1. What were some of the problems and difficulties of Pfizer that lead to the consideration of using inventory models?
2. List some of the advantages resulting from the use of inventory models.

SUMMARY

In this chapter we presented several decision models that are often helpful in establishing cost effective order quantities and reorder point decisions. First, we considered cases where the demand for the product occurs at a stable or constant rate. In analyzing these inventory systems, total cost models were developed that include ordering costs, inventory holding costs, and in some cases, backordering costs. Then minimum-cost formulas for the order quantity Q were presented. A reorder point r was established by considering the lead-time demand for the item.

In addition, we discussed inventory decision models where a constant demand could not be assumed, including instances where demand is described by a probability distribution. A critical issue with probabilistic demand models is obtaining a probability distribution that realistically approximates demand for the item. A solution procedure was presented for order quantity and reorder point decisions with probabilistic demand. In addition, a solution procedure was presented for the single-period probabilistic inventory model. Simulation was suggested as a method for analyzing inventory decision problems when the models presented in the chapter did not approximate the characteristics of the inventory system being studied.

In closing this chapter, we reemphasize that inventory and inventory systems can be an extremely expensive component of a firm's operation. Operations managers must be aware of the cost of inventory systems when considering how to make the best possible operating policy decision.

KEY TERMS

Economic order quantity (EOQ)
Constant demand rate
Lead-time demand
Cycle time
Quantity discounts
Lead-time demand distribution
Service level
Single-period inventory models

REVIEW/ DISCUSSION QUESTIONS

1. List the important assumptions behind the EOQ model.
2. What is meant by *constant demand rate*?
3. How is the annual inventory holding cost expressed in the EOQ model?
4. Discuss the sensitivity of the EOQ model with respect to changes in the model parameters.

5. Discuss some practical aspects of inventory decision making that are not taken into account by the EOQ model.

6. Describe the general procedure for finding optimal order quantities using the quantity discount inventory model.

7. How does the economic production lot-size model differ from the EOQ model?

8. What types of costs are associated with backorders?

9. What are some of the problems associated with using EOQ for determining lot sizes with dynamic demand?

10. Describe the periodic order quantity approach to lot sizing.

11. Describe the method of part-period balancing.

12. Describe the Silver-Meal approach to dynamic lot sizing.

13. What is meant by a *service level* in inventory management? Why is it not necessarily desirable to attempt to attain a 100 percent service level?

14. Discuss at least three situations in which the single-period inventory model is applicable.

15. Explain how simulation can be used to analyze inventory problems.

PROBLEMS

1. Suppose that R&B Beverage Company has a soft-drink product that has a constant annual demand rate of 3600 cases. A case of the soft drink costs R&B $3. Ordering costs are $20 per order and inventory holding costs are charged at 25 percent of the cost per unit. There are 250 working days per year and the lead time is 5 days. Identify the following aspects of the inventory policy.
   a. economic order quantity
   b. reorder point
   c. cycle time
   d. total annual cost

2. A general property of the EOQ inventory model is that total inventory holding and total ordering costs are equal or balanced at the optimal solution. Use the data in Problem 1 to show that this result is observed for this problem. Use Equations (13.1), (13.2), and (13.5) to shown in general that total inventory holding costs and total ordering costs are equal whenever Q^* is used.

3. The reorder point [see Equation (13.6)] is defined as the lead-time demand for the item. In cases of long lead times, the lead-time demand and thus the reorder point may exceed the economic order quantity Q^*. In such cases the inventory position will not equal the inventory on hand when an order is placed and the reorder point may either be expressed in terms of inventory position or inventory on hand. Consider the economic order quantity model with $D = 5000$, $C_0 = \$32$, $C_h = \$2$, and 250 working days per year. Identify the reorder point in terms of inventory position and in terms of inventory on hand for each of the following lead times.
   a. 5 days
   b. 15 days

c. 25 days

d. 45 days

4. The XYZ Company purchases a component used in the manufacture of automobile generators directly from the supplier. XYZ's generator production operation, which is operated at a constant rate, will require 1000 components per month throughout the year. Assume ordering costs are $25 per order, unit cost is $2.50 per component, and annual inventory holding costs are charged at 20 percent. The company operates 250 days per year and the lead time is 5 days.

   a. Compute the EOQ, total annual inventory holding and ordering costs, and the reorder point.

   b. Suppose that XYZ's management likes the operational efficiency of ordering in quantities of 1000 units and ordering once each month. How much more expensive would this policy be than your EOQ recommendation? Would you recommend in favor of the 1000-unit order quantity? Explain. What would the reorder point be if the 1000-unit quantity were acceptable?

5. Tele-Reco is a new specialty store that sells television sets, videotape recorders, video games, and other television-related products. A new Japanese-manufactured videotape recorder costs Tele-Reco $600 per unit. Tele-Reco's inventory carrying cost is figured at an annual rate of 22 percent. Ordering costs are estimated to be $70 per order.

   a. If demand for the new videotape recorder is expected to be constant with a rate of 20 units per month, what is the recommended order quantity for the videotape recorder?

   b. What are the estimated annual inventory holding and ordering costs associated with this product?

   c. How many orders will be placed per year?

   d. With 250 working days per year, what is the cycle time for this product?

6. Nation-Wide Bus Lines is proud of its 6-week bus driver training program that it conducts for all new Nation-Wide drivers. A 6-week training program costs Nation-Wide $22,000 for instructors, equipment, and so on, and is independent of the number of new drivers in the class as long as the class size remains less than or equal to 35. The Nation-Wide training program must provide the company with approximately five new fully trained drivers per month. After completing the training program, new drivers are paid $1600 per month but do not work until a full-time driver position is open. Nation-Wide views the $1600 per month paid to each idle new driver as a holding cost necessary to maintain a supply of newly trained drivers available for immediate service. Viewing new drivers as inventory-type units, how large should the training classes be in order to minimize Nation-Wide's total annual training and new driver idle-time costs? How many training classes should the company hold each year? What is the total annual cost associated with your recommendation?

7. Cress Electronic Products manufactures components used in the automotive industry. Cress purchases parts for use in its manufacturing operation from a variety of different suppliers. One particular supplier provides a part where the assumptions of the EOQ model are realistic. The annual demand is 5000

units. Ordering costs are $80 per order and inventory carrying costs are figured at an annual rate of 25 percent.

a. If the cost of the part is $20 per unit, what is the economic order quantity?

b. Assume 250 days of operation per year. If the lead time for an order is 12 days, what is the reorder point?

c. If the lead time for the part is 7 weeks (35 days), what is the reorder point?

d. What is the reorder point for part (c) if the reorder point is expressed in terms of inventory on hand rather than inventory position?

8. Assume that the following quantity discount schedule is appropriate:

Order Size	Discount	Unit Cost
0 to 49	0%	$30.00
50 to 99	5	28.50
100 or more	10	27.00

If annual demand is 120 units, ordering cost is $20 per order, and annual inventory carrying cost is 25 percent, what order quantity would you recommend?

9. Apply the EOQ model to the following quantity discount situation:

Discount Category	Order Size	Discount	Unit Cost
1	0 to 99	0%	$10.00
2	100 or more	3	9.70

$D = 500$ units per year, $C_0 = \$40$, and an annual inventory holding cost of 20 percent are given. What order quantity do you recommend?

10. Keith Shoe Stores carries a basic black dress shoe for men that sells at an approximate constant rate of 500 pairs of shoes every 3 months. Keith's current buying policy is to order 500 pairs each time an order is placed. It costs Keith $30 to place an order. Inventory carrying costs have an annual rate of 20 percent. With the order quantity of 500, Keith obtains the shoes at the lowest possible unit cost of $28 per pair. Other quantity discounts offered by the manufacturer are as follows:

Order Quantity	Price per Pair
0–99	$36
100–199	32
200–299	30
300 or more	28

What is the minimum cost order quantity for the shoes? What are the annual savings of your inventory policy over the policy currently being used by Keith?

11. In the EOQ model with quantity discounts we stated that if the Q^* for a price category is larger than necessary to qualify for the category price, the category cannot be optimal. Use the two discount categories in Problem 9 to show that this is true. That is, plot the total cost curves for the two categories and show that if the category 2 minimum cost Q is an acceptable solution, we do not have to consider category 1.

12. All-Star Bat Manufacturing, Inc., supplies baseball bats to major and minor league baseball teams. After an initial order in January, demand over the 6-month baseball season is approximately constant at 1000 bats per month. Assuming that the bat production process can handle up to 4000 bats per month, the bat production setup costs are $150 per setup, the production cost is $10 per bat, and assuming that All-Star uses a 2 percent monthly inventory holding cost, what production lot size would you recommend to meet the demand during the baseball season? If All-Star operates 20 days per month, how often will the production process operate, and what is the length of a production run?

13. Assume that a production line operates such that the production lot-size model of Section 13.3 is applicable. Given D = 6400 units per year, C_0 = $100, and C_h = $2 per unit per year, compute the minimum-cost production lot size for each of the following production rates:
    a. 8000 units per year
    b. 10,000 units per year
    c. 32,000 units per year
    d. 100,000 units per year
    Compute the EOQ recommended lot size using Equation (13.17). What two observations can you make about the relationship between the EOQ model and the production lot size model?

14. Wilson Publishing Company produces books for the retail market. Demand for a current book is expected to occur at a constant annual rate of 7200 copies. The cost of one copy of the book is $14.50. Inventory holding costs are based on an 18 percent annual rate, and production setup costs are $150 per setup. The equipment the book is produced on has an annual production volume of 25,000 copies. There are 250 working days per year and the lead time for a production run is 15 days. Use the production lot-size model to compute the following values:
    a. minimum-cost production lot size
    b. number of production runs per year
    c. cycle time
    d. length of a production run
    e. maximum inventory level
    f. total annual cost
    g. reorder point

15. A well-known manufacturer of several brands of toothpaste uses the production lot-size model to determine production quantities for its various products. The product known as Extra White is currently being produced in

production lot sizes of 5000 units. The length of the production run for this quantity is 10 days. Because of a recent shortage of a particular raw material, the supplier of the material has announced a cost increase that will be passed along to the manufacturer of Extra White. Current estimates are that the new raw material cost will increase the manufacturing cost of the toothpaste products by 23 percent per unit. What will be the effect of this price increase on the production lot sizes for Extra White?

16. A manager of an inventory system believes that inventory models are important decision-making aids. While often using an EOQ policy, the manager has never considered a backorder model because of the assumption that backorders were "bad" and should be avoided. However, with upper management's continued pressure for cost reduction, you have been asked to analyze the economics of a backordering policy for some products that can possibly be backordered. For a specific product with $D = 800$ units per year, $C_0 = \$150$, $C_h = \$3$, and $C_b = \$20$, what is the economic difference in the EOQ and the planned shortage or backorder model? If the manager adds constraints that no more than 25 percent of the units can be backordered and that no customer will have to wait more than 15 days for an order, should the backorder inventory policy be adopted? Assume 250 working days per year.

17. If the lead time for new orders is 20 days for the inventory system discussed in Problem 16, find the reorder point for both the EOQ and the backorder models.

18. The A&M Hobby Shop carries a line of radio-controlled model racing cars. Demand for the cars is assumed to be constant at a rate of 40 cars per month. The cars cost $60 each, and ordering costs are approximately $15 per order, regardless of the order size. Inventory carrying costs are 20 percent annually.
    a. Determine the economic order quantity and total annual cost under the assumption that no backorders are permitted.
    b. Using a $45 per unit per year backorder cost, determine the minimum-cost inventory policy and total annual cost for the model racing cars.
    c. What is the maximum number of days a customer would have to wait for a backorder under the policy in part (b)? Assume that the Hobby Shop is open for business 300 days per year.
    d. Would you recommend a no-backorder or a backorder inventory policy for this product? Explain.
    e. If the lead time is 6 days, what is the reorder point for both the no-backorder and backorder inventory policies?

19. The demand for a particular product over the next 12-week period will be as follows: 500, 400, 300, 200, 100, 0, 0, 100, 200, 300, 400, and 500 units. The cost per order is $500.00 and the inventory-holding cost is $2.00 per unit per week.
    a. What is the average weekly demand?
    b. Using your answer to part (a), assume the EOQ constant-demand rate assumption holds and compute the EOQ. What is the total cost under this policy, assuming the inventory-holding cost is charged on the basis of the inventory carried at the end of each weekly period?
    c. Reduce inventory-carrying cost to zero by ordering each week exactly what is demanded for the week. What is the cost of this inventory policy?

20. For the situation described in Problem 19, determine the lot-sizing policy using periodic-order quantity, part-period balancing, and Silver-Meal heuristics.

21. Floyd Distributors, Inc., provides a variety of auto parts to small local garages. Floyd purchases parts from manufacturers according to the EOQ model and then ships the parts from a regional warehouse direct to its customers. For a particular type of muffler, Floyd's EOQ analysis recommends orders with $Q^* = 25$ to satisfy an annual demand of 200 mufflers. There are 250 working days per year and the lead time averages 15 days.
   a. What is the reorder point if Floyd assumes a constant demand rate?
   b. Suppose that an analysis of Floyd's muffler demand shows that the lead-time demand follows a normal distribution with $\mu = 12$ and $\sigma = 2.5$. If Floyd's management can tolerate one stockout per year, what is the revised reorder point?
   c. What is the safety stock for part (b)? If $C_h = \$5$/unit/year, what is the extra cost due to the uncertainty of demand?

22. For Floyd Distributors in Problem 21, we were given $Q^* = 25$, $D = 200$, $C_h = \$5$, and a normal lead-time demand distribution with $\mu = 12$ and $\sigma = 2.5$.
   a. What is Floyd's reorder point if the firm is willing to tolerate two stockouts during the year?
   b. What is Floyd's reorder point if the firm wants to restrict the probability of a stockout on any one cycle to at most 1 percent?
   c. What are the safety stock levels and the annual safety stock costs for the reorder points found in parts (a) and (b)?

23. A product with an annual demand of 1000 units has $C_0 = \$25.50$ and $C_h = \$8$. The demand exhibits some variability such that the lead-time demand follows a normal distribution with $\mu = 25$ and $\sigma = 5$.
   a. What is the recommended order quantity?
   b. What are the reorder point and safety stock if the firm desires at most a 2 percent probability of stockout on any given order cycle?
   c. If a manager sets the reorder point at 30, what is the probability of a stockout on any given order cycle? How many times would you expect to stockout during the year if this reorder point were used?

24. The B&S Novelty and Craft Shop in Bennington, Vermont, sells a variety of quality handmade items to tourists. B&S will sell 300 hand-carved miniature replicas of a Colonial soldier each year, but the demand pattern during the year is uncertain. The replicas sell for $20 each, and B&S uses a 15 percent annual inventory holding cost rate. Ordering costs are $5 per order, and demand during the lead time follows a normal distribution with $\mu = 15$ and $\sigma = 6$.
   a. What is the recommended order quantity?
   b. If B&S is willing to accept a stockout roughly twice a year, what reorder point would you recommend? What is the probability that B&S will have a stockout in any one order cycle?
   c. What are the safety stock and annual safety stock costs for this product?

25. The J&B Card Shop sells calendars with different Colonial pictures shown for each month. The once-a-year order for each year's calendar arrives in September. From past experience the September-to-July demand for the cal-

endars can be approximated by a normal distribution with $\mu = 500$ and $\sigma = 120$. The calendars cost $1.50 each, and J&B sells them for $3 each.

a. If J&B throws out all unsold calendars at the end of July (that is, salvage value is zero), how many calendars should be ordered?

b. If J&B reduces the calendar price to $1 at the end of July and can sell all surplus calendars at this price, how many calendars should be ordered?

26. The Gilbert Air-Conditioning Company is considering the purchase of a special shipment of portable air conditioners manufactured in Japan. Each unit will cost Gilbert $80 and it will be sold for $125. Gilbert does not want to carry surplus air conditioners over until the folowing year. Thus all supplies will be sold to a wholesaler, who has agreed to take all surplus units for $50 per unit. Assume that the air conditioner demand has a normal distribution with $\mu = 20$ and $\sigma = 8$.

a. What is the recommended order quantity?

b. What is the probability that Gilbert will sell all units it orders?

27. A popular newsstand in a large metropolitan area is attempting to determine how many copies of the Sunday paper it should purchase each week. Demand for the newspaper on Sundays can be approximated by a normal distribution with $\mu = 450$ and $\sigma = 100$. The newspaper costs the newsstand 35¢ a copy and sells for 50¢ a copy. The newsstand does not receive any value from surplus papers and thus absorbs a 100% loss on all unsold papers.

a. How many copies of the Sunday paper should be purchased each week?

b. What is the probability that the newsstand will have a stockout?

c. The manager of the newsstand is concerned about the newsstand's image if the probability of stockout is high. The customers often purchase other items after coming to the newsstand for the Sunday paper. Frequent stockouts would cause customers to go to another newsstand. The manager agrees that a 50¢ loss of goodwill cost should be assigned to any stockout. What are the new recommended order quantity and the new probability of a stockout?

28. A perishable dairy product is ordered daily at a particular supermarket. The product, which costs $1.19 per unit, sells for $1.65 per unit. If units are unsold at the end of the day, the supplier takes them back at a rebate of $1 per unit. Assume that daily demand is approximately normally distributed with $\mu = 150$ and $\sigma = 30$.

a. What is your recommended daily order quantity for the supermarket?

b. What is the probability that the supermarket will sell all the units it orders?

c. In problems such as these, why would the supplier offer a rebate as high as $1? For example, why not offer a nominal rebate of, say, 25¢ per unit? What happens to the supermarket order quantity as the rebate is reduced?

29. Bushnell's Sand and Gravel (BSG) is a small firm that supplies sand, gravel, and topsoil to contractors and landscape firms. BSG maintains an inventory of high-quality screened topsoil, which is used to supply the weekly orders for two companies: Bath Landscaping Service and Pittsford Lawn Care, Inc. The problem for BSG is to determine how many cubic yards of screened topsoil to have in inventory at the beginning of each week in order to satisfy the needs of both of its customers. BSG would like to select the lowest-possible inventory level that would have a .95 probability of satisfying the combined

weekly orders from both customers. The demand distributions for the two customers are as follows:

	Weekly Demand	Relative Frequency
Bath Landscaping	10	.20
	15	.35
	20	.30
	25	.10
	30	.05
Pittsford Lawn Care	30	.20
	40	.40
	50	.30
	60	.10

Simulate 20 weeks of operation for beginning inventories of 70 and of 80 cubic yards. Based upon your limited simulation results, how many cubic yards should BSG maintain in inventory? Discuss what you would want to do in a full-scale simulation of this problem.

30. Domoy Motors, Inc., purchases a certain model automobile for $5778. In order to finance the purchase of cars of this model, Domoy must pay an 18 percent annual interest rate on borrowed capital. This interest rate amounts to approximately $20 per car per week. Orders for additional cars can be placed each week, but a minimum order size of five cars is required on any given order. It currently takes 3 weeks to receive a new shipment of cars after the order is placed. The cost of placing an order is $50. If Domoy runs out of cars in inventory, a shortage cost of $300 per car is incurred. Currently Domoy has 20 cars of this model in inventory. Historical data showing the weekly demand are given below. Assuming an order quantity of 15 cars and a reorder point of 10 cars, perform a 12-week simulation of Domoy's operation. Use the first 12 two-digit random numbers from row 2 of Appendix C. Show your simulation results in a table.

Number of Sales	Number of Weeks
0	2
1	5
2	8
3	22
4	10
5	3
	Total 50

Wagner Fabricating Company is reviewing the economic feasibility of manufacturing a part that it currently purchases from a supplier. Forecasted annual demand for the part is 3200 units. Wagner operates 250 days per year.

CASE PROBLEM

Wagner's financial analysts have established a cost of capital of 14 percent on the use of funds for investments within the company. In addition, over the past year $600,000 has been the average investment in the company's inventory. Accounting information shows that a total of $24,000 was spent on taxes and insurance related to the company's inventory. In addition, it has been estimated that $9000 was lost due to inventory shrinkage, which included damaged goods as well as pilferage. A remaining $15,000 was spent on warehouse overhead, including utility expenses for heating and lighting.

An analysis of the purchasing operation shows that approximately 2 hours are required to process and coordinate an order for the part regardless of the quantity ordered. Purchasing salaries average $28 per hour, including employee benefits. In addition, a detailed analysis of 125 orders showed that $2375 was spent on telephone, paper, and postage directly related to the ordering process.

A 5-day lead time is required to obtain the part from the supplier. An analysis of demand during the lead time shows that lead-time demand is approximately normally distributed with a mean of 64 units and a standard deviation of 10 units. Service-level guidelines indicate that one stockout per year is acceptable.

Currently the company has a contract to purchase the part from a supplier at a cost of $18 per unit. However, over the past few months, the company's production capacity has been expanded. As a result, excess capacity is now available in certain production departments and the company is considering the alternative of producing the parts itself.

Forecasted utilization of equipment shows that production capacity will be available for the part being considered. The production capacity is available at the rate of 1000 units per month, with up to 5 months of production time available. It is felt that with a 2-week lead time, schedules can be arranged so that the part can be produced whenever needed. The demand during the 2-week lead time is approximately normally distributed with a mean of 128 units and a standard deviation of 20 units. Production costs are expected to be $17 per part.

A concern of management is that setup costs will be significant. The total cost of labor and lost production time is estimated to be $50 per hour, and it will take a full 8-hour shift to set up the equipment for producing the part.

Develop a report for management of Wagner Fabricating that will address the question of whether the company should continue to purchase the part from the supplier or should begin to produce the part itself. Include the following factors in your report:

1. An analysis of the inventory holding cost, including the appropriate annual inventory holding cost rate.
2. An analysis of ordering costs, including the appropriate cost per order from the supplier.
3. An analysis of setup costs for the production operation.
4. A development of the inventory policy for the following two alternatives:
   a. ordering a fixed quantity Q from the supplier
   b. ordering a fixed quantity Q from in-plant production
5. Include the following in the policies of 4(a) and 4(b) above:
   a. quantity Q
   b. number of order or production runs per year
   c. cycle time
   d. reorder point

e. amount of safety stock
f. expected maximum inventory level
g. average inventory level
h. total annual inventory holding cost
i. total annual ordering cost
j. total annual cost of the units purchased or manufactured
k. total annual cost of the purchase policy and the total annual cost of the production policy

6. Make a recommendation as to whether the company should purchase or manufacture the part. What is the saving associated with your recommendation as compared with the other alternative?

Aggregate
Production Planning
and Master Scheduling

<p>roduction planning and master scheduling involves determining future production levels over a time horizon of several months to one year. The production plan establishes an intermediate-range goal for the company's products and capacity utilization in total, while the master schedule provides the input for detailed scheduling and control at the operational level.

Top-management involvement in production planning is essential, especially with regard to establishing manufacturing, marketing, and financial plans. From a manufacturing perspective, for instance, the production plan assists in determining what intermediate capacity is required and what capacity adjustments need to be made. From marketing's perspective, the production plan determines the amount of product that will be available to meet demand. Finally, from the viewpoint of finance, the production plan identifies funding needs and establishes the basis for making budgeting decisions.

Poor production planning can lead to excessive inventory levels and increased carrying costs or backorders and reduced customer service. Good production planning is important in helping a firm to achieve its productivity and customer service goals.

This chapter covers the fundamental concepts and techniques used in production planning and master scheduling. This provides the basis for material requirements planning, which is discussed in the next chapter. The supplement to this chapter introduces *linear programming,* a quantitative tool that has applications to production planning and scheduling.

14.1 THE PRODUCTION-PLANNING PROCESS

Figure 14.1 illustrates the essential elements of the production planning and scheduling process. The elements focused on in this chapter are aggregate production planning, master production scheduling, rough-cut capacity planning, and final assembly scheduling. Material requirements planning (MRP), short-range scheduling, and related capacity issues are discussed in subsequent chapters.

Accurate demand estimation is a necessary input to production planning. Demand estimation should include not only forecasts of future product demand (see Chapter 3), but also actual orders for which commitments have been made, service and spare-part requirements, warehouse inventory requirements, and inventory level adjustments, as determined by the strategic business plan. As we noted in Chapter 3, more accurate forecasts can be made for aggregate groups of items, particularly over long time horizons. Since production plans are made for up to one year's time, demand and production/inventory levels are usually expressed by aggregate measures of capacity such as dollars, tons, gallons, machine hours, or units of product groups.

Aggregate production planning is the development of monthly or quarterly production requirements for product groups or families that will meet the estimates of demand. Manufacturing, marketing, and financial managers are responsible for the development of the production plan. Gross capacity considerations must be taken into account during production planning. If production to

FIGURE 14.1

The Production
Planning and
Scheduling
Process

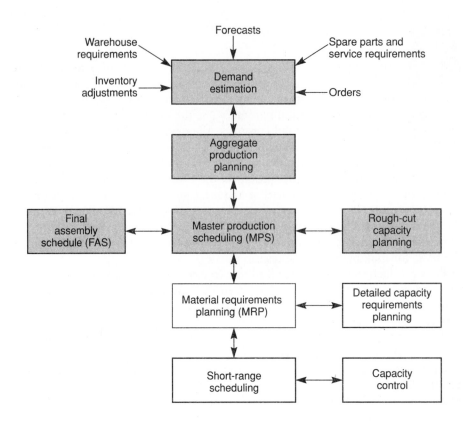

satisfy demand cannot be achieved within existing resource limitations, then management may have to make intermediate-range capacity adjustments. If long-term trends are evident, then management may also wish to consider strategic resource changes.

Once an aggregate production plan is made, it must be disaggregated into time-phased requirements for individual products. This time-phased plan is called the **master production schedule (MPS)**. The MPS usually provides weekly product requirements over a 6- to 12-month time horizon. The master production schedule is not a forecast but rather a schedule of when production should be completed in order to satisfy demand. The MPS is used by operating personnel to make detailed plans for the procurement of materials, the production of components, and the final assembly of the finished goods.

Rough-cut capacity planning involves the analysis of the MPS to determine if sufficient capacity is available at critical points in the production process. Rough-cut capacity planning focuses on specific operations such as final assembly, painting, or finishing to determine where bottlenecks will probably occur. This provides a rapid determination of the feasibility of the master production schedule. Often adjustments to the MPS are made as a result of this analysis. Rough-cut capacity planning generally covers a 3-month time horizon.

The **final assembly schedule (FAS)** is a statement of the final products that are to be assembled from MPS items. The FAS is usually not prepared as far in advance as the MPS. In some firms, the MPS and FAS are identical; in others they are distinct schedules. For example, final products may differ only by labeling, packaging, painting, or finish. The MPS would be concerned only with the basic items, while the FAS would involve the individual differences among final products.

Note the hierarchical nature of the planning process in Figure 14.1. Plans are developed and passed down the hierarchy to the next level, leading to the ultimate goal of production on the shop floor. (Nonshaded areas will be discussed in subsequent chapters.) Plans made at each level must be consistent with those developed at the next higher level. Thus the MPS must be consistent with the aggregate production plan; the material requirements plan must be consistent with the MPS; and short-range schedules must be consistent with the material requirements plan.

Production planning is an important component of manufacturing strategy. The aggregate production plan specifies production requirements for an intermediate-range time horizon. There must be sufficient capacity to meet these requirements. Management objectives and philosophy determine how capacity is managed. This is particularly important when demand is highly seasonal. Some questions that management must consider are: To what extent will inventory be used as a buffer against uncertain demand? Will customer demand be managed through planned backorders? Will the labor force fluctuate through planned layoffs and rehiring as demand fluctuates, or will excess capacity be carried during periods of low demand? The answers to such questions affect profitability, customer service, and the flexibility to introduce new products and change product mix. Thus, the alternatives considered in production-planning activities should support the overall goals and objectives of manufacturing in relation to the corporate strategy.

14.2 AGGREGATE PRODUCTION AND CAPACITY PLANNING

The first step in the production-planning process is to translate demand forecasts into planned monthly production levels. Aggregate planning focuses on overall capacity because it is concerned with product groups as opposed to individual products. Aggregate capacity measures, such as barrels per month, units per month, or labor hours per month, are used in specifying the plan. For instance, a sport-shoe manufacturer might consider broad product lines such as tennis shoes, aerobic shoes, and high-top basketball shoes in developing an aggregate production plan. Individual styles, colors, and sizes are not considered at this level.

If the demand is relatively constant, it is not difficult to develop a production plan. First, we must determine a time horizon, commonly one year, and obtain a sales forecast over this period. Next, minimum inventory levels must be established in order to provide desired levels of customer service. The inventory level at the beginning of the planning horizon must be identified, and the desired inventory level at the end of the horizon must be determined. The total production required over the planning horizon is the total sales forecast plus or minus any desired change in inventory. The required monthly or weekly production rates are then easily determined. For example, suppose that an automotive parts company has a current inventory of air filters of 80,000 and wishes to reduce this level to 50,000 over the next year. The demand forecast calls for sales of 500,000 filters. The total production required is then 500,000 − 30,000 (the net change in inventory level), or 470,000. Thus an average of about 39,167 (470,000 ÷ 12) filters per month need to be manufactured. Producing a constant amount each month is an acceptable strategy *provided that* demand is also relatively constant. When demand is seasonal or fluctuates significantly over the planning period, production must be more carefully planned or shortages and/or high inventory levels may result.

<table>
<tr><td>

Strategies for
Meeting
Fluctuating
Demand

</td><td>

There are a variety of strategies for dealing with fluctuating or seasonal demand. These methods effectively change intermediate-range capacity. As we have seen, long-range trends are addressed through changes in facilities and capital equipment. Short-range capacity decisions, in reaction to machine breakdowns, absent employees, and so on, are the subject of shop floor control in Chapter 16.

There are four types of aggregate planning strategies: production rate changes, work force changes, inventory smoothing, and demand shifting. The choice of strategy depends on corporate policies, practical limitations, and cost factors.

Production Rate Changes

One of the most common approaches for increasing the production rate without changing existing resources is through planned overtime. Generally, this requires wage premiums to be paid. Alternatively, during slow periods, hours can be reduced. However, layoffs and reduced pay can seriously affect employee morale.

The production rate may also be altered by subcontracting during periods of peak demand. This would probably not be a feasible alternative for some companies, but it is an effective strategy for industries that manufacture a large portion of their own parts, such as the machine-tool industry. When business is brisk, components can be subcontracted, and when business is slow, the firm may act as a subcontractor to other industries that may be working at capacity. In this way, a stable work force is maintained.

Work Force Changes

This usually involves changing the size of the work force through hiring and layoffs. Hiring additional labor usually results in higher costs for the personnel department and for training. Layoffs result in severence pay and additional unemployment insurance costs, as well as low employee morale. Also, seniority "bumping" practices may change the skills of the work force and result in inefficient production. A stable work force may be obtained by staffing the plant for peak production levels, but then many workers may be idle during low-demand periods, yet still get paid.

In many industries changing work force levels is not a viable alternative. However, in firms that consist primarily of assembly operations with low-skill requirements, this may be a cost-effective approach. The toy industry is a good example. Accurate forecasts for the Christmas holiday season cannot be made until wholesale buyers have placed orders, usually around midyear. Toy companies maintain a minimal number of employees until production is increased for the holidays. Then they hire a large number of part-time workers in order to operate at maximum capacity. As another example, the U.S. Postal Service hires extra mail carriers during the holiday season in order to increase its capacity. In general, service facilities must meet demand through work force capacity changes as the other alternatives are simply not feasible.

</td></tr>
</table>

Inventory Smoothing

Inventory can be built up during slack periods and held for peak periods. Though this is often done, inventory-carrying costs are increased, and sufficient warehouse space must be available. For some products, such as perishable commodities, this alternative cannot be considered. A related strategy is to carry backorders or to tolerate lost sales during peak demand periods. This may be unacceptable if profit margins are low and competition is high.

Another typical strategy for smoothing inventory is to produce other products with seasonal peaks just the opposite of current products. Companies that produce home-heating equipment are usually in the air-conditioning business as well. Thus marketing and product mix have a direct impact on the decisions involved in aggregate planning.

Demand Shifting

Various marketing strategies may be employed to influence demand. For example, higher prices can be charged to reduce peak demand, whereas low prices, coupons, and increased advertising can be used to reduce inventories and increase demand during slack times. For example, mowers and other garden tools can often be purchased at the lowest prices during the winter months, and airlines and other vacation industries offer reduced rates between Labor Day and Christmas and in late winter.

These strategies and their relevant costs are summarized in Table 14.1.

The major costs associated with implementing a production plan include costs of production, inventory holding and stockout, and capacity change. Production costs typically have a fixed cost component for setup and a variable cost per unit produced. (See, for instance, the development of the production lot-size model in Chapter 13.) Inventory-holding and stockout costs are usually directly proportional to the amount of inventory and stockouts, as we discussed in Chapter 13. Capacity-change costs often take on different forms. There may be a fixed cost associated with, for example, hiring an additional employee, as well as a variable cost for wages paid. If overtime is used, then only variable costs may be appropriate.

Cost Considerations

Strategy	Cost Factors
Production rate changes	
Overtime	Wage premiums
Undertime	Opportunity losses
Subcontracting	Additional overhead
Work-force changes	
Hiring and laying off	Training costs and separation pay
Inventory smoothing	
Build inventories	Carrying costs
Allow shortages	Backorders and lost sales costs
Demand shifting	
Pricing strategies	Lower profit margins
Advertising promotions	Administrative costs

TABLE 14.1

Aggregate Planning Alternatives

PLANNING FOR SEASONAL DEMAND

Let us consider the situation faced by Golden Breweries, a producer of Golden Brew and Golden Delight beers. Table 14.2 gives a monthly aggregate demand forecast over the next year. Note that for Golden Breweries, the demand forecast fluctuates quite a bit over the year, with seasonal peaks in the summer and winter holiday season.

How should Golden Breweries plan production for the next 12 months in the face of fluctuating demand? Let us suppose that Golden Breweries has a normal production capacity of 2200 barrels per month and a current inventory of 1000 barrels. If they produce at normal capacity each month, then we have the production/inventory schedule given in Table 14.3. In this table, the inventory column represents the inventory at the end of the month. To calculate the inventory level, note that

$$\text{Beginning inventory} + \text{production} - \text{demand} = \text{ending inventory} \quad (14.1)$$

For example, in February we have

$$1700 + 2200 - 1000 = 2900$$

At this constant production rate, Golden Breweries will build up an inventory of 3200 barrels in March and suffer lost sales of 500 barrels in August, one of the peak demand months for beer consumption. Incurring shortages and carrying high inventories may not be a good business policy. Another possible difficulty with this schedule is the fact that there may not be sufficient storage space available for inventories as large as 3200 barrels.

A production plan is often illustrated graphically. Figure 14.2 shows a graph of cumulative production, along with the cumulative demand. This information is taken from Tables 14.2 and 14.3. Note that a shortage occurs when the cumulative production curve falls *below* the cumulative demand curve. Also, note that the distance between the curves represents the accumulated inventory each month or the amount of lost sales. To avoid shortages, the cumulative production

TABLE 14.2

Demand Forecast for Golden Breweries

Month	Demand (Barrels)	Cumulative Demand
January	1,500	1,500
February	1,000	2,500
March	1,900	4,400
April	2,600	7,000
May	2,800	9,800
June	3,100	12,900
July	3,200	16,100
August	3,000	19,100
September	2,000	21,100
October	1,000	22,100
November	1,800	23,900
December	2,200	26,100
	26,100	

Month	Cumulative Demand	Production	Cumulative Product Availability	Ending Inventory	Lost Sales	TABLE 14.3
January	1,500	2200	3,200*	1700*	0	**Production/**
February	2,500	2200	5,400	2900	0	**Inventory Plan at**
March	4,400	2200	7,600	3200	0	**Full Capacity**
April	7,000	2200	9,800	2800	0	
May	9,800	2200	12,000	2200	0	
June	12,900	2200	14,200	1300	0	
July	16,100	2200	16,400	300	0	
August	19,100	2200	18,600	0	500	
September	21,100	2200	21,300†	200	0	
October	22,100	2200	23,500†	1400	0	
November	23,900	2200	25,700†	1800	0	
December	26,100	2200	27,900†	1800	0	

*We assume that there are 1000 barrels left in inventory in December. This is added to production in January.

†Adjusted for lost sales. Since there are no backorders, the inventory level cannot become negative. Thus in September, we essentially begin anew with zero inventory. We must add the lost sales to the cumulative production in order to maintain the correct relationship: cumulative production − cumulative demand = current inventory level. If backorders are allowed, then inventory values would be negative and we would not have to make any adjustments.

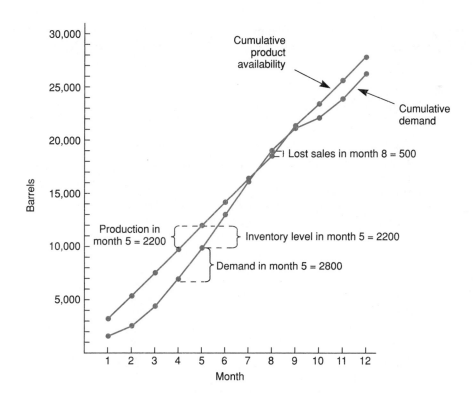

FIGURE 14.2

Golden Breweries' Full-capacity Aggregate Production Plan

curve must always lie above the cumulative demand curve. This type of graphical method is often used to construct alternative production plans.

Next, the costs involved in the Golden Breweries example are considered. Assume that the production cost is $70 per barrel, inventory-holding costs amount to $1.40 per barrel per month of ending inventory, lost sales have an opportunity cost of $90 per barrel, overtime costs $6.50 additional per barrel, and there is a $5 per barrel charge to change the production rate. Cost of undertime (production below full capacity) is $3.00 per barrel. The cost for the production plan shown in Table 14.3 is given in Table 14.4.

Now, let us propose an alternate plan (shown in Table 14.5) in order to reduce springtime inventories and meet all the forecasted demand. This is graphed in Figure 14.3, where no lost sales will occur, since the cumulative production curve lies above the entire cumulative demand curve. The cost of this plan is shown in Table 14.6. This represents an increase of approximately $2480 over the original plan. However, the anticipated lost sales have been eliminated.

Needless to say, there are countless numbers of alternate strategies that could be employed. Since many costs change simultaneously, it is difficult to assess the impact of the overall cost effects. Thus trial-and-error approaches may be less than satisfactory, although they are widely used in practice. Quantitative techniques are often used in aggregate planning problems to develop good strategies.

14.3 QUANTITATIVE METHODS FOR AGGREGATE PLANNING

The key variables in aggregate planning are production levels, inventory levels, and work force size. Various approaches have been proposed over the years to

TABLE 14.4 Cost Calculation for the Production Plan Shown in Table 14.3

Month	Production	Production Cost	Ending Inventory	Inventory Cost	Lost Sales	Lost Sales Cost	Rate Change Cost
January	2,200	$ 154,000	1700	$ 2,380	0	—	—
February	2,200	154,000	2900	4,060	0	—	—
March	2,200	154,000	3200	4,480	0	—	—
April	2,200	154,000	2800	3,920	0	—	—
May	2,200	154,000	2200	3,080	0	—	—
June	2,200	154,000	1300	1,820	0	—	—
July	2,200	154,000	300	420	0	—	—
August	2,200	154,000	0	0	500	$45,000	—
September	2,200	154,000	200	280	0	—	—
October	2,200	154,000	1400	1,960	0	—	—
November	2,200	154,000	1800	2,520	0	—	—
December	2,200	154,000	1800	2,520	0	—	—
Total	26,400	$1,848,000		$27,440		$45,000	$0

Total cost = $1,920,440

Month	Production	Inventory	Lost Sales	Cumulative Product Availability
January	1500	1000	0	2,500*
February	1500	1500	0	4,000
March	1500	1100	0	5,500
April	2800	1300	0	8,300
May	2800	1300	0	11,100
June	2800	1000	0	13,900
July	2800	600	0	16,700
August	2800	400	0	19,500
September	2200	600	0	21,700
October	2200	1800	0	23,900
November	2200	2200	0	26,100
December	1500	1500	0	27,600

*Initial inventory = 1000

Table 14.5

Alternate Production/ Inventory Plan

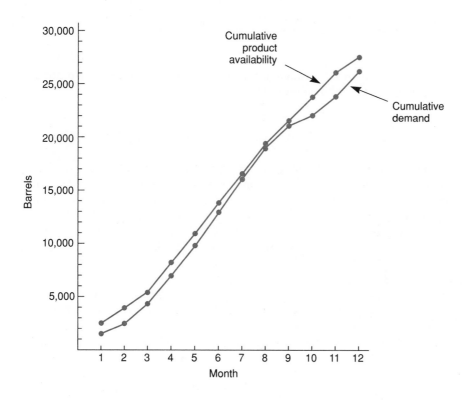

FIGURE 14.3

Alternate Production Plan for Golden Breweries

determine minimum-cost production plans. One method, linear programming, is very general and is used by many large corporations. This technique is discussed in the chapter supplement. Here, we discuss the use of a transportation model for aggregate planning. The transportation model is useful when various sources of production are available (for example, regular time, overtime, and subcontracting), when production and inventory costs are linear, and when there is a

TABLE 14.6 Cost Calculation for the Production Plan Shown in Table 14.5

Month	Production	Production Cost	Ending Inventory	Inventory Cost	Rate Change Cost*	Overtime Cost	Undertime Cost
January	1,500	$ 105,000	1000	$ 1,400	$ 3,500	—	$2,100
February	1,500	105,000	1500	2,100	—	—	2,100
March	1,500	105,000	1100	1,540	—	—	2,100
April	2,800	196,000	1300	1,820	$ 6,500	$ 3,900	—
May	2,800	196,000	1300	1,820	—	3,900	—
June	2,800	196,000	1000	1,400	—	3,900	—
July	2,800	196,000	600	840	—	3,900	—
August	2,800	196,000	400	560	—	3,900	—
September	2,200	154,000	600	840	3,000	—	—
October	2,200	154,000	1800	2,520	—	—	—
November	2,200	154,000	2200	3,080	—	—	—
December	1,500	105,000	1500	2,100	3,500	—	2,100
	26,600	$1,862,000		$20,020	$16,500	$19,500	$8,400

Total cost = $1,926,420

*Cost of changing production rate, $5/unit.

limited capacity for each production source in each time period. We illustrate this approach in the following example.

<table>
<tr><td>

EXAMPLE

</td><td>

A TRANSPORTATION MODEL FOR AGGREGATE PLANNING

The Snow Sporting Goods Company is a producer of a variety of recreational equipment. The demand forecast for one product, snow skis, over the five winter months is 5000, 12,000, 11,000, 7500, and 5000 units (a set of skis). Suppose the production cost per unit made on regular time is $50, and is $54 for each unit produced on overtime. The skis can also be subcontracted at a cost of $57 per unit. Inventory-holding costs are $6 per unit each month and no backorders are allowed. In each month, 9000 units can be produced on regular time, 1800 units can be produced on overtime, and up to 2500 units can be subcontracted.

The transportation tableau in Figure 14.4 shows the structure of the problem. Each row corresponds to a source of production in a particular month. The numbers in the right-hand margin are the capacities. For example, row 1 shows that up to 9000 units can be produced on regular time in period 1; row 2 shows that up to 1800 units can be produced on overtime in period 1; row 3 shows that up to 2500 units can be produced by a subcontractor in period 1; and so on for periods 2, 3, 4, and 5. The columns correspond to the periods in which the production can be used. The numbers at the bottom of each column represent the demand for that period. Several cells have been crossed out. This is because production in one period cannot be used to satisfy demand in an earlier period (for instance, demand in period 2 cannot be satisfied by production in period 4) under the assumption of no backorders. Costs shown in the upper right-hand corner of each cell are calculated as follows: If a unit is produced in period t and held until period k, then the cost is the sum of production in period t plus holding costs for period t, $t + 1$, ..., $k - 1$. For instance, the cost of producing in regular time in period 1 and holding until period 4 is $50 + 6 + 6 + 6 = 68$.

</td></tr>
</table>

This indicates production in period 1 (overtime) and holding until period 2

Production period		Demand period 1	2	3	4	5	capacity
1	Regular time	50	56	62	68	74	9000
	Overtime	54	60	66	72	78	1800
	Subcontract	57	63	69	75	81	2500
2	Regular time		50	56	62	68	9000
	Overtime		54	60	66	72	1800
	Subcontract		57	63	69	75	2500
3	Regular time			50	56	62	9000
	Overtime			54	60	66	1800
	Subcontract			57	63	69	2500
4	Regular time				50	56	9000
	Overtime				54	60	1800
	Subcontract				57	63	2500
5	Regular time					50	9000
	Overtime					54	1800
	Subcontract					57	2500
	Demand	5000	12,000	11,000	7500	5000	

FIGURE 14.4
Transportation Tableau for the Snow Ski Example

The problem now can be easily solved.[1] Starting in period 1, we attempt to satisfy demand using the cheapest cost alternative available, as long as capacity is available. The cheapest source in column 1 is regular time production in period 1. Since there is a capacity of 9000 units available and a demand of 5000, we produce 5000 units. Once the demand in a period is satisfied, we move on to the next period. In period 2, the cheapest source is regular time production in period 2. However, the demand is 12,000 units and only 9000 units can be produced without exceeding capacity. Thus we produce 9000 and then must find the *next*-cheapest alternative with available capacity for the remaining 3000 units. This is to produce 1800 using overtime in period 2 and the remaining 1200 units using regular time in period 1. Next, we move on to period 3, and so on until all demand is satisfied. The final solution is given in Figure 14.5 and summarized in Table 14.7. The numbers in each cell show the amount of production to be scheduled for each source in each period.

14.4 MASTER SCHEDULING AND ROUGH-CUT CAPACITY PLANNING

The aggregate production plan represents a firm's aggregate measure of manufacturing output. Implementing it requires a disaggregation of the plan into individual products. The master production schedule (MPS) is the final statement

[1]The transportation solution procedure introduced in the supplement to Chapter 7 is not necessary here. Because of the special nature of the problem, we can show a much simpler solution procedure.

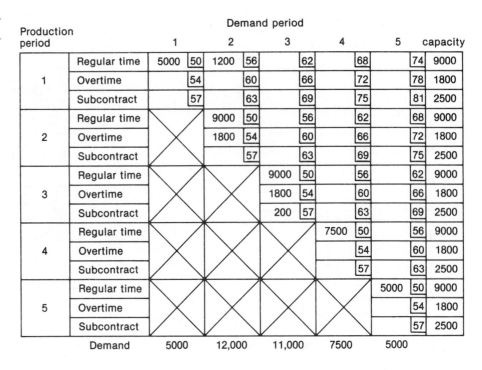

FIGURE 14.5

Transportation Tableau: Optimal Solution for the Snow Ski Example

TABLE 14.7   Solution to the Snow Ski Planning Problem

Period	Demand	Regular Time Production	Cost	Overtime Production	Cost	Sub-Contract	Cost	End-of-Period Inventory	Cost
1	5,000	6200	$ 310,000	0	$ 0	0	$ 0	1200	$7200
2	12,000	9000	450,000	1800	97,200	0	0	0	0
3	11,000	9000	450,000	1800	97,200	200	11,400	0	0
4	7,500	7500	375,000	0	0	0	0	0	0
5	5,000	5000	250,000	0	0	0	0	0	0
			$1,835,000		$194,400		$11,400		$7200

Total cost = $2,048,000

of how many finished items are to be produced and when they are to be produced. It is a *production plan,* not a *sales plan.* The master schedule must consider the total demand on a factory's resources and the capacity of the plant and its suppliers to meet those demands. All planning for materials, labor, and equipment are derived from the MPS. Typically, the master schedule is developed for weekly time periods over a 6- to 12-month horizon. An example of a partial MPS is shown in Figure 14.6.

The purpose of the master schedule is to translate the aggregate plan into a separate plan for individual items. It also provides a means of evaluating alternative schedules in terms of capacity requirements, provides input to the material requirements planning (MRP) system, and helps managers generate priorities for scheduling by setting due dates for the production of individual items.

End item		1	2	3	4	5	6	7	8
	A		200		200		350		
	B	150	100		190			120	
	⋮	⋮	⋮	⋮	⋮	⋮	⋮	⋮	⋮
	X			75		75	75		60
Totals (Aggregate production plan)		500	800	350	600	280	750	420	300

FIGURE 14.6

A Portion of an MPS

Developing a master production schedule is usually a very complex problem, especially for products with a large number of operations. For example, at Dow Corning, there are 12 master schedulers, who are responsible for scheduling 4000 packaged products over a 26-week time horizon.[2] In process industries with only a few different operations, master production scheduling is somewhat easier.

The MPS is developed somewhat differently depending on the type of industry (make-to-stock versus make-to-order) and number of items produced (few or many). For make-to-stock industries, a net demand forecast (that is, after on-hand inventory is subtracted) is used. If only a few final products are produced, then the MPS is a statement of the individual product requirements. For many items—for instance, more than 500—it is impractical to develop an MPS on an individual product basis. In this case, individual products are usually grouped into product families, and some method of proportionately decomposing the plan into a schedule for individual items is employed. A common approach is to apportion using historical percentage of sales.

For make-to-order industries, order backlogs provide the needed customer-demand information; thus the known customer orders determine the master production schedule. In industries where a few basic components are assembled in many different combinations to produce a large variety of end products, the MPS is usually developed for the basic components and not the end products. An example is automobiles, in which basic components are engines, transmissions, body components, and so forth. The final assembly schedule is used for the actual finished products. In order to illustrate the basic concepts of master production scheduling let us return to the Golden Breweries example.

DEVELOPING A MASTER PRODUCTION SCHEDULE

EXAMPLE

Let us suppose that Golden's management has decided to use the production plan in Table 14.5. Since the company produces two products, Golden Brew and Golden Delight, the master scheduler must translate the aggregate production plan into a weekly schedule for each product. Golden's beer is produced in cases of twenty-four 16-ounce cans (3 gallons). Each barrel holds 32 gallons; the product mix, which is determined by historical sales data, is relatively constant,

---

[2]W. L. Berry, T. E. Vollmann, and D. Clay Whybark, *Master Production Scheduling: Principles and Practice,* American Production and Inventory Control Society, Inc., 1979.

a 70–30 percent split between Golden Brew and Golden Delight. With this information, we can project the monthly production for each product for the first 7 months as follows:

Month	Aggregate Production		Product Mix	
	Barrels	Cases	Golden Brew (Cases)	Golden Delight (Cases)
January	1500	16,000	11,200	4800
February	1500	16,000	11,200	4800
March	1500	16,000	11,200	4800
April	2800	29,867	20,907	8960
May	2800	29,867	20,907	8960
June	2800	29,867	20,907	8960
July	2800	29,867	20,907	8960

To simplify our calculations, we assume there are 4 weeks in each month. Then the average weekly production required is given in Table 14.8. At Golden's plant, only one product at a time can be produced, since they share common facilities such as mixing equipment, bottling, capping, and case packing. Using a master schedule as determined by Table 14.8 would probably not be economical, since there would be frequent changeovers of products and thus high setup costs. One method of reducing the number of product changeovers is to produce in large batch sizes. Table 14.9 shows a possible master schedule in which products are alternated on a weekly basis.

Rough-cut Capacity Planning

In the Golden Breweries example, we have not determined whether there is sufficient capacity available on a short-term basis to be able to achieve the master production schedule. We previously stated that under normal conditions, the plant has a capacity of 2200 barrels per month, or 5867 cases per week. With overtime, the capacity can be increased to 2800 barrels per month, or 7467 cases

TABLE 14.8   Average Weekly Production Requirements for Golden Breweries

	Week												
Product	1	2	3	4	5	6	7	8	9	10	11	12	13
Golden Brew	2800	2800	2800	2800	2800	2800	2800	2800	2800	2800	2800	2800	5227
Golden Delight	1200	1200	1200	1200	1200	1200	1200	1200	1200	1200	1200	1200	2240

	Week												
Product	14	15	16	17	18	19	20	21	22	23	24	25	26
Golden Brew	5227	5227	5227	5227	5227	5227	5227	5227	5227	5227	5227	5227	5227
Golden Delight	2240	2240	2240	2240	2240	2240	2240	2240	2240	2240	2240	2240	2240

per week. These restrictions are due to the physical limitations of the production equipment. From Table 14.9, we see that up to week 12, we are able to produce within capacity. Beyond this, the planned schedule for Golden Brew cannot be achieved within the limitation of 7467 cases per week. We would therefore say that this master schedule is *infeasible*. This is the essence of rough-cut capacity planning—namely, converting the MPS into capacity needs for key resources and then determining if the master schedule is feasible with respect to capacity limitations. If it is not feasible, then the master scheduler must revise the MPS to stay within capacity constraints. In some cases, it may even be necessary to revise the aggregate production plan. Table 14.10 shows a feasible master schedule, developed by trial-and-error, which meets the capacity limitations in each month. Note that as in Table 14.10, two product changeovers each month must be made. For example, in weeks 14 and 15, Golden Delight will be produced and, early in week 15, a changeover will be made to Golden Brew. This will be produced

TABLE 14.9   A Master Schedule for Golden Breweries

	Week												
Product	1	2	3	4	5	6	7	8	9	10	11	12	13
Golden Brew	5600	0	5600	0	5600	0	5600	0	5600	0	5600	0	10,454
Golden Delight	0	2400	0	2400	0	2400	0	2400	0	2400	0	2400	0

	Week												
Product	14	15	16	17	18	19	20	21	22	23	24	25	26
Golden Brew	0	10,454	0	10,454	0	10,454	0	10,454	0	10,454	0	10,454	0
Golden Delight	4480	0	4480	0	4480	0	4480	0	4480	0	4480	0	4480

TABLE 14.10   A Feasible Master Production Schedule for Golden Breweries

	Week												
Product	1	2	3	4	5	6	7	8	9	10	11	12	13
Golden Brew	5600	0	5600	0	5600	0	5600	0	5600	0	5600	0	7467
Golden Delight	0	2400	0	2400	0	2400	0	2400	0	2400	0	3892	0

	Week												
Product	14	15	16	17	18	19	20	21	22	23	24	25	26
Golden Brew	0	5974	7467	7467	0	5974	7467	7467	0	5974	7467	7467	0
Golden Delight	7467	1493	0	0	7467	1493	0	0	7467	1493	0	0	7467

until week 18, when a changeover to Golden Delight will be made, and so on. Hence rough-cut capacity planning is an iterative process in conjunction with master production scheduling as shown in Figure 14.7. Often, several iterations are necessary before a realistic master schedule is produced.

Capacity profiles are usually developed by department or work center. One method of rough-cut capacity planning is called *capacity planning using overall factors*. This technique allocates capacity requirements to individual departments or work centers on the basis of historical data on work loads.

EXAMPLE	CAPACITY PLANNING USING OVERALL FACTORS

Consider the MPS for two end products, A and B, as shown in Table 14.11.[3] Suppose that item A requires .95 labor hours per unit, and item B requires 1.85 labor hours per unit. Then, in period 1, the total capacity requirement (expressed in labor hours) is calculated as

$$(33 \text{ units of A})(.95 \text{ hours/unit}) + (17 \text{ units of B})(1.85 \text{ hours/unit})$$
$$= 62.8 \text{ hours}$$

Now suppose that these items are manufactured in three work centers. Table 14.12 shows historical data on the number of labor hours worked in each work center during the past year. These data show that 60.3 percent, 30.4 percent, and 9.3 percent of the total labor hours were reported at work centers 1, 2, and 3, respectively. Applying these percentages to the total capacity requirement estimates (such as 62.8 hours for period 1), we obtain an estimate of the labor capacity required in each work center. These results are shown in Table 14.13.

Capacity planning using overall factors requires only a minimal amount of data and is used in a number of manufacturing firms. However, because it does not use detailed product and process data such as bills of materials, it provides only approximations of actual capacity requirements at individual work centers. Other techniques, beyond the scope of this text, can be used to obtain more accurate capacity estimates.

It is a good idea to check planned inventory levels in relation to an MPS. We may use Equation (14.1) on a weekly basis to do this. Using the projected demand from Table 14.2 and translating this into cases per week, we arrive at Table 14.14,

FIGURE 14.7

Rough-cut Capacity Planning and Master Scheduling

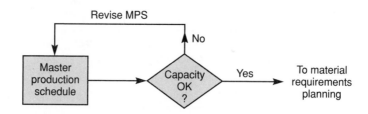

[3]Adapted from William L. Berry, Thomas G. Schmitt, and Thomas E. Vollmann, "Capacity Planning Techniques for Manufacturing Control Systems: Information Requirements and Operational Features," *Journal of Operations Management*, 3, no. 1 (1982), 13–24. Reprinted with permission, The American Production and Inventory Control Society, Inc.

End Product	Time Period												
	1	2	3	4	5	6	7	8	9	10	11	12	13
A	33	33	33	40	40	40	30	30	30	37	37	37	37
B	17	17	17	13	13	13	25	25	25	27	27	27	27

TABLE 14.11

Master Production Schedule

Work Center	1st Quarter	2nd Quarter	3rd Quarter	4th Quarter	Total	Percentage of Total Labor Hours
1	125	90	150	140	505	60.3%
2	55	60	80	60	255	30.4%
3	18	15	20	25	78	9.3%
					838	

TABLE 14.12

Historical Data on Labor Use

Work Center	Historical Work Center Percentage	1	2	3	4	5	6	7
1	60.3%	37.87	37.87	37.87	37.41	37.41	37.41	45.07
2	30.4%	19.09	19.09	19.09	18.86	18.86	18.86	22.72
3	9.3%	5.84	5.84	5.84	5.78	5.78	5.78	6.96
Total plant capacity		62.80	62.80	62.80	62.05	62.05	62.05	74.75

Work Center	Historical Work Center Percentage	8	9	10	11	12	13	Total Hours
1	60.3%	45.07	45.07	51.32	51.32	51.32	51.32	566.33
2	30.4%	22.72	22.72	25.87	25.87	25.87	25.87	285.49
3	9.3%	6.96	6.96	7.91	7.91	7.91	7.91	87.38
Total plant capacity		74.75	74.75	85.10	85.10	85.10	85.10	939.20

TABLE 14.13

Rough-cut Capacity Requirements

which shows the projected short-term fluctuations in inventory for both products and can be used in assessing the feasibility of the master schedule from the viewpoint of safety stock.

It is clear from this simple example that master production scheduling can be a complicated process. Let us summarize some of the observations we made through the Golden Breweries example. First, the master production schedule should relate to the aggregate production plan; that is, the planned monthly schedule should equal the aggregate plan when totaled over all products. Second, rough-cut capacity planning assists the master production scheduler in developing a feasible schedule by identifying potential production bottlenecks. Often, the MPS must be revised several times until it is feasible. Third, other ways of evaluating a

Using the Master Schedule

Table 14.14

Inventory
Analysis for
Golden
Breweries'
Master
Production
Schedule

	Golden Brew			Golden Delight		
Week	Demand	Production	Inventory*	Demand	Production	Inventory*
1	2800	5600	10,267	1200	0	2000
2	2800	0	7,467	1200	2400	3200
3	2800	5600	10,267	1200	0	2000
4	2800	0	7,467	1200	2400	3200
5	1867	5600	11,200	800	0	2400
6	1867	0	9,333	800	2400	4000
7	1867	5600	13,066	800	0	3200
8	1867	0	11,199	800	2400	4800
9	3547	5600	13,252	1520	0	3280
10	3547	0	9,705	1520	2400	4160
11	3547	5600	11,758	1520	0	2640
12	3547	0	8,211	1520	3892	5012
13	4853	7467	10,825	2080	0	2932
14	4853	0	5,972	2080	7467	8319
15	4853	5974	7,093	2080	1493	7732
16	4853	7467	9,707	2080	0	5652
17	5227	7467	11,947	2240	0	3412
18	5227	0	6,720	2240	7467	8639
19	5227	5974	7,467	2240	1493	7892
20	5227	7467	9,707	2240	0	5652
21	5787	7467	11,387	2480	0	3172
22	5787	0	5,600	2480	7467	8159
23	5787	5974	5,787	2480	1493	7172
24	5787	7467	7,467	2480	0	4692
25	5973	7467	8,961	2560	0	2132
26	5973	0	2,988	2560	7467	7039

*Initial inventory = 1000 barrels (7467 cases of Golden Brew and 3200 cases of Golden Delight)

master production schedule include the number and cost of setups or product changeovers and short-term inventory fluctuations.

The MPS is important, since it forms the basis for future production-planning activities. Therefore, it must be adaptive to changes in the environment. Seldom will forecasted demands be realized or production plans be adhered to perfectly. As each week passes, operations managers must compare scheduled production with actual results. This may result in changes to the MPS—master production scheduling is a full-time job! Too many changes, however, indicate that master production scheduling is not being performed correctly and can result in poor productivity and low levels of customer service. In the next chapter, we examine how the MPS is used in the planning of component production.

Aside from resource planning and as an input to material control, the master production schedule has other important applications. First, the MPS simplifies the task of making customer delivery promises by specifying what is to be produced and when it is to be produced. Through proper coordination between marketing and manufacturing, delivery performance to customers can be improved. Second, the MPS can be used for budgeting purposes by financial personnel since it indicates changes in inventories of finished goods and, indirectly, materials and components. Since requirements will be known by time period, budgets for labor and supplies can be developed through capacity planning data.

Earlier in this chapter we noted that the FAS is a schedule of the individual end products to be assembled from MPS items. The MPS is used to produce orders for component parts. The FAS must guarantee that these components are available when needed. The development of a FAS is constrained by the availability of items scheduled on the MPS, inventory, lead-time requirements, and the capacity of the assembly process. The FAS represents the final commitment for production, and the authorization is usually held back until the latest possible time to allow flexibility and better customer service.

The Final Assembly Schedule

14.5 CAPACITY PLANNING IN SERVICE ORGANIZATIONS

The most important distinction between manufacturing goods and the provision of services that affects capacity planning is the fact that services are produced and consumed simultaneously. One cannot build inventories during periods of slack demand in the same manner as in manufacturing. However, the other strategies that we have discussed for meeting fluctuating demand in manufacturing, namely, production rate changes, work force changes, and demand shifting, can be applied to various service operations.

In service operations, strategies that change the production rate and work force level in response to changing demand are commonly referred to as "chase-demand" strategies. The use of part time or seasonal employees is quite common in service organizations. For example, fast-food restaurants employ large numbers of part-time employees with varying work schedules in order to match capacity to demand. Retailers use part-time workers during the holiday season. Amusement parks and resort hotels use full-time seasonal employees during peak seasons. Chase-demand strategies are good ways to reducing cost while maintaining high levels of service.

A second method of effectively adjusting service capacity is to shift work to slack periods. For example, hotel clerks prepare bills and perform other paperwork at night when check-in and check-out activity is light. This leaves more time to service customers during the daytime.

Increasing customer participation in the service process increases capacity and reduces the demand on the physical resources of the organization. Examples of this strategy include self-service gasoline pumps, bagging groceries by customers, and self-service salad bars in restaurants.

A fourth method is capacity sharing. Fire stations in neighboring townships or villages do this routinely. Hospitals also employ this strategy. Every hospital, for example, need not purchase every expensive and specialized piece of equipment. A consortium of several hospitals might be set up in which each hospital focuses on a particular specialty and services are shared. A blood bank is another example of capacity sharing.

Another means of meeting fluctuating demand in service organizations is to shift demand. Differential pricing schemes to increase demand during normally nonpeak hours are common. For example, bars and restaurants offer happy hours; telephone rates are reduced during evenings and weekends to stimulate demand; movie theaters offer special matinee prices, and so on.

New service packages are often developed to utilize idle capacity during off-peak times. For instance, many fast-food restaurants have introduced breakfast service, and many hotels offer special weekend packages. As another example, The Kings Island amusement park in Cincinnati developed "Winterfest" several years ago, featuring ice skating and holiday shopping.

Similar to manufacturing, service organizations must manage capacity and "plan production." While the approaches differ in many ways, the goal is the same: to maintain a level of service that meets the strategic goals of the organization at a low cost.

P/OM IN
PRACTICE

The following two cases illustrate production planning in practice. American Olean Tile Company employs a hierarchical production-planning system that integrates planning and decision making across corporate and plant level organizations. Rowntree MacKintosh Canada Ltd. incorporates consideration of quality, personnel, capital, and customer service levels in its production planning.

PRODUCTION PLANNING FOR AMERICAN OLEAN TILE COMPANY[4]

T he American Olean Tile Company (AO) manufactures a wide variety of ceramic tile products. These products range from indoor and outdoor tile for walls and tile for residential and heavy commercial floors to tiles for elaborate mural designs. The company operates eight factories throughout the United States that supply approximately 120 sales distribution points (SDPs), which are combinations of marketing sales territories and company-owned warehouses. AO produces three basic lines of tile products: glazed tile, ceramic mosaics, and quarry tile. The production process begins with crushing and milling and leads to firing of the tile in large kilns.

Expansion and growth of the distribution network prompted AO's management to develop new production-planning approaches. A hierarchical production-planning system was developed to improve the integration of the annual plan, short-range scheduling, and inventory control. The quarry tile division was the first to be addressed. The product line was grouped into 10 product families, each of which comprised several hundred items. Figure 14.8 shows AO's production-planning and scheduling framework for the quarry tile division.

The planning process began with an annual, subjective sales forecast for total quarry division sales expressed in terms of square feet of tile. The director of market planning, in consultation with other top managers, generated this sales projection based upon a combination of economic trends and specific quarry market developments. This forecast was al-

[4]Reprinted by permission of Matthew J. Liberatore and Tan Miller, "A Hierarchical Production Planning System," *Interfaces*, 15, no. 4 (July-August 1985): 1–11. Copyright 1985 The Institute of Management Sciences, 290 Westminster Street, Providence, Rhode Island 02903, USA.

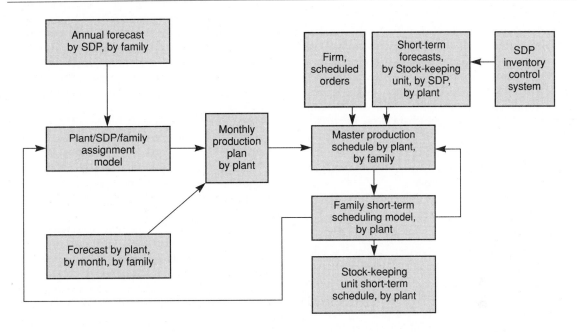

located to each product family and apportioned to the SDPs based on the ratio of their annual total sales to the total of all quarry tile sales during the previous year. Some adjustments were then made by the planning and marketing staffs.

A monthly production plan was then developed by plant-level production personnel based on these assignments and seasonal inventory targets and demand patterns. The monthly production plan, scheduled orders received from large customers, and short-range demand forecasts generated at each SDP were combined into a master production schedule by product family at each plant. The planning horizon for the MPS was the upcoming quarter, and the length of the planning period was typically 1 to 2 weeks.

Process industries tend to schedule capacity first and then materials. This differs from fabrication and assembly industries, which schedule material use first. AO uses a short-range scheduling model, which first determines the assignment of production lines by planning period to meet the master schedule while minimizing the total variable manufacturing, setup, and inventory costs. Then a short-range production schedule and associated material requirements for each plant are established.

The use of this hierarchical planning and scheduling system has helped to improve coordination and communication between departments and has substantially reduced production and distribution costs, saving between $400,000 and $750,000 per year. As a whole, the system significantly enhances American Olean's ability to position itself more competitively in the marketplace. The system suggested significant changes in product family mixes and uncovered comparative cost advantages in terms of delivered cost from each plant. The process of developing the system stimulated closer coordination between the marketing and manufacturing departments in meeting the needs of sales territories.

In summary, the hierarchical production-planning system offers an approach that integrates decision making and communication across corporate and plant-level organizations.

QUESTIONS

1. Explain how the forecast is used in planning. Is it an aggregate forecast?
2. What were the inputs and outputs of the monthly production plan developed by plant-level personnel?

AGGREGATE PLANNING AT ROWNTREE MACKINTOSH CANADA LTD.[5]

R owntree MacKintosh Canada Ltd., has factories around the world—in Canada, Australia, South Africa, and Ireland—and other facilities in several countries. The company exports confectionery and grocery products, (e.g., candy bars, boxed chocolates, cookies, and peanut butter) to over 120 countries. The Canadian factory, where from 500 to 800 people are engaged in manufacturing, sales, and distribution activities, is located in Toronto. The factory manufactures 16 major brand items which generate 75 distinct product lines.

Production planning is influenced by several considerations.

- *Quality:* High-quality standards are maintained. The company operates under the rules of the Federal and Provincial Health Departments. An important quality consideration is the age of the product when it reaches the consumer. It is essential to ensure that products reach the consumer within well-defined, acceptable time periods to ensure freshness.
- *Personnel:* It is stated company policy and practice to maintain a stable work force. This limits the plant's ability to adjust capacity since capacity can only be significantly changed by adding or reducing the number of people employed. Short-term capacity can be increased with overtime and/or with part-time employees.
- *Capital Restrictions:* Amount of inventory investment has become a major concern, and inventory levels must be kept low to meet restrictions on capital investment.
- *Customer Service Levels:* The nature of the industry makes it necessary to strive for 100 percent customer service. The desire to minimize inventory investment is often in conflict with the need to react to a changing environment.

These four considerations make production planning difficult for the company. We shall focus on one of the major brand items that has a highly seasonal demand: boxed chocolates. Figure 14.9 shows a typical sales and inventory pattern. Boxed choc-

olates are produced in three types, with a total of nine distinct end items: Black Magic, in 2 lb, 1½ lb, 1 lb, and ½ lb boxes; Rendezvous, in 14 oz boxes; and Dairy Box, in the same four sizes as Black Magic.

Forecasting is accomplished by dividing the year into 13 periods of four weeks each. Sales planning provides an end-item forecast, by period, for the full 13 periods. This estimate is updated every four weeks, reflecting the latest information on available inventories and estimated sales for the next 13 periods.

Aggregate planning is performed by first converting all end items to a poundage figure. The planning task is to calculate levels of production that will best meet the quality, capital, customer service, personnel, and capacity goals and restrictions. To assure quality, the plan cannot exceed an inventory level of 18 weeks sales. Constraints on personnel determine the ability to adjust production rates. The daily production rate with one regular shift is 9,000 lb. The following table gives the production alternatives for one period (20 days' production):

Hours Worked	Output per Day	Output per Period	Work Force
8	9,000	180,000	regular shift
12	13,500	270,000	regular + part time
13	14,900	298,000	regular + part time
14	16,300	326,000	regular + part time
15	17,600	352,000	regular + part time
16	19,000	380,000	two full shifts

The master production plan must determine the timing of production rate changes to meet all requirements. The effect of the learning curve during the period when production is increased must also be considered. Table 14.15 illustrates a typical aggregate production plan. Notice that production is substantially increased in period 5 and decreased in period 12 to account for the seasonality of demand (the low production in period 8 is the result of a vacation shutdown). Minimum acceptable inven-

[5]Adpated from Martin S. Visagie, "Production Control in a Flow Production Plant," APICS 1975 Conference Proceedings, p. 161–166. Reprinted with permission, The American Production and Inventory Control Society, Inc.

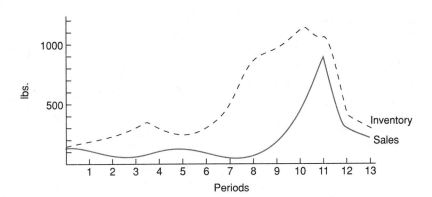

FIGURE 14.9
Typical Sales and
Inventory Pattern

1000

500

lbs.

Inventory

Sales

Periods

TABLE 14.15 Typical Aggregate Production Plan

Period	Estimated Stock	Estimated Production	Estimated Sales
1	145,201	180,000	155,310
2	169,891	180,000	101,190
3	248,701	90,000	120,630
4	218,071	90,000	135,825
5	172,246	247,000	102,750
6	316,496	380,000	61,140
7	635,356	361,000	62,550
8	933,806	95,000	34,440
9	994,366	361,000	107,790
10	1,247,576	380,000	462,600
11	1,164,976	321,000	1,034,610
12	451,366	180,000	337,260
13	294,106	90,000	238,905
		2,955,000	2,955,000

New forecasts provide production control personnel the ability to incorporate the latest information into the original master production schedule and make any required changes. If poundage output can be maintained, the main adjustments are in the actual product mix.

The information from the aggregate production plan is used by purchasing to negotiate long term contracts with various suppliers. It is also used to provide printing suppliers with the necessary information to schedule their production and to develop a tentative schedule of delivery dates. It is used to generate a forecast of what accounts payable will be, and to provide a forecast for delivery frequency of bulk products.

QUESTIONS

1. Explain how the considerations of minimizing inventory investment, quality of products, and customer service are related.
2. The estimated production in periods 7 through 13 shows considerable variability. State what the work force requirements in each period will be. Should the company anticipate any problems?
3. Explain how Rowntree's personnel policies affect the aggregate production plan.

tory levels are maintained for customer service. Inventory levels in the plan are controlled to meet the quality standards.

The aggregate plan becomes the input for more detailed scheduling on a weekly and daily basis.

SUMMARY

In this chapter, we discussed the production-planning process: translating forecasts and other demand data into a monthly aggregate production plan and using this production plan and rough-cut capacity analysis to develop a master production schedule (MPS). The MPS states the anticipated schedule of final product completion and serves as the input to material requirement planning systems (see Chapter 15) for component production.

Aggregate planning is complicated by seasonal fluctuations in demand. Strategies for modifying capacity include production rate changes, work force changes, inventory smoothing, and demand shifting. Managers must consider the various costs of such strategies in developing an aggregate plan. Various quantitative methods are available for assisting managers to develop production plans and master schedules. It is important to keep in mind that the final MPS must be *realistic;* that is, the firm must be capable of achieving the MPS given its capacity limitations. Otherwise, it will be difficult to control production, and poor productivity will be the result. Rough-cut capacity-planning techniques are used for this purpose.

KEY TERMS	Aggregate production planning	Rough-cut capacity planning
	Master production scheduling (MPS)	Final assembly schedule (FAS)

REVIEW/ DISCUSSION QUESTIONS

1. Describe the essential elements of the production-planning and scheduling process.

2. What is *aggregate production planning*? How does it differ from *master production scheduling*?

3. Discuss the role of inventory in aggregate production planning.

4. What costs need to be considered in aggregate production planning? Why?

5. What factors should be considered in choosing a planning horizon?

6. How frequently should the aggregate production plan be updated?

7. Why is aggregate production planning much more difficult when demand is seasonal?

8. Explain the various strategies available for meeting fluctuating demand. What are the costs involved?

9. Under what conditions can the transportation model for aggregate planning be used?

10. What is a *master production schedule*? Why is it important?

11. Explain how a master production schedule is constructed. For what does a master scheduler look?

12. What is the purpose of rough-cut capacity planning?

13. Explain how capacity planning by overall factors is performed.

14. How does capacity planning in service organizations differ from capacity planning in manufacturing organizations?

PROBLEMS

1. Consider the following six-month demand forecast:

Month	Jul	Aug	Sept	Oct	Nov	Dec
Demand Forecast	850	900	1000	850	600	450

a. Compute the cumulative demand for each month and the average demand per month.
b. If the production for each month is set equal to the average demand, compute the net ending inventory for each month, assuming that the ending inventory for June is 150 units, and that all shortages are backordered.
c. Draw a graph of cumulative production and cumulative demand.

2. A manufacturer of stamped metal parts has a sales forecast for the next 5 weeks of a particular part.

Week	1	2	3	4	5
Forecast	2000	2500	3000	3000	3500

Beginning inventory equals 13,000 units and the firm wishes to maintain this level at the end of the planning period.
a. What weekly production rate is necessary?
b. Prepare a graph of ending inventory level over time using your answer to part a.
c. Suppose the company wishes to reduce its inventory level to 10,000 units. How would the production plan change?

3. The projected aggregate demand of a certain product is given for the next 12 months. What is the minimum level of constant production necessary to meet demand and incur no stockouts? Assume an initial inventory of 150. Show your results on a graph.

Month	1	2	3	4	5	6	7	8	9	10	11	12
Demand	480	530	500	480	470	520	450	480	500	530	570	600

4. Chapman Pharmaceuticals, a large manufacturer of drugs, has an aggregate demand forecast for a liquid cold medicine.

Month	J	F	M	A	M	J	J	A	S	O	N	D
Liters (1000s)	180	120	75	60	20	15	15	15	30	70	90	150

a. If the firm has a capacity of 80 thousand liters per month, show by means of a graph the sales level, production level, and inventory level over the next 12 months if the initial inventory is 190,000 liters.
b. What is the minimum level of production necessary to maintain a non-negative inventory?
c. Develop a plan that includes overtime for which inventory levels are held to at least a 100,000 liter level each month.

5. For Chapman Pharmaceuticals in Problem 4, suppose that inventory holding costs are $25 per 1000 liters per month, regular time production costs are $350 per 1000 liters, and overtime premiums add an additional 20 percent. Compute the cost of the production plans developed in parts (a) and (c) in Problem 4.

6. Refer to Chapman Pharmaceuticals in Problems 4 and 5. Suppose that normal capacity is 80,000 liters per month and a maximum of 20,000 liters can be

produced in overtime. If the initial inventory in January is 150,000 liters and there are no other inventory restrictions, construct a transportation tableau for this problem and determine the minimal-cost production plan.

7. Determine a more cost-effective production plan than in Table 14.5 for Golden Breweries that incurs no shortages.

8. Given the following monthly demand pattern and unit production cost of $1.20, overtime costs of $1.30 per unit, and subcontracting costs of $1.40 per unit, compute the cost of a level production strategy and also a strategy of setting production levels equal to the monthly demand. The inventory holding cost is $0.20 per unit per month. In the case of level production strategy, assume a desired ending inventory of 24,000. The beginning inventory for both cases is 20,000 units. The capacity for regular production is 24,000 units and there is an overtime capacity of 2000 units and a subcontracting option up to 2000 units.

Month	1	2	3	4	5	6	7	8	9	10	11	12
Demand (1000s)	24	22	26	20	20	20	22	23	24	26	28	28

9. The Westerbeck Co. manufactures several models of washers and dryers. The projected requirements over the next year for their automatic washers are

Month	Jan	Feb	Mar	Apr	May	Jun	Jul	Aug	Sep	Oct	Nov	Dec
Requirement	800	1030	810	900	950	1340	1100	1210	600	580	890	1000

Current inventory is 100 units. The firm's current capacity is 960 units per month. The average salary of production workers is $1300 per month. Overtime is paid at time and one-half up to 20 percent additional time. Each production worker accounts for 30 units per month. Additional labor can be hired for a training cost of $250, and existing workers can be laid off at a cost of $500. Any increase or decrease in the production rate costs $5000 for tooling, setup, and line changes. This does not apply, however, to overtime. Inventory-holding costs are $25 per unit per month. Backorders cost $75 per unit short. Determine at least two different production plans, trying to minimize the cost of meeting the next year's requirements.

10. Microdevices makes a memory expansion board for microcomputers. The company has the following orders over the next 6 months:

Month 1:	2000	Month 4:	4500
Month 2:	5000	Month 5:	2000
Month 3:	8000	Month 6:	8000

Monthly production capacities are 5000 units on regular time and 1000 units on overtime, and up to 2000 can be subcontracted each month. Production costs are $20 per unit on regular time and $25 per unit on overtime; the cost per unit for the components subcontracted is $28. Inventory-holding costs are charged at the rate of $1.00 per unit per month.

Use the transportation model to develop a production schedule for Microdevices over the next six months.

11. Refer to Problem 10. At the end of month 2, Microdevices received a new order for 2000 additional components in month 4 and 5500 additional units in month 5. Also, due to slow demand, the subcontractor has offered to produce components for Microdevices at a cost of $22 per unit. Develop a revised production schedule for Microdevices for months 3 through 6.

12. The demand for a certain manufactured product during the next four months is expected to be 175, 235, 270, and 220 units, respectively. The cost of manufacturing with regular, overtime, and subcontract options and the capacities are given below. Use the transportation method to determine the least-cost production plan and compute the costs.

Options	Cost of Manufacturing	Capacity per week
Regular production	75	50
Overtime production	85	12.5
Subcontract operations	100	25

The holding cost is 10 percent of manufacturing cost per month.

13. The demand for a certain product over a 6-month period is as follows:

Month	1	2	3	4	5	6
Demand	1475	1300	1325	1150	1500	1275

The firm has the option of regular production at a cost of $12 per unit, subcontracting at a cost of $18 per unit, and overtime production at a cost of $16 per unit. The holding cost is given as 20 percent of the cost of manufacturing per month. The capacities over the 6-month period are as follows:

Period	Regular Production	Overtime Production	Subcontracting
1	800	150	150
2	850	200	150
3	900	200	150
4	900	200	200
5	950	250	200
6	950	250	200

The beginning inventory is 575 units and desired ending inventory at the end of 6 months is 200 units. Find the least-cost production plan using the transportation method. Also compute the total cost of this production plan.

14. An electronics firm produces two types of printed circuit boards for computer assembly. Based on current and anticipated orders, the projected demand over the next 8 weeks is:

				Week				
Type	1	2	3	4	5	6	7	8
A	15	20	30	30	20	20	10	20
B	10	5	0	0	10	20	20	20

Circuit board A is produced in lots of 50, and B in lots of 30. Current inventories of each type are 20 and 10, respectively. Safety stocks of 10 and 5 are carried for boards A and B. Develop a master schedule based upon this information.

15. Can you improve the master schedule for Golden Breweries in Table 14.10 by eliminating some product changeovers during the first 12 weeks, while still maintaining the aggregate plan? If so, then analyze the short-term inventory fluctuations for your new schedule.

16. A firm manufacturing three types of hydraulic cylinders has the following aggregate production plan over the next 3 months.

    Jan: 1500 cylinders
    Feb: 1475 cylinders
    Mar: 1450 cylinders

The product mix is usually of the ratio of 25%: 30%: 45% among wheel, master, and slave cylinders, respectively. The production capacity is 380 cylinders per week. Formulate a feasible master production schedule with weekly time periods. The initial inventories are 50, 60, and 90 units respectively, and are also the safety stocks for the three types of cylinders.

17. A firm producing three products has developed the following 3-month aggregate production plan, along with marketing estimates of the monthly product mix because of seasonal fluctuations. Initially there are 300 units of product A, 100 units of product B, and 75 units of product C in inventory. The weekly capacity of the plant is 220 units. Develop a feasible master production schedule for this situation, providing for a safety stock of 25 units for each product.

		Planned	Product Mix		
Month	Projected Requirements	Production Level	A	B	C
July	650	850	.40	.25	.35
August	975	850	.40	.35	.25
September	1000	850	.30	.50	.20

18. The CammShaft Company subcontracts production for major automotive manufacturers. Three standard end items are produced, and a six-month master production schedule is as shown.

Item/Month	1	2	3	4	5	6
A	140	180	200	150	120	100
B	100	100	150	150	100	100
C	200	250	250	250	300	300

Products A, B, and C require .60, 1.20, and 1.00 labor hours per unit, respectively. Over the past year, the fabrication department reported 1950 labor hours, whereas the assembly department reported 1050 labor hours. Determine the rough-cut capacity requirements for each department and the total plant for the next six months.

A small manufacturer of marine radios has the following quarterly sales data for **CASE PROBLEM** the past 7 years:

		Quarter			Total
Year	1	2	3	4	Sales
1	60	150	100	40	350
2	100	180	150	70	500
3	140	260	230	120	750
4	190	280	250	180	900
5	220	340	280	210	1050
6	240	360	300	200	1100
7	280	400	350	270	1300

a. Sketch a graph of this time series. If a linear trend appears to exist, determine the trend equation.
b. Show the four-quarter, moving-average values for this time series. Plot this along with the original time series. Using the moving average, compute seasonal factors for the four quarters.
c. Develop a quarterly forecast for next year using the techniques discussed in Chapter 3.
d. The plant has a capacity to manufacture 130 radios per month. Develop three alternate monthly production plans for the next year, assuming there are 80 radios currently in inventory. Show your results graphically and in tabular form. Include a discussion of safety stock, overtime, rate changes, and so on. What if forecasts are off by 10 percent on the low side? Which of your plans would appear to be best?
e. For what long-range capacity requirements should the company be preparing?

L inear programming is a mathematical procedure that is often helpful in finding the best solution to a variety of managerial problems. Two operations management problems where linear programming and its variations have been used successfully are aggregate production planning and the transportation problem. For example, consider a manufacturer who wants to develop a production schedule and an inventory policy that will satisfy sales demand in future periods. Ideally, the recommended schedule and policy will enable the company to satisfy demand and at the same time *minimize* the total production and inventory costs. As another illustration, consider the transportation problem that arises when a company has warehouses located throughout the United States. Given a set of customer demands for its products, the company would like to determine which warehouse should ship how much product to which customers so that the total transportation costs are *minimized*.

A close scrutiny of these two applications shows some common features. In both cases, we are concerned with minimizing some quantity. In the first, we are interested in minimizing production and inventory costs; in the second, we are interested in minimizing transportation costs. All linear programming problems involve the minimization or maximization of some quantity. In linear programming terminology, the *minimization* or *maximization* of some quantity is referred to as the *objective* of the problem.

The second property common to all linear programming problems is that there are restrictions, or **constraints**, that limit the extent to which the objective can be pursued. In the aggregate planning problem, the manufacturer is restricted by the constraints requiring product demand to be satisfied and by the constraints indicating limited production capacities. In the transportation problem, the minimum-cost shipping schedule is constrained by the supply of product available at each warehouse and the requirement that demand be satisfied. Thus constraints are another general feature of every linear programming problem.

Although we have not defined linear programming in a formal manner, we have nonetheless been able to describe some typical problems where linear programming has been applied, and as a result recognize two properties that are common to all linear programs: the objective and the constraints. In the following discussion, we illustrate how linear programming can be used to solve problems of the above nature.

THE SOFTWATER, INC., PRODUCT MIX PROBLEM

Softwater, Inc., manufactures and sells a variety of chemical products used in purifying and softening water. One of its products is a pellet that is produced and sold in 40- and 80-pound bags. A common production line packages both products, although the fill rate is slower for 80-pound bags.

Softwater is currently planning its production schedule for the peak summer season. The company wants to develop and solve a linear programming model that will assist in this scheduling decision.

One of the critical inputs to the production-scheduling decision is the demand estimate. The company has orders for 20,000 pounds over the next week. Currently, they have 4000 pounds in inventory. Thus Softwater should plan on an aggregate production of at least 16,000 pounds. They expect to be able to sell more if they can produce more. Softwater has a sufficient supply of pellets to meet this demand but has limited amounts of packaging materials available, as well as a limited amount of time on the packaging line. Softwater's problem is to determine how many 40- and 80-pound bags to produce to maximize profit given limited materials and time on the packaging line. In order to develop a linear programming formulation of this problem, we start by defining the objective function.

The Objective Function

Every linear programming problem has a specific objective. For Softwater, Inc., the objective is to maximize profit. We can write this objective in a more specific form by defining variables to represent the number of each type of bag produced. Let

x_1 = the number of 40-pound bags produced

x_2 = the number of 80-pound bags produced

Softwater's profit will come from two sources: (1) the profit made by producing x_1 40-pound bags and (2) the profit made by producing x_2 80-pound bags. If Softwater makes $2 for every 40-pound bag produced, the company will make $2x_1$ dollars if x_1 40-pound bags are produced. Also, if Softwater makes $4 for every

80-pound bag produced, the company will make $4x_2$ dollars if x_2 80-pound bags are produced. Denoting total profit by the symbol z and dropping the dollar signs for convenience, we have

$$\text{Total profit} = z = 2x_1 + 4x_2 \quad (14S.1)$$

The solution to Softwater's problem is the *decision* that will maximize total profit. That is, Softwater, Inc., must determine the values for the variables x_1 and x_2 that will yield the highest possible value of z. In linear programming terminology we refer to x_1 and x_2 as the *decision variables*. Since the objective—maximize total profit—is a *function* of these decision variables, we refer to $2x_1 + 4x_2$ as the **objective function**. In linear programming terminology, we say that Softwater's goal, or objective, is to maximize the value of its objective function. Using *max* as an abbreviation for *maximize*, the objective is written as follows:

$$\max z = 2x_1 + 4x_2$$

Suppose Softwater decided to produce two hundred 40-pound bags and three hundred 80-pound bags. Using Equation (14S.1), the corresponding profit is

$$z = 2(200) + 4(300)$$
$$= 400 + 1200$$
$$= 1600 \text{ dollars}$$

What if Softwater decided upon a different production schedule, such as four hundred 40-pound bags and four hundred 80-pound bags? In this case, the profit is

$$z = 2(400) + 4(400)$$
$$= 800 + 1600$$
$$= 2400 \text{ dollars}$$

Certainly the latter production schedule is preferable in terms of the stated objective of maximizing profit. However, it may not be possible for Softwater to produce four hundred 40-pound bags and four hundred 80-pound bags. For instance, there might not be enough materials or enough time available on the packaging line to produce these quantities. Indeed, Softwater can consider only production alternatives that meet the aggregate demand utilizing no more packaging materials than are available and no more packaging time than is available on the packaging line.

In the Softwater, Inc., problem, any particular production combination of 40- and 80-pound bags is referred to as a **solution** to the problem. However, only those solutions that satisfy *all* the constraints are referred to as **feasible solutions**. The particular feasible production combination or feasible solution that results in the largest profit will be referred to as the *optimal* production combination or, equivalently, the **optimal solution**. At this point, however, we have no idea what the optimal solution is because we have not developed a procedure for identifying feasible solutions. The procedure for determining the feasible solutions requires us to first identify all the constraints of the problem.

The Constraints

Every 40- and 80-pound bag produced must go through the packaging line. In a normal work week, this line is up and running for 1500 minutes. The 40-pound bags, for which the line was designed, each require 1.2 minutes of packaging time; the 80-pound bags require 3 minutes per bag. The total packaging time required to produce x_1 40-pound bags is $1.2x_1$ and the time required to produce x_2 80-pound bags is $3x_2$. Thus the total packaging time required for the production of x_1 40-pound bags and x_2 80-pound bags is given by

$$\text{Total packaging time} = 1.2x_1 + 3x_2$$

Since there are only 1500 minutes of packaging time available, it follows that the production combination we select must satisfy the constraint

$$1.2x_1 + 3x_2 \leq 1500 \qquad (14S.2)$$

This constraint mathematically denotes the requirement that the total packaging time used cannot exceed the amount available.

Softwater has 6000 square feet of packaging materials available; each 40-pound bag requires 6 square feet and each 80-pound bag requires 10 square feet of these materials. Since the amount of packaging materials used cannot exceed what is available, we obtain a second constraint for the linear programming problem.

$$6x_1 + 10x_2 \leq 6000 \qquad (14S.3)$$

The aggregate production requirement is for the production of 16,000 pounds of softening pellets per week. Since the small bags contain 40 pounds of pellets and

the large bags contain 80 pounds, we must impose the following aggregate demand constraint:

$$40x_1 + 80x_2 \geq 16,000 \qquad (14S.4)$$

We have now specified mathematical relationships for three constraints. Are there any other constraints we have forgotten? Can Softwater produce negative quantities of either product? Clearly, the answer is no. In order to prevent the decision variables x_1 and x_2 from having negative values, the two constraints

$$x_1 \geq 0 \quad \text{and} \quad x_2 \geq 0 \qquad (14S.5)$$

must be added. These constraints ensure that the solution to our problem will contain nonnegative values for the decision variables and are thus referred to as the **nonnegativity constraints**. Nonnegativity constraints are a general feature of all linear programming problems and will be written in the following abbreviated form:

$$x_1, x_2 \geq 0$$

Mathematical Statement of the Softwater, Inc., Problem

The mathematical statement, or formulation, of the Softwater problem is now complete. We have succeeded in translating the objective and constraints of the real-world problem into a set of mathematical relationships referred to as a **mathematical model**. The complete mathematical model for the Softwater problem is as follows:

$$\max z = 2x_1 + 4x_2 \qquad \text{(profit)}$$

subject to

$$
\begin{aligned}
1.2x_1 + 3x_2 &\leq 1500 \quad \text{(packaging line)} \\
6x_1 + 10x_2 &\leq 6000 \quad \text{(materials availability)} \\
40x_1 + 80x_2 &\geq 16,000 \quad \text{(aggregate production)} \\
x_1, x_2 &\geq 0 \quad \text{(nonnegativity)}
\end{aligned}
$$

Our job now is to find the product mix (that is, the combination of x_1 and x_2) that satisfies all the constraints and, at the same time, yields a value for the objective function that is greater than or equal to the value given by any other feasible solution. Once this is done, we will have found the optimal solution to the problem.

This mathematical model of the Softwater problem is called a **linear program**. The problem has the objective and constraints that we said earlier were common properties of all linear programs. But what is the special feature of this mathematical model that makes it a linear program? The special feature that makes it a linear program is that the objective function and all **constraint functions** (the left-hand sides of the constraint inequalities) are *linear* functions of the decision variables.

Mathematically speaking, functions where each of the variables appears in a separate term and is raised to the first power are called **linear functions**. The objective function $(2x_1 + 4x_2)$ is linear, since each de-

cision variable appears in a separate term and has an exponent of 1. If the objective function were $(2x_1^2 + 4\sqrt{x_2})$, it would not have been a linear function and we would not have had a linear program. The amount of packaging time required is also a linear function of the decision variables for the same reasons. Similarly, the functions on the left-hand side of all the constraint inequalities (the constraint functions) are linear functions. Thus the mathematical formulation of the Softwater problem is referred to as a linear program.

GRAPHICAL SOLUTION OF LINEAR PROGRAMS

Let us begin the graphical solution procedure by developing a graph that can be used to display the possible solutions (x_1- and x_2-values) for the Softwater problem. The graph (Figure 14S.1) has values of x_1 on the horizontal axis and values of x_2 on the vertical axis. Any point on the graph can be identified by the x_1- and x_2-values, which indicate the position of the point along the x_1- and x_2-axes, respectively. Since every point (x_1, x_2) corresponds to a possible solution, every point on the graph is called a *solution point*. The solution point where $x_1 = 0$ and $x_2 = 0$ is referred to as the *origin*.

The next step is to show which of the possible combinations of x_1 and x_2—that is, solution points—correspond to feasible solutions for the linear program. Since both x_1 and x_2 must be nonnegative, we need only consider points where $x_1 \geq 0$ and $x_2 \geq 0$. This is indicated in Figure 14S.2 by arrows pointing in the direction of production combinations that will satisfy the nonnegativity constraints, namely, those points in the first quadrant. In all future graphs, we assume that

FIGURE 14S.2 The Nonnegativity Constraints

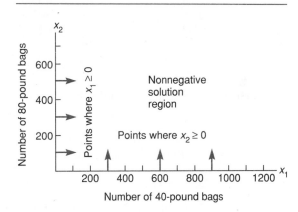

the nonnegativity relationships hold and we draw only the portion of the graph corresponding to nonnegative x_1- and x_2-values.

Earlier we saw that the inequality representing the packaging line constraint was of the form

$$1.2x_1 + 3x_2 \leq 1500$$

To show all solution points that satisfy this relationship, we start by graphing the line corresponding to the *equation*

$$1.2x_1 + 3x_2 = 1500$$

The graph of this equation is found by identifying two points that lie on the line and then drawing a line through the points. Setting $x_1 = 0$ and solving for x_2, we see that the point $(x_1 = 0, x_2 = 500)$ satisfies the above equation. To find a second point satisfying this equation, we set $x_2 = 0$ and solve for x_1. Doing this, we obtain $1.2x_1 + 3(0) = 1500$; hence, $x_1 = 1250$. Thus a second point satisfying the equation is

FIGURE 14S.1 Graph of Solution Points for the Two-Variable Softwater, Inc., Problem

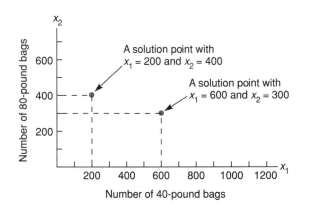

$(x_1 = 1250, x_2 = 0)$. Given these two points, we can now graph the line corresponding to the equation

$$1.2x_1 + 3x_2 = 1500$$

This line, which will be called the *packaging constraint line,* is shown in Figure 14S.3. For purposes of identification, we label this line "PL" to indicate that it represents the packaging line constraint.

Recall that the inequality representing the packaging line constraint is

$$1.2x_1 + 3x_2 \leq 1500$$

Can you identify all the solution points that satisfy this constraint? Since we have the line where $1.2x_1 + 3x_2 = 1500$, we know any point on this line must satisfy the constraint. But where are the solution points satisfying $1.2x_1 + 3x_2 < 1500$? Consider two solution points, $(x_1 = 200, x_2 = 200)$ and $(x_1 = 600, x_2 = 500)$. You can see from Figure 14S.3 that the first solution point is below the constraint line and the second is above the constraint line. Which of these solutions will satisfy the packaging line constraint? For the point $(x_1 = 200, x_2 = 200)$, we see that

$$1.2x_1 + 3x_2 = 1.2(200) + 3(200) = 240 + 600$$
$$= 840$$

Since the 840 minutes is less than the 1500 minutes available, the $x_1 = 200$, $x_2 = 200$ production combination, or solution point, satisfies the constraint. For $x_1 = 600$, $x_2 = 500$, we have

$$1.2x_1 + 3x_2 = 1.2(600) + 3(500) = 720 + 1500$$
$$= 2220$$

Since the 2220 minutes is greater than the 1500 minutes available, the $x_1 = 600$, $x_2 = 500$ solution point

does not satisfy the constraint and is thus an unacceptable production alternative.

Are you ready to answer the question of which solution points satisfy the packaging line constraint? Your answer should be that any point *below* the packaging line constraint line satisfies the constraint. You may want to satisfy yourself by selecting additional solution points above and below the constraint line and checking to see if the solutions satisfy the constraints. You will see that only solution points on or below the constraint line satisfy the constraint. In Figure 14S.4, we indicate all such points by shading the region of the graph corresponding to the solution points that satisfy the packaging line constraint.

Next let us identify all solution points that satisfy the packaging materials constraint

$$6x_1 + 10x_2 \leq 6000$$

We start by drawing the constraint line corresponding to the equation

$$6x_1 + 10x_2 = 6000$$

As before, the graphing of a line is most easily done by finding two points on the line and then connecting them. Thus we first set x_1 equal to zero and solve for x_2, which yields the point $(x_1 = 0, x_2 = 600)$. Next we set x_2 equal to zero and solve for x_1, which gives the second point $(x_1 = 1000, x_2 = 0)$. In Figure 14S.5 we have drawn the line corresponding to the materials constraint. For identification purposes, we label this line "M." Using the same approach as for the packaging line constraint, we realize that only points on or below the line satisfy the materials availability constraint. Thus, in Figure 14S.5, the shaded region corresponds to all feasible production combinations or feasible solution points for packaging materials availability.

FIGURE 14S.3 The Packaging Line Constraint

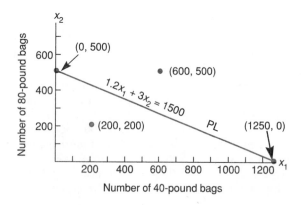

FIGURE 14S.4 Feasible Region for the Packaging Line Constraint

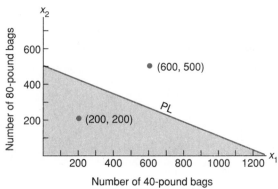

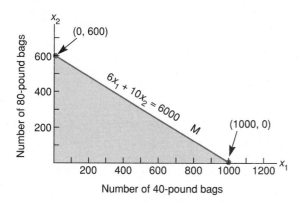

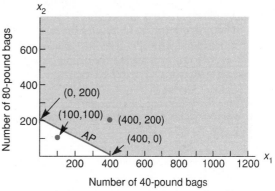

In a similar manner, we determine the set of all feasible production combinations for the aggregate production constraint. This constraint is $40x_1 + 80x_2 \geq 16,000$. If we graph the equation

$$40x_1 + 80x_2 = 16,000$$

by first setting $x_1 = 0$ and solving for x_2, we obtain the point ($x_1 = 0, x_2 = 200$). Next, setting $x_2 = 0$ and solving for x_1, we obtain the point ($x_1 = 400, x_2 = 0$). We label this line "AP." Note that this constraint contains the symbol for greater than or equal to. If we choose a point on either side of the line, such as (100, 100) and (400, 200), we find that

$$40(100) + 80(100) = 12,000$$

and

$$40(400) + 80(200) = 32,000$$

The point (100, 100) does *not* satisfy the constraint $40x_1 + 80x_2 \geq 16,000$; however the point (400, 200) does satisfy it. Therefore, the feasible region for this constraint is given by the shaded region in Figure 14S.6. Note that this extends without bound in the first quadrant above the constraint line.

We now have three separate graphs showing the feasible solution points for each of the three constraints. In a linear programming problem, we need to identify the solution points that satisfy *all* the constraints *simultaneously*. To find these solution points, we draw our three constraints on one graph and observe the region containing the points that do in fact satisfy all the constraints simultaneously. This combined-constraint graph is shown in Figure 14S.7. The shaded region in this figure includes every solution point that satisfies all the constraints. Since solutions that satisfy

FIGURE 14S.7   Feasible Solution Region for the Softwater Problem

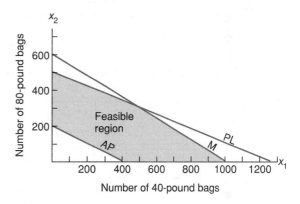

all the constraints are called *feasible solutions,* the shaded region is called the *feasible solution region,* or simply the *feasible region.* Any point on the boundary of the feasible region or within the feasible region is a *feasible solution point.* You may want to check points outside the feasible region to satisfy yourself that these solution points violate one or more of the constraints and are thus infeasible or unacceptable.

Now that we have identified the feasible region, we are ready to proceed with the graphical solution method to find the optimal solution for the Softwater, Inc., problem. Recall that the optimal solution for any linear programming problem is the feasible solution that provides the best possible value of the objective function. We could arbitrarily select feasible solution points (x_1, x_2) and compute the associated profit $2x_1 + 4x_2$. However, the difficulty with this approach is that there are too many feasible solutions (actually an infinite number), and thus it would not be possible to evaluate all feasible solutions. Hence this trial-and-error procedure would not guarantee that the optimal solution could be obtained. Thus we would like a systematic way of identifying the feasible solution that does in fact maximize the profit for Softwater, Inc.

Let us start this final step of the graphical solution procedure by drawing the feasible region on a separate graph. This is shown in Figure 14S.8.

Rather than selecting an arbitrary feasible solution and computing the associated profit, let us select an arbitrary profit and identify all the feasible solution points (x_1, x_2) that yield the selected profit. For example, what feasible solution points provide a profit of $1200? That is, what value of x_1 and x_2 in the feasible region will make the objective function $2x_1 + 4x_2 = 1200$?

The expression $2x_1 + 4x_2 = 1200$ is simply the equation of a line. Thus all feasible solution points (x_1, x_2) yielding a profit of $1200 must be on the line. We learned earlier in this section how to graph a constraint line. The procedure for graphing the profit or objective function line is the same. Letting $x_1 = 0$, we see that x_2 must be 300, and thus the solution point $(x_1 = 0, x_2 = 300)$ is on the line. Similarly, by letting $x_2 = 0$, we see that the solution point $(x_1 = 600, x_2 = 0)$ is also on the line. Drawing the line through these two solution points identifies all the solution points that have a profit of $1200. A graph of this profit line is presented in Figure 14S.9. From this graph, you can see that there are an infinite number of feasible production combinations that will provide a $1200 profit.

Since the objective is one of finding the feasible solution point that has the highest profit, let us proceed by selecting higher profit values and finding the feasible solution points that yield the stated profits. For example, what solution points provide $1500 profit? What solution points provide a $2100 profit? To answer these questions, we must find the x_1- and x_2-values on the following lines:

$$2x_1 + 4x_2 = 1500$$

and

$$2x_1 + 4x_2 = 2100$$

Using the previous procedure for graphing profit and constraint lines, we have drawn the $1500 and $2100 profit lines on the graph in Figure 14S.10. While not all solution points on the $2100 profit line are in the feasible region, at least some points on the line are, and thus it is possible to obtain a feasible production combination that provides a $2100 profit.

FIGURE 14S.9 $1200 Profit Line for the Softwater Problem

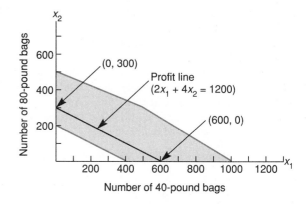

FIGURE 14S.8 Feasible Solution Region for the Softwater Problem

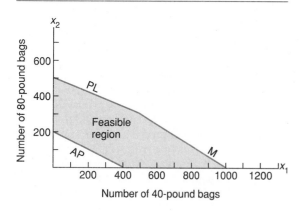

FIGURE 14S.10 Selected Profit Lines for the Softwater Problem

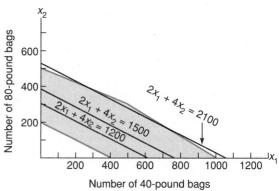

Can we find a solution yielding even higher profits? Look at Figure 14S.10 and see what general observations you can make about the profit lines. You should be able to identify the following properties: (1) The profit lines are *parallel* to each other; and (2) higher profit lines occur as we move farther from the origin.

These properties can now be used to determine the optimal solution to the problem. By continuing to move the profit line farther from the origin so that it remains parallel to the other profit lines, we can obtain solution points that yield higher and higher values for the objective function. However, at some point, we will find that any further outward movement will place the profit line outside the feasible region. Since points outside the feasible region are unacceptable, the point in the feasible region that lies on the highest profit line is the optimal solution to our linear program.

You should now be able to identify the optimal solution point for the Softwater, Inc., problem. Use a ruler or the edge of a piece of paper and move the profit line as far from the origin as you can. What is the last point in the feasible region that you reach? This point, which is the optimal solution, is shown graphically in Figure 14S.11.

The optimal values of the decision variables x_1 and x_2 are the x_1- and x_2-values at the optimal solution point. Depending upon the accuracy of your graph, you may or may not be able to read the *exact* x_1- and x_2-values from the graph. The best we can do with respect to the optimal solution point in Figure 14S.11 is to conclude that the optimal production combination consists of approximately five hundred 40-pound bags and three hundred 80-pound bags. As you will see later, the actual x_1- and x_2-values at the optimal solution point are indeed $x_1 = 500$ and $x_2 = 300$. Later,

we show how to compute these exact optimal solution values.

Summary of the Graphical Solution Procedure for Maximization Problems

As you have seen, the graphical solution procedure is one method of solving two-variable linear programming problems such as the Softwater, Inc., problem. The steps of the graphical solution procedure for a maximization problem are outlined below:

1. Prepare a graph of the feasible solution points for each of the constraints.
2. Determine the feasible solution region by identifying the solution points that satisfy all the constraints simultaneously.
3. Draw a profit line showing all values of the variables x_1 and x_2 that yield a specified value of the objective function.
4. Move parallel profit lines toward higher profits (usually away from the origin) until further movement would take the profit line completely outside the feasible region.
5. The feasible solution point that is touched by the highest-possible profit line is the optimal solution.
6. Determine, at least approximately, the optimal values of the decision variables by reading the x_1- and x_2-values at the optimal solution point directly from the graph.

Solving a minimization problem graphically requires modification of Steps 4 and 5. In Step 4 the objective function is moved in a parallel fashion to lower and lower values. In Step 5 the feasible solution point that is touched by the lowest possible objective function line is the optimal solution.

FIGURE 14S.11 Optimal Solution for the Softwater Problem

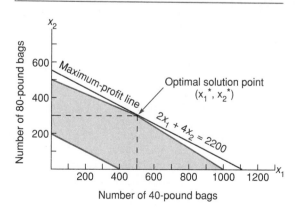

Number of 40-pound bags

Extreme Points and the Optimal Solution

Suppose that the profit for the Softwater, Inc., 40-pound bag is reduced from $2 to $1 per bag, while the profit for the 80-pound bag and all the constraint conditions remain unchanged. The complete linear programming model of this new problem is identical to the previous mathematical model, except for the following revised objective function:

$$\max z = x_1 + 4x_2$$

How does this change in the objective function affect the optimal solution to our Softwater, Inc., problem? Figure 14S.12 shows the graphical solution of the Softwater, Inc., problem with the revised objective function. Note that since the constraints have not changed,

FIGURE 14S.12   Optimal Solution to the Softwater Problem with an Objective Function of $x_1 + 4x_2$

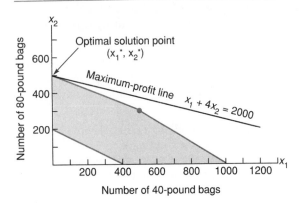

Number of 40-pound bags

FIGURE 14S.13   The Five Extreme Points of the Feasible Region for the Softwater Problem

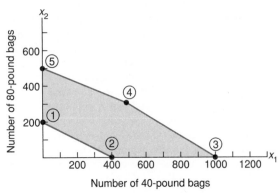

Number of 40-pound bags

the feasible solution region has not changed. However, the profit lines have been altered to reflect the new objective function.

By moving the profit line in a parallel manner away from the origin, we find the optimal solution point shown in Figure 14S.12. The exact values of the decision variables at this point are $x_1 = 0$ and $x_2 = 500$. Thus the reduced profit for the 40-pound bags has caused a change in the optimal solution. In fact, as you may have suspected, we are cutting back the production of the lower profit, 40-pound bags and increasing the production of the higher profit, 80-pound bags.

What have you noticed about the location of the optimal solutions in the two linear programming problems that we have solved thus far? Look closely at the graphical solutions in Figures 14S.11 and 14S.12. An important observation that you should be able to make is that the optimal solutions occur at one of the vertices, or "corners," of the feasible region. In linear programming terminology, these vertices are referred to as the *extreme points* of the feasible region. Thus the Softwater, Inc., problem has five vertices, or five extreme points, for its feasible region (see Figure 14S.13). We can now state our observation about the location of optimal solutions as follows:

The optimal solution to a linear programming problem can be found at an extreme point of the feasible solution region for the problem.

This is a very important property of all linear programming problems because it says that if you are looking for the optimal solution to a linear programming problem, you do not have to evaluate all feasible solution points. In fact, you have to consider *only* the feasible solutions that occur at the extreme points of the feasible region. Thus for the Softwater, Inc., problem, instead of computing and comparing the profit for all feasible solutions, we can find the optimal solution by evaluating the five extreme-point solutions and selecting the one that provides the highest profit. Actually the graphical solution procedure is nothing more than a convenient way of identifying an optimal extreme point for two variable problems.

To help convince yourself that the optimal solution to a linear program always occurs at an extreme point, select several different objective functions for the Softwater, Inc., problem and graphically find the optimal solution for each case. You will see that as you move the profit lines away from the origin, the last feasible solution point—the optimal solution point—is always one of the extreme points.

What happens if the highest profit line coincides with one of the constraint lines on the boundary of the feasible region? This case is shown for the objective function $2.4x_1 + 6x_2$ in Figure 14S.14. Does an optimal solution still occur at an extreme point? The answer is yes. In fact, for this case the optimal solution occurs at extreme point ④, extreme point ⑤, and any solution point on the line joining these two points. This is the special case of *alternate optimal solutions*.

Finding the Exact Location of Graphical Solution Extreme Points

Let us consider extreme point ④ of the Softwater problem, as shown in Figure 14S.15. In the graphical so-

FIGURE 14S.14 Optimal Solution Points for the Softwater Problem with an Objective Function of $2.4x_1 + 6x_2$

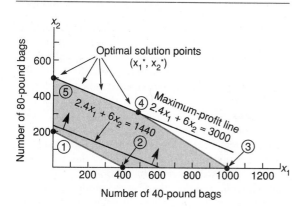

Number of 40-pound bags

FIGURE 14S.15 Feasible Region for the Softwater Problem

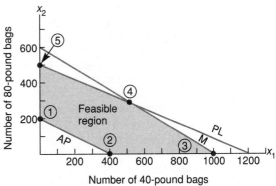

Number of 40-pound bags

lution procedure, extreme point ④ was identified as the optimal solution to the original Softwater problem. However, we had difficulty reading the exact values of x_1 and x_2 at extreme point ④ directly from the graph. Actually, the best we could do was to arrive at approximate values for the decision variables.

Referring to Figure 14S.15, note the constraint lines that determine the exact location of extreme point ④. The packaging line constraint line and the materials constraint line combine to determine this extreme point. That is, extreme point ④ is on both the packaging line constraint line

$$1.2x_1 + 3x_2 = 1500 \qquad (14S.6)$$

and the materials constraint line

$$6x_1 + 10x_2 = 6000 \qquad (14S.7)$$

Thus the values of the decision variables x_1 and x_2 at extreme point ④ must satisfy both Equations (14S.6) and (14S.7). Using Equation (14S.6) and solving for x_1 gives

$$1.2x_1 = 1500 - 3x_2$$

or

$$x_1 = 1250 - \frac{5}{2}x_2 \qquad (14S.8)$$

Substituting this expression for x_1 into Equation (14S.7) and solving for x_2 provides the following:

$$6\left[1250 - \frac{5}{2}x_2\right] + 10x_2 = 6000$$

$$7500 - 15x_2 + 10x_2 = 6000$$

$$-5x_2 = -1500$$

$$x_2 = 300$$

Using $x_2 = 300$ in Equation (14S.8) and solving for x_1 provides

$$x_1 = 1250 - \frac{5}{2}(300)$$

$$= 1250 - 750$$

$$= 500$$

Thus the exact location of extreme point ④ is $x_1 = 500$ and $x_2 = 300$. Since we have previously observed that the optimal solution occurs at this extreme point, we now know the optimal production quantities for Softwater are five hundred 40-pound bags and three hundred 80-pound bags. This is, of course, what we had identified earlier by reading the approximate values on the graph.

In any graphical solution of a two-decision-variable linear programming problem, the exact values of the decision variables at the optimal solution can be determined by first using the graphical procedure to identify the optimal extreme point and then solving the two equations in two variables associated with the optimal extreme point.

MANAGERIAL USE OF THE SOFTWATER, INC., MODEL

This supplement shows a graphical solution method that can be used for solving linear programs with two variables. More complex examples require a computer for solution. Most computer manufacturers have linear programming software as a standard feature on their systems, and there are even linear programming packages available for use on microcomputers. In this section we address the question of what information the solution provides to operations managers.

The solution to the Software, Inc., problem is to produce five hundred 40-pound bags and three hundred 80-pound bags during the next week. By substituting these values into the objective function, we see that a profit of 2(500) + 4(300) = $2200 can be achieved. The solution gives financial managers information on anticipated profits and production managers the information required to develop specific plans for equipment utilization. For instance, if we substitute the optimal solution into each of the constraints, we determine how much of each department's capacity will actually be used:

Packaging line: 1.2(500) + 3(300) = 1500 min

Materials
  availability: 6(500) + 10(300) = 6000 sq ft

Aggregate
  production: 40(500) + 80(300) = 44,000 lb

We see that the amount of time used on the packaging line and the number of square feet of materials used are at their limits. Also, Softwater has exceeded its aggregate production constraint by 44,000 − 16,000 = 28,000 pounds. This difference is called *surplus*. If Softwater produces according to this plan, they will have excess production, which (as was pointed out earlier) could easily be sold or carried in inventory for the following week. However, these results must be interpreted carefully. For example, a breakdown in the packaging line will decrease the amount of productive time available, and thus the planned production could not be achieved. In addition, no inventory-holding costs are included; such a high excess production, if not sold, will decrease profitability. Also, it is assumed that customers will not care whether or not they receive 40- or 80-pound bags. The actual product mix has not been considered in this model. Despite these shortcomings, the linear programming model and solution have provided Softwater's management with information on how best to utilize its resources. Other considerations can be taken into account in more detailed operational planning.

LINEAR PROGRAMMING FOR AGGREGATE PLANNING: GOLDEN BREWERIES REVISITED

Linear programming is one of the most widely used quantitative methods. The reason for this is that computer software packages are available that permit efficient solution of problems involving several thousand variables and constraints. These software packages also have components that facilitate data handling and report generation. Thus managerial reports can be constructed directly as output of a computer run to solve a linear programming problem. Before these software packages can be used, however, we must formulate a mathematical statement of the linear programming problem to be solved.

In this section, we show how a linear programming formulation of a problem involving several variables and constraints can be developed. The formulation we develop can easily be solved on the computer and illustrates the power of linear programming as a method for dealing simultaneously with a multiplicity of decisions and requirements. The problem with which we deal is the Golden Breweries aggregate planning example, discussed in this chapter. We shall see how linear programming can aid the operations manager in making good decisions concerning the choice of a production plan.

In order to formulate the linear programming model, we define the following variables, which are all measured in numbers of barrels:

X_t = production in period t

I_t = inventory held at the end of period t

L_t = number of lost sales incurred in period t

O_t = amount of overtime scheduled in period t

U_t = amount of undertime scheduled in period t

R_t = increase in production rate from period $t − 1$ to t

D_t = decrease in production rate from period $t − 1$ to t

Material-balance Constraint

The constraint that requires beginning inventory plus production minus sales to equal ending inventory is called a *material-balance equation*. In the case of Golden Breweries, it is possible for demand to exceed sales. This happens when there is a stockout and we have lost sales. Thus, in words, the material-balance equation for Golden Breweries in month t is

$$\begin{pmatrix} \text{ending} \\ \text{inventory} \\ \text{in} \\ \text{month } t-1 \end{pmatrix} + \begin{pmatrix} \text{production} \\ \text{in} \\ \text{month } t \end{pmatrix} - \begin{pmatrix} \text{demand} \\ \text{in} \\ \text{month } t \end{pmatrix}$$

$$+ \begin{pmatrix} \text{lost sales} \\ \text{in} \\ \text{month } t \end{pmatrix} = \begin{pmatrix} \text{ending} \\ \text{inventory} \\ \text{in} \\ \text{month } t \end{pmatrix}$$

Note that the ending inventory in month $t-1$ is also the beginning inventory in month t. Each term in the material-balance equation is a variable, except for demand; demand is a constant given by the demand forecast. Putting the demand constant on the right-hand side of the equation and using our previously introduced variable definitions, we can write the material-balance equation as follows:

$$X_t + I_{t-1} - I_t + L_t = \text{demand in month } t$$

The beginning inventory for the aggregate planning problem is 1000 barrels; therefore, the material balance equations for a 12-month planning horizon are the following ($t = 1$ corresponds to January).

$$X_1 - I_1 + 1000 + L_1 = 1500$$
$$X_2 - I_2 + I_1 + L_2 = 1000$$
$$X_3 - I_3 + I_2 + L_3 = 1900$$
$$X_4 - I_4 + I_3 + L_4 = 2600$$
$$X_5 - I_5 + I_4 + L_5 = 2800$$
$$X_6 - I_6 + I_5 + L_6 = 3100$$
$$X_7 - I_7 + I_6 + L_7 = 3200$$
$$X_8 - I_8 + I_7 + L_8 = 3000$$
$$X_9 - I_9 + I_8 + L_9 = 2000$$
$$X_{10} - I_{10} + I_9 + L_{10} = 1000$$
$$X_{11} - I_{11} + I_{10} + L_{11} = 1800$$
$$X_{12} - I_{12} + I_{11} + L_{12} = 2200$$

Overtime/Undertime Constraint

Since the normal production capacity is 2200 barrels per month, any deviation from this amount represents overtime or undertime. The number of units produced on overtime and the number of units produced on undertime is determined by the following equation for month t:

$$O_t - U_t = X_t - 2200$$

Of course, we cannot have both overtime and undertime in the same month. If $X_t > 2200$, then O_t equals the excess production over normal capacity ($X_t - 2200$). If $X_t < 2200$, then U_t equals the amount of under-capacity production ($2200 - X_t$).

We need a separate overtime/undertime constraint for each month in the planning horizon. The 12 constraints needed are

$$X_1 - O_1 + U_1 = 2200$$
$$X_2 - O_2 + U_2 = 2200$$
$$X_3 - O_3 + U_3 = 2200$$
$$X_4 - O_4 + U_4 = 2200$$
$$X_5 - O_5 + U_5 = 2200$$
$$X_6 - O_6 + U_6 = 2200$$
$$X_7 - O_7 + U_7 = 2200$$
$$X_8 - O_8 + U_8 = 2200$$
$$X_9 - O_9 + U_9 = 2200$$
$$X_{10} - O_{10} + U_{10} = 2200$$
$$X_{11} - O_{11} + U_{11} = 2200$$
$$X_{12} - O_{12} + U_{12} = 2200$$

Production-rate-change Constraints

In order to determine the necessary decreases or increases in the production rate, we write a constraint of the following form for each period:

$$X_t - X_{t-1} = R_t - D_t$$

Note that $X_t - X_{t-1}$ is simply the change in production rate from period $t-1$ to period t. If the difference between the production rate, X_t, and the rate in the previous period, X_{t-1}, is positive, then the increase R_t equals $X_t - X_{t-1}$ and the decrease D_t equals zero; otherwise D_t equals $X_{t-1} - X_t$ and R_t equals zero to reflect the decrease in production rate. Obviously, R_t and D_t cannot both be positive. We need one production-rate-change constraint for each month in the planning horizon. Letting X_0 denote the production rate in the last month's production, we obtain the following 12 constraints:

$$X_1 - X_0 = R_1 - D_1$$
$$X_2 - X_1 = R_2 - D_2$$
$$X_3 - X_2 = R_3 - D_3$$
$$X_4 - X_3 = R_4 - D_4$$
$$X_5 - X_4 = R_5 - D_5$$
$$X_6 - X_5 = R_6 - D_6$$
$$X_7 - X_6 = R_7 - D_7$$
$$X_8 - X_7 = R_8 - D_8$$
$$X_9 - X_8 = R_9 - D_9$$
$$X_{10} - X_9 = R_{10} - D_{10}$$
$$X_{11} - X_{10} = R_{11} - D_{11}$$
$$X_{12} - X_{11} = R_{12} - D_{12}$$

Objective Function

As indicated in the main part of the chapter, the following costs are applicable for the Golden Breweries aggregate production planning problem:

Type of Cost	Cost
Production	$70 per barrel
Inventory-holding	$1.40 per barrel per month
Lost-sales	$90 per barrel
Overtime	$6.50 per barrel
Undertime	$3 per barrel
Production-rate-change	$5 per barrel

The objective function calls for minimizing total costs. It is given by

$$
\begin{aligned}
z = {} & 70(X_1 + X_2 + X_3 + X_4 + X_5 + X_6 \\
& + X_7 + X_8 + X_9 + X_{10} + X_{11} + X_{12}) \\
& + 1.4(I_1 + I_2 + I_3 + I_4 + I_5 + I_6 \\
& + I_7 + I_8 + I_9 + I_{10} + I_{11} + I_{12}) \\
& + 90(L_1 + L_2 + L_3 + L_4 + L_5 + L_6 \\
& + L_7 + L_8 + L_9 + L_{10} + L_{11} + L_{12}) \\
& + 6.5(O_1 + O_2 + O_3 + O_4 + O_5 + O_6 \\
& + O_7 + O_8 + O_9 + O_{10} + O_{11} + O_{12}) \\
& + 3(U_1 + U_2 + U_3 + U_4 + U_5 + U_6 \\
& + U_7 + U_8 + U_9 + U_{10} + U_{11} + U_{12}) \\
& + 5(D_1 + D_2 + D_3 + D_4 + D_5 + D_6 \\
& + D_7 + D_8 + D_9 + D_{10} + D_{11} + D_{12}) \\
& + 5(R_1 + R_2 + R_3 + R_4 + R_5 + R_6 \\
& + R_7 + R_8 + R_9 + R_{10} + R_{11} + R_{12})
\end{aligned}
$$

Linear Programming Solution

This rather small aggregate planning problem involves 84 variables and 36 constraints. It was solved in a few seconds using the computer program MPSX. This is a general-purpose linear programming code written by IBM. The solution is given in Table 14S.1 and graphed in Figure 14S.16. We see that the minimal cost is $1,796,670. This represents a decrease of $126,250,

TABLE 14S.1 Linear Programming Solution to Golden Breweries Aggregate Planning Problem

Month	Production	Production Cost	Inventory	Inventory Cost	Rate-change Cost	Overtime Cost	Undertime Cost
January	2200	$ 154,000	1700	$ 2,380	—	—	—
February	2200	154,000	2900	4,060	—	—	—
March	2200	154,000	3200	4,480	—	—	—
April	2200	154,000	2800	3,920	—	—	—
May	2325	162,750	2325	3,255	625	$ 812.50	—
June	2325	162,750	1550	2,170	—	812.50	—
July	2325	162,750	675	945	—	812.50	—
August	2325	162,750	0	—	—	812.50	—
September	2000	140,000	0	—	1625	—	$ 600
October	1400	98,000	400	560	3000	—	2400
November	1400	98,000	0	—	—	—	2400
December	2200	154,000	0	—	4000	—	—
		$1,757,000		$21,770	$9250	$3250	$5400
			Total cost = $1,796,670				

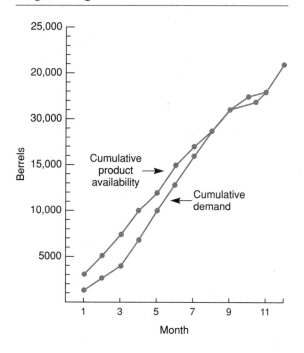

or 6.57 percent, over the plans presented in Tables 14.4 through 14.6. This plan, however, might make an operations manager nervous, since zero inventory is planned for August, September, November, and December. If this is unacceptable, we could add constraints to the model of the form

$$I_t \geq l_t$$

where l_t represents the minimum amount of inventory that should be carried each month—that is, safety stock. The new model could then be solved and the solution examined for acceptability. This suggests that building linear programming models—indeed, any quantitative model—is an iterative process. Solutions to a first model often suggest modifications which lead to an improved model. Thus quantitative methods should not be taken at face value. Nevertheless, they are quite flexible in modeling many different practical situations.

Though this linear programming model took some time to develop, it can be saved in a data file on a computer and used on a routine basis. As demands, costs, or planned inventory levels change, we need only make a few modifications to the model and resolve the problem. Thus the linear program could easily be incorporated into a decision support system for aggregate planning.

SUMMARY AND KEY TERMS

Summary

In this supplement, we showed how linear programming can be used to solve production-planning problems. We saw how the problem-formulation process translates a verbal description of a problem into a mathematical statement of the problem. The mathematical statement is called a model; if the objective function and all the constraint functions are linear, the model is a linear program.

We studied in some detail the formulation and graphical solution process for linear programs involving only two variables. The concluding section of the supplement then showed how a linear programming formulation of the aggregate production-planning problem can be a valuable aid to the operations manager. Such an aid is particularly useful when the problem involves large numbers of variables and constraints. Computer software is now available that make the optimal solution of such models routine.

Key Terms

Constraint
Objective function
Solution
Feasible solution
Optimal solution
Nonnegativity constraints
Mathematical model
Linear program
Constraint function
Linear functions

PROBLEMS

1. Graphing constraint lines is an essential step in the graphical method. Show a separate graph of the constraint lines and feasible solutions for each of the following constraints:

a. $3x_1 + 2x_2 \leq 18$
b. $12x_1 + 8x_2 \geq 480$
c. $5x_1 + 10x_2 = 200$

2. Show a separate graph of the constraint lines and feasible solutions for each of the following constraints:
  a. $3x_1 - 4x_2 \geq 60$
  b. $-6x_1 + 5x_2 \leq 60$
  c. $5x_1 - 2x_2 \leq 0$

3. Solve the following linear program:

$$\max\ 5x_1 + 5x_2$$
$$\text{s.t.}$$
$$1x_1 \qquad\qquad \leq 100$$
$$1x_2 \leq 80$$
$$2x_1 + 4x_2 \leq 400$$
$$x_1, x_2 \qquad \geq 0$$

4. Consider the following linear programming problem:

$$\max\ 2x_1 + 3x_2$$
$$\text{s.t.}$$
$$1x_1 + 2x_2 \leq 6$$
$$5x_1 + 3x_2 \leq 15$$
$$x_1, x_2 \qquad \geq 0$$

Find the optimal solution. What is the value of the objective function at the optimal solution?

5. Consider the following linear programming problem:

$$\max\ 3x_1 + 3x_2$$
$$\text{s.t.}$$
$$2x_1 + 4x_2 \leq 12$$
$$6x_1 + 4x_2 \leq 24$$
$$x_1, x_2 \qquad \geq 0$$

  a. Find the optimal solution.
  b. If the objective function were changed to $2x_1 + 6x_2$, what would the optimal solution be?
  c. How many extreme points are there? What are the values of x_1 and x_2 at each extreme point?

6. Par, Inc., is a small manufacturer of golf equipment and supplies. Par has been convinced by its distributor that there is an existing market for both a medium-priced golf bag, referred to as a standard model, and a high-priced golf bag, referred to as a deluxe model. The distributor is so confident of the market that if Par can make the bags at a competitive price, the distributor has agreed to purchase all the bags that Par can manufacture over the next three months. A careful analysis of the manufacturing requirements resulted in Table 14S.2, which shows the production time requirements for the four required manufacturing operations and the accounting department's estimate of the profit contribution per bag.

The director of manufacturing estimates that 630 hours of cutting and dyeing time, 600 hours of sewing time, 708 hours of finishing time, and 135 hours of inspection and packaging time will be available for the production of golf bags during the next 3 months.

  a. Assuming that the company wants to maximize profit, how many bags of each model should Par manufacture?
  b. What is the profit Par can earn with the above production quantities?
  c. How many hours of production time will be scheduled for each operation?
  d. What is the slack time in each operation?

7. Refer to Problem 6. Suppose that the selling price for the Par, Inc., standard bag must be reduced by $7 due to competitive pressures. No other costs or prices are affected.
  a. What are the optimal production quantities for Par, Inc.?
  b. What constraint lines combine to form the optimal extreme point?

8. Suppose that the management of Par, Inc., (Problem 6) encounters each of the following situations:
  a. The accounting department revises its estimate of profit contribution for the deluxe bag to $18 per bag.
  b. A new low-cost material is available for the standard bag, and the profit contribution per standard bag can be increased to $20 per bag. (Assume that the profit contribution of the deluxe bag is the original $9 value.)

TABLE 14S.2		Production Time (Hours)				Profit per Bag
Production Time Requirements for Problem 6	Product	Cutting/ Dyeing	Sewing	Finishing	Inspection/ Packaging	
	Standard	7/10	1/2	1	1/10	$10
	Deluxe	1	5/6	2/3	1/4	$ 9

c. New sewing equipment is available that would increase the sewing operation capacity to 750 hours. (Assume that $10x_1 + 9x_2$ is the appropriate objective function.)

If each of the above conditions is encountered separately, what are the optimal solution and profit contribution for each situation?

9. The Erlanger Manufacturing Company makes two products. The profit estimates are $25 for each unit of product 1 sold and $30 for each unit of product 2 sold. The labor-hour requirements for the products in each of three production departments are summarized below.

Department	Product 1	Product 2
A	1.50	3.00
B	2.00	1.00
C	.25	.25

The production supervisors in the departments have estimated that the following number of labor hours will be available during the next month: 450 hours in department A, 350 hours in department B, and 50 hours in department C. Assuming that the company is interested in maximizing profits, answer the following:

a. What is the linear programming model for this problem?
b. Find the optimal solution. How much of each product should be produced, and what is the projected profit?
c. What is the scheduled production time and slack time in each department?

10. M&D Chemicals produces two products that are sold as raw materials to companies manufacturing bath soaps, laundry detergents, and other soap products. Based on an analysis of current inventory levels and potential demand for the coming month, M&D's management has specified that the total production for products 1 and 2 combined must be at least 350 gallons. Also, a major customer's order for 125 gallons of product 1 must be satisfied. Product 1 requires 2 hours of processing time per gallon and product 2 requires 1 hour of processing time per gallon; for the coming month, 600 hours of processing time are available. Production costs are $2 per gallon for product 1 and $3 per gallon for product 2.

a. Determine the production quantities that will satisfy the requirements specified above at minimum cost.
b. What is the total product cost?
c. Identify the amount of any surplus production.

11. Refer again to the M&D Chemicals situation in Problem 10. Suppose, because of the use of some new equipment, that the production cost for product 2 is reduced to $1.50 per gallon.
a. What are the optimal production quantities for M&D Chemicals?
b. What constraint lines combine to form the optimal extreme point?

12. Car Phones, Inc., sells two models of car telephones: model x and model y. Records show that 3 hours of sales time are used for each model x phone that is sold, and 5 hours of sales time for each model y phone. A total of 600 hours of sales time is available for the next 4-week period. In addition, management planning policies call for minimum sales goals of 25 units for both model x and model y.
a. Show the feasible region for the Car Phones, Inc., problem.
b. Assuming the company makes a $40 profit contribution for each model x sold and a $50 profit contribution for each model y sold, what is the optimal sales goal for the company for the next 4-week period?
c. Develop a constraint and show the feasible region if management adds the restriction that Car Phones must sell at least as many model y phones as model x phones.
d. What is the new optimal solution if the constraint in part (c) is added to the problem?

13. Photo Chemicals produces two types of photograph developing fluids. Both products cost Photo Chemicals $1 per gallon to produce. Based on an analysis of current inventory levels and outstanding orders for the next month, Photo Chemicals' management has specified that at least 30 gallons of product 1 and at least 20 gallons of product 2 must be produced during the next 2 weeks. Management has also stated that an existing inventory of highly perishable raw material required in the production of both fluids must be used within the next 2 weeks. The current inventory of the perishable raw material is 80 pounds. While more of this raw material can be ordered if necessary, any of the current inventory that is not used within the next 2 weeks will spoil; hence the management requirement that at least 80 pounds be used in the

next 2 weeks. Furthermore, it is known that product 1 requires 1 pound of this perishable raw material per gallon and product 2 requires 2 pounds of raw material per gallon. Since Photo Chemicals' objective is to keep its production costs at the minimum possible level, the firm's management is looking for a minimum cost production plan that uses all the 80 pounds of perishable raw material and provides at least 30 gallons of product 1 and at least 20 gallons of product 2. What is the minimum cost solution?

14. Reconsider the Par, Inc., situation in Problem 6. Suppose that management adds the requirements that at least 500 standard bags and at least 360 deluxe bags must be produced.
   a. Graph the constraints for this revised Par, Inc., problem. What happens to the feasible region? Explain.
   b. If there are no feasible solutions, explain what is needed to produce 500 standard bags and 360 deluxe bags.

15. Management of High Tech Services (HTS) would like to develop a model that will help allocate technicians' time between service calls to regular contract customers and new customers. A maximum of 80 hours of technician time is available over the 2-week planning period. In order to satisfy cash flow requirements, at least $800 in revenue (per technician) must be generated during the 2-week period. Technician time for regular customers generates $25 per hour. However, technician time for new customers only generates an average of $8 per hour because in many cases a new customer contact does not provide billable services. To ensure that new customer contacts are being maintained, the time technicians spend on new customer contacts must be at least 60 percent of the time technicians spend on regular customer contacts. Given the above revenue and policy requirements, HTS would like to determine how to allocate technicians' time between regular customers and new customers so that the total number of customers contacted during the 2-week period will be maximized. Technicians require an average of 50 minutes for each regular customer contact and 1 hour for each new customer contact.
   a. Develop a linear programming model that will enable HTS to determine how to allocate technicians' time between regular customers and new customers.
   b. Graph the feasible region.

c. Solve the appropriate simultaneous linear equations to determine the values of x_1 and x_2 at each extreme point of the feasible region.
   d. Find the optimal solution.

Note to Student. The following problems have been designed to give you an understanding and appreciation of the broad range of problems in P/OM that can be formulated as linear programs. They are more challenging than the previous problems because most require more than two decision variables to formulate the problem correctly. However, you will need access to a linear programming computer package in order to develop the solution and make the requested interpretations.

16. *Product mix.* Better Products, Inc., is a small manufacturer of three products. The products are produced on two machines. In a typical week, 40 hours of time are available on each machine. Profit contribution and production time in hours per unit are as follows:

	Product		
	1	2	3
Profit/unit	$30	$50	$20
Machine 1 time/unit	0.5	2.0	0.75
Machine 2 time/unit	1.0	1.0	0.5

Two operators are required for machine 1. Thus 2 hours of labor must be scheduled for each hour of machine 1 time. Only one operator is required for machine 2. A maximum of 100 labor hours is available for assignment to the machines during the coming week. Other production requirements are that product 1 cannot account for more than 50 percent of the units produced and that product 3 must account for at least 20 percent of the units produced.
   a. How many units of each product should be produced in order to maximize the profit contribution? What is the projected weekly profit associated with your solution?
   b. How many hours of production time will be scheduled on each machine?

17. *Overtime planning.* Hartmann Company is trying to determine how much of each of two products

should be produced over the coming planning period. The only serious constraints involve labor availability in three departments. Shown below is information concerning labor availability, labor utilization, and product profitability.

| | Product | | Hours of Labor Available |
	1	2	
Profit unit	$30.00	$15.00	—
Dept. A hours/unit	1.00	0.35	100
Dept. B hours/unit	0.30	0.20	36
Dept. C hours/unit	0.20	0.50	50

a. Develop a linear programming model of the Hartmannn Company's problem. Solve it to determine the optimal production quantities of products 1 and 2.

b. Suppose that 10, 6, and 8 hours of overtime may be scheduled in departments A, B, and C, respectively. The cost per hour of overtime is $18 in department A, $22.50 in department B, and $12 in department C. Formulate a linear programming model that can be used to determine optimal production quantities if overtime is made available. What are the optimal production quantities, and what is the revised profit? How much overtime do you recommend using in each department? What is the increase in profit if overtime is used?

18. *Quality assurance.* Hilltop Coffee manufactures a coffee product by blending three types of coffee beans. The cost per pound and the available pounds of each bean are as follows:

Bean	Cost/Pound	Available Pounds
1	$0.50	500
2	0.70	600
3	0.45	400

Consumer tests with coffee products were used to provide quality ratings on a 0-to-100 scale, with higher ratings indicating higher quality. Product quality standards for the blended coffee require a consumer rating for aroma to be at least 75 and a consumer rating for taste to be at least 80. The individual ratings of the aroma and taste for coffee made from 100 percent of each bean are as follows:

Bean	Aroma Rating	Taste Rating
1	75	86
2	85	88
3	60	75

It can be assumed that the aroma and taste attributes of the coffee blend will be a weighted average of the attributes of the beans used in the blend.

a. What is the minimum cost blend of the three beans that will meet the quality standards and provide 1000 pounds of the blended coffee product?

b. What is the bean cost per pound of the coffee blend?

19. *Blending problem.* Ajax Fuels, Inc., is developing a new additive for airplane fuels. The additive is a mixture of three liquid ingredients: A, B, and C. For proper performance, the total amount of additive (amount of A + amount of B + amount of C) must be at least 10 ounces per gallon of fuel. However, because of safety reasons, the amount of additive must not exceed 15 ounces per gallon of fuel. The mix or blend of the three ingredients is critical. At least 1 ounce of ingredient A must be used for every ounce of ingredient B. The amount of ingredient C must be greater than one-half the amount of ingredient A. If the cost per ounce for ingredients A, B, and C is $0.10, $0.03, and $0.09, respectively, find the minimum cost mixture of A, B, and C for each gallon of airplane fuel.

20. *Labor planning.* G. Kunz and Sons, Inc., manufactures two products used in the heavy equipment industry. Both products require manufacturing operations in two departments. Production time in hours and profit figures for the two products are as follows:

	Product 1	Product 2
Profit/unit	$25	$20
Dept. A hours	6	8
Dept. B hours	12	10

For the coming production period, Kunz has a total of 900 hours of labor available, which can be allocated to either of the two departments. Let b_1 be the hours assigned to department A and b_2 be the hours assigned to department B. Find the production plan and labor allocation (hours assigned in each department) that will maximize profits.

21. *Production routing.* Lurix Electronics manufactures two products that can be produced on two different production lines. Both products have their lowest production costs when produced on the more modern of the two production lines. However, the modern production line does not have the capacity to handle the total production. As a result, some production will have to be routed to an older production line. Table 14S.3 shows the data for total production requirements, production line capacities, and production costs.

Formulate a linear programming model that can be used to make the production routing decision. What are the recommended decision and the total cost? (Use notation of the form x_{11} = units of product 1 produced on line 1.)

22. *Make or buy.* The Carson Stapler Manufacturing Company forecasts a 5000-unit demand for its Sure-Hold model during the next quarter. This stapler is assembled from three major components: base, staple cartridge, and handle. Until now Carson has manufactured all three components. However, the forecast of 5000 units is a new high in sales volume, and it is doubtful that the firm will have sufficient production capacity to make all the components. The company is considering contracting a local firm to produce at least some of the components. The production time requirements per unit are given in Table 14S.4.

After considering the firm's overhead, material, and labor costs, the accounting department has determined the unit manufacturing cost for each component. These data, along with the purchase price quotations by the contracting firm, are as follows:

Component	Manufacturing Cost ($)	Purchase Cost ($)
Base	$0.75	$0.95
Cartridge	0.40	0.55
Handle	1.10	1.40

a. Determine the make-or-buy decision for Carson that will meet the 5000-unit demand at a minimum total cost. How many units of each component should be made and how many purchased?

b. Which departments are limiting the manufacturing volume?

c. Suppose that up to 80 hours of overtime can be scheduled in department A. What do you recommend?

23. *Equipment acquisition.* The Two-Rivers Oil Company near Pittsburgh transports gasoline to its distributors by trucks. The company has recently received a contract to begin supplying gasoline

TABLE 14S.3
Production Data for Problem 21

	Production Cost/Unit		Minimum Production Requirements
	Modern Line	Old Line	
Product 1	$3.00	$5.00	500 units
Product 2	$2.50	$4.00	700 units
Production line capacities	800	600	

TABLE 14S.4
Production Time Requirements per Unit for Problem 22.

	Production Time (Hours)			Total Department Time Available (Hours)
Department	Base	Cartridge	Handle	
A	0.03	0.02	0.05	400
B	0.04	0.02	0.04	400
C	0.02	0.03	0.01	400

distributors in southern Ohio and has $600,000 available to spend on the necessary expansion of its fleet of gasoline tank trucks. Three models of gasoline tank trucks are available.

Truck Model	Capacity (gallons)	Purchase Cost ($)	Monthly Operating Costs* ($)
Super Tanker	5000	$67,000	$550
Regular Line	2500	55,000	425
Econo-Tanker	1000	46,000	350
*Includes depreciation			

The company estimates that the monthly demand for the region will be 550,000 gallons of gasoline. Due to the size and speed difference of the trucks, the different truck models will vary in terms of the number of deliveries or round trips possible per month. Trip capacities are estimated at 15 per month for the Super Tanker, 20 per month for the Regular Line, and 25 per month for the Econo-Tanker. Based on maintenance and driver availability, the firm does not want to add more than 15 new vehicles to its fleet. In addition, the company would like to make sure that it purchases at least three of the new Econo-Tankers to use on the short-run, low-demand routes. As a final constraint, the company does not want more than half of the new models to be Super Tankers.

a. If the company wishes to satisfy the gasoline demand with a minimum monthly operating expense, how many models of each truck should be purchased?

b. If the company did not require at least three Econo-Tankers and allows as many Super Tankers as needed, what would the company strategy be?

24. *Multiperiod planning.* The Silver Star Bicycle Company will be manufacturing both men's and women's models for their Easy-Pedal 10-speed bicycles during the next 2 months, and the company would like a production schedule indicating how many bicycles of each model should be produced in each month. Current demand forecasts call for 150 men's and 125 women's models to be shipped during the first month and 200 men's and 150 women's models to be shipped during the second month. Additional data are shown in Table 14S.5.

Last month the company used a total of 4000 hours of labor. The company's labor relations policy will not allow the combined total hours of labor (manufacturing plus assembly) to increase or decrease by more than 500 hours from month to month. In addition, the company charges monthly inventory at the rate of 2 percent of the production cost based on the inventory levels at the end of the month. The company would like to have at least 25 units of each model in inventory at the end of the 2 months.

a. Establish a production schedule that minimizes production and inventory costs and satisfies the labor-smoothing, demand, and inventory requirements. What inventories will be maintained, and what are the monthly labor requirements?

b. If the company changed the constraints so that monthly labor increases and decreases could not exceed 250 hours, what would happen to the production schedule? How much will the cost increase? What would you recommend?

25. *Labor balancing.* The Williams Calculator Company manufactures two kinds of calculators: the TW100 and the TW200. The assembly process requires three people. The assembly times are as follows:

	Assembler		
	1	2	3
TW100	4 min	2 min	3½ min
TW200	3 min	4 min	3 min
Maximum hours available per day	8	8	8

Model	Production Costs	Labor Required for Manufacturing (Hours)	Labor Required for Assembly (Hours)	Current Inventory
Men's	$40	10	3	20
Women's	$30	8	2	30

TABLE 14S.5

Data for Problem 24

The company policy is to balance workloads on all assembly jobs. In fact, management wants to schedule work so that no assembler will have more than 30 minutes more work per day than other assemblers. This means that in a regular 8-hour shift, all assemblers will be assigned at least 7½ hours of work. If the firm makes a $2.50 profit for each TW100 and a $3.50 profit for each TW200, how many units of each calculator should be produced per day? How much time will each assembler be assigned per day?

Material Requirements Planning

I nventories that support the production process are called *manufacturing inventories*. Since manufacturing inventories serve a different purpose than finished goods inventories, different management techniques are required. **Material requirements planning,** or **MRP,** is a technique used to plan for and control manufacturing inventories. MRP is actually a new name for an old concept that has been made practical because of the ability of computers and MRP software packages to carry out the calculations required in a fast and efficient manner.

Figure 15.1 is a flow chart of the production-planning and scheduling process introduced in the previous chapter. The master production schedule lists the finished products that must be produced to meet anticipated demand. Many of these products consist of individual parts or subassemblies that must be manufactured or purchased. The data that shows the makeup of each product is given in the bill of materials, which we discussed in Chapter 8. Using these data, MRP determines the requirements and schedule for (1) manufacturing the components and subassemblies, and/or (2) purchasing the materials needed in order to meet the requirements of the master production schedule. Essentially, MRP uses the master production schedule to project the requirements for the individual parts or subassemblies. These requirements are compared with on-hand inventory levels and scheduled receipts on a time-phased basis so that lots can be scheduled to be produced or received as needed. The purpose of MRP is to ensure that materials and all the individual parts and subassemblies are available in the right quantities and at the right time so that finished products can be completed according to the master production schedule.

The key inputs to an MRP system are the master production schedule, inventory records, and bills of materials for each product that is manufactured. The primary output of an MRP system is a report which provides (1) the purchasing department with a schedule for obtaining raw materials and purchased parts, and (2) the production managers with a detailed schedule for manufacturing the product and controlling manufacturing inventories.

Although it is difficult to conceptualize without going into more detail, we must point out that MRP is more than simply a method of projecting the requirements of the individual components of a product. An *MRP system* has three major functions: control of inventory levels, assignment of priorities for components, and determination of capacity requirements at a more detailed level than the process of rough-cut capacity requirements planning. In this chapter we present the basic concepts and applications of MRP.

15.1 DEPENDENT DEMAND AND THE MRP CONCEPT

In Chapter 12 we discussed inventory management for *independent demand* items such as finished goods. Forecasts of demand for finished goods are needed. This chapter focuses on planning and controlling manufacturing inventories such as raw materials, components, and subassemblies that are used in the production of finished goods. The demand for such items is *dependent* on a number of finished

FIGURE 15.1 The Production-planning and Scheduling Process

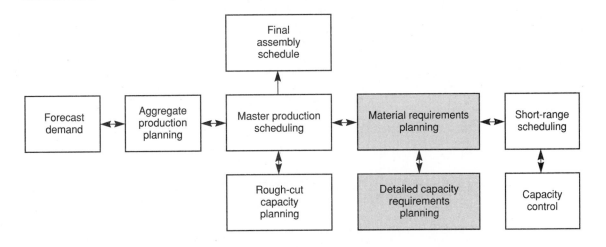

goods that are scheduled to be produced, and can be derived from the master production schedule.

In order to illustrate dependent demand and the MRP concept, consider the Finger Lakes Celebration Doll Co. The company purchases unpainted ceramic dolls that are carefully hand-painted in their upstate New York factory. Suppose that product demand for one of Finger Lake's popular Birthday Celebration Dolls consists of independent demand from many customers. Since this independent demand occurs somewhat randomly, the total demand rate is often fairly constant, and the assumptions needed to support the use of the production lot-size model are reasonable. (See Chapter 13.)

The finished-product inventory level is shown at the top of Figure 15.2. When production (that is, painting) of the finished doll is initiated (point *A* on the time axis), the unpainted dolls are withdrawn from inventory in order to meet production needs. The inventory level for unpainted dolls is shown at the bottom of Figure 15.2. When the unpainted-doll inventory level falls below its reorder point, an order is placed with the supplier. The shipment is received at point *B* and the inventory is replenished. However, note that the unpainted doll is not needed again until the next production run for the finished product which is scheduled to occur at point *C*. Clearly, the investment in the unpainted doll inventory from points *B* to *C* is unnecessary. We can eliminate this unnecessary component inventory by "backing up" from point *C* according to the purchase lead time so that the unpainted dolls will arrive just at time *C*. This situation is illustrated in Figure 15.3. Note that the unpainted-doll inventory level and corresponding inventory investment is less in Figure 15.3 than it is in Figure 15.2.

What makes this process difficult to implement is that many products consist of dozens or hundreds of components, many of which are successively dependent on others. Therefore, there must be accurate data and a reliable computer system to perform the many calculations that are required. The reduction of computer costs and development of software over the past two decades have made MRP an important part of many production systems.

FIGURE 15.2

Finished-product and Purchased-part Inventory Levels Without an MRP System

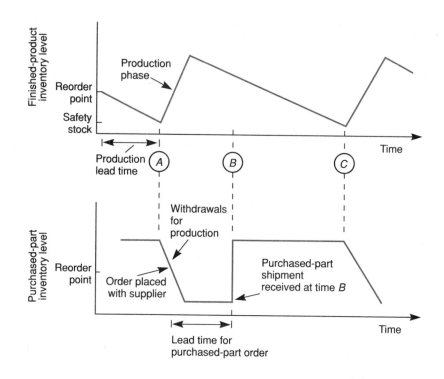

Table 15.1 presents some results of a survey conducted by Anderson, et al. on the type of industries that use MRP and the characteristics of their manufacturing processes.[1] From Table 15.1, we see that MRP is being used in all types of industries and is especially predominant in the machine tool, electronic, and transportation equipment industries. These are characterized by a combination of make-to-order and make-to-stock products and assembly/fabrication manufacturing.

15.2 INFORMATION SYSTEM DESIGN FOR MRP

Because a large amount of data must be stored and processed in an MRP system, a computerized information system is the basis for any successful MRP implementation. An MRP information system must include components which contain the data in the master production schedule (MPS) and the bill of materials (BOM), as well as computer software that can access and process this data in order to produce the reports needed by production and purchasing. Since material requirements planning begins with the master production schedule, our discussion of the MRP information system begins with the MPS.

---

[1]John C. Anderson, Roger G. Schroeder, Sharon E. Tupy, and Edna M. White, "Material Requirements Planning Systems: The State of the Art," *Production and Inventory Management,* Fourth Quarter, 1982, Journal of the American Production and Inventory Control Society, Inc.

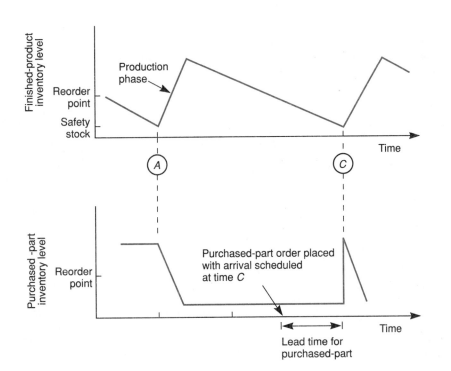

Recall that the MPS provides a statement of the number of finished products to produce in each time period, generally weekly. Consider, for example, the MPS for the Spiecker Manufacturing Company, a major producer of outdoor home power equipment. A portion of their MPS is given in Figure 15.4; thus, for example, 1250 14-inch snowblowers are scheduled to be made during week 15. Given this master production schedule, operations managers must determine when the various components that make up the product should be manufactured or purchased. First we need a list of the components in the product. This is usually defined by the bill of materials.

Recall from Chapter 8 that the bill of materials (BOM) is a structured parts list; however, it differs from an ordinary parts list in that it shows the hierarchical relationship between the finished product and its various components. An example of a BOM for the Spiecker Manufacturing Company is shown in Figure 15.5. This figure shows the bill of materials for a 14-inch snowblower. The finished product is shown at the top of the hierarchy (level 0). It consists of one main housing assembly, one wheel assembly, one engine assembly, and one handle assembly. Also, recall from Chapter 8 that the components at each level of the BOM hierarchy are "parent items" for those at the next level. Thus, for example, the wheel assembly (level 1) is the parent item for the level 2 components, blade assembly and wheels. From the BOM, we can determine exactly how many components are needed in order to produce the quantity of finished products stated in the master production schedule.

Bill of Materials

TABLE 15.1

Industry
Application of
MRP

Industry Representation			
Industry	Total Companies	MRP Companies	% MRP
Food	16	8	50
Tobacco	1	0	0
Lumber and wood	5	1	20
Paper	12	4	33
Chemicals	15	8	53
Petroleum and coal	5	1	20
Rubber and plastic	15	7	47
Primary metal	1	0	0
Fabricated metals	95	47	49
Machinery	166	108	65
Electric-electronic	90	68	76
Instruments	34	24	71
Transportation equipment	67	50	75
Misc. manufacturing	61	46	75
Apparel	5	2	40
Furniture	10	5	50
Printing and publishing	6	3	50
Leather	0	0	0
Stone, clay, glass	4	2	50
Other manufacturing	54	24	44

Plant Characteristics			
	Total Response (%)	MRP Companies (%)	Non-MRP Companies (%)
Type of products			
Make-to-order	16.3	14.1	20.1
Make-to-stock	13.3	13.7	12.9
Both	70.4	72.2	67.0
	100.0	100.0	100.0
Type of manufacturing			
Assembly	7.1	7.2	7.5
Fabrication	9.7	6.3	17.0
Both	83.2	86.5	75.5
	100.0	100.0	100.0
Type of process			
Job shop	41.3	38.8	45.8
Continuous process	11.5	9.1	17.6
Assembly line	22.8	22.4	24.5
Combination	24.4	29.7	12.1
	100.0	100.0	100.0

Source: Production and Inventory Management, Fourth Quarter, 1982, Journal of the American Production and Inventory Control Society, Inc.

Figure 15.5, of course, is greatly simplified. The actual BOM is exploded so that every individual part is identified in its assembly hierarchy. In an MRP system, the file containing the bill of materials is sometimes called the *product-structure file.*

FIGURE 15.4

Portion of
Master
Production
Schedule for
Spiecker
Manufacturing

Item . . .	End of week					
	11	12	13	14	15	16 . . .
•						
•						
•						
12-inch snowblower	0	250	750	250	250	0
14-inch snowblower	1000	0	500	1500	1250	250
•						
•						
•						

FIGURE 15.5   A Portion of the BOM for the 14-inch Snowblower

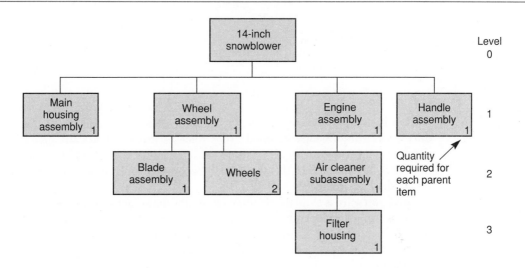

Inventory status information must be maintained on each item in the bill of   **Inventory Files**
materials. Typical data elements in an inventory file are

Part number
On-hand quantity
On-order quantity
Cost data
Procurement lead time

This file must be linked to production and purchasing in order to update orders,
receipts, and issues from stock.

A schematic diagram of an MRP information system is given in Figure 15.6. The   **The MRP**
BOM, inventory files, and MPS are the primary inputs to the MRP computer   **Information**
software. The ouput from MRP calculations is the determination of the amount   **System**
of each BOM item required, along with the dates they are needed. This infor-

FIGURE 15.6
**An MRP
Information
System**

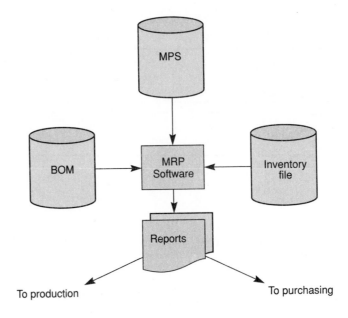

mation is used to plan order releases for purchased parts and for in-house production of components. Planned order releases are automatically generated by the MRP information system, along with orders that should be rescheduled, modified, or canceled. In this way, MRP becomes a tool for operational planning by production managers.

MRP software is available from many major manufacturers of computer equipment as well as independent software developers. Usually, the MRP software is only one module in a total manufacturing package that includes forecasting, order entry, bills of materials and inventory file maintenance, and shop floor control modules.

15.3 MRP CALCULATIONS

In MRP terminology, time periods, which are called **buckets**, are usually 1 week in length. Although small buckets such as 1 week are good for scheduling production over a short time horizon they may be too precise for long-range planning. Thus, larger buckets are often used as the planning horizon gets larger. For the Spiecker Manufacturing problem, we assume that all buckets are 1 week in length.

The MPS in Figure 15.4 calls for the final assembly of 1250 units of the 14-inch snowblower during week 15 of the current planning period. We shall use this to illustrate the MRP calculations. Similar calculations must be performed for *every* end item and week on the MPS. We first consider the question of *when* to schedule production or purchase orders for assemblies or components in order to meet this MPS.

Suppose that the time required to assemble the four main assemblies of the snowblower is 1 week (this is called the final-assembly lead time). Then 1250 units each of the main-housing assembly, wheel assembly, engine assembly, and handle assembly must be completed no later than the end of week 14. The accompanying table gives the production lead times for the remaining components and assemblies.

Component or Assembly	Lead Time (Weeks)
Main housing assembly	3
Wheel assembly	1
Blade assembly	2
Wheels	1
Engine assembly	4
Air cleaner subassembly	1
Filter housing	2
Handle assembly	1

Figure 15.7 shows when the production of each component or assembly must be carried out in order to complete the final assembly by week 15. This figure was developed by "backing up" from the time the component or assembly is required by the amount of the lead time. This process is called **time phasing**. For instance, to have the main housing assembly ready by the end of week 14, pro-

---

FIGURE 15.7   Time-phased Assembly Schedule

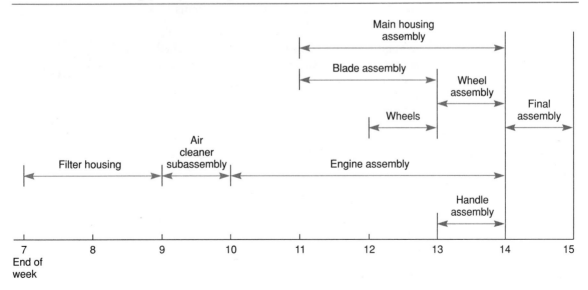

duction must be started by the end of week 11, since the lead time is 3 weeks. Time-phasing calculations for the engine assembly, which consists of three BOM levels of components, are as follows:

	End of Week	
Complete order for engine assemblies:	14	
Minus lead time for engine assemblies:	4	
Place an order for engine assemblies:	10	← Order engine assemblies
Complete order for air cleaner subassemblies:	10	
Minus lead time of air cleaner subassemblies:	1	
Place an order for air cleaner subassemblies:	9	← Order air cleaner subassemblies
Complete order for filter housings:	9	
Minus lead time of filter housings:	2	
Place an order for filter housings:	7	← Order filter housings

The next question we consider is *how many* components or assemblies to produce. Since 1250 of the 14-inch snowblowers are required in week 15, we can compute the *gross requirements* of each component or assembly using the BOM. The gross component requirement is the quantity of the component needed to support production at the next higher level of assembly. For example, the gross component requirement for the filter housing is the number of filter housings required to meet the number of air cleaner subassemblies needed; the gross component requirement for the air cleaner subassembly is the number of air cleaners needed to meet the requirement for the engine assembly; and so on.

Gross requirements, however, must be adjusted by the number of units in inventory and the scheduled receipts. *Scheduled receipts* are those orders that have already been placed and are due to be delivered. (In our illustration we assume, for simplicity, that all scheduled receipts are zero.) Table 15.2 gives the current inventory levels for each component or assembly.

The formula for computing the net requirements is

$$\begin{pmatrix} \text{Net component} \\ \text{requirement} \end{pmatrix} = \begin{pmatrix} \text{gross component} \\ \text{requirement} \end{pmatrix} - \begin{pmatrix} \text{scheduled} \\ \text{receipts} \end{pmatrix} - \begin{pmatrix} \text{number of} \\ \text{components} \\ \text{in inventory} \end{pmatrix}$$

TABLE 15.2

On-hand Inventory for the Spiecker Manufacturing Example

Component or Assembly	Inventory
Main housing assembly	400
Wheel assembly	200
Blade assembly	800
Wheels	2300
Engine assembly	450
Air cleaner assembly	250
Filter housing	500
Handle assembly	400

The computations of net requirements for each component or assembly are given as follows:

Quantity of snowblowers to be produced:	1250	(level 0)
Gross requirements, main housing assembly:	1250	(level 1)
Less main housing assemblies in inventory:	400	
Net requirements, main housing assembly:	850	
Gross requirements, wheel assembly:	1250	(level 1)
Less wheel assemblies in inventory:	200	
Net requirements, wheel assemblies:	1050	
Gross requirements, blade assembly:	1050	(level 2)
Less blade assemblies in inventory:	800	
Net requirements, blade assembly:	250	
Gross requirements, wheels:	2100	(level 2)
Less wheels in inventory:	2300	
Net requirements, wheels:	(200)	← (0 required)
Gross requirements, engine assembly:	1250	(level 1)
Less engine assemblies in inventory:	450	
Net requirements, engine assembly:	800	
Gross requirements, air cleaner subassembly:	800	(level 2)
Less air cleaner subassemblies in inventory:	250	
Net requirements, air cleaner subassembly:	550	
Gross requirements, filter housing:	550	(level 3)
Less filter housings in inventory:	500	
Net requirements, filter housing:	50	
Gross requirements, handle assembly:	1250	(level 1)
Less handle assemblies in inventory:	400	
Net requirements, handle assembly:	850	

Note that, although the net requirement for the engine assembly is 800, MRP uses the dependent demand information to show that only 550 air cleaners and 50 filter housings are needed.

We can organize the calculations shown and the time-phasing information into a table called an *item record*, as shown in Figure 15.8. The time phased net requirements are referred to as *planned order releases*. Lot-sizing techniques, such as the ones introduced in Chapter 13, are usually used to group planned order releases into production lots to reduce setups. The components are scheduled so that they are made available only when required for the next higher level of assembly. If the BOM is exploded into detailed part requirements, a complete schedule for shop orders and purchase requisitions is available.

The calculations shown are only for *1 week* of the MPS. Clearly the total number of calculations is enormous; thus a computer is essential. Fortunately, because of modern computer technology, we find that what was an unmanageable problem for earlier manual approaches is now routinely handled by an MRP system.

MRP systems must be capable of adapting to changes in forecasts, lead times, product structures, and so on. There are two fundamental approaches for updating net requirements in response to such changes. In the **regeneration approach,**

Regeneration Versus Net Change Systems

FIGURE 15.8 MRP Item Record Illustrating Time Phasing

					End of Week				
	7	8	9	10	11	12	13	14	15
Snowblower: lead time, 1 week									
Gross requirements									1250
Scheduled receipts									0
On-hand inventory									0
Net requirements									1250
Planned order releases								1250	
Main housing: lead time, 3 weeks									
Gross requirements								1250	
Scheduled receipts								0	
On-hand inventory								400	
Net requirements								850	
Planned order releases					850				
Wheel assembly: lead time, 1 week									
Gross requirements								1250	
Scheduled receipts								0	
On-hand inventory								200	
Net requirements								1050	
Planned order releases							1050		
Blade assembly: lead time, 2 weeks									
Gross requirements							1050		
Scheduled receipts							0		
On-hand inventory							800		
Net requirements							250		
Planned order releases				250					
Wheels: lead time, 1 week									
Gross requirements							2100		
Scheduled receipts							0		
On-hand inventory							2300		
Net requirements							(200)		
Planned order releases							0		
Engne assembly: lead time, 4 weeks									
Gross requirements								1250	
Scheduled receipts								0	
On-hand inventory								450	
Net requirements								800	
Planned order releases				800					
Air cleaner subassembly: lead time, 1 week									
Gross requirements				800					
Scheduled receipts				0					
On-hand inventory				250					
Net requirements				550					
Planned order releases			550						
Filter housing: lead time, 2 weeks									
Gross requirements			550						
Scheduled receipts			0						
On-hand inventory			500						
Net requirements			50						
Planned order releases	50								
Handle assembly: lead time, 1 week									
Gross requirements								1250	
Scheduled receipts								0	
On-hand inventory								400	
Net requirements								850	
Planned order releases							850		

the entire materials plan is recalculated periodically—for instance, each week—based on current information. This method usually consumes a large amount of computer time. In the **net change approach,** the MRP system recalculates requirements *whenever necessary* but only for those components affected by a change. Both approaches are effective; however regeneration is easier to implement because the recalculations are done periodically. On the other hand, regeneration is less responsive; information is only current at the time the calculations are done. Although net change is more difficult to implement, it is highly responsive to changes in requirements and provides more timely information. Table 15.3 summarizes the differences between the two approaches.

15.4 USES AND BENEFITS OF MRP

The outputs available from an MRP information system provide timely and useful information to production and inventory managers. The three principal uses of MRP are for

1. planning and controlling inventory
2. detailed capacity planning
3. priority planning on the shop floor

The calculations performed by MRP yield planned order releases for purchased parts and manufactured components. In this fashion, MRP assists operations managers in planning and controlling inventories by answering the basic questions

Inventory Planning and Control

TABLE 15.3   Regeneration Versus Net Change Systems

Key System Characteristics	Regeneration	Net Change Approach
Frequency of replanning	Limited—weekly or less	High—daily or continuous
Planning trigger	The entire master schedule on a regular basis	Changes in the status of the master schedule or specific parts
Extent of explosion	Every item in the master schedule	Only items with status changes
Processing mode	Batch	On-line or batch
Validity of requirements data over time	Deteriorates between batch processes	No deterioration because of continuous file updating
Data processing efficiency	Highly efficient	Relatively inefficient
Response time to change	Limited by infrequency of replanning	Quick because of frequent replanning or on-line updating
Ability to purge inaccurate requirements planning	Yes	No
Files that can be updated	Inventory data only	Inventory data and requirements data
Number of operating phases	Two—periodic requirements planning and intraperiod file updating	One—combined updating and requirements planning

Source: Gene J. D'Ovidio and Richard L. Behling, "Material Requirements Planning," in *Handbook of Industrial Engineering,* Gavriel Salvendy, ed. New York: John Wiley & Sons, 1982, p. 11.6.13. Copyright © 1982 by John Wiley & Sons. Reprinted by permission of John Wiley & Sons, Inc., © Copyright 1982.

of what to order, how much to order, when to order, and when delivery should be scheduled.

Although the Spiecker Manufacturing example did not illustrate it, MRP usually applies some lot-sizing technique (for example, part-period balancing or periodic-order quantity) to combine the net requirements for several periods into realistic, planned order releases. This is necessary when the net requirements for an individual item are spread out over many time periods. Lot sizing is usually performed by MRP prior to determining the planned order releases by backing up, or offsetting, the lead time.

Capacity Requirements Planning

In Chapter 14 we discussed how rough-cut capacity-planning techniques are used to determine the feasibility of a master production schedule. MRP is insensitive to capacity limitations. It simply determines what materials and components are required in order to meet the MPS. **Capacity requirements planning** (CRP) is the process of determining how much labor and machine resources are required to accomplish the tasks of production on a more detailed level, based on all component parts and end items in the materials plan. CRP requires detailed input information for all components and assemblies such as MRP planned order releases, on-hand quantities, current status of shop orders, routing data, and time standards.

The process of CRP is similar to that of rough-cut capacity planning. The difference is that the MRP system establishes the exact order quantities and timing for each component part, whereas the MPS simply states the schedule of end items. In addition, rough-cut capacity planning examines key equipment or work centers; that is, bottlenecks. CRP examines many more work centers, and thus provides more detailed information.

Capacity requirements are computed by multiplying the number of units scheduled for production at a work center by the unit-resource requirements and adding in the setup time. These requirements are then summarized by time period and work center. To illustrate CRP calculations, suppose that the planned order releases for a component are as follows:

Time Period	1	2	3	4
Planned Order Release	20	0	25	25

Assume that the component requires 1.10 hours per unit of labor in a particular work center and 1.5 hours of setup time; the capacity requirement in period 1 is

$$(20 \text{ units})(1.10 \text{ hours/unit}) + 1.5 \text{ hours} = 23.5 \text{ hours}$$

Similarly, in periods 3 and 4, we have

$$(25 \text{ units})(1.10 \text{ hours/unit}) + 1.5 \text{ hours} = 29 \text{ hours}$$

Such information is usually provided in a *load report,* as illustrated in Figure 15.9. If sufficient capacity is not available, then decisions must be made regarding overtime, transfer of personnel between departments, subcontracting, and so on. The master production schedule may also have to be revised in order to meet available capacity. This requires that the MRP program be run again. The integration of capacity requirements, master scheduling, and MRP is often called a *closed-loop MRP system.* This is illustrated in Figure 15.10. In this way, capacity requirements planning provides a feedback between master scheduling and MRP.

Priority Planning

Each order in a plant is prioritized by assigning a due date to it. Once the priorities of *orders* are established, then individual operation schedules can be derived. This is discussed in the next chapter. The role of MRP in priority planning is to establish valid order priorities when orders are released to the shop and to keep them up-to-date. Priority control is accomplished through **expediting** and *de-expediting*; that is, rescheduling production orders to either make them move faster or hold them up, respectively. For instance, in the Spiecker Manufacturing problem, assume that during the manufacture of the filter housing component, a machine breakdown occurs that will delay production of the housings for 1 week. Perhaps the only alternative management has for maintaining the current schedule is to hire an outside contractor to produce the remaining number of required filter housings; however, the increased costs associated with using an outside contractor are significant. What should management do?

Before reaching a decision regarding the use of an outside contractor, management should analyze the effects that a 1-week delay in the production of the filter housings would bring about. Because an MRP system maintains information on all items in inventory, this data can now be made available to management. For example, the MRP system would examine the bill of materials in order to determine the impact a 1-week delay in the filter housing would have in terms

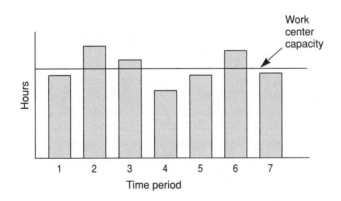

FIGURE 15.9

A Sample Load Report

FIGURE 15.10 Closed-loop MRP System

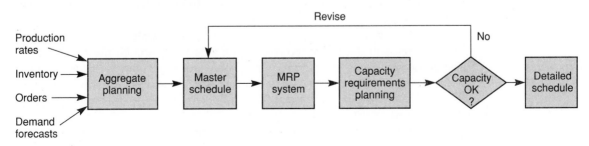

of the production schedule for all other components. In addition, if management elects to delay production by 1 week, all components affected by the change would then be updated by the MRP system to reflect new production schedules.

Thus MRP assists operations managers in making decisions regarding the rescheduling of orders and the cancellation or suspension of orders on the master production schedule as priorities change. In a factory with many hundreds of orders, this is nearly impossible to do manually; however, it is routine for computerized MRP systems. In addition, the MRP information system allows managers to obtain reports on projected inventory levels, vendor delivery performance and lead times, and exceptions such as late orders, high scrap, and so on.

MRP also provides benefits in other areas of the firm. For example, purchasing can achieve improved vendor relations and better utilization of time. Receiving can reduce labor requirements through improved scheduling of work by knowing when shipments will arrive. Marketing can achieve better customer relations through more reliable delivery, and finance can improve planning and control.

15.5 PLANNING AND IMPLEMENTING MRP

A significant amount of preplanning is required in order to apply MRP. A comprehensive review of a company's existing manufacturing system should include an examination of

1. Operating policies: organization and staffing, customer service objectives
2. Materials management systems: master scheduling, capacity planning, production control, inventory control
3. Customer demand: forecast accuracy, variability
4. Purchasing and manufacturing operations: volumes, lead times, performance to schedule

Such an examination will help to identify areas that must be improved before MRP can be implemented.

Because MRP necessitates a comprehensive change in a firm's approach to manufacturing, it requires a high level of discipline throughout the organization. Many MRP systems have been successful, but others have failed. Failures can usually be attributed to one of two causes: lack of accuracy and realism in data and information, and inadequate planning and implementation.

Accuracy and Realism

The old computer adage "garbage in, garbage out" is especially true for MRP systems. Inaccuracies in inventory records, bills of materials, and master schedules can lead to inaccuracies in the output of the MRP system. If these sources of error are not controlled for, the results can be disastrous for the firm.

Accurate inventory records are necessary for any successful implementation because errors in inventory records will be amplified through the MRP system. The consequences of errors will be the failure to order material needed and/or the ordering of unnecessary material. Inaccurate inventory records will also lead to inaccuracies in the MRP calculations of net requirements and eventually cause the system to malfunction.

With inaccurate records, management will be continually responding to crises caused by parts shortages and other inconsistencies, and the end result will be that the integrity of the MRP system will be lost. In looking for sources of such difficulties we find that inaccurate inventory records are often caused by the lack of formal receiving procedures, unlocked storerooms, inappropriate forms and material information systems, and lack of audit procedures.

Effective performance of MRP requires accurate bills of materials. For products with frequent design changes, maintenance of accurate BOMs is a must. Errors in bills of materials can cause the MRP system to signal a need for materials that are not actually required, or to not plan orders for required items. Usually such inaccuracies are the result of missing BOMs for some items and/or lack of control and communication with regard to design changes.

Quigley suggests three sampling tests for checking accuracy.[2]

1. Take a finished product that is boxed and ready to ship. Disassemble it and verify the bill of materials for that product. This must be 100 percent correct.
2. Sample three parts from inventory. Check the on-hand level against inventory records. These should be within 1 to 2 percent of each other.
3. Obtain a status report from production control on current production, current targets, and next month's plan. Ask for the same information from materials control and assembly. These should be in agreement.

Referring back to Figure 15.6, we see that tests 1 and 2 are used to verify accuracy of the input files to the MRP system. Test 3 is performed to ensure that proper coordination between departments at the front and back ends of production is taking place. Such checks should be made periodically if an MRP system is to operate successfully. Good physical inventory control, such as cycle counting (described in Chapter 12), is one method for assuring inventory accuracy.

Since the MPS drives the MRP system, it too must be accurate and realistic. Schedules that call for production of quantities that exceed the capacity of the plant or those which do not include all items that are actually produced will obviously lead to problems. An unrealistic master production schedule is often reflected in large numbers of overdue orders, excessively high amounts of indirect labor performed by direct labor employees, or too many late jobs which must be expedited. Such problems can be minimized by careful attention to aggregate planning and the use of capacity requirements in a closed-loop system.

Planning and Implementation

When a company decides to implement MRP, it undertakes a very complex project. The typical amount of time required to operationalize a system is 12 to 15 months, and costs vary from $500,000 to $1.5 million.[3] The success of MRP depends on good computer software and close cooperation among all groups in the organization that will affect or be affected by MRP. Typically, a project team consisting of personnel from manufacturing, data processing, marketing, accounting, and purchasing will be in charge of the project. This is an excellent opportunity to use project management techniques for coordinating activities (see Chapter 18).

Education and training provide a crucial role in implementing an MRP system. Lack of understanding of the MRP concept and the function of the MRP system

[2]Philip E. Quigley, "Pre-MRP Planning: Make These Three Tests Before Implementing," *Industrial Engineering*, 12, no. 2 (February 1980): 36–37.

[3]"Putting Theory to Work in the Shop," *Datamation*, 26, no. 10 (October 1980): 125.

can prove disastrous. Education should include personnel at all levels and should be actively supported by top management. Training programs should provide all users of the system with a thorough knowledge of the techniques and concepts of MRP and a sense of shared responsibility for its success. Good training can help alleviate many of the behavioral problems that often arise when any type of change occurs. Many MRP experts feel that education represents more than half the effort required for success. Once an MRP system is operational, training and support must continue to ensure long-run success.

15.6 MRP IN SERVICE ORGANIZATIONS

Provision of services often has features analogous to manufacturing. For example, in a restaurant, meals can be thought of as end items. The service required to assemble an order can be defined in terms of a bill of materials, lead times, and so on. For labor-intensive services, the analogy to the BOM would be a "bill of labor." However, not all possible end items can be defined because of the greater customization and uncertainty needs. For service organizations that offer more structured services, concepts of MRP can be useful.

For example, the MRP concept can be applied to planning capacity requirements in colleges and universities. In determining how many sections of a course to schedule, universities need to know the projected number of students that will need to take that course. In this illustration, the end items are graduates in each major. The number of graduates can be forecasted on a short-range basis from current demands, projections of high school graduates, employment trends, and so on. From this information, a master schedule can be constructed.

The curriculum, described for each major, constitutes the bill of materials. The prerequisite structure of courses defines the product structure in the BOM. This can then be exploded by semester or quarter to give a schedule of time-phased course requirements. College department heads and deans can use this information to plan capacity in terms of faculty, teaching assistants, classrooms, computer facility requirements, and the like.

In one of the P/OM in Practice cases, we show how requirement-planning-systems concepts can be used to improve the management of an expensive surgical inventory.

15.7 MANUFACTURING RESOURCE PLANNING (MRP II)

The use of an MRP-based system to plan all the resources of a manufacturing company is called **manufacturing resource planning,** or **MRP II.** MRP II includes strategic financial planning as well as production planning through the use of simulation capabilities to answer what-if questions. The principal attributes of MRP II are described by Melnyk et al.[4] MRP II is a *top-down system,* beginning

---

[4]S.A. Melnyk, R.F. Gonzalez, and S.J. Anderson, *Manufacturing Resource Planning: Insights into a New Corporate Way of Life,* APICS Rsearch Report 82-8, March 1983, American Production and Inventory Control Society.

with the formulation of strategic business plans that are formalized and restated as functional strategies. MRP II uses a *common data base* to evaluate alternative policies. Manufacturing data can be converted into financial data, and formal procedures exist to maintain accuracy and introduce changes in the data. *What-if* capabilities are routinely used to evaluate alternative plans. The system is capable of generating detailed resource requirements for evaluation purposes. MRP II is a *total company system,* in which functional groups interact commonly and formally and make joint decisions. Finally, the system is *user-transparent.* Users at all levels understand and accept the logic and realism of the system and need not work outside the formal system.

A COMMERCIAL MRP II SYSTEM

MRPS: Manufacturing Resource Planning System,[5] developed by CINCOM Systems, Inc., is a commercial MRP II system that was based on a five-point design philosophy.

1. The system must be adaptable, extendable, and modifiable to meet changing conditions.
2. The system must be functionally complete, yet flexible, so that it can be fine-tuned to a changing environment.
3. The system must be modular, so that it can be implemented in a step-by-step fashion.
4. The system must be on-line, interactive, and user-friendly.
5. All modules must offer the most contemporary functional features accompanied by complete documentation.

The structure of MRPS is shown in Figure 15.11. It includes the vertical dimension of production planning, master production scheduling, MRP, and shop-floor control. The system also expands horizontally to include inventory control, purchasing, and other planning considerations.

The system consists of a foundation module and four planning modules. The foundation module provides basic record maintenance and establishes the system framework with the necessary information data base. The four planning modules are as follows:

- *MMPS—manufacturing material planning system.* This system provides the essential MRP calculations and reports for production planning and control.
- *MPSS—master production scheduling system.* This module provides a base to plan, coordinate, and control material and production activities. It develops resource planning data and can simulate the impact of planned changes to forecasts, orders, resources, or capacities.
- *PPCS—production planning and control system.* Detailed work schedules are created for the shop floor. Detailed capacity requirements planning and control, priority dispatching, and work-in-process reporting are included.
- *VAPS—vendor analysis and purchasing system.* This module is designed to interface with production and streamline purchasing by providing data for the control of vendors, delivery schedules, and price variances.

---

[5]*MRPS: Manufacturing Resource Planning System,* CINCOM Systems, Inc., 2300 Montana Ave., Cincinnati, Ohio 45211, (513) 662-2300.

FIGURE 15.11

The Structure of MRPS

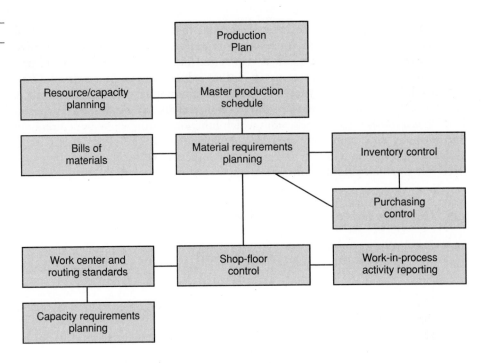

The system is also designed for data processing flexibility. It can operate on a mainframe computer, a stand-alone minicomputer, or in a distributed environment. Processing can be performed in a batch mode or on-line.

How Exxon Office System used MRPS illustrates the value of such a system.[6] The Qyx Division of Exxon Office Systems is a manufacturer of electronic typewriters and is located in Lionville, Pennsylvania. Qyx management recognized early that future growth would strain manufacturing operations and that a more effective control system needed to be implemented. The Qyx typewriter consists of hundreds of parts, the majority of which are purchased. There is also a heavy concentration in product improvements and value engineering. Thus it is critical that the shop be provided with the right parts, in the right quantities, and at the right time.

Qyx was a new company and had no formal manufacturing-control system. A team representing various functional areas of the company was created to develop a plan for a closed-loop MRP system. Three important objectives were identified:

1. Minimize inventory investment.
2. Maximize customer service.
3. Optimize plant efficiency.

---

[6]Adapted from "Controlling Growing Manufacturing Ops with CINCOM's MRPS," *Production & Inventory Management Review*. Reprinted with permission from P&IM Review, July 1981. Copyright 1981 by T.D.A. Publications, Inc.

For each of these objectives, the appropriate roles of material management, manufacturing, engineering, accounting, and data processing were studied. From this study a list of specifications that were required in a total system was developed. MRPS was chosen as the system that best met the needs at Qyx.

The key to implementing the system, as with all projects in operations management, was commitment and teamwork at all levels of the organization. In just 7 months after the project was initiated, the system was fully implemented. In the 6 months after implementation, many intangible and financial benefits were noted. Among these were

- a 30 percent reduction in inventories
- an improvement in inventory accuracy from under 50 percent to 95 percent
- higher accuracy in bills of materials
- reduction in outstanding purchasing commitments
- reduction in overdue purchase orders
- improvement in on-time deliveries
- reduction in inbound freight charges
- reduction in overtime.

In addition to the tangible financial benefits, the company was provided with more timely and accurate information with which to work and plan. This increased morale and productivity in the company.

MRP II systems accrue the benefits of ordinary MRP systems, including reduced manufacturing inventories, fewer stockouts, and improved delivery. As a strategic planning system, however, the use of MRP II has demonstrated other unique benefits.[7] One firm, whose business objectives included level employment, used MRP II to convince marketing personnel that it was necessary to smooth the sales plan so that manufacturing could level its labor requirements. Another firm used the simulation capability to formulate contingency plans to minimize the adverse effects of strikes on the firm's operation. Using MRP II to identify strike-induced capacity shortages and to schedule vendors to make up projected capacity shortfalls, the firm was able to meet all its commitments and deliveries during a 13-week strike. In a third firm, the use of MRP II enabled the lead times for new product development and introduction to be reduced. The system linked the material-planning and product-engineering groups during the development process and was able to achieve better coordination.

P/OM IN PRACTICE

Two examples illustrate the application of MRP systems. The first describes implementation of a computerized MRP system at Southwire Company where employee education plays a key role. The second describes a requirements-planning system for Houston's Park Plaza Hospital. This example shows how MRP applies in the service sector.

---

[7] S. A. Melnyk, and R. F. Gonzalez, "MRP II: The Early Returns are In," *Production and Inventory Management*, 26, no. 1 (1985): 124–137.

MRP AT THE SOUTHWIRE COMPANY[8]

S outhwire is a major manufacturer of utility cable and building wire. Beginning with one small plant in 1950, Southwire grew at an annual rate of 25 percent to its present size which involves nine major production facilities with worldwide distribution.

Southwire had been using computerized data bases to control finished-goods inventory, sales order entries, and certain raw materials and parts. Manufacturing inventories, however, were controlled manually with "a mish-mash of safety stock levels

and gut feelings," according to the manager of corporate production control. With expanding volume and a complex mix of products, manual methods were no longer adequate. A special committee, appointed to study production-control problems, decided to implement a computerized MRP system.

Figure 15.12 illustrates the essentials of the Southwire MRP system. Demand for finished goods is generated by customers and from the company's distribution warehouses and entered in an on-line order entry system. The computer checks the de-

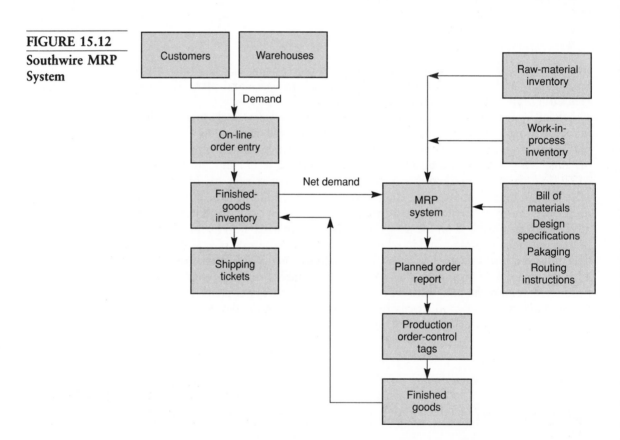

FIGURE 15.12
Southwire MRP System

Source: Adapted from Boyer, "Production Control: MRP Ends Guessing at Southwire." Reprinted with permission from *Industrial Engineering* magazine, March 1977. Copyright Institute of Industrial Engineers, 25 Technology Park/Atlanta, Norcross, GA 30092.

---

[8]Adapted from Charles H. Boyer, "Production Control: MRP Ends Guessing at Southwire," Reprinted with permission from *Industrial Engineering* magazine, March 1977. Copyright Institute of Industrial Engineers, 25 Technology Park/Atlanta, Norcross, GA 30092.

mand against a finished-goods inventory file. Those goods in stock are allocated to the demand and a shipping ticket is automatically printed. The demand not covered by finished goods available for shipment becomes the net demand input to the MRP system. The output from MRP is a planned order report, which acts as a master production schedule. This report shows

- product description
- source (make or buy)
- order number
- amount
- release and due date
- manufacturing time
- lead time

The MRP module then compares work-in-process inventory with net demand requirements and determines what materials must be ordered and when, in order to meet production requirements. Production-control personnel use this report to initiate production. The production orders contain manufacturing and packaging instructions, bills of materials, routing instructions, and design specifications. As the finished goods are produced, on-line terminals are used to enter this information in the inventory file.

As discussed in this chapter, the effective implementation of MRP requires accurate records. During the initial investigation of using MRP, the work-in-process (WIP) inventory accuracy was only about 69 percent. This had to be improved in order to make MRP successful. Southwire had 700 different end products with about seven components on each

BOM. To ensure inventory accuracy, a tagging system was implemented to track the manufacturing inventory carefully after it entered the plant. However, the first outputs from the system were, in the manager's words, "garbage." The problem was quickly discovered. The tags were not taken seriously by the employees. As a result, the number and type of tags turned in from the shop floor did not match the inventory used. To correct this, an educational improvement program was implemented to emphasize the importance of the tag system. Tags are now accounted for at release, when they are turned in, and once during every shift. As a result, WIP accuracy jumped to 96 percent, which was considered the minimum acceptable level.

Employee education beyond the tagging problem was crucial to system development. Several teaching aids, including videotape presentations and seminars, were used to demonstrate the advantages of MRP and to gain support. Convincing supervisors not to stockpile inventory was not easy, but it was well worth the effort. Since start-up of the system, the number of unique stock items in WIP inventory has been reduced 50 percent, and planning, rescheduling, and updating has been significantly improved.

QUESTIONS

1. What were the reasons that lead to Southwire's decision to implement a computerized MRP system?
2. Were record inaccuracies a problem in implementing the MRP system? Explain.
3. Briefly describe the role that employee education played in the implementation of the MRP system.

A REQUIREMENTS-PLANNING SYSTEM FOR HOUSTON'S PARK PLAZA HOSPITAL[9]

Park Plaza Hospital is a privately owned 374-bed facility with a surgical suite of nine operating rooms. These operating rooms are reserved at least one week in advance by physicians with surgery privileges at the hospital. Thus, at any point in time, the schedule of planned operations for the next 7 days is known with some certainty, whereas anything beyond this horizon is far less certain. After an operation has been entered on the surgical schedule, it must be confirmed on two other occasions:

[9]Adapted from E. Steinberg, B. Khumawala, and R. Scamell, "Requirements Planning Systems in the Health Care Environment." Reprinted with permission from *Journal of Operations Management*, 2, no. 4 (1982): 251–259, Journal of the American Production and Inventory Control Society, Inc.

first, 72 hours beforehand, and second, 48 hours prior to the actual operation. This scheduling process permits the assignment of staff (nursing, orderlies, etc.) and the selection of the necessary supplies and equipment for the specific procedure. The patient is generally admitted to the hospital some 12 hours prior to the operation.

Surgery is, for the most part, performed during normal working hours (7 A.M. to 5 P.M.), Monday through Friday and some Saturdays. As for the operations themselves, they generally average about 45 minutes. Obviously, however, different operations take different amounts of time and furthermore, there is no set time for any procedure as they differ from case to case and physician to physician. This lack of definitive durations for the procedures is further complicated by evidence that physicians perceive that they work more quickly than they actually do.

As a result, the surgical schedule, for any given operating room on any given day (and hence, for the seven-day planning horizon) is not entirely fixed. The schedule includes such information as: date, operating room number, scheduled time, patient name, patient room number, operation, physician, estimated time, and anesthesia.

Supplies for any operation fall into three general categories.

1. Disposable items that can be used only once.
2. Reusable instruments that are recycled and used again; i.e., they are cleaned, sterilized and placed back into inventory (for example, pickups, clamps, and so on).
3. A limited number of high-technology instruments—this limited supply results from the prohibitive costs of these instruments (for example, a CAT-scan, heart-lung machine, and so on).

In addition, the required stock for any operation not only differs with the particular procedure, but also by physician—each having their preference as to the instruments and disposable supplies to be used for a given procedure. Supplies and instruments are drawn from inventory by the use of a Physician's Preference Sheet that lists these requirements by procedure and by physician. The goal of the requirements-planning system for Park Plaza is to ensure that these required supplies arrive at the proper place (the correct operating room), at the proper time, correctly assigned by surgical procedure and physician preference, and with the maintenance of appropriate and accurate inventory levels.

In order to demonstrate the application of requirements planning to the surgical suite, a nomenclature that relates to the hospital environment is required. Table 15.4 shows the nomenclature used and indicates how it parallels the terminology employed in manufacturing applications. We next define each system component in the context of the surgical suite and describe the role of each in the system.

The first component of the system is the 7-day horizon surgical schedule, the analog of a master production schedule. In this case, however, each product is defined as a specific physician performing a specific procedure. This definition is necessary since two physicians performing identical procedures may desire different surgical kits. Therefore, each physician may fill out his or her preference sheet differently. Thus, if we have k physicians, each performing n procedures, we may identify as many as $k \times n$ separate products.

Unlike the conventional MPS, where the end items are physical products, here the end items represent procedures performed by a specific physician, and each end item has a quantity of only one. However, in both cases, the end item remains the target of the material flow and the output of the process.

The surgical requirements file—the analog of the BOM—contains the materials and supplies needed for the various procedures (or level 0 end items). In the traditional MRP system, the bill of materials file defines the final product in terms of its components; in the surgical suite such components are the supplies required for a particular surgical procedure in accordance with physician preference. Thus, the items on the Physician's Preference Sheet are defined as level 1 components that must be ready for use (sterilized if appropriate) in the procedure.

TABLE 15.4   MRP Terminology

Application	
Manufacturing	Health Care
Master production schedule	Surgical schedule
Bill of materials	Surgical requirements file
Inventory	Inventory item file

Extending this concept one step further, all items that require sterilization are considered level 2 subassemblies with lead times equal to their required time for sterilization (this time ranges from five minutes to, as mentioned, 16 hours) and recycling. While this concept means that inventory records must be kept on two levels, such a scheme provides an effective method for handling items that must be sterilized. Sterilization units may be viewed as machine centers with limited capacity. One of the outputs of the system is a projected load for sterilization and a schedule of release of sterilized items to projected inventory.

The procedure for systems operation is shown in Figure 15.13. The system operation begins with an inquiry to the surgical schedule. If capacity is available in the surgical schedule, the procedure is to update the schedule by inserting the operation in the appropriate spot. The schedule is then exploded through the surgical requirements file to generate gross requirements for all necessary materials and supplies. Note that a specific product (a particular physician performing a specified procedure) is iden-

tified, which is traceable to a single Physician's Preference Sheet. The gross requirements thus generated are netted against the projected on hand inventory for all items required. A sample record for a reusable component is shown in Table 15.5.

The key data base elements of the system are the Surgical Schedule File, Inventory Item File, and Surgical Requirements File.

The Surgical Schedule File should contain all posted surgeries for a specific day and time in each operating room. It includes such data as

- Operation number
- Scheduled date and time
- Operating room number
- Patient room number
- Patient name
- Procedure(s)
- Anesthesia
- Physician name

The Inventory Item File is a time-phased inventory record of surgical supplies and instruments required by one or more procedures. Particular care must be

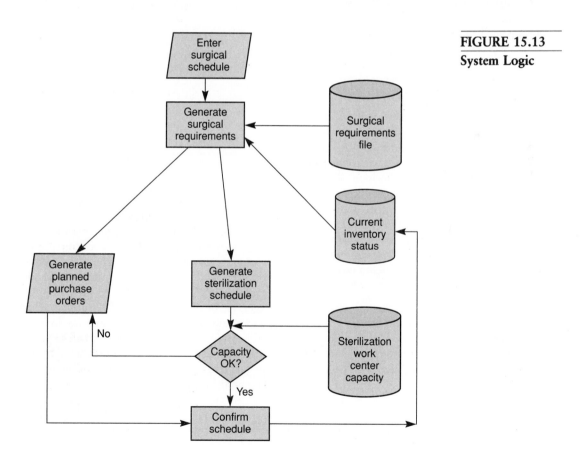

FIGURE 15.13
System Logic

TABLE 15.5 Item Record for Reusable Part

ITEM: Blade, #10
Sterilization lead time: 2 periods
Procurement lead time: 1 period

Period	0	1	2	3	4	5	6	7	8	9	10	11	12
Gross requirements		5	5	10	10	10	15			5	10		
Scheduled receipts													
Projected sterilized				5	5	10	10	10	10	5		5	10
Projected on-hand	15	10	5	0	0	0	0	10	20	20	10	15	25
Net requirements					5		5						
Planned order receipts					5		5						
Planned order release			5		5								

taken in this file to distinguish between disposable and reusable items. Data contained in this file includes

- Unique item number
- Description of the item
- Level
- Gross requirements
- Quantity on hand (current, allocated, projected available)
- Scheduled receipts
- Planned order releases
- Standard inventory ordering data (lot size, order point, lead time, vendor information)
- Recycling time (if applicable)

The Surgical Requirements File is the functional equivalent to a single item bill of materials for a procedure.[10] This file identifies quantities of each item that are needed for a procedure as well as the specific size and/or brand of the item. The file is divided into two parts: the common items and the preference items. The common items represent the materials used by *all* physicians when performing a procedure. On the other hand, the preference items reflect physician differences in surgical material requirements. Collectively, these items establish the inventory requirements of a specific procedure in the following manner:

- Level 0 element number (procedure identifier).
- Lower-level element numbers of common items.
- Lower-level element numbers of preference items (for each physician associated with Level 0 element number).

TABLE 15.6 Surgical Requirements for a Bronchoscopy

Common materials
 Bronchoscopy set, rigid
 Suction tubing
 Telescope, right angle
 Telescope, forward oblique
 Glass slides
 Fixative
 Specimen trap
 Table cover
 Towels
Preference items
 Dr. **********
  Flexible bronchoscope
  Gloves, size 6½ brown
 Dr. **********
  Gloves, size 7½
  Local set

Table 15.6 outlines the two parts of the surgical requirements file for a bronchoscopy. Observe that the upper portion shows the common inventory items used and the lower portion depicts the additional inventory items *preferred* by a specific physician.

In the environment for which the system was developed, the chief nurse of the surgical suite operates as the medical analog to the materials manager. He or she is in charge of all surgical scheduling and equipment sterilization activities and is reponsible for inventory management of all required medical supplies for the surgical suite including all tools, instruments and equipment (excluding medication) required for all procedures.

This is a sampled in the file assume that all items have been prepared for surgery. Therefore, the distinction between component levels is not important.

The storeroom, sterilization facilities, and operating rooms themselves are located in one contiguous area under the nurse's control. In this area, an inventory of more than 2000 items used in conjunction with the various surgical procedures, is maintained. Inventory balances are updated by an on-line transaction-driven batch-processing system that provides a complete inventory status report for the 2000 items each week. In addition, a query-driven system provides access to the current level of inventory on hand for each item.

The entire system is designed to be operated by nursing personnel. Its success and acceptance stem from two factors:

1. Generation of reliable schedules and insurance of adequate supplies. The reduction of problems in this area leads to greater physician satisfaction and a more harmonious relationship with nursing personnel.
2. Simplicity of operation. The system outputs include a daily schedule of surgical procedures, a list of items to be picked from storeroom, a list of items for outside purchase, and a sterilization schedule.

The application of requirements planning to the surgical suite demonstrates how job shop-related techniques can be employed in a nonmanufacturing environment with resource and time constraints but without a physical final product. It provides hospital administrators with a better vehicle to understand and control the investment in material and supplies in this rapidly increasing cost area. Furthermore, the use of MRP-based technology insures that materials will be available when needed, protects against the overcapitalization of inventory, and aids in formulating and adjusting reordering policies.

QUESTIONS

1. In a surgical context, what is the counterpart of a "product" in a traditional manufacturing environment? Briefly explain how this term is defined.
2. What is the analog of the BOM called and how is it defined?
3. What person in the surgical suite is the analog to the materials manager in a traditional manufacturing environment? Briefly describe this person's duties.
4. What are the primary factors that determine the success and acceptance of requirements planning in the surgical suite?

SUMMARY

In essence, an MRP system is implemented as a computerized data processing and information system, whose function is to monitor the status of production and inventory. By recognizing the dependent nature of demand inherent in most manufacturing environments and the subsequent importance of timing, MRP offers a better alternative to production and inventory control than do traditional types of reorder-point models.

The inputs to an MRP system include the master production schedule, bill-of-materials file, and inventory file. MRP uses this information to determine time-phased gross and net requirements for manufacturing inventory. MRP assists operations managers in planning and controlling inventory levels, planning priorities of orders, and in capacity planning. MRP concepts are also often useful in service organizations.

The effective implementation of MRP requires accuracy of inventory records, bills of material, and realistic master schedules. Behavioral problems often account for failures of MRP systems. Thus managers involved in MRP must have a quality-assurance perspective and be able to deal effectively with people at all levels of the organization.

Currently, there are many firms that offer computer programs that will carry out the calculations required to implement the MRP approach. Although the use of any of these software packages can greatly simplify the development of an MRP system, the development can be an expensive and time-consuming project.

Properly implemented, however, the MRP approach can provide significant inventory planning and control advantages for the firm.

MRP II, or manufacturing resource planning, extends the use of MRP to strategic business planning. MRP II helps to coordinate manufacturing, finance, and marketing functions so that strategic business goals can be achieved.

KEY TERMS

Material requirements planning
  (MRP)
Bucket
Time phasing
Regeneration approach
Net change approach

Capacity requirements planning
  (CRP)
Expediting
Manufacturing resource planning
  (MRP II)

**REVIEW/
DISCUSSION
QUESTIONS**

1. What is the role of MRP in the production planning and scheduling process?

2. What are the major functions of an MRP system?

3. Explain the difference between *independent* and *dependent demand.*

4. How can the use of MRP reduce unnecessary inventory holding?

5. What are the components of an MRP information system?

6. What is the function of the bill of materials in an MRP system?

7. Explain how net component requirements are calculated?

8. Explain the concept of *time phasing.*

9. What are the differences between the *regeneration approach* and the *net change approach* in MRP?

11. What is *capacity requirements planning?* How does it interface with MRP?

12. Of what value is MRP in areas of a firm other than production?

13. Discuss the importance of accuracy and realism in implementing MRP.

14. Why is MRP difficult to implement in an organization?

15. How can the MRP concept be applied in a service organization? Can you provide a new example not discussed in this chapter?

16. What is *manufacturing resource planning?* How does it differ from MRP?

PROBLEMS

1. For the Spiecker Manufacturing example discussed in this chapter, determine the net requirements for the engine assembly, the air cleaner subassembly, and the filter housing if the number of units in inventory are 500, 375, and 250, respectively. Assume that 1250 units of the 14-inch snowblower are still required in week 15.

2. For the Spiecker example, determine the effect on time phasing if lead times are 5 for the engine assembly, 2 for the air cleaner subassembly, and 3 for the filter housing.

3. An electrical appliance A consists of three major subassemblies: B, C, and D. One unit of A is comprised of 2 units of B, 1 unit of C, and 3 units of D. The subassembly B consists of 2 untis of D, 1 unit of E, and 1 unit of F. The subassembly C consists of 2 units of E. The subassembly D, consists of 1 unit of E and 1 unit of F. A second major appliance G consists of 3 units of D and 4 units of F.

   a. Draw the bill of materials for products A and G.

   b. If 50 units of A and 25 units of G are required for the month of May, compute the requirements of all components and subassemblies.

4. In Problem 3, suppose that 100 units of A and 50 units of G are required for the month of June. At the end of May, we have the following stock on hand:

Item	A	G	B	C	D	E	F
Stock on Hand	50	25	50	20	350	0	175

   Calculate the requirements for all components and subassemblies.

5. C&D Lawn Products manufactures a rotary spreader for applying fertilizer. A portion of the BOM is shown in the figure below.

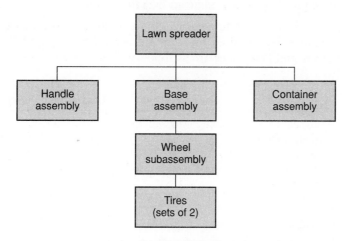

   If 3000 lawn spreaders are needed to satisfy a customer's order, determine the net requirements for the base assembly, wheel subassembly, and tires. Assume that 1000, 1500, and 800 of each component are currently in inventory.

6. In Problem 5, assume that the lead time for the base assembly, wheel subassembly, and tires are 2, 4, and 5 weeks, respectively. If all components must be completed no later than week 15 of the current production period, determine when orders must be placed to meet the production schedule.

7. The parts used in the manufacturing of a yo-yo are shown in the accompanying figure. One thousand yo-yos are needed by week 10. Current inventory levels and lead times are as follows:

Part	Inventory (Units)	Lead Times (Weeks)
Wooden peg	100	1
String	500	1
Sides	200	5
Cartons	—	3

In addition it is known that 200 sides have already been ordered and will arrive at week 6. When all the parts are available, it will take 1 week to assemble 1000 yo-yos.

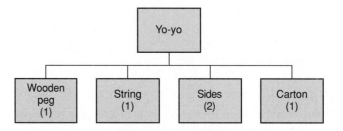

a. Determine the net requirements for all components.
b. Use time phasing to determine an overall schedule.

8. The parts used in the manufacturing of a toy car are shown in the accompanying figure. Five hundred toy cars are needed by week 12. Current inventory levels and lead times are as follows:

	Inventory (Units)	Lead Times (Weeks)
Toy car	100	2
Body assembly	125	5
Hood	—	3
Top	100	2
Base	175	4
Side	200	3
Trunk	300	2
Wheels	800	3

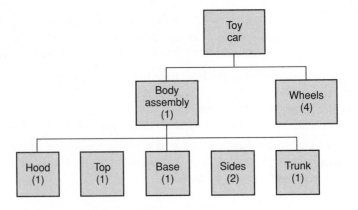

a. Determine the net requirements for all components.

b. Use time phasing to determine an overall schedule.

9. Given the following product structure and the gross requirements schedules for final assemblies A and G, complete the table for item F below. The lead time for F is 2 weeks. Assume that the scheduled receipts, on hand and lead times for B and D are all zero.

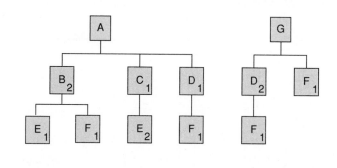

	Weeks							
	4	5	6	7	8	9	10	11
A	100	0	100	0	100	0	100	0
G	0	50	0	50	0	50	0	50

Item F:

	Weeks							
	4	5	6	7	8	9	10	11
Gross requirements								
Scheduled receipts	200	100	400	100	175	100	150	150
On Hand	100							
Net requirements								
Planned order release								

10. The following MRP table pertains to a low-level purchased item. Complete the table, assuming a lead time of 2 weeks.

	Weeks								
	10	11	12	13	14	15	16	17	18
Gross requirements	150	0	175	0	150	0	175	0	150
Scheduled receipts	125	0	150	0	175	0	125	0	0
On Hand	75								
Net requirements									
Planned order release									

A plant stand consists of the following parts:

1. Four long legs
2. Four short legs
3. Eight cross bars
4. Four middle glass retainers

5. Four top glass retainers
6. Two glass shelves
7. Sixteen screws (to fasten crossbars)
8. Four leg caps

The stand is illustrated in Figure 15.14a. The assembly chart is given in 15.14b.

FIGURE 15.14

Plant Stand and Assembly Chart

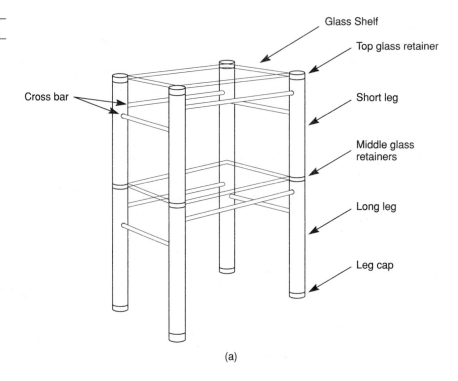

(a)

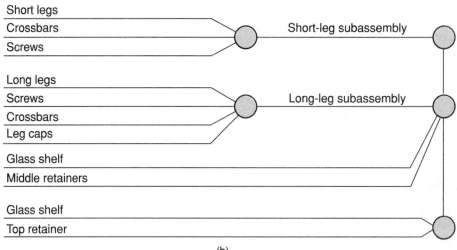

(b)

a. Construct a structured BOM for this product.

b. Current on-hand inventories and lead times (days) are given in the table below.

Component	On-hand Inventory	Lead Time (Days)
Finished stand	200	3
Short-leg subassembly	200	5
Long-leg subassembly	150	5
Long leg	1800	6
Short leg	1800	6
Crossbar	6000	5
Middle retainer	500	2
Top retainer	400	2
Glass shelves	250	6
Screws	5000	1
Leg caps	6000	2

Develop a time-phased material-requirements plan for all components if the master schedule calls for 300 units on day 5, 400 on day 10, 300 on day 15, and 300 on day 20.

Operations Scheduling and Production-Activity Control

M aster scheduling and material requirements planning are tools that assist operations managers in planning production. In manufacturing organizations once work orders have been released to the shop floor, first-line supervisors face the problem of detailed day-to-day scheduling and control of production in response to the higher level master scheduling and MRP plans. Thus, these activities are operational in nature and provide feedback to upper levels of management.

In Chapter 8, we defined five types of production systems: continuous flow, mass production, batch, job shop, and project systems. The scheduling of continuous-flow processes and mass production processes generally present little difficulty, since the systems are usually in continuous operation. Scheduling for these systems is incorporated into the design of the systems, as we discussed in Chapter 9. Project scheduling is accomplished and controlled using network techniques like PERT/CPM, described in Chapter 18. In this chapter, we focus on the remaining two production systems: batch processing and job shops. For batch processing, scheduling involves the simultaneous determination of the quantity produced and the sequence of products. In job shops, there is a great variety of low-volume items, each with different production requirements and routings. Job shops present the most difficult type of scheduling problem. We also examine the production-control function in a manufacturing organization. Finally, we examine control issues and discuss two types of scheduling problems common in service organizations: labor scheduling and vehicle scheduling.

16.1 THE SCOPE OF PRODUCTION-ACTIVITY CONTROL AND SCHEDULING

The goals of production-activity control are to

1. Meet customer service objectives. This implies, among other things, that all orders should be completed on time to meet delivery promises.
2. Minimize production costs. The control system should minimize work-in-process inventory and unnecessary machine setups.
3. Maximize resource utilization. The system should strive to achieve high labor and machine productivity by minimizing idle time, and reducing in-plant congestion.

Oftentimes these goals are in conflict and operations managers must find the appropriate balance. However, quality should not be sacrificed in order to meet any of these goals. Since quality requires a long-term commitment, the above goals often present a dilemma to managers who are evaluated on short-term results. Thus, continued vigilance is necessary to ensure that a long-term commitment to quality is not sacrificed to meet short-term goals.

Through the process of production-activity control the operations manager seeks to plan and control priorities of manufacturing orders and to plan and control capacity utilization. Figure 16.1 illustrates the production activity-control function in manufacturing. The output from material requirements planning (MRP) provides a detailed schedule of when materials, components, assemblies, and end

FIGURE 16.1
The Production
Activity-control
Function

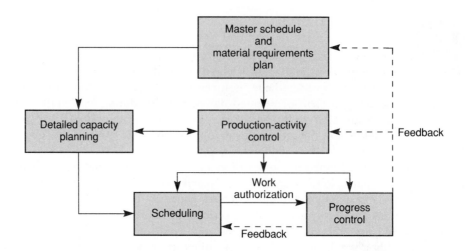

products are required and, in turn, when they should be produced. It is the responsibility of production activity-control personnel to successfully implement this plan. Doing so requires effective *scheduling* and *progress control*.

The scheduling function, with input from MRP, assigns priorities to manufacturing orders, and allocates work to specific work centers. In addition to input from the MRP system, the development of good schedules requires knowledge of the process routings of the manufactured goods, capacities of the various workstations, and data describing the status of the shop floor at any moment of time. A schedule specifies the timing and sequence of production, and the amount of work scheduled for completion at any work center during any time period.

Schedules must be realistic; that is, they must be achievable within the capacity limitations of the manufacturing facility. Problems arising from machine breakdowns, delays, material shortages, and so on, will require schedule revisions. Therefore, the scheduling function must be capable of rapidly responding to changes in the manufacturing environment.

Two important components of the scheduling function are *dispatching,* which controls the allocation of jobs to workstations, and the *transportation of materials* between workstations. Dispatchers are responsible for coordinating individual work center schedules and controlling material movement. When an operation is to be performed, the required material must be dispatched to the proper location at the proper time. Dispatchers require up-to-date information on the status of the current schedule and work centers. Dispatching involves real-time decision making to ensure that the schedule is adhered to as closely as possible. When problems arise, dispatchers must resequence jobs within the constraints of the schedule.

Physical transport of materials is necessary to implement a schedule and respond to dispatching decisions. Material handling devices must be available when necessary. Automated technology such as bar coding allows easy identification of parts and better control and coordination.

All these activities must be performed and monitored on a real-time basis. *Progress control* involves making sure that materials and tools are available when they are needed, making adjustments to short-term capacity limitations, tracking work-in-process, supervising labor, handling machine breakdowns, expediting rush orders, checking output quantities and scrap with planned requirements, and helping to solve quality problems. A good production activity-control system is necessary to provide the data and information that production supervisors require. This includes up-to-date information on work-in-process, manufacturing order status, actual output, and measures of efficiency, utilization, and productivity. Such information provides feedback to the planning process for possible adjustments of the master production schedule and material requirements plans.

Scheduling is also important in service organizations. For example, nurses must be scheduled in a hospital, and trucks must be scheduled for deliveries for a furniture distributor. Although our principal focus will be on manufacturing, we shall also discuss some techniques useful in service organizations. Since scheduling forms the basis for production-activity control, we next discuss some methods of scheduling work in different production environments.

16.2 BATCH-PRODUCTION SCHEDULING

Many make-to-stock manufacturers produce different products on common facilities. For example, a soft-drink manufacturer may produce several different flavors at one facility, or a soap company may package several different sizes on the same packaging lines. In these situations, products are generally produced in batches. The decisions faced by managers of such production systems are how much to produce in each batch and choosing the sequence, or order, in which the batches are made.

The batch quantity (which can be equivalently characterized by the length of time for a production run) and the frequency of production affect inventory levels and setup costs. A setup cost is incurred each time a changeover for a new product is required. With longer production runs, more inventory is carried and fewer setups are incurred. The optimal batch quantity can be computed using the economic production lot-size model discussed in Chapter 13. However, when several products share common facilities, this batch size must be modified because product sequencing will also affect cost. For instance, the setup cost may vary depending on the sequence of product changeovers, as in the case of changing a packaging line from small to medium size versus small to large size, or going from cola to lemon-lime versus cola to diet cola. This section is limited to the discussion of inventory considerations. A technique that is often used in batch-processing situations is *scheduling by runout time*.

SCHEDULING BY RUNOUT TIME

EXAMPLE

Suppose that a consumer-products company produces five different sizes of a laundry soap at one plant. Lot sizes and demand data are given in Table 16.1. The first question to ask is whether or not sufficient capacity exists to meet the demand for all products. To produce the weekly demand for the small size requires $150/833 = .18$ weeks. Similarly, the medium size requires $250/1000 = .25$ weeks; the large size, $150/750 = .20$ weeks; the jumbo size, $100/900 = .11$ weeks; and the giant size, $100/600 = .17$ weeks. Thus to meet the total weekly demand requires $.18 + .25 + .20 + .11 + .17 = .91$ weeks of production time. This

TABLE 16.1

Lot Size and Demand Data for Five Laundry Soap Products

Size	Economic Lot Size	Production Time (Weeks)	Production Rate (Units/Week)	Demand (Units/Week)	Current Inventory
Small	1000	1.2	833	150	800
Medium	800	.8	1000	250	600
Large	1500	2.0	750	150	2000
Jumbo	1800	2.0	900	100	2500
Giant	600	1.0	600	100	525

leaves machinery idle 9 percent of the time. The idle time can be used for set up and maintenance. When sufficient capacity does not exist, shortages will occur. This means that the aggregate plan is inconsistent with the capacity available.

Suppose that the company adopts a "cyclic" schedule of producing the economic lot size for each product in rotation. From Table 16.1 we see that it would take a total of $1.2 + .8 + 2.0 + 2.0 + 1.0 = 7$ weeks to produce the economic lot sizes of all products. Let us see what would happen during that time. For the small size, we begin with an inventory of 800 units. If we produce 1000 units, we will have a total of 1800 units available to satisfy the demand during the 7 weeks until we produce the small size again. Since 7 weeks' demand is $7(150) = 1050$, we see that we will be able to cover the demand and have some inventory remaining when the next production cycle begins.

Now consider the medium size. With an initial inventory of 600, if we produce 800 units, we will have 1400 units available to satisfy the 7 weeks' demand. However, 7 weeks' demand is $7(250) = 1750$. The cyclic economic lot size schedule will lead to shortages. An alternative is to use runout time as a scheduling rule.

The **runout time** (R) for a product is defined to be

$$R = \frac{\text{inventory level}}{\text{demand rate}}$$

The runout time is the length of time that inventory will be available to satisfy demand. If runout times are calculated for each product, then we schedule the product with the smallest runout time first.

The runout times in weeks for each product are calculated as follows:

Size	Runout Time
Small	800/150 = 5.33
Medium	600/250 = 2.4
Large	2000/150 = 13.33
Jumbo	2500/100 = 25
Giant	525/100 = 5.25

In choosing the size with the smallest runout time, we would schedule the medium size first. From Table 16.1, the lot size of 800 will take .8 week to produce. At the end of .8 week, the updated inventory levels are found by subtracting .8 week's demand from the current levels. This yields

Size	Inventory
Small	$800 - 150(.8) = 680$
Medium	$600 - 250(.8) + 800 = 1200$
Large	$2000 - 150(.8) = 1880$
Jumbo	$2500 - 100(.8) = 2420$
Giant	$525 - 100(.8) = 445$

Next, we use these updated inventory levels to compute new runout times and select the next product to run.

Size	Runout Time
Small	$680/150 = 4.53$
Medium	$1200/250 = 4.8$
Large	$1880/150 = 12.53$
Jumbo	$2420/100 = 24.2$
Giant	$445/100 = 4.45$

Thus, the giant size is scheduled next.

Notice that in using the smallest runout time, we are not scheduling all products in a rotating sequence, but instead we schedule them one at a time in response to current inventory levels and anticipated demand. This is, then, a dynamic approach. This approach does not consider inventory-holding costs, stock-out costs, or setup costs. Even using this rule, shortages may occur. (More sophisticated mathematical models exist, but these are beyond the scope of this text.) Managers should carefully examine projected inventory levels for all products to see if they are being depleted too fast or building up to unnecessarily high levels. Production schedules can be adjusted, if necessary, by aggregate planning approaches such as overtime, undertime, or other capacity-change strategies. There must be good communication between tactical and operational levels of management in making such decisions.

16.3 JOB SHOP SCHEDULING

In a pure job shop, there are several jobs to be processed, each of which may have a different routing among departments or machines in the shop. The two important decisions an operations manager must make involve scheduling and sequencing the jobs. Technically speaking, **scheduling** is the process of assigning starting and completion times to jobs. **Sequencing** involves the determination of the order in which jobs are processed. In practice, this distinction is not often made, however, and the term scheduling is used to mean both the timing and sequencing of jobs.

In general, job shop scheduling is very difficult. However, some special cases lend themselves to simple solutions. Although these special cases are not commonly found in practice, they provide understanding and insight into more difficult practical problems. The special cases considered in this chapter are

1. *Scheduling on a single processor.* Several jobs must be scheduled at one work center.
2. *Scheduling in a flow shop.* Several jobs may require many processing steps, but all have the same sequence.

Let us first discuss the major criteria that are used to evaluate schedules.

Scheduling Criteria

There are four principal criteria used to evaluate schedules for job shop problems. These are listed in Table 16.2. The **makespan** is defined to be the time to process a given set of jobs. **Flowtime** is the amount of time a job spends in the shop. If jobs have **due dates** (promised delivery times), then **tardiness** is defined as the amount of time by which the completion time exceeds the due date, and is equal to zero if the job is completed before the due date. **Lateness** is the difference between the completion time and the due date (positive or negative).

Minimizing makespan aims to achieve high utilization of equipment and resources by getting all jobs out quickly. Minimizing flowtime reduces work-in-process inventory. With the tardiness criteria, appropriate objectives are to minimize the number of tardy jobs or the value of the maximum tardiness. In either case, customer service is the prime consideration. We will see examples of each of these criteria in use as we discuss different job shop scheduling problems.

Sequencing on a Single Processor

The simplest scheduling problem is that of processing n jobs on a single processor. This type of problem arises in many situations. For example, in a serial production system, the bottleneck machine or work center controls the output of the entire system. Thus, it is critical to schedule the bottleneck machine efficiently. In other cases, such as in a chemical plant, the entire plant may be viewed as a single processor. Another reason for studying the single processor scheduling problem is that it is a component of more complex systems and thus provides insight

TABLE 16.2

Common Scheduling Criteria

Criteria	Definition	Objectives
Makespan	Time to process a set of jobs	Minimize makespan
Flowtime	Time a job spends in the shop	Minimize average flowtime
Tardiness*	The amount by which completion time exceeds the due date of a job	Minimize number of tardy jobs or minimize the maximum tardiness
Lateness	The difference between completion time and due date	Minimize average lateness or minimize maximum lateness

*If a job is completed before its due date, then tardiness is zero.

about more complex problems. For the single processor sequencing problem, a very simple rule finds a minimal average flowtime sequence: *Process the jobs in order of shortest processing time first.* This is often called the **shortest processing time,** or **SPT** rule.

SEQUENCING BY SHORTEST PROCESSING TIME

EXAMPLE

Consider a shop that has one maintenance mechanic to repair machines that have failed. We can think of the mechanic as the processor and the machines awaiting repair as the jobs. Let us assume that six machines are down, with estimated repair times given below and that no new jobs arrive.

Job	Processing Time (Hr)
1	8
2	4
3	7
4	3
5	6
6	5

No matter what sequence is chosen, the makespan is the same, since the time to process all the jobs is the sum of the processing times. Therefore, we use average flowtime as the criterion to minimize. Using the SPT rule, we use the sequence 4-2-6-5-3-1. The flowtimes for each job are

Job	Flowtime
4	3
2	3 + 4 = 7
6	7 + 5 = 12
5	12 + 6 = 18
3	18 + 7 = 25
1	25 + 8 = 33

Thus the average flowtime for these six jobs is (3 + 7 + 12 + 18 + 25 + 33)/6 = 16.33. This means that the average time a machine waits to be repaired will be about 16 hours.

It has been proven that SPT gives the smallest average flowtime and average lateness for any scheduling rule that might be chosen. A disadvantage of the SPT rule, however, occurs in a heavily loaded shop. If new jobs arrive frequently, those with long processing times are continually pushed back and may remain in the shop a long time. Thus it is advantageous to consider sequencing rules that take into account the due dates of jobs.

Scheduling with Due Dates

A popular and effective rule for scheduling on a single processor is the *earliest due date* rule, that is, sequence the jobs in order of earliest due date first. This rule minimizes the *maximum* job tardiness and *maximum* job lateness. However, it will not minimize the average flowtime or the average lateness as does SPT.

<table>
<tr><td>**EXAMPLE**</td><td>

SEQUENCING BY EARLIEST DUE DATE

Suppose that five jobs have processing times and due dates as given below:

Job	Processing Time	Due Date
1	4	15
2	7	16
3	2	8
4	6	21
5	3	9

If the jobs are sequenced in the order 1-2-3-4-5, then the flowtime, tardiness, and lateness for each job are calculated as follows:

Job	Flowtime	Due Date	Tardiness	Lateness
1	4	15	0	−11
2	4 + 7 = 11	16	0	−5
3	11 + 2 = 13	8	5	5
4	13 + 6 = 19	21	0	−2
5	19 + 3 = 22	9	13	13
Average	13.8		3.6	0

If we use the shortest processing time rule to schedule the jobs, we obtain the sequence 3-5-1-4-2. The flowtime, tardiness, and lateness are shown below.

Job	Flowtime	Due Date	Tardiness	Lateness
3	2	8	0	−6
5	2 + 3 = 5	9	0	−4
1	5 + 4 = 9	15	0	−6
4	9 + 6 = 15	21	0	−6
2	15 + 7 = 22	16	6	6
Average	10.6		1.2	−3.2

Note that the maximum tardiness is 6 and the maximum lateness is also 6. Using the earliest due date rule, we obtain the sequence 3-5-1-2-4.

</td></tr>
</table>

Job	Flowtime	Due Date	Tardiness	Lateness
3	2	8	0	−6
5	2 + 3 = 5	9	0	−4
1	5 + 4 = 9	15	0	−6
2	9 + 7 = 16	16	0	0
4	16 + 6 = 22	21	1 ← Maximum	1 ← Maximum
Average	10.8		0.2	−3.0

The maximum time that any job is tardy or late is 1 day; however the average lateness is worse than the SPT rule.

The procedures we have presented for sequencing jobs are based on scheduling *forward* from the current date. We will not know when the jobs are completed until the schedule is finished. If due dates are to be met and tardiness cannot be tolerated, then time phasing is often done backward. For instance, in the five-job problem we have been discussing, we must start each job by the time indicated below if we are to meet the required due dates.

Job	Due Date	Latest Start
1	15	11
2	16	9
3	8	6
4	21	15
5	9	6

Meeting such deadlines might require overtime or subcontracting if sufficient capacity is unavailable. Backward scheduling is typical of the aircraft industry (when due dates are established by government contracts) and in MRP systems.

A **flowshop** is a job shop in which all jobs have the same routing. In this section, we consider a simple flowshop with only two operations. We assume that each job must be processed first on machine 1 and second on machine 2. Processing times for each job on each machine are known. In contrast to sequencing jobs on a single processor, the makespan can vary for each different sequence. Therefore for the two-machine flowshop problem, it makes sense to try to find a sequence with the smallest makespan.

An algorithm was developed by S. M. Johnson in 1954 to find a minimum makespan schedule.[1]

Two-machine Flowshop Problem

Johnson's Rule

1. List the jobs and their processing times on machines 1 and 2.
2. Find the job with the smallest processing time (on either machine).

---

[1] S.M. Johnson, "Optimal Two- and Three-Stage Production Schedules with Setup Times Included," *Naval Research Logistics Quarterly*, 1, no. 1 (March 1954).

3. If this time corresponds to machine 1, sequence the job *first;* if it corresponds to machine 2, sequence the job *last.*
4. Repeat Steps 2 and 3, using the next smallest processing time and working *inward* from both ends of the sequence until all jobs have been scheduled.

SEQUENCING WITH JOHNSON'S RULE

Hirsch Products is a small manufacturer that produces certain custom parts, which first require a shearing operation and then require a punch press operation. Hirsch Products currently has orders for five jobs, which have processing times (days) estimated to be as follows:

Job	Shear	Punch
1	4	5
2	4	1
3	10	4
4	6	10
5	2	3

The five jobs that are awaiting processing may be sequenced in any order but must first be sheared. Therefore we have a flowshop situation. .

Suppose that the jobs are sequenced in the order 1–2–3–4–5. This schedule can be represented by a simple bar chart. A *bar chart* (a variation of a *Gantt chart,* which is formally introduced in Chapter 18) shows the schedule of each job on each machine along a horizontal time axis. The bar chart for the sequence 1–2–3–4–5 is given in Figure 16.2. This shows, for instance, that job 1 is scheduled on the shear for the first four days; job 2, for the next four days, and so on. We construct a bar chart for a given sequence by scheduling the first job as early as possible on the first machine (shear). Then, as soon as the job is completed, it can be scheduled on the punch press, provided that no other job is currently in progress. First, note that all jobs follow each other on the shearing machine. However, because of variations in processing times, the punch press is often idle while awaiting the next job. The makespan is 37, and the flowtimes for each job are as follows:

Job	Flowtime
1	9
2	10
3	22
4	34
5	37

Thus the average flowtime is (9 + 10 + 22 + 34 + 37)/5 = 22.4.

Applying Johnson's rule to the Hirsch Products example, we find that the smallest processing time occurs for job 2 on the punch press.

Job	Shear	Punch
1	4	5
2	4	①
3	10	4
4	6	10
5	2	3

Since the minimum time is on the second machine, job 2 is scheduled last:

$$\underline{}\ \ \underline{}\ \ \underline{}\ \ \underline{}\ \ \underline{2}$$

Next, for the remaining jobs, we pick the second-smallest processing time. This is 2, which corresponds to job 5 on machine 1. Therefore, job 5 is scheduled first

$$\underline{5}\ \ \underline{}\ \ \underline{}\ \ \underline{}\ \ \underline{2}$$

In the next step, we have a tie between job 1 on the shear and job 3 on the punch press. When ties occur, either job can be chosen. If we pick job 1, we then have

$$\underline{5}\ \ \underline{1}\ \ \underline{}\ \ \underline{}\ \ \underline{2}$$

Continuing with Johnson's rule, the last two steps yield

$$\underline{5}\ \ \underline{1}\ \ \underline{}\ \ \underline{3}\ \ \underline{2}$$
$$\underline{5}\ \ \underline{1}\ \ \underline{4}\ \ \underline{3}\ \ \underline{2}$$

The bar chart for this sequence is shown in Figure 16.3. The makespan is reduced to 27 and the average flowtime is also improved from the original schedule, having a value of 18.2.

The General Job Shop Scheduling Problem

In the most general job shop situation, we must sequence n jobs on m machines. Each job may have a unique routing. If so, there are up to $(n!)^m$ possible schedules. For example, when $n = 5$ and $m = 4$, there are over 200 million schedules! These problems are too difficult to solve optimally and heuristic methods must be used.

Before addressing this problem, it is important to understand the assumptions on which all the previous procedures have been based. We have implicitly assumed that all jobs are available at the same time and that no new jobs arrive during processing. This situation does not usually arise in practice. Jobs arrive intermittently, and scheduling decisions must be made over time. We call these *dynamic* scheduling problems. In these situations, scheduling decisions at each

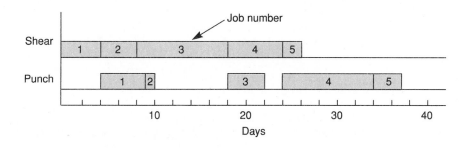

FIGURE 16.2

Bar Chart for Sequence 1-2-3-4-5

machine are usually made by considering only those jobs that are awaiting processing when that machine becomes available. *Priorities* are assigned to the jobs awaiting processing and are used to select the next job to be processed. The assignment of priority rules and selection of jobs for processing is often called **dispatching** and forms the basis for production control in practice.

16.4 PRIORITY DISPATCHING RULES

Dispatching rules used in dynamic job shop situations are usually based on either the attributes of the job, such as processing time or number of operations, or on the characteristics of the shop itself at a particular point in time. The former class of rules are called *static* rules, since job priorities can be calculated before any production activity begins. The latter class of rules are called *dynamic,* since job priorities may change over time depending on the progress of a job in relation to others.[2] Priorities using dynamic rules can only be calculated at the time a machine loading decision is made. Some of the different priority dispatching rules that have been suggested are listed in Table 16.3.

Since jobs arrive intermittently over time, we must usually resort to simulation in order to evaluate a dispatching rule. We illustrate how this can be done through a small example. The example also illustrates how such rules are used in practice.

EXAMPLE

SIMULATION OF DISPATCHING RULES

Lynwood Manufacturing is a small job shop with a lathe, drill press, milling machine, and grinder. Jobs arrive as customers place orders. For simulation purposes, the job arrivals must be specified. This is usually done through analysis of historical data. Let us assume that four jobs will arrive in the near future with characteristics given in Table 16.4.

We also need a method of depicting the status of the shop at any point in time. We do this through the illustration shown below.

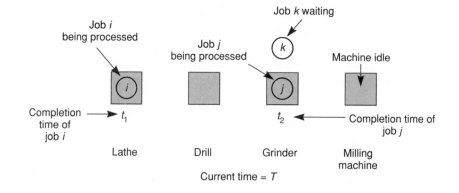

---

[2]Do not be confused over the use of the terms *static* and *dynamic*. In the previous section these terms referred to the way in which jobs arrive at a shop. Here they refer to the type of dispatching rule used.

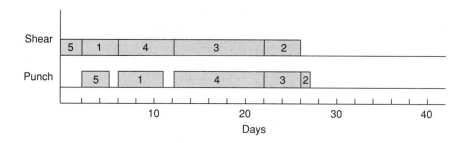

FIGURE 16.3

Bar Chart for Sequence 5-1-4-3-2

TABLE 16.3

Priority Dispatching Rules for Job Shops

Rule	Type	Description
1. Earliest release date	Static	Time job is released to the shop
2. Shortest processing time	Static	Processing time of operation for which job is waiting
3. Total work	Static	Sum of all processing times
4. Earliest due date	Static	Due date of job
5. Least work remaining	Static	Sum of processing times for all operations not yet performed
6. Fewest operations remaining	Static	Number of operations yet to be performed
7. Work in next queue	Dynamic	Amount of work awaiting the next machine in a job's processing sequence
8. Slack time	Dynamic	Time remaining until due date minus remaining processing time
9. Slack/remaining operations	Dynamic	Slack time divided by the number of operations remaining
10. Critical ratio	Dynamic	Time remaining until due date divided by days required to complete job

In this illustration, each machine is represented by a box; jobs being processed or waiting are denoted by circles above the box. Beneath each box is listed the completion time of any job that is being processed by that machine.

Figure 16.4 is a flow chart of the simulation process. In simulating the behavior of the Lynwood Manufacturing job shop over time, we increment time by 5 units because the processing times are given in multiples of 5. Further, we assume that the time to move jobs between machines is negligible.

We shall begin the simulation at time $T = 0$ and use the least-work-remaining rule to schedule jobs. At time 0, jobs 1 and 2 arrive. Job 1 is immediately scheduled on the lathe, and job 2 is assigned to the drill press. The status of the shop at time 0 is

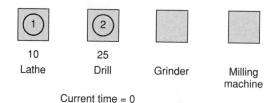

There are only two events that can occur. Either a new job arrives, or some job completes processing on a machine. If nothing occurs during a time interval,

TABLE 16.4

Job Data for Lynwood's Job Shop

Job	Arrival Time	Processing Sequence (Processing Time)*
1	0	$L(10)$, $D(20)$, $G(35)$
2	0	$D(25)$, $L(20)$, $G(30)$, $M(15)$
3	20	$D(10)$, $M(10)$
4	30	$L(15)$, $G(10)$, $M(20)$

*For instance, job 1 must be processed first by lathe, second, by drill press, and third, by the grinder with times 10, 20, and 35, respectively.

L = Lathe; D = Drill; G = Grinder; M = Mill

we simply move on to the next. For the Lynwood example, nothing occurs at time 5, but job 1 finishes on the lathe at time 10. Since job 2 is still on the drill press, job 1 will wait. The status of the shop at this time is:

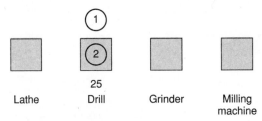

Current time = 10

Nothing happens at time 15. Next, at time 20, job 3 arrives and joins the queue at the drill press:

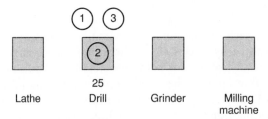

Current time = 20

At time 25, job 2 completes work on the drill press. A decision must be made whether to schedule job 1 or 3 next. The work remaining for job 1 is 20 + 35 = 55, while for job 3, the total remaining processing time is 10 + 10 = 20. Thus job 3 is scheduled next and job 2 moves to the lathe.

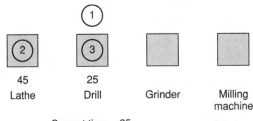

Current time = 25

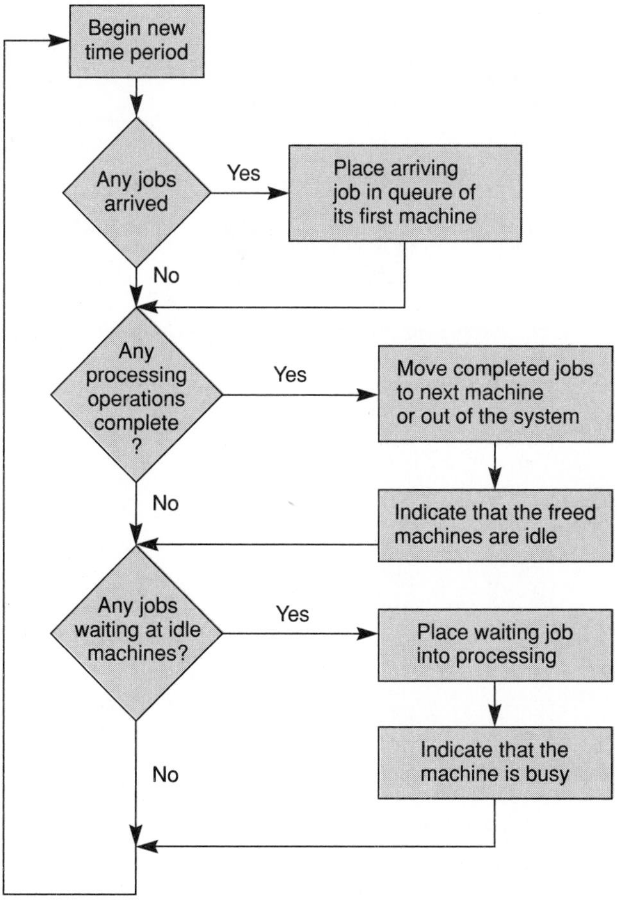

FIGURE 16.4
Flow Chart for
Simulating
Lynwood
Manufacturing
Job Shop

Continuing in this fashion, we trace the status of the shop over time, as shown in Figure 16.5, until all four jobs are completed.

We may construct a bar chart of the result of this scheduling process, shown in Figure 16.6. Statistics regarding machine utilization and job waiting times and completion times can now be computed easily and used as measures to compare various dispatching rules. A summary is provided in Table 16.5. Simulations such as these also give the manager an idea of where bottlenecks might occur or where more capacity needs to be added.

Obviously, in order to obtain any useful results about the performance of dispatching rules, simulations must be conducted over longer periods of time and for more realistic shop configurations. Extensive studies have been conducted to analyze these rules.[3] There is no single best dispatching rule to use for job shop

Selecting a Dispatching Rule

---

[3]A survey of results can be found in J.H. Blackstone, D.T. Phillips, and G.L. Hogg, "A State-of-the-Art Survey of Dispatching Rules for Manufacturing Job Shop Operations," *International Journal of Production Research*, 20 (1982): 27–45.

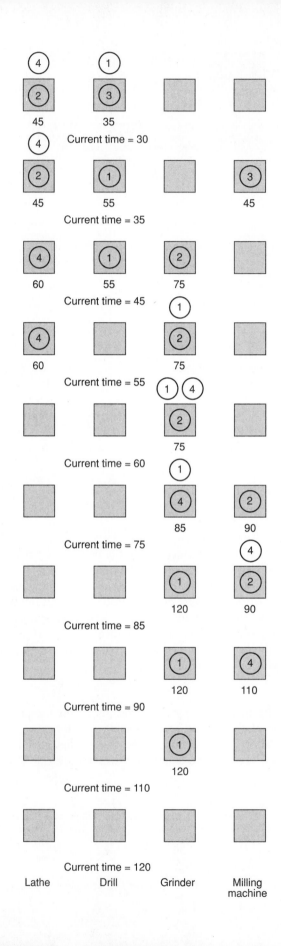

FIGURE 16.5

Simulation of Lynwood Manufacturing Problem

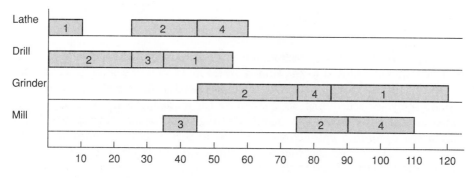

FIGURE 16.6

Bar Chart for Lynwood's Job Shop

Job	Waiting Time	Completion Time	Machine	Idle Time*
1	55	120	Lathe	75
2	0	90	Drill	65
3	25	45	Grinder	45
4	65	110	Mill	75

*Makespan minus processing time

TABLE 16.5

Simulation Results Using Least Work Remaining for Lynwood's Job Shop

scheduling, since these rules are very much dependent on the shop configuration and sequence of job arrivals. However, the simulation studies have shown that shortest processing time, though very simplistic, is among the best rules. In general, SPT results in fewer jobs waiting in queues than many of the other rules. However, jobs that do wait (those with longer processing times) usually wait a long time. This can be avoided by modifying the rule to place higher priorities on jobs that have been waiting an extensive amount of time. Slack time and slack time per remaining operation, rules 8 and 9 in Table 16.3, are among the best dynamic rules.

When due dates are important, the critical-ratio (rule 10 in Table 16.3) is very useful. The critical ratio is the ratio of the demand time of a job to the supply time. For instance, if it takes 8 days to make an order and it is needed in 10 days, the critical ratio is $10/8 = 1.25$. If this index is greater than 1, the job is ahead of schedule; if equal to 1, the job is on time; and if less than 1, the job is behind schedule. The use of this index permits managers to see easily the status of all jobs and place priorities accordingly. The earliest due date has also been shown to be an effective rule.

One of the important factors that affects whether we choose to use a static, as opposed to a dynamic, rule is the amount of information gathering required. With a static rule, priorities can be placed on the route card when it is issued. Dynamic rules require constant feedback from the shop floor and recalculation of priorities. Often this requires a computer system for efficient data processing. The cost of implementing such a system may indeed outweigh the benefits derived from using a dynamic scheduling rule.

Dispatching rules can be used only as guidelines. Machine breakdowns, material problems, absenteeism, and so on are problems that must be resolved by rescheduling and expediting. The experience and knowledge of supervisors and operations managers is critical in day-to-day shop operations.

OPT (**optimized production technology**) is a production planning and scheduling tool that was introduced to the United States in 1979 by Creative Output, Inc., (COI) of Milford, Connecticut. OPT can be viewed from several perspectives: as a philosophy for scheduling; as a language for modeling manufacturing operations; as a software system for manufacturing resource planning; as a tool for developing optimized production schedules; and as a tool for coordinating the efforts of marketing, engineering, and manufacturing to realize the *common* goals of an organization.

The OPT software provides a detailed description of the production system in a *product network* (see the case problem at the end of this chapter for an illustration of a product network) that reflects the reality of the manufacturing process. The network shows exactly how a product is made using information commonly found in a company's BOM (bill of materials) and routing files. Each operation is defined by specifying the resources used, setup times, and run times. In addition, the model allows for specification of desired stock levels at each operation, maximum stock limits, minimum batch quantities, scheduled delays, order quantities, and due dates. Resource descriptions must also be specified; these include the relative efficiency of various resources, available overtime, and additional resources required for setting up the operation.

OPT is based on a set of rules that define the philosophy advanced by COI. Many of these rules revolve around the concept of a *bottleneck* or constrained resource. The concept of a bottleneck was introduced in Chapter 9. Recall that the bottleneck in a system is an operation that limits the throughput (total sales) of the entire system. The rules stated by COI are as follows:

1. *Balance flow, not capacity.* That is, we should not attempt to keep all the resources busy but should focus on maintaining a smooth flow of material. This has been an effective rule in assembly lines and process industries but has not traditionally been used in job shops and repetitive manufacturing.

2. *The level of utilization of a nonbottleneck is determined not by its own potential but by some other constraint in the system.* Nonbottleneck resources should not be operated to their inherent capacity but should be scheduled and operated in a manner consistent with other constraints, such as bottlenecks in the system. It clearly makes no sense to have nonbottleneck operations produce more than the bottleneck operations can absorb. This only increases inventory and operating expense.

3. *Utilization and activation of a resource are not synonymous.* This is an intuitive rule if we consider utilization as the degree to which we *should* use a resource to reach the strategic goal of profitability and define activation as the degree to which we *can* use a resource.

4. *An hour lost at a bottleneck is an hour lost for the entire system.* The OPT philosophy stresses the importance of maintaining 100 percent utilization on bottleneck resources in order to maximize output.

5. *An hour saved at a nonbottleneck is just a mirage.* Since the capacity of a system is limited by the bottleneck resources, saving time at a nonbottleneck does not affect the throughput of the system.

6. *Bottlenecks govern both throughput and inventory in the system.* COI argues that work-in-process inventories are a function of the amount of work required to keep the bottlenecks busy; inventories can be controlled by where the bottlenecks are located.

7. *The transfer batch may not, and many times should not, be equal to the process batch.* The transfer batch is the amount of product transferred from one operation to another; and the process batch is the amount processed at any operation between changeovers. Many manufacturers would state that lot splitting and overlapping of batches should be avoided. The OPT philosophy states that flexibility in how batches are processed is essential to speeding the flow of product from raw material to finished goods. The OPT logic is derived from observing assembly lines; there the amount moved between operations is a transfer batch of one, whereas the process batch (the amount produced between changeovers) is much larger.

8. *The process batch should be variable, not fixed.* OPT process batches are a function of the schedule and should not be fixed over time and from operation to operation. When different numbers of parts are manufactured on different equipment, the process batch needs to be varied in order to maintain a smooth and rapid flow of materials to customers.

9. *Schedules should be determined by looking at all the constraints simultaneously. Lead times are the result of a schedule and can not be predetermined.* Although MRP assumes predetermined lead times, OPT suggests that lead times are not fixed but are variable. Consider the production of two parts needed for an assembly. Part A requires processing on machines X and Y, with times of 20 hours and 5 hours, respectively. Part B requires processing on machines X and Z, with times of 6 hours and 15 hours, respectively. Whereas the lead times of parts A and B appear to be 25 and 21, note that since both require processing on machine X first, if part A is initially released to the shop, its actual lead time will be 25 hours, whereas B's will be 41. If part B is released first, its actual lead time will be 21 hours, whereas A's will be 31. Hence, the lead time is a function of the schedule.

The OPT software uses these principles to guide the creation of a schedule. The first step is to determine where the bottlenecks of the system lie. Once these have been identified, the network is split into two parts: a critical resource portion, which contains the bottleneck operations up through final assembly to customer orders; and a noncritical resource portion. The critical resource portion of the network is scheduled forward in time to maximize throughput at the bottleneck operation while simultaneously maintaining the smooth flow of parts. Critical resources are loaded at 100 percent of their available capacity. Finally, the noncritical resource portion of the network is scheduled backward in time in a manner similar to MRP but only to "support" operations performed by critical resources. That support takes the form of strategically established inventory buffers to ensure maximum utilization of critical operations even in the event of machine malfunction. Additionally, because these few buffers contain what little inventory remains in the system, they provide a focal point for improving quality and directing engineering changes where such improvements will have the greatest impact on the financial well-being of the company.

OPT has many advantages. Among these are[4]

1. A simplified technique for production scheduling.
   - Schedules are not time consuming to develop
   - Schedules do not require much data
   - Less accuracy is required in the data
   - Less computer processing capability is required
   - Less personnel time is required to analyze the schedule
2. User portion less complex
   - The internal mathematical technique contains sophistication that makes the system user's job easier
   - User knowledge requirement is small
3. Rapid projection of schedule
   - Quick schedules allow for the quick modification of the schedules and therefore more flexibility
   - Schedule changes can occur in a few hours rather than days
   - Quick schedule development allows for simulation capability
4. Plant production analysis occurs
   - Bottlenecks in the production process are specifically defined
   - Improvements are easily made on the bottlenecks because of their clear definition
   - Simulation can be used to test variations in plant output and how this will affect the plant load
   - Capacity changes can be simulated
5. Other advantages
   - Actual manufacturing resources are taken into account
   - Production output is maximized and work-in-process (WIP) inventory is minimized
   - A ten percent or greater increase in production output is possible
   - A twenty percent or greater reduction in WIP inventory is possible
   - Smaller batch sizes are calculated based on profitability rather than on EOQ

As one may expect, several disadvantages also exist in using OPT.

1. Plant reorganization required
   - Conceptual reorganization would be required
   - Data processing systems would be replaced
   - Management style will need to be changed
   - New reporting systems will need to be learned
   - Equipment changes and movement may be necessary in order to facilitate using OPT efficiently
2. Costing and accounting systems disrupted
   - Efficiency can no longer be calculated
   - Job cost control data is restricted in some areas
   - Performance evaluations no longer exist

---

[4]Plenert, Gerhard, and Thomas D. Best, "MRP, JIT, and OPT: What's 'Best'?" *Production and Inventory Management*, 27, no. 2, (1986):22–29. Reprinted with permission, The American Production and Inventory Control Society, Inc.

3. Users disrupted
   - Users will need to be retrained
   - New reports will need to be developed for data processing and accounting to handle the new information base
4. Other disadvantages
   - OPT is more complex than other manual methods
   - A tighter schedule is produced than other methods, allowing less ability to accommodate production errors
   - The financial analysis system has been changed

A number of corporations are using OPT and have reported some significant benefits.[5] For example, one company used it to verify capacity analysis and operating plans for a "factory of the future." Plant management was able to eliminate several million dollars of planned equipment purchases, reduce the plant staffing by 50 percent, and cut planned cycle time by 25 percent. Another used OPT scheduling to reduce its manufacturing lead time and finished goods inventory by 50 percent, even though the number of manufactured end items of its product line increased by 35 percent. In yet another case, a small auto parts manufacturer planned to add 30 to 40 workers to meet a sudden increase in demand. An OPT simulation showed that the demand could be met by running a number of operations 6 or 7 days a week and adding very few workers. The savings in benefit costs alone totaled nearly $100,000.

OPT represents a new approach to operations planning and scheduling. The underlying concepts are relevant to many production environments and can be applied even without the OPT software.

16.6 PROGRESS CONTROL

As Murphy's law states, if something can go wrong it will, and this is especially true with schedules. Thus it is important that progress be monitored on a continuing basis. Production controllers must know the status of orders that are ahead of schedule or behind schedule, orders that are short of material, work centers that are backlogged, changes in inventory, labor turnover, and sales commitments for shipments.

Short-term capacity fluctuations also necessitate changes in schedules. Factors affecting short-term capacity include absenteeism, labor performance, machine failures, tooling problems, and material shortages. These invariably occur and are unavoidable. Some alternatives available to operations managers for dealing with capacity shortages are overtime, short-term subcontracting, alternate production routing, or reallocations of the work force.

Bar charts are useful tools for monitoring production. An example is shown in Figure 16.7. The shaded areas indicate completed work. This chart shows, for example, that job 4 has not yet started on machine 2, job 1 is currently behind schedule on machine 3, and jobs 2 and 5 are ahead of schedule. Perhaps needed

[5]Adapted from *OPT Management System,* Creative Output, Inc., Milford, CT.

FIGURE 16.7
Bar Chart for
Monitoring
Schedule Progress

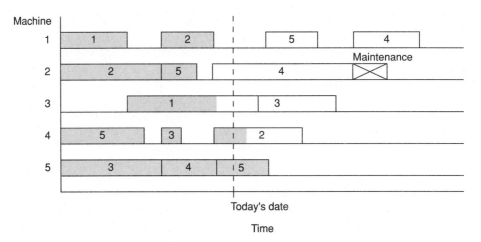

material has not yet been delivered for job 4 or machine 3 has experienced a breakdown. In any event, it is up to production control personnel to revise the schedule or to expedite jobs that are behind schedule. Many other types of graphical aids are useful and commercially available (see Photo 16.1). Many companies have production personnel whose sole purpose is to expedite "hot jobs," those with top priority for completion. Their task is to find ways of handling rush orders, to track down orders that are late and, in essence, to determine the true priorities of jobs for scheduling. Too much expediting, however, can create

PHOTO 16.1

A small New York manufacturer uses a magnetic board to schedule its jobs over a 3-month horizon and track progress. The file cards on the left show the company name and order information and act as a record for each job that passes through the plant. Courtesy of Methods Research Corp., 1108 Pollack Ave., Ocean, NJ 07712.

much disruption in a plant—if a high percentage of jobs are hot, then there is a problem. Excess expediting can be avoided by proper scheduling and capacity planning. If hot-job lists can be reduced, then the need for overtime to complete jobs that are behind schedule is also reduced. This can also lower setup costs, since operators are not required to tear down a running job in order to run a hot one and will improve productivity and quality since workers will not be pressured.

Computerized information systems are used extensively for production control in large plants. It is not uncommon for a manufacturing facility to consist of hundreds of work centers or machines and process thousands of different parts. The sheer complexity of scheduling in such firms requires a computerized approach. A typical information system is illustrated in Figure 16.8. Three primary inputs to a production control system are the *route file, work center file,* and *shop order file.* The route file contains the routing information for each customer's

Computerized Production-control Systems

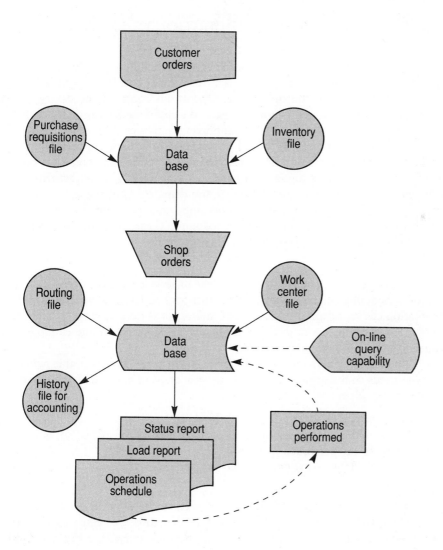

FIGURE 16.8

Information System for Production Scheduling and Control

order, including part numbers, operations performed, standards, and so on. The work center file includes capacity information, and the shop order file contains the data on each customer's order. Typical outputs include *load reports, shop schedules,* and *order status reports.* Updates may occur on a daily basis or even every few hours. This involves a lot of data collection and processing, and maintenance of accuracy is vitally important. Automatic identification systems are being used more frequently to accomplish this. Many systems have on-line query capabilities whereby a salesperson can check on the status of a customer's order or establish a projected delivery date.

In order for a computerized control system to work efficiently, it needs accurate information and support of management. The users of the system also need to be trained and educated. The P/OM in Practice case study involving Western Electric's Semiconductor Production-Control System illustrates some of the problems, solutions, and behavioral implications in the design and implementation of a computerized production-control system.

16.7 SCHEDULING AND CONTROL IN THE PRODUCTION OF SERVICES

The production of services provides some unique scheduling problems. The principal objective is making sure that the service is made available to the customer at the right time and in the right place. Operations control is necessary in two principal areas of activity. The first area is the interface between the customer contact portion of a service and its supporting activities. Examples are the interface between order entry and food preparation in a fast-food restaurant, and the interface between bank tellers and a bank's computer system. This type of operations control is analogous to operations control in a manufacturing environment. The second involves scheduling and dispatching of the service delivery system to the customer. Two of the most important problems in this category are personnel scheduling and vehicle scheduling. These problems are examined and some techniques are presented for solving them.

Personnel Scheduling

Personnel scheduling problems are prevalent in service organizations. Examples include scheduling telephone operators, turnpike toll booth operators, airline reservation clerks, hospital nursing staff, police, fast-food employees, and many others. Some of the most difficult problems involve scheduling employees of transportation services, such as airlines and buses.

The objective of a personnel scheduling problem is to match available personnel with the needs of the organization. The general steps in approaching a personnel scheduling problem are

1. determine the quantity of work to be done
2. determine the staffing required to perform the work
3. determine the personnel available
4. match available personnel to staffing requirements and develop a work schedule.

The first step, determining the quantity of work to be done, is often facilitated by graphing the demand over time. If service demands are relatively level over time, then it is usually easy to schedule personnel on standard weekly work shifts.

If the work load varies within a shift, as is the case for telephone operators or toll gate operators, then the problem becomes one of scheduling shifts to meet the varying demand.

Determining the staffing required must take into account worker productivity factors, personal allowances, sickness, vacations, and so on. Personnel availability is a function of time off because of sickness and vacation, the part-time labor pool in some cases, temporary summer employees, or other sources of labor.

The matching of personnel to staffing requirements is the most difficult step. Different approaches are required for different problem situations because of the nature of constraints. We examine a problem of scheduling personnel with consecutive days off in the face of fluctuating requirements.

SCHEDULING CONSECUTIVE DAYS OFF[6]

EXAMPLE

The Sam Brent Bridge has nine manual toll booths in addition to several automatic collectors. Based on statistics of traffic flow, it was determined that the minimum personnel requirements on each day of the week are those given below.

Day	Mon	Tue	Wed	Thur	Fri	Sat	Sun
Minimum Personnel	8	6	6	6	9	5	3

We wish to schedule the employees so that each has two consecutive days off and all labor requirements are met. We proceed as follows. First, we choose the set of smallest requirements with at least two consecutive days. That is, we pick the days with the smallest demand, next smallest, and so on, until there are at least two consecutive days. We then circle the requirements for the two consecutive days. From the table above, we choose Sunday first and then Saturday. We stop, since these are consecutive days. Thus we have

Employee Number 1

Day	Mon	Tue	Wed	Thur	Fri	Sat	Sun
Requirements	8	6	6	6	9	⑤	③

Assign employee 1 to work on all days that are *not* circled, that is, Monday through Friday. Now subtract 1 from the requirements of each day worked. This gives us

Day	Mon	Tue	Wed	Thur	Fri	Sat	Sun
Requirements	7	⑤	⑤	⑤	8	⑤	③

We now repeat the procedure with this new set of requirements. We obtain

Employee Number 2

Day	Mon	Tue	Wed	Thur	Fri	Sat	Sun
Requirements	7	5	5	5	8	5	3

---

[6]This approach is suggested by R. Tibrewala, D. Phillippe, and J. Browne, "Optimal Scheduling of Two Consecutive Idle Periods," *Management Science*, 19, no. 1 (September 1972): 71–75.

When there are several alternatives, as in this case, we do one of two things. First, we try to choose a pair of days with the lowest requirement. If there are still ties, then we choose the first available pair. In this case, we again use Saturday and Sunday as days off for employee 2, since this pair has the smallest requirement. Subtracting 1 from each working day's requirement, we now have

Day	Mon	Tue	Wed	Thur	Fri	Sat	Sun
Requirements	6	4	4	4	7	5	3

Circling the smallest requirements until we obtain at least two consecutive days yields:

Employee Number 3

Day	Mon	Tue	Wed	Thur	Fri	Sat	Sun
Requirements	6	④	④	④	7	5	③

The only pairs from which we could choose are Tue–Wed or Wed–Thur, so we choose Tue–Wed by the tie-breaking rule, leaving

Day	Mon	Tue	Wed	Thur	Fri	Sat	Sun
Requirements	5	4	4	3	6	4	2

Continuing with this procedure, we obtain the following sequence of requirements (circled numbers represent the lowest requirement pair selected).

Employee Number	Mon	Tue	Wed	Thur	Fri	Sat	Sun
4	5	4	4	3	6	④	②
5	4	3	③	②	5	4	2
6	3	2	3	2	4	③	①
7	②	①	2	1	3	3	1
8	2	1	①	⓪	2	2	0
9	①	⓪	1	0	1	1	0
10	1	⓪	⓪	0	0	0	0

The employee schedules we obtain are summarized in Table 16.6. Even though some requirements are exceeded, the solution procedure minimizes the number of workers required. A more difficult problem that we do not address is that of determining a schedule of rotating shifts so that employees do not always have the same 2 days off. This is a more practical situation.

16.8 VEHICLE SCHEDULING

In Chapter 7, we discussed the importance of physical distribution. The day-to-day scheduling of vehicles is an important operational concern. Many companies own their own fleets of trucks to handle their transportation needs. This gives

TABLE 16.6

Toll Bridge Employee Schedule

Employee Number	Mon	Tue	Wed	Thur	Fri	Sat	Sun
1	x	x	x	x	x		
2	x	x	x	x	x		
3	x			x	x	x	x
4	x	x	x	x	x		
5	x	x			x	x	x
6	x	x	x	x	x		
7			x	x	x	x	x
8	x	x			x	x	x
9			x	x	x	x	x
10	x			x	x	x	x
Total	8	6	6	8	10	6	6

them more control over customer service, dispatching of shipments, and selecting routes. In addition, lower costs can often be realized because of the elimination of common carrier charges. Typical industries that manage large fleets of vehicles include dairy, produce, gasoline, beer, and soft drink, as well as service organizations such as municipal sanitation departments, schools, and the postal service. Scheduling and routing of vehicles is an important problem to managers of these organizations.

The general vehicle-scheduling problem can be described as follows. We are given a number of customers with known delivery requirements and locations. A fleet of trucks with limited capacity is available. What customers should be assigned to different routes to minimize the total time or distance traveled? Other constraints may also be present. For instance, there may be union rules about the total time a driver can be on the road at one time, or customer deliveries may only be made over specific time intervals, such as only in the mornings, because of dock availability. Other routing problems are variations of this general situation. School buses must be routed to stop at various locations to pick up school children. Snow-removal equipment must be assigned to streets so that all major roads are treated in the shortest possible time.

Computerized routing assists beer distributors in minimizing their travel time during beer deliveries. Anheuser-Busch, for instance, provides routing systems to its wholesalers.[7] The routing system takes into account a distributor's sales volume, number of accounts, and driving distances, as well as special requests from retailers who want to receive their beer deliveries at a certain time of the day. By reducing travel time, wholesalers can spend more productive time servicing their accounts. In addition, increased efficiency may help wholesalers avoid the significant manpower, vehicle, and other delivery costs of assigning additional routes, while still maintaining the highest quality of service available. Computerized routing is also useful when a wholesaler is planning to add a satellite warehouse location. The routing system can determine the best site for the new

---

[7]William L. Rammes, "Making Friends is Our Business," in *When America Does It Right: Case Studies in Service Quality,* Jay W. Spechler, ed., Norcross, GA: Industrial Engineering and Management Press, 1988, p. 29–37.

facility based on the number and location of existing accounts, distribution costs, and related factors.

A procedure that is often used in vehicle-routing applications is the *Clarke-Wright savings approach*.[8] This technique is used in determining routes from a central depot or warehouse to n delivery points or customers. Generally there are time or capacity restrictions associated with the problem that preclude the use of only one route from the depot to all customers and back.

We assume that travel times between all pairs of customers and the depot (customer zero) are known, and let t_{ij} be the travel time between customer i and customer j. The procedure begins with an initial solution in which each customer is serviced individually from the depot as shown in Figure 16.9. This initial solution, therefore, has n routes between the depot and each customer.

Notice that such a solution is very inefficient since the vehicle must return to the depot after servicing each customer. An alternative is to *combine* routes in order to eliminate unnecessary return trips. For example, suppose that the routes to customers i and j are combined into one route (see Figure 16.10). The combined route can be completed in less time than the original route if

$$t_{0i} + t_{0j} + t_{ij} < 2t_{0i} + 2t_{0j}$$

or

$$0 < t_{0i} + t_{0j} - t_{ij} = s_{ij}$$

The term on the right hand side, s_{ij}, is called the *savings* associated with joining customers i and j on the same route. If the savings is positive, then it is beneficial to join the customers.

The steps of the Clarke-Wright solution procedure for a given set of travel times and customer requirements are as follows:

1. Compute the savings for all pairs of customers. The savings for customers i and j is

$$s_{ij} = t_{0i} + t_{0j} - t_{ij}$$

2. Choose the pair of customers with the largest savings and determine if it is feasible to link them together. If so, then construct a new route by joining them. If not, discard this possibility and choose the pair with the next-largest savings.

3. Continue with Step 2 as long as the savings is positive. When all positive savings have been considered, stop.

EXAMPLE

VEHICLE ROUTING USING THE CLARKE-WRIGHT SAVINGS APPROACH

In order to illustrate the application of the Clarke-Wright savings approach, let us consider a hypothetical beer distributorship.

Mike and Kevin's beer distributorship has received orders from seven customers for delivery on the next day. The number of cases required by each

---

[8]G. Clarke and J. W. Wright, "Scheduling of Vehicles From a Central Depot to a Number of Delivery Points," *Operations Research,* 11 (1963): 568.

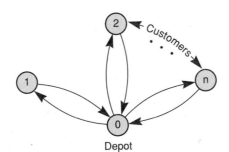

FIGURE 16.9
Initial Routes

Depot

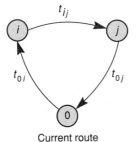

Current route

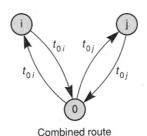

Combined route

FIGURE 16.10
Calculation of Savings

customer is given in Table 16.7. The time it takes to travel from one customer to another is shown in Table 16.8. We assume that the travel time from 1 to 2 is the same as that from 2 to 1, and so on, so only the lower portion of the matrix is filled in. The van that M&K uses has a capacity for 80 cases. M&K wants to route the trucks so that all deliveries are made in 8 hours and so that fuel costs are as low as possible.

We start with an initial solution in which each customer is serviced alone from the warehouse (which is denoted as "customer" 0). The initial set of routes is

$$0-1-0$$
$$0-2-0$$
$$0-3-0$$
$$0-4-0$$
$$0-5-0$$
$$0-6-0$$
$$0-7-0$$

Letting t_{ij} represent the time required to travel from customer i to customer j, the total time required is

$$2(t_{01} + t_{02} + t_{03} + t_{04} + t_{05} + t_{06} + t_{07})$$
$$= 2(20 + 57 + 51 + 50 + 10 + 15 + 90)$$
$$= 586 \text{ minutes}$$

This solution takes approximately 9.8 hours; hence, all shipments cannot be made in one day using this solution.

We want to now construct new routes that *improve* the current solution. For instance, if customers 1 and 2 are linked together (which is not possible, however, since their demand together is greater than the van's capacity), the total distance

TABLE 16.7

Customer Requirements for M&K Beer Example

Customers	Number of Cases
1	46
2	55
3	33
4	30
5	24
6	75
7	30

TABLE 16.8

Travel Times (t_{ij}) in Minutes (0 Represents the Warehouse)

					Customer			
Customer	0	1	2	3	4	5	6	7
0	—							
1	20	—						
2	57	51	—					
3	51	10	50	—				
4	50	55	20	50	—			
5	10	25	30	11	50	—		
6	15	30	10	60	60	20	—	
7	90	53	47	38	10	90	12	—

saved is $t_{01} + t_{02} - t_{12} = 20 + 57 - 51 = 26$ minutes. The return trip from each customer is eliminated, but the added link between customers 1 and 2 is included. The first step is to compute the savings for all pairs of customers. This is done in Table 16.9.

The next step is to choose the pair of customers with the largest savings, and if no constraints are violated by joining them on the same route, then we should join them together. We then take this new solution and again try to join the pair of customers with the next-largest savings, as long as no constraints are violated. We continue on in this fashion until all remaining s_{ij} are negative, at which point it is no longer profitable to consider joining customers.

To illustrate, we see that the largest savings is 130. If customers 4 and 7 are joined, the total demand on the route is 60, which is below the van's capacity. Therefore, the new set of routes is

$$0-1-0$$
$$0-2-0$$
$$0-3-0$$
$$0-4-7-0$$
$$0-5-0$$
$$0-6-0$$

Next we try to join customers 3 and 7, since this represents the next-largest savings. Note that this increases the demand on the route to 93, which violates the van capacity constraint. Thus we discard this idea and choose the next-largest savings, 100. Combining customers 2 and 7 again violates the capacity constraint and so does the next (combining 7 and 6). Similarly, if we consider customers 2 and 4, with the next-largest savings of 87, we again violate the van capacity

	Customer						
Customer	1	2	3	4	5	6	7
1	—						
2	26	—					
3	61	58	—				
4	15	87	51	—			
5	5	37	50	10	—		
6	5	62	6	5	5	—	
7	57	100	103	130	10	93	—

TABLE 16.9

Savings Matrix for the Clarke-Wright Method

constraint. Again the next largest savings of 62 (combining 2 and 6) violates the van capacity. However, the next-largest savings is 61, and customers 3 and 1 may be joined because their combined capacity is 79. Continuing in this fashion, we obtain the final set of routes.

Route	Time
0–4–7–0	150
0–3–1–0	81
0–2–5–0	97
0–6–0	30

The total time required is reduced to 358 minutes, or about 6 hours, a savings of about 3.8 hours over the original schedule.

P/OM IN

PRACTICE

In this section we present applications from Western Electric and Mobil Oil Corporation which describe current practices in production-activity control. The Western Electric example focuses on a production-control system for semiconductor manufacturing.

The Mobil Oil example describes a computerized real-time vehicle scheduling system. These examples show the important role of scheduling and production-activity control in operations management, both in manufacturing and source.

WESTERN ELECTRIC'S SEMICONDUCTOR PRODUCTION-CONTROL SYSTEM[9]

I n the manufacture of semiconductors, it is difficult to achieve consistent electrical and mechanical

characteristics. Because of the nature of semiconductor processing, the percentage of good parts pro-

---

[9]Adapted from E. H. Heilman, R. W. Loy, and W. F. Byers, "Production Control System for Semiconductors." Reprinted with permission from *Industrial Engineering* magazine, August 1976. Copyright © Institute of Industrial Engineers, Inc., 25 Technology Park/Atlanta, Norcross, GA 30092.

duced, referred to as *manufacturing yields,* may vary from one group of materials to another. Because of this, there is constant uncertainty as to the amount of in-process inventories required for machine loading and estimation of deliveries.

A second problem arises because electrical properties of materials can be significantly changed without changing the physical appearance. Thus it is difficult to keep track of various products during processing. At Western Electric's Reading Works, several hundred different types of semiconductors are made. In view of these problems, Reading developed a computerized production-control system to replace an inadequate manual system.

However, the system designers recognized that computerization is often misunderstood or resented by both shop employees and shop management. Thus it was important to take into account several basic considerations: user's feelings, solution requirements, data collection, and accuracy.

Behavioral considerations are critical. It is important that the users feel comfortable with the level of sophistication that a computerized system provides in order to gain acceptance of the system. For instance, the system calculates current production yields from raw data provided by the shop. This information is used by shop management to plan future production. Although the planning function can also be computerized, this was *not* done, so that shop supervisors' experience and judgment could be integrated with the computer-calculated information.

Successful systems development must consist of a coordinated effort between the designers *and* the users. Many production-control systems have failed because of a lack of communication between designers and users. In the Reading project, users saw the need for providing fast and accurate data collection, while the designers saw the need for providing flexibility for changing needs and greater sophistication as the system matured. User involvement was assumed by including first- and second-level shop supervision on the development team, as well as production-control managers, information systems specialists, and industrial engineers.

Data collection methods utilized punched cards, since there was no need for real-time response. This, however, was unsatisfactory for the new system. Furthermore, the system in use permitted shop operators to punch their own cards. It was found that shop training and system modifications could be better coordinated by one person, and this was already being done informally under the current sys-

tem. This concept led to the establishment of a special terminal operator in each area, whose duties were to collect production records and enter them into the computer.

In order to provide for the desired accuracy of data, several steps were taken. The hardware and software used were selected to provide error-detection capability. Terminal operators were responsible for prescreening of data, and a checklist of the previous day's entries were provided for post-entry screening. Also, shop supervisors were responsible for their employee's accuracy in data recording and entry.

The production data collected is used to update three major system files and produce shop reports. These files contain the operations for each manufactured part, the location of all in-process inventories and summarized production data for specific time periods. The responsibility for file maintenance was given to the production-control department. The information that the system provides consists of

1. *Daily inventory status:* tracking and expediting specific products
2. *Yield calculations:* shop planning and production scheduling
3. *Calculation of potential good product*
4. *Production status:* current customer orders and expected future shipments
5. *Labor efficiency:* individual and department
6. *Absence reporting*

Daily reports are distributed to first-line supervisors and selected shop personnel, whereas summaries are prepared for higher level management on a daily, weekly, or monthly basis for tactical planning purposes.

The new system has helped to alleviate some of the problems associated with semiconductor manufacturing and has also reduced clerical effort required for effective production control. It is worthwhile to point out that this system provides information, not decisions. The production-control department can use the information in order to make better decisions.

QUESTIONS
1. Discuss why Western Electric decided to computerize their production control system.
2. Explain the role of user involvement in successful systems development.
3. What steps were taken to ensure quality?

COMPUTER ASSISTED DISPATCHING OF TANK TRUCKS FOR MOBIL OIL CORPORATION[10]

In the spring of 1985, a nationwide system for dispatching and processing customer orders for gasoline and distillates began full operation at Mobil Oil Corporation. This is a completely integrated, highly automated system that controls the flow of $4 billion annual sales from initial order entry to final delivery, confirmation, and billing. The entire process is overseen by a handful of people in a small office in Valley Forge, Pennsylvania, but it now operates more efficiently than the old system in all respects: it provides better customer service, greatly improved credit, inventory, and operating cost control, and significantly reduced distribution costs. Central to this new system is CAD (computer assisted dispatch), designed to assist human dispatchers in real-time as they determine the means by which ordered product will be safely and efficiently delivered to customers.

Under the best of conditions, dispatching is hard work. The dispatcher must attend to myriad details concerning customer, vehicle fleet, and product status. Dispatching petroleum tank trucks involves following intricate rules that govern safe and efficient operation. The costs of distribution are very sensitive to dispatching decisions, and even small errors in judgement can severely disrupt daily operations.

When considering the dispatching problem, one must take into account the following aspects, as illustrated in Figure 16.11. An area may have several terminals (sources of product). Each terminal may have different products available, and the same product may have a different cost at each terminal. Although over 20 products may be distributed, three grades of motor gasoline constitute most of the volume.

The trucks available include Mobil's own trucks and hired trucks. The trucks may have different capacities and different numbers and sizes of separate bulk cargo compartments, and different cost structures. Assigning orders as loads on trucks may require adjustment of the ordered quantities of products so that they fit into the truck compart-

ments. Further, equipment compatability must be considered, and the routes must reflect the various weight jurisdictions through which the trucks pass, as well as the cost of road and bridge tolls.

The objectives of the dispatching process are to minimize the cost of delivered product, to balance the work load among the company trucks, and to load the maximum weight on a truck while adhering to all laws and proper loading rules. These conflicting objectives must be met within the constraints of maintaining customer service levels. The following set of decisions must be made:

- from which terminal to supply each order
- assignment of orders to delivery trucks
- adjustment of order quantities to fit truck compartments
- loading the trucks to their maximum legal weight
- routing the trucks and sequencing the deliveries

These decisions must take into account truck cost; product cost, availability, specific gravity, and temperature; equipment compatibility; weight jurisdiction; and delivery policy. Because of the complexity of the decisions and the interaction among them, human dispatchers usually seek acceptable solutions. They may be guided by simple decision rules that perform reasonably well on the average but poorly in specific situations. In such an environment, dispatchers cannot be expected to look for very low-cost solutions. In fact, they are not even aware of all the needed data.

The CAD system that was developed to automate the dispatching process makes the following major business decisions:

1. *Own versus hired transportation:* By considering the availability and cost of proprietary, dedicated contract carrier, and common carrier trucks, the system reduces costs and balances work load among trucks. The cost of overtime and undertime of trucks and drivers is also a consideration.

[10]Adapted from Gerald G. Brown, Carol J. Ellis, Glenn W. Graves, and David Ronen, "Real-Time, Wide Area Dispatch of Mobil Tank Trucks," *Interfaces*, 17, no. 1, (1987): 107–120. Copyright 1987 The Institute of Management Sciences, 290 Westminster Street, Providence, Rhode Island 02903, USA.

FIGURE 16.11   Small Area Dispatch

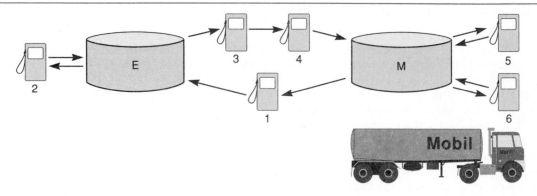

A small area dispatch in which terminal M is a truck domicile, and terminal E i s not. Customer 1 is used as a relay load to terminal E so that customer 2's order may be delivered economically from there. Customers 3 and 4 constitute a split load (a mulitple stop, route delivery). This simplified illustration ignores limited product availability, one-way streets, weight and load restrictions, bridge and road tolls, truck shift limits, and other realistic features encountered in practice.

2. *Sourcing:* The inclusion of all terminals in the area results in dynamic sourcing of orders, which allows differences in laid-down product costs at the various terminals to be considered in concert with transportation costs to further reduce costs.

3. *Vehicle Loading:* Fitting the orders well on the trucks keeps customers happy. Loading to maximize product weight increases the delivered quantities per load while adhering to weight limits and safe loading rules.

4. *Routing:* Delivery time and mileage trip standards are maintained for frequently used routes between terminals and customer locations. A georeference system estimates trip time and mileage for other routes and, incidentally, provides an independent means of auditing trip standards. Routing takes into account weight jurisdictions under way and road and bridge tolls, thus assuring good sequencing of loads for each truck.

The overall objectives of the system are to minimize all costs, maintain service levels, and remain safe and legal.

CAD cannot completely replace the human dispatcher because many crucial aspects of the dispatching process are not quantifiable. To achieve ideal results, CAD must support human judgment. By relieving human dispatchers of the routine dispatching tasks, CAD allows them to concentrate on the qualitative aspects of the specific dispatching situation and to quickly see the economic impact of manually overriding CAD's recommended solutions. Accordingly, CAD provides for trial-and-error dispatching, inviting experimentation and digression with user-friendly on-line model support. CAD also automatically logs off-line every version of every dispatch for later use in evaluating new ideas and alternatives and gauging individual dispatcher performance.

CAD supports many features unique to the problems at hand. If the product in a customer's tank is nearly exhausted or if little excess storage space remains in the tank, the dispatcher may specify restrictions on gallonization (limits on increasing or reducing the ordered quantities to fit truck compartments) that are strictly honored by CAD. Weight jurisdictions and loading rules vary within and between cities and states. Sometimes these rules can change daily: frost laws in some northern states reduce the gross weight limits on short notice to minimize road damage in thawing conditions. Ice and slush clinging to trucks can increase their weight significantly. CAD accommodates such details with minimal direction.

The development of CAD took over two years. It involved a large effort to make the system user-friendly and to create interfaces with existing corporate systems and data bases. The computerization of the manual dispatching process required management to formalize many delivery policy decisions. Different dispatchers have different attitudes about dispatching and different methods. Comput-

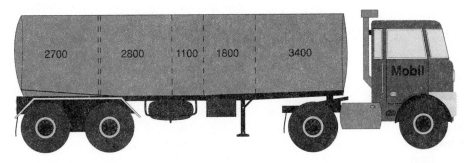

FIGURE 16.12
Tank Truck Loading Example

2700   2800   1100   1800   3400

Mobil

erizing the system compelled management to standardize its delivery policy, and the system automatically enforces that policy.

The CAD system was fully implemented during the first half of 1985, and with its implementation, Mobil has finished consolidating three manual centers into one automated center dispatching about 50,000 orders for light products per month.

The productivity of dispatching personnel has increased more than twofold, on the basis of the number of orders delivered per person.

The costs of communications and computer operation have been higher than originally forecasted, but so have the savings. Annual net cost savings for product distribution of well over $2 million have been realized. As dispatchers become better aquainted with their new tools, ever greater benefits are expected.

QUESTIONS

1. To see some of the difficulties associated with tank truck loading, consider the following simplified example. Examine Figure 16.12. The compartments are to be filled and different products cannot be mixed in the same compartment. You are allowed to adjust the volume of each product that is loaded on the truck, if necessary, in order to fit within the compartment capacities. In no case, however, can you adjust the total volume by more than plus or minus 400 gallons.

Three orders received are given in Table 16.10. In each case, the total volume and truck capacity is 11,800 gallons.

TABLE 16.10   Orders for Tank Truck Loading Example

Product	Order 1 (Easy to Fit)	Order 2 (Not So Easy)	Order 3 (Hard)
Super	2900	3500	2900
Regular	3400	1100	4000
Unleaded	5500	7200	4900

Show how each order can be loaded on the truck. Why is order 3 much harder to load?

2. Explain the benefits that the CAD system provided for Mobil Oil Corporation. Why can it not completely replace the human decision maker?

SUMMARY

We saw that scheduling and production control form the basis for implementation of a firm's production plan. Day-to-day scheduling decisions are more difficult in batch processing and job shop systems than in continuous-flow, mass-production, or project systems. Except for specific cases, the general job shop scheduling problem cannot be optimally solved. Operations managers must resort to heuristic rules, called priority dispatching rules, for scheduling jobs at work facilities.

Production control includes detailed capacity planning, scheduling, and daily or hourly progress control of production. For many plants, production-control systems are computerized and rely on new technology, such as automatic data capture, to provide fast and accurate information from the shop floor.

In service organizations, many other types of scheduling problems exist. Two of the most common are personnel scheduling and vehicle routing and scheduling.

We presented simple procedures that provide good solutions to these types of scheduling problems.

KEY TERMS

Runout time
Scheduling
Sequencing
Makespan
Flowtime
Due date
Tardiness

Lateness
Shortest processing time (SPT)
Flowshop
Dispatching
OPT (optimized production technology)

REVIEW/ DISCUSSION QUESTIONS

1. What are the goals of production-activity control?

2. What are the objectives and activities of scheduling?

3. What is the purpose of progress control?

4. Explain how runout time is used to schedule batch production processes. What are the limitations of using a cyclic schedule for this problem?

5. How does scheduling differ from sequencing?

6. List and define the common criteria used to evaluate schedules in job shops.

7. Compare the effectiveness of the shortest processing time and earliest due date rules with respect to the scheduling criteria in Table 16.2 for the single machine scheduling problem.

8. In the single machine scheduling problem, explain why the schedule chosen will not affect makespan.

9. How does flowshop differ from a job shop?

10. Why is the general (n machine) job shop scheduling problem so difficult to solve?

11. What is the difference between static and dynamic dispatching rules?

12. List several dispatching rules. How can one evaluate a rule to determine its effectiveness?

13. Why is bottleneck operation critical to the OPT philosophy?

14. In the discussion of OPT, the following statement is made: "An hour lost at a bottleneck is an hour lost for the total system." Explain the meaning of this statement.

15. List some of the advantages and disadvantages of OPT.

16. Explain the need for expediting. Can it ever be avoided?

17. Discuss the structure and use of computerized production-control systems.

18. List some examples of personnel scheduling in service organizations.

19. What are the general steps in solving personnel scheduling problems?

20. Discuss how Anheuser-Busch has used computerized routing systems to assist beer distributors.

21. Explain how the Clarke-Wright technique is used in vehicle routing problems.

1. Using the example of batch scheduling in Section 16.2, suppose that the demands for the five products are 250, 300, 500, 800, and 300 units per week, respectively. Show that
   a. demand greatly exceeds available capacity
   b. using the runout time method, shortages will eventually occur.

2. A soft-drink manufacturer bottles six flavors on a single machine. Relevant data are given next.

Flavor	Economic Lot Size (Gallons)	Bottling Time (Hours)	Demand (Gallons/ Day)	Current Inventory
Cola	7500	32	3000	5000
Orange	4000	17	1000	3000
Diet cola	5000	21	2000	4500
Lemon-lime	2000	8	800	1500
Ginger ale	3000	13	700	2000
Club soda	3500	15	1200	2100

Using the smallest runout time rule, which flavor would be produced first? What will be the resulting inventory levels? Assume 3 shifts per day.

3. A detergent manufacturer uses a single facility for filling and packaging all of its 4 major types of detergents. The inventory at the beginning of a particular week, the average demand, the production rate and lot size are given below (in ounces). If runout time is used for scheduling this activity, how would the activity be scheduled during the first 4 weeks?

Product	Inventory	Weekly Demand	Production Rate/Week	Lot Size
Brand A, Size A	10000	5000	20000	10000
Brand A, Size B	12000	4000	5000	5000
Brand B, Size A	15000	3000	12000	6000
Brand C, Size A	6000	1000	2000	1000

4. The following 6 jobs are to be scheduled on a single machine.

Job	1	2	3	4	5	6
Processing Time (Min)	240	120	210	90	180	150

   a. Suppose the jobs are processed in numerical order. Compute the average flowtime after each job is completed.
   b. In what order would the jobs be processed using the SPT rule? Compute the average flowtime after each job is completed. Compare this answer with your answer to part (a).
   c. In what sense does SPT minimize the average flowtime? Why would this rule be preferred?

5. Five jobs are waiting to be processed on a single machine. Use the shortest processing time rule to sequence the jobs. Compute the flowtime, tardiness, and lateness for each job. Also, compute the average flowtime, average tardiness, and average lateness for all jobs.

Job	Processing Time	Due Date
1	7	20
2	3	8
3	5	7
4	2	4
5	6	17

6. Schedule the jobs in Problem 5 using the earliest due date rule. How do the performance measure compare with the SPT rule?

7. Tony's Income Tax Service personnel can estimate the time required to complete tax forms using standards for each particular form which must be filed. These are as follows:

Form	Standard Time (Min)
1040 short	10
1040 long	15
Schedule A	15
Schedule B	5
Schedule G	10
Schedule C	15
Schedule SE	5
Form 2106	10

One morning, five customers are waiting:

Customer	Forms
A	1040 long, schedules A, B
B	1040 long, schedules A, B, SE, 2106
C	1040 short
D	1040 long, schedules A, B, G
E	1040 long, schedules A, B, C, 2106

a. If these customers are processed on a first-come-first-served basis, what is the flowtime of each and the average flowtime?
b. If SPT is used, how will the flowtimes change?

8. A student at a state university has four assignments due in class the following day. The class times are as follows:

Class	Time
Finance 216	8 A.M.
Marketing 304	12 P.M.
P/OM 385	10 A.M.
Psychology 200	4 P.M.

Each class lasts 1 hour and no other classes are scheduled. It is now 12 midnight and the student estimates that the finance, marketing, P/OM, and psychology assignments will take 4, 3, 5, and 6 hours, respectively. How should this student schedule the work? Can all of it be completed?

9. Kinko's copies operates with a single xerox copier. At the beginning of a particular day the following jobs were awaiting processing:

Job	Job Content
1	500 forms regular size 250 forms large size
2	100 forms regular size 400 forms large size
3	1000 forms regular size
4	1500 forms large size
5	1200 forms regular size 300 forms large size

Regular forms take on the average about 10 seconds to complete while the larger ones take 12 seconds. If processing is always by job, calculate the flowtime of each job and the average flowtime for
a. first-time-first-served rule
b. SPT rule.
What is the makespan in both cases?

10. A small consulting group of a computer systems department has seven projects to complete. How should the projects be scheduled? The time in days and project deadlines are given below.

	Project						
	1	2	3	4	5	6	7
Time	4	8	12	16	10	14	8
Deadline	12	24	60	28	24	36	48

11. On Monday, Baxter Industries currently has the following jobs awaiting processing in two departments:

	Time Required (Hours)	
Job	Mill	Drill
216	8	4
327	6	10
462	10	5
519	5	6
258	3	8
617	6	2

a. Develop a minimum makespan schedule using Johnson's rule. Graph the results on a bar chart.

b. Assuming an 8-hour workday, suppose that two new jobs arrive on Wednesday morning with the following requirements:

Job	Mill	Drill
842	4	7
843	10	8

How should the schedule be changed?

12. A simple manufacturing process involving machined components consists of 2 operations to be done on 2 different machines. At the beginning of a particular week, the status of the queue was as follows:

Job Number	Number of Components	Scheduled Time on Machine 1 (Min per Piece)	Scheduled Time on Machine 2 (Min per Piece)
101	200	2.5	2.5
176	150	1.5	0.5
184	250	1.0	2.0
185	125	2.5	1.0
201	100	1.2	2.4
213	100	1.2	2.2

The processing on machine 2 necessarily has to follow processing on machine 1. Schedule these jobs to minimize the makespan. Illustrate the schedule arrived at through a bar chart.

13. Compute the number of possible schedules for a general job shop with n jobs and m machines for each of the following cases:
    a. $n = 3$, $m = 2$
    b. $n = 2$, $m = 3$
    c. $n = 3$, $m = 3$
    d. $n = 4$, $m = 4$

14. For the Lynwood job shop data in Table 16.4, simulate the first-come-first-served, shortest processing time and total work-dispatching rules. Draw a bar chart schedule for each and critically compare these rules with the least-work-remaining rule simulated in the chapter.

15. The following seven jobs with due dates arrive at a two-machine flowshop in the following sequence:

			Processing Time	
Job	Arrival Time	Due Date	Machine 1	Machine 2
1	0	6	1	3
2	1	6	4	1
3	2	12	5	4
4	4	8	3	1
5	6	15	1	3
6	8	16	4	2
7	10	20	1	5

   a. Apply the slack-time dispatching rule to schedule these jobs. When each job arrives, what is the critical ratio of all jobs?
   b. Construct a bar chart for the schedule. How much idle time is there for each machine? What is the lateness of all jobs?

16. Given the following 6 jobs which arrive during the first 10 days of August, along with the due dates and processing times on 2 sequential machines, schedule the jobs using the slack time dispatching rule. Compute the waiting times and completion times, machine utilization, etc. (Illustrate the process.) Also compute the critical ratio when each job arrives.

			Processing Time	
Job	Arrival Date	Due Date	Machine 1	Machine 2
1	July 31	Aug. 10	5	3
2	Aug. 1	Aug. 27	2	7
3	Aug. 3	Aug. 15	4	5
4	Aug. 4	Aug. 20	3	6
5	Aug. 5	Aug. 30	8	7
6	Aug. 9	Nov. 15	6	9

17. A hospital emergency room forecasts the following minimal requirements for nurses on a daily basis:

Day	Mon	Tue	Wed	Thur	Fri	Sat	Sun
Minimum Personnel	3	2	2	4	6	7	4

Each nurse should have two consecutive days off. How many full-time nurses are required?

18. A supermarket outlet has the following minimal personnel requirements during various days of the week. It is required that each employee has to have 2 consecutive days off. How many regular employees are required to meet this schedule?

Day	Mon	Tue	Wed	Thur	Fri	Sat	Sun
Minimum Personnel	4	4	5	6	6	5	4

19. T. Urtles Parcel Service delivers small packages overnight in most major cities. On Wednesday morning at 8 A.M., 15 packages are ready to be delivered. To keep their promised delivery, all parcels must arrive by noon. The time required to travel between the depot and various customers is given in Table 16.11. Use the Clarke-Wright algorithm to develop a schedule for Urtles' delivery trucks.

20. A manufacturer has to supply seven of its subcontractors with materials on a daily basis for certain parts produced on a high-volume basis. A 100-ton truck is usually available in the mornings between 8 A.M. and 12 noon. The travel distances of the 7 subcontractors from the manufacturer is given in

TABLE 16.11

Travel Times for Problem 19

From	To 0	1	2	3	4	5	6	7	8	9	10	11	12	13	14	15
0	—															
1	14	—														
2	32	20	—													
3	56	44	10	—												
4	16	85	40	60	—											
5	72	31	29	16	40	—										
6	36	47	51	28	26	62	—									
7	19	21	65	43	52	36	48	—								
8	29	36	41	40	20	10	12	46	—							
9	78	32	51	46	31	12	16	17	58	—						
10	96	63	35	41	26	17	9	16	16	21	—					
11	43	41	18	36	42	37	41	23	18	19	10	—				
12	28	65	25	45	81	97	61	35	30	29	18	50	—			
13	17	42	22	14	37	62	14	48	54	34	17	21	19	—		
14	64	19	25	21	36	17	28	28	50	42	50	33	27	15	—	
15	50	35	14	20	62	75	32	32	45	26	34	11	58	34	25	—

the matrix below. Solve this vehicle routing problem using Clarke-Wright savings method.

Vendor	Amount of Materials to Be Supplied (Tons)
1	80
2	20
3	70
4	20
5	80
6	30
7	40

From	To							
	0	1	2	3	4	5	6	7
0	—							
1	20	—						
2	30	25	—					
3	35	20	35	—				
4	20	15	25	15	—			
5	10	20	15	20	30	—		
6	20	35	55	70	60	50	—	
7	80	40	30	60	20	10	5	—

CASE PROBLEM[11]

You are in the business of manufacturing and selling one assembly. The assembly is made from four different parts, each of which has from three to five manufacturing operations on three common machining centers (Figure 16.13). There is a 60-minute setup prior to each operation for each part. Each part has a work-in-process (WIP) inventory value of $100 the moment it is started at the first operation. Assembly and shipment occur instantaneously as soon as a matched set of parts is available. Demand for your assembly is unlimited, as is your raw material supply. When you start, no WIP inventory exists in the system, and the three machines are not set up.

The objective is to produce as much as possible. The best schedule is the one that generates the most throughput without violating any of the following constraints:

1. The schedules must be realistic (for instance, you cannot run two parts on the same machine simultaneously).
2. Inventory can never exceed $50,000 (500 parts).
3. A minimum of 140 assemblies must be shipped on a cumulative basis each week.

[11]"The OPT Quiz." Reproduced with permission of Creative Output, Inc.

FIGURE 16.13

Product Routing for Case Project

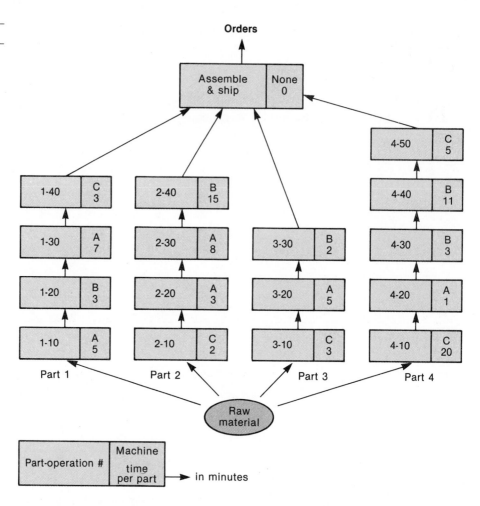

4. At least 680 assemblies must be shipped by the end of the first 4 weeks.
5. There are only 40 days (8 weeks) of production time available, and you may work 24 hours a day.

Develop a schedule that meets these constraints, showing the results on a bar chart.

Just-in-Time Production

T he Japanese have captured a sizable share of world markets for many products because of the significant progress they have made in manufacturing. Among the reasons for this success are the Japanese style of management, the development and adaptation of any new technologies, and the use of new methods for material management and control. This chapter covers the Japanese approach to material management and control, known as **just-in-time** (**JIT**). JIT is more than a new way of handling material management; it represents a philosophy whose objective is to eliminate all sources of waste, including unnecessary inventory and scrap in production.

17.1 THE JUST-IN-TIME CONCEPT

In order to understand how JIT evolved, it is necessary to examine some of the characteristics of Japan and its people. Japan is approximately the size of California, and 80 percent of the land is mountainous. Since Japan has a much larger population than California, it is easy to understand the space limitations they face as a country. In addition, since Japan has few natural resources, the Japanese people tend to avoid waste as much as possible in every aspect of their lives. In manufacturing, for example, inventory is considered waste, and scrap, even more wasteful. Since land is expensive, factory layouts and material flow must be efficient; indeed, there is little land available for large warehouses to store inventory. Thus Japanese production systems have evolved around the principle of reducing waste; in production, this takes the form of reducing both time and inventory.

In Chapter 9, we described several types of manufacturing processes. One of the most common types was mass production, sometimes called *repetitive manufacturing*. Automobiles, appliances, and many other products are made in this way. In repetitive manufacturing, the same or similar operations are repeated over and over, with an uninterrupted flow of materials through the sequence of operations. Through repetitive manufacturing, inventories and lead times can be reduced over such types of production as batch or job shop, thus leading to increased productivity and lower cost. However, it takes careful design and commitment by both management and workers for repetitive manufacturing to be effective. The Japanese have recognized this potential in developing JIT.

The JIT production concept was developed by the Toyota Motor Company of Japan, and later adopted by other Japanese companies. Today many American firms are employing JIT procedures. It has been estimated that the percentage of companies in America using JIT will increase from 25 percent in 1987 to over 55 percent by 1992.

The fundamental principle of JIT is to produce the right units in the right quantity at the right time, or "just-in-time." This sounds very similar to the basic idea of material requirements planning (MRP). However, in MRP, the idea is to *make available* items when and where they are needed. In JIT, the items are *produced* only when they are required. The objective of JIT is to create a smooth and rapid flow of all products from the time materials and purchased parts are received until the time the final product is shipped to the customer. Ideally, the number of parts produced in a plant or purchased from outside suppliers at any one time should be just enough to produce one final unit of the product. Inventories are not needed, or at least minimized.

Several steps are taken to achieve the objectives of JIT. U-shaped work cells are designed to optimize material flow through the plant, one worker is assigned to multiple machines, equipment setup times are reduced, and quality control is emphasized. JIT is the integration of these techniques into an organized, focused system. JIT is simply a return to basics, attempting to use human resources and machines in a way that will eliminate waste.

JIT is viewed as a major component of competitive strategy. Successful Japanese manufacturers, using JIT, have focused energies on the manufacturing process, improving it through more efficient machine and plant layout, reducing setup times to near zero, developing mistake-proof operations, and using simple scheduling techniques. JIT results in reduced costs, improved quality, and smoother production flow.

17.2 THE COMPONENTS OF JIT

There are four components of JIT systems that work together to provide important benefits for production. These components are *layout and production methods, Kanban, total quality control,* and *suppliers.*

In order for a JIT system to function effectively, fundamental changes in traditional production systems must take place. These changes require a modification of the design of the layout and material flow process. In addition, setup times must be reduced.

Poor equipment layout is one of the major causes of inefficiency in manufacturing. In a typical U.S. manufacturing environment, material is transported from a supplier's truck to a warehouse, later transported from the warehouse to the plant, and then stored in a holding area or even restocked in another warehouse. In a common process layout, material is often transferred between departments during the manufacturing operations. Unnecessary costs are incurred in the form of inventory, material handling, production delays, and so forth.

With JIT, the production layout must provide a smooth flow, in which material introduced at one end of the process moves without delay to finished product. Thus, the layout should be in a straight line or U-shaped cells involving group technology that we introduced in Chapter 9.

Group technology combines several machines that perform different tasks into a single work center so that these tasks can be performed without moving large lots of in-process inventories. For example, the pieces of equipment are located close together and are connected by short roller conveyors. As a result, materials or parts can flow one piece at a time from machine to machine. Inventory is reduced to minimal levels, and operators can move one piece at a time without the need for forklifts or other bulk material handling equipment. In addition, a group layout allows workers to work on more than one machine at a time, thus

Layout and Production Methods

increasing efficiency. In this case, workers must be trained to operate several different machines in a JIT environment. Automation, such as robots, is often used for routine operations in work cells. This allows the worker to be free to attend to multiple machines while robots transfer or load parts.

An example illustrating the benefits of improved layout can be seen at Omark's Guelph, Ontario, plant, which makes chain saws. The distance that the product had to travel within the plant was 2620 feet in November 1982 and flow time was 21 days. Within two years, the distance was reduced to 173 feet and the time to 3 days by moving metal-forming machines together and eliminating much of the work-in-process (WIP) inventory. Omark's ultimate marketing strategy is to fill orders from the factory and eliminate finished-goods warehouses altogether.[1]

On the production floor, careful coordination between processes must exist. Processes withdraw parts from the preceding processes at the time needed and in the necessary quantities. If such withdrawals occur in an uncontrolled atmosphere, the preceding stations will acquire large inventories in order to allow for peak demands. Therefore it is critical that a JIT system minimize fluctuation in production demand. This is accomplished by making finished product lot sizes as low as possible, ideally, one.

Another factor affecting production flow is the setup time for the various production operations. In order to maintain small lot sizes, frequent changeovers between products must be made. This can be quite costly if setup times are large. Therefore, in order to compensate for large setup times, large lot sizes are produced. This results in large work-in-process inventories which remain idle between each step of the process, high levels of indirect labor and overhead to account for inventory and to transport the materials. Therefore setup times must be reduced as much as possible for JIT to work effectively.

The ability to produce in smaller lot sizes also increases the firm's flexibility to meet customer orders—one of the critical determinants of competitive strategy. In addition, machines will not be overworked and can be properly maintained, thus avoiding unanticipated breakdowns and improving quality.

Japanese manufacturers using JIT have reported remarkable reductions in setup times. For example, Yammar Diesel reduced a machining line tool setting from 9.3 hours to 9 minutes, and Toyo Kogyo reduced a ring-gear cutter tool setting from over 6 hours to 10 minutes. Similar results have been achieved in the United States. A chain saw manufacturer reduced setup time on a punch press from over 2 hours to 3 minutes, and a Midwestern manufacturer was able to cut equipment setup time on a 60-ton press from 45 minutes to 1 minute. This was accomplished through process improvements such as storing the required tools next to the machine, using conveyors to move the tools in and out of the machine, and improving the labeling and identification. Previously, the setup tools were poorly identified, poorly organized, and stored far from the machine, requiring a forklift to transport them. The new changeovers or setups can be performed by the machine operator with no indirect assistance.

Production scheduling approaches support the JIT concept. Master production schedules are constructed for 1 to 3 months, and Japanese manufacturers attempt to level or smooth the production schedule on a daily basis; that is, they attempt

---

[1]Richard J. Schonberger, "Just-in-Time Production Systems: Replacing Complexity with Simplicity In Manufacturing Management," *Industrial Engineering,* 16, no. 10 (October 1984): 52–63.

to produce the same quantity of each end item every day. This approach to production allows a smooth flow of parts throughout the factory and minimizes expediting, rework, and other delays. In addition, employees become used to the same schedule; consequently, disruptions are less likely to occur. To accomplish this, no changes in the master production schedule are permitted over a time that typically varies from 1 week to 1 month.

The driving force behind JIT production is coordination of successive production activities. An automobile, for instance, consists of thousands of parts. It is extremely difficult to coordinate the transfer of materials and components between production operations to realize the JIT concept—that is, to have materials and assemblies arrive at precisely the right time. At Toyota, the process is viewed in reverse: Employees at one operation go to the source of the required parts, such as machining or subassembly, and *withdraw* the necessary units when needed. Then, the process from which parts are withdrawn produces the necessary number of items to replace those just withdrawn. As the process from which parts were withdrawn replenishes the items it transferred out, it draws upon the output of *its* preceding process, and so on. This process begins at final assembly and works backward through all work stations in the production process, continuing even to subcontractors and suppliers.

Kanban

A key component of just-in-time production in Japan is an information system called **Kanban**, which is a Japanese word for *card*. The type of units required by a process and the number required are written on Kanbans and used to initiate withdrawal and production of items through the production process. A Kanban system is illustrated in Figure 17.1. There are two kinds of Kanbans: a withdrawal

---

FIGURE 17.1   Steps Involved in Using the Two Kanbans

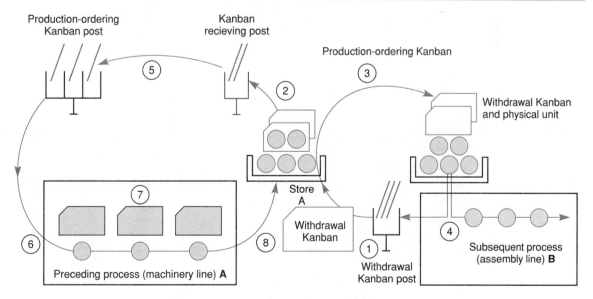

Reprinted with permission from *Industrial Engineering* magazine, May 1981. Copyright Institute of Industrial Engineers, 25 Technology Park/ Atlanta, Norcross, GA 30092.

Kanban and a production-ordering Kanban. The system operates as follows. The carrier of process B goes to the store of process A (Step 1 in Figure 17.1) with the withdrawal Kanbans and empty pallets, after a sufficient number have accumulated. When the necessary number of parts are withdrawn, the worker detaches production-ordering Kanbans, which were attached to the inventory, and places these at the Kanban receiving post, leaving the empty pallets (Step 2). For each production-ordering Kanban detached, a withdrawal Kanban is put in its place (Step 3). When these units are used, this withdrawal Kanban is placed in the withdrawal Kanban post (Step 4). In process A, the production-ordering Kanbans are collected and placed in the production-ordering Kanban post (Step 5). These Kanbans provide the authority to produce the parts (Step 6), and the Kanbans move physically with the parts throughout the operations in process A (Step 7). The completed parts are placed in inventory, along with their production-ordering Kanbans (Step 8). In this fashion, many individual processes are interconnected. Production orders and withdrawal quantities under Kanban are approximately 10 percent of the daily demand. With such small lot sizes, it is unnecessary to warehouse in-process inventory, thus minimizing holding costs.

The amount of WIP inventory is equal to the number of Kanban cards issued times the size of the standard container used. The following equation is used to calculate the initial number of Kanban cards required:

$$\text{Number Kanban cards} = \frac{D(T_w + T_p)(1 + \alpha)}{C}$$

where

D = the average daily production rate as determined from the MPS

T_w = the waiting time of Kanban cards in decimal fractions of a day (that is, the waiting time of a part)

T_p = the processing time per part, in decimal fractions of a day

C = the capacity of a standard container

α = a policy variable determined according to the efficiency of work centers using the part

For example, suppose that $D = 50$ parts/day, $T_w = .20$, $T_p = .10$, $C = 5$, and $\alpha = 1$. Then the number of Kanban cards is calculated as

$$\frac{50(.20 + .10)(1 + 1)}{5} = 6$$

Once the system is running, supervisors may pull Kanban cards from the system as they observe that certain work centers can function with less WIP. As D changes from month to month, the number of cards will be increased or reduced appropriately. Since the number of cards is directly proportional to the amount of in-process inventory, both managers and production workers strive to reduce the number of cards in the system through reduced lead time $(T_w + T_p)$ or through other improvements.

Note that Kanban "pulls" parts from the preceding workstation beginning at final assembly; thus the entire manufacturing operation is synchronized to the final assembly schedule. JIT prohibits the source of production from "pushing" inventory forward only to wait idle if it is not required.

The Kanban system just described above is a *dual-card* system. Although the dual-card system is used by Toyota in producing automobiles, very few other companies use this particular approach. A more common approach is the single-card Kanban system that signals requirements from the preceding production stage. This system has been adopted by many Western manufacturers, often as simple visual systems. Schonberger[2] cites some examples.

- In General Electric's lamp division, which consists of multiple plants in the state of Ohio, truck drivers from component plants collect Kanban cards and empty containers when they unload. The card signals which components are to be delivered next trip.
- At a Hewlett-Packard plant, the signal for a subassembly shop making computer-system modules to send another plastic tub of parts forward is removal of the present plastic tub of parts from a sensing platform.
- At another Hewlett-Packard facility, an empty "Kanban square" outlined in yellow tape is the visual signal for the preceding workstation to forward another disk-drive unit.

Total Quality Control

JIT cannot function properly if production has a high rate of defective items. Implementation of JIT requires painstakingly careful attention to quality, both in purchasing and in production. Since lot sizes are small and there is no safety stock to back up nonconforming items, any quality problem disrupts the flow of materials throughout the plant.

With JIT, more attention must be paid to *preventing* poor quality. Japanese production workers are their own quality inspectors; knowing that a problem can stop the entire system provides the incentive to produce good-quality parts consistently. Purchased items are not inspected; they are expected to be defect free when they are received. Japanese manufacturers take great pains to ensure that supplier quality is perfect, even to the extent of helping suppliers solve their own quality problems. Manufacturers work to develop mutual trust and confidence with their suppliers often using only one supplier for a given item rather than several, as has been the practice in the United States.

Group layouts help promote higher quality. With one-piece production flow, inspection methods must be incorporated as part of the operator's responsibilities, and production defects must be identified immediately and corrected. To assure that no defective parts are allowed to flow in the system, the Japanese use two methods: **bakayake** and **yo-i-don**. Bakayake involves the use of automatic stopping devices on machines if quality deteriorates. For example, during a milling process, holes may be drilled into the tooling plate, allowing a small amount of compressed air to pass through. If the work piece does not rest properly on the tooling plate because of the presence of a chip, the flow of compressed air will not be stopped and the machine can be automatically shut off.

Yo-i-don involves the manual stoppage of production if difficulties are encountered. For example, if a problem is discovered by an operator, the operator may signal for assistance by activating an *andon,* or yellow warning light. If the problem is not corrected within, say, one minute, a red light will automatically come on, a siren will sound, and the entire production line will stop. Managers and workers will immediately rush to the scene and try to locate the source of the problem and correct it.

Other common means of improving quality, such as the use of quality control circles and statistical process control are employed.

---

[2]*Ibid.*

Suppliers

The material flow cycle begins with suppliers; thus to maintain a smooth production flow, suppliers must make just-in-time deliveries. Instead of receiving one large shipment that must be counted, inspected, and stored before issuance to the production floor, suppliers make smaller deliveries on a daily basis or more frequently to accommodate that day's production schedule. This is one reason why suppliers are often located in close geographical proximity to a manufacturer. In North America, where industry is frequently geographically dispersed, transportation delays often make it difficult to achieve this type of vendor support.

In a true JIT environment, shipments will be received in standardized containers, each containing standardized quantities. This way, there is no reason to unpack and count all incoming goods. This eliminates potential damage through handling and saves space. This standardization is carried through the entire production process. With a good supplier-manufacturer relationship and supplier-certification program, quality inspection at receiving is unnecessary, which further reduce delays and costs.

In the past, suppliers were considered adversaries and safety stock was maintained as insurance against poor supplier performance. JIT requires a trusting partnership between the supplier and the manufacturer to deliver on-time and with zero defects. To build such relationships requires a reduction in the number of suppliers that are typically used. All U.S. companies that have implemented JIT have reduced the number of suppliers to five or fewer for a given part. Without this reduction, JIT purchasing becomes unmanageable. A single or few sources of supply allows the manufacturer to work more closely with the suppliers, thus improving design and product quality, and reducing costs.

In return for the extra effort that suppliers make to accommodate JIT manufacturers with more frequent deliveries, standardized shipments, and better quality, suppliers are rewarded with long-term contracts. Hewlett-Packard, for instance, has given its JIT suppliers 18- to 36-month contracts with the potential for renegotiation every 6 to 13 months in exchange for quality improvement or cost reduction. Long-term contracts encourage supplier loyalty and reduce the risk of an interrupted supply of parts. If the manufacturer increases market share, then larger orders will be received by the supplier.

17.3 BENEFITS OF JIT

The purpose of JIT is to improve profits by reducing costs and improving quality. The most obvious benefit from using JIT is a reduction in WIP inventory. Besides reducing inventory investment, lower costs of facilities, equipment, and labor are realized. There is less need for sophisticated inventory control systems and WIP tracking; thus production control is highly simplified. JIT encourages participation of the workforce in problem solving by encouraging workers to reduce setup times and solve quality problems. Better quality, in turn, results in less wasted material, fewer labor hours on rework and hence higher productivity, and fast feedback on defects. Figure 17.2 illustrates this cause-and-effect chain.

Using the principles of JIT, Toyota reduced its production time from 15 days to one day. At the same time, Toyota found that every time the work-in-process inventory level halved relative to production volume, labor productivity increased,

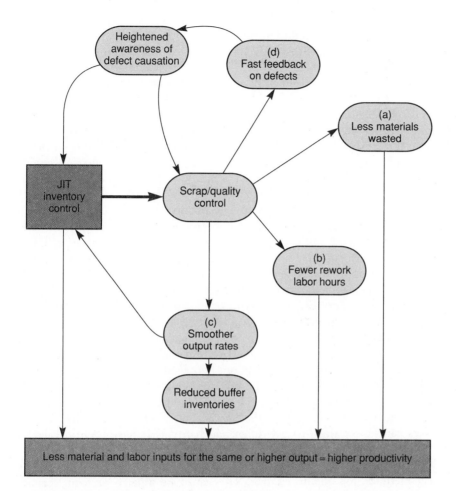

FIGURE 17.2
Effects of JIT
Production
Management

Source: R. J. Schonberger, "Some Observations on the Advantages and Implementation Issues of Just-In-Time Production Systems." Reprinted with permission, 1, no. 1 (1982), *Journal of Operations Management,* Journal of the American Production and Inventory Control Society, Inc.

about 40 percent over a ten-year period. Other Japanese manufacturers of automobiles, motorcycles, and electronic products reported similar results. In the United States, a motor-control manufacturer reduced production time from 8 weeks to 1 week; inventory level was halved; floor space required was halved; and indirect labor costs were reduced significantly.

17.4 IMPLEMENTATION OF JIT

As can be seen from the previous discussions, implementation of JIT requires many internal and external changes for an organization. The necessity of reconfiguring the physical layout of the manufacturing process, making changes in production control methods, and making changes in supplier relationships have been discussed. These steps cannot be accomplished overnight. Toyota took 20 to 30 years to develop and refine its efficient production system. With today's knowledge and the experiences of others, however, a company should be able to implement JIT within two years if the process is completed properly—with a clear set of objectives and a carefully designed implementation plan—and with the commitment and involvement of all employees, from top management to the line operators.

JIT must be initiated from the top, with full support of all managerial levels. A company must be willing to make fundamental changes in the way it operates. Prior to implementation, a basic *understanding* of JIT is necessary in order to take full advantage of a firm's resources, both physical and human. A company must ask some difficult questions such as: How will performance be measured? Who will perform equipment setup? Who is responsible for quality control? Management must realize that short-term profits may be sacrificed for significantly larger long-term gains. This is contrary to the bottom-line attitudes of Western management, but is essential for successful implementation of JIT.

JIT requires a change in management and employee relationships. Management must openly support the system and respond to criticism from workers. Thus, participative management practices are essential for gaining acceptance and successful implementation. Employee motivation is a critical factor for productivity and quality improvement. If JIT is developed in an atmosphere of mutual trust and cooperation, morale can be improved dramatically.

Workers are a vital element of JIT; therefore, management must invest heavily in training. The Japanese have always put people ahead of profits. Their concept of "lifetime training" enables them to take full advantage of the JIT environment. Training is focused on how to perform a job more efficiently and with better quality. Experiences with JIT in the United States have shown that American workers can be retrained to get rid of bad habits that have been learned from the typical American manufacturing environments.

Workers must be trained in new problem-solving techniques, including statistical methods for quality control. They must be able to perform their own preventive maintenance and minor repairs to maintain smooth production flow. They need to be able to operate a variety of types of machines and equipment. These requirements are often contrary to union practices.

In a traditional Western manufacturing facility, there is a high subdivision of labor and strict adherence to union job classifications. For example, union contracts may prohibit a milling machine operator from being assigned to operate a drill press. However, in order to obtain a smooth work flow, workers must be able to switch from one machine to the next and to perform their own setups and maintenance. This concept of a multifunction worker helps to eliminate inventory between processes, to reduce the number of workers required, and to create a larger sense of involvement and participation in the total production process. Hence, full support of labor unions is required. One way of doing this is to seek union help, for example, through a union-management committee.

Most JIT programs begin with a pilot implementation. For example, one specific product or process might be selected for JIT. Before implementation, a plan must be developed in which specific goals are established and milestones benchmarking success are agreed upon. During implementation, progress in reducing inventories, setups, and other resources should be monitored on a regular basis to ensure that improvements are taking place. Helpful techniques of project management are presented in the next chapter.

Krajewski et al. summarize the important factors that create an atmosphere that is amenable to JIT production.[3] These are:

1. small lot production
2. single-digit setups
3. 100 percent quality
4. high machine reliability
5. balanced work flow between stations
6. stable master-production schedule
7. low-cost automation
8. one worker – multiple machine
9. group technology
10. focused factories
11. few bill-of-material changes
12. vendor reliability
13. short vendor lead times
14. daily schedule performance
15. flexible work force
16. short manufacturing cycle times
17. high volume demands
18. quality circles
19. bottom-up management

Clearly, every company cannot create an identical environment, much of which is due to cultural influences and geography in Japan. However, several lessons can be learned from the Japanese experience. For example, new equipment and automation can be studied in order to reduce setup times. A total systems approach to balance production rates in different operations can be considered. Quality problems can be addressed and preventive maintenance activities can be redesigned. This is not to say that JIT production cannot work in America, but operations managers need to take a fresh look at current practices and tradition.

17.5 JIT VERSUS MRP: A COMPARISON

JIT and MRP systems have similar objectives: to reduce inventory investment and improve productivity and customer service. Yet they are significantly different. MRP systems are designed to construct a realistic materials plan given the constraints and restrictions in the plant; JIT strives for constant improvement, not accepting any restrictions as given. MRP uses sophisticated computer-processing systems and generates a large amount of paperwork; JIT uses visual control and is simple to implement. MRP allows a highly variable master production schedule (MPS), whereas JIT uses a level schedule. Table 17.1 provides a comprehensive

---

[3]L.J. Krajewski, B.E. King, L.P. Ritzman, N. Weiner, and D.S. Wong, "A Comparision of Japanese and American Systems for Inventory and Production Management, A Simulation Approach," *Proceedings 13th Annual Meeting, American Institute for Decision Sciences,* (1981): 109–111. Published by the American Institute for Decision Sciences (currently the Decision Sciences Institute).

summary of the differences between a Kanban-driven JIT system and MRP (for both repetitive and job shop manufacturing).

In assessing manufacturing resource planning (MRP II), Walter Goddard, a leading consultant in inventory management, drew two conclusions.[4]

1. Kanban can succeed only where the user produces highly repetitive products. MRP II, however, works equally well for highly engineered one-of-a-kind environments, make-to-stock products, and finished-to-order products.
2. MRP II has better tools than Kanban, but these tools are more costly. With Kanban, material planning, capacity planning, and dispatching are done manually; no sophisticated computer system is required.

However, MRP II is broader in scope than the Kanban system. It can help plan other activities, such as tooling and maintenance requirements, assist in financial planning, and act as a simulator to answer what-if questions. Thus MRP II integrates many functions besides manufacturing within an organization. In essence, MRP II can be used as a strategic business-planning system, as well as a system for operational control.

Some of the significant differences between Toyota's philosophy and American philosophy include the treatment of inventory, setups and lot sizes, quality, and lead times. At Toyota, inventory is viewed as a liability, not an asset, and all efforts are aimed at reducing it. In American firms, inventory is viewed as protection. Frequent setups and small lot sizes are characteristic of Japanese production efforts at reducing inventory. In America, setups are viewed as a necessary evil and nearly no effort is spent on finding ways to make setups less costly. Quality goals at Toyota are zero defects; in America, some scrap is always expected, although it should be minimized. Finally, short lead times eliminate scheduling problems at Toyota, whereas longer lead times are sought after in American production, and inevitably the Peter Principle takes effect. However, despite these significant differences in production control philosophy, the key factors behind the Japanese success are teamwork and education. These are perhaps the most important lessons that can be learned from studying the Japanese success.

Some efforts have been made to incorporate features of Kanban into MRP systems. Yamaha Motors has created a structure called PYMAC (Pan Yamaha Manufacturing Control) that combines features of MRP and Kanban into one system called *Synchro MRP*.[5] This system was developed for high-volume manufacturing with a broad line of products. The company prepares the final assembly schedule, then MRP is used to generate work center production schedules.

Micro Kanban is another method of combining MRP and Kanban.[6] In this case, Kanban is added as an addition to an already installed MRP system. MRP is used to schedule and plan the purchasing and delivery of materials, then a microcomputer-based Kanban system generates production and moves Kanbans. Feedback information is returned to the MRP system for any necessary replanning or rescheduling of operations.

---

[4]Walter E. Goddard, "Kanban versus MRP II—Which is Best For You?", *Modern Materials Handling* (November 5, 1982): 40.

[5]Robert W. Hall, *Driving the Productivity Machine: Production Planning and Control in Japan*, Falls Church VA: American Production and Inventory Control Society, 1981.

[6]Mehran Sepehri, "Micro Kanban, A control Supplement to MRP," *P&IM Review and APICS News*, January, 1985, p. 48–52.

TABLE 17.1 Comparing MRP versus Kanban as Production Planning and Control Systems

Production Planning and Control Function	Kanban (Repetitive Manufacturing)	American MRP System (Repetitive Manufacturing)	MRP System (Job Shop Manufacturing)
Primary intent of system	Productivity improvements by promoting flow control 1. small lot sizes 2. short setup times 3. minimum inventories 4. coordinating just-in-time production 5. providing production status visibility to workforce (morale)	Productivity improvement by 1. scheduling parts runs in sequence 2. reducing inventories to planned levels 3. reducing lead times.	Productivity improvement by 1. maintaining valid job order priorities 2. reducing inventories to planned levels 3. reducing lead times. 4. projecting work center loads for capacity planning.
Production planning	Done in aggregate units to be built because of uniformity of product.	Usually done in aggregate units to be built because of uniformity of product.	Often done in standard hours because of non-uniformity of product. Useful for make-to-order or assemble-to-order production.
Master production scheduling	Short planning horizon.	Usually a short planning horizon, but longer than with Kanban.	Long planning horizon.
1. Planning horizon	Short (months)	Longer (usually one year)	Longer (usually one year or more)
2. Time fence	Short (typically 1 month)	Short (typically 2–3 months)	Longer (usually over 3 months)
	Clearly defined because all end items generally have similar lead times.	Clearly defined because most items have similar lead times.	May not be as clearly defined. Different heterogenous products may have different lead times. Frequently do not key MPS on end items.
3. Nature of MPS	A summary in daily buckets of the final assembly schedule.	Almost always based on the final assembly schedule. May need to plan material requirements prior to setting firm final assembly schedule.	Sometimes based on final assembly schedule. Frequently based on assembly schedules at sub-assembly stages using modular bills of material.
4. Leveling the MPS	Level by setting the final assembly line rates and by setting the model sequence in final assembly so that every day's schedule is identical inside a rigid time fence (one month at Toyota).	Try to level production rates between different stages of production. Use parts banks between stages to absorb imbalances. Balance individual lines.	Level only the total work-load based on feedback from capacity projections. Little attempt to balance work flows in nonrepetitive manufacturing.
Capacity planning and control			
1. Production planning stage: resource-requirements planning	Projection of line and work-center rates. Projection of labor requirements.	Projection of line and work-center rates. Projection of labor requirements.	Projection of work-center loads and labor requirements.
2. Master production scheduling stage: rough-cut capacity planning.	Projection of line and work-center rates. Feedback from departments on proposed schedule feasibility.	Projection of line and work-center rates. Overplan run lengths to prevent shortages.	Projection of work-center loads from unit load profiles. No time offsetting.

Production Planning and Control Function	Kanban (Repetitive Manufacturing)	American MRP System (Repetitive Manufacturing)	MRP System (Job Shop Manufacturing)
3. Capacity-requirements planning	Not done	Rarely done	Sometimes done. Project work-center loads, time-offset, by projections based on MRP.
4. Capacity-control stage	Work-center rates increase or decrease to keep up with final assembly. Keep enough reserve capacity at work centers so that they can catch up if they are behind.	Usually focus activity on keeping final assembly running. Adjust run rates and use parts banks to do this.	Production control or purchasing smooths temporary overloads and under-loads when releasing orders. Input/output control.
Explosion of MPS to dependent items			
1. Bill of material structure	Planning bill is the same as a final assembly bill. The explosion is needed only to determine the quantities required.	Planning bill is the same as a final assembly bill only if all planning can be done by time offsetting from the end of the line. Planning bills must usually allow for inventory netting between steps of production—not the same as a final assembly bill.	The planning bill must reflect the stages at which inventory is held between different order releases for fabrication or subassembly.
2. Lot sizing	Run multiples of standard container sizes. Strive to put no more than 10% of one day's requirements in a container.	Often thought of as run lengths converted to daily schedules $$\text{Daily rate} = \frac{\text{requirements}}{\text{\# of work days}}$$	Lot sizing allows for trade-off between inventory holding cost and set up cost. Often simplified by using lot-for-lot or fixed lot sizes.
3. Lead time offsets	Elementary. Work centers run the same schedule every day during the frozen schedule period. Change layout and cut setup time to run smoothly. Emphasize frequent, fast deliveries.	Time offsets are needed to sequence runs at different stages and provide lead times to other plants and suppliers at a distance.	Time offsets are needed because of irregular work flow. Need to backschedule the issuance of job orders from the time materials are needed. Must allow lead time for queues at work centers.
Production activity control (Shop floor control)			
1. Issuance of work to plant floor	Parts schedules and Kanban cards are issued to work centers according to routing. Cards may be prepared by computer or manually.	Schedules developed by MRP are released to the plant floor. Usually some manual review.	Sometimes require jobs at a work center to be run in a scheduled sequence but rarely. Usually the worker selects jobs based on their priority and on other plant circumstances.
			MRP suggests orders to be released by production control. Orders are rarely released automatically, but only after manual review.
2. Priority communication	The Kanban card system identifies what is really needed at downstream work centers.	Priority communicated by daily schedules and by parts bank levels.	Daily dispatch reports given priority information and due dates on each order in queue at each work center.

3. Priority updating	The Kanban card system ties all priorities to the final assembly lines.	MRP updates due dates or schedules. Schedules tie fabrication runs and subassembly runs to final assembly.	MRP updates due dates for released orders and planned orders. Other information may be used for centralized updating of priorities of all open orders each day.
4. Floor reporting "Paperwork"	Little paperwork except for cards. Very basic labor reporting, usually by department.	Many variations. Report production counts. System may assign counts to a run number (job number) for MRP purposes. Use cumulative system, etc. to simplify reporting.	Reporting of moves, labor, scrap and other costs are done by the job order. Material is issued from inventory by job order. Completed work is returned to inventory by job order.
Inventory control	Avoid use of stockrooms. Keep material at work-center stockpoints.	Usually have trouble following job shop practice. Issue in bulk to the floor so material handlers can pick at will from floor stock, etc. Inventory systems usually depend heavily on production counts for receipts and backflush for issues.	Keep inventory off the floor in stockrooms as much as possible. Return parts to inventory at the end of each routing through the shop floor.
1. Inventory accuracy	Use Kanban cards and standard containers so each transaction is for a standard quantity. Errors are usually detectable because of small inventory volume on the floor, disruption, etc.	Keep accurate balance by 1. issue by count from stockrooms 2. cycle count to verify balances and identify sources of error 3. usually relieve inventory records by backflush. Reconcile discrepancies. 4. Use standard containers for most items.	Keep accurate balance by 1. transaction discipline: count in and count out of closed stockrooms 2. cycle count to verify balances and identify sources of errors 3. Use standard containers, scales, etc., to simplify counting.
2. Inventory levels	Minimize WIP inventory by withdrawing Kanban cards from floor. Changes are made in operations to get to minimum possible WIP inventory.	Use MRP planning and control to avoid unneeded inventory or inventory built too soon. Try to balance operations to minimize parts banks between operations.	Use MRP planning and control to avoid unneeded inventory, inventory built too soon, and shortages. Accept a planned level of WIP inventory consistent with ability to reduce lead times.
Engineering change control	With Kanban, engineering changes must be manually executed on the plant floor. Changes are simplified by the use of "functional specifications" for parts, and by making EC's at schedule change times when possible.	Engineering changes are planned using MRP. Often use date effectivity for control.	Engineering changes are planned and executed using the planned orders from MRP and job orders for control. Often use date effectivity to coordinate.
Vendor control	Schedule vendors almost as one's own plant. Sometimes send Kanban cards to vendors to signal that deliveries are wanted.	Use purchase orders. Major use of blanket purchase orders. Often send vendors a delivery schedule.	Use purchase orders with due dates. Often send vendor forecasts of orders planned for them. "Buy capacity" of vendors with blanket purchase orders.

Source: Robert Hall, *Driving the Productivity Machine: Production Planning and Control in Japan*, pp. 25–28. Reprinted with permission, The American Production and Inventory Control Society, Inc., 1981.

Two illustrations of JIT are presented. The first concerns the implementation of JIT in an American production facility for Toyota Motor Manufacturing. However, JIT principles are not limited to manufacturing. The second case describes the improve-

ments that can be made by implementing JIT in a service environment. This example involves mail-order processing of customer orders. In reading this case, think of excess orders as an analogy to work-in-process inventory.

IMPLEMENTING JIT IN AN AMERICAN TOYOTA MOTOR FACILITY[7]

T he Toyota Motor Manufacturing (TMM) plant in Long Beach, California, a wholly owned subsidiary of Toyota, is an excellent example of JIT implementation in the United States. Begun in 1972, TMM fabricates, assembles, and paints four models of truck beds for Toyota light trucks. Annual production exceeds 150,000 units, and the plant employs about 375 people in a 300,000-square-foot production area in 14 buildings.

JIT was gradually introduced in the plant. Implementation started in the assembly area and gradually expanded to other manufacturing functions as well as a selected number of suppliers over a two-year period. A group of managers, each of them assigned to a specific JIT responsibility, started a pilot model and planned the detailed JIT implementation.

Implementation resulted in many initial problems, including an immediate loss in manufacturing volume. As one problem was fixed, many others surfaced. Fortunately, Toyota understood that problems would occur in the short run but that time spent in solving them would translate into significant long-term benefits and cost savings.

Kanban is used at the Toyota Long Beach plant to control the flow of material and production operations. It is understood that Kanban, by itself, is only a small piece of total JIT planning and control system. The environment created by the Kanban attention and JIT philosophy is mostly responsible for continuous improvements in manufacturing and reduction of the WIP inventory.

Although an MRP is used for overall production planning, Kanban is the primary source for shop floor control. The Kanbans are traveling paper tickets containing detailed information used to provide control requirements and even to satisfy the accounting and IRS needs, in contrast to many Japanese plants where Kanban is a simple (usually triangular) piece of metal with limited information.

The tickets are constantly modified to cover all necessary information and to travel over the most appropriate routes. The Kanbans currently cover a single or few operations. The objective is to modify the system allowing Kanbans to travel in longer routes over many operations.

In one instance, Kanbans are combined with bar coding to obtain rapid access to inventory level information and to facilitate work in process cycle counting. Many types of Kanbans are used to trigger different operations or to order the raw material. The Kanbans are placed on hooks on a board stationed at the entrance of each area. The hook board is the staging area for the Kanbans, which circulate between the suppliers and the warehouse, the warehouse and the press department, and so on.

TMM cycles 4000 to 5000 Kanbans per day, which requires an immense amount of manual sorting and placing on the proper hooks each day. The company uses a single Kanban method of recirculation whereby the Kanban represents both the authority to produce and also the move and identification ticket. The hook board is color coded, as are the Kanbans, to indicate raw material or other stages

[7]Adapted from Mehran Sepehri, "How Kanban System is Used In An American Toyota Motor Facility." Reprinted from *Industrial Engineering* magazine, Feb. 1985. Copyright Institute of Industrial Engineers, 25 Technology Park/Atlanta, Norcross, GA 30092.

of manufacturing. The motto is, of course, "no Kanban—no production."

An attempt is made to decrease the number of Kanbans each month in order to drive down constantly the in-process inventory and to increase the inventory cycles. The objective is to reduce the lot sizes to one and WIP inventory to zero.

However, the schedule is not as rigid as in many other plants. A small safety stock is considered acceptable to allow for some flexibility in shifting the sequence of the operations or the mixture of the products. It also allows the plant to meet the schedule without exhausting the supply and interrupting the line. In the paint and stamping operations, the nature of manufacturing calls for a certain quantity per production run. In this case, a number of Kanbans are accumulated before they trigger the production of the previous operation.

The master schedule is used to calculate the number of Kanbans. The calculations are simple and mostly manual. The products are made to order, which is anticipatory order due to the difficulty of coordination with Japan in terms of the precise timing and destination of the orders. Additional flexibility is built in to allow for change of priorities. Ideally, the truck should arrive in time for the bed to be assembled and then shipped to the dealers and delivered to the customers. Study teams are constantly working to coincide the orders without sacrificing the flexibility and the ability to deliver the trucks to the customers.

Kanban is an example of the Toyota philosophy, which is to provide management by sight or visual control everywhere possible. This is done through color, light boards, hook boards, charts and graphs at any opportunity. These visual controls facilitate immediate identification of problems such as shortage or excess of parts as well as any other unusual occurrence.

Visual controls are also extended to testing and shipping areas. They are easy to understand and inexpensive and allow for immediate detection. There is a control chart for each critical operation graphing the performance of that operation versus the acceptable level. A buzzer is used to indicate a problem or a failure in a function. An unusually long buzzer should warn the supervisor that the machine is out of sequence and additional help should be dispatched.

A computerized board in the assembly area contains many colored lights indicating the status of machines and orders. Another board provides information on the scheduled versus the actual production as well as the reason for the variance. It provides workers with an immediate feedback and general awareness to assist them in taking corrective action and avoid variances.

Toyota attributes its success to the simultaneous materialization of the JIT system and respect for human beings. The workers are made aware that the purpose of process improvement activities is not to eliminate their jobs but to utilize them more effectively and, thus, to help guarantee their jobs.

The sole purpose of reducing costs is to obtain a better market competitive edge and, thereby, to maintain the need for production in the long run. The resulting benefits are shared by all and are not credited to only a few. The workers can really believe the JIT system is the ultimate solution, which eliminates all waste from the manufacturing floor and places a higher value on their work. JIT depends on teamwork for continuous improvements and on a full understanding of the workers who should support and maintain it.

At TMM, many workers voluntarily belong to quality circles, which meet weekly in paid overtime. The company initially established a circle in the press area and then in the paint and the maintenance areas. The overall trend has been a rapid growth in the number of quality circles, the number of suggestions and the quality and complexity of suggestions. The quality circles were a great source of problem solving in preparation for JIT implementation.

The quality circles are most effective in implementing the changes that workers often tend to oppose. Implementing a JIT system requires making many drastic changes in manufacturing. Quality circles may be used to educate the workers and to communicate to them the need for JIT production control. Quality circles may also be used to implement and support the required changes very quickly.

They usually solve a number of smaller problems while they are working on the main problem. The workers submitting suggestions are well recognized by management. The rewards, which are not necessarily financial, have strengthened the workers' attitudes.

The company has firmly maintained the policy of retaining any worker whose job is eliminated in productivity improvement process by transferring his or her employment to other areas. The workers start to believe in their intelligence and the value of teamwork. The company, on the other hand, recognizes all the good suggestions and provides opportunities for trying the new ideas.

Prior to the JIT system, the amount of raw material and work-in-process inventories and also of finished goods in the shipping area was of great concern to management. Another major shortcoming was the hidden problems in quality and material-handling procedures. A worker may have produced several hours of defective units before they could be discovered. There was no mechanism for the problems to be identified and resolved immediately to avoid excessive loss.

The immediate improvement from the implementation of JIT was the reduction of inventory and WIP, which resulted in a major reduction in carrying and handling costs. The average WIP inventory was lowered by about 45 percent and the raw material inventory was reduced by approximately 24 percent in one year.

The warehousing cost of material was reduced by about 30 percent; the carrying and control costs were also lowered accordingly. The policy was clear: Don't buy, don't move and don't produce unless there is an immediate need. The suppliers were initially concerned, but were soon encouraged to rely on a continuous JIT order and deliver accordingly.

As the inventory was drained, the overloaded buildings were emptied and many hidden problems in handling and moving the material surfaced. The warehouse was reorganized and the additional space was utilized for other productive purposes. Improvements in handling procedures resulted in lower movement distances and fewer needs for equipment.

The material was delivered directly to the point of use. About 30 percent of the forklifts were eliminated as the average movement time and distance were reduced. In the production area, the number of presses was reduced by 30 percent. The same operations were performed with approximately 20 percent reduction in labor, and the production volume per shift was increased by 40 percent in less than 2 years. Such improvements were the direct results of JIT production and many simply by the workers rather than the results of any additional financial investments.

The most noticeable improvements are in worker attitudes and awareness. They are proud of their work and pleased with the positive changes. There is a feeling of unity and participation, and an improved sense of awareness about the environment and how to cope with problems. The environment offers continuous challenge in the sense that there is no reserved inventory to comfort the production. As a problem arises in the sequence, the line comes to a halt immediately. The workers are constantly stimulated to discover problems, and to fix them.

The absenteeism rate and nonproduction time are substantially reduced. The labor turnover and interdepartmental conflicts are diminished. The effects are translated into the process and result in productivity improvements. The outgoing product quality is improved and, therefore, the warranty costs and replacement parts are reduced substantially. The plant was recently given a safety award (only four awards were granted in 5 years) as the number of internal problems and accidents were reduced.

The JIT production and material flow system played a major role in reducing manufacturing costs and increasing production productivity at Toyota Motor Manufacturing, USA. Additionally, beyond all the cost savings, the JIT environment provided a framework for problem solving and teamwork which resulted in better worker attitude and international competitive position.

QUESTIONS
1. How was JIT introduced in the Long Beach Toyota plant? Why do you think it was done in this fashion?
2. How was the Toyota philosophy of providing management by sight or visual control implemented in this plant? What advantages does this have?
3. What benefits were derived from implementing JIT?

AN APPLICATION OF JIT TO MAIL ORDER PROCESSING[8]

S emantodontics is a direct marketing company that sells nationally by catalog to dentists. One of Semantodontics major product lines is personalized printed products. This product line was creating a

---

[8]Adapted from Ronald G. Conant, "JIT in a Mail Order Operation Reduces Processing Time From Four Days to Four Hours," *Industrial Engineering*, 20, no. 9, (1988) 34–37. Copyright Institute of Industrial Engineers, 25 Technology Park/Atlanta, Norcross, GA 30092.

larger than normal number of customer complaints, resulting in an increasing number of calls to the customer service department. A study of the reason for customer service calls indicated that 64 percent of all calls involved two questions: "What is this charge on my statement?" and "Where is my order?"

After some investigation, it was revealed that both of these questions were related to the long lead times required to produce personalized printed products. Customers often waited three or more weeks, and often, statements were mailed at the end of the month showing charges on the customer's account for or-

ders invoiced but not yet printed. Therefore, the company began to study the process involved in meeting customer orders.

Figure 17.3 shows a flow chart that describes the order filling process. In the first step, telephone orders were taken over a 12-hour period each day. These were collected at the end of the day and checked for errors by the supervisor of the phone department, usually the following morning. Depending on how busy the supervisor was, the one-day batch of print orders would often not get to the data-processing department until after 1:00 P.M.

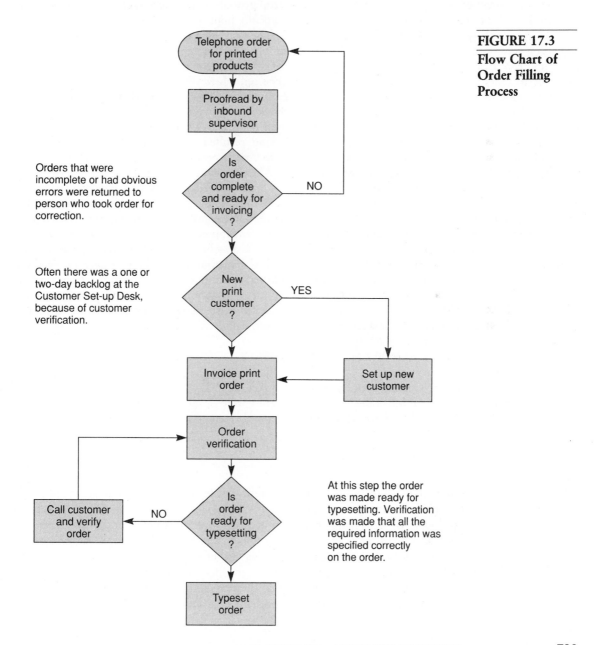

FIGURE 17.3
Flow Chart of Order Filling Process

Orders that were incomplete or had obvious errors were returned to person who took order for correction.

Often there was a one or two-day backlog at the Customer Set-up Desk, because of customer verification.

At this step the order was made ready for typesetting. Verification was made that all the required information was specified correctly on the order.

In the data processing step, the telephone orders were invoiced, still in one-day batches. Then the invoices were printed and matched back to the original orders. This step usually took most of the next day to complete. At this point in the process, if the order was for a new customer, it was sent to the person who did customer verification and setup of new customer accounts on the computer. Setting up a new account often would delay an order by a day or more.

The next step involved order verification and proof reading. Once invoicing was completed, the orders with invoices attached were given to a person who verified that all the required information was present and correct to permit typesetting. If there was a question at this time about an order, it was checked by computer or by calling the customer. It was common for this step to have a two-day backlog of orders waiting for verification.

Finally, the completed orders were sent to the typesetting department of the printshop. Using current methods, an order for an existing customer took at least four days to flow from the order taker to typesetting. Often a new customer's order took an additional day or two longer. In addition, there were often more than a one-day backlog of orders at each step in the process.

This operation provided a classic application of the JIT philosophy that lot sizes should be reduced as much as possible. In the telephone department, a system was developed to make the order batches smaller in size. Under this new system, the daily telephone orders are divided into three batches. The telephone supervisor reviews these smaller batches promptly and sends them to the data processing department three times daily, at 9:00 A.M., 12:00 noon, and 3:00 P.M.

In the data-processing department, each batch of orders is invoiced. After the printing of the invoices, the smaller batch size improved productivity of the matching operation by making it easier to match an invoice to its original order. It was also determined that the "new customer setup" procedure was the bottleneck for about 20 percent of the orders. Customer verification required looking up the customer in various directories or checking with the customer by telephone. This often took a day or more to complete. After a careful review, it was determined that verification of each customer was an unnecessary step in the process for telephone orders because the person taking the order had already talked with the customer. By removing this part of the setup procedure, new customer setup time was dramatically improved to only a few minutes.

The third step of the process, print order verification, had always been thought to be the bottleneck. Even with smaller batch sizes, delays were still expected. However, the person in this position began working faster to complete each batch before the next one arrived. Getting smaller batches rather than having a two-day backlog and always being behind, resulted in increased job satisfaction as well as increased productivity.

After implementing the JIT principles, the average order arrived at the typesetting department less than four hours after the order was taken. This resulted in a significant reduction in the typesetting and printshop backlog. A large percentage of print orders is now being processed, printed, and shipped in less than four days. The customer receives the finished order in less than two weeks. After the first month of using the new system, Semantodontics observed a 20 percent reduction in the customer service calls.

QUESTIONS
1. Why did Semantodontics study the customer order process?
2. How were JIT principles applied to the order processing function? What benefits were realized?

SUMMARY Japanese manufacturers have been highly successful in implementing an approach to material management and control known as just-in-time. JIT is based on producing or delivering required parts and materials when and where they are needed. When used effectively, JIT results in less inventory, reduces scrap, achieves higher quality and in general, provides higher productivity.

The components of JIT are layout and production methods, an information system referred to as Kanban, total quality control, and excellent relationships with suppliers. Each of these components must be considered in order to provide little or no in-process inventory and a smooth flow of product from one end of the process to the other. Problems with any component will limit the success and contribution of the JIT philosophy.

The reported benefits of JIT are numerous. Examples of benefits include better customer service, better quality, lower inventories, lower costs, less scrap, and smoother output rates. Team work and coordination between management and labor is critical in obtaining the benefits of a successful JIT system. Implementation of JIT in a typical American manufacturing environment will require cooperation, planning, and a change in traditional work habits of both management and labor. However, indications are that benefits of JIT are worth the efforts to make these changes.

		KEY TERMS
Just-in-time (JIT)	bakayake	
Kanban	yo-i-don	

1. What cultural differences in Japan led to their high acceptance of JIT?
2. What is the JIT production concept? How does it differ from MRP?
3. Discuss the four components of JIT systems.
4. What aspects of facility layout and production methods support the JIT philosophy?
5. What is the importance of setup times in JIT?
6. Explain how a Kanban system operates.
7. Discuss the importance of total quality control in successful JIT operation.
8. What do the Japanese terms *bakayake* and *yo-i-don* mean?
9. What is the role of suppliers in JIT systems?
10. Discuss the benefits of JIT. How does JIT lead to higher productivity?
11. What factors are necessary for JIT to be successfully implemented in an organization?
12. Discuss the differences between JIT and MRP for repetitive manufacturing.

CHAPTER

18

Project Planning
and Management

A t all organizational levels, managers are responsible for planning, scheduling, and controlling projects that consist of numerous activities performed by a variety of personnel. Some projects may be so large and complex that the manager cannot keep all the information pertaining to the plan, schedule, and progress of the project in his or her head. Therefore, a systematic approach to project management is necessary. At the strategic level, projects that require project management techniques include the development of new products and processes or the construction of a new plant. At the tactical level, an example is the preparation of corporate annual reports or the preparation of environmental impact statements. At the operational level, the routine maintenance of complex equipment requires careful project planning and management in order to minimize downtime.

In this chapter we present several methods that are useful in planning, scheduling, and controlling complex projects.

18.1 THE SCOPE OF PROJECT PLANNING AND MANAGEMENT

There are three factors influencing project-management decisions: *time, resources,* and *cost*. Managers responsible for complex projects look for procedures that can help them determine how long a project is expected to take and when specific activities should be started and completed. This enables a deadline to be established and provides a measure for controlling the progress of the project. In most projects, some activities are critical and must be completed *exactly* on schedule or the entire project will be delayed. For other activities, there is some freedom in scheduling.

Managers must also determine the resources, such as people and equipment, available for the project and how they should be allocated among the various activities. Improper management of resources can significantly delay a project. Finally, the cost of the project must be controlled. Managers seek ways in which cost can be minimized in order to meet a deadline. Cost is closely related to the allocation of resources throughout the project.

Although project management activities are carried on by many functional managers, organizations often have specific people designated as *project managers*. Project managers differ from functional managers in several respects. The functional manager participates in the determination of resource needs and the development of project plans. The functional manager also recruits, trains, and assigns personnel to the project, provides guidance, and assesses the quality of the results. The project manager leads the project activities, plans and tracks progress of the work, and provides direction to project personnel. Typically, project managers are found in technical areas such as research and development, engineering design, and installation of computer systems. However, the methods used in project management can be successfully applied by functional managers in many of their normal activities.

Project managers are usually generalists, with wide backgrounds and experience. In addition to managing the project, the project manager must manage the relationships among the project team, the parent organization, and the client. In this regard, the project manager's ability to facilitate is more important than his or her ability to supervise. The project manager must also have the technical expertise needed to resolve disputes among functional specialists. In general, successful project managers possess four-key skills: a bias toward task completion, technical and administrative credibility, interpersonal and political sensitivity, and leadership.

Two of the more useful tooks that have been developed to assist project managers in their scheduling efforts are PERT (project evaluation and review technique) and CPM (critical-path method).

While PERT and CPM have the same general purpose and utilize much of the same terminology, the techniques were actually developed independently. PERT was introduced in the late 1950s specifically for planning, scheduling, and controlling the Polaris missile project. Since many jobs or activities associated with the Polaris missile project had never been attempted previously, it was difficult to predict the time to complete the various jobs or activities. Consequently, PERT was developed with an objective of being able to handle uncertainties in activity completion times.

On the other hand, CPM was developed primarily for scheduling and controlling industrial projects where job or activity times were considered known. However, CPM offered the option of reducing activity times by adding more workers and/or resources, usually at an increased cost. Thus a distinguishing feature of CPM was that it enabled time and cost trade-offs for the various activities in the project.

In today's usage, the distinction between PERT and CPM as two separate techniques has largely disappeared. Computerized versions of the PERT/CPM approach often contain options for considering uncertainty in activity times as well as activity time-cost trade-offs. In this regard, modern project planning, scheduling, and controlling procedures have essentially combined the features of PERT and CPM such that a distinction between the two techniques is no longer necessary.

Although PERT and CPM provide the computational procedures used for scheduling projects, the process of project planning and management is more of an art. Let us now see how this process is performed and how PERT/CPM can be used effectively.

18.2 THE PROJECT-PLANNING PROCESS

The project-planning process involves determining a specific set of activities that must be performed and when they should be completed in order to meet an organization's goals. There are a number of basic questions that must be addressed in order to develop a useful plan. What results do we want and by when? Why do we want them? How should we go about getting them? Who should be involved? Where should the work be done? When should the activities be completed? The first two questions define the objective and its rationale, whereas the remaining questions define the details of the plan itself. These questions can be logically structured into a step-by-step planning framework that provides the basis for project management. This methodology can be described as follows:

1. *Project definition.* For the project that needs to be done, determine what activities must be completed and the sequence required to perform them.
2. *Resource planning.* For each activity, determine the resources needed: personnel, time, money, equipment, materials, and so on. If any training is needed, make sure the personnel are properly trained.
3. *Project scheduling.* Specify a time schedule for each activity.
4. *Project control.* Establish the proper controls to determine progress. Develop alternative plans to anticipate problems in meeting the planned schedule.

Projects are often late because of failure to perform these four tasks.

Let us consider a specific example to illustrate the process of project planning. R.C. Coleman stores and distributes a variety of food products that are sold in grocery stores and supermarkets. The company receives orders directly from the individual outlets, with a typical order requesting the delivery of several cases of anywhere from 20 to 50 different products. In the company's current warehouse operation, order-picking personnel fill each order and the goods move to the warehouse shipping area. Because of the high-labor cost and relatively low productivity of hand order-picking, the company has decided to automate the warehouse operation by installing a computer-controlled order-picking system. The proposed system will include a conveyor for moving goods from storage to the warehouse shipping area.

The R.C. Coleman Automated-warehouse Project

R.C. Coleman's director of material management has been named the project manager in charge of coordinating the selection and installation of the automated-warehouse system. In the following sections, we address the various tasks of project definition, resource planning, project scheduling, and project control that the director of material management will face in the role of project manager.

18.3 PROJECT DEFINITION

The first step in the project-planning process is to define the individual activities and the sequence in which they must be performed. This is by far the most difficult task in project management and requires a good deal of experience and knowledge of the project, as well as good communication with all individuals in the organization that may be involved. In order to do this effectively, we need to distinguish between an activity and an event. **Activities** are tasks that *consume* time; **events** are *points* in time that represent the start or completion of a set of activities. Projects may be defined completely in terms of activities; however, most managers usually think in terms of both activities and events. Events are often thought of as milestones by which to measure the progress of a project. Thus it is often convenient to specify events and then define the activities necessary to accomplish the events. However, it is necessary to have a complete set of project *activities* in order to proceed with the planning process.

IDENTIFYING ACTIVITIES AND EVENTS

In the R.C. Coleman project, the director of material management—after consulting with members of the engineering staff and warehouse management personnel—compiled the following initial list of activities (tasks that consume time) and events (points in time) associated with the project.

- Begin project (event)
- Determine equipment needs (activity)
- Obtain vendor proposals (activity)
- Select vendor (activity)
- Design new warehouse layout (activity)
- Design computer interface (activity)
- Order system (activity)
- Warehouse layout complete (event)
- Interface computer (activity)
- Installation complete (event)
- Train system operators (activity)
- Test system (activity)
- Automated-warehouse system ready for operation (event)

This list was reviewed and discussed several times in order to be sure that no activities were omitted from the project-definition step. In particular, certain items on the list, such as the event "warehouse layout complete," implied that the activity "layout warehouse" needed to be added to the activity list. Similarly, the event "installation complete" signaled the additional activity of "install system." Finally after several trials, the project manager developed the final list of activities shown in Table 18.1.

Note that associated with the project activities in Table 18.1 is a set of activities in the column labeled "immediate predecessors." The **immediate predecessors** for a particular activity are the activities that *must be completed prior* to the start of the given activity. For instance, the information in Table 18.1 tells us that we can start work on activities A and B anytime, since these activities do not depend on the completion of prior activities. However, activity C cannot be started until both activities A and B have been completed. Likewise, activity H cannot be

TABLE 18.1

Activities for the R.C. Coleman Automated-warehouse Project

Activity	Description	Immediate Predecessors
A	Determine equipment needs	—
B	Obtain vendor proposals	—
C	Select vendor	A, B
D	Order system	C
E	Design new warehouse layout	C
F	Layout warehouse	E
G	Design computer interface	C
H	Interface computer	D, F, G
I	Install system	D, F
J	Train system operators	H
K	Test system	I, J

started until activities D, F, and G have been completed. The immediate-predecessor information is important in identifying the sequence in which the activities must be performed.

Once all activities and immediate predecessors have been identified, we construct a graphical representation of the project called a **project network**, or **PERT/CPM network**. A project network consists of numbered circles that are interconnected by arrows. The circles are called **nodes** and the arrows connecting the nodes are called **branches** or **arcs**. In project networks the arcs correspond to activities and the nodes correspond to events. Every arc must have a starting node and an ending node. A project network portrays the predecessor relationships among the activities.

CONSTRUCTING A PROJECT NETWORK

EXAMPLE

Let us construct a project network for the R.C. Coleman project in Table 18.1. We begin with a node corresponding to "Begin project." The activities that leave this node are those with no immediate predecessors. From Table 18.1 these activities are A and B. Thus the beginning of the network appears as follows:

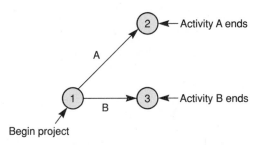

Node 2 represents the event "Activity A ends," and node 3 represents the event "Activity B ends."

Next, we see that activity C must follow the completion of both activities A and B. Clearly activity C cannot start at both nodes 2 and 3. To get around this, we use an arc that does not correspond to an actual activity in the project, but simply indicates a predecessor relationship. Such an arc, shown with a dashed line, is called a **dummy activity**. In a PERT/CPM network, dummy activities play an important role in guaranteeing that the immediate predecessor requirements are maintained. To show that activity C cannot begin until both activities A and B are completed, we draw the network as follows:

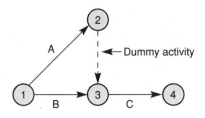

Next, we see that activities D, E, and G all have activity C as their immediate predecessor. This results in the following network:

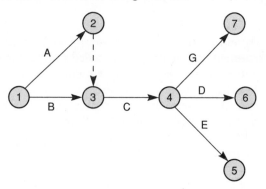

We continue to add activities, making sure to maintain the proper predecessor relationships. Figure 18.1 shows the completed project network. Notice that we have a second dummy activity from node 6 to node 7. To see why, consider the following portion of the network with the dummy activity from nodes 6 to 7 removed.

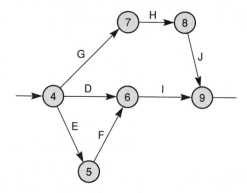

Now look carefully at the immediate predecessor for activity H. The network shows this to be only activity G; however, Table 18.1 shows that the actual immediate predecessors for activity H should be activities D, F, and G. Using the dummy activity from node 6 to 7 maintains D, F, and G as the immediate predecessors for activity H.

Let us look at another version of this portion of the network where we attempt to maintain the immediate-predecessor relationships without using a dummy activity.

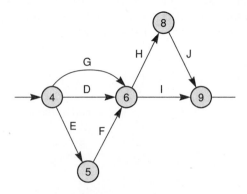

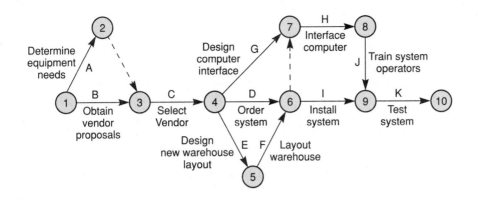

FIGURE 18.1

PERT/CPM Network for the R.C. Coleman Project

A close look at this portion of the network shows we still have problems accurately describing the desired relationships. Now activity H correctly shows the immediate predecessors D, F, and G. However, what are the immediate predecessors shown for activity I? Table 18.1 indicates that they should be activities D and F only. However, without using the dummy activity, the above network incorrectly shows D, F, *and* G as the immediate predecessors for activity I. Thus we see that dummy activities are often necessary to depict the predecessor relationships in a project correctly.

In addition, note that the portion of the network just given shows both activity G and D starting and ending with the same nodes. Computer procedures for analyzing PERT/CPM networks often require activities to be uniquely defined by two node numbers. Thus referring to the activity only by nodes 4 and 6 in this portion of the network would make it unclear as to whether we were referring to activity D or G. Note that this was the reason the dummy activity from node 2 to 3 was added in Figure 18.1, thus making activity A uniquely defined by nodes 1 to 2 and activity B uniquely defined by nodes 1 to 3.

While it is difficult to describe all cases where dummy activities might be desired, the best approach is to attempt to develop the PERT/CPM network without dummy activities. Insert dummy activities whenever two or more activities have the same starting and ending nodes and insert dummy activities wherever they are necessary in order to preserve the correct immediate-predecessor relationships for the project.

We should also point out that project networks can be drawn in which *nodes* correspond to *activities* and arcs are used only to represent precedence relationships. These networks are called *activity-on-node* networks. Figure 18.2 shows an activity-on-node network for the R.C. Coleman project. Activity-on-node networks have the advantage that dummy arcs are never necessary; thus, they are usually easier to conceptualize. The major disadvantage, however, is that events do not have an explicit graphical representation on an activity-on-node network as they do on activity-on-arc networks. The selection of which approach to use—activity-on-arc or activity-on-node—is a matter of choice, and both approaches are commonly used. We prefer to use the activity-on-arc representation so that both activities and events have a clear graphical interpretation.

Now that the project definition phase of the R.C. Coleman automated-warehouse project has been completed (See Table 18.1 and Figure 18.1), the next task is to define the resources that will be required for each activity.

FIGURE 18.2
Activity-on-node
Representation
for the R.C.
Coleman Project

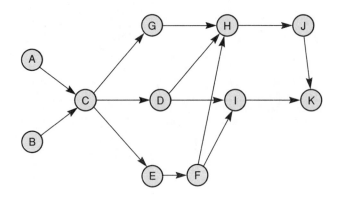

18.4 RESOURCE PLANNING

Once a network for the project has been established, information is needed on the resources required to complete each activity. For scheduling purposes, the most important resource requirement is *time*. This is necessary in order to calculate the duration of the entire project and to schedule the specific activities. Accurate estimates of activity time are essential for successful project management. Errors in estimates of activity time will cause errors in scheduling and errors in project completion-date projections.

Uncertain
Activity Times

In many situations, activity times can be estimated accurately. For example, in projects such as construction or maintenance, a manager may have sufficient experience or historical data to provide activity time estimates that are fairly accurate. In addition, the nature of these activities may have low variability, and thus times would be relatively constant. In other cases, activity times are uncertain and perhaps best described by a range of possible values. In these instances the uncertain activity times are treated as random variables with associated probability distributions.

The most common method of dealing with uncertain activity times is to obtain three time estimates for each activity. The three estimates are

- **Optimistic time,** *a.* The activity time if everything progresses in an *ideal* manner.
- **Most probable time,** *m.* The most likely activity time under normal conditions.
- **Pessimistic time,** *b.* The activity time if we encounter significant breakdowns and/or delays.

The three estimates enable the manager to make his or her best guess of the most likely activity time and then express uncertainty by providing estimates ranging from the best (optimistic) possible time to the worst (pessimistic) possible time.

EXAMPLE

COMPUTING THE MEAN AND VARIANCE OF ACTIVITY TIMES

In the R.C. Coleman project, the project manager gathered information from warehouse personnel, industrial engineering, and other sources and developed

TABLE 18.2

Optimistic, Most
Probable, and
Pessimistic
Activity Time
Estimates in
Weeks for the
R. C. Coleman
Project

Activity	Optimistic Time (a)	Most Probable Time (m)	Pessimistic Time (b)
A	2	3	4
B	3	4	11
C	1	2	3
D	4	5	12
E	3	5	7
F	2	3	4
G	2	3	10
H	2	3	4
I	2	3	10
J	1	2	3
K	1	2	3

the time estimates listed in Table 18.2. Using activity A as an example, we see that this activity will require from 2 weeks (optimistic) to 4 weeks (pessimistic), with the most likely time being 3 weeks.

In order to schedule these activities, we need to determine the **average**, or **expected time** for each activity. The expected time t is computed using the following formula:

$$t = \frac{a + 4m + b}{6} \qquad (18.1)$$

Thus for activity A, we compute the expected time to be

$$t = \frac{2 + 4(3) + 4}{6} = \frac{18}{6} = 3 \text{ weeks}$$

Using the three time estimates of $a = 3$, $m = 4$, and $b = 11$ for activity B, Equation (18.1) provides the following expected time:

$$t = \frac{3 + 4(4) + 11}{6} = \frac{30}{6} = 5 \text{ weeks}$$

Figure 18.3 shows the probability distribution for acitivity B. Note that different values of a, b, and m will result in a different shape for the activity time distribution. The fact that varying the values of a, b, and c provides considerable flexibility in determining the shape of this distribution is one of the major reasons it is used in PERT/CPM.

For uncertain activity times, we can use the common statistical measure of the *variance* to describe the dispersion or variation in the activity time values. We compute the variance of the activity times from the following formula:[1]

$$\text{Variance of activity time} = \left(\frac{b - a}{6}\right)^2 \qquad (18.2)$$

---

[1]The variance equation is based on the notion that a standard deviation is approximately ⅙ of the difference between the extreme values of the distribution: $(b - a)/6$. The variance is simply the square of the standard deviation.

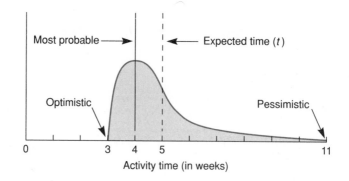

FIGURE 18.3

Activity Time Distribution for Activity B of the R.C. Coleman Project

Most probable ⟶

⟵ Expected time (t)

Optimistic

Pessimistic

0   3 4 5   11

Activity time (in weeks)

As you can see, the difference between the pessimistic (b) and optimistic (a) time estimates greatly affects the value of the variance. With large differences in these two values, management has a high degree of uncertainty in the activity time. Accordingly, the variance given by Equation (18.2) will be large.

Referring to activity A, we see that the measure of uncertainty—that is, the variance of this activity, denoted by σ_A^2—is

$$\sigma_A^2 = \left(\frac{4-2}{6}\right)^2 = \left(\frac{2}{6}\right)^2 = .11$$

For activity B, we have an optimistic time of 3 weeks but a pessimistic time of 11 weeks. Thus activity B has a greater uncertainty in completion time than activity A. The variance measure for activity B is

$$\sigma_B^2 = \left(\frac{11-3}{6}\right)^2 = \left(\frac{8}{6}\right)^2 = 1.78$$

The expected times and variances for all R.C. Coleman project activities can be computed by using the data in Table 18.2 and Equations (18.1) and (18.2). These values have been computed and are shown in Table 18.3.

Additional Resource Requirements

Besides time, a variety of other resources may be required for project activities. These might include

- executives, managers, and supervisors
- professional and technical personnel
- capital
- materials
- equipment and tools
- clerical services

The project manager must determine how many of these resources are required, if they are available, and where in the organization they can be obtained. The project manager's job is to bring these resources together at the proper times in order to perform the activities of the project. The determination of when activities are to be performed is called scheduling and is the next task in the project planning process.

Activity	Expected Time (Weeks)	Variance σ^2
A	3	.11
B	5	1.78
C	2	.11
D	6	1.78
E	5	.44
F	3	.11
G	4	1.78
H	3	.11
I	4	1.78
J	2	.11
K	2	.11

TABLE 18.3

Expected Times and Variances for the R.C. Coleman Activities

18.5 PROJECT SCHEDULING

A schedule enables a manager to assign resources effectively and to monitor progress and take corrective action when necessary. There are several scheduling tools available in project management. We focus first on the more common graphical tools and then we will illustrate how schedules can be determined from the PERT/CPM network itself.

A very useful tool for graphically depicting a schedule is a **Gantt chart**, named after Henry L. Gantt, one of the pioneers of scientific management. Gantt charts enable the operations manager to know exactly what activities should be performed at a given time and, more importantly, to monitor daily progress of a project so that corrective action may be taken when necessary.

CONSTRUCTING A GANTT CHART

EXAMPLE

To construct a Gantt chart, we list the activities on a vertical axis and use a horizontal axis to represent time. Figure 18.4 shows the initial layout of the Gantt chart for the R.C. Coleman project. The symbols used in a Gantt chart are defined as follows:

Symbol Number	Symbol	Description
1.	$\ulcorner$	Scheduled starting time for activity
2.	$\urcorner$	Scheduled completion time for activity
3.	▭	Completed work for an activity
4.	⋈	Scheduled delay or maintence
5.	∨	Current date for progress review

FIGURE 18.4

Gantt Chart Construction

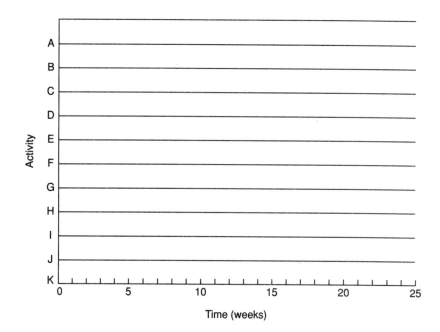

The network describing the precedence relationships among project activities (Figure 18.1) and the estimated times in Table 18.3 assist us in constructing a Gantt chart for this project. We assume that each activity will be scheduled as early as possible. The resulting schedule will be an "early start" schedule. For instance, activities A and B can begin at time 0. For these activities, we place symbol number 1 at time 0 and symbol number 2 at the completion times of 3 and 5, respectively. The top portions of these symbols are joined by a lighter line to indicate the duration of the activity. Activity C cannot begin until A is completed; thus this activity is scheduled to begin at time 5. After activity C is completed at time 7, activities G, D, and E can be scheduled. Continuing in this fashion we may construct the Gantt chart shown in Figure 18.5.

From Figure 18.5 we see that the entire project is scheduled to be completed in 22 weeks. What happens if an activity is delayed? Suppose, for example, activity E is delayed by 1 week. Because E is a predecessor of F and the starting time of F is the same as the completion time of E, then F is forced to begin 1 week later. This forces a delay in activity H, which in turn delays activities J and K. In addition, activity I is also pushed back 1 week. The Gantt chart for this new schedule is shown in Figure 18.6.

The effect that delays in one activity have on other activities can be better seen by referring to the project network in Figure 18.1. A *path* in the network is a sequence of activities, performed *in order*, that starts at the beginning node

(node 1 in the R.C. Coleman network) and ends with the completion node (node 10 in the R.C. Coleman network). Examples of paths are shown below.

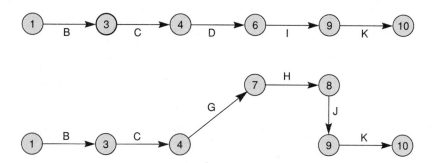

Whenever the scheduled completion time for some activity is the same as the scheduled start time for a successor activity along a path, then any delay in the activity will force a delay in that successor activity. If this holds true for *all* activities on some path from the start of the project to the end, then the activities on this path are called **critical activities**, and the path is called the **critical path**. Critical activities are those for which any delay will push back the completion date of the entire project. For the R.C. Coleman project, the critical activities are B, C, E, F, H, J, and K and the dummy activity from node 6 to node 7.

Let us show how to calculate the critical path directly from the network and also show how to obtain some other important scheduling information.

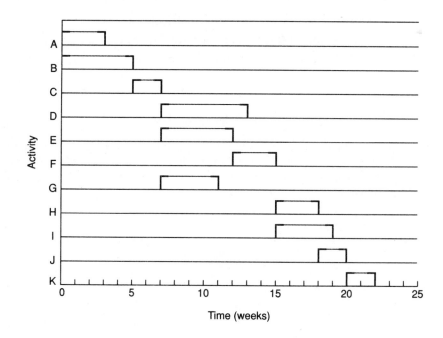

FIGURE 18.5

Early Start Schedule for R.C. Coleman Project

FIGURE 18.6

Early Start
Schedule with
Activity E
Delayed 1 Week

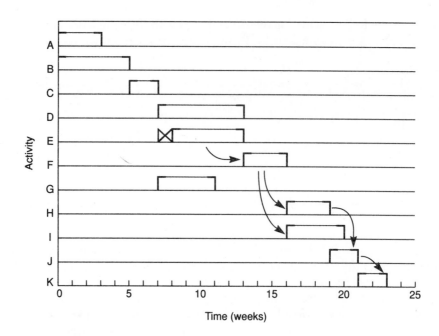

Time (weeks)

FINDING THE CRITICAL-PATH

Figure 18.7 shows the R.C. Coleman project network with expected activity times labeled on the arcs. Note that dummy activities have an expected activity time of zero. The following discussion presents a step-by-step procedure for finding the critical path.

Starting at the network's origin (node 1) and using a starting time of 0, compute an *earliest start* and *earliest finish* time for each activity in the network. Letting

$\qquad$ ES = earliest start time for a particular activity
$\qquad$ EF = earliest finish time for a particular activity
$\qquad$ t = expected activity time for the activity

the following expression can be used to find the earliest finish time for a given activity:

$$EF = ES + t \qquad (18.3)$$

For example, for activity A, ES = 0 and t = 3; thus the earliest finish time for activity A is EF = 0 + 3 = 3. We write the earliest start and earliest finish times directly on the network in brackets next to the letter of the activity. Using activity A as an example, we have

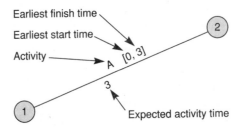

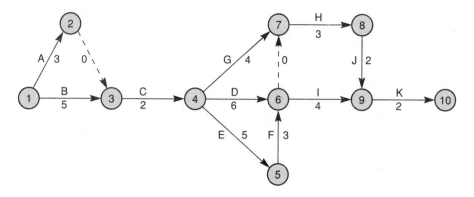

FIGURE 18.7
R.C. Coleman
Project with
Expected Activity
Times

Because activities leaving a node cannot be started until *all* immediately preceding activities have been completed, the following rule can be used to determine the earliest start times for activities.

Earliest Start Time Rule

The **earliest start time** for an activity leaving a particular node is equal to the *largest* value of the earliest finish times for all activities entering the node.

Applying this rule to the portion of the network involving nodes 1, 2, 3, and 4, we obtain the following:

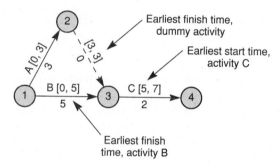

Note that applying the earliest start time rule at node 3 shows that the earliest start time for activity C is equal to the largest value of the earliest finish times for the two entering activities, B and the dummy activity.

Proceeding in a *forward pass* through the network, we can establish an earliest start and an earliest finish time for each activity. The R.C. Coleman network with ES and EF values is shown in Figure 18.8. Note that the earliest finish time for activity K, the last activity, is 22 weeks. Thus the earliest completion time for the entire project is 22 weeks.

We now continue the procedure for finding the critical path by making a *backward pass* calculation. Starting at the completion point (node 10) and using a latest finish time of 22 for activity K, we trace back through the network computing a *latest start* and *latest finish* time for each activity. We use a latest finish time of 22 for activity K because we are concerned about finishing the project as quickly as possible. This is not necessary, and we might use a different target date for project completion in performing the subsequent calculations.

FIGURE 18.8
R.C. Coleman
with Earliest
Start and Earliest
Finish Times
Shown Next to
Activities

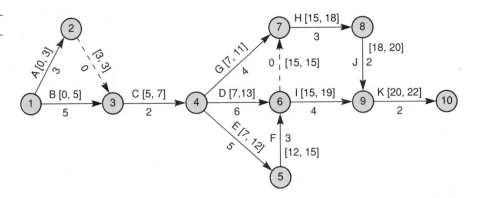

Letting

LS = latest starting time for a particular activity

LF = latest finishing time for a particular activity

the following expression can be used to find the latest start time for a given activity

$$LS = LF - t \qquad (18.4)$$

Given an LF = 22 and t = 2 for activity K, the latest start time for this activity can be computed as LS = 22 − 2 = 20.

The following rule is necessary in order to determine the latest finish time for any activity in the network.

Latest Finish Time Rule

The **latest finish time** for an activity entering a particular node is equal to the *smallest* value of the latest starting times for all activities leaving the node.

Logically, the above rule states that the latest time an activity can be finished is equal to the earliest (smallest) value for the latest start time of following activities. The complete network with the LS and LF backward-pass calculations is shown in Figure 18.9. The latest start and latest finish times for the activities are written in parentheses directly under the earliest start and earliest finish times.

Note the application of the latest finish time rule at node 4. The latest finish time for activity C (LF = 7) is the smallest value of the latest start times for the activities that leave node 4; that is, the smallest LS value for activities G (LS = 11), D (LS = 9), and E (LS = 7), which is 7.

After obtaining the start and finish activity times as summarized in Figure 18.9, we can find the amount of slack or free time associated with each of the activities. **Slack** is defined as the length of time an activity can be delayed without affecting the completion date for the project. The amount of slack for each activity is computed as follows:

$$Slack = LS - ES = LF - EF \qquad (18.5)$$

For example, we see that the slack associated with activity A is LS − ES = 2 − 0 = 2 weeks. This means that activity A can be delayed up to 2 weeks (start anywhere between weeks 0 and 2) and the entire project can still be completed in 22 weeks. This activity is not a critical activity and is not part of the critical path. Using Equation (18.5), we see that the slack associated with activity C is LS − ES = 5 − 5 = 0. Thus activity C has no slack time and must be held to the 5-week start time schedule. Since this activity cannot be delayed without affecting the entire project, it is a critical activity and is on the critical path. In general, the critical-path activities are the activities with zero slack.

The start and finish times shown on the network in Figure 18.9 provide a detailed schedule for all activities. That is, from Figure 18.9, we know the earliest and latest starting and finishing times for the activities. Putting this information in tabular form provides the activity schedule shown in Table 18.4. Note that by computing the slack associated with each activity, we see that activities B, C, E, F, H, J, and K each have zero slack, and hence these activities form the critical path in the R. C. Coleman network. Table 18.4 also shows the slack, or delay, that can be tolerated for the noncritical activities before these activities will cause a project delay.

For the operations manager, this means that critical activities must be carefully monitored and controlled if the project is to be completed on schedule. Delays in noncritical activities are not as important and consequently these activities do not require such close control. PERT/CPM calculations easily enable us to determine critical activities and the amount of slack in noncritical activities.

The Gantt chart schedule that we constructed earlier is the same as the earliest start-earliest finish schedule given in Table 18.4. The critical-path calculations

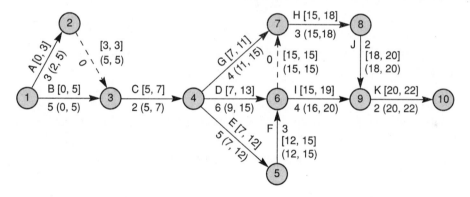

FIGURE 18.9

R.C. Coleman Project with Latest Start and Latest Finish Times in Parentheses

Activity	Earliest Start	Earliest Finish	Latest Start	Latest Finish	Slack (LS − ES)	Critical Path
A	0	3	2	5	2	
B	0	5	0	5	0	✓
C	5	7	5	7	0	✓
D	7	13	9	15	2	
E	7	12	7	12	0	✓
F	12	15	12	15	0	✓
G	7	11	11	15	4	
H	15	18	15	18	0	✓
I	15	19	16	20	1	
J	18	20	18	20	0	✓
K	20	22	20	22	0	✓

TABLE 18.4

Activity Schedule in Weeks for the R.C. Coleman Project

provide additional information to the project manager regarding latest start, latest finish, and slack times.

Variability in the Project Completion Date

While we treated the activity times as fixed at their expected values during the critical-path calculations, we are now ready to consider the uncertainty in the activity times and determine the effect this uncertainty, or variability, has on the project completion date. Recall that the critical path determines the duration of the entire project. For the R. C. Coleman project, the critical path of B, C, E, F, H, J, and K resulted in an expected project completion time of 22 weeks.

Just as the critical-path activities govern the expected project completion date, variation in critical-path activities can cause variation in the project completion date. Variation in noncritical-path activities will ordinarily have no effect on the project completion date because of the slack time associated with these activities. However, if a noncritical activity were delayed long enough to expend all of its slack time, then that activity would become part of a new critical path, and further delays would extend the project completion date. Variability leading to a longer than expected total time for the critical-path activities will always extend the project completion date. On the other hand, variability in critical-path activities resulting in a shorter critical path will enable an earlier than expected completion date, unless the activity times on the other paths become critical. The PERT procedure uses the variance in the critical path activities to determine the variance in the project completion date.

EXAMPLE

PROBABILITY CALCULATIONS FOR PROJECT COMPLETION TIMES

If we let T denote the project duration, then T, which is determined by the critical activities B-C-E-F-H-J-K in the R. C. Coleman problem, has the expected value of

$$T = t_B + t_C + t_E + t_F + t_H + t_J + t_K$$
$$= 5 + 2 + 5 + 3 + 3 + 2 + 2 = 22 \text{ weeks}$$

Similarly, the variance in the project duration is given by the sum of the variance of the critical path activities. Thus the variance, σ^2, for the completion time of the R. C. Coleman project is given by

$$\sigma^2 = \sigma_B^2 + \sigma_C^2 + \sigma_E^2 + \sigma_F^2 + \sigma_H^2 + \sigma_J^2 + \sigma_K^2$$
$$= 1.78 + .11 + .44 + .11 + .11 + .11 + .11 = 2.77$$

This formula is based on the assumption that all the activity times are independent. If two or more activities are dependent, the formula provides only an approximation to the variance of the project completion time. The closer the activities are to being independent, the better the approximation.

Since we know that the standard deviation is the square root of the variance, we can compute the standard deviation, σ, for R. C. Coleman project completion time as follows:

$$\sigma = \sqrt{\sigma^2} = \sqrt{2.77} = 1.66$$

A final assumption of PERT is that the distribution of the project completion time T follows a normal, or bell-shaped, probability distribution.[2] Thus, T follows the distribution shown in Figure 18.10. With this assumption we can compute the probability of meeting a specified project completion date. For example, suppose that management has allotted 25 weeks for the R.C. Coleman project. While we expect completion in 22 weeks, what is the probability that we will meet the 25-week deadline? Using the normal probability distribution from Figure 18.10, we are asking for the probability that $T \le 25$. This is shown graphically as the shaded area in Figure 18.11. The z-value for the normal distribution at $T = 25$ is given by

$$z = \frac{25 - 22}{1.66} = 1.81$$

Using $z = 1.81$ and the tables for the standard normal distribution (see Appendix B), we see that the probability of the project meeting the 25-week deadline is .4649 + .5000 = .9649. Thus, while variability in the activity time may cause the project to exceed the 22-week expected duration, there is an excellent chance that the project will be completed before the 25-week deadline. Similar probability calculations can be made for other project deadline alternatives.

The procedure that we have described is only approximate since we have *assumed* that the distribution of T is normally distributed. Moreover, this method assumes that only one critical path exists; if there are two or more critical paths, this method tends to underestimate the project completion time. Also, when several paths are close (in terms of time) to the critical path, caution should be exercised when interpreting the results since randomness in activity times may cause one of the other paths to be critical. Simulation is often used in such

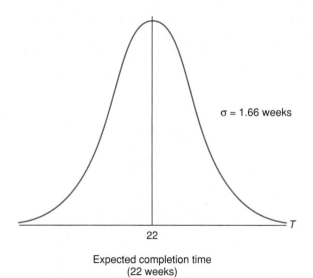

σ = 1.66 weeks

22

Expected completion time
(22 weeks)

FIGURE 18.10

PERT Normal Distribution of the Project Completion Time Variation for the R.C. Coleman Project

[2]The use of the normal probability distribution as an approximation is based on the central limit theorem, which indicates that the sum of independent activity times follows a normal distribution as the number of activities becomes large.

situations to gain a clearer perspective on project completion times and critical activities.

Computer packages can be helpful in analyzing project networks, identifying a critical path, and determining the project completion time. Figure 18.12 shows the computer output for the R.C. Coleman project using *The Management Scientist* microcomputer software package. Input data included the immediate predecessor, optimistic, most probable, and pessimistic time information. As shown in Figure 18.12, the output includes the expected activity times, variance of activity times, the complete activity schedule, the critical path, the expected project completion time, and the variance of project completion time.

18.6 PROJECT CONTROL

Up to now we have simply discussed the process of *project planning*. Because of the uncertainty of task times, unavoidable delays, or other problems, projects will rarely, if ever, progress on schedule. Managers must monitor performance of the project and take corrective action when needed (see Photo 18.1). A typical progress report is shown in Figure 18.13. The manager needs to be able to evaluate planned versus actual results, any changes in the situation, problems that are facing the project now and in the future, and action needed to correct these problems or avoid future ones. Schedules should be revised periodically using actual times when they become known.

<table>
<tr><td>**EXAMPLE**</td><td>### USING A GANTT CHART FOR PROGRESS CONTROL</td></tr>
</table>

Let us return to the R.C. Coleman project. Figure 18.14 illustrates a typical Gantt progress chart at week 9. Note that symbol number 3 (the color block) is used to denote the actual progress of activities at a given point in time. We see that activities A, B, and C have already been completed, activity D is ahead of schedule,

FIGURE 18.11

Probability of an R.C. Coleman Project Completion Date Prior to the 25-week Deadline

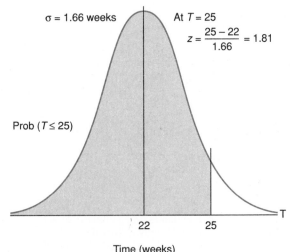

$\sigma = 1.66$ weeks

At $T = 25$

$$z = \frac{25 - 22}{1.66} = 1.81$$

Prob $(T \le 25)$

22   25   T

Time (weeks)

ACTIVITY	EXPECTED TIME	VARIANCE
A	3	0.11
B	5	1.78
C	2	0.11
D	6	1.78
E	5	0.44
F	3	0.11
G	4	1.78
H	3	0.11
I	4	1.78
J	2	0.11
K	2	0.11

FIGURE 18.12

The Management Scientist Computer Software Solution for the R.C. Coleman Project Scheduling Problem

*** ACTIVITY SCHEDULE ***

ACTIVITY	EARLIEST START	LATEST START	EARLIEST FINISH	LATEST FINISH	SLACK	CRITICAL ACTIVITY
A	0	2	3	5	2	
B	0	0	5	5	0	YES
C	5	5	7	7	0	YES
D	7	9	13	15	2	
E	7	7	12	12	0	YES
F	12	12	15	15	0	YES
G	7	11	11	15	4	
H	15	15	18	18	0	YES
I	15	16	19	20	1	
J	18	18	20	20	0	YES
K	20	20	22	22	0	YES

CRITICAL PATH: B–C–E–F–H–J–K
EXPECTED COMPLETION TIME = 22
VARIANCE OF PROJECT COMPLETION TIME = 2.77

activity E has not yet begun, and activity G is right on schedule. A progress chart such as this allows the manager quickly to see the status of a project. It also provides the information required to revise the schedule. For instance, since E is a critical activity and since it is currently late, the project will be delayed unless the times for future activities can be shortened. This might be done by adding more resources to certain activities, working overtime, and so on. These are the decisions that a project manager must make on an ongoing basis in order to control a project. Techniques for controlling projects which consider resources and costs are discussed in the next section and in the supplement to this chapter.

18.7 PLANNING AND SCHEDULING WITH LIMITED RESOURCES

In the early-start schedule we developed in Figure 18.5, no consideration was given to resources. We assumed that there were sufficient resources available for all activities that are scheduled at the same time. Usually, however, there are limited resources such as labor and equipment, that must be shared among the

PHOTO 18.1

A large Midwest electronics equipment manufacturer uses this Rotate-A-Panel system to schedule, plan, and control each of its projects over a 2-year period. The first panel lists function, person responsible and percentage complete of each function using Magnetic Card Holders with Flexcard Inserts. Panels 2, 3, and 4 show the estimated and actual time for each function using red and white PF-7 Magnetic Rubber. Courtesy of Methods Research Corp., 1108 Pollack Ave., Ocean, NJ 07712.

activities. Determining how to allocate limited resources is a difficult problem. Two major objectives involving resource allocation are

1. minimizing project duration subject to resource constraints
2. resource leveling, or smoothing, over time.

MINIMIZING PROJECT DURATION WITH RESOURCE LIMITATIONS

In order to illustrate how a project manager can make decisions that minimize project time when resource limitations occur, let us consider activity F in the R.C. Coleman project. This activity involves the layout of the warehouse, including subtasks such as moving stock to a temporary storage area, removing existing storage racks, shifting the office location, painting new aisle and safety markers, and so on. A network that provides the detailed information for specific activities that must be undertaken in order to layout the warehouse is shown in Figure 18.15. The number of days required to complete each activity and the

FIGURE 18.13

Typical Progress
Report

Project name: _____
Date: _____

PERIODIC PROGRESS REPORT

1. What results have we attained so far? _____
2. ☐ Are we ahead of schedule?   ☐ On schedule?   ☐ Behind schedule?
3. Has the objective changed or been modified? _____
4. Has the situation changed or been modified? _____
5. What unanticipated problems are we now facing? _____
   _____
6. What changes need to be made? _____
   _____
7. Whose approval is needed for these changes? _____
   _____
8. Action steps for me to take. _____
   _____
   _____
   _____
9. What additional problems are anticipated? _____
   _____
   _____
   _____

Source: Improving Management Skills: A Workbook. Copyright © S.J. Mantel, J.M. McKinney, and R. Riley 1977, used by permission.

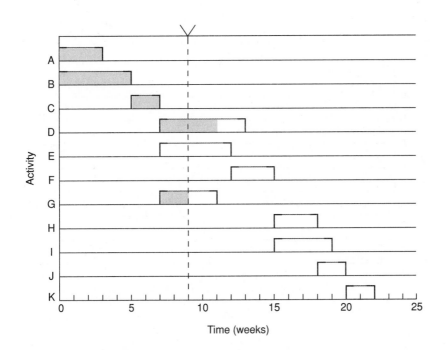

FIGURE 18.14

Progress Chart
for the R.C.
Coleman Project

number of people needed are shown in parentheses on the arcs of the network. For example, (3, 4), written below the arc corresponding to a, indicates that activity a requires 3 days with 4 people working together. Activity b requires 6 days with 2 people working together, activity c requires 2 days with 1 person, and so on. We assume that the tasks or activities do not require special training, so that any employee may work on any activity. Because of the importance of the automated-warehouse project, the warehouse-layout activity will operate on a seven-day-week basis. Thus the critical path defined by activities b, d, e, f, and h provides the expected completion time of 21 days, or 3 weeks.

Figure 18.16 shows a Gantt chart using a schedule based on the earliest-start times. Using this Gantt chart, we may now construct a *resource-loading chart*, showing the amount of resource, that is, the number of people, required at any point in time for the particular schedule. For the R.C. Coleman problem this is done by adding the number of people required for all activities at each point in time. The resource-loading chart for the schedule in Figure 18.16 is shown in Figure 18.17. The maximum value of 6 tells us that 6 people are required in order to complete the project by its scheduled time of 21 days.

Suppose, however, that only 5 employees are available. The only way of accommodating this constraint is to delay certain activities; if these are critical, then the project duration must be extended. Finding the minimum project time that will meet this constraint is a very difficult problem. Although there are a

FIGURE 18.15

Network for the Warehouse-layout Subtask

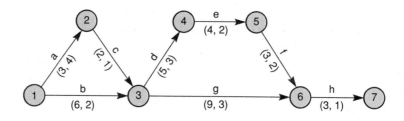

FIGURE 18.16

Gantt Chart for the Early Start Schedule for Warehouse-layout Subtask

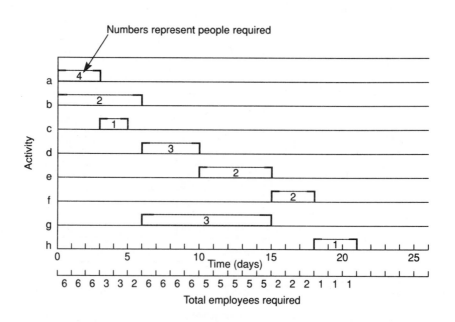

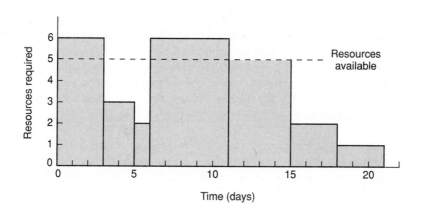

FIGURE 18.17

Resource Loading Chart for Warehouse-layout Subtask

number of quantitative techniques that can be used to find the optimal solution, they are beyond the scope of this text. Instead, a **heuristic,** or "rule of thumb," which will often provide a good solution—but may not always yield the best possible one—can be used. Heuristics are often used to solve difficult problems because they are usually easy to implement and often give satisfactory solutions.

There are a variety of different heuristic rules that can be applied. Some of these are

1. Schedule the task with the shortest time first.
2. Schedule the task with the longest time first.
3. Schedule tasks with the least variability in time first.

Let us illustrate rule 1 for the R.C. Coleman example. At the start of the project, a and b cannot be scheduled simultaneously because only 5 employees are available. Using heuristic 1 we would schedule activity a first because it has the shortest time. Because of the resource constraint, activity b cannot be scheduled at the same time as activity a; therefore, we schedule activity b immediately after activity a is completed. The partial Gantt chart at this point looks as follows:

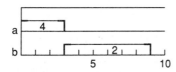

Now, c is the only activity that can be scheduled next. Because it must follow a and requires only one person, it can be scheduled to start at the same time as b:

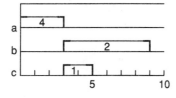

Next, we must choose to schedule either activities d or g. Again, because their combined resource requirements exceed 5, we choose to schedule activity d first because it has a shorter time. Continuing in this manner, we arrive at the schedule given in Figure 18.18. The other rules can be applied in a similar manner, although we cannot tell in advance which will give the best results. Observe that the time to complete the warehouse layout was lengthened to 26 days due to the resource limitation. In the R. C. Coleman project, the warehouse-layout activity was critical. Therefore, lengthening the time to lay out the warehouse will lengthen the entire project duration.

In other situations we might be interested in *leveling*, or smoothing, resources over time. In essence, we try to level the resource-loading chart by rescheduling tasks that are not critical. We cannot reschedule critical activities because this would increase the project time.

| EXAMPLE | RESOURCE LEVELING |

To illustrate the **resource-leveling** process, consider the network shown in Figure 18.19. Suppose this represents the subtask of interfacing the automated warehouse systems computer with Coleman's central computer. If sufficient resources are available, we may wish to balance the work load among the employees working on this task. The early-start schedule is shown on the Gantt chart on

FIGURE 18.18

Revised Schedule with Resource Limit

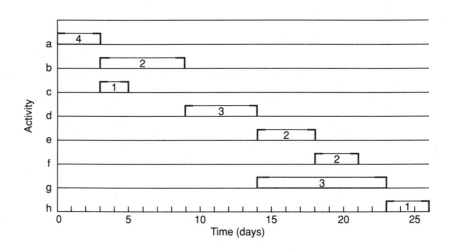

FIGURE 18.19

Network for the Computer Interface Subtask

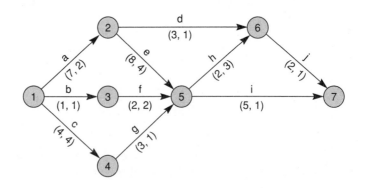

Figure 18.20, with the accompanying resource-loading chart in Figure 18.21 The maximum resource requirement is eight employees which occurs near the start of the project. The way to smooth the resource requirement is to shift noncritical activities. This is basically a trial-and-error procedure. As a general guideline, we look at the peaks and valleys in the resource-loading chart and attempt to reschedule noncritical activities in order to provide a more stable level of resource requirements.

By inspecting the schedule in Figure 18.20, we see that activities b and f can be rescheduled after activity c without delaying the subtask. In addition, slack on activities g and d allows them to be scheduled later. This revised schedule is shown in Figure 18.22 and its resource-loading chart in Figure 18.23. We see a much smoother level of resource requirements over the duration of this subtask.

Gantt charts provide an invaluable visual aid in rescheduling tasks with resource requirements. Many types of magnetic boards that enable manual sched-

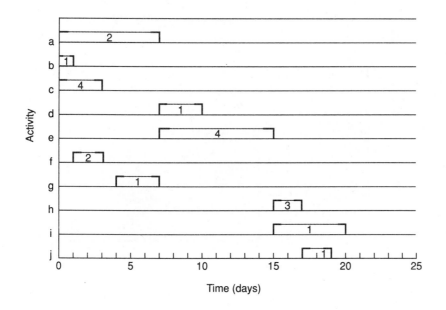

FIGURE 18.20

Gantt Chart for the Early Start Schedule for Computer Interface Subtask

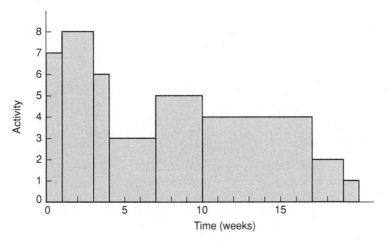

FIGURE 18.21

Resource Loading Chart for the Computer Interface Subtask

FIGURE 18.22

Revised Schedule for Computer Interface Subtask

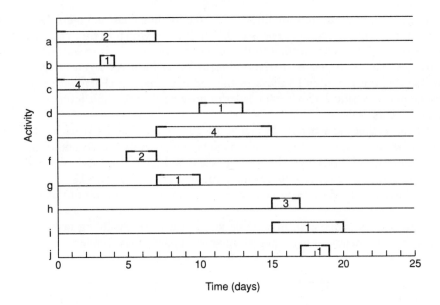

FIGURE 18.23

Resource-loading Chart for the Computer Interface Subtask (Revised Schedule)

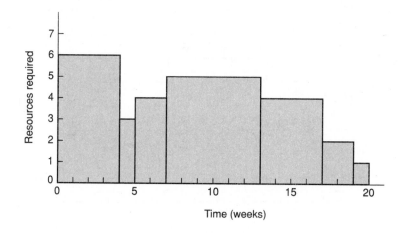

uling to be done quickly and easily are available from supply firms. In addition, computer software for applying heuristic scheduling rules is often available or can easily be written by experienced programmers.

P/OM IN PRACTICE

We present two examples of project management. In the first case, we show an example of a project network for a hospital relocation project and discuss some of the implementation issues involved. The second case describes a control system for Bechtel Power Corporation. From these cases you can see that considerable effort is involved in planning, scheduling, and controlling projects. The project networks and Gantt charts are merely tools for assisting project managers.

RELOCATING A HOSPITAL[3]

S t. Vincent's Hospital and Medical Center moved from a 373-bed hillside facility in Portland, Oregon to a new 403-bed facility located 5 miles away in a suburban area. Due to construction delays, much of the new equipment ordered for installation in the new hospital was delivered to the old hospital and put into use. Thus, when construction on the new facility was completed, a large volume of equipment had to be moved from the old to the new facility.

A large variety of planning considerations had to be taken into account. Army vehicles and private ambulances would be used to move patients; local merchants would be affected by the move; police assistance would be required, and so on. In order to coordinate these and other activities, a project network was constructed and used as the basic planning tool for activities that occurred 8 months prior to the move. A portion of this network is shown in Figure 18.24. The actual network contained dozens of activities and events.

The network was developed by first establishing major milestones (events) that must be reached. Activities necessary to accomplish these events were added until the final project definition was complete. Close cooperation with hospital department heads early in the planning process was essential in order to determine individual moving needs and open channels of communication. Critical activities were determined by using a computer program. Lists of

---

FIGURE 18.24   A Portion of St. Vincent's Hospital Project Network (Heavy Arrows Denote Critical Activities)

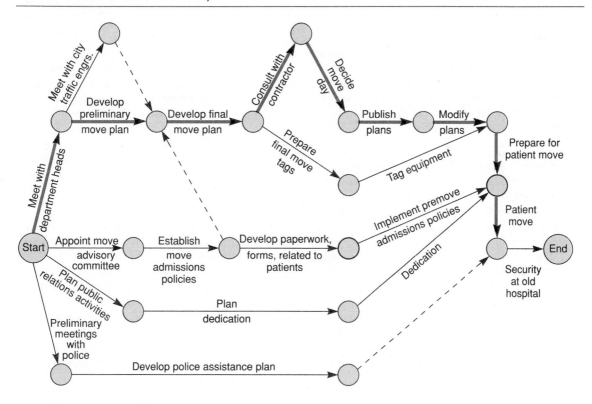

---

[3]Adapted from R. S. Hanson, "Moving the Hospital to a New Location." Reprinted with permission from *Industrial Engineering* magazine, November 1972, Copyright Institute of Industrial Engineers, 25 Technology Park/Atlanta, Norcross, GA 30092.

activities, scheduled times, and graphical bar charts were automatically provided by the computer program. The input times were updated during the move to show progress and to determine any needs for reallocation of resources.

Although many modifications to plans were made during the process, the basic planning document, the project network, remained unchanged. According to the user, "It remained the constant framework around which all other plans were based and developed. The time spent in the early development of sound plans proved a wise investment."

It is important to realize that the activities shown in Figure 18.24 need to be broken down in more detail for actual implementation. For example, in the activity "patient move," managers would have to determine which patients to move first (for example, intensive care), equipment that must be in place in order to support each class of patient, and so on. Again, this illustrates the hierarchical nature of planning and decision making. Figure 18.24 provides an overall planning structure, but each activity must be implemented by managers at lower levels of the organization.

This example illustrates how project-management techniques can be valuable tools in planning and operationalizing a complex project. Without such planning, the welfare of the hospital patients could have been in serious jeopardy.

QUESTIONS
1. Develop a list of activities and immediate predecessors using the network shown in Figure 18.24.
2. Is there sufficient detail in the network shown in Figure 18.24 to actually implement the project? Explain.

PROJECT CONTROL FOR BECHTEL POWER CORPORATION[4]

I n the Betchel Power Corporation, project-control activities begin as soon as company management and the client define the job requirements, the scope of work, overall schedules, and the project's magnitude. Important control documents are prepared and are used to monitor the project during its planning and implementation phases. These include

- *Scope of Services Manual*, which establishes a baseline for identifying changes in services and a definition of engineering, home office support, and field nonmanual services that will be performed by the company.
- *Division of Responsibility Document*, which describes the responsibilities of the company, the client, and the major suppliers.
- *Project Procedures Manual*, which defines the procedures involved in interface activities among the company, the client, and the major suppliers with respect to engineering, procurement, construction, preoperational services, quality assurance, quality control, project control, and communication.

- *Technical Scope Document*, which describes the project's physical plant, establishes the design basis, and provides input to the civil/structural, architectural, plant design, mechanical, electrical, and control systems disciplines.
- *Project Activity Control Guide*, which aids in the administration of project activities by identifying and time-phasing the development and execution of project plans, programs, procedures, controls, and other significant activities required for effective operation of the project.

After the project has been defined and the preliminary control documents prepared, the project manager and his team develop the project-control system that will be used through the remainder of the project. The main objectives of the project-control system are to develop a monitorable plan that reflects expected performance of the contract work and to establish a work-control system that provides the information necessary for the team, the company management, and the client to identify problem areas and initiate corrective action.

[4]Adapted from F.A. Hollenbach, "Project Control in Bechtel Power Corporation," in *Project Management Handbook*, David I. Cleland and William R. King, eds. New York: Van Nostrand Reinhold, 1983.

The control system includes

- A project plan covering expected scope, schedule, and cost performance.
- A continuous monitoring system that measures the performance against the plan through the use of modular monitoring tools.
- A reporting system that identifies deviations from the plan by means of trends and forecasts.
- Timely actions to take advantage of beneficial trends or correct deviations.

The first objective in project control is the development of a well-conceived project plan that adequately defines the project scope, schedule, and cost. This plan is developed in four stages as the project evolves. It begins with a proposal schedule and cost estimate based on the scope obtained from the client showing type, size, location, and required services. Following project award, a front-end schedule is implemented to identify activities for the first 12 to 18 months. The process plant layout, major equipment, and key operating parameters are developed during this period.

The trend base schedule and estimate are established as the second stage plan. It is used to establish early project budgets (such as engineering and home office costs) for reporting and control.

A trend program, based on this plan, is implemented to provide a mechanism for identifying changes in project technical scope, scope of services, and the current plan of engineering, procurement, and construction. A monthly trend report is developed for the project team, company management, and client management. The trend program also identifies scope changes for potential contract changes. It extends through the life of the project.

In the third stage, the preliminary plan is developed on the basis of a project technical scope document containing actual project data. It updates the trend base schedule and estimate and ensures that the current plan is consistent with the scope of work.

The more comprehensive project plan is the fourth stage. Based on established minimum criteria, it forms the basis for all detailed cost and schedule budgets; therefore, it is necessary that the company and the client concur that the defined scope accurately reflects what will be built. This plan is usually the basis for contractual cost and schedule goals.

Each plan has as its basis for cost, schedule, and material control a definition of the technical scope of the project and the scope of services to be provided. Milestone dates to be achieved and project procedures to be followed by the client, the company, and major suppliers are also identified.

The project plan is scheduled in a hierarchal and sequential manner. The milestone summary schedule, comprising about 50 lines of major project milestones, is the basic schedule. It is expanded into engineering, construction, and startup summary schedules of approximately 500 activities each. Intermediate and detail schedules follow. The intermediate schedules contain about 3000 activities. As each plan develops, the elements of scope, schedule, and cost are integrated by a standard numbering system and are displayed in budgets that are used as a frame of reference for continuous monitoring.

Manual or computerized continuous monitoring tools are used to monitor project progress and identify potential deviations from established budgets. These tools monitor engineering and home office manhours and cost, quantities, schedules, commitments, and the cost of project materials as well as contracts/subcontracts and construction performance.

Work process flow charts and quantity take-offs are used to monitor the design, procurement, and installation of commodities; to identify commodity status; and to identify responsibilities for work functions. These flow charts depict the information flow from conceptual design through construction and startup. Deviations from the project plan are identified and reported to management for corrective action. This continuous monitoring of quantities is called quantity tracking and is generally computerized.

After the project plan has been prepared, forecasts are made semiannually that reflect the current scope, schedule, and cost of the project. They are the bases for planning the remaining work and updating the schedule. They provide an up-to-date evaluation of project costs and a current basis for project monitoring and control.

The project plan, budgets, continuous monitoring tools, trending/change control, and forecasting produce the necessary information needed by mangement to evaluate the current situation and take appropriate action. Client management reports, prepared periodically, include project status, an executive summary, a production summary, and detailed reports about cost, commitments, subcontracts, and work progress.

Project planning and monitoring identify beneficial trends and detrimental deviations; however, the action taken by the company-client team is the most critical aspect of the control cycle.

1. What control documents are prepared in order to monitor the project during planning and implementation?

2. What is the purpose of the project control system? What components make up this system?

3. Briefly describe the four stages of the project plan.

SUMMARY

In this chapter we discussed the process of project planning and management. This process consists of four steps: project definition, resource planning, project scheduling, and project control. The objective of the project-definition step is to define the set of activities that must be performed and the order in which they must be completed. The time required to accomplish each activity and any other resource requirements must also be specified. Project scheduling involves using this information to determine starting and finishing times for each activity. To assist the project manager in scheduling, Gantt charts and the PERT/CPM procedure are useful tools. Resource limitations often also have to be taken into account during the scheduling process, and this is one of the most difficult tasks of project management. Heuristic techniques are often used for resource leveling. Finally, monitoring of project progress is one of the most important responsibilities of the project manager, since plans rarely stay on schedule.

KEY TERMS

Activities
Events
Immediate predecessors
Project network or PERT/CPM
  network
Nodes
Branches
Arcs
Dummy activity
Optimistic time
Most probable time

Pessimistic time
Average or expected time
Gantt chart
Critical activities
Critical path
Earliest start time
Latest finish time
Slack
Heuristic
Resource leveling

**REVIEW/
DISCUSSION
QUESTIONS**

1. Discuss the three major factors that influence project management decisions.

2. Describe the role of the project manager. What skills should he or she possess?

3. Discuss the key elements of the project-planning process.

4. What is the difference between an event and an activity?

5. Why is a network diagram used in project management?

6. Explain the use of dummy activities in a project network.

7. Explain what *optimistic time, most probable time,* and *pessimistic time* estimates are. How would you estimate these times for a specific activity?

8. Explain why Gantt charts are a useful aid to a manager.

9. What is a *critical path*? Describe, in your own words, the procedure for finding the critical path.

10. What is the effect of uncertainty of activity times on the total project completion time?

11. Discuss the importance of project control.

12. What is a resource-loading chart and how is it used in project management?

13. Describe the procedure used for resource leveling.

14. The local chapter of the Operations Management Association is planning a dinner meeting with a nationally known speaker and you are responsible for organizing it. How could the methodology discussed in this chapter be useful?

15. Find an application of project management in your own life (for example, in your home, fraternity, business organization, etc.). List the activities and events that comprise the project and draw the precedence network. What problems did you encounter in doing this?

PROBLEMS

1. The Mohawk Discount Store chain is designing a management-training program for individuals at its corporate headquarters. The company would like to design the program so that the trainees can complete it as quickly as possible. There are important precedence relationships that must be maintained between assignments or activities in the program. For example, a trainee cannot serve as an assistant to the store manager until after obtaining experience in the credit department and at least one sales department. The activities shown in the following table are the assignments that must be completed by each trainee in the program.

Activity	Immediate Predecessor
A	—
B	—
C	A
D	A, B
E	A, B
F	C
G	D, F
H	E, G

Construct a project network for this problem. Do not attempt to perform any further analysis.

2. Consider the PERT/CPM network shown below.

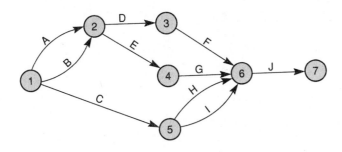

a. Add the dummy activities that will eliminate the problem of activities having the same starting and ending nodes.

b. Add dummy activities that will satisfy the following immediate predecessor requirements:

Activity	Immediate Predecessor
H	B, C
I	B, C
G	D, E

3. Construct a PERT/CPM network for a project having the following activities.

Activity	Immediate Predecessor
A	—
B	—
C	A
D	A
E	C, B
F	C, B
G	D, E

The project is completed when both activities F and G are completed.

4. The following estimates of activity times (days) are available for a small project:

Activity	Optimistic Time	Most Probable Time	Pessimistic Time
A	4	5	6
B	8	9	10
C	7	7.5	11
D	7	9	10
E	6	7	9
F	5	6	7

Compute the expected activity completion times and the variance for each activity.

5. Given the following project network, construct an early-start schedule using a Gantt chart.

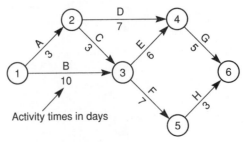

Activity times in days

6. Construct an early-start schedule using a Gantt chart for the following project network:

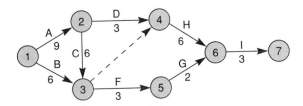

7. Consider the project network shown below.

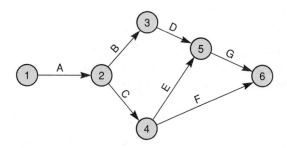

The appropriate managers have made estimates of the optimistic, most probable, and pessimistic times (in days) for completion of the activities. These times are as given

Activity	Optimistic Time	Most Probable Time	Pessimistic Time
A	1	4	7
B	2	3	10
C	4	4	10
D	3	5	7
E	1	7	7
F	2	9	10
G	2	3	4

a. Compute the expected activity times and the variances.
b. Construct an early-start Gantt chart.
c. Which activities are critical?

8. Doug Casey is in charge of planning and coordinating next spring's sales management training program for his company. Doug has listed the activity information for this project in Table 18.5.
a. Draw the project network for this problem.
b. Compute expected activity times.
c. Construct an early-start Gantt chart.

TABLE 18.5 Data for Problem 8

Activity	Description	Immediate Predecessors	Times (Weeks) Optimistic	Times (Weeks) Most Likely	Times (Weeks) Pessimistic
A	Plan topic	—	1.5	2	2.5
B	Obtain speakers	A	2	2.5	6
C	List meeting locations	—	1	2	3
D	Select location	C	1.5	2	2.5
E	Speaker travel plans	B, D	0.5	1	1.5
F	Final check with speakers	E	1	2	3
G	Prepare and mail brochure	B, D	3	3.5	7
H	Take reservations	G	3	4	5
I	Last-minute details	F, H	1.5	2	2.5

9. Maffei Manufacturing Co. is planning to install a new flexible manufacturing system. The activities that must be performed, their immediate predecessors, and estimated activity times are shown below.

Activity	Description	Immediate Predecessors	Estimated Activity Time (Days)
A	Analyze current performance	—	3
B	Identify goals	A	1
C	Conduct study of existing operation	A	7
D	Define new system capabilities	B	6
E	Study existing technologies	—	2
F	Determine specifications	D	9
G	Conduct equipment analyses	C, F	13
H	Identify implementation activities	C	3
I	Determine organizational impacts	H	4
J	Prepare report	E, G, I	2
K	Establish audit procedure	H	2

Draw the PERT/CPM network and find the critical path.

10. Consider the following project network (the times shown are in weeks).

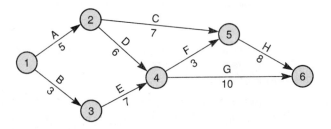

a. Identify the critical path.
b. How long will it take to complete this project?

   c. Can activity D be delayed without delaying the entire project? If so, how many weeks?

   d. Can activity C be delayed without delaying the entire project? If so, how many weeks?

   e. What is the schedule for activity E (that is, start and finish times)?

11. Colonial State College is considering building a new multipurpose athletic complex on campus. The complex would provide a new gymnasium for intercollegiate basketball games. In addition, it would provide expanded office space, classrooms, and intramural facilities. The activities that would have to be undertaken before beginning construction are shown below. Activity times are stated in weeks.

Activity	Description	Immediate Predecessor	Time
A	Survey building site	—	6
B	Develop initial design	—	8
C	Obtain board approval	A, B	12
D	Select architect	C	4
E	Establish budget	C	6
F	Finalize design	D, E	15
G	Obtain financing	E	12
H	Hire contractor	F, G	8

   a. Develop a PERT/CPM network for this project.

   b. Identify the critical path.

   c. Develop a detailed schedule for all activities in the project.

   d. Does it appear reasonable that construction of the athletic complex could begin 1 year after the decision to begin the project with the site survey and initial design plans? What is the completion time for the project?

12. Suppose that the following estimates of activity times (weeks) were provided for the network shown in problem 10.

Activity	Optimistic Time	Most Probable Time	Pessimistic Time
A	4	5	6
B	2.5	3	3.5
C	6	7	8
D	5	5.5	9
E	5	7	9
F	2	3	4
G	8	10	12
H	6	7	14

What is the probability that the project will be completed within

   a. 21 weeks?

   b. 22 weeks?

   c. 25 weeks?

13. Consider the project network given below.

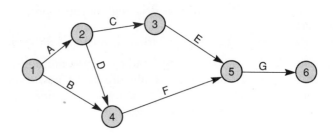

The appropriate managers have made estimates of the optimistic, most probable, and pessimistic times (in days) for completion of the activities. These times are as follows:

Activity	Optimistic Time	Most Probable Time	Pessimistic Time
A	5	6	7
B	5	12	13
C	6	8	10
D	4	10	10
E	5	6	13
F	7	7	10
G	4	7	10

a. Find the critical path.
b. How much slack time, if any, is there for activity C?
c. Determine the expected project completion time and the variance.
d. Find the probability that the project will be completed in 30 days or less.

14. A competitor of Kozar International, Inc., has just started marketing a new instant developing film for home movies. Kozar has had a similar product under study in its R&D department, but has not yet been able to begin production. Because of the competitor's action, Kozar's top management has asked for a speed up of R&D activities such that the Kozar instant film can be produced and marketed at the earliest possible date. The PERT/CPM network for the Kozar film project is shown below. The activity time estimates in months are also given below.

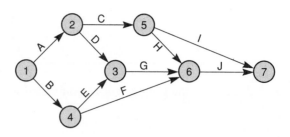

Activity	Optimistic Time	Most Probable	Pessimistic Time
A	1	1.5	5
B	3	4	5
C	1	2	3
D	3.5	5	6.5
E	4	5	12
F	6.5	7.5	11.5
G	5	9	13
H	3	4	5
I	2	3	4
J	2	2.5	6

a. Develop an activity schedule for this project and define the critical activities.

b. What is the probability the project will be completed such that Kozar may begin marketing the new product within 1½ years? 2 years?

15. The product development group at Landon Corporation has been working on a new computer software product that has the potential to capture a large market share. Through outside sources, Landon's management has learned that a competitor is working to bring a similar product to market. As a result Landon's top management has increased its pressure on the product development group. The group's leader has turned to PERT/CPM as an aid to the scheduling of the activities remaining before the new product can be brought to the market. The PERT/CPM network developed is shown below:

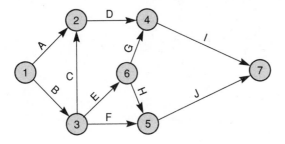

The activity time estimates in weeks are given below.

Activity	Optimistic Time	Most Probable Time	Pessimistic Time
A	3	4	5
B	3	3.5	7
C	4	5	6
D	2	3	4
E	6	10	14
F	7.5	8.5	12.5
G	4.5	6	7.5
H	5	6	13
I	2	2.5	6
J	4	5	6

a. Develop an activity schedule for this project and identify the critical path activities.

b. What is the probability that the project will be completed so that Landon Corporation may introduce the new product within 25 weeks? 30 weeks?

16. For the R.C. Coleman project, suppose that management had originally started with the schedule given in Figure 18.4. After 13weeks, the status of the project is as follows:

> Activity A was completed in 6 weeks.
> Activity B took 4 weeks to complete.
> Activity C was completed in 2 weeks.
> Activity D was delayed 4 weeks.
> Activity H is anticipating a 1-week delay.

What is the status of the remainder of the project and what revised schedule should be followed?

17. Astronauts on the next space shuttle flight are performing a variety of scientific experiments, many of which depend on the results of previous experiments. Some experiments require both astronauts working together; others can be performed by either one. The sequence of experiments is given by the accompanying network, along with the time required and number of astronauts needed. Use both the shortest time first and longest time first rule to schedule these experiments. Compare your results.

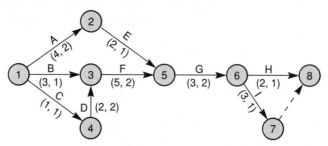

(Hours required, astronauts required)

18. Consider the following network with resource requirements:

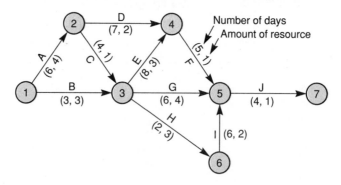

a. Smooth the resource requirements over the minimum project duration.

b. If the project can be delayed by as much as 10 days, can a better leveling of resources be obtained?

CRASHING
AND PERT/COST

I n this supplement we present two additional techniques for project management. The first technique, crashing, deals with establishing tradeoffs in time and cost for a project; the second, PERT/Cost, is a method for planning and scheduling project costs over time when budget considerations are important.

CONSIDERING TIME-COST TRADE-OFFS

We now consider an approach to project scheduling that provides the project manager with the capabilities of adding resources to selected activities in an attempt to reduce activity times, and thus project completion times. Since added resources, such as more workers, overtime, and so on, generally increase project costs, the decision to reduce activity times must take into consideration the additional cost involved. In effect the project manager has to make a decision that involves trading off decreased activity time against increased project cost.

In order to illustrate this aspect of project management, let us reconsider the warehouse-layout activity for the R.C. Coleman project. The network showing the subtasks that must be performed in completing this activity is shown in Figure 18.15. Recall that the critical path of the network consists of subactivities b, d, e, f, and h, and indicates that 21 days will be required to complete the warehouse layout.

Now suppose that the entire R.C. Coleman project is behind schedule and that it has become imperative for the warehouse layout activity to be completed within

18 working days. By looking at the length of the critical path (21 days), we realize that it is impossible to meet the new completion time unless we can shorten selected activity times. This shortening of completion times, which is usually achieved by adding resources such as labor and/or overtime, is referred to as **crashing**. However, since the added resources associated with crashing usually result in added project costs, we want to identify the least-cost ways to crash and then crash only the amount necessary to meet the specified completion date. In effect, the project manager makes time-cost decisions that reduce completion times but add cost to the project.

In order to determine just where and how to crash activities of any project-management network, we need information on how much each activity can be crashed and how much the crashing process costs. One way to accomplish this is to ask management for the following information on each activity:

1. Estimated activity cost under the normal or expected activity time.

2. Activity completion time under maximum crashing (that is, shortest possible activity time).
3. Estimated activity cost under maximum crashing.

Let

τ_n = normal activity time

τ_c = crashed activity time (at maximum crashing)

C_n = normal activity cost

C_c = crashed activity cost (at maximum crashing).

We can compute the *maximum* possible activity time reduction M due to crashing as follows:

$$M = \tau_n - \tau_c \qquad (18S.1)$$

On a per unit time basis (for example, per day), the crashing cost K for each activity is given by

$$K = \frac{C_c - C_n}{M} \qquad (18S.2)$$

For example, if activity a in Figure 18.14 has a normal activity time of 3 days at a cost of $500, we have τ_n = 3 and C_n = 500. Suppose that maximum crashing of this activity indicates that for a cost of $800 the activity could be completed in 1 day. This information provides τ_c = 1 with C_c = 800. Thus, using Equations (18S.1) and (18S.2), we see that activity a can be crashed a maximum of M_c = 3 − 1 = 2 days at a crashing cost of

$$K_a = \frac{800 - 500}{2} = \frac{300}{2} = \$150 \text{ per day}$$

We make the assumption that any portion or fraction of the activity crash time can be achieved for a cor-

FIGURE 18S.1   Time-cost Relationship for Activity a

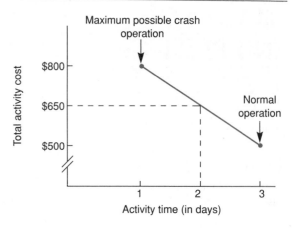

responding portion of the activity crashing cost. For example, if we decided to crash activity **a** by only 1 day, we assume that this can be accomplished with an added cost of $150, which results in a total activity cost of $500 + $150 = $650. Figure 18S.1 shows the graph of the time-cost relationship for activity **a**.

The complete normal and crash activity data for the R.C. Coleman project are given in Table 18S.1.

Crashing Activities at Minimum Cost

Now, the question is which activities should be crashed and how much these activities should be crashed in order to meet the 18-day completion deadline with a

---

TABLE 18S.1   Normal and Crash Activity Data for the R. C. Coleman Warehouse-layout Activity

Activity	Normal Time τ_n	Crash Time τ_c	Normal Cost C_n	Crash Cost C_c	Maximum Crash Days $(M = \tau_n - \tau_c)$	Crash Cost Per Day $K = \dfrac{C_c - C_n}{M}$
a	3	1	$ 500	$ 800	2	$150
b	6	3	800	950	3	50
c	2	1	900	1100	1	200
d	5	3	500	800	2	150
e	4	3	400	500	1	100
f	3	*	600	—	—	—
g	9	5	1000	1320	4	80
h	3	*	300	—	—	—

*These activities cannot be crashed.

minimum added cost. Your first reaction might be to consider crashing the critical-path activities b, d, e, f, or h. Table 18S.1 shows us that activities f and h cannot be crashed. However, activity b can be crashed up to a maximum of 3 days at a cost of $50 per day. This crashing decision would reduce the b-d-e-f-h path to the desired 18-day completion; the total added cost is $150. While this looks like a good decision, it is important to realize that crashing some activities may cause other activities to form a new critical path. For example, if b is crashed from 6 to 3 days, a-c-d-e-f-h will become the new critical path with a completion time of 20 days; hence this new critical path will not meet the 18-day completion time. Thus care has to be taken in making the crashing decision.

Let us reconsider the crashing decision for the warehouse-layout network. This is shown in Figure 18S.2. If we crash b by more than 1 day ($50 per day), we must also crash a and/or c simultaneously. Since the cost of crashing a and c are relatively high, let us try to crash other activities on the current critical path. Because the cost to crash activity d is $150 per day and the cost to crash activity e is $100 per day, suppose that we decide to crash the less-expensive activity e. Since activity e can be crashed for a maximum of 1 day, the final day of crashing then comes from activity d ($150). Checking other paths in the network, we find crashing each of the activities b, d, and e ($50 + $150 + $100) by one day enables us to meet the 18-day completion time with a total added cost of $300.

In reaching these crashing decisions, we took a trial-and-error approach, testing the desirability of each crashing decision by inspecting the network to determine how it would affect other activities in the project. While this is possible in rather small networks, it is difficult to use this approach for projects with larger networks. Fortunately, computerized mathematical procedures are available for making optimal crashing decisions in a project network. Input information for the crashing procedure requires only the data from Table 18S.1, along with the specification of the desired total completion time. We show how this is done with a linear programming model.

A Linear Programming Model for the Crashing Decision

One approach that can be used to determine the optimal crashing decision is based upon a linear programming model of the problem. First recall that an event refers to the completion of all the activities that lead into a node. Since we have seven nodes or events in the warehouse-layout activity example, the linear programming approach requires us to define seven-decision variables to identify the time of occurrence for each event. In addition, we will need six-decision variables to represent the amount of crash time used for each of the six activities that can be crashed. Thus we define the following decision variables:

x_i = time of occurrence of event i

y_j = amount of crash time used for activity j

Note that the normal time project cost of $5000 (obtained by summing the column of normal costs in Table 18S.1), does not depend upon what crashing decisions we will make. As a result, we can minimize the total project cost (normal costs plus crashing costs) by minimizing the crashing costs. Thus, in general, the linear programming objective function becomes

$$\min 150\, y_a + 50\, y_b + 200\, y_c + 150\, y_d + 100\, y_e + 80\, y_g$$

Note that since the x_i variables indicate event occurrences, they do not result in any costs; thus these decision variables have zero coefficients in the objective function.

The linear programming constraints that must be developed include constraints which describe the network, limit the activity crash times, and result in meeting the desired project completion time. Of these, the constraints used to describe the network are perhaps the most difficult. These constraints are based on the following conditions:

1. The time of occurrence of event i (x_i) must be greater than or equal to the activity completion time for all activities leading into the node or event.

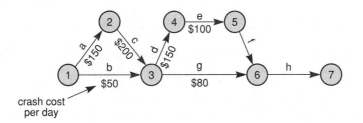

FIGURE 18S.2

Warehouse-layout Network

2. An activity start time is equal to the occurrence time of its preceding node or event.
3. An activity time is equal to its normal time less the length of time it is crashed.

Using an event occurrence time of zero at node 1 ($x_1 = 0$), we can create the following set of network description constraints:

Event 2: amount of crash time for activity a

$$x_2 \geq 3 - y_a + 0$$

where

$$x_2 = \text{time of occurrence for event 2}$$
$$3 - y_a = \text{actual time for activity a}$$
$$0 = \text{start time for activity a } (x_1 = 0)$$

or

$$x_2 + y_a \geq 3$$

Since two activities enter event or node 3, we have the following two constraints:

Event 3:

$$x_3 \geq 6 - y_b + 0$$
$$x_3 \geq 2 - y_c + x_2$$

or

$$x_3 + y_b \geq 6$$
$$x_3 + y_c - x_2 \geq 2$$

Event 4:

$$x_4 \geq 5 - y_d + x_3$$

or

$$x_4 + y_d - x_3 \geq 5$$

Event 5:

$$x_5 \geq 4 - y_e + x_4$$

or

$$x_5 + y_e - x_4 \geq 4$$

Event 6:

$$x_6 \geq 3 + x_5$$

(Note that activity f cannot be crashed so y_f does not appear here)

$$x_6 \geq 9 - y_g + x_3$$

or

$$x_6 - x_5 \geq 3$$
$$x_6 + y_g - x_3 \geq 9$$

Event 7:

$$x_7 \geq 3 + x_6$$

or

$$x_7 - x_6 \geq 3$$

The maximum allowable crash time constraints are

$$y_a \leq 2$$
$$y_b \leq 3$$
$$y_c \leq 1$$
$$y_d \leq 2$$
$$y_e \leq 1$$
$$y_g \leq 4$$

To account for the desired project completion of 18 days, we add the constraint:

$$x_7 \leq 18$$

Adding the nonnegativity restrictions and solving this linear programming model using *The Management Scientist* we obtain the following solution:

$x_2 = 3$	$y_a = 0$
$x_3 = 5$	$y_b = 1$
$x_4 = 9$	$y_c = 0$
$x_5 = 12$	$y_d = 1$
$x_6 = 15$	$y_e = 1$
$x_7 = 18$	$y_g = 0$

objective function = $300

We see that this is the same solution that we obtained using the heuristic procedure that was previously described. This is only a coincidence; in general, the heuristic procedure will not provide the optimal solution.

PLANNING AND SCHEDULING PROJECT COSTS (PERT/COST)

The project management procedures we have discussed emphasized the *time* aspect of a project and provided information that can be used to schedule and control individual activities so that the entire project is completed on time. While project time and the meeting of a scheduled completion date are primary considerations for almost every project, there are many situations in which the *cost* associated with the project is just as important as time. In this section, we show how the technique referred to as **PERT/Cost** can be used to help plan, schedule, and control project costs. The ultimate objective of a PERT/Cost system is to provide information that can be used to maintain project costs within a specified budget.

The budgeting process for a project usually involves identifying all costs associated with the project and then developing a schedule or forecast of when the costs are expected to occur. Then at various stages of project completion, the actual project costs incurred can be compared to the scheduled or budget costs. If actual costs are exceeding budgeted costs, corrective action may be taken to keep costs within the budget.

The first step in a PERT/Cost control system is to break the entire project into components that are convenient in terms of measuring and controlling costs. While a PERT/CPM network may already show detailed activities for the project, we may find that these activities are too detailed for conveniently controlling project costs. In such cases related activities under the control of one department or subcontractor are often grouped together to form what are referred to as **work packages.** By identifying costs of each work package, a project manager can use a PERT/Cost system to help plan, schedule, and control project costs.

Since the projects we discuss in this chapter have a relatively small number of activities, we find it convenient to define work packages as having only one activity. Thus in our discussion of the PERT/Cost technique we treat each activity as a separate work package. Realize, however, that in large and complex projects we would almost always group related activities so that a cost-control system could be developed for a more reasonable number of work packages.

In order to illustrate the PERT/Cost technique for project cost control, let us consider the research and development project network for the Preston and Granger Company shown in Figure 18S.3. The specific project involves an effort to develop a suds-producing additive for a dishwashing detergent. We are assuming that each activity in the network is an acceptable work package and that a detailed cost analysis has been made on an activity basis. The activity cost estimates, along with the expected activity times, are shown in Table 18S.2. In using the PERT/Cost technique we assume activities (work packages) are defined such that costs occur at a constant rate over the duration of the activity. For example, activity B, which shows an estimated cost of $30,000 and an expected 3-month duration, is assumed to have a cost rate of $30,000/3 = $10,000 per month. The cost rates for all activities are provided in Table 18S.2. Note that the total estimated, or budgeted, cost for the project is $87,000.

Using the expected activity times, we can compute the critical path for the project. A summary of the critical path calculations and the resulting activity schedule is shown in Table 18S.3. Activities B, D, and F determine the critical path and provide an expected project completion time of 8 months.

We are now ready to develop a budget for the project that will show when costs should occur during the 8-month project duration. First let us assume that all activities begin at their earliest possible starting date. Using the monthly activity cost rates shown in Table 18S.2 and the earliest start times, we can prepare the month-by-month cost forecast as shown in Table 18S.4. For example, using the earliest start date for activity A as 0, we expect activity A, which has a 2-month duration, to show a cost of $5000 in each of the first 2 months of the project. By similarly using the earliest starting date and monthly cost rate for each activity, we are able to complete Table 18S.4 as shown. Note that by summing the costs in each column, we

FIGURE 18S.3 Network for the Preston and Granger Research and Development Project

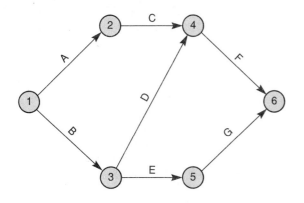

TABLE 18S.2 Activity Time and Cost Estimates

Activity	Expected Time (Months)	Budgeted or Estimated Cost	Budgeted Cost per Month
A	2	$10,000	$ 5,000
B	3	30,000	10,000
C	1	3,000	3,000
D	3	6,000	2,000
E	2	20,000	10,000
F	2	10,000	5,000
G	1	8,000	8,000
	Total project budget = $87,000		

TABLE 18S.3 Activity Schedule	Activity	Earliest Start	Latest Start	Earliest Finish	Latest Finish	Slack	Critical Path
	A	0	3	2	5	3	
	B	0	0	3	3	0	✓
	C	2	5	3	6	3	
	D	3	3	6	6	0	✓
	E	3	5	5	7	2	
	F	6	6	8	8	0	✓
	G	5	7	6	8	2	

obtain the total cost anticipated for each month of the project. Finally, by accumulating the monthly costs, we can show the budgeted total cost schedule provided all activities are started at the *earliest* starting times. In a similar manner, we can develop the budgeted total cost schedule when all activities are started at the *latest* starting times. (Table 18S.5 shows these results.)

Provided the project progresses on its PERT/CPM time schedule, each activity will be started somewhere between its earliest and latest starting times. This implies that the total project costs should occur at levels between the earliest start and latest start cost schedules. For example, using the data in Tables 18S.4 and 18S.5, we see that by month 3, total project costs should be between $30,000 (latest starting date schedule) and $43,000 (earliest starting date schedule). Thus, at month 3 a total project cost between $30,000 and $43,000 would be expected.

In Figure 18S.4, we show the forecasted total project costs for both the earliest and latest starting time schedules. The shaded region between the two cost curves shows the possible budgets for the project. If the project manager is willing to commit activities to specific starting times, a specific project cost forecast or budget can be prepared. However, based on the above analysis, we know that such a budget will have to be in the region of feasible budgets shown in Figure 18S.4.

Controlling Project Costs

The information that we have developed thus far is helpful in terms of planning and scheduling total project costs. However, if we are going to have an effective cost-control system, we need to identify costs on a much more detailed basis. For example, information that the project's actual total cost is exceeding the budgeted total cost will be of little value unless we can identify the activity or group of activities that are causing the cost overruns.

TABLE 18S.4 Budgeted Costs for an Earliest Starting Date Schedule (Thousands of Dollars)

Activity	Month							
	1	2	3	4	5	6	7	8
A	5	5						
B	10	10	10					
C			3					
D				2	2	2		
E				10	10			
F							5	5
G						8		
Monthly cost	15	15	13	12	12	10	5	5
Total project cost	15	30	43	55	67	77	82	87

TABLE 18S.5 Budgeted Costs for a Latest Starting Date Schedule (Thousands of Dollars)

Activity	Month							
	1	2	3	4	5	6	7	8
A					5	5		
B	10	10	10					
C						3		
D				2	2	2		
E						10	10	
F							5	5
G								8
Monthly cost	10	10	10	7	7	15	15	13
Total project cost	10	20	30	37	44	59	74	87

The PERT/Cost system provides the desired cost control by budgeting and then recording actual costs on an activity (that is, work package) basis. Periodically throughout the project's duration, actual costs

FIGURE 18S.4 Feasible Budgets for Total Project Costs

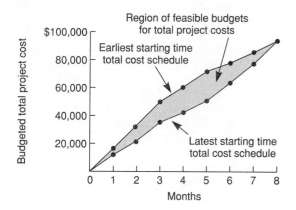

TABLE 18S.6 Activity Cost and Percent Completion Data at the End of Month 4

Activity	Actual Cost	% Completion
A	$12,000	100
B	30,000	100
C	1,000	50
D	2,000	33
E	10,000	25
F	0	0
G	0	0
Total actual cost = $55,000		

for all completed and in-process activities are compared to the appropriate budgeted costs. The project manager is then provided with up-to-date information on the cost status of each activity. If at any point in time, actual costs exceed budgeted costs, a cost overrun has occurred. On the other hand, if actual costs are less than the budgeted costs, we have a condition referred to as a *cost underrun*. By identifying the sources of cost overruns and cost underruns, the manager can take corrective action where necessary.

Now at any point during the project's duration, the manager can use a PERT/Cost procedure to obtain an activity cost status report by collecting the following information for *each activity:*

1. Actual cost to date
2. Percent completion to date

While a PERT/Cost system will require a periodic—perhaps biweekly or monthly—collection of the above information, let us suppose we are at the end of the fourth month of the project and have the actual cost and percent completion data for each activity, as shown in Table 18S.6. This current status information shows that activities A and B have been completed, activities C, D, and E are in process, and activities F and G have not yet been started.

In order to prepare a cost status report we will need to compute the value for all work completed to date.

Let

V_i = value of work completed for activity i

p_i = percent completion for activity i

B_i = budgeted for activity i

The following relationship is used to find the value of work completed for each activity.

$$V_i = \left(\frac{p_i}{100}\right) B_i \qquad (18S.3)$$

For example, the values of work completed for activities A and C are as follows.[1]

$$V_A = \left(\frac{100}{100}\right) (\$10,000) = \$10,000$$

$$V_C = \left(\frac{50}{100}\right) (\$3,000) = \$1,500$$

Cost overruns and cost underruns can now be found by comparing the actual cost of each activity with its appropriate budgeted value.

Letting

AC_i = actual cost to date for activity i

and

D_i = difference in actual and budgeted value for activity i

we have

$$D_i = AC_i - V_i \qquad (18.4)$$

---

[1]Equation (18S.3) and the succeeding calculations are based on the PERT/Cost assumption that activity costs occur at a constant rate over the duration of the activity. For details regarding this assumption see J. D. Wiest and F. K. Levy, *A Management Guide to PERT/CPM*, 2nd ed., Englewood Cliffs, N.J., Prentice-Hall, 1977.

A positive D_i indicates the activity has a cost *overrun*, while a negative D_i indicates a cost *underrun*. A value of 0 indicates that actual costs are in agreement with the budgeted costs.

For example,

$$D_A = AC_A - V_A = \$12,000 - \$10,000 = \$2,000$$

shows that activity A, which has already been completed, has a $2000 cost overrun. However, activity C with $D_C = \$1000 - \$1500 = -\$500$ is currently showing a cost underrun, or savings, of $500. A complete cost-status report such as the one shown in Table 18S.7 can now be prepared for the project manager.

This cost report shows the project manager that the costs to date are $6500 over the estimated, or budgeted, costs. On a percentage basis, we would say the project is experiencing a ($6500/$48,500) × 100 = 13.4% cost overrun, which for most projects is a serious situation. By checking each activity, we see that activities A and E are causing the cost overrun. Since activity A has been completed, its cost overrun cannot be corrected; however, activity E is in process and is only 25% complete. Thus activity E should be reviewed immediately. Corrective action for activity E can help to bring actual costs closer to the budgeted costs. The manager may also want to consider cost reduction possibilities for activities C, D, F, and G in order to keep the total project cost within the budget.

While the PERT/Cost procedure just described can be an effective cost-control system, it is not without possible drawbacks and implementation problems. First, the activity-by-activity cost-recording system can require significant clerical effort, especially for firms with large and/or numerous projects. Thus the personnel and other costs associated with maintaining a PERT/Cost system may offset some of the advantages. Second, questions can arise as to how costs should be allocated to activities to work packages. Overhead, indirect, and even material costs can cause cost allocation and measurement problems. Third, and perhaps most critical, is the fact that PERT/Cost requires a system of cost recording and control that is significantly different from most cost-accounting systems. Firms using departments or other organized units as cost centers will need a substantially revised accounting system to handle the PERT/Cost activity-oriented system. Problems of modifying accounting procedures and/or carrying dual accounting systems are not trivial matters.

TABLE 18S.7 Project Cost-Status Report at Month 4

Activity	Actual Cost (AC)	Budgeted Cost $\left(V = \dfrac{P}{100}B\right)$	Differences (D)
A	$12,000	$10,000	$2,000
B	30,000	30,000	0
C	1,000	1,500	−500
D	2,000	2,000	0
E	10,000	5,000	5,000
F	0	0	0
G	0	0	0
Totals	$55,000	$48,500	$6,500*

*Total project cost overrun to date

SUMMARY AND KEY TERMS

Summary

In this supplement we presented methods for reducing project completion times by crashing selected activities under increased, but known, costs. We also described how PERT/Cost can be used to help plan, schedule, and control project costs. In each of these situations, computer programs are used in actual implementation due to the complexity of the computations required.

Key Terms

Crashing
PERT/cost
Work package

PROBLEMS

1. Consider the following network with activity times shown in days:

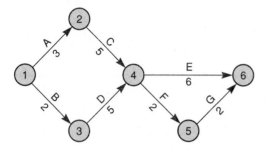

The crash data for this project are as follows:

Activity	Normal Time	Crash Time	Normal Cost ($)	Crash Cost ($)
A	3	2	800	1400
B	2	1	1200	1900
C	5	3	2000	2800
D	5	3	1500	2300
E	6	4	1800	2800
F	2	1	600	1000
G	2	1	500	1000

a. Find the critical path and expected project duration.

b. What is the total project cost using the normal times?

c. If a project must be crashed, a logical or common sense approach is to crash the least expensive critical activity in order to shorten the critical path. Assuming management desires a 12-day project completion, which critical path activity would be crashed using the least expensive critical activity philosophy?

d. As the critical path activities are crashed, other paths may become critical, requiring further crashing decisions. Use the crashing decision made in part (c), compute the new critical path, and make additional crashing necessary to meet the 12-day project completion date. What is the activity schedule and total project cost required to meet the 12-day completion date?

2. Office Automation, Inc., has developed a proposal for introducing a new computerized office system that will improve word processing and interoffice communications for a particular company. Contained in the proposal is a list of activities that must be accomplished in order to complete the new office system project. Information about the activities is shown in Table 18S.8. Times are in weeks and costs are in thousands of dollars.

a. Show the network for the project.

b. Develop an activity schedule for the project using normal times.

c. What are the critical path activities and what is the expected project completion time?

d. Assume that the company wishes to complete the project in 26 weeks. What crashing decisions would be recommended in order to meet the completion date at the least possible cost? Work through the network and attempt to make the crashing decisions by inspection.

e. Develop an activity schedule for the crashed project.

f. What is the added project cost to meet the 26-week completion time?

Table 18S.8 Data for Office Automation, Inc. (Problem 2)

Activity	Description	Immediate Predecessors	Normal Time	Crash Time	Normal Cost ($)	Crash Cost ($)
A	Plan needs	—	10	8	30	70
B	Order equipment	A	8	6	120	150
C	Install equipment	B	10	7	100	160
D	Set up training lab	A	7	6	40	50
E	Training course	D	10	8	50	75
F	Testing system	C, E	3	3	60	—

3. Consider the following project network and related data:

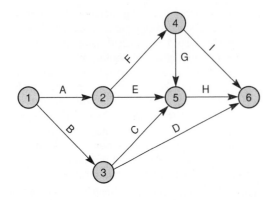

Activity	Normal Time	Crash Time	Normal Cost ($)	Crash Cost ($)
A	3	2	8,000	9,000
B	8	6	600	1,000
C	6	4	10,000	12,000
D	5	2	4,000	10,000
E	13	10	3,000	9,000
F	4	4	5,000	5,000
G	2	1	1,200	1,400
H	6	4	3,500	4,500
I	2	1	700	800

a. Find the critical path and the minimum project duration time.
b. If a deadline of 17 time periods is imposed, what activities should be crashed, what is the crashing cost, and what are the critical activities of the crashed network?

4. Consider the following network with activity times shown in days:

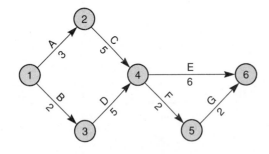

The crash data for this project are as follows:

Activity	Normal Time	Crash Time	Normal Cost ($)	Crash Cost ($)
A	3	2	800	1400
B	2	1	1200	1900
C	5	3	2000	2800
D	5	3	1500	2300
E	6	4	1800	2800
F	2	1	600	1000
G	2	1	500	1000

a. Find the critical path and the expected project duration using normal times.
b. What is the total project cost using the normal times?

5. Refer to Problem 4. Assume that management desires a 12-day project completion time.
a. Formulate a linear programming model that can be used to assist with the crashing decisions.
b. What are the activities that should be crashed?
c. What is the total project cost for the 12-day completion time?

6. A project involving the installation of a computer system consists of eight activities. The immediate predecessors and activity times in weeks are as follows:

Activity	Immediate Predecessor	Time
A	—	3
B	—	6
C	A	2
D	B, C	5
E	D	4
F	E	3
G	B, C	9
H	F, G	3

a. Draw the PERT/CPM network for this project.
b. What are the critical path activities?
c. What is the project completion time?
d. Assume that the project has to be completed in 16 weeks. Crashing of the project is necesssary. Relevant information follows:

Activity	Normal Time	Crash Time	Normal Cost ($)	Crash Cost ($)
A	3	1	900	1700
B	6	3	2000	4000
C	2	1	500	1000
D	5	3	1800	2400
E	4	3	1500	1850
F	3	1	3000	3900
G	9	4	8000	9800
H	3	2	1000	2000

Formulate a linear programming model that can be used to make the crashing decisions for the above network.

e. Solve the linear programming model and make the minimum-cost crashing decisons. What is the added cost of meeting the 16-week completion time?

f. Develop a complete activity schedule using the crashed activity times.

7. Consider the following project network and related data:

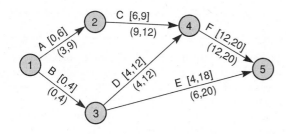

Activity	Normal Time	Crash Time	Normal Cost ($)	Crash Cost ($)
A	6	4	10,000	14,000
B	4	3	5,000	8,000
C	3	2	4,000	5,000
D	8	3	1,000	6,000
E	14	6	9,000	13,000
F	8	4	7,000	8,000

The critical path of the above network is B–D–F; the project duration is 20 time periods.

a. If a deadline of 18 time periods is imposed, what activities should be crashed, what is the cost of crashing, and what are the critical activities of the crashed network?

b. Given the *original* network (before crashing), develop a PERT/Cost budget for total project cost over the first 6 periods of the project's duration. What should the range be for expenditures after 5 weeks of the project?

8. Consider the project network shown below.

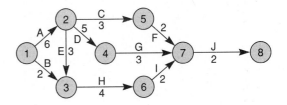

Suppose that expected activity costs are as follows:

Activity	Expected Cost (Thousands of $)
A	90
B	16
C	3
D	100
E	6
F	2
G	60
H	20
I	4
J	2

Develop a total cost budget based on both an earliest start and a latest start schedule. Show the graph of feasible budgets for the total project cost.

9. Consider the project management network shown:

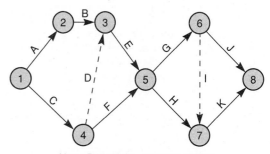

Note: D and I are dummy activities

Pertinent time and cost data are as follows:

Activity	Expected Time (Weeks)	Variance	Budgeted Cost ($)
A	3	.3	6,000
B	2	.5	4,000
C	8	2.0	16,000
D	0	.0	0
E	6	1.0	18,000
F	4	.2	20,000
G	5	.4	15,000
H	1	.1	2,000
I	0	.0	0
J	5	1.0	5,000
K	6	.6	12,000

a. Develop an activity schedule for the project.
  i. What is the critical path?
  ii. What is the expected completion date?
  iii. What is the probability of meeting a desired 6-month (26-week) completion date?

b. Develop a PERT/Cost budget for total project costs over the project's duration. What should the range be for expenditures after 12 weeks of the project?

10. Referring to the network in Problem 9, suppose that after 12 weeks of operation the following data are available on all completed and in-process activities:

Activity	Actual Cost ($)	Percent Completion
A	5,000	100
B	4,000	100
C	18,000	100
E	9,000	50
F	18,000	75

Is the project in control based on both time and cost considerations? What corrective action, if any, is desirable?

CASE PROBLEM

The R.A. Hamilton Company in Evergreen Park, Illinois, has manufactured home workshop tools for a number of years. Recently, a member of the company's new-product research team submitted a report suggesting the company consider manufacturing a heavy-duty cordless electric drill that could be powered by a special rechargeable battery. Because no other manufacturer currently had such a product, management hoped that the new product could be manufactured at a reasonable cost and that its portability would make it extremely attractive.

Hamilton's top management would like to initiate a project to study the feasibility of this idea. The end result of the feasibility project will be a report rec-

TABLE 18S.9 Activities and Times for the R.A. Hamilton Project

Activity	Description	Immediate Predecessors	Times (Weeks) a	m	b
A	R&D product design	—	3	7	11
B	Plan market research	—	2	2.5	6
C	Manufacturing process study	A	2	3	4
D	Build Prototype model	A	6	7	14
E	Prepare market questionnaire	A	2	3	4
F	Develop cost estimates	C	2.5	3	3.5
G	Preliminary product testing	D	2.5	4	5.5
H	Market survey	B, E	4.5	5.5	9.5
I	Pricing and forecast report	H	1	2	3
J	Final report	F, G, I	1	2	3

ommending the action to be taken for this new product. The project manager has identified a list of activities and a range of times necessary to complete each activity. This information is given in Table 18S.9.

1. Develop a complete PERT/CPM analysis for this project. Include in your report the project network, calculation of expected times and variances, critical activities, and minimum project-completion date. In addition, construct an early start Gantt chart and compute probabilities for completing the project by weeks 18, 20, 22, and 24. Discuss how this information can be used by the project manager at the R.A. Hamilton Company.

2. The costs for each activity are given in Table 18S.10. Develop a total cost budget based on both an earliest start and a latest start schedule. Show the graph of feasible budgets for the total project cost. Also, prepare a PERT/Cost analysis for each of the three points in time in parts a, b, and c. For each case, show the percent overrun or underrun for the project to date and indicate any corrective action that should be undertaken. Why is this information important to the project manager? (*Note:* If an activity is not listed below, assume that it has not been started.)

TABLE 18S.10 Activity Costs for the R.A. Hamilton Project

Activity	Expected Cost (Thousands of Dollars)
A	90
B	16
C	3
D	100
E	6
F	2
G	60
H	20
I	4
J	2

a. At the end of the fifth week

Activity	Actual Cost (Thousands of $)	Percent Completion
A	62	80
B	6	50

b. At the end of the tenth week

Activity	Actual Cost (Thousands of $)	Percent Completion
A	85	100
B	16	100
C	1	33
D	100	80
E	4	100
H	10	25

c. At the end of the fifteenth week

Activity	Actual Cost (Thousands of $)	Percent Completion
A	85	↑
B	16	
C	3	
D	105	
E	4	100
F	3	
G	55	
H	25	
I	4	↓

Quality Control

T hroughout this book the importance of quality in the design and operation of manufacturing and service organizations has been stressed. While it is imperative that quality be designed and built into these systems, to ensure that quality standards are being adhered to, quality control is a necessary function. In this chapter several methods for controlling quality in both manufacturing and service organizations will be discussed. In doing so we will examine some of the quality-control practices that have helped make Japan a leader in the manufacturing of high-quality products.

19.1 THE QUALITY-CONTROL FUNCTION

Quality control is concerned with the prevention, detection, and correction of product or service defects that would make the product or service unfit for use. Thus, quality control has several objectives:

1. to ensure that purchased materials and components meet predetermined quality standards
2. to maintain conformance to design specifications throughout the manufacturing process or during the delivery of a service
3. to achieve the highest possible quality level for the final product or service
4. to improve productivity by reducing scrap and rework in manufacturing, as well as reduce the number of complaints and returns from customers
5. to reduce the internal and external failure costs that arise when quality standards are not achieved.

To accomplish these objectives, organizations must develop quality control systems.

Control is the process of comparing actual results to goals and objectives and taking corrective action when necessary. Any control system has three components: (1) a standard or goal, (2) a means of measurement of accomplishment, and (3) comparison of actual results with the standard along with feedback to form the basis for corrective action. Figure 19.1 shows the role of a quality-control system in the model of a production system that we introduced in Chapter 1.

To ensure that raw materials and purchased parts meet the stated quality standards, incoming shipments of these goods are usually inspected. The purpose of such inspection is to determine whether or not the raw materials and purchased parts are of acceptable quality and thus can be used in production. In this context, acceptable quality means meeting the standards developed during the product-design effort. Inspections of raw materials and purchased parts which result in the acceptance or rejection of the entire shipment can lead to higher quality in manufacturing, since the supplier knows that poor-quality lots will be returned at the supplier's expense. The quality-control technique that is used is referred to as *acceptance sampling.*

During the production process, work-in-process is inspected to uncover possible problems in equipment, methods, people, and so on. As tools wear out, for instance, they need to be replaced in order to manufacture the item properly. Therefore, it is necessary to examine the production output over time to see if any changes have occurred. *Statistical process control* is a widely used technique for monitoring work-in-process.

Finally, after the finished product is completed, an inspection is usually performed. This may be a mechanical or electronic test for performance or a visual inspection for appearance. Final inspection is necessary in order to minimize external failure costs of poor quality, as we discussed in Chapter 2. Various sampling techniques are also useful at this point.

Quality control also plays an important role in service organizations. Since customer satisfaction is one of the major goals in the delivery of services, quality control is a vital function. In a hospital, for instance, a simple checksheet can be used for attribute inspection of cleanliness. Each item in a patient's room can be checked as either satisfactory or unsatisfactory, and the results used as a measurement tool for efficiency and to identify problems that require correction. Restaurants, hotels, and other service organizations keep close watch on the quality of their services.

The analogy of raw material, work-in-process, and finished-goods inspection can also apply to services. A travel agency, for example, often previews resorts, cruise ships, and so on prior to recommending them to clients. While working with a client, the agent might check to see if tickets arrive on time or if any other assistance is needed. Finally, the agent might check with the client after his or her return.

FIGURE 19.1

The Use of Quality Control in Production

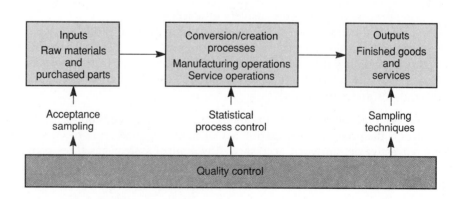

In designing a quality-control system, one must determine which quality characteristics are important to monitor, how they should be measured, and what standards will distinguish acceptable quality levels from unacceptable levels. The inspection of incoming materials, work-in-process, or final products plays a fundamental role in this process.

19.2 INSPECTION AND MEASUREMENT

Inspection and measurement form the basis for detecting quality-control problems. To determine the quality of a polished chrome faucet, a simple visual inspection may be done, or to measure the diameter of a ball bearing, a micrometer or some other measuring device might be used. In a service application, an audit is used to inspect and measure the quality of an accounting function.

The purposes of inspection are to determine whether or not products conform to specifications, identify and separate nonconforming items from the production process, and report any deficiencies. However, before the turn of the twentieth century, inspection was not a separate function in the production system. Craftspeople served as fabricators *and* inspectors and were entirely responsible for the quality of their products. As mass production techniques and interchangeable parts were introduced, the need for inspection became critical in order to ensure that the final product could be assembled correctly. Thus, separate job classifications for inspectors became common in industry. The task of the inspection department was to seek out defective items in production and remove them to be scrapped or reworked before they were to be shipped to customers. Thus, inspectors were conceived of as "policemen" who were to catch "lawbreakers"—the operators and others who contributed to poor quality products.

The nature of these inspection activities was contrary to the improvement of quality. Inspection was used as a screening activity that removed nonconforming products from production but did not seek to improve the causes of poor quality. This historical role of inspectors is still being used in many companies today. Not only does it often result in poor quality, but it can also result in negative interpersonal relations. Inspectors are often promoted from the ranks of production workers and have close associations with shop personnel. When a part borders on being defective, an inspector may tend to err in favor of the operators to preserve their friendship and protect them from criticism or even loss of jobs because of consistently poor quality production. Conversely, the operators, believing that the inspection department will catch any nonconforming parts may not take their own roles in producing quality products very seriously.

Just as there are never enough police officers to patrol every highway, there are never enough inspectors to inspect every part and catch every defect. As a result, the Japanese approach to total quality control, in which quality is everyone's responsibility, states that conformance to specifications must be ensured by those who make the parts or deliver the service. The nature of the inspection job drastically changes when this concept is applied. The operator becomes the inspector in the process of producing the product. Interestingly, this process is similar to the role that individual craftspeople had before the industrial revolution. The inspector is no longer a policeman but becomes a technical consultant, auditor, and coach. In this revised approach to inspection, the inspection department is responsible for assisting production personnel in developing effective processes, procedures, and practices for controlling and monitoring quality.

Many manufacturers do not inspect incoming materials purchased from outside suppliers because they work closely with their suppliers and verify that the suppliers consistently produce products of acceptable quality. This practice has been the norm in Japan for many years, and many more companies in the United States are following this practice. However, many reasons exist why inspection will continue to remain an important activity in quality assurance.

1. Quality conformance may be required by government regulations.
2. Customer requirements specify an independent inspection activity.
3. Critical parts or materials require close scrutiny by an independent inspection function to prevent economic losses from defective items.
4. Centralized inspection is needed to accomplish testing using expensive inspection equipment in a timely and cost-effective fashion.
5. Inspection and testing activities require specialized skill or in-depth training for the person performing the work.
6. Strategically placed inspection personnel may be able to give early warnings of potentially catastrophic situations before they cause major damage.
7. Management audit and review requirements may necessitate an impartial inspection and quality assurance function.

In such circumstances, the traditional role of inspection will continue to play a major part in assuring overall quality.

Type of Inspection

The type of inspection performed depends on the characteristic being evaluated or measured. An *attribute* is a characteristic that assumes one of two values; for instance, present or not present, conforming or not conforming, within specification or out of specification, complete or incomplete. An example of an **attribute measurement** would be the visual inspection of the color of an item from a printing press in order to determine whether or not the color is acceptable. Another example involves the determination of whether or not the correct ZIP code was used in shipping an order. A third example is deciding if the diameter of a shaft falls within the specification limits of $1.60 \pm .01$ inch.

The second type of measurement is called **variable measurement**. In this context, variables refer to those characteristics that can be measured on a continuous scale; for instance, length or weight. With variable measurement, we are concerned with the *degree* of conformance to specifications. Therefore, rather than determining whether or not the diameter of a shaft meets a specification of $1.60 \pm .01$ inch, we are concerned with measuring the actual value of the diameter.

Attribute inspection is usually simpler than variable inspection for several reasons. The inspection itself can be made more quickly and easily, less information needs to be recorded, and administration of the inspection is easier. In a statistical sense, attribute inspection is less efficient than variable inspection. Thus attribute inspection requires a larger sample size than variable inspection to obtain the same amount of statistical information about the quality level of the part, product, or service. The difference can become significant when inspection is time consuming or expensive.

In determining where to locate inspection stations, one must consider trade-offs between the explicit costs of detection, repair, or replacement and the implicit costs of unnecessary additional investment in a nonconforming item if inspection is not performed. While the location decision is fundamentally based on economics, it is a complex one, since it involves the trade-off between prevention and appraisal costs and failure costs as discussed in Chapter 2. It is not always easy or possible to quantify these costs.

Route sheets, operation process charts, and assembly charts developed during manufacturing planning show the steps that are performed in manufacturing a product. They are used as a basis for identifying locations to perform inspections. Inspections might be located before or after any or all operations. How does one decide? Several rules of thumb have been proposed for the location decision. The more popular rules are as follows:

- Locate inspection stations after operations likely to generate a high proportion of defectives.
- Locate inspection stations after the finished product is completed.
- Locate inspection stations before all processing operations, such as before every machine or assembly operation.
- Locate inspection stations before relatively high-cost operations or where significant value is added to the product.
- Locate inspection stations before processing operations that may make the detection of defectives difficult or costly, such as operations that may mask or obscure faulty attributes; for example, painting.

No one rule is best in all situations. Simulation, economic analysis, and other quantitative tools often are used to evaluate a particular design of inspection activities.

One important decision in inspection planning is the amount of inspection to be performed. Several factors should be considered: the type of product to be inspected, the quality characteristics to be examined for conformance, the quality history of the producer, the cost of inspection, and the effect of inspection on the product (for example, destructive testing). The decision is usually to use either one hundred percent inspection or some type of sampling procedure.

One hundred percent inspection is the inspection of every unit that is produced. For critical quality characteristics, such inspection is usually required. While it provides the best assurance of conformance to specifications, it is not always perfect, because of such problems as human error, faulty measuring equipment, and use of incorrect standards. One hundred percent inspection is often not practical because of the time, effort, and costs involved. Clearly, it cannot be used when testing is destructive. With automated inspection techniques, one hundred percent inspection is becoming more economical and feasible.

Sampling procedures involve inspecting only a portion of a production lot. They are useful in dealing with large quantities of noncritical quality characteristics. Sampling is more economical than one hundred percent inspection but is subject to a higher degree of risk. The lower costs of sampling inspection must be weighed against the risk of greater cost incurred by permitting nonconforming products to be accepted. In practice, however, it has been shown that sampling procedures are often superior to one hundred percent inspection, because of their ability to overcome systematic forms of human error. As a result, sampling procedures form the basis for most quality control procedures used in practice. Specific sampling methods for process control and inspection of incoming material or finished products are discussed in later sections of this chapter.

Accuracy and Precision

Accuracy relates to measuring the correct value. Accuracy is defined as the amount of error in a measurement in proportion to the total size of the measurement; that is, the relative error. One measurement is more accurate than another if it has a smaller relative error. For example, suppose that two instruments measure a dimension whose true value is 0.250 inch. Instrument A may read 0.248 inch, while instrument B may read 0.259 inch. The relative error of instrument A is $(.250 - .248)/.250 = .008 = 0.8$ percent, while that of instrument B is $(.259 - .250)/.250 = .036 = 3.6$ percent. Thus, instrument A is said to be more accurate than instrument B.

Precision relates to the variance of repeated measurements. For example, a measuring instrument having a low variance is said to be more precise than another having a higher variance. Note that a measurement system may be precise but not necessarily accurate at the same time. For instance, in the example above, suppose that each instrument is used to measure the dimension three times. Instrument A may record values of .248, .246, and .251, while instrument B may record values of .259, .258, and .259. Although instrument B is more precise than instrument A (it has less variance), instrument A is more accurate.

The relationships between accuracy and precision are summarized in Figure 19.2. The figure illustrates four possible frequency distributions of ten repeated measurements of some quality characteristic. In Figure 19.2(a), the average measurement is not very close to the true value. Moreover, there is a wide range of values around the average. In this case, the measurement is neither accurate nor precise. In Figure 19.2(b), even though the average measurement is not close to the true value, there is a small range of variation. Thus, we say that the measurement is precise but not accurate. In Figures 19.2(c) and (d), the average value is close to the true value—that is, the measurement is accurate—but in 19.2(c) the distribution is widely dispersed and therefore not precise, while the measurement in 19.2(d) is both accurate *and* precise. Thus, it is vital that all instruments used for quality measurements be properly calibrated and maintained in good working order.

Human Factors Issues and Automated Inspection

Many inspection tasks are performed manually. Because inspection is not an easy task, it is highly subject to error; therefore, error rates of 10 to 50 percent are not uncommon. To provide an experiment that will illustrate this, ask three people to proof a lengthy manuscript for typographical errors. Rarely will everyone discover all errors, much less the same ones. The same is true of complicated industrial inspection tasks, especially those involving detailed microelectronics.

Inspection tasks that are performed manually are affected by several factors.

■ *Complexity.* The number of defects identified by an inspector decreases with more parts and less orderly arrangement.

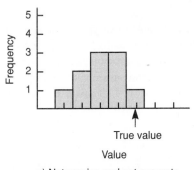

a) Not precise and not accurate

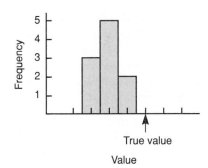

b) Precise but not accurate

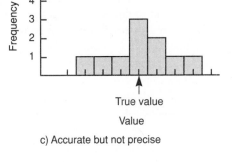

c) Accurate but not precise

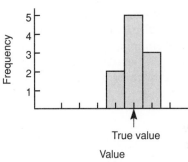

d) Accurate and precise

FIGURE 19.2
Accuracy versus
Precision

- *Defect rate.* When the product defect rate is low, inspectors tend to miss more defects than when the defect rate is higher.
- *Repeated inspections.* Different inspectors do not miss the same defects. Therefore, if the same item is inspected by a number of different inspectors, a higher percentage of total defects will be caught.
- *Inspection rate.* The inspector's performance degrades rapidly as the inspection rate increases.[1]

As a result of understanding these factors, there are several ways to improve inspection.

- Minimize the number of quality characteristics considered in an inspection task. Five to six different types are approximately the maximum limit that the human mind can handle well at one time.
- Minimize disturbing influences and time pressures.
- Provide clear, detailed instructions for the inspection task.
- Design the workspace to facilitate the inspection task and provide good lighting.

Microprocessors and advanced electronics are now making automated inspection possible. Automated visual inspection systems can recognize and identify, classify,

---

[1]Douglas H. Harris and Frederick B. Chaney, *Human Factors in Quality Assurance,* New York: John Wiley & Sons, 1969.

sort, and inspect objects. For instance, automated visual inspection systems can check snack food packages for the proper amount of food or check the seals on each package. Such systems are fast and capable of inspecting 2 to 10 objects per second. Robots are also beginning to be used for quality inspection. General Electric, for example, uses a robotized X-ray inspection station to manipulate objects in front of an X-ray machine in order to keep inspectors from being exposed to radiation.[2]

| Statistics in Quality Control | As we have noted, many variations in output occur naturally by chance. This variation is often described through the use of an appropriate probability distribution. For instance, in measuring attributes, the outcomes may assume only one of two values. In this case, the binomial distribution is an appropriate model. In measuring variables, we often assume that the measures are described by the normal distribution. Probability and statistical theory provide a powerful means for determining whether variations in quality are due to chance or to assignable causes. In the remainder of this chapter, we see how statistical tools can be used in quality control. |

19.3 ACCEPTANCE SAMPLING

The purpose of acceptance sampling is to make a decision about whether to accept or reject a group of items based on specified quality characteristics. The group of items in question is usually called a **lot**. Each lot should consist of homogeneous units of product; that is, the items should be similar in nature but would not be identical under detailed inspection. Items produced from the same batches of raw material, components, or assemblies; on the same production line with the same molds, dies, and personnel; and during a unit of time such as an hour, day, or shift are considered to be homogeneous. Nonhomogeneous lots may bias the results of the acceptance scheme and may make it difficult to discover causes of poor quality. Also, large lots are preferable to small ones, since it is usually more economical to inspect them with sampling techniques.

The general acceptance sampling procedure is shown in Figure 19.3. A lot is received from a supplier or from final assembly. Items from the lot are inspected for quality characteristics, and the results are compared with acceptance criteria. If these criteria are satisfied, the lot is accepted and sent to production or shipped to the customers; otherwise, the lot is rejected. The determination of whether to accept or reject a lot is often called **lot sentencing**. We emphasize that this is the true purpose of acceptance sampling; it is not appropriate to use acceptance sampling to attempt to determine the percentage of the lot that do not conform to standards or the average value of a quality characteristic. Other statistical sampling techniques are appropriate in such cases.

The rejection of a lot brings up the questions of the lot's disposition, remedial action to be taken, rework time, difficulty in meeting delivery schedules, and

---

[2]"Inspection: A New Role for Robots," *Quality Progress* (August 1982): 50.

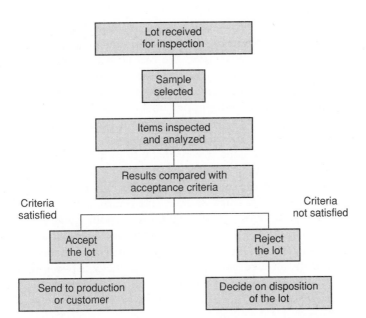

FIGURE 19.3

Acceptance Sampling Procedure

Lot received for inspection

Sample selected

Items inspected and analyzed

Results compared with acceptance criteria

Criteria satisfied

Criteria not satisfied

Accept the lot

Reject the lot

Send to production or customer

Decide on disposition of the lot

additional financial burdens on the supplier. The most common alternatives are (1) to keep the lot (often at a reduced price to compensate the buyer for lower quality) and remove nonconforming items during production or (2) to return the rejected lot to the supplier. The first alternative is not a good one, although if no other sources of product are available, it may be preferable to a production stoppage. With the second alternative, the supplier must pay the shipping cost, and the rejected lot will be screened, defective units will be reworked or replaced, and the lot will be resubmitted by the supplier. The extra burden placed on the supplier often provides good motivation to improve quality!

Since acceptance sampling is based on statistical principles, it provides an assessment of risk in the decision. In addition, acceptance sampling is relatively inexpensive and particularly well suited to destructive testing situations. It takes less time than one hundred percent inspection, thus reducing the inspectors' workload. It also requires less handling and therefore decreases the chance of damage. Finally, acceptance sampling generally does not lead to inspector fatigue as does one hundred percent inspection. Acceptance sampling is also a very flexible method; the amount of inspection can be varied depending on the quality history of the items being inspected. Since entire lots are rejected, there is economic and psychological pressure on vendors to improve quality rather than simply replace the nonconforming items.

In deciding whether or not to use sampling inspection, one must first ask the question, What would be the result of allowing a nonconforming item to continue through production or on to the consumer? If the result might be a safety hazard, costly repairs or correction, or some other intolerable condition, the conclusion would probably be to use one hundred percent inspection. If the sampling plan is properly chosen and implemented, lots of good quality will be accepted more often than rejected, and lots of poor quality will be rejected more often than accepted. It must be remembered, however, that with sampling, there is always a risk that nonconforming items will be accepted as good.

Risk in Acceptance Sampling

In any sampling procedure, there exists the risk of making an incorrect decision. That is, based upon a sample of the items in a lot, we might accept a lot of poor quality or reject a lot of good quality. We can view acceptance sampling as a statistical test of hypothesis: The null hypothesis is that the lot is of "good" quality, and the alternate hypothesis is that the lot is of "poor" quality. We will define the notions of "good" and "poor" quality more precisely later. A type I error refers to rejecting the null hypothesis when it is true, while a type II error refers to accepting the null hypothesis when it is false.

In quality control terminology, the probability of a type I error—rejecting a lot of good quality—is commonly referred to as the **producer's risk**. Type I errors create a risk for the producer, because a customer may erroneously reject a lot of good quality based on a small sample and return it to the producer. The probability of a type II error—accepting a lot of poor quality—is called the **consumer's risk**. In a similar fashion, a consumer may test a lot and erroneously accept it as good. Later, when the product is put into the production process, it is discovered that the lot is of poor quality. The analogy between these common statistical and quality-control terminologies is summarized in Table 19.1.

The traditional value used for the producer's risk is 0.05. The use of this value means that management is willing to risk at most a 5 percent chance that a lot of good quality will be rejected by the acceptance sampling plan and returned to the producer; in other words, there is at least a 95 percent chance that a good quality lot will be accepted. The consumer's risk is usually set at 0.1. The use of this value means that management is willing to risk at most a 10 percent chance that a lot of poor quality will be accepted by the sampling plan and thus will find its way into production. Alternatively, a consumer's risk of 0.1 also means that there is at least a 90 percent chance that a poor quality lot will be rejected. Published acceptance sampling tables often use these values in defining sampling plans. However, with the current focus on quality, these levels are unacceptable in most plants today. Computer programs now allow the selection of much smaller values of producer and consumer risks in defining a sampling plan.

Sampling Plans for Attribute Inspection

Assume that we have a lot of items that we must determine whether to accept or reject. Recall that the objective of attribute inspection is to determine whether or not a particular characteristic of the lot assumes one of two values; for example, conforming or nonconforming. A **sampling plan** for attribute inspection is a decision rule that can be used to determine whether or not to reject the lot based upon the number of nonconforming items in a sample of items from the lot. To make this decision we must specify a sample size (n) and an acceptance number

TABLE 19.1

Statistics and Quality Control

Statistical Concept	Notation	Quality-control Concept
Null hypothesis	H_0	Lot is of good quality
Alternate hypothesis	H_1	Lot is of poor quality
Reject H_0 when H_0 is true	Type I error	Reject a good lot
Accept H_0 when H_0 is false	Type II error	Accept a bad lot
Probability of type I error	α	Producer's risk
Probability of type II error	β	Consumer's risk

(c). Then, if the number of nonconforming items in the sample is less than or equal to c, we accept the lot. If the number of nonconforming items is greater than c, we reject the lot. This type of sampling plan is called a *single-sampling plan* and is illustrated in Figure 19.4.

A variety of other sampling plans are often used. For instance, in a *double-sampling plan*, illustrated in Figure 19.5, two sample sizes, n_1 and n_2, and two acceptance numbers, c_1 and c_2 with $c_1 < c_2$, are specified. First, a sample of n_1 items is taken. If the number of nonconforming items, x_1 is less than or equal to c_1, then the lot is accepted. If the number nonconforming is greater than c_2, then the lot is rejected. If $c_1 < x_1 \leq c_2$, a second sample of n_2 items is taken. If the total number of nonconforming items in both samples $(x_1 + x_2)$ exceeds c_2, the lot is rejected; otherwise it is accepted.

Double-sampling plans, as well as other designs, can often reduce total sampling costs. However, a discussion of these approaches is beyond the scope of this text. Thus, we will restrict our discussion to single-sampling plans.

COMPUTING LOT ACCEPTANCE PROBABILITIES

EXAMPLE

To illustrate the concepts and development of sampling plans for quality-control decisions, consider a problem faced by Robertson Electronics, a manufacturer of missile guidance systems for the U. S. Air Force. Robertson Electronics purchases an important component that must withstand high temperatures. To check incoming shipments of this component, Robertson subjects a sample of the components to temperatures much higher than those anticipated; each component tested either survives the test or fails it. Because of the stress put on them during testing, each of the components tested cannot be used in the manufacture of the missile guidance systems. Each time a shipment of components arrives, the quality-control manager must decide whether or not to accept the lot.

Suppose that 10 components are sampled ($n = 10$) from a very large lot of components that have just been received. Assume that management decides to

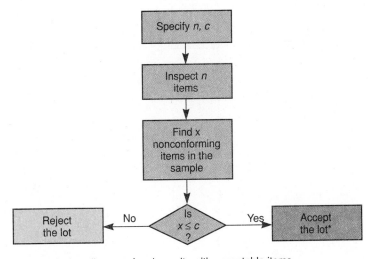

FIGURE 19.4

Single Sampling Plan Logic

*after replacing all nonconforming units with acceptable items

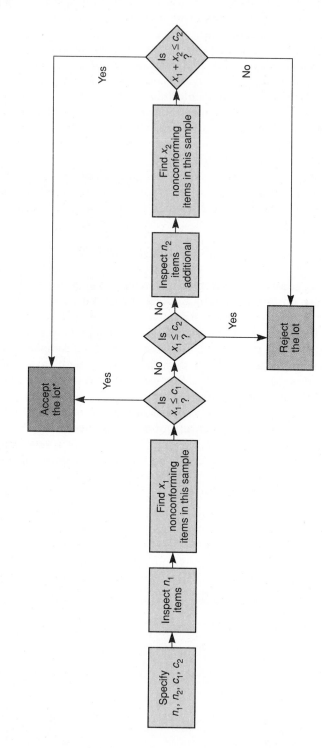

FIGURE 19.5   Double-sampling-plan Logic

*after replacing all nonconforming units with acceptable items accept the lot only if no nonconforming items are found in the sample; that is, $c = 0$. Although we do not know the actual percentage of nonconforming components in the lot, let us assume that this value is 5 percent. What is the probability that the lot will be accepted using this particular sampling plan? Since each component tested will either survive the test or fail it, and since the lot size is relatively large, the number of failures in the sample of 10 can be described by the binomial probability distribution. Recall from statistics that the binomial probability function is

$$f(x) = \binom{n}{x} p^x (1 - p)^{n-x} = \frac{n!}{(n - x)!x!} p^x (1 - p)^{n-x}$$

where in the context of acceptance sampling, p denotes the probability that any one component will fail the test and x is the number of failures observed in the sample of n components. For the Robertson Electronics problem, the probability of x failures in a sample of 10 components is given by

$$f(x) = \binom{10}{x} (.05)^x (.95)^{10-x}$$

Note that $f(0)$ represents the probability that 0 components will fail and hence the lot will be accepted; this probability is calculated as follows.

$$f(0) = \binom{10}{0} (.05)^0 (.95)^{10-0}$$

$$= \frac{10!}{(10 - 0)!0!} (1)(.95)^{10}$$

$$= (1)(1)(.95)^{10} = .5987$$

(Recall that 0! is defined to be 1.) Similarly, if the actual percentage of nonconforming items is 10 percent, the probability of accepting the lot is

$$\binom{10}{0} (.10)^0 (.90)^{10} = .3487$$

Table 19.2 gives the probability of acceptance for various values of p. When the acceptance number (c) is greater than or equal to 1, we find the probability of accepting the lot by *summing* the binomial probabilities from 0 to c. For instance, suppose that $c = 1$ and that 5 percent of the items in the lot are actually nonconforming. Then the probability of accepting the lot is $f(0) + f(1)$, since the lot is accepted if *at most* one defective item is found. Thus, for the Robertson Electronics problem the probability the lot is accepted when $c = 1$ is .5987 + .3151 = .9138. Instead of using formula (19.1) to compute the binomial probabilities, tables have been developed that provide the binomial probabilities for various values of n, p, and x. In Appendix D we show a table which contains probabilities for the binomial distribution for selected values of n, p, and x.

Using Table 19.2, we can develop a graph of the probability of accepting the lot given the percent defective in the lot. Figure 19.6 shows the curve we obtained. This curve is called an **operating characteristic**, or **OC curve**. OC curves are

Operating
Characteristic
Curves

TABLE 19.2	Percent Defective in the Lot (%)	Probability of Accepting the Lot
Probability of Accepting the Lot for the Robertson Electronics Problem: $n = 10, c = 0$	1	.9044
	2	.8171
	3	.7374
	4	.6648
	5	.5987
	10	.3487
	15	.1969
	20	.1073
	25	.0563
	30	.0282

unique for a specific sampling plan and enable us to determine the producer's and consumer's risks. To do this, we need to specify an **acceptable quality level (AQL)** and **lot tolerance percent defective (LTPD)**. The AQL is the maximum percent of nonconforming items that is considered acceptable. For instance, a company may be willing to accept lots with at most 2 percent nonconforming items. The LTPD is the percent nonconforming associated with what is considered to be a bad lot. For example, 10 percent nonconforming may be considered "bad" for a particular application. Not all lots with AQL values will be accepted, nor will all lots with LTPD values be rejected every time. The producer (vendor) would like good lots accepted with a high probability. The consumer (buyer) would like to reject bad lots most of the time; thus the consumer wishes to have a low probability of accepting bad lots. Suppose that for Robertson Electronics AQL = 2 percent and LTPD = 10 percent. From the OC curve in Figure 19.6, we see that if the percent nonconforming is actually 2 percent, the probability of accepting the lot is approximately .82. Thus the probability of *rejecting* this good lot is $1 - .82 = .18$. This is the producer's risk. On the other hand, if the actual percent nonconforming is actually 10 percent (LTPD), then the probability of accepting the lot is about .35. This represents the consumer's risk. Figure 19.7 illustrates these relationships in general.

As AQL decreases, so does α, the probability of rejecting a good lot. Similarly, as LTPD increases, then β—the probability of accepting a bad lot—decreases. The AQL is mutually agreed upon between the producer and consumer and is a useful negotiating tool in purchase contracts. A smaller AQL reduces the producer's risk but also requires tighter control in manufacturing. Thus economic analysis is important in determining quality specifications and contracts.

EXAMPLE

SELECTING AN ACCEPTANCE SAMPLING PLAN

How is a sampling plan actually chosen? Recall that we mentioned that there is a unique OC curve for every value of n and c. Figure 19.8 illustrates OC curves for some alternate sampling plans for the Robertson Electronics problem. To determine an appropriate plan, the quality-control manager must select values for the AQL, LTPD, α, and β. From Figure 19.7, we see that these values specify two points on the OC curve, namely, (AQL, $1 - \alpha$) and (LTPD, β). There is a unique OC curve that passes through these two points; thus, the values of n and

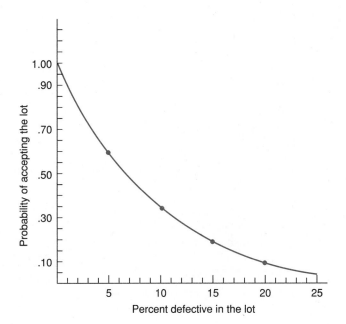

FIGURE 19.6

Operating Characteristic Curve for $n = 10, c = 0$

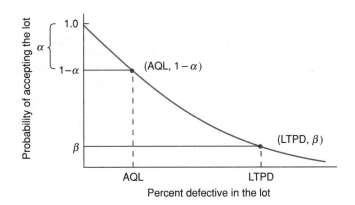

FIGURE 19.7

OC Curves and Risk

c for this OC curve determine the sampling plan. For example, suppose that a quality control manager specifies AQL = 3 percent, LTPD = 15 percent, α = .25, $(1 - \alpha = .75)$, and $\beta = .2$. Finding the two points (3%, .75) and (15%, .2) in Figure 19.8, we see that the OC curve corresponding to $n = 10$, $c = 0$ passes through these points. Thus $n = 10$, $c = 0$ is the appropriate sampling plan to choose.

We do not have to plot all possible OC curves to choose a sampling plan. Fortunately, there are published tables that can be used to choose one. One of the most commonly used tables for attribute sampling is *MIL-STD-105D, Sampling Procedures and Tables for Inspection by Attributes,* published by the Department of Defense. Industry has accepted these tables as the standard in nearly all situations involving attribute sampling.

FIGURE 19.8

OC Curves
Alternate
Sampling Plans
for Robertson
Electronics

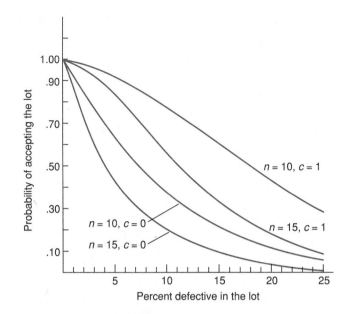

**Average
Outgoing
Quality**

The **average outgoing quality** (AOQ) is the average quality of outgoing product, including all accepted lots plus all rejected lots after they have been effectively screened and nonconforming items have been removed and replaced by conforming items. Thus, in AOQ sampling plans, rejected lots must be one hundred percent inspected and all nonconforming items replaced. The resulting lots will have zero nonconforming items. However, lots that are accepted will still have some percentage of nonconformities. The *average* quality of outgoing lots will nevertheless be better than the quality of the incoming lots. In this section we show how to compute average outgoing quality using OC curves.

To illustrate this, suppose that the percentage of nonconforming items in each of the incoming lots is 4 percent, and the sampling plan is designed so that there is a 90 percent chance of accepting the lot and a 10 percent chance of rejecting the lot. Note that if the lot is rejected, each nonconforming item in the lot is removed and replaced by a conforming item. This step is called *rectification*. Hence, 90 percent of the time we will accept a lot, resulting in 4 percent of the items that we use being nonconforming, and 10 percent of the time we will reject the lot, resulting in 0 percent of the items that we use being nonconforming. In the long run, then, the average percentage of nonconforming items used is

$$(.90)(.04) + (.10)(0) = .036 \text{ or } 3.6\%$$

Thus, we say that the average outgoing quality is 3.6%. Similarly, if 12 percent of the items in each lot are nonconforming and the sampling plan is designed so there is a 5 percent chance of accepting the lot, the AOQ is

$$(.05)(.12) + (.95)(0) = .006 \text{ or } 0.6\%$$

In this case we see a significant improvement between the percentage of nonconforming items incoming and outgoing.

The average outgoing quality limit (AOQL) is the maximum AOQ for all possible incoming qualities for a given sampling inspection plan.

We can use OC curves to compute the average outgoing quality (AOQ) and to determine the average outgoing quality limit (AOQL) for sampling plans in which rejected lots are rectified. The AOQ for incoming lots whose fraction of nonconforming items is p is computed using the expected value formula

$$AOQ = P_a\,p + (1 - P_a)\,(0) = P_a\,p$$

where P_a is the probability of accepting a lot with quality level p. The first term corresponds to lots that are accepted. The second term corresponds to lots that are rejected; these lots will have zero nonconformities after screening and will be rejected with probability $1 - P_a$. The formula follows from the definition of expected value.

COMPUTING AVERAGE OUTGOING QUALITY

EXAMPLE

Let us compute the AOQ for Robertson Electronics using Table 19.2. Recall that this table is based on a sampling plan in which we accept the lot only if no nonconforming items are found in the sample of 10 items. The following table shows the AOQ corresponding to the different values of p.

p	P_a	$P_a\,p$ = AOQ
0.01	.9044	.0090
0.02	.8171	.0163
0.03	.7374	.0221
0.04	.6648	.0266
0.05	.5987	.0299
0.10	.3487	.0349
0.15	.1969	.0295
0.20	.1073	.0215
0.25	.0563	.0141
0.30	.0282	.0085

Thus, for instance, if $p = 0.05$, the average outgoing quality—after screening rejected lots—will be 2.99 percent. If we plot AOQ versus p, we obtain the graph shown in Figure 19.9. Note that the curve achieves a maximum value around $p = 0.10$. It can be shown that the maximum AOQ actually occurs for $p = 0.09$ and is equal to 0.0350. This is the value of AOQL. Therefore, *in the long run* (and this is important to remember), the average outgoing quality of all lots will not exceed 0.0350.

The formula given above assumes that the lot size is very large relative to the sample size. To account for smaller lot sizes of size N, the formula should be modified to be

$$AOQ = P_a\,p - n/N$$

For the Robertson example, N was assumed to be relatively large, therefore the difference is negligible.

In contrast to defining sampling plans based on specified values of producer and consumer risks, AOQ plans assure the manufacturer that no matter what

FIGURE 19.9

Average
Outgoing Quality
Curve for
Robertson
Electronics

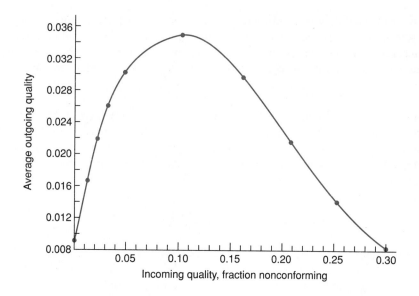

the incoming percentage nonconforming is, the long-run average outgoing quality level will never exceed AOQL.

19.4 ACCEPTANCE SAMPLING FOR VARIABLES

As we have seen, sampling plans for attributes are based on the binomial distribution, since the items inspected can be classified as either good or bad. For variable measurements, operations managers are interested in the *degree* of conformance to specifications. Thus, rather than basing a decision rule on the number of nonconforming items in a sample, we determine a range for the sample mean over which the lot is accepted. Values outside this range dictate rejection. We illustrate variables sampling inspection through the following example.

EXAMPLE

FINDING A DECISION RULE FOR LOT ACCEPTANCE BY VARIABLES

Barrett Laboratories, a major manufacturer of pharmaceuticals, buys an expensive chemical in 3-pound containers for use in producing certain drugs. Since the chemical is very expensive, Barrett Labs would like to make sure that the mean weight of the containers they receive is at least 3 pounds. The chemical is ordered in lots of 360 containers, and 36 containers are sampled for inspection. From past history, the chemical manufacturer knows that the standard deviation of its filling machines is relatively constant at .18 pounds. The mean weight may vary due to the fill settings of the packaging equipment, but it averages approximately 3 pounds.

The management of Barrett Labs would like a 99 percent chance of concluding that the chemical supplier is meeting the specifications when the true mean is 3 pounds or more. In other words, they want only a 1 percent chance of rejecting a lot whose mean weight is actually 3 pounds or more; thus the producer's risk, α, is .01. To conduct the test, 36 containers are sampled at random and weighed. The results are averaged to obtain a sample mean. Barrett Labs needs to know how small this value can be before they can reasonably conclude that the average weight per container for the entire lot is less than 3 pounds.

From statistics, we know that random samples taken from a population generate a sampling distribution for the sample mean, $\bar{x}$. We further know that the mean of the sampling distribution is equal to the population mean, μ, and the standard deviation is given by $\sigma_{\bar{x}} = \sigma/\sqrt{n}$, where σ is the population standard deviation. With a sample size of 36, the central limit theorem allows us to assume that the sampling distribution is approximately normal. For this example with $n = 36$ and $\sigma = .18$, we have $\sigma_{\bar{x}} = .18/\sqrt{36} = .03$. The sampling distribution of $\bar{x}$ is shown in Figure 19.10.

With a producer's risk of 1 percent, we are saying that the probability of rejecting a good lot (having mean equal to 3) should be .01. The decision rule is based on the critical value c such that if the sample mean is less than c, Barrett Labs can conclude that the chemical manufacturer is not meeting its contract. In terms of the normal distribution, we seek a value of c for which the area under the curve to the left of c is .01 (Figure 19.11). We know that any normal distribution can be expressed in terms of a standard normal distribution (mean = 0, variance = 1) by computing

$$z = \frac{\bar{x} - \mu}{\sigma_{\bar{x}}}$$

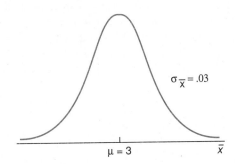

FIGURE 19.10

Sampling Distribution of $\bar{x}$ for the Barrett Laboratories Example When $\mu = 3$

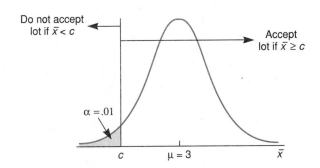

FIGURE 19.11

Sampling Distribution of $\bar{x}$ Showing Producer's Risk

where z is a standard normal random variable. Thus the z-value corresponding to the critical value c is

$$z_{.01} = \frac{c - 3}{.03}$$

or, equivalently, $c = 3 + .03z_{.01}$. Here $z_{.01}$ refers to the standard normal probability distribution value with a .01 area in the lower tail. Using Appendix B, we find that $z_{.01} = -2.33$. This is negative because the tail area we are concerned about is in the lower tail of the distribution. Thus the critical value for the sample mean is

$$c = 3 + .03(-2.33) = 2.93$$

Barrett's decision rule is to reject the lot if the sample mean is less than 2.93.

We may also compute the consumer's risk and construct OC curves for variables inspection. Suppose, for instance, that the chemical supplier is underfilling the containers by an average of 2 ounces. Since 2 ounces is equivalent to $\frac{2}{16} = .125$ pounds, this degree of underfilling corresponds to a mean filling weight of $3 - .125 = 2.875$ pounds. If $\mu = 2.875$, we want to know the probability that a sample mean $\bar{x}$ will be greater than or equal to the critical value of 2.93, leading us to conclude that the lot is of acceptable quality. This probability is the consumer's risk β. This is shown in Figure 19.12. Since the mean is 2.875, the corresponding z-value at $c = 2.93$ is

$$z = \frac{2.930 - 2.875}{.03} = 1.83$$

From Appendix B, we find that the tail area to the right of $z = 1.83$ is .0336.

We may determine the probability of accepting the lot for various values of μ. This is given in Table 19.3. Plotting these values gives the OC curve shown in Figure 19.13. This provides the same basic information as for attributes inspection. Again, there are published tables and charts that assist quality-control personnel in selecting sampling plans when α, β, a good-quality level, and a poor-quality level (analogous to AQL and LTPD) are predetermined.

19.5 ECONOMICS OF SAMPLING AND INSPECTION

Economic criteria play an important role in determining whether or not to inspect work in process between various production operations and also in choosing

FIGURE 19.12

Consumer's Risk When $\mu = 2.875$

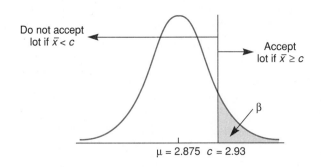

PART THREE   TACTICS AND OPERATIONS IN P/OM

Actual μ	$z = \dfrac{2.93 - \mu}{.03}$	Probability of Acceptance
2.8500	2.67	.0038
2.8750	1.83	.0336
2.9000	1.00	.1587
2.9250	.17	.4325
2.9375	− .25	.5987
2.9500	− .67	.7486
2.9750	− 1.50	.9332
3.0000	− 2.33	.9900
3.0100	− 2.67	.9962
3.0200	− 3.00	.9986
3.0500	− 4.00	1.0000

TABLE 19.3

Probability of Acceptance for Barrett Labs

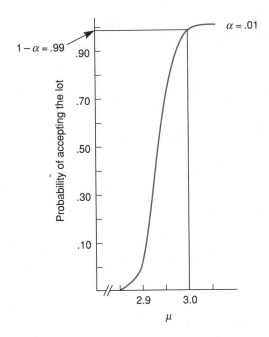

FIGURE 19.13

OC Curve for Barrett Labs

sampling plans. Since there may be hundreds of production operations, it would not be economical to inspect work-in-process after each operation, nor would it be appropriate to wait until final inspection because of possible high rework or scrap costs.

USING BREAK-EVEN ANALYSIS FOR THE ECONOMICAL INSPECTION DECISION

EXAMPLE

Let us consider the decision between having 100 percent inspection versus no inspection after one operation; for instance, an intermediate assembly operation for an electronic calculator. To make this decision, we compare the inspection cost to the penalty cost incurred if a nonconforming item is missed. Suppose that it costs an average of \$.25 per unit for the inspector's time, equipment, and overhead. If a nonconforming part is assembled at this stage of production, the calculator will not work properly during final inspection. Rejected calculators must be disassembled and repaired; the work involved averages \$8 per unit. The problem now becomes one of establishing a break-even point for the quality level. Figure 19.14 illustrates the costs involved and the break-even point. For a lot size of, for example, 100 items, one hundred percent inspection costs 100(.25), or \$25. The cost of no inspection depends on the quality level, that is, the fraction nonconforming. If the fraction nonconforming is p, then $100p$ units require rework at a cost of \$8 each. Thus the average cost of no inspection is $800p$. The break-even point is found by setting

$$25 = 800p$$

Thus

$$p = .03125$$

Hence, if the fraction nonconforming is greater than .03125, then it is more economical to inspect each assembly. In general, the break-even point, in terms of fraction nonconforming, is the ratio of the inspection cost per unit (.25) to the unit cost of not inspecting (8).

If the value of p is known, then the best policy is to use either no inspection or 100 percent inspection. However, when there is a probability distribution associated with p, then a sampling plan can be used to first test the lot of assemblies for acceptance. If the lot is accepted, then all nonconforming items will be found in final inspection; if the lot is rejected, then 100 percent inspection can be performed and the nonconforming items replaced with good parts. We may develop a simple model of the total cost for a particular sampling plan. Define

$$C_I = \text{inspection cost per unit}$$
$$C_R = \text{rework cost per unit}$$
$$P_a = \text{probability of accepting the lot}$$
$$N = \text{lot size}$$
$$n = \text{sample size}$$

The total cost is composed of the cost of sampling plus the cost of inspecting a rejected lot plus the cost of rework. Inspection cost is simply nC_I. If a lot is rejected, then $N - n$ units must still be inspected, at a cost of C_I. Since the probability that a lot will be rejected is $1 - P_a$, the expected cost is

$$(N - n)C_I(1 - P_a)$$

Finally, if an accepted lot has a true fraction defective p, then $(N - n)p$ defectives will be found later, incurring a cost of C_R each. By multiplying by P_a, the expected cost is

$$(N - n)pC_RP_a$$

The total cost is then

$$\text{TC} = nC_I + (N - n)C_I(1 - P_a) + (N - n)pC_RP_a$$

P_a can be found from the OC curve for a particular sampling plan.

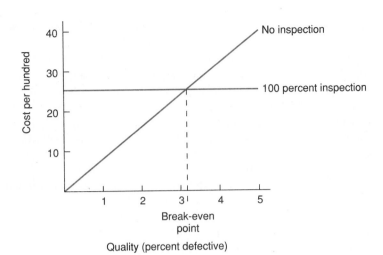

FIGURE 19.14
**Break-even Point
for Quality
Inspection**

COMPUTING THE EXPECTED COST OF A SAMPLING PLAN   EXAMPLE

To illustrate the use of this model, let us assume that $N = 500$, $p = .05$, $C_I = 2$, and $C_R = 10$. We use the OC curves in Figure 19.8 from the Robertson Electronics problem. For the plan $n = 10$, $c = 0$, with $p = .05$ we have $P_a = .60$ and

$$TC = 10(2) + (500 - 10)(2)(1 - .6) + (500 - 10)(.05)(10)(.6)$$
$$= 559$$

For the plan $n = 10$, $c = 1$, with $p = .05$, we have $p_a = .91$ and

$$TC = 10(2) + (500 - 10)(2)(1 - .91) + (500 - 10)(.05)(10)(.91)$$
$$= 331.15$$

Since there are numerous plans from which to choose, a computer can be used to find a plan with the minimum expected cost. This involves selecting different values for n and c in order to find the combination that yields the smallest expected cost.

19.6 STATISTICAL PROCESS CONTROL

Despite the effort spent in designing quality into a product or service, machine tools will invariably wear out, vibrations will cause machine settings to fall out of adjustment, purchased materials will be defective, and human operators will make mistakes. Any or all of these factors can result in the output of a production process not conforming to specifications. Fortunately, such problems can be corrected; tools can be replaced, adjustments to machines can be made, materials can be returned, and operators can be better trained. For this reason, we call such causes of poor quality **assignable causes**. On the other hand, there are many other environmental factors that cause variations in the output of a production process. For instance, the diameters of precision-manufactured ball bearings show slight differences due to natural variations in materials, temperature, and humidity, tooling materials, and many other factors. These differences combine in a random fashion to produce variations in output that are due *purely to chance*. Such causes of variation are called **common causes**. The main objective of quality control is to determine if variations in output are due to common causes or because of assignable causes. If assignable causes are found, then it is the responsibility of the operations manager to bring the process back to an acceptable level of quality by taking corrective action. Variation due to assignable causes can normally be eliminated through operator or management action such as adjusting a machine or removing a bad batch of material. Variation due to common causes can be reduced only through technological improvements such as buying a new machine or using a better material.

If the output of a production process is governed only by common causes, then we say that the process is *in statistical control* (or simply *in control*), and no changes or adjustments are necessary. When assignable causes are present, then the process is said to be *out of control* and needs to be corrected. Production personnel need to be able to determine when a process is in or out of control in order to maintain adequate levels of productivity and quality. Doing this is equivalent to making a statistical test of hypothesis.

In process control, the null hypothesis is that the process is in control, while the alternative hypothesis is that the process is out of control. The risk of adjusting a process already in control is equivalent to making a type I error and not correcting a process that is out of control is a type II error (see Table 19.4).

Traditionally, process-control decisions have been based on a policy of *detection*—that is, after-the-fact product inspection by quality-control personnel not associated with production. The problem with this approach is that a large quantity of nonconforming products might have already been made, and unnecessary costs will be incurred to correct any mistakes. Additionally, the quality-control inspector would not know if nonconformance was caused by assignable causes or whether the process is simply not capable of producing to specifications. This can easily result in behavioral problems between manufacturing and quality personnel and low employee morale. An alternative is to maintain an ongoing control over the process by the person who knows it best—the operator. This approach of *process,* rather than *product,* inspection is a prevention-oriented strategy and is best accomplished by statistical process control.

Statistical process control is a methodology using graphical displays known as control charts for assisting operators, supervisors, and managers to monitor quality of conformance and to eliminate assignable causes of variability in a process. Specifically, control charts allow one to determine the capability of a process to meet specifications, to predict the yield from a production process, and to detect undesirable process changes early so that they can be corrected, thus reducing the amount of nonconforming product manufactured.

TABLE 19.4

Decisions and Risks in Process Control

	Process State	
Decision	In Control	Out of Control
Adjust process	Type I error	Correct decision
Leave alone	Correct decision	Type II error

It is simply good management to try to reduce the variation of any quality characteristic. Low variation means greater uniformity of product, higher productivity because of reduction of scrap and rework, and improved competitive position. This last point is worthy of note from the viewpoint of business strategy. If two companies produce the same product, the one that can demonstrate more consistent uniformity and quality will likely receive more business. In the automotive industry today, for example, suppliers are *required* to provide evidence of statistical process control to their customers. The survivors in this competitive market will be those with demonstrated quality.

Control charts were first proposed by Dr. Walter Shewart at Bell Laboratories in the 1920s. Dr. Shewart was the first to make a distinction between common causes and assignable causes in process variation and developed the concept of a control chart to separate them. More recently, the control chart has been a principal tool in assisting the Japanese in quality and productivity efforts. As a result of the Japanese success, there has been a renewed interest in the use of control charts throughout the United States.

Control Charts

A **control chart** is a graphical tool for describing when a process is in control or out of control; thus, it provides a graphical aid for determining when to search for assignable causes of variation and take corrective action. Figure 19.15 illustrates the general structure of a control chart. The horizontal axis is centered on the process mean and corresponds to time; the vertical axis represents the value of the attribute or variable. UCL and LCL denote the *upper control limit* and the *lower control limit,* respectively. These limits are chosen so that there is a high probability (generally greater than .99) that sample values will fall between these limits if the process is in control.

The natural variability of process output is often described by the normal distribution. From statistics, we know that 99.7 percent of normal distribution values fall within three standard deviations (σ) of the mean (μ). This is illustrated in Figure 19.16. Thus if a process is in control, we expect about .3 percent of the output to fall outside of the 3σ range. For large samples ($n \geq 30$), the central limit theorem states that the sampling distribution of the sample mean, $\bar{x}$, is approximately normally distributed, with mean μ and standard deviation $\sigma_{\bar{x}} = \sigma/\sqrt{n}$. This holds true even if the process output itself is not normally distributed

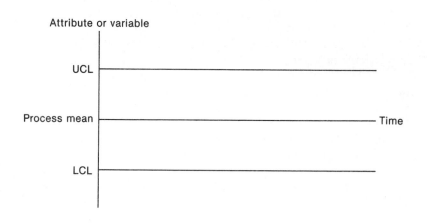

FIGURE 19.15
Control Chart Structure

FIGURE 19.16

**Three σ Range
for Normally
Distributed
Process Output**

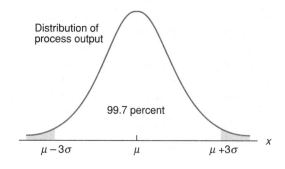

FIGURE 19.17

**Distribution of
Sample Means of
Process Output**

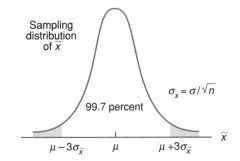

(see Figure 19.17). If the process output is normally distributed, however, the sampling distribution of $\bar{x}$ will be normally distributed for any sample size. Therefore, if a process is in control, 99.7 percent of the *sample means* lie within $3\sigma_{\bar{x}}$ of the true process mean. Hence, upper and lower control limits are usually chosen to be $\mu + 3\sigma_{\bar{x}}$ and $\mu - 3\sigma_{\bar{x}}$, respectively.

Some of the important benefits that can come from properly using control charts can be summarized as follows.

- Control charts are simple and effective tools to achieve statistical control. They lend themselves to being maintained at the job station by the operator. They give the people closest to the operation reliable information of when action should be taken, and when action should *not* be taken.
- When a process is in statistical control, its performance to specification will be predictable. Both producer and customer can rely on consistent quality levels, and both can rely on stable costs of achieving that quality level.
- After a process is in statistical control, its performance can be further improved to reduce variation.
- Control charts provide a common language for communications about the performance of a process—between the two or three shifts that operate a process; between line production (operator, supervisor) and support activities (maintenance, material control, process engineering, quality control); between different stations in the process; between supplier and user; between the manufacturing/assembly plant and the design engineering activity.
- Control charts, by distinguishing assignable from common causes of variation, give a good indication of whether any problems are likely to be correctable locally or to require management action. This minimizes the confusion, frustration, and excessive cost of misdirected problem-solving efforts.

Recall that attribute data assumes only two values, such as good or bad, pass or fail, and so on. Although attributes cannot be measured, they can be counted, and are useful in many practical situations. However, one drawback in using attribute data is that large samples (one hundred or greater) are necessary in order to obtain valid statistical results.

For attribute measurements, we are usually concerned with monitoring and controlling the fraction of nonconforming items. The type of control chart that is used is called a p-chart, where p represents the fraction of nonconforming items found in a sample. If we take, for example, M samples of n pieces of output over a long period of time during which the process was known to be in control, we can calculate the fraction nonconforming in each sample as y/n, where y is the number of nonconforming items in a particular sample. If we let p_i be the fraction nonconforming in the ith sample, then the average fraction nonconforming for the M samples is

$$\bar{p} = \frac{p_1 + p_2 + \cdots + p_M}{M}$$

From the central limit theorem, we expect a high percentage of samples to have a fraction nonconforming within three standard deviations of $\bar{p}$. Since an estimate of the standard deviation is

$$s_{\bar{p}} = \sqrt{\frac{\bar{p}(1 - \bar{p})}{n}}$$

we expect a high percentage of samples to have a fraction nonconforming within 3 standard deviations of $\bar{p}$, so we set

$$\text{UCL} = \bar{p} + 3s_{\bar{p}}$$

and

$$\text{LCL} = \bar{p} - 3s_{\bar{p}}$$

If LCL is less than zero, then a value of zero is used. The following example illustrates the construction of a p-chart.

CONSTRUCTING A CONTROL CHART FOR ATTRIBUTES

EXAMPLE

The operators of automated sorting machines in a post office must read the zip code on a letter and divert the letter to the proper carrier route. Over 1 month's time, 25 samples of 100 letters were chosen and the number of errors were recorded. This is summarized in Table 19.5. The fraction defective in each sample is simply the number of errors divided by 100. Adding the fraction defectives and dividing by 25 yields $\bar{p} = .55/25 = .022$. The standard deviation is computed as

$$s_{\bar{p}} = \sqrt{\frac{.022(1 - .022)}{100}}$$

$$= .01467$$

TABLE 19.5
Sorting Errors in
a Post Office

Sample	Number of Errors	Sample	Number of Errors
1	3	14	3
2	1	15	4
3	0	16	1
4	0	17	1
5	2	18	2
6	5	19	5
7	3	20	2
8	6	21	3
9	1	22	4
10	4	23	1
11	0	24	0
12	2	25	1
13	1		

Thus UCL = .022 + 3(.01467) = .066 and LCL = .022 − 3(.01467) = −.022. Since the LCL is negative, and since the actual fraction nonconforming cannot be less than zero; the LCL is set equal to 0. The control chart is shown in Figure 19.18; the points plotted are the data shown in Table 19.5. Although no values above the UCL or below the LCL were observed for this example, the occurrence of such values might indicate operator fatigue or the need for more experience or training.

Control Charts for Variables

The charts that are most commonly used for variable data are the $\overline{X}$-chart and R-chart (or *range* chart). The $\overline{X}$-chart is used to depict the variation in the centering of the process, and the R-chart is used to depict the variation in the ranges of the samples. The range is often used instead of the standard deviation because it is much easier to compute—it is simply the difference between the largest and smallest values in a sample.

To construct a control chart for variable data, we take M samples of n observations and compute the mean $\overline{X}_i$ and range R_i for the ith sample. Next, we compute the overall mean

$$\overline{\overline{X}} = \frac{\overline{X}_1 + \overline{X}_2 + \cdots \overline{X}_M}{M}$$

and overall range

$$\overline{R} = \frac{R_1 + R_2 + \cdots + R_M}{M}$$

The R chart is constructed first, since the control limits for the $\overline{X}$-chart depend on the average range. If the R-chart is out-of-control, then the $\overline{X}$-chart will not provide good information.

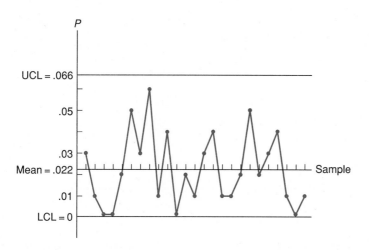

FIGURE 19.18
Control Chart for the Post Office Example

To compute control limits for the R-chart, we use factors D_3 and D_4 from Table 19.6; these factors depend on the size of the sample. Such tables are widely available[3] and make it easy to compute limits using $\overline{R}$. The control limits are

$$\text{UCL} = D_4\overline{R}$$
$$\text{LCL} = D_3\overline{R}$$

To compute the control limits for the $\overline{X}$-chart, we use the factor A_2 in Table 19.6. Then, assuming that the R-chart is in control, control limits for the $\overline{X}$-chart are calculated as

$$\text{UCL} = \overline{\overline{X}} + \overline{R}$$
$$\text{LCL} = \overline{\overline{X}} - A_2\overline{R}$$

CONSTRUCTING A CONTROL CHART FOR VARIABLES

EXAMPLE

The Goodman Tire and Rubber Company periodically tests its tires for tread wear under simulated road conditions. To study and control its manufacturing processes, the company uses $\overline{X}$- and $\overline{R}$-charts. Twenty samples, each containing three radial tires, were chosen from different shifts over several days of operation. The results are shown in Table 19.7. The average range is computed as

$$\overline{R} = \frac{R_1 + \cdots + R_{20}}{20} = 11.4$$

and the overall mean is

$$\overline{\overline{X}} = \frac{\overline{X}_1 + \cdots + \overline{X}_{20}}{20} = 29.17$$

---

[3]Complete tables can be found in most books on quality control—for example, James R. Evans and William M. Lindsay, *The Management and Control of Quality,* St. Paul: West, 1989.

TABLE 19.6

Factors Used in Quality-control Calculations

Sample Size, n	D_3	D_4	A_2	d_2
2	0	3.27	1.88	1.128
3	0	2.57	1.02	1.693
4	0	2.28	.73	2.059
5	0	2.11	.58	2.326
6	0	2.00	.48	2.534
7	.08	1.92	.42	2.704
8	.14	1.86	.37	2.847
9	.18	1.82	.34	2.970
10	.22	1.78	.31	3.078

TABLE 19.7

Tread-Wear Results for Goodman Tires

Sample (i)	Tread Wear*			Average ($\bar{X}_i$)	Range (R_i)
1	31	42	28	33.67	14
2	26	18	35	26.33	17
3	25	30	34	29.67	9
4	17	25	21	21.00	8
5	38	29	35	34.00	9
6	41	42	36	39.67	6
7	21	17	29	22.33	12
8	32	26	28	28.67	6
9	41	34	33	36.00	8
10	29	17	30	25.33	13
11	26	31	40	32.33	14
12	23	19	25	22.33	6
13	17	24	32	24.33	15
14	43	35	17	31.67	26
15	18	25	29	24.00	11
16	30	42	31	34.33	12
17	28	36	32	32.00	8
18	40	29	31	33.33	11
19	18	29	28	25.00	11
20	22	34	26	27.33	12

*Hundredths of an inch

Since $n = 3$, the control limit factors for the R-chart are $D_3 = 0$ and $D_4 = 2.57$. The control limits therefore are

$$\text{UCL} = D_4 \bar{R} = 2.57(11.4) = 29.3$$

$$\text{LCL} = D_3 \bar{R} = 0(11.4) = 0$$

For the $\bar{X}$-chart, $A_2 = 1.02$; thus the control limits are

$$\text{UCL} = 29.17 + 1.02(11.4) = 40.8$$

$$\text{LCL} = 29.17 - 1.02(11.4) = 17.5$$

The R- and $\bar{X}$-charts for the sample data are shown in Figures 19.19 and 19.20, respectively.

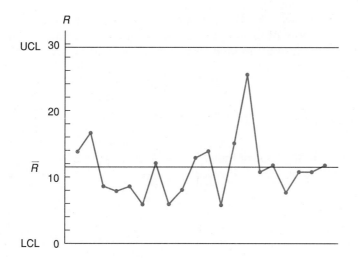

FIGURE 19.19

R-chart for Goodman Tires

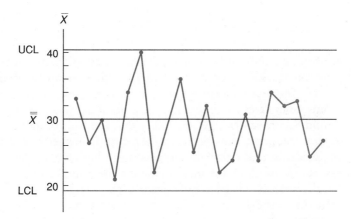

FIGURE 19.20

X-chart for Goodman Tires

We summarize the procedure for constructing control charts as follows. For attributes, take M samples of size n and compute p_i, the fraction nonconforming in the ith sample. Generally M should be approximately 25 to 30 and n is usually at least 100. Next calculate

Summary of Control-chart Construction

$$\bar{p} = \frac{p_1 + p_2 + \cdots p_M}{M}$$

and

$$s_{\bar{p}} = \sqrt{\frac{\bar{p}(1 - \bar{p})}{n}}$$

The control limits are then

$$\text{UCL} = \bar{p} + 3s_{\bar{p}}$$
$$\text{LCL} = \bar{p} - 3s_{\bar{p}}$$

For variables data, we take M samples of size n (usually between 3 and 5) and compute $\overline{X}_i$, the mean of the ith sample, and R_i, the range of the ith sample. The average range and average sample mean are computed by

$$\overline{R} = \frac{R_1 + R_2 + \cdots + R_M}{M}$$

$$\overline{\overline{X}} = \frac{\overline{X}_1 + \overline{X}_2 + \cdots + \overline{X}_M}{M}$$

Using Table 19.6, the control limits for the R-chart are

$$\text{UCL} = D_4\overline{R}$$

$$\text{LCL} = D_3\overline{R}$$

The control limits for the $\overline{X}$-chart are

$$\text{UCL} = \overline{\overline{X}} + A_2\overline{R}$$

$$\text{LCL} = \overline{\overline{X}} - A_2\overline{R}$$

Interpretation of Control Charts

The location of points and patterns of points in a control chart enable one to determine, with only a small chance of error, whether or not a process is in statistical control. The first indication that a process may be out of control is a point that is outside the control limits. If such a point is found, the operator or supervisor should first check for the possibility that the control limits were mis-calculated or that the point was plotted incorrectly. If neither one is the case, there is strong evidence that either the process mean has shifted, the variability of the process has changed, or the measurement system has changed. A second indication that the process may be out of control is the presence of a large number of points on one side of the center line. This might indicate an equipment problem, a change in materials, new operators, or a change in measurement technique or tools. Eight points in a row on one side of the center line, 10 of 11, or 12 of 14 should signal an investigation. If this occurs *below* the center line on the range chart, it indicates a potential improvement in the process. This should be carefully investigated to determine if indeed a change for the better has occured and why.

In general, about two thirds of the points should lie within the middle one-third of the region between the upper and lower control limits. If this is not true, a possible cause is that the samples consist of two or more different sources. For instance, a mix of two different materials might have been used, or the samples may have been chosen from a machine having two different spindles. Two rules of thumb used to detect such out-of-control states are (1) two of three consecutive points which fall in the outer one-third region between the center line and one of the control limits and (2) four of five consecutive points which fall within the outer two-thirds region. Examples of these guidelines are illustrated in Figure 19.21.

A third characteristic to look for in a control chart is any pattern or trend. A common pattern is an increasing or decreasing trend. As tools wear down, for example, the diameter of a machined part will gradually become larger. Changes in temperature or humidity, general equipment deterioration, dirt buildup on fixtures, or operator fatigue may cause such a trend. About six or seven points in a row that all increase or decrease in value should be considered as out of

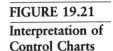

FIGURE 19.21
Interpretation of
Control Charts

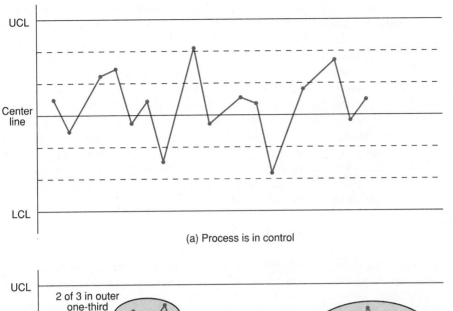

(a) Process is in control

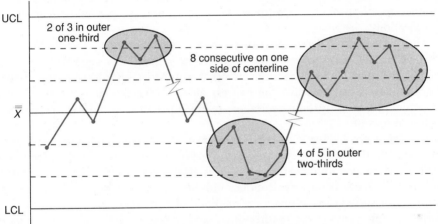

(b) Examples of out of control indicators

control. A wave or cycle pattern is also unusual and should be suspect. This might be a result of seasonal effects of material deliveries, temperature swings, maintenance cycles, or periodic rotation of operators. Again, if an out-of-control condition is indicated, one should first check for errors in constructing the control chart. Although the numbers of samples are limited, the control charts for both examples in this section appear to be in control.

19.7 APPLICATIONS OF CONTROL CHARTS

Control charts have three basic applications: (1) to establish a state of statistical control, (2) to determine process capability, and (3) as monitoring devices to signal the existence of assignable causes in order to maintain a state of statistical control.

The post office and Goodman Tire examples illustrated how to construct control charts to determine if a process is in a state of statistical control. If any special causes are found when initially constructing a control chart, managers and quality assurance personnel must investigate the underlying causes and eliminate them. Only after a process has been brought in control can we determine its capability to consistently produce output that conforms to specifications.

Recall that process capability was introduced in Chapter 8 in our discussions of process design. Process capability refers to the total variation that comes from the common causes. The data from control charts can be used to determine process capability. If we assume that the distribution of process output is normally distributed, then we can estimate the process standard deviation, σ (not the standard deviation of the *sample* mean, $\sigma_{\bar{x}}$), by dividing the average range by a constant d_2, which can be found in Table 19.6. That is

$$S = \frac{\bar{R}}{d_2}$$

The process capability is then given by $\bar{\bar{X}} \pm 3S$. This can be compared with the product specifications to determine whether or not the process can meet the specifications.

After a process is determined to be in control, the control charts should be used on a daily basis to monitor production, identify any special causes that might arise, and make corrections as necessary. More importantly, the control charts tell us when to leave the process alone. Unnecessary adjustments to a process result in nonproductive labor, reduced production, and increased variability of output.

It is more productive if the operators themselves take the samples and chart the data. In this way, they can react quickly to changes in the process and immediately make adjustments. To do this effectively, training of the operators is essential. Many companies conduct in-house training programs to teach operators and supervisors elementary methods of statistical quality control. Not only does this provide the mathematical and technical skills that are required, but it also gives the shop-floor personnel increased quality consciousness.

Control charts are designed to be used by production operators rather than by inspectors or quality control personnel. Under the philosophy of statistical process control, the burden of quality rests with the operators themselves. This is why the range is used in place of the standard deviation: shop-floor personnel can easily make the necessary computations to plot points on a control chart. Only simple calculations are required.

It is not uncommon for improvements in conformance to follow the introduction of control charts on the shop floor, particularly when the process is labor intensive. Apparently, broadening the job responsibilities of the operators often produces positive behavioral modifications (as first demonstrated in the Hawthorne studies). Under such circumstances, it is advisable to periodically revise control limits and determine new process capability as improvements take place.

Applications of Control Charts in Service Organizations

Although control charts were first developed and used in a manufacturing context, they are certainly applicable to service organizations. In this section we will describe briefly applications of control charts in service organizations.

There are many different types of service organizations: banks, hotels, hospitals, restaurants, trucking companies, insurance companies, and so on. However, they all share common features that differ from manufacturing. These include direct contacts with the customer, large volumes of transactions and processing, and often large amounts of paperwork. It is easy to see that there are many sources of error in recording transactions and in processing. It is not unusual to see a newspaper report of a large error in billing that amounts to thousands or hundreds of thousands of dollars.

To monitor and control quality in service organizations, the principles of control charts introduced in this chapter can be used quite effectively. The key is defining the quality measurements that need to be monitored. Many of the standards used in service industries form the basis for quality-control charts. Table 19.8 lists just a few of the many potential applications of control charts for services.

19.8 QUALITY IMPROVEMENT

Acceptance sampling and control charts are only two methods for improving quality. Many managers believe that once such controls are implemented, their quality problems are over. In fact, their problems may have just begun! Generally, when a quality-control system is implemented, problems that have been covered up for a long time are discovered. Even after months and years of operation, a good quality assurance program will continue to reveal areas for improvement. Every manager's true goal should be the continual improvement of quality. In this section we discuss two of the more widely used techniques for quality problem identification: cause-and-effect diagrams, and Pareto diagrams.[4]

An effective problem-solving tool that can be used in quality improvement is the cause-and-effect diagram, also known as the *Ishikawa* (after its originator Dr. Karoru Ishikawa) or the *fishbone* diagram. Any manufacturing process can basically be divided into four major categories (causes) that have an impact on a quality characteristic (effect). Hence the name *cause-and-effect diagram*. The four categories that are usually employed in conjunction with these diagrams are *man, machine, method,* and *material*. These are traditionally called the *4ms* in the manufacturing process. In these diagrams, the 4ms are usually subdivided into finer categories. Figure 19.22 illustrates a generic cause-and-effect diagram. Cause-and-effect diagrams make understanding the manufacturing process easier for production workers, especially when attempting to solve a particular quality problem.

Cause-and-effect Diagrams

A CAUSE-AND-EFFECT DIAGRAM FOR A SOLDERING OPERATION

EXAMPLE

To illustrate a cause-and-effect diagram for a specific problem, consider a soldering operation that occurs in a printed circuit board manufacturing operation.

[4]The descriptions of these techniques are paraphrased from *Statistical Quality Control for Manufacturing Managers* by William S. Messina, New York: John Wiley & Sons, 1987, 10–13. Permission granted through the American Society of Quality Control.

TABLE 19.8
Control-chart
Applications in
Service
Organizations

Organization	Quality Measure
Hospital	Lab-test accuracy
	Insurance-claim accuracy
	On-time delivery of meals and medication
Bank	Check-processing accuracy
Insurance Co.	Claims-processing response time
	Billing accuracy
Post Office	Sorting accuracy
	Time of delivery
	Percent of express mail delivered on time
Ambulance	Response time
Police department	Incidence of crime in a precinct
	Number of traffic citations
Hotel	Proportion of rooms satisfactorily cleaned
	Checkout time
	Number of complaints received
Transportation	Proportion of freight cars correctly routed
	Dollar amount of damage per claim
Auto service	Percent of time completed as promised
	Number of complaints

The quality characteristic monitored in this operation is the solder balls. The presence of solder balls can adversely affect the performance of the circuit board. Figure 19.23 shows the cause-and-effect diagram. The horizontal line represents the main stem of the cause-and-effect diagram, and at the end of this stem we state the *effect* for which we want to determine possible causes. In this case, the effect is solder balls.

From the main stem we have drawn lines which represent the main causes of solder balls. These are the machine, the solder, the flux, the components, and preheat. For each of these main causes, specific causes can be identified; for example, the causes of solder balls because of preheat are time and temperature. You can see now why a cause-and-effect diagram is often called a fishbone diagram.

Pareto
Diagrams

The Pareto principle has widespread applications in quality improvement. It can be stated as follows: "A few process characteristics [vital few] cause most of the quality problems, whereas most process characteristics [trivial many] account for a small portion of the quality problems on the manufacturing line." The Pareto principle is often stated as "the vital few and the trivial many."

This application to quality was discovered by Dr. J.M. Juran and has seen far-reaching applications outside manufacturing. The principle is important because immediate focus is given to the vital few process problems. Working on reducing the number of nonconformances associated with these vital few characteristics is where the greatest quality improvements can be achieved. In the terminology of Juran, they are called the *vital few projects*. The Pareto diagram is an important problem-solving tool.

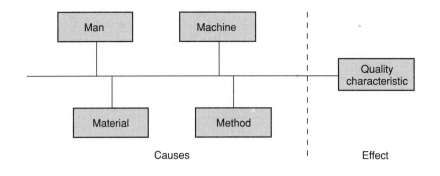

FIGURE 19.22

Generic Cause-and-effect Diagram

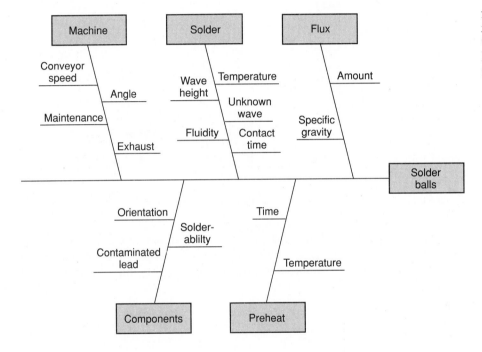

FIGURE 19.23

Cause-and-effect Diagram for Solder Balls

PARETO ANALYSIS FOR SOLDER DEFECTS

EXAMPLE

To illustrate how the Pareto diagram can be used to improve quality, the soldering process discussed in the previous section will be used. During a week's production, a total of 2000 printed circuit boards (PCBs) are manufactured. The following solder nonconformities were observed: pinholes, unwetted, blowholes, unsoldered, insufficient solder, and shorts. Studies showed that 800 of the 2000 PCBs had the following solder nonconformities: 440 had insufficient solder, 120 had blowholes, 80 were unwetted, 64 were unsoldered, 56 had pinholes, and 40 had shorts. The Pareto diagram of these results is shown in Figure 19.24.

After this study was completed, the manufacturing manager used the Pareto diagram to present the results to the engineering personnel responsible for developing the soldering process. It clearly showed that more than half of the soldering nonconformities were due to insufficient solder on the PCB; thus, effort

FIGURE 19.24

Pareto Diagram
of Solder Defects
before Process
Change

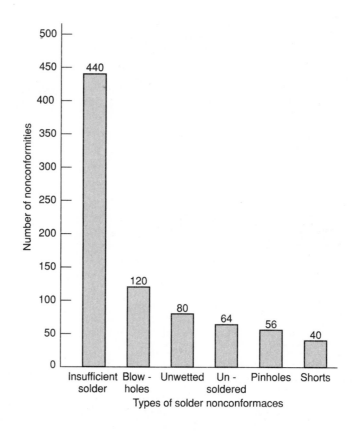

was concentrated there. Figure 19.25 is the Pareto diagram after a process change
was implemented on line. As a result of this process change, the number of solder
nonconformities dropped from 40 to 15 percent, a quality improvement of 62.5
percent.

In this section we present two examples of statistical
quality control. In the first example we discuss how
the Dow Chemical Company has used statistical
quality control to improve operations in their chemical process areas. In the second example, Corning

Glass has adapted statistical quality control in a
unique fashion at several of its electronic plants. In
both cases, significant savings and benefits in operations were realized through the application of
quality-control procedures.

USING SQC FOR PROCESS IMPROVEMENT AT DOW CHEMICAL COMPANY[5]

T he magnesium department of the Dow Chemical Company in Freeport, Texas has produced mag-

nesium, a silvery light metal, for the past 70 years.
This was the first major group in Texas Operations

---

[5]Adapted from Clifford B. Wilson, "SQC + Mg: A Positive Reaction," *Quality Progress,* April 1988,
pp. 47–49.

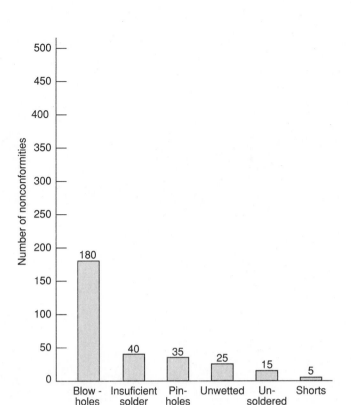

FIGURE 19.25
Pareto Diagram
of Solder Defects
after Process
Change

to train all its technical people and managers in the use of statistical quality control (SQC) techniques, following the example set by the automobile industry.

Some of the earliest successful applications of SQC were in chemical process areas. Figures 19.26 and 19.27 show the improvement in the drier analysis after SQC and retraining were implemented. In addition to the fact that the process control required significant improvement, it was found that differences between operators existed. The blackened circles in Figure 19.26 represent one operator in question; the open circles represent the other operators. On examination, it was found that the operator had not been properly trained in the use of SQC even though this operator had been performing the analysis for two years. There was an immediate improvement in the consistency of the analysis between the operators after retraining.

The use of control charts in the control room made the operators realize that their attempts to fine tune the process introduced a great deal of unwanted variation. A comparison of the before and after range charts shows the improvement (see Figure 19.27).

As with many chemical and manufacturing operations, when the variability of the feedstock to one operation is reduced, it is possible to reduce the variability of the basic operation. With tighter control over the concentration of magnesium hydroxide from the filter plant, Dow was able to exert much tighter control of the subsequent neutralization operation. As seen in Figure 19.28, the differences are substantial. The upper control limit on the second range chart is about where the center line is on the first range chart. A similar situation exists on the $\bar{x}$ charts. These improvements resulted without any additional instrumentation or operators.

Another application involved the casting operation. On primary magnesium, for example, Dow calculated a process capability index C_{pk} of meeting minimum magnesium content of 99.8 percent purity and found it to be over 10, based on over 10,000 samples. Thus, there has been little incentive to use control charts in this operation because of the comfortable level of compliance. However, ingots are also graded according to their surface quality. Using control charts, Dow found that the process was in control but that the number of rejects was much

FIGURE 19.26   Before and After x-Bar Charts on Drier Analysis

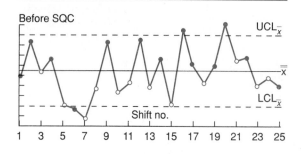

FIGURE 19.27   Before and After Range Charts on Drier Analysis

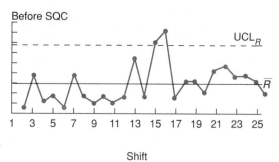

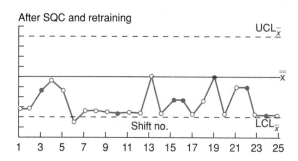

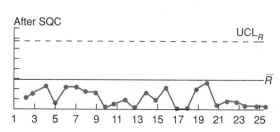

FIGURE 19.28   x-Bar and R-charts on Neutralizer Excess Alkalinity Before and After SQC

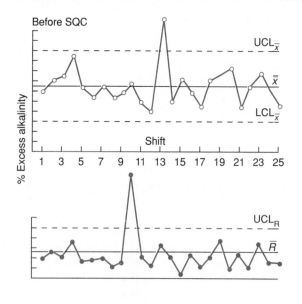

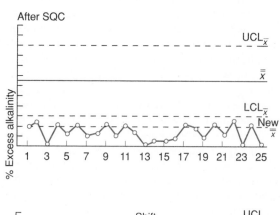

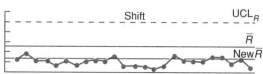

higher than desired. After several months of analysis and modifications, this process was improved.

Dow Chemical Company has experienced success everywhere that SQC has been used in the magnesium process. Documented savings of several hundred thousand dollars per year have been realized, and new applications are continually being discovered.

QUESTIONS
1. Briefly describe how SQC techniques were used to make improvements in the drier analysis.
2. Briefly describe how Dow Chemical used SQC techniques in the casting operations.

PROCESS CONTROL MANAGEMENT AT CORNING GLASS[6]

Corning Glass has adapted statistical quality control in a unique fashion at several of its electronic plants in the United States and in Europe. They call their approach "Process Control Management" or PCM. The burden of continuous checking is placed on the operators themselves, and processes that continually produce excellent quality products are seldom checked by quality-control personnel. Data obtained from several operations are fed into the system and tabulated to produce a picture of current operations. These data are available to production, quality control, and engineering for analysis and evaluation. QC may then increase its monitoring of processes that are questionable, while reducing involvement with those running with consistent excellence. Annual savings has been estimated to be more than $200,000 in direct labor and $300,000 in yield improvement.

Analysis is based on past experience, historical data, process-capability studies, and other statistical methods. Each machine in a process is categorized into one of four quality levels, which are identified by a color code. Level 1 denotes a problem-free, excellent machine or process, identified by the color blue. Most of the machines of a process should enter into this category. The manufacturing costs are low and requirements for the next operation or for final release to the customer are satisfied. Under level 1, it is necessary only to verify that changes have not occurred. Full trust is given to production personnel at this level, and it is assumed that the process will continue in full control and produce quality parts under constant operator verification. Quality-control personnel will make only occasional random checks on these processes.

In level 2, the machine or process is classified as workable and is identified by the color green. This level requires that the process inspector be directed to the same machine more often than required by level 1. The machine chosen and the frequency of visits by QC personnel is higher. Production personnel still exercise full control, but QC monitors the processes more closely to detect deterioration and trends toward a level 3 classification.

Level 3 denotes borderline operation. The identifying color is yellow. The inspectors are directed to step up the monitoring of machines. Very tight control is required and every effort is expended to bring the offending machines back into the relative safety of level 2.

In level 4, machines designated out of control (color red) are immediately shut down and repaired. Parts produced to determine acceptability after the machine is repaired are segregated into lots for special consideration by QC. Maximum support is provided by QC whenever machines reach this level.

Conventional control charts and process-capability studies are used to designate the levels. Figure 19.29 is an example of a p-chart and the color codes. In this way, operators can immediately detect changes in the process and alert quality-control personnel. Quality-control support is directed from the process-control monitor console, which may be operated manually, computer-supported, or fully computerized. This support provides continuously adjusted levels of machines and processes and directs QC personnel to the next machine to be checked.

Corning has found the system to be beneficial in many ways. It maintains and improves quality by motivating production department personnel and

[6]Adapted from "Process Control Management," by Basile A. Denissoff, *Quality Progress*, 13, no. 6 (June 1980): 14–16. © 1980 American Society for Quality Control. Reprinted by permission.

FIGURE 19.29   An Example of Quality-level Settings

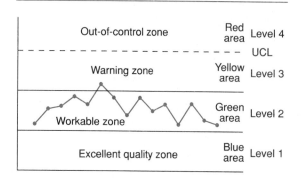

charging them with the responsibility for making acceptable products without sacrificing yield. It has improved interdepartmental communicaions by developing a feeling of teamwork. Each plant has its own adaptation of PCM to fit its specific needs.

QUESTIONS

1. What does Corning Glass call their approach to statistical quality control? What benefits have been achieved using this process?
2. Explain the method for categorizing machines or processes.
3. What type of control chart is shown in Figure 19.29? Briefly explain how this chart is used.

SUMMARY

In this chapter we addressed the operational aspects of quality control. The most important quality-control techniques include sampling inspection and control charts. Sampling inspection is used to determine the quality of purchased or manufactured lots without having to inspect each individual item. Control charts are most often used to determine if the variability of a process is because of chance or the result of assignable causes that can be corrected. Sampling inspection and control charts are used for attributes, which assume only one of two possible values, and for variables, which are measured as continuous values.

The Japanese have approached quality control with the philosophy that everyone in a firm is responsible for quality. The unique environment developed by Japanese industry since 1950 has allowed this concept of total quality control to become a reality, and is being carefully evaluated in the West today.

KEY TERMS

Attribute measurement
Variable measurement
Lot
Lot sentencing
Producer's risk
Consumer's risk
Sampling plan
Operating characteristic (OC) curve

Acceptable quality level (AQL)
Lot Tolerance percent defective (LTPD)
Average outgoing quality (AOQ)
Assignable causes
Common causes
Control chart

REVIEW/ DISCUSSION QUESTIONS

1. What are the general objectives of quality control?
2. Describe the components of any control system.
3. Describe the role of quality-control inspection throughout the overall production system.
4. What is the purpose of inspection and measurement? Why will inspection continue to remain an important activity in quality control?

5. Discuss the distinction between variable and attribute measurement.

6. What are the advantages and disadvantages of attribute versus variable inspection?

7. List the major rules used for locating inspection stations.

8. What are the advantages of sampling inspection over 100 percent inspection?

9. How does accuracy differ from precision?

10. Discuss the importance of human factors in inspection tasks. How can inspection be improved by taking human factors into account?

11. What is the purpose of acceptance sampling?

12. Describe the general acceptance sampling procedure.

13. Define the terms *producer's risk* and *consumer's risk*. What relationship do these concepts have to type I and type II errors in statistical hypothesis testing?

14. What is a sampling plan? Describe how single and double sampling plans operate.

15. What is an *operating characteristic curve*? How can an OC curve be used to specify a sampling plan?

16. Discuss the concept of *average outgoing quality*. Why do we compute the AOQL?

17. What types of economic trade-offs are usually considered in quality control?

18. Discuss the difference between assignable causes and common causes. Which of these should management be more concerned with?

19. What do we mean when we say that a process is *in statistical control*?

20. What is *statistical process control* and what benefits can be gained from using it?

21. Describe the various types of control charts and their applications.

22. Discuss how to interpret control charts. What types of patterns indicate a lack of control?

23. What is the purpose of a process capability study?

24. List some applications of control charts in service organizations.

25. Discuss the use of cause-and-effect diagrams and Pareto analysis in quality control.

26. Choose a personal or business problem that you face (not necessarily quality-related). Construct a cause-and-effect diagram for this problem. Has it helped you to focus better on the problem?

1. For a single sampling plan with $n = 25$ and $c = 0$, find the probability of accepting a lot that has a fraction nonconforming of 2%. Of 6%.

2. For a single sampling plan with $n = 100$ and $c = 4$, find the probability of accepting a lot that has a fraction nonconforming of 3%. Of 7%.

3. Verify the OC curves in Figure 19.8 for $n = 10, c = 1; n = 15, c = 0$; and $n = 15, c = 1$ by computing the probability of acceptance for values of p between 0 and .25 in increments of .05.

4. Draw an OC curve for the Robertson Electronics example for a plan with n = 15 and c = 3. Show the effect of increasing n in increments of 5 up to 30. Show also the effect of increasing c in increments of 1 up to 6.

5. A domestic manufacturer of watches purchases quartz crystals from a Swiss firm. These are bought in lots of 1000. Twenty crystals are sampled at random and inspected for defects.
   a. Construct OC curves for acceptance numbers of 0, 1, and 2.
   b. If the AQL is established as .01 and LTPD = .08, what are the producer and consumer risks for each plan considered in part a?
   c. If a sample of 15 crystals is chosen, how do your answers in parts a and b differ?

6. In Problem 1, find the producer's and consumer's risk if AQL = 2% and LQL = 6%.

7. In Problem 2, find the producer's and consumer's risk if AQL = 3% and LQL = 8%.

8. Find the average outgoing quality for a plan with n = 100, c = 4, and p = 4%. What is the average outgoing quality limit?

9. Find the average outgoing quality for a plan with n = 80, c = 3, and p = 5%. What is the average outgoing quality limit?

10. The average lifetime of a hydraulic valve is 10,000 hours of normal operation with a variance of 1.44 million. For a sample size of 25, what is the probability that the average lifetime of the sample is greater than 10,500 hours? Less than 9350 hours?

11. The proportion of chemical A in a base material from which it is extracted is expected to be 0.4 on the average, with a standard deviation of 0.15.
    a. If a sample of size 35 is chosen, what should be the decision rule to accept an incoming lot assuming a producer's risk of 0.05?
    b. If the actual proportion is 0.3, what is the consumer's risk?

12. The cost to inspect a credit card statement in a bank is 25 cents, while correction of a mistake later amounts to $500. What is the break-even point in errors per thousand transactions for which one hundred percent is no more economical than no inspection?

13. The watch manufacturer in Problem 5 has the option of inspecting each crystal. If a bad crystal is assembled, the cost of disassembly and replacement after the final test and inspection is $1.40. Each crystal can be tested for $.08. Perform a break-even analysis to determine the percent nonconforming for which 100% inspection is better than no inspection at all.

14. For the situation in Problem 13, if the true fraction defective is 4 percent, determine the total cost of the sampling plans considered in Problem 5(a).

15. Twenty-five samples of 100 items each were inspected and 68 were found to be defective. Compute control limits for a p-chart.

16. Over several weeks, 20 samples of 50 packages of synthetic-gut tennis strings were tested for breaking strength; 38 packages failed to conform to the manufacturer's specifications. Compute control limits for a p-chart.

17. The fraction nonconforming for an automotive piston is given below for 20 samples. Two hundred units are inspected each day. Construct a p-chart and interpret the results.

Sample	Fraction Nonconforming	Sample	Fraction Nonconforming
1	.04	11	.07
2	.05	12	.09
3	.03	13	.05
4	.02	14	.04
5	.02	15	.03
6	.04	16	.04
7	.04	17	.03
8	.06	18	.05
9	.04	19	.02
10	.08	20	.04

18. One hundred insurance claim forms are inspected daily over 25 working days and the number of forms with errors are as recorded. Construct a p-chart. If any points occur outside the control limits, assume that assignable causes have been determined. Then construct a revised chart.

Day	Number Nonconforming	Day	Number Nonconforming
1	2	14	2
2	1	15	1
3	2	16	3
4	3	17	4
5	0	18	0
6	2	19	0
7	0	20	1
8	2	21	0
9	7	22	2
10	1	23	8
11	3	24	2
12	0	25	1
13	0		

19. A production process, sampled 20 times with a sample size of 8 gave the following $\overline{X}$ and $\overline{R}$ values:
$$\overline{\overline{X}} = 28.5, \overline{R} = 1.6$$

a. Construct the R and $\overline{X}$ charts for this process given that for a sample size of 8, $D_3 = 0.14$, $D_4 = 1.86$, $A_2 = 0.37$, and $d_2 = 2.847$.

b. At a later stage, 6 samples produced the following results for $\overline{X}$: 28.001, 28.25, 29.13, 28.72, 28.9, 28.3. Is the process in control?

c. Is the following set of sample results indicative of the process being out of control: 28.3, 28.7, 28.1, 28.9, 28.01, 29.01? Why or why not?

20. Twenty-five samples of size 5 resulted in $\overline{\overline{X}} = 5.42$ and $\overline{R} = 2.0$. Compute control limits for $\overline{X}$- and R-charts and estimate the standard deviation of the process.

21. Use the following sample data and construct $\overline{X}$- and R-charts. Assume that the sample size is five.

Sample	$\bar{X}$	R	Sample	$\bar{X}$	R
1	95.72	1.0	11	95.80	.6
2	95.24	.9	12	95.22	.2
3	95.18	.8	13	95.56	1.3
4	95.44	.4	14	95.22	.5
5	95.46	.5	15	95.04	.8
6	95.32	1.1	16	95.72	1.1
7	95.40	.9	17	94.82	.6
8	95.44	.3	18	95.46	.5
9	95.08	.2	19	95.60	.4
10	95.50	.6	20	95.74	.6

22. Develop $\bar{X}$- and R-charts for the following data:

Sample	Observations				
	1	2	3	4	5
1	3.05	3.08	3.07	3.11	3.11
2	3.13	3.07	3.05	3.10	3.10
3	3.06	3.04	3.12	3.11	3.10
4	3.09	3.08	3.09	3.09	3.07
5	3.10	3.06	3.06	3.07	3.08
6	3.08	3.10	3.13	3.03	3.06
7	3.06	3.06	3.08	3.10	3.08
8	3.11	3.08	3.07	3.07	3.07
9	3.09	3.09	3.08	3.07	3.09
10	3.06	3.11	3.07	3.09	3.07

23. For Problem 22, estimate the process capability by first computing the sample standard deviation and then computing $\bar{R}/d_2$. Why is there a difference?

24. Discuss the interpretation of each of the control charts presented in Figure 19.30.

25. In the final inspection of a product, the following defects were discovered out of 2600 units inspected:

Surface scars: 32
Cracks: 23
Incomplete: 48
Misshapen: 4
Other: 8

Draw a Pareto diagram for these defects. What quality improvement strategy is suggested?

CASE PROBLEM Gotfryd Hydraulics, Inc., is a manufacturer of hydraulic machine tools. They have had a history of leakage trouble resulting from a certain critical fitting.

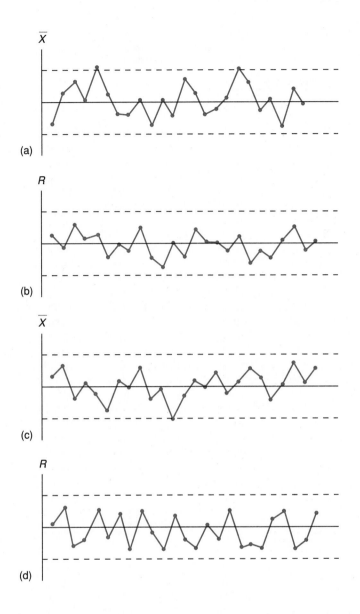

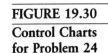

FIGURE 19.30
Control Charts
for Problem 24

(a)

(b)

(c)

(d)

Twenty-five samples of machined parts were selected, one per shift, and the diameter of the fitting was measured. The results are given in Table 19.9.

a. Construct control charts for this data ($D_4 = 2.28$, $D_3 = 0$, and $A_2 = .73$ for $n = 25$).

b. It was discovered that the regular machine operator was absent when samples 4, 8, 14, and 22 were taken. How will this affect the results in part *a*?

c. Table 19.10 represents measurements taken during the next 10 shifts. What information does this provide to the quality-control manager?

TABLE 19.9

Data for Case Problem—First Twenty-five Shifts

	Diameter Measurement (cm) Observation			
Sample	1	2	3	4
1	10.94	10.64	10.88	10.70
2	10.66	10.66	10.68	10.68
3	10.68	10.68	10.62	10.68
4	10.03	10.42	10.48	11.06
5	10.70	10.46	10.76	10.80
6	10.38	10.74	10.62	10.54
7	10.46	10.90	10.52	10.74
8	10.66	10.04	10.58	11.04
9	10.50	10.44	10.74	10.66
10	10.58	10.64	10.60	10.26
11	10.80	10.36	10.60	10.22
12	10.42	10.36	10.72	10.68
13	10.52	10.70	10.62	10.58
14	11.04	10.58	10.42	10.36
15	10.52	10.40	10.60	10.40
16	10.38	10.02	10.60	10.60
17	10.56	10.68	10.78	10.34
18	10.58	10.50	10.48	10.60
19	10.42	10.74	10.64	10.50
20	10.48	10.44	10.32	10.70
21	10.56	10.78	10.46	10.42
22	10.82	10.64	11.00	10.01
23	10.28	10.46	10.82	10.84
24	10.64	10.56	10.92	10.54
25	10.84	10.68	10.44	10.68

Table 19.10

Data for Case Problem—Next Ten Shifts

	Observation			
Additional Sample	1	2	3	4
1	10.40	10.76	10.54	10.64
2	10.60	10.28	10.74	10.86
3	10.56	10.58	10.64	10.70
4	10.70	10.60	10.74	10.52
5	11.02	10.36	10.90	11.02
6	10.68	10.38	10.22	10.32
7	10.64	10.56	10.82	10.80
8	10.28	10.62	10.40	10.70
9	10.50	10.88	10.58	10.54
10	10.36	10.44	10.40	10.66

CONCLUSION

I n a brief concluding chapter, we return to the important issue that was raised in Part I of this book: the need to improve productivity and quality in order to compete in today's international marketplace. Specifically, we discuss a new philosophy of manufacturing—*world-class manufacturing*—and its potential for meeting the challenges of the twenty-first century.

Competitive Advantage and World-Class Manufacturing

T hroughout this book we have discussed a wide variety of topics and issues in P/OM. We began by noting the serious threat to American industrial competitiveness. The increasing trade deficit, low rates of productivity growth, and a declining position in high-technology international markets all point to the severe competitive problem that America faces. The world economy and the state of technology are changing. These changes have important implications for production and operations management.[1]

In discussing the scope of P/OM we focused on several major themes, including quality, productivity, customer service, profitability, flexibility, technology, and people, primarily as related to manufacturing. These factors determine the competitive advantage that a business will have in today's international economy.

One of the important ways in which the competitive pressure that America faces can be resolved is through manufacturing. We must rethink and reorganize our approach to manufacturing to recapture a dominant position in the world economic system. New manufacturing technologies such as CIM and new managerial philosophies such as JIT and TQC can provide the cost efficiencies and productivity improvements that are needed. Without downplaying the importance of services, in this brief concluding chapter we make some final comments about how manufacturing should be addressed to assure our future growth and survival.

20.1 MANUFACTURING FOR COMPETITIVE ADVANTAGE[2]

Nearly everyone agrees that the needs and skills required to manage a manufacturing or service firm in today's global environment are different than they were ten years ago, and will change even more ten years into the future. Markets are rapidly changing; traditional approaches to marketing no longer suffice. Information technology is becoming an important tool for communications and as a competitive weapon. More sophisticated design and manufacturing procedures are necessary to meet consumer desires. These issues have placed increasingly more difficult demands on production and operations.

In years past, production was studied as a science, not as a system. We tended to compartmentalize the business organization and to optimize, or more correctly, suboptimize, the individual components. The lack of integration of business functions has, over the years, limited the effectiveness of production to meet its true goals and potential. We obviously need to look at production in a much different manner today.

Operations must be viewed as a *total system*. The entire production process—from individual work centers through suppliers and customers—must be in-

---

[1]We recommend reading Stephen S. Cohen and John Zysman, *Manufacturing Matters,* New York: Basic Books, Inc. 1987, to better understand the importance of manufacturing to the future growth and survival of the American economy.

[2]The ideas presented in this section have been adopted from Thomas G. Gunn, *Manufacturing for Competitive Advantage,* Cambridge, MA: Ballinger Publishing Co., 1987. The student is encouraged to read this book in order to gain a broader view of the integration of the various components of P/OM.

volved. Plans and decisions must be coordinated, not only vertically throughout the organization, but horizontally across multiple functions.

The consulting firm of Ernst & Young (formerly Arthur Young) has addressed these issues in a manufacturing context, through a framework called Manufacturing for Competitive Advantage.[3] Figure 20.1 illustrates this framework. This framework provides a logical, yet easy-to-understand frame of reference for managers to consider when planning for and implementing a program to achieve competitive advantage.

This framework begins with a strategic vision that defines the overall business objectives that the business is striving to attain. This vision must incorporate the global markets in which the business competes, and its global competitors. To compete in today's global markets, manufacturers must make significant reductions in inventory and significant improvements in quality. It is suggested that top competitors should have 80 to 100 inventory turnovers per year and fewer than 200 defective parts per million for any product. Many U.S. manufacturers only obtain 1 to 4 inventory turnovers per year and do not even measure defective units per million.

The four critical resources that must be managed effectively are quality, human resources, technology, and planning. We have dwelled on quality throughout this book, illustrating on numerous occasions the benefits that the Japanese have achieved through quality commitment. A company's competitive progress depends on how fast its employees can learn and adapt to change. The crisis in mathematics education in the United States is but one unnerving indicator of the difficulties we face in the future in this regard. Performance and measurement systems, incentive and reward systems, personnel policies and procedures, and training programs must all reinforce the goals of the future, not the practices of the past. Proven technology can provide significant benefits when properly implemented. Finally, planning must become a way of life, focusing on the long term, rather than short term performance.

The next level in the Manufacturing for Competitive Advantage framework is integrated manufacturing. It is important to realize that manufacturing consists of the entire range of activities from product and process design all the way through distribution and after sale service and support. No activity can be performed without affecting some other part of this spectrum. Suppliers must be integrated throughout the process. Communication with customers is required in each of these functions to better understand their requirements and expectations.

Finally, the "pillars" that support the integrated manufacturing plane, computer-integrated manufacturing (CIM), total quality control (TQC), and just-in-time (JIT) are the bases on which a modern manufacturing capability must be built. Any overall program must address all three.

While this framework provides a structure for management, no company has yet completely implemented all components, though many have made great progress. Companies that have achieved progress in this area have been properly called *world class manufacturers*. Some of the benefits that have been realized in specific components of this world class manufacturing structure are listed.

- Through computer aided design, AVCO Lycoming Division reduced gear drafting time from several days to thirty minutes.

---

[3]Thomas G. Gunn, *Manufacturing for Competitive Advantage,* Cambridge, MA: Ballinger Publishing Co., 1987.

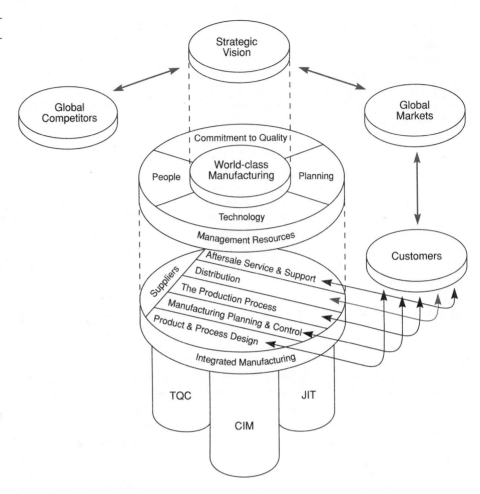

- Milwaukee Gear Co., used computer aided process planning for a $750,000 annual reduction in costs.
- Collins Transmission Systems Division, Rockwell International reduced costs 30 percent, lead time 70 percent, and investment payback one year through group technology.
- Atlas Copco increased inventory turns by 30 percent, decreased inventory by 40 percent, and improved on-time deliveries from 70 to 93 percent by implementing MRP.
- Tektronix, Inc., saved over $2 million annually, decreased space requirements by 160,000 square feet after a 30-percent sales increase, and realized a three-year payback from a $14 million automated warehouse.
- Cummins Engine Co., reduced inspection time for a diesel engine block from 40 hours to 35 minutes by employing vision systems.
- A flexible manufacturing system reduced work-in-process time from 2 months to 1 day at a Renault Vehicles Industries plant.

- Hewlett-Packard used a corporate TQC program to reduce its supplier products' incoming part failure rate from over 2000 parts per million in 1982 to 100 parts per million by 1985.
- Harley-Davidson used a combined TQC-JIT program to reduce work in process inventory by $22 million, reduce machine setup times by 75 percent, increase productivity by 30 percent, and reduce scrap and rework by 60 percent in just a five-year period.

There are many more examples. We cite these as an illustration of the specific benefits that can be achieved from only *one* focused improvement in the entire manufacturing program. Just imagine what could be achieved through attention to the entire Manufacturing for Competitive Advantage framework! Consider the strategic implications of simply reducing new product development lead time by 50 percent. How would that enable a company to capture new markets? Or, what if the order-to-ship time can be reduced ten-fold? What advantage can this have over the competition? What if quality costs can be decreased to less than one percent of sales? Management needs to consider such questions in the course of defining its business strategy.

20.2 PLANNING AND IMPLEMENTATION FOR WORLD-CLASS MANUFACTURING

Gunn recommends a three-step process for establishing a planning frame of reference. The first step is self-assessment. A company must understand its current manufacturing capabilities. This involves examining current costs, products, facilities, information technology, employee skills, processes, quality, material flow, supply and distribution channels, capacity, inventory turns, and lead times—all the elements that we have studied throughout this book. The next step is assessing the competition. Some questions to be considered include: What kind of systems do they have? Do they use total quality control and just-in-time? How do they use information technology? The third step is to determine the future course of action. What capabilities are needed for the future? What proven technologies, philosophies, and practices exist? How can these be exploited for achieving competitive advantage?

Specific objectives should then be developed along with the means of achieving them. For example, one objective might be to increase raw material and work-in-process inventory turns from two to ten over the next year. Means of achieving this objective might be to apply JIT techniques to minimize setup times and lot sizes, obtain greater supplier involvement, and reduce manufacturing lead time. A second objective might be to reduce quality costs from 12 percent of sales to 1.5 percent in five years. This might be achieved by implementing a statistical quality control program, improving production equipment capability, and improving product and process design.

Central to the entire process is a focus on human resources. People devise strategies and make systems work, however, they are often completely ignored. Significant cultural changes must take place in a firm when new technologies and procedures are introduced. Managers must consider organization structure and staffing, performance measurement systems, incentive and reward systems, education and training, and communication systems in planning the transition. For example, since CIM is removing barriers between design and manufacturing, why not create a position of vice-president of design *and* manufacturing? How many firms still reward managers on volume rather than quality? How can teamwork be promoted better within the organization?

The trend toward world class manufacturing is making significant changes in tradition. The scope of production jobs is increasing. Workers must have a greater understanding of the big picture of manufacturing, including overall system maintenance and reconfiguration of flexible manufacturing systems. To accomplish these trends requires significant changes in worker attitudes and skills through education and training. Companies can *not* afford to sacrifice long-term objectives for short-term profits. It has been noted that IBM spends about $2000 per worker per year to educate and train all of its employees; Xerox spends about $1700 per worker per year. In contrast, the average manufacturer spends only about $100 per worker. Consider a $600 million per year company that has a quality cost of 5 percent of sales. They are spending $30 million per year for poor quality. If the company would spend $1000 per employee per year to educate and train its workers—$6 million—and decrease its cost of quality by only 20 percent, it would pay back the training program in only one year. Sadly, many companies are unwilling to recognize and make this type of commitment.

Tompkins Associates, Inc. a leading engineering consulting firm in facilities planning, material handling, integrated automation, warehousing, and distribution systems proposes 20 essential elements which will be required of all survivors in the world of manufacturing by 1995.[4] These are

1. *Manufacturing costs.* Significant reductions in the total costs of manufacturing will be necessary to stay in business.
2. *Manufacturing and marketing.* Manufacturing and marketing will become integrated and function as a team.
3. *Product development.* Although the costs of product development will continue to increase, a drastic compression will occur from the time a product is developed until it is manufactured.
4. *Global marketplace.* Product lives will be shorter, and therefore it will be necessary to amortize the product development costs over higher production volumes. Firms must address the global marketplace to obtain these higher volumes.
5. *Customer lead times.* Significant reductions in customer lead times will be expected with product being manufactured to order and not to stock.
6. *Product lot sizes.* Production lot sizes approaching 1 and setup times approaching 0 will be the trend.
7. *Production and inventory control.* Production and inventory control systems will be decentralized and more responsive to the needs of the shop floor, and schedules will be met.
8. *Uncertainty.* All uncertainty will be minimized, and discipline will be increased.
9. *Balance.* More important than the speed of any operations will be the balance of series of operations. High turnover shift equalizers will exist

---

[4]Courtesy of Tompkins Associates, Inc. Reprinted by permission.

after several operations, and high turnover production sequence buffers will exist before several operations to facilitate this balance.

10. *Inventories.* Drastic reductions in raw and WIP inventories will occur.
11. *Quality.* Product quality, vendor quality, and data integrity will approach 100 percent, as quality will be viewed as every employee's and every vendor's job.
12. *Maintenance.* Tremendous increases in the mean time between manufacturing process failures will be expected, as preventative and predictive maintenance will be wholeheartedly utilized.
13. *Flexibility.* Manufacturing facilities, operations, and personnel will become more flexible.
14. *Material flow.* There will be an increased emphasis on efficient material flow, and continuous process manufacturing will be the norm.
15. *Material tracking and control.* Enhanced material tracking and control systems will be required, and automatic identification techniques will become the norm.
16. *Human resources.* Every manager will be dedicated to creating an environment in which every employee is motivated and happy.
17. *Team players.* Customers, vendors and vendors' vendors, etc. will be integrated with the manufacturing operation, and will be treated as team players.
18. *Simplification.* All of manufacturing will be simplified.
19. *Integration.* Islands of automation, islands of knowledge, islands of education, and organizational islands will cease to exist as these islands are integrated.
20. *Understanding.* Manufacturing management will stop embracing manufacturing gimmicks, fads, and acronyms moving towards a true understanding of the manufacturing process.

We see that the visions of world class manufacturing proposed by both Ernst & Young (formerly Arthur Young) and Tompkins Associates share many similarities. Achieving these objectives will not be easy; they require commitment, cooperation, and hard work. Nevertheless, they are crucial to the future survival of today's manufacturing industries.

20.3 FINAL REMARKS

As a student reading this book, your major area of interest is probably *not* P/OM. However, we hope that you have come to recognize the critical importance of P/OM in the total scheme of business, and that you will better appreciate and support the operations function as you enter the world of business.

APPENDIXES

APPENDIX A Values of e^{-iN}

To find $e^{-1.5}$, choose $N = 15$ and $i = 1$.

N	.01	.02	.03	.04	.05	.06	.07	.08	.09	.10	.11	.12
1	0.990	0.980	0.970	0.961	0.951	0.942	0.932	0.923	0.914	0.905	0.896	0.887
2	0.980	0.961	0.942	0.923	0.905	0.887	0.869	0.852	0.835	0.819	0.803	0.787
3	0.970	0.942	0.914	0.887	0.861	0.835	0.811	0.787	0.763	0.741	0.719	0.698
4	0.961	0.923	0.887	0.852	0.819	0.787	0.756	0.726	0.698	0.670	0.644	0.619
5	0.951	0.905	0.861	0.819	0.779	0.741	0.705	0.670	0.638	0.607	0.577	0.549
6	0.942	0.887	0.835	0.787	0.741	0.698	0.657	0.619	0.583	0.549	0.517	0.487
7	0.932	0.869	0.811	0.756	0.705	0.657	0.613	0.571	0.533	0.497	0.463	0.432
8	0.923	0.852	0.787	0.726	0.670	0.619	0.571	0.527	0.487	0.449	0.415	0.383
9	0.914	0.835	0.763	0.698	0.638	0.583	0.533	0.487	0.445	0.407	0.372	0.340
10	0.905	0.819	0.741	0.670	0.607	0.549	0.497	0.449	0.407	0.368	0.333	0.301
11	0.896	0.803	0.719	0.644	0.577	0.517	0.463	0.415	0.372	0.333	0.298	0.267
12	0.887	0.787	0.698	0.619	0.549	0.487	0.432	0.383	0.340	0.301	0.267	0.237
13	0.878	0.771	0.677	0.595	0.522	0.458	0.403	0.353	0.310	0.273	0.239	0.210
14	0.869	0.756	0.657	0.571	0.497	0.432	0.375	0.326	0.284	0.247	0.214	0.186
15	0.861	0.741	0.638	0.549	0.472	0.407	0.350	0.301	0.259	0.223	0.192	0.165
16	0.852	0.726	0.619	0.527	0.449	0.383	0.326	0.278	0.237	0.202	0.172	0.147
17	0.844	0.712	0.600	0.507	0.427	0.361	0.304	0.257	0.217	0.183	0.154	0.130
18	0.835	0.698	0.583	0.487	0.407	0.340	0.284	0.237	0.198	0.165	0.138	0.115
19	0.827	0.684	0.566	0.468	0.387	0.320	0.264	0.219	0.181	0.150	0.124	0.102
20	0.819	0.670	0.549	0.449	0.368	0.301	0.247	0.202	0.165	0.135	0.111	0.091
21	0.811	0.657	0.533	0.432	0.350	0.284	0.230	0.186	0.151	0.122	0.099	0.080
22	0.803	0.644	0.517	0.415	0.333	0.267	0.214	0.172	0.138	0.111	0.089	0.071
23	0.795	0.631	0.502	0.399	0.317	0.252	0.200	0.159	0.126	0.100	0.080	0.063
24	0.787	0.619	0.487	0.383	0.301	0.237	0.186	0.147	0.115	0.091	0.071	0.056
25	0.779	0.607	0.472	0.368	0.287	0.223	0.174	0.135	0.105	0.082	0.064	0.050
26	0.771	0.595	0.458	0.353	0.273	0.210	0.162	0.125	0.096	0.074	0.057	0.044
27	0.763	0.583	0.445	0.340	0.259	0.198	0.151	0.115	0.088	0.067	0.051	0.039
28	0.756	0.571	0.432	0.326	0.247	0.186	0.141	0.106	0.080	0.061	0.046	0.035
29	0.748	0.560	0.419	0.313	0.235	0.176	0.131	0.098	0.074	0.055	0.041	0.031
30	0.741	0.549	0.407	0.301	0.223	0.165	0.122	0.091	0.067	0.050	0.037	0.027

N	.13	.14	.15	.16	.17	.18	.19	.20	.21	.22	.23	.24
						i						
1	0.878	0.869	0.861	0.852	0.844	0.835	0.827	0.819	0.811	0.803	0.795	0.787
2	0.771	0.756	0.741	0.726	0.712	0.698	0.684	0.670	0.657	0.644	0.631	0.619
3	0.677	0.657	0.638	0.619	0.600	0.583	0.566	0.549	0.533	0.517	0.502	0.487
4	0.595	0.571	0.549	0.527	0.507	0.487	0.468	0.499	0.432	0.415	0.399	0.383
5	0.522	0.497	0.472	0.449	0.427	0.407	0.387	0.368	0.350	0.333	0.317	0.301
6	0.458	0.432	0.407	0.383	0.361	0.340	0.320	0.301	0.284	0.267	0.252	0.237
7	0.403	0.375	0.350	0.326	0.304	0.284	0.264	0.247	0.230	0.214	0.200	0.186
8	0.353	0.326	0.301	0.278	0.257	0.237	0.219	0.202	0.186	0.172	0.159	0.147
9	0.310	0.284	0.259	0.237	0.217	0.198	0.181	0.165	0.151	0.138	0.126	0.115
10	0.273	0.247	0.223	0.202	0.183	0.165	0.150	0.135	0.122	0.111	0.100	0.091
11	0.239	0.214	0.192	0.172	0.154	0.138	0.124	0.111	0.099	0.089	0.080	0.071
12	0.210	0.186	0.165	0.147	0.130	0.115	0.102	0.091	0.080	0.071	0.063	0.056
13	0.185	0.162	0.142	0.125	0.110	0.096	0.085	0.074	0.065	0.057	0.050	0.044
14	0.162	0.141	0.122	0.106	0.093	0.080	0.070	0.061	0.053	0.046	0.040	0.035
15	0.142	0.122	0.105	0.091	0.078	0.067	0.058	0.050	0.043	0.037	0.032	0.027
16	0.125	0.106	0.091	0.077	0.066	0.056	0.048	0.041	0.035	0.030	0.025	0.021
17	0.110	0.093	0.078	0.066	0.056	0.047	0.040	0.033	0.028	0.024	0.020	0.017
18	0.096	0.080	0.067	0.056	0.047	0.039	0.033	0.027	0.023	0.019	0.016	0.013
19	0.085	0.070	0.058	0.048	0.040	0.033	0.027	0.022	0.018	0.015	0.013	0.010
20	0.074	0.061	0.050	0.041	0.033	0.027	0.022	0.018	0.015	0.012	0.010	0.008
21	0.065	0.053	0.043	0.035	0.028	0.023	0.018	0.015	0.012	0.010	0.008	0.006
22	0.057	0.046	0.037	0.030	0.024	0.019	0.015	0.012	0.010	0.008	0.006	0.005
23	0.050	0.040	0.032	0.025	0.020	0.016	0.013	0.010	0.008	0.006	0.005	0.004
24	0.044	0.035	0.027	0.021	0.017	0.013	0.010	0.008	0.006	0.005	0.004	0.003
25	0.039	0.030	0.024	0.018	0.014	0.011	0.009	0.007	0.005	0.004	0.003	0.002
26	0.034	0.026	0.020	0.016	0.012	0.009	0.007	0.006	0.004	0.003	0.003	0.002
27	0.030	0.023	0.017	0.013	0.010	0.008	0.006	0.005	0.003	0.003	0.002	0.002
28	0.026	0.020	0.015	0.011	0.009	0.006	0.005	0.004	0.003	0.002	0.002	0.001
29	0.023	0.017	0.013	0.010	0.007	0.005	0.004	0.003	0.002	0.002	0.001	0.001
30	0.020	0.015	0.011	0.008	0.006	0.005	0.003	0.002	0.002	0.001	0.001	0.001

APPENDIX B   Areas for the Standard Normal Distribution

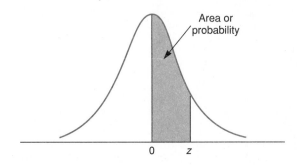

Area or probability

Entries in the table give the area under the curve between the mean and z standard deviations above the mean. For example, for $z = 1.25$ the area under the curve between the mean and z is 0.3944.

z	0.00	0.01	0.02	0.03	0.04	0.05	0.06	0.07	0.08	0.09
0.0	0.0000	0.0040	0.0080	0.0120	0.0160	0.0199	0.0239	0.0279	0.0319	0.0359
0.1	0.0398	0.0438	0.0478	0.0517	0.0557	0.0596	0.0636	0.0675	0.0714	0.0753
0.2	0.0793	0.0832	0.0871	0.0910	0.0948	0.0987	0.1026	0.1064	0.1103	0.1141
0.3	0.1179	0.1217	0.1255	0.1293	0.1331	0.1368	0.1406	0.1443	0.1480	0.1517
0.4	0.1554	0.1591	0.1628	0.1664	0.1700	0.1736	0.1772	0.1808	0.1844	0.1879
0.5	0.1915	0.1950	0.1985	0.2019	0.2054	0.2088	0.2123	0.2157	0.2190	0.2224
0.6	0.2257	0.2291	0.2324	0.2357	0.2389	0.2422	0.2454	0.2486	0.2518	0.2549
0.7	0.2580	0.2612	0.2642	0.2673	0.2704	0.2734	0.2764	0.2794	0.2823	0.2852
0.8	0.2881	0.2910	0.2939	0.2967	0.2995	0.3023	0.3051	0.3078	0.3106	0.3133
0.9	0.3159	0.3186	0.3212	0.3238	0.3264	0.3289	0.3315	0.3340	0.3365	0.3389
1.0	0.3413	0.3438	0.3461	0.3485	0.3508	0.3531	0.3554	0.3577	0.3599	0.3621
1.1	0.3643	0.3665	0.3686	0.3708	0.3729	0.3749	0.3770	0.3790	0.3810	0.3830
1.2	0.3849	0.3869	0.3888	0.3907	0.3925	0.3944	0.3962	0.3980	0.3997	0.4015
1.3	0.4032	0.4049	0.4066	0.4082	0.4099	0.4115	0.4131	0.4147	0.4162	0.4177
1.4	0.4192	0.4207	0.4222	0.4236	0.4251	0.4265	0.4279	0.4292	0.4306	0.4319
1.5	0.4332	0.4345	0.4357	0.4370	0.4382	0.4394	0.4406	0.4418	0.4429	0.4441
1.6	0.4452	0.4463	0.4474	0.4484	0.4495	0.4505	0.4515	0.4525	0.4535	0.4545
1.7	0.4554	0.4564	0.4573	0.4582	0.4591	0.4599	0.4608	0.4616	0.4625	0.4633
1.8	0.4641	0.4649	0.4656	0.4664	0.4671	0.4578	0.4686	0.4693	0.4699	0.4706
1.9	0.4713	0.4719	0.4726	0.4732	0.4738	0.4744	0.4750	0.4756	0.4761	0.4767
2.0	0.4772	0.4778	0.4783	0.4788	0.4793	0.4798	0.4803	0.4808	0.4812	0.4817
2.1	0.4821	0.4826	0.4830	0.4834	0.4838	0.4842	0.4846	0.4850	0.4854	0.4857
2.2	0.4861	0.4864	0.4868	0.4871	0.4875	0.4878	0.4881	0.4884	0.4887	0.4890
2.3	0.4893	0.4896	0.4898	0.4901	0.4904	0.4906	0.4909	0.4911	0.4913	0.4916
2.4	0.4918	0.4920	0.4922	0.4925	0.4927	0.4929	0.4931	0.4932	0.4934	0.4936
2.5	0.4938	0.4940	0.4941	0.4943	0.4945	0.4946	0.4948	0.4949	0.4951	0.4952
2.6	0.4953	0.4955	0.4956	0.4957	0.4959	0.4960	0.4961	0.4962	0.4963	0.4964
2.7	0.4965	0.4966	0.4967	0.4968	0.4969	0.4970	0.4971	0.4972	0.4973	0.4974
2.8	0.4974	0.4975	0.4976	0.4977	0.4977	0.4978	0.4979	0.4979	0.4980	0.4981
2.9	0.4981	0.4982	0.4982	0.4983	0.4984	0.4984	0.4985	0.4985	0.4986	0.4986
3.0	0.4986	0.4987	0.4987	0.4988	0.4988	0.4989	0.4989	0.4989	0.4990	0.4990

APPENDIX C   Random Digits

63271	59986	71744	51102	15141	80714	58683	93108	13554	79945
88547	09896	95436	79115	08303	01041	20030	63754	08459	28364
55957	57243	83865	09911	19761	66535	40102	26646	60147	15702
46276	87453	44790	67122	45573	84358	21625	16999	13385	22782
55363	07449	34835	15290	76616	67191	12777	21861	68689	03263
69393	92785	49902	58447	42048	30378	87618	26933	40640	16281
13186	29431	88190	04588	38733	81290	89541	70290	40113	08243
17726	28652	56836	78351	47327	18518	92222	55201	27340	10493
36520	64465	05550	30157	82242	29520	69753	72602	23756	54935
81628	36100	39254	56835	37636	02421	98063	89641	64953	99337
84649	48968	75215	75498	49539	74240	03466	49292	36401	45525
63291	11618	12613	75055	43915	26488	41116	64531	56827	30825
70502	53225	03655	05915	37140	57051	48393	91322	25653	06543
06426	24771	59935	49801	11082	66762	94477	02494	88215	27191
20711	55609	29430	70165	45406	78484	31639	52009	18873	96927
41990	70538	77191	25860	55204	73417	83920	69468	74972	38712
72452	36618	76298	26678	89334	33938	95567	29380	75906	91807
37042	40318	57099	10528	09925	89773	41335	96244	29002	46453
53766	52875	15987	46962	67342	77592	57651	95508	80033	69828
90585	58955	53122	16025	84299	53310	67380	84249	25348	04332
32001	96293	37203	64516	51530	37069	40261	61374	05815	06714
62606	64324	46354	72157	67248	20135	49804	09226	64419	29457
10078	28073	85389	50324	14500	15562	64165	06125	71353	77669
91561	46145	24177	15294	10061	98124	75732	00815	83452	97355
13091	98112	53959	79607	52244	63303	10413	63839	74762	50289
73864	83014	72457	22682	03033	61714	88173	90835	00634	85169
66668	25467	48894	51043	02365	91726	09365	63167	95264	45643
84745	41042	29493	01836	09044	51926	43630	63470	76508	14194
48068	26805	94595	47907	13357	38412	33318	26098	82782	42851
54310	96175	97594	88616	42035	38093	36745	56702	40644	83514
14877	33095	10924	58013	61439	21882	42059	24177	58739	60170
78295	23179	02771	43464	59061	71411	05697	67194	30495	21157
67524	02865	39593	54278	04237	92441	26602	63835	38032	94770
58268	57219	68124	73455	83236	08710	04284	55005	84171	42596
97158	28672	50685	01181	24262	19427	52106	34308	73685	74246
04230	16831	69085	30802	65559	09205	71829	06489	85650	38707
94879	56606	30401	02602	57658	70091	54986	41394	60437	03195
71446	15232	66715	26385	91518	70566	02888	79941	39684	54315
32886	05644	79316	09819	00813	88407	17461	73925	53037	91904
62048	33711	25290	21526	02223	75947	66466	06232	10913	75336

Reprinted from Page 44 of *A Million Random Digits With 100,000 Normal Deviates,* by the Rand Corporation. New York: The Free Press, 1955. Copyright 1955 by The Rand Corporation. Used by permission.

APPENDIX D Binomial Probabilities

Entries in the table give the probability of x successes in n trials of a binomial experiment, where p is the probability of a success on one trial. For example, which six trials and p = .40, the probability of two successes is .3110.

		p									
n	*x*	.05	.10	.15	.20	.25	.30	.35	.40	.45	.50
1	0	.9500	.9000	.8500	.8000	.7500	.7000	.6500	.6000	.5500	.5000
	1	.0500	.1000	.1500	.2000	.2500	.3000	.3500	.4000	.4500	.5000
2	0	.9025	8100	.7225	.6400	.5625	.4900	.4225	.3600	.3025	.2500
	1	.0950	.1800	.2550	.3200	.3750	.4200	.4550	.4800	.4950	.5000
	2	.0025	.0100	.0225	.0400	.0625	.0900	.1225	.1600	.2025	.2500
3	0	.8574	.7290	.6141	.5120	.4219	.3430	.2746	.2160	.1664	.1250
	1	.1354	.2430	.3251	.3840	.4219	.4410	.4436	.4320	.4084	.3750
	2	.0071	.0270	.0574	.0960	.1406	.1890	.2389	.2880	.3341	.3750
	3	.0001	.0010	.0034	.0080	.0156	.0270	.0429	.0640	.0911	.1250
4	0	.8145	.6561	.5220	.4096	.3164	.2401	.1785	.1296	.0915	.0625
	1	.1715	.2916	.3685	.4096	.4219	.4116	.3845	.3456	.2995	.2500
	2	.0135	.0486	.0975	.1536	.2109	.2646	.3105	.1536	.3675	.3750
	3	.0005	.0036	.0115	.0256	.0469	.0756	.1115	.0256	.2005	.2500
	4	.0000	.0001	.0005	.0016	.0039	.0081	.0150		.0410	.0625
5	0	.7738	.5905	.4437	.3277	.2373	.1681	.1160	.0778	.0503	.0312
	1	.2036	.3280	.3915	.4096	.3955	.3602	.3124	.2592	.2059	.1562
	2	.0214	.0729	.1382	.2048	.2637	.3087	.3364	.3456	.3369	.3125
	3	.0011	.0081	.0244	.0512	0.879	.1323	.1811	.2304	.2757	.3125
	4	.0000	.0004	.0022	.0064	.0146	.0284	.0488	.0768	.1128	.1562
	5	.0000	.0000	.0001	.0003	.0010	.0024	.0053	.0102	.0185	.0312
6	0	.7351	.5314	.3771	.2621	.1780	.1176	.0754	.0467	.0277	.0156
	1	.2321	.3543	.3993	.3932	.3560	.3025	.2437	.1866	.1359	.0938
	2	.0305	.0984	.1762	.2458	.2966	.3241	.3280	.3110	.2780	.2344
	3	.0021	.0146	.0415	.0819	.1318	.1852	.2355	.2765	.3032	.3125
	4	.0001	.0012	.0055	.0154	.0330	.0595	.0951	.1382	.1861	.2344
	5	.0000	.0001	.0004	.0015	.0044	.0102	.0205	0.369	.0609	.0938
	6	.0000	.0000	.0000	.0001	.0002	.0007	.0018	.0041	.0083	.0156
7	0	.6983	.4783	.3206	.2097	.1335	.0824	.0490	.0280	.0152	.0078
	1	.2573	.3720	.3960	.3670	.3115	.2471	.1848	.1306	.0872	.0547
	2	.0406	.1240	.2097	.2753	.3115	.3177	.2985	.2613	.2140	.1641
	3	.0036	.0230	.0617	.1147	.1730	.2269	.2679	.2903	.2918	.2734
	4	.0002	.0026	.0109	.0287	.0577	.0972	.1442	.1935	.2388	.2734
	5	.0000	.0002	.0012	.0043	.0115	.0250	.0466	.0774	.1172	.1641
	6	.0000	.0000	.0001	.0004	.0013	.0036	.0084	.0172	.0320	.0547
	7	.0000	.0000	.0000	.0000	.0001	.0002	.0006	.0016	.0037	.0078
8	0	.6634	.4305	.2725	.1678	.1001	.0576	.0319	.0168	.0084	.0039
	1	.2793	.3826	.3847	.3355	.2670	.1977	.1373	.0896	.0548	.0312
	2	.0515	.1488	.2376	.2936	.3115	.2965	.2587	.2090	.1569	.1094
	3	.0054	.0331	.0839	.1468	.2076	.2541	.2786	.2787	.2568	.2188
	4	.0004	.0046	.0185	.0459	.0865	.1361	.1875	.2322	.2627	.2734
	5	.0000	.0004	.0026	.0092	.0231	.0467	.0808	.1239	.1719	.2188
	6	.0000	.0000	.0002	.0011	.0038	.0100	.0217	.0413	.0703	.1094
	7	.0000	.0000	.0000	.0001	.0004	.0012	.0033	.0079	.0164	.0312
	8	.0000	.0000	.0000	.0000	.0000	.0001	.0002	.0007	.0017	.0039

						p					
n	x	.05	.10	.15	.20	.25	.30	.35	.40	.45	.50
9	0	.6302	.3874	.2316	.1342	.0751	.0404	.0207	.0101	.0046	.0020
	1	.2985	.3874	.3679	.3020	.2253	.1556	.1004	.0605	.0339	.0176
	2	.0629	.1722	.2597	.3020	.3003	.2668	.2162	.1612	.1110	.0703
	3	.0077	.0446	.1069	.1762	.2336	.2668	.2716	.2508	.2119	.1641
	4	.0006	.0074	.0283	.0661	.1168	.1715	.2194	.2508	.2600	.2461
	5	.0000	.0008	.0050	.0165	.0389	.0735	.1181	.1672	.2128	.2461
	6	.0000	.0001	.0006	.0028	.0087	.0210	.0424	.0743	.1160	.1641
	7	.0000	.0000	.0000	.0003	.0012	.0039	.0098	.0212	.0407	.0703
	8	.0000	.0000	.0000	.0000	.0001	.0004	.0013	.0035	.0083	.0176
	9	.0000	.0000	.0000	.0000	.0000	.0000	.0001	.0003	.0008	.0020
10	0	.5987	.3487	.1969	.1074	.0563	.0282	.0135	.0060	.0025	.0010
	1	.3151	.3874	.3474	.2684	.1877	.1211	.0725	.0403	.0207	.0098
	2	.0746	.1937	.2759	.3020	.2816	.2335	.1757	.1209	.0763	.0439
	3	.0105	.0574	.1298	.2013	.2503	.2668	.2522	.2150	.1665	.1172
	4	.0010	.0112	.0401	.0881	.1460	.2001	.2377	.2508	.2384	.2051
	5	.0001	.0015	.0085	.0264	.0584	.1029	.1536	.2007	.2340	.2461
	6	.0000	.0001	.0012	.0055	.0162	.0368	.0689	.1115	.1596	.2051
	7	.0000	.0000	.0001	.0008	.0031	.0090	.0212	.0425	.0746	.1172
	8	.0000	.0000	.0000	.0001	.0004	.0014	.0043	.0106	.0229	.0439
	9	.0000	.0000	.0000	.0000	.0000	.0001	.0005	.0016	.0042	.0098
	10	.0000	.0000	.0000	.0000	.0000	.0000	.0000	.0001	.0003	.0010
11	0	.5688	.3138	.1673	.0859	.0422	.0198	.0088	.0036	.0014	.0005
	1	.3293	.3835	.3248	.2362	.1549	.0932	.0518	.0266	.0125	.0054
	2	.0867	.2131	.2866	.2953	.2581	.1998	.1395	.0887	.0513	.0269
	3	.0137	.0710	.1517	.2215	.2581	.2568	.2254	.1774	.1259	.0806
	4	.0014	.0158	.0536	.1107	.1721	.2201	.2428	.2365	.2060	.1611
	5	.0001	.0025	.0132	.0388	.0803	.1321	.1830	.2207	.2360	.2256
	6	.0000	.0003	.0023	.0097	.0268	.0566	.0985	.1471	.1931	.2256
	7	.0000	.0000	.0003	.0017	.0064	.0173	.0379	.0701	.1128	.1611
	8	.0000	.0000	.0000	.0002	.0011	.0037	.0102	.0234	.0462	.0806
	9	.0000	.0000	.0000	.0000	.0001	.0005	.0018	.0052	.0126	.0269
	10	.0000	.0000	.0000	.0000	.0000	.0000	.0002	.0007	.0021	.0054
	11	.0000	.0000	.0000	.0000	.0000	.0000	.0000	.0000	.0002	.0005
12	0	.5404	.2824	.1422	.0687	.0317	.0138	.0057	.0022	.0008	.0002
	1	.3413	.3766	.3012	.2062	.1267	.0712	.0368	.0174	.0075	.0029
	2	.0988	.2301	.2924	.2835	.2323	.1678	.1088	.0639	.0339	.0161
	3	.0173	.0853	.1720	.2362	.2581	.2397	.1954	.1419	.0923	.0537
	4	.0021	.0213	.0683	.1329	.1936	.2311	.2367	.2128	.1700	.1208
	5	.0002	.0038	.0193	.0532	.1032	.1585	.2039	.2270	.2225	.1934
	6	.0000	.0005	.0040	.0155	.0401	.0792	.1281	.1766	.2124	.2256
	7	.0000	.0000	.0006	.0033	.0115	.0291	.0591	.1009	.1489	.1934
	8	.0000	.0000	.0001	.0005	.0024	.0078	.0199	.0420	.0762	.1208
	9	.0000	.0000	.0000	.0001	.0004	.0015	.0048	.0125	.0277	.0537
	10	.0000	.0000	.0000	.0000	.0000	.0002	.0008	.0025	.0068	.0161
	11	.0000	.0000	.0000	.0000	.0000	.0000	.0001	.0003	.0010	.0029
	12	.0000	.0000	.0000	.0000	.0000	.0000	.0000	.0000	.0001	.0002
13	0	.5133	.2542	.1209	.0550	.0238	.0097	.0037	.0013	.0004	.0001
	1	.3512	.3672	.2774	.1787	.1029	.0540	.0259	.0113	.0045	.0016
	2	.1109	.2448	.2937	.2680	.2059	.1388	.0836	.0453	.0220	.0095
	3	.0214	.0997	.1900	.2457	.2517	.2181	.1651	.1107	.0660	.0349
	4	.0028	.0277	.0838	.1535	.2097	.2337	.2222	.1845	.1350	.0873
	5	.0003	.0055	.0266	.0691	.1258	.1803	.2154	.2214	.1989	.1571
	6	.0000	.0008	.0063	.0230	.0559	.1030	.1546	.1968	.2169	.2095
	7	.0000	.0001	.0011	.0058	.0186	.0442	.0833	.1312	.1775	.2095
	8	.0000	.0000	.0001	.0011	.0047	.0142	.0336	.0656	.1089	.1571
	9	.0000	.0000	.0000	.0001	.0009	.0034	.0101	.0243	.0495	.0873

		p									
n	x	.05	.10	.15	.20	.25	.30	.35	.40	.45	.50
13	10	.0000	.0000	.0000	.0000	.0001	.0006	.0022	.0065	.0162	.0349
	11	.0000	.0000	.0000	.0000	.0000	.0001	.0003	.0012	.0036	.0095
	12	.0000	.0000	.0000	.0000	.0000	.0000	.0000	.0001	.0005	.0016
	13	.0000	.0000	.0000	.0000	.0000	.0000	.0000	.0000	.0000	.0001
14	0	.4877	.2288	.1028	.0440	.0178	.0068	.0024	.0008	.0002	.0001
	1	.3593	.3559	.2539	.1539	.0832	.0407	.0181	.0073	.0027	.0009
	2	.1229	.2570	.2912	.2501	.1802	.1134	.0634	.0317	.0141	.0056
	3	.0259	.1142	.2056	.2501	.2402	.1943	.1366	.0845	.0462	.0222
	4	.0037	.0349	.0998	.1720	.2202	.2290	.2022	.1549	.1040	.0611
	5	.0004	.0078	.0352	.0860	.1468	.1963	.2178	.2066	.1701	.1222
	6	.0000	.0013	.0093	.0322	.0734	.1262	.1759	.2066	.2088	.1833
	7	.0000	.0002	.0019	.0092	.0280	.0618	.1082	.1574	.1952	.2095
	8	.0000	.0000	.0003	.0020	.0082	.0232	.0510	.0918	.1398	.1833
	9	.0000	.0000	.0000	.0003	.0018	.0066	.0183	.0408	.0762	.1222
	10	.0000	.0000	.0000	.0000	.0003	.0014	.0049	.0136	.0312	.0611
	11	.0000	.0000	.0000	.0000	.0000	.0002	.0010	.0033	.0093	.0222
	12	.0000	.0000	.0000	.0000	.0000	.0000	.0001	.0005	.0019	.0056
	13	.0000	.0000	.0000	.0000	.0000	.0000	.0000	.0001	.0002	.0009
	14	.0000	.0000	.0000	.0000	.0000	.0000	.0000	.0000	.0000	.0001
15	0	.4633	.2059	.0874	.0352	.0134	.0047	.0016	.0005	.0001	.0000
	1	.3658	.3432	.2312	.1319	.0668	.0305	.0126	.0047	.0016	.0005
	2	.1348	.2669	.2856	.2309	.1559	.0916	.0476	.0219	.0090	.0032
	3	.0307	.1285	.2184	.2501	.2252	.1700	.1110	.0634	.0318	.0139
	4	.0049	.0428	.1156	.1876	.2252	.2186	.1792	.1268	.0780	.0417
	5	.0006	.0105	.0449	.1032	.1651	.2061	.2123	.1859	.1404	.0916
	6	.0000	.0019	.0132	.0430	.0917	.1472	.1906	.2066	.1914	.1527
	7	.0000	.0003	.0030	.0138	.0393	.0811	.1319	.1771	.2013	.1964
	8	.0000	.0000	.0005	.0035	.0131	.0348	.0710	.1181	.1647	.1964
	9	.0000	.0000	.0001	.0007	.0034	.0116	.0298	.0612	.1048	.1527
	10	.0000	.0000	.0000	.0001	.0007	.0030	.0096	.0245	.0515	.0916
	11	.0000	.0000	.0000	.0000	.0001	.0006	.0024	.0074	.0191	.0417
	12	.0000	.0000	.0000	.0000	.0000	.0001	.0004	.0016	.0052	.0139
	13	.0000	.0000	.0000	.0000	.0000	.0000	.0001	.0003	.0010	.0032
	14	.0000	.0000	.0000	.0000	.0000	.0000	.0000	.0000	.0001	.0005
	15	.0000	.0000	.0000	.0000	.0000	.0000	.0000	.0000	.0000	.0000
16	0	.4401	.1853	.0743	.0281	.0100	.0033	.0010	.0003	.0001	.0000
	1	.3706	.3294	.2097	.1126	.0535	.0228	.0087	.0030	.0009	.0002
	2	.1463	.2745	.2775	.2111	.1336	.0732	.0353	.0150	.0056	.0018
	3	.0359	.1423	.2285	.2463	.2079	.1465	.0888	.0468	.0215	.0085
	4	.0061	.0514	.1311	.2001	.2252	.2040	.1553	.1014	.0572	.0278
	5	.0008	.0137	.0555	.1201	.1802	.2099	.2008	.1623	.1123	.0667
	6	.0001	.0028	.0180	.0550	.1101	.1649	.1982	.1983	.1684	.1222
	7	.0000	.0004	.0045	.0197	.0524	.1010	.1524	.1889	.1969	.1746
	8	.0000	.0001	.0009	.0055	.0197	.0487	.0923	.1417	.1812	.1964
	9	.0000	.0000	.0001	.0012	.0058	.0185	.0442	.0840	.1318	.1746
	10	.0000	.0000	.0000	.0002	.0014	.0056	.0167	.0392	.0755	.1222
	11	.0000	.0000	.0000	.0000	.0002	.0013	.0049	.0142	.0337	.0667
	12	.0000	.0000	.0000	.0000	.0000	.0002	.0011	.0040	.0115	.0278
	13	.0000	.0000	.0000	.0000	.0000	.0000	.0002	.0008	.0029	.0085
	14	.0000	.0000	.0000	.0000	.0000	.0000	.0000	.0001	.0005	.0018
	15	.0000	.0000	.0000	.0000	.0000	.0000	.0000	.0000	.0001	.0002
	16	.0000	.0000	.0000	.0000	.0000	.0000	.0000	.0000	.0000	.0000
17	0	.4181	.1668	.0631	.0225	.0075	.0023	.0007	.0002	.0000	.0000
	1	.3741	.3150	.1893	.0957	.0426	.0169	.0060	.0019	.0005	.0001
	2	.1575	.2800	.2673	.1914	.1136	.0581	.0260	.0102	.0035	.0010
	3	.0415	.1556	.2359	.2393	.1893	.1245	.0701	.0341	.0144	.0052
	4	.0076	.0605	.1457	.2093	.2209	.1868	.1320	.0796	.0411	.0182

n	x					p					
		.05	.10	.15	.20	.25	.30	.35	.40	.45	.50
17	5	.0010	.0175	.0668	.1361	.1914	.2081	.1849	.1379	.0875	.0472
	6	.0001	.0039	.0236	.0680	.1276	.1784	.1991	.1839	.1432	.0944
	7	.0000	.0007	.0065	.0267	.0668	.1201	.1685	.1927	.1841	.1484
	8	.0000	.0001	.0014	.0084	.0279	.0644	.1134	.1606	.1883	.1855
	9	.0000	.0000	.0003	.0021	.0093	.0276	.0611	.1070	.1540	.1855
	10	.0000	.0000	.0000	.0004	.0025	.0095	.0263	.0571	.1008	.1484
	11	.0000	.0000	.0000	.0001	.0005	.0026	.0090	.0242	.0525	.0944
	12	.0000	.0000	.0000	.0000	.0001	.0006	.0024	.0081	.0215	.0472
	13	.0000	.0000	.0000	.0000	.0000	.0001	.0005	.0021	.0068	.0182
	14	.0000	.0000	.0000	.0000	.0000	.0000	.0001	.0004	.0016	.0052
	15	.0000	.0000	.0000	.0000	.0000	.0000	.0000	.0001	.0003	.0010
	16	.0000	.0000	.0000	.0000	.0000	.0000	.0000	.0000	.0000	.0001
	17	.0000	.0000	.0000	.0000	.0000	.0000	.0000	.0000	.0000	.0000
18	0	.3972	.1501	.0536	.0180	.0056	.0016	.0004	.0001	.0000	.0000
	1	.3763	.3002	.1704	.0811	.0338	.0126	.0042	.0012	.0003	.0001
	2	.1683	.2835	.2556	.1723	.0958	.0458	.0190	.0069	.0022	.0006
	3	.0473	.1680	.2406	.2297	.1704	.1046	.0547	.0246	.0095	.0031
	4	.0093	.0700	.1592	.2153	.2130	.1681	.1104	.0614	.0291	.0117
	5	.0014	.0218	.0787	.1507	.1988	.2017	.1664	.1146	.0666	.0327
	6	.0002	.0052	.0301	.0816	.1436	.1873	.1941	.1655	.1181	.0708
	7	.0000	.0010	.0091	.0350	.0820	.1376	.1792	.1892	.1657	.1214
	8	.0000	.0002	.0022	.0120	.0376	.0811	.1327	.1734	.1864	.1669
	9	.0000	.0000	.0004	.0033	.0139	.0386	.0794	.1284	.1694	.1855
	10	.0000	.0000	.0001	.0008	.0042	.0149	.0385	.0771	.1248	.1669
	11	.0000	.0000	.0000	.0001	.0010	.0046	.0151	.0374	.0742	.1214
	12	.0000	.0000	.0000	.0000	.0002	.0012	.0047	.0145	.0354	.0708
	13	.0000	.0000	.0000	.0000	.0000	.0002	.0012	.0045	.0134	.0327
	14	.0000	.0000	.0000	.0000	.0000	.0000	.0002	.0011	.0039	.0117
	15	.0000	.0000	.0000	.0000	.0000	.0000	.0000	.0002	.0009	.0031
	16	.0000	.0000	.0000	.0000	.0000	.0000	.0000	.0000	.0001	.0006
	17	.0000	.0000	.0000	.0000	.0000	.0000	.0000	.0000	.0000	.0001
	18	.0000	.0000	.0000	.0000	.0000	.0000	.0000	.0000	.0000	.0000
19	0	.3774	.1351	.0456	.0144	.0042	.0011	.0003	.0001	.0002	.0000
	1	.3774	.2852	.1529	.0685	.0268	.0093	.0029	.0008	.0002	.0000
	2	.1787	.2852	.2428	.1540	.0803	.0358	.0138	.0046	.0013	.0003
	3	.0533	.1796	.2428	.2182	.1517	.0869	.0422	.0175	.0062	.0018
	4	.0112	.0798	.1714	.2182	.2023	.1491	.0909	.0467	.0203	.0074
	5	.0018	.0266	.0907	.1636	.2023	.1916	.1468	.0933	.0497	.0222
	6	.0002	.0069	.0374	.0955	.1574	.1916	.1844	.1451	.0949	.0518
	7	.0000	.0014	.0122	.0443	.0974	.1525	.1844	.1797	.1443	.0961
	8	.0000	.0002	.0032	.0166	.0487	.0981	.1489	.1797	.1771	.1442
	9	.0000	.0000	.0007	.0051	.0198	.0514	.0980	.1464	.1771	.1762
	10	.0000	.0000	.0001	.0013	.0066	.0220	.0528	.0976	.1449	.1762
	11	.0000	.0000	.0000	.0003	.0018	.0077	.0233	.0532	.0970	.1442
	12	.0000	.0000	.0000	.0000	.0004	.0022	.0083	.0237	.0529	.0961
	13	.0000	.0000	.0000	.0000	.0001	.0005	.0024	.0085	.0233	.0518
	14	.0000	.0000	.0000	.0000	.0000	.0001	.0006	.0024	.0082	.0222
19	15	.0000	.0000	.0000	.0000	.0000	.0000	.0001	.0005	.0022	.0074
	16	.0000	.0000	.0000	.0000	.0000	.0000	.0000	.0001	.0005	.0018
	17	.0000	.0000	.0000	.0000	.0000	.0000	.0000	.0000	.0001	.0003
	18	.0000	.0000	.0000	.0000	.0000	.0000	.0000	.0000	.0000	.0000
	19	.0000	.0000	.0000	.0000	.0000	.0000	.0000	.0000	.0000	.0000
20	0	.3585	.1216	.0388	.0115	.0032	.0008	.0002	.0000	.0000	.0000
	1	.3774	.2702	.1368	.0576	.0211	.0068	.0020	.0005	.0001	.0000
	2	.1887	.2852	.2293	.1369	.0669	.0278	.0100	.0031	.0008	.0002
	3	.0596	.1901	.2428	.2054	.1339	.0716	.0323	.0123	.0040	.0011
	4	.0133	.0898	.1821	.2182	.1897	.1304	.0738	.0350	.0139	.0046

n	x	.05	.10	.15	.20	.25	.30	.35	.40	.45	.50
20	5	.0022	.0319	.1028	.1746	.2023	.1789	.1272	.0746	.0365	.0148
	6	.0003	.0089	.0454	.1091	.1686	.1916	.1712	.1244	.0746	.0370
	7	.0000	.0020	.0160	.0545	.1124	.1643	.1844	.1659	.1221	.0739
	8	.0000	.0004	.0046	.0222	.0609	.1144	.1614	.1797	.1623	.1201
	9	.0000	.0001	.0011	.0074	.0271	.0654	.1158	.1597	.1771	.1602
	10	.0000	.0000	.0002	.0020	.0099	.0308	.0686	.1171	.1593	.1762
	11	.0000	.0000	.0000	.0005	.0030	.0120	.0336	.0710	.1185	.1602
	12	.0000	.0000	.0000	.0001	.0008	.0039	.0136	.0355	.0727	.1201
	13	.0000	.0000	.0000	.0000	.0002	.0010	.0045	.0146	.0366	.0739
	14	.0000	.0000	.0000	.0000	.0000	.0002	.0012	.0049	.0150	.0370
	15	.0000	.0000	.0000	.0000	.0000	.0000	.0003	.0013	.0049	.0148
	16	.0000	.0000	.0000	.0000	.0000	.0000	.0000	.0003	.0013	.0046
	17	.0000	.0000	.0000	.0000	.0000	.0000	.0000	.0000	.0002	.0011
	18	.0000	.0000	.0000	.0000	.0000	.0000	.0000	.0000	.0000	.0002
	19	.0000	.0000	.0000	.0000	.0000	.0000	.0000	.0000	.0000	.0000
	20	.0000	.0000	.0000	.0000	.0000	.0000	.0000	.0000	.0000	.0000

Reprinted from *Handbook of Probability and Statistics with Tables* by Burington and May, Second Edition, McGraw-Hill Book Co., Inc., 1970, by permission of the author's trustee.

GLOSSARY

ABC classification A grouping of inventoried items into three classes—those accounting for a large dollar value but relatively small percentage of items, those accounting for a small dollar value but a large percentage of items, and those in between.

Acceptable quality level (AQL) The maximum percent nonconforming considered acceptable.

Activities Specific jobs or tasks that are components of a project.

Aggregate production planning The establishment of aggregate production and inventory levels over a medium range time horizon.

Analog model While often physical in form, a model that does not have a physical appearance similar to the real object or situation it represents.

Anthropometric data Data regarding physical characteristics of human beings.

Anticipation inventory Inventory built-up during an off-season in order to meet peak demand.

Applied research Research oriented toward commercial application.

Appraisal costs Quality costs expended on maintaining quality levels through measurement and analysis of data in order to detect and correct problems.

Arcs Same as branches.

Assembly chart A graphical representation of the order of assembly of a product.

Assembly drawing An exploded view of the individual components of a product and their relationship to one another.

Assignable causes Causes of poor quality because of problems with materials, equipment, or operators that can be corrected.

Attribute measurement A measurement that assumes only one of two possible values.

Backward pass A calculation procedure for PERT/CPM that moves backward through the network to determine the latest start and latest finish times for each activity.

Balance delay The amount of idle time on an assembly line.

Beta distribution A probability distribution often used to describe activity times.

Blanket contract A purchase contract for a large quantity of material with no specified delivery dates. Instead, release orders are sent out as needed.

Branches The lines connecting the nodes which represent activities in the network.

Break-even analysis The economic analysis that uses total cost and total revenue to determine the volume (break-even point) that must be sold in order to recover all costs. Sales volumes above the break-even point will provide a profit for the firm.

Break-even point Point at which total cost equals total revenue.

Bucket A term denoting a time period used in the master schedule.

Business logistics The management of materials and goods from the point of origin to the point of consumption.

Capacity The highest reasonable output rate which can be achieved with the current product specifications, product mix, work force, plant, and equipment.

Capacity requirements planning (CRP) A system for determining if a planned production schedule can be accomplished with available capacity and, if not, making adjustments as necessary.

Causal-forecasting methods Forecasting methods that relate a time series value to other variables that are believed to explain or cause its behavior.

Cell A section of a transportation tableau corresponding to a route between a specific origin and a specific destination.

Center-of-gravity method A quantitative approach to locating a facility that minimizes the distance or cost of transportation weighted by the volume of goods moved.

COFAD Computerized facilities design; a computer-based system for facility layout and material handling.

Common causes Variation in output due purely to chance.

Computer-aided design (CAD) The use of a computer to interact with a designer in developing and testing product ideas without actually building prototypes.

Computer-aided manufacturing (CAM) Computer control of the manufacturing process.

Computer-integrated manufacturing system (CIMS) The union of hardware, software, database management, and communications to plan and control production activities.

Consolidation Bringing together the orders of several customers at a warehouse rather than shipping direct from several factories.

Constant demand rate An assumption of many inventory decision models, which states that the same number of units are taken from inventory in each period of time.

Constraint An equation or inequality that rules out certain combinations of variables as feasible solutions.

Constraint function The left-hand side of a constraint relationship (that is the portion of the constraint containing the variables).

Consumer's risk The probability of accepting a bad lot.

Continuous-review system An inventory system in which the inventory level is continuously monitored and, when the level drops below the reorder point, an order is placed.

Control chart A graphical means of depicting sample characteristics over time, used for process control. Control charts are usually constructed for fraction defective, means, and ranges.

Controlling The process of monitoring and evaluating performance and correcting any problems as necessary.

Conversion process A process that changes the inputs of a production system into outputs or products.

Corporate strategy Definition of the businesses in which a corporation will participate and plans for the acquisition and allocation of resources among these businesses.

Cost of capital The cost a firm incurs, usually as interest payments on borrowed funds or dividend payments on stocks, in order to obtain capital for investment. The cost of capital, which may be stated as an annual percentage rate, is part of the holding cost associated with maintaining inventory levels.

CRAFT Computerized relative allocation of facilities technique; a computer-based system for facility layout.

Crashing The process of reducing an activity time by adding resources and hence usually cost.

Critical path The longest sequence of activities or path in a project management (PERT/CPM) network. The time it takes to traverse this path is the estimated project duration.

Cycle counting The process of taking a physical count of each item once during its replenishment cycle.

Cycle time (1) The length of time between the placing of two consecutive orders. (2) The time required to produce one item on an assembly line.

Cyclical component The component of the time series model that results in periodic above-trend and below-trend behavior of the time series lasting more than one year.

Delphi method A subjective forecasting technique for arriving at group consensus in an anonymous fashion.

Deseasonalized time series A time series that has had the effect of season removed by dividing each original time series observation by the corresponding seasonal factor.

Development Translating research ideas into actual products.

Directing The process of turning plans into realities by assigning specific responsibilities to employees.

Dispatching The assignment of priorities and selection of jobs for processing.

Due date A promised delivery date.

Dummy activity A fictitious activity with zero activity time used to represent precedence or used whenever two or more activities have the same starting and ending nodes.

Dummy destination A destination added to make total supply equal to total demand in a transportation problem. The demand assigned to the dummy destination is the excess of the actual supply over the actual demand.

Dummy origin An origin added to make total supply equal to total demand in a transportation problem. The supply assigned to the dummy origin is the excess of the actual demand over the actual supply.

Earliest finish time The earliest time at which an activity may be completed.

Earliest start time The earliest time at which an activity may begin.

Economic analysis Using costs, selling price and demand figures determine the profitability and return on investment of a new product or service.

Economic order quantity (EOQ) The order quantity that minimizes the total inventory costs in the most fundamental inventory decision model.

Efficiency The fraction of time that a machine or worker operates.

Ergonomics (human-factors engineering) A field of study concerned with the physical capabilities of human beings in the design of tools, instruments, and workplaces.

Event An event occurs when all the activities leading into a node have been completed.

Expected activity time The average activity time.

Expediting Rescheduling production in order to process certain orders faster than planned.

Exponential probability distribution A probability distribution used to describe the pattern or service times for some waiting lines.

Exponential smoothing A forecasting technique that uses a weighted average of past time series values in order to arrive at smoothed time series values which can be used as forecasts.

External failure costs Quality costs that occur after poor-quality products or services reach the customer.

Fabrication The process of modifying the physical characteristics of materials.

Failure rate Number of failures per unit time.

Feasible solution A solution that satisfies all the constraints.

Feedback The process of monitoring the outputs of a production system and using this information for control and corrective purposes.

Final assembly schedule (FAS) A statement of the final products that are to be assembled from MPS items.

Fixed-position layout A layout in which the construction of a large product is accomplished in one place.

Fixed-time simulation model A simulation approach that increments time in fixed intervals.

Flexible manufacturing system (FMS) Two or more computer-controlled machines linked by handling devices.

Flow-blocking delay Delay incurred when a production stage completes a unit but cannot release it to the next stage.

Flow-process chart A description of the sequence of operations in a production process. These generally are operation, inspection, movement, storage, and delay.

Flowshop A job shop in which all jobs have the same routing.

Flowtime The time a particular job spends in the shop.

Fluctuation inventory Inventory maintained in order to reduce the number of stockouts resulting from fluctuations in demand or lead time.

Forecast An estimate of future demand.

Forecast error The difference between a time series value and its corresponding forecast.

Forward pass A calculation procedure for PERT/CPM that moves forward through the network to determine the early start and early finish times for each activity.

Gantt chart A graphical representation of a schedule used to plan and monitor progress.

Goodwill cost A cost associated with a backorder, a lost sale, or any form of stockout or unsatisfied demand. This cost may be used to reflect the loss of future profits due to the fact a customer experienced an unsatisfied demand.

Group layout A layout in which machine groups are arranged to process families of parts with similar characteristics.

Group technology A concept for identifying and classifying part families so that efficient mass-production-type layouts can be designed for items usually manufactured by a process layout.

Hard technology Technology involving the application of computers, sensors, robots, and other mechanical and electronic aids.

Heuristic A procedure for arriving at a solution to a problem that is not guaranteed to give the optimal solution, but usually a very good one.

Hierarchical planning and decision making A structure for classifying plans and decisions by the organizational level at which they are made.

Human factors The biomedical, psychosocial, training, and performance considerations associated with a product.

Iconic model A physical replica or representation of a real object.

Immediate predecessors The activities that must immediately precede given activity.

Internal failure costs Quality costs that result from unsatisfactory quality that is found prior to the delivery of a product or service to the customer.

Inventory Any idle resource that is waiting to be used.

Inventory-holding or inventory-carrying costs All costs associated with maintaining an inventory investment: cost of the capital investment in the inventory, insurance, taxes, warehouse overhead, and so on. This cost may be stated as a percentage of the inventory investment or a cost per unit.

Inventory position The amount of inventory in stock plus any amount on order but not yet received minus backorders.

Irregular component The component of the time-series model that reflects the random variation of the actual time series values beyond what can be explained by the trend, cyclical, and seasonal components.

Job The set of tasks that an individual performs.

Job design The determination of specific job tasks and responsibilities, the work environment, and work methods.

Just-in-time (JIT) An approach to material management and control designed to produce or deliver parts and materials when required in production.

Kanban A Japanese word for card. Kanban refers to an information system for implementing JIT.

Lack-of-work delay Delay incurred when a production stage completes a unit and no units are waiting to be processed.

Latest finish time The latest time at which an activity must be completed without holding up the complete project.

Latest start time The latest time at which an activity must begin without holding up the complete project.

Lead time The time between the placing of an order and its receipt in the inventory system.

Lead-time demand The number of units demanded during the lead-time period.

Lead-time demand distribution In probabilistic inventory models, this is the distribution of demand that occurs during the lead-time period.

Learning curve A curve that describes the relationship between the production time per unit and the number of units produced.

Life-cycle curve A graph of sales volume over time for a product.

Linear equations or functions Mathematical expressions in which the variables appear in separate terms and are raised to the first power.

Linear program A mathematical model with a linear objective function, a set of linear constraints, and nonnegative variables.

Lot-size inventory Inventory purchased or manufactured in lots in order to take advantage of economies of scale.

Lot tolerance percent defective (LTPD) The percent defective (nonconforming) associated with a poor quality lot.

Makespan The time required to process a set of jobs.

Management science/operations research (MS/OR) The application of scientific methodology to managerial decision making.

Manufacturing resource planning A comprehensive system that coordinates MRP with shop floor control, inventory, and other aspects of material management.

Manufacturing strategy (1) A term used to denote the operation's strategy in a manufacturing organization. (2) The set of goals and policies that guide manufacturing decisions.

Master production schedule (MPS) A time-phased statement of how many individual items are to be produced. The MPS is obtained by disaggregating the aggregate production plan.

Material management The area of P/OM concerned with the acquisition, storage, handling, and movement of materials and finished goods from procurement to distribution to customers.

Material Requirements Planning (MRP) A computerized data processing system whose function is to schedule production and to control the level of inventory for components with dependent demand.

Mathematical model (1) A representation of a problem where the objective and all constraint conditions are described by mathematical expressions. (2) Mathematical symbols and expressions used to represent a real situation.

Mean absolute deviation (MAD) A measure of forecast accuracy. MAD is the average of the sum of the absolute value of the forecast errors.

Mean arrival rate   The expected number of customers or units arriving or entering the system in a given period of time.

Mean service rate   The expected number of customers or units that can be serviced by one server in a given period of time.

Mean squared error (MSE)   One approach to measuring the accuracy of a forecasting model. This measure is the average of the sum of the squared differences between the forecast values and the actual time series values.

Micro Kanban   A combination of Kanban where a microcomputer system generates production and move kanbans within the larger MRP structure.

Minimum-cost method   A procedure used to find an initial feasible solution to a transportation problem.

Model   A representation of a real object or situation.

Modified distribution (MODI) method   A procedure for determining the per unit cost change associated with shipping over an unused route in the special-purpose solution procedure for a transportation problem.

Modular design   The design of components that can be assembled in a variety of ways to meet individual consumer needs.

Monte Carlo simulations   Simulations that use a random-number procedure to create values for the probabilistics components.

Most probable time   Time estimate for the most likely activity.

Motion study   The analysis of a manual task in order to improve productivity.

Moving averages   A method of forecasting or smoothing a time series by averaging each successive group of data points. The moving averages method can be used to identify the combined trend/cyclical component of the time series.

MTM (methods-time measurement)   A system of predetermined motion-time data used to develop standards for highly repetitive tasks.

Multifactor productivity   The ratio of total output to a subset of inputs.

Multiple-activity chart   A graphical representation of simultaneous activities of machines and/or people.

Multiple-channel waiting line   A waiting line with two or more parallel identical servers.

Net change approach   A method in which MRP outputs are updated only for components that have changes.

Network   A graphical description of a problem or situation consisting of numbered circles (nodes) interconnected by a series of lines (branches or arcs).

Nodes   The intersection or junction points of a network.

Nonnegativity constraints   A set of constraints that requires all variables to be nonnegative.

Objective function   All linear programs have a linear objective function that is either to be maximized or minimized. In most linear programming problems the objective function will be used to measure the profit or cost of a particular solution.

Operating characteristics (OC) curve   A plot of the probability of acceptance of a lot as a function of the percent of nonconforming items. OC curves are unique for a sampling plan.

Operational plans and decisions   Short-range plans and decisions aimed at directing and controlling productive operations, conducted at the lower levels of an organization.

Operation chart   A chart used to describe simultaneous motions of hands when performing a task.

Operations   The set of all activities that are associated with the production of goods and services.

Operations strategy   Sets parameters for how the firm's resources will be converted into goods and services that meet the design specifications.

OPT (optimized production technology)   A planning and scheduling tool based on a set of rules for scheduling bottleneck operations in a product network.

Optimal solution   A feasible solution that maximizes or minimizes the value of the objective function.

Optimistic time   Time estimate based on the assumption that the activity will progress in an ideal manner.

Ordering cost   The fixed cost (salaries, paper, transportation, and so on) associated with placing an order for an item.

Organizing   The process of bringing together all the resources necessary to accomplish a task.

Packaging and shipping   The departments responsible for preparing material for shipment and loading it onto transport vehicles.

Pallet   A portable platform, usually made of wood, used for stacking and moving materials.

Partial factor productivity   The ratio of total output to a single input.

Parts list A list of part numbers, names, specifications, and other information used in manufacturing.

Periodic-review system An inventory system in which the inventory level is reviewed at fixed time intervals. If the inventory level is below the reorder point at time of review, then an order is placed for enough stock to raise the inventory position to a given level.

PERT/Cost A technique designed to assist in the planning, scheduling, and controlling of project costs.

Pessimistic time Time estimate based on the assumption that the most unfavorable conditions will occur.

Pipeline inventory Inventory in transit.

Planning The process of establishing what guidelines and actions should be pursued and when they should be completed in order to meet the goals of the organization.

Poisson probability distribution A probability distribution used to describe the random arrival pattern for some waiting lines.

Prevention costs Quality costs expended in an effort to keep nonconforming products or services from occurring and reaching the customer.

Process capability The range over which the natural variation of a process occurs.

Process layout A layout in which machines or activities are arranged by function.

Process technology The methods and equipment used to manufacture a product or deliver a service.

Procurement The acquisition of goods and services, including purchasing, stores, traffic, receiving, and inspection.

Producer's risk The probability of rejecting a good quality lot.

Product-development process Idea generation, initial screening, initial design and development, economic analysis, prototype testing, and final-product and process design.

Product layout A layout in which equipment is arranged based on the sequence of operations performed on a product or group of products.

Production The process of converting, or transforming, resources into goods and services.

Production line A fixed sequence of production stages.

Production/operations management (P/OM) The management of the operations involved in producing goods and services and of the interface with supporting functions in the organization.

Production system The collection of inputs, conversion/creation processes, outputs, feedback mechanisms, and managers involved in production.

Productivity Measures to what extent the resources of an organization are being used effectively in transforming inputs to outputs; in other words, productivity is the ratio of output of a production system to the input.

Productivity index The ratio of a productivity measure in some time period to the base period.

Productivity indicator A ratio such as the number of employees to the number of customers served; these types of ratios are often used to measure progress and achievement in service organizations where no tangible goods are produced.

Product-process matrix A framework for analyzing the relationship between process technology and product structure.

Pseudorandom numbers Computer-generated numbers developed from mathematical expressions that have the properties of random numbers.

Purchase requisition A document generated by production or inventory control authorizing the purchase of material.

Purchasing The function of acquiring raw materials and supplies at low cost and to meet the needs of production.

Pure research Research performed with the objective of developing new knowledge.

Quality The totality of features and characteristics of a product or service that bears on its ability to satisfy given needs.

Quality assurance Refers to the entire system of policies, procedures, and guidelines established by an organization in order to achieve and maintain quality.

Quality circle A group of workers who work closely together to identify and solve problems related to quality and productivity.

Quality control Involves making a series of planned measurements in order to determine if quality standards are being met.

Quality-cost index Computed by dividing a cost over a current time period by a base-period value.

Quality costs Any costs that would not occur if perfect quality could be achieved.

Quality engineering The concept of designing quality products and processes and predicting potential problems prior to production.

Quantity discounts Discounts or lower unit costs offered by the manufacturer when a customer purchases larger quantities of the product.

Queue A waiting line.

Queuing theory The operations research term for the study of waiting lines.

Receiving The function of controlling and accepting inbound shipments of materials.

Regeneration approach A method in which MRP outputs are updated on a periodic basis for all components.

Reliability (1) The probability that a process or system will perform satisfactorily over a specified period of time. (2) The probability that a product or process will perform satisfactorily over a period of time under specified operating conditions.

Reorder point The inventory level at which a new order should be placed.

Resource leveling The process of developing a schedule in which the amount of resources required is relatively constant over time.

Resource-requirements planning The process of determining the types and amounts of resources that are required to implement an organization's strategic plan.

Robot A programmable machine designed to handle materials or tools in the performance of a variety of tasks.

Rough-cut capacity planning Analysis of the master production schedule to determine its feasibility with respect to capacity limitations.

Route sheet A document that provides complete information for manufacturing an item. This usually includes part number, operations required, and machines to be used.

Runout time The ratio of current inventory level to the demand rate of an item.

Safety stock Another term for fluctuation inventory.

Sampling plan The specification of a sample size and an acceptance number when sampling from a lot.

Scoring model A procedure for quantitatively evaluating several different criteria by assigning numerical values to attributes of the criteria.

Seasonal component The component of the time series model that shows a periodic pattern over one year or less.

Sequencing The determination of the order in which a facility is to process a set of jobs.

Service level The probability of no stockouts during the lead time.

Simulation A technique used to describe the behavior of a real-world system over time. Most often this technique employs a computer program to perform the simulation computations.

Simulator The computer program written to perform the simulation calculations.

Single-channel waiting line A waiting line with only one server.

Single-period inventory models Inventory models in which it is assumed that only one order is placed for the product, and at the end of the period, the item has either sold out or there is a surplus of unsold items that will be sold for a salvage value.

Slack In a project network, the length of time an activity can be delayed without affecting the project completion date.

Smoothing constant A parameter of the exponential-smoothing model that provides the weight given to the most recent time series value in the calculation of the forecast value.

Soft technology Technology involving the application of computer software and other techniques that support managers of manufacturing and service organizations.

Solution Any set of values for the variables.

SPT (shortest processing time) A scheduling rule that chooses jobs in order of shortest processing time first.

Standardization The process of specifying product characteristics such as dimensions, composition, quality, or performance.

Stepping-stone method A procedure for identifying which routes will receive flow adjustments when a shipment is made over an unused route in the special-purpose solution procedure for the transportation problem.

Stores The department that physically maintains all inventoried items.

Strategic business units (SBUs) Families of products having similar characteristics or methods of production.

Strategic planning The determination of long-term goals, policies, and plans for an organization.

Strategic plans and decisions Long-range plans and decisions involving product lines, facilities, and equipment, conducted at the highest levels of an organization.

Synchro MRP A combination of MRP and Kanban which is used in high-volume manufacturing with a broad line of products.

Tactical plans and decisions Intermediate-range plans

and decisions involving resource allocation and utilization, conducted at the middle levels of an organization.

Tardiness   The amount by which completion time exceeds the due date.

Technology   The set of processes, tools, methods, and procedures used in the production of goods and services.

Therblig   One of 17 elementary human motions such as grasp, select, assemble, and so on.

Time phasing   Adding the dimension of time to inventory status data.

Time series   A set of observations measured at successive points in time or over successive periods of time.

Time standard   The amount of time required to perform a task by a trained operator working at a normal pace and using a prescribed method.

Time study   The development of standards through stopwatch observation.

Total productivity   The ratio of total output to total input.

Traffic and physical distribution   The management of transportation. This includes the selection of carriers as well as scheduling vehicles.

Transportation problem   The problem of determining how much to ship from each origin to each destination in order to minimize total distribution costs.

Transportation tableau   A table showing origins, destinations, routes, costs, supplies, and demands in a transportation problem. The tableau is used to facilitate the solution algorithm calculations.

Trend   The long-run shift or movement in the time series observable over several periods of time.

Utilization factor   Probability that the server is busy.

Validation   The process of determining that a simulation model accurately represents the real-world system that it is designed to simulate.

Value analysis   (1) The process of trying to reduce product costs by substituting less expensive materials, redesigning nonessential parts, and so on. (2) The review of product costs to evaluate their contribution to product value.

Value engineering   The process of trying to minimize product costs during the product design phase by being sure that each element serves its necessary function.

Variable measurement   Measurement of a physical quantity or any characteristic that takes on continuous values.

Work center   A uniquely defined group of workers or machines.

Work package   A natural grouping of interrelated project activities for purposes of cost control. A work package is a unit of cost control in a PERT/Cost system.

Work sampling   A method of randomly observing work over a period of time in order to obtain a distribution of activities performed.

REFERENCES

GENERAL REFERENCES

Adam, E.E., Jr., and R.J. Ebert: *Production and Operations Management*, 2d ed., Englewood Cliffs, N.J.: Prentice-Hall, 1982.

Anderson, D.R., D.J. Sweeney, and T.A. Williams: *An Introduction to Management Science*, 5th ed., St. Paul: West Publishing Co., 1988.

Buffa, E.S., and J.G. Miller: *Production—Inventory Systems, Planning and Control*, 3d ed., Homewood, Ill.: Richard D. Irwin, 1979.

Chase, R.B., and N.J. Aquilano: *Production and Operations Management*, 4th ed., Homewood, Ill.: Richard D. Irwin, 1985.

Dervitsiotis, K.N.: *Operations Management*, New York: McGraw-Hill, 1981.

Dilworth, J.B.: *Production and Operations Management: Manufacturing and Non-manufacturing*, 3d ed. Random House, New York, 1986.

Fearon, H.E., W.A. Ruch, P.G. Decker, R.R. Reck, V.G. Reuter, and C.D. Wieters: *Fundamentals of Production/Operations Management*, St. Paul: West Publishing Co., 1979.

Fitzsimmons, J.A., and R.S. Sullivan: *Service Operations Management*, New York: McGraw-Hill, 1982.

Greene, J.H., ed.: *Production and Inventory Control Handbook*, New York: McGraw-Hill, 1970.

Mayer, R.R.: *Production and Operations Management*, 4th ed., New York: McGraw-Hill, 1982.

Meredith, J.R., and T.E. Gibbs: *The Management of Operations*, John Wiley, New York, 1980.

Monks, J.G.: *Operations Management/Theory and Problems*, 2d ed., New York: McGraw-Hill, 1982.

Moore, F.G., and T.E. Hendrick: *Production/Operations Management*, 7th ed., Homewood, Ill.: Richard D. Irwin, 1977.

Plossl, G.W., and O.W. Wight: *Production and Inventory Control, Principles and Techniques*, Englewood Cliffs, N.J.: Prentice-Hall, 1967.

Riggs, J.L.: *Production Systems: Planning, Analysis and Control*, New York: John Wiley, 1976.

Schonberger, R.J.: *Operations Management*, Plano Texas: Business Publications, Inc., 1981.

Schroeder, R.G.: *Operations Management*, 2d ed., New York: McGraw-Hill, 1985.

Timms, H.L.: *Introduction to Operations Management*, Homewood, Ill.: Richard D. Irwin, 1967.

Wight, O.W.: *Production and Inventory Management in the Computer Age*, Boston: Cahners Publishing Co., 1974.

INTRODUCTION TO PRODUCTION/OPERATIONS MANAGEMENT (Chapter 1)

Amrine, H.T., J.A. Ritchey, and O.S. Hulley: *Manufacturing Organization and Management*, Englewood Cliffs, N.J.: Prentice-Hall, 1966.

Cohen, Stephen S. and John Zysman: *Manufacturing Matters*, New York: Basic Books, Inc. 1987.

Gunn, Thomas G.: *Manufacturing for Competitive Advantage*, Cambridge, Mass.: Ballinger Publishing Co., 1987.

Johnson, L.A., and D.C. Montgomery: *Operations Research in Production Planning, Scheduling, and Inventory Control*, New York: John Wiley, 1974.

Meal, Harlan C.: "Putting Production Decisions Where They Belong," *Harvard Business Review*, 62 (March-April 1984): 102–110.

Mills, P.K., and D.J. Moberg: "Perspectives on the Technology of Service Operations," *Academy of*

Management Review, 7, no. 3 (1982): 467–478.

Thomas, Dan R.E.: "Strategy is Different in Service Businesses," *Harvard Business Review*, 56, (July-August 1978): 228–235.

Thurston, P.H.: "The Concept of a Production System," *Harvard Business Review*, 41, 1963.

Wild, Ray: *Operations Management: A Policy Framework*, Oxford: Pergamon Press, 1980.

PRODUCTIVITY AND QUALITY (Chapter 2)

Blake, R.R., and J.S. Mouton: *Productivity: The Human Side,* New York: AMACOM, 1981.

Blank, L., and J. Solorzano: "Using Quality Cost Analysis for Management Improvement," *Industrial Engineering,* 10, no. 2 (February 1978): 46–51.

Burch, E.E., Jr.: "A Conceptual Framework for Understanding Productivity," *Industrial Management* (May-June 1979): 1–4.

Burnham, D.C. "Productivity: An Overview," in G. Salvendy, Ed. *Handbook of Industrial Engineering,* New York: John Wiley & Sons, 1982.

Campanella, Jack, and Frank J. Corcoran: "Principles of Quality Costs," *Quality Progress* (April 1983): 16–22.

Case, K.E., and L.L. Jones: *Profit Through Quality: Quality Assurance Programs for Manufacturers,* American Institute of Industrial Engineers Monograph Series AIIE-QC&RE 78-2, 1978.

Caskey, C.C.: *The Flexible Manager,* Kissimmee, Fla.: Cody Publications, Inc., 1980.

Devaney, C. William: "Keeping Current with Manufacturing Technology," *Price Waterhouse Review,* 29, no. 2 (1985): 29–30.

DeWitt, F.: "Productivity and the Industrial Engineer," *Industrial Engineering,* 8, no. 1 (January 1976): 20–27.

Edosomwan, J.A. "The Challenge for Industrial Managers: Productivity and Quality in the Workplace," *Industrial Management,* September-October, 1987, 25–27.

Enrick, N.L., and H.E. Mottley, Jr.: "Management of Quality in the Manufacturing System," *Industrial Management,* 20, no. 3, (May-June 1978): 4–8.

Fein, M.: "Improving Productivity by Improved Productivity Sharing," *The Conference Board RECORD,* 13, no. 7 (July 1976): 44–49.

Fesmier, R.J.: "Productivity—and Manufacturing Control," *Production and Inventory Management,* (Fourth Quarter 1978): 37–46.

Hawaleshka, O. and A. Mohamed, "Evaluation of Productivity and Technology Measures in Manufacturing Industries," *Engineering Management International,* 4, 2, (April 1987): 133–142.

Hines, W.W.: "Guidelines for Implementing Productivity Measurement," *Industrial Engineering,* 8, no. 6 (June 1976): 40–43.

Midas, Michael T., Jr.: "The Quality/Productivity Connection," *Quality,* 21, no. 2 (February 1982): 22–23.

Mundel, M.E.: "Measures of Productivity," *Industrial Engineering,* 8, no. 5 (May 1976): 24–26.

Osborn, R.W.: "Theories of Productivity Analysis," *Datamation* (September 1981): 212–216.

Page, Harold S.: "A Quality Strategy for the '80s," *Quality Progress,* 16, no. 11 (November 1983): 16–21.

Riggs, J.L.: "Improved Productivity Needs Leadership—YOURS!," *Industrial Engineering,* 10, no. 11 (November 1978): 45–49.

Ross, J.E.: *Managing Productivity,* Reston, Va.: Reston, 1977.

Ross, J.R.: "Productivity and Quality—The Inseparable Pair," *Institute of Industrial Engineers 1982 Fall Industrial Engineering Conference Proceedings,* pp. 81–88.

Ross, J.E. and E. Shaw, "Improving the Productivity of Service Organizations," *Industrial Management,* September-October, 1987, 21–24.

Santora, A.: "Quality Circles: When and How," *Production and Inventory Management Review,* 2, no. 2 (February 1982): 20–22.

Shell, R.L., and D.S. Shupe: "Productivity: Hope for City Woes," *Industrial Engineering,* 8, no. 12 (December 1976): 26–29.

Sink, D. Scott, and J. Bert Keats: "Productivity and Quality: What Is the Connection?" *1982 Fall Industrial Engineering Conference Proceedings,* Norcross, Georgia: Institute of Industrial Engineers, pp. 277–283.

Sullivan, Edward, "Quality Costs: Current Ideas," *Quality Progress* (April 1983): 24–25.

Sumanth, D.J.: "Productivity Indicators Used by Major U.S. Manufacturing Companies: The Results of a Survey," *Industrial Engineering,* 13, no. 5 (May 1981): 70–73.

Terry, G.R.: *Principles of Management,* 5th ed., Homewood, Ill.: Richard D. Irwin, 1968.

Thompson, P.G. DeSousa, and B.T. Gale, "The Strategic Management of Service Quality," *Quality Progress,* 18, no. 6, (June, 1985): 20–25.

van Gigch, John P.: "Quality—Producer and Consumer Views," *Quality Progress,* 10, no. 4 (April 1977): 30–33.

Wilson, P.N.: "Productivity Improvement Takes Hold in Banking," *Industrial Engineering,* 11, no. 9 (September 1979): 25–27.

FORECASTING AND TIME SERIES ANALYSIS (Chapter 3)

DeSalvia, D.N.: "Exponential Smoothing: A Pragmatic Approach to Production Planning," *Production and Inventory Management* (First Quarter 1968): 15–29.

Georgoff, David M., and Robert G. Murdick: "Manager's Guide to Forecasting," *Harvard Business Review,* January/February 1986, 110–120.

Gips, J., and B. Sullivan: "Sales Forecasting—Replacing Magic With Logic," *Production and Inventory*

Management Review, 2, no. 2 (February 1982): 25.

Muir, J.W., and T. Newberry: "Management's Role in a Forecasting System," *American Production and Inventory Control Society 1981 Conference Proceedings,* pp. 16–19.

Plossl, G.W.: "Getting the Most from Forecasts," *Production and Inventory Management* (First Quarter 1973): 1–15.

P/OM AND STRATEGIC PLANNING (Chapter 4)

Buffa, Elwood S.: *Meeting the Competitive Challenge: Manufacturing Strategy for U.S. Companies,* Homewood, Ill.: Dow Jones-Irwin, 1984.

Fine, Charles H., and Arnoldo C. Hax: "Manufacturing Strategy: A Methodology and an Illustration," *Interfaces,* 15 (November-December 1985): 28–46.

Hales, H. Lee: "Time Has Come for Long-Range Planning of Facilities Strategies in Electronic Industries," *Industrial Engineering,* 17, no. 4 (April 1985): 29–39.

Hayes, Robert H., and Steven C. Wheelwright: *Restoring Our Competitive Edge: Competing Through*

Manufacturing, New York: John Wiley, 1984.

Hill, T. J.: "Manufacturing Implications in Determining Corporate Policy," *International Journal of Operations and Production Management,* 1, no. 1, 1981, 3–11.

Kimes, Sheryl E.: "Towards a Theory of Service Operations Strategy," *Proceedings 1987 Annual Meeting of the Decision Sciences Institute,* p. 935–937.

Skinner, Wickham: *Manufacturing in the Corporate Strategy,* New York: John Wiley, 1978.

Thomas, Dan R.E.: "Strategy is Different in Service Businesses," *Harvard Business Review* (July-August 1978): 228–235.

PRODUCT DESIGN AND SELECTION (Chapter 5)

Baker, N.R., E.P. Winkofsky, L. Langmeyer, and D.J. Sweeney: "Idea Generation: A Procrustean Bed of Variables, Hypotheses, and Implications," *TIMS Studies in the Management Sciences,* 15 (1980): 33–51.

Ben-Arieh, D., C.A. Fritsch, and K. Mandel: "Competitive Product Realization in Today's Electronic

Industries," *Industrial Engineering,* 18, no. 2 (February 1986): 34–42.

Case, K.E., and L.L. Jones: *Profit Through Quality: Quality Assurance Programs for Manufacturers,* QC&RE Monograph Series No. 2, Institute of Industrial Engineers, 1978.

Gedye, R.: *A Manager's Guide to Quality and Reli-*

ability, New York: John Wiley, 1968.

Goslin, L.N.: *The Product Planning System,* Homewood, Ill.: Richard D. Irwin, 1967.

Harris, J.S.: "New Product Profile Chart," *Chemical and Engineering News,* 39, no. 16 (1961): 110–118.

Huchingson, R.D.: *New Horizons for Human Factors in Design,* New York: McGraw-Hill, 1981.

Levitt, T.: "Exploit the Product Life Cycle," *Harvard Business Review,* 43 (November-December 1965): 81–94.

Pessemier, E.A.: *New Product Decisions,* New York: McGraw-Hill, 1966.

Richardson, P.R., and J.R.M. Gordon: "Measuring Total Manufacturing Performance," *Sloan Management Review,* 21 (Winter 1980): 47–58.

Sachs, W.S., and G. Benson: *Product Planning and Management,* Tulsa, Okla.: Penwell Publishing Co., 1981.

RESOURCE-REQUIREMENTS PLANNING (Chapter 6)

Ahrens, R.: "Basics of Capacity Planning and Control," *American Production and Inventory Society 1981 Conference Proceedings,* pp. 232–235.

Aley, P.N., and G.H. Zimmer: "Capacity Planning," *Industrial Engineering,* 6, no. 4 (April 1974): 16–19.

Hirschmann, W.B.: "Profit from the Learning Curve," *Harvard Business Review,* 42, no. 1 (January-February 1964).

Khan, M.B.: "How Large a Staff for a Service Organization," *Industrial Engineering,* 10, no. 8 (August 1978): 32.

Patterson, R.T.: "Should You Expand Your Restaurant?," *Food Service Marketing* (July 1981): 16–19.

Reed, R., Jr.: *Plant Layout, Factors, Principles, and Techniques,* Homewood, Ill.: Richard D. Irwin, 1961.

FACILITY LOCATION AND DISTRIBUTION SYSTEM DESIGN (Chapter 7)

Beltrami, E.J.: *Models for Public Systems Analysis,* New York: Academic Press, 1977.

Geoffrion, A.M.: "A Guide to Computer-Assisted Methods for Distribution Systems Planning," *Sloan Management Review,* 16 (Winter 1975): 17–41.

Geoffrion, A.M., and T.J. Van Roy: "Caution: Common Sense Planning Methods Can Be Hazardous to Your Corporate Health," *Sloan Management Review,* 20 (Summer 1979): 31–42.

Heskett, J.L.: "Logistics—Essential to Strategy," *Harvard Business Review,* 55 (November-December 1977): 85–96.

Schmenner, R.W.: "Look Beyond the Obvious in Plant Location," *Harvard Business Review,* 57 (January-February 1979): 126–132.

PROCESS TECHNOLOGY AND SELECTION (Chapter 8)

Fillmore, W.E.: "Material Handling Analysis Is Approached from Traditional Points of View," *Industrial Engineering,* 13, no. 4 (April 1981): 52–57.

Huang, P.Y., and Ghandforonsky, P.: "Procedures Given for Evaluating, Selecting, Robots," *Industrial Engineering,* 16, no. 4 (April 1984): 44–48.

Reed, R., Jr.: *Plant Layout,* Homewood, Ill.: Richard D. Irwin, 1961.

Webster, D.B.: "From Receiving to Shipping—An Overview of In-Process Material Handling Systems," *Industrial Engineering,* 13, no. 4 (April 1981): 72–79.

PROCESS DESIGN AND FACILITY LAYOUT (Chapter 9)

Abou-Zeid, M.R.: "Group Technology," *Industrial Engineering,* 7, no. 5 (May 1975): 32–39.

Fitch, J.C., and W.P. Bryce, Jr.: "Developing Automation Applications: How to Identify and Implement High Yield Projects," *Industrial Engineering,* 13, no. 11, (November 1981): 47–56.

Fry, Timothy D., Martin G. Wilson, and Michael Breen: "A Successful Implementation of Group Technology and Cell Manufacturing," *Production and Inventory Management,* 28, no. 3, (1987): 4–6.

Groover, M.P., and J.E. Hughes, Jr.: "Job Shop Automation Strategy Can Add Efficiency to Small Operation Flexibility," *Industrial Engineering,* 13, no. 11 (November 1981): 67–76.

Kinney, Hugh D. Jr. and Leon F. McGinnis: "Design and Control of Manufacturing Cells," *Industrial Engineering,* 19, no. 10, (October 1987): 28—38.

Malstrom, E.M., and R.L. Shell: "Projections for Future Manufacturing Work Force Productivity," *Proceedings, 25th Annual Joint Engineering Management Conference,* The American Institute of Industrial Engineers, 1977, pp. 41–47.

Mariotti, J.J.: "Assembly Line Design: Choosing and Setting Up Conveyor Systems," *Industrial Engineering,* 13, no. 8 (August 1981): 52–56.

Shell, R.L.: "The Impact of Automation on Work Measurement," *Proceedings, Fall Industrial Engineering Conference,* Institute of Industrial Engineering Conference, Institute of Industrial Engineers, 1982, pp. 348–353.

AUTOMATION AND ADVANCED TECHNOLOGY (Chapter 10)

Bedworth, D.D., and J.E. Bailey: *Integrated Production Control Systems,* New York: John Wiley, 1982.

Blois, K.J.: "Matching New Manufacturing Technologies to Industrial Markets and Strategies," *Industrial Marketing Management,* 14 (1985): 43–47.

Goldhar, Joel, and Mariann Jelinek: "Computer Integrated Flexible Manufacturing: Organizational, Economic, and Strategic Implications," *Interfaces,* 15, no. 3 (May-June 1985): 94–105.

Groover, M.P., J.E. Hughes, and N.G. Odrey: "Productivity Benefits of Automation Should Offset Work Force Dislocation Problems," *Industrial Engineering,* 16, no. 4 (April 1985): 50–59.

Huang, Philip Y. and Chin-Sheng Chen: "Flexible Manufacturing Systems: An Overview and Bibliography," *Production and Inventory Management,* 27, no. 3, (1986): 80–90.

Link, P.: "CAD/CAM: A Much Needed Overview," *Production & Inventory Management Review and APICS News,* (October 1982): 40.

Lohrashi, Ardeshir: "Effects of Robotics on Production and Operations Management," unpublished paper, presented at the ORSA/TIMS National Meeting, Denver, October 1988.

Longmire, R.C.: "Robots Are Joining the Work Force," *Production & Inventory Management Review and APICS News* (October 1982): 54–58.

Mitchell, Roger H., and Vincent A. Mabert: "Robotics: Myths and Realities for Smaller American Manufacturers," Working Paper, WPS 86-29, College of Administrative Sciences, Ohio State University, February 1986.

Rifkin, Glenn: "A Look at Robotics in the U.S.," *Computerworld* (October 7, 1985): 10.

Suresh, N.C., and J.R. Meredith: "A Generic Approach to Justifying Flexible Manufacturing Systems," Department of Quantitative Analysis and Information Systems, University of Cincinnati (undated).

Takevchi, H., and A. Schmidt: "The New Promise of Computer Graphics," *Harvard Business Review,* 58, no. 1 (January-February 1980): 122–131.

White, Ken W.: "Vision Systems See Beyond Basic Inspection," *Quality Progress,* 21, no. 12, (1988): 56–60.

Wiley, David T.: "Automation Technology: Past, Present, and Future," *Production and Inventory Management,* 27, no. 4, (1986): 10–19.

JOB DESIGN AND WORK MEASUREMENT (Chapter 11)

Alexander, D.C.: "A Business Approach to Ergonomics," *Industrial Engineering,* 17, no. 7 (July 1985): 32–39.

Barnes, R.M.: *Motion and Time Study, Design and Measurement of Work,* 6th ed., New York: John Wiley, 1968.

Cross, K.F.: "The Factory of the Future Depends on Successful Integration of Automation and Job Design," *Industrial Engineering*, 18, no. 1 (January 1986): 14–18.

Heese, L.A.: "Wage Incentives Eliminate 'Zombie Time'," *Industrial Engineering*, 9, no. 10 (October 1977): 26–27.

Huchingson, R.D.: *New Horizons for Human Factors in Design*, New York: McGraw-Hill, 1981.

McGuire, T.R.: "Standards for Radiology are Made Easier," *Industrial Engineering*, 12, no. 4 (April 1980): 37–39.

McQuade, W.: "Easing Tensions Between Man and Machine," *Fortune* (March 19, 1984): 58–66.

Murrell, K.F.H.: *Human Performance in Industry*, New York: Reinhold Publishing Co., 1965.

Rice, R.S.: "Survey of Work Measurement and Wage Incentives," *Industrial Engineering*, 9, no. 7 (1977): 18–31.

Van Cott, H.P., and R.G. Kinkade, eds.: *Human Engineering Guide to Equipment Design*, U.S. Government Printing Office, 1972.

Wygant, Robert M.: "Improving Productivity with Financial Incentives," *Engineering Management International*, 4, (1987): 87–93.

MATERIALS AND INVENTORY MANAGEMENT (Chapter 12)

Ammer, D.S.: *Materials Management*, Richard D. Irwin, Homewood, Ill., 1974.

Berry, W.L.: "Lot Sizing Procedures for Requirements Planning Systems: A Framework for Analysis," *Material Requirements Planning*, APICS, 1973.

Burch, J.D.: "Cycle Counting and Inventory Accuracy," *Production & Inventory Management Review and APICS News*, 1, no. 9 (September 1981): 66.

Castaldi, J.: "The State-of-the-Art: Automated Storage and Retrieval Systems," *Production and Inventory Management Review and APICS News* (April 1982): 20.

Chentnik, C.G.: "Inventory: Controlling Its Costs," *Transportation and Distribution Management* (May-June 1976).

Coyle, J.J., and E.J. Bardi: *The Management of Business Logistics*, 2d ed., West Publishing Co., St. Paul, 1980.

Enrick, N.L.: *Inventory Management*, San Francisco: Chandler Publishing Co., 1968.

Leenders, M.R., H.E. Fearon, and W.B. England: *Purchasing and Materials Management*, 7th ed., Richard D. Irwin, Homewood, Ill., 1980.

Plossl, G.W., and O.W. Wight: *Production and Inventory Control*, Englewood Cliffs, N.J.: Prentice-Hall, 1967.

Silver, E.A., and Peterson, R.: *Decision Systems for Inventory Management and Production Planning*, 2nd ed., New York: John Wiley, 1985.

Warehouse Operations, General Services Administration, Federal Supply Service, February 1969.

Wight, O.W.: *Production and Inventory Management in the Computer Age*, Boston: Cahners Publishing Co., 1974.

AGGREGATE PRODUCTION PLANNING AND MASTER SCHEDULING (Chapter 14)

APICS Training Aid: Master Production Scheduling, American Production and Inventory Control Society, Washington, D.C.

Berry, W.L., T.E. Vollmann, and D.C. Whybark: *Master Production Scheduling, Principles and Practice*, American Production and Inventory Control Society, 1979.

Goodrich, T.H.: "The Basics of Master Production Scheduling," *American Production and Inventory Control Society, 1981 Conference Proceedings*, pp. 90–91.

Proud, J.F.: "Controlling the Master Schedule," *Production and Inventory Management*, 22, no. 2 (Second Quarter 1981): 78–90.

MATERIAL REQUIREMENTS PLANNING (Chapter 15)

Blasingame, J.W., and J.K. Weeks: "Behavioral Dimensions of MRP Change: Assessing Your Organization's Strengths and Weaknesses," *Production and Inventory Management*, 22, no. 1 (First Quarter 1981): 81–95.

Blumberg, D.F.: "Factors Affecting the Design of a Successful MRP System," *Production and Inventory Management*, 21, no. 4 (Fourth Quarter 1980): 50–62.

Campbell, R.J., and T.M. Porcano: "The Contributions of Materials Requirements Planning (MRP) to Budgeting and Cost Control," *Production and Inventory Management*, 20, no. 2 (Second Quarter 1979): 63–71.

Conlon, J.R.: "Is Your Master Production Schedule Feasible?," *Production and Inventory Management*, 17, no. 1 (First Quarter 1976): 57–63.

Cox, J.F., and R.R. Jesse, Jr.: "An Application of Material Requirements Planning in Higher Education," *Decision Sciences*, 12, no. 2 (April 1981): 240–260.

Donelson, W.S., II: "MRP—Who Needs It?," *Datamation* (May 1979): 185.

D'Ovidio, Gene J. and Richard L. Behling: "Material Requirements Planning," in *Handbook of Industrial Engineering*, Gavriel Salvendy, Ed. New York: John Wiley & Sons, 1982.

Hall, R.W.: "Why the Excitement About Repetitive Manufacturing," *Production and Inventory Management Review and APICS News*, 1, no. 8 (August 1981): 14–18.

Heizer, J.: "Inventory System Design for Restaurants," *Production and Inventory Management*, 22, no. 1 (First Quarter 1981): 57–64.

Higgins, M.J.: "Material Requirements Planning: What Is It and Why Use It?," *Distribution* (January 1980).

Jones, J.: "The Use of Materials Requirements Planning (MRP) in a Food Service Installation," *Production and Inventory Management*, 20, no. 2 (Second Quarter, 1979): 1–15.

Khumawala, Basheer M., Charles Hixon, and Japhet S. Law: "MRP II in the Service Industries," *Production and Inventory Management*, 27, no. 3, (1986): 57–63.

Mehra, S., and M.J. Reid: "MRP Implementation Using an Action Plan," *Interfaces*, 12, no. 1 (February 1982): 69–73.

Monden, Y.: "Adaptable Kanban System Helps Toyota Maintain Just-In-Time Production," *Industrial Engineering*, 13, no. 5 (May 1981): 29–46.

Monden, Y.: "What Makes the Toyota Production System Really Tick?," *Industrial Engineering*, 13, no. 1 (January 1981): 36–46.

"Putting Theory to Work in the Shop," *Datamation* (October 1980): 125–136.

Rossman, D.D.: "Materials Requirements Planning in a Small Tire Manufacturing Company," *Production and Inventory Management*, 18, no. 1 (First Quarter 1977): 88–103.

Schuchts, D.R.: "Give MRP a KISS: Keep It Smooth and Simple," *Production and Inventory Management*, 20, no. 3 (Third Quarter 1979): 68–80.

Schultz, T.: "MRP to BRP: The Journey of the 80's," *Production and Inventory Management Review and APICS News*, 1 (October 1981): 29.

Wantuck, K.A.: "The ABC's of Japanese Productivity," *Production and Inventory Management Review and APICS News*, 1, no. 9 (September 1981): 22–28.

OPERATIONS SCHEDULING AND PRODUCTION ACTIVITY CONTROL (Chapter 16)

Aley, P.N.: "Priority Scheduling Reduces Inventory," *Industrial Engineering*, 8, no. 1 (January 1976): 14–18.

Baker, K.R.: *Introduction to Sequencing and Scheduling*, New York: John Wiley, 1974.

Browne, J.: "Production Activity Control—A Key Aspect of Production Control," *International Journal of Production Research*, 26, no. 3, (1988): 415–427.

Browne, J.J., and R.K. Tibrewala: "Manpower Scheduling," *Industrial Engineering*, 7, no. 8 (August 1975): 22–23.

Burgess, William J. and Robert E. Busby: "Personnel Scheduling," in *Handbook of Industrial Engineering*, Gavriel Salvendy, ed., New York: John Wiley & Sons, 1982, pp. 11.9.1–11.9.16.

Clarke, G., and J. Wright: "Scheduling of Vehicles from a Central Depot to a Number of Delivery

Points," *Operations Research,* 12, no. 4 (July-August 1964): 568–581.

Fischer, W.A.: "Line of Balance: Obsolete After MRP?," *Production and Inventory Management,* 16, no. 4 (Fourth Quarter 1975): 63–77.

Fox, Bob: "OPT—An Answer for America, Part IV, Leapfrogging the Japanese," *Inventories and Production,* 3, no. 2 (March-April 1983).

Fox, Robert E.: "Main Bottleneck on the Factory Floor?," *Management Review* (November 1984).

Garwood, D., and J. Civerolo: "A Checklist for a Dispatch List," *Production and Inventory Management Review,* 1, no. 10 (October 1981): 24.

Graves, S.C.: "A Review of Production Scheduling," *Operations Research,* 29, no. 4 (July-August 1981): 646–675.

Hutchings, H.V.: "Shop Scheduling & Control," *Production and Inventory Management,* 17, no. 1 (First Quarter 1976): 64–93.

Jacobs, F. Robert: "OPT Uncovered: Many Production Planning and Scheduling Concepts Can be Applied With or Without the Software," *Industrial Engineering,* 16, no. 10 (October 1984).

New, C.C., "Job Shop Scheduling: Who Needs a Computer to Sequence Jobs?," *Production and Inventory Management,* 16, no. 4 (Fourth Quarter 1975): 38–45.

Shachter, H.I.: "Shop Floor Control: How Much Is Enough," *Production and Inventory Management Review,* 1, no. 12 (December 1981): 29.

JUST-IN-TIME PRODUCTION (Chapter 17)

Ansari, Ahsanuddin: "Survey Identifies Critical Factors in Successful Implementation of Just-in-time Purchasing Techniques," *Industrial Engineering,* 18, no. 10, (1986): 44–50.

Burnham, John M.: "Some Conclusions about JIT Manufacturing," *Production and Inventory Management,* 28, no. 3, (1987): 7–11.

Esparrago, Romeo A., Jr., "Kanban," *Production and Inventory Management,* 29, no. 1, (1988): 6–10.

Hall, R.: *Driving the Productivity Machine: Production Planning and Control in Japan,* American Production and Inventory Control Society, Falls Church, Va., 1981.

Hannah, Kimball H.: "Just-in-time: Meeting the Competitive Challenge," *Production and Inventory Management,* 28, no. 3, (1987): 1–3.

Jamrog, Mark R.: " 'Just-in-time' Manufacturing: Just in Time for U.S. Manufacturers," *Review,* 32, no. 1, (1988): 17–30.

Lee, Sang M. and Maling Ebrahimpour: "Just-in-time Production System: Some Requirements for Implementation," *International Journal of Operations and Production Management,* 4, no. 4, (1984); 3–15.

Nellemann, D.O., and L.F. Smith: "Just-In-Time vs. Just-in-Case," *Production and Inventory Management,* (Second Quarter 1982): 13–21.

Reda, Hussein M.: "A Review of 'Kanban'—The Japanese 'Just-in-time' Production System," *Engineering Management International,* 4, (1987): 143–150.

Roan, C.T.: "Purchasing's Role in Manufacturing Control," *Inventories and Production Magazine* (May-June 1981): 9–13.

Schonberger, R.J.: "Some Observations on the Advantages and Implementation Issues of Just-In-Time Production Systems," *Journal of Operations Management,* 1, no. 1 (November 1982): 1–10.

Suzaki, Kiyoshi: "Japanese Manufacturing Techniques: Their Importance to U.S. Manufacturers," *Journal of Business Strategy,* 5, no. 3, (1985): 10–20.

PROJECT PLANNING AND MANAGEMENT (Chapter 18)

Cleland, D.I., and D.F. Kocaoglu: *Engineering Management,* New York: McGraw-Hill, 1981.

Hajek, V.G.: *Project Engineering,* New York: McGraw-Hill, 1965.

Johnson, J.R.: "Advanced Project Control," *Journal of Systems Management* (May 1977): 24–27.

Mantel, Samuel J. and Jack R. Meredith: "IEs are Best Suited to Challenging Role of Project Manager," *Industrial Engineering,* 18, no. 4, (1986): 54–60.

Mantel, S.J., R. Riley, and J. McKinney: *Improving Management Skills, A Workbook,* New York: Penton Publishing Co., 1979.

Miller, W.B.: "Fundamentals of Project Management," *Journal of Systems Management* (November 1978): 22–29.

Rogers, L.A.: "Guidelines for Project Management Teams," *Industrial Engineering,* 6, no. 12 (December 1974): 12–19.

QUALITY CONTROL (Chapter 19)

Baker, J.T.: "Automated Preventive Maintenance Program for Service Industries and Public Institutions," *Industrial Engineering,* 12, no. 2 (February 1980): 18–21.

Brown, T.H.: "Quality Control," *Harvard Business Review,* 1951.

Case, K.E., and L.L. Jones: *Profit Through Quality: Quality Assurance Programs for Manufacturers,* AIIE Monograph QC&RE-78-2, Norcross, Georgia, AIIE, 1978.

Cheng, P.C.: "Managerial Control of Maintenance Cost," *Industrial Management,* (March-April 1979): 12–15.

Dhavale, D.G., and G.L. Otterson, Jr.: "Maintenance by Priority," *Industrial Engineering,* 12, no. 2 (February 1980): 24–27.

Duncan, A.J.: *Quality Control and Industrial Statistics,* 3d ed., Homewood, Ill.: Richard D. Irwin, 1965.

Evans, J.R. and W.M. Lindsay, *The Management and Control of Quality,* St. Paul: West Publishing Co., 1989.

Fetter, R.B.: *The Quality Control System,* Homewood, Ill.: Richard D. Irwin, 1967.

Gedye, R.: *A Manager's Guide to Quality and Reliability,* London: John Wiley, 1968.

Grant, E.L., and R.S. Leavenworth: *Statistical Quality Control,* 5th ed., New York: McGraw-Hill, 1980.

Halpern, S.: *The Assurance Sciences,* Englewood Cliffs, N.J.: Prentice-Hall, 1978.

Juran, J.M.: *Quality-Control Handbook,* New York: McGraw-Hill, 1951.

Mayer, Raymond R.: "Selecting Control Chart Limits," *Quality Progress,* 16, no. 9 (September 1983): 24–26.

Peterson, C.: "Selecting a Product Quality Level," *Industrial Engineering,* 2, no. 8 (August 1970): 23–26.

Squires, Frank H.: "What Do Quality Control Charts Control?," *Quality* (November 1982): 63.

INDEX

Voice-recognition systems, 421
Vroom, Victor, 458